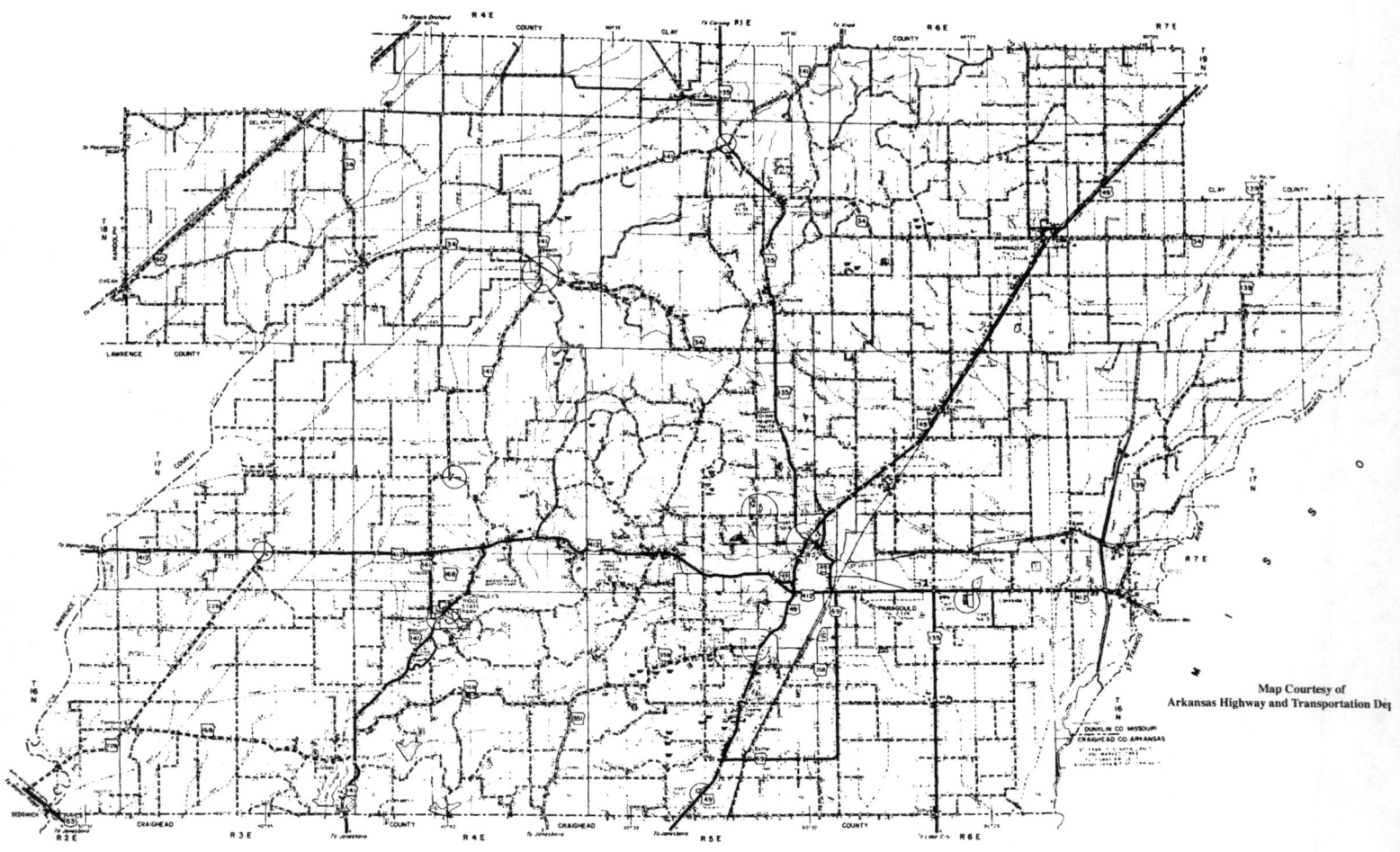

# Greene County, Arkansas Highways

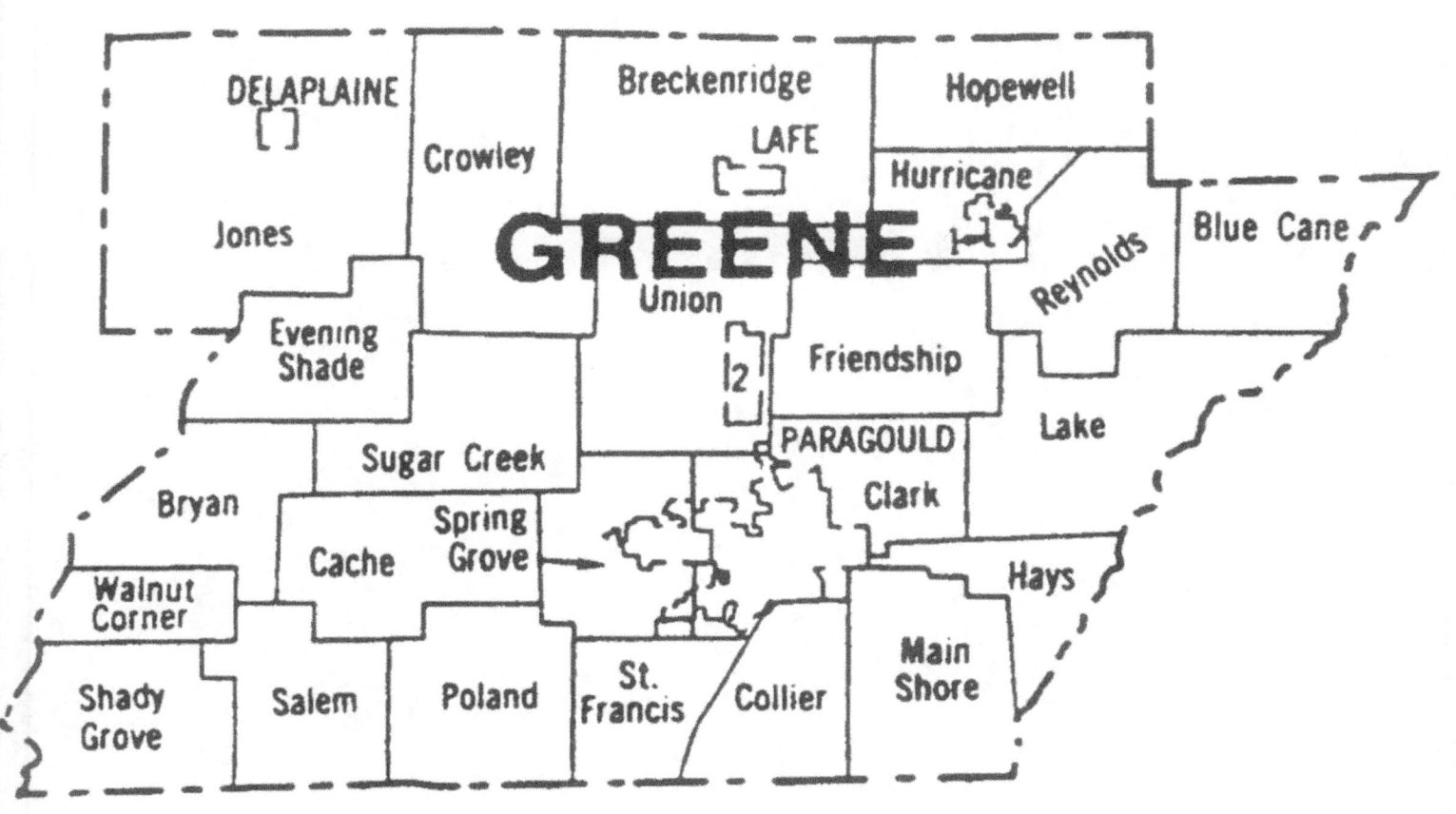

Greene County, Arkansas Townships

# Greene County, Arkansas

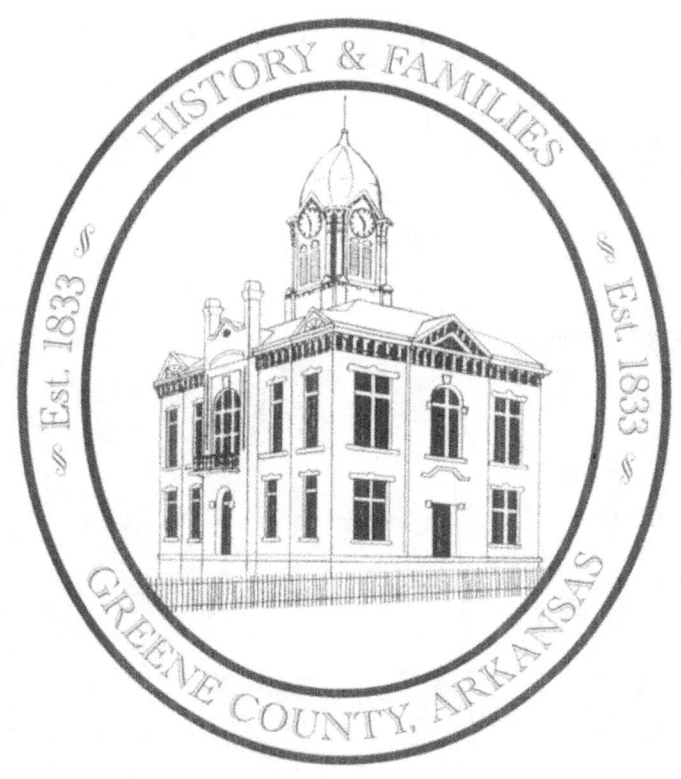

# History and Families

TURNER PUBLISHING COMPANY

**Turner Publishing Company**
Publishers of America's History

Book Commitee Chairman: Claire Jenkins
Publishing Consultant: Douglas W. Sikes
Book Designer: Emily K. Sikes

Copyright © MMI
All rights reserved.
Publishing Rights: Turner Publishing Company

Library of Congress Catalog No.: 2001097436

ISBN: 978-1-68162-174-6

Limited Edition, First Printing 2002 A.D.
Additional copies may be purchased from
Turner Publishing Company and the Greene
County Historical and Genealogical Society.

This book or any part thereof may not be reproduced by any means, mechanical or electronic, without the prior written consent of the Greene County Historical and Genealogical Society and Turner Publishing Company. This publication was produced using available information. The Publisher regrets it cannot assume responsibility for errors or omissions.

# Contents

Dedication .................................................................................... 4

Book Committee ........................................................................ 5

History of Greene County ........................................................ 10

Communities ............................................................................ 15

Local Government .................................................................... 25

Businesses ................................................................................ 28

Organizations ........................................................................... 59

Churches .................................................................................. 64

Schools ..................................................................................... 91

Historic Homes ........................................................................ 125

Memorials ................................................................................ 134

Family Histories ...................................................................... 139

Index ......................................................................................... 364

# DEDICATION

*Francis Bland*

A person who was very instrumental in the publication of this book, Francis Bland, has given more to this community than anyone we know.

Bland was born Aug 25, 1918 to Herbert and Alvina Bland and now lives one block from where he was born. He graduated from Paragould High School in 1936 and from Hendrix College, Conway, in 1940, with a degree in chemistry.

It is said, "behind every successful man, stands a good woman," which is certainly true of the mate whom Francis married, Winnie Landrum, on July 9, 1941. Winnie has been a great support to Francis in all his endeavors. They are the proud parents of four children: Donna, Herbert Francis III, John, and Denise.

Some of his achievements include:
Started a Little League program in 1951 and was the first coach
Started a Babe Ruth program in 1954
Rotary Club "Citizen of the Year" in 1954
President, Paragould Rotary Club 1954-1955
Paragould School Board 1954-1964 and was board president
President, Arkansas Soft Drink Association 1956
Dr Pepper Company Marketing Award Advisory Board 1964-1975
Chairman of the Eight-Mile Creek flood control program since 1974
Greene and Clay County Bar Association "Liberty Bell" award in 1976
Paragould "Centennial King" 1983
"Spirit of America" award winner from Crowley's Ridge College in 1983
Kiwanis Club "Citizen of the Year" 1989
American Legion Community Award 1993
Greene County Historical and Genealogical Society President 1994-1995
Grand Marshal, Paragould Annual Christmas Parade 1995
Paragould-Greene County Chamber of Commerce "Lifetime Member" award 1996
"American Legion" award for contributions to American Legion Baseball
Dr Pepper Bottlers' Association Board of Directors
Parks and Recreation Commission Founding Member and Chairman
Sunday School teacher and board member of First United Methodist Church
United Way volunteer
Francis is presently the President and Chairman of the Board of Dr Pepper Bottling Company of Paragould, AR.
Eight-mile creek was re-named "Francis Bland Floodway" in November 1999 and Civitan Club dedicated the "Francis Bland Floodway" sign
Bland was voted into the Babe Ruth Hall of Fame in January 2000
He is state president of Babe Ruth Baseball
He helped raise funds and build new baseball and softball parks in Paragould, with the parks being named "Francis Bland Community Baseball Parks"

In Bland's spare time you will find him at the Lipscomb History and Genealogy room of the Greene County Library, assisting anyone who needs help with family history research.

Francis, we love you and it is with much love and affection that we dedicate this Greene County History Book to you.
*Greene County Historical and Genealogical Society*

# BOOK COMMITTEE

*Francis Bland*

I, Francis Bland, was born and have lived all my life in Paragould, AR. I, along with my family and my business, have attempted to help make our community a better place because we have been here. I have been active in the Greene County History and Genealogical Society for many years. We have 300 members, many who give of themselves to make our organization helpful to people living in our community and to others from all over the country who had lived here or their families who had at one time lived in Greene County. I am a member of the Greene County Book Committee. Here's hoping you will find the book gives you information that will be of help to you.

*Catherine Gerdes*

*Edward G. Gerdes*

Catherine Gerdes is a native of Greene County. She graduated from Lafe High School in 1948 and Arkansas State University in 1953. She taught elementary school for 30 years, most of the years at Bono (Westside) in Craighead County, AR.

She and her husband, Edward G. have two sons Randall and Mark. The entire family has been interested in history and genealogy.

Edward G. Gerdes grew up in the northern Greene/Southern Clay county area in the Lafe community. Ed is a graduate of Arkansas State University, a WWII USCG veteran and a military retiree having completed his military service as an administrative technician with the Army National Guard. He has done extensive research into the Civil War units and personnel.

*Bettye Sparks Busby*

Bettye Sparks Busby was born and reared in Dunklin County, MO 12 miles from Paragould, AR. After six years at the University of Missouri she returned to Kennett, MO. In 1963 she married Ethan Busby, a Greene County native and moved to Paragould. She has always been a history buff and is now classified as a "genealogy nut". Bettye works in the Lipscomb room, Greene County Library. She has served as President, Treasurer, Vice President, program chairman and many other offices in the Greene County Historical Society. Bettye and Ethan have six children and 13 grandchildren. Running and genealogy take up most of the Busby's spare time along with grandchildren.

*Betty Jo (Martin) Clayton*

The youngest of three children, I was born Aug 28, 1937 in Paragould, Greene County, AR to Edna E. (Haggard) and John Raymond Martin. I attended Woodrow Wilson Elementary School and graduated from Paragould High School in 1955. After two years of college at Arkansas State Teacher's College in Conway, AR I began my working career in the clerical field at our family business, Martin Wholesale Radio Supply. Following the closing of our business in 1989 I took care of my father, who lived with me, until his death. I then worked for three and one-half years at Darling Store Fixtures factory before retiring in Oct 1994.

A handsome young man by the name of Robert William Clayton caught my eye in the summer of 1958 and we were married April 9, 1959 at St. Mary's Catholic Church in Paragould. Bob died at the age of 44, leaving me to raise our four children:
1. Robert W. Jr.
2. Steven
3. Patricia
4. Michael

God guided me through those tough years and later blessed me with four grandchildren.

During my "active" years, I was very involved with St. Mary's church and school organizations, served as a Girl Scout Leader three years and a board member of the Crowley's Ridge Girl Scouts Council two years, serving as secretary one of the terms.

My favorite hobbies are making Christmas ornaments, as well as other handcrafts and family genealogy. I bought my first computer at age 62 and am still trying to overcome the frustrations of learning to use it. I currently am a member of Greene County Historical and Genealogical Society and volunteer in the library research room, which I dearly love doing.

I have lived my entire life in Paragould and Greene County. I love this town and have never desired to live anywhere else. This is the best place in the United States to live and raise a family!

*Lynda Heath Bryant*

Lynda Heath Bryant was born in Jonesboro, Craighead County, AR and lived in Marked Tree, Poinsett County, until 1945. Paragould and Greene County have been her home since that time. As a child, she looked forward to Decoration Day and loved to visit the cemeteries where her grandparents and great grandparents are buried. Afterwards, she would sit and listen to her aunts talking while the other children were outside playing. Lynda has always been interested in family and genealogy. She is married to Jimmy Ray Bryant, a native of Greene County. Her husband, three daughters and three grandchildren are the joys of her life. Lynda is secretary/treasurer, co-manager and co-owner of Heath Funeral Home and is currently serving as president of the Greene County Historical and Genealogical Society.

*Claire (Walker) Jenkins*

Randall K. and Claire (Walker) Jenkins, both Paragould natives, were married in 1950. Randall has always been in the building supply business and Claire is a secretary. Their three children are Randall Wayne (July 23, 1960 St. Peters, MO), Polly Ann Medici (Oct 9, 1963 Carlsbad, CA) and Patricia Jean Garner (Nov 30, 1965 Paragould). Claire has served as book committee chairman.

*Anita Phillips*

Anita Phillips was born in Memphis TN, and graduated from Rector High School, Rector, AR. She received BME and MSE from Arkansas State University; taught junior and senior high choral music and served as choir director for a United Methodist church. Currently volunteering at the Lipscomb Room (Greene County Library), member of Greene County Scholarship committee, pianist at Pruett's Chapel United Methodist church, member of Greene County Historical and Genealogical Society and serves on the book committee of Greene County Family History Book.

*Clara Lovelady*

Clara Clifton Lovelady was born and reared in Greene County, AR. She was only away from Arkansas two years while beginning her teaching career in 1955 at Marston, MO. She returned to Arkansas and was employed by the Delaplaine School district for 30 years. She is a member of the Greene County Historical and Genealogical Society and feels it is a privilege to be able to serve on the Greene County History Book Committee and hopes that the book will be a treasure to the people of Greene County.

She is married to Billy Lovelady and they live in the Beech Grove community where the Lovelady's settled in the 1850s.

*1999 – President Bettye Busby, President-elect Lynda Heath Bryant, Recording Secretary Ruth Woodside, Board Members Francis Bland, Anita Phillips and Clara Lovelady*

## Greene County Historical and Genealogical Society

The first historical society in Greene County was organized in 1933 known as the Crowley's Ridge Historical Society, which was to have preserved the history of eight northeastern Arkansas counties. J. M. Futrell was listed as president; H. L. Ponder, vice president and George M. Moreland as historian. Records of this group or their activities have not been kept.

The Greene County Historical Society was organized in 1964, with the assistance of Mrs. W. L. "Dot" Skaggs, Mrs. R. P. Calvert and Mrs. Pearl Morrow, all natives of Greene County. Mrs. Skaggs underwrote the publishing cost of the first issue of the Greene County History quarterly in the fall of 1964. In lean years Mrs. Morrow was known to attend the Marmaduke Picnic and sell issues of the publication and also on the streets of Paragould. She would solicit members at the same time. Due to the death of many of the older members of the society, whose support had kept the organization active, the waning interest of the public and the failure to find new leadership after the departure of Dr. D. W. Starnes, who was president, the society was forced to disband.

The first officers of the society were: Raymond Frey, president; Alfred Holland, vice president; Mrs. W. L. Skaggs, secretary; J. W. Thompson, treasurer. The membership committee included Mrs. Pearl Morrow and J. Sam Thompson.

The Greene County Historical and Genealogical Society was reorganized on Sept 14, 1987. The society inherited $800 from the previous Greene County Historical Society. Officers were: Dr. Bennie Mitchell, president, Dr. Omer E. Bradsher, vice president; Mary Esther Herget, second vice president; Dawn Linden, secretary and Barbara Hazzard, treasurer.

At the present time, 1999, we have over 250 members and publish nine newsletters and four quarterlies each year. Current officers are: Lynda Heath Bryant, president; Bettye Sparks Busby, vice president; Ethan Busby and Charles White, program chairmen; Frances A. Morris, treasurer; Ruth Woodside, recording secretary; Clara Lovelady, corresponding secretary; Louise Richardson, publicity chairman and Kitty Sloan, newsletter editor.

Today the members of the society are active in their community, preserving the history and assisting the S. S. Lipscomb Genealogy Room at the Greene County Library. We have volunteers almost every afternoon to assist those persons who are researching their families. Books are purchased as funds allow. The society has purchased a new Xerox copier and computer for the room. We are proud to sponsor the Greene County History and Family Book and are looking forward to its completion. We hope that it will be beneficial to family researchers in the years to come. We wish to express our thanks to the many people who have worked long hours in seeing that this book is completed.

Goinesville, Greene County, Arkansas

# General History and Communities

# History of Greene County

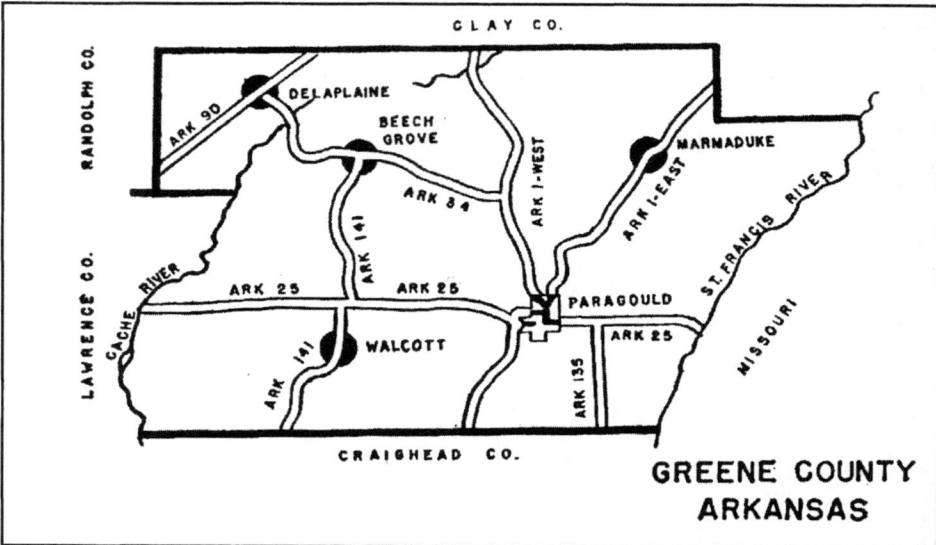

*Highways of Greene County*

Composing a land area of 579 miles, Greene County is located in Northeast Arkansas. The area is bounded on the north by Clay County, on the east by a portion of the State of Missouri, on the south by Craighead County and on the west by Lawrence and Randolph Counties.

In 1811-12 a great national cataclysm, known as the New Madrid earthquake, laid waste a large part of the area that would become Greene County. The three great quakes, now judged to have been of an intensity geologist call "total destruction", affected a three-state area and for years was a scene of desolation and delayed the settlement by several decades. The earth sank in places 15 to 20 feet and rose in others, destroying the channel of the St. Francis River and causing the St. Francis swamps on the eastern boundary. Long narrow lakes appeared, causing a series of islands. Fissures channeled great pockets of sand forced from the earth and fields. The natural drainage pattern was upset and it was to take years of drainage projects to make it suitable for tilling. However, there were still beautiful high timbered slopes of the ridge.

In the spring of 1821 Benjamin Crowley, a 65-year old surveyor and a holder of a New Madrid certificate, left his home in Kentucky in the company of his two older sons and several slaves, seeking suitable land on which to settle with his wife and eight children. They crossed the Mississippi at Cairo and came down the Missouri Line into Lawrence County and stopped at Davidsonville. They stopped there long enough to plant a crop and then proceeded down the ridge, which was to bear the Crowley name. When the party reached a large spring, which had been used for many years by Indians for their pow-wows, the elder Crowley is reported to have said to his sons, "this is good enough". He had located a choice spot on the ridge, at these springs which are now a part of Crowley's Ridge State Park, about 12 miles west of Paragould.

Crowley returned to Davidsonville, harvested his crop and sent his sons and his slaves back to his selected site to build a dwelling and a stockade. The family was sent for and arrived on Christmas day to move into their new home. Thus began the history of Greene County.

It was in the Crowley home that the first post office was located. Isaac Brookfield, the young Methodist missionary from New Jersey, organized the first church there. When news of Crowley's discovery was sent back to friends and relatives in Kentucky, others began arriving to make homes on the Ridge. In 1883 a new county was organized in the Crowley home. Brookfield became the first judge and is credited with naming the county after General Nathaniel Greene, one of Washington's most trusted generals.

In 1836 Arkansas achieved statehood. The county seat was located at a place called Paris, because it was centrally located. The original county included what are now Clay County and a part of Craighead County.

When the national highway was put through in 1848, the county seat was moved to a small village, which they named Gainesville, where the county seat remained until 1883. At this point, a new town came into existence.

*Submitted by Greene County Historical & Genealogical Society*

## Nathanael Greene: County Namesake

By the time Greene County, AR was created in 1833, at least 10 other states had named counties to honor Nathanael Greene (1742-1786), a military hero of the American Revolution.

The general's name traveled west with American settlers, starting in the Piedmont where Greene earned his reputation as "Savior of the South" and where many of the families who settled Greene County, AR began their own journeys west.

Greene was active in the War for Independence from beginning to end. Only two generals served the American cause all eight years of the war; Greene was one, George Washington the other. Greene is considered second only to Washington as a military strategist. Even British commander Lord Cornwallis complained, "Greene is as dangerous as Washington."

Greene was fifth-generation American. His Quaker family emigrated from England to Massachusetts with some Puritans and then to Rhode Island with Roger Williams in the 1630s seeking religious freedom. But Nathanael's decision to fight for political freedom led to his being "read out" of the pacifist Society of Friends.

Involved in early anti-British protests in New England, Greene took up arms in April 1775, joining other area militiamen gathered outside Boston as news of Lexington and Concord provoked the start of the colonial revolu-

*This marker was placed on the north side of the Greene County Community Center in 1976 to help celebrate the American Bicentennial.*

tion. He never looked back. Greene crossed the Delaware with Washington, shared the winter at Valley Forge, presided at the trial of British spy John Andre, tried to keep the Continental Army supplied as quartermaster general and skillfully outmaneuvered the British to help set the trap for Cornwallis at Yorktown.

Even after the British surrender in 1781, Greene kept his troops together for two years until the Treaty of Paris officially ended the war, paying them out of his own pockets.

Financial problems are said to have contributed to his early death in 1786, less than three years after the official peace. He died on the Mulberry Grove plantation outside Savannah, GA, that had been given to him by a grateful legislature and which he refused to work with slave labor. A tall marble obelisk marks his burial site in a public square in Savannah.

The only physical monument to the general in Greene County, AR, is a 1976 marker at the Jaycee Flag Plaza on the north side of the Greene County Community Center off Twelfth Street. It reads:

Dedicated to the 200th anniversary of the Declaration of Independence, this plaza honors General Nathanael Greene, the Revolutionary War hero 'ready at all times to bleed in my country's cause.' He served the cause of independence for eight years, commanding with distinction in major battles from Trenton to Eutaw Springs. 'We fight, get beat, rise and fight again,' he said of the strategy, which won America its freedom. His name survives in Greene County and this plaza is dedicated with the hope that his memory will endure as well."

*Submitted by Kitty Sloan*

## Greene County 1888 Courthouse

On Sept 1, 1884 voters decided 943 to 737 to move the county seat from Gainesville to the new railroad town of Paragould. It was decided that the new county seat would have a new majestic brick courthouse. Construction began in 1887. W. F. Boon and S. R. McGinnis were awarded the contract to build the new courthouse at a cost of $14,700.

Original plans did not include a bell in the clock tower, but the public wanted one, so donations provided the additional $1000 needed. The courthouse was completed on April 3, 1888.

In 1918 the building was remodeled when W. A. Branch was county judge. The exterior brickwork was reported to be deteriorating and needed attention to preserve the building. Stucco for exterior finishing had just been introduced in Paragould and was yet something of a novelty. It was decided to plaster the red brick with gray stucco at a cost of $15,000 and to add a wing to the west side. There was a great deal of controversy over the action and Griffin Smith, then editor of the Paragould Daily Press, wrote an editorial protesting it as "an error in judgment", but to no avail. The original design was further diminished in 1968 when the clock tower, the building's distinctive feature, was judged unsafe and removed.

Need for additional space caused two box-like wooden "doghouses" to be built on both the east and west walls. The iron fence disappeared many years ago; portions of it reappeared to grace the lawns of several private homes. The south expanse of Court Square had been cut with concrete and iron railings for the building of a civil defense shelter.

*Greene County 1888 Courthouse*

## New Greene County Courthouse

July 14, 1995 a groundbreaking ceremony was held for the new Greene County courthouse. The new courthouse was being funded largely by a one-cent sales tax passed by voters in August. Most county offices had been moved from the old courthouse to the new by the end of December 1996. County Judge David Lange occupied his office in the new courthouse two weeks before newly elected County Judge Jerry Shipman took office.

## Old 1888 Greene County Courthouse Saved

There were mixed emotions as to whether the old courthouse should be torn down or restored. Mary Ann Schreit believed the old courthouse should be restored as it was in 1888. She also believed the clock tower should be replaced on top and appealed for help in accomplishing this. Her appeal led to the formation of the Greene County Preservation Society and the rest, as they say, is history.

In 1995 Schreit and the courthouse society received the award for Outstanding Achievement in Preservation Advocacy from the Historic Preservation Society of Arkansas.

Funds have been raised and grants applied for. The second floor of the old courthouse has been restored. The old gray stucco has been removed. The brick has been tuck-pointed and restored to its original state and plans call for restoring the first floor and landscaping. A commemorative brick sidewalk will be built, each brick inscribed with a name or a message designated by the donor. The old iron fence has been reclaimed and will be replaced around the courtyard.

As you drive down Court Street and see this beautiful red brick building, a part of our history, you will want to say "thank you" to those people who have spent so many hours and hard work to preserve this building. As funds become available, other phases of this restoration will take place.

At the present time some of the oldest Greene County records are stored in the "bomb shelter" in the basement of the old courthouse. Greene County Genealogical and Historical Society members spent more than a year cleaning and repairing these records. They get requests weekly from people who are researching their family history for information that is in the records.

The new courthouse is modern and meets our present needs. But it is still a great blessing to have the 1888 courthouse, a part of our ancestors' and our lives, still standing.

*Submitted by Greene County Historical & Genealogical Society*

## Greene County Liberty Memorial

The Greene County Liberty Memorial, located at the northeast corner of the old Greene County Courthouse, honors the 133 local men who died in military service in five 20th century wars – WWI, WWII, Korea, Vietnam and the Persian Gulf.

The original memorial, dedicated on Nov 11, 1924, features a bronze replica of the Statue of Liberty atop a marble pedestal. Engraved on the back of the pedestal is the dedication, "To the men of Greene County who served in the World War and in memory of those who made the Supreme Sacrifice 1917-1918." Listed individually are the names of the 40 men who died in The Great War that we now call WWI. On the front of the pedestal is the inscription:

"Let us hold in honored memory those men from Greene County who gave their lives that mankind might hope for a better world".

The bronzed statue – about 1/20th the size of Bartholdi's colossal Lady Liberty – was crafted by Chicago artist John Paulding, who created at least 21 other WWI memorials in 17 other states. The Statue of Liberty had been a rallying symbol during the war, often used in war bond drives and other home front support activities. The memorial was one of the first projects undertaken in 1921 by the local post of a new veterans' organization, the American Legion. The county government provided $1000 of the $2000 cost. The other half was raised through the sale of Memorial Certificates at $1 each.

Almost 5,000 people attended the 1924 dedication, which was preceded by a parade of floats, bands, automobiles and marchers through downtown Paragould.

Unfortunately, "the war to end all wars" didn't. In 1948, Adams-Jackson American Legion Post No. 17 initiated plans to add marble wings to the pedestal so that the names of the 78 soldiers and sailors killed in WWII could be added.

Eventually, 15 more names were engraved – two from Korea, 11 from Vietnam and two from the Persian Gulf.

*Greene County Liberty Memorial: the bronze Statue of Liberty repleca atop a central marble pedestal was placed at the courthouse in 1924 as a memorial to "The Great War." Marble wings were added after World War II.*

The monument continues to be the centerpiece of patriotic ceremonies sponsored by the American Legion and the Veterans of Foreign Wars every Memorial Day and Veterans Day.

In the 1990s, a photograph of the Liberty Memorial was included in *Stone and Steel: A Sculptural Tour of Arkansas,* a map published by the Arkansas Historic Preservation Program, a state agency of the Department of Arkansas Heritage.

In 1998, a grant from the Smithsonian Institution's national Save Outdoor Sculpture project funded a professional assessment of the monument's conservation needs, which include removing corrosion from the bronze statue and repairing cracks and joints in the marble base. The estimated cost of the conservation work is $19,000, which is still under consideration for grant funding. A Greene County Liberty Memorial Fund has been set up at First National Bank to raise the local match.

Because the memorial is on the grounds of the old Greene County Courthouse, it will also be included in the landscaping plans of the Greene County Courthouse Preservation Society.

## Greene County in Wartime

When their government called for soldiers and sailors to go to war, Greene Countians have always responded. This was also true during the War Between the States. Greene County furnished at least 10 companies to the confederate government plus many more individuals who joined other units from other localities.

Some of the units that were supplied by Greene County were:

Kuykendall's Co 1st AR Vols (30 day)
Co D, 5th AR Inf Regt
Co E, 5th AR Inf Regt
Co H, 5th AR Inf Regt
Co D, 25th AR Inf Regt
Co F, 30th (Hart's) Inf Regt
Joel Anderson's Co, Cockes's Inf Regt
Three companies of Maj. Davies' Cav BN
An unknown number of companies of Col Kitchen's 7th MO Cav Regt.

Greene County fared much better during that war than did most of her sister counties in Arkansas. There were no major battles fought in the area and only minimal troop movements across the county occurred. Casualty lists are not available for this war.

A list of those who served in subsequent wars would fill volumes; therefore, we list only the casualties as inscribed on the Memorial on the courthouse lawn as follows:

WWI
Adams, Ranzie
Austin, Lon
Barnett, Charles S.
Bonds, Jimmie
Boone, Arlin
Bowlin, Luther F.
Brooks, William B.
Brown, Chesser W.
Brown, Don P.
Brown, Jack
Chestnut, James
Childers, Wilmer L.
Chitwood, Adla S.
Clayton, Oscar R.
Costen, Fred C.
Cothern, Earl D.
Crow, Arthur P.
Cupples, Hubert L.
DeBoe, John
Depew, Clarence W.
Dixon, Elbert E.
Dollar, Walter
Easter, Richard
Fitzgerald, Amos
Fletcher, Olen
Foster, Wesley
Good, Jack
Hopper, George A.
Howe, John
Jackson, Adams
Layman, Hollie J.
Meador, Walter
Noel, John H.
Riley, Charlie
Stover, Isaac A.
Sutton, Jessie J.
Walters, Arlie E.
Watson, John W.
Watwood, Murry M.
Weatherford, Alvie C.

WWII
Ahlf, Robert G.
Atchison, Willis D.
Baker, Victor W.
Barron, Donald E.
Baty, Wesley A.
Beaver, Allen R.
Bishop, Earl L.
Blagg, Jim C.
Blankenship, Harley L.
Bridges, Jack D.
Bridges, Paul H.
Browning, James E.
Bruce, Woodrow L.
Butler, James S.
Cathey, Henry N.
Clayton, Kenneth M.
Cobb, Guy W. Jr.
Craft, Clayton O.
Crawford, Woodson B.
Dowdy, Dewey
Eaker, William C.
Eubanks, John A.
Fahr, Herschel S.
Farmer, Ezra F.
Faulkner, John N.
Finley, Billy G.
Ford, William P.
Freeman, Leslie H.
Gardner, Walter S.
Hall, Wilson M.
Hass, Crillon A.
Hathcock, Walter C.
Henley, Wayne R.
Henson, Archie,
Hilburn, Melvin
Hopkins, Richard J.
Hunter, Major L.
Jackson, Verla F.
Jenkins, Elbert W.
Johnson, Eugene
Johnson, Robert T.
Kennedy, Harold P.
Lawson, Dillard D.
Livingston, Lloyd L.
Lovelady, Milbern F.
Maxwell, Newell O.
McMurtry, E. H. Jr.
Miller, Woodrow
Moore, Emmett L.
Myer, Urban E.
Myers, Rudy S. Jr.
Ogles, Hubert G.
Parkinson, Roy F.
Parrish, Vowell G.
Payne, James J.
Payne, Thomas L.
Peeler, Willie L.
Pierce, Robert E.
Robertson, Joseph M.
Robeson, Claude C.
Rowe, C. L.
Rowe, Sidney L.
Schmuecker, Roman E.
Shatley, Lois A.
Spain, George W.
Staggs, James C.
Straub, Virgil A.
Sullinger, William A.
Tillman, Norman M.
Trantham, Forrest A.
Vines, Arel
Walker, Birt F.
Walker, Robert F.
Williams, Jeff L.
Williams, Robert L.
Wilson, Dallas W.
Wogman, Jimmie W.
Yates, John G.

KOREAN WAR
Cooper, Russell
Collier, S. T.

VIETNAM WAR
Clark, Timothy Eugene
Cleveland, Hardy Edward
Cook, John Edward
Crow, Kenneth Leland
Harvey, Randall Lloyd
Huffine, Dennis Willard
Lyles, J. L.
McCord, David W.
Prince, Ronald
Taylor, Danny Gene
West, Mounce Edward
Whitton, Teddy Gene

PERSIAN GULF (DESERT STORM)
Mason, Steven G.
Mitchem, Earnest F. Jr.

## Greene County Library

The Greene County Library traces its roots back to Jan 1, 1936, when the Paragould Public Library opened under the sponsorship of the local Business & Professional Women's club. The club paid rent and utilities for a second-floor room in the 100 block of West Court Street. The salary of librarian Nona Dixon and her successor Pearl Diggs was paid through federal New Deal jobs programs until 1943.

After 17 years of struggling to survive on donations, volunteer help, severely limited hours, meager federal aid, rent-free space from the city of Paragould and sometimes $50 a month from the county quorum court, the public library became tax-supported with the Nov 1952 passage of a special one-mill county wide property tax earmarked solely for the library. A second women's group, the local chapter of the American Association of University Women, spearheaded the library tax campaign.

Library funding was a statewide problem that led to the 1946 adoption of an initiated amendment to the state constitution allowing the local-option county library tax. After lengthy discussion, a proposed Greene County library tax was put on the ballot in 1950; it failed 2,011 to 2,765. With increased determination and the campaign slogan "So Much for So Little," the AAUW brought the proposal back to the ballot in the next general election two years later and won 2,783 to 1,618.

From an original collection of 600 donated books, the library has grown to fill its 14,000 square foot building with about 50,000 fiction, non-fiction and reference books, magazines, newspapers, microfilm, microfiche, audio cassettes, compact discs and videotapes.

The library's main funding continues to come from the one-mill library tax, although it also receives a small share of the county sales tax adopted in 1982. And provisions of the Arkansas constitution have continued to impact the library, including county government reorganization after Amendment 55 in 1974; the massive property tax changes wrought by Amendment 59 after 1980 and, in recent years, regular threats to the entire system of funding public services with property taxes.

In the midst of all challenges, the Greene County Library has survived and has even been able to expand services, especially children's programming, Internet public access and, since 1983, its local history/genealogy department, the S. S. Lipscomb Room.

The Wright Memorial Library building at 120 N. 12th Street was dedicated April 28, 1974. Built at a cost of more than $300,000, it was the first Greene County Library location to be designed specifically for library use. It is named for Rupert C. Wright and Georgia O. Wright, publishers of the Paragould *Daily Press* from 1921 to 1951, whose bequest helped fund its construction.

Past locations, Paragould Public Library: (1) 1936 to 1949, rented a second-floor room and sometimes a separate reading room in the 100 block of West Court Street; above Trail Blazer Café. Site of the building is now a bank drive-through. (2) 1949 to 1953, rent-free space provided on third floor of Paragould City Hall, the former Dickson Memorial Hospital. Lower floors of this building are still standing, but third and fourth floors were removed in 1957.

Past locations, Greene County Library: (1) April 1953 to Aug 1954, rented a five-room first-floor apartment in the Dillman Building, just west of the post office. The house was razed when the post office building was enlarged in 1966. (2) Aug 1954 to March 1962, rented old Emerson Funeral Home on northwest corner of Poplar and Second Streets. The site is now a vacant lot. (3) March 1962 to April 1974, owned Partain Building at 110 E. Poplar. The building was torn down in 1999.

Librarians, Paragould Public Library: Nona Dixon, Jan 1936 to July 1941; Pearl Diggs, July 1941 to Dec 1943 and also 1945 to 1948; Pauline Hooper, 1948 to Jan 1951; Lindel Hooper, 1951 and Rubye Branom, 1951 to 1953.

Librarians, Greene County Library: Minnie Gay, June 1953 to Sept 1953; Myrtle Deason, Sept 1953 to Nov 1955; Minnie Gay, Dec 1955 to Aug 1961; Nadene Lee, "for a few months" 1961; Kathleen Sharp, June 1962 to July 1979; Nancy Evans, Sept 1979 to May 1988; Paullean Capps, June 1988 to May 1998 and Sandra Rogers, July 1998 to present.

As of Aug 2, 2000.
*Submitted by Kitty Sloan*

*The Greene County Library moved into its new home, the Wright Memorial Library building, in 1974.*

*Greene County Library, Paragould, Arkansas*

*Sandra Rogers, Greene County Librarian*

# COMMUNITIES

## Beech Grove

The community of Beech Grove is located 13 miles west of Paragould in the northwest central part of the county.

The first settlers, the Jess Williams family, came to this area soon after the Crowleys settled on the ridge. The Frairs were also among the early settlers and the first school was called the Frair School, which was established about 1840 in an early Methodist log church.

A grove of beech trees surrounding the log church gave the community of Beech Grove its name.

Others settling in the same area were the Breckenridges, who have long been associated with this community. They established the first mercantile business in Beech Grove. Andrew Breckenridge established the first cotton gin in Beech Grove, which was a treadmill type of gin. From that time until recent years there was a cotton gin in Beech Grove.

The first post office was opened in 1880 in the store of J. Henry Breckenridge, son of Andrew. This store was considered the center of the community life. Besides offering a selection of groceries and other things, Breckenridge maintained a funeral parlor and also sold caskets. He donated the town five acres on which to build the first schoolhouse and also land for the cemetery.

There was also a telephone exchange operated by Mattie Robinson and her sister.

At one time Beech Grove was a thriving little community with three or four stores, a blacksmith shop, a post office, four churches, a cotton gin and a high school. The high school consolidated with the Greene County Tech District in 1949. The elementary school did not move until the 1960s.

In 1973, Beech Grove was noted for having the World Bass Masters Classic Championship Fisherman, Rayo Breckenridge.

Other early settlers in the area included the Craigs, Davises, Jettons, Loveladys, Meadows, Scobeys, Smelsers, Stallcups, Taylors and Whitlocks.

Today Beech Grove still has a post office and three churches still meet.

## Beliew

Many Greene Countians today well remember "Uncle Charlie" Beliew. Few citizens in the county have been better known, or more respected. And although his descendants are scattered throughout the county, years of search and inquiry have revealed that very little was known of Uncle Charlie's past. After numerous interviews with old-timers from the Lafe area, as well as a search of county records and U. S. Census records, the following information was obtained.

Charles Cooper Beliew was born in Gibson County, TN on Oct 25, 1868. He was orphaned at an early age and was taken to live with his uncle and aunt, Aaron and Nancy Beliew. He came with them from Dresden, TN to Greene County in 1886. Aaron Beliew had purchased 40 acres of land from the St. Louis Iron Mountain Railroad (Section 21,

*The Post Office and Store in the Beech Grove Community, ca. 1902*

Twp. 18 North, Range 5 East) on July 10, 1886 and another 40 acres adjoining this on Aug 9, 1897. Mr. Beliew donated one acre of this for establishing a Christian Church and adjacent cemetery. The remaining 79 acres were sold to Mr. L. P. Johns on Dec 4, 1901. Both Nancy and Aaron Beliew died shortly after 1901 and were the first persons buried in the country churchyard. Both the church and the cemetery were referred to as "Beliew Hill".

Beliew Hill Church was a Christian church located at the southeast corner of the cemetery. The old Beliew Church was approximately 200 yards down from the southeast corner of the cemetery. Here, Uncle Charlie grew up and eventually bought much of the land in the area. Only small white concrete markers, bearing no inscriptions, mark the graves of Aaron and Nancy Beliew. For many years the two graves were covered with a brick mausoleum, but this gradually crumbled and was removed from the cemetery. Exact location of the graves is included in the Cemetery Census located in the Lipscomb Room of the Greene County Library.

On May 17, 1891, Charlie Beliew was married to Sarah Emmaline Jamison, long known by friends and relatives as "Aunt Liney". To them were born four children: Hattie, who died at three days of age; Enos, who married Laura Swindle; Hoyt, who first married Beulah Tarrance; later, Pat Breckenridge and Lillie May, who died at the age of 17, shortly after being married to Obe Owen.

The Beliew family remained in the Union-Breckenridge Township area for a number of years, continuing to farm. However, they later moved to Rector, where "Uncle Charlie" died on July 18, 1958. "Aunt Liney" died Oct 10, 1962.

## Center Hill

Center Hill is thought to have had its first settlers in the early 1830s, soon after the Crowleys settled on the Ridge in 1822. The Austins were listed in the county's first tax records in 1833.

The Dovers, Cravens, Hamptons, Grooms, Turners and Stevensons were also among some of the early settlers of Center Hill.

The old Spring Grove Church, which probably started in the 1850s and was located on a 40-acre tract owned by Joe Austin, became known as Center Hill Baptist Church when a new church building was constructed on a different site.

The naming of the church came about because of its location. It was suggested that the church be called "Cedar Hill" because of the many cedars growing in the area. However, others felt it should be called "Center Hill" since it was centrally located between two creek bottoms.

Fire destroyed the Spring Grove Church and many records in 1880. The new church was constructed about a mile from the original site in 1883. The church building was also used as a school and was known as Spring Grove School.

The Center Hill Community is located two miles west of Paragould and was merged with the city in 1974. It became Paragould's fourth ward. The area of the addition comprised about 1000 acres. In 1986, it was extended to include Tech High School and its campuses.

## Coffman

The Coffman Community, located in the southeastern part of Greene County, is said to have first been settled in 1880 by Ross Coffman, who came to Arkansas from Indiana.

Mr. Coffman first purchased 400 acres at one dollar per acre, later he became the owner of 3,000 acres, most of which he cleared. However, later he disposed of approximately one-third of his holdings because it was too expensive to farm in that early day.

Coffman brought a sawmill from Indiana, which he erected on his farm. He also had a brickyard and a cotton gin. A tall windmill, was for many years, a landmark on his farm and it was used for power to generate electricity. The Coffman home was one of the first in the county to have running water and a bathroom. People would come from miles around to view this modern feature.

There was also a gristmill, owned by Mark Overman, in the community.

At the time Coffman settled in Greene County that area was a wooded wilderness. There was a boat landing, named Mitchell Point, on the St. Francis River to the south of the Coffman farm. Steamboats from as far away as Helena, AR would dock there. The landing was eventually abandoned, but during prohibition days, it was claimed to be a rendezvous for moonshiners.

The first schoolhouse, a small one-room structure, was built in 1895. In 1922, a two-room house was built and used until 1939, when the district was consolidated with Lakeside District and the Lakeside School built.

A tornado hit the community in the spring of 1911 and destroyed most of the fruit trees and leveled many of the houses and barns.

Robb's Chapel Baptist Church was built in 1924, adjacent to the schoolhouse, on land donated by Mrs. Ina Robb. Services were formerly held in the schoolhouse.

Until 1922, the main road to Coffman ran diagonally through the woods from Paragould and it was necessary to lay a timber or log base to keep it passable. In 1922 a new road was built, although in bad weather this road was not easy to travel. In 1939, the road was resurfaced by the WPA and has since become a good road maintained by the county.

Early settlers in the Coffman Community besides the Coffman family included the following: J. W. Latherman, Tom Hopkins, Frank Dover, J. J. Montieth, Marion Holligan, John Robinson, Nick Hoyer and Arthur Wadley.

## Commissary

This information was taken from the *Greene County Historical Quarterly, Volume 2, 1966,* by Mrs. Jeff Morrow:

The community of Commissary, located about 12 miles northwest of Paragould, was originally known as Jackson's Commissary.

Richard Jackson, a member of a pioneer Greene County family, had purchased extensive timber holdings in that part of the county and built a saw mill and opened a store to take care of the mercantile needs of the workers. In a short time, a community was established.

The date of the establishment of the sawmill as Commissary must have been around 1885, which was the date the branch line of the Cash Valley Railroad was built. A branch line rant to Jackson's sawmill; there was another line to Johnson's sawmill on the Daniel Futrell farm and one south of Big Rocks to a gravel pit. The line to the gravel pit was taken up in 1896.

Besides the Jackson's store, there were stores owned by Sam and Will Morrow (later owned by Charlie Chadwick), Gamewell Gregory and Lee White. Other businesses included a blacksmith shop, a gristmill and cotton gin. The telephone switchboard was located at Catwalk's and was operated by Nora Catwalk.

Some of the pioneer families near Commissary were: Wod Bowlin, T. R. Rogers, Clarks, Bateys, Brattons, Futrells, Halls, Autreys, Andrews, Smelsers, Morrows, Smiths, Johns and Taylors.

Some of the doctors in that vicinity included Doctors Shoals, Biggs, Gregory, Cupp, McKinzie, Dickenson and Farley.

## Delaplaine

Located in the northwestern corner of Greene County early settlers of Delaplaine found remains of a French-Indian trading post. When the St. Louis-Iron Mountain Line extended into Arkansas in 1873 a station stop was established at this cross roads and called Grey's Station; later officially given the French name De La Plaine (of the plains). This rail line served the entire county for passenger and freight services. James W. Wray published the county's first newspaper at Delaplaine in 1873.

There were few settlers prior to Civil War, but it was the timber industry in the late 1870s thru the turn of the century that promoted population growth. A large timber mill at Brookings on Black River used a wooden rail line to Mollus Crossing about a mile north of Delaplaine and flat cars pulled by oxen took

*Delaplaine Depot, 1912*

*Epsaba Cemetery*

the giant logs two miles thru the forest to the main line.

The town was incorporated in April 1912. A fire destroyed the main part of town April 16, 1922. Delaplaine had been a boomtown prior to this time. The timber industry was supplanted by agriculture; cotton and later rice and soybeans became the principle crops. Cotton ginning vanished in the late 1950s and was replaced by a soybean and rice elevator now operated by Riceland Foods.

In 1937 10 schools united to form the Delaplaine School District, providing a high school for this area.

## Epsaba

Dennis Cole who migrated to Greene County from North Carolina via Tennessee settled Epsaba Community in the early 1870s. He and his family came by wagon train pulled by mules and oxen.

When Dennis first arrived in the area in the late 1850s he began farming in the Cache River bottomland where he found flooding to be a problem. Soon he moved to Pine Hill on Crowley's Ridge where he homesteaded a section of land. Other families moved to the community, built homes and started farming.

They raised tobacco, corn, livestock food and some cotton. There was also a sawmill, a gristmill, a sorghum mill and a blacksmith shop. The families raised all of their own food. They corded the wool from sheep to make sweaters, socks and caps. They made coffins out of pine as needed. Influenza and colds were treated with sugar and kerosene. Putting tallow on a poultice on the chest was the treatment for pneumonia.

Dennis built a home from logs for his family and gave two acres of his land for a church and a school. Being the oldest man in the community, he was given the honor of naming the community. Recalling a church in North Carolina by the name of Epsaba, taken from the *Holy Bible*, he decided on this name for the community and the church. "Thou shalt no more be termed forsaken; neither shall thy land be termed desolate; but thou shalt be called Hephzibah and thy land Beulah; for the Lord delighteth in thee and thy land shall be married." Isaiah 62:4. The church, which was the center of the community, was rebuilt twice. It was first destroyed by fire and next it was demolished by a tornado. The last building was converted to a residence and is no longer standing.

John Thomas Cole, oldest son of Dennis, gave two acres of his land for the establishment of the Epsaba Cemetery. Founded in 1872, it is still in use today. The first burial was an infant of a relative by the name of Stanford. Later John Cole's son, Ned Rochelle Cole, designated Epsaba Cemetery as a community cemetery, not just a family cemetery. About 180 people are buried there, including three soldiers who fought for the Confederate States of America. Veterans of more recent wars are buried there also.

The Epsaba Community, started by courageous, hard-working people who lived simple lives, still exists in records but more in the memories and hearts of the descendants of those early pioneers.

*Submitted by Rochelle Robert Penny*

## Finch

Finch Community is located about 10 miles southwest of Paragould. "Finch" was the name of the first schoolmaster to conduct a school in that area. It must have started before 1878, because a post office was granted in August of that year, under the name of Finch, with Albert A. Arnold as postmaster.

In the earlier days, the area in which Finch is located was blessed with several good creeks and springs, such as Poplar, Village and Thompson Creeks. Village Creek was so named because an Indian village once stood on its banks. Thompson Creek was named for the Lawrence Thompson family, early settlers of that area and Poplar Creek was so named because of the poplar timber growing on its banks.

Among the first settlers on Village Creek was Sterling Newsom. Legend says that Sterling built the first treadmill cotton gin at Finch, in cooperation with Bill Cone.

Following is a list of postmasters at Finch, who also were often storekeepers. The first was Arnold; Obediah Newsome, December 1880;

*Second Epsaba Church Building*

*Finch baseball team, 1904*

James Herren, April 1882; William Cone, May 1882; James Newsome, January 1888; Arthur Lovelace, January 1891; Thomas Anthony, November 1897 and the last was Joseph Thompson, October 1900.

Some of the early storekeepers were: David Edwards, Tom Fletcher, Jim Pillow, Jim Hyde, Ezra Newman, Tom and Lawrence Newberry, Gove and Florence Fletcher, Tom Gill, Gaylen Levine, Tom Horton, Ed Thompson, O. H. Payne, Erving Ellington, Tom Hargrove, Willie Wood and Carol Payne.

Finch was a thriving community in its early days.

## Fontaine

If you come to the intersection of Arkansas Highways 228 and 168 in southwest Greene County, it is hard to imagine you are at the center of the once bustling community of Fontaine, a place inhabited by Native Americans for thousands of years. In its heyday, the first half of the 20th century, Fontaine boasted three churches, a school, two general stores, a post office, a cotton gin and grain elevator, sawmills, a railroad, blacksmiths, a baseball field, a place where movies were shown weekly, a cemetery and even a 'canning kitchen' during the depression. Arkansas Highway 228 from Sedgwick is built on the bed for the tracks of the old Cache River Valley Railroad. Before it was paved, it was unusual to travel this road without seeing several railroad spikes in the road. Countless flat tires ensued.

Even though cotton was king, probably the first rice produced in Greene County was grown on the "company farm" by W. C. Sloan, owner and operator for 50 years of the 3,400-acre farm that was the heart of the community. None of the 22 houses that were standing on this farm as late as 1960 survives today.

Many families can trace their heritage to Fontaine, probably none more so than the Scotts. Some of the many other family names include Bass, Birmingham, Childers, Cook, Fielder, Gaither, Gleghorn, Goodson, Hancock, Hefner, Jumper, Lee, Martin, Pratt, Shelton, Simpson and Songer.

Today, the area surrounding Fontaine is farmed intensively. Cotton is no longer king, now it is rice. Not much remains from the heyday, only the churches and the cemetery.

## Gainesville

Historians tell us that about 1842 Gainesville was already a well-developed village. For over 40 years, Gainesville was the only community of any size in Greene County and was the center of county business.

The first county seat was located at Paris and remained there until around 1840. The exact location of Paris is uncertain. Different points in the county competed for the relocation of the county seat. The one where Gainesville was situated gained the location, hence the name, "Gainesville".

According to Goodspeed's History of Greene County, a log courthouse and jail were constructed, but was soon abandoned and replaced by a three-story frame courthouse. The

*Gainesville Depot*

county offices were located on the first floor, the courtroom on the second floor and a Masonic hall on the third. That building, along with a portion of the county records, was burned in 1874. A storeroom was rented for a courthouse, but it was also destroyed, along with the remaining records, that same year.

Another storeroom was found for a temporary court office, but in 1876, it also burned along with the accumulated records. All of these fires were judged to be arson set by persons seeking to destroy records of evidence uncovered by a grand jury that had indicted them.

A one-story frame courthouse was erected and was used until 1884, when the county seat was moved from Gainesville to its present site at Paragould.

## Halliday

This information was taken from a story submitted to the Greene County Historical Society Quarterly by Hazel Files:

The Halliday Community was named for one of the officials of the St. Louis Southwestern Railroad, later known as the "Cotton Belt" Railroad. It is believed to have started in about 1880.

The small town of Halliday was located in a

*Late 1940's – Greene County natives Charles L. Hunt and wife, Georgia (Price) Hunt with daughter, Jo Nell, wait to board the train near Scheer's General Store in Lafe.*

helpers for cutting trees and hauling timber to the mills. This gave employment to many men.

In its early days, there was a one-room school at Halliday. When the attendance increased, a second room was added and another teacher was hired. There was not a church in Halliday. However, there were some in walking distance.

Some names of early settlers were: Action, Adams, Buchanan, Carmack, Demoss, Dollins, Glisson, Lewis, Malin, Jayes, Noel, Roberts, Stout, Warbritton, Watson, Willbanks and Zolliner. Around 1912 Dr. Hudgens came to Halliday and set up his medical practice.

## Hooker

At one time Hooker was a busy community. It was a flag stop on the Helena branch of the St. Louis Iron Mountain Railroad, located near Lafe. The community became known as Hooker Switch and is still often called by that name, though the railroad has been gone for many years, as well as the sawmill.

John Hooker, a Union Army Civil War veteran, migrated with his family from Indiana in

*Bierbaum Flour Mill*

huge timber belt and offered a living and a way of life to timber workers and their families.

It was definitely a mill town. The Wrape family established a huge stave mill, from which a spur tract extended from a switch out to the mill. The logs were shipped to finishing mills.

There was a sawmill where the logs were cut into lumber. This, too, was shipped out to factories.

The Glissons owned a handle mill, producing axe and hammer handles. These were also shipped out to be finished in factories in either St. Louis or Memphis.

Each mill worked a large crew of men and

1881. He acquired land near the railroad where he built a house and erected a sawmill.

A small station was built near the mill, as were several homes when other families moved in. There were at one time two general stores, one operated by Ed Sheer and another by Carl Bishop. About anything could be purchased at these stores.

There was a school at Hooker from 1916 to 1938, at which time it consolidated with the Lafe School District.

The first Sunday school was organized in 1900 and was called the Union Sunday School, because it welcomed young people of all denominations. In 1907 the Baptists constructed a building, which is still in use and is known as the Big Creek Baptist Church.

After the sawmill closed and the railroad ceased operation, the little settlement did not have much reason to exist.

In 1936, Clifford and Ollie Winn opened and operated a grocery store until 1974, at which time they sold it to Alvin and Pat Howe. The store closed in 1980.

## Lafe

In 1886, Mr. Herman Toelken, a German immigrant, came south from his home in New Haven, Franklin County, MO seeking a new life for his family. He got off the train at Gainesville, AR with an axe and with 35 cents in his pocket.

In an effort to establish himself, he began cutting railroad ties and selling them to the railroad company. As soon as he had saved enough money he paid the railroad company $40 for 40 acres one and one-half miles east of the present town of Lafe. He built a little log shack and sent for his family in New Haven. His wife, the former Lina Ommen and their children, came on the train to Gainesville, bringing with them a dresser, a chifferobe, a bedstead and some chairs. After having paid for having the family and furniture hauled to the cabin, he again found himself with only 75 cents. Again, by cutting and selling railroad ties, he saved enough money to buy a yoke of oxen for hauling the ties. Then, seeing the abundance of good land in the area, he began advertising in a Minneapolis newspaper, the "Germania," for other German Lutherans to come and settle in the community. In fact, several had already arrived prior to the end of 1886.

In the meantime, more settlers had arrived and settled closer to the railroad. Mr. W. C. Newberry operated a large sawmill, located in the area, and as more houses and stores sprang up, the settlement became commonly referred to as "Newberry". On Dec 9, 1889, Mr. Carl Gilg submitted an application to the U. S. Postal Service for establishment of a post office at Newberry, AR. He described Newberry as a "flag station" on the St. Louis Iron Mountain Railroad. Records indicate that the name "Newberry" was considered by the Postal Department, but not accepted. Mr. Gilg was asked to submit another name for consideration. In selecting the name, Mr. Gilg decided to combine portions of the names of each of his three daughters, Louise, Lilly and Mary with the name subsequently becoming "Loulyma". The application listed number of inhabitants as 12. It was accepted and the official name of the little town became Loulyma.

Lolulyma would never have survived with the railroad, but it was also the railroad that caused it to disappear from the map. There was constant confusion since freight continued to come to Newberry, with the mail addressed to Loulyma. On Mar 1, 1901, Mr. Lafayette "Lafe" Mueller became postmaster at Loulyma. Determined to end the confusion, he proposed that a new name be submitted for the town. Townspeople in turn honored him by suggesting the short, yet appropriate name, "Lafe". The name was submitted and was accepted by the Post

Office Department, thus officially on May 21, 1902, the little village acquired its present name of Lafe.

### Lydia's Early Memories Of Lafe

Lafe, AR is my home. I loved the 118 acres of the farm I grew up on. It was rather hard to chop and pick cotton, but that was the way children earned money, to buy clothes and things they needed. We milked lots of cows and had the cream separated from the milk. We gave the separated milk to the hogs and sent the cream in five-gallon cans to the St. Louis Market.

Before 5:00 p.m. a Missouri Pacific train stopped at Lafe and brought mail to the post office and picked up full cans of cream and packages to be shipped. Often there would be a shipment of hundreds of baby chicks. What a noisy chirping sound would be in the post office until people picked up their orders of chicks.

During WWII several trains would go through Lafe carrying soldiers. We loved to wave at these boys as they passed through Lafe. I wrote to lots of soldiers from Lafe. It was so exciting to get letters from them. Some of these dear boys never came back; they gave their lives for their country.

My sister and I carried as many as 18 dozen eggs to stores at Lafe to exchange for groceries and money. We also carried fryer chickens to the store to be sold. They were called "spring chickens" – I guess because they were raised from baby chickens in the spring.

We loved to go fishing in the creek and we would catch lots of perch. My dad loved to eat them, even if they weren't very big.

In those days we didn't buy very much from the store except flour, sugar, baking powder and kerosene for the lamps. There were five stores in Lafe at the time. There were five churches in and around Lafe. There were several doctors and they made house calls at the time. Some doctors traded out their bill for potatoes, pork or anything their patients had to trade.

We had no iceboxes or refrigerators in those days. We had to eat the food we cooked for that day. We had lots of canned foods –400 to 500 quarts of fruits and vegetables.

The 1930s were very rough during the depression years. It was hard to have food and clothing or pennies in our pockets. We didn't get a new dress except Christmas or Easter. We didn't have battery radios until the 1940s.

Lafe people had lots of fun. We had ball teams. At night they would have parties, playing games and have singing games. One game was "Happy is the Miller boy that lived by the Mill." At the school we had plays and musicals. At noon when you worked in the field you could hear neighbors' dinner bells ringing all over the country. "Come home – it's dinnertime." Often we would be working in the fields and hear church bells ringing, which meant someone had passed away.

Families who were wealthy finally got a car, which was an A model or 1927 Chevrolet.

Children made their toys out of sticks and cans because they only got toys at Christmas. Those were good old days – but hard times, too.

God helped us through those days and we can look back at the memories we love.

*Submitted by Lydia Tritch*

## Light

The community of Light was settled by and named for Warner Light who owned land and brought his family to live there in approximately 1885. As an earlier small community, it was called Cache and was located in Cache Township, which was one of the three original townships formed before 1840. Today it is in Bryan Township.

A post office was granted in the name of Cache in 1881, but was withdrawn the next year, probably because of population decrease. That area off the ridge and toward the Cache Bottoms was thinly settled because the temperamental Cache River turned it into a slough. Today an extensive drainage system keeps overflow from happening.

The Lights were stockmen from Georgia. As he acquired more land, the name of Cache was gradually dropped and became known as Light.

The Cache Bottoms were heavily covered with valuable hardwood timber and in 1897 a short line known as the Cache Valley Railroad, a branch from the Frisco Railroad in Craighead County, was built into Greene County from Sedgwick and the line ended in Light. This was a tramline to carry timber from the Cache forests to the mills along the route. One of the largest companies operating in the area was that of Herget-Stout Company.

A large sawmill had been built at Light and also a commissary, which provided provisions to the timber workers. Among the men working at the mill was J.E. Newberry, who lived at Walcott and operated a mule breeding business during the months the mill was closed. He moved to Light around 1912 and bought interest in a store owned by Lawrence Dacus and became its manager. A second post office had been granted to Light in 1901 and was located in the store. The post office still maintains service today, although under a different arrangement.

Through the years Light has been home to restaurants, a theater, schools, churches, groceries and gas stations and beauty shops. J. E. Newberry married Rosa Biggs in 1898 and one of their daughters; Laura married Vance Cupp in 1922. In 1933 a cotton gin was built and managed by Vance and his family until 1979 when grain-wheat, corn, beans and milo – took first place in farming in that area. The gin was closed and a grain business took over which is known as Vance Cupp and Sons, Inc. and is managed by Vance Cupp Jr. one of the five children of Vance and Laura. The general store and station is owned and managed by another son, James M. Cupp.

A school was established in 1906 and remained until 1949 when it consolidated with Greene County Tech School District.

*Source: Mueller History of Greene County*
*Submitted by Evangeline (Cupp) Cothren*

## Lorado

Lorado, located just above the Craighead County line, five miles south of Walcott, was one of the earlier settlements of Greene County. However, it seems it did not really flourish until about 1900. A post office was established in 1848 and was there until 1913. For some time it was a well-defined community with about 200 inhabitants. At one time there were two general stores, two gristmills, two blacksmiths, an axe-handle business, a cotton gin and a telephone exchange.

It seems there was always a doctor in residence, with Dr. J. D. Blackwood being the last to practice there. Other doctors who at one time lived and practiced there included Doctors Estes, Russell and Lamb.

Among some of the early settlers were the Adams, Blackwoods, Burtons, Catheys, Dennises, Estes, Lambs, Nutts, Russells and Willcoxens.

Business tended to follow railroads and when the railroad was put through Greene County it missed Lorado; hence, the community began to die. However, there are still several families living in the community.

## Marmaduke

*Goodspeed's History of Greene County, AR,* published in Oct 1889 stated that "Marmaduke, a town of about 200 inhabitants on the "Cotton Belt" Railroad, 12 miles northeast of Paragould, contains four stores, a blacksmith shop, cotton gin and press, a church, a schoolhouse, a sawmill and a boarding house. From here a tramway is run a mile out on the St. Francis River, where other mills are located. The village was first laid out in 1882 by the Railroad Company."

Many pioneers had settled the road to Gainsville and about 1847, according to historical documents, there was already a store where the Delta Cotton Co-Op is located and two log cabins.

Mrs. Emma Barton Moore was born Jan 31, 1876, in a log cabin where the Methodist Church is now located and the other cabin was on the corner across from the post office. These cabins were on the way to Gainsville where the early settlers received their mail and purchased supplies. The settlement had begun.

Naming The Town

According to one account:

The town of Marmaduke was named for Major-General John Sappington Marmaduke of the Confederate Army, who later became the governor of the state of Missouri. The general's name was bestowed upon the town to commemorate a camp that was established by General Marmaduke for his troops.

Another factor in naming the towns along this new branch line seemed to be related to the names of the men connected with the railroad or to men with interests in the railroad construction (as in the case of Paragould.) John S. Marmaduke had served on the Missouri Railway Commission from 1875 until 1880 and no doubt would have served as a resource of information in developing the new line and probably gave information regarding the terrain and accessibility. Too, it seems reasonable that many railway employees and personnel would have heard of the exploits of Marmaduke during the Civil War.

Marmaduke became an incorporated town with ordinance number one, naming the governing officers, the manner of their elections, qualifications, powers and duties, meeting

*In 1905 the Vaile Donaldson Company, a large corporation, purchased the Huckabay business interests along with several other mills near Marmaduke.*

times, salaries, jurors and witness fees on Aug 2, 1909 and this Ordinance was signed by E. P. Holt, mayor of the town. Attest. by J. H. Boone, Recorder.

One resident recalled, "that in 1914, Marmaduke had two drugstores, three banks, three good restaurants, two churches, the Methodist and Baptist, as the Church of Christ was located about two miles out of town, two "dime stores", two barber shops and a hotel and boarding house. Marmaduke was a good-sized town in 1914. There were wooden walks downtown and everyone owned a cow those days because you couldn't buy milk in stores." The timber kept the people here and business booming. A lumber mill, a stave mill, a sawmill and the large lumber and cut timber distributors provided employment for the residents. The number of available employees included many young women in the stave mills and the work was hard and hours, long.

In an interview in 1982, with the former postmaster, Elmer McHaney stated that Marmaduke was a busy place when he first came. "There were four blacksmiths, all the mail was rural delivery, either buggy or horseback. There was the Vale Donaldson. Company, the Band Mill and the Stave Mill, which worked many people. There were 25 bootleggers, three cotton gins and three banks, The Marmaduke Bank, The Farmers Bank and the Farmers Union Bank. There were four or five doctors but none could make much of a living. Dr. Hudgeins, Dr. Clopton, Dr. Hawkins and Dr. Kennedy. There was a general store, the Racket Store (general merchandise), The Bertig Company and a drugstore. There was a café and old "Dad" Wilson was the mayor of the town".

Currently the population of Marmaduke is 1100 plus with a good school system, two factories, the Anchor (plastics) Company and the American Rail Car Company. The town continues with the same type of government as elected officers for mayor and city council.

*Submitted by Mona L. Fielder*

## Providence

One of the oldest and certainly the most recognizable areas in Northern Greene County is the Providence Community. Providence Baptist Church is said to be one of the oldest churches in Greene County. "*A Brief History of the Bethlehem Missionary Baptist Association*", published in 1944, states that Providence Church was established in 1874. ("*Statistics Records of Arkansas*", Volume II, Church Records, gives its date of organization as even earlier, in 1866). At any rate, it was initially located one mile south of Gainesville. In 1885, the membership voted to move the church to its present site, two miles east of Lafe, alongside what is now Highway # 34. The first building was destroyed by fire in the late 1890s. Another large wood frame building was then constructed and remained until the 1950s, when it was replaced with the present brick structure.

Charter members of the old original church were listed as Hezekiah Wright, Mrs. Hezekiah Wright, Newton Wright, Jasper Wright, Squire Bohannan, James Lax, Mrs. James Lax, Benjamin Lax, Elijah Haneline, Mrs. Elijah Haneline and Mrs. Tabitha Rutledge.

Providence Church, perhaps because of its convenient centralized location, has always enjoyed good attendance. Highway 34, now paved from Lafe to Marmaduke, runs along the southern edge of the property, rather than the north side as the old county road had run.

Providence School is one that will be long remembered by many people in northern Greene County. The first school was located on land owned by Mr. Lige Tigg and became known as the Tigg School. This was located approximately three-fourths mile southeast of the present church building. The teachers at Tigg School included Tom Jackman and Powell Middleton.

In 1905 a new school was constructed north of this school. It was still approximately one-half mile east of the church and on the opposite side of the road. It then became known as the Providence School.

Some of the instructors here included: Mrs. Lee Ramsey, Miss Clara Ruth Grimes, Professor C. E. Bond, Ruth Thompson, Mr. Luther Starnes, Mr. Gerald Starnes and Mr. John Marshall Starnes. The school consolidated with Lafe in 1946.

The first seat of the Greene County government was located in Providence Community at Paris, AR. There are no remains of Paris. Government matters were said to have been conducted in the home of Mr. Bohannon.

## Scatter Creek

From several tiny tributaries in Union township, approximately two and one half miles southwest of Lafe, Scatter Creek is formed, then channels due north into Breckenridge Township. Shortly after it passes to the west of Hooker, a canal ditch drains it into Cache River. Scatter Creek community generally refers to the area due west of Lafe. It was never a village as such, but did boast of a good church and school. Both were located near where Scatter Creek Road turns directly south. The first school was a one room frame building located across the road from Scatter Creek Methodist Church. The school burned in 1911 and a new one was built. Those known to have taught school there include: Lela Bishop, Dick Poole, Albert Jackson, a Miss Garner, Orley Johnston, Myrtle Weddington, Clara Meadows, Roy Walden, Irvin Butler, Elsie Livesay and Verla Gerdes. The school held classes for all 12 grades in the later years and at one time had an enrollment of 94 pupils.

Scatter Creek School consolidated with Lafe in 1944. The church then purchased the building and services were held there. A Methodist Church had been built in Lafe approximately 15 years previously and most of the members left Scatter Creek to attend services in Lafe. However, membership dwindled there, too, and services were finally discontinued. On Nov 14, 1968 the building was purchased by members of Hurricane Methodist Church and placed alongside Highway 34, about one-half mile north of old Hurricane and just across the line from Breckenridge Township.

## Stanford

The Stantford Smith family was one of the earliest settlers in this community. They came to this area around 1852 and acquired 160 acres of "wild land" along sugar creek, which was at that time a spring fed swift stream. His farm was near the present location of Stanford. From the beginning cotton was an important part of the economy. Mr. Smith owned and operated the first cotton gin in this area. It was probably powered by a water wheel on sugar creek. The second T in Stantford's name was dropped and for over 100 years the community has been called Stanford. Mr. Smith and his son David were skilled carpenters and built many of the homes in this area.

Other pioneer families that have owned cotton gins were: John Herren, W. C. Gramling and sons Jesse and Earl and B. A. Robb. Both Gramling and Robb gins became farmer owned and established the Stanford Co-op Gin Corporation.

In 1901 a post office was established. This same year Dr. George Self began a much needed and appreciated medical practice here and was later elected Greene County Judge. He practiced in Stanford for 40 years.

Hunts Chapel Methodist Church was organized in 1917. Also a church of Christ was built at an early date. Earl Gramling described Stanford before WWII as being a very active little community.

Some of the early settlers were: Smith, Herren, Gramling, Shewmaker, Robb, Self and Gardner.

## Stonewall

Stonewall was never more than a small neighborhood that is located on the north-central boundary of Greene County, and began as one of the many flag stops on the Knobel-Helena branch of the Iron Mountain Railroad, to service several sawmills in the vicinity.

Application was made by Joseph Collins to the Post Office Department in January 1884, requesting the establishment of a post office under the name of Collinsville. The application was returned pending the selection of another name, since there was already a Collins and a Collins Bluff in the State.

The community had been referred to as Stonewall because of levee walls made of large stones that the railroad had constructed on either side of the river to prevent flooding of the tracks. The name "Stonewall" was submitted and accepted, and on February 5, 1884 the post office was established, with Mr. Collins as postmaster.

Since Stonewall was adjacent to Cache River it was a favorite hunting and fishing ground. Local farmers once supplemented their income from hunting and fishing. For a short period around 1900 a group of St. Louis sportsmen maintained a hunting lodge at Stonewall.

For a few years (ca. 1908) there was a box factory owned by a firm from Kalamazoo, Michigan that manufactured crates for strawberries. A sawmill was operated in conjunction with the factory. They both closed in 1915.

Stonewall's first school was a one-room school built in 1909 with Harry Layman as first teacher. They consolidated with Lafe in 1950.

## Tokio

The Tokio Community was located between Rector and Marmaduke. It seems that the J. N. "Newt" Merideth family was a big part of the community.

Mr. Merideth operated a sorghum mill in the Tokio Community on the Merideth farm adjoining the Tokio Church that Mr. Merideth donated for church and school purposes.

In 1937 the Tokio School District consolidated with the Marmaduke School District. After the consolidation of the school the building continued to be used as a church building and other community activities.

## Walcott

The Crowley family made the first settlement in Greene County in this area in 1822. Benjamin Crowley's plantation extended near where Walcott is now located.

Legend states that the first post office was established in the Crowley home in 1832 and mail addressed to Crowley, AR. In 1841 George Croft was listed as postmaster at Walcott. This post office was established and closed several times, probably due to political changes.

There is a legend concerning a Walls family that lived in this area. It is said that a Mr. Walls placed a cot in his yard and enjoyed reclining outside. People began referring to the area as Wall's cot, giving the town its name.

Walcott became a flourishing town from 1900 to 1920. It was incorporated in 1908 to enforce an ordinance prohibiting animals to be pastured within the town's limits. There were several general stores, a drug store, blacksmith shop, movie theatre, cotton gin, bank and sawmill. "Ole timers" state that it was a "lively" little town.

Some of the early settlers were: Crowleys, Gramlings, Campbells, Fielders, Hutchins, Peevehouse, Wall, Lamb, Land, Croft, Blackwood, Borrow, Sibert, Steinberg and Robinsons.

Crowley's Ridge State Park was developed by the Civilian Conservation Corps from

*Merideth Sorgum Mill in the Tokio Community in Greene County Arkansas, 1905*

*John L. and Cora Goins, April 12, 1982 (Dad's last Easter on Big Rocks); Grandchildren in background.*

*Descendants of Benjamin Crowley who attended the homecoming: L-R: Cora Goins, second great granddaughter of Benjamin Crowley; Eula (Crowley) Hughes, second great granddaughter of Benjamin Crowley; Clint Gramling, fourth great grandson; Vickey (Gramling) Brents, fourth great granddaughter; Judy (Hughes) Gramling, third great granddaughter; Nathan C. Gramling, fifth great grandson.*

1933-1935 under the leadership of Belle Hodges Wall of the Paragould Chamber of Commerce and W. R. Heagler, engineer and camp superintendent of the CCC boys. A beautiful park is now maintained in the area settled by the Crowley family.

## Big Rocks

A historic and scenic spot in Greene County is located north of Stanford off Highway 141. The Big Rocks have been a meeting place and ideal picnic site for school children, friends and family. This historic spot has been in the Goins family for the past 90 years when William Preston Goins purchased the land from Nancy Smith in 1910.

This massive rock out cropping with giant boulders stacked haphazardly together, some perched on each other as high as a two-story building. The Big Rocks have been a meeting and picnic spot, especially on Easter for years. Picnickers would come in wagons and buggies, on horseback and on foot, bring baskets of food as well as feed for the horses. There are flat tables rocks to lay the dinner on.

One rock has a hole through it and is called the Needle's Eye through which children like to play as they crawl over the giant rocks. The Big Rocks is on a Scenic Byway and is the highest spot on Crowley's Ridge. The highest rock commands a spectacular view of lush green fields stretching as far as the eye can see.

The picnics have long been discontinued, but the Goins family and friends still gather there every Easter for their traditional egg hunt.

*Submitted by Louise Goins Richardson*

## Crowley's Ridge, Jones Ridge and Big Rock

Situated in Greene County are some very unusual geological formations. Foremost of these is Crowley's Ridge. Two others in this area are Jones Ridge and Big Rock.

Crowley's Ridge was created during the Ice Age when glaciers centered over the Great Lakes area. As they retreated to the north their outwash formed Crowley's Ridge. Through the ages it eroded into hills and valleys. As you near the lower end of the Ridge to the south you encounter loess soil, which was deposited by the wind. Some of this soil was so dense, it is not as badly eroded as other parts of Crowley's Ridge. Huge boulders and much petrified wood have been found in places on the ridge. At my home a well digger encountered, at a depth of 54 feet, a log he was unable to bore through. Crowley's Ridge is a good source of sand and gravel. Also, it is covered with oak and pine timber.

The second geological oddity is Jones Ridge. This is a low ridge running east and west for about five miles. It was probably caused from an upheaval of the earth's surface many years ago. It is extensive, but in no way comparable to Crowley's Ridge. Many stone artifacts have been found on Jones Ridge. In order to see this phenomenon of nature, follow Highway 34 toward Delaplaine, cross Cache River and look to the east.

The third oddity in this area is a place known as Big Rock. It is about 10 miles west of Paragould and a short distance north of Highway 412. Big Rock used to be a popular place for school picnics to be held. Located nearby is Sugar Creek that used to be a good creek in which to fish but now has almost disappeared and is only a small stream. The little village of Stanford is the closest settlement. At Big Rock one can see rocks larger than a house. A glacial outwash almost covered a mountain there.

## Homecoming: Crowley's Ridge State Park, May 20, 1989

An unveiling of the new Shilo cemetery sign and rededication of the Bell Hodges Wall Amphitheater was held at Crowley's Ridge State Park. A special historical pageant was presented on Saturday night, directed by Dr. Jay Springman.

A special community church service was held on Sunday and representatives from a number of local churches were featured.

Among those buried in the old Shilo Cemetery are: Benjamin Crowley and wife; Larkin Wiley and wife, daughter and son; Mr. Pevehouse and wife; U. P. K. Luster's child. Jake Sutfin and wife; John Wesley Willingham and two daughters; Abe Tennison and wife: Stanton Smith and wife; Mrs. Cynthia Hester; Samuel Crowley and wife; Alfred Smith; Margaret Smith; R. Deason and wife; Poke Autry; Pete Russel; Tom Boyd; Bill Smith; Bill Sutfin; Billy Tennyson; Jonathan Sutfin; Charles Sutfin and Mrs. Esinger.

*Submitted by Judy Gramling*

## Crowley's Ridge Story

The pioneers, sporting long dresses and bonnets, coonskin hats and suspenders, sat along the rows of benches in the amphitheater, waiting for their moment in history.

But first came the American Indians, with their chiefs dressed in full regalia and their women and children preparing to make pottery, tan hides and prepare dolls.

It was all part of a practice session for "The Crowley's Ridge Story," an historical drama to be presented June 2, 1990 at the Belle Hodges Wall Amphitheater at Crowley's Ridge State Park. Admission to the event, scheduled to begin at 8 p.m., is free.

During a practice session last week, Wanda Lee Vaughn, writer-director for the program, told cast members they had managed to accomplish an intended purpose with the rehearsed segment. "You did weave a little magic," she told them. "This is what we want to do ... weave a little magic."

In the midst of weaving that magic, the cast from Greene, Clay, Craighead, Randolph and Lawrence counties will weave parts of the past together into a dramatic presentation chronicling the history of the ridge and its people.

In addition to contributions from Vaughn, Larry Clifford and Rick and Brenda Lane are contributing writers and directors. Ruth Hall is costume and technical director for the Redman segment. Jim Vaughn is narrator and sound director. Eddie DeBoard is lighting director and Lola Gray is publicity director.

*New Shiloh Cemetery sign*

*June 2, 1990 – Crowley's Ridge Story (L to R): Clint, Ann, and Nathan Gramling*

Charlotte Thompson portrays Belle Hodges Wall, the chamber of commerce secretary who dreamed of seeing a park established on the ridge, and Joe Linam plays W.R. Heagler, the Civilian Conservation Corps engineer instrumental in the park's founding and the first park superintendent.

Terry Waits portrays George Moreland, a writer for the Memphis *Commercial Appeal* who helped Wall. Rick Lane portrays Benjamin Crowley, the settler for whom the ridge was named.

Several of the Crowley family descendants will be part of the presentation. Among them: Judy Gramling portrays Annie Crowley, who was her great-great-great-grandmother and Nathan Gramling, the great-great-great-great-great-grandson of Ben Crowley, is expected to dance to "Froggie Went A Courtin'" in one of the pioneer scenes.

Crowley isn't the only one with descendants in the cast. American Indians also seem to be well-represented. Enid Thomen, who portrays a native American doing bead work in The Redman segment, notes most of the cast members in that portion are descendants of native Americans.

All are parts of the Crowley's Ridge story.

*Submitted by Judy Gramling, permission of the* Paragould Daily Press

## Meadow's Grove

On the south side of State Road 141, about half way between Hooker and Beech Grove, lies a small cemetery by the name of Meadow's Grove. Mr. Dave Meadows, his wife Barbra and some of their children moved to the area from Moline, IL in the mid-1850s purchased 43 1/2 acres of land and built their home.

Dave and Barbra Meadows had five sons: Bartholomew, Henderson, Nathaniel, Hamilton and Buchanan. Buchanan died in 1858 as an infant and was buried just north of the home. Within the next 28 years, Mr. and Mrs. Meadows and the other four sons had all died, three sons dying in their early 20s and one at age 34.

Nathaniel Meadows and his wife both died at early ages, leaving a small son David H., who was taken to live with the A. G. Breckenridge family. He later married and continued to farm in the same general area. He and his wife Amanda, were the parents of six children: Fannie, Winnie, Clara, Ella, Elgin and Cecil. Fannie was married to John Dowler.

In the late 1800s a school was built just north of the Meadow's Grove Cemetery, at the foot of the hill and appropriately named Meadow's Grove. Fannie Meadows was one of the teachers in the little school. In 1914 the Meadow's Grove district was split, with one portion being consolidated with Beech Grove. The little Meadow's Grove School was no longer centrally located in the remaining district and was too small and inadequate to accommodate the growing number of students. In 1916, another school was built about two miles east of Meadow's Grove, on land donated by Harris Earp. Because Mr. Alvin Jackson had the largest number of children attending the school it was named "Jackson College" by Mr. Grover Eaker. Some of the teachers at Jackson College included: Vera Davidson, Della Breckenridge, Charles Wells, George Butler, Clara Starnes and Hester Starnes.

Mr. Jackson and Mr. Avery Cunningham both served as school directors. The school (Meadow's Grove District) consolidated with Gum Grove and Beech Grove in 1928.

## The Oldest Known Working Well in Greene County

In the spring of 1988 while my cousin Inez Morrow Clark and I were visiting her sister and my cousin, Judy Morrow Mock, in her home in Poplar Bluff, MO, she loaned me many important papers belonging to my Grandmother and Grandfather Goins. My Grandmother Goins and my Aunt Pearl Goins Morrow have carefully preserved them through the years.

These papers included their tax receipts from 1880 to 1900; also, two warranty deeds, which are as follows:

One deed reads: Captain Joel C. Anderson sold Francis R. Clark twenty-five acres of land in Township 17 North of Range 5 in 1880 (June 15) for $72.50. Recorded in Deed Book 1, Page 765, at Gainsville, AR, Aug 2, 1881.

The other deed reads: Francis L. Clark bought 40 acres Aug 3, 1887 from the St. Louis Iron Mountain and Southern Railway, in Township 17 Range 5 for $180. Record Book 6, Page 212, recorded Feb 14, 1888.

W. P. Goins' tax receipts show he bought 40 acres in Section 3, Township 16, Range 6 when he first moved to Arkansas from Illinois.

I took these deeds to Francis Bland and learned Francis R. Clark was his great uncle for whom his father, Herbert Francis and he were named. Also, Captain Joel C. Anderson (a Captain in the Civil War) was Winnie Bland's great grandmother's cousin. Captain Joel C. Anderson trained to be a soldier in England. He was the son of John Anderson and grandson of John Anderson, a Revolutionary War soldier. Winnie Bland did the research on this family.

In the Greene County Courthouse Francis found the deed where my grandfather and grandmother Goins purchased the land from Francis R. Clark. This supports the fact that my grandparents purchased 104 1/2 acres in 1889 from Francis R. Clark for $2,000. as recorded in Deed Book 7, Page 428.

In 1891 Grandpa bought two more acres in Township 17, Range 5. His tax receipts show all but two acres of this land in Section 22, Township 17; Range 5 was sold to Albert Louis Schnivving in 1893.

David Allen Goins (a great grandson of William Preston Goins), Francis Bland and I went searching for the property located on Mount Carmel Road. We walked over the property lines looking for the house place. While searching we talked with Mrs. Herbert Walden and discovered she now owns and resides on the land that was the house place.

There we made an interesting discovery when we learned Mrs. Walden is still using a well dug by Francis R. Clark, who was "a well digger in 1880." Francis and David Allen drew a bucket of water from the well and we all drank good, fresh water from the oldest known working well in Greene County. Mrs. Walden then watered her flowers with the rest of the water.

Mrs. Walden is an interesting conversationalist. She now has city water and every convenience, but maintains the well. It is enclosed in her glassed in back porch and is still in good condition.

Our visit with her was enjoyable. She described the log cabin, which was on the property when they moved there. It is not clear whether Joel Anderson or Francis R. Clark built the cabin.

The log cabin as described by Mrs. Walden is exactly like the one my grandfather built on his farm when he moved in 1897 to what was known as "Cache Bottoms" after closing the meat market in Paragould. He accepted the "Donation Act" of 160 acres of land, which today is still owned by the Goins family.

Mrs. Walden said there isn't an original picture of the cabin. She said that using rollers they moved the house, which they had lived in while their new house was being built on the former house place.

*Submitted by Louise Goins Richardson*

# Local Government

## Greene County Government

Greene County has nine elected officials. Seven of them are full time positions. Six of the officials have offices in the county courthouse, situated on Court Street in uptown Paragould.

County Judge: Jerry Shipman is the county administrator, presiding officer at the monthly Quorum Court meetings, supervisor of road department operations and presiding officer at county court sessions.

Levi Pillow, administrator of the road department, assists Shipman by directing the county's Office of Emergency Services.

Sheriff: Dan Langston, works from the department offices at the Greene County Jail located on North Rockingchair Road. He is responsible for law enforcement in the rural areas of the county as well as operation of the jail.

David Lange, Greene County Jail Administrator, oversees the day-to-day operation of the facility.

County: Linda Heritage. Heritage issues marriage licenses and is responsible for maintaining voter registration, tax, marriage license, quorum, county and probate court records.

Circuit Clerk: Ellen Johnson. Johnson maintains circuit (criminal and civil divisions), chancery and juvenile court records as well as deed records.

Treasurer: Donna Napier. Napier manages all the county funds, issuing payment for county bills and employee salaries and is responsible for maintaining county financial records.

Tax Assessor: Diana Simons. Simons maintains county assessment records and up-to-date assessments on all real estate and personal property in the county, with the exception of utilities and transportation companies. The State Assessment Coordination Division handles those assessments.

Tax Collector: Larry Kidd. Kidd collects the taxes due each year and maintains collection records.

Coroner: John Lowe. This is a part-time position. He conducts death scene investigations (murder, natural causes and accidents) and investigates all unattended deaths.

County Surveyor: Marvin Jernigan. This is a part time position.

Quorum Court: Greene County has 11 justices of the peace who represent the various townships in the county. The justices make up the county's Quorum Court. The legislative body, presided over by the county judge, meets in the chancery courtroom of the county courthouse on the second and fourth Monday nights of each month.

Justices of the Peace are:
District One: Jessie Dollars
District Two: Brent Arant
District Three: Jerry Cunningham
District Four: Omer David Overbay
District Five: Jim Diggs
District Six: Don Lambert
District Seven: Tommy Kueter
District Eight: Charles Richey
District Nine John Lynn
District 10: Bill Lovelady
District 11: Larry Faulkner

## City Government of Paragould

The Paragould City Hall, located at 302 West Court Street, houses several municipal offices as well as the police department. This building was the former City Light and Water office before they moved to their new headquarters on Jones Road.

Mayor Mike Gaskill is the city's top executive officer. Other elected or appointed officials at city hall include: City Clerk Goldie Wise, City Treasurer Laveda Smith, Sherry Childress, personnel and Americans with Disabilities Act Coordinator, Brian Gray, City Inspector/Code Enforcement officer, Police Chief Dennis Hyde and City Attorney Randy Philhours.

Paragould's governing body is composed of an eight-member city council. Council members are:
Ward One:
 Position One: Mark Rowland
Position Two: Sharon Joy
Ward Two:
Position One: Darrell Taylor
Position Two: Dale Coy
Ward Three:
Position One: Randy Aden
Position Two: J. W. Dortch
Ward Four:
Position One: Jim Inness
Position Two: Frank Gatlin.
Other city departments are:
Public works: Sandra Medsker, director
Fire Department: Eddie Brown, fire chief
City Light, Water and Cable: Larry Watson, chief executive.

Airport Commission Committee: Dr. Bill Morgan, Ed Tolleson, Dr. John Perry, Rick Dickinson and Tom Graber. City Beautiful Commission members: Darrell Taylor, Kenneth Hamilton, Virginia Highfill, Mary Ann Schreit, Bill Block, Bryant Marshall, Frankie Gilliam and Ray Lindsey. Arkansas Methodist Hospital Commission members: Roy McSpadden, Alfred Herget, Rex Bouldin, Pat Case and Mayor Mike Gaskill. Paragould Housing Commission Board members: Dr. Ron Hall, Weldon Chesser, Dorothy Green, Rex Bouldin and Pam Daniels. Paragould Planning Commission members: Mike Finch, Breck Freeman, Tommy Marlar, Bob Branch, Melvin Wamock, Edgar Byers and Glen DePriest.

*Submitted by Greene County Historical & Genealogical Society*

*Greene County, AR Quorum Court In Session, Judge Jerry Shipman, presiding. Members shown: Tommy Kueter, Judge Shipman, Don Lambert, Jim Diggs, Omer Overbay, ec. Cindi Rudi*

*Officer Arvin Volner*

*Mr. Kimbrough's (at left) first store, 1910.*

# Businesses, Organizations, Churches, Schools, Historic Homes and Memorials

# BUSINESSES

## American State Bank

American State bank was originally established in Wilson, AR in 1908 as the Bank of Wilson, but has officially been a part of Greene County since 1998. However, the roots of the northeast Arkansas bank run much deeper in the Paragould and Greene County area.

Frank Oldham, chairman of American State Bank, was formerly the chairman of Security Bank of Paragould. Steve Gramling, David Dudley and Judy Dacus were all previously with the former Security Bank as well. However, they are all currently officers with American State Bank. Joe Wessell, Community Bank President for Greene County, is another lifelong resident of Greene County and Security Bank alumnus. Hundreds of years of banking experience are vested in the hands of the personnel who provide banking services for Greene County residents.

In 1997, Mr. Oldham had begun the process of obtaining a new Greene County bank charter, following the sale of Security Bank to Union Planters Bank in 1994. Members of the R. E. Lee Wilson family in Mississippi County suggested an alternative. At their urging, the $25 million Bank of Wilson's charter was moved to Jonesboro and a banking office was established in Paragould under the new name: American State Bank.

The bank opened a loan production office in Paragould during the fall of 1998. Soon afterward, construction began on the $2 million permanent banking facility at the corner of Linwood Drive and Mockingbird Lane. Further expansion in Greene County followed, with the opening of a temporary office in Marmaduke during the fall of 1999. The permanent Marmaduke facility opened for business during the summer of 2000. An additional banking facility in Paragould also opened on West Kingshighway in August of the same year.

The involvement of Joe Wessell and the entire Greene County banking staff in their community demonstrates the "personal touch" brought to their daily customer service duties. Employees are also encouraged to come up with new and innovative ways of serving the customer. It is this kind of "thinking outside the box" that American State Bank strongly believes is a key to their success, not only in Greene County, but in northeast Arkansas.

The men and women of American State Bank are eager to improve the level of service they are able to provide to all bank customers. Mr. Wessell recognizes the important role banks have in the economic well being of Paragould and Greene County. American State Bank is able to make local lending decisions promptly and efficiently, which benefits not only the customer, but also Greene County as a whole.

American State Bank has additional offices in Craighead and Mississippi Counties as well as Greene County. The home office is located in Jonesboro and there are two additional banking facilities also in Jonesboro. Other American State Bank offices are located in Osceola, Wilson and Keiser in Mississippi County. Assets are now approaching $200 million.

In recent years, the banking industry has undergone many changes and the impact of technology has literally changed the way banks operate. With expansion into Internet banking, as well as a nationwide network of automated teller machines, American State Bank's presence now extends outside traditional banking boundaries. With the increasing number of personal computers in homes, more and more people are becoming used to conducting their banking using a computer. American State Bank has been a leader in utilizing this new technology. An example is American State Bank's web site. By visiting the bank's web site, an individual has the opportunity to learn about the bank's history, locations, products and services offered as well as finding links to other web sites. This is a great tool that enables anyone with access to a computer to find answers to a variety of banking questions, without the need to visit a specific bank office.

Another service which is gaining in popularity is Internet banking. American State Bank customers can perform a variety of banking transactions using this computer service. The bank has made plans to introduce additional computer-related services such as Internet bill paying in the immediate future. American State Bank believes that in the long run the customer will benefit from all these changes, while still realizing the importance and necessity of maintaining personal banking relationships with customers. American State Bank wants to reinforce the partnership between technology with old-fashioned person service and good customer relations. It is also essential to keep in mind the importance of American State Bank's role in the community and how vital it is to the bank's success to adapt and change with the advent of new technology, while maintaining sound banking practices. The motto of American State Bank says it all: Customer Service is Priority One.

American State Bank will continue to grow and prosper in the 21st century, along with Greene County. American State Bank is poised and ready to meet the challenges ahead while keeping in mind the rich history of the past.

# Bank of Paragould

Bank of Paragould opened its doors for business in October 1998. The company operated from a temporary facility located on site while its new bank was under construction. The bank moved into its new facility in March of 2000. The bank also established and opened a new branch location in Marmaduke around this same time. The bank has also purchased property for a future branch location at McDaniel Road and Highway 49 South.

The bank, even though only a few years old, is owned by Security State Bancshares, Incorporated a "family owned" Bank Holding Company established in the early 1930s. Bank of Paragould is proud to be a community bank located in Paragould. The bank has experienced excellent growth the first two years of operations. The bank attributes its success to concentrating its efforts on good customer service, fast local decisions and a variety of unique products. Some of the products include No-Closing-Cost Home Loans and Home Equity Loans, High Rate Money Market Accounts, Industrial Free Checking with No-Bounce Banking, Vintage Gold Seniors Account and Much More.

Bank of Paragould is Greene County's Real Community Bank maintaining its charter in Paragould, AR.

*Marmaduke Branch, 7281 Hwy 34 East*

*Main Bank, 3005 W. Kingshighway*

# City Light And Water

The story of City Light and Water dates back to 1898. But now what is City Light and Water was officially created in 1984. The Paragould City Council voted to have City Light and Power absorb Paragould Water Works.

Efforts for a public water distribution system began in 1898 when the city council helped instigate the formation of water improvement district number one. A bond issue of $28,000 financed the construction. In 1915, water improvement district number two was created and issued $25,000 in bonds to provide service in new areas. South of Kingshighway, in 1923, the two districts combined and formed district number three. A bond issue of $132,000 financed construction of a plant on East Poplar and enlarged the distribution system.

In 1891, the Paragould Electric Light and Power Company was organized by a group of Paragould's most prominent businessmen. After its 20-year contract was up in 1911, the Crystal Ice Company became the town's supplier of electricity. The city council then later gave the franchise for electricity to Arkansas Utilities Company and its successors Missouri Utilities Company, Arkansas-Missouri Power Company.

Feb 2, 1933 Paragould voters approved construction of their own electric utility. Six years separated the approval of voters and the actual start of generation on Jan 17, 1939. The plant went into service at 2:45 p.m. with operator J. C. Holland making the first entry in the power plant log.

Paragould's electric cost became lower in 1966 when the utility connected with Southwestern Power Administration. Today, the utility buys peaking power from Southwestern Power Administration and base load from the Grand River Dam Authority. During the year the utility also buys and sells on the open market with several utilities and marketers. In 1984, water and sewer were combined by Mayor Charles Partlow to form City Light and Water; the utility has added tens of millions of dollars of improvements since then. Today, the utility provides electric, water, sewer, cable and Internet services.

In June of 1990 the utility added a 16-megawatt turbine generating plant. The new capacity was added in addition to the old generating plant in downtown Paragould.

In 1990, the utility built a cable system and competed with a private cable company until April of 1998 when it was bought out by the city utility. In 1998, the utility became the Internet provider for the area and today also serves wireless Internet and data transfer with a division called grnco.net.

A water treatment plant was built in 1998. In the year 2000 the utility contracted to build a 10 million dollar expansion of the wastewater treatment plant and a 12 million dollar additional generating plant. The utility can generate over 35 megawatts of power.

Original Light Plant Commissioners were J. C. Ford, Joe Shelby H. W. Woosley, L. V. Stedman and R. W. Meriwether. The utility managers have been Dan Pepper, J. C. Holland, John McDaniel and Larry Watson.

The utility headquarters are on 39 acres on Jones Road, built in 1990.

Source: information taken in part from *History of City Light and Water* by Kitty Sloan

## Dr Pepper Bottling Co.

On April 18, 1926, R. A. "Red" Reynolds, J. M. Marvin Reynolds and their half brother, Herbert Bland, opened the doors of the Mellow Moon Bottling Company in Paragould. Prior to this time Red and Marvin had been operating a café in Paragould and Herbert was selling and making ice cream for the Ideal Bottling Works of Paragould.

With an initial investment of $1,800 the three brothers began the bottling operation in a building measuring 14x35 feet, manufacturing only Mellow Moon flavor drinks. It was strictly a three-man operation, with the Reynolds twins bottling all the drinks at the rate of 100 cases a day. Herbert Bland was the only salesman, traveling a six county area.

In 1929 the franchise to bottle Dr Pepper was acquired and the name was changed to Dr Pepper Bottling Company, while the brothers continued to bottle their private brand of Mellow Moon flavors. In 1959 the Seven-Up Bottling Company of Paragould was purchased and the operation was merged into the existing business. The name was then changed to Dr Pepper Seven-Up Bottling Company.

A modern building was completed in 1967 featuring high-speed equipment for bottling the soft drinks. One bottling line can produce as many as 7,000 cases per day.

Another bottling line was added in 1974, allowing the manufacture of 32 ounce and 2-liter beverages at the rate of 4,000 cases per day. Within the past 12 years we have added a can line that will produce 1,000 cans per minute.

At this time the third generation of Blands is employed at Dr Pepper Seven-Up. The company operates over 70 trucks.

The ethics set forth by Herbert, Marvin and Arvin, three brothers, are still followed by their families.

*Submitted by Francis Bland*

# First National Bank

### FOUNDERS AND LEADERS

Dr. Calvin Wall probably delivered quite a few babies during his 27-year medical practice. But he was likely most proud of his own progeny, six children and one bank. The bank we know today as First National Bank. Dr. Wall was the founding president when the bank first opened its doors on March 22, 1889. The bank was incorporated with capital stock of $30,000 in 1889 and capital was increased in 1903 to $50,000. From 1901 to 1967 the National Bank of Commerce also provided strong financial leadership to Greene County. In 1967 First National Bank and National Bank of Commerce merged to form one institution. During the past 111 years many strong leaders have risen to the challenge of guiding this community's leading financial institutions. Others who have served First National Bank or National Bank of Commerce as either president or chairman are: (from earliest to latest) Ad Bertig, J. M. Lowe, J. D. Block, Eli Meiser, H. S. Trice, W. F. Kirsch, W. L. Gatz, A. H. Wrape, J. R. Ford, Cecil Mitchell, Larry Brewer, J. C. Vaughn, Norman Kelley, G. L. Lieblong, current President Kelly Wright and current Chairman William E. Brewer.

### SMALL BEGINNINGS

The original location for First National Bank was at the corner of Pruett and Emerson Streets. According to *Goodspeed's History* the bank's "neat" brick building was not complete until July 1, 1889. Extensive improvement was made to the building and in 1909 it was called "one of the handsomest bank buildings in the state". Our original building, after over 111 years of service stands tall in the year 2000 as the home of Arnold's Jewelry. Between 1929 and 1961 First National Bank operations were located one block north of its original site at the corner of Pruett and Court Street. Since 1961 First National Bank's main office has been located at the corner of Second and Court Street, just one block from either of its prior locations. The bank undertook extensive remodeling and expansion of the main office facilities from 1971 to 1973.

### CHANGE-GROWTH-PROGRESS

The growth of Paragould and the mobility of our customers have required significant growth of First National Bank's facilities and services. In 1979 First National Bank opened its West Branch office located at 201 Linwood Drive in Paragould. In 1995 the Reynolds Road drive up branch at 2701 W. Kingshighway in Paragould was opened. In 1998 First National Banks first banking office outside of Greene County was opened at 3500 East Johnson Avenue in Jonesboro. In 2000 First National Bank's Paragould Reynolds Road Office at 2701 West Kingshighway was expanded to include a full service lobby with new accounts and lending officers. Through the years significant technological advancement has given rise to many new banking services including telephone banking, automatic teller machines, debit cards and Internet banking. Personal service has always been and will continue to be the foundation of our financial dealings.

### STRENGTH-STABILITY-SERVICE

Since 1889 our top priority has been to provide a safe, secure bank for our growing community. Bauer Financial Incorporated and VeriBanc are two independent bank research firms that rate all banks in the United States for safety and soundness. First National Bank is proud to have received the highest ratings from both of these firms for the past 11 years. Less than eight percent of all United States banks have earned the Bauer five star rating 11 consecutive years. According to the Federal Deposit Insurance Corporation as of June 30, 1999, First National Bank of Paragould ranked 25th largest of more than 200 banks based in Arkansas. Through sound management, integrity, hard work and a vision for the future, the directors, officers and employees of First National Bank are preparing the bank for another century of service to Greene County.

*Dr. Calvin Wall*

*Original location, corner of Pruett and Emerson Streets*

*Present site of the bank, corner of Second and Court Streets.*

# Gazaway Ace Home Improvement Center

In the late '50s, B. C. Gazaway built several small houses in Paragould, AR and had no trouble selling them. He quit his factory job and built a few more modest houses and sold them. In order to store the lumber and millwork for this construction he built a lumber shed on Reynolds Road, across from his home. The lumber shed soon evolved into a small retail business selling building materials. B. C. sold his interest in the company to his son, Moud, in 1970. After a few years, Moud built a more substantial office and warehouse on the same property. Doris Wells was hired as bookkeeper. Her son, Bob Wells had just graduated from Greene County Tech and was employed part-time while he attended Arkansas State University. He graduated from ASU and began to work fulltime in 1977. Tommy Bowers, also an ASU graduate, joined the lumber company a short time later in 1979. The town of Paragould maintained a steady growth and new homes and businesses were being built. Gazaway Lumber steadily increased its market share.

Property on the corner of what is now West Kingshighway and Carroll Road was secured in 1980. This property had special significance because B. C. Gazaway and his wife, Viva, had built a house on this site back in 1948. Moud recalls living there as a boy. The memories include riding horses, camping out by the creek, walking across the highway to go to the service station for soda pop and witnessing the era of Collin's Drive-In movie which could be seen from their front porch. They lived there until 1957 when the family of six bought a house "in town".

The present hardware store and warehouse

*Gazaway lumber shed, Reynolds Road, Paragould, Arkansas*

were built in 1985, after several years of clearing the seven and one half acre corner. The company became affiliated with Ace Hardware and Allied Building Stores. Several storage buildings were built and the inventory was increased. Computer sales tickets replaced the hand written tickets of the past. Equipment was purchased to handle and deliver the building materials. These improvements helped the staff to give the customer high quality products and service.

Gazaway Lumber Company became a manufacturer of trusses in 1980. However, the Truss Plant suffered a fire in 1990. On the night of the fire, smoke could be seen for miles and fire trucks had to get water from a hydrant across the highway, which held up traffic for quite awhile.

The Truss Plant was rebuilt and supplies customers in Northeast Arkansas and Southeast Missouri. More recently, a Door Shop has been added which builds door units for special orders. Gazaway Ace Home Improvement Center now has 45 employees. Sales are over $7,000,000 annually. The main store area features a paint department, service desk, rental department, contractors counter, lighting and electrical department, a plumbing department, hardware, millwork and cabinet design specialties.

In 1991, Moud and Sharon's son, Todd joined the company. He is the purchasing agent and wears many hats. He and his wife, April, are parents of a son, Ben.

*Gazaway Home Improvement Center, October 25, 2000, corner of Carroll Road and W. Kingshighway, Paragould, Arkansas*

# Goodwin, Moore, Colbert, Broadaway and Gray, LLP

Jefferson Davis Block founded Paragould's oldest law firm in 1889. The firm is the second oldest continuing business in Greene County and one of the oldest law firms in the state.

It has a rich history of service to the community, the state and the bar of the State of Arkansas.

## J. D. Block

Jefferson Davis Block moved his law practice from Cross County to Paragould in Greene County in 1889 when Paragould was only six years old. Mr. Block was 28 that year. He was already well established in political circles in Northeast Arkansas, having served a term in the Arkansas House of Representatives in 1887 and 1888 and having been elected prosecutor for the Second Judicial District for a term beginning in 1889. His duties as prosecuting attorney brought him to Greene County where he met Lena Hicks, the daughter of a pioneer Paragould physician, whom he wooed and married. The date of his move to Paragould is established through the date of his marriage, June 12, 1889.

Mr. Block was described as a very effective trial lawyer with a charming personality. He also did a great deal of real estate title work. During the early days of his practice, much of the eastern part of Greene County was swampland. Mr. Block was a participant in extensive litigation that took place between the United States of America and the owners of title to these lands. He acquired large farming interests, which are still owned and managed by his family.

Mr. Block is also reported to have had a marvelous memory, particularly of any Arkansas Supreme Court decisions which he might have read.

Following his service as prosecuting attorney, Mr. Block was instrumental in the early development of Paragould. He participated in the formation of a bank, which became the National Bank of Commerce and was serving as its president at the time of his death. National Bank of Commerce's main competitor, First National Bank, was organized only three months prior to Mr. Block's arrival in Paragould. The two banks later merged to form the current First National Bank of Paragould, which is the oldest business in Greene County.

Mr. Block's public service was concluded when he was chosen as a delegate to the Arkansas Constitutional Convention in 1918. After participating in its deliberations for some time, he concluded that nothing constructive was going to come from the Convention and resigned. J. M. Futrell, later governor of Arkansas, succeeded him as a delegate. Mr. Block was correct in his forecast of the ineffectiveness of the 1918 convention.

When Mr. Block died in 1929 at the age of 67, the mayor of Paragould declared a day of public mourning and all businesses in the city closed during his funeral. The local newspaper, the Daily Press, waxed eloquent in its account of his contributions:

"He had a remarkable faculty for remembering names and faces as a result of which he knew and was probably known to more people that any other lawyer in the northeast part of the State.

He believed in the practice of his profession on the highest plain and had small consideration for those without due observance of the ethics of their profession."

Mr. Block's son, M. F. Block, practiced briefly with the firm before forming a highly successful insurance company which is still operated by his son, William J. "Bill" Block and his grandson, William J. "Jeff" Block Jr. Another of J. D. Block's grandsons, Steven H. Block, is a lawyer and CPA in Dallas, TX.

Mr. Block was the sole participant in what has to be the most "dramatic" event in the firm's 110-year history. As part of his duties as prosecuting attorney, he represented an unwed mother in a paternity case. The putative father became enraged at the lady and Mr. Block. He walked into Mr. Block's office one day while Mr. Block and the mother were in conference, pulled a gun, fired one shot at Mr. Block, one shot at the lady and then turned gun on himself. The late Joe Coates of Paragould, a teenager at the time, was the second person on the scene after the shooting. He recalls, "Mr. Block was lucky. He was just nipped in the burr of the ear. The lady was struck in the mouth and was taken to the hospital. The man died right in the office."

Mr. Block was a solo practitioner until 1894, when he formed a partnership with Frank Hugh Sullivan, a Paragould attorney who, earlier that year, married Susie Hicks, the sister of Lena Hicks Block.

Mr. Sullivan moved to St. Louis in 1898, where he achieved considerable success as an appellate advocate and a master of the English language.

In retirement Mr. Sullivan moved to Biloxi, MS, where he died in 1966 at the age of 97.

## William F. Kirsch

Mr. Block continued to practice alone until 1909 when he formed a partnership with William F. Kirsch. Mr. Kirsch was also blessed with a brilliant legal mind, having graduated first in his class from the Washington University School of Law in St. Louis, MO.

Although Mr. Kirsch was a native of Belleville, IL, he became acquainted with Paragould as a result of his father's service as superintendent of the Paragould Brick Factory and his own stints as a summer worker in the brick factory.

Mr. Kirsch's association with the law firm lasted almost 60 years. He, too, was an active real estate title lawyer and became an investor in farmlands, which have remained in his family through the years. He was active in drainage law, organizing and representing some of the drainage districts, which are still operating in Northeast Arkansas.

In addition to his law practice, he was heavily involved as a board member, officer and later, president of the National Bank of Commerce.

Mr. Kirsch was an effective trial lawyer. He cut back his trial practice extensively after Maurice Cathey returned from the military service in the mid-40s, but still participated in some of Mr. Cathey's trials, usually making the closing argument.

Mr. Kirsch remained associated with the firm until his death in 1967 and was still participating in firm activities when Ray Allen Goodwin joined the firm in 1965. Despite his age, Mr. Kirsch still kept his early morning hours, as Goodwin quickly learned. In trying to impress his new bosses with his work habits, Goodwin started coming to the office earlier than the 8:30 opening time in hopes of arriving before the senior partners. Coming earlier each morning on successive days, Goodwin finally gave up when he came to the office at 6:30 a. m. and found Mr. Kirsch already there.

Mr. Kirsch was an eloquent orator and was the featured speaker in many of the city and county's civic celebrations.

Mr. Kirsch and his wife, Jessie had two children, Mary Elizabeth Kirsch and William F. Kirsch Jr. The junior Mr. Kirsch practiced briefly with the firm in 1950, then moved to Memphis where he became a partner in one of the city's most prominent law firms, Heiskell, Donelson, Bearman, Adams, Williams and Kirsch, where he practiced until his death in 1989.

## Maurice Cathey

Maurice Cathey became associated with Mr. Kirsch on Jan 1, 1933 and remained with the firm until his retirement in 1985. His practice spanned parts of six decades, during which time both the law firm and the legal profession underwent massive changes.

Mr. Cathey as a child knew Mr. Kirsch, as his father was first a deputy clerk and later circuit clerk for Greene County and had many contacts with Mr. Kirsch and others members of the Bar.

Mr. Cathey graduated from Washington University School of Law in 1931 at the age of 21 and remained in St. Louis as an associate with a St. Louis firm. The practice in St. Louis was not very satisfactory. "We were in the very depths of the Depression and lawyers were a dime a dozen in St. Louis," Mr. Cathey said. When he was approached by Mr. Kirsch about coming back to Paragould, he agreed to do so, at the princely salary of $65.00 per month.

Mr. Cathey was a tireless worker and believed that the majority of lawsuits were won through diligent preparation and thorough research. He attempted to instill these principles in the lawyers who followed him into the firm.

Until an aneurysm diminished his hearing, Mr. Cathey was known as one of the top trial lawyers in Northeast Arkansas. He also became a probate specialist and helped write the Probate Code in 1949.

It was Mr. Cathey who guided the firm into its continuing support of the organized Bar. He served as president of the Greene County and Northeast Arkansas Bar Associations. Then, after having served on almost every major committee of the Arkansas Bar Association, he became its president in 1966. It was during Mr. Cathey's tenure that the *Arkansas Lawyer*, the bar association's quarterly journal came into existence.

Mr. Cathey firmly believed in the duty of the legal profession to provide pro bono service. His most famous pro bono representation was that of an English girl, Valerie Swindle, in a child custody case. The request for an Arkansas attorney came through the British Consulate in St. Louis. Over a period of 20 months, he was involved in four hearings in the Greene County Chancery Court, two cases in the Supreme Court of Arkansas, a petition for certiorari to the Supreme Court of the United States, a trial in the Circuit Court of St. Louis County and an immigration proceeding to avoid deportation of the client. The case received international publicity and resulted in the young mother's gaining custody of her daughter and returning to England. When Mr. Cathey visited Great Britain in 1969; he was a special guest of the British government at a luncheon in the House of Commons and at one of its sessions.

He served his community as director and vice president of what is now First National Bank, as chairman of the administrative board of the First United Methodist Church, as a member of the executive board of Arkansas Methodist Hospital and as president of the Paragould Rotary Club.

Mr. Cathey retired from the practice in 1985 and died in 1990. His wife, Ina, who died in March 2000, and two children, Ann Gregg of Conway and Donald M. Cathey, who died August 1999, survived him.

### Gerald P. Brown

Gerald Parker Brown came to the law firm in 1951 following a WWII tour of duty with the United States Marines and a distinguished educational career at the University of Arkansas where he graduated Phi Beta Kappa.

When Mr. Brown joined the firm, Mr. Cathey anticipated that he would become an "office lawyer" because of his scholarly background. Mr. Cathey was wrong. Mr. Brown became one of the top trial lawyers in Northeast Arkansas. He was especially effective with juries in the Eastern District of Clay County, where he was born, raised and attended high school.

Brown continued in the active practice of law until 1975, at which time he took a "temporary" appointment as chancellor in the Twelfth Chancery Circuit, followed by a "temporary" appointment as circuit judge in the Second Judicial Circuit. Brown decided at this point that he would like to continue on the bench and was then elected circuit judge, a position he held until his retirement at the end of 1986. In 1979, the Arkansas Trial Lawyers Association honored Brown as Trial Judge of the Year

In his early days in the practice, Brown was very active in the organization of the Paragould Youth Baseball leagues. He served as president of the Paragould Kiwanis Club and on three different occasions served as chairman of the board of the Arkansas Methodist Hospital. He served as president of the Greene-Clay Bar Association and the Northeast Arkansas Bar Association and was a member of the first House of Delegates of the Arkansas Bar Association.

Since his retirement from the bench, he has continued his community service by working on a voluntary basis with students of all ages in an attempt to give them a better understanding of the judicial system. He has been honored by the Arkansas Judicial Council with its Community Service award and by the Paragould-Greene County Chamber of Commerce with its Life Citizen award.

Brown and his wife, Lottie, still live in Paragould. They have three children, Ronald J. Brown, a Virginia attorney; Clifford Allen Brown, who resides in Great Britain (The Browns enjoy house-sitting at this son's home) and a daughter, Celia "Bunny" Brown Lee, who lives in Paragould.

Donis B. Hamilton, a native of Russellville, practiced with the firm from January 1968 until May 1993. He and his wife, the former Bonnie Mack of Little Rock, still live in Paragould. They have one daughter, Audra Hamilton, who is also an attorney and practices in Tulsa, OK.

### Current Partners

The current partners in the firm, Ray Allen Goodwin, Harry Truman Moore, Roger U. Colbert, Brad Broadaway, Angela Bowden Gray and Michael W. Langley, have followed their predecessors' examples in service to the community and the Bar.

Goodwin's earliest 'connection' with the firm came shortly before his birth when his mother was working as secretary of the Greene County chapter of the Red Cross. Mr. Cathey was chairman of the Red Cross at that time, but gave Mrs. Helen Goodwin a sufficient amount of time off from her duties to deliver her oldest son, Ray Allen.

Goodwin began his undergraduate career at the

*Standing: Harry Truman Moore, Ray Allen Goodwin, Roger U. Colbert. Seated: Brad Broadaway, Angela Bowden Gray and Michael W. Langley*

University of the South (Sewanee) upon completion of six months of active duty military service with the United States Army following his high school graduation in 1956. Later he transferred to and received his undergraduate degree from Hendrix College. He attended laws school at Southern Methodist University where he served, as editor in chief in the *Journal of Air Law and Commerce,* was a member of Delta Theta Phi legal fraternity and the Barristers. His practice with the firm began Aug 15, 1965. He assumed many of the firm's managerial duties sooner than anticipated when Brown ascended to the Bench in 1975.

He probably has the most "general" practice of any of the current members of the firm and holds the firm records for the largest recoveries in personal injury litigation and commercial litigation.

He has served the community as president of the Rotary Club, chairman of the Northeast Arkansas Regional Library Board and the Greene County Library Board during the planning, construction and opening of the present public library facility, chairman of the board and Sunday school teacher at First United Methodist Church, a member of the Arkansas Methodist Hospital Association and as a member of the judicial and legal advisory committee for the design and construction of the present Greene County Courthouse. He has served on the Arkansas State Library Commission by appointment of then-Governor David Pryor. He has been a member of the board of governors of the Hendrix College Alumni Association. In 1994, Goodwin received the lifetime achievement award from the Paragould Rotary Club. He is a Paul Harris Fellow.

Ray has served as a member of many of the committees of the Arkansas Bar Association over the years, including a stint as chairman of the Committee for Legal Services to the Deaf for which he received the Association's Golden Gavel Award in 1986. He was instrumental in changing the bylaws of the Association to permit lay people to serve on bar committees. He has served as a member of the trial practice committee for the Second Judicial District and is a member of the board of directors of Legal Services of Northeast Arkansas. In June 2000, he was elected to the House of Delegates of the State Bar. By gubernatorial appointment, he has served as a special justice of the Supreme Court of the State of Arkansas.

He was named one the Best Lawyers in Arkansas by the Arkansas Times in 2000.

He is married to the former Kay Evelyn Monk of Hot Springs. Ray and Kay have two children, Mark Allen Goodwin and James Allen Goodwin.

Moore, a native of Walnut Ridge, came to the law firm in 1975 after having received degrees from Arkansas State University in 1969 and University of Arkansas Law School. He was named a "Distinguished Alumnus" of ASU in 1997.

His practice has included the formation of several regional water distribution districts, representation of drainage districts and financial institutions and social security claimants. A large portion of his practice is in the area of domestic relations. He has served as a participant in several programs presented by the Family Law Section of the Arkansas Bar Association and has been awarded seven "Best of CLE" awards. He is a former chairman of that section.

In 1998 and 2000 he was selected by the Arkansas Times as one of the "Best Lawyers in Arkansas" in the family law area and he was selected for the 1999-2000 and 2001-2002 editions of the "Best Lawyers in America" as a family law practitioner.

In 1996 Moore became the second lawyer in the firm's history to serve as President of the Arkansas Bar Association. This followed service as president of the Greene-Clay Bar Association, president of the Northeast Arkansas Bar Association, in the state bar's House of Delegates and Executive Council and many other bar committees.

Moore served as chairman of the Young Lawyers Section of the Arkansas Bar Association in 1981-82, during which time the YLS received two first place awards from the Young Lawyers Division of the American Bar Association. He continues to serve on several bar association committees. He was appointed as one of the initial members of the Arkansas Continuing Legal Education Board and has served on the Supreme Court Child Support Committee, as a director of the Arkansas Bar Foundation and on the Arkansas IOLTA board. He has also served by appointment as Special Chief Justice of the Arkansas Supreme Court.

From 1997 to 2000 he served as the representative of the Arkansas Bar Association in the House of Delegates of the American Bar Association. In July 2000, he became the State Delegate for Arkansas to the American Bar Association and in such position chairs the Arkansas delegation to the ABA House of Delegates and serves on the ABA's 67 person nominating committee. In June 2000, he received the prestigious Carpenter Award for his service to the Arkansas Bar Association.

His community activities include past service as chairman of the Paragould Parks and Recreation Commission and president of the Paragould-Greene County Area Chamber of Commerce. He chaired the Chamber's Industrial Committee for two years and as a result of his efforts in obtaining new industry for Greene County, was named as "Volunteer of the Year" by the Industrial Developers of Arkansas.

He has served as president of the Arkansas State University Alumni Association, as an elder and trustee of the First Presbyterian Church and as a member of Grace Presbyterian Church. He serves as counsel to the Presbytery of Arkansas.

He has been active in political affairs, having served as treasurer of the Democratic Party of the State of Arkansas. Prior to attending law school, he was an aide to Congressman Bill Alexander and later was campaign manager for many of Alexander's re-election bids. He was an Arkansas Traveler for the 1992 Clinton for President Campaign and legal counsel for Gore 2000 in the State of Arkansas.

He is married to the former Linda Lou Lipscomb of Blytheville. Linda Lou was formerly the speech pathologist on staff at Arkansas Methodist Hospital and is currently self-employed as an etiquette consultant.

Roger Colbert is a native of Campbell, MO. He graduated from Arkansas State University in 1981 with a Bachelor of Arts degree and from the University of Arkansas at Little Rock School of Law in 1984. Roger currently serves on the Board of Directors of the Arkansas State University Indian Club, the fund-raising entity for the athletic department. He is a member of the initial board of directors for the Endowment Foundation of Greene County, which was recently selected as an affiliate of the Arkansas Community Foundation. Roger presently serves on the Paragould-Greene County Chamber of Commerce, Inc. Board of Directors and has served on the Chamber's Economic Development-Industrial Committee for the past five years.

Roger is married to the former Kelly Gerber of Mountain Home, AR and the father of two daughters, Graycen and Bailey. Kelly is employed as a speech pathologist by the Paragould School District.

Roger's practice is concentrated in the areas of real estate, debtor-creditor and commercial law.

Brad Broadaway joined the firm in 1988. He is the current managing partner. One of his first duties as managing partner was to create the firm website. He attended Rhodes College in Memphis, TN, arch rival to Goodwin's Sewanee. He graduated from the University of Arkansas School of Law as a member of the Arkansas Law Review.

Brad's past bar activities have included the Young Lawyers Division Executive Committee and chair of the Disaster Relief Sub Committee. He is currently a member of the Committee for Persons with Disabilities, which holds a special interest as one of his children is disabled.

Brad is married to his high school sweetheart, Mary Lile Broadaway, who is an attorney in private practice in Paragould. They have two children, Jack and Whit.

Angela Bowden Gray originally hails from Russellville, AR. She joined the firm in 1995 and became a partner in January 1998. She graduated magna cum laude from Arkansas Tech University in Russellville, where she received the Margaret Young Award as the outstanding female senior. She obtained her Juris Doctorate from the University of Arkansas at Little Rock School of Law. While attending law school, Angela was a member of Delta Theta Phi and an active participant in Young Democrats of Arkansas.

She has been a member of the Paragould Rotary Club, a graduate of Leadership Paragould and is the immediate past president of Junior Auxiliary of Paragould. She also serves as member of the Paragould Housing Authority Board.

Angela is married to Terry Gray, a farmer and commodities broker. They have one son, Houston.

Michael W. Langley joined the firm in 1998. He is originally from Jonesboro and attended Ole Miss and UALR. He is a member of the Rotary Club and serves on the board of directors for Habitat for Humanity. He participated in the Paragould Leadership program. He was president of the Literacy Council and is currently president of the Greene-Clay Bar Association. He is active in the Democratic Party and is currently the second vice chair of the Democratic Party of Arkansas. He is also active in the Chamber of Commerce and is currently serving on the Transportation Committee and the Legislative Affairs Committee. He was recently involved as campaign manager in a successful local election

He is married to the former Beck Cook of Paragould and has one daughter, Tapp Ellen.

# Heath Funeral Home

When Verlyn L. and Helen G. Heath purchased the Irby Funeral Home in Paragould in 1945, they began a business which has been serving Greene County and the surrounding area for over 55 years.

Heath Funeral Home, founded in 1945 at 221 West Main Street, later merged with the A. J. Emerson Funeral Home in 1952 when Emerson retired and sold the business to the Heath family. 25 years after the Heath Funeral Home was opened, in 1970, as a result of growing pains experienced by both the community and the business, the Heath family was extremely proud to announce the formal opening of the present facility located at 321 West Garland.

Verlyn instilled in his family and employees that each family served is important and should be provided with a "Sincere Personal Service". He saw this business start from the bare minimum and develop into a very successful service to the public. He always appreciated the folks in this area who had given him the opportunity, especially in the early years, to prove himself.

Mr. and Mrs. Heath retired in 1984 turning the management of Heath Funeral Home over to their son, Verlyn G. "Butch" Heath and their daughter, Lynda Heath Bryant. Butch's wife, Jan and Lynda's husband, Jimmy, are both licensed funeral directors, as well as Butch and Jan's sons, Zac and Jeremy. Jim and Lynda's daughter, Melanie, is also a licensed funeral director and an embalmer. Verlyn died Jan 6, 1995, the year of the 50th anniversary of the business he loved. He would be very proud to know that a third generation of his family is now following in his footsteps and striving to give care and concern to each family served.

*Heath Funeral Home, 1945 - 1970*

*Heath Family – front row, L to R: Verlyn L. and Helen G. Heath; back: Jimmy Bryant, Lynda Heath Bryant, Veryln G. "Butch" Heath and Jan Heath.*

*Heath Funeral Home, 1970 - present*

# J & S Woodcrafts, Inc.

J & S Woodcrafts, Incorporated is a classic American success story and a beaming testimony of the free market economy. J & S Woodcrafts, Incorporated was started by Jasper and Shirley Wright in 1985 in the basement of their home.

The business specializes in wood products using a unique process to combine photography with craftsmanship. Gun Racks are the company's chief line, although they also manufacturer clocks, pictures, displays and organizers. All products are designed with the outdoor sportsman in mind.

Using a chemical process which coats photo prints in a glass-type finish, the company mounts nature and landscape prints in sturdy wooden frames. The end product is sturdy, useful and exceptionally beautiful with pictures of deer, elk, duck and wild turkey in their natural surroundings.

Shirley Wright worked at the Wal-Mart store in Paragould and persuaded her husband to take a shot at breaking into the Wal-Mart market. They gave J & S Woodcrafts, Incorporated their first big break. Jasper Wright attributes a lot of credit to Wal-Mart. Since the chain store picked up on their products, other large companies have followed suit.

Wayne Wright, brother of Jasper Wright, was the first to come aboard and Wayne's son, Perry Wright, soon followed. Jasper and Shirley's daughters, Susan and Jennifer, also helped with the business in various areas. The expansion of product lines has made work at the plant more stable and allows J & S Woodcrafts, Incorporated, to keep a present staff of 12 to 15 core employees year-round.

In 1987, John Lane became a partner with Jasper Wright and the pressure of overseeing every aspect of the business eased. Sharing a mutual love for wildlife and the outdoors, Jasper and John set out on a mission to expand their horizons and cater their products to the wildlife and outdoor industries.

John Lane, who comes from years of experience in local industries with a strong marketing and purchasing background, was able to purchase parts wholesale and initiate market drives to keep the business thriving.

In 1993 J & S Woodcrafts, Incorporated purchased approximately 10 acres of land and built a 16,500 square foot manufacturing and office facility. Business grew steadily and in 1996 an additional 15,000 square feet of manufacturing space was added. In 1999, with business continuing to grow, it became necessary to add an additional 15,000 square feet, for a total of 46,500 square feet of manufacturing, warehouse and office space, which is occupied at present, nestled in the beautiful hill country atop Crowley's Ridge in Northeast Arkansas.

Every year we are refining and expanding our product- something for everyone. For the hunters there are gun racks, archery racks, ammo boxes, organizers, etc. For those of you who just love the great outdoors there are beautiful scenic clocks, key racks and pictures. For the fishing enthusiast, we offer an eight-place rod rack to organize your rod and

reels. For the avid collector we offer the Commemorative Coin Holder and Fishing Lure Display.

J & S Woodcrafts, Incorporated would like to thank the people of Greene County for their support for the past 15 years and their continued support as they look toward the future. While J & S Woodcrafts, Incorporated has grown over the past decade, we still cherish and uphold those good ol' country values that have gotten us where we are today: honesty, hard work, quality products and customer satisfaction.

# Northeast Arkansas Tribune

"Community newspaper debuts," a banner headline proclaimed in a sample issue of the Northeast Arkansas Tribune published Aug 18, 1989. The story beneath the headline said the new publication, a twice-weekly tabloid, would be mailed to every home in Paragould.

The stories in the sample issue were true, but the ads were dummies, intended only to show what potential customers could expect. The official debut for the new publication produced at 2210 W. Kingshighway was Aug 25, 1989.

J. V. Rockwell, the Tribune's owner, dedicated the new publication to covering local news and issues and many of the stories, which appeared in the early issues of the Tribune, are still relevant today. Jeff Hankins, the Tribune's founding editor and general manager, oversaw coverage of events ranging from church news to work on securing funding to help tame Eight Mile Creek.

While the name has changed, the waterway still finds its way into Tribune headlines.

The Tribune assumed its current format on March 16, 1990, several months after the debut.

"The larger, more standard size will give us the chance to use larger photographs and more local community news," a page one story proclaimed. The paper also went high-tech and began publishing color photographs and company officials increased the number of copies coming off of the presses in Corning to expand the paper's circulation outside Greene County. "We're excited about our progress and we hope our readers and advertisers will also be pleased," the story proclaimed.

During the 1990s, Hankins departed to join Arkansas Business Week. However, the Tribune continued to spread its wings, adding Associated Press service, including photos. A third edition was added and rumors circulated around Paragould that the Tribune would soon be a daily publication. Those rumors were laid somewhat to rest when veteran publisher Owen Lusk assumed the helm.

Lusk realized the Tribune had abandoned its mission of providing local news to local people. To put the paper back on track, he dropped one issue per week and canceled the Associated Press wire services. Lusk's decisions returned the Tribune to its roots, making it again a twice-weekly publication focused on local people and events.

Growth has followed and 22,450 copies of the Wednesday edition are distributed throughout Greene County, Craighead County and Dunklin County, MO. Working to produce that paper and the Friday edition, which is available in racks and on subscription basis, are 17 employees, up seven from the crew which launched the enterprise. Another factor adding to the local economy are the independent contractors, which have replaced the U. S. Postal Service as the paper's method of delivery. Having a positive impact on the region's economy is a trend company officials expect to continue.

*The* Tribune *prints 22,450 copies on Wednesday*

*The* Tribune *is located at No. 1 Stout Spur Shopping Center*

*A sample of the first edition of the* Tribune *ever printed*

# Razorback Concrete Company

Razorback Concrete Company was founded in 1965 with headquarters in West Memphis, Arkansas. Plants are now located in fourteen Arkansas cities, including the Paragould plant at 412 Airport Road. Founder of the company was the late W. K. "Bill" Ingram and the Board of Directors includes Kent Ingram, President; Keith Ingram, Vice President; and Magalene Ingram, Secretary-Treasurer.

Razorback Concrete has built a reputation for outstanding service as well as the innovative use of new ready-mix technologies. These include the use of ultra-thin white topping for street paving, the first central mix plant in Eastern Arkansas, the first to use flowable fill, among many other state-of-the-art concepts.

The Paragould plant was purchased in 1989 from Express Ready Mix, owned by J. D. Hamilton of Paragould. Nineteen people are employed at this location.

In 1985 the company founded RazorRock Materials, a sand and gravel mining operation that now has five branch locations, including one in Paragould.

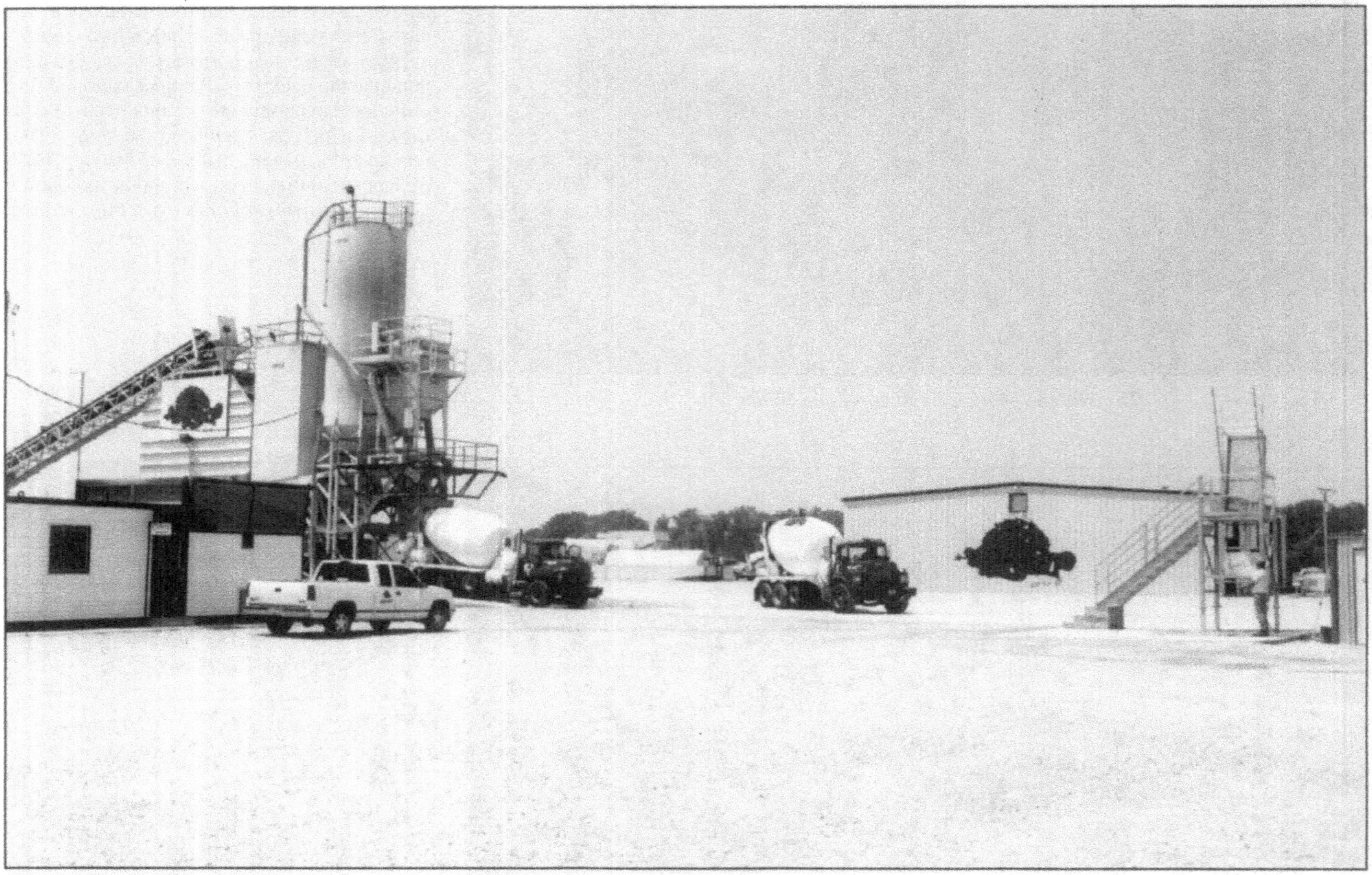

# Ed Roleson Jr., Inc.

Ed Roleson Jr. founded Falstaff Distributing Company in 1943. In 1948 he moved his family to Paragould from Jonesboro, due to Craighead County voting dry.

Ed Roleson Jr.'s business was located on Kingshighway, doing business as Falstaff Distributing Company.

In 1962 he moved his business to Chestnut and Railroad, what is known as The Old Feed Mill.

In 1979 Ed Roleson Jr. moved into a new facility at 400 West Baldwin Street, doing business as Ed Roleson Jr., Inc. The founder Ed Roleson Jr. was born Feb 15, 1911 – deceased Oct 17, 1979.

In 1979 Michael W. Roleson became president and John Ed Roleson, secretary and treasurer

New upgrade on equipment, as we participated in the 1983 Paragould Centennial Parade.

Third Generation will be our sons, Shawn Edward Roleson, merchandiser and John Edward Roleson Jr., presalesman of Ed Roleson Jr. Inc.

At the present, Ed Roleson Jr., Inc. has 10 employees and three office employees with a total of 65 years experience. Larry Holcomb, general manager, 25 years; Carol Roleson, secretary, 24 years and Angela Hale, secretary, 16 years.

Ed Roleson Jr., Inc has 12 vehicles and five trailers, servicing Mississippi, Poinsett and Greene Counties.

Ed Roleson Jr., Inc. will have been in business for 57 years in the year 2000.

*Ed Roleson Jr., founder*

*Second Generation: Michael and John Roleson*

*Third Generation: Shawn Edward and John Edward Roleson*

*Employees Larry Holcomb, Carol Roleson, and Angela Hale*

*Mr. Roleson's first established distributing company*

*1979 – Grand opening of Ed Roleson Jr.'s new facility*

*Ed Roleson Jr. at his business on Chesnut and Lake Street*

*1983 Centennial Paragould Parade*

# Tenneco Automotive – Monroe

The Tenneco Automotive (old Monroe Auto Equipment Company) plant located in Paragould, AR was dedicated Oct 14, 1970. This facility was the third domestic plant for Tenneco Automotive, increasing the company's manufacturing capacity by 65 percent. Built at a cost of more than 12 million, the Paragould Plant is over 400,000 square foot steel and concrete building located on a 49.5-acre tract on highway 49B north.

The Paragould plant produces a complete line of shock absorbers, load levelers, stabilizers, air adjustable shocks and strut units primarily for the replacement automotive markets.

Striving for the perfect product is our goal at Tenneco Automotive. We are constantly striving to produce new technologically advanced products of superior quality. Several new designs and types of shocks were first put into production here in Paragould.

Paragould started making the air adjustable shock absorber in 1971. We are very proud of the fact that we were the first plants in the United States to produce this type of shock absorbers.

The North American Aftermarket Distribution Center was completed in November 1989. It is over 380,000 square foot steel and concrete building. Product is shipped in from and out to all of North America.

The Sensa-Trac strut product line began production in 1992 and is another step in our goal to give the public a superior product at a fair price. SensaTrac is the most advanced product available today. A new Strut line was added in 2000, bringing the current employment rate to over 1,100 employees.

Tenneco Automotive is not only in the business of making ride control and exhaust products; we are also very involved in community affairs. Over the years, Tenneco Automotive has led the community in the Greene County Community Fund Drive. Each year, we sponsor many youth activities such as little league baseball, youth girls' softball and several youth and adult bowling reams. We support the youth of our community 100% because they are the future of our community.

Tenneco Automotive is a leader in new and exciting products, in helping to develop the future leaders of our community, of the preferred place of employment in our area and the effort of everyone to strive for perfection. Tenneco Automotive of Paragould will continue, as it always has, to lead the way into the future.

## Adams Nursery and Landscaping

Seeing a need for a full-service nursery and landscaping business, Neal Adams set out in the fall of 1989 to develop just that kind of company. With the help of his parents, Larry and Rita Adams, Neal opened "Bushes and Blooms Nursery and Landscaping" for business March 1, 1990, at 311 Carroll Road. In August 1990, Steve Adams joined his brother in the business. To reflect the personal service Neal and Steve give their customers, Bushes and Blooms became "Adams Nursery and Landscaping" in the spring of 1994.

A significant change occurred in the fall of 1995 when Adams Nursery and Landscaping moved to 215 North 23rd Street. By moving, the nursery was able to see an expansion of greenhouse space, an increase in tree and shrub selection and the addition of new product lines.

The spring of 1997 brought yet another change: Jamie, Neal's wife, joined the company full-time to oversee the growing operation. The most important aspect of Adams Nursery is family involvement. Even Opal Mangrum, Neal and Steve's grandmother, helps in the greenhouse. The full and part-time staff of Adams Nursery and Landscaping has achieved their goal of providing the surrounding area with quality plants, helpful information and a friendly atmosphere.

## Allen Engineering Corporation

In January of 1964 Dewayne Allen and a friend opened a ready-mix concrete business in Piggott, AR. At that time, Dewayne, a civil engineer, was working for a paving contractor in Illinois. By 1968, Allen ready-mix operations had been established in Piggott, Corning and Paragould and the Allens moved to Arkansas for Dewayne to become involved in the business full time. After two years of teaching, Mary Ann, Dewayne's wife, also joined the business and managed the offices.

In 1973, Fred Allen, Dewayne Allen's father, was fatally injured in an accident at an Allen gravel pit. The trauma of that incident prompted the eventual sale of the ready-mix and sand and gravel operations during the period of 1973-1975.

Dewayne Allen became acquainted with a concrete finishing tool (truss screed) during a short period of employment in Houston, TX, in 1976. In 1977, Allen Engineering Corporation began manufacturing screed at the location of the former Paragould ready-mix operation. Dewayne Allen designed and sold the equipment and Mary Ann Allen ran the office. By 1979, AEC had its first patent and by 1980, AEC was selling concrete finishing equipment through a distributor network nationally and internationally.

Allen Engineering Corporation celebrated its 35th anniversary in 1999. AEC's complete line of concrete finishing and placing equipment for industrial floors which includes screeds, walk-behind trowels, riding trowels, spreaders, sprayers and tools, is recognized worldwide for its innovations and superior quality. AEC's Paragould operation employs 160+ workers and there are 16 outside salesmen located throughout the U. S., Mexico and England. Within the last decade, the second generation of Allens (Jay and John) has become active in the business. Jay heads up the sales and marketing division and helps with the daily family business management. John is working in the field in customer service.

With the boys in place at Allen Engineering, Dewayne has recently been concentrating on a concrete paving equipment line for bridge and highway work. This equipment brings him back to the type of jobs he left in Illinois in 1968, highway paving, and that is not a coincidence! It's where his civil engineering heart is!

*Submitted by Mary Ann Allen*

## American Railcar

American Railcar Industries is an affiliate of ACF Industries, Incorporated which has a long history in the United States. About 1875, the first railroad tank car, a "tub car", was constructed at Milton, PA and in 1889 a tank car company was formed there.

In 1899 13-railroad equipment manufacturers located in various parts of the country merged to form the American Car and Foundry Company. Their reputation rapidly spread abroad and in 1905 more than 100 motor and trailer subway cars were shipped to England for use in London's underground system.

An American Railcar plant opened in Paragould in July 1995 and in Marmaduke in August 1999. They employ 370 persons in Paragould and 140 in Marmaduke.

## Arkansas Methodist Hospital

The story of the Arkansas Methodist Hospital is one of hope and disappointment, of success and failure. It is the story of raw determination and discouragement and finally, a story of accomplishment.

*The third generation of the Allens include little Daniel and Jessica, children of Jay and Lesle Allen. From Jay in marketing and sales to John in customer service, the Allen name remains a working presence. Founders Dewayne and Mary Ann Allen complete the Allen family portrait.*

*ARI manufactors and assembles covered hopper railcars at its Paragould, AR Plant*

*First railroad tank car – "tub car"*

The first date in the history of the hospital cannot be fixed, for it was the date when it was conceived in the minds of the public that the people of the Paragould trade territory were entitled to a hospital that could provide the highest possible standards of care. By the late 1930s the Dickson Memorial Hospital, which was originally built to accommodate only about 20 inpatients, was no longer adequate. With the exception of the few hospitals in Jonesboro and Poplar Bluff, MO, few of the small local hospitals which now dot the map were in existence at the time. It was estimated at this time that the service area was near 100,000 people. There was little question that new facilities were needed.

On Nov 18, 1940, the Paragould City Council passed a resolution granting Mayor W. C. Middleton power to sign all the papers necessary to secure government aid in the construction of a modern hospital and on May 12, 1941 the non-profit Community Hospital Corporation was formed. This original organization accepted generous donations from many individuals and firms who held the hope that the hospital could be completed and made ready for operation. Although records of this original association are not available, later estimates by the Hospital Commission of local contributions were between $85,000 and $90,000. The WPA contribution was twice that amount.

The Paragould City Council authorized the mayor to sign an agreement on June 16, 1941, between the city and A. N. McAninch, a Little Rock architect, for the proposed municipal hospital. Mr. Joseph R. Bertig purchased the land for the hospital in July of that year and donated it to the city as a memorial to his father and mother. Site development and construction began soon afterward.

The original plans calling for the completion of the hospital with local donations and WPA labor was disrupted by an unforeseeable event: WWII. The war limited the resources available and forced the stopping of the project at a time when it was more than 75 percent complete. The WPA was dissolved in 1942 and local funds were exhausted by the summer of 1943. The work completely stopped and the Community Hospital Corporation was left with outstanding debts of nearly $4,000.

For a period of four years the incomplete structure stood vacant. Weather and vandalism took their toll and equipment and materials stored in the building were damaged. While the community's attention was focused on war efforts, the hospital project was overrun with weeds.

At the end of the war, interest was again renewed in the hospital's completion. On March 10, 1947, the residents of Paragould voted approval by an eight to one margin of a $150,000 bond issue for the completion of the facility. In the meantime, the Arkansas General Assembly passed Act 322 of 1947. The act allowed cities that owned or operated municipal hospitals to create hospital commissions for the purpose of operation and management on a non-profit basis. Immediately on March 31, the city council created the Community Hospital Commission, which consisted of Houston Garner, George Barnhill, Joseph D. Wessell, W. H. Trice and Joseph Kirchoff.

When the original Community Hospital Board was formed in 1940, it was composed of Maurice Block, Chairman; Al Wrape, R. A. Reynolds, Joe Bertig, Houston Garner and Earnest Gardner. On Sunday, Oct 16, 1949, the residents of Paragould and the surrounding area attended the dedication of the newly completed Paragould Community Hospital. The Board of Trustees for the Community Methodist Hospital Association was as follows: J. D. Hamilton, chairman; Joseph Bertig, vice-chairman; George Lockwood, treasurer; Ralph Haizlip, secretary; James E. McDaniel, finance chairman; Dr. Rufus D. Haynes, budget chairman; Ray Meriwether, building chairman; Maurice Cathey, legal advisor; Ted Rand, public education chairman; Jay Kirchoff, school of nursing chairman and Eugene Lopez, hospital administrator.

Other members of the association were Don Richardson, Piggott; Charles Stuck, Jonesboro; Terry Rainwater, Walnut Ridge; J. M. Crews, Memphis; Leslie Stratton Jr., Memphis; Rev. A. N. Storey, superintendent Methodist district, Rt. Rev. Paul E. Martin, bishop of Arkansas-Louisiana district; John Bearden, Leachville; E. A. Ellis, Rector; Paul Oliver, Corning; Francis Bland, Ross Ford, Russell Mack, Robert Gardner, Marlan Phillips, Cecil Mitchell, Bill Hammond, Orris Collins, Rupert Blalock, Ray Goodwin, Donald Cox, R. A. Reynolds, W. L. Gatz, Dr. Charles Bowers, Eugene Kirchoff, Ewing Freidman and M. F. Block.

Community Methodist Hospital, now Arkansas Methodist Hospital has had many additions and renovations during the last 50 years of service. The newest project, Phase IV, held its dedication service June 4, 2000. The size of the hospital with this latest project doubled the size of the facility and offers many more state-of-the-art services to the community and surrounding area.

Source: Information researched through hospital archives.
*Submitted by Casey Brue and Kitty Witcher*

# M. F. Block Insurance, Incorporated

We believe that this business is the oldest enterprise in Greene County still owned and managed by the same family.

In July 1914, Maurice F. Block formed M. F. Block & Company, a general insurance agency specializing in property and casualty insurance. In 1917 he joined the French Foreign Legion and served in France, later being transferred to the American Expeditionary Forces. At the end of WWI, he returned and became recognized in Arkansas as one of its leading insurance agents. He was the organizer, the guiding hand and the "boss "until his death in 1965.

The agency expanded in April 1952 with the addition of William J. "Bill" Block joining his father. Bill earned both the CPCU and CIC designations, which indicated knowledge and professionalism in his chosen field. Upon his father's death in 1965, Bill became the owner and CEO of the firm.

In 1967, the agency was incorporated, the ampersand dropped and the name changed to M. F. Block Company.

In 1972, Stanley C. Wright came on board. He holds the CIC designation, is vice-president of the agency and for 27 years has been a most important member. In addition, Stan has served with distinction in the State Insurance Association as a teacher and committeeman. Then in 1974, Jeff Block joined the business and became the third generation Block to serve Greene Countians in the business of insurance. He too holds the profes-

*Arkansas Methodist Hospital*

sional designation of CIC, is a graduate of the USF&G School for agents in Baltimore, MD and has served on three different insurance company counsels as well as an officer and/or director of many local boards and organizations.

The year 1979 was a big one for our company, for in that year we purchased the Ford & Herget Insurance Agency. This agency had been in operation for over 30 years, was well managed and had developed a good book of business. After the sale, Alfred Herget, one of the founders and the manager of Ford & Herget, joined M. F. Block Co. With his knowledge and help the agency continued to grow. Alfred retired in 1988 after over 40 years of service to his clients and to the insurance companies he represented.

Mergers and acquisitions were the trend in the 70s, 80s and 90s. So M. F. Block Co. reached out again to acquire another insurance agency. The year was 1994 and the agency was the Security Insurance Agency of Paragould. At this time Mary Poe, with 21 years insurance experience and former manager of Security, joined our growing agency.

So that the name might better explain our business, in 1998 we became "M. F. Block Insurance, Inc." It was that same year that Bill Block retired after 46 years and Jeff Block became president and CEO.

Through the years, the agency has expanded so that all lines of insurance are offered and today there are eight licensed agents working to serve you.

The year 1999 marked our 85th year of continuous insurance service by the same family. Three generations saying, "thank you" for your friendship and your business.

## Child Art Studio

Child Art Studio has been developing Paragould's photographic memories since 1945.

Founded by B. E. "Brownie" Holoneck and R. G. Knight, Child Art Studio has long specialized in children's portraits. But the CAS lens expanded decades ago to include everyone in the family, especially high school seniors.

In 1947, Bill Hunter and Burk Brinton purchased the two-year-old studio. Hunter bought out his partner in 1954 and for another 33 years continued documenting weddings, senior classes, special occasions and three generations of children.

In 1987, Hunter retired and sold the studio to John Kennett, an award-winning professional photographer who had re-located to Paragould from Texas. Kennett has continued to keep Child Art Studio on the leading edge of photographic technology.

Kennett is a member of Professional Photographers of America, the Southwest Photographers Association and Professional Photographers of Arkansas.

While keeping a steady focus on the future, Kennett and Child Art Studio also maintain a deep respect for the past. The CAS building at 211 N. Pruett St. in Paragould's historic downtown business district has received praise from the City Beautiful Commission and Kennett serves on the charter board of Main Street Paragould.

Kennett and his wife Dot are the parents of Lori and Matthew. The family lives in the Historic Beisel-Mitchell House at 420 W. Court Street, a distinctive Spanish Colonial Revival residence built in 1930. Through Kennett's efforts, the house was listed on the National Register of Historic Places in 1996.

*Submitted by John Kennett*

## City Barber Shop

Ray Thomason was born Sept 27, 1944 in Greene County Arkansas, the seventh son of Jack and Vestal Thomason and the grandson of S. O. Thomason and Bessie (Stevenson) Thomason and also Johnathan and Sarah (Kee) Smith.

Ray Thomason has been the owner and operator of the City Barber Shop, which officially opened for business on Thanksgiving Day 1966.

Ray purchased the shop on May 20, 1976. Since then to the best of his memory some of the barbers he has employed over a period of 23 years are as follows: Lloyd Gilliam, Wylie Maxwell, Don Morrow, Sandy Thomason, Don Sisk, and Glenn Pillow.

As of the printing of this book on the History of Greene County, AR, his son Jason Thomason is in training college located in North Little Rock, AR at the Arkansas College of Barbering and Hair Design.

The art of the old-fashioned barbershop is

*M. F. Block Insurance, Incorporated*

*Child Art Studio*

on the decline because of cost of Barber College compared to cosmetology. A student can attend beauty school for about one fourth the cost of Barber College. Only two barber colleges are in the state, both located in Little Rock.

I can truly say that barbering has been very educational and I've made a modest living, although we sometimes make it look easy, it's not. I have just started my 35th year.

## The Collins Theatre

The Collins Theatre, formerly the Capitol Theatre, is 74 years old. It has a proud history in the community and provided a wide range of entertainment, from Broadway shows to Vaudeville performances, to first-rate movies.

The Collins' is now being used by the community for a wide range of cultural and general entertainment events, beauty pageants, fashion shows, dramatic plays, summer musicals, gospel music, country and western music and other events.

Some of the well-remembered vaudeville acts include: Edgar Bergen, Yodeling Jimmy Rogers, Tex Ritter, Roy Acuff, Ernest Tubb and in later years, the Kentucky Headhunters, a group including the Phelps' Brothers from Cardwell, MO.

Bertig Realty Company built the Capitol Theatre and its grand opening was Oct 15, 1925. John A. Collins was named manager. In 1936 the Collins' family purchased the Capitol and became the sole owners-operators. The community is indebted to the Orris F. Collins' family for making this theatre available to the public, with the forming of Collins' Theatre Foundation, Inc. in 1990.

Even though times have changed, many oldsters remember Capitol Theatre and the 25-cent movies (15 cents for matinees) and a nickel for a large sack of popcorn.

*Submitted by Greene County Historical & Genealogical Society*

## The Corner Café

Our first café was built with the ambitions of a wealthy Tennessee man, W. E. Baird, who came to Paragould in the early 1880s. According to local legend, Baird is said to have remarked, "There'll be a nice town here someday." And so he began to build.

He built a saloon-restaurant on the corner, the first brick residence in Paragould and other buildings on the block that became known as the "Baird block" of South Pruett Street. Upon his death, sometime around 1894, Baird left his estate to his family in Lebanon, TN.

Baird's original Corner Café building was destroyed by fire in Feb 1913. Shortly thereafter, his nephew, Nute Baird, constructed the present two-story red brick structure and by Sept 10, 1913, the Corner Café once again opened its doors for business.

The Corner Café's management changed hands many times throughout its history. Managers included Peck McBride, Sam Rogers and C. C. Crutchfield in the late 1920s, followed later by Gid Elmore. Clyde Hicks and Calvin Yeargain operated the café in the early 1940s. Clyde Hicks died in 1942. Calvin Yeargain continued to operate the café and his daughter, Carol Yeargain Tomlinson, is contributor of the photo made in 1941.

Following the Yeargain's management, Barney Elmore and Alex Fletcher owned the café and then at the end of WWII they sold it to Jack Hyde. Later, Herbert Lundy and Bess and Dess Daughhetee owned and operated it and added air conditioning, which made it the first air-conditioned café in town. Mr. Lundy noted that the other merchants in Paragould were concerned that the air conditioning would ruin their business. According to Bess Daughhetee, some of the customers just came in to keep cool.

In the 50s, prices for the café's home-style cooking ranged from a dollar seventy-five for a T-bone steak dinner to 25-cents for a cheeseburger.

The upstairs story housed 18 boarding rooms and Dr. Fred Porter, a local veterinarian, had a room upstairs which also served as his office. There were 36 beds, one bathtub, three sinks and a lounge. The cost of lodging was one dollar for a night or five dollars for one week.

Paragould's train depot was across Main Street from the café. The majority of the guests were railroad workers who worked long, hard hours away from family and friends. Also, across the street were the 200 Cab Company and the bus depot.

The Lundys sold the café to Mrs. "Tic" Tillman of Jonesboro. Then Earl Sidebottom operated it for two years and Agnes Smith op-

*Ray Thomason in front of the City Barber Shop on September 28, 1998*

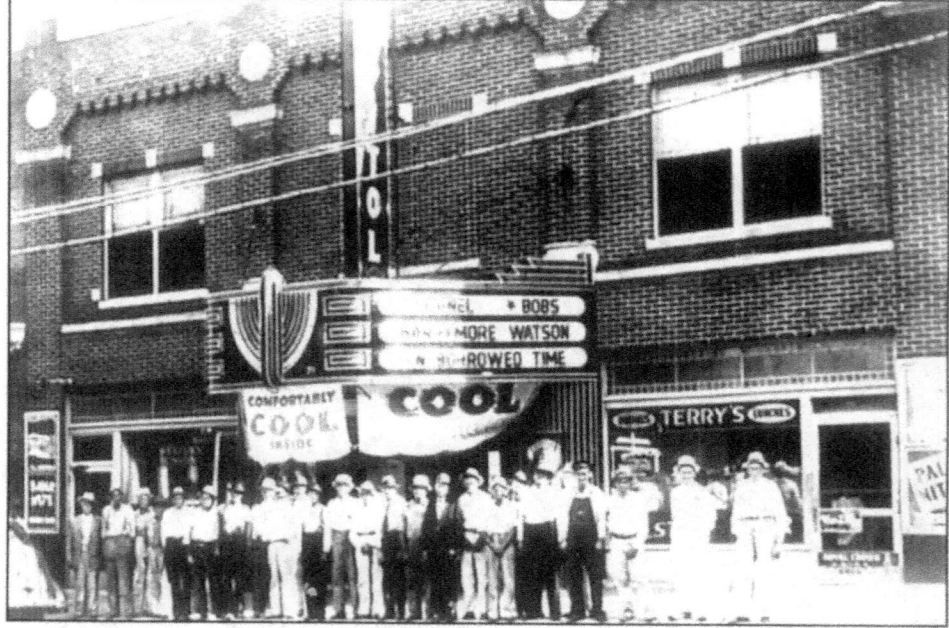

*The Collins Theatre*

erated it and eventually closed it – a place called home by countless railroad workers who came into town with empty stomachs and aching muscles – a place in Paragould's history known as the Corner Café.

*Submitted by Greene County Historical & Genealogical Society*

## Dickson Memorial Hospital

On Feb 1, 1907, the dream of Dr. Aaron Graham Dickson became a reality. Dr. Dickson was an eminent surgeon who began his practice in Paragould in 1890. He studied in Berlin, Vienna and London and had been urged by colleagues to set up a practice in Memphis. The strong bonds which he felt with Paragould and Greene County couldn't be broken and he remained here for more than 15 years before his vision of a modern hospital was realized. His sister, Letha Dillman, assisted in financing the construction of the hospital, according to his plans. Dr. Dickson died only two years later in 1909 and to maintain the hospital, his wife found it necessary to incorporate and sell stock.

The Dickson Memorial Hospital continued to serve this area for 42 years. When the new Community Methodist Hospital was opened in 1949, Dickson shut its doors and took an honored place in Paragould history.

In 1950 City Hall was moved into the old hospital building and H. L. Bogan was contracted to remove the top two floors, including the building's distinctive mansard roof. The city hall later moved next door to the building vacated by City Light and Water. At the present time the fate of the building is being discussed. Some would like to see it restored and a museum located in the building. Other uses are also being considered.

*Submitted by Greene County Historical & Genealogical Society*

## Dollins Furniture

Ed and Bertha Dollins farmed in the Bard community for several years. They moved to Paragould and started a grocery store on Pruett Street. Apparently, it did not thrive and they went into the furniture business in 1933.

Their two sons, Chalma and J. C., eventually joined the business.

After serving in the Navy during WWII, Chalma and his wife Noma bought the furniture store. Danny and his wife, Linda, continued to run the business. Chalma and Danny were members of the Chamber of Commerce.

Dollins Furniture served as a gathering place for local people to visit each other. Chairs were placed out in front for people to sit down and spread the latest gossip.

Dollins Furniture won many outstanding sales awards. The furniture store served the community for more that 50 years.

*Submitted by Sandra Dollins Hollis*

## Faustenia's

Miss Faustenia Barksdale began a long career in retail merchandising with her first part-time job. She along with her parents, James E. and Lucy Barksdale and older sister Jessie, moved to Paragould from Newborn, TN. As a high school teenager, she worked during the summer for S. L. Joseph Company.

Upon graduation, Miss Barksdale accepted fulltime employment at S. L. Joseph Company, learning the retail business. Eventually, she became manager and buyer for the fabric department. She remained with the Joseph Company when it sold to Mr. O. M. Atkins in the late 1930s.

*Corner Café, 1941 – Clyde C. Hicks, manager; Blanche Hunt Holiway, cook; others unknown. (Photo courtesy of Carol Yeargain Tomlinson)*

*Dickson Memorial Hospital*

*Dollins Furnature – Seated: Ed Dollins; standing: Danny Dollins, Chalma Dollins*

Known as Miss Faustenia, she realized a lifelong dream when she opened her own women's apparel shop in Sept 1946. Fashion conscious women of Northeast Arkansas found the latest styles and trends on display at "Faustenia's", located at 202 South Pruett Street in Paragould.

Miss Faustenia traveled regularly to New York, then later to the Dallas Fashion Mart, where she purchased merchandise that included a complete inventory of fine women's apparel. She continued these market trips and enjoyed serving her clientele until 1970, when health problems limited Miss Faustenia's full participation in day-to-day operation of the store. Her nephew, Alvin B. Samuel and his wife, Carolyn, assisted her in managing the business until her death in May 1971.

The store closed with a dispersal sale in March 1973 and with it an era in retail business of Paragould.

*Submitted by Mrs. Alvin B. Samuel*

## Greene Acres Nursing Home

Greene County has seen many changes since the days of the poor farm. On Nov 25, 1957 the Greene Acres Nursing Home held their formal dedication. Donald Cox was president of the Paragould Chamber of Commerce and was the keynote speaker on this great day. He gave credit to J. Ed Thompson, county judge in 1954, who had an idea and desire to do something for the residents who then lived in what was called the "County Poor Farm". Judge Thompson invited 15 civic, service and fraternal organizations of Paragould and Greene County to select one from their group to serve on a committee to see what could be done. With these good citizens of Greene County working together, Greene Acres Nursing Home was built and opened in 1957.

Greene Acres continued to operate on Linwood Drive (Hwy. 49S) until Aug 5, 1995. After five years of planning and two years of construction, Greene Acres Nursing Home was ready to move into its new 125-bed facility. Larry McFadden was administrator at this time. This new facility is located at 2402 Country Club Road. The home sits on four acres. This is a very nice and modern facility.

*Submitted by Bettye Busby*

## Old Gulf Station

Ruby Phillips and Bill Phillips, owners of this old station, say the structure hasn't changed since it was built in 1927. The station has been placed on the National Register of Historical Places. This station is significant because it is the best example of a historic Greene County gas station. It is designed in the Craftsman style of architecture, with Mediterranean style influences.

The Phillips' family bought the station in 1945 and the family operated it until Paul Phillips retired in 1969. Mr. Phillips died in 1975. In the days of this station, it was called "service station" and lived up to its name—service. When you pulled into this business, you got full service: windows washed, oil checked, flats fixed, or tires aired up. This was all done

*Greene Acres Nursing Home, 2402 Country Club Road, Paragould, AR. Date opened Aug 5, 1995.*

*Greene Acres Nursing Home opening day Nov 25, 1957*

*Old Gulf Station, corner of Main and South Third Streets*

with a smile and friendliness that we often miss in this day and time. Bill and Ruby Phillips are the present-day owners of this historic station.

*Submitted by Greene County Historical & Genealogical Society*

## Hamilton Hardware

On Feb 8, 1968 Jean and Kenneth Hamilton purchased the Craver Hardware Store at 207 South Pruett Street from Homer and Beatrice Craver, changing the name to "Hamilton Hardware".

The Hamiltons stocked a large variety of items needed for do-it yourself projects. Plumbing, electrical, lawn and garden, housewares, tools and fasteners were some of the types of products they supplied. Hamiltons prided themselves in giving personal knowledgeable service. They thought themselves fortunate to have had competent and helpful employees, which included Sam Jones, Nicky Wigginton, Ray Bishop, Stan Robbins, Frank Wright and the Hamilton's son, David. They enjoyed the relationship they had with their customers and being in the hardware business.

Jean and Kenneth sold the store in February 1999 to the Bill Orr family of Oak Grove, AR and retired after 31 years in business.

## Harris Barber Shop

The Harris Barber Shop is located at 223 South Pruett Street, next to the old Corner Café. The construction of the building was completed on Sept 10, 1913 and the barbershop was opened at the same time by George Taylor and Victor Clark.

I graduated from Eaton Barber College in Little Rock, AR and began working at the shop on Aug 10, 1949 along with the other barbers in the shop: Otto Bonham, Winston Cunningham and Joe Pace.

In 1952 Jeff Harris purchased the barbershop. He and Joe Pace operated the shop until 1955 and then Neil Jordan worked with them until 1960. At that time Jim Higgins began working at the shop. Joe Pace left and opened his own shop in 1971. Randal Pruett of Cardwell, MO began working in 1987. Jim Higgins got seriously ill and died in 1997.

On Aug 10, 2000 Harris celebrated 51 years of grooming men's hair and is confident that Harris Barber Shop is one of the oldest shops in Arkansas.

The shop was fortunate to have the best shoe shine boy in town. Beginning in 1946 until 1970, Jethro "Chuck" Clark could put a shine on a pair of shoes that would just glisten and he had so much business he had to have a helper. He hired Larvardis Burton. Larvardis is the father of Lavar Burton, who starred in the movie *Roots* as Kunta Kinte. Larvardis now works at Disney World in Orlando, FL.

Al Buck and Jeff Harris are now the only two barbers working at the Harris Barber Shop.

*Submitted by Greene County Historical & Genealogical Society*

## Bobbie Houston's Café

Bobbie Parker Houston was born in Greene County, AR July 14, 1902. She was the youngest daughter of Jessie Andrew Jackson Parker and Mary Bell Huffines who came to Arkansas from Kentucky in a covered wagon with two small daughters Sarah and Margarie. After they arrived in Arkansas Jessie, Cecil and Bobbie Mae were born. Jessie A. Jackson Parker bought land in Bryan Township in Light and farmed.

*Farewell to Hamilton Hardware – Pictured (L to R): David, Jean, and Kenneth Hamilton*

*Harris Barber Shop*

*James and Bobbie Houston, 1964*

*Bobbie Houston's Café*

Bobbie Mae married James Calvin Houston from Randolph County Dec 26, 1920 at her parent's home in Light. He came to Light to work in the cotton harvest and worked for Bobbie's father. He fell in love with Bobbie. Six girls were born to them: Sylvia, Thelma, Lois, Nadean, Alma and Earline.

Bobbie's mother died so she and James lived with her father and farmed the land. Later James and Bobbie bought land east of Light, built a house and farmed the land.

In the spring of 1946, Bobbie bought the café located at Light on the north side of Highway 25. She operated the café until the building burned in May 1956. A building on the west of her caught fire and the whole row burned.

This café was a favorite gathering place for people of all ages. It was open seven days a week. It had a jukebox and part of the time a pinball machine in it. The young people played cards, games and worked puzzles. The women brought their crochet, mending and quilt top piecing to work on while they talked during the day. People came on Saturday evenings from Walcott, Stanford, Walnut Corner, Paragould and other surrounding towns. They had to come early to get a close parking place. She served the regular menu of burgers, sandwiches, candy, cakes, pop and other snacks. She served plate lunches during the harvest time.

Before daylight, the Wonder Bread truck delivered bread, buns and cakes. He left them in an unlocked box beside the door with a ticket for the amount of money due him. That night when Bobbie closed the café, she left a new order and the cash for the previous order in the box. No person ever took a cupcake or a dollar from the box. She was so loved that people would do nothing to hurt her.

Bobbie and James lived at Light until he died in 1971. Bobbie then moved to Paragould. She died in Fort Worth, TX May 13, 1987. They are buried at Mt. Zion Cemetery.

*Submitted by Thelma McMillon*

## Jenkins Lamp and Shade Manufacturing, Inc.

In 1941, the late Isaac E. Jenkins and his wife, Gladys Yeager Jenkins, moved to Paragould from Kansas City, MO and opened Jenkins Variety Store on Pruett Street. In 1962 they sold the variety store and founded Jenkins Lamp Company at their residence on Friendship Road, north of Paragould. Initially the Jenkins' used their garage as an assembly area and used a large barn on the property as a warehouse facility. Table lamps were sold to furniture stores in a two-state area, Arkansas and Missouri.

The product line in 1962 was composed of ceramic bases with parchment shades. Pricing started at $3.95 each and topped out at $5.95. Delivery was included at those prices! Isaac used a station wagon to deliver products to his customers.

In 1972, upon their retirement, the Jenkins' sold the business to their son-in-law, Jack Cox and their daughter, Jean Jenkins Cox. Jack Cox is the grandson of Christopher Huffman Cox and James Lexander Lan, whose family biographies are contained in this book.

The Coxes built a concrete and steel structure at 412 Unity Road in 1972 and expanded the building in 1983. The business was incorporated in 1996 and continues today in its assembly, wiring and lampshade manufacturing operation.

Jenkins' Lamp has outside sales people and now distributes its product line by way of company-owned trailers and commercial carriers to customers located primarily in a 10 state area. The company product line consists of a full line of portable table and floor lamps made of wire metal castings, steel, wood, poly-risen and solid brass parts. Jenkins' lamps are distributed by better home furnishing businesses, decorators and gift shops.

The Coxes and Jenkins' Lamp Company consider Paragould and Greene County to be home.

## Keasler Body Company

Keasler Body Company "got started by accident," but has adapted and changed with the times to become one of Paragould's oldest family-owned businesses.

Lawrence Keasler, 79, who lives across U. S. 412 West from the business in the Center Hill area of Paragould, said his parents moved to Paragould from southern Illinois in 1913.

His father, Jim Keasler, was a blacksmith by trade and also owned a gristmill. In 1925 he bought a brand new Ford Model "T" Roadster. "He built a body for it to go into town and haul sacks of horseshoe nails, horseshoes and blacksmith coal," Keasler said.

A nearby grocery store owner saw Keasler's new wooden truck bed and inquired about it. He wanted one, so he built him one and then another man wanted one. And the business grew from there.

Keasler said his father wasn't one to fight progress and it didn't take him long to realize that the future was in building truck beds – not shoeing horses. He could see that it was a coming thing.

The elder Keasler "turned a lot of heads" in Greene County when he built a truck bed that could be used to haul a team of mules.

The business was originally located about one mile west of the current site at 4207 West Kingshighway. His father moved the business to the current site in 1934.

Keasler's wife of 59 years, Mary, who also worked in the business for many years, said the old wooden truck beds "were strong enough for cattle to walk up on."

Prior to WWII, all of the beds were made from native pine and oak from Northeast Arkansas. During those times, Keasler said his father operated a sawmill to process the logs to his exact specifications. His father had a natural talent for designing and building a product to meet a particular need.

The main truck beds they sold at that time were for hauling livestock. They also built a truck bed that could haul a bale of cotton.

The business closed for a short time during WWII when no new trucks were available for sale and all of the labor force had been drafted into the armed services.

Gradually, all of the quality timber was harvested from Greene County and the surrounding area. They bought some trailer loads of timber for a while, but it got hard to get quality material.

After the war, virtually all of the material switched to steel. Some of the products are now made of lightweight aluminum.

Over the years, Keasler Body Company has built a wide variety of truck beds and enclosed vans to haul a wide variety of products – everything from bulldozers to live baby chicks. They have sold Keasler Body products all across the United States. They have also moved into the business of selling and installing a variety of pre-manufactured truck beds.

One of their truck beds has even made the movies – a Keasler bed was on the catfish-hauling truck that was in the movie, "The Firm."

In 1985, Keasler and his wife sold the business to their youngest daughter, Becky Rieck, her husband, Haley Rieck and Gene Parkinson. "I told them I was going across the street and going home," Keasler said. But he worked for another year or so and now comes over to loaf during the morning and afternoon breaks.

They now employ about eight workers. "We never dreamed of it being more than a one-man operation, but it has really grown," he said.

## Kirk and Brazil Construction Company

Kirk and Brazil Construction Company, a general contractor specializing in industrial and commercial buildings, is a highly service oriented design-build organization that gives full attention to their clients' projects. They have been performing quality general construction for industrial and commercial building projects since 1979 in northeast Arkansas and southeast Missouri with in-house design capabilities or as a team member with design professionals.

Charles C. Brazil, owner and president of Kirk and Brazil Construction Company traces the roots to Earl Kirk, Incorporated, a John Deere dealership owned by his father-in-law, the late Earl Kirk.

A "building division" of that enterprise began as Earl Kirk Construction Company in 1958, primarily constructing grain bins and farm buildings.

Charles Brazil, a registered professional engineer and a native of Newport, AR who has a bachelor's degree in electrical engineering and a master's degree in engineering from the University of Arkansas, first bought a portion of the construction company in 1973. He increased his holdings in the company to 50 percent in 1979 and formed Kirk and Brazil Construction Company. He and his wife, Donna Kirk Brazil, who serves as secretary-treasurer, are the sole owners.

Offices were located at the John Deere dealership on U. S. Highway 412 E. until 1978, when they were moved to the present location at 302 Airport Road.

Earl Kirk Construction and Kirk and Brazil Construction Company have been significant in the growth of Paragould and Greene County as well as several other areas in northeast Arkansas and southeast Missouri. The list of industrial plants, shopping centers, churches and other building by the companies takes up four typed pages, including Paragould Jr. and Sr. High Schools.

The formation by Earl Kirk of the industrial park north of town was instrumental in attracting industry to Paragould. It took Earl Kirk several years to establish a 100-acre industrial park by buying small pieces of property. The industrial park was also supplied with water and sewer lines as well as electrical lines.

The land remained unused for about 10 years, until Modern Packaging, the first company to locate there, broke ground in October 1988. In early 2000 Kirk and Brazil Construction Company doubled the size of this building and added new offices converting the facility to Walsh Heartland, LLC.

The presence of the industrial park was also instrumental in securing the local Prestolite plant, the second company to locate there in 1989. Many other plant facilities have been built since that time in the industrial area.

## Northeast Arkansas Regional Library

The Northeast Arkansas Regional Library is an administrative entity that oversees the five public libraries in Clay, Greene and Randolph counties. The Greene County Library in Paragould is the headquarters library for the system. Other NEARL branches are located at Corning, Piggott and Rector in Clay County and Pocahontas in Randolph County.

Until 1998, the Greene County librarian also served as director of the Northeast Arkansas Regional Library, a position for which the Arkansas State Library requires a master's degree in library science. But after Paullean Capps retired in May 1998, the two positions were split. Sandra Collar Rogers was hired as Greene

*Hal Hubener, regional librarian*

County librarian, beginning in July 1998. Hal Hubener took over the job of regional librarian in January 2000.

A five-member regional library board makes decisions that affect all five libraries, administering the state funds allotted to the region and overseeing cooperative programs such as inter-library loan and the computer automation of check-out procedures and collections management. But each county is still independently governed by a separate county library board, with five members serving staggered terms. County board members are appointed by the county judge, subject to the approval of that county's quorum court.

The Greene County Library has been part of a regional system since 1963 when it joined with its northern neighbor to form the Greene-Clay Regional Library. When Randolph County joined the system in 1965, the name was changed to the Northeast Arkansas Regional Library. Earlier regional librarians were Kathleen Sharp, 1963-1979 and Nancy Evans, 1979-1988.

### S.S. LIPSCOMB ROOM FOR ARKANSAS HISTORY AND GENEALOGY

When the Greene County Library moved into its new home in 1974, a 750 square-foot space was designated as the "Arkansas Room." But there wasn't much to put in it until 1982 when the foundation established by the late Samuel Scott Lipscomb provided more than $100,000 to establish and endow a special library collection. The grant resulted from a proposal submitted by library director Nancy Evans.

Foundation gifts of more than $50,000 purchased the initial collection, furnishings and equipment for the S. S. Lipscomb Room for Arkansas History and Genealogy, which was dedicated May 14, 1983. Another $50,000 was invested with the Arkansas Community Foundation. The investment income provides several thousand dollars each year so the library can continue to add to the Lipscomb Collection.

Growth of the collection and its ever-increasing use have led to two major spurts in the amount of library space dedicated to the Lipscomb holdings. Soon after its 10th anniversary in 1993, the room was doubled in size when a wall was removed that had separated the Lipscomb Room and the old audiovisual section. In March 1999, not long after its 15th year, the Lipscomb Room was re-located to a 2,500 square foot area that had once been the children's department, a glass-enclosed space more than three times the size of the original Lipscomb Room.

With an emphasis on local research materials such as newspaper microfilm, census indexes and cemetery listings, the collection has attracted visitors with Greene County roots from more than half of the 50 states. Thousands of area residents have used the collection to document their family trees and research local history.

The county histories published by Vivian Hansbrough in 1946 and Myrl Rhine Mueller in 1984 as well as the *Fathers of the Ridge* series of more than 700 family profiles compiled by George Rowland have provided a starting place for almost all later research. The set of Paragould Daily Press microfilm donated by former newspaper publisher Fred A. Wulfekuhler provides a keyhole to past local events. Many of the other Greene County materials were compiled by members of the Greene County Historical and Genealogical Society, especially by Charles and Helen Wood, who personally surveyed all 78 known cemeteries in the county during the late 1980s.

Continuing today, all genealogy researchers are encouraged to add their names to our Roots Registry and to contribute to the Family File, a genealogy collection that now fills three cabinet drawers.

Among its many features, the Lipscomb Room also has census microfilm for all of Arkansas; materials on most of the southeast states from which early Greene County settlers migrated and a special section on the Civil War, emphasizing military activity west of the Mississippi River.

The Lipscomb Room enjoys an unparalleled reputation for service, thanks to a reliable crew of volunteers, most of them affiliated with the Greene County Historical and Genealogical Society, which has been a major support group for the room since GCHGS was organized in 1988. Volunteers assist researchers, answer mail requests and help keep the room organized. The Lipscomb Room volunteer program, spearheaded by Charles and Helen Wood, was one of the First GCHGS projects.

Three of the original volunteers are still with us – Flo Hazzard, Dawn Linden and Fran Morris. Other regulars include Betty Clayton, Sara Flowers, Maxine Harris, Robert Harris, Clara Lovelady and Anita Phillips. Our newest volunteers are Norma Addison, Gerlene Jackson, Mary Smith Johnson and Millie Wyatt. Sonya Hester, Ellen Lacey and Vernon Lacey continue to serve as substitute volunteers as needed and as available.

Past volunteers have included Erin Boulton, Aleen Bozarth, the late Rose Bradsher, Darla Eaker, Elwanda Gates, the late Joe Gonser, Scott Hill, Annette O"Neal and Gerald Scott Jr.
*Submitted by Kitty Sloan*

## Paragould Doors

Paragould Doors was started in 1986 by Wayne and Pauletta (Pillow) Glenn under the name Shamrock Enterprises and was located at 1413 E. Kingshighway. In 1990 the name was changed to Paragould Overhead Doors. In 1996 the establishment was moved to 3211 E. Kingshighway where it is located today. Pauletta Glenn taught school at Paragould High School and coached volleyball and track when she married Wayne in 1987. Wayne Glenn had moved here from Dexter, MO, where he had been in the grain bin, irrigation and building of steel buildings. This is where he learned his trade of installing garage doors. In 1986 and 1987 they sold and installed garage doors together after work or on the weekends until they built the business to the point that it required full-time help. Pauletta went full-time in the summer of 1988. Today the business is well established and competitive with other larger companies. Wayne died in July of 1999, but Pauletta and her son-in-law, Steven Boggs along with the occasional help of her son, Chris Glenn and daughter, Cara Killian, continue to run the business.
*Submitted by Pauletta Glenn*

## Peoples Bank

Peoples Bank is owned by Spring River Bank Shares, which is a two-bank holding company that was founded in 1988. It owns Peoples Bank in Imboden and purchased Peoples Bank in Paragould in September 1991 from RTC. Paragould's main office is located at 300 West Emerson Street, with branch offices at 201 Reynolds Road and 801 East Ninth Street in Rector.

The Board of Directors includes Charles Luter, President/CEO, Warren (Chip) Luter, Vice President, Tim Wells, Vice President, Arthur Pillow, Rex Bouldin, George Cook, Preston Clark, Moud Gazaway and Gregg Sain. Officers are: Charles Luter, President/CEO, Warren (Chip) Luter, Vice President; Tim Wells,

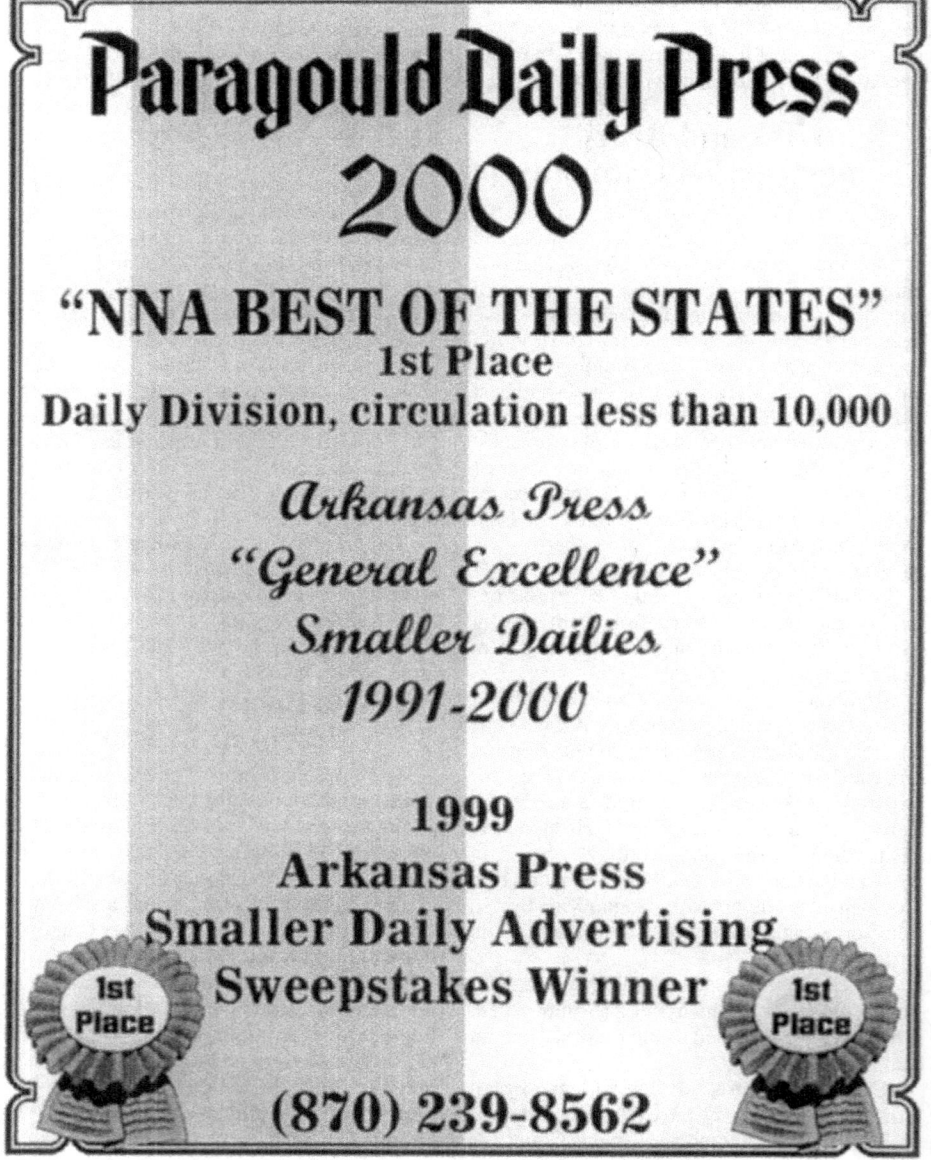

Vice President; Crete Rhodes, Vice President/Cashier; Sherry Dills, Vice President/Branch Manager; Lora Laubach, Business Development Officer; and Cheryl Poindexter, Mortgage Loan Officer.

Peoples Bank has grown from 20 million in 1991 to 130 million in 2000. Our expansions include the Reynolds Road branch, which was built in 1996; and the Rector branch, currently being expanded, will double in size. Rector has grown from 6 million to 25 million.

Today's services include: checking accounts, savings, money market, certificates of deposit, Christmas Club, loans, debit card, credit card, internet banking and bill pay, IRA's, and Peoples' Access (24-hour banking).

We have recently purchased land on Highway 49 South to build a new main bank.

## Don Perkey's Shoes

In 1958, Don and Loree' Perkey moved to Greene County and decided to open a new business. In May 1958 the doors of the Sample Shoe Store were opened at 219 South Pruett Street. Don and Loree' were the proud new owners. City Light and Water had previously owned the building.

A lot of work was done to make the local shoe store the place to shop in downtown Paragould. Don Perkey, assisted by his father-in-law, Othar Campbell, built all of the store's fixtures, painted and got everything ready for the open shoeboxes to be displayed. Don made a trip to the St. Louis Shoe Market and the Dallas Shoe Market to stock the shelves of the new business. As stock began arriving, Loree' coded and marked the shoes, using the store's current system, getting all of the merchandise ready to go on the shelves.

On July 4, 1983, the Perkeys moved their business to its current location at 203 South Pruett, formerly Western Auto. At this time, the name of the business was changed from Sample Shoe Store to Don Perkey's Shoes, Inc. Over the years, shoe styles may have changed, but the way Don and Loree' Perkey treat their customers has never changed. The customer has and will always take top priority with the local couple.

Don Perkey's Shoe Store, Inc. has a staff of employees eager to help as customers walk through the doors. The Perkeys are proud of their five employees including: Reba Bridges, an employee for 17 years; Laveda Barnhart, an employee for five years; Bea DeLuryea and Jacob Landrum, employees for three years and Jan Cody an employee for two years.

For nearly 43 years, the Perkeys have served customers in Greene County and surrounding areas. The couple has placed shoes on three generations.

*Submitted by Don Perkey*

## Security – Union Planters Bank

Security Bank was established in 1906 and has played an important role in Greene County's development. We're proud of our past. We're proud of what the people in Greene County have helped us do. We'll continue to look for the future, to put our faith in the strength of our fellow-Greene Countians.

*Don Perkey's Shoes employees, L to R: Don Perkey (owner), Laveda Barnhart, Reba Bridges, Jan Cody, Fran Wagster, and Bea DeLuryea; insert: Jacob Landrum*

Security Bank and Trust Company was incorporated July 24, 1906 with capital stock of $100,000 divided into 1,000 shares of $100 each. I. C. Legitt was president.

In 1931, the bank was reorganized as The Security Bank and Trust Company, Paragould. James W. Alexander was elected president. By the end of 1931, assets had climbed to almost $443,000.

In 1960 James E. Alexander was chairman and E. R. Browning became president. Assets were $6 million. In 1964 E. R. Browning was chairman and W. W. Misenhimer became president. The year 1965 saw the bank's name changed to Security Bank.

When Marlin D. Jackson was elected president and chairman on Jan 13, 1970, assets were a little over $12 million. During his 13-year presidency, assets grew to over $70 million. On April 13, 1983, Frank Oldham Jr. was elected chairman and president.

When Dr. Oldham assumed the responsibilities of chairman of Mid South Bancshares, Inc (the holding company of Security Bank) in July 1985, Bill Fisher became president of Security Bank. At that time total assets had grown to approximately $80 million. Assets continued to increase and were approximately $102 million when Steve Gramling was elected president May 11, 1992.

In December 1994, Security Bank was acquired by Union Planters Bank, Memphis, TN. At that time the Paragould Branch had total assets of Approximately $112 million. On April 13, 1998, Bill Fisher returned to the bank as president.

The Paragould Branch of Union Planters Bank is one over 800 banking offices located in 12 states. We serve over 1.5 million customers and bring you the best of both worlds in that we are closely focused on each community we serve; yet we have the products and services of one of the nation's largest banks with approximately 35 billion in total assets.

## Shamco Metal Recycling

Prior to 1838, there was a company called Paragould Hide and Metal. A gentleman named Thomas O. Smallen owned this company. Mr. Smallen also had a scrap metal business in Pocahontas, AR. He may have even been from Pocahontas.

William Samuels, of Cape Girardeau, MO purchased the land, building, equipment and inventory from Mr. Smallen in 1938. Mr. Samuels and his eldest son, Bernard, moved to Paragould in 1938 to operate the business. He changed the name to Samuels' Hide and Metal Company, Incorporated.

William, whose background was in the ladies' ready to wear retail business, had no experience in the scrap metal business. However, his son Bernard, had worked for sometime for his uncle in Cape Girardeau in this type of business.

After settling in Paragould, William moved his wife and his two other sons to Paragould. He had two daughters who were living together in St. Louis. After WWII started, his son Bernard went into the service. His youngest daughter had married a gentleman from St. Louis named Samuel Buchman.

Samuel went into the Army and his daughter, Selma, moved to Paragould while her husband was away. During the war, almost everything was rationed. William had been buying tires and inner tubes and when they became scarce he was able to sell them and he did quite well growing his business. As the war ended, Bernard rejoined the business. His oldest son, David, had finished high school and started in the business. Selma's husband, Samuel Buchman, returned from the war, came to Paragould and began working for his father-in-law in the business.

By 1947, the business could not support four families, so Samuel Buchman moved to Caruthersville, MO and opened a satellite scrap yard called Buchman Iron and Metal Company.

He sold this business in 1952 when it was apparent that he was needed back at Samuels' Hide and Metal Company, Incorporated.

The company had a growing spurt from the early 50s to the early 60s. The volume of material increased along with the number of employees. Also, new production equipment was added during this time.

In 1964, David Samuels decided to leave the family business, so he moved to St. Louis, MO. William Samuels passed away in 1966, leaving Bernard Samuels and Samuel Buchman as the owners and operators of the business. In the summer of 1973 Samuel Buchman's son Martin, entered the business and in 1977 Martin bought out his father. In 1980 Martin and his brother-in-law, John Havens, purchased the remaining business from Bernard Samuels. In 1995, after careful consideration, it was decided to change the name of the company. There were several reasons for this. First, there will most likely never be a Samuels involved in the business again; second, the company will never again be in the hide and fur business and lastly the name did not really express what the company began. Internally, the company was called Shamco, which is the acronym for Samuel's Hide and Metal Company. So to preserve the history of the company, Shamco was decided upon. Recycling was a catchword of the 90s, even though metal recycling is what the company had done since its inception in 1938, so recycling best described the business. Hence, SHAMCO METAL RECYCLING became the new name.

As you can see, our history dates back to sometime before 1938. Today we are a metal recycling company serving industry and the public. We recycle in excess of 14,000 tons of ferrous scrap and 750,000 pounds non-ferrous scrap per year. Our facility has grown over the years occupying approximately 10 acres of land. We are a modern facility with a considerable investment in scrap hauling and scrap processing equipment. Over the years we have shipped scrap for export to Taiwan and Mexico. Our U. S. markets have been from Colorado to Southern Texas to Chicago, Pittsburgh and Birmingham. Almost all of the ferrous scrap now goes within the State of Arkansas; most within 65 miles of our facility.

We currently employ 15 people. With all the changes over the years some things never change. Even with our modern processing equipment some of our raw material is still processed in the same manner that it was in 1938. We have had a good 60 plus years and look forward to the challenges and opportunities in the years to come.

## Sunlite Casual Furniture

Transnational Capital Venture – Mr. Haim Zitman and Mr. Joseph Eiger are the owners of Sunlite Casual Furniture.

The 239,000 square feet manufacturing plant with office space of 14,352 square feet was built 1979 in Paragould, AR by the founding owner, Arkla Industries, producing gas grills.

Other previous owners:
1984-Purchased by Preway.
1989-Re-purchased by Arkla Industries.
1992-Purchased by Sunbeam.
1997-Purchased by U. S. Industries.
1998-Purchased by Transnational Capital Ventures.

Significant changes or advances:
1995-Installed wrought iron furniture line.
1996-Gas grill lines removed.
1996-Second wrought iron furniture line installed.
1997-Started consolidation of all furniture manufacturing-completed early 1998.

Growth and Expansions:
1982-Arkla added 16,000 square feet to plant for powder paint system.
1987-Preway added 9,600 square feet to offices.
1995-Sunbeam added 200,000 square feet warehouse

Today's products and services include wrought iron, aluminum and steel outdoor furniture, which are popular.

Future plans are continual growth and expansion for our products in the marketplace.

## Stacy & Company Hair and Nail Salon

Stacy & Company Hair Salon was established in 1989. The salon, Sandy and Friends owned by Sandy West at that time, was bought into around 1987 by Trent Stacy, of Peach Orchard, AR. Sandy and Friends Salon relocated to Brookside Plaza on W. Kingshighway in 1988. In 1989 Trent bought Sandy out, she left the business and he changed the name of the shop to Stacy & Company. Patsy Clark purchased Stacy & Company in 1994, when Trent moved to Memphis, TN. (Patsy had originally owned Clarkdales, a previous salon with Dale Tyler in 1984. She sold out in 1987.)In 1995 Pat relocated the shop a second time due to increase in business. The shop is now located at 100 N. Rockingchair Road, Ste. 11 in the Rockingchair Village. Now Stacy & Company Hair and Nail Salon with the addition of her daughter, Rebecca Clark a Nail Technician, employs five other hair dressers: Pat, now Pat Gatlin, Denise Flanery, Sheila Stubblefield, Jamie Taylor and Pat's other daughter Whitney Blankenship. Stacy & Company is a full service salon, specializing in cuts, colors, perms, waxing, all artificial nails, manicures and pedicures.

## Teleflora

Teleflora is an innovative company dedicated to providing exciting products, cutting edge technology and exceptional service to the flowers-by-wire industry.

We at Teleflora are proud to be a contributing part of Greene County and this great community.

*The Trading Barn*

*1989 Christmas advertisement (Brookside Plaza location) – Seated L-R: Denise and Ryan Flanery, Santa, Sheila Stubblefield with Brynne Wortham. Top L-R: Pat Gatlin, Trent Stacy, Whitney (Clark) Blankenship and Rebecca Clark.*

## Trading Barn

The old trading barn as it was called, was a strong barn until 1935 when it was hit by a tornado. It withstood this heavy cable wire pulling it up straight again. It was used in a 20 acre peach orchard to cradle peaches, then selling these different sizes and grades.

Later it was made into a trading barn. Selling whatever farmers had to sell but especially cows, goats, horses and mules.

Most barns now are made of metal and design of the barns is a thing of the past. Years ago every farmhouse had a barn like this. Now barns are not needed as much as then. There are fewer cattle put into barns. Cows are not put up into barns as then. There were stalls to put cows into milk. Children now don't know what fresh milk is, milk that is unpasteurized.

I believe if this barn could talk it would house lots of history stories to tell.

The old trading barn is located between Hooker and Beech Grove, Highway 141 North in Greene County.

*Submitted by Kim Tritch*

## Turner Holdings, L.L.C. – Turner Dairies, Inc.

Turner Dairies started as a local farm dairy in Covington, TN early in the 1900s. The Turner family milked cows and delivered the product to their customers in town seven days each week in horse drawn wagons. In Jan 1946, P. A. Turner and W. H. Turner pasteurized the first gallon of milk at Turner Dairies and the commercial dairy processing and delivery enterprise was started. Early delivery vehicles were surplus WWII Army ambulances and later "previously owned milk trucks".

From those humble beginnings, the company has grown to sales of over $200,000,000 and employs over 1000. Ice cream novelties are sold over the entire Southeastern United States. Nationally branded milk and ice cream products are distributed along with the Quality Chekd Dairy products manufactured at one of Turner's four modern plants. Well over 90% of their sales are in products manufactured by Turner in their own plants. Products are sold under the Turner, Forest Hill and Coleman brands on over 250 company routes.

Turner belongs to the Quality Chekd Products Association. Quality Chekd is a member owned cooperative whose 42 members account for over 2.5 billion dollars in milk and dairy product sales in the United States and Canada. Association members must meet quality standards that exceed government requirements for safety and quality. Turner is a past recipient of Merit Awards of quality in both production and marketing from the Association.

Full service milk and ice cream routes provide the majority of Turner's sales. Significant sales are also in drop shipment of Turner and other label products. In addition to the routes, Turner processes the milk used in Aunt Jemima frozen French toast for The Quaker Oats Company, soft frozen yogurt mix for Miss Karen's frozen yogurt and other contract-manufactured products in both the milk and ice cream products.

Quality Assurance is provided by state certified labs at each plant staffed with certified lab technicians. Turner is a regular competitor and winner, in Tennessee State Fair dairy judging as well as Quality Chekd Dairy Products Association awards competitions.

## Union Station 1909–1976

Hotels and other businesses quickly surrounded Union Station, built in 1906. This was a brick building that served passengers and freight customers of both the Cotton Belt and the Iron Mountain Railroads. At first, the two lines had separate depots. The Iron Mountain called its station "Parmly" for several years. A joint depot was built sometime before 1895. Like any train station, it was the scene of many goodbyes, but none as spectacular as when Paragould answered the call and turned out in force to send "her brave soldier boys" off to fight WWI.

With the decline in train travel, the depot fell on hard times. Despite efforts to save it by the Paragould-Greene County Bicentennial Celebration Commission and the Greene County Fine Arts Council, the depot was sold to "be torn down for materials" in 1976. A Cotton Belt spokesman explained, "The land is of value; the building is not". A parking lot is now located at this site, but part of the depot's tile floor remains, a simple reminder of another Greene County landmark.

*Submitted by Greene County Historical & Genealogical Society*

## The Vandervoort Hotel

The really great hotel in Paragould was the Vandervoort, built by L. L. Vandervoort while the town, still in the glow of prosperity, was a

*The Vandervoort Hotel*

*Union Station Paragould, Arkansas*

great timber-manufacturing center. Opened Dec 1, 1915, it was a modern handsome four-story brick building of 75 rooms. It stood where the First National Bank is now located, at Second and West Main. Designed by architects Yeager and Cairs, it duplicated on a smaller scale the famous Chisca Hotel of Memphis.

The Vandervoort is nostalgically remembered as the scene of many memorable social gatherings, weddings, dinners, dances and banquets. It was a social center of Paragould and Cardwell, MO. Each spring for years, Junior-Senior banquets were held in the ballroom.

Many young men started their business careers working at the hotel, as shoeshine boys, waiters, bus boys, etc. Ethan Busby, a local businessman, remembers his first job was shining shoes at the Vandervoort.

Gus Wright purchased the Vandervoort in 1957. It was kept open for several years, and then sold to First National Bank for a building site. At the time the hotel closed, the office of the Chamber of Commerce was housed there, as were the Deluxe Beauty Salon and Massengill's Barber Shop.

*Submitted by Greene County Historical & Genealogical Society*

## Watson Brothers

The Watson brothers- Earby and Henry – owned Watson's Brothers General Merchandise in Halliday, AR. Earby bought Henry's share of the business in early 1925 and stayed in that business until 1939. At that time he moved to his farm in Holly Grove Community. Earby fought in France during WWI. He was married to Leora (Casebolt) Watson. The Watson family came to Arkansas from Greenville, TN.

Earby Watson died January 1, 1967, and Leora in March of 1975. Henry Watson was married to Lizzie Zolner and they had one son, Henry Carroll Watson. Both Henry and Lizzie are deceased.

## Watson's Fashion Boutique

Earby Leroy and Patty S. Watson were owners of Watson's Fashion Boutique, 109 North Pruett Street in Paragould, from March 1985 through January 1996. Leroy's father and grandfather had both operated businesses, so he kept the tradition going.

Leroy Watson is married to Patty S. (Bivins) Watson. They have one son, Dan Watson and one daughter, Susan K. Watson. They have three grandchildren: Nathan, Andrew and Kelsey Watson.

The Watson's opened their first store at 110 South Pruett Street, known as "Watson's Music and Gift Gallery." Later in 1988 they bought the building at 109 North Pruett Street, renaming it, "Watson's Fashion Boutique". They sold it to Paulette Bivens on Jan 16, 1996.

The Watsons are members of Greater Vision Pentecostal Church. They are now enjoying traveling, fishing and working in their church.

## White Printing Company, Incorporated

During the 1930s the late Mr. and Mrs. James W. Roney owned and operated the Roney Printing and Gift Shop located in the south half of the building at 221 South Pruett Street, Paragould, AR. The north half of the building was occupied by Mr. Will Burrow who owned the Burrow Shoe Repair Shop.

In 1946 the late Mr. and Mrs. Calvin White bought the Roney Printing and Gift business and Mr. Burrow moved out of the north half of the building giving the Whites more room to expand the new business. After remodeling the building, Mr. White, along with Mr. Hugh Copeland, operated the printing business in the south half of the building and Mrs. White ran the office and gift shop in the north half of the building. At this time Mr. White bought more modern equipment, such as printing presses, a hand-powered paper cutter and a linotype-typesetting machine.

Named "White Printing Company" the business continued to grow and Mr. White was looking for more help. In August 1947 he contacted Mr. Charles Northen and asked Mr. Northen, who, having just completed three years in the Air Force was working in a drug store under the G. I. Bill (on the job training), if he would like to change vocations and learn to operate the linotype machine. Mr. Northen said "yes" and began, Aug 8, 1947, under the tutorship of Mr. White and a Gregg Typesetting Manual, as an apprentice.

In 1949 Mr. White rented the building located at 113 W. Emerson Street, formerly occupied by Mid-West Dairy, to provide more space for the growing business. Mr. Copeland, who was an employee, suggested that Holcomb Transfer Company could assist in moving the heavy equipment to the new location. While loading the linotype machine a skid broke and the linotype fell to the ground, breaking into many pieces. The Dr Pepper Bottling Company provided a power lift to complete the move.

Upon moving to the new location, several pieces of new equipment were purchased: a Miehle vertical cylinder press, a Heildleberg automatic platen press, a flat bed cylinder press and a hand-fed paper cutter that was all power, along with several other pieces of equipment for the bindery department

Repairing the linotype took approximately six weeks, during which time Mr. A. M. Owen, who owned and operated a print shop across the street, was kind enough to lend his linotype machine for several print jobs. Soon after the move Mr. White's son, Wallace returned from the armed services and began work as a printer and shop foreman. In the early 1950s Wallace left the print shop to become part owner and editor of the Paragould Daily Press, at which time Mr. White pro-

*Watson Brothers in 1923: Earby, standing by the gas pump and Henry next to the car. Note that gas is priced at 16 cents a gallon.*

*Patty and Leroy Watson of Watson's Fashion Boutique*

moted Charles Northen to the job of shop foreman in which capacity he remained until his retirement.

Business was good and many new jobs were being done with the new equipment, such as: the Paragould High School "*Echo*", for Ms. Clara Stepp's / Vivian Hansbrough's journalism class, shoe box labels for the Ed White Shoe Company with the Happy-Go-Lucky four color label; check books, letterheads and envelopes for the Bertig Company's 24 cotton gins and office supplies for city and county offices as well as for the Emerson Electric Manufacturing Company, E. & W. Shirt Factory, Foremost Dairy, M. F. Block Insurance Company, Ford and Herget Insurance Company and the Dr Pepper Bottling Company just to name a few.

One of the most delicate and difficult jobs was the publication of the Greene County Poll Tax Book. This was an alphabetical list of all the registered voters in Greene County and was published by White Printing Company until the State Legislarture abolished it.

In March 1964, Messrs. John W. McKenzie, Frank J. Schreit and Charles Northen purchased the business from Mr. and Mrs. White, who consented to the use of their name for the new business (White Printing Company, Incorporated). Mr. McKenzie was named president and general manager; Mr. Schreit was the secretary/treasurer and Mr. Northen was the print shop foreman. Ms. Linda (Jetton) McClure, who was an office employee of the Whites at the time, continued as bookkeeper and office manager.

In the 1970s, the business was in need of a much larger offset press. John McKenzie and Charles Northen flew to Cincinnati, OH, to the Harris Manufacturing Plant to see one of the newest 25" Harris Offset Presses in operation. An order was placed for a new Harris Press of which only 25 had been manufactured and sold at this time.

The L. A. Darling and Monroe Auto Equipment factories became very good customers, both always needing much printing and lots of office supplies.

The printing department played a big part in several area publications during that period: *The Buffalo Island Fair catalogue, The Arkansas Methodist Hospital Auxiliary's Belles and Beaux program, the Paragould Centennial Cookbook* (five reprints) and several church books and publications. Especially noteworthy were *"The History, Morgan's Baptist Church, 1771-1971, Moneta, Virginia"* and the *history of the East Side Baptist Church of Paragould, AR.*

With the increase in business in both the printing and office supplies departments, more space was needed to expand into. Fortunately, the building next door, east of the print shop became available in the early 1970s, which was rented for the office supplies business. More equipment was added as well as inventory of office supplies. An outside salesman was added to cover Northeast Arkansas and Southeast Missouri, where additional business added to the success of the firm. Office supplies were delivered overnight and most print jobs were delivered within one week's time.

*Printshop foreman Charles Northern sitting at the old linotype machine shortly before his retirement in 1984.*

Charles Northen retired from White Printing in December 1984 and Leon Eagan became the print shop foreman later on. John McKenzie retired as general manager in April 1986 and Mr. Johnnie Fleeman became general manager in his place.

On Dec 24, 1990, the Bertig (Graber Store) building caught fire and the ensuing blaze destroyed that building as well as the office supply building of White's and several other downtown buildings. Only through the valiant efforts of the Paragould Fire Department were the print shop building and the printing equipment therein saved, on that freezing cold, ice-covered night.

Thanks to their efforts and the efforts and loyalty of the company's employees the print shop was back in the printing business within one week, at its West Emerson Street location. The office supply department was relocated into new premises at 100 W. Main Street within two weeks and despite the complete loss of all customer records due to the fire, sales and collections from all customers continued uninterrupted.

On April 29, 1991, the company acquired Mr. Charles Northen's interest in the White Printing Company, Incorporated, leaving the families of Messrs. McKenzie and Schreit as 100% owners of all of the company's common stock.

At the end of February 1998, Johnnie Fleeman retired as general manager and he was succeeded by Mr. Joe Schreit, son of Frank Schreit, as general manager. Also at which time new print shop equipment, including a Hamada multicolor press and a Konica digital image setting system, costing more that $15,000 was purchased and installed.

On June 30, 1999, Leon Eagan retired and was succeeded by his son, Richard Eagan, as the foreman of the print shop, which now has five full time employees.

Messrs. Neil Laffoon and Brent Arant now serve as outside salesmen for both the printing and office supply departments. Mr. Jeff Jones serves as assistant manager; Ms. Linda McClure is the assistant secretary/treasurer and Ms. Jennifer Schreit is the accounting/computer manager.

Both Joe Schreit and Richard Eagan are young men by the writer's standards and have been handed the responsibility of carrying on the traditions of White Printing Company of highest quality workmanship and service, established by those who have served the company before them, into the new millennium.

## Wyatt Brothers Furniture, Incorporated

W. A. Wyatt Sr. established Wyatt's Furniture Store on Pruett Street in 1914, after working at a local drug store where he was known as "The best fountain man in town". He came to Paragould from Rector to further his education at Parrish Business College.

W. A. Wyatt married Maud McHaney, a member of a prominent Greene County family who owned extensive real estate. Their two-story home was located on top of a hill (across from the current Paragould High School) overlooking large acres of farmland.

He later was joined by his brother Richard "Jack" Wyatt forming Wyatt Brothers Furniture Incorporated.

W. A. Wyatt and Maud had one son, W. A. "Bill" Wyatt Jr. born Jan 6, 1916.

Bill Wyatt married the former Miss Margaret Juanita Chunn, daughter of John and Gelena Chunn, from Jonesboro on April 6, 1937. Juanita had one brother, Dr. Ellsworth

Chunn, an award-winning violinist, educator, war hero (Bataan and Corregidor prisoner of war for four years) and chief of bureau of textbooks for California under Governor Ronald Reagan. Later Ellsworth became president general of the Sons of The American Revolution and president of The Decendents of George Washington's Army at Valley Forge.

Bill was a graduate of the New York School of interior design, the American Conservatory of Music of Chicago, IL and Draughon's Business College in Memphis, TN. He was the past president of the Arkansas Furniture Association, past president of the Paragould Rotary Club.

He was a graduate of Arkansas State College (University) with a degree in music and was an accomplished musician and vocalist. He was very well known for his singing ability.

Juanita played piano in Jonesboro including the daily KBTM radio broadcast with Ernest Johnson where they played twin pianos and did dramatic skits and both later played professionally in Chicago. Ernest later played with Red Skelton during the war. Juanita once played on the world's smallest piano in the lounge of the Richard's Restaurant in the loop in downtown Chicago, the meeting place for many celebrities (Mae West, Jean Harlow, etc) who signed the guest book there. She also played at the Normandy Lounge in the world famous Aragon Ballroom Building, home of many of the "Big Bands" of the day and was listed in the who's who in Chicago among entertainers to see and hear.

Before WWII, Bill joined his father and uncle in the furniture store in downtown Paragould. He left to enlist in the U. S. Navy and was stationed in Farragut, ID where he was later joined by his wife and family and lived in Spirit Lake, ID.

After the war Bill and Juanita returned to Paragould and the furniture business and took over the store upon the passing of Bill's father and uncle. Later they attended the New York School of Interior Design and the University of Tennessee School of Interior Design and added interior design services to Wyatt Brothers Furniture, Incorporated and changed the name to Wyatt's Interiors. The building located at 108 North Pruett was later sold to Security Bank and the store was relocated on East Kingshighway. After 70 years of operation the store was sold and Bill continued as a real estate broker at Wyatt's Real Estate.

Bill and Juanita had four sons, William Calvin Wyatt (optometrist in Pocahontas), John

*Left to Right: W. A. Wyatt, Jr. (Bill), Jack Wyatt, and W. A. Wyatt, Sr.*

Robert Wyatt (pharmacist in Paragould), Richard Allen Wyatt (banker and real estate developer in Jonesboro) and James David Wyatt (deceased). They have six grandchildren: Courtney Sue Wyatt (Mrs. Lane McMurry), John Robert Wyatt Jr., David Allen Wyatt, Richard James Wyatt, Matthew Lee Wyatt (Deceased) and Stephanie Kay Wyatt.

Bill and Juanita were both accomplished entertainers and were involved with the "Belles 'n Beaux" for many years, church special musical performances and performed in many programs throughout the south and on their many trips abroad.

*Submitted by Mrs. William Wyatt*

# ORGANIZATIONS

## Arkansas Methodist Hospital Auxiliary

Having opened the hospital on a shoestring budget with much substandard equipment, Eugene Lopez, administrator, found it necessary in early 1950 to call on the wives of the Medical Staff and Hospital Association for assistance. He told them that the hospital could not continue to operate unless it had more operating funds and unless more of the patients paid their bills.

On July 7, 1950, the Hospital Auxiliary came into being under the leadership of Obion Gatz. Immediately assigned money-raising goals – this group put on plays at school (one dime per child), got dealers to donate merchandise (including a new Ford car) and held raffles, bake sales and card parties. The group of ladies who became the building blocks for the Hospital Auxiliary were: Obion Gatz, Walta Mildred Haynes, Ellen Wessell, Frances Collins, Maxine Rand, Marie Meriwether, Ann Light, Kathleen Bowers, Ina Cathey, Frances Pennington, Lottie Reynolds, Marcie Haizlip and Thelma Mitchell.

They raised the necessary cash ($12,000) and established a fund to pay the bills of indigent patients and started an annual theater production (Belles 'n' Beaux). The new auxiliary also visited factories and businesses and made talks to encourage people to sign up for hospital insurance so when they became patients their bills would be paid. This was in addition to helping with simple chores inside the hospital – filling water pitchers, distributing mail, etc., to help the nursing staff.

By 1960, the auxiliary had contributed around $60,000 to the hospital. Many of the hospital originators credit the auxiliary with saving the hospital during its many early financial crises.

Today with the auxiliary well into their 50th year of service, they are busy with the sale of their new cookbook and have honored some of the organization's oldest members who continue to serve. Upon entering into the millennium they eagerly await the move into the gift shop and reception area in the new addition of the hospital where they can better serve patients and visitors.

*Submitted by Greta K. Witcher*

## Fox Hills Country Club

In 1915 a small group of men led by Perry House and Sol Bertig started the Paragould Country Club, now known as Fox Hills County Club. They purchased 120 acres of land and Fox Hills now occupies the middle 42 acres. The first project was to build a clubhouse, which was used until the early 1970s. In 1915 three holes for golf were laid out but there were no greens. The infant club operated for several years with more parties than golf and went bankrupt in 1922. Guy Cotton purchased the west 40 acres and Eli Meiser the east 40 acres. The local chapter of the Ku Klux Klan purchased the middle 40 acres, which included the clubhouse and spring and used both for meetings. In 1926 the Ku Klux Klan disbanded and deeded the 40 acres to Paragould to be used for recreational purposes. The city council rented part of the land to a man who farmed it for a few years.

In 1928 Monte F. McCullough, Arthur Jackson, Elmer Stuart and Franklin Wilbourn asked the mayor and city council for permission to build a golf course. They were met with a "cool" reception since several council members felt that golf was "a rich man's game". But they were persistent in meeting with the council, which gave them permission to build in 1929.

A man from Scotland, Scottie Thornton, was hired and work on a six-hole course began. A black man from Auvergne, near Newport, AR was later hired to build the sand greens and the six-hole course was played for the first time in 1930.

In 1932, with the help of the WPA in clearing out woods, three more holes were added. It was a short course, but sporty because of many water hazards.

The course was constantly plagued by a lack of money. Dues were $25 a year (no monthly dues) and only 40 members in 1954. Membership increased to 87 in 1955 and in 1956 to 111.

In 1956 "sand greens" became outdated and a few members started building grass greens, also lengthening the course since two acres had been purchased from Guy Cotton. The greens grass was Tifton 328, the first in Arkansas to have this type green. It was necessary to lay water lines to each hole also; all of this work was done by interested members in 1956 and 1957 and the total cost to buy the water lines, Tifton grass etc was only $3500.

In 1957 James Hart, one of Paragould's best golfers, was hired to manage and maintain the course.

In 1956 the officer format was changed to a board of directors and also changed the name from Paragould Country Club to Fox Hills Country Club.

In 1961 20 acres were purchased where the present clubhouse, swimming pool and driving range are now located.

More detailed information about Fox Hills is available in the Lipscomb Room of the Paragould-Greene County Library.

*Submitted by Alfred G. Herget*

## Kingsway Club

Kingsway Club was built in 1935 by Walter and Bea Cole and opened on December 18. A contest to name the club was won by Harlan Trice, who won the prize of $5.00. Located at 1250 West Kingshighway in Paragould, AR the building was constructed of logs, with native

*January 1950 – The first picture of the Hospital Auxiliary, made inside the hospital*

cypress wood used on the interior. It had a wooden dance floor of 1,000 square feet, no air conditioning and heated with pot-bellied wood stoves. Music for dancing was provided by a jukebox. The Coles commanded good behavior and a strict dress code, requiring suit and tie for the men and dresses for the ladies.

Joe and Martha Coates bought the club in June 1943 on its good reputation, continuing the strict rules of the former owners. Joe booked the Jack Staulcup Orchestra and featured them on a regular basis from 1943 to 1985. Other "Big Band" groups were also engaged over the years. Radio Station KBTM broadcast the bands from Kingsway over the radio. The average age of patrons was 40 to 50, many being regulars who loved to come there to dance. Joe said Elvis Presley wanted to play at Kingsway, but he turned Elvis down numerous times because he did not want a bunch of screaming people in his club.

In 1952 Joe changed his club from a "night club" to a "supper club" and began offering a dinner menu. Kingsway Supper Club introduced the Filet Mignon steak to Greene County in the early 1950-s and Rooster Fries about 1970. The club had its own famous "house" salad dressing, a garlic-flavored French dressing. The recipe is in some local cookbooks and is still being used by home cooks today.

Some of the special guests and events at Kingsway were fashion shows, governors, Miss Arkansas contestants in 1951, Miss America of 1950 and the original Paragould Lions Club organized and met there.

The dress code was relaxed in 1969 to accommodate the casual styles of the time. Joe married Mikie Lou Highfill in 1976 and they worked together running the club until retirement. Joe said the busiest years were from 1945 through 1951 and the worst was 1952, the year he changed to a "supper club". Jack Staulcup Orchestra was on hand in June 1978 to help Joe celebrate his 35 years of ownership of the club.

Joe and Mikie Lou retired in 1980 and leased the club to Mary Hughes. In December 1983 Joe sold the club to Fred and Mary Orick, who sold it to Bob Rider in November 1985. When the club changed ownership, the "style" changed, featuring country music bands and catering to the young generation. A 50$^{th}$ anniversary of the Kingsway Club was celebrated at the club Dec 18, 1985. The club burned two days later.

Joe Coates died Oct 30, 1997 at the age of 89. Joe and Kingsway Supper Club will continue to live on in the memories of "the older generation" who are still living.

Source: Mikie Lou Coates
*Submitted by Betty Clayton*

# Knights of Columbus

Local Council # 1713 was organized and instituted on Nov 30, 1913. There were 47 members welcomed into this council on this date, by a team from Pine Bluff for first and second degrees, with the third degree being conferred by a team from Little Rock. At that time the grand knight was John Kirchoff his deputy was Dr. J. F. Morris. Other officers were J. J. Raley, J. M. Alvey, R. F. Wrape, F. L. Jakubik, A. Goodman, Rev. R. J. Jenne and F. J. Chapman.

Charter members included: E. Abell, James Carroll, H. H. and John Knoppe, J. P. Nolan, Jeff, Omer and H. T. Raley, Leo and R. C. Schmucker and R. F. and A. H. Wrape to name a few.

Father Michael J. McGivney in New Haven, CT chartered the Knights of Columbus on Mar 29, 1882. As the priest explained to the small group of men, his purpose of calling them together was manifold: To help Catholic men remain steadfast in their faith through mutual encouragement; to promote closer ties of fraternity among them and to set up an elementary system of insurance for its members. The membership embodied knightly ideals of spirituality and service to church, country and fellowmen. Present day membership includes

*Exterior view of the original Kingsway Supper Club*

some 8500 councils of 1.45 million Catholic men world wide, dedicated to the ideals of Columbianism: Charity, unity, fraternity and patriotism.

The current council leadership consists of: Pat Quinn, grand knight. Pat Schultz, deputy grand knight. Art Pickard, financial secretary. Dan Quinn, treasurer and Dean Graves, John Haffey, Max Steyer, David Pigue, Dean Inman, Rev. Jos. Kay and Jim Deroe. The local council boasts continuous operation since its inception.

*Submitted by Urban Dohogne*

## Paragould Business and Professional Club

Mrs. Belle Wall, Emily Meiser, Ruth Simpson, Mrs. R. Laird and Wint Mack were the ladies credited with starting the first ladies club, which later became known as Business and Professional Women. The club was formed in July of 1919 with 14 charter members. In October of 1919 when the national organization of Business and Professional Women was formed in St. Louis, MO., they became affiliated with them.

In 1921-22 they organized a Christmas tree for the needy and 150 baskets of food were given out on the courthouse lawn. Arkansas was organized as a state federation that year and sent Emily Meiser to a national meeting in Portland, OR.

On July 4, 1924, they hosted a picnic to create interest for better workingwomen. Over 100 attended to hear attorney William F. Kirsh speak in support of B.P.W.

1925 Paragould hosted the state convention at the Vandervoort Hotel with 13 of the 17 Arkansas clubs represented by 40 ladies. Emily Meiser was elected state president. The student loan fund in the amount of $60.00 was established for girls wanting to go to college. The amount to be repaid, interest free, after they finished school.

1927-28 Faustina Barksdale was club president and came up with the first club handbook ever made in Arkansas. A baby clinic was started and 25 babies were examined. The state convention was again held in Paragould with a full week of activities. $57.00 was raised for storm victims in Lorado. Club pins were initiated at a program explaining the pin and every member was urged to purchase one.

1929 the local club sponsored and organized clubs in Jonesboro and Piggott, then in 1930 the Corning Club.

The depression years hurt. Some members dropped out and even some clubs. Our club didn't have the Christmas tree, but the Capitol Theater opened its doors to BPW and for admission, people brought clothes and food to be distributed to the needy. Districts were organized, Paragould being in District # 2 with Blytheville.

1929-30 colors of green and gold were adopted and by-laws revised to conform to state and national by-laws.

1932 the first cotton queen was sponsored by BPW. 2,000 visitors attended the event.

1934 state convention was again in Paragould hosted by District # 2. The cedar chest full of linens was started as a fundraiser and continued until 1974.

1935 the annual Garden Party was replaced by a Cotton Carnival dance. Another fundraiser was the New Years breakfast dance and a fashion show of the hour and Thanksgiving dance.

1936 Mary Turner was elected state president. The public library was started with BPW paying rent and utilities. WPA paid the salary of librarian Nona Dixon, a BPW member.

1938 advocated women's right to serve on jury. As a result, four women were selected with one being a BPW member. Ladies' dollar days were started sponsored by BPW, Chamber of Commerce and local merchants. This continued until 1942.

1941 the attack on Pearl Harbor brought about some changes. This marked the end of the library as WPA folded. But within a month BPW members volunteered their time to keep it open from three to five each afternoon. In 1945 the quorum court allocated $50 per month for salary.

1942 Essie Butler was elected state president (the youngest ever at that time). A program was set up by BPW to make surgical dressings for war victims. Club members purchased $211,781 in war bonds.

1946 ERA was adopted by the club in their drive for women voters.

1948 Chamber of Commerce was reorganized with two BPW members on the board. This was the first year to send a girl to "Girl's State."

1949 BPW members served as greeters at the new hospital's open house. They also worked with the Girl Scouts.

1950 was the first year to sponsor a float in the Christmas parade.

1952-53 The first scholarship of $200 was given to a high school senior. Jo Willie Dickey was appointed to the board of Greene Acres Nursing Home, a position she held 'til her death.

1953-54 BPW gave $500 to furnish a room in the new hospital and gave silverware to American Legion for their new building.

1955 they sponsored a contestant in the annual "Belles and Beaux" production. Became more active in the Good-Fellows, now that it had been taken over by all civic clubs. Accepted the club collect that is still used today.

1957-58 BPW furnished a room in Greene Acres in memory of deceased members.

1959-60 they gave another $200 to Greene Acres and helped to start a special school for retarded children by furnishing bookshelves and room dividers.

1963-64 they furnished signs at two entrances to the city.

1966-67 they gave $500 to the community center fund. Hosted a reception for Candy Stripers at A.M.H.

1972-73 helped in construction of new library and sponsored an open house when it was finished.

1977-78 gave $250 each to two high school graduates for college. The fundraiser changed that year from the cedar chest of linens to a TV set. They also sponsored a 'young careerist' candidate for the next six years.

Since then the scholarship has been increased to $650 and is available to women wanting to go back to school. Nellie Murphy served as state president for 1998-99 and Bobbye Brengard is now our local club president.

## Paragould Country Club

After being involved at Fox Hills Country Club, Paragould, in changing the sand greens to grass greens and lengthening this nine hole course, Alfred G. Herget concluded that Paragould needed a new 18 hole golf course for several reasons, the main two being that the City of Paragould owned the land and the other that the course was too small. This was in 1956 and times were so poor there was nothing to do but wait. Herget wrote a six-page letter detailing reasons for a new course but stashed it away for future use. He did look for golf course sites however and picked out the Everett Rogers stock farm as the best location.

In 1965 the Everett Rogers stock farm was offered for sale and listed with a Jonesboro real estate agent. Herget found out about this and called Mr. Rogers who informed him that he thought the farm had been sold to a man originally from Osceola but who now lived in California with Dot Records. Herget practically begged Mr. Rogers to talk with him and he agreed and an appointment was made.

The first meeting was in June 1965, the first of several pleasant meetings between Mr. Rogers and Herget. As the meetings continued Mr. Rogers began to like the idea of a golf course and even suggested the name of "Twin Trees County Club" if the deal went through. In the meantime, because the potential buyer lived in California and was so busy Mr. Rogers broke off this deal. Later Mr. Rogers called Herget to state that he would sell his farm if we could agree on the price and a few other details. In the meantime Herget had contacted enough people to get 15 to pledge $1000 each if the deal went through.

In Aug 1965 Herget met with Mr. and Mrs. Rogers and they agreed to sell the 160-acre farm for $350 an acre or $56,000. Also, in the meantime the 15 who had pledged got others to pledge and we had $61,000 and on Sept 17, 1965 the deal was closed.

Herget had asked Elmer Hazlewood, a recent retired merchant to help build the course since Herget also had a business to run. Mr. Rogers had an employee Allan Bullinger, who he would no longer need and recommended we hire Allan, which we did. On April 1, 1967 we started building the golf course with practically no equipment or money. We had earlier paid Walter "Junie" Dowell to design the 18-hole course; however, because of no money we could build only nine holes to start. Alvin Samuel and Herget picket out the clubhouse site. The first green to be built is now number 18. The nine original greens are what are now three, four, five, six, seven, 15, 16, 17 and 18. Because the equipment used to build the greens was owned by Herget and what he could borrow from Harold Wade and Everett Rogers the total cost, including water to these nine greens was only about $26,600. The grass greens for these nine holes is Dwarf Tifton Bermuda and because of the excellent maintenance and hard work by Allan Bullinger this course became known as the best nine hold golf course in Arkansas. Elmer Hazlewood and Allan Bullinger deserve a lot of credit, which they never received.

In 1981 the other nine greens were built by

H. L. "Chic" Hill and are present holes numbers one, two, eight, nine, 10,11,12,13 and 14.

The first nine holes were opened for play in late July 1967. The clubhouse was built in 1968 and opened in Dec 1968.

More information regarding Paragould Country Club is in Lipscomb Room of library.
*Submitted by A. G. Herget*

## Paragould Lions Club

The Paragould Lions Club, formed in April 1947, is one of the oldest Civic Clubs in Paragould. The Manila Lions Club sponsored the club. A group of 31 businessmen attended the organization meeting on April 29, 1947 at the Vandervoort Hotel. The club actually received its charter of June 6, 1947.

According to official records, Horace Whitsitt was the first president of Paragould Lions Club. The current president is Jeff Boone. The presidents came from all facets of life: physicians, attorneys, school administrators and all areas of the business community.

The Paragould Lions Club has changed through the years. One major change was the addition of women to its organization. Bonnie Abbott was one of the first women in the club. The Lions Club aggressively recruits women to the organization. Recently a "special event" was staged to draw female visitors to the meeting, there were 35 ladies present. Hopefully, the club will benefit numerically

The Paragould Lions Club stages various programs to raise money. Among them are flag programs, broom sales and entertainment events at the Collins Theater.

The Paragould Lions Club has also provided two district governors, Ron Hall and Jimmy Grooms. Roy Whitten, a 47-year veteran of Lions Club, has served as vice district governor. Among the current members, Bob Singleton and Bonnie Abbott have served on the governor's council as zone chairman. Lion Singleton also served on the board of directors of Lions World Services for the Blind.

The Lions Club is known worldwide for its sight conservation program and the Paragould Lions Club is very active in supporting those efforts. Additionally, "setting out flags" has been a major effort for many years. Providing scholarships for area students, helping Greene Countians pay for eyeglasses and the efforts in Boys' State and Girls' State are also a few of the works of Paragould Lions Club.

The Leo Club was formed many years ago by the local Lions Club. This Club, under the oversight of the Paragould Lions Club and Paragould High School, is composed of civic-minded high school youth who work with the local Lions Club in various activities, including broom sales and raising funds for such activities as Lions World Services for the Blind. In its earlier years former Paragould High School Principal Gary Washington was very active in the organization. Jeff Boone from the local Lions Club has been active in assuring the growth of the Leo Club. Some of them attend the meeting each Monday.

The Paragould Lions Club is proud to have numerous WWII veterans, as well as veterans from the Korean conflict and the Viet Nam war among the current membership. Some of these were actually combat veterans. When it was formed in 1947 the club had numerous WWI veterans. These military veterans feel that their active service with the Paragould Lions Club is, in a way, a continuation of the service they performed when they wore the U. S. Military uniform.

Dale Morgan was only 22 years old when he joined the Paragould Lions Club in 1948, less than one year after the club's formation. He recently celebrated 51 years of service, all with the Paragould Lions Club. He has fond memories of the club's first two presidents, Horace Whitsitt and Lee Ward. According to Morgan, both made him feel welcome. He stated that Whitsitt was very generous with financial support (many times anonymously) to the Lions Club.

The Paragould Lions Club has met in various locations since its inception in 1947 at the Vandervoort Hotel. The club met at Ogle's Café', Lamb's Café, Ember Glo Restaurant and Bonanza, where it currently meets at noon on Monday.

Through the years the Lions Club has been active in local disaster relief. One example was the March 1, 1947 tornado that hit Greene County. Through efforts by the Paragould Lions Club District 7-0 $9,000 was made available in disaster relief to the Marmaduke area. In addition, several members of the local Lions Club assisted in the cleanup as well as making individual monetary contributions. As several individual Lions members stated, serving mankind is not a burden, but an opportunity to uphold the Lions' tradition, WE SERVE.

The Lions Club is continually taking applications for those in need of help in their sight preservation efforts. Bob Singleton has for many years served as chairman of the Paragould Lions Club sight preservation efforts, getting referrals primarily from optometrists, Mission Outreach and school nurses. In order to qualify, an applicant must state how much money they need and certain information about household income. If they have received assistance in the past two years, they are ineligible. The local club helps buy eyeglasses and provide other services, including surgery relating to vision problems. Those who cannot be served by area physicians are often referred to Mid South Lions Sight and Hearing Service, in Memphis, TN. After more than 12 years coordinating the "sight" effort, Singleton is still going strong.

The Paragould Lions Club looks forward to its continuation of serving mankind. When all is said and done out motto is still, WE SERVE.

*Seated, L to R: J. M. Williams, Pete Gregory, Jimmy Grooms, Karl Potter, Horace Whitsett, Claude Abney, Nixon Jenkins, Cecil Gould, Gordon Schaff. Standing: Avon Schug, Don Herron, Tom Watson, Bob Martin, Paul Hooper, Jack Blacksher, Unknown, Unknown, Lee Ward, Bud McCalister.*

*Past Presidents of the Paragould Lions Club*

# Churches

## All Saints' Episcopal Church

All Saints Mission had its beginning in 1949 when the Reverend John D. Pettus, Rector of St. Mark's Jonesboro, began holding weekly *Bible* classes in private homes. Ladies met in the afternoon; men met in the evening. From this humble beginning both groups grew in size and enthusiasm. By 1950 the group was organized as All Saints Mission Paragould of the Episcopal Diocese of Arkansas.

Initially services were held at the First Christian Church but were soon moved to the First Presbyterian Church. In 1952, due to continued growth and commitment of early members, the Rt. Rev. Mitchell, Bishop of the Episcopal Diocese of Arkansas, with a loan of $5000 secured the deed to the property at 10th and Main Streets for the purpose of building a church. Owen Fitzgerald finalized plans, drawn up in a rough draft by the Rev. Pettus. Under the supervision of James Fitzgerald, the project manager, members of the mission did much of the work. The church was finished in November 1952 and dedicated by Bishop Mitchell. James and Mary K. Fitzgerald were the first to be confirmed in the new church building. The mission continued to grow and in 1959 a parish hall was completed.

The mission has remained a community focal point. Their annual bazaars were a "must-see" event. In 1981 a Lenten program of "Sermons and Soup" was established. At present the church building serves also as a meeting place for several self-help groups.

*All Saints' Episcopal Church*

# Beech Grove United Methodist Church

The Beech Grove United Methodist Church was founded in 1850 by Rev. H. M. Grande. Charter members were A. J. Breckenridge and wife, Elizabeth, Joe Friar and wife Nancy, Henry Lovelady and wife Sarah, George Taylor and wife Naomi, Jess Williams and wife Evaline and Daniel Breckenridge and wife. These charter members were converted at a camp meeting, held at Camp Ground Methodist Church.

These families built the first church south of Beech Grove near the Beech Grove Cemetery. The church was built of logs, with a chimney, puncheon floors and split-log seats. The Civil War slowed the progress of the church, but in the 1860s a great revival occurred and the church grew.

In 1876, a box building, 24 x 36 feet, was built near the spot of the first church. The membership had grown to close to 50 persons.

A third church was built, under the leadership of L. C. Craig, pastor in 1897-1898. This was a frame building, 30 x 50 feet, with a tower and a bell, weighing 500 pounds. The church was located closer to Beech Grove, across the road from the two school buildings, a short distance east of Beech Grove, with the Beech Grove creek in the background.

A tabernacle, 50 x 60 feet, was built on the south side of the church, with a raised platform for the pulpit and benches for the choir. An altar reached across the front of the platform and sawdust covered the floor area. This tabernacle was used during the summer months for services, day and night and especially for the two weeks of summer revivals each year.

The congregation of the church became a part of the organized Methodist Church South. J. H. Breckenridge served as Sunday School Superintendent for more that 20 years. Wooden benches were used for seating and kerosene lamps and hanging white gasoline lanterns provided lighting. A large black, wood-burning stove served to heat the building. This church burned in 1938.

In that same year construction began on a new church, a short distance north of Beech Grove on four acres of land donated by Mr. and Mrs. J. E. Winn. People of the church and other persons in the community furnished much of the labor in the construction, even the digging of a full basement.

The church building was stucco, 50 x 56 feet. J. E. Winn was Sunday School Superintendent for 10 years. The church was dedicated by Bishop Charles C. Selectman on Sunday, June 21, 1942. A few years later, under the leadership of Rev. Charles Reed, pastor, an educational building 40 x 50 feet, was added to the north side of the church. Over the years and under the guidance of many pastors, renovations were made on the parsonage, the church, the basement and the educational building

Rev. George Srum came to pastor our church in 1974 and stayed 17 years. Olen Boyd served as Sunday School Superintendent during this period for over 30 years.

In 1982 the congregation decided that a need was great for repairs of the church building. The decision was made that more than necessary repairs were needed. After much thought, deliberation and many hours of prayer, "the dream" began with a complete renovation of church, educational building and grounds. On July 12, 1993 "the dream" became a reality. The church congregation today is very proud of its beautiful place of worship, which represents gifts, labor, love and a spirit of dedication for all our members and many friends who gave freely.

The Beech Grove United Methodist Church, in the small community of Beech Grove, is located on Highway 141. Dr. Wayne Gould is now serving his ninth year as pastor. Under his ministry, we have grown spiritually. F. D. Williams is our Sunday School Superintendent, faithfully filling that position for a number of years.

We worship here with people we love dearly and consider our congregation a caring and spiritual family. We welcome all who enter our doors with open arms as we strive to win more people to Christ.

*Beech Grove United Methodist Church*

# Browns Chapel Baptist Church

On Saturday before the 2nd Sunday of August, 1890, the Brothers and Sisters in Christ met in the Lord's name and organized themselves into a church with a desire to love the Lord and give their best to God.

The land for this great church was donated by Jonathan Jones.

Their Love was reflected in a resolution adopted in 1891 to collect offerings for missions. In November of 1891 their first offering of State and Associational missions was taken, which was 40 cents.

In July of 1892, the church scripturally followed God's leadership and elected the first Deacon, J. T. McDaniel. The first pastor of this great church was G. H. Holker.

As God continued to add to the church it was necessary for the church to expand. In October of 1903, they added a 30' x 42' building. The church building was added to many more times over the next 83 years.

On December 28, 1986, the church was completely destroyed by fire. In what seemed to be our darkest hour, Jesus Christ did shine through by allowing a new church building to be dedicated in May of 1987, debt free. People in the church, community, and people that had early roots at Browns Chapel donated time, money and prayers. During all the construction, no money was asked for, God provided it all.

As the church grew, a need for an Educational Building arose. In July, 1989, a 50' x110' addition was made to the church. This building was also debt free upon completion. Once again, the Lord provided all the necessary money, through the prayers of his people.

In March, 1990, the sanctuary was enlarged to accommodate the growth which the Lord provided. And in January, 1999, the need for a larger sanctuary arose again.

Also in 1999, a 40' x 125' Family Life Center was built behind the church. This building project was completed with the Lord's help and the church remained debt free.

The church has a total membership of over 800 and an average attendance of 425. Brother Royce Boling has been pastor of Browns Chapel since April, 1980.

The desire to love and worship the Lord is what makes Browns Chapel Baptist Church so great.

*Browns Chapel Baptist Church*

# Camp Ground United Methodist Church

Camp Ground United Methodist Church is located seven miles northwest of Paragould, AR at 1976 Greene 628 Road. This road was once known as Old Greensboro Road and was a connecting link between Greensboro in Craighead County and Gainesville in Greene County. A major tributary of Jack's Creek curves through church property and forms the western and southern borders of the present churchyard. Continuous flowing springs are found in the churchyard and creek bank. As late as the early 1960's these springs served as a water source for some area residents in dry weather.

According to church tradition and some *Annual Conference Journals* the church was established in 1815. Although the first permanent settlers arrived in Greene County in 1822, circuit riders are said to have preached to hunters, trappers and Indians camped at the springs as early as 1815. The church was certainly in existence before the Green Mission Circuit began in 1839. As early as 1842, county camp meetings were being held at this location. People around the county would come by wagon and horseback and camp at the springs while their meetings took place. The meetings generally lasted from one to three weeks in the late summer or early fall.

Camp Ground Church has had at least six different names. The first known name was Green Mission. Later it was called Greensboro Chapel because of its location on Old Greensboro Road. In 1844, the Methodist church was divided because of the slavery issue; churches in states favoring slavery were called Methodist Episcopal (ME) Church, South. By the early 1850's the church was called Straughan's Chapel ME Church South. Pressley G. Straughan, thus the name, Straughan's Chapel, donated the land where the church is located. The original deed was lost in the fire that destroyed the Gainesville Courthouse in 1874. When trustees of the church petitioned the court for a replacement deed, they stated the land had been deeded to the church prior to 1858, the most probable date 1855 when Mr. Straughan received his patent on the land.

The Civil War began April 12, 1861 with the firing on Fort Sumter. In early July 1861, the Fifth Arkansas Infantry Regiment of the Confederate States of America was officially organized at Camp Ground. Companies C, D, E and H were made up of men from Greene County. The soldiers camped near the springs located in the churchyard and trained there and on the land adjacent to church property. After the soldiers departed, the church was known as Camp Ground ME Church, South. This name continued in use until the United Methodist Church was formed in 1968. Since that time the church's name has been Camp Ground United Methodist Church.

There have been three known church buildings. The first two were made of logs, with split log benches and had dirt floors. They were located across the creek, west of the present church buildings and springs. It is believed the first church building was constructed in 1816-1817. No date is known for the building of the second structure. The church also served as a school building before the schoolhouse was built. After the completion of the third church building, the second log church was sold to a local resident who dismantled it and moved the logs to his farm to use in the construction of a barn.

The third church was constructed in 1889. It was built on the eastern side of the creek near the springs. This building was a wood frame structure with four windows on each side and two doors in the front. As was the custom of the time, the men entered the church through the door on the right and were seated in the pews on the right side of the building. Women and children entered by the left door and were seated on the left. The floor joists were hand-hewn oak beams measuring a foot square. The rafters were also hand-hewn from oak. These rafters and joists are in excellent condition still today. This structure is the oldest part of the present day sanctuary.

An addition to the sanctuary was completed in 1924 that provided classrooms and more sanctuary space. In 1953, a vestibule was added to the church. The two doors in the front of the church were eliminated and a new central double door was added. The 1955 addition provided a needed fellowship hall that was enlarged in 1977. The present fellowship hall was built in 1986. Upon its completion, renovations were begun on the sanctuary and old fellowship hall; this work created new classrooms, an office and a storage room. The sanctuary acquired a new chancel area, stained glass windows and new pews resulting in the church as we now see it.

The church is nestled in a beautiful wooded setting. At one time, giant oaks surrounded the church. Although several of the more than 300-year-old trees remain, injury, disease and death have required the removal of five of the massive oaks, forever changing the churchyard as we once knew it.

We must always be mindful of the hardships and sacrifices faced by our early church members. Because of their faith and love they came on foot, horseback and in wagons to worship the Lord. Their commitment laid the foundations on which we build. Our church today is alive, filled with joy, love and the Spirit of God. With a rich past and an active vibrant present, Camp Ground looks forward to doing the will of our Lord by serving Him and future generations. Reaching out to spread the word and love of God, we realize we are truly blessed as we follow in the footsteps of those dedicated early Christians who planted this church in this place.

*Submitted by Madeline Prater*

*Camp Ground ME Church, South Singing School Aug 1917*

*Camp Ground United Methodist Church as it appears today*

# First Baptist Church of Paragould

In the 1880s Paragould was a thriving railroad town, enjoying economic growth from many sources. These were rough exciting years filled with hope and expectations for the influx of people from east of the Mississippi River.

Rev. J. K. Pate and a few Baptist believers saw the need for a Baptist Church to meet the spiritual needs of this fast growing town. On May 25, 1885, Pate and a small group gathered in the newly erected Methodist meeting house and formally organized themselves into a church.

For over a century, First Baptist Church has been looked to and thought of as the "Mother Church" of Baptist churches in Paragould. Several of the local churches were started as missions of First Church.

The preaching and teaching of the *Bible* as the inerrant Word of God and missions have been the hallmark of Baptist faith down through these years.

The church, now located at Third and Poplar, has grown in spite of depressions, wars and other difficulties. New buildings have been erected, programs expanded and staff members added as the need arose.

Looking for new and different ways to minister to the community, the church in 1930 started broadcasting the Sunday morning service over radio station KBTM. For the past 21 years, the Sunday school lesson and both Sunday church services have been televised live for the homebound members and the entire community.

Nurturing the youth of the church has always been a priority for the leadership. "Children's Sermon" is a part of the regular morning worship service. A floor of the educational building is equipped with recreational activities for the youth.

The commitment to young people is reflected in a scholarship program, which provides grants to many of the church's college students. These funds come from the estates of S. S. Lipscomb, Georgia Wright, Robert Rose and Tennie Barnhill.

Through the years, First Church has been among the top churches in Arkansas in gifts to the Cooperative Program, the Baptist Colleges and Universities and other Baptist mission work across the state.

Who knows what the 21st Century will bring? First Baptist Church will continue to strive to meet the spiritual needs of people through the preaching of the Gospel. With a vision just as the founding fathers had so long ago, it will be the challenge, for this and future generations, to continue to build on the foundation laid by all those who have gone before.

Pastors of First Baptist Church
J. K. Pate 1885
J. W. Bell 1885-1886
A. S. Hall 1886-1889
J. S. Edmonds 1889-1890
J. B. Wise 1890-1893
J. H. Paey 1894- 1898
J. N. Hartley 1899-1902
A. B. Bohannon 1902-1905
H. C. Rosemond 1905-1907
T. T. Thompson 1907-1909
W. C. McPherson 1909-1910
W. C. Wood 1911-1917
C. A. Dickey 1917-1918
Ben L. Bridges 1918-1929
Roy Hurst 1929-1931
Edgar Williamson 1931-1937
Homer Reynolds 1937-1940
I. M. Prince 1940-1948
D.C. Applegate 1948-1952
L. D. Farrell 1952-1954
Jarry Autrey 1954-1957
James Yates 1957- 1961
P.E. Claybrook 1962-1969
C. A. Johnson 1969-1978
Winfred Bridges 1978-1988
Coy Samples 1989 – 1991
C. A. Johnson 1992-1993
Keith Brickell 1994-1999

*First Baptist Church of Paragould*

# First Presbyterian Church

Twenty-two charter members started First Presbyterian Church Dec 29, 1918. Rev. Thomas H. Watkins was commissioned to organize the church. The original meeting place was his home at 324 West Garland Street.

In January of 1919 a lot was purchased at the corner of Seventh and Main Streets. A building was started in May 1921. At times, this sanctuary was shared with Lutheran and Episcopal congregations. A manse was acquired in 1925. The 1926 Paragould High School class held commencement exercises in the church.

Various improvements were made during the 1930s and in the 1950 decade a large annex was built with kitchen and meeting facilities. Later, an addition was included with a small chapel and offices.

The Presbyterian Church has hosted community groups including Boy Scouts, Brownie Scouts, Greene County Fine Arts Council rehearsals, art workshops and Historical Genealogical Society meetings. Our members have reached out into the community serving on boards and councils. An annual college scholarship is awarded from an estate gift.

To date, 16 pastors have served the church either as interim or elected leaders. With pastoral guidance, a six-member board of elders governs the church. In addition to worship and church school on Sunday mornings, there are *Bible* study groups, special observances and social gatherings.

In 1997 an eight-acre plot of ground was purchased at Rosewood Circle and Kingshighway for a new sanctuary. Plans are being made to relocate the Presbyterian Church in a fast growing area of the city.

*First Presbyterian Church*

# First United Methodist Church of Paragould

First United Methodist Church was the first congregation established in Paragould. It began with the first service preached in February 1883. Rev. F. E. Taylor who was pastor of the Greensboro Circuit, Jonesboro District, White River Conference of the Methodist Episcopal Church, South, was invited to preach. He held a service in an unfinished store building on the south side of Main Street about where the Collins Theater now stands.

According to an eyewitness, Dr. F. M. Scott, this was the beginning of Methodism in Paragould. Rev. Taylor continued to visit the new town and conducting services in a small building belonging to John F. Dover, located on West Emerson Street.

In the summer of 1883, following a protracted meeting, the First Methodist Church was organized. The original members were: Dr. John M. Davis, Mrs. John M. Davis, John N. Johnston, Mrs. John N. Johnston, David King, Mrs. David King, E. P. Holt, Mrs. E. P. Holt, Mrs. Mattie Hammonds, Miss Nannie Davis, Dr. F. M. Scott, Mrs. R. M. Scott and Mr. King.

On Aug 18, 1883, W. S. Pruett deeded to this church a parcel of land. The land was lot two in block six of the town of Paragould. A building was erected in the fall of 1883. Other denominations were given use of the new building. C. T. Stallcup, a layman in the church, who later was appointed as its pastor, established the first Sunday School in 1884.

The church began as part of the Jonesboro Circuit, but by 1887 was a station church. About this time a parsonage was built. It was the first building of its kind in Paragould. It was located on Third and Main Streets.

The church rapidly outgrew the original frame structure and a new location at Third and Emerson Streets was obtained. A new brick church building was begun in 1892. In 1903, just 20 years after the establishment of First United Methodist Church, A. C. Griffin organized the East Side Methodist Church. The church was later renamed in his honor, Griffin Memorial Methodist Church. That congregation built a frame building on East Court Street.

In 1925-26 a new church building was constructed at Fourth and Main Streets. The lot was given by Mrs. Sarah Wyse Cook, who also gave the lot across the street for a new parsonage at 320 West Main. The total cost of the new building was $125,000, which included a $10,000 pipe organ. The first service was held Nov 26, 1926. This continues to be the home for First United Methodist Church.

In 1978, the congregation completed a major addition to the church building. It added a Fellowship Hall, Chapel and elevator to connect four floors of the existing building. In the 90s two major renovation projects were completed to modernize the church and equip it for service in the new century.

First United Methodist Church has from the beginning opened its doors to other community groups and in some cases other denominations whose churches were destroyed by fire. The congregation continues to grow and provide leadership and a Christian witness to the people of Paragould. Its members have had leading roles in many of the projects that benefit the community as a whole. The Arkansas Methodist Hospital, Mission Outreach and Ministerial Alliance are all outstanding local examples of leadership provided, in part, by the people of First United Methodist Church.

*Submitted by Rev. Michael Morey*

*First United Methodist Church of Paragould*

# Pine Knott Church of Christ

Benjamin H. Crowley, in the Paragould newspaper, "Soliphone," Nov 20, 1906, related that the first church of Christ in Greene County, AR was located at Pine Knott. It was established in 1841. Key men instrumental in the establishment of this congregation were James Hyde, Newell Greenway, B. C. Treadway, L. C. Thompson and Res McClure. The congregation was formed when James Hyde deeded 40 acres for a church and a cemetery. B. C. Treadway also deeded land to the church where the old cemetery is located. The first building was built of logs with a dirt floor. A few years later, a wood frame building replaced the log building and was used until it burned, around 1900. A larger wood frame building was built and lasted until 1967 when the current brick building was constructed. The Pine Knott Church has always been known for its vivacious singing. Many great song leaders have come and gone, some of them were:

1. Limb Lenderman
2. Fate Lemmons
3. Dave Greenway
4. Tom Hopper
5. Evan Lemmons
6. Louis Treadway
7. Monroe Lemmons
8. Early Johns
9. Clennie Johns.

One man who has had a profound influence upon Pine Knott's singing for the last 50 years has been, of course, Lawrence Treadway. Mr. Early Johns held a two-week singing school at Pine Knott every winter for years. The first preacher at Pine Knott was Uncle Jimmy Hyde. His sons became gospel preachers and their influence spread throughout the country. Many great preachers have stood in the pulpit at Pine Knott and proclaimed the "Unsearchable Riches of Christ." Some of them were:

1. J. D. Tant
2. Monroe Lemmons
3. Alexander Douglas
4. J. D. Barber
5. Joe Blue
6. R. L. Colley
7. J. E. Green
8. John M. Higgins
9. William Hopper
10. Christian Lyle
11. Frank Gould
12. Harbert D. Hooker
13. Boyd Morgan
14. Marshall Conner
15. Winston Burton.

No church could function long with scriptural guidance and supervision. Some of the early Pine Knott elders were:

1. John Higgins
2. John Pillow
3. Newal Greenway
4. B. C. Treadway
5. Orestus McClure
6. Oss Herren
7. Bill Hopper
8. Jack Burton
9. Robert Newsom
10. Oscar Austin
11. Ted Ford
12. B. C. Ford
13. Adrian Denham

The Pine Knott cemetery is also one of the oldest in Greene County with many founders of the church and their families buried there. Several relatives of the forefathers still live in the area and worship at this congregation of the Lord's Church.

*Submitted by Nadine (Treadway) Jamison*

*June 1981 – 150 year Homecoming of the Pine Knott Church of Christ*

# Pruett's Chapel Methodist Church

The Pruet brothers, Charles, Willis S. and Robert returned to their farms in Greene County in the Pleasant Grove community after the end of the Civil War. They attended the Pleasant Grove Methodist Church, which was built on land donated by the Pruet family. It was organized in 1858 and was a one-room log structure with split-rail seats located in a grove of trees, adjacent to the cemetery. This was one of at least 17 organizations of the Methodist Episcopal Church South located in Greene County prior to the Civil War.

The building was used as a community church and there was a school known as Maple Grove on the property. The church, school and cemetery were all located just north of what is now Finch Road.

In 1858 Reverend R. W. Anderson was the circuit rider for the Paragould circuit, which included Mt. Carmel, Pleasant Grove, New Bethel and Wood's Chapel in Greene County and Greensboro and Pine Log in Craighead County.

A membership book shows Robert and Willis S. Pruet took the vows of the Methodist Church that year. Charles joined in 1860.

According to Mrs. Edna Driskell, a niece of Charles Pruet, the first person interred in the cemetery was Caroline Pruet's brother, a Mr. Nelson. Mrs. Pruet later donated five acres of land for the cemetery.

In 1879 Charles and Caroline Pruet with Robert and Elizabeth M. Stewart Pruet deeded one acre of land for a church about one mile north of the Pleasant Grove structure. This church is on what we know as Pruett's Chapel Road. The cemetery entrance, however, remained on Finch Road.

The two families donated most of the funds for construction of the frame building and its furnishings. Robert and Elizabeth gave the pulpit furniture to the congregation. The name of the church and school was then changed to Pruet's Chapel. The family name was spelled "Pruet" on early deeds, but the spelling of Charles Pruet's name on Caroline's tombstone was spelled "Pruett", probably by mistake. Eventually, the latter spelling was used.

Both Charles and Robert Pruet and their wives are buried in the family plot at Pruett's Chapel Cemetery.

In 1974 the old frame building was moved to the back of the church property and sold as a dwelling. A new brick structure was erected just behind the site of the old building.

The new church sanctuary was consecrated when Reverend J. Albert Gatlin was pastor. On Nov 28, 1982, the congregation held dedication services, having paid the debt incurred for the new building. Reverend Bob Burnham was pastor at that time.

In May 1992, a groundbreaking ceremony for construction of a new parsonage was held jointly with members of Christ United Methodist Church who share the charge. By November, the three-bedroom brick home was completed and occupied by Reverend Ted Winberry and his wife. In April of 1993, Pruett's Chapel share of the mortgage was retired.

Among the early ministers was Reverend A. C. Griffin who had the longest record of service, beginning in 1873 and then at different times until 1907. He received over 1,000 members into the Methodist Church during his career. He is quoted as saying he was quite proud of the construction of the first parsonage during his tenure at Pruett's Chapel.

With over 100 years of ministry and service to God and its community, Pruett's Chapel United Methodist Church stands as a monument of faith. While we remember the past, we also rejoice in the future. Although times have changed, it is wonderful to know that God remains the same. He never stops reaching out and caring for His people and by grace we all can find forgiveness and the assurance of eternal life with Him.

Pastors who served the Pruett's Chapel Methodist Church 1858-1995:
1. 1858: R. W. Anderson, circuit rider for the Paragould District
2. 1873, 1890, 1892, 1893, 1895, 1900, 1901, and 1907: Rev. A. C. Griffin who was said to have taken over a thousand people into the Methodist Church.
3. 1886: J. S. Watson
4. 1889-1891: T. B. or F. B. Watson
5. 1895-1899: W. M. Watson
6. 1899-1900: W. B. Roe
7. 1900-1902: A. C. Griffin
8. 1903-1905: I. H. Russel
9. 1906: W. M. Watson
10. 1907: A. C. Griffin
11. 1908: J. S. Watson
12. 1909: C. L. Castleberry
13. 1910: T. R. Allen
14. 1912-1915: H. E. May
15. 1916-1917: W. J. Williamson
16. 1918: P. W. Emmer
17. 1918-1919: S. G. Watson
18. 1920
19. 1921-1924: C. L. Castleberry
20. 1925-1926: R. C. Boone
21. 1927-1928: G. C. Taylor
22. 1929-1930: W. J. Jordan
23. 1930-1932: C. J. Wade
24. 1933-1934: E. Marlar
25. 1935-1936: M. A. Cherry
26. 1937-1938: W. E. Benbrook
27. 1939-1940: Earl DuBois
28. 1940-1941: J. W. Simmons
29. 1941-1942: J. H. Holt
30. 1943-1944: David Dillon
31. 1945: J. L. McDaniel
32. 1946-1948: W. T. Lingo
33. 1948: Nath Mabry
34. 1949-1951: Robert Montgomery
35. 1952
36. 1953-1954: Alvin Gibbs
37. 1954-1957: Elvis Wright
38. 1957-1959: Marvin Thompson
39. 1960
40. 1961-1962: Jim West
41. 1963-1965: Sherman Waters
42. 1966-1967: S. Woodrow Woods
43. 1968-1970: Eugene Bain
44. 1971-1972: Felix Holland
45. 1973: Wayne Gould
46. 1973: Robert Montgomery
47. 1974-1976: J. Albert Gatlin
48. 1976-1978: Harry Price
49. 1978-1980: Bobby Bell
50. 1980-1982: Allen Rainey
51. 1982-1984: Bob Burnham
52. 1984-1988: Cleve Yarbrough
53. 1988-1989: Michael Hollowell
54. 1989-1990: Everett Isom
55. 1991-1992: Ted Winberry
56. 1993-1996: G. Robert Bailey
57. 1996-1999: Mark Ashcraft
58. 2000: Dustin Carpenter

*Submitted by Anita Phillips*

*Pruett's Chapel Cemetery tombstones from left: Irene (second wife), Charles Pruet and Caroline Pruet (first wife). Tall tombstone is Robert Pruett's with information about first and second wives on each side.*

*Pruett's Chapel United Methodist Church 2000*

# St. Mary's Church in Paragould, Arkansas

One of Paragould's earliest Catholic settlers was John Staudt, owner of the Commercial Hotel, where Rev. John Eugene Weibel first celebrated Mass and began to organize St. Mary's parish. At that time, Father Weibel was pastor of the Pocahontas parish.

During the years from 1883 to 1887 Father Weibel occasionally said Mass in Paragould among many other places. From 1888 to 1889 Father Weibel resided in Jonesboro. Father George Gleisner, Pocahontas, attended the Paragould parish. Father Weibel moved back to Pocahontas in 1889.

On April 25, 1890, the famous Father O'Reilly gave a talk in the courthouse at Paragould, entitled "Marriage and Divorce" in order to raise funds for the new Catholic church to be built there and also to instruct the public. A very interesting comedy was also presented. The proceeds of both were satisfactory.

Father Weibel, having resumed the pastorate of St. Mary's church in 1889, purchased four lots in Pruett's M Addition located on Second and Highland Streets for $300.00. They later succeeded in buying the Presbyterian Church, which stood on Poplar and Second Streets, a frame building for $625. The Presbyterian congregation had had the church built but upon completion of the building, refused to pay the contractor more than $400. The contractor had invested more that $600 in materials alone, not counting labor cost. Cash was paid to the builder.

The building stood on land owned by the Presbyterian congregation. Though the Catholics had a more suitable location and had offered a hundred dollars bonus, they could not make a trade with the other church. The church had to be moved to the Catholic property. This was a difficult task because of uneven terrain and a pond between the two places. It was also feared that the church's high tower would be damaged. Finally, a man was found who guaranteed his contract to move the church for $170. Three days later the church stood in its new location. Nothing was damaged, neither the church nor the tower.

According to a report, Catholic services were conducted for the first time in this church in May 1890 for a parish with about 70 Catholics. Among them were the Brinkmans, Wrapes, Englishs, Staudts, Bleiers, Weyers, Islers, Kerchoffs, etc.

The new church was 46 x 30 feet, with a fine tower of approximately 60 feet. A sanctuary 18x20 foot was planned for later. The parish was still very small, but made great sacrifices and all debts were paid. The location of the church was in the center of the town, but not in the business district.

On Oct 27, 1890, the Rt. Rev. Bishop Fitzgerald dedicated St. Mary's Church.

About 1895 a considerable addition was added to the rear of St. Mary's Church and Father Joseph McQuaid bought three fine bells for the church and these bells are still in use.

After several other priests had served St. Mary's Parish, Father Joseph M. Hoflinger arrived in Paragould on Jan 6, 1915. At that time, St. Mary's showed indebtedness in excess of $10,000 but Father Hoflinger immediately set out to liquidate that debt. Six years later that goal was accomplished.

The dream of Father Hoflinger and his congregation was to build a new permanent church. Next on the agenda was a building fund. With Bishop's sanction, he began placing savings in various building and loan associations. In 1929, however, the depression disrupted those plans. Banks and loan associations closed and the outlook was glum. There seemed little hope that the dream would be realized, since the "papers" he held were almost worthless. He received offers to sell the "papers" at 10 cents on the dollar, but he rejected those offers and waited for better times. And the better times came, enabling Father to redeem his "papers" at 100 cents on the dollar –full value. In 1935 construction began on the new church. The white frame church had served the parish since 1890. The present red brick church cost $50,000. It is of Italian renaissance architecture, with stained glass windows and a rear bell tower.

Msgr. Joseph Hoflinger's pastorship of 41 years brought many improvements to the parish. St. Mary's has had three school buildings. The newest, "Hoflinger Hall" was blessed by Bishop Albert L. Fletcher on Feb 10, 1957. The present rectory was purchased in about 1959. In August 1982 kindergarten was added. A Parish Hall was begun in July 1982 and was used for the first time Jan 3, 1983 and dedicated on April 17, 1983. A building and property were purchased in 1999 across the street from the parish hall to house the ever-growing preschool. Parishioners renovated the building and a beautiful playground was constructed. This parish still continues to grow and prosper.

*Original St. Mary's Church property: Church, School, and Convent.*

*St. Mary's Church*

# Seventh and Mueller Church of Christ

On Oct 17, 1948, 150 Christians from the Second and Walnut congregation met at Seventh and Mueller Streets and formed a new congregation. Emmett Smith preached that day and remained 17 years. Doug Kostowski, Claude Lewis and Eddie Lewis followed him. Other preachers serving in specialized ministries include: J. T. Ashby, Stanley Freeman, Jim Short, Norman Childs, Sonny Childs, Joe Cabrera and Roger Utter. Present ministers include: Larry McFadden, Willie Sandlin, Art Smith, Jim Short, Roy Thomas and Telpher Campbell.

Previous elders include: Roy Greenway, Buck Hurd, Melvin Eubanks, I. E. Lemmons, Travis Blue, Hayden Carter, Allen Berry, Gus Eubanks, John L. Watson, W. T. Watson, Claude Lewis, Noel Jetton, Raymond Meadows, Boyd Leath, Ed Woodward, John McDaniel, Maurice Hurd, Johnnie Wilkins, Terry Wilkins and Vance Greenway. Present elders are: Duane Towell, Jerry Carlile, Larry Watson, Tommy Arnold and Rick Watson.

Mission work is supported in Central America, Greece and Africa. The church fulfills the Great Commission through World Bible School, Bible Correspondence Courses, Home Bible Studies, summer camp, benevolence, a bus ministry and group campaigns.

Our benevolence program is administered through the Compassion Outreach Ministry and Children's Homes, Inc., which began in 1956 and cares for children under the supervision of our elders. James Balcom is director.

The church has always supported Christian education, aiding in the founding and growth of Crowley's Ridge Academy and Crowley's Ridge College.

*Aerial view of the Seventh and Mueller Church of Christ*

# Shiloh United Methodist Church

Shiloh Church was organized in 1888 as part of the White River Conference of the Methodist Church. A two-story building was constructed on land donated by James W. and Virginia Thompson. A warranty deed, dated May 10, 1890, listed J. P. Cox and M. L. S. Anderson as trustees.

The land eventually went into litigation and was sold at an auction. A quitclaim deed, granted Jan 1897 by J. D. and Lena Block, gave the land to be used solely for church purposes. The trustees at this time were J. P. Cox, R. C. Burton and Virgil Hale.

The building was used also as a lodge and school but, since a minister came only one Sunday a month, a Sunday school was begun to fill the void on the remaining Sundays.

The Sunday school superintendent arrived early each week to carry in wood and build a fire in winter or raise the windows in summer to cool the room. Then he rang the church bell, calling everyone to worship, according to Nath Mabrey who was a superintendent for many years.

All members contributed to the preacher's salary. Church leaders went by horse and buggy to each home to collect money or donations such as chickens, meat, vegetables and fruit, home-canned goods, or sorghum molasses.

Over time, improvements were added. One of the most appreciated was the addition of window screens. By 1905, the church had a reed organ played by Mrs. Pearl Wills.

As the congregation grew, the first building was torn down and another erected by 1915. The congregation met in the old Palestine School until the new building was completed.

To help finance the building, people donated money or goods such as corn, chickens or animals to be sold. Cash was scarce in those days but people were generous with their time and effort. The congregation numbered in the 60's then with the Reverend H. E. May as pastor.

As the membership grew, the church was enlarged and improvements made. The Ladies' Sunday school class was innovative in their approach at raising money. They had a cotton patch on the Mabrey farm and used the money to buy a piano, which is now in the fellowship hall.

The congregation grew to over 200 members and on Dec 13, 1964, groundbreaking ceremonies were held for a third building. This was exactly 76 years after the church organized on Dec 13, 1888. On Sept 5, 1965, the first service was held and the following January, a service for the laying of the cornerstone was conducted. A box placed in the cornerstone contained, among other things, a list of preachers since 1888, a Cokesbury hymnal, a Kennedy half-dollar and quarter and the names of the couple first married in the new church.

Exactly 82 years to the day that Shiloh was organized, the new church building was dedicated to the glory of God. Eventually a special place was built into a new, lighted church sign for the old church bell, which had been used for many years to call the faithful to worship.

A new parsonage was built in 1973. Then Shiloh became a full-time pastorate, after having previously shared a pastor first with Pruett's Chapel and then Christ United Methodist Church.

A fellowship hall with kitchen was added providing a place for potluck dinners and ice cream suppers. Church members also served Thanksgiving dinner to the public for many years and now they hold a fish fry yearly.

The members want future generations to know that God has been and is a vital part of this church. We will continue doing His will and serving His people to pass down the Christian heritage we have received.

The following is a list of Methodist ministers who served at Shiloh:

1888-1892 I. A. Vernon
1892-1896 William M. Watson
1896-1900 John Edison
1900-1902 Brother Rowe
1902-1905 A. C. Griffith
1905-1907 Ira Russell
1907-1909 John S. Watson
1909-1911 Charles L. Castleberry
1911-1912 Thomas A. Rowen
1912-1916 H. E. May
1916-1918 W. J. Williams
1918-1920 Samuel G. Watson
1920-1921 A. W. O'Bryant
1921-1924 C. L. Castleberry
1924-1926 William P. Emrah
1926-1927 Paul Boon
1927-1929 G. C. Taylor
1929-1930 Floyd G. Villines
1930-1931 William J. Jordan
1931-1933 Charles Jackson Wade
1933-1935 Elbert Marlar
1935-1937 Marvin A. Cherry
1937-1939 William E. Benbrook
1939-1940 Earl DuBois
1940-1941 J. W. Simmons
1941-1943 James H. Holt
1943-1945 R. B. Howerton
1945-1948 W. T. Lingo
1948-1952 Robert Montgomery
1952-1953 John F. Wilson
1953-1955 Alvin Gibbs
1955-1957 Elvis Wright
1957-1960 Marvin Thompson
1960-1962 Jim West
1962-1965 Sherman Waters
1965-1967 Woodrow Woods
1967-1971 Eugene Bain
1971-1972 Felix Holland
1972-1974 Joe Kennedy
1974-1976 David Moose
1976-1977 Ray Edwards
1977-1979 Chris Cooper
1979-1982 Leonard D. Nash
1982-1983 Von Dell Mooney
1983-1984 Louis See Jr.
1984-1986 Harlin Shelton
1986-1988 Bruce Wallace
1988-1993 Michael Sutton
1993-1996 Robert L. Hager
1996-1997 Willis Osban
1997-1999 Don Wilson
1999 -Jim Chaplain

*The remodeled second church*

*First Shiloh church about 1900*

*Current building with fellowship hall on right and the old Shiloh church bell by sign at left*

# Warren's Chapel Methodist Episcopal Church, South

Rev. David Broiles organized the Warren's Chapel Methodist Episcopal Church South, in 1857. It first met in the homes of the members. The first church building was located near the present site of Crowley's Ridge State Park.

The exact date when the church moved to its present location in not known, however, the church was already standing when the deed was given for the five acres of land on Oct 20, 1876. Benjamin H. Crowley, his wife Elizabeth Jane and Lucy Mellon gave land where the present church and cemetery now stand.

The trustees of the church were Darrel Owen, William R. Gregory and J. R. Gramling. It was the White River Conference.

The first record of membership known is Aug 11, 1879. There were four (4) members on roll; they were George A. Gramling, George B. Harris, D. C. Moore and James F. Wall. There is no record of the pastor for 1879. There is also no record of the pastors since the Rev. David Broiles in 1857 until the Rev. A. C. Griffin in 1882. However it got its name from Rev. Warren.

In the early beginning of the church, there were 142 members on roll. There were 123 Methodists and other faiths as well.

The first Sunday school record began May 21, 1893. J. W. Watson was the pastor.

There have been four church buildings at the present location. The first one was of logs. The second was built of lumber and was destroyed by a tornado. The third building was about 50 years old when it was torn down in Dec 1956. And a new church was built. Church members and friends donated labor to build it, which cost around $4000 when completed. The members planted cotton on land donated by J. E. Cline to raise the money.

The church was dedicated on May 19, 1957. Rev. Elbert Brunner was pastor.

There have been many improvements since then. A new addition with kitchen and bathrooms in the early 1980's.

We have many from the congregation who provided music up through the years. The first musical instrument in the church was an organ. Mrs. Clara Kuykendall was organist sometime between 1901 and 1930's with Mable Wise being the first pianist. Faye Cline, in the late 40's and 50's and many more on up to now. We once again have an organist, Nina Brewer, who plays for us. In her absence we have some piano players coming on.

We have had many pastors since then, many were just starting out as young preachers. Our present pastor is one of those young men, Rev. Everett Isom. Today we have 40 members. Most of the present members are descendants or related to the first trustees of the church. The Tedders and Amorines are descended from Benjamin H. Crowley, the Cotherns descended from William R. Gregory. The Shipman, Lenderman, Gander, Cline, Jackson and Reed families are descended from J. R. Gramling.

The trustees today are also descendants of the first trustees. They are Luther Cline, Lester Cline, Mattie Tedder, Wynbourn Reed, James and Emma Shipman.

*Submitted by Mrs. Emma Shipman*

*This was the third church building. It was torn down in late December 1956. It was said to have been 50 years old.*

*The present day church building, October 8, 2000.*

# West View Baptist Church

West View Baptist Church was organized on Mar 6, 1960 with 92 charter members. The first formal service was held in the Highfill building, located at East Kingshighway and South 8th Ave., on February 20 of that year. Reverend Guy Whitney was called to serve as our first pastor.

In April 1960, our church purchased an acre of ground on the corner of N. 7th and W. Morgan Streets in the northwest corner of Paragould. Construction of the first two units of the church complex was begun in May 1960 and on Aug 6, 1960, we moved into the new building. In May 1962, construction was begun on the third unit of the church complex.

In May 1967, our church purchased an additional acre of ground and in March of that year a parsonage was purchased at the corner of 10th and Morgan Streets.

March 1967 brought the resignation of Brother Guy Whitney. Brother Sedric Wesson served as pastor until his resignation October 1968. Brother J. R. Hull was called as pastor in December 1968.

On July 7, 1969 the church voted to construct a new auditorium to be used for the glory of God. Construction was completed and the first services were held in the new sanctuary on March 15, 1970. On April 12 the auditorium was dedicated to the Lord with the dedicatory message being brought by Brother Guy Whitney the first pastor of West View.

In June 1973 Brother Hull resigned as pastor. Brother Eugene Webb served as interim pastor until the church was led to call Brother Ledell Bailey who came to West View in Nov 1973.

On Sept 5, 1979 our church voted to build a building that would include a pastor's study, music director's office, secretary office and a preschool department. It was later decided to finance this construction by a bond program. This building program completed the original master plan adopted by the church at its beginning.

The church called Bro. Gary Fulton to be their pastor in Sept 1981. He served at West View until the Lord called him to the mission field in 1992.

In 1982 our church, through faith, raised approximately $6,000 through special offerings to purchase needed office equipment and choir robes.

In 1983 our church voted in regular business meeting to remodel our education building. This was to be done on faith and through special offerings we raised approximately $15,000 of the $17,500 required to complete this project.

In 1983 our church began an ongoing Evangelism Training Program, Continuing Witness Training and many have been won to Christ by our trained lay people since this began.

In 1984 our church voted in regular business session to remodel our fellowship hall area. Through faith we raised approximately $17,000 by special offerings to accomplish this project.

We organized a Senior Adult Organization in 1984, which will prove to be a successful ministry to our church.

In March 1985 we called Brother Ronnie Winn as youth and music director.

In Oct 1988 the church voted to purchase a 30-passenger bus. Payments were to be made through love offerings or general fund. The cost was $47,000.

On Feb 8, 1989 our church voted to build a combination storage and bus garage. The cost of the building was $9,472.45.

In March 1992 Brother Gary Fulton resigned as pastor. In April 1992 Ron Sanders served as interim pastor until the church was led to call Brother Bengy Massey who came to West View in July 1992.

On April 29, 1992 voted to make improvements to the parsonage. The cost of the improvements was $12,600.

On March 5, 1993 the church voted to build five classrooms, halls, two bathrooms on the north of present auditorium, with one classroom on the second floor, the roof to be level with the auditorium. Tommy Clubb was the contractor and cost for additions was $73,108.

On Aug 11, 1993 the church voted to purchase 19 acres of land adjacent to church ground for $90,000. We had been negotiating with Mr. Thompson for years to purchase part of the 19 acres. The Lord opened the door for the church to purchase all 19 acres.

On Dec 4, 1994 the church voted to purchase a 19-passenger bus. The cost was $11,750.

On April 12, 1995 a motion was made at regular business meeting to proceed with the plan to build a new church facility.

In Dec 1996 Brother Bengy Massey resigned as pastor. In Feb 1997 Brother Raymond Atwood served as interim pastor until the church was led to call Brother Randy Vanover who came to West View in Sept 1997.

In May 1997 the church added a part-time music director, Gary Pyland. Brother Ronnie Winn took the position as full youth director.

In June 1997 Gary Pyland resigned as music director.

In July 1997 the position of secretary changed from part-time to fulltime secretary.

In Jan 1998 David King came as part-time music director.

March 9, 1997 report on the new building: The new facility seats 561 (bottom) 65 (choir) and 125 balcony. The church went through a Together We Build Program and the church members pledged $300,000.

Summer of 1997 breaking ground for the new building began. The total cost of the new facility was $1,100,000. On Aug 30, 1998 the auditorium was dedicated to the Lord with the dedicatory message being brought by Brother Gary Fulton.

In May 1997 the parsonage was reported sold for $58,000.

In June 1999 Brother Randy Vanover resigned as our pastor and Brother David King resigned as music director in July 1999.

In Aug 1999 Brian Horn was called to be our part-time music director.

In Sept 1999 Brother Robert Wring began serving as our interim pastor and is with West View at the present time. During the years of 1960-2000 West View received 574 by baptism. Our present membership is 614. Our 40th Anniversary was Mar 6, 2000.

On March 11, 2001 West View voted to call Bro. Leon Johnson from Waynesboro, TN as our new pastor.

As we face the future, West View Baptist church looks forward with hope and courage, anticipating great things from God and determined to attempt great things for Him. With God's help we shall be "about the Master's business" continuing the task that is ours as we await our Lord's return.

# Wood's Chapel United Methodist Church

On July 24, 1861 William H. Wood deeded two acres to the Methodist Church for the sum of one dollar. The church was called Wood's Chapel Episcopal Methodist Church South. Trustees were William H. Wood, James R. Wood and Hezekiah Highfill. A. Rev. Glassgo was the pastor.

The church was made of hewn logs with one large door and a fireplace on one end, but no windows. The fireplace furnished heat and was a source of light with coal oil lamps, lanterns and candles. Seats were made of hewn logs, smooth on one side with pegs driven in auger holes on the round side, secured to the floor with wooden pegs.

The charter members were:
1. William Wood
2. Thomas Wood
3. Sallie Wood
4. James Wood and wife,
5. Durant Wood
6. Mike Wood
7. Reverend Hezekiah Highfill and wife, Sarah
8. Mary Highfill
9. Mollie Wood
10. Harris Powell and wife, Anna Powell
11. Sallie Powell
12. Bettie Powell
13. Flora Ann McDaniel
14. Fannie Lloyd
15. Robert C. Bowlin
16. Mr. Hutchins

The church building was used as a school for a short time but burned during the 1890's. The new church, built in 1898 across the road, was much larger with two single front doors and a single door at the back. The steep roof was covered with wood shingles. The white church had windows down both sides and was heated with a wood stove. The church has been remodeled several times by lowering the roof and replacing the wood shingles with tin. The building now has a composition roof. Electricity was installed in the 1940's and a basement later added, along with a steeple, a new side entrance and a small paved parking area.

Music has always been a very important part of the worship service. Mrs. Osa Virgin remembered Wood's Chapel as a singing church. After working hard all week, people looked forward to the fellowship and singing on Sunday.

James Alexander McDaniel was the song leader beginning in the 1890's. It is said he never missed church except when he attended Methodist conference meetings.

Singing schools were quite popular. One, taught by Bud Diggs, lasted a week with 100 to 115 people attending. Songs were sung using the Southern Harmony songbook, which had many old favorites, still sung today.

In 1914 the Soliphone had a contest as an advertising promotion and Wood's Chapel won by collecting the most coupons. The prize was a church organ, which was used until it "played out" according to Mrs. Virgin. Then the piano was used again.

From the beginning the congregation has been supportive of the church and its ministry. In a fourth Quarterly Conference report of the Gainesville Circuit in 1867, Wood's Chapel donated $1, a large sum in those days, for the support of the ministry. When asked about pastoral candidates, it was recorded that Henry D. Wood was "recommended by the society at Wood's Chapel as a suitable person to be licensed to preach."

Membership has varied over the years, beginning with 20 charter members. Services are still held every Sunday and though small in number, the congregation feels the Lord has blessed them in many ways. Members agree with the sentiments of early, long-time member Samuel McDaniel, who said "On these benches and in this building, fathers and mothers assembled to worship God according to the dictates of their consciences and never since that day has this church been abandoned and we would like that this church, like the influence of its early members, live on forever".

Those who have served as ministers for Wood's Chapel Methodist Church are:
1. 1861-1862-Brother Glassgo
2. 1863-1865-H. M. Grenade
3. 1866 - John C. Clayton
4. 1867- John Webb
5. 1868 – John Potter
6. 1869 - John Webb
7. 1870-1871 - D. B. Warren
8. 1871-1872 - Dock McWorter
9. 1873 – A. S. Hillburn

*Young Men's Class ca. 1916 – L to R: Henry Highfill, Clyde Wood, Vernice Jones, Paul McClerkin, Herbert Farrell, Adrian Diggs, Alex Wood, Enos Courtney, "Big" Granger McDaniel, Frank Wood, Charlie Wood, Jack Diggs, Harvey Farrell, Jim McDaniel, Thebert Jones and Paul Jones.*

*Young Ladies Class, Alice Highfill, teacher – Row 1: Tennie Woods, Edith Woods, Oma McDaniel, Eula Jones, Minnie McDaniel, Marie Jackson, Maggie Woods. Back Row: Unknown, unknown, Edna Mae Diggs, Callie McDaniel, Grace McCauley, Jessie Shields*

10. 1874 (first six months) - Colia Ford
11. 1874 (second six months) - N. Ford
12. 1875 - J. S. Hillburn
13. 1876-1879 - A. C. Griffin
14. 1880 – R. G. Britton
15. 1881-1882 – J. T. Suttle
16. 1883-1884 F. E. Taylor
17. 1885 – W. R. Foster
18. 1886-1887 – John S. Foster
19. 1888 – I. H. Vernon
20. 1889 – W. W. Anderson
21. 1890-1891 – T. B. Williamson
22. 1892-1895 – A. C. Griffin
23. 1896-1899 – W. M. Watson
24. 1900 - W. B. Row
25. 1901-1902 — A. C. Griffin
26. 1903 – W. C. Toombs
27. 1904-1905 – I. H. Russell
28. 1906 - W. M. Watson
29. 1907-1908 – J. S. Watson
30. 1909 – C. L. Castleberry
31. 1910 – T. R. Allen
32. 1911 – G. A. Bowen
33. 1912-1915 – H. E. May
34. 1916-1917 – W. J. Williams
35. 1918-1919 – S. G. Watson
36. 1920 – A. W. Obriant
37. 1921-1923 – C. L. Castleberry
38. 1924-1925 – O. W. Emrah
39. 1926 – R. C. Boone
40. 1927-1929 – G. C Taylor
41. 1930 – Floyd G. Williams
42. 1931 – W. J. Jordon
43. 1931 – A. M. Alsey
44. 1931 – C. J. Wade
45. 1932-1933 – C. J. Wade
46. 1934-1935 – Elbert Marlar
47. 1936- 1937 – M. A. Cherry
48. 1938-1939 – W. E. Benbrook
49. 1940 – Earl DeBois
50. 1941 – J. W. Simmons
51. 1942-1943 – J. H. Holt
52. 1944-1946 – Robert B. Howerton
53. 1947-1948 – W. T. Lingo
54. 1949-1951 – Robert Montgomery
55. 1952- John F. Wilson
56. 1952-1954 – Marvin Gibbs
57. 1955- Elvis Wright
58. 1956-1959 – Marvin Thompson
59. 1960-1962 – Jim West
60. 1962-1964 – Sherman Waters
61. 1965-1968 – Woodrow Woods
62. 1969-1970 – Eugene Bains
63. 1971-1972 – Felix Holland
64. 1972-1973 – Charles Southerland
65. 1973-1974 – Jo A. Gatlin
66. 1974-1975 – Larry Spear
67. 1975-1976 – J. H. Holt
68. 1976-1982 – Marvin Thompson
69. 1982-1984 – Harmon Whitehurst
70. 1983-1993 – John Soward
71. 1993-1994 – John Zolk
72. 1994-1996 – James Lann
73. 1996-1997 – Lay Speaker
74. 1997-1998 – Nancy Rainwater
75. 1998- Robert DeBaun

Sources: This article was partly based on an interview with Mrs. Osa Virgin by Mack Hamblin and a history of Wood's Chapel as remembered by Samuel McDaniel. Also used were a *History of Greene County* by Vivian Hansbrough and a Wood's Chapel church history prepared by members of the church, Methodist conference minutes.

*Wood's Chapel United Methodist Church, 2000*

## Center Hill Church of Christ

141 people met at Crowley's Ridge Academy on Jan 2, 1961 to begin the Center Hill Church of Christ. From that very first meeting, there has been a determined effort to serve the Lord and our community.

Work was begun immediately on the building on land donated by Hayden and Nora Carter. Men of the congregation did the work. The first meeting in the new building was the second Sunday of October in 1961. Five additions have been added to the building since that time, the latest being completed in early 1990.

Travis Blue and Hayden Carter were installed as the first elders of the congregation and also delivered the first sermons. Those serving as elders currently are: Larry Bills, Vernon Lacey, Charles Long and Alfred Rowe.

For the first two years men of the congregation and preachers of the area filled the pulpit. In the fall of 1962 Boyd Morgan began preaching on a regular basis. Don Smith began full time work in July of 1967. Albert Lemmons who began work in 1974 followed him. Art Smith worked with the congregation from January 1977 until March of 1980. Mike Brooks started his work in June of 1980 and served until August of 1992. Mark Howell served as co-minister from 1982 until 1986. Michael Cox began his work with Center Hill in January of 1993 and is the current pulpit minister for Center Hill. John Massey served as Center Hill's first full time youth minister. Gary Cremeens is now Center Hill's full time youth and family minister.

Mission work has been one of the major priorities of the Center Hill Church of Christ. Beginning with the first month, approximately 50% of the contribution has been used for this area of work.

Through the years the church has experienced many spiritual feasts with great meetings, Vacation *Bible* schools, workshops, etc. With all these as stepping-stones, the future looks very bright for the Center Hill Church of Christ now and into the new millennium.

---

## Delaplaine Baptist Church

In 1919 as the boys were returning home from WWI, two men John Andis and Carl Ferrell discussed holding a revival in the unused upper story of the Delaplaine School building with the hopes of getting a church started. An old pump organ was borrowed and carried up the stairs, where a dear old lady, Mrs. Luther Gates played for the revival. Brother Cooper, a retired minister, agreed to come to conduct the meetings and several of the men nailed scrap lumber together for some rough benches for the congregation to use. Then came a disturbing rumor. The rough element of the town said when the Baptist preacher came they would ride him out of town on a rail. The first night of the revival several uniformed men were scattered among the congregation and needless to say the 'rough necks' made no disturbances during the entire revival. Mr. Carl Ferrell led the singing during the 10-night revival. The Sunday following the meetings, the group went to Black River where 60 new converts were baptized. These new converts along with several older Christians formed the nucleus for the new church. Now a new church building was needed. Mr. Luther Gates donated a lot and several businessmen gave materials. There was no expense for labor as volunteers mixed gravel and cement by hand while others nailed the building together. This building was in use until 1972, and then it was replaced by the new brick building that is in use today.

*Submitted by Mr. & Mrs. Ed Wilkinson*

*Delaplaine Baptist Church (built ca. 1922), 1950's (Photo courtesy of Mr. and Mrs. Ed Wilkinson)*

## East Side Baptist Church

East Side Baptist Church, formerly known as Second Missionary Baptist Church of Christ, was organized in Paragould on May 27, 1912. It was constituted with 72 charter members. The first services were held in a tent erected on two lots where the first permanent building was located at the corner of East Poplar Street and North Sixth Avenue.

Bro. George O. Light was elected as the Sunday School Superintendent of the new church. Mrs. Luna Williams Smith was elected as the first church organist. Rev. G. A. Crocker accepted the call as the first full-time pastor in September of 1912.

The building committee closed the deal on the two lots where the tent was located on June 16, 1912 for a cost of $250. Early financial goals included the building of the new church sanctuary and the pastor's salary of $600 per year.

At the close of WWI, our nation had come through a time of heartbreak and devastation and many families had lost loved ones. The families began to turn to the church for support. The church saw attendance and offerings increase.

January 25, 1931 was the first known recording of the name "East Side Baptist Church". The church continued to prosper with ordination of deacons, retirement of financial debts, supporting missions and cooperative programs. Funds were separated into building fund and general fund.

In 1941, a parsonage was provided for the pastors. On May 7, 1947, they voted to establish a mission known as Lake Street Mission Church with Rev. Joe Hester as the pastor.

In May 1966, the church approved a $75,000 bond issued to erect a new sanctuary. It was completed in 1967. Rev. Jesse Holcomb was the pastor during this building project.

During the 1970's, East Side purchased three lots for future expansion. Other expansions included additional educational rooms, remodeling of the sanctuary, adding a balcony and enlarging the choir loft. The church was growing and more land was purchased as it became available.

On December 15, 1985, the members of East Side Baptist Church were devastated to find out that God's beautiful sanctuary had been destroyed by fire. Churches all over the community were very gracious by offering their facilities for services. Starting in January, the congregation was able to hold two Sunday morning services. The building of a new sanctuary and additional educational space began after the placement of more land. The "Together We Build" program was the beginning of a new era in the work of East Side Baptist Church.

Pastors who have served at East Side in its recent history include Jim Fowler 1975-1990, Bruce Swihart 1990-1995 and Charles F. DeVane Jr. 1997-present.

## Finch Baptist Church

Finch Baptist Church was organized in 1872 as "Pleasant Grove Baptist Church" and was a member of the Gainesville Association until the church changed its name to "Finch Baptist Church" in 1953. The original 13 members met in a cotton gin on the Newsom farm located northeast of present building until a log building was erected. The log building served until 1906, when a new building was built. This building remained until 1970 when the present modern brick building was completed. The present building will seat 350 in worship, with a choir for 50, a kitchen and fellowship hall that will seat 80, two offices, 10 classrooms and a basement. The church is located nine miles west of Paragould on Highway 358.

In 1876, a small child who belonged to a family passing through the community died and was buried near the church. A short time later Sterling Newsom died and was buried there also, the land belonged to Newsom.

*Finch Baptist Church*

## Liberty Church of Christ

Liberty Church of Christ was one of the five pioneer churches of Christ in this area. These pioneer Christians saw a need for a church building and on Sept 17, 1877, the deed was made for the church. Liberty is located on Crowley's Ridge about 15 miles north of Jonesboro, AR and about 10 miles southwest of Paragould, AR on Highway 351.

According to records from 1877 to 1888, there were 23 male and 24 female members. Two of the female members died in 1880. The preacher was W. L. Wood, great grandfather of current minister Gene Wood (1979 to present, 1999). At present we have two elders and three deacons.

The first building was built in 1877, the second 1923 and the third and one currently in use, 1963. The Liberty Church is involved in many areas of the Lord's Work. We are constantly working to spread the glorious Gospel of our Lord Jesus Christ. We have been blessed through the years with many young people that have gone from Liberty to be an influence and help in the places they worship. Many are serving as elders, deacons, ministers and song leaders. Many of our young ladies are wives of the same. A special invitation is extended to any and all that would come and visit with us.

*Submitted by G. Wood*

## St. Mary's Cemetery

St. Mary's Cemetery is located on Highway 49 half a mile south of U. S. Highway 412.

According to the Warranty Deed, the cemetery property was purchased in July 1898 from W. J. McDonald and his wife for the sum of $120 cash in hand paid by Joseph Bliss Alois Martin and Bernhard Kirchoff, Trustees for the Congregation of St. Mary's Catholic Church of Paragould.

Before the turn of the century there were three marked graves, all in 1898. 26 more parishioners had been laid to rest within the next 10 years.

The first monument in St. Mary's Cemetery was a cedar tree, which is still standing at the head of the grave of John Joseph Kueter who died July 7, 1898. Years later, a stone monument was put at his gravesite.

Nikolaus Staudt, who died on Aug 6, 1898, was the second burial. The third burial in 1898 was Mary Peterson. Two priests are buried here. Very Rev. Monsignor Joseph M. Hoflinger, who served St. Mary's Parish for over 41 years, died Jan 19, 1959 and Rev. Stephen F. Jacklin died July 21, 1960.

There is also a small monument near the entrance, which reads:

*Baby*
*Before I formed you in the womb, I knew you. Jeremiah 1:5*
*In loving memory of the innocent victims of abortion*
*Knights of Columbus Council #1713*

A large concrete crucifix erected by Miss Anna Staudt in the year 1907 overlooks the cemetery.

*The entrance to Saint Mary's Cemetery on Highway 49*

*The crucifix donated by Miss Anna Staudt*

## Walcott Baptist Church History

The Walcott Baptist Church was organized on the second Sunday in May 1887. The first meeting place was in the Walcott School House, a box building then located on the corner of Highway 141 and the Old Walcott Road. The church originated as a mission of the Mt. Zion Baptist Church. In 1916 the church built its first log building on the property where the church building now stands. For many years the church had an old fashion tabernacle where revivals and camp meetings were held every year. This was removed from the property in 1942. A large white frame building was built in 1927. This remained the church's building until May 2, 1976 when the new 325 seat capacity church building was erected. In July 1994 our new Family Life Center was completed. The church is located in a growing community and has unlimited potential. Our pastor, Bro. Rudy Ring says our church can make a world of difference, one person at a time.

*Walcott Baptist Church*

## Bard Methodist Church

The Bard Methodist church was built in 1923. The first pastor was Brother Garland Taylor. During the period of the early 1930's at the Bard Church, Sam Roberts was serving on the committee who chose the elders of the church. The average attendance was about 30.

In 1933 or 1934 the church was used as a high school as they had no room in the schoolhouse. The church caught fire and since the parsonage was empty, it was used the rest of the school year.

The first wedding in the Bard Church was Kathryn Brandon and Owen Hoskins. They were married in 1947. The last weddings in the church were, Pauline Smoot and Bill Hill on Oct 15, 1961 and Ellen Smoot to John Felty on June 2, 1962, both by Brother Charles Crossno.

## Clark's Chapel Church, School and Cemetery

Clark's Chapel Cemetery is located on Highway 351 in south Greene County. Joseph Clark donated the original land for the Clark Chapel Cemetery in 1865. The first two graves were two unknown Union soldiers returning from the Civil War.

P. W. Boyd and Nancy Boyd deeded to Methodist Episcopal Church South at Clark's Chapel six acres in 1899. Trustees were G. Greenway, J. C. McMillon and G. F. Miller.

Rev. G. H. Faulkner organized Missionary Baptist Church of Christ at Clark's Chapel Aug 1908 with charter members as follows:
1. P. N. McNiel
2. Dove McNiel
3. Dove Emer Schivner
4. J. A. Duffell
5. Emerine Duffell
6. Grover Duffell
7. O. H. Payne
8. Caroline Payne
9. Callie Levins
10. Docie Ellington
11. Mrs. M. E. Winn.

M. S. Lenderman and M. C. Lenderman, his wife, deeded two acres to trustees of the Missionary Baptist Church at Pleasant Hill in 1913.

P. G. Ellington, unmarried, deeded one acre to Pleasant Hill Baptist Church and Clark's Chapel School District 25 in 1935.

W. Ellington donated one acre in approximately 1937.

M. A. West and Vestal West deeded one-quarter acre to J. E. Thompson, Willie Wood, Leroy Walden and Alton Pegg, deacons of Clark's Chapel Baptist Church in 1967.

Ralph and Nora Blackford deeded one acre for the parsonage to Clark's Chapel Baptist Church in 1979.

The present trustees of Clark's Chapel Cemetery include:
Arburn Graftenreed
Donald Johnston
N. J. McMillon
Wesley Winn
Verbadean Ellington, secretary.

## Christ United Methodist Church

The Christ United Methodist Church was brought into being by the merger of the Bard, New Liberty and Morning Star Methodist Churches. Each of the three churches came to realize that individually they could not survive, so they met one Sunday night in 1961 at Morning Star to discuss a union of the three churches. This meeting set the stage for Christ United to become a reality.

Brother Lloyd Conyers, our district superintendent, was receptive to the plan and along with our Pastor Charles Crossno, they both worked diligently in the months that followed to put the plan together. A committee of three men from each church was appointed to supervise construction. O. V. "Orie" Smoot, James "Jack" Smoot and Alvin Cupp represented Bard. Norman "Perry" Toombs, Herman Toombs and Clarence Thomason represented New Liberty; Morning Star's representatives were Griffin Cothern, Charles Lewis and Eugene Widmer.

Early in the planning it was agreed that the church would be located on Highway 25 East. Procuring a site proved to be no small task, but through the diligent effort of Brother Crossno he eventually obtained the present location. On Nov 9, 1962 the Morning Star Church building was moved to this location to be the new sanctuary and the fellowship hall was added.

A committee made up of one person from each of the three churches, was appointed to choose a name for the new church.

## Grace United General Baptist Church

Grace United General Baptist Church was organized May 2, 1971 when First General Bap-

*Christ United Methodist Church*

*Clark's Chapel School group, ca. 1938*

tist Church on East Vine Street joined with a church from Cardwell, MO.

They had purchased, with financial assistance from the General Baptist Home Mission Board, Calvary Full Gospel Church.

Dr. Ollie Latch was the speaker for the morning worship. His message was entitled "The Open Door". It was a wonderful challenge as God had truly opened the door of opportunity.

The organizational service was held that afternoon with several ministers present: Rev. O. E. Hargrave, Secretary of General Baptist Home Mission Board, Rev. Leland Duncan, a member of the General Baptist Home Mission Board, Rev. James Dortch, Pastor of Kennett, Mo. General Baptist Church, Dr. Ollie Latch, Pastor of Bethany General Baptist Church, Malden, MO and Rev. Cecil Winberry of Moweaqua, IL.

50 people presented themselves for membership that afternoon. Charter membership was offered through June 1, 1971 reaching a total of 71 members.

Trustees for the new church were R. C. Copeland, John Parker and Chester Jones. Deacons were Adolph Cupp and R. C. Copeland. The pastor elected was Rev. Cecil Winberry.

There were three major building expansions the first 10 years.

The church recently completed a remodeling job on the exterior of the building.

Pastors have been: Cecil Winberry, Ollie Latch, Charles Crisp, Dale Money, Junior McGinnis, Royce Schanda and our present pastor Rev. Richard Stevenson.

*Submitted by Wanda Gray and Erymie Camren*

## Griffin Memorial United Methodist Church

The Griffin Memorial United Methodist Church was organized in 1903 following a series of cottage prayer meetings led by the Reverend Alonzo C. Griffin. It had 12 charter members.

Rev. A. C. Griffin, the founding pastor, was born in the State of Alabama in 1845. He joined the White River Conference in 1875 and served for 42 years in the Methodist ministry.

For many years the church was known as East Side Methodist Church. In the mid 1940s, the church changed its name to Griffin Memorial Methodist Church in honor of its founding pastor. Paragould Methodism actually began in 1883 and the East Side Church was organized some 20 years later to meet the needs of the eastern part of the city. Records indicate that Mr. Richard Jackson donated one acre of land for the site of the Griffin Church.

The present sanctuary was built in 1953 under the pastoral leadership of the Reverend J. Harmon Holt at a cost of $40,000. It was expanded in the early 1970s, along with the construction of a complete educational building and fellowship hall, under the leadership of the Reverend J. Albert Gatlin.

For nearly a century Griffin Memorial has remained a vital part of the work of Christ in Paragould, offering warmth, friendliness and ministry in our community.

*Submitted by Nancy Estes*

## Immanuel Baptist Church

On Oct 11, 1939 the First Baptist Church Paragould, AR established a mission, known as South Side Mission, in a framed store building at 812 South Fifth Street in Paragould. Mrs. Lottie Reynolds, a long time member of First Baptist Church was instrumental in organizing South Side Mission and remained with it until it became an independent Baptist church.

In 1942, because of continued growth, the South Side Mission constructed a new building at the site of the present church at 607 West Mueller Street.

On Feb 20, 1955 South Side Mission was

*Immanuel Baptist Church, 1998*

*Griffin Memorial United Methodist Church*

*Grace United General Baptist Church*

organized as Immanuel Baptist Church and with 110 charter members, called Pastor Emmitt Pipkins as its first pastor.

In 1963 a new church building was constructed at its present location. Since the church continued to grow a new addition was built and all of the property on Mueller St. between S. 6th St. and S. 7th St. was acquired and a parsonage was constructed.

Over the years additions have been added to the church to meet the needs of a growing church and to serve the spiritual needs of the local community.

In 1955 when Immanuel Baptist Church was first established it began with an operating budget of approximately $5,700. Today it has an operating budget of approximately $149,000 and employs a full time pastor, a part time assistant and full time secretary.

Immanuel Baptist Church is a friendly, Christ led, Bible teaching church and welcomes all who enter our door.

## Light Baptist Church

100 years ago, in 1895, Cache Valley Baptist Church was organized. In the late 1940's the name was changed to Light Baptist Church, as we know it today. In looking back over the last 100 years of dedication to Christ by this church, many things come to mind. The fact that this church has been around for 100 years is a statement about God's guidance and provision and about Christians willing to follow God.

Remembering the past 100 years, perhaps one of the first things that comes to mind is the many members who have gone on to be with God. There have been some wonderful, godly men and women who have passed through this church. Spending time with current members can show evidence of the appreciation for each of these people. When current members can recall favorite verses of scripture and favorite songs of these members, God has truly touched our lives with these people.

We could remember many financially tough times when God has provided. A time when different members each week would cover any expenses for the week that the offering could not cover. When people are willing, God will provide. Now we have a beautiful church building, a nice Fellowship Hall and a "brand new:" parking lot and best of all NO DEBT. God is continuing to provide.

We could look at all the families who have grown up in this church. Many families for several generations have been a huge part of this church. The joys of parents watching their kids grow up in the church, coming to know Christ and then serving in the church as well.

We could look at how this church has supported missions over the years. The church giving generously to Home Missions, Foreign Missions, State Missions, Assoicational Missions and Children's Homes. Not only giving financially but also spiritually as well in prayer time. God will continue to use that and bless it. While helping missionaries in other places, members have been missionaries themselves here through Vacation Bible Schools, Sunday school, Discipleship Training, and Revivals and by being examples in the community for Christ.

We could also remember the many pastors who have come through here. From Brother Thomas Williams in 1895 all the way to Brother David McClung in 1995. There have been approximately 40 pastors who have led here over the last 100 years. Each one has left memories and I'm sure has taken many with him. Whether experienced or not, this church has supported the pastor. This can only be described as a true love for God.

The one element that seems to color every aspect of the life of this church over the last 100 years has to be a love for God. This has been evident in many ways over the years remaining constant. This love for God led to a love for other church members. Whenever troubles arose from a death in the family, to a house burning down, to loved ones suffering in the hospital the church has been here to help; whether it was helping financially with what they could give or helping through prayer and close friendship. A love for God that has been demonstrated to members of the community outside our church. A love for God that welcomes new people in with open arms. This love has shown itself in many ways. We all can remember special times.

God has truly blessed this church over the last 100 years. Through good times and bad, He has provided. As we celebrate 100 years of service, we recognize that God has allowed us to be a part of his divine plan for a long time. This has been both a challenge and a blessing. God is now looking for this church to carry on with this same purpose and love from here until Christ comes, whether it be another 10 years, 100 years, or 1000 years. I pray God will continue to bless and use us.

*Submitted by Brother David McClung*

*Marmaduke Methodist Church*

*Corinth Church*

## Marmaduke Methodist Church

The founding father of the Methodist Church was the circuit rider of long ago. Each circuit rider had his own group of churches he ministered to. Braving weather, wild animals and trails for roads he visited each church once a month. Most of the time the service was held in homes, blacksmith shops, school houses or brush arbors. Thus is the beginning of our church. According to church conference record books First Methodist Episcopal Church South was established in 1874 by a circuit rider holding services in homes. Then in 1882, the railroad, following the lead of General John S. Marmaduke, came to lay out the roads and establish the town of Marmaduke. Land donated by Edmond Holt just west of the present General Baptist Church became the location of the first church building that bore the name. Charter members were Rev. E. N. Bickley, Mrs. M. A. Thompson, Mrs. Mollie Holt, Mrs. Ellen Parker, Mrs. Ellen Jackson and Mrs. Lucinda Conger. C. C. Cupples was the first member to be taken in by profession of faith. Other early members were Mrs. Lula Holt, D. W. Cribbs, John W. Moore, Mrs. Margaret Vowell, Mrs. W. L. Skaggs, Joseph J. Thompson, Mrs. Annie Thompson, Mrs. Mary Frieland and Mrs. Zera Simpson was the first child baptized. In 1925 the church moved to its present location on the corner of Highway 49 and Highway 34. In the 1960s all Methodist churches underwent a name change and we became Marmaduke First United Methodist Church. At present the Marmaduke church is the home church of a three church circuit, which includes Ramer's Chapel of the Marmaduke area and Woods Chapel of the Paragould area.

## Morning Star Methodist Church

The original Morning Star Church building was purchased from the Gainesville Baptist Church in 1906. Brother Alonzo McKelvey was the first pastor. During this period of 57 years between 1906 and 1963, this little community church dwindled to a pretty low ebb and almost withered to extinction during the mid-thirties. During this time, the old building was in need of extensive repairs. It was then that Claud Clark, a leading citizen of the community, organized a non-denominational group that met in the Morning Star school building a quarter of a mile down the road. After our school system consolidated, the community came to realize this meeting place could only be a temporary arrangement. It was then that the good people of the community put forth a lot of effort and set about remodeling the old run down structure.

According to the secretary's minutes of Nov 3, 1929, Brother J. C. Crenshaw was the pastor. The opening song was *"Since Jesus Came Into My Heart"*, morning offering was 92 cents and the weather was fair.

During the late 40's and early 50's there were

*Oak Grove Methodist Church and members – Row 1: Jess Hollis, Mary Hutchison, unknown, Hazel Brooks, John Hollis, Olga Pannell, Lois Baldridge, unknown, unknown, unknown. Row 2: Mattie Miller, Juanita Miller (on lap), unknown woman and child on lap, Mollie Hampton and Clifton Walden at her knee, Shirley McKelvey, unknown woman and child, Laura Hollis, Ada Pannell holding Helen Pannell, R. S. Stutes, Roy Miller, Roy Swindle, Clete Baldridge, Clete Baldridge's father. Row 3: Henry Miller, James R. Miller, Minnie Mae Miller, unknown couple, unknown couple, unknown couple, John Hollis holding Margarite (child), Levi "Dot" Pannell, Clyde Baldridge, Cumi Baldridge, Carly Baldridge, Lillie Stutes, Willie Ellen Miller, Erva Swindle, Belva McKelvey. Row 4: unknown tall woman, Naomi Pannell, Charlie Pannell, unknown, unknown, J. Alfred Walden (tall man), unknown, unknown, unknown, Mary McKelvey, unknown Swindle, unknown. (Submitted by Diane Hart Blossom)*

100-110 on roll and the average attendance was around 45-50. In 1952 the old church building was completely razed and for several months services were held in Charles Lewis' house on Goldsmith Road.

On Nov 9, 1962 the Morning Star Church was moved to its present location on Highway 412 East, when Morning Star, Bard and New Liberty consolidated to form Christ United. Brother Charles Crossno was our pastor when the big move was undertaken.

## New Liberty Methodist Church

Liberty Methodist Church was founded in 1875 and was supplied by a circuit rider until about 1920, at which time it was admitted to the North Arkansas Conference. Lonzo McKelvey was pastor. Then it became New Liberty. It remained in this low land location until 1939. A team of horses and members of the church then moved it to a higher location on the Hoyer farm. New Liberty was remodeled in 1942 into a stucco building and remained there until it was united with Bard and Morning Star in 1963 to become the present Christ United. Charles Crossno was pastor. Members of New Liberty who are still carrying on at Christ United are the Baldwins, Howards, Hoyers, Hopkins, Thomasons and Toombs.

## Owens' Chapel

Owens' Chapel Church and Cemetery both have a small claim upon the history of Northeast Arkansas and Greene County. Owens' Chapel Cemetery and the former Owens' Chapel Methodist Church is located about four miles west of Paragould on U. S. Highway 412, then north about one half mile to County Road 606, then left again about one half mile. Both were named after the Owens family. There is little doubt that these were of the earliest established in the area.

James Owens migrated from the state of Virginia to Kentucky, and then moved to Arkansas in 1840. The Owens immediately sensed the urgency of a church and cemetery. As in a lot of early churches their buildings also served as a schoolhouse in the communities. Records indicate that the church building was sold to Mr. Caleb Harris (1866-1932) in 1929. Mr. Harris and two of his sons, Virgil and Marlin, began the removal and dismantling of the building Jan 3, 1930. Materials from the church building were used in the building of a farm dwelling and located on Sugar Creek west of Stanford, upon lands owned by the Harris family.

About 1988 the District Board of Trustees of the Methodist Churches declared the cemetery as being abandoned and recommended that the five-acre cemetery plot be sold at public auction and the proceeds be designated as mission funds. Upon learning about the action being taken by church officials a grandson of Mr. Caleb Harris pursued the issue and purchased the cemetery. Even though it is privately owned, the owner still considers it to be public property.

Many of the most prominent folk of Greene County are buried in the cemetery. Some of the marked graves bear the names of Owens, Cothren, Gramling, Gregory, Spillman, Jetton, Eubanks, Huffman, Harris and Watson, just to name a few.

The entire community is urged to honor their ancestry by helping maintain the burial grounds and making their resting-place neat and attractive. In doing so we send a strong message, "We love our heritage".

*Submitted by J. B. Harris (1927-)*

## Pleasant Hill Methodist Church

The first building for the church was constructed in the late 1800s and was blown away by a tornado in 1908. Another building was built in 1909. Another tornado hit the church in 1929 and blew off the spiral roof and badly damaged the building. The main carpenters for the building were Sammy Horton, Frank Cathey and Alf Carr. Others were Billy Horton, Henry Adams and several more whose names are now unknown.

Such families as the Hortons, Catheys, Adams, Carrs, Berrys, Farrars, Tennisons, Jones, Tillmans, Miles, Blackwoods, Jumpers, Dacuses and Rheas have played important roles in the church.

A new building was constructed in 1966.

This was copied from an article in the Jonesboro Sun, dated March 23, 1966, at the groundbreaking service for the new church.

## Ramer's Chapel United Methodist Church

*Ramer's Chapel United Methodist Church*

Ramer's Chapel is located eight miles northwest of Marmaduke off highway 34. It was organized in March 1894 with eight charter members. E. W. Scott was the primary leader in organizing the church.

The eight charter members were:
1. T. J. and Sarah Ramer
2. George W. and Ann Ramer
3. J. W. and Nancy "Nanny" Beaton
4. L. R. and Tula Butler

T. J. Ramer was the donor of the land on which the church and cemetery are located. T. J.'s brother, George, is remembered for selling his last cow to pay for finishing the church building.

The church today is still thriving after over 100 years in existence. Many of the members today are direct descendents of the charter members. Four ministers have come from the Ramer's Chapel membership:
1. George W. Ramer, charter member
2. Buel Starnes, nephew of charter member Nannie Starnes Beaton
3. Wayne Gould, great-grandson of charter members George W. and Ann Ramer
4. Dolphie Hampton

The present treasurer and administrative board chairman, Gerald Smith, is the great-grandson of charter members T. J. and Sarah Ramer, who were also the donors of the land. Gerald's wife Velma Stephens Smith is the granddaughter of charter members J. W. and Nanny Beaton.

## Robbs Chapel Baptist Church

In 1914 the Oscar S. Barger, Albert Johnson, Hart and Green Beck families met together and called Reverend T. B. Emmons to come and preach once a month to the little congregation. Reverend Emmons preached for the congregation through 1916 and 1917. This group named themselves the Mt. Pleasant Baptist Church. Mr. and Mrs. Albert Johnson and daughter Bufie brought letters from New Friendship Baptist Church. Mr. and Mrs. Green Beck brought letters from Fairview Baptist Church. Mr. and Mrs. E. A. Hinman, Mr. and Mrs. Oscar S. Barger and daughter Vera all joined the church on statements of fact. The church was organized in 1918 and continued meeting in the one room Mt. Pleasant School located on the old

Mitchell Road about one fourth mile from where Robbs Chapel Church sits now.

Ennis C. Johnson was the first deacon ordained and that was in 1918. The Reverend T. B. Emmons was pastor through 1918. In 1919, the Reverend E. D. Cooper was called and stayed through the year 1920.

Reverend T. H. McDonald was pastor in 1921-22. Reverend Ed Lidel was pastor through 1923. Reverend James Hammond was called in 1924 and stayed through 1927. Ennis C. Johnson was ordained as a minister in 1923.

It was in the year 1926 that Drew Robbs and wife donated the land where the church still stands. Labor Day 1926, these families met and cut logs: Ennis Johnson, Albert Johnson and Reverend A. O. Collier. Others helped and hauled the logs to the mill along with Paul Kibler. Other loggers that lived in the community hauled the lumber to the church site. Mrs. Minnie Ford also donated needed lumber. The church was built just north of the present site and was renamed Robbs Chapel Baptist Church.

These men were called and served:
Reverend J. H. Hughes 1928-1929
Reverend R. C. Rogers 1930-1933
Reverend J. O. Miles 1934-1939
Reverend R. C. Rogers 1940-1946

Robbs Chapel was affiliated with Gainsville Association but changed and joined the Greene County Missionary Baptist Association in 1925. Reverend Robert Johnson became pastor followed by Reverend Richardson, Reverend Clarence Young, Reverend T. F. Stroud and Reverend Gwin Renshaw. The church became a "full time church" at this time. The present church building was constructed in 1952. The sanctuary has four adjacent classrooms and four other rooms upstairs.

There were other pastors in the following years some of which were students of Southern Baptist College in Walnut Ridge. Reverend Sam Stewart was called followed by Reverend C. E. Moses and Reverend Alfred Psalmonds. While Brother Psalmonds was pastor, a fellowship hall, kitchen and two bathrooms were built.

In later years, Reverend Wilbur Griggs came as pastor and finally Reverend John Slatton was called in 1983 and is still serving in 1999. There were many families through the years that were strong contributors to this church. These were:

The Bargers, Harts, Becks, Johnsons, Rileys, Bentons, Thurmonds, Monteiths, Frees, Wadleys, Craftons, Tarrys, Colliers, Bolings, Kieffners, Cupps, and Roy Dyer.

*Submitted by Peggy Collier Jackson*

## St. John's Lutheran Church

St. John's Lutheran church was first started in 1886 with a small band of German settlers. It was at "Upper Lafe" under the name of St. Peters Evangelical Lutheran church. Rev. Ernest Bangester was the first full time pastor. He helped organize the church. Later the church was moved to Lafe, AR. The first building was built in 1881. In 1911 another church was built at Lafe and given the name of St. John's Lutheran church. In 1947 another new church was built at Lafe and dedicated on Dec 19, 1948. A new wing was added in 1982.

In 1911 the church had no electricity so oil

*Robbs Chapel, 1926–1952. The new building was built in 1952.*

*St. John's Church buildings: 1948 and 1911*

*St. John's Lutheran Church, Lafe, Arkansas*

*Present Schugtown Methodist Church*

*St. Paul Church, the beginning of Schugtown Church*

*Schugtown United Methodist Church*

lamps were used. These lamps hung between each window. A chandelier was hung from the ceiling in the center of the church holding about 10-12 lamps on a wheel. A vacuum cleaner motor was put on the old pump organ. 1900 organ was then easier to play.

The old school has had about 20-30 pupils in fourth through 7th grades. Religion was taught and Bible passages and 10 commandments were memorized. Each night I had to learn a lot of Bible passages. Which I am glad now I have the memory of them.

We took our lunch buckets and ate our lunch out beside the school. When we were mean we were taken out to the wood shed for a whipping. We respected the pastor and teacher for their discipline.

We were so glad for the new church, which had a basement and kitchen. We did have our dinners on tables outside beside the old school house. We had big 20-gallon crocks of tea with 25 or 50 pounds of ice in it.

We played softball between the church and school on a big ball diamond.

I remember when members came to church in fancy buggies and wagons.

In that time, they believed women were supposed to cover their heads in church so the women all wore hats. Before the hats women wore bonnets.

Those were the days and I recall them with sweet memories.

*Submitted by Orin Tritch*

## Schugtown Church

The history of the Schugtown Church is not very long because it is a young church.

Many years ago there was a church in that community located on the corner of the Phelps' land, just in front of the Andy Schug home. This church ceased active service around 1925 and there was no church or Sunday school to take its place. This condition remained for many years.

In 1929 Miss Elsie Calvert, a young teacher, came to the Schugtown community to teach school. Two years later she married John Schug. The young Mrs. Schug was not content to live in a community where there was no church or Sunday school. She secured permission from the school board to have a Sunday school in the schoolhouse. Ministers from different denominations were invited to preach at various times. The Presbyterians sent ministers regularly and also the Baptists.

Dr. E. W. Potter, district superintendent of the Jonesboro district, of the Methodist Church became interested in the community and sent Rev. W. J. LeRoy to hold a revival meeting. At the close of the revival, July 25, 1938, a church was organized with the following charter members: George Cook, Mildred Cook, Elsie Schug, Tommy Higgins, Chatty Higgins, Mrs. Viola Higgins, Mrs. Vina McDaniel, Luther Lawrence, Rosa Lawrence, Hassie Wineland, Edith Cox and Betty Dowell.

In 1937, the Schugtown School (St. Paul) was consolidated with the Dixie School. This left a two room building to be donated to the church by Wiley Norton and the church then bought a half-acre of ground from him. The schoolhouse building was then turned around and moved onto the plot that was purchased. This move required a great deal of labor and since there was no money in the church treasury, the labor had to be donated.

This modest little building served the community for a time, but the steady growth of the church made it necessary to build a new church more suited to a growing community. A tent was borrowed from the district superintendent of the Methodist Church at Paragould, the Rev. Lynn Wade. Then the little building that had served so well was torn down.

Meetings were held in the tent until the new building was constructed. Mrs. John Schug again took the burden of supervision until at last an $8,000 church building was ready to be dedicated to God. The dedication services on April 30, 1950, represented an important day to the members of this little church. It marked the culmination of many years of effort to establish solidly a community church at Schugtown.

After several years of planning, in 1985 the aging white stucco structure that served the Schugtown community so faithfully was razed and replaced with a modern metal structure. The same spirit of love and cooperation that had bound the church together during the two previous construction projects once again united the effort to better the little Methodist Church that has been a central part of this little town for over a half century.

## Third Avenue Baptist Church

The following is a brief history of the Third Avenue Baptist Church located on the corner of Third Avenue and Locust Street.

On June 9, 1943 in conference upon recommendation from the board of deacons, the First Baptist Church voted to establish a mission Sunday school on East Kingshighway.

The first meeting was held June 13, 1943 in the store building, southeast corner of South Fourth Avenue and Kingshighway to organize the Sunday school. After a few Sundays, Mr. J. H. Grooms was selected as the first Sunday school superintendent along with teachers, J. H. Grooms, Mrs. Riley Johnson, Mrs. Rose Mayberry, Mrs. J. E. Beasley, Mrs. W. G. Nutt and Mrs. Chas Dreman.

On Dec 8, 1943 the board of deacons voted to let the workers of the mission with J. H. Grooms the chairman to select a name for the mission. The name East Side Mission was selected and it was voted to construct a mission building.

Feb 13, 1944 the first services were conducted in the new building, which is the present location of the Third Avenue Baptist Church.

On Feb 18, 1945, Reverend I. M. Prince, pastor of the First Baptist Church, held revival at the East Side Mission.

Sept 19, 1945, the Mission called Reverend David Patton as the first Mission pastor.

Aug 18, 1948 in a short business meeting it was voted to change the name to Third Avenue Baptist Chapel and on Wednesday May 9, 1951 all arrangements of making the chapel into a church were completed and a letter from the First Baptist Church was issued for all persons wanting to move their membership to sign, thus becoming charter members of the new Third Avenue Baptist Church.

On May 23, 1951 the list was sent to the First Baptist Church of 100 persons wishing to become charter members of the Third Avenue Baptist Church. On Sunday May 27, 1951 in an organization service the Third Avenue Baptist Chapel, a mission of the First Baptist Church of Paragould, became a full time missionary church and was named the Third Avenue Baptist Church.

At this service the songs were led under the direction of Mr. J. H. Grooms, Reverend Jeff Rousseau led prayer. Reverend D. C. Applegate, pastor of the First Baptist Church, discussed the responsibilities of becoming a church and read the church covenant. Later Reverend Applegate spoke on the declaration of faith, along with the names of the charter members. A motion was made by J. A. Perciful that we of Third Avenue Chapel who have requested membership from First Baptist Church of Paragould, AR vote to organize ourselves into a missionary Baptist Church, independent and cooperating with the Southern Baptist convention. Mr. J. N. Trozler seconded the motion, the vote carried.

Mr. J. H. Grooms made a motion and Paul Benoit seconded it, the motion carried that Reverend Curtis Bryant be called as pastor of the new Third Avenue Baptist Church.

Reverend Jeff Rousseau, Pastor of the East Side Baptist Church gave the message from Acts Chapter three.

Mr. J. H. Grooms began at the very beginning of the mission program and continued working and serving God after the mission became a church. On Oct 1, 1952, Mr. Grooms felt his work was done and returned to the First Baptist Church. Thanks to people like Mr. Grooms and his love for the Lord, missions are started and will continue to serve the Lord until He calls His church home in heaven.

Through the years there have been 20 called men of God to serve as pastors of the Third Avenue Baptist Church:

Reverend Curtis Bryant, Reverend Clarence DeSpain, Reverend Ira L. Henderson, Reverend H. G. Rhea, Reverend Jack Mick, Reverend Stanley Smith, Reverend Hal Gallop, Reverend Arnold Clayton, Reverend Coy Richardson, Reverend Dub Clemets, Reverend Orval Coln, Reverend James Moore, Reverend R. L. Spain, Reverend Don McBride, Reverend James Moore, Reverend Bob Ivy, Reverend Donnie Smith, Reverend Clyde Cook, Reverend Glen Swigert and the Reverend Bob Lee.

Over the years God has called a lot of young men to preach his word. One example, on July 30, 1950, Van Booth joined Third Avenue Baptist Church by baptism. On Feb 11, 1951, the church licensed him to preach God's word. In Sept 1951 Reverend Van Booth was ordained to preach the word of the Lord.

This is just one example of how God has used Third Avenue Baptist Church to carry out his Great Commission; "Go ye therefore and teach all nations, baptizing them in the name of the father and of the son and of the holy ghost; teaching them to observe all things whatsoever I have commanded you and lo, I am with you always, even unto the end of the world. Amen."

The Lord has kept his promise to the Third Avenue Church.

Glory to His name!

*1906 – Tokio Church*

# Education in Greene County

By law, the 16th section of each township was set aside for the establishment of a school. Often, depending on the location of homes, this 16th section would be "traded" for an area where a majority of students lived. There were no compulsory attendance laws, no uniform textbooks and no required number of days during which classes were held. The curriculum was limited to writing, reading and arithmetic, with some geography and history, depending upon the capabilities of the teacher. These schools were called subscription schools, because the parents of those attending had to pay. Many of these schools were held in church buildings, while others consisted of one or two rooms. By today's standards they were woeful, indeed, but they served their purpose by providing a place for the education of the early settlers in Greene County. Today Greene County has four school districts: Paragould, Greene County Tech, Deleplaine and Marmaduke. There are also two private schools: St. Mary's and Crowley's Ridge Academy. Black River VoTech and Crowley's Ridge Junior College maintain campuses in the county.

Paragould School District and Greene County Technical District each have an average enrollment 2700 students and each operates on budgets of about $14 million. Deleplaine has an enrollment of more than 350 students and its budget is about $1.2 million while Marmaduke's enrollment is more than twice as large with about 750 students and an operating budget of $4 million.

Today's modern schools had their beginnings in the tiny one-room buildings of more than a century ago. While many of the records of these schools have been lost to time, we have located and identified a few of the older ones.

The Campground School, of which a painting is shown, was a small one-story building, located just south of the Campground Methodist Church. Some of the fam-

*Campground School*

*1934 Oak Grove High School Sophmore class*

ily names appearing on the Campground School roll were Blalock, Taylor, Stevenson, McKelvey, Thompson and Holifield.

The Epsaba School was located near the Epsaba Cemetery on Highway 34. It was a one-room building with one teacher teaching all the children. Reba Blalock Roberts said while she was teaching there the building began to lean toward the downside of the hill. She and the students wondered if the building would fall while having class. Some men in the neighborhood met one day and simply propped the building up into its original position with logs they had cut and there it stood for years to come.

The Mt. Carmel School was located at what is now the intersection of Reynolds Road Extended and Fairview Road on the Northwest corner. Students from the families of Walters and Walden attended this school.

The Oak Grove school was located across highway 135 from the present day Oak Grove Baptist Church. Shown are pictures of Oak Grove in 1934 and the graduating class of 1936. This building is still in use today, however, the district has consolidated with the Paragould District and now houses the fifth and sixth grades only.

The school called Miller served patrons of the communities of Coffman and Mitchell Point Landing east of Paragould and near the St. Francis River. This building was two stories. The first floor was two classrooms and the second floor served as a lodge hall for the community. The school building was located where today's Mulberry Church of Christ now stands. A drawing of the school is shown. John Lane and Reba Blalock Roberts were teachers at Miller in the late 1930s.

The Landrum School was located just west of highway 135 North and north of the Campground Road. The picture at right was taken on the north side of the school about 1900. Beginning with the back row: Ike Brummett, Monroe Agee, unknown, Claud Agee, Amber Smith, unknown; third row: teacher Charlie West, Charlie Anderson, small girl is unknown, Lizzie Agee, Neeley Cotton, Maud Agee, unknown, Tula Burton, Beatrice Agee, Ed McGowan; Second row: unknown Lashley, Unknown, Unknown, Amy Spence, Audra Stevenson Blalock, unknown Lashley, unknown, Iva Stimson Walters, Onie Riley, unknown Thurman; bottom row: boy just in front of teacher is unknown Lashley, Hubert Stimson, Luster Stimson, Unknown Lashley, Luther unknown, Arthur Dodge, Tommy McGowan, Cannon "Buck" Stimson and E. B. "Buddy" Stimson.

*Submitted by Gretta Jernigan*

*Miller School*

*Oak Grove High School class of 1936*

*Landrum School*

# Crowley's Ridge College

Crowley's Ridge College is a two-year college with a strong Christian heritage and a reputation of providing a quality liberal arts education to its local community and religious fellowship. Anticipating an increased demand for higher education, CRC was founded in 1964 as the "Baby Boomers" reached college age. College and media materials indicate the college was founded with great support from the religious and local community – Arkansas Governor Orval Faubus participated in groundbreaking ceremonies.

CRC is located in Paragould, AR, near the crest of Crowley's Ridge. The scenic campus covers 115 acres of rolling hills densely covered by pine trees.

For roughly its first decade, CRC operated under the same governing board as Crowley's Ridge Academy, a K-12 Christian academy established in 1953. In 1975, the two institutions legally separated and now operate under separate charters and boards.

The driving force behind the college was founding President Emmett F. Smith Jr. Dr. Smith's vision for Christian education in Northeast Arkansas was stimulated, in part, from the previous existence of two Christian Schools: MONEA Christian College, located in Rector, AR and Croft College located in rural Greene County. Both institutions had ceased operation by the 1930's but Smith and other founders believed strongly that a need for Christian higher education existed in the area.

The college has had a varied academic history. True to its mascot of the Pioneers, CRC began with an innovative system as an "accelerated institution of higher education." The academic year was divided in two sessions, each having 24 weeks. The sessions were divided into two 12-week semesters each comprising two six-week terms. Under this system, it was possible to earn 64 semester hours credit in 48 weeks of residence, thus completing the A. A. degree in one calendar year. The accelerated program was discontinued in 1974 in favor of a four-semester system. The academic year remained 48 weeks, consisting of four 12-week semesters. In 1980 the four-semester system was replaced with a standard semester system, under which CRC currently operates.

Four presidents have served CRC. Emmett Smith held that position from 1964 through 1973. Albert Lemmons served from 1973-1975. Dr. Smith returned as Chancellor to lead the college until 1979. Joe K. Alley became CRC's third president until 1982. From 1982 to 1985 and 1986 to 1987, CRC operated directly under the board's fiscal oversight with the vice president for operations, Phillip Wilkerson, supervising day-to-day operations. Alan Carter served as executive vice president during 1985 and 1986. Hired in 1987, Larry M. Bills has been the longest serving president.

While students took advantage of the unique educational opportunities and many alumni became civic, religious and educational leaders, CRC also experienced some challenging time during its first 20 years. None of these times were so difficult as the reorganization of the college in the summer of 1986. However, this proposed closing and the subsequent reorganization one week following did not mark the end of the college but a new beginning.

Support for the college's mission was galvanized in 1986. The dedication of college constituencies to its mission became abundantly clear as students, parents of students, faculty, staff, alumni and other supporters donated substantial amounts of money and time to continue the operation of the college. The board reorganized and classes began in the fall of 1986 as scheduled.

In 1987, Bills was named as the college's fourth president. According to college publications, he included improving endowment and obtaining regional accreditation among his goals. Following this course, in 1991 the college was enjoying its most stable position to date in preparing to seek affiliation with the North Central Association of Colleges and Schools. The fiscal stability came to an unanticipated end when federal congressional action resulted in CRC students being ineligible to receive federal funds for financial assistance. The action came as a surprise to CRC, which for almost three decades had been a part of the Federal Student Aid Program. Subsequent legislation made provisions for affected colleges such as CRC to be reinstated into the federal financial assistance program by becoming candidates for accreditation with a recognized body within two years from Dec 20, 1993. Similar to the challenges of 1986, the loss of federal financial assistance energized support from those who believe in CRC's mission.

Although a longtime goal of the college, efforts toward becoming affiliated with an accreditation body were intensified by elimination of the TCAA option for federal financial assistance. The process precipitated substantial changes in the college operation and especially the education it offers students. A $2.1 million gift in Oct 1994 enabled the college to set about a course to improve its governance, human resources, educational programs and learning resources.

In 1995, the college took its first step toward affiliation with NCA when a visiting team recommended and the commission subsequently approved, Initial Candidacy at the Associate Degree level. A 1995 visiting team stated a unanimous opinion that CRC would meet each of the criteria for accreditation within the period of candidacy and financial assistance eligibility was restored. Realizing a long-time goal that was included in the first catalog in the mid 1960s, CRC was granted accreditation by NCA in the summer of 2000.

Throughout its history, CRC and Greene County have been good partners. CRC alumni often make Greene County their home and CRC employees are involved in civic and volunteer organizations. CRC sponsored events, such as Spirit of America, have featured such well known speakers as basketball legend Julius Irving, radio celebrity Paul Harvey, comedian Jerry Clower, White House Press Secretary Jody Powell, Emmy Award winner Art Linkletter and television commentator Howard K. Smith.

CRC was founded not only with the intention of providing higher education opportunities for students, but also to support the work of area Churches of Christ and families. Its board, administration and faculty remain committed to that end. Reflecting the values of its local community, CRC is bridging the gap from a strong heritage to a promising future.

*Orval Faubus, Arkansas governor and Emmett Smith Jr., CRC president at the groundbreaking ceremony for Crowley's Ridge College, January 28, 1964.*

*The natural beauty of the Crowley's Ridge College campus provides an ideal setting for a Christian education. Devotionals enhance the spiritual growth and academic opportunities.*

# St. Mary's School

The first Catholic school in Paragould was opened by Sister Agnes, an Olivetan Benedictine Sister. More than a century later what began as St. Gertrude's Select School continues to educate young students today. The school is now known as St. Mary's and students in preschool through sixth grade are educated at the private parochial school.

St. Gertrude's classes began in 1890 – the first local private school and the first local school to provide instrumental and vocal music instruction, according to various written accounts of the school's history.

The school operated its first two years in the back of St. Mary's Catholic Church. It had one teacher and 34 students that year, growing to 82 students and two teachers, Sister Cecilia and Sister Beatrice, the second year. German was taught, as well as English, mathematics, history, social studies, penmanship and religion. The better part of the school's enrollment included students not of Catholic faith; at that time there were only 20 children in the parish and only 73 Catholics in Paragould.

One account stated that Father Joseph McQuaid, the first resident pastor, considered it his main priority to construct a facility for classes. According to Father McQuaid's plan, the new schoolhouse materialized in a beautiful two story practical wooden building furnished with three adequate schoolrooms and two living rooms for the Sisters.

The small frame school served the students until 1906, when a two-story concrete block building was constructed for $10,000. Many of us today have fond memories of that school. It included three large classrooms on the first floor. We entered into a large hall as we came in through the front door on the south end of the building. The door to the left led to the third, fourth and fifth grade room while directly across the hall was the sixth, seventh and eighth room. At the north end of the hall was a door leading to the first and second grade room. To the right in front of that door was a very wide stairway leading to the second floor, which contained a huge auditorium with a large stage on the north end. Each student at some time played in the rhythm band. However, the highlight of the school year for many had to be the school plays performed on that stage. Every student was included. A narrow stairway on the north end of the building came up in the back of the stage. This made it easy to dress for the plays in the room below and enter the stage without being seen by the audience. There was a piano in the auditorium and one in each classroom. The auditorium was also used for many other activities. Several learned to square dance there. It came in very handy when the weather was too bad to play outside.

In 1956, the present brick school was built and named Hoflinger Hall in honor of Monsignor Joseph M. Hoflinger, who had served St. Mary's Church, school and the community since Jan 6, 1915. A gable roof was added to the school in August of 1983.

The statue of Our Lady of Fatima that stands in the alcove in front of the school is dedicated to Virgil Straub, who was killed in WWII. His close friend, Emit Logan, donated the statue in Virgil's memory. The two friends, knowing they would be in danger of losing their lives, promised each other that if either one was killed, the survivor, in thanksgiving for his safe return, would have a statue of St. Mary placed outside the school to encourage devotion to the mother of Jesus. Emit kept his promise and the statue stands there still.

Until 1963 the school offered instruction up to grade eight, but seventh and eighth grade were dropped that year. Almost 20 years later in August 1982 a kindergarten was added. A preschool was added in 1989. A building and property were purchased in 1999 across the street from the parish hall to house the ever-growing preschool. The parishioners renovated the building and a beautiful playground was constructed.

Although there are no longer Sisters teaching full time at the school, St. Mary's strives to provide quality Catholic education for each student.

*St. Mary's School*

*St. Mary's School, 1906-1956*

*St. Mary's School 1956-present*

## Alexander School

The Alexander community was named after Robert L. Alexander who moved to Paragould in 1896 and purchased large sections of land in the areas of Bark Camp and Bowlin Islands in extreme northeastern Greene County.

A one-room schoolhouse was then constructed on Bark Camp Island, possibly around 1910 and was Alexander School. About 1915, a two-room school was built about one- and- a- quarter miles away on Panther Island, near the Alexander Baptist Church. Later, some school classes had to meet in the church building for at least a year, due to overcrowding.

In 1931, a brick schoolhouse with eight grades was built about one- fourth mile south from the original one-room school at Bark Camp. The Alexander clubhouse is now located on these grounds.

Eventually the Reddick, Hartsoe, Brighton and Alexander schools consolidated to form District #4. The first person to graduate from the Alexander school was Ralph Thompson, who graduated about 1934.

Source: *"St. Francis River Bottoms Area"* by C. W. Starnes, MD. *GCHGS Quarterly Vol 6, # 1, 1971)* and conversations with James Bradburn and Dan Hester

## Bard School

The first school at Bard opened in 1903 in a converted sheep shed for three months' term of six grades. Miss Dot Thompson, later Mrs. W. L. Skaggs, was the first teacher, receiving $100 for the summer term.

Mrs. Skaggs recalled that the first schoolhouse was replaced in the fall of 1903. Another structure was built in 1916 and when Lakeside District was organized, the students were moved to the newer school.

Source: *"Greene County's Boom Towns"* by Myrl R. Mueller *(GCHGS Quarterly, Vol. 2, No. 1, Winter, 1966).*

## Beech Grove School

The first school in the Beech Grove vicinity was established in 1840 and was called Friars' School. It had a puncheon floor, split-log seats and a fireplace. Four other area schools followed this one: Meadows Grove, Jackson College (so- called because the founders hoped one day it would become a college), Gum Grove and New Home.

The early school had eight grades and only one teacher. In 1930, Henry Breckenridge donated five acres and Beech Grove High School with 12 grades finally became a reality.

The first graduating class in 1934 had only one graduate, Woodrow Davidson. The following year graduates included: Vera Norman, Elmo North and Allen and Talmadge Stallcup.

In 1949, grades 10 through 12 moved to Greene County Tech High School. Grades one through nine joined them at Tech in 1966.

That same year Reverend Bennie Parmenter bought the school building, tore it down and built two houses in Rector with material saved from the school.

Mrs. Zelma Moore, a longtime teacher, owned five acres in the vicinity of the Beech Grove School and at one time her son, Morris Moore, had an apartment in the old school gym.

Source: *A History of Beech Grove"* by Elaine Boyd *(GCHGS Quarterly, Vol 11, # 2, 1998).*

## Bobo School

Bobo School was located in the extreme southwest corner of Poland Township. It consolidated with Walcott about 1947 or 1948.

The community and school were named for an early settler in the area.

Some of the teachers at the Bobo School were Buel Adams, Nora Adams, Mont Barrow, Clevie Battey, Fred Berryhill, Clevie Blackwood, Kate Blackwood, Mack Bobbit, Clyde Brown, Elsie Calvert, Omie Tennison Casey, Porter Cathey, Lou Cothern, Mrs. Frank Dickenson, Walter Ellington, Ruby Fahr, Henry Gibson, Willie Hardiman, Nellie Sea Heath, Bill Hendrix, Mont Hickman, John Honey, Lester Horton, Glenda Jackson, Ivan Jackson, Virginia Tyner and Ocil Jackson Williams.

Others who taught there included Ellie Lamb, Lee Levins, Julie Lloyd, Harry Martin, Jeff McClure, James McGlothern, Almus McNiel, Roy

*Alexander School 1927, Ina Adams, teacher. Back Row (L to R): Ivan Mercer, Tom Hill, Alvie Jones, Cecil Wilcox, Joe Newsom, Erby Newsom, Alva McMillon, Sterl Thomason, Barney Howard, Gene Brandon. Second Row: Juanita McMillon, Jody Robinson, Tomazine Elmore, Erphy Rippy, Dorothy Rippy, Margaret Blackburn, Pauline Newsom, Sylvia Lovelady, Sterline Thompson. Third Row: Ralph Noel, Earl Bishop, unknown Davis, Lawrence Pace, Paul Howard, James Blackburn, James Wynn. Bottom Row: Faustina Robinson, unknown, Lurline Bishop, Fostine Newsome. Taken at the old two-room schoolhouse, approximately 500 feet north of Alexander Baptist Church. (Picture courtesy of Steve Wood.)*

*Bard School: Hazel Jameson, Lena Johnson, Russell Shatley, unknown Nettles, Beatrice Nettles, Cash Carver, Dorris Carmack, Lou unknown, Ray Johnson, Mildred unknown, Inez Bateman, Muril Shatley. (Picture courtesy of Daniel Hester)*

Mounce, Mary Odell, Eula Odell, Mose Rhea, Kathaline Schaff, Jim Schyboard, Billie Heath Short, Jim Thompson, Sam Thompson, Edward Turner, Frank Watson, Goldie Willcockson, Ocil Jackson Williams, Parten Williamson, Charlie Winn, Charley Wood and Leander Wright.

Source *GCHGS* article by Mack Thompson on Poland Township.

## Brighton School

Brighton was a station on the Paragould Buffalo Island Railway located about four miles due east of Paragould toward the St. Francis bottoms.

A factory was established there, which manufactured a variety of containers for packaging food items. The company also had one of the largest lumber operations in eastern Arkansas. By 1908, there was a sizable business district and the community included a depot, a Baptist church and a one-room schoolhouse. At one time, the population may have been about 300 residents.

In 1908 the factory was forced to close and the building abandoned. The post office closed in 1917, reopened in 1919, then closed permanently in 1921.

Source: *A History of Greene County, Arkansas* by Myrl Rhine Mueller.

## Brown's Chapel School

The Brown's Chapel School was located in the southwest part of Greene County next to the Brown's Chapel Baptist Church. By 1891, the school was a one-room building and by 1902 there were 86 pupils enrolled in the school.

W. A. Branch, who attended school there and taught eight years there as well, received $30 per month for his teaching, remaining at the school from 7 a. m. to 5:30 p. m.

One person recalls attending Brown's Chapel in the mid-1920's when a cloth curtain was hung down the center of the room to divide the younger students from those who were older.

Beginning in 1944, the pupils of Brown's Chapel school held an annual reunion on the last Thursday evening in March. From 400 to 1000 people attended the exhibitions at this reunion. Former pupils gave nursery recitations, put on plays, had spelling bees, played the fiddle and in other ways duplicated the program of the last day of school. Men and women aged 50 or 60 who would not make a speech in public, would take their turn in the school exhibition.

## Brushy Ridge School

Brushy Ridge is the area in the far northeast corner of Greene County. There are three settlements in this area: Mounds, Fritz and White Oak.

Mounds was named because of the Indian burial mounds in the area. Thomas Hancock

*Bobo School early 1940's, Lester Horton, teacher. Students pictured include: Alma Rhea, Billy Chamberlin, Ruby Heath, Amy Heath, Eva Heath, Marie Rhea, Emma Dee Rhea, Jack Forkum, Becky Pierce, Princess May Payne, Earnest Rhea, Alton Pegg, Leon Dunnam, Norman Forkum, Hazel Forkum, Jim Pierce, James Chamberlin, Edna Pierce, Agness Williams, O'Neal Hughes, Fay Hughes, Patsy Chamberlin, J. R. Williams. (Picture courtesy of Mrs. Alma Harris)*

*Beech Grove School about 1947. (Picture courtesy of Phyllis Adams)*

taught the first school there in a tent in the summer of 1907. A building constructed later in 1907 on land belonging to Judge Kasserman was, in fact, near a very large Indian mound.

According to a history of Brushy Ridge written by H. M. Manchester, the teachers at this school from 1907-1917 included Miss Randleman, Tom Ross, Maymie Pattishall, Mint Farrel, Richard Poole, Lee Clarida, Kate Clarida, Pearl Owens, H. M. Manchester, C. E. Bond, Fay Cooper and Hughey Gibbs.

Mr. Manchester taught at Mounds beginning in 1914, employed by J. L. Lamand, Walter and John Evans, school board members. There were approximately 60 children, four "grown" boys and three "grown" girls enrolled in the 1914 school term. Mr. Manchester also taught a night school class during the winter of 1915 for the benefit of the older people. There 11 adults in this class.

Those who taught at Mounds beginning in 1918 include Mary McKelvey, Clessie Smith, Frank Layer, Gus Marshall, Mr. Brewer, Mr. Faulkner, Sadie Lam, W. K. Kelley, Mr. and Mrs. Willie French and Wesley Beaton.

One student of Mr. Kelley's recalled his standing before the class and calling upon the students to stand and recite the day's lesson. He always knew when they made a mistake even though he never looked at a book.

One event the students eagerly awaited each day was the passing of the "train" on the "dummy" line. The railroad went right by the school with loads of logs to be sawed into lumber at the sawmill. This created an interesting diversion from the classes each day.

School board members in 1918 were John W. Bandfield, John Betts and Grover Rippy.

Later teachers included Woodrow Thorne, Mary Thorne, John Starnes, Mary Lucille Sprague, Doyle Washington and Walter Moore.

Alexander school had hoped to consolidate both Mounds and White Oak schools. Petitions were circulated and by an extremely small margin, both consolidated instead with Marmaduke in 1949.

## Caldwell Chapel School

Caldwell Chapel is located near the Greene-Craighead County line, about 10 miles north of Jonesboro and one mile east of Highway 141. The road along the north side of the school property is the county line, but students from both Greene and Craighead Counties attended the school. The school and cemetery property consist of five acres.

The 40 acres of land on which Caldwell Chapel School and Cemetery is located was purchased from the federal government by Devaney Burrow on May 1, 1861. The certificate transferring this land was signed by President Abraham Lincoln or by his secretary, William Osborn Stoddard.

On Oct. 5, 1870, Devaney Burrow sold this property to William Baugh. On Aug. 12, 1885, William Baugh and his wife, Frances Harvey Baugh, sold five acres of land to the trustees, one of whom was Joseph Caldwell. Some restrictions were included on the deed which reads: "To have and to hold so long as it is kept for the use and benefit of the Methodist Church and School and burying ground and with the privilege of other denominations preaching there so that their appointments do not conflict with the Methodist. Reserving the right to use water out of well on said premises."

The Caldwell's Chapel School District (Greene County School District # 17) was not established until June 2, 1911. A subscription school or other type of school may have been held on the premises prior to 1911.

The one-room schoolhouse that was erected in 1911 burned in 1928. Prater Lindley built a new one-room school building, which is still standing. In 1946, the school consolidated with the Walcott School District. The building is now used once each year as a meeting place for the annual school reunion.

Some teachers at Caldwell's Chapel were: Clevie Cathey, unknown McCord, Lon Bobbit, Jeff Willcockson, Edward Turner, Albert Kiltz, Armour Lamberth, Walter Erwin, Homer Hopgood, a Miss Dickson, Arthur Willcockson, Basil Dacus, N. J. McMillon and Garland Arrington.

Source: *Caldwell's Chapel History* by R. L. Dunnam

*Blue Cane School, 1935 – Students of 1935 included from Left: Front: Clois Miller, J. W. Worley, Joe Stokes, Adell Foster, J. R. (unknown), Luvene Morris Hamm, Duane Edwards, Junior French, Leon Morris, Donald Presson, Olita Presson, (unknown) Sanford, Lanell Edwards and Barbara Rust. Second Row: Dallas Miller, Elmer Clardy, Joe Worley, Buell Clardy, Delbert Foster, Alva Bradly, Gerldean Kiestler, Marie Stokes, Hattie Sanford, Kathryn Sanford, Flov Burns, Wanda Presson and Jeannette Foster. Third Row: Edith Cole (big room teacher), Wilma Walker, Rita Fae Mobbs, Lerene Cullen, Fredonia Mobbs, Claudine Fluty, Mary Presson, Gearldean Gordon, Faye Worley, Ava Cullen, Devon Clardy, Glen Stokes, Buren Cullen and Helen Ellis (little room teacher). Back row: Clyde Lamb, Doyne Fowler, Jack Edwards, James Clardy, Lee Presson, Landon Hill, Clois Stokes and Avery Edwards. (Picture courtesy of Doyne Rasberry)*

*Brighton School, Nov 27, 1908. (Picture courtesy of Daniel Hester)*

*Barton School 1904, Mr. Bounds, teacher. (Picture courtesy of Doyne Rasberry)*

*Brown's Chapel School, about 1914 – Arthur Jones, Teacher (Picture courtesy of Mrs. Muragatha Scott)*

## Clark's Chapel School

Clark's Chapel is located one mile north of the Greene-Craighead County Line. The Baptists built a church and school on the east side of what is now Highway 351. The school operated until 1940 when it consolidated with Greene County # 1 School District.

According to a school news report from March 31, 1909, in the newspaper, "The Paragould Soliphone" Clark's Chapel school turned out two "full-fledged" teachers that winter: Dock Boyd and M. H. Ellington. Both passed the teachers' exam and procured licenses, according to the two school reporters.

The following December, Mollie McClure and Nealia Wood, reporters and their teacher Dock Boyd, reported a number of students absent for various reasons. The 26 students in the arithmetic class were all doing good work, as were those in the advanced grammar classes. The students were curious as to which teachers were going to be attending the teachers' association meeting at Hot Springs the last of the month.

According to Mack Thompson's list, some teachers of the Clark's Chapel School were: Grace Boone, Dock Boyd, Albert Buckanan, Earl Clayton, Lloyd Cole, Earl Day, Harry Day, Olive Driskel, Lester Edwards, Edgar Ellington, Hervie Ellington, Hurdle Ellington, Henry Gibson, Chester Gilliam, Monroe Greenway, Henry Grooms, Melinda Grooms, Lester Horton, Mary Ida Hopkins, Ivan Jackson, Leo Jackson, Liddie Winn Johnson, Harold Johnston, Ester Norton Jones, William Kelley, Jones Lamb, John Lawless, Sam Lloyd, Charlie Long, Will Majors, Harry Martin, Jeff McClure, Mary Jane McDaniel, Minnie McDaniel, Selma McDaniel, Woodrow McDaniel, Essie McHaney, Meda Haney, Jim McLaughlin and Minnie McMillon.

Others were Almus McNeil, Affie Myers, Roy Pack, Vester Phillips, Dick Poole, Mable Yopp Pyle, M. R. Richardson, Ed Robinson, Cora Rogers, George Rogers, Harold Rogers, Sterling Rogers, Jim Thompson, Mack Thompson Sr., Sam Thompson, Ocie Virgin, Gerturde Willcockson, Agnes Williamson, Charlie Winn, Henry Wood and Lena Zimmerman.

Source: *GCHGS Quarterlies (Vol. 7, # 3, 1994 and Vol. 8, # 3, 1995)* and the Paragould "Soliphone".

*Brushy Ridge School, about 1915 – Family names represented in this picture are Vincent, Vowell, Evans, Smoot, Little, Rippy, Gilmore, Wilson and Lam. (Picture courtesy of Mrs. Sadie Cox)*

*Caldwell Chapel School, about 1914 – Top Row: Leffie Guest, Mamie Coleman, Lisa Chapman, Teacher Clevie Cathey, Mandy Powers, Ethel "Bessie" Dunnam, Doris Evans, Pearl Richards. Fourth Row: Mary Ida Little, Mattie O'Dell, William Hunt, Jenning Williams, John Smith, Ed Williams, Robert "Bob" Dunnam, Fred Caldwell, Unknown, Emlie Lindly. Third Row: Unknown, Burl Tompkins, Oliver Caldwell, Unknown, Jake Caldwell, Luin Coleman, Eskio Booten, Loyd Chapman, Allen Powers, Albert Hunt, Elmer Baugh, Elmo Williams. Second Row: Fred Williams, Alma Jones, Retha Baugh, Pansey Jones, Velma Berry, Ollie Adams, Lorrene Berry, Bertha Cook, Vestal Powers. First Row: John Williams, Clyde Lindly, Avery Williams, Basil unknown, Jennings Baugh, Butch Harlow, Ollie unknown, Unknown, unknown Jones, Unknown, Porter Jones, unknown. (Picture courtesy of Mr. and Mrs. R. L. Dunnam)*

## Commissary School

Commissary is one of the earliest sections settled in Greene County, located west of Paragould.

There were two buildings located on the north side of Commissary Road, which was where Greene County Roads 602 and 603 meet. One was the church building and the other was the school.

The youngest children met outside under the trees and were taught by the preacher, Mr. Starlin. On rainy days, they used the church building for class. The older students met inside the school building. Another teacher at Commissary was Albert Buchanan.

Family names of students who attended this school include Buchanan, Farley, Futrell, Wallis, Breckenridge, Owen, DeHart, Norwood, Rowe, Goins, Taylor and Jetton.

Source: Information provided by Cathy Rowe.

## Connelly School

Connelly School was located in the northwest corner of Greene County.

## Cooper School

Cooper School was located in Greene County near the old Ahlf Store at Hopewell.

Many of the students were absent on March 3, 1921 to help plow and sow spring oats when the picture was taken by Joe Phillips, photographer.

## Cotton Belt School

No one seems to know what year George Washington "Uncle Wash" Riley came to Greene County or how he acquired around 300 acres of land located about one mile due north of the Paragould Landfill just off of Highway 49 North. This farm in later years was known as the Bass Place, Riley Cunningham Farm, Barker Farm, and the Bramlett or Bowden Farm.

We do know that George Riley was a charter member of Unity Baptist Church in 1879 and around 1890 gave the southeast corner of his property and Riley Corner Schoolhouse came into being. The school was used until it burned in 1903. (Some people in the community felt the school fire was a result of arson).

A vote was taken and by a margin of one vote, it was decided to move the school site to a location three-fourths mile due south by the railroad (just across the railroad from the Paragould Landfill). The name was changed to Cotton Belt School, which became the school of district 42, with a one-room building ready for the fall term of 1904.

The following is an attempt to list the teachers of Cotton Belt School in the order they served at the school. The first teacher, Oscar Harvey, was from Marmaduke and no one seems to know how many terms he taught, but he began teaching in 1904. Then came Lawrence Hyatt, Cordelia Hart, Silvester Campbell, W. K. Kelly, Lillian Howell, C. E. Bond and a Mr. Justice.

By 1912 another room was added along with a bell tower to "take up books". Ora Walker and his future wife, Iva Hodge, were hired for the first term in the two-room school at Cotton Belt.

The following is an attempt to list the teachers who served the Cotton Belt School (although not in perfect order) in the two-room building. Ora Walker and Iva Hodge served in 1912, and then came Ruth Hodge, Ruth Barton, Bert Dover, Harry Beckwith, Pearl Stevens, Martha Charles, Blanche Pratt and Mary Faulkner.

By 1920 there was a summer term of school. Those serving as teachers after this time included Estelle Buchanan, Lucy (Green) Sanders, Ruth Spence, Kate Remeley, Ralph Taylor, Ora Walker (second time), Bill Holmes, Lillian Howell (second time), Author Trantham, Martha Charles (second time), Joy Bond, Lee Haas, Sarah McDaniel, Mack Blackwood, Scott Noel, Lorene Taylor, Erba Butler, Vera Williams, Javine Faulkner, David Smith, Tom Payne, Bernice Phillips, Cecil Shearer, Eula (McGowan) Kingston, Margaret Blount and Pearl Newberry.

Cotton Belt School consolidated with Oak Grove School District in the 1940's. The old two-room building was torn down in 1946 and no one seems to know what became of the "school bell" that hung in the bell tower and rang for so many years.

Source: Information gathered by J. P. Cunningham who started to school there in 1920.

*Clark's Chapel School, 1905 – Back Row: Gardner Ellington, Perry Holland, Henry Wood, teacher (salary in 1905 was $40 a month), Dr. Boyd, Charlie Winn, Dr. W. E. Ellington, Dr. Edgar Cleveland Linderman, Osbon Ellington. Second Row: Albert Winn, Charley Howe, Lizzie Taylor, Myrtle Winn, Mollie Isom, Lydia Lynn, Albert Robinson, M. M. McNeil, Maude Tomason, Dora Miller, Emma Jernigan, Nellie McClure, Lettie Tennison, Maybelle Ward, Charlie Robinson, Sank McNeil, Finnis Ward, Clifford Tennyson, Mrs. S. E. Wynn. Third Row: Dovie McNeil, Gracie Tennison, Martha Tomason, Mollie McNeil, Ello Iison, Foler Iison, Bertie Gibson, Isa Gibson, Gus Ellington, Dexter Jarrett. Front Row: Jeff McNeil, Harve McNeil, Morris Tennison, Sammie Winn, Emmett Jernigan, Bea Jarett, Joe Winn, Etta Winn.*

## Croft School

Dr. George B. Croft, one of the earliest settlers and probably the first physician to arrive in Greene County, donated the land for Croft School, for the "use and benefit of a Christian

*Commissary School, 1910 – Chephus Autrey, teacher (Picture courtesy of Daniel Hester)*

College or Seminary of learning". The school was also known as Croft College, because the people had hoped it would someday become a college, although this never did occur.

The school was actually established after the death of Dr. Croft's widow, Sarah who died in 1901. Since much of the Croft money had been depleted by the time of her death, the sale of produce from the farm was to be used to maintain the school. The farm was not very productive and the school's existence was a struggle.

In 1906, the Campbellite denomination split. One group, the Church of Christ, took over the Croft church and school.

Among the early teachers were Professor Johns and brothers, A. D. and Neely Gardner.

The school closed in 1939.

Source: *GCHGS QUARTERLY (VOL. 9, # 3, 1996)* article on Dr. Croft researched by Louise Goins Richardson

## Cross Roads School

Cross Roads School was located nine miles west of Paragould on what is now U. S. Highway 412.

*Submitted by Anita Phillips*

## Crowley's Ridge Academy

Crowley's Ridge Academy was the result of a long time dream of Emmett Smith. Mr. Smith had a vision of beginning a private Christian school in Greene County. Mr. Smith, along with original board members John L. Watson, Vance Greenway, Monroe Lemmons, Brad Brumly and Earl Taylor made this dream become a reality.

The first day of classes at CRA was Sept 21, 1953. 39 students composed the first group on that Monday morning. By June 1954, enrollment had grown to 115 students. There were two graduating seniors that year.

CRA has always had a strong faculty and staff. Teachers for that first school year were Ileta Buchanan, Mattie Geer, Dwight and Kitty Hesson, Aquailla Fuchs, Elmo Hall, Forrest Grady, Paul Vining, Wayne Hemmingway and Emma and Emmitt Smith.

From its beginning, CRA has had a mission to provide a quality education in a Christian environment. Students attended *Bible* classes and chapel each day. This has encouraged many CRA graduates to become missionaries, elders, deacons, *Bible* class teachers and dedicated servants in the church. Crowley's Ridge Academy has also done an excellent job over the years of preparing students for college.

The original building housed six classrooms, an office and a lunchroom. CRA has grown to 20 classrooms, two gymnasiums, seven offices, a library, a bus barn and shop and a 600-seat auditorium. The PALS pre-school is also housed on campus.

With an active and dedicated board of trustees, along with an experienced and caring faculty and staff, great accomplishments are expected at Crowley's Ridge Academy during the coming years.

## Denman School

Denman School was located in the northwest corner of Greene County.

## Evening Shade School

Evening Shade School was a one-room school that started in 1911. It was located about five miles north of Stanford on what is now 230 Road.

There were eight grades with a total number of students some years reaching 50 to 55

*Cooper School March 3, 1921 – Mrs. Zola Pruett, teacher (Picture courtesy of Doyne Rasberry)*

*Cotton Belt School (Picture courtesy of Doyne Rasberry)*

*Connelly School – Russell Starr, teacher. Row One: Doris Jean Lance, Doris Getson and Alma Russell. Row two: Herschel Webster, John Like and Lee Henry Russell. Row three: Alice Marie Hand, Mary Ellen Martin and Wilma Lovell. Row four: Carrie Martin, Zella Mae Martin and Leveta Like. Row five: Verna Like, Lucille Martin and Russell Starr, teacher. (Picture courtesy of Mr. and Mrs. Ed Wilkinson)*

students taught by only one teacher. There were two long seats, one on each side of the room at the front, for the class that was in session. The remainder of the students were in their seats, some being helped by older students, while others studied on their own.

Recess and lunch period were always a time of enjoyment, where each student, along with the teacher, participated in a number of games such as wolf-over-the-ridge, whip-pop, marbles, anti-over, rabbit, drop the handkerchief and softball.

Students walked from miles around, many times when water was over the roads. One man, John Clifton, would hitch his team and wagon and take children to school.

Some teachers and substitute teachers include:

1. Tony Farley
2. Melinda Grooms
3. Daphine Johns
4. Hurt Faulkner
5. Hazel Ragsdall
6. Rupert Blalock,
7. L. V. Clifton
8. Juanita Johns
9. Laura Bone
10. Melba Jackson
11. Flossie McClure
12. Ed Williams
13. Mozell Faulkner
14. O. P. Killian
15. Artie Hall
16. Osmer Garner
17. Gracie Garner
18. Ezra Garner
19. Carl Garner
20. Miss Alma Gilbert
21. Tom Crowley
22. Opal Cooper
23. Lessie Howard
24. Mollie Hall
25. Eula Farley
26. Jess Gramling
27. Bill Smith
28. Harry Starling
29. Earl Tatum
30. Thad Crowley
31. Jeptha Futrell

The school closed in 1946 when it consolidated with Stanford School District.

Source: Information provided by Mrs. Clara Lovelady

*Cotton Belt School reunion, 1984 (Picture courtesy of J. P. Cunningham)*

*Croft School early 1900's (Picture courtesy of Mrs. Louise Richardson)*

*Cross Roads School, September 1916 – Sam Blackwood, teacher (Picture courtesy of Paragould* Daily Press*)*

*Denman School, about 1916 – Carl Ferrell, teacher. First Row: Denman Trout, Lou Ella Neal, Carrie Gunter, Unknown, Bessie Fossett, Lou Ella Reid, Evelyn Trout and Argyle Neal. Second Row: Tom French, Vernon Bracken, Harvey Reid, Marvin Hodge, Chacey Eveland, Ernest Lacey, Arthur Young, Mabel Bracken, Silas Gunter and Matthew Hodge. Third Row: Clyde James, Otis Forehand, Suzy Forehand, Lydia Lacey, Joseph Gunter, Blanche Dalton, Glenna Walton and Carl Ferrell (teacher). (Picture courtesy of Mr. and Mrs. Ed Wilkinson)*

*Crowley's Ridge Acadamy*

*Evening Shade School, 1940. Row 1: Cleo Morrow, Carl Davis, Harrold Morrow, Herman Holland, Billy Lashley, Edward Morrow, Leo Busby, unknown, Benny Lee White, Fred Orick, Ethan Busby, Herman Farley, Lindy Busby. Row 2: Martha Jane Bronson, Laura Jean Bone, Gwelyn Mears, Carrie Bone, Jessie Martin, Drelline Copeland, Burnes Mears, Eunice Orick, Mary Alice Busby, Grace Orick, Reba Morrow, Jessie Bell Farley, Clara Clifton. Row 3: Earl Clifton, Warren Busby, J. M. Smith, Charlie Busby, Brown Copeland, David Smith – teacher, James Smith, Dickie Davis, unknown, unknown, Laven Morrow. (Picture courtesy of Mrs. Clara Lovelady)*

# Evening Star School

Settlement of the Evening Star community is thought to have been in the late 19th century. The community is located four and one-half miles east of Delaplaine, in the northwest corner of Greene County. From 1903 to 1915 the area was known as Black Jack, AR and there are those who still use that name. At one time a Mr. Frasure was known to have been the postmaster prior to changing the name to Evening Star.

Most of the early pioneers worked in the timber industry. Many hewed and sold ties and stave bolts. The ties were hauled to Bradshaw bridge, made into rafts and floated down Cache River to a mill in Sedgwick, AR. The stave bolts were hauled by wagon to the Iron Mountain line at Delaplaine and shipped from there.

In the early days many people moved in and out of the community as it was at that time not well suited to agriculture. There was a sawmill and shingle mill in the area about 1900. Among the early settlers were the Cliftons, Rowen, Frasure, Mitchell, Vines, Carmikle, Pridemore, Garner, Grey, Orick, Clark and Ellis families.

Source: History by F. A. Clifton

*Evening Star School, about 1934 – Lucille Faulkner, teacher. Row 1: Claudie Rooker, J. E. Mitchell, Raymond Wagner, Emory Clifton, Bobby Ray Kellim, Floyd Vines, Charles Carter and Harrison Wagner. Row 2: Wanda Moore, Grace Johnson, Furia Johnson, Eileen Hawk, Lucille Faulkner (teacher), Essie May Devore, Ethel Carter, Velma Cambell, Almeda Wagner and Norma Lee Johnson. Row 3: Troy Smith, Fredrick Carter, Fermond Clifton, Alfred "Pete" Downs, Melvin Wagner, Voy Smith and Herman Devore. (Picture courtesy of Mr. and Mrs. Ed Wilkinson)*

# Finch School

The Finch community is southwest of Paragould in Poland Township.

Finch was the name of the first schoolmaster to conduct a school in the area. It is not known if the school was held in a church, home or abandoned building. It must have started before 1878 because a post office was granted in August of that year under the name of Finch.

It would have been a subscription school, then actually a private school and was probably known as "the Finch School".

The school identified the area and when a name was selected to submit to the Post Office Department, Finch was chosen. The county school system was not organized until much later and the first date in the County Education Office for a public school at Finch is 1910.

Finch school consolidated with Walcott in 1941. It was in the area where the church and cemetery were located, perhaps in a separate building.

Two students from area schools served as reporters and submitted news to the Paragould Soliphone on a regular basis. These reports sometimes gave insight to the life and times of the early 1900s.

On Jan 20, 1909, Florence Newberry and Joisa Edwards reported Henry Wood as their teacher, with five new pupils and three visitors that week. Three members of one family were absent on account of home duties. On Feb 12, 1909, the students reported they had only two more weeks of school and hoped to do a great deal of work before the close of the term. Records show that the teacher, Henry Wood, received $40 that term.

Other teachers in the Finch School according to a list compiled by Mack Thompson included:

1. Stella Edwards Bostic
2. Mr. Bowers
3. David Faulkner
4. A. M. Finch
5. Tom Fletcher
6. Della Foliger
7. Minnie Gibson
8. Mun Greenway
9. Ostell Greenway
10. Roy Greenway
11. Tom Gill Sr.
12. Mildred Grimes
13. Mary Ida Herren
14. Lester Horton
15. John W. Hyde

Source: A history of Poland Township compiled by Mack Thompson (GCHGS Quarterly, Vol. 8, # 3, 1995), A History of Greene County by Myrl Rhine Mueller, Paragould Soliphone.

*Evening Star School, 1913*

*Fritz School, May 13, 1932 (Picture courtesy of Mrs. Sadie Cox)*

*Fairview Penmanship Class – R. E. L. Stricklin, teacher, is shown standing at the penmanship chart by a tree. Mr. Stricklin had beautiful Spencerian handwriting and taught several penmanship classes. This picture was made about 1900 in the Fairview area west of Paragould, where Fairview Baptist Church now stands. (Picture courtesy of Mrs. Paul Stricklin)*

# Fritz School

The Fritz community was located in the far northeast part of Greene County called Brushy Ridge, just north of the Mound community.

The Frets schoolhouse was built in the early part of 1903. It was named in honor of W. H. Frets, who donated the land for a schoolhouse. Eventually the spelling of the name was changed to Fritz.

The first school at Fritz was taught by Mr. Staggs in the summer of 1903. According to Mr. H. M. Manchester in his history of Brushy Ridge, the teachers at Fritz from 1904 to 1915 included Agnes Cox, Jacob Pitman, Ola French, Vernon Smith, Leona Burroughs, James Evans, Otto Brewer and P. C. Cooper.

Those who taught after 1915 included P. C. Cooper, George M. Dodd, Mrs. Bertha Glass, C. E. Bond, H. M. Manchester, Elmer Holifield, Wesley Beaton, Mrs. George A. French, Linley Vowell, Cleo Hill, Issac Runyan, Lillian Vincent, Mr. and Mrs. Willie French, Sadie Lam, Pauline Holifield, Miss Sikes and Milo Miller who taught from 1936 to 1939.

A newspaper article from April 16, 1929, lists Fritz school as the first-place winner in the two- and three- room school division of Greene County elementary school athletic contests held at Harmon playfield.

In 1932-33, the Fritz students again placed first among several county schools in the athletic events as well as the literary contests. The categories of the literary competition included recitations, spelling and addition, posters judged on penmanship and language, and choral events including vocal solos by both boys and girls. The Fritz school choir composed of eight girls and four boys finished in first place.

In 1939, a petition was circulated by Herman Braden and Bill Vowell to consolidate the Fritz School with Marmaduke. All 17 people in the community who held poll tax receipts were contacted and the Fritz school was consolidated. The White Oak School two miles east of Fritz consolidated with Marmaduke in 1949.

Source: a history of the Fritz community compiled by H. M. Manchester.

# Halliday School

The Halliday School originated about 1900. Lev Buchanan gave an acre of land for the one-room school building with the understanding that the land remained property of the school district as long as needed. If it was ever abandoned, the land would return to the Buchanan heirs.

The school was about one-quarter of a mile west of Halliday and set back from the road in a grove of trees. There was enough space here for a large playground for the students.

Among the early teachers were two sisters, Miss Agnes and Miss Tennie Williamson, hired by school director Frank Glisson so that when one was sick, the other sister could fill in.

Another early teacher was Estel Buchanan who lived near the school. She arranged "entertainments" which were quite popular. They included exhibitions, plays, speeches, pantomimes and debates. These events gave the community a place to gather socially other than at church.

Other teachers at Halliday include Claud Bradsher from Marmaduke who taught during the 1910 school term, George Rogers, Carl McDonald, Tom Payne and Agnes Barker Maxwell. Inez Barker filled in after her sister Agnes died in Sept 1929.

In Aug 1914, a special election was held to enable the school to qualify for a revolving loan to finance the addition of a second room when the attendance had sufficiently increased. Officials who held the election were A. L. Buchanan, M. Malin, J. F. Dollins and I. H. Trantham. Following the addition of the second room, two teachers were hired, one for the primary grades one through four who met in the old room and another for the advanced grades five through eight who met in the new room.

Halliday consolidated with Marmaduke schools sometime in the 1946-1950 period. The old school was then abandoned.

*Harvey's Chapel School 1931-1932. Back Row: Hollis Boone, Odell Graves, Gaylon Gouge, A. C. McBride, Imogene Brooks, Doyle Fitch, Unknown, Gale Fred. Row Two: Lucille Jones, Paul Lee Archibald, Bernice Clark, Charles Jones, Annie Fitch, Wilbur Graves, and Pauline Brown. First Row: Jib Cudd, Pluma Smith, Maurice Cudd, Winford Hamett, Elsie Archibald, Buddy Henderson, Gerald Henderson, Olen Cudd, Jackulen Brooks. (Picture courtesy of Doyne Rasberry)*

*Finch School about 1938 – Front Row: Tommy Carr, Leland Gill, Leon McClure, Dora Hampton, William Hampton, Betty Smith, Anna Bell Sims, Dorothy Hampton. Second Row: Granville Hampton, Junior Strope, Lindy Carr, Dillon Cole, Effie Grace Martin, Junior Gill, Alicetine Sims, Lola Smith, Bertha Mae Hampton and Margaret Denham. Third Row: Obie Newsome, Bob Treece, Darrell Gill, Almarie Cox, Iris Hyde, Earl Carr, Robbie Smith, Ruth Woods, Bernice Denham, Helen Fletcher. Back Row: Teacher Dolford Payne and Henry Carr. (Picture courtesy of Steve Wood)*

Shortly after this consolidation a tragic accident occurred. A school bus, loaded with children on their way home from school, was sideswiped by a large lumber truck on a highway bridge between Halliday and Marmaduke. Five children were killed and several were injured.

Source: Articles in the *GCHS Quarterlies* written by Hazel Files concerning her remembrances of Halliday.

## Jones Ridge School

Jones Ridge School was located in the northwest part of Greene County.

## Landrum School

Landrum School was north of Paragould in Union Township near what is now known as Fairview Road.

## Miller School

Miller School was located in extreme southeast Greene County in Mainshore Township. The school was located five miles south on Highway 135 and a mile east of Road 919 and was only two or three miles from the St. Francis River. It was named for Sam and Jake Miller, early property owners in the Miller community.

Miller School was a two-story building with an entrance hall to two downstairs rooms, called the "Big Room" and the "Little Room". There was a huge hall on the second floor with access to the "Bell Tower Room" on the northeast corner of the building.

The bell rang at 8 a.m. and could be heard miles away. Each room in the school had a long wood stove and on cold days the teachers would slide the desk and chairs around it.

In 1937 Frank Service Key, a carpenter, removed the top floor and lowered the ceilings of the classrooms. The bell tower was removed at that time also.

The hall was generally used by some fraternal organization and possibly for political rallies. Della Carpenter Key Bridges remembers the hall once being used for dancing by the community as they entertained soldiers during WWI.

Mozelle Blackwood taught the "Little Room" in the 1930's and Rupert Blalock, the principal, taught the "Big Room", grades five through eight. Mrs. Reba Stimson also taught second, third and fourth grades at Miller in the 1930's.

Source: *"Miller School of Mainshore Township"* by Betty Key (*GCHGS Quarterly, vol. 8, # 3, 1995*).

*Submitted by Betty Key*

## "In Remembrance of Morning Star School"

By Mozelle Blanton, GCHGS *Quarterly (Vol. 1, # 4, 1988)*

On July 2, 1988 a reunion was held to honor the former students, patrons and teachers of Morning Star School and commemorate the closing of the school doors for the last time, 50 years ago. The reunion was held at Christ United Methodist Church on Highway 412, east of Paragould.

The Morning Star School was opened about 1899. Although located not very many miles from Paragould, a loyal group of people established homes there and developed their own independent community. At that time the roads east of Paragould were very poor and transportation was by horse and wagon, so the school and church became the heart of the community and tied together the social, political and business activities.

The one-room, one-teacher school was heated with a wood stove and there was no electricity. Water was from a hand pump set on a concrete slab in the schoolyard. The teacher was obligated to sweep the classroom floor and keep the schoolroom clean.

In those days a teacher in Greene County was permitted to teach only three years in the same school. They were paid in warrants, which were cashed at a discount and sometimes holders received only half of the value.

The Cotton Belt Railroad passed through Morning Star. Teachers living in Paragould commuted to and from school on morning and evening trains. Many prominent Greene County people taught at Morning Star School. Among them were W. A. Branch, who became county superintendent; his daughter Lorene Williams; Robert Rose and Maudine Rose. Rupert Blalock, Paragould businessman started his teaching career there. Vaniece Lewis, a "graduate" of the school, returned as a teacher.

In 1938 the rural county schools were consolidated into districts. The small communities were unhappy to see their neighborhood schools closed but realized it would broaden educational opportunities. Morning Star was consolidated with the schools at Bard, Big Island, Coffman and Light, to become Lakeside School. In 10 years Lakeside became a part of the Tech School District.

In time the old Morning Star School Build-

*Halliday School about 1914 (Picture courtesy of Patrick Zollner)*

*Landrum School 1901 – Row one: Winn Shepherd, Rafe Agee, Luster Stimmson, Erva Stimson, Buddy Stimson, Unknown, Jess Lynch, Otis Shephert, Author Dodge, Luther Brummett, Tommy McGowan, Freddy Shehorn, Edna Shehorn, Amy Brummett, Lily Agee, Mara Gilbert, Ona Brummett, Clara Stutts. Row two: Mrs. Sudie Stimson, Mrs. Benton, Mrs. Hammond, Mr. Cole Burton, Unknown, William Brummett, Mr. Shehorn, Jimmy Stimson, Other Newsom, Bert Lynch, Jim Merideth, Annie Lashley, Meda McHaney, Mrs. Jane Burton, Katherine Brummett, Eunice Landrum, Mrs. Jane Wetherly, Roy Swindle, Mac Stell. Row three: Betty Haygood, Ollie McGowan, Ed McGowan, Lutor Dodge, Arrie Stutes, Thurmand Gilbert, Maude Agee, Rosa Merideth, Lula Burton, Leona Shepherd, Maude Bullin, Mrs. Gilbert, Zula Burton, Estel McHaney, Molly Laconure. Row four: Charlie Lynch, Rosa Lynch, Unknown, Bun Stutes, Gorda Forbus, Tom Duley Smith, Anderson, Joe Bech in door, Arther Brummett, Moss Agee, Ortha Newsom, Issac Brummett, Claude Agee, Ambeis Smith, Ed Brummett, Lou Landrum, Edith Landrum. (Picture courtesy of Mrs. Molly Emmons)*

*Jones Ridge School about 1911 – Claude Roy Rooker, teacher (Picture courtesy of Mr. and Mrs. John Wilkinson)*

ing was razed, the pump taken out and the railroad abandoned, yet the spirit that bonded the community together still lived.

It was fitting that the reunion and memorial service were held at Christ United Methodist Church, because the church auditorium, once the auditorium of the school, was moved and added to the present building.

## Newberry School

Newberry was a two-room schoolhouse sitting on two acres of land. In later years, only one room was used. Newberry consolidated with the Marmaduke School District in 1948.

To reach Newberry turn left off Highway 49, north of Paragould, onto Road 515. Go one and one-half miles west to Road 520, turn right and go one-half mile, over a culvert. Newberry School was located on the right.

## New Home School

New Home School was approximately four miles west of Marmaduke, Arkansas.

## North End School

In 1922, patrons of Mt. Carmel and Morning Star communities, located in the extreme north edge of Paragould, petitioned the court to create a North End School District to serve the north section of the town. Until 1946, this section existed as a separate school district and then became a part of the Paragould Special School District #1.

In Nov 1952, the old school building was replaced with an ultramodern building, containing three classrooms, three restrooms, and an office, coatrooms, a kitchen and janitor quarters, all arranged in a large central corridor.

In 1964 and 1965, portable classrooms were added, followed in 1968 by a cafetorium and more classrooms in 1976.

The school was called Oakwood, a name chosen by Mrs. Vivian Hollis, principal.

Source: *A History of Greene County* by Myrl Rhine Mueller

*Marmaduke School – This is Marmaduke's first school, built in 1884, which burned in 1913. (Picture courtesy of Doyne Rasberry)*

*Miller School 1933-34. Row one: Vernon Higgins, Robert L. Davidson, Johnny Fletcher, unknown, James Thomas, unknown, unknown, unknown, unknown, Kenneth Ellington, Martin Lemmons, Cletus Hoyer. Row two: Betty Key, Marcella Hoyer, Maxine Jackson, Katherine Mayberry, Annabelle Hopkins, Wynona Higgins, Dorothy Higgins, Vaudine Jackson, Helen Fletcher, Novalee Smith, Betty Jean Thompson, Laveta Thomas and Evelyn Ellington. Row three: Angelo Cummins, Harold Jackson, Johnny Mangrum, Buddy Day, unknown, unknown, Joe Lemmons, unknown, Wilma Skaggs, Alene Hoyer, Freuda Ellington, Gearidene Norton, unknown, unknown, unknown and Thomas Walter Davidson. Row four: Unknown, George Batey, unknown, unknown, Randall Ellington, unknown, Winston Cummins, Sam Hopkins, Toby Day, unknown, unknown, unknown Spillman and Sherman Ellington. The teacher was Mozelle Blackwood and Rupert Blalock was the principal-teacher. (Picture courtesy of Betty Key)*

## O'Kean School

O'Kean School District # 74 was formed in April 1888 by a division of District # 66 (Gumstump). School was held in a large one-room building until 1927 when a new $4000 two-room school building was completed at O'Kean. The first year, however, the only teacher there was Professor Tom Bottom.

Teachers in the old building at O'Kean included Lee Rice, Mr. Higgins, Della Crotts, Lura Glisson, Marvin Green and Mrs. Coleman.

Other teachers were George Purdy 1928-29, Ralph Staten, Elsie Staten, Mary Staten, Elsie Hart, Eileen Ingram, Eula Jones, Louise Bode, Carolyn Getson, Ethel Caldwell, Essie Bennett Ford and long-time teachers, Tom and Gladys Bottom.

On Dec 29, 1948, O'Kean District # 74 and Sanders District # 94 consolidated with Delaplaine District # C-7, which is located seven miles north of O'Kean and is in Greene County. Most O'Kean students who were able to pay tuition, bus fare and other fees attended school there before consolidation.

The Haney school building located two miles north of O'Kean in Greene County was moved to O'Kean making this a three-room school. The upper grades were bused to Delaplaine while the lower grades remained at O'Kean.

Some teachers during this time were: Leon Lee, Geraldine Stayton, Amos Gillean, Pauline Schimming and Marvene Carter Lance from 1952 until the remaining students were moved to Delaplaine classrooms in 1962.

The Haney School building was sold and moved to be used as a private dwelling. The O'Kean School building was sold and converted to a Pentecostal church building. Later it also was sold to be used as a private dwelling.

Source: *O'Kean School* by Mary Hibbard (*Randolph County Historical and Genealogical Review, Winter, 1999*).

*Submitted by Mary Hibbard*

## Old Bethel School

The Old Bethel School was located about two miles west of Finch. This was originally a Methodist Church built in 1880 when the church was established.

*Newberry School about 1946 – Lee Hass, teacher. Front Row: Unknown, Reynolds, Ernestine Austin. Row two: Wayne "Tuffy" Eubanks, Janie Eubanks, Patsy Childers, Betty West, Glen Austin, Wilburn Jackson, Denzil Reynolds, Merritt "Pooch" Jackson, David Terry. Row three: Myrtle West, Alan Jackson, Melvin Terry, Anna Beth Austin, Raymond Reynolds, Lee Hass (teacher), Betty Weaver, J. D. Tuggle, J. C. Ball. (Picture courtesy of Faye Hufford)*

*New Home School, 1936 – teacher, Buren Arnold (Courtesy of Doyne Rasberry)*

The first building, also used as a schoolhouse was destroyed about 1900 in a tornado. A one-room frame building was erected in 1901 and was used for church services and school sessions.

In 1925, the school consolidated with Tech District and church services was discontinued in 1926.

Some teachers at this school, according to a list compiled by Mack Thompson, included: Will Barnhill, Clevie Blackwood, Kate Blackwood, Mack Blackwood, J. D. Blackwood, Stirl Blackwood, W. J. Blackwood, Lon Bobbit, Carol Bobo, Ben Boling, Lou Cothern, Thad Cothern, Stella Edwards, Dallas Faulkner, Doc Fields, Harvey Forschy, Nellie Heath, John Honey, Ivan Jackson, Eli Lamb, Luther Martin, Tom McHaney, Will Newberry, Alice Tillman Ramsey and Jim Sibert.

Sources: *Mueller's "History of Finch Community"*, Mack Thompson's article on Poland Township *(GCHGS QUARTERLY)* and the Paragould Soliphone.

*North End School 1914*

*O'Kean School 1946-47. First Row: Jackie Todd, Billy Joe Walker, Joe Todd, Walter Lee Ball, Eddie Halstead, Sonny Ford, Leon Judd (behind Sonny), Nelbert Kifer, Loyd Judd, Ray Ball. Second Row: Norma Alice Martin, Joann French, Bobbie Harris, Thelma Mae Rogers, Henrietta Brandon, Doris Jean Perkins, Janice Parker, Lois Getson, Blanche Ball, Norma Lou Getson, Wavie Arthur, Jerry "Hogtail" Ogden, Arthur, Billy Rickey, Gracie Harris, David Ball, Ann Carolyn Harris, Emit Ray Stone, Irene Brandon, Junior Wayne Ball, Helen Sue Getson, Loyd Rickey. Third Row: Imogene Ogden, Frankie Henson, Dowell Bennett, Glen Heral, Vernie Walker, Carolyn Getson, Betty Lou Martin, Evelyn Judd, Jean Rickey, Lorene Judd, Mary Ruth Martin, Mary Heral, Lillian Heral, Alvie Atkins, Tommy Getson, Frank Haynes, Jimmy Ray Getson, Fern Dillingham, Ralph Atkins, Bobby Gray, Eugene Rogers. Fourth Row: Patsy Brandon, Charles Henson, Ellen Craig, Cletis Rickey, Lorene Judd, Shirley Getson. Fifth Row: Cecil Loyd Ragsdell, Jim Martin, Henry Lee Gates. Teachers: Tom and Gladys Bottom. (Picture courtesy of Mary Hibbard)*

## Old Dixie School

Dixie School was originally in Greene County prior to about 1890, but the building was moved about two miles south of Rector on what is now Airport Road. According to Mr. Oscar Barker of Rector, the building was moved one side at a time on wagons using oxen.

In the background of this picture, made about 1902, the wheels of the buggy driven to the scene by photographer Joe Phillips, can be seen. Behind the buggy, part of the seven-rail fence is visible. Mr. Barker said in those days a legal fence had seven rails and any other type might bring difficulties over damage from stray livestock.

In the schoolyard were a big hickory tree and a large oak, later damaged by a sleet storm, from whose twisted limbs wonderful swings were suspended.

In the photo are 52 pupils and three visitors, although Mr. Barker said on some days there were as many as 120 pupils. The teacher was Louis Becker.

*Submitted by Betty Key*

*Old Bethel School 1898 – Luther Martin, teacher (Photo courtesy of Mack Thompson)*

## Palestine School

Palestine School building has been converted to a dwelling house and still stands at the intersection of Greene County Roads 626 and 628. It is located a short distance northwest of today's Mountain Home Cemetery and Church of Christ building.

*This picture of the one-room Oak Grove School was taken in 1902. Students were, front row, left to right: Roger Bramlett, Leonard McKelvey, Boone McNutt, Homer Walden, Inez Smith, Curni Cole, Naomi Faulkner, Iler Tanner, Mabel Winder, Nannie Tanner, Lola Wyse and Willie Pannell. Second row: Jess Walden, Chester Hampton, Orman Faulkner, Bob May, Lloyd McWhirter, Floyd Walden, Roy Miller, Charlie Benton, Ray Winder, Dollie Lacewell, Lillian Winder, Lillie Miller, Amy Sammons, Albertine Gardner and Grace Faulkner. Third row: Will Lake, Charlie Pannell, Ed May, Joe Warren, Dan Warren, Harley Warren, John Winder, May Miller, Gladys Walden, Kathleen Gardner, Mandy Benton and Sallie Faulkner. Back row: Roy Walden, Tom Benton, Lee Hampton, Willie Hampton, Eddie Walden, Elmer May, Jake Lacewell, Clarence Warren, Tom Hedgepeth, Alfred Walden, Harry Walden, Governor Faulkner, Calvin May and Tom Tanner. The teacher was Estelle McHaney. (Courtesy of the Paragould Daily Press)*

*Old Dixie School, about 1902. Front Row: The first eight pupils are unknown, Bertha Mitchell, Ada Jones, Maud Davidson, Mary Chandler, Unknown, Unknown, Gertie Chandler, unknown, Jim Carter, Unknown. Second Row: Minnie Morris, Meron Morris, Uncle Dan Mitchell, John Barker, George Barker, Lee Bertchit, Arthur Morris, Joe Chandler, Unknown, Unknown, Unknown. Third Row: Merry Jones, Joe Dunigan, Goldie Wills, Uway Terry, Ethel Abney, Sadie Wells, Eva Chandler, Louis Becker (teacher), Hattie Davidson, John Morris, Joe Chandler, Unknown, Unknown, Unknown. Back Row: Dollie Phillips, Beadie Abney, George Elenander, visitor, Joe Rowden, Uylis Abney, visitor, Frank Mitchell, Connie Finch, Oscar Barker, Arthur Finch, Bob Davidson, Oscar Finch, John Carter, visitor.*

*Palestine schools about 1912-13 (Picture courtesy of Mrs. Paul Stricklin)*

*Pine Knot School, about 1933 – Albert Buchanan, teacher. Top Row: Ted Ford (teacher), Albert Buchanan, Kenneth Lovelace, R. L. Sims. Row two: J. C. Lovelace, Ray Lovelace, Morrow, Cloyce Lemons, Orlan Hyde, Unknown, Johnny Austin, B. C. Ford, Carrie Treadway, Ellen Treadway, Jewel Ford, Mildred Austin. Bottom Row: Monedith Ford, Curtis Newsom, Unknown, Unknown, Norma Hodley. (Picture courtesy of Mrs. Curtis Newsom)*

*L to R: Pleasant Hill School and Pleasant Hill Methodist Church about 1920s (Picture courtesy of Mr. and Mrs. Glen Adams)*

## Pine Knot School

Pine Knot was one of five different district schools located in Poland Township. This school was well known in the early days because of its location in a predominately Church of Christ community.

It is thought that the first school was built shortly after the Pine Knot Church was constructed on the opposite side of the road. The school was one long building with only a single room. This was replaced by another building, also one room, with two doors and a porch across the front. The school went only through the eighth grade. Eventually, the church was rebuilt on the site of the school building.

Pint Knot School closed about 1945 with some students going to Walcott and the rest to Greene County School on what is now Highway 49 South.

According to a list compiled by Mack Thompson, a partial list of teachers at Pine Knot included Betty Austin, Dave Barnhill, Albert Buchanan, Lawrence Cooper, Donald Cox, Lillie Crockett, Jim Darels, Bud Dover, Dallas Farley, Tony Farley, Elsie Green, Mathel Lemmons, Monroe Greenway, Newell Greenway, Ostell Greenway, Laura Hight, Charlie Hodley, John Honey, Richard Howard, Lester Horton, W. P. Hutchins, Carl Hyde, Ernest Hyde and Frankie Hyde.

Other teachers were Cecil Kennedy, Will Majors, Agnes McClure, Jeff McClure, Edna McElweece, Hardy Newsom, Arthur Pillow, Mr. Paff, Virl Roberts, Rachel Simpson, Garland Smith, Onie Stevenson, Angus Thompson, Jim Thompson, Chester Wells, Ida Willcockson, Ike Willcockson and Becky Ellen Wilson.

Source: Article on Poland Township by Mack Thompson (*GCHGS Quarterly*) and information provided by Mrs. Sadie Toler.

## Pleasant Hill School

Sometime in the 1800s the Pleasant Hill School was a log cabin located in the Lorado Community on land originally owned by Indians. Either a storm or a fire destroyed this log cabin and a two-story structure was built across the road.

This first two-story school was destroyed by a

*Ramer's school about 1941, Freeda Simmons Knight, teacher (Picture courtesy of Mr. and Mrs. Ed Gerdes)*

*Post Oak School, grades five through eight, about 1936 (Picture courtesy of Mrs. Nita Smith)*

storm in 1908 and a second two-story structure was built. The upstairs was used by the Woodmen of the World Lodge for their meetings. Mr. Basil Dacus, who taught at Pleasant Hill from 1933 to 1936, was a member of that lodge. Robert Dennis was another member. Many of the students recall lodge members keeping a wooden goat upstairs that had a wooden crank.

Around 1928 or 1929, a storm destroyed the school and the church across the road. The structure which replaced it had two rooms and was used until the Pleasant Hill School consolidated with Walcott around 1950.

The schoolhouse was also used for voting purposes and when the building was no longer used as a school, it was used as a building for the Lorado community as well as a place to vote.

Source: Pleasant Hill Methodist Church history

## Post Oak School

Post Oak School, located one mile south of Marmaduke, was formerly known as Post Oak Knoll. The old school building had been about one mile north on a knoll. To reach the school site, turn east on "Peck's Speedway", go two miles, turn right, going another mile. Mt. Hebron Baptist Church was across the road from the school.

Post Oak School was a two-room school with grades one through eight.

Teachers of grades one through four in the 1930s included Mrs. Georgia Brewington and Mrs. Alma Smoot, both of Marmaduke. Teachers of grades four through eight in the 1930s included Luther Starnes of Marmaduke and Will Rowland of Paragould.

Source: Information provided by Mrs. Nita Smith.

## Pruett's Chapel School

Pruett's Chapel School was originally called Maple Grove and was located just off Finch Road next to the Pleasant Grove Methodist Church. When Charles and Robert Pruet and their wives donated land for a new church on what is now Pruett's Chapel Road, the church was then renamed in honor of the Pruet family. A new school built next to the Pruett's Chapel Methodist Church then became known as Pruett's Chapel School.

*Reddick School (Picture courtesy of Doyne Rasberry)*

*Pruett's Chapel School class with Pruett's Chapel Church on the left, ca.1900's*

The first known teacher was a Professor Spars who taught around 1887-88. An incomplete list of teachers at Pruett's Chapel is as follows: Professor Phoff, Sally Mills, Lena Watson, Neal Gardner, Will Barnhill (1902), William Kelley (1901-02 and later), Della Mack (about 1898-1901), Monroe Honey, Professor Jones, Ambrose Scaggs, C. D. Morris, Bun Stutz, Tennie Williamson, Agnes Williamson, George Baldridge, Will Branch, Beulah Diggs, Paul McClerkin, Edna McElwee, Valeria Brown, Pearl Owens, Cora Rogers, Minnie McDaniel, Ike Willcockson, Letha Phillips, Vivian Kelley, Jack Boone, Grace Jarvis, Ted Rogers, Helen Brown, John Batton, Nan Yopp, Donald Cox, Sadie Cox and Gene Garner.

During the last term in 1926, Sadie Lam taught the primary grades one through four and Gene Garner taught the advanced grades five through eight. There were approximately 100 students enrolled at that time. School directors were Arthur Jones and Dr. George P. Bridges.

Several schools consolidated to form Greene County High, which was built on the Paragould-Jonesboro Highway. The one and two-room schools which first closed and consolidated were Village, Old Bethel, Wood's Chapel and New Hope. At the end of 1926-27 term, the school at Pruett's Chapel closed, followed later by Bethel Station.

*Submitted by Anita Phillips*

## Ramer's School

At the end of the 1890s the population in northern Greene County along Crowley's Ridge had increased to the point that another school was needed in the community. Land was donated and a large one-room school was built one mile north of Ramer's Chapel Church, which was about five miles northwest of Marmaduke.

Some of the families whose children attended this school were Arnold, Fricke, Gerdes, Gibbs, Gould, Hampton, Henley, Henson, Herons, McDowell, Ragle, Ramer, Reed, Rutledge, Stephens and Wyatt.

Teachers at Ramer's School included Paul Lee Archibald, Buren Arnold, Delbert Dortch, Edward Gerdes, Lee Hass, Mrs. Anna Jones, Miss Jones, Freeda Simmons Knight, Mrs. Lee Ramsey, Eulean Staires, John Marshall Starnes, Lerlean Starnes, Luther Starnes, Thelbert Stephens, Arthur Trantham and Luther Vowell.

*Submitted by Mr. & Mrs. Ed Gerdes*

## Reddick School

The old Reddick School was located near Mounds in Greene County.

## Scatter Creek School

Scatter Creek community generally refers to the area due west of Lafe in Greene County.

The first school was a one-room frame building located across the road from Scatter Creek Methodist Church. The school burned in 1911 and a new one was built.

Those known to have taught school there include Lela Bishop, Dick Poole, Albert Jackson, Miss Garner, Orley Johnston, Myrtle Weddington, Clara Meadows, Roy Walden,

*Scatter Creek School, 1905*

*Stonewall School, 1915 – Miss Ollie Miller, teacher*

*Stanford School about 1942 – Izetta Vaughn, teacher (Picture courtesy of Mrs. Louise Richardson)*

Irvin Butler, Elsie Livesay and Verla Gerdes.

The school held classes for all 12 grades in the later years and at one time had an enrollment of 94 pupils.

Scatter Creek School consolidated with Lafe in 1944. The Methodist Church then purchased the building.

Source: *GCHGS Quarterly (Vol. 8, # 1-4, 1973).*

## Stonewall School

Stonewall's first school was a one-room box school built in 1909. Prior to 1912, the school was also used as a community church by all faiths.

The first teacher was Mr. Harry Laymond and Mr. McCurtry was one of the first school directors. Other teachers included Ollie Miller Clopton, Estelle Miller Yeargin, C. O. Bond, Verna Price, Eric Price, Clifford Winn, Pauline Huckabay and Zelma Robinson.

Stonewall consolidated with Lafe in 1950.

Source: *GCHGS Quarterly (Vol. 8, # 1-4, 1973) The History of Stonewall* by C. W. Starnes, MD.

## Southside School

Until 1907, the Southside School was a two-story structure with a basement in which a cafeteria was installed. In 1926, Southside School became the L. W. Baldwin Elementary School. The name was to have honored a railroad company vice-president in anticipation of his company locating a railroad enterprise in Paragould, but this did not occur. The initials L. W. were later dropped from the school's name.

Because of overcrowding, six classrooms were added in 1954.

The old two-story building was destroyed in 1967 by a tornado. The students were temporarily sent to various schools in the district. In some instances, it was necessary to hold two classes in one classroom. The building was rebuilt in two separate structures and two classrooms were added to those built in 1954.

Source: *A History of Greene County* by Myrl Rhine Mueller

## Stanford School

The earliest school remembered by this present generation is the Old Gunnell School, which was about one mile from the location of the present school. That school building was struck by lightning and burned. Then the first building was built at the present site in 1914 on land donated by Mr. Carol Hunt. It was at first a one-room school building and was later converted to two rooms and eventually to three rooms. This school only went to the eighth grade and students going to high school had to go to Paragould.

In 1940, the present school building was constructed and Stanford became a senior high school. In 1940 and 1941, several school districts consolidated to form the new Stanford

*Southside School about 1918 – Mrs. Camp, teacher. Top Row: Tyler Smith, Red Pierce, Cleyburn Myham, J. Herbert Woodard, Ralph Payne, Joe Taylor, Leonard Waldrum, unknown, Juanita Nesler Maxwell, Eva Briggs, Unknown, Unknown, Unknown, Reba Thompson, Imogene Springles McDonald, Amelia Light Weatherly, Alfreda Wilcockson. Second Row: Unknown, Unknown, Donald Yantis, Unknown, Ray McAllister, Burnus Payne, John Campbell Lady, Jimmie Stearns, Earl Armstrong, Vada Albright, Louise Hester, Unknown, Bonida Dollins, Helen Blake, Unknown, Unknown, Bonita Phillips, Unknown. Third Row: Otis Ward, John Spencer, Eugene Beisel, Boone, James Walker, Harold Cruse, Unknown, Iola Camp, Unknown, Bernice Woodson, Minnie Jean Wolf, Sadie Graham, Virginia Thompson, Louise Treadway, Charlene White, Pauline Riggsbee, Mary Lou Stricklin. Fourth Row: Unknown, Eugene Amos, Jay Ensor, Grapel Williams, Unknown, Smith, Mrs. Camp (teacher), Frances Yopp, Ann Roleson, Martha Dover, Edith Smith, Unknown, Veva Sims Phillips, Maurine Oliver. Fifth Row: Bronc Morrison, Cosmo Wilson, Alfred Knox, Raymond Fry, Cecil Walker, Winston Harris, Bennie Rosenthal, Hazel Bogan, Marie Hampton, Violet Adams DeBons, Bonnie Holcomb, Alberta Woods, Louise Bridges Cox. Front Row: Victor Lloyd, Henry Sub Greene, Henry Goldman, Robert Gross, Lester Freeman. (Picture courtesy of Mrs. Marlan Phillips)*

Consolidated School. Those districts were: Rice, Pruett, Commissary, Pumpkin Center, 44, Cross Roads, Evening Shade, Corner and New Home. Then in May 1941, the first class graduated from Stanford High School.

Source: *History of Stanford School* by Alfred Rowe, GCHGS Quarterlies. Information provided by Louise Richardson.

## Toddsvile School

To reach Toddsville School, turn off Highway 49, north of Paragould, onto Road 526. Toddsville was located on the northeast corner of the first crossroad, which is at the intersection of Road 526 and Road 509.

## Tokio School

Mr. J. N. Merideth donated land for Tokio School to the community around 1900. The one-room building erected was used as a school and for community activities.

The Tokio School District consolidated with the Marmaduke School in 1937.

Source: *Picture History of Marmaduke* compiled by Doyne Rasberry.

## Tower School

Tower School was located in the northwest part of Greene County.

## Upper Lafe School

The Upper Lafe School was not in the 1915 list of Greene County Schools, so it was probably formed about the time of WWI. It was located on the hill road to Knob (presently County Road 441) and was about four miles north of Lafe. It was a one room-eight grade school that served until the early 1940s when it was consolidated with Lafe High School. Some of the patrons of this school were the families of: Arnold, Bill, Brewer, Brown, Dover, Fricke, Gatewood, Gerdes, Haller, Helton, Hendrix, Hopper, Howe, Huckabay, McBee, Mifflin, Miller, Newton, Phillips, Rusher, Ramer, Reeves, Scheer, Thomas, Tritch, Ward, Watley and Wegner.

## Village School

Village School was just two miles down Pekin Road in Paragould, near Village Creek.

*Tokio School 1910-11, Otto Brewer, teacher (Picture courtesy of Roxann Thompson)*

*Toddsville School about 1936 – Mrs. Georgia Brewington, teacher. Front Row: Doyle McPherson, Ethridge Owens, Ralph Dooley, Smith, Ralph Wilson, Lonnie Wilson, George Terry, Gene Terry. Row two: Harold McPherson, Laveta Cupples, Patty Sue Haneline, Aliene Anderson, unknown, Jarvis, Louis Simpson, Letha Crafton, Jarvis, Mrs. Georgia Brewington, teacher. Row three: Anderson, James Powers, Louise Stanford, Eula Dean Terry, Corene Parks, Inez Parks, Lavern Dooley, Romsine Manor. (Picture courtesy of Faye Hufford)*

# Walcott School

Walcott School District # 40, which included part of Mt. Zion community, was organized July 17, 1882. From 1882 until 1907, Walcott Baptist Church services and Walcott School classes were held in the same building.

In 1907, a three-room school was built to accommodate grades one through ten.

Woodmen of the World # 134 contributed money to build an upstairs onto the school, which they used for their monthly meetings.

Construction of a new school began in 1929. The new school, Consolidated District # 2, included Old Bethel, Cedar Grove, Buck Horn, Cross Roads, Bobo, Finch, Mt. Zion schools and half of the Pine Knot School. In March 1930, Professor Thomas Worlds along with four other teachers plus all the students marched from the old school over to the new red brick building. The other four teachers were Izetta Vaughn, Mike Blackwood, Hazel Dacus and Margaret Detrich.

Walcott consolidated with Greene County Tech High School in 1948.

Teachers included Mrs. Hazel Dacus, Harry Martin, Bernice Peavyhouse, Opal Landrum, Eula Hughes, Lucille Lemons, Thad Crowley, Helen Beasley, Lerline Higgins and Tolly Cooper.

The first graduation was in May 1932. The four graduates were Mavis Short Downs, Luther Cline, Vincent Cline and Ivan Smothers.

Walcott, Greene County High, Lakeside and Alexander were all consolidated into one big school and became Greene County Tech High School in 1947-48. Beech Grove came into this consolidation the following year.

Source: Information given to Gerlene Jackson by L. V. Jones of Walcott, AR.
*Submitted by Gerlene Jackson*

# Walnut Grove School

Walnut Grove School was located in Greene County between Stanford and Evening Star.

# Walnut Ridge School

Walnut Ridge School was located two miles east of Marmaduke, on Highway 34 on the left side of the highway. It was a two-room school with grades one through eight.

# White Oak School

There were three settlements in the far northeastern part of Greene County known as Brushy Ridge: Mounds, Fritz which was two miles to the north, and White Oak, two miles due east of Fritz.

Mr. John Seay who moved to the White Oak community in 1905 recalled helping to cut and haul logs to build the first wooden schoolhouse in White Oak in 1906. In 1939 he sold a portion of his land for the construction of the new brick school there.

The first teacher at the old White Oak school was Mr. Mack Manchester. Mr. Milo Miller and Mrs. Duma McCluney were teaching there when the new one was built. Teachers at the new school included Mr. Miller, Luther Starnes, Mrs. Thelma Hoggard.

Later teachers included Wesley Beaton, Christine Williams, Mrs. Opal (Williams) Reynolds, Ethel Landrus, Ruth Mildred Wimberly, Mrs. Lorene Houston and Mr. Lee Hass.

Alexander had hoped to consolidate both White Oak and Mounds schools. Petitions were circulated and by extremely narrow margins, patrons of both schools voted to consolidate with Marmaduke in 1949.

Source: *History of White Oak* by H. M. Manchester

# Wood School

Wood School was southwest of Marmaduke, approximately halfway between Marmaduke and Gainesville.

# Wood's Chapel School

Wood's Chapel School was located just over a mile from Wood's Chapel Church, on the west side of what was known as "Turtle Back Hill."

*Tower School about 1936 – Row one: Wanda and Wanus Flannery, Christine and Eugene Lee, Ruby and Cecil Varner, Herman Tinsley, Larry Tower, Buddy Farrar, Vonda Pitcher and Dolly Varner. Row two: Earl and Ruby Lee, Dorothy Flannery, Juanita Lee, Leon Lee and Cleo Pitcher. Row three: Tanker Eugene, Odell Bennett, Lester Flannery, Willy and Opal Lee, Oral Lee, and Chester Summers. Row four: Kenneth Varner, Hubert Lee, Marvie Flannery, Agnes Price and Irene Lee. Row five: Frank Pitcher and Almeda Farrar. (Picture courtesy of Mr. and Mrs. Ed Wilkinson)*

*Village School 1914 – Bill Turner and Elva Houston, teachers (Picture courtesy of Mr. and Mrs. Bill Jones)*

*Walcott School 1938-39. Kneeling: Cloyce Woodson. Row one: unknown, Evangeline Cupp, Queen Virginia Newberry, Nancy Rogers, Goldie Wilcox, Jewel Bobo, Jerry Ponder. Row two: Charles Carney, J. C. Cothren, Woodrow Faught, Lucille Rogers, Superintendent H. A. Carney, Helen Underwood, Bedford Bunch and Ronnie Short. (Picture courtesy of L. V. Jones)*

*Walnut Grove School about 1912 – Monte Barrow, teacher (Picture courtesy of Gerald Scott)*

**ABOVE:** *Walnut Ridge School -- Mr. and Mrs. Lawson Swindle, teachers (Picture courtesy of Mrs. Nita Smith)*
**LEFT:** *Wood School August 24, 1906 -- Charles Webb, teacher (Picture courtesy of Doyne Rasberry)*

*White Oak School group picture 1933-34. Top Row: Raymond Hill, Garlon Lamb, Edward Floyd, George Floyd, Pauline Greene, Ruth Fagg, Freeda Parish, Oneida Beaton, Audrey Fagg and Ellen McGue. Second Row: Bill Floyd, Armunda Floyd, Gladys Parish, Seueda Wofford, Joe Fagg, Pauline McGee, Emma Crum, Lamma Walls, Audie Floyd, Nouella Floyd, Earline McGee, D. C. Smith, Glen Fagg, Derwood Dowdy, R. L. Hill, Willard Pascal, Teacher, Mary Lee Read, Teacher's helper Freeda Hill and Elbert Reynolds. Third Row: Billie Robinson, Doyle Reynolds, Shorty Smith, Bobby Robinson, Junior Eagle, Leverel Parish, J. B. Ward, Quara Hill, Dortha Dean Seay, Hazel Ward, Ollie Dowdy, Wanda Lee Eagle. (Picture courtesy of Freeda Gregory)*

*Wood's Chapel School about 1915 – Charlie Wood, teacher (Picture courtesy* GCHGS Quarterly, Vol. 9, # 1, 1996)

*WWII veterans who were taking agricultural classes at Marmaduke High School 1946 through 1949-50. C. G. Liddell, teacher (Picture courtesy of Mrs. Nita Smith)*

# Historic Homes of Greene County

## Barry - Kitchens
*508 West Court Street (formerly 444 West Court Street)*

T.B. Kitchens purchased this property in 1855 from Willis S. Pruet. 33 years later the Kitchens sold one-half of block 28, Pruet Second Addition to their only child, B. M. Kitchens and his wife, Medora Hampton Kitchens. They began to build their dream home immediately. Blueprints were prepared by John D. Almond of Little Rock, AR. Construction began in 1920 and when the Kitchens moved into the home in 1922, it was only partially completed. The house was finished in stages, as money was available. The home is a lovely English style, with two stories and a partial basement.

Having no living relatives, the Kitchens' bequeathed their beloved home to Glenda and Albert Barry, who inherited the property in 1983. Glenda had been employed by the Kitchens' family for 25 years and was a loyal employee and friend.

The Barry's kept most of the house as they received it, with the exception of the kitchen, which they modernized to suit their living style and the installation of the electric heating and air system.

*Submitted by Greene County Historical & Genealogical Society*

## Bell - Hale
*206 South Seventh Street*

An example of the bungalow style of carpenter craftsmanship, this home was built in 1906 by John B. Hale, a well-known merchant and cotton buyer and Sarah Hale. Mr. and Mrs. Tony Hale McDonald moved there in 1977 and remodeled it extensively. Present owners are Jim and Marty Bell.

*Submitted by Greene County Historical & Genealogical Society*

## J. D. Block
*827 West Kingshighway*

J. D. Block, a prominent Paragould attorney and banker, built this home, once located at 827 West Kingshighway, in 1904. Situated on a spacious estate bounded by Vine, Eighth and Ninth Streets, it was perhaps the most handsome home ever built in the city. The three-story, 14 room home was constructed off buff brick, with a slate roof and wooden columns.

In 1964 after the death of Block's daughter, Mildred Smith, the house was razed and replaced by a grocery store and parking lot. Bill Block, a grandson of J. D., also an insurance executive, built a modern brick home on the Vine Street side of the original estate. Mr. Block recently sold the house and lots to Arkansas Methodist Hospital. The hospital is expanding and buying property in the surrounding area.

*Submitted by Greene County Historical & Genealogical Society*

## Blossom - Mack
*611 West Main Street*

This home is classic Revival Style and was built by Winston Mack in 1920. Winston's father, Clyde Mack, founded the Clyde Mack Clothing store and his son, Winston, helped him operate the store. Clyde Mack also had a home on West Main. Tom and Diane Blossom, only the second owner of the property, purchased this home in 1978.

*Submitted by Greene County Historical & Genealogical Society*

## Branch - Wrape
*701 West Emerson Street*

Louis P. Wrape built this Georgian style home for himself and his new bride, Nora G. Wrape. They continued to own the property for 30 years and on April 24, 1941 sold it to Eugene Kirchoff. In 1950 Sol S. Steinberg and Hallie Steinberg purchased the home and occupied it until their deaths. Robert and Jo Ann Branch purchased the home on May 22, 1961. At the present time their son, Jeff and his wife, Sherry are the occupants.

*Submitted by Greene County Historical & Genealogical Society*

## J. Marion Futrell
*130 South Fourteenth Street*

The home of Junius Marion Futrell, who served two terms as governor of Arkansas 1932-1936. The home was built prior to 1908. Futrell died in Paragould in 1955. The home is now vacant and First National Bank owns the property.

*Submitted by Greene County Historical & Genealogical Society*

## Glenn - Skaggs
*801 West Emerson Street*

This home is Benedict style and was built in 1907. Past owners are the W. L. Skaggs' family and Ed and Alta Hamilton. Mrs. Skaggs was one of the pioneer women educators of Greene County. She taught in Greene County for more that 50 years. Her husband, W. L. Skaggs, was at one time superintendent of Paragould Schools. Present owner is Pauletta Glenn. There are still books from the first Greene County Library in this house.

*Submitted by Greene County Historical & Genealogical Society*

## Goodson - Atkins
*210 South Seventh Street*

This home was built in 1910 for the Olin Atkins' family. The architect was doing work at what is now Arkansas State University and drew up plans for this English Tudor house at the same time. In 1935 the house was remodeled. The home has had only three owners: the Atkins, Dwight Williams' family and at the present time is owned by David and Sharon Goodson.

*Submitted by Greene County Historical & Genealogical Society*

## Hammond
*313 West Highland*

The original address of this home when it was built was 412 West Depot, later changed to 313 West Highland Street. The home was built in the early 1900s by Frazier Hammond's father and has stayed in the family since that time. Frazier and Neva Hammond occupied the home for many years. Later their daughter, Martha Hammond Wade and her family lived in the home and her son, Glen Wade, now occupies it.

*Submitted by Greene County Historical & Genealogical Society*

## Harris - McKenzie
*706 West Court Street*

This house was built for Dr. J. G. McKenzie, who was born in Aberdeen, Scotland and received his medical education in that country. As a youth, he was given opportunity for extensive travel, having a brother who was chief engineer on a boat plying between Liverpool and New Orleans and an uncle who was captain of a vessel that made voyages to the Orient and around the Horn. He came to the United States, first stopping in Cotton Plant and then moved to Greene County.

His first wife was Cynthia Pevehouse from a pioneer family and he established a practice near Crowley and Walcott. He was appointed postmaster of Crowley in 1885. The date he built this house has never been established. Comparing the style of architecture with other homes in Paragould, about 1895 to 1900 is the date placed on the construction of this home. Mrs. Pauline Sheridan, Dr. McKenzie's stepdaughter, who had lived at the residence since 1932, previously occupied it. David and Janie Harris purchased the house in 1993.

*Submitted by Greene County Historical & Genealogical Society*

## Heath - Grizzard
*314 West Main Street*

This home was built by R. C. Grizzard in 1908 and was sold at public auction in April 1946. Mrs. Verlyn L. Heath, who is only the second owner, presently owns it. The front of the house was remodeled in 1960.

*Submitted by Greene County Historical & Genealogical Society*

## Heath - Mack
*617 West Main Street*

Clyde A. Mack, who founded Clyde Mack Mercantile Company, built this house in 1906. It is a blend of Queen Anne and Classical architectural style. It features leaded, prism windows in the three front rooms. Light fixtures, which were originally in the front hall, are now in the kitchen. Former owners are Dr. Jack and Shirley Richmond; current owners are the Butch and Jan Heath family.

*Submitted by Greene County Historical & Genealogical Society*

**Barry - Kitchens**
*508 West Court Street (formerly 444 West Court Street)*

**Bell - Hale**
*206 South Seventh Street*

**J. D. Block**
*827 West Kingshighway*

**Blossom - Mack**
*611 West Main Street*

**Branch - Wrape**
*701 West Emerson Street*

**J. Marion Futrell**
*130 South Fourteenth Street*

**Glenn - Skaggs**
*801 West Emerson Street*

**Goodson - Atkins**
*210 South Seventh Street*

**Hammond**
*313 West Highland*

**Harris - McKenzie**
*706 West Court Street*

**Heath - Grizzard**
*314 West Main Street*

**Heath - Mack**
*617 West Main Street*

## Higgins - Owens
*720 West Court Street*

The house was built about 1910, perhaps by W. R. Owens, on land owned by W. H. Ritter (cashier and trustee of Greene County Bank from 1892 until 1901). This Victorian bungalow was owned by Lewis and Clara Linke; Artie Houston Garner; Sam Lipscomb; Arthur Pillow and at the present time by Mr. and Mrs. Joe Higgins.

In 1929 the house was sold to the State of Arkansas for non-payment of taxes due (at this time it was owned by Lewis and Clara Linke). Clara Linke paid the back taxes ($88.66) and reclaimed the property in 1932.

*Submitted by Greene County Historical & Genealogical Society*

## Highfill - Knox
*416 West Main Street*

Alfred and Maggie Knox lived in this home at 416 West Main Street. Knox purchased this lot west of First Methodist Church in 1889, the year he married Maggie. Six years later, 1895, he borrowed $750.00 to build a home. Charles W. Highfill purchased the property from Knox in 1917 and today it is the home Paul and Lola Highfill.

*Submitted by Greene County Historical & Genealogical Society*

## Hoskins - Meriwether
*306 South Third Street*

An example of bungalow design, this two-story frame house features a slate roof and stained glass windows at the front entrance. It is most noted as one of three adjacent homes once belonging to the Meriwether family, prominent early landowners and hardware store owners in Greene County.

This house was built by Bill Greticher around 1908-1912 and was purchased in 1928 by Ray Meriwether. The house remained in his family until 1976, when Van Ray and Ruth Hawkins purchased it. The Richard Hoskins' family occupies the house at the present time.

*Submitted by Greene County Historical & Genealogical Society*

## Hughes - Little
*319 West Court Street*

W. S. Pruet, who later sold the land to C. Verbeyck, once owned the lot this home sits on. This is a two-story frame home, whose builder is not known. Previous owners were J. W. Crawford and Elwyn and Juanita Little. Mr. Little was county school supervisor and Mrs. Little taught school at Greene County Tech for many years. Joseph D. Hughes recently purchased the home for use as a law office.

*Submitted by Greene County Historical & Genealogical Society*

## Jackson - Herget
*206 South Fourth Street*

This home, built in 1890, was designed by Little Rock architect Thomas Harding for Richard Jackson and is a fine example of Queen Anne architecture. According to family legend, Jackson, a Gainesville merchant and timber man, would not allow framing with knots to be used in its construction. Phil and Mary Esther Herget are the third generation of the family to live there. Since 1977, they have painstakingly restored the house and have furnished it with family treasurers. This home was placed on the national register on July 23, 1992.

*Submitted by Greene County Historical & Genealogical Society*

## Kennett - Beisel - Mitchell
*420 West Court Street*

This home was proposed for National Register of Historic places by the Arkansas Historic Preservation Program's State review board on June 5, 1966.

Located at 420 West Court Street in Paragould, the two-story, partial basement, and wood frame structure was built in 1930 by E. N. Beisel, from St. Louis, MO, who had moved to Paragould to manage a wood-veneer mill. J. V. Landrum had owned the land and sold it to Dr. Hopkins. Mr. Beisel duplicated the Spanish Colonial Type home after traveling in the west and viewing this type home being built.

Stained glass windows are made from wine bottles. The living room wood-burning fireplace has brown ceramic tile imported from Mexico. The tile is imprinted with Mayan hieroglyphics that supposedly depict the gathering of grain.

The kitchen has been updated, but the upstairs bathrooms still have the original fixtures.

Other owners have been Cecil and Thelma Mitchell, their son, Robert, John and Patty Stage, Pat Boling and the present owners, John and Dot Kennett, who purchased the home in 1993.

*Submitted by Greene County Historical & Genealogical Society*

## Luter - McPherson
*631 West Main Street*

This unique home was built in the early 1930s. The original owners were thought to have been Harry J. and Cora McPherson. Mr. McPherson was Paragould's postmaster during this time and his wife was a teacher. Other owners have been Hank Broyles, Rex Ellington and the present owners, the Charles Luter family.

*Submitted by Greene County Historical & Genealogical Society*

## McClure - Highfill
*701 West Highland*

In 1937 Claude and Elizabeth Highfill purchased the Eakers property at the west end of Highland Street where it intersects North Seventh Street, not for the house or its land, but for the home site. Situated seven blocks west of the Greene County Courthouse, the location was on the fashionable outskirts of town. Claude had the Eakers' two-story house dismantled, saving much of the lumber for use in the construction of the large home he and Elizabeth built for their family. Their children were Martin, Melvin, Betty and J.C.

The Highfills' new home, an excellent example of Craftsman style architecture, was under construction for a year. Preacher Thomas was the contractor and he and his crew worked with NO power tools! Even the concrete in the basement was hand mixed and transported in a wheelbarrow. The pay was 50 cents a day! The total cost of construction was $15,000.

Each room is a complete wooden box: ceiling, floor and walls. Inside each "box" the interior walls, ceilings and floors were added. The exterior walls have five layers of building materials: bricks, wood sheeting, insulation, another wooden wall (forming the "box") and finally wallboard. The interior walls each have four layers. Much of the lumber used to build these "boxes" was from the original Eakers house.

Many of the home's original features have been preserved. These include newel posts (which were from the Eakers' house); a telephone nook built into a hall wall; mortise locks, escutcheons and glass doorknobs; mantel and floors-oak on the main floor and pine on the top floor.

Perhaps the most unique features of the home are Preacher Thomas' hand carved designs on the wallboards and ceiling throughout the house; his only tool was a small carving knife! Most of the wall enhancements are fairly simple, except for one room, the walls of which are carved in 19 arches. Most of the ceilings are simple; every ceiling, however, is different. Three of the elaborate ceilings and two of the more simple ones remain, as do the arched walls.

The house has about 5000 square feet. There are 50 windows and five exterior doors. On the two top floors, there are six bedrooms, three baths, living and dining rooms and a kitchen with breakfast room. In the full basement there is a second kitchen, library, family room, office, exercise room, craft room, laundry room, bath, shop, and furnace room. There are also both front and back porches.

In 1969, Gary and Marilyn McClure bought the Highfill home for $17,369.59. The McClures had three children, Leianne, Lucinda and Mike at the time they purchased the property and later a fourth child, Tim, was born.

In 1987, Marilyn McClure died. The three older children were all working out-of-state or away in college, so Gary and young son Tim rambled around the large old home alone together. Through the years, however, frequently visiting children and their growing families again filled the home with joy and laughter.

In 1997, Gary married Beverly Ann Newsom. She and her daughter Ruth and family have joined an ever-growing number of grandchildren in the McClure family and the lovely old home at Seventh and Highland is again filled with love and happiness.

## Morgan - Block
*612 West Main Street*

Architect, C. M. Jones built this home for M. F. Block in 1921. The house partially burned in 1936, but it was restored. Dr. O. E. Bradsher and the present owners, Dr. and Mrs. William Morgan, are the only other owners.

*Submitted by Greene County Historical & Genealogical Society*

**Higgins - Owens**
*720 West Court Street*

**Highfill - Knox**
*416 West Main Street*

**Hoskins - Meriwether**
*306 South Third Street*

**Hughes - Little**
*319 West Court Street*

**Jackson - Herget**
*206 South Fourth Street*

**Kennett - Beisel - Mitchell**
*420 West Court Street*

**Luter - McPherson**
*631 West Main Street*

**McClure - Highfill**
*701 West Highland*

**Morgan - Block**
*612 West Main Street*

**Nunn - Trice**
*302 West Highland*

**Owen - Merriwether**
*126 North Seventh Street*

**Philhours - Bertig**
*506 West Main Street*

## Nunn - Trice
*302 West Highland*

This home was built in the early 1900s for W. H. Trice, whose sons, Bill and Harlan Trice, were born there. The house was later used as upstairs and downstairs apartments, Bill occupying one and Harlan the other.

Second owner of the house was St. Mary's Catholic Church and it was used for the nuns' convent. At one time there were 10 nuns living there. Most were teachers at St. Mary's School, while others did the household chores. Present owners, Eugene and Tollie Sue Nunn, bought the house from the Catholic Church in 1977. They are currently adding an addition to the home.

*Submitted by Greene County Historical & Genealogical Society*

## Owen - Merriwether
*126 North Seventh Street*

Dr. Marcus L. Merriwether, who moved from Gainesville to Paragould about 1886 or 1887, originally built this house. He was one of the promoters and organizers of the city government. The house was built about 1888 – 1890.

A brick building still standing at the rear of the property was built first and used as a home while the main building was under construction. The building, which was later used as the doctor's office, includes a fireplace. Originally there was a separate building at the rear for a "summer kitchen". In the yard there are three enormous pine trees, which from their size and height are undoubtedly the oldest in the city and were probably original forest trees when Dr. Merriwether planned his home. There is also a rare fringe tree in the yard.

Mr. and Mrs. Alpha Owen and their family came to Paragould in 1913 and purchased the home in 1924. The property, now occupied by Dorothy Owen, has been in the Owen family since that time.

*Submitted by Greene County Historical & Genealogical Society*

## Philhours - Bertig
*506 West Main Street*

The Ad Bertig family built this house in 1876. They had two children, Jeanne and Joe. When Joe married, he and his wife, Elsa, made their home there. Only four families have occupied this house. Saul Bertig had an identical house on the lot to the west, which later burned. Behind the Joe Bertig house there was a small house where two maids from Switzerland lived. Mr. and Mrs. Randy Philhours own this home at the present time.

*Submitted by Greene County Historical & Genealogical Society*

## W. S. Pruet
*644 West Kingshighway*

This home was located at 644 West Kingshighway and was the oldest house in Paragould at the time it was dismantled. W. S. Pruet built the home in the 1860s on farmland he owned, which for many years after Paragould was incorporated was the boundary line of the city limits. The house was built at the location, which is now known as 627 West Garland Street.

The home was constructed of logs, which were later covered with wood siding and painted white. The main house was built separate from the kitchen, where meals were prepared and garden produce was processed. When the house was moved to Junction Street – now West Kingshighway – the upstairs was finished and a kitchen became part of the main house.

Mr. Pruet had planned to move the house up on the hill (which is the corner of Vine and Seventh Streets), but the movers claimed the equipment had broken down and the house was left at the location.

Mary Deakin Horton was born in the house when it was located in the Garland Street area. She and her parents moved into the house with her grandfather, W. S. Pruet, when she became school age.

*Submitted by Greene County Historical & Genealogical Society*

## Robbins - Kirsch
*213 West Garland Street*

This home was built in the early 1900s, probably by A. A. Robbins. William F. Kirsch purchased the home in 1930 and lived at the residence until his death in 1967. Kirsch's daughter, Mary Elizabeth Brenneisen of Hillsborough, CA still owns the property and it is being rented.

*Submitted by Greene County Historical & Genealogical Society*

## Stidham - Landrum
*500 West Court Street*

J. V. and Ella Landrum, grandparents of Winnie Bland, built this home in 1889. It is assumed to be the oldest standing residence in Paragould. This is because the original log cabin built by Willis Pruet in 1869 has been dismantled and is stored under a tarpaulin near the Branch, Thompson, Philhours and Warmath law firm.

In 1889 the house was described as "one of the finest residences in Paragould and Greene County".

In 1890 the Landrums sold the house to Dr. Calvin, a physician and banker. Dr. Mike and Lisa Jarman were owners when Dan and Kim Stidham traded a lot near the Paragould Country Club as part of the purchase price for the property. This house was involved in a similar trade more than a century ago between Landrum and Dr. Wall.

Other owners have been David and Beverly Fletcher, 1980-1990; Dr. Michael and Lisa Jarman, 1990-1994 and Dan and Kim Stidham, present owners, who purchased the home in 1994.

*Submitted by Greene County Historical & Genealogical Society*

## Taylor
*602 West Highland*

This home was probably built in the 1930s and at one time served as the Methodist Church district parsonage. Other owners have been Earl and Matilene Kirk, Charles and Donna Brazil and the present owner, Michael Taylor.

*Submitted by Greene County Historical & Genealogical Society*

## Washington – Owens
*400 West Poplar Street*

This classical Revival house built for Dr. W. R. Owens, features specially built doors, brass hardware, hardwood floors and a leak proof basement for coal storage. The large serving butler that was originally installed between the kitchen and dining room is now hanging in the kitchen. In 1913, the house was sold to James E. Wilbourn, founder of J. E. Wilbourn & Sons, wholesale grocers. The Wilbourns lived there 50 years. Past owners were Frank and Mary Pineda. Mary Ann Washington is the present owner.

*Submitted by Greene County Historical & Genealogical Society*

## White - Hays
*611 West Court Street*

Built in 1892 by A. B. Hays, the cyclone of Dec 1892 ripped off the east end of the house, blowing out everything in the parlor except the piano. Past occupants has been the Bob Gardner family and Charles and Fayetta Boggs. The home was sold to Dr. Robert White in 1999, whose wife plans to make it Paragould's first "Bed and Breakfast".

*Submitted by Greene County Historical & Genealogical Society*

## Young - Cox
*510 South Seventh Street*

This American Four Square style home was built in 1903. Dr. Rufus Markham, M.D. of Gainesville, had purchased the 10 acres that included this property. George Cox became owner in 1904. George was the son of Moses Cox of Gainesville, who was murdered by William Lindley with a bowie knife. George and Emma Cox are listed in the 1908 City Directory of Paragould as being in the hardware business and in 1920 as owning the Cox Land Company.

C. V. and Bertha Lloyd owned the house from 1934 to 1972, when Larry and Mary Lou Gist bought it. Present owners are Robert and Patricia Young, who purchased the home in 1984 and have completely restored it, using historically accurate materials. The house is known as "Gypsy Hill" because Gypsies camped on the land before its development.

*Submitted by Greene County Historical & Genealogical Society*

**W. S. Pruet**
*644 West Kingshighway*

**Robbins - Kirsch**
*213 West Garland Street*

**Stidham - Landrum**
*500 West Court Street*

**Taylor**
*602 West Highland*

**Washington – Owens**
*400 West Poplar Street*

**White - Hays**
*611 West Court Street*

**Young - Cox**
*510 South Seventh Street*

**J. D. Block**
*827 West Kingshighway*

# MEMORIALS

## Wiley Adams Jackson

Wiley Adams Jackson was born Nov 3, 1898 in Clinton, Hickman County, KY. He died July 1918 in France.

His parents were: Wiley E. Jackson, born 1870 – died March 26, 1906 in Clinton, KY. His mother was Mary Katherine "Mollie" Adams, born Feb 22, 1876, died March 17, 1953 in Amarillo, TX.

Wiley E. Jackson and Mollie Adams were married, Aug 11, 1892. They had the following children: Alta Beatrice, Wiley Adams and Dola Ann Jackson.

After the death of Wiley E. Jackson, the family moved to Greene County, AR. They settled first in the Halliday Community where Mollie Jackson's parents were living. Mollie's parents were J. C. Adams and Ann Mary Campbell Jackson.

The family later moved to Paragould where Mr. Adams operated a grocery store at 401 E. Lake Street. The 1920 Paragould City Directory shows Mollie Jackson living with her parents at 405 East Lake Street.

Some local residents said they remembered Adams Jackson working at his grandfather's grocery store when he was a young boy.

Adams Jackson was the first man from Greene County to die in WWI. He had been in France less than a week when his death occurred. At some unknown time his remains were moved to Arlington National Cemetery, Washington, D. C. There is a monument on the lawn of the Greene County Court House. A.O.U.W. Lodge placed this marker.

Information provided by: Richard Jackson Lawson, Enid, OK and Sue Benton Todd, Lubbock TX.

*Submitted by Shirley L. Moss*

*Adams Jackson is surrounded by his immediate family in this early photograph. Clockwise is his father Wiley E. Jackson, sister Alta Beatrice Jackson, mother Mary Catherine Adams Jackson and sister Dola Ann Jackson.*

*This stone marker notes that Adams Jackson was killed in battle at Soissons, France, on July 21, 1918. It was placed at the Greene County Courthouse by the AOUW-The Ancient Order of United Workmen – a local fraternal group.*

## George Taylor F. Johnson

**CIVIL WAR MEDAL OF HONOR HERO**

How did a United States naval hero of the Civil War come to spend his final years in Greene County and be buried at Paragould's Linwood Cemetery in 1893? For now, it's one of the mysteries of local history.

And that's only part of the mystery: His original Navy veteran's grave marker identifies him only as G. F. Johnson, born Nov 15, 1830, died Oct 7, 1893. But it was as George Taylor that he served as an armorer aboard the U.S.S. Lackawanna and was awarded the Medal of Honor for his actions during the Battle of Mobile Bay in Aug 1864. He single-handedly put out a fire that could have caused the ship's stored ammunition to explode. As a result, he suffered for the rest of his life from wounds he received that day.

That the G. F. Johnson in Linwood Cemetery and George Taylor, the Medal of Honor recipient, were the same person is verified by documents from the National Archives. Yet none of those documents explains the mystery. Nor do any answer the question asked by the Medal of Honor historian who first notified the Lipscomb Room about this heroic local connection: What middle name does the initial "F." stand for?

Buried beside G. F. Johnson is his wife of almost 40 years, Elizabeth W., who died April 10, 1895. Their son, George W. Johnson was listed as a merchant in the 1900 census of Greene County. He and his wife Nora had five children, but only one daughter survived. The daughter, Nettie Johnson Tansil, was listed with her parents and her son George E. Tansil in the 1910 census here. But no other trace of the family has yet been found in Greene County or elsewhere, although it is known that the daughter, Nettie Johnson Tansil Johnson Morrison Snetsinger, was living in Illinois when her father died there in 1940. George W. Johnson was brought back to Paragould to be buried in Linwood Cemetery with his wife Nora, who had died here in 1926 and a son who died in 1898. Their plot is not adjacent to the elder Johnsons.

A modern bronze military marker identifying George Taylor F. Johnson's Medal of Honor status was added to his gravesite in the 1990s through the efforts of GCHGS members Francis Bland, Paul Hampton and others.

*Submitted by Kitty Sloan*

*This modern bronze marker was placed at the foot of G. F. Johnson's grave in the 1990s, after GCHGS became aware of his Medal of Honor status.*

# William Fenton Kimbrough, Sr.

### Memorial To My Dad

William Fenton Kimbrough, Sr…"Bill"…Dad…"River Boat Bill"…Grandpa born Sept 9, 1918 on to the next fishing adventure Aug 17, 1999.

My dad lived almost 81 years and he lived those years HIS WAY. He taught me what was important in life and how to live life to its fullest. I, along with my wife, Rhonda and my kids, Bill 28, Marissa 17, Josh 14 and Daniel 11 had just started to learn all that he had to teach us. If we lived a million years we would not be able to repay him for all he taught us about life.

Bill married Nadine "Deano" Bishop in 1941 just after he joined the Coast Guard at the beginning of WWII. He was stationed at the Scituate, MA, where he became the second in command. At the end of WWII, Bill was torn between staying the New England or returning to Paragould where his mother lived. Because he felt a great responsibility to take care or his mother he did return to Paragould along with his wife and son, me, William Fenton Kimbrough Jr. Deano passed away in 1991 but Bill remained her husband until the day he passed away in August 1999 and this is something that is rare in today's world.

There are no words to explain the greatness of this man, his effect on me and others he knew. He taught me to fish, hunt, the joys of the outdoors and how to get along with people. As I get older the lessons I learned from him are only now starting to be clear to me. Everyone who knew him will miss him and no one will ever be able to replace him. He was one of a kind!

Bye Dad…I Miss You…We All Miss You…We will fish together again someday.

*Submitted by William Fenton Kimbrough, Jr.*

*William Fenton Kimbrough, Sr.*

# Leona Shepherd McGee

My grandmother, Leona Shepherd McGee was the daughter of Thomas Riley Shepherd and Mary M. I. "Belle" Meredith Shepherd and the wife of Eli Alonza McGee. Leona was born 1886 in the Fairview community of Paragould but moved to Harrisburg in 1903 and continued living in Harrisburg until her death in 1963. I was a little girl of 11 when my grandmother died. A gentleman by the name of Rhea Gardner attended visitation at the funeral home and told me he knew Leona when she was a young lady. He said she was the prettiest girl in Harrisburg! This picture taken before her 18th birthday in 1903 does prove that Leona was indeed a beautiful young lady. Not only was she pretty on the outside but the inside too, and a very lovely older woman as well.

In 1979 I had an oil painting made of Leona from this 1903 black and white photo and presented it to my father, Tommy McGee, for Christmas. It hangs proudly in my living room today.

*Submitted by Judy McGee*

*Leona Shepherd McGee*

## Mrs. Pearl Goins Morrow

The present Greene County Historical and Genealogical Society is indebted to the late Mrs. Pearl Morrow, who worked long and hard to see that the history of Greene County was not lost or forgotten. She walked the streets of Paragould to sell the quarterlies and attended the Marmaduke Fourth of July picnic each year to solicit members and sell publications. She was largely responsible for keeping the former Greene County Historical Society solvent. She was a great public relations' representative and spent many hours calling prospective members, collecting dues and generally keeping interest alive. The society was dear to her heart. She also contributed many articles for publications.

Mrs. Morrow was born in 1898 to William Preston and Lydia Elizabeth Goins, pioneer family of Greene County. She married Jeff Morrow on Sept 30, 1917 and they were the parents of eight children: Inez Morrow Clark, Janice Morrow Mock, Lewis Preston Morrow, Golvia Morrow Metheny, June Carolyn Morrow Rizzotto, John D'wight Morrow, Leah Katie Morrow Smith and Letha Faye Morrow, who died in infancy.

We, the Greene County Historical and Genealogical Society, would like to say thank you to members of Mrs. Morrow's family who continue to be members of the society and are carrying on their mother's work.

*Submitted by Greene County Historical & Genealogical Society*

*Mrs. Pearl Goins Morrow*

Rowe Family

*Family Histories*

**ACUFF** – Alfred Acuff was born in Paragould, AR on March 18, 1917, the son of Edward Otho and Ida Mae (Hall) Acuff. He died on Nov. 3, 1991 and was interred in Memorial Gardens Cemetery.

Alfred was first married to Edith Bird of Paragould. Two children, Myrna Lou Acuff and Nelson Wilson Acuff, were born out of the union. After what proved to be a stormy marriage, they were divorced.

On June 23, 1943, Alfred married Martha Ellen Edmiston, the daughter of Frank and Tennie (Lumley) Edmiston of Hickory Ridge, AR. When lightening killed Martha's father, her mother was not able to support the children. At about age nine, Martha and her siblings were sent to the Children's Home in Morrilton, AR. The home, supported by the church of Christ, provided care for the children until they were returned to the mother. Martha had reached the age of about 17 by this time.

*Alfred W. and Martha E. (Edmiston) Acuff.*

Alfred and Martha's marriage produced four children: Eddie Earl Acuff, who died in infancy, David Wilson Acuff, who married Elizabeth Eubanks, Marsha Diann Acuff, who married Frank Reddick and Deborah Lynn Acuff, who married Donald McDaniel.

Alfred was drafted into the army during WWII and trained as an anti-aircraft gunner at Fort Bliss, TX. Just before the assigned ship date to the Pacific Theater, Alfred broke his glasses. He was not able to deploy until he received his replacement glasses. New orders were cut and he was ordered to the Panama Canal Zone, where he spent the rest of his army tour.

After his discharge, Alfred returned to Paragould and went to work for the Missouri Pacific Railroad as a line crewman. He spent much of the time working out of the "Paragould Round House" and was later assigned to crew work in Monroe, LA. During the latter period, he greatly missed his family but would drive home to see them on weekends when he was able to. Alfred retired from the railroad after 28 years of service.

Martha was somewhat of a fixture around Paragould for quite some time. For many years, she worked as a salesclerk at the Belk Simpson store in the downtown area. Later, she worked for Woolworth's as a clerk. Forced to quit work because of health problems, she spent her remaining years as a housewife. Martha died on May 17, 1996 and was buried next to Alfred at Memorial Gardens.

Alfred and Martha were simple people who lived each day to the fullest. They were deeply religious and believed in strong family values. Alfred enjoyed fishing, camping and gardening, while Martha liked to shop, watch TV and listen to St. Louis Cardinals baseball on radio. Their children and grandchildren were the highlight of their lives and served as the focal point for their love. Alfred and Martha are truly missed.

*Submitted by David Acuff*

**ADAMS** – David Adams was born about 1797 to Thomas and Ann (Vaughn) Adams in what became Williamson County, Tennessee. His father died in the last quarter of 1799 leaving a widow and seven minor children.[1]

David's maternal grandfather, David Vaughn, who resided at Guiliford, North Carolina, during the American Revolution, assisted in establishing American Independence while acting in the capacity of patriot, "furnishing supplies and providing material aid."[2]

On September 11, 1816, David married Betsey Fielder. By 1830, possibly earlier, David and Betsey had moved to Lauderdale County, Alabama, at which time nine children under 15 years old were in the household.[3] David supported his burgeoning family as a miller on Bumpass Creek. Subsequent census records reflect that David and Betsey were the parents of at least 10 children:

James A., born 1821, married Martha P. Johnson.
Silvester, born 1825, married Martha Haine.
John H., born 1826, married Martha J. Price.
Reuben, born 1828, married first Sarah Lamb, second Melissa Emeline Earle and third Orlena B. Gatlin.
Elisha, born 1831, married first Melinda Caroline Scott, second Ettha Purvine, third Elizabeth C. Morrison and fourth Josephine Unknown.
Josephus, born 1832, married Martha W. Fowler.
Mary "Polly" Ann, born 1836, married John Caswell Price.
Betty Elizabeth, born 1838, married Bill Martin.
Isabella, born 1839, married William Price.
Nancy B., born 1842.

After Betsy's death around 1843, David married Vicie W. Haynes. That marriage produced five children:

Henry Jackson, born 1845, married Columbia Long.
Sarah "Sally," born 1846, married Joseph Franks.
David, born 1848, married first Coretha Jane Owen and second Nancy Cupp.
Daniel, born 1849, married Nancy Busby).
Tennessee "Tennie," born 1850, married first John Bettis, second William Cupp, and third William Nutt.

*Eight children of David, all of whom migrated to Green County, Alabama, starting shortly before 1860. The picture was taken before 1907 because Silvester (back row, far left) died in that year. Sill Vesta Adams, born April 1822; John Adams, born December 1826; Joseph Adams, born June 1828; Nancy Adams, born February 1842; Henry Adams, born June 1845; Sallie Adams, born November 1846; David Adams, born July 1848; and Tennie Adams, born June 1850.*

By 1860, Silvester (aka Sil Vesta), John, Reuben and Josephus (aka Joseph S.) were living in southern Greene County. By 1870 other siblings had arrived and sometime before 1880 David and Vicie joined their children and lived near Joseph(us) who, by that time, was found in Powell Township of Craighead County.

Of the 15 known children of David, 10 of them ultimately made their way to Northeast Arkansas, most settling in and around Lorado and Walcott. It is presumed that Betty died in Lauderdale County. James settled and flourished in Hardin County, Tennessee. Elisha went further west to Lamar County, Texas. Daniel went to Tishomingo County. Mississippi. Isabella has not been found after her marriage in 1856 to William Price.

Seven sons of David were of the age called upon to serve the Confederacy during the War between the States, and they proudly answered the call. Serving were: Silvester, John H., Josephus, Reuben, Elisha and Henry.[4] Henry served all four years in the 27th Ala. Infantry and saw considerable action. Elisha was a 2nd Lt. in the 27th Texas. Cavalry and was captured in 1863. Joseph enlisted in the 8th Arkansas Infantry Batt'n. Reuben and John were members of Kitchen's Arkansas Cavalry. Silvester served with the Missouri 8th Cavalry. It is believed that Silvester, Reuben and John participated in Price's raid into Missouri. Silvester's son, William Case, also served in the 8 Mo. Cav. James was also of the age to serve but his service records have not yet been found.

The offspring of those who migrated from Alabama to Greene County took spouses from neighboring families, some of whom were: Barfield, Bo(w)ling, Brown, Bryant, Cathey, Cooper, Cowen, Cupp, Daniel(s), Dillon, Dickson, Dixon, Edwards, Elder, Gatlin, Good, Hargrove, Horton, Johnson, Johnston, Kirby, McCullars, McDaniel, Mounce, Nelson, Nutt, Owen, Parham, Roberts, Ryan, Sims, Smith, Swindle, Trice, Weatherly and Wyatt.

Records reveal that most of these early Adamses enjoyed long, full lives. They were laid to rest in cemeteries near their homes along the Greene-Craighead county line, primarily Pleasant Hill, Mount Zion and Pine Log.[5]

[1] Tennessee Tidbits 1778-1914, Vol. 1, compiled by Marjorie Hood Fisher, 1986. Easley, SC:Southern Historical Press, Inc.

[2] Military Service Record #817, Revolutionary Army Accounts, Vols. 40-60, Book A (Vol 40), p. 259.

[3] 1830 Lauderdale County Census, page 216 (30), certified November 4, 1830 by John W. Byrn. Assistant to the Marshall, of the Northern District of Alabama.

[4] Confederate Service and Pension Records

[5] Cemetery records, S.S. Lipscomb Room, Greene County Library.

*Submitted by Debra Walker*

**ADAMS** – Guy Leroy Adams, born November 28,1880, married Sarah Viola "Ola" Trice, born August 23,1882; see Trice Family, on December 31, 1907. Guy Adams was the son of Jesse Adams and Mary Catherine Fulk Adams of Texas and Oklahoma. His siblings were Elmer, Nora, Jessie, and Paul Adams. Guy and Ola's, daughter, Elizabeth Jane, was born May 15, 1918, in Paragould. Guy Adams died February 12, 1964, and Ola Adams died February 1, 1969; both are buried in the Linwood Cemetery in Paragould. On April 24, 1945, Elizabeth Adams married Walter Lemuel Beall (born May 26, 1917 in Washington, D.C., the son of Arthur Beall and Lyndall Fallon Beall) in San Antonio, Texas, but they made their home in the Washington, D.C. area. Their three children were: John Walter, born December 16, 1945, Patricia Martha "Tiffy," born September 1, 1947, and Janet Lisabeth, born October 13, 1951. Walter Beall died December 1980 and is buried in suburban Washington, D.C. (Virginia). Elizabeth Adams remarried to Gerard McNiff, born December 17, 1917, on September 25, 1982, in Montgomery County,

Maryland, and died September 24, 1990. She is buried in the Gate of Heaven Cemetery in Montgomery County.

John Walter Beall married Marilyn Beal, born in Ohio on October 5, 1947, in Gaithersburg, Maryland, on July 29, 1989. His stepchildren by that marriage are Jay and Mary Beal. Tiffy Beall married James Monroe Pollock, born January of 1941 in Central Florida, in Rockville, Maryland, April of 1971, and their daughter, Janet Lynette Pollock, was born April 1, 1972, in Nashville, Tennessee. Tiffy and James divorced June 28, 1973, and Tiffy married William Allen Barnett, born June 4, 1951, in Lawrenceburg, Tennessee, on April 22, 1988, in Nashville, Tennessee. She and William Barnett divorced February 6, 1996.

**ADAMS** – Leo Nealon Adams was born July 1, 1925 in Opal, AR. a small rural area in the hill country between El Paso and Beebe, AR. He was the son of Orn and Emma Belle (Neal) Adams. His maternal grandparents were Afton and Sally (Anderson) Neal from Humboldt, TN. His great grandparents, Mr. and Mrs. John Neal, were from Kentucky. His paternal grandparents were Francis Marion and Nancy Belle (McCardle) Adams from Danville, IL.

Leo was the sixth of 12 children: Jessie Merle, Berle Noel, Nettie Lorene, Loyd Hazen, Marion Afton, Leo Nealon, Oren Lee, Horace Eugene, Bonnie Louise, Charles Dean, Rose Marie and Tulula Faye.

The Adams family was a close-knit, hard working family. In 1937 the family left the central part of Arkansas and moved to Monette, AR. in Craighead County. The children were loaded up in the back of a truck and moved to the L. D. Yates' farm place. Leo's dad was a sharecropper and his mother, Emma was a homemaker and the children worked on the farm. The children attended school at Monette Public Schools. In the mid 1940's the family moved to Leachville and worked on the farm for Hershel and Virgil Johnson.

*Leo Nealon Adams*

Hoeing and picking cotton was a way of life in rural Northeast Arkansas and so was playing basketball. The city of Leachville has long had a reputation as a "basketball town." The Adams' brothers were all gifted athletes. Leo's brothers and sisters spent many nights playing basketball in the school gymnasium.

At the age of 17, Leo and his friend, Floyd Cornish, joined the United States Navy. Leo piloted a P. T. boat during WWII. Following the war he returned home to Leachville and met Dorothy Sue Potter, a waitress at a local café. On Sept. 20, 1947, Leo and Dorothy were married. He attended G. I. School and worked for the city. A friend encouraged his interest in law enforcement. He served as a policeman in Manila, AR for two years and he served as Chief of Police and Constable in Leachville and Mississippi County deputy sheriff for 19 years. His wife, Dorothy, worked 12 years at Brown Shoe Company. Leo and Dorothy had three children: Phyllis (9-28-50), Terry (2-28-53) and Donna (4-10-54). In 1969 their oldest daughter, Phyllis DeLean Adams married Ronnie Lee McFarland and they established their home in Leachville. Ronnie and Phyllis have two children, Jennifer Lee and Blake Lee McFarland.

Leo and Dorothy and their two younger children moved to Paragould, AR. in 1970. A new company in Paragould, Monroe Equipment Company, offered employment opportunities for the family. Leo was employed at Monroe. He began working at Monroe during the final phases of construction before the plant actually began production. Leo worked in the maintenance department. He and wife, Dorothy were employed at Monroe for 22 years. The family lived in several residences before purchasing their home at 517 South Fifth Street. Leo's son, Terry Adams, married Gina Gramling. They had three sons: Chad, Jeff and Brad Adams. His daughter, Donna, married Glen Allen Brooks. Both families reside in Paragould.

At the age of 63, Leo was forced to retire due to serious health problems.

Leo Adams was an ordained deacon of the Second Baptist Church. His love of God, family and country was evident to everyone that met him. He was a giant of a man with a soft voice and gentle spirit. His spirit lives on in the hearts of family and friends. On Jan. 14, 1993, Leo Nealon Adams passed away at St. Bernards Regional Medical Center in Jonesboro, AR. Dorothy, his faithful and loving wife of 45 years was by his side.

*Submitted by Dorothy Adams*

**AINLEY** – Charles F. and Wyona Ainley moved to Paragould and Greene County March 1, 1957. Prior to the move, Charles served in the Merchant Marines in the U. S. Army during WWII, graduated from Memphis State University, worked as a chemist and graduated from the University of Tennessee School of Dentistry. After graduating from Arkansas State Teachers College, Wyona taught Home Economics and the sixth grade. Both Charles and Wyona graduated from Corning High School in 1944 and 1950, respectively.

Charles started his dental practice on Pruett Street and Wyona was a full time mother to their son, Alan, who was nine months old. Neal was born the following year on April 12, and Lauren joined the family on Jan. 25, 1960. Nine years later another daughter, Carol was born on Jan. 7th.

All four children were active in school, church, sports, scouting, music programs and other activities. Their parents supported all of their efforts. The older children graduated from Paragould High School and Carol was in the first graduating class of Ridgecrest High School.

*Dr. and Mrs. Charles F. Ainley's 25th Wedding Anniversary, June 16, 1979*

Alan graduated from Ouachita Baptist University and Baylor Dental School. He also studied as an exchange student in Japan for one year and had one year of study at the University of Tennessee. He started his dental practice in Paragould in 1984.

Neal attended the University of Arkansas and graduated from the University of Central Arkansas. He also has a degree from Southern Methodist University in Banking. He worked for the State of Arkansas as a bank examiner, was president of Perry County Bank and owns A. J.'s Convenience Store in Paragould.

Lauren attended Ouachita Baptist University and graduated from the University of Missouri. She obtained her master's degree from Vanderbilt University. She is an Environmental Engineer at the Corps of Engineers, having worked previously for the Environmental Protection Agency and the University of Tennessee.

Before graduating from Baylor University, Carol passed the certified public accountant examination and then worked for Ernst and Young Accounting Firm and Marketing Specialists. Additionally, she obtained a juris doctor from Southern Methodist University School of Law and is currently working in the area of corporate law.

Charles is a deacon at East Side Baptist Church where he teaches a men's Bible class and is a member of the sanctuary choir. He has been a member of the local Kiwanis Club since 1957, was the MO-AR District Award winner in 1965 and was given the George F. Hixson Fellow Award in 2000. He also belongs to the Paragould Area Chamber of Commerce and served as its president in 1976. He was district chairman of Osage District Boy Scouts and served as a board member of the Arkansas Baptist Child Care Services for 11 years. For 13 years, he was on the board of the Paragould Special School District. Governor Huckabee appointed Dr. Ainley to the Arkansas appraiser's board.

In Dr. Ainley's professional life, he served as president of the Northeast Arkansas District Dental Society, president of the Arkansas State Dental Society and is a member of the American College of Dentists, Pierre Fauchard Academy, International College of Dentists and the Federation Dentair International.

While caring for her family, Wyona was also active in volunteer work. She taught a Bible class, held positions in parent-teachers groups, had leadership roles in scouting, was co-chairman of the United Way Fund Drive and was a charter member and helped organize the Greene County Literacy Council. Starting in 1992 she was chairman for the election of Mike Huckabee in his campaign for U. S. Senate, Lieutenant Governor of Arkansas and the Governor of Arkansas. Mrs. Ainley was appointed to serve on the State Job Training Coordinating Council by Governor Huckabee.

After the children were grown she became an image consultant and reached the level of senior director in BeautiControl.

*Submitted by Wyona Ainley*

**ALLEN** – Dewayne Allen was born in Piggott, Arkansas, the son of Fred and Thelma (Toombs) Allen. He graduated from Piggott High School in 1956 and left to seek employment. On a hitchhiking trip back to Arkansas after applying for work in Rockford, Illinois, Dewayne was given a ride from Hayti, Missouri, to Piggott by Mr. MacDonald Pine, a contractor from Springfield, Illinois. At the conclusion of that short ride Mr. Pine offered Dewayne work in his seeding contracting company. The following Monday Dewayne was in Springfield working for Mr. Pine. After a years employment, Pine and Company arranged to send Dewayne to junior college and then on to the University of Illinois from which he graduated with a civil engineering degree in 1962.

In Springfield in 1961, through a blind date, Dewayne met Mary Ann Brass from Petersburg,

Illinois, and then a senior at MacMurray College in Jacksonville, Illinois. They were married in March 1962. After each graduated from college, Dewayne continued to work in construction with Pine and Company and Mary Ann taught high school English. In September 1963 their son Jay MacDonald was born. In 1965 Dewayne took a job with a highway paving company in Belleville, Illinois, and in 1964 he also started a ready-mix business in Piggott with a Piggott friend, Warner Hardin.

By 1968 there were three Allen ready-mix plants in Piggott, Corning and Paragould, Arkansas, and also a sand and gravel plant in Knob, Arkansas, so the family left their jobs in Illinois and moved to Piggott. Dewayne worked the Allen businesses and Mary Ann taught English at Piggott High School, Dewayne's alma mater.

By 1971 it was apparent that teaching and contracting seasons did not match so Mary Ann stopped teaching and began working in the Allen businesses. In 1973 tragedy struck when Dewayne's father, Fred, who also worked in the businesses, was killed in an accident at one of the Allen gravel pits. The trauma of that incident prompted the beginning of selling out the ready-mix and sand and gravel businesses. By 1976 Dewayne had a job in Houston and the family of three moved there.

*The third generation of the Allens include little Daniel and Jessica, children of Jay and Lesle Allen. From Jay in marketing and sales to John in customer service, the Allen name remains a working presence. Founders Dewayne and Mary Ann Allen complete the Allen family portrait.*

It was in Houston that Dewayne Allen became acquainted with the concept of a concrete finishing screed. By 1977 the Allen were back at the Paragould, Arkansas, ready-mix facility and making concrete screeds. This venture has grown into a manufacturing business that in 1999 employed 160 plus workers. Allen Engineering Corporation manufactured a complete line of concrete placing and finishing equipment and markets this line (through distributors) throughout the world.

In 1978 the family was blessed with the addition of John Dewayne, 15 years and 15 days younger than his brother Jay. Now 21 years later, all four Allens are active in the business.

Jay has expanded the family by marrying Lesle Chandler in 1993 and they are proud parents of Jessica, born in 1995, and Daniel, born in 1997. So the third generation of the J. Dewayne Allen family is now beginning.

**ALLRED** – Randy Allred and Eugene Allred, both lifelong residents of Greene County, are descendants of Calvin Allred, who was born in Blountville, AL. in 1837. Calvin joined the Confederate Army in Blount County, AL. when he was a 25-year-old single farmer. He was in the 48th Alabama volunteer infantry regiment. He was wounded in action in Jan. 1863. He took part in many of the major Civil War battles throughout Virginia and Georgia. He was discharged from service in 1865 and lived in Tennessee from 1865 until 1890. Calvin married Sarah Maxwell in 1868. In 1890, Calvin and his son, Jim traveled to the Cash River Bottoms in Lawrence County, AR. They decided to settle there to make a living and returned to Tennessee the following year for the rest of the family. Calvin farmed in this area during the years from 1890 until his death.

*Brothers Eugene and Randy Allred, descendants of Calvin Allred who first came to this area in the 1890s*

His son, Enoch Allred, was 13 years old at the time they moved to AR. Enoch married Atha George, the daughter of J. D. and Mary Amanda George and settled in Greene County.

Enoch also was a farmer and, for a while around 1910, he ran a country store in the Commissary community. His children were, Margie (Allred) Neiswonger, Mary (Allred) Johnson, Minnie (Allred) Shelton, Dick Allred, Jim Allred, Bonnie (Allred) Morrison and Edward Allred.

Jim Allred married Rellie Wheeler and raised their family in Greene County, near the Okean community. Their children were Margie (Allred) Varner, John Allred, Jerry Allred, Eugene Allred, Larry Allred, Randy Allred and Kathy (Allred).

A century passed before the next descendant (in the line of Enoch Allred) served their country in a time of war. Eugene Allred served in the Vietnam War from 1963-1969. He was wounded in action in 1967. The Greene County Tech High School honored Eugene for his valor and service to America by inducting him into the Veterans Hall of Fame. His picture hangs on the hallways of the high school. Eugene currently (2000) lives in the Walcott community with his wife, Glenda (Hall), who was raised around Fontaine and Light. Their children and grandchildren are: Emma (Allred) married to Boyce Cate and Edward Allred married to Deanna (Noles); Lowin Cate, Rebeckha Cate, Boyce Edward Cate, Katlyn Allred and Madison Allred.

Randy Allred and his wife Jannena (Cossey), a schoolteacher at Greene County Tech, also live at Walcott. Their children are Jim Allred and Julie (Allred) who is married to Jody Blankenship.

*Submitted by Jan Allred*

**ANDERSON** – Hardin Wallace Anderson (1868-1920) and Addie (Cole) Anderson (1872-1917) lived in the Gainesville, Arkansas area. The family worked in timber. One of the elderly cousins related this story of how living was during this time.

The girls of the family helped Addie do the family's cooking and laundry. They were taught very young - as early as four years old. They stood on old buckets or boards so they would be tall enough to reach objects to be able to help. Of course, everything was done by hand.

The boys of the family learned to help Hardin in the timber business. I do remember my Dad, Telfair Thomas Anderson (1901-1984) saying that he helped Grandpa Anderson in the logging business. The girls would stay home to help cook for all the workers. I specifically remember him telling of the hard freeze of the winter of 1917-1918. He said it started snowing, "freezing over" – in November, and didn't start thawing until April. The family took jobs away from home and at the time the men were able to move the logs, but the mules had

*H. W. "Sandy" and Addie Cole Anderson family photo, 1914. Front row: Telfair Thomas, H. W., Addie, Everett, Marrona, Jeff (hidden behind H. W.). Back row: Pearl and son, Lena, and Ruth Anderson.*

trouble standing up on Cache River The river was frozen so hard that it would hold up most of the loads.

*Submitted by Ruth Ann Smith*

**ANDERSON** – Joel C. Anderson was born September 19, 1826, in Benton County, Tennessee, the son of John and Elizabeth Anderson. Joel grew up with three other brothers: William Carroll, Isaac and Enoch; and four sisters: Catherine, Marian, Elizabeth and Seany. Joel was about 18 years old when he joined the other volunteers from Tennessee during the War with Mexico. He received five bullet wounds during his service and was discharged as a private in May 1845. He returned home and worked on his father's farm.

On October 19, 1854, Joel married Mary Ann Duncan, daughter of Charles Duncan in Benton County, Tennessee. Joel's brother, Isaac Anderson, was justice of the peace and performed the marriage. Mary Ann was born November 25, 1829, in Rockingham County, North Carolina. While liv-

*Joel C. and Mary Ann (Duncan) Anderson*

ing in Benton County, Tennessee, they had two children: Cordelia Antonette born October 29, 1855, and Washington Alonzo born November 4, 1857. The family moved to Greene County, Arkansas, about 1859 where Joel bought 80 acres of land to farm. He also set up a blacksmith trade. His third child, Eldorado Josephine, was born on February 16, 1860. Other relatives also followed Joel and Mary to Greene County (i.e, Robert Duncan, Enoch Anderson, Mariam and Catherine Swindle, Swift Anderson and his Landrum cousins).

With the outbreak of the Civil War, Joel was elected captain of a group of 100 volunteers from Greene County who were known as Captain Anderson's Company. They became a part of the 1st Regiment, 30 day Volunteers Arkansas Infantry. Joel served in other confederate units including Company L of the 6th Arkansas Infantry Regiment.

During the war Joseph E. Johnson Anderson was born on May 4, 1862. After the war three other children were born in the Clarke Township, John Harrison on September 24, 1865, Uratus Likergus on March 22, 1868, and Charles Layfaett on May 23, 1871. Joel served as elections judge in 1876 and 1878 for Clark Township. He also served as school director for District 12 for three years 1877-1880. Joel died on January 23, 1891. Mary Ann died April 16, 1908. Both are buried in the Fairview Cemetery, Paragould, Arkansas.

Washington Alonzo Anderson, the second child of Joel and Mary Ann Anderson, married Isabelle Tyner on June 5, 1882, in Paragould, Arkansas. Isabelle was born on December 22, 1864, in Carbondale, Illinois. She was one of five children of Lewis Washington Tyner and Nancy Jane Hastings. Wash and Nancy Jane's other children were: Alonzo "Lon," Oliver Perry, Jane, Joshua and Minnie Alice Tyner. Alonzo farmed in Greene County until 1896, then moved his family to Texas and settled in Buffalo Springs, Clay County. After Oklahoma became a state they moved into Jefferson County, Oklahoma, where Washington worked as a share cropper. Washington Alonzo and Isabelle had 16 children: Osmer Cicero, Lenard Bruce, Omer Paul, Benjamin Franklin, George Marcus, Forrest Likergus, John Fredrick, Maslin Dewitt (all born in Greene County, Arkansas) Willie Ray, Mary Alice, Ona Belle, Clara Barton, Washington Alonzo Jr., Charles Ray, Ruth Velma and Laurence Neil Anderson. Isabelle died on December 9, 1934, and 11 months later Washington Alonzo died on October 10, 1935, in Ringling, Oklahoma.

*Submitted by Gary Anderson*

**ARNOLD** – Hester Lucy Newsom, the daughter of Sterling and Nancy H. Newsom was born in 1843 in Tippah County, MS. Lucy, along with her three brothers and two sisters, would grow up on the family farm, located in the Finch community, Greene County, AR., after her parents settled there in 1855.

Lucy married Tillman A. Webb, circa 1861, after the death of his first wife, Margaret Rebecca. He entered the Confederate army in March 1862 and would die and is buried in Verona, MS, on Aug. 12 1862. On Nov. 7, 1862, Lucy gave birth to their only child, a daughter, she would name Tilman Ann Webb.

Being a widow at age 19, with a small child to raise, she married Robert A. Arnold, a highly decorated and seriously wounded southern soldier, upon his return from serving in the Confederate army. From this marriage she would give birth to their six children: S. Francis 1867; M. Catherine 1869; Robert Jr. 1871; Caldona 1873; Richard Walter 1875 and Alonzo "Lon" Price 1881.

In August 1872, Lucy along with husband, father and 10 other residents of the Finch community, mostly kinsfolk, organized a Baptist church, called The Pleasant Grove Missionary Baptist Church. The name of the church would later be changed to The Finch Baptist Church.

In 1882, Robert and Lucy received a Homestead Original Land Patent for 80 acres of land. The property is located approximately one mile due west of the Finch Baptist Church. Today, the homestead is still known as the Bob Arnold place by the "old timers" in the Finch community.

*Hester Lucy Newsom Webb Arnold; Walter, standing; baby (Lon); c. 1881.*

Around 1888 Robert and Lucy, with their family, moved to Lawrence County. AR and settled in the Richwood Township. There she would pass away around 1891. It is assumed she was buried in the Sanders Cemetery, located in Lawrence County, since Robert would be buried there circa 1913.

*Submitted by Daniel A. Hester.*

**ARNOLD** – Robert A. Arnold, the son of Absalom and Mary (Cobal) Arnold, was born in 1839 in Bedford County, TN. The Arnold family migrated to Arkansas in 1859 and settled near the Finch community.

With the coming of the Civil War, Robert enlisted in Company D, 5th Arkansas Infantry Regiment, Confederate States Army, at Old Greensboro on June 7, 1861. He would emerge four years later severely wounded and highly decorated.

During the Battle of Perryville, on Oct. 8, 1862, Robert received a gunshot wound to the mouth. The bullet ripped eight teeth from their sockets and tore off the end of his tongue.

On Dec. 31, 1862, during the Battle of Stones River, Robert was again wounded.

*Robert A Arnold*

This time he received a gunshot to his arm.

In the heated battle at Liberty Gap, on June 24, 1863, Robert was shot in the right temple. The resulting wound would affect his nerves, according to his veterans pension application filed many years later.

At bloody Chickamauga, on Sept. 23, 1863, Robert was wounded by a gunshot through the spine. The injury caused much weakness to his back later in life.

For his gallantry during the battle of Chickamauga, Robert was presented the highest military honor awarded a soldier by the Confederate States of America. His name was entered on the ROLL OF HONOR.

Again, during the battle of Kennesaw, in June 1864, Robert was struck in the left breast with a piece of bombshell. The exploding bombshell fractured two ribs, which later caused weakness of his heart.

In the battle of Atlanta, on July 21, 1864, during a heavy engagement with the Federals, Robert was lying in a ravine to escape the deadly cannon fire. It was during the bombardment when a lead projectile struck an overhanging tree branch, glanced off and struck him in the back of the head, rendering him unconscious. Being taken for dead, he was removed from the battlefield by the grave detail. As Robert was being lowered into the grave, a passing doctor stopped and examined him. To determine if Robert was still breathing, the doctor placed a mirror under Robert's nose. Robert's breath caused the mirror to fog up, which indicated he was still alive. The doctor saw he was not dead and proceeded to treat the wound by placing a silver dollar over the hole in the skull. Robert thereafter would say, " that he was always worth a dollar". The wound destroyed the hearing in his right ear.

Returning to Greene County, Robert married Hester Lucy Newsom Webb. Moving to Lawrence County, AR, circa 1893, Robert settled in the Richwood Township. There he would make his home and serve faithfully in the Richwood Baptist Church as superintendent and labor as a Star Route mail carrier to supplement his veterans pension.

Robert died around 1913. He was buried in Sanders Cemetery in Lawrence County, AR.

*Submitted by Daniel A. Hester*

**ATKINS** – Olin McCord Atkins was born on May 25, 1892, in Crossland, KY, "on the Tennessee side", a border town. His parents were Andrew Lee Atkins, who had come from Henry County, TN and Sarah Captola Province Atkins, a music teacher and a native of McKenzie in Carroll County. They were married in 1881.

Olin's grandfather, William James Atkins, was born in North Carolina in 1816 of parents born in that state. Tradition has it that he made several trips on horseback to Kentucky and Tennessee and finally settled in Henry County, TN during the 1840s. William James held the title of "Squire" which indicated that he was a local judge or justice of the peace. He traveled on horseback from his home to the county seat in Paris to conduct business. He died in 1902 at age 86, when Olin was 10 years old.

Olin's father, Andrew Lee, had a tobacco business and worked for his cousin, Columbus Atkins, in a Crossland store. The family later moved to Henry County where Andrew operated a tobacco farm. Andrew and his wife were members of the Cumberland Presbyterian Church. Olin, the first of five brothers, was born in the 1890s: Olin, Wendell, Euel, Andrew and Thomas. In 1900 the father's health began to fail and he took Olin on a trip to Colorado for the benefits of "mountain air" and later on an excursion train to Florida, the warm climate making an impression on him for life. The father and youngest brother died the next year when Olin was nine years old. The family moved to land formerly owned by his mother's family, the Province farm, near McKenzie, TN, where the boys grew up.

Many humorous tales are told about the four brothers and their escapades, including staging their own "circuses". They rode horseback and attended a nearby country school. For Olin, a lifelong belief in education began.

At the age of 16 Olin began working at a general store in McKenzie, later joined by his brother, Wendell.

*Olin and Ethel Myrick Atkins after his retrun from World War I, 1919, in McKenzie, Tennessee.*

Part of their job was to unload flour and tobacco barrels from railroad cars and serve as night watchmen, sleeping in a storeroom in the rear of the building armed with a revolver.

Olin was later employed at the Reynolds' department store in Henry, TN, one of a small chain, where he worked for several years. Here he met his future wife, Ethel Eva Myrick, a piano teacher and church organist. They were married on May 31, 1917 at the Methodist church in Martin, TN. Soon after the marriage he was inducted into the army, stationed in North Carolina, where scores of soldiers died during the devastating influenza epidemic that winter. He was later sent to France with a New

Jersey regiment and served until the armistice in 1918.

Ethel Eva Myrick was born Oct. 14, 1890, the last of five children born to Samuel Thomas Myrick and Mary Margaret Hooper Myrick in Martin, TN. After his first wife's death her father married Grace Hunt, who was commonly known as "Mama Grey". They lived in a two-story frame home at 403 McGill Street on the outskirts of the city.

A large tobacco barn for drying and an orchard were situated behind the house, along with other service buildings.

Father Myrick was a tobacco farmer and a devout Methodist, descended from generations of Methodists with roots in northern Wales. An ancestral "Meyrick" home still exists there, named "Bodogan Hall", in Anglesley Isle,

*O. M. Atkins in the 1960's. Photograph by Child Art Studios from a group taken of First National Bank board of directors.*

North Wales, continuously occupied by a member of the Myrick family for over a 1000 years. Tobacco was raised on land some distance from the home. Ethel studied music at McFerrin College in Martin.

*210 South Seventh Street, home of Mr. and Mrs. O.M. Atkins, completed in 1936, where they resided for fifty years. Pen and ink drawing by artist Ralana Forbis in 1982. Judge and Mrs. David Goodson and family currently reside in this home.*

During the 1920s O. M., as he became to be known, joined the Stovall chain of department stores in Mayfield, KY. Mr. T. J. Stovall, the founder, became a father figure to him and was to be his friend and benefactor for life. Throughout the 1920s and 30s depression years, O. M., together with Stovall's son, Roy, bought, operated and sold retail business inventories in Kentucky, Missouri, Arkansas, Texas, Arizona and California. It was also during these years that the Atkins received information from a St. Louis wholesale firm, the Diamond Feinstein Company, regarding the offering for sale of a major retail business in Paragould, the S. L. Joseph Company. The following year he accepted the offer and the Atkins family moved to Paragould. In 1936 a two-story brick home was built at 210 South 7th Street, designed by Little Rock architect A. N. McAninch and occupied by the family for almost 50 years. Joseph's store was owned and operated by O. M. Atkins for the next 15 years, leading up to and during WWII. In the late 1930s, after the death of S. L. Joseph's widow in Germany, O. M. purchased a group of Joseph properties at an auction held on the Greene County courthouse lawn, which included the building, which housed the department store. In the mid 1940s he leased the building to the Butler Brothers department store chain of Chicago, IL and later to the Belk Corporation based in Charlotte, N. C.

During the following 20 years he was engaged in commercial construction and real estate development. He also co-founded Van-Atkins department store chain with former associate Earl Van-Hook who had returned from service in WWII.

O. M. served 37 years on the board of directors of the former National Bank of Commerce and the current First National Bank of Paragould and was a member and former chairman of the City Light Plant Commission from 1942-1953. He was a long-time member of First United Methodist Church, Paragould Rotary club, Paragould Chamber of Commerce and the Greene County Industrial Development Commission.

Among the local civic and philanthropic causes supported by Mr. and Mrs. Atkins was a college scholarship program founded in their name in the 1940s and administered by the National Honor Society at Paragould High School. In 1962 the first publicly owned library building was purchased on East Emerson Street in Paragould with gifts from Mr. and Mrs. Atkins, Mrs. Jean Bertig Kempner and Mrs. W. F. Kirsch, with addition of a bequest from the Adrian Coleman estate.

Ethel Myrick Atkins was a devout and lifelong member of the Methodist Church and a lover of music. For years she was a member of the Dorian Music Club, which sponsored visiting artists and music education, the Paragould Garden Club and the Fortnightly Club. She was known to nurture as her own, all children with whom she came in contact.

For O. M. Atkins the state of Florida, which he loved as a boy, remained his favorite destination during the winter months and he and his wife made annual visits to the warmer climate. For as long as he lived, these always included stops in Tampa to visit his benefactor, Mr. Stovall, who had retired there.

The Atkins' family continued to live at their home on South 7th Street until Ethel died in 1974 and Olin, in 1982, at the age of 90 years. They were survived by their son, Robert Myrick Atkins of Gainesville, FL and two daughters, Mrs. Sara Grey Moseley Batesville AR and Mrs. Mary Ann Schreit who resides with her husband, Frank Joseph Schreit Jr. on Pruett's Chapel Road in Paragould.

They are also survived by nine grandchildren: Mary Ann Moseley Critz of Little Rock; Helen Susan Moseley Farris of Batesville; John Presnell Atkins and Robert Olin Atkins, both of Gainesville, FL; Margaret Ainsley Atkins of Marietta, GA; Eva Myrick Schreit Blackshear of Springfield, MO; Sara Grey Schreit Morgan of Conway; Anna Province Schreit Smith of Jonesboro and Frank Joseph Schreit III who lives at Winston Place in Paragould.

**BAILEY** – A Cantwell family, on their way to Kansas from South Carolina, stopped on the Mock Farm at Old New Hope near Warm Springs, AR. where the father, DeWitt Cantwell, died. The family made Warm Springs their home.

The Bailey family had been at Warm Springs from 1800. Moses Bailey had two sons, Isaac and Elijah. Elijah chose Sarah Cantwell for his wife. Their children were DeWitt, Dona, Icy, Ollie Si and Fannie.

DeWitt married Rhoda Whittenberg, daughter of Isaac and Nancy Whittenberg. Rhoda had a son, Clarence. They raised their six children at Warm Springs. As the children grew older, they moved to give the children a better education. They lived at Shannon, Elnora and Richmond communities before moving to Light.

They cut trees and built a home on the forty acres two miles northwest of Light, AR. The oldest daughter, Erma, had gone to MI. Her daughter is Jacqueline Fairchild.

Claud married Irene Spikes. They lived with his dad and near the Pumpkin Center with son Cloyce and daughter Brenda.

Claud moved his family to Michigan and worked at Buick Motors until he retired. Jewell became a nurse. She got a job as health nurse of Fulton County. She married O. A. Wood of Salem.

*Grandpa DeWitt Bailey and Grannie Rhoda Bailey in front of home, 1953.*

Notra went to Michigan to visit Erma. Erma had married John Bingham. Notra married his cousin, Edgar Bingham. They had three children when they came back to Light to live, where they had three more children. Their children are Bill, Norma, Eva, Burl, John and Walter. Eva died of diphtheria.

Notra and Edgar sold their farm and bought a farm at Griffithville. They spent the rest of their lives there. Cloyd married Helen Allen. They lived near Pumpkin Center. Their children are Cleatus, Harold, Corene, Elaine and Evely. Cloyd and Helen moved to Walnut Ridge, AR.

Earl married Nelsie Miller; their children are J. D., Carl, Boyd, Patricia, William, Jerry, Beverly and Marilyn. They lived with DeWitt and Rhoda a couple of years before buying their own place. They were married 59 years. Nelsie died of a stroke. Earl was killed in an automobile accident three years later, on Feb. 14, 2000.

*Submitted by Mrs. Pat Myrick*

**BAILEY** – Earl Bailey helped build Pruett Freewill Baptist Church, West Light Church of Christ and many houses. When electricity came to western Greene County, Earl was busy wiring houses so people could have electric lights. Earl worked at the D. D. Kennemore Gin. He also worked for the Weight Division at Hoxie, AR.

In 1955 Earl built a three-bedroom home for his family. He purchased Bailey Lumber Company and worked there until retirement. Earl and his wife, Nelsie, had eight children.

J. D. choked to death on a bean at 18 months old. Carl married Margie Galbreath. They have three children. Jeanne married Stan Mize. Emanual married Judy Jones. Lisa married Jeff Fry. The three grandchildren are Michael, Brandi Mize and Carleton Bailey.

Boyd married Peggy White. They have four children. Angie married Junior Hancock. Keith and Jimmy live in IL. Jimmy is married to Lisa Drake. Lance married Debbie White and their daughters are Casey and Taylor. Angie and Junior have Sami Jo and Jodi Rae. "Pat" married Tommy Myrick. They lived and farmed at Fontaine two years. They moved to the Stanford

Community where they have farmed 40 years. Their children are Tim, Dan, Latricia and Karrie.

Tim and Kim have one son, Todd Lashley Myrick. Dan and Tonya (Smith) had three children: Andrew, Aaron and Anna. Anna was stillborn.

Latricia has three daughters, Lexi Jordan, Ashlie and Alison. Alison is married to Thomas Wortham. He has two children, Ryan and Brittany, by a former marriage.

*Earl and Nelsie Bailey, Carl, Boyd, Patricia "Pat", William "Billy", Jerry, Beverly, and Marilyn.*

Karrie is married to Tim Clark. Their son is Patrick Garrett. Tim has a son, Logan.

William "Billy" married Patricia Kemp. Their children are Marlin, Linda and Greg. Marlin married Liz Breckenridge and they have three sons: Brandon, Justin and Dakota. Linda married Michael Westhouse. They have two daughters, Bailey and Madison. Greg and Crystal have no children.

Jerry was drafted into the army and served in Vietnam. He married Connie Tillman and their daughters are Dee Dee and Cherie. Beverly married Bobby Tedder. Their children are Bobby Jr. and Beth. Bobby married Kathy Kueter. Beth married Jason Gosha. Breanna and Brittany are the granddaughters.

Marilyn married Gerald Nathan Crafton and their children are Tony and Tonya. Tony married Shelly Rogers. Tonya married Brian Held and has two children, Sabrina and Nathaneal.

Carl, Boyd, Pat and Billy walked to Pruett School, which consolidated with Stanford in 1951. All of Earl and Nelsie's children graduated from Stanford High School.

*Submitted by Mrs. Pat Myrick*

**BALLARD** – They have been referred to as the Intrepid Ballards. These Ballards of Greene County, Arkansas, are descendants of the first 13 families that settled and established a place known as Fancy Farm, Kentucky. Eugene "Virgie" Ballard arrived in Greene County around 1918 with his wife and 10 children. Virgie supported his family by working for the Wrape Heading Mill, making the tops and bottoms for the "tight" barrel, usually referred to as a whiskey barrel.

*"Virgie" family picture: Virgie and Ollie Pearl with Linna, Gertrude, Imma, Dora, Carl, Troy and Ruby.*

They continued the practice of their faith at St. Mary's Catholic Church under the direction of Monsignor Hofflinger, which has a history in itself, as documented by TV crews from Little Rock upon the death of Monsignor Hofflinger.

Eugene "Virgie" Ballard is grandson of Stephen Bland Ballard and son of William "Proctor" Ballard. Virgie married Ollie Pearl Goins daughter of Andrew Goins and Winnie Richardson. Of this union were born 11 children:

Mary Gertrude born September 22, 1891; married Thomas Norval Grogan, a watch maker, and they had three children: Agnes, Thomas Woodrow and Melvin.

Augusta Imma born August 9, 1893, married Sylvester Layton. They had six children: Dora Maude born August 2, 1895, married Clarence Henry McCarroll and produced six children.

Anna Olinna, born October 4, 1897, married Herbert Williams on March 2, 1918, and they had five children.

Carl William, born February 2, 1900. Carl worked for Wrape Heading Mill and the Eli Shirt Factory in Paragould, Arkansas. Carl is best remembered for his prize winning flower gardens. On January 11, 1927, he married Susie Margaret Pierceall, daughter of William Roy Pierceall and Mattie K. Ivie. Carl and Susie had three daughters: Rosemary, born October 17, 1918; Betty Ann, born April 15, 1932, died June 16, 1945; and Sue Carolyn born May 19, 1937.

*Carl Ballard with wife Susie and daughters, Rosemary, Betty Ann and Sue Carolyn.*

James Osie born June 20, 1903, died September 14, 1904.

Joseph Troy born June 20, 1905, died February 3, 1983.

Agnes Ruby born March 7, 1907, married Joseph Downs. They had two sons: Joseph and Jimmy.

Frances Olivia born January 20, 1911, married Sylvester Eastman. They had two sons: Richard Eugene and Charles Robert.

Hazel Arnellia, born March 19, 1914, died October 10, 1917.

Alvin "Leo" born January 9, 1917. Leo built crystal radios, using empty cigar boxes, for his mom and dad and his brother Carl's family. It was the first radio they had and were totally amazed by the sound it produced.

After serving in World War II he returned to Paragould and became known for his expertise in painting and wallpaper hanging. Leo married first, Venia Mae Jones daughter of Henry Jones and Mary Gray in 1937. They had two daughters: Betty Jean, born December 18, 1938; and Shirley Ann, born January 20, 1941. His second marriage was to Pauline Crowell. To this union four children were born: Brenda Kay, born May 8, 1949; Glenda Fay, born June 2, 1950; Alvin

*Alvin "Leo" Ballard with wife Venia Mae and daughters Betty Jean and Shirley Ann.*

Leo Jr., born June 8, 1952; and Sherry Sue, born May 20, 1958. All of Virgie's children are gone now with only the grandchildren and great-grandchildren to carry on along with all the cousins.

*Submitted by Betty Haley*

**BANDY** – A. L. (Ayers, Adolpheus?) was born Nov 1834 in North Carolina, married Susan M. Pruet, born 1841 in Tennessee, daughter of Willis S. Pruet Sr. and Mary E. "Polly" Williams Pruet.

A. L. and Susan Bandy came to Greene County before 1860, probably from Roane County, TN as Susan's parents are there on 1850 Federal Census. Susan (Pruet) Bandy died July of 1870 and A. L. remarried to Nancy (unknown), born 1836 in North Carolina.

Susan and A. L. Bandy had four known children:
1. M. A. F. "Mollie" Bandy (1858)
2. Adolpheus (1860) married April 20, 1879 to Ella C. Pulley (Adolpheus was listed as D. L.).
3. Charles N. Bandy, born Aug 16, 1862 married Nov. 9, 1881 to Jennie McElwee, born Feb 1, 1865, daughter of Samuel S. and Hannah Holden McElwee. Jennie McElwee Bandy died Dec 24, 1901 and Charles N. Bandy died Aug 1, 1883. Had at least one daughter, Bertie Bandy, born April 1, 1883, died June 28, 1962, who married J. C. Shelby.
4. Pinky L. Bandy born 1865, died Dec 11, 1906 married Aug. 17, 1884 to Ida M. Paul.

Believe that F. B. Bandy, born about 1838, North Carolina, was a brother to A. L. Bandy.

**BARGER** – Oscar Schuffle Barger, born of immigrant parents who came down the Ohio River in the late 19th century into the Paducah, Kentucky, area and settled. Oscars' parents crossed the river into Illinois settling in Eddyville, Polk County, Illinois. There Oscar met and married Nora Gossage, daughter of a Union Civil War veteran Henry Gossage. Nora was also a member of the Daughters of the American Revolution.

The young couple moved to Greene County and were parents of Vera Schuffle Barger, Ray Schuffle Barger, Clifford Schuffle Barger, Harold Schuffle Barger and Donald Schuffle Barger.

Oscar moved his family to the thriving community of Coffman in eastern Greene County. He and other members of his family were charter members of Robbs Chapel Church, a Southern Baptist membership.

*Oscar Schufle Barger family, from left: Harold S. Barger, Donald S. Barger, Ray S. Barger, Nora S. Barger, Clifford S. Barger (in back), Vera S. Barger and Oscar S. Barger.*

While living in Coffman Vera married Charles Herbert Monteith in 1916. It was Herbert Monteith and D. J. Cunningham who crisscrossed Greene County convincing their neighbors to give easements across their land so that rural Greene County could have electricity. It was accomplished in 1930 when Craighead Electric Coop-

145

erative became a reality. Both men served on the Cooperative Board of Directors as long as they lived.

Herbert Monteith, Roy Dyer, Raymond Frey, Jim Eubanks, Tom Hill Sr. and B. D. Bone worked to form a Farmers Cooperative for better marketing and better purchasing of agricultural needs. They also participated in a managerial capacity of the Coop.

Oscar Schuffle Barger then moved his family into Paragould where he worked at Wrapes' Heading Mill. He moved amidst neighbors of the Reynolds family, the Blands, the Havens, the De Bons and the Kimbroughs.

The children attended High School in Paragould. Ray S. Barger graduated from high school and studied as an electronic engineer. During World War II he was cleared by a security check in order to work with Dr. Werner Von Braun. During the 1960s he worked out of Tinker Air Field in Oklahoma City to dismantle the minute man missiles that were stored in sites on our south eastern coast.

Clifford S. Barger followed a chautauqua trail performing with monologues and dramatic pieces.

Harold S. Barger joined Graver Tank Company in Chicago, Illinois. He built several oil tanks throughout the United States, Europe and New Zealand. He also designed the geodesic bird building for Anheuser Busch theme park in Tampa Florida.

Donald S. Barger became a C. L. U. with New York Life Insurance company. He was also a Spanish interpreter for Railway Express in Miami, Florida.

The Oscar Schuffle Barger family was a part of Greene County in the early years of the 20th century but we cannot mention one without another of the citizens of this county for they are all woven into the warp and woof that makes the human tapestry of our country.

**BARNHILL** – Adah Josephine Barnhill was born in Tennessee in 1857 to Caswell Hall Barnhill, born March 23, 1828, in Blount County, Tennessee, and Sarah Jane McDonough, born January 31, 1836, in Knox or Blount County, Tennessee. They married January 12, 1853, in Knoxville, Knox County, Tennessee. They had George Houston and Adah Josephine in Tennessee and Arminta Elizabeth, Leah A. and Sarah Jane "Sally" in Greene County, Arkansas. She died November 21, 1868, the day after "Sally" was born, in Greene County and is buried in Pruett Chapel Cemetery.

Caswell Hall Barnhill then married Epsy Jane Jones. Born to them: Epsy Arkansas, William Caswell, Jonathan C., David King and Joseph Hall. He died July 2, 1879, and is buried in Pruett Chapel Cemetery.

In 1873 Adah Josephine married James Thomas Hicks (1851-1882)

*Caswell Hall Barnhill, father of Adah Josephine Barnhill.*

in Arkansas. To this union was born Mary Lavena (1875-1908); Charles Ezra (1877-1880); and Sarah Louisa (1880-1974).

In 1889 Adah Josephine married Pleasant Green Light (1831-1889) in Greene County, Arkansas. Their children were: Wake Orville (1884-1963); Dewitt (1886-1886); Willie Izora (1887-1889); Addie Lee (1889-1922); Tennessee D. "Tennie" (1889-1973) twins.

In 1892 she married Zackaris Taylor Anderson of Alabama (1850-1910). Born to them were: Robert Edgar (1893-?); Susie Audrey (1895-?); Ella Blanch (1901-1961).

Adah Josephine died December 14, 1911, and is buried at Walcott, Arkansas. Thomas William Rickey and a brother Charles Louis came from Ohio to near O'Kean to visit a sister Lizzie Jane "Jennie" and George Erwin. After some time, they both married here; Charles Louis Rickey to Edie Elizabeth Connelly on January 1, 1889, and Thomas William Rickey to Mary Lavena Hicks on November 20, 1899, in Greene County. George and "Jennie" returned to Ohio.

"Tom Will" and Mary had a daughter Odessa Gustava born October 15, 1900. He became ill with cancer and returned to his parents in Scioto County, Ohio, where he died December 22, 1901. Mary and Odessa returned to her mother near O'Kean where daughter Willie Felicia Rickey was born June 21, 1902. Odessa died that year.

Mary did housekeeping in other homes to support herself and baby. She later married John Rummel (born in Germany). They had Josephine Prudence born December 21, 1904. He left while Josephine was still a baby. Mary died from measles and pneumonia February 4, 1908. Willie was reared by Charles and Edie Rickey; Josephine by Ira and Louisa Hicks Gray. Willie reminded her children that she was born on longest day of the year and Josephine on shortest day.

Willie married William Edward Heral on September 21, 1925. They had Wanda Louise (1926-1983); Viola Maxine (1927-); Albert Ray (1928-); Cecil James (1930-1987); Rose Mary (1931-); Alice Lillian (1933-); Arthur Glen (1934-). The first three were born in Greene County and last four in Lawrence County. Of the surviving five children, all but Glen live in same or adjoining county of their birth. Willie died December 31, 1958, of cancer as did Wanda in 1983, both age 56. W. E. died October 16, 1970.

*Submitted by Bill and Mary Hibbard*

**BARNHILL** – Caswell Hall Barnhill came to Greene County, AR from Blount County, TN in 1859. His wife, Sara Jane McDonaugh and two children came with him to St. Francis Township. C. H. acquired several acres and started a farm. He also was a timber and timberland trader and built wagons in the community.

At the outbreak of the Civil War, C. H. traveled to Pocahontas to enlist in Co. H. of the 5th Arkansas Infantry. He fought in several battles, including Chickamauga, GA and Corinth, MS before being captured at Paint Rock, AL and sent to a federal prison camp at Louisville, KY. While in the camp, C. H. was given the option of spending the rest of the war in prison or "galvanizing" and going west to fight Indians for the Union. He chose to go west and was given a bounty of $60.00 and a blue uniform. He was mustered in to Co. B, Independent Battery C, 1st Kentucky Light Artillery. On one muster roll, C. H. was listed as killed in action at Little Rock, AR. Whether he became lost or jumped the train, C. H. wound up back in Greene County where he bought a horse and joined Co. E., Davies Battalion, Arkansas Cavalry. He was apparently captured again at Mound City, Kansas and sent to a prison camp at Rock Island, IL. Major General G. M. Dodge paroled him on May 25, 1865 in Wittsburg, AR.

In 1868, his wife, Sara Jane, died leaving five children, George Houston (1855), Ada Josephine (1857), Elizabeth Armentia (1861), Leah A. (1866) and Sara Jane (1868) for C. H. to raise. Sometime in 1869, C. H. married a young lady named Mary Jane Jones, daughter of Jonathon Shelby Jones and Bethany Williams Jones of Bibb Co. Alabama. They had five more children together: Epsey Arkansas (1870), William Caswell (1872), Jonathon C. (1875), Henry O. (1876) and David King (1877) and one on the way when C. H. died on July 2, 1879. Joseph Hall Barnhill was born Feb. 5, 1880. On July 10, 1884, Mary Jane married L. G. Latimer. There were no children from this marriage.

J. H. taught school for a few years in the community before returning to farming. He and his wife, Virgie Ida Mae Spence, were married on March 12, 1905 and had nine children:
1. Clarence Franklin (1906)
2. Bertie Mae (1908)
3. Olive Marie (1911) the sole survivor of a set of twins
4. Woodrow Franklin (1913)
5. Thomas Charles (1915)
6. Mabel (1917) the only survivor of a set of triplets, Mabel lived only 30 days.
7. Joseph Leonard (1919).

J. H. had 160 acres off what is now Pekin Road or Arkansas Highway 69. He and other members of the family helped blast stumps to make the road passable. The family sold produce, peaches, sorghum, eggs and hay. They would take the peaches to Missouri and sell door to door. They were also traded for bananas at the farmers markets. Joseph Hall Barnhill died on April 6, 1970 and is buried at Browns Chapel Cemetery in Paragould, AR.

*Submitted by Tony Barnhill Gerdes*

**BARNHILL** – Floyd R. Sr. was an avid historian and genealogist. He enjoyed entertaining his family via monologues on these subjects. The following is Dane Barnhill's recollection of one of those sessions.

My grandfather, Caswell Hall Barnhill, came to Greene County in 1859. He established the old Barnhill homestead two miles southwest of what was to become Paragould, AR when it was incorporated in 1893. The Barnhill's journeys to Greene County trace back to Ireland. The following information will relate directly to Greene County and its history.

Grandpa Hall was born on March 23, 1828, in Blount County, TN. In January 1853 he married Sara Jane McDonough, an Irish girl, with whom he had two children, George Houston and Ada Josephine Barnhill, before moving to Arkansas.

Sara Jane, his wife, was born on Jan. 31, 1836. George Houston, was born Sept. 22, 1855 and Ada Josephine was born October 11, 1957.

I have in my possession two items that Grandpa Hall brought with him to Arkansas, a daguerreotype likeness of himself and the complete works of William Shakespeare, including his will. The book was so well read that the back was gone. Grandpa had bound it together with leather, using an awl to make holes in the book. This would indicate that he was a well-educated man.

Upon Grandpa's arrival in Greene County and the establishment of the old homestead, Grandpa and Sara Jane had another girl, Elizabeth Araminta Barnhill, born in 1861, prior to his enlistment in the Confederate Army.

In the summer of 1861 Caswell Hall Barnhill joined the Fifth Arkansas Infantry as a private in Company H. This became part of the Arkansas Brigade, formed at Pittman's Ferry on the Current River under General William J. Hardee.

I've been fortunate to have co-authored *The Fighting Fifth Arkansas*. This book documents the struggles of the Fifth Arkansas and the South.

This could not have been accomplished without the aid of family, friends and data I have acquired through decades of research.

After the War Between the States, Grandpa Hall returned home to develop his claim and raise his family in Greene County. Sara Jane and Caswell had two more girls, Leah A. Barnhill, born Feb 26, 1866 and Sara Jane Barnhill Jr. Nov. 20, 1868. Sara Jane Sr. passed on Nov. 21, 1868.

Caswell Hall Barnhill then married your grandmother, Espy Jane Jones, in 1869. I have been told the story that the Jones family came to Greene County by way of boat from Bibb County, AL. Starting from around Centreville, AL and continuing down the Cahaba River, into the Alabama and from there on the Tombigbee and Mobile rivers into Mobile Bay. They then traveled south to the Gulf of Mexico, west to the Mississippi River, where they went north to NE Arkansas and Greene County.

August 26, 1870 was the birth of Grandpa's sixth and first of six children to start another branch of the Barnhill family. This child was Espy Arkansas Barnhill, or "Aunt Kansas", as many family members called her. Later in life, she married Steven Winchester Spencer.

William Caswell Barnhill, your father, was born June 1, 1872. Jonathan C. Barnhill was born in 1875, passing in 1893. Henry O. Barnhill was born on April 17, 1876. He died just short of eight months of age on Dec. 13, 1876. David King Barnhill was born Dec. 2, 1877. He married Cora Dela Johnson. Joseph Hall Barnhill was born Feb. 5, 1880. He married Virgie Ida Spencer.

Never having the opportunity to see his last son, Caswell Hall Barnhill, progenitor of all Greene County, Arkansas Barnhills, passed away on July 2, 1879. My father was only seven at the time of his father's death. My father recalled Masons dropping twigs of cedar in the open grave of Grandpa Hall, a Mason himself. When Grandpa passed away, he had managed to accumulate many parcels of land scattered throughout Greene County. Quite a bit of land was wooded and the rest was farmland. Caswell Hall was, by no means, rich. Trying to provide for 11 children, caring for his farms and building wagons is what I believe led to an early grave at the age of 51.

William Caswell Barnhill and Maude Lile Kirby were married Aug. 2, 1903. They would have three children: Carl Alphonso Barnhill, born Jan. 4, 1906; Floyd Raymond Barnhill Sr., born Oct. 14, 1907 and Donald Bruce Barnhill, born Sept. 25, 1921. Donald died Mar. 2, 1933.

Growing up on our farm, my brother, Carl Alphonso and I, besides other chores, always had an acre of land or a calf that was our responsibility.

During the winter months, we would walk to school and back before tending to all the things that went with life on the farm. In the summer time, we would walk to Sycamore Bend on a nearby creek. Afterwards, we would journey back.

Carl had a little Western Bronco that was a single foot'n dude. Every time a rope was tied around his neck and to a post, he would break the rope. Alphonso got tired of this bronco's little game. He thought he would teach him a lesson. One day we tied a one-inch hay rope around his neck and tied it to a tree. I thought that horse was going to break his neck trying to break that rope. He would sit down on that rope and pull and pull, but never was able to break that rope. That broke him of breaking ropes.

My mother was a hard working woman. She would start her day by milking the cows and feeding the chickens before fixing breakfast for the family. There was a butter churn that sat next to the fireplace and we all took many a turn at churning until chunks of marbled butter came to the top. Mom made some of the best homemade butter that you ever tasted and always had a few regular customers requesting her butter.

There was an old hickory smoke house behind the house that my dad would use to smoke hogs that we raised. He would begin by removing the backbone of the hog and then separating the meat to begin the process of making sausage. The sausage meat would be put in a large kettle and placed over an open fire in the back yard.

For hours at a time, my father would sit there and stir the meat, from which he would get a couple of gallons of lard and the cracklings for making crackling bread. At this point, dad would season and cook the sausage, taking many samples until the right combination was found. Will Barnhill had a reputation for having some of the best sausage and hams in Paragould.

Donald Bruce Barnhill was 14 years my junior at the time of his birth and only reached 12 years of age at the time of his death on March 2, 1933. Apparently my father was a little slow at having Donald's illness diagnosed and the young lad died of a ruptured appendix. Ultimately I believe this caused ill feeling between my parents and led to their divorce. Although they would later remarry, afterwards things were never really the same.

Carl Alphonso Barnhill, my older brother, would marry Laneal Patton on March 5, 1932. They would go to have six children of their own: Carl Patton Barnhill, born June 18, 1933; Charles Edwin Barnhill, born May 11, 1935; Harrel "Dan" Barnhill born Jan. 22, 1937; Fredrick Ray Barnhill born June 22, 1943; Ann Carol Barnhill born June 25, 1944 and Darrel Wayne Barnhill, born Oct. 5, 1951.

At the time that I was courting my future wife, Wilma Powers, I was employed by Beards Temple of Music as an announcer for KBTM. On evenings that I intended to call on Wilma, I would sign off by playing our song so she would know that I would be calling on her. After 52 years, I can honestly say that all has not been total marital bliss, but I can't say that I could have made a better choice in a mate.

On June 2, 1922, Wilma Paralee Powers and I were married. We would have two children. On Sept. 20, 1934, William Arnold Barnhill was born at the McClure Clinic on North Second Street in Paragould, AR. Floyd Raymond Barnhill Jr. was born Nov. 15, 1938 at 703 East Johnson in Jonesboro, AR.

My eldest son, William Arnold Barnhill, would go on to marry Connie Sue Jones of Jonesboro, AR. they would have two children, MeLeisa Lynn Barnhill on Aug. 11, 1958 in New Orleans, LA and Dane Christopher Barnhill, born on Oct. 14, 1964, my birthday, in Little Rock, AR. On July 19, 1977, Bill and Connie divorced. Bill then married Zada McGill of North Little Rock, AR.

Floyd Raymond Barnhill Jr. would marry Sharon Ann Warner of Belleville, IL in East St. Louis, MO, on Nov. 26, 1962. They also would have two children: Floyd Raymond Barnhill III, was born on Jan. 5, 1968 in Springfield, MO and Mindy Warner Barnhill was born on March 23, 1970, in Springfield, MO.

I really don't consider myself a very religious man, but I am a member of The First Baptist Church located on Main Street here in Jonesboro, AR. I guess you could say that I have been very blessed for being able to tell you my roots because I feel the past is not only a part of our history, but an anchor to our present that can open a gateway to our future.

At this point in my story, I would be remiss if I didn't interject this piece of information.

Just after my oldest granddaughter's eighth birthday, I received a call from her Uncle Jupe wanting to know if MeLeisa had received her birthday present. I informed him that she had gotten it and proceeded to let her know the proper way to acknowledge such gifts. I sent this letter to her.

"MeLeisa:

"Congratulations! You are becoming a big girl, old enough to acknowledge gifts of kindness with manners and etiquette, to respond with notes of gratitude saying thank you. I once had a little pig that, when I would feed it, would always grunt in appreciation. It was his way of saying thank you. Now, I know that you and your mother and father would not want a little pig to have better manners than you, so I'm sending this little thank you note for you to sign and send to your Uncle Jupe. Always remember that little pig that said thank you."

POSTSCRIPT

I am certain Dad would approve Dane's recollection.

*Submitted by Floyd R. "Jupe" Barnhill Jr.*

**BARR** – Thomas Jackson Barr was born January 10, 1817, to Alexander and Nellie McCaskay Barr, in Williamson County, Tennessee. Thomas married Sarah Winford Smith, January 18, 1841, in Henderson County, Tennessee. Children of Thomas and Sarah were: Garlan Alexander born July 23, 1843; Martha Ann born January 9, 1844; Kenson McVay born August 16, 1846; Terrell Filmore born August 11, 1848; Thomas Guadaloupe born March 2, 1851; Samuel Carson born March 17, 1853; Robert Trimble born September 17, 1857; Dorcas Elmonia born January 6, 1861; and Sarah Isabelle born August 22, 1863.

*From left: Kenson, James and Vernon Barr*

After the Civil War Thomas had a letter from a friend, Levi Stewart, telling him of the great opportunities in Johnson County, Texas. Six weeks before Christmas the Barrs left Tennessee with 13 wagons and 20 outriders for Texas. Stopping in Memphis to buy supplies for a store Thomas planned on opening in Texas. They boarded the Dixie Belle for Helena, Arkansas, crossing the Red River at Fulton, Arkansas, and stopped in Sherman, Texas, because of some of their colored people contacted malaria. Months later after arriving in Cleburne, Texas, Thomas started his home. Years later he added more rooms. This house built in 1869, still stands and was visited by Bettye Sparks Busby and Katherine Barr Carson in 1998.

Two of Thomas and Sarah's children that were married left Texas and settled in Greene County, Arkansas, and Dunklin County, Missouri. Kenson McVay Barr had married a Greene County teacher, Josephine Shaver, daughter of Daniel and Sophia Dorsey Shaver. They lived in the Gainesville Community. On the 1870 Greene

County census, Union Township the Barrs are living next door to the Shavers. Another son, Terrell Fillmore Barr had moved to Senath, Missouri, where his wife Martha Brewer Barr's family had moved from Tennessee. The Kenson Barrs left Greene County in 1880 and lived in Palo Pinto, Texas.

In later years we find Vernon L. Barr, a grandson of Kenson and Josephine living in Marmaduke. Preaching at the local Baptist Church. In a history printed by Eastside Baptist Church, Paragould, (Through the Years 1912-1987) Vernon L. Barr of Marmaduke had been hired as the pastor of Eastside on May 13, 1938. His salary was $40.00 a month, to preach part-time. Vernon L. Barr died at age 77 in Dallas, Texas. He attended the University of Kansas and received his Doctorate of Theology from Texas Baptist Institute. He was survived by one son Don; one daughter Charlene; and one sister Katherine Carson.

Thomas Jackson Barr.

In recent years through genealogy research several of the Barr cousins have met and keep in touch. They are Bettye Sparks Busby, Paragould, Arkansas; Katherine Barr Carson, Fort Worth, Texas; Ella Barr Franklin, Lexington, Tennessee; Kay Barr Frank, Las Vegas, Nevada; Barbara Barr Stanley, Eugene, Oregon; and Finis Barr, Steeleville, Missouri.

*Submitted by Katherine Barr Carson*

**BARRON** – Porter Franklin Barron born Jan. 28, 1863 in Tennessee, son of William A. and Dilly Ann (Spain) Barron, married March 14, 1886, in Greene County, AR to Laura E. Stuart, born Aug 10, 1869 in AR, daughter of James Wilson and M. R. E. (Smith) Stuart. Porter Franklin and Laura Barron had 16 known children.

1. William W. Barron, born Nov. 1888 in Arkansas, married Aug. 11, 1914 to Bessie G. Stuart.
2. Ethel Barron, born May 1889.
3. Charlie Cline Barron, born Sept. 19, 1891 in Arkansas, married Nov. 5, 1911 to Hester A. Byrd, born Oct. 10, 1891. Charlie Cline died June 12, 1941 and Hester died July 9, 1975. They had two known sons: Rex Barron, born 1914 in Arkansas and Clarence Barron, born 1915 in Arkansas.
4. Thomas P. Barron, born Dec 17, 1892 (TS says 1894) in Arkansas, died Aug. 21, 1954, married July 12, 1913 to Ada Jones, daughter of James W. and Elizabeth Pearl Jones. Moved to Detroit, MI.
5. Jacob A. "Jake" Barron, born July 1893 in Arkansas, married in 1914 to Marie Young, born 1896 in Indiana. Moved to Illmo, MO.
6. Joseph Lee Barron, born July 2, 1896 in Arkansas, married Dec. 3, 1916 to Martha Janet Davenport, born May 6, 1898, daughter of John and Mary A. Davenport.
7. Earnest C. Barron, born April 1889 in Arkansas, married (1) Frankie Laster and (2) Christine (unknown). Moved to St. Louis, MO.
8. Bertha Barron, born Sept 1899 in Arkansas, married April 22, 1925 to R. L. Smith and moved to Detroit, MI then Florida.
9. George M. Barron, born 1902, married April 5, 1921 to (1) Nora Bray, born 1904, daughter of Elsie Bray. Divorced. Married (2) Alice Thurman, daughter of John and Pearl Thurman. Moved to St. Louis, MO.
10. Charlsie E. Barron, born 1904 in Arkansas married Clarence Olive Bonhan and moved to Springfield, MO.
11. Wakeman L. Barron, born 1905 in Arkansas moved to St. Louis, MO.
12. Ruth L. Barron, born 1906 in Arkansas married Oct. 19, 1927 to Adrian Rogers and moved to Baltimore, MD, then Detroit before moving to Holly Branch, MS.
13. James L. Barron, born 1908 in Arkansas, married Juanita Smith and moved to Detroit, MI.
14. Mary Margaret Barron, born 1910, died 1937 and is buried at Woods Chapel Cemetery.
15. Myron B. Barron, born 1913, married 1934 to Beatrice Barnhill, born 1916, daughter of David and Cora Barnhill and moved to St. Louis, MO.
16. Beachy R. Barron, born 1915, married Robert Rogers, son of T. W. and Sallie Rogers and moved to Detroit, MI before moving to Holly Branch, MS.

Most of the Barron Family is buried at Woods Chapel Cemetery near Paragould, Greene County, AR.

*Submitted by Carolyn Metheny.*

**BARRON** – William A. and Dilly Ann (Spain) Barron came to Greene County from Henderson County, TN before 1870. William A. Barron was born Oct 21, 1836 in Tennessee and died March 12, 1894. Dilly Ann Spain Barron was born Jan. 5, 1837 in North Carolina and died Jan. 9, 1923. Both are buried at Woods Chapel Cemetery near Paragould, AR.

William A. and Dilly A. Barron had eight known children:
1. Sarah Frances, born July 1861 in Tennessee, married March 13, 1890 to John C. Wood.
2. Porter Franklin, born Jan. 28, 1863 in Tennessee, married March 14, 1886 to Laura E. Stuart.
3. John T., born 1865 in Tennessee, married Nov. 27, 1890 to M. H. Wright.
4. Emily C., born 1867 in Tennessee, married July 30, 1885 to Henry Jasper McDaniel.
5. Mary E., born 1870 in Arkansas married Dec. 23, 1894 to John C. Willcockson.
6. William Jacob, born 1872 in Arkansas, married (1) Dec. 26, 1895, Sarah Lovina Norton (2) May 10, 1908, Virgie Colbert
7. James C., born 1874 in Arkansas, married Jan. 13, 1890 to Alice Jones
8. Susan, born 1877 in Arkansas, married March 6, 1898 to A. F. Harrell.

William A. Barron is believed to be the son of John Barron (1815 TN). Unknown at this time is the name of his mother.

*Submitted by Clarence Barron*

**BASS** – John Logan Bass, born November 8, 1865, near Dresden, Tennessee, died December 26, 1943, at the home of his daughter, Ruth Pillow, in Paragould, Arkansas, and is buried in Pine Knott Cemetery beside his wife and father. Logan's parents were Gilford Peter and Mary Elizabeth Hughes Bass. She passed away before they moved to Greene County. Grandparents were David and Harriet Nancy Smith Bass from Giles County, Tennessee. Logan married Octavia Elizabeth Herren born February 26, 1876, died February 18, 1901. She was the daughter of Asa Augustus and Abigail Clark Herren and granddaughter of James Herren. Their children were: Ruth Abigail who married Arthur (NMI) Pillow; William Henry who married Clara Susan in Santa Ana, California; Mary "Mamie" who married Charlie Rowe; Martha E. married Fred Roberts; and Bertha who married William Thompson. Logan and his father moved to Greene County near Asa Herren on Finch Road and Pine Knott Church in the late 1850s from Dresden, Tennessee. A tree fell on his leg causing him to be crippled, so he wore a shoe with a built-up sole. He was sent to Martin, Tennessee, to learn bookkeeping so that he could make a living. He excelled in that and also had beautiful penmanship. After moving to Greene County he farmed because he didn't like being inside.

Octavia became very ill before Bertha was born and Peter (his father) was also ill. Peter went to Asa Herren's store and bought some laudanum, which he took. Then, he went to a back storeroom and hanged himself, because he didn't want to be a burden. Octavia passed away a few days after Bertha was born. Logan had a nervous breakdown, and could not care for his children.

Logan, Peter and Octavia were members of the Church of Christ, so members of the church and relatives took all of the children and reared them. Henry went to his grandfather Asa Herren. Joe and Hester Higgins took Ruth. Dave and Annie Greenway took Mary. Walker and Sarah Clark Hyde reared Martha, and a Mr. and Mrs. Lemmons took Bertha.

John Logan Bass

Logan had sandy, red hair and was about five feet five inches tall. He was very thin, humble, and had a twinkle in his eyes. He would talk to himself as he combed his beard, and never said an unkind word about anyone. He worked in his daughters' gardens every spring and fall. All of his daughters welcomed him into their homes. His son lived in Santa Ana, California, while his daughters lived in Greene County. He worked as a bookkeeper for Arthur Pillow for a while, but didn't like the work or living in the city, so he quit. When he went visiting, he would wear as many clothes as he could put on, then carry the rest in his suitcase with all of his patent medicine.

Everyone who knew him, spoke well of him. He lived as good a Christian life as he could.

*Submitted by Dera Hunter*

**BEAN** – Henry Bean, born April 5, 1900, the son of James Alexander Bean, May 7, 1855-December 27, 1935, and Roda Ellen Lamb, August 29, 1860-May 8, 1940, both of Gallatin County, Illinois, lived in Blytheville, Arkansas, when he met and wed on February 5, 1921. They met at a simple neighborhood come-as-you-are social with singing and dancing. Mary Agnes Furgerson was smitten by this handsome, green-eyed, dark-haired young gentleman. Agnes said, "That one's mine even it he never will be!" Henry and Agnes had a good time. The man Agnes put her claim on soon became her husband after a whirlwind romance. They loved each other all their lives.

Henry played the violin by ear and made the sweetest music playing old Irish ballads and folk songs. Henry liked to eat sorghum molasses with butter on bread. He was good at fixing things, and fixed almost anything he set out to fix. During his lifetime he had many different jobs. He worked at the Howell Girls' Dairy Farm where they threw the calves over the fence to die as they only kept the heifers.

From Blytheville they moved to Oklahoma, where Henry did odd jobs. James Bean, Henry's father, enjoyed lavishing his grandchildren with gifts. Fall 1928,

*Henry and Agnes Bean*

they took a train back to Paragould, Arkansas. Henry sharecropped, but he hated it. Henry hired on at the Wrape Stave Mill and tried to organize the workers. He got fired for his trouble. Then he farmed again with John Ritchey, his new father-in-law.

One day at noon, Henry's son, Joseph, asked Agnes why she put ashes in his plate. Agnes looked up and saw that the ceiling was on fire. She got the children out while screaming fire at the top of her lungs. Henry and John heard her two miles away, and came running. They soon made short work of that fire.

Their children went to St. Mary's Catholic Parochial School, and were Regina, Jospeh, Dottie, Marie, Morine, Tom, Nancy and Michael. Four of their 12 children died.

In 1941 Henry went to work for the Western Pacific Railroad and was stationed at Black Rock Desert, Utah. Then, he got a job in the shipyards, and they were in Berkeley, California, for five years. They lived in Nevada City and Grass Valley, California, through the rest of the 1940s and 1950s. In the early 1960s, they lived on a farm in Sutherlin, Oregon, but Agnes got homesick so they returned to Arkansas. First living at Beech Grove, and then moving to a small farm owned by Henry's lifelong friend "Shorty Ross". While here Henry had a massive stroke. He passed away April 9, 1969, in Oak Grove, Greene County, Arkansas. Henry was laid to rest in St. Mary's Catholic Cemetery, Paragould, Arkansas. Agnes died May 5, 1982, and was laid to rest alongside Henry.

*Submitted by John Rainwater*

**BEATON** – Collin Beaton (1833) married March 25, 1855 to Susannah French (1832) in Benton County, TN. They came to Greene County, AR about 1861 with their three sons: Christopher (1856), James Wright (1858) and John (1860). They settled in the Gainesville area with the intention of farming. The civil war changed things as Collin was called into service July 18, 1862 with Co F, 30th AR Inf Regt and Oct 15, 1862 sent to Camp Hope at Austin, AR. He died at Austin during an epidemic of measles, etc. He was buried at Camp Nelson, a Confederate cemetery at Cabot, AR. Susannah later married James D. Eastep of the Ramer's Chapel Community. Nothing is known of her later years.

James Wright Beaton (Jan 21, 1858- Dec. 17, 1926) married Jan.

*James and Nancy P. Beaton*

6, 1884 to Nancy Paralee Starnes (July 17, 1868) daughter of Marshall and Paralee Starnes.

James and Nancy were charter members of the Ramer's Chapel Methodist Church and are buried in the Ramer's Chapel Cemetery. Their children were: Emma (1885), Georgia Annie (1887), Nancy Belle (1894), Hettie (1896), Walter (1901), Berlie (1905) and John Wesley (1908).

Nancy Belle (1894) married July 16, 1913 to James Clayborne Stephens (Aug. 11, 1886). Both are buried in Ramer's Chapel Cemetery.

*Submitted by Ed and Catherine Gerdes*

**BEISING** – Frank Joseph Beising was born in Cincinnati, O in 1856 to German immigrants of Catholic faith. Frances Rosa (Alleman) was born to another German couple in 1866 in Ohio. Frank and Rosa were married in 1886 in Napoleon, Ripley County, IN. They came to Paragould, Greene County, AR in 1887. There they produced three children: August Nicholas "Gus", Joseph John and Mary Florence "Flora" Beising.

Frank bought property in 1887 and continued to buy and sell real estate throughout his lifetime in Paragould, including grocery stores at three different locations: 223 N. Pruett, 538 East Court and 320 East Lake. He proved to be a very successful businessman and well known around town.

Frank first appears on records of St. Mary's Catholic Church in 1891, although he probably had been an active member since his arrival. He was one of several major contributors toward the purchase of three bells for St. Mary's bell tower, which are still in use. Rosa converted to Catholicism in Sept. 1895.

*Frank J. Beising in front of his first grocery store in Paragould located then at 223 N. Pruett St. about 1895.*

After 15 years of marriage, Frank and Rosa divorced in 1901, after one year of separation. Rosa married again Aug. 29, 1902 to Peter T. Schneider. Frank also married again to Mrs. Ola Hawkins, Nov. 17, 1901.

Iola Maud (Flora), daughter of Martha (Miller) and John Flora, was born in 1876 in St. Joseph, MO. Her first marriage was to William F. Hawkins, who was born in Missouri in 1869. They were divorced in 1900. Their two children, Eva and Joseph Francis, died as children and are buried in Linwood Cemetery in Paragould beside Ola's mother, Martha Snyder.

Frank and Ola had two children, born in Paragould. Edward Joseph was born June 14, 1901, married Hazel Dover in 1922 and had three children: Willidene, Edmonia and Frank. They eventually left Paragould. The second child was Catherine Frances "Katie", born Nov 26, 1904. She married Jerome Gilbert Clayton in St. Mary's Church Jan. 10, 1924. Jerome, one of seven children born to Gregory and Anna (Mackey) Clayton, was born in Beech Grove, McLean County, KY, Sept. 30, 1897 and came to Arkansas with his family in 1903 in a covered wagon. Jerome and Katie had seven children, all born in Paragould: Jerome Jr., Mary Catherine, Francis Eugene, Robert William, Patricia Ann, James Alan and Sharon Lea. Katie graduated from eighth grade at St. Mary's School. She worked at Bertig Department Store until she got married and was a homemaker the remainder of her life.

Frank Beising died June 16, 1925 at age 68, having lived in Paragould 38 years. In addition to his wife Ola and their five children, two sisters in Cincinnati, O, survived him. It is unknown how many siblings he had in his original family. His three children from the first marriage probably were still living but the obituary did not list them.

Ola eventually used all the assets Frank left her and became a "housekeeper" and took in "washings" for her income. Ola died a Catholic, having converted Dec. 8, 1925. She died Jan. 8, 1941 at age 64 at the home of her daughter, Katie Clayton.

Frank and Ola are buried in St. Mary's Cemetery in Paragould.

*Submitted by Mrs. Betty J. Clayton*

**BIRMINGHAM** – The Birmingham family has lived through four generations at Fontaine.

M.C. Birmingham moved his family from Strawberry, Arkansas, to Fontaine in 1921 and began a small farming operation with his family of five children and his wife Minnie Jane.

M.C. Birmingham died in 1954 and Murvel, his oldest son, and his wife Iva, continued farming as Murvel had never left the farm.

Murvel and Iva had four children and they worked hard making the farm produce a living for their family and adding acres as the years flew by.

Murvel passed away in 1975 and Iva died in 1996 passing the farm to their daughter Doris. Doris and her husband Benny Martin are currently farming the family farm. Doris, like her father, has never left the farm.

Benny and Doris have two children: Chrystal Hamilton who teaches third grade at Cedar Park Elementary in Trumann, Arkansas. She is a graduate of Arkansas State University with a degree in early childhood/elementary education. She is married to Michael K. Hamilton who is the Agricultural County Extension Agent for Poinsett County. Michael also is a graduate of Arkansas State University with a degree in general agriculture.

Brandon Martin is a senior at Arkansas State University majoring in agri business. He received his degree in May 2000 and plans to continue his education further toward a master's degree. Brandon is currently farming with his mother and father and also farms for himself. He plans to continue the farming operation after his parent's retirement.

He was also named the "State Star Farmer" in 1995 a very high honor given by the state of Arkansas. He has always been very active in anything dealing with agriculture. He received numerous awards and was president of the Greene County Tech FFA.

In years to come, the way things look, we may be looking at a fifth generation of Birmingham farming.

**BLACKSHEAR** – Jack Ligon Blackshear Sr., son of Arvil Hurt Blackshear and Maggie Hunt Ligon Blackshear, was born November 29, 1915, in Hamilton, Texas.

My acquaintance with Paragould began in the late 1920s when my father was sent here by his employer, Dan Kempner of the H. Kempner Cotton Company of Galveston, Texas, on the insistence of Jeane Bertig Kempner, wife of Dan Kempner and sister of

Joe Bertig. Ad Bertig, Jeane and Joe's father, had made losing investments for others and himself, and committed suicide, leaving Joe with few liquid assets.

His goal was to save and preserve the Bertig Brothers' many interests, which included New First National Bank (now First National Bank), Hurt Grocer Company, Arbyrd Compress Company, American Securities Company, Bertig Cotton Company of Memphis, Tennessee, and mainly The Bertig Company of Paragould which operated approximately 27 cotton gins in Northeast Arkansas and Southeast Missouri.

*Arvil Hurt Blackshear, 1890-1957*

My father had his work cut out for him and needed a responsible person to head these businesses. With Cecil Mitchell's help, who at that time was head of the New First National Bank, they contacted William L. Gatz in Jonesboro, Arkansas, who agreed to the proposition for a substantial salary. The choice proved to be providential. My father continued to oversee the operation annually.

In 1938 I graduated from college with a degree in business administration, and my father asked me to accompany him to Paragould for his annual audit that year in August. Joe Bertig (who continued in name as President of The Bertig Company) and William L. "Bill" Gatz, CEO, asked me to remain and work in one of the companies. I selected Hurt Grocer Company and to learn this business I started in the office as a bookkeeper and as the years passed owned the company.

In 1939 I met my wife-to-be, Hildegarde Bebout, in Caruthersville, Missouri. We were wed March 24. Together, we were blessed with three fine sons, now grown: Jack Jr. (doctor of internal medicine), William C. "Bill" (stock broker) and Robert H. (doctor of anesthesiology). We gave our sons a Christian education and they all graduated from Hendrix College.

I am a charter member of the Lions Club (inactive), Mens' Bridge Club; served the Boy Scouts of America as Commissioner of the Clay-Greene District; was an organizer of the Greene County Association for Retarded Children; and in 1960 was Rotary Club's selection for Citizen of the Year. The Community Vision award was given me by the Greene County Community Fund for 1962-1992.

I served my country during World War II as a Marine in the First Marine Division. Paragould is a wonderful place to work and raise a family, and I owe this great experience to my father who passed this life in 1957. At the time of his death he was president and director of Galveston Cotton Company, vice president and director of the U. S. National Company, director of the Merchants and Planters Compress and Warehouse Company in Galveston, vice president and director of American Securities Company, Paragould; president and director of The Bertig Cotton Company, Memphis, Tennessee; director of Arbyrd Compress Company of Arbyrd, Missouri, director of Hurt Grocer Company and trustee of H. Kempner Cotton Company, Galveston, Texas.

*Submitted by Jack Blackshear*

**BLALOCK** – William Macon Blalock was born February 6, 1849, Graves County, Kentucky, to Sam T. and Rebecca Simms Blalock who were both born in North Carolina, as were their parents. On February 29, 1870, he married Nancy Jane Newton, three years younger than Macon and at least a foot shorter, for she was a tiny woman, called "Little Grandma" by her grandchildren. Macon and Nancy built a large Victorian styled house in southern Graves County, Kentucky, near the home of his parents. To this marriage were born 10 children: Rosa Lee, married Scott Marshall; Charlie Oliver, married Sally Shelby; Cappie, married Magney Roach; Walter Macon, married Beulah Green; Leonard Sullivan, married Audra Kathleen Crawford; Josephine, married Joseph Lacewell; Lucy Jane, married Harry Walden; Bessie Estelle, married Wakemon Anderson; William Bernard, married Audra Stevenson; and Inis Jewell, married Luster Stimson.

Around the turn of the century Macon and Nancy, accompanied by their younger children, moved across the Mississippi into Arkansas, where they erected a large log cabin with two rooms on one side and one large room on the other side with a "dog trot" (large open hall) between them. The west end of the hall was screened and the family took their meals there in warm weather. The house was situated on land that is presently occupied by the Oak Grove Baptist Church. There Macon farmed as well as owning and managing a prosperous sorghum mill.

*Macon and Nancy Jane Newton Blalock.*

In the winter of 1912-1913 their son, Leonard, moved his wife Audra and children Kathleen and Rupert to Greene County. They stayed with the elder Blalocks awaiting their furniture shipment and on Macon's birthday, February 6, 1913, a daughter, Reba Adell was born. A short time later Leonard and Audra settled their family in the Camp Ground Community where they built a new home. Seven years later another son, Warren Crawford Blalock, was born. The children were sent to a subscription school and the family attended church at the Camp Ground Methodist Church.

After farming for several years, and having seen his three older children married–Kathleen married Robert Riley and moved to Michigan; Reba married John D. Edward Stimson; and Rupert married Vera Stevenson–Leonard died and was buried at Friendship Cemetery near the graves of his parents. Warren went off to college and later to military service; Rupert, having taught for many years, became Greene County Tax Collector; and Reba taught elementary school in Greene County. During WWII, Rupert also became active in the military where he and Warren were fortunate to find themselves stationed near each other in both Africa and Europe. Reba and her family moved to California where she worked in an aircraft plant. Finding herself alone on a large farm, Audra sold the property and moved to West Emerson Street in Paragould, where she lived until her death in 1974.

After the end of the war, Rupert and Warren, interested in rice farming and cotton, bought and operated several cotton gins in the county. Warren married Ruth McBride. Rupert became interested in real estate and became a broker, establishing his own firm. Reba returned to Paragould and remarried Buford Roberts. She returned to the teaching career, which the war had interrupted. She retired after having taught more than 35 years in several Greene County school districts.

Today these four Blalock children are all deceased: Kathleen did in 1987, Warren in 1993, Rupert in 1997 and Reba died in March 1999. They are survived by many children, grandchildren and great-grandchildren who are ever thankful for their ancestor's interest in education, religion and politics with the general idea that each of us should strive to make Greene County and the world a better place for having been here.

*Submitted by Ray Jernigan*

**BLAND** – The Greene County Blands first settled in Paragould in 1891, coming from Crockett County, TN. Our oldest known had come from Amherst County, VA. My great-great-great-grandfather, Jesse Bland married Sarah "Sally" Newman on May 11, 1801, in Amherst County. Sarah was the daughter of John Newman who fought in the Revolutionary War.

Also living in Amherst on May 7, 1767, were two Blands, John and Charles. On this date, surveys were made on each of their lands. Each of them had plots on each side of the Pedlar River. On Sept. 1 and 20, 1808, Jesse and Sally bought land on the Pedlar. Since there were 41 years between the 1767 and 1808 land transactions, I would think that either John or Charles could be the father of Jesse. A John Bland of the County and Parish of Amherst, VA, pledged a white horse, two feather beds, furniture, 16 heads of hogs, household furniture, one lot of uninspected tobacco, a bay mare and her two colts and other appurtenances belonging to the promises made by the said John Bland to James and Robert Donald and Company.

*Herbert and Alvina Bland*

Joseph Newman, born about 1735, was the father of John Newman. Joseph appeared in the January Court of Amherst County in 1777 and had a Johnson Been charged with mistreating his son, John. In the 1780 Court Records of Amherst County I found the following information: "Joseph Newman personally appeared in Court and made satisfactory proof that he served as a soldier in one of the Virginia Regiments till properly disbanded in the year 1755 under the command of General Braddock, and that he nor any person for him hath obtained a Warrant for the Land allowed by the King of Great Britain in 1763, which is ordered to be certified to the Register of the Land Office of the State." General

Braddock was sent by the King's son of Great Britain to America to head an army to drive the French and Indians form Fort Duquesne. Two British Regiments of 500 men each, the 44th and 48th, were sent from Ireland in Jan. 1755 to Virginia. Braddock sailed from Great Britain to Virginia in Feb. 1755. On his arrival he enlisted 200 Virginia Militia soldiers with each of the British Regiments. Braddock and his 1400 men marched from Virginia to Duquesne, arriving July 8, 1755. The battle was fought that day with Braddock and 977 soldiers were killed. There 482 soldiers who survived. George Washington, a young militia colonel and my Joseph Newman both made it back to Virginia.

In Jan. 1777 Joseph's son, John, enlisted in the army and was on his way to Georgia. He was placed in 2nd Georgia Regiment of the Georgia Line under Colonel Samuel Elbert. He was in several marches, including the Florida Expedition under the command of General Howe. John was with his company at the Battle of Savannah fought on Dec. 29, 1778, during which his right arm was shot off near his shoulder by a British cannon ball. After the fighting was over he was taken prisoner by the British and kept in Savannah on board a prison ship some 15 miles below the town of Savannah. He remained there until the last of Aug. 1779 when he was exchanged and delivered over to the American Troops at Augusta, GA. There he applied to General McIntosh for a discharge. "D—you," said the General, pointing to the declarant's shoulder, "you have a better discharge than I can give you. I have no right to discharge you as you were enlisted for during the war." At that time John was doing nothing for the service, was receiving no clothing or pay, nor had he received any since the Battle of Savannah. John then applied to General Elbert for a discharge, who told him he could not give one until the war was over. John left Augusta about the first of Dec. 1779. After walking about 350 miles he reached home in Amherst County about Christmas. In 1784 this declarant received from General Samuel Elbert a discharge as a private soldier. On Dec. 17, 1794, John Newman received the following grant from the State of North Carolina: Grant Number 286 – Know ye that we have granted unto John Newman 1000 acres of land in our Middle District on the head waters of Harpeth River." In 1786 this part of North Carolina became Tennessee. On Sept. 12, 1815, Jesse and Sally Bland sold their land in Amherst County to Samuel Turner – 228 acres for $100.00. At this time the Jesse Bland family, together with the Newmans, moved to Rutherford County, TN and settled on the land that John Newman had been granted for his service in the Revolutionary War.

Proof that Jesse was the father of my great-great-grandfather John Bland is a Court document from the September Court Term of Amherst County in 1812 stating that "John Bland," an infant by Jesse Bland, his father and next friend against William and Madison Ware, his infant son, for trespass and assault and battery. Case dismissed and plaintiff not further prosecuting."

Jesse and son John were in Rutherford County, TN, in 1820. They were both listed together in an estate settlement of a doctor in Rutherford County. It seemed that they were both indebted (separately) for monies they owed the deceased doctor.

Jesse had another, Charles who married Nancy Cates in 1825. At that time he was living next to his grandfather, John Newman. Charles paid taxes in Rutherford County through 1849. His grandfather died there in 1842. In 1850 Charles was living next to his brother, John, in Haywood County, TN.

Jesse and his son John were living in the late 1820s in Gibson County, TN, where both families were still living in 1830. In 1833 Jesse sold his land in Gibson County to Daniel Cherry. This was the last information I found on Jesse. I suppose that he died at this time. His wife Sally moved to Shelby County, TN, where she died in 1838. On May 16, 1842, Court Order 738 stated that Jesse Jr., William and Eleanor Bland would give Power of Attorney to their brother, Cornelius, to go back to Rutherford County to obtain a settlement for their mother, Sally Bland, deceased, for her part of the estate of her father, John Newman, who died in 1842. My great-great-grandfather, John Bland, sold his land in Gibson County in 1844 and moved to Cageville (Alamo) in Haywood County, TN.

In the 1850 Census of Haywood County, John was listed as a Baptist Minister. He and wife, Elizabeth, were both 46 and both were born in Virginia. Their children were Calvin, 24; Charles, 15; William, 12; Sophronia, 10 and Amanda, 4. Eliza married Thomas Laman on Jan. 6, 1848. John's brother, Charles Bland, with his family in Haywood County lost two sons in 1861, Solomon and Allen, in the Battle of Shiloh. John died in 1856. His will was dated July 8, 1856.

Charles N. Bland, second son of John Bland, was my great-grandfather. He first married Elizabeth (Baird) Lewis on Jan. 30, 1860. Elizabeth was the daughter of James E. Lewis. Their children were: John Charles born about 1863; Parallee born about 1866; William "Dock" born about 1868; Sarah L. born about 1872; Ephriam Thomas "E. T." "Robert", born Nov. 11, 1875; and Alice born about 1879. Charles' second wife was Fanny White. They married in Jan. 1897. Charles and Fanny had two sons: Joseph C., born 1897 and Fulton M., born April 1900. Charles must have died in the latter part of 1900. The 1900 census was taken in June 1900 and Charles was still living. Fanny married a second time to W. B. Lea in 1901. We haven't been able to find Joseph or Fulton.

John Charles Bland, the first child of Charles, is my grandfather. He married Louisa Jane Lewis Aug. 23, 1881. They had four children: Lenora, born June 22, 1882, married John H. Pritchett; Estell (1885-1887); Herbert Francis Sr., born Sept. 3, 1890, married Alvina Lydia Poppe, born Dec. 4, 1895, in 1916 in Kettlersville, OH.

Herbert Sr. and Alvina had three children: H. Francis Bland Jr., who married Winifred Landrum on July 9, 1941, in Paragould. Winifred was the daughter of Horace and Margaret (Barrett) Landrum

The second child was Mary Lou Bland who married Jacob M. Williams.

The third child was Robert "Bob" Bland, who married Anna Lou Alstadt.

Francis and Winifred have four children: Donna, Herb (H.F. III), John Arvin and Denise.

Donna married Bill Williams and they have two daughters, Kathy and Nancy. Kathy married Dan Kostopulos. Nancy married Jason White. Their children are Madison and Mahlon.

Herb married Kay Denton. They have two daughters, Sara (who married Patrick Burnett) and Amy and one son, Jason Bland.

John married Joyce Horton. Their children are Julie, Jacob and Joseph.

Denise Bland married Frank Bednar.

**BLAND** – Robert "Bob" Preston Bland, son of Herbert and Alvina Poppe Bland, was born June 16, 1923 in Paragould, AR. He was the brother of Herbert Francis Bland Jr. and Mary Lou (Bland) Williams. On Aug. 3, 1947 he married Anna Lou "Ann" Alstadt, born March 15, 1927 in Rector, AR to Henry Lee and Bertha Ann Roberts Alstadt.

*Bob and Ann Bland 1976*

Bob and Ann's first child, Robert Preston Bland Jr., was born July 17, 1948 in Fayetteville, AR. He was married in Aug. 1969 and the couple had one child, Robert "Rob" P. Bland III, born Sept. 25, 1972 in Paragould. On July 29, 1989 Preston married Donna Frances Ratton, born July 23, 1952 in Memphis, TN. Donna is the daughter of Ralph and Joan Collins Ratton of Paragould.

Bob and Ann's second child, Barbara Ann, was born Dec. 18, 1951 in Paragould. On Nov. 2, 1979 She married Riley Allen VanHorn, born Aug. 1, 1954 in Blytheville, AR to Betty Louise Carter VanHorn and Sherwood Allen VanHorn. Barbara and Riley have two children: Anna Allyn VanHorn, born April 11, 1981 in Paragould and Jonathan Riley VanHorn, born Sept. 20, 1982 in Paragould.

**BLOCK** – Maurice Block (1819-1875) the great-grandfather of the writer of this family history, is the first Block about whom we have any knowledge. He was born in Germany. and spent his youth until 15 years of age with his parents. His father wished him to learn the baker's trade, but this being unsatisfactory to Maurice, he left home and went to Paris, France. At age 21 he married Bettie Bloon. In 1842 the family came to the United States through the port of New Orleans where they stayed for four or five years. Two sons were born of this union, Lasso and Nathan. While in New Orleans Mrs. Block was stricken with yellow fever and died. Soon after her death Mr. Block took the children and moved to Memphis. Lasso died in 1849. Nathan or L. N., as he was later known, joined the Confederate Army at age 15 and became somewhat of a hero by removing his commanding officer's body from the battlefield while the battle was still raging.

In 1849 Maurice Block married Anna Woubilman, a native of Germany. From this marriage were born 10 children, seven sons and three daughters. Two sons and one daughter died at an early age. The other children were reared in Cross County, Arkansas. During the Civil War days of 1861 Maurice Block was thought by some to be a Northern sympathizer. Confederate soldiers burned 139 bales of his cotton and a large quantity of seed cotton amounting in all to nearly 300 bales. The family had been warned that this might happen and so Mrs. Block had taken the straw out of the bed ticks and by filling them with cotton, saved about two bales. Later, Mr. Block was able to run the blockade around Memphis and sold the cotton for $1.20 a pound.

Jefferson Davis Block (1861-1929) was the seventh child of Maurice and Anna. He was born in Poinsett County, Arkansas. In his youth he clerked in his father's store, farmed with his older brother and spent time working on the boats then navigating the St. Francis River. J. D. or Jeff, as he was also called, studied law, became an attorney and began his law practice in Cross County. In 1886 he was elected to the state legislature and had the distinction of being its youngest member. Later he was elected as the prosecuting attorney for the district which included Greene County. It was in Paragould that he met and in June 1889 married Lena Hicks (1867-1961), the daughter of Dr. and Mrs. William Hardaway Hicks of Paragould. He did not seek re-election as prosecuting attorney but rather established his own law practice in Paragould in 1889.

*The J.D. and Lena Block home constructed in 1904 at 827 West Kingshighway and rased in 1963.*

From his early years, Jeff learned to love the land and held farming in high esteem. Through the early 1900s, he bought and cleared a large tract of land east of Marmaduke. Much of this land was subject to flooding with one parcel known as Bagwells Lake. However, today it is considered a good farm. This land, almost 100 years later, is still owned by his heirs.

Jeff was an attorney who had many friends and was held in high regard in his chosen profession. The law practice that he started has been in continuous operation since its formation so many years ago and is now known as Goodwin, Moore, Colbert & Broadaway. Jeff Block died in July 1929 and is buried in Linwood Cemetery, Paragould.

There were two children born of the marriage of Jeff and Lena: Maurice F. Block (1890-1965) and Mildred Block Smith (1895-1972).

Maurice, or Morris as he was called, graduated from Washington University School of Law and entered practice with his father and William F. Kirsch. After a few years he determined that law was not for him. World War I was raging and he decided to join the French Army as America was not yet in the fight. He served in France in the French Army for a year before joining the American Expeditionary Forces. While in France, he met Constance Scudder (1890-1939) of St. Louis, who was in France with the Red Cross. After a courtship back in the states, they were married in April 1920.

In 1914 Mr. Block had purchased a small insurance agency which was managed by Mr. T. B. Kitchens until Morris returned from service in France. Morris was intelligent and blessed with a quick mind. He was almost immediately successful in the insurance business and was recognized by his colleagues throughout the state as one of its leading agents. He enjoyed his work so much that he spent 50 years serving his clients.

Morris Block would have been a successful architect, engineer or contractor, for he loved building things and was very good at it. He donated much time and effort toward bringing the Ely-Walker shirt factory, Paragould's first factory in many years, to the community in 1937. He was then placed in charge of the construction of the building they were to occupy. In 1939 and the early 1940s, he was a prime mover for a new hospital building. With the help of many and the WPA, he organized and started the original building of what is now known as the Arkansas Methodist Hospital. World War II interrupted construction and the building was not finished until 1949.

Morris loved stories and had many of them to tell including being in Chicago with a case of "moonshine" whiskey, requested by the president of one of the insurance companies he represented, on St. Valentine's Day. The St. Valentine's Day, the day one gang massacred another gang over territorial whiskey rights. There he was with a case of moonshine whiskey during prohibition days in Chicago where people were being murdered over whiskey. Needless to say, he left Chicago as soon as possible.

After an interesting and successful life, Maurice F. Block died in January 1965 and was buried in Linwood Cemetery, Paragould.

Maurice and Constance Block had two children: Ann Block Powell (1923-) of Houston, Texas and William J. "Bill" Block (1925-) of Paragould. Bill attended Paragould schools until his mother's death in 1939. Then his sophomore, junior and senior years were spent at Western Military Academy. World War II was raging and Bill volunteered for the army, entering service in January 1944. He was discharged as a 1st lieutenant in September 1946. After graduating from the University of Arkansas in 1950, he was called back into service during the Korean Conflict. Upon his discharge in April 1952, Bill returned home and joined his father in the insurance business. During his career, he received the professional insurance designations of CPCU and CIC. He was active in church and civic affairs having served on many boards and commissions. His efforts in these endeavors were recognized by the Paragould Rotary and Kiwanis Clubs, the Chamber of Commerce and the Arkansas Methodist Hospital.

In 1950 Bill and Katherine Harrel (1927-) of Lewisville, Arkansas, were married and from this union two sons were born: William Jefferson "Jeff" Block (1951-) and Steven Harrel Block (1954-).

Jeff graduated from Paragould High School and four years later from Centre College, Danville, Kentucky. In 1974 he joined his father in the insurance business, thus entering the business his grandfather began in 1914. He too is active in the life of his community having also served on many boards and commissions and in many ways to help make Paragould "a better place to live." In 1974 he married Gay Chaney (1954-). From this marriage were born two children: Toby Jefferson Block (1979-), now a student at Hendrix College and William Chaney Block (1980-) now attending the University of Florida.

Steve graduated from Paragould High School, received his Juris Doctor in law from the University of Arkansas and a masters in tax law from Southern Methodist University. He chose to enter the accounting field, attained the CPA designation and worked with the Arthur Young Accounting Firm in Dallas rising to the position of a partner. In 1999 he accepted a position as chief financial officer for Hillwood Development Corporation, Dallas, Texas. In 1984 Steve and Patrice Sandusky (1954-) of Dallas, Texas, were married. They have two children: Elizabeth Catherine Block (1984-) and Bryan Davis Block (1987-).

This is a very brief picture of this Block family for the past 180 years. Regretfully, space did not permit a discussion of the Block women, Anna, Lena, Mildred, Ann, Katherine and Patti, each of whom played a very important and meaningful role in the development and lives of their husbands and their children.

*Submitted by Bill Block*

**BOBO** – Alfred P. Bobo was born about 1814 in the Spartanburg District of South Carolina to Elisha and Lucy Dean Bobo. By 1820 the family was residing in Bedford County, Tennessee. Several families including siblings of both parents had migrated from South Carolina to Tennessee during this time period.

It is believed Alfred returned to South Carolina about 1835. He married Elizabeth R. Hobby, daughter of Zachariah and Rhoda Bobo Hobby. Census records show that most of their children were born in South Carolina. In 1857 the family left the Palmetto State to settle in Greene County, Arkansas. They resided in St. Francis Township where he farmed and raised stock on 160 acres of land. A.P. Bobo served as coroner of Greene County from 1858 until 1860.

Goodspeed wrote in 1898 that A.P. and Elizabeth were parents of seven children with four living at that time. They were: Mary Prince, Virginia Swindle and Spotana Love who resided in Texas and North Carolina. Their son Elisha Madison Bobo remained in Greene County until his death. The 1860 census lists another son L.L., age 11. Dr. W.C. and V.E. Barnes resided in that household. She may have been a daughter as she is listed in a later census as V.E. Bobo. A.P. Bobo died in 1868. His widow Elizabeth and daughters M.C. and S.P. resided in the household of son L.L. in the 1870 census. Elizabeth was deceased by 1880.

Another daughter has been identified as Medora. Brent H. Holccomb's book, *Marriage and Death Notices from Upper SC Newspapers 1843-1865* included an article from the June 23, 1859, issue concerning her death. " Died at the residence of her husband, in Green County, Arkansas, on the 2d May, Mrs. Medora Rudisill, in the 24th year of her age...daughter of Capt. A.P. Bobo, formerly a citizen of Spartanburg. With her husband, left this native state last fall...member of the Baptist Church ...left two children and a husband."

Alfred, Elizabeth, Lafayette and Johnnie Bobo are buried in Fairview Cemetery. Medora Rudisal and infant Florence Rudisal are also buried there. No dates or other information is given.

My husband's grandfather Reverend J.D.J. Faulkner said that Mr. and Mrs. Bobo were charter members of Fairview Baptist Church. The church was organized in 1857, the year the Bobo Family settled in Greene County. The information was given to Vivian Hansbrough when she wrote *History of Greene County Arkansas*.

Son Elisha M. Bobo built a house near his parents. On March 14, 1861, he married Elizabeth Miller. To this union were born nine children. They were: Middleton, Ella, Granville, Olive, Victoria, Arthur Evan, Jacob, Alice and Ida.

In 1898 Goodspeed wrote that he owned about 154 acres of land with 80 in cultivation, 40 of which he had cleared himself. His farm is well stocked with horses, cattle, hogs and fine sheep. He belongs to the Agricultural Wheel. He and his wife and family are active members of the Methodist church.

Elisha M. and Elizabeth are buried in the Old Bethel Cemetery.

**BOBO** – Elizabeth Miller Bobo was born December 7, 1841. She was married to Elisha M. Bobo March 14, 1861. They were Lisha and Lizzie to family and friends. She was already pregnant when he joined the 5th Regiment Arkansas Infantry in October 1861. Though wounded twice he fought for the South until the war ended. (I was told that he hated Abe Lincoln!)

Middleton, their first child, was born March 3, 1862. He was my grandfather. His daughter Lucy Bobo Hart was my mother. Lizzie and the baby lived with his family while Lisha was away. They lived in the hills about three miles from Walcott, Arkansas. She never heard from him while he was gone. Not knowing if he was alive or dead she watched the road for his return when the other men were making their way home.

After his return they cleared land, built a log house and farmed. In 15 years she had nine children. She was now 36 years old. All this time miles from nowhere and practically no medical help available. She contended with summer heat, winter cold, floods, mosquitos, malaria, typhoid and T.B.

E.M. and Elizabeth Miller Bobo family. Children: Alice Jones, Ella Cox, Olive Newberry, Granville, Middleton and Jake Bobo with families.

They raised sheep, used a spinning wheel to make it into yarn then knit socks and such (I wonder how many pairs they had), sewed all their clothes, washed clothes on a board and ironed with irons heated in a fireplace. It must have been an awful job considering the long full dresses they wore.

All cooking was done in the fireplace, used kerosene lamps, raised geese for pillows and feather beds, used bulk cotton (probably hand picked out the seed) carded into bats to fill quilts which were all hand sewn. Maybe sewed clothes by hand as well. Got water from a well or cistern, made her own soap and lived with outdoor plumbing.

Her only leisure was going to church but since Sunday was visiting day Lizzie probably worked harder than ever, cooking for a slew of people.

She most likely milked her cow or cows, as that was considered part of a wife's chores. Of course gardened, dried and canned everything she could—no refrigeration. If she went any place it was by horse and buggy or wagon.

She saw so many of her family buried! From gravestones, the information is: son Arthur E. January 6, 1894, age 23; daughter Victoria April 11, 1895, age 25; son Middleton's wife, Sarah E. December 5, 1901, age 36 leaving eight daughters age 2 to 18; Middleton and Sarah E.'s daughters Viana April 22,1905, age 17; Nora June 9, 1905, age 20; Cora May 28, 1908, age 24; Eva Bobo McClain and her infant about 1910 age 20(?); son Middleton drowned May 7, 1916, age 54; son Granville, October 10,1918, age 51; Granville's wife Mary Alice October 29, 1918, age 46; son Middleton's daughters Lela about 1919 age 20(?) of T.B. and Nettie about 1920 age (?); Lizzie's husband Lisha April 21,1921, age 80. These are just the ones we know about.

Elizabeth Miller Bobo died March 1,1930, at age 88. This was 10 days before my brother Bill Hart was born. Great Grandma Lizzie had lived through the Civil War and its aftermath, World War I and part of The Great Depression. She lived more years than any of her children and grandchildren most likely. Her obituary listed survival of four children, 26 grandchildren, 67 great-grand children and three great-great-grandchildren.

I wonder what she would think of her liberated great-granddaughters, and her great-great-granddaughters Darlene, Sharon, Pam, Holly, Charlene, Joyce, Flo, Sue and Brenda just in our family alone.

After Cora's death Grandma Lizzie helped raise Middleton's girls. Lela, his youngest, died of T.B. four years after his death. I wonder where she lived and who took care of her. Grandma was nearly 80 then. In those days people with T.B. stayed home with their families.

When Lizzie's ninth child Ida was born she was 36 years old. Number seven child Jake and number eight Alice were born less than a year apart two years earlier. She was about 60 when Middleton's family started dying. How could she bear to see so many of the people that she loved buried!

Proverbs chapters 31 verses 10-19-27 reads "Who can find a virtuous woman? For her price is far above rubies.- She layeth her hands to the spindle and her hands hold the distaff. She looketh well to her household and eateth not of the bread of idleness." (I'm sure she never did!) The dictionary: Virtuous - good, moral, righteous, chaste, pure. I am sure Great-Grandma Lizzie qualified. I am proud to be one of her many descendants as I write her story in 1984.

The first log house built by Elisha probably became too small as their family grew. At some point Aunt Caroline said a new house was built. It was still standing when I visited the area in 1935. I believe it to be same house in old pictures. I don't know when it was no longer used as a dwelling. Probably after Lisha's death in 1921. Lizzie probably moved into Jake's home then. There was a wide open hall in the center with rooms on both sides. Likely kitchen and living room on one side, bedrooms on the other. The hall was a cool place to sit in summer and like ice in winter when they dashed across it to other side.

An apple tree they had still grew and had fruit as I was told. It grew in the back yard near a well that still had good water. The house looked forlorn at that time as Uncle Jake used it to store bales of hay in.

An unpaved country road running east and west ran past the one room Bobo School. They must have donated the land for a school and all the Bobo kids went there. Cora and Nora both served as teacher there during the years. It was still used as a school when I was there. One of Olive Bobo Newberry's grandsons was the teacher then and had only a few students. The school was on the right side of the road.

**BOHANING** – Washington Green Bohaning, was born in the state of Tennessee in 1821. Nothing is known of his parents or other family. Mr. Bohaning arrived in Arkansas in the mid 1840s by wagon train from western Kentucky.

On March 27, 1845, he was married to Cassandra Jane Jones. W.G. and Cassandra were residents of Cache Township, Randolph County, Arkansas.

Mr. Bohaning was actively involved in his community. In 1849 he was a member of the Greene County "Internal Improvement Commission."

By 1850 he was widowed and living in the household of Charles G. Jones, a merchant of Jones Ridge. Also in the household was a daughter Louisa Jane Bohaning age 1, and two orphans Henry and William Glasscock.

Washington Green Bohaning.

W.G. subsequently married Malinda N. Shaver, daughter of Daniel and Mary Murray Shaver.

Their children were: Nancy Ann born 1851; William G. born 1854; James F. born 1855; Daniel Jefferson born 1857; Mary Ella born 1859; Green Lee born 1860; Elmona born 1862; and Estella born 1864.

Mr. Bohaning purchased land in 1859 in Township 18 just east of Lafe and at another site just north of Hooker.

In 1861, at the outbreak of the Civil War, W.G. raised the first full Company of soldiers, mostly from Greene County, Arkansas for the First Regiment of Arkansas Confederate Infantry. Mr. Bohanning was elected captain. The unit in conversion to Confederate Service became Company D, Fifth Arkansas Infantry. By November 1861 Company D was stationed in the Bowling Green and Scottsville areas of Kentucky.

Captain Bohaning wrote a letter to Colonel D.C. Cross attesting to the ill health that had affected many in his Company. In 1862 the Confederate Army withdrew from Bowling Green, Kentucky. By May 1862, the Arkansas Fifth was encamped at Corinth, Mississippi. On May 19, 1862, W.G. was not reelected captain in a reorganization of the Arkansas Fifth. He returned home to Gainesville, Arkansas. Private W.G. Bohaning was paroled as a prisoner of war at Wittsburg, Arkansas, on May 25, 1865, W.G. was in Company F, Arkansas 30th Cavalry.

Following the war W.G. served as a justice of the peace. Mr. Bohaning was appointed, along with H.W. Glasscock as director of School District #5 in 1877. A school house for District #3 was erected on land owned by Mr. Bohaning in Section 13 Township 18N, Range 5 E.

Mr. Bohaning was a charter member of the Providence Baptist Church and served as a messenger to the Gainesville Association for several years.

By 1880 Mr. Bohaning and family were residing in Delaplaine, Arkansas. He and his son-in-law Varner Giles, were hotel keepers.

W.G.'s health was failing. On March 18, 1880, he was appointed postmaster at Delaplaine. Mr. Bohaning died on March 19, 1880, of typhoid - malaria. He was attended by Doctor Camp.

W.G. Bohaning was a resident of Greene County for 35 years. He was a stalwart individual who contributed to its development. His oldest living descendent is Marvin Charles Bohaning of Louisville, Kentucky, "Charlie" was born November 30, 1906, in Blytheville, Arkansas, and was a veteran of World War II.

**BOMAR** – Enos Bertrum Bomar and his wife, Zettie Lavadel (Ferguson) Bomar and six children came to Greene County from Benton County, TN around 1912. They had seven more children after coming to Greene County. They first lived at Gainesville, later moving to Paragould and got a job on the Missouri-Pacific Railroad, where he was an engineer until his retirement.

Enos Bertrum Bomar was born in Benton County, TN, Nov. 26, 1883. He died Jan. 4, 1974 in Greene County. His ancestors came from England around 1728. They helped settle South

Carolina, Tennessee, and Kentucky. They were all Whigs and fought for America in the Revolutionary War.

Zettie Laveda Ferguson was born in White County, TN on March 15, 1890 and died Oct. 14, 1951 in Greene County. Her family came from Scotland and settled in Tennessee in the Cumberland Mountains.

*Enos Bertram Bomar and Zettie Laveda Ferguson Bomar*

Zettie's father, Lemul Ferguson, was 17 or 18 when the Civil War started. He enlisted in the Confederate Army on Jan. 14, 1862. He fought under Captain Lawson M. Burfoot in Company A of the Second Regiment of the Virginia Artillery. Her uncle was the famous Captain Champ Ferguson, the Confederate guerilla fighter of the Cumberland Mountains. He was a scout for Morgan's men and a member of Fighting Joe Wheeler's Cavalry. He fought throughout the war, only to be captured after the war ended and was formally tried before a military court in Nashville, TN. The South loved him; the Union hated him. He was the only soldier to be put on trial after the war ended. The Union Army hanged him on Oct. 20, 1865 in Nashville, TN.

My father was the fifth child of Enos and Zettie Bomar, Clarance Aubry Bomar, born Feb. 16, 1909 in Benton County, TN. He was six years old when he came by wagon to Greene County from Tennessee. He married Mae Bell Bean. She was born May 27, 1912 in Saline County, IL. Her family came to Greene County around 1919 or 19120 from Eldorado, IL. Logan Forest Bean and his wife, Minnie Bell Maxfield, brought seven children with them from Illinois and had four more after moving to Greene County. He had been a Marshall in Eldorado before coming to Arkansas. His ancestors were farmers and silversmith. One of them made the Bean Rifle. He died April 4, 1926 in Greene County. His wife died Nov. 3, 1948 in California.

Clarance Aubry Bomar and Mae Bell Bean had eight children. They raised their family in Greene County. He was a brakeman on the Missouri Pacific Railroad, where he worked until he retired. Clarance Aubry Bomar was born Feb. 16, 1909 in Benton County, TN and died April 10, 1992 in West Memphis, AR. Mae Bell Bean was born May 27, 1912 in Eldorado, IL and died Dec. 25, 1991 in West Memphis, AR.

*Submitted by Betty Ragsdell*

**BOWLIN** – John H. Bowlin was born on June 13, 1818, in Spartanburg County, South Carolina. He married Lucinda Hogan on August 14, 1845, at Spartanburg County. Lucinda was born on November 22, 1820, in South Carolina. Twin daughters, Adaline and Angeline Bowlin were born to John and Lucinda at Spartanburg County on March 20,1846. By 1850 the family was living in East Armuchee, Walker County, Georgia. Four children were born in Georgia–James William Bowlin, born March 30, 1850; Mary Jane Bowlin, born May 8,1852; John Morgan Bowlin, born October 27,1854; and a daughter, E.W.C. Bowlin born January 1856-died February 1860. In 1856 the Bowlin family moved by horse and oxen drawn wagons, northwest through Tennessee, the trip taking three weeks, to Greene County, Arkansas. They settled near Walcott. Benjamin Franklin Bowlin, born February 27, 1857, was the first of John and Lucinda's nine children to be born in Greene County. William Pinkney Bowlin, born August 31, 1860; Sarah Elizabeth "Sadie" Bowlin, born April 26, 1862, were also born in Greene County.

John H. Bowlin joined the Fifth Missouri State Guard as a private in Confederate States Army (CSA) Civil War. He was killed at the bloody Battle of Pea Ridge in Benton County, Arkansas, on March 8, 1862 at the age of 44.

Lucinda (Hogan) Bowlin, supported her large family by farming and taking in boarders. Lucinda died on March 23,1890, at Walcott, Greene County, Arkansas, at the age of 69. She and seven of her children, Adaline, James William, John Morgan, E.W.C., Benjamin Franklin, William Pinkney and Sarah Elizabeth are buried at Mt. Zion Cemetery in Greene County. Angeline is buried at Center Hill Cemetery in Greene County and Mary Jane is buried at Linwood Cemetery in Greene County. Lucinda and the nine children all died in Greene County.

1. Adaline (1846 South Carolina -1903 Arkansas) married James Henry Willcockson on January 6, 1868, at Greene County. (1845 Tennessee -1916 Arkansas) Four children: Anna Lee Willcockson, married William P. Martin; William Carroll Willcockson, married Nora Alice Jackson Edwards; Robert Alexander Willcockson, married first Nancy C. Eayson, married second Nancy Caroline Clements; Lawrence Jefferson Willcockson, married first Lavinia Ryan, married second Ida Hester Kennedy, married third Bessie Horton; married fourth Ginny Gibson. James Henry was the son of William Willcockson (1821 Tennessee -1860 Texas) and Mary Rose (1825 Tennessee -1860 Texas).

2. Angeline (1846 South Carolina -1922 Arkansas) married Nimrod R. Hampton in 1865 at Greene County. (1846 Missouri -1906 Arkansas) Ten children: Mary Ann Hampton, married Edward Edrington; Ida E. Hampton; Laura J. Hampton; Ella Hampton, married Robert Cammon; Emma L. Hampton; Benjamin F. Hampton; Bertie A. Hampton; Eva L. Hampton, married George W. Rowland; Thomas L. Hampton, married Lula M, Fox; John J. Hampton, married Verdie J. Little. Nimrod was the son of Isaiah Hampton (1797 North Carolina) and Jallie McDaniel (1802 Kentucky-1880 Arkansas).

3. James William "Bud" (1850 Georgia - 1896 Arkansas) married Sinie L. Willcockson in 1870 at Greene County (1850 Tennessee -1918 Arkansas) Seven children: James Edward Bowlin, married Caldonia Ryan; Benjamin Wilson Bowlin, married Eldorado Elizabeth Mayness; Thomas Alonzo Bowlin, married Eva Lou Key; Hendrix "Tinker" Bowlin, married Fannie Lou Langley; Cleveland "Cub" Bowlin, unmarried; Rosa Bowlin, married W. Tom Clements; Lily Bell Bowlin, married Robert M, Lamb. Sinie L. was the daughter of William Willcockson and Mary Rose.

4. Mary Jane (1852 Georgia-1938 Arkansas) married Thomas Riley Willcockson on December 6, 1868, at Greene County. (1848 Tennessee -1925 Arkansas) Ten children: Dovie Caldonia "Callie" Willcockson, married Sterling P. Rousseau; Lucy Lovena Willcockson, married William Pleasant Dennis; Mildred Ardena Willcockson, married first Edwin Goodloe, married second E.G. Harper Tinsley; Monty Mack Willcockson, married Clara Reiser; Idella Willcockson; Charley Willcockson. Sudie Willcockson, married Minton McHaney; Myrtle Willcockson; Minnie Allen Willcockson, married Edward Walter Stanley; Holland Willcockson, married first John Dover, married second W. Telfair Stedman. Thomas Riley was the son of Samuel Willcockson (1817 Tennessee -1887 Arkansas) and Frances Willard Gibson (1818 Kentucky-1895 Arkansas).

5. John Morgan (1854 Georgia-1935 Arkansas) married first Mary L. Hutchins on November 10, 1874, at Greene County (1856 Arkansas -1900 Arkansas) Four children: Cora B. Bowlin, married John Lawrence Dacus; William Robert "Bob" Bowlin, married first Ollie Esther Ross on April 12, 1896, at Greene County. Ollie Esther (1879 Arkansas -1913 Arkansas) was the daughter of Lewis W. Ross and Charity E. Dennis; married second Vera White about 1914 at Greene County. Lilie M. Bowlin and Lewis Bowlin died as infants. Mary L. was the daughter of William H. Hutchins (1829 Tennessee - 1877 Arkansas) and  Mary Cupp (1832 Georgia -1878 Arkansas). John Morgan, married second Mary (Clements) Short (1865-1951), widow of J.N. Short. Mary Clements was the daughter of Samuel Clements and Katy Hutchins. Mary L. (Hutchins) Bowlin and Mary (Clements) Short-Bowlin were both  granddaughters of Wiley Hutchins and Charlotte Pearce who were among the earliest settlers of what is now Greene County.

6. Benjamin Franklin (1857 Arkansas -1927 Arkansas) married first Alta Elizabeth Walden on October 21, 1886, at Greene County (1870 Alabama -1900 Arkansas) Six children: Mattie Bowlin, married Jim Lands;  Luther Franklin Bowlin, married Mary N. Annice;  Dora Bowlin, married Park Newsom; Holland Bowlin, married Joseph R. Tucker; Adaline Bowlin, married William G. Nutt; Ray Vaughn Bowlin, married first T. Mae Lawrence, married second Margaret Watson. Alta E. was the daughter of George Peter Walden (1841 Georgia) and Lucinda E. McDow (1848 Georgia) Benjamin Franklin, married second Lou I. Allison (1867 Tennessee -1954 Arkansas) Two children: Roy I. Bowlin, married Rosalee Elliot; Ervie P. Bowlin, married Mary Blackwood.

7. William Pinkney (1860 Arkansas - 1926 Arkansas) married Emily Frances Boozer on December 19, 1880, at Greene County (1862-1912 Arkansas). Six children: Luveny "Lizzie" Elizabeth Bowlin, married Neal S. Adams; Bertha Lee Bowlin, married Willie Wade Martin; Nanny Ray Bowlin, married first E.J. Ryan, married second Guv. Faulkner; Orro John Bowlin, married William Earl Tillman; Dora Frederick Bowlin, married Jim Carpenter; William Troy Bowlin, unmarried. Emily Frances was the daughter of Frederick Boozer (1826 Georgia - 1894 Arkansas) and E.J., died 1873 to 1880.

8. Sarah Elizabeth (1862 Arkansas - 1943 Arkansas)  married Andrew Jackson Willcockson on February 10, 1881, at Greene County (1855 Arkansas - 1894 Arkansas) Five children: Wake Wilson Willcockson, married first Laura Lee Odia Seay, married second Daisy Selma Bobo; Della Willcockson, married Robert Perkins Blackwood; Maudy Willcockson, married Charley Thomas Doyle;  Lucy Elcey Willcockson, died as an infant; Arthur William Willcockson, married Pearly Izora Ryan. Andrew Jackson was the son of William Willcockson and Mary Rose.

Dozens of descendants of John H. and Lucinda (Hogan) Bowlin still live in North East Arkansas.

**BOYD** – Paul Boyd's history starts in Tennessee. Looking in the 1850 Macon County, TN census we find a William Boyd, age 45. In his household there is Nancy 39, Robert 19, John 17, William 15, Mary 12, Andrew 10, Frances 8, George 6, Martin 4 and P. W. 1.

The story as told by Paul Whitfield's oldest son.

William and his family left Tennessee for Arkansas. They crossed the Mississippi River in southeast Missouri, William became ill at the crossing and they camped out by the river. William later died there and was buried by the river. The mother and children went on to Arkansas with other wagons.

Now we look at the 1860 census of Greene County, AR we find:

Mary, W. P. C. (William) 24; A. J. (Andrew) 19; Francis M. 17; G. W. (George) 15; Martin W. 13; Paul W. 11 and D. F. L. (David Feenie L.) 5. So the family must have moved between 1850 and 1860.

We have found no record of Robert Boyd. John Boyd married a Sophia A. – children are: William F. Boyd; Pinkney C. Boyd; William F. C. Boyd; Mary Boyd; Andrew J. Boyd; Frances M. Boyd; George W. Boyd.

Martin W. Boyd born Oct. 12, 1846 in Tennessee, died May 27, 1885 in Greene County, AR. Married Martha J. Macmillan, born Nov. 11, 1842 in South Carolina. Died Feb. 4, 1911 in Greene County, AR, children are One J. Boyd (1869), Alice (1871), Clara Boyd (1877).

Selma Boyd born Jan. 9, 1880 in Greene County, AR, died June 18, 1970, married George S. Self, born 1876 in Arkansas, died 1903 in Greene County, AR.

Paul Wheatfield Boyd: born Oct. 31, 1848 in Tennessee, died Jan. 12, 1909 in Greene County, AR, married Nancy Anne Clark, born April 27, 1848 in Gibson County, TN, died Feb 24, 1928 in Greene County, AR (see family of Joseph Clark), children are: Ida Boyd (1872); Joseph Arthur Boyd (May 2, 1874); Sallie Boyd (May 1876); Aubrey Boyd (April 1879); Alex Markum Boyd (March 30, 1882); Elmer Cleveland Boyd (Nov. 8, 1885); Dock Leslie Boyd (Feb. 26, 1887); Annie Boyd (Jan. 1, 1890).

Note: Joseph Arthur Boyd was on the first Oak Grove Board when the District consolidated to one school. His name can be found on front of the original building with other board members of that time. Dock Leslie became a doctor, he served the community of Bard until he opened his office in Blytheville, AR. David Feenie L. Boyd, (Jan. 3, 1855 TN-Oct. 14, 1933 OK) married Matte, (Oct. 8, 1858-Nov 1, 1878 AR). Children are: Thomas Sanford Boyd (Oct. 18, 1878). David's third wife, Nancy Goodwin was born and died in Arkansas. Children are: Cleo Boyd; Selmer Ashly Boyd (July 27, 1877); Lon Boyd (Nov. 13, 1889); Audie Boyd (1897); Arville Boyd (1897).

Paul Wheatfield Boyd and Nancy Anne lived and farmed on land owned by Nancy Anne's father Joseph Clark. Their oldest son Arthur farmed the same land after Paul could no longer farm. The land later on was so poor it was said you could not raise an umbrella on it.

Arthur and his family moved to the bottoms known then as Panther Island.

*Submitted by Joseph D. Sanders, grandson of Arthur Boyd*

**BRANCH** – William Andrew Branch, was born April 26, 1884, the son of John H. and Mary F. (Burton) Branch in the Wood's Chapel Community, Greene County, Arkansas. He attended Wood's Chapel School and Brown's Chapel School. He attended Ouachita College and returned to teach school in Greene County including school at Brown's Chapel. For 34 years he was a teacher or school administrator in Greene County.

On September 25, 1910, he married Beulah Diggs, daughter of John T. and Fannie (Lamb) Diggs of Browns Chapel Community. They had nine children: William Owen "Buster" Branch, Lorene (Branch) Williams, Frances (Branch) Walls, Thomas Edwin Branch, James D. Branch,

*The family of John Hugh and Francis Burton Branch: Harrison Branch, children, and housekeeper, Sally Beasly, Grover, Marvin, Sarah, Charlie, Oscar, Alice Branch Highfill, Henry Highfill, and children, John and Tennie, W. A. Branch, John and Margaret Branch (Sis) and children, Albert, Cora Estelle, Carrie, and Selma.*

Walter J. "Bud" Branch, Robert B. Branch, Jean (Branch) Lane, and Ben F. Branch.

W.A. Branch was the county judge in Greene County from 1916-1921. During this time he led in the movement to remodel and enlarge the courthouse. A vault was added to the west side of the courthouse to provide secure storage space for county records. Also, the exterior of the courthouse was covered with stucco. From 1924-1926 he was the county school superintendent. From 1933-1940 he was the county school examiner. He was the postmaster at the Paragould Post Office from 1940-1954.

The primary interest of W.A. Branch was in improved education. He foresaw this in consolidated schools. In 1946 there were 26 schools in Greene County. Under the leadership of W.A. Branch, Lloyd Howell and E.W. Little, the consolidation of Greene County Technical School District was brought about and the school was opened in November 1947. With the consolidation of schools making up the Greene County Technical School District Number one, this left seven schools in Greene County, Arkansas.

W.A. Branch died in 1957 and is buried at Wood's Chapel Cemetery. There is constructed at Brown's Chapel Church, a small school to serve as a replica of the school which W.A. Branch taught at Brown's Chapel.

**BRANDON** – George Washington Brandon married Ida Lucinda Elmore on Nov. 8, 1888 in Pickens County, AL. George, an avid hunter and fisherman, wanted to come to Greene County because he had heard of the good hunting and fishing in the Cache River Bottoms. They came to Greene County by train from Reform, AL sometime between 1894-1897.

After living in the Larado area for a while, George and Ida homesteaded land in Light, AR. According to their daughter, the late Dicie Brandon Gatlin, her father built a shanty on the homestead because you had to have some sort of house built very quickly in order to keep the property. Dicie recalled her mother talking about cooking in a lean-to kitchen out back. George built a very nice barn that stood for many years on the property at Light. They traded the property in Light for a house (shown in the photo) and land near Lorado. According to Dicie Gatlin, Ida would bake pound cakes so big; she baked them in a dishpan. George would have to help her stir the cakes. She would take them to community get-togethers and there were never any leftovers. The house in the photo burned and the family Bible, which was kept on a table in the hallway, was destroyed. It is said that Ida tried to go in to get the Bible, but was held back. Much of the family records were destroyed. George died in 1914 and Ida died in 1940. They are buried in the Finch Cemetery.

The children of George Washington Brandon and Ida Lucinda were Maud, Richard Grover, Florence, George Lee and Dicie. Three children Annie, Kittie and Julian Ann died at very young ages. Maud and Florence moved away after marrying. Grover, Lee and Dicie lived most of their lives in Greene County.

Dicie Brandon Gatlin lived many years in Greene County. She was an accomplished seamstress and operated a custom drapery shop in her home. She and her husband, Sam, lived on Pruett's Chapel Road and were active in Pruett's Chapel Methodist Church. She died in March 2000 and is buried with her husband in Linwood Cemetery.

Lee's son, Eugene and his wife, Bertie, still live in Paragould. They have two children, Larry and Diana.

*Home place of George W. Brandon. From left: George W. Brandon, Ida Brandon, Florence Brandon Funk holding her older sister Maude's son, Edward Chadwick, Richard Grover, George Lee, and Dicie Bell Brandon Gatlin.*

Richard "Grover" Brandon served in WWI. He was inducted on April 1, 1918 to the 22nd Company, 6th Training Battalion, 162nd Depot Brigade, United States Army. He later married Rena May Carraway from Shelby, MS. She was the daughter of John Turner Carraway and Alice Jane Nunnery. After living in Mississippi and Lorado for a short while, Grover and Rena settled on a 40-acre farm in the Bard Community. They were active in the Bard Methodist Church where Rena taught children's Sunday school classes. Grover, a skilled blacksmith and woodworker, made tools, furniture and baskets. He built the little wooden chairs for her Sunday school classroom at the Bard Methodist Church. They grew cotton and soybeans and also raised cattle, hogs and chickens. Grover died in 1947 and Rena continued to farm the land. She loved to watch the planting and harvesting of her crops. She was also a dedicated gardener. She later was remarried to Ben Gaskill. Ben died in 1990 and Rena died in 1992. She is buried, with most of the Brandon family, in the Finch Cemetery.

Grover and Rena Brandon had three daughters: Kathryn Jane, Carolyn Grace and Mary Lou.

Kathryn Brandon married Owen Hoskins from Monette. They have three sons: Richard, Steve and Frank. Richard and his wife, the former Rebecca Rowe of Clarksdale, MS and daughter, Katy, live in Paragould. Steve and his wife, the former Margaret McMenamin of Greene County have one daughter, Frankie Ann. Frank lives in Milton, FL.

Carolyn Brandon married Bill Ford from the Coffman Community in Greene County. His mother was Jewell Lovelace and his father was William Rudy Ford. Carolyn and Bill had four children: Ann, deceased 1959, Rena, Andy and Marilynn who all live in Paragould. Rena is married to Davey Joe Jackson. They have on son, Kyle. Andy has one daughter, Shea, who also lives in Paragould. Marilynn married Philip Brasher. They have one daughter, Carly. Bill died in July of 1977. He and Ann are buried in Linwood Cemetery. Carolyn later remarried to Bruce Highfill.

Mary Lou Brandon married Larry Gist from Cardwell, MO. Larry served in the U. S. Air Force and their family lived throughout the United States and overseas. Larry died in 1993 and Mary Lou died in 1998. Their three children are Donna Moore, Angela Shilcutt and Brandon Gist. Their grandchildren are: Audrey Moore; Brandi Gist; Tyler and Jarrod Shillcut.

George Washington Brandon came to Greene County because of its opportunities for hunting and fishing. It is interesting to note that many of his descendents, who continue to live in Greene County, are also avid hunters and fishermen and women, who still enjoy the outdoors, waterfowl and wildlife of Greene County.

*Submitted by Rena Jackson*

**BRAZIL** – The history of Donna (Kirk) Brazil in Greene County began May 25, 1941, with my birth at Dickson Memorial Hospital in Paragould. I was the second daughter born to Matilene and Earl Kirk, who came to Greene County in 1939.

I attended public schools and graduated from Paragould High School, home of the Bulldogs. During high school I participated in a work-study program, Distributive Education and was employed at Faustenia's Dress Shop on Pruett Street.

*Brazil Family- Donna, Charles, Sara and Suzanne 1984*

My college years were spent at the University of Denver (Colorado) and the University of Arkansas, where I graduated with a BSBA in Marketing.

Marriage in 1965 to Charles Brazil, son of Lois Hinson Brazil and the late James Crawford Brazil of Searcy, took us to Yuma Proving Ground, AZ. Charles was a 2nd lieutenant in the U. S. Army stationed with the U. S. Army Test Command. After the completion of his military service, we moved to Pine Bluff, AR, where Charles, a graduate of the University of Arkansas with a degree in electrical engineering, was employed with Arkansas Power & Light Co. for eight years. Our first daughter, Sara was born in Pine Bluff, (Jefferson County) AR. in 1970.

Opportunity to join my father, Earl Kirk, in his business, brought us back to Paragould in 1973. We moved into the family home, a former Methodist District parsonage at 602 W. Highland Street, where my family had lived for 23 years previously. We lived there another 20 years before building a home on McDaniel Road.

*Kirk–Brazil Family Home*

My husband, Charles, became active in civic affairs, purchased the business which became Kirk & Brazil Construction Co. and our second daughter, Suzanne, was born in Jonesboro, (Craighead County), AR in 1975.

Our children had the privilege of growing up in a small, safe friendly town and were involved in similar activities that I experienced growing up. They graduated from Ridgecrest High School. Sara furthered her education at Hendrix College in Conway, AR and the University of Tennessee, graduating with a doctor of pharmacy degree. She now lives in Memphis, TN with her husband Ken Haynes and son, Matthew.

Suzanne graduated from the University of Arkansas with a degree in Kinesiology and moved to the Pacific Northwest, where she has enjoyed skiing and snowboarding. She is currently living in Bellingham, WA.

*Submitted by N. D. J. Brewer Family, Courtesy of Eugene Walden*

**BREWER** – John Clifton (Cliff) Brewer, was born July 29, 1904, the son of James F. and Emma Williams Brewer. Emma's parents were William Thomas and Arbella E. Hayes Williams. The Brewer and Williams families traveled by wagon from Gibson County, Tennessee, to the Marmaduke area in Greene County about 1884. Cliff attended school at Oak Grove and Normal School. He enlisted in the United States Navy in 1922 at Little Rock. Except for a brief time he remained in the Navy over 29 years until retirement in 1953. He advanced from fireman to lieutenant during this time. His career included 17 years of foreign and sea duty.

*Clifton Brewer family: Jim, Jewel and Clifton.*

On February 10, 1925, he married Jewel Faulkner while home on leave. She was born January 25, 1906, to Reverend J.D.J. and Mary Rutledge Faulkner. They eloped and were married at Arkansas State College in Jonesboro. Her parents learned of the marriage when they read it in the newspaper. Jewel traveled by train to join Cliff in San Diego, California. Her father placed her in the care of railroad people who were members of the Masonic Lodge. They passed her along the line until she arrived in San Diego. This began an exciting and sometimes lonely marriage of 53 years until Cliff's death on December 12, 1978.

Their son "J" Kenneth "Jim" was born June 29, 1926, in San Diego. Cliff was at sea abroad the *U.S.S. Somers* when Jim was born. Like many Navy wives Jewel followed Cliff's ship when possible. They lived in San Diego, Bremerton, Washington, Norfolk, Virginia; Ocracoke, North Carolina, New Orleans, Louisiana; Philadelphia, Pennsylvania and two separate tours in the Panama Canal Zone. During the early years of marriage Cliff's ships were often at sea for several months at a time. Jewel and Jim returned to Paragould to be with her parents at those times. They drove alone across the United States in 1933 when there were few paved roads and fewer tourist courts. Cliff was abroad the *U.S.S. New York* as it changed ports from the California to Virginia.

He transferred to shore duty in the commissary at Norfolk for three years. In 1937 he went abroad he *U.S.S. Yorktown* to serve his last shipboard duty.

On December 7, 1941, the family was stationed in the Panama Canal Zone. Jewel and Jim were evacuated along with other dependents soon after Pearl Harbor was bombed. They returned to Paragould remaining until 1944 when Jewel joined Cliff at Ocracoke and their son enlisted in the United States Navy. During World War II and until retirement Cliff served as a supply and disbursing officer.

Following retirement Cliff earned a real estate license at Long Beach City College. He sold real estate several years in California.

The couple returned to Greene County for the remaining years of their lives. They were members of Imanuel Baptist in Paragould. Cliff was a Mason. Jewel died June 6, 1991. They are buried in Memorial Gardens.

**BREWER** – Nathaniel D. J. Brewer was born Nov. 20, 1816 in North Carolina. I believe that his father was James W. Brewer. A Carroll County, TN estate settlement for James W. was recorded in 1839. No heirs were listed but 1840 Carroll census shows that Nathaniel's household included one female near his age, one older female and a young male child. His first child (1838) was named James W. Brewer. The mother of Nathaniel's oldest children James, Martha Jane (1840) and John F. (1843) is unknown. Records found in the family Bible of son John show a Nancy Brewer listed with these three children.

Alcey Brewer was born Nov. 8,1822. The same records identify her as the third wife of N.D.J. Brewer. They were married in Carroll County in 1847. The children born to this union were Nancy E. "Nannie"(1848); William Franklin "Frank" (1849); J. Newton "Newt" (1850); Thomas Marion T. "Tom"(1851); Joseph R. "Joe" (1853); George H. "Buck"(1854) and Edmond Jones "Abe" (1855).

Records from Holly Springs Baptist Church of Carroll County show N.D. J. becoming a member by letter in 1843. His dismissal date is 1886. That was the year he moved from Tennessee to Greene County, AR. Some families of allied lines were also members of the church. They included Carey, Hammett, Birdwell and Hatch.

The oldest one, James W., died in 1879 while serving as pastor of Mount Nebo Baptist Church. And his wife, Mary McCall Brewer, are buried in nearby Spellings Cemetery.

*N. D. J. Brewer family*

By 1880 sons, John, Tom and their families migrated to Hurricane Township in Greene County. Nathaniel and Alcey moved to the Marmaduke area in 1886 with several family members. In 1900 NDJ and Alcey lived in the home of their youngest son, Abe and his wife Eliza A. Cary. She was the daughter of William and Georgean Johnson Cary.

Another child, Nannie, married Felix Cary, son of William and Caroline Hammett Cary. Felix and Nannie reared her brother "Buck's" children. My great-grandfather, John F. Brewer, married Sarah M. Cary, daughter of Samuel and Mary Minerva Akin Cary. She was a cousin to Eliza A. and Felix. John's second wife was Ellen Boyd.

Marriages of N.D.J.'s other children included Martha Jane to John Wesley Hammett; Frank to Margaret Birdwell; Newt to Nancy J.; Tom to (1) Margaret Lenzy (2) Mary Lax (3) Ida Margaret Butler and Joe to Permelia. Buck's spouse is not known.

Nathaniel D. J. Brewer died in 1906 and his wife Alcy, in 1910. They are buried in Wright Cemetery near Marmaduke. Many of their descendents currently reside in Greene County.

My grandfather, James F. "Jim" Brewer, was the son of John and Sarah Cary Brewer. He married Emma Williams, daughter of William Thomas and Arabella Hays Williams. They were the parents of Clarence; Earle, my father John Clifton; Beulah; Alvin and Dathel.

Jim's second wife was Lula Butler. They were parents of Lorene; Leonard; Melvina; Jackie and Bonnie.

*Submitted by "J" Kenneth Brewer*

**BREWER** – Thomas M. T. Brewer was born on Oct. 22, 1852 to Nathaniel D. J. Brewer and his second wife, Alcie Elizabeth, in Benton County, TN. Tom had nine brothers and sisters, James W.; Martha Jane; John F.; Nancy E.; William Franklin; J. Newton "Newt"; Joseph R.; George H. and Edmond Jones "Abe". On Nov. 24, 1870 Tom married Margaret "Milly" Lenzy in Tennessee and they had three children, John Wesley, Dave W. and Sarah Bell "Sis". Tom and his family (including his parents and many of his siblings) moved to Greene County, AR. After moving to Arkansas, Tom married his second wife, Cordelia Anderson Dover, on Dec. 17, 1883. Tom and Cordelia had one son, Elsay Seaburn Brewer, born in 1884. Then came wife number three, Mary Ida Butler Lax. It is thought that Tom met her while cutting logs to clear land near the St. Francis River. Mary had two children from a previous marriage, Hubert and Marcia Lax. Tom and Ida Margaret Butler (she is thought to be the same as Mary Ida Butler Lax) married on Feb. 1, 1890 and had six children, Ezra Herman; Van; Alcie Elizabeth; Ellen Leona; Alvie and Christine. Ida Margaret Butler Brewer died in Aug. 1908 when Christine was still a baby and her older half brother, "Big" Dave and his wife, Jenny, raised Christine. Tom had a sorghum mill. He would travel around the Gainesville area and get permission from a cane farmer to set up his mill on the farmer's property. People from the area would bring their sorghum cane to Tom's mill to be made into molasses. Two mules would walk in a circle pulling the grinder around the wagon, which squeezed juice out of the sorghum cane. It was then boiled over a fire to make molasses and put into barrels or jugs after it was cooked. Then Tom would pack up and move to a different area. Tom was a Methodist. He loved to walk and even though he used a cane he would refuse to ride when people offered. He usually wore moleskin pants with black and gray stripes. After his last wife died, Tom moved from place to place and stayed with his son, Van, a lot. Van took over the Sorghum Mill operation. Tom liked to visit his grandchildren and would usually show up with candy canes in his pocket for them. In his last years he lived with his youngest daughter, Christine Walden. Tom smoked a pipe and raised his own strong smelling tobacco while living with Christine. He was not a big man, probably only about 5 feet 6 inches tall. He was very talkative and loved to tell jokes and talk about his past and his family. It is said he had a temper, but no one can ever remember him using bad language. He passed away on Dec. 9, 1938 at the age of 86 years. He is buried at the Gainesville Cemetery.

*Submitted by Sandra Krupa*

*Man second from right is Tom M.T. Brewer and his sorghum molassas mill. Man left of Tom is Bud Payne. Man right of Tom is Van Brewer. Young boy and man on far left unknown.*

**BRIDGES** – George P. Bridges, the firstborn son of Silas Wright Bridges and Melvina Palestine Phillips, born April 5, 1885 at Shiloh in Poinsett County, moved to Pruett's Chapel in 1892 after his fathers death in 1891. His Phillips' relations had located there in 1883.

He attended school at Pruett's Chapel and at Lorado and entered Louisville University Medical School from a school in Marmaduke

In 1908 he passed the state board and was licensed to practice his profession before completing his medical education in Louisville. The 1910 census shows him living in the Main Shore community with his wife Lura Thomas and younger brother Clarence in the household. He received his medical degree from the University of Louisville in 1914 and moved his practice into Paragould at 110 West Court Street, over Walden-Blount's Drug Store, where he worked until three days before his death.

Around 1920 he built a home on the Jonesboro Road about a quarter of a mile south of Linwood, which was sold by a family member in 1995 and dismantled before 1996.

George Bridges and his wife Lura were the parents of three boys, the oldest of whom died at birth. Lloyd Bowen Bridges, born Sept. 17, 1911, married Louise Kimbrough and had Frances Ann, who married Bill McKelvey. Thurman Joseph Bridges married May Ruth Gilbert and had Mary Jo, Betty Nell, Perry and Larry

*39 Linwood Dr. looking north, fall 1979*

George P. Bridges, the son of Silas and Melvina Phillips Bridges, grandson of George S. Bridges and Lucinda Scott and the great grandson of Joseph Bridges of North Carolina, Alabama and Poinsett County, AR died Nov. 22, 1950 and is buried with his mother and wife at Linwood Cemetery. His father, Silas Bridges, is buried at Shiloh in Poinsett County.

*Submitted by Betty Key*

**BRIDGES** – My grandfather, Thomas Grover Bridges, was the third of four children of Silas Wright Bridges and Melvina Palestine Phillips Bridges. He was born Dec. 26, 1888 in Poinsett County, AR. His brother George Perry was born April 5, 1885; sister Lela Mae, Dec. 14, 1886 and brother Clarence Gilbert, Oct. 25, 1890. They were born in a small house cobbled together with planks and logs eight miles south of Harrisburg on the Bay Village Road.

The Bridges and the Phillips families lived contemporaneously in Poinsett County for more than a decade, but the Bridges were much earlier settlers. Silas Bridges' grandfather was probably Joseph Bridges, one of the first white émigrés to Poinsett County. Joseph migrated from Jefferson County, AL in about 1838 with his wife Margaret Condry Bridges. They had married Nov. 23, 1818 in Jefferson County when he was 18 years old and had had at least three children before they came to Arkansas. Two of them were likely Lewis W. Bridges and George S. Bridges, next door neighbors in Mitchell Township, Poinsett County, in 1850. By 1850 Joseph Bridges had either died or moved away from Arkansas.

George S. Bridges was Silas Bridges' father. George was born Nov. 26, 1826 in Alabama and married Lucinda B. Scott, who was born about 1831 in Kentucky. George and Lucinda had 12 children: Mary S. (1850); Margaret S. (1852); Samantha (1853); Matilda (1855); Silas Wright (Oct. 21 1857-Dec. 14, 1891); George (1858-before 1870); Josephine (1860); William (Nov. 5, 1863- July

*L-R Back row: Lela Mae and George P. Bridges; Caroline Dover; Melvina Bridges holding Clarence G. Bridges; Thomas G. Bridges (Courtesy Arkansas History Commission).*

18, 1903); Joseph Shelby (Jan. 29, 1867-March 23, 1899); Lucinda Ada (1870); John Leo (1871) and James R. (March 18, 1874-Oct. 4, 1900).

On Sept. 19, 1857 George S. Bridges applied for a 40-acre land grant in Section 8, Township 9 North, Range 4 East, which is in present-day Cross County near Hydrick. President Buchanan officially granted the land July 1, 1859. The family moved briefly to Fulton County, AR after 1857 and was recorded there in Bennett's Bayou Township in 1860, two doors down from Lucinda's relatives, the Scott's. Family history has it that George Bridges was a scout for the Confederacy and was in Fulton County reconnoitering the Yankees.

*Melvina Bridges (far right); George P. Bridges (holding an umbrella) Lela Lam, fourth from right (Courtesy Arkansas History Commission).*

By 1865 the George Bridges family was back in Poinsett County and in the 1870 census was recorded in Scott Township. When George Bridges died in Oct. of 1877 the family owned 80 acres in the southwest corner of Section 15, Township 10 North, Range 4 East. He was buried nearby in the Shiloh Cemetery southeast of Harrisburg.

His son Silas married Melvina Palestine Phillips on March 20, 1883. Silas was 28 years old and Melvina was only 17. She was born Sept. 30, 1867 in Alabama, the oldest of seven children of John Perry Phillips (Aug 6, 1837- March 9, 1883) and Caroline Malinda Dover (June 25 1842-Feb 15, 1907). The Phillips family had moved to the Farm Hill community south of Harrisburg in late 1868 from Blount County, Al. After John Perry Phillips' death Caroline moved to Pruett's Chapel community in Greene County to be near three of her brothers: William Franklin, John Bailey and Andrew L. Dover. She died of pneumonia at their home two miles west of Paragould, on Feb. 15, 1907 and was buried in Pruett's Chapel Cemetery.

Silas Wright Bridges died in Poinsett County Dec. 14, 1891 of 'kidney colic." He was buried at the Shiloh Cemetery in Harrisburg near his father. After his death Melvina and her children followed her mother to Pruett's Chapel community, where she supported her family by taking in washings. On Sept. 22, 1894 she sold their former home in Poinsett County and its surrounding 80 acres of land in Section 16, Township 10 North, Range 4 East to Silas' brother, William B. Bridges. Melvina and her family stayed in the Pruett's Chapel community until she married John A. "Con" Ray Nov. 25, 1903 and moved to the St. Francis River bottoms. The children attended the old Miller school. By 1910 Melvina had left John Ray. He divorced her April 6, 1911 for deserting him. Sometime before 1920 she moved to the George Bridges farm located approximately eight miles southeast of Paragould in the Main Shore Township. She spent most of her later years in Paragould at the home of her daughter; Lela Lam. Melvina died June 18, 1954 and was buried in Linwood Cemetery, near her son George.

George Perry Bridges graduated from medical school in Louisville, KY in 1914 and practiced in Paragould, AR until his death Nov. 22, 1950. He was married to Lura Lee Thomas and had three children: a male infant who was born and died Sept. 30, 1910, Thurman Joseph and Loyd Bowen.

Lela Mae married James P. Lam Aug. 21, 1904. They spent most of their lives in Greene County and had four children: Sadie, Dortha, Hester and twin sister Estie. James died March 31, 1961 and Lela April 30, 1971.

Clarence Gilbert first married Esta Ola Miller and had six children: Lulene; Bernice; Alvin Edward; Orvin Derry; Opie Lorraine and Reedie Mozelle. He later married Helen Burch. Clarence was first a fireman and then an engineer for the Missouri-Pacific Railroad. In 1965 he wrote *Us Bridges*, a book about the family and growing up in Greene County. He was residing in Walnut Ridge, AR when he died Sept. 12, 1970.

Thomas Grover Bridges graduated from Northwestern University School of Pharmacy in Evanston, IL in 1913. He first worked at Scott Drug Company in Paragould and later bought his own drug store in Corning, AR, the Bridges Drug and Jewelry Company, which he sold to buy a cotton gin in Reyno, AR. He traded this gin for one in Datto, AR and later traded that for the Crystal Drug Company in 1932. He did a stint in the army from May 1918 to Nov. 1919, serving in France in WWI. He married Lily Pearl Hosey Dec. 25, 1920 in Corning, Clay County, AR. They had three children: Thomas Grover Jr., who died March 8, 1941 at the age of 16 from injuries suffered in a diving accident at Current River Beach; Peggy Jean Bridges (April 13, 1923- April 12, 1972) and my father, Ronald Perry Bridges, who was born April 17, 1927. Thomas Grover Bridges died on March 24, 1978 and Lily Pearl on Feb. 6, 1987. Both are buried in the Corning Cemetery next to Peggy Jean and Thomas Grover Jr. Ronald Perry and his wife Betty Jane Drilling Bridges and their descendants live in Heber Springs, Cleburne County, AR.

*Submitted by Janet Claire Porterfield*

**BROOKFIELD** – Cynthia Jane Brookfield was the youngest daughter of the Rev. Isaac Brookfield and Nancy Campbell who first settled in Greene County, AR with their large, loving family of four boys and two girls. Being the daughter of a very famous pioneer preacher, it would be hard to find any one to live up to your father's example. But Cynthia Jane found just that man. Rev. Samuel Clark had come here from Ohio to become one of the early pioneer missionaries in Northeastern Arkansas. Rev. Clark had worked with Rev. Isaac Brookfield in the missionary field, prior to Isaac's death on Feb. 25, 1845.

Here is an account of what took place that morning:

It was a Friday

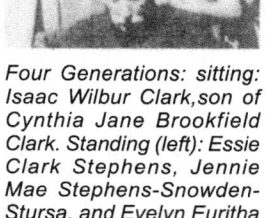

*Four Generations: sitting: Isaac Wilbur Clark, son of Cynthia Jane Brookfield Clark. Standing (left): Essie Clark Stephens, Jennie Mae Stephens-Snowden-Stursa, and Evelyn Euritha Snowden-Stursa.*

morning at sunrise, when Isaac motioned to be raised up. He put his feet out of the bed, as Cynthia Jane sat behind him with a pillow bracing his back. Nancy sat by his left side and Mr. Ramsey held his head. Nancy noticed that his breathing seemed unusually easy, but she saw that he was sinking fast. She called to the rest of the family to come in as he closed his eyes on all terrestrial objects and died.

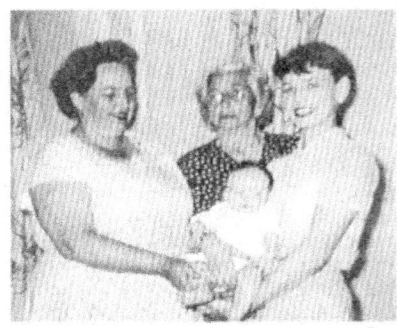

*March 1956 "Four Generations". Left: Jennie Mae Stursa, Essie Clark Stephens, Evelyn Euritha Sharkey, Jack Douglas Sharkey.*

Nancy lost her beloved husband and Cynthia Jane lost the father she had always looked up to and loved deeply. This experience brought mother and daughter closer together than at any other time in their lives.

After a sufficient mourning period, Cynthia Jane and Rev. Samuel Clark were finally married on Aug. 7, 1845. Also in that year, the Methodist Church in Arkansas split with the original Methodist Episcopal Church over the slavery issue. When the Southern Methodist Church was established, Sam Clark's stand against slavery caused him to be "located", a polite way of asking him to leave the ministry.

Rev. Sam Clark took his wife, Cynthia Jane and moved to Ohio where they lived on a farm near the rest of the Clark family for the next several years. When needed, he continued his work in the Methodist ministry.

Their family consisted of five boys, Samuel Asbury born Jan. 25, 1848; Thomas Newton born May 17, 1852, both of whom died within three days of each other in Oct. 1852. The three surviving boys were William Fisk born June 27, 1852 and died April 6, 1884; Isaac Wilbur born Jan. 3, 1855 and died Jan. 15, 1942 and James Bascum born April 2, 1857 and death date unknown.

In 1856, Sam and Cynthia came back to Bolivar, AR to help Cynthia's mother, Nancy Brookfield with her farm.

Sam Clark died Feb 11, 1859. His years as a circuit rider had taken its toll.

During the height of the Civil War, Cynthia Jane died on Feb. 12, 1863. She left behind her three little orphans, William, Isaac and James, who were taken in by the Brookfield family.

Cynthia is buried with her mother, father and husband in the Brookfield Cemetery located near Bolivar, Poinsett County, AR.

*Submitted by Evelyn Euritha Wagner*

**BROOKFIELD** – The name Isaac Brookfield must be associated with the beginnings of Greene County. In the year 1819, Rev. Isaac Brookfield left New Jersey and made his way to St. Louis, where he secured a horse and rode into the wilds of Arkansas to become the first missionary to the Indians and whites. The minutes of the Methodist Conference for 1821, as recorded in the Congressional Library,

Washington, show that he was first located at Hot Springs and a year later was sent to Spring River Circuit, with headquarters at Davidsonville.

The Brookfields are of English descent and were friends of John Wesley, founder of the Methodist church. It was through Wesley's influence that they came from England to America, where Isaac Brookfield's father became a glass manufacturer in New Jersey. William H. Brookfield, Lord Tennyson and the poet Browning were schoolmates at Oxford. These gentlemen, along with Mrs. Wm. H. Brookfield, formed a literary cult and a book was published of their activities under the title, "*Mrs. Brookfield and Her Circle.*" A copy of that book is in the possession of Isaac Brookfield's great-great-great-granddaughter, Evelyn Euritha Wagner.

*The Rev'd William Henry Brookfield at the age of 40. From the painting by Samuel Lawrence.*

While living in Davidsonville, Brookfield married Nancy Campbell, the daughter of Judge James Campbell of Lawrence County, March 23, 1823.

Brookfield assisted in the preparation of petition to be submitted to the Territorial Assembly requesting the creation of the county. It was approved Nov. 5, 1833.

The Methodist circuit riders, like Isaac Brookfield, received no stipend for their services and were only supported with lodging and board by church members. They were not only evangelist; they also taught and organized, baptized, married and consoled the bereaved. Usually they were men of some literacy and were often asked to assist a largely uneducated people in writing letters and preparing legal papers.

Since the establishment of churches was Brookfield's mission in northeast AR with the support of Benjamin Crowley and other early settlers on the Ridge, Brookfield organized the first church in Greene County in the Crowley home prior to the organization of the county in 1833. He served as the county judge until l835.

About the year 1825 he was engaged in mercantile pursuits at or near the town of Davidsonville, His dry goods were shipped from New York and required six months to reach their destination. Groceries were usually purchased at New Orleans. In 1834 he removed to what is now Poinsett County, locating a few miles east to the present town of Harrisburg, where he remained until his death Feb. 25, 1845. His church was called Spring Valley.

Isaac and Nancy had six children: Moses Asbury, born Feb. 8, 1824; Narcissus, born July 13, 1825; Cynthia Jane, born Sept. 26, 1827(this writer's great-great-grandmother); James Campbell Brookfield, born July 14, 1829; Joshua Soule Brookfield, born May 11, 1832 and Isaac Newton Brookfield, born Nov. 28, 1834.

Though Rev. Isaac Brookfield died at a relatively young age, his political and religious influence left an indelible mark on northeast AR.

*Submitted by Evelyn Euritha Wagner*

**BROOKS-TROXLER** – Maude Willodene (Fletcher) Brooks-Troxler was born Sept. 19, 1909 in the Finch community, a rural area of Paragould, AR. She was the daughter of Lonnie "Bud" and Phrona Fletcher and the paternal granddaughter of Ruben and Alce Dora Fletcher and the maternal granddaughter of Murray and Mary York.

Maude, called Willodene by her family and friends, was the youngest of six children (five girls and one boy). Tragically, when Willodene was only three weeks old her father was accidentally killed in a dynamite explosion.

Willodene was raised in the Finch community. She lived in a three room, tin roof house deep in the woods. The family cooked on a wood stove, burned kerosene lamps, drank water from the well and traveled by horse and buggy. Willodene attended Finch School through the second grade and completed the sixth grade at Baldwin Elementary School.

The country life provided fun and adventure for Willodene and her brothers and sisters. They enjoyed working together and playing together. During the summer months the children would fish and play ball at the sawmill yard and during the winter months they enjoyed snow sledding. One of Willodene's prized possessions was her organ. Playing the organ was entertaining for her and her family.

*L-R: Maude Willodene Fletcher, Albenteen Fletcher, Alex Fletcher, Juanita Wood Turpin, Alce Dora Fletcher, Ruben Fletcher holding Bill Hester, George Wood, Taylor Fletcher (Standing) Myrtle Fletcher, Harmon Fletcher, Bill Elmore, Mattie Bell Fletcher Elmore, Barney Elmore, Maude Fletcher Wood, Vanette Elmore Kirchoff, Henery Wood. (In back by door) Evie Fletcher.*

Christmas was a festive time of the year. The family would decorate the Christmas tree with red berries and stringed popcorn. Everyone would enjoy a big dinner and sing Christmas carols. The children would hang their stockings on the mantle and Santa filled them with fruit and hard candy.

At the age of 15, Willodene went to work at the Box Factory. While working at the Box Factory, she met 15 year-old Charlie Brooks. Charlie invited her to the movies and after one date they were a steady couple. Never having dated anyone else, Willodene and Charlie were married. Interestingly, the couple was married in Paragould on Mueller Street behind the cemetery standing in the road. A justice of the peace performed the ceremony and a friend, Ora Hensley, witnessed the special event.

Willodene and Charlie lived with Willodene's mother and continued to work at the Box Factory. On Sept. 10, 1927, their only child, James Edward Brooks was born in a house on East Vine Street. James Edward " Ed" Brooks was raised in Paragould. He worked for Wrapes Heading Mill and Hurt Grocery. He married Joyce Shipp and they had two sons, David Jerome and Glen Allen Brooks.

Later in life, Willodene married James Nicholas Troxler; James "J. N." was employed and later retired from Missouri Pacific Railroad. Willodene and J. N. were married 40 years. J. N, Troxler died in 1994. Maude Willodene (Fletcher) Brooks/Troxler died in April 1991 at the age of 81 in the Arkansas Methodist Hospital in Paragould, AR.

*Submitted by Donna Brooks*

**BROWN** – Gerald Parker Brown was born August 19, 1920, in Chalk Bluff Township, Clay County, Arkansas. He attended a one room school grades one through eight, and rode a plow horse seven miles to attend Piggott High School. On January 14, 1942, he joined the United States Marine Corps where he met and married Lottie Balk of Hoboken, New Jersey, also a Marine, on May 31, 1945. To this, union were born three children: Ronald, Clifford, and Celia "Bunny."

Gerald Brown was awarded a B.A. degree from the University of Arkansas in 1948, and an L.L.B. degree in 1951. He practiced law with William F. Kirsch and Maurice Cathey for 25 years and then served as chancery judge and circuit judge of the Second Judicial Circuit for 15 years. Following his retirement, he performed volunteer

*Standing: Judge Gerald Brown and Ronnie; front: Bunny (Brown) Lee, Lottie and Cliff.*

work for several organizations and active in preserving and restoring the 1888 Greene County Courthouse. He served on the board of the Arkansas Methodist Hospital for 47 years. Lottie Brown was volunteer director at the hospital for many years and chaired the Memorial Committee of the American Cancer Society for 35 years.

Ronald obtained a B.A. degree from Tulane University in New Orleans, and L.L.B. degree from the University of Virginia Law School. He practices law in Leesburg, Virginia. He has a daughter, Sara Elise Brown McKinnon, who lives in Memphis.

Clifford also obtained a B.A. degree from Tulane, did postgraduate work in Russian language at the Institute of Foreign Languages in Monterey, California, and the University of Arizona. He is a systems engineer in the Satellite Division of the Lockheed Corporation in San Jose, California.

Bunny Brown Lee received a B.A. degree from Sweet Briar College in Amherst, Virginia. She is a financial advisor with Morgan Stanley Dean Witter. Her husband, Stephen Lee, is a native of Forrest City, Arkansas, and has a B.A. degree from Harvard University. They reside in Paragould with their two daughters, Emily and Anna Caroline.

**BROWN** – Oscar Tolbert Brown, December 4, 1880-May 8, 1946, was born in Arlington, Kentucky, and followed the timber trade. He married at Leesville, Louisiana, January 28, 1903, Dosha Warren, September 21, 1881-April 12, 1967, the daughter of William N. and Letitia Absher Warren of Patterson, Missouri, via Lee County, Virginia.

They settled in the Upper Lafe Community in about 1922 and were buried in Providence Cemetery.

Their children were: Ollie (1903), Calvin (1907), Floy Maye (1909) and Virgil (1914).

Ollie married Louis Gerdes; Calvin married Mayne Valentine; and Virgil married Cletis Huckabay. Floy Maye died as an infant.

**BROWN** – Parmer Sanford Brown was born Sept. 23, 1830 in Herkimer County, NY. In the 1850 census, he is found in Granby Township, Oswego County, NY with Rosetta Davis whom he married in 1849. Then in 1864, after the death of their youngest son, Charles and in the dead of winter, the family followed Indian trails in Canada and crossed over frozen lakes and rivers to reach Clinton County, MI. They farmed until 1872, when he divorced Rosetta and married Madora Page, a 16-year-old neighbor. They moved to Kansas in 1874 and later, in 1880, to Indiana. He came to Arkansas from Indiana in October of 1894 and settled on "flat woods" near Imboden on the present day Lucus farm on Perry Toles Road, where they farmed and cut crossties for the railroad. Madora was a mid wife and raised eight children to adulthood. Sanford, who was in ill health in 1894, went back to Indiana to sell the farm. There, he took ill and died on Sept. 21, 1895. Madora married James Lee Tate on March 10, 1898. She died Jan. 1928 and is buried at Kelley's Cemetery near Black Rock.

Among their children was Joseph A. Brown, born Feb. 8, 1892 in Indiana. He married Nettie Oldham of Lawrence County, AR. The Oldham family came to Arkansas from Pendleton County, Kentucky around 1848. Nettie's great-great-grandfather, Jessie Oldham of Madison County, KY, was with Daniel Boone at Fort Boonesboro in 1775 during the Indian uprising and was also credited for the first recorded corn crop grown in Kentucky. Jessie's son, Tyree Oldham, was also at Fort Boonesboro and moved to Pendleton County, KY in 1814. Tyree was an industrious man, running a tavern, a ferry across the Licking River at Falmouth, KY and also a gristmill. In 1824, he built a Victorian style manor house and at the time, owned 21 slaves on the 1000-acre plantation that he bought from Henry Clay. Most of Joseph's children moved on to other parts, but his son Virgil stayed. He lived most of his life in Lawrence County farming in Randolph and Lawrence Counties in Arkansas and running a dairy up on flat woods north of Smithville. Virgil married Mary Hibbard and they raised six children. Around 1992, Virgil and Mary moved to Paragould because of Virgil's failing health.

Virgil and Mary's children are: Ancil; Allen; Sharon; Jerry; David and Michael. Two of their children live in Paragould. Michael moved to Paragould in June of 1972 to attend Crowley's Ridge College. There he met and later married Pauletta Wheeler, daughter of Russell and Aline Wheeler. Michael currently works at Tenneco Automotive in Paragould, in Human Resources and has traveled world wide for the company. Along with Human Resources, Michael works in the area of training and development. Allen moved to Paragould around 1996 and is a retired truck driver and is currently driving a school bus for Greene County Tech.

*Submitted by Michael Brown*

**BROWN** – Thomas Fulton Brown, of Marion County, South Carolina, with wife Mary migrated to Georgia circa 1845 where they remained until their death. They settled at Lawrenceville, Gwinnett County where seven more children were added to the four born in South Carolina.

One of these was John Fulton Brown who married Sarah E. Smith, daughter of Allen and Rebecca Lockridge Smith, October 13, 1872, in Gwinnett County. This marriage produced eight children. One, Ralph Cornelius Brown, is the subject of our story.

Ralph C. Brown, the progenitor, of this Brown family arrived in Arkansas with his grandfather Allen Smith from Gwinnette County, Georgia. First settling in the Brookland area of Craighead County he later worked in Jonesboro then moved to the Dixie Community where he had purchased a farm. He lived here until his death in 1946.

On April 7, 1923, Ralph C. "Corny" Brown married Bertha E. Randal Adams at Lake City, Arkansas. They became the parents of five children: Mattie Lou, William Scott, Mamie Elizabeth, Dessie Lee and Sarah Helen all of them reaching maturity.

*Brown family circa 1933. Front row: Elizabeth, Dessie and Helen. Back row: Mattie, Ralph C., Scott and Bertha.*

Upon the death of Ralph, Bertha continued to live on the farm until her youngest child, Helen, graduated from Dixie High School then she moved to Paragould where she purchased a house. Bertha moved to California, in 1963, living there until her death in 1977 and is buried in Lemoore Cemetery, Lemoore, California.

Mattie Lou married Herdle Brown in 1940 and they lived in the Greene County area for several years where three of their four children were born. In the late 1940s they moved to California where they and all the children yet live. Herdle died in 1991 and is buried in Lemoore. Mattie presently lives in Hanford, California.

Scott, who was a policeman in the Paragould Police Department for a number of years before, joined the Arkansas State Police, is now retired and living in Hope, Arkansas. He married Peggy Shirley and they have three boys: Reggie, born 1950 who died at birth and Ricky and Nicky all born in Paragould.

Mamie Elizabeth married Burlice White in 1945 at Paragould and lived in the Schugtown area before moving to Poinsett County. They have four children: Patricia, Katherine and Ralph were born in Greene County, Bertha Mae was born in Tyronza. This family later moved to California. Elizabeth died in 1982 and is buried in Lemoore, California. Burlice, now retired, lives at Hornersville, Missouri.

Dessie Lee, upon graduation from Dixie High School, married Joe Cupp, son of Jeff and Belle McClure Cupp. Two of their five children were born at Paragould while Joe pursued a BS degree in agriculture. Upon Joe's graduation they moved to Butler County, Missouri, where Joe worked in the county agent's office five years. While here the family increased by three before they moved to Union, Missouri. The children are Sherry now living in Washington, Missouri; Ronnie splits his time between Union and Philippine Islands; Randy lives at home; Steve and family are in Tampa, Florida, and Bruce Edward born 1958 died at one day of age and is buried Poplar Bluff, Missouri.

Last is Sarah Helen who married Charles Wood in 1951 and they moved to Michigan where they remained for 35 years, returning to Greene County in 1986. While in Michigan they had three children, a daughter Phyllis who lives in Greene County and two sons Michael and Richard who still live in Mt. Morris, Michigan. (See Charles and Helen Wood article).

*Submitted by Helen Brown Wood*

**BROWNING** – Eugene Rutledge Browning was born on December 3, 1893, in Piggott, Arkansas, to James Kitchen Browning, born on November 12, 1869, in Franklin County, Illinois and died on October 14, 1926, in Piggott, Arkansas, and Augusta Mae Spraggins, born May 27, 1874, in Greenway, Arkansas and died November 6, 1948, in Clarksville, Arkansas. James and Augusta are buried in the Memorial Gardens Cemetery in Piggott.

Eugene's first known ancestors are John Browning and Alice Maltravers in the 1300s in England. His first ancestor to come to America was Captain John Browning who sailed from Gravesend, England, on the *Abigail* landing on the Collegelands, Virginia, in 1622. He later married Elizabeth Dameron. Eugene married Bessie Lee Sanford, born on December 2, 1895, in Waco, Texas to Edward Owen Sanford and Caroline Lee Haddon, on November 29, 1917, in Alexandria, Louisiana. Some of the surnames of Mrs. Browning's ancestors include Rhea, Haddon, Jones, Fuller, Phillips, Hill, Duke, Spivey and possibly Littleton, Martiau, Berkeley and Thomas. Her father Edward was born in Louisville, Kentucky, on November 13, 1873, and died on March 4, 1918, in St. Louis, Missouri. Her mother, Caroline, was born in Grimes County, Texas, on January 26, 1870, and died on November 22, 1935, in Austin, Texas. Her parents were married on June 24, 1891, in Austin, Texas. They are both buried in the Oakwood Cemetery in Austin. She had one brother, Edward Ross Sanford Sr. born January 29, 1893, in Waco, Texas, and died March 13, 1956, in Kansas City, Missouri. He married Virginia Herrick in Sedalia, Missouri, on March 1, 1911. They had one son, Edward Ross Jr. (deceased) who married Mary Grace Spurlock (deceased). Edward Ross Jr. had three children: Michael (deceased), Patricia, and Eugene (deceased).

*State Senator James Kitchen Browning, Eugene Rutledge Browing and Augusta Mae "Gussie" (Spraggins) Browning.*

Edward Owen Sanford's parents were Chester Sanford born in New York and Sarah E. Rhea born in Tennessee. Caroline's parents were Sterling Abernathy Haddon born in Hardin County, Tennessee and Mary Emily "Mollie" Jones born in St. Clair County, Alabama.

Eugene and Bess had two children: Eugene Sanford "Squif," born December 28, 1918, in Austin, Texas and died February 2, 2000, in Bridgeton, Missouri, and James Edward, born October 7, 1920, in Piggott, Arkansas and died on December 31, 1944, in Heiderscheidt, Luxembourg. Eugene and Bess moved to Paragould around 1924. He was employed at the Security Bank and Trust Company until he retired as president of the bank. He was an avid golfer and Bess was very active in the Episcopal Church. Bess attended the University of Arkansas in Fayetteville and was a member of the Tri Delta Sorority as well as being a Phi Beta Kappa. Prior to their marriage Eugene went with Pershing's troops in the 153rd Infantry as a First Lieutenant to fight Pancho Villa in Mexico. Eugene died in Paragould on January 12, 1974, and Bess died in Normandy, Missouri, on October 14, 1975. They are both buried in the Linwood Cemetery in Paragould.

The first Browning of this line to come to Arkansas was James Kitchen Browning. His parents were James K. Browning and Rebecca Allen. His grandparents were John Browning and Nancy Kitchen who came from North Carolina through Tennessee and were among the first settlers of Franklin County, Illinois. James graduated from Benton Township High School in 1888, attended Ewing College, and then moved to Piggott. He sold insurance, worked for the Bank of Piggott, was the superintendent of schools for Clay County, was on the board of trustees for the University of Arkansas in Fayetteville, and was a state senator for Arkansas. He was encouraged to run for governor of the state, but declined due to ill health. He married Augusta Mae "Gussie" Spraggins on February 22, 1893, in Piggott. Gussie was the daughter of George Washington Spraggins and Virginia C. Watson and the granddaughter of Nathaniel S. and Lucy Catherine Spraggins. Nathaniel is buried in the Scattersville Cemetery near Rector and Virginia is buried in the Memorial Gardens Cemetery in Piggott.

Gussie's mother was born in Lauderdale County, Tennessee, the daughter of James M. and Willia Watson. Her father was born in Poinsett County, Arkansas. Gussie and James had four other children in addition to Eugene all born in Piggott. They were Ethel Mae born in May of 1898 and died May 2, 1958, in Birmingham, Alabama; Everett born May 10, 1901, and died June 22, 1964, in Yountville, California; Ruth Barrett born December 15, 1902, and died July 7, 1971, in Dubuque, Iowa; and Pauline Elizabeth born January 12, 1911, and died December 27, 1989, in Houston, Texas. Ethel married John T. Batten of Paragould; Everett married Hiwanda Howard; Ruth married William P. Walsh; and Pauline married Dr. Donald Hamm. Ethel and Ruth did not have any children. Everett had two daughters, Hiwanda "Teddy" and Pauline "Cissy," both deceased. Pauline had two sons, Kyle (deceased) and Mike. Other surnames connected to the Browning family are Whittington, Crockett, Huston, Jordan, Crews, Curry, Duncan, Bryant, Berkeley, Throckmorton, Purnell, Constable, Coddrington, Harding, Tovey, Parsons, and FitzNicoll.

From left: Eugene Rutledge Browning, Captain Eugene Sanford Browning, Bessie Lee (Sanford) Browning, and Nina Louise "Jill" (Lawson/Rockwood) Browning.

Eugene Sanford Browning attended the University of Arkansas in Fayetteville and was a member of the Sigma Chi Fraternity and the Blackfriar Fraternity. He enlisted in the army after college and was in the 501st Parachute Battalion for eight months before becoming a pilot in the Army Air Corps. He was a member of the 12th Air Force, 446th Bomb Squad, 321st Bomb Group, and 57th BombWing. He flew 52 missions in B-25's in North Africa, Sicily, and Italy. He received the Air Medal and eight Oakleaf Clusters and was a captain when he was discharged. He remained in the reserves until 1957. After the war he went to work for the Metropolitan Life Insurance Company and was a regional supervisor for the Group Division in St. Louis when he retired in 1980. James Edward Browning attended the University of Arkansas and then West Point, graduating 26th in his class. At the University he was a Sigma Chi and a member of the Pershing Rifles. James was attached to the intelligence staff under Patton in the Infantry, 3rd Army, 80th Division. He was a first lieutenant and was killed in action while on patrol at the Battle of the Bulge. James and Eugene are buried in the Linwood Cemetery.

Robert Eugene Browning.

James never married. Eugene married Nina Louise "Jill" Lawson/Rockwood in Atlanta, Georgia, on June 5, 1941. Jill was born on September 21, 1923, in Little Rock, Arkansas. She was the daughter of John Francis Lawson and Lou Evie Johnson both from Paragould, and the stepdaughter of John Rockwood from New York. She had one brother, James Franklyn "Jack" Lawson, born on August 2, 1921, in Paragould and died on June 2, 1987, in Atlanta, Georgia. He married Sarah Landrum. Eugene and Jill had two children: Robert Eugene born on November 2, 1943, in Emory, Georgia; and Elizabeth Louise born on January 3, 1947, in Richmond, Virginia. Robert graduated from Paragould High School and the University of Arkansas in Fayetteville. He then enlisted in the Air Force. Elizabeth graduated from Kirkwood High School in Kirkwood, Missouri, and then the University of Missouri in Columbia. She earned a masters degree in secondary education at the University of Missouri in St. Louis and now teaches social studies at the high school level in St. Louis County. Jill died on October 2, 1993, in Chesterfield, Missouri, and Robert died on February 4, 1994, in Glendale, Missouri. They are both buried in the Linwood Cemetery. Elizabeth resides in Glendale, Missouri.

**BRYANT** – Jimmy Bryant and Lynda Heath were married June 20, 1964 at St. Mary's Catholic church in Paragould, AR. They have three daughters, Kimberly Ann Bryant born May 9, 1966, Tanya Lynn Bryant born April 4, 1968 and Melanie Heath Bryant born May 21, 1971. Kim is a youth minister and also works for Heath Funeral Home. Tanya and her husband, Scott Ellington, live in Jonesboro, where she is a trust office and assistant vice president for Union Planters Bank. Her children are Jordan Lee McBride, Bradley Heath McBride and Jack Ellington. Melanie works at Heath Funeral Home, where she is a licensed embalmer and funeral director.

First Lieutenant James Edward Browning.

Jimmy Ray Bryant was born April 27, 1937 in Light, Greene County, AR, the only child of Lester Thomas and Emma Bernice Bryant. He attended school in Light and is a 1955 graduate of Greene County Tech. He worked part time as a meat cutter for Kroger. Following graduation Jimmy was a pitcher with the Arkansas Travelers Baseball Team, a farm club of the Detroit Tigers in 1955 and 1956. After a shoulder injury, he attended the University of Mississippi before going to work for Emerson Electric Company on Aug. 3, 1958 until his retirement in the summer of 1999. During those 41 years he worked himself up through the ranks where he worked in quality control as a supervisor from Sept. 1965. He spent a good part of two years in Venezuela where he opened a joint venture plant with Motor Veenca called Veenca. He has also held an Arkansas Funeral Directors License since 1980. Jimmy has always felt that the youth are our future and has enjoyed helping with youth activities. He, along with Joe Wessell, Mike Holsten and Peck Bryant founded the Pee Wee basketball program for girls in Paragould. He was active as a parent in many school activities for his girls through the years and has served on the Williams Baptist College Athletic Board since 1992.

Lynda Kathryn Heath was born Feb. 10, 1941 in Jonesboro, AR the daughter of Verlyn L. and Helen Heath. She lived in Marked Tree before moving to Paragould with her family in 1945. Lynda attended St. Mary's School, Paragould High School and is a graduate of Arkansas State University with a BSE degree in elementary education. She taught second grade at Baldwin Elementary School until the birth of her first child. She did private tutoring at home for nearly 10 years until she started working part time at Heath Funeral Home. She received her Arkansas Funeral Directors license in 1976 and her Missouri license in 1977. In 1984 Verlyn and Helen Heath retired, turning the management of Heath Funeral Home over to their son, Verlyn G. "Butch" Heath and their daughter, Lynda as co-managers. Lynda has been active in community activities including, Hospital Auxiliary, PTA, Athletic and Band Boosters, Chamber of Commerce, church activities, Rotary and the Greene County Historical and Genealogical Society. She has also enjoyed serving all offices for Northeast Arkansas Funeral Directors Club, Arkansas Funeral Directors Association, Arkansas Club of Burial Associations, Memorial Insurance Company as well as six years for Arkansas Burial Association Board and five years on the National Funeral Directors Association Board of Directors.

Jimmy and Lynda Bryant

Of the many blessings given to Jimmy and Lynda, the things they cherish most are their family and the opportunity to serve others.

**BRYANT** – Lester Thomas "Peck" Bryant was born July 15, 1914 in Rice, Greene County, AR, the son of John Thomas and Mary Magaline (Blair) Bryant.

Emma Bernice "Niece" Lands was born July 26, 1919 in Light, Greene County, AR, the daughter of Ira Eugene and Willie (Cooper) Lands.

Peck and Niece were married Oct. 5, 1935

in Greene County. Their only child, Jimmy Ray Bryant, was born April 27, 1937 at their home in Light, Greene County, AR.

During his lifetime Peck has had many different careers. He was a farmer, served in the U.S. Navy on a submarine during WWII, was a game warden with the Arkansas Game and Fish Commission, worked with the Arkansas State Police in the Weight and Standards Division, served as night chief of police in Paragould and worked for Emerson Electric Motor Division in Paragould for 32 years.

*Lester and Bernice Bryant*

He still found time to help young people. He was one of the founders of the Pee Wee basketball program for local girls and the AAU basketball team for girls in the area. He enjoyed helping and watching them grow into young adults. He doesn't miss many local basketball games, even today. At 86, he stills bowls two nights a week. He bowled in a summer league with his daughter-in-law, Lynda, before she ever met his son, Jimmy. He was recently inducted into the Paragould Bowling Association's Hall of Fame.

Niece worked at Loretta's Dress Shop, Ima's, The Laundromat and at Nettle's Beauty Shop. She was a wonderful cook. Anyone who ever had the fortune of eating any of her dishes always looked forward to going back to her house for more. Niece loved taking care of her grandchildren and her great-granddaughter, Jordan. She enjoyed helping anyone when she could. Bernice Bryant died on Sept. 8, 1991 at her home in Paragould.

One highlight of Peck's life was in the spring of 1998 when he received a plaque from Williams Baptist College women's coach and athletic director, Carl Halford recognizing his outstanding support of the school over the years. The formation of the Peck and Niece Bryant/Emerson Electric Athletic Endowment was announced. Jim and Lynda Bryant and their family established a $10,000.00 endowment for the athletic department at Williams Baptist College in honor of Peck and Niece. "On the Thursday before my mom died on a Saturday," Jim said, 'we were talking and she said' Do something for your dad after I'm gone.' "Obviously, I didn't know she was going to die right away and she didn't either. I asked her what she meant and she said,' When the time comes, you'll know.' Well, she was right; Dad loves that little school so much, this just jumped right out at me." A reception was held after the games, with the players, WBC representatives and family and friends attending.

No one knows how many people's lives have been touched and helped by this couple.

*Submitted by Lynda Bryant*

**BRYANT** – Hall of Fame Bowler Peck Bryant says at 86, that he'll bowl in the Senior Citizen League when he gets old enough. He still bowls in regular league play twice weekly. Peck carries a 175 average on Tuesday nights and 177 on Wednesday nights. He once bowled a 287 with 10 consecutive strikes. Peck was inducted into the Paragould Bowling Association's Hall of Fame in March 2000.

Peck was born Lester Thomas Bryant July 15, 1914. On Oct. 5, 1935, he married Emma Bernice Lands. One son, Jimmy Ray Bryant, was born April 27, 1937 in Greene County.

1942 sent Peck, Bernice and Jimmy to Coronado, CA where Peck was stationed as a patrolman for the Navy. Later he served on the island of Guam. He tells a story of confused Japanese soldiers surrendering at the base several months after the war had ended.

Around 1946 Peck returned to GreeneCounty and resumed a job with the Arkansas Game and Fish Commission. One fall when the Mississippi River flooded, Peck and another Game Warden, Tom Fears, were sent to rescue and feed wild turkeys. At the time, they were the only wild turkeys in Arkansas. The turkeys had congregated on an island most easily reached from Tunica County, MS. While traveling down the Old Mississippi by motorboat, Peck and Tom encountered such a great storm with towering waves that it overturned their boat. Peck and Tom had to swim in hip boots. Once both men reached a branch, Peck buckled his belt around it, fired three shots from a wet pistol and hoped someone had heard them. Later he fired his last two shots. They clung to the branch for five hours. Peck was worried about hypothermia, but with his belt fastened, knew he would not drown. He fired his gun two last times.

The distress shots had been heard but the storm and river were too dangerous to risk more lives. When the rescuers finally came in another boat, Peck insisted that the men help Tom first.

Once on land Peck and Tom had nothing dry to wear. A clothing store owner opened his shop on Sunday and allowed both men to pick out shoes, socks, shirts, pants, underwear and anything else they wanted. The shop owner would only take $5.00 from each man.

Later Peck worked for the Arkansas State Police in the Weight and Standard Division. Around 1954 Peck became the night chief of police in Paragould. In 1958 he began work at Emerson Electric in Paragould. He retired in 1980.

Peck and his son Jim were two of the founders of the countywide AAU Basketball Team and two founders of Paragould School District's first girls Pee Wee basketball program.

Jim married Lynda Kathryn Heath, the daughter of Verlyn L. and Helen Heath of Paragould, on July 20, 1963. Peck has three granddaughters: Kimberly Ann Bryant, Tanya Lynn Bryant Ellington, and Melanie Heath Bryant. He has three great grandchildren: Jordan Lee McBride, Bradley Heath McBride and Jack Ellington.

*Submitted by Kim Bryant*

**BRYSON** – John Pinkney Bryson was born 1858 and died 1919 in Perry County, Tennessee, to Eli and Nancy Ann Bryson. He married Martha Jane Austin (1862-1917) in Benton County, Tennessee, in 1880. She was born in Benton County to John Austin and Anne Mariah Barnes. Martha's grandfather, William Barnes, was a Methodist Circuit Riding Preacher. Six of John and Martha's children were born in Benton County, Tennessee. They came to Arkansas around 1900 in a covered wagon and may have stayed in Obion County, Tennessee, before moving on. According to oral history, they waited for the Mississippi River to freeze over, to cross it and the surrounding swamp area. They followed Martha's mother, Anne, who had married Frank Ellinor and moved to Arkansas around 1890. John and Martha bought a farm at Pine Hill, near Gainesville and on the old Jacksonport Military Road. Their neighbors were Daniel Owens and the Coles. They built a log house near the creek and spring that was on their property. John planted every kind of fruit tree and berry plants that he could find. John was a full-blooded Irishman who loved music and played the accordion. He had his own quartet - Jeff, Arvin, Eula and Iona. Jeff and Arvin played the guitar and Laura played the pump organ. Martha was half-Cherokee Indian and was a hard worker. She was a typical pioneer woman. She picked cotton by day, took the seeds out of it at night, and made thread out of it on her spinning wheel and made bed covers and clothing for her family. John, Martha, and a child are buried at Gainesville Cemetery as well as Anne Ellinor and other family members.

Their children were:

Nancy Ann born September 28, 1881, married Perry Hedges, and had three children: Charles, Alfred and Mae. She died in 1933 in California.

*John P. Bryson and Martha Austin Bryson and their children. Standing: Nancy. Sitting from left: Dora, Robert, Laura and Jeff.*

Robert Edward Lee born October 12, 1885, married Hattie Mae Oma Owens. They had four children: Virgie Vida Ruby, Lola Clara Dell, Elvis G. and Titus James. They lived north of Paragould, near Halliday, where he was a member of the school board. Robert and Hattie are buried at Epsada Cemetery.

Laura Louvernia born December 17, 1889, married William Aaron Jackman. They had nine children: John, Orman Buel, Lorene, Albert Ulyesses, Hattie Oreatha Jane, William Charles, Eula Mae, Laura Verna and Henry. After World War II, all of the children left this area, except for Eula Mae who married Houston Johnson of Arbyrd, Missouri, where they lived until recently. Laura and Bill are buried at New Friendship Cemetery.

Dora Isadora Victoria born September 28, 1891, married Leonard "Bun" Cole. They lived near Lafe and had four children, Mary Marie, Violet Angeline, Ernest Thomas and Artie Jefferson. Dora and Leonard are buried at Belieu Hill Cemetery.

Jefferson Franklin born February 16, 1893, married Mary Ezell Barrow. They lived in Paragould. He was a World War I veteran and retired from the Paragould Water Works. She had two children by a previous marriage, Delbert and Robert Barrow. She and Jeff had two children: Vestal Mae and Edward Lee. Jeff and Mary are buried at Warren's Chapel Cemetery.

Ulyesses Arvin born January 12, 1895, went back to Tennessee and married Clara Myers. They remained in Tennessee and had a son, Cecil Lee.

Eula Arizona born June 20, 1901, married William Henry McCord. They moved to Arizona in the early 1950s. Their children were Anna Mae, Betty Lou, Thomas LeRoy, Donald Leon, William Raymond, Alice Faye and Jerry Allen. Their descendants all live in Arizona.

Hattie Iona born May 17, 1904, married Melvin Dured Mann.

John James born October 22, 1906, married Dona Huddleston. They lived mainly in St. Louis, Missouri. Their two children, James Alvin and

Bobby live in Flint, Michigan. John and Martha had three children who died young: Sarah Rose Zendy, Dickey May and "Dee."

**BURGESS** – James Oscar Burgess, of Galveston, Texas, and Florence Higdon Burgess of Hardin County, Illinois, moved from Eagle Creek, Illinois, in 1910 and settled in the Gainesville Community where they farmed. They brought with them their children: Gilbert, Frankie, Rena, Carrie and Mary. Nellie and Gene were later born in Greene County.

*Attending the wedding of Nellie to Ralph Dodge are, back row: James, Florence, Rena, Nellie, Gib and Frankie. Front row: Gene, Mary and Carrie.*

After several business start-ups, including building a motel in Arizona, Gilbert became successful in the fabric business in McAllen, Texas.

Frankie was married to Bill Shepard for a time and later moved to Flint, Michigan and worked at the AC plant until her retirement.

Rena married Carl Pranger and worked at Eli Walker from its start until her retirement.

Carrie married Hubert Toalson, a railroad man, and lived in Hannibal, Missouri, until her death.

Mary and Tom lived in North Paragould for over 40 years after their marriage.

Nellie and Ralph Dodge operated Dodge's Store in Halliday until it's closing.

Gene Burgess, the only remaining sibling now lives in Chile.

**BURKEEN** – Jessie was the son of Stanford Burkeen and Sarah Evans. He was born in Tennessee on March 18, 1852. The family moved to Greene County in 1869. He married Eliza Jane Anders, who was born in Arkansas 1850-1918, on October 11, 1874, by John Chandler at his home. William Franklin Morrow and P.N. Anders were witnesses. Jessie and Eliza Jane had eight children. Four of these had issue.

Mary Alice 1875-1951, married Logan Smith. They had 10 children: Sudie, Jack, Hettie, Nettie, Walker, Jim, Cora, Rebecca Jane, Clinnie and David.

Malinda 1880-1916 married Jasper Morrow. They had four children: Gordon, Thelma, Jessie and Darrell.

Nancy 1882-1961 married Isaac Morrow, had one son Ezra. Isaac died and she married Ollie Langrum. They had one son, Oren. Ollie died and she married James Smith. They had one son Macon.

*Jessie Burkeen born March 18, 1852, died March 27, 1915, married October 11, 1874, Greene County, Arkansas, to Eliza Jane Anders Burkeen. Both are buried in Greene County.*

John Burkeen 1884-1885

Charley Burk-een 1887-1947 married Mary Gregory. They had one son Frank. Mary died and Charley married Meg Carter. They had Earnest, Estelle, Liza Jane, C.E. and Earley.

Lieu 1890-1891 (no information on Lieu).

Rebecca Jane 1878-1900.

The 1910 census of Randolph County, Arkansas list this family living there. His occupation is listed as a miller. He ran a grist mill there powered by the water from Five Mile Springs. He also farmed. They moved back to Greene County after a short stay in Randolph County and started farming.

Jessie Franklin died March 17, 1915, of Lobar pneumonia. Eliza Jane died 1918 with congestive heart failure. Both are buried in the Morrow Cemetery, Greene County, Arkansas.

Jessie worked in the timber when his children were small. At one time they moved to the Boston Mountains in Pope County, Arkansas. The hills were so steep that when they were pulling the wagons up the mountains they would have to block the wheels on the wagons to keep them from rolling back down the hill and the men pushed the wagons to help the animals pull the wagons up.

There were bear, wolves, panthers and all kinds of wild animals plentiful there. Once when the family had killed a hog and had the fresh meat in the cabin the wolves tried to get into the cabin. Jessie was gone. Eliza Jane had to keep throwing hot scoops of fire out side to keep the wolves away. They turned their table over and put it against the fireplace so the wolves wouldn't come down the fireplace.

Once Mary Alice went to a neighbor's for a bucket of honey. A bear got after her. She ran to the river and grabbed hold of a tree. The bucket of honey went into the river. The bear went away.

If their fire went out they would have to go borrow fire from the neighbors. The Burkeens were hard working Christian people. Many of their descendants still reside in Greene County.

**BURROUGHS** – Leonard Bryan Burroughs was a native of McKenzie, TN prior to moving to Paragould, Greene County, AR in 1919. He caught the eye of Wilma "Totsie" Snowden. They were married Sept. 7, 1921. Their only son, Leonard Bryan Burroughs, was born May 12, 1923 in Paragould, Greene County, AR. Leonard was retired head of the Paragould Sanitation Department and a member of the Masonic Lodge. He was a member of the Methodist church of Paragould. Leonard died Nov. 18, 1971; he was 71 years old. When Leonard died, he left besides Totsie and his son Leonard Bryan Burroughs Jr., his grandson Lynn Burroughs, his brother Joe Burroughs of McKenzie, TN, two sisters, Mrs. Mary Connell, also of McKenzie and Mrs. Buna Hall of Memphis, TN. Totsie never remarried, there could never be another Leonard Burroughs like her Leonard Burroughs!

*Leonard Bryan Burroughs 1919-1971*

*Submitted by Evelyn Euritha Wagner*

**BURROUGHS** – Leonard B. Burroughs Jr. was born May 12, 1923 in Paragould, AR. "Jr" was the only son of Leonard B. Burroughs, Sr. and Wilma "Totsie" (Snowden) Burroughs. "Jr" was a lifelong member of the First Baptist Church of Paragould and member of the Masonic Lodge # 368.

He met and married Betty Sue Payne, the daughter or Marion Thomas "Tom" and Carmon Payne of Halliday, Greene County, AR, June 22, 1947.

They had one son, Micky Lynn Burroughs, born Sept. 16, 1959 in Paragould, AR. Betty Sue is a devoted mother and grandmother. She is the essence of southern ladies.

Jr. was a sexton at Linwood Cemetery, Greene County Coroner for 14 years and a former employee of Mitchell Funeral Home. He died March 26, 1980, at the age of 57 years, after a long battle with cancer. His wife and mother still feel the loss to this day. Betty Sue never remarried.

*June 1947, Leonard Bryan and Betty Sue Payne Burroughs.*

*Submitted by Evelyn Euritha Wagner*

**BURROUGHS** – Micky Lynn Burroughs was born Sept. 16, 1959, the son of Leonard Bryan Burroughs, Jr. and Betty Sue Payne. His grandparents were Leonard Bryan Burroughs, Sr. and Wilma "Totsie" Snowden Burroughs. His great-grandparents were Albert Sidney Snowden and Beulah Nancy Chandler-Kennemore-Snowden.

*Betty Sue, Alex, Bryan, Zackery, and Mickey Lynn Burroughs.*

Micky Lynn Burroughs "Lynn" attended Paragould High School. He met and married Betty Claire Watson. They have three sons: Bryan Neal Burroughs, born May 15, 1990 and twins, Alex and Zackery Burroughs, born Aug. 4, 1992. All of the boys are active in athletics. Betty died in Aug. 2000.

Lynn Burroughs was a long-time employee of Life and Casualty Insurance Agency prior to opening his own business, Paragould Laundry and Dry Cleaners. He has two locations: The original business, located at 409 North Pruett Street, was opened in 1905 and is probably the oldest family-owned business in Paragould. Lynn purchased it in Nov. 1989 and has since opened a second location. The laundry was recently voted " best dry cleaners" in a Paragould *Daily Press* survey.

*Submitted by Evelyn Euritha Wagner*

**BUSBY** – John Busby was born in Tennessee to Jack Busby and Sallie Glover. Date of birth was 1865. He married Sally Webb and moved to Hickman County, Kentucky. Their children were: Jessie born August 1886 in Tennessee; Maud born June 1889 in Kentucky; Earnest born August 1890; John H. born April 1892; Dora B. February 1894; Bessie born October 1895; Wils born February 1897; Calvin born 1900; Melvin born in Missouri (Dunklin County) 1901; and Armon born 1905.

By the year 1901 the Busby family were living in Dunklin County, Missouri, near Holcomb. Then in 1920 we find John Sr. living and buying property in Greene County, Arkansas. John and Sally's son, John D. Busby was killed in France on October 6, 1918, while fighting in World War I.

Our father, Calvin Busby, married Thelma Morrow, daughter of Jasper Morrow and Malinda Burkeen, on August 27, 1922. Seven sons and two daughters were born into this family. The two daughters died in infancy.

Newell Eugene was born September 2, 1924. He married first Maxine Campbell and second Laure Wilhelm.

Warren Henry was born April 29, 1927, and married Deanie Waddell in Alabama.

Elmon Leo was born September 30, 1929, and married Alene Gladish in Paragould, Arkansas.

Ethan C. Busby was born May 22, 1931, and married first Norma Greer and second Bettye Sparks Overbay.

Lindy Lee Busby was born April 28, 1933, and married Nicole Scheer in Paris, France.

Billy Gene born April 25, 1938, in Paragould and married Winnia Lou Bullington.

*Seated: Hettie and Roxie Busby, Thelma and Eugene Busby. Standing: John Busby Sr., Melvin and Calvin Busby.*

*Thelma Busby family. Seated: Thelma Busby. Standing: Billy Gene, Lindy Lee, Ethan, Leo, Warren and Eugene Busby.*

John Calvin Busby was born October 5, 1941, and died in Paragould, Arkansas on December 31, 1949.

John Busby died February 2, 1928, in Paragould of liver cancer. He was buried in Stanfield Cemetery near Holcomb, Missouri. At the present time, of seven sons born to Calvin and Thelma Busby, only two survive, Lindy Lee of Jonesboro, Arkansas, and Ethan Busby of Paragould, Arkansas.

Eugene died in Lake Havasu, Arizona, on January 19, 1998. Warren died in Paragould on July 27, 1993. Elmon Leo died September 15, 1991, in Paragould. Billy Gene died September 17, 1990, in Baptist Hospital, Memphis, Tennessee of lung cancer. John Calvin died December 31, 1949, in Paragould, Arkansas.

Lindy Lee Busby and Nicole Busby have two daughters, Carol and Rebecca.

Ethan Busby has one son, Ethan "Randy" Busby Jr., and two daughters, Sandra Jean and Brenda Kay. He has been married to Bettye Sparks Overbay for 36 years. Bettye has three children, Clarence Overbay III, Omer David Overbay II, and Lea Ann (Overbay) Vanaman. Bettye and Ethan have 13 grandchildren. Ethan is still in the appraisal and insurance business in Paragould with his office located in the Rhine Building, 120 N. 2nd Street. Bettye works in the S.S. Lipscomb genealogy room at the Greene County Library.

**BUTLER** – John Wesley Butler, Sr. was born Sept. 3, 1840 in Wilkes County, GA, believed to be the son of Bennett Butler and Francis Jones Butler. He married Nancy Ann Dukes Jan. 5, 1860 in Tuscaloosa County, AL. She was born July 9, 1843 in Georgia. John W. and Nancy had nine living children: Mary Jane; Nancy Andelite: John W. Jr.; Emmitt; Andrew; Sara E; Jasper H.; Ader and Tinnie.

*Otto, Vernon, Ellie Ethel, John Wesley Jr., Rosa Jane holding Arvel Wesley, Lucy Ellmira, Earl Gilbert, and Floyd Shelby, taken about 1908.*

John W. Sr. and Nancy made their way through Tennessee, living for a while in Obion County, up through Arkansas and settled in Paragould, AR in the 1880s. While John W. Sr. and Nancy stayed in Paragould, Emmitt, Andrew and Jasper moved to St. Louis, MO with the remainder of their adult children moving to southeast Missouri.

While John W. probably farmed at times, it cannot be determined exactly what his occupation was during his lifetime. The later generations felt he must have been a storekeeper or other such type clerical job. All his sons dressed in suits (not always with a tie) and it seemed they must have had the influence of their father in their manner of dress.

It is believed that John W. Sr.'s siblings were Albert, Henry, William and James M., born Jan. 1846 in Alabama. James married Sarah Elizabeth Dukes (probably a sister or cousin of Nancy Ann Dukes, wife of John W. Sr.) about 1867 in Alabama. James and Sarah's children: Moses M. born Nov. 1869; Noah Athlene, born March 1870; Austin, born 1872; James "AB", born May 21, 1873; Marion, born Dec. 1875; Crawford "C.C" born about 1876; John W. born Feb. 1877; Elizabeth, born 1877 and Allie "Alabama".

John W. Jr. spent some time in Paragould before going to southeast Missouri. He married Marthy Hopkins about 1885 and they had one child, Otto Lee. Marthy died soon after Otto's birth and John W. remained single until Jan. 18, 1891, when he married Rosa Jane Whitehead (daughter of John and Mary Whitehead) in southeast Missouri. John and Rosa had 14 children, Larry Mey, born July 1892; Leathey Gertrude, born Nov. 1893; Vernon, born June 2, 1895; Hattie, born Oct. 1896; Ellie Ethel, born April 1898; Clarence Evert, born July 1900; Lucy Ellmira, born March 1902; Floyd Shelby, born July 1904; Earl Gilbert, born Aug. 1906; Arvel Wesley, born April 1908; Hubert Ottis, born Feb. 1910; Jewell Gilbert, born Nov. 19ll and Rufus Harold, born Oct. 1913. Lucy Elmira died Nov. 1908 and Floyd, Ellie, Otto, Earl and Arvel died between May and July 1910. John W. Jr. and Rosa Jane are shown in the attached picture with seven of the children. Rosa Jane died Dec. 24, 1933 and John W. Jr. died Oct. 29, 1946. They are buried in McGrew Cemetery, Senath, Mo.

John W. Sr. and Nancy Ann lived their remaining years in Paragould. Nancy died Jan. 3, 1906 and he died Aug. 13, 1916. They are buried in Wood's Chapel Cemetery.

The descendants of this pioneering family are proud of the tenacity and fortitude they showed in traveling by covered wagon to forge westward and explore new country.

*Submitted by Millie Wyatt*

**BYRD** – Jasper Anthony Byrd, worked at the Lion Oil Company, was born September 30, 1889, in Clay County, Arkansas, and died December 23, 1968, aged 68 in Paragould, and was buried at the Linwood Cemetery. He was the son of Lod Byrd, born about 1871 in Arkansas and Mary Francis Langley, a homemaker, born about 1871 in Arkansas. Jasper married Isable "Belle" May Whitworth about 1912 in Paragould.

*Jasper Anthony Byrd September 30, 1889 to December 23, 1968.*

Isabel was born May 1895 in Arkansas and died May 1913 aged 19 in Paragould and was buried north of Paragould in a local Cemetery. Isabel was the daughter of William "Willie" Whitworth, farmer laborer, was born June 1861 in Arkansas and Delia Whitworth, a homemaker, born May 1873 in Missouri and died before 1910. Isabel had two brother, James R. Whitworth, born 1903 in Arkansas and Henry B. Whitworth, born 1905 in Arkansas. Jasper and Isabel had one daughter Lottie Mae Francies Byrd.

*Lottie Mae Byrd Morgan December 19, 1912 to June 13, 1977. Circa July 1958.*

Lottie was born December 19, 1912, at Ponset County, Arkansas, and taken in July to be raised by the Philips family after Isabel's death in May. The Philips lived in Ponset County at the time.

Lottie married Harry Edwin Morgan on June 25, 1932, in Paragould. Lottie died June 13, 1977, age 64 in Fort Smith, Arkansas, and was buried at Linwood Cemetery.

**CADENHEAD** – Clayton V. Cadenhead was born May 16, 1882, in Batesville, Mississippi, to Billy and Margaret Cadenhead. After his father died in 1885 he came to Greene County with his mother, one brother, Fisher Cadenhead, and two sisters, Lena Cadenhead Cole and Dora Cadenhead Crockett.

When they moved to Greene County they lived west of Greene County on the Joe T. Faulkner farm. Clayton worked for Mr. Faulkner and lived with his mother, Margaret Fitzgerald Cadenhead, until he married Mary Elizabeth Bone in 1913. She was the daughter of J. J. and Sarah Bone, and the granddaughter of Col. Ben Johnson.

In 1995 there was a memorial service for Col. Johnson at Owens Chapel Cemetery. Clayton worked for Arkansas Utilities Ice Company for 30 years.

In 1937 he opened Cadenhead's Grocery on Fourth Avenue. He sold the store in 1946 and retired. Mary E. Cadenhead had a curtain laundry on Fourth Avenue. I doubt that there were many area people who didn't have their curtains done at her business.

Clayton and Mary had four daughters: Marie, Imogene, Nadine and Wilma; four grandchildren, and six great-grandchildren.

Clayton died in March 1963; Mary died October 1981.

**CAMPBELL** – Othar and Oletta Campbell are familiar names in Greene County. The couple owned and operated Campbell's Café from 1957 to 1976. They were also farmers for many years.

Othar Lee Campbell was born Sept. 6, 1906, the son of Mattie Janes and William Thomas Campbell. Mattie Janes was born on Nov. 10, 1874 and died on June 15, 1910. William Thomas Campbell was born Sept. 16, 1874 and died Sept. 1, 1925. After the death of Othar's mother in 1910, William Thomas Campbell married Louisa Hooten on Aug. 31, 1911. The couple had six children: Vivian Campbell Crider; Janie Evelyn Campbell (who died Sept. 15, 1915); Lillian Campbell Mock, Wanda Campbell Hawk (who died April 1, 1992) and Velma Campbell Robert.

Oletta Inez Varvil Campbell was born Feb. 11, 1913 and died July 4, 1998. She was the daughter of Myrtle Mae Rooker and Joseph Otto Varvil. The Varvils had five children including Oletta: Howard, Reuben and Joseph Jewell Varvil and Pansy Varvil Vines.

Othar and Oletta Campbell were married on Jan. 1, 1930. They had one daughter, Loree Campbell Perkey.

Seated – Othar and Oletta Campbell. Standing – Donna Rae Helverings, Don and Loree Perkey and Patti Ernst

The Campbell's farmed the L. G. Staub land at Evening Star for many years. The couple were members of Evening Star Church of Christ. Othar Campbell served on the Delaplaine School Board and was a member of Farm Bureau. Oletta Campbell was a lunchroom supervisor for Delaplaine School District from 1951-1957.

Shortly after the Campbell's married, they started farming in the Evening Star area. They raised cotton, soybeans, corn and cane, among other things. In 1954, the Chamber of Commerce named the Campbell's Farm Family of the Year

On Aug. 1, 1957, the couple purchased Lamb's Café, located at 103 North Pruett. It was always Oletta's dream to own her own café. She loved to cook. Nothing made her happier than fixing a huge meal for family or friends. Campbell's Café was a special place for all who remember the restaurant.

In 1963, Lennie Stamps sold the property where the café was located to the Sterling Five and Dime Store. Campbell's Café moved up the street to 115 North Pruett, where it remained as long as Othar and Oletta owned the business. Over the years, the Campbells had some wonderful employees who helped them with their business. Lorene McDaniel was a former waitress at the café, along with Amy Shirley. Mrs. Charlie Smith helped Oleta with some of the cooking.

A group of men known as 'the early risers' always came for breakfast. Others made it part of their morning to stop by the café on their way to work.

Hamburgers, hot dogs, chili and fries were favorites among the lunchtime crowds. However, most who ate at Campbell's Café agreed that the homemade pies and cobblers were the reason to stop by for lunch.

Along with running the café, Othar Campbell was employed in the shipping department at Eli Walker until he retired in 1971. Othar Campbell then helped his wife run the business, until health problems caused the couple to sell the café in Jan. 1976 to Robert and Opal Watkins.

*Submitted by Patti Ernst*

**CARPENTER** – From 1869 to 1885 four of the six sons of Absalom Carpenter and his wife Jane McGuire of Franklin County, Alabama, removed to northeast Arkansas, locating along the St. Francis River at Lester, west at Greenboro and into north Craighead County along the Greene County line. Later members of this clan eventually settled in Lake City, Lunsford, Bay and Bowman.

Hamilton "Ham" Carpenter born 1834 in Elbert County, Georgia, and Frederick S. Carpenter born 1840 in Elbert County came in the fall of 1869 and appear on the 1870 Census. Ham with teenage children and Fed with a 10 year old son by Julia McGuire who he married in Murray County, Georgia, a younger wife and an infant. William Carpenter and his wife Louise Green came in 1878 with two married sons and their families.

My great-grandfather John Elbert Carpenter born 1836 in Elbert and his wife Charlotte Cothren born September 19, 1839, were in Franklin County 1880, removing to Mississippi after the death of Jane Carpenter and on to Poinsett County where John Carpenter died. Lottie Carpenter was in the household of her daughter in the 1900 census of Greene County, along with her youngest son, Cicero Holloway Carpenter who was my maternal grandfather. He is listed as a hired-hand of his brother-in-law George Parson. Before he settled in Greene he was in Bowie County, Texas, riding horses and chasing cows. The weekly edition of the *Kansas City Star* serialized *The Virginian* in the late 1930s and he relived his youth. *The Virginian* was his *Gone With The Wind*.

Fed Carpenter had gone on to Oklahoma Territory by 1900, but William, Ham and John have many descendents in Greene and Craighead Counties.

The Bogan children are descendents of Millie Carpenter Knight, daughter of William and has other descendents around Lunsford, Bay and Truman.

Mansfield Barrow and his sister Bonita Barrow and the descendents of Ray Carpenter of Dixie are descendents of Ham known to this researcher.

Betty Carpenter Winn Langston, granddaughter of Joshua E. "Dot" Carpenter and Emma Hess descend from John and Lottie Carpenter.

*Barbara Vaudine Carpenter Rankin daughter of Christopher Columbus Carpenter and Eunice Green, circa 1931. Granddaughter of John and Charlotte Cothren Carpenter.*

The children of George Parson and his wife Lue Ada Carpenter are his descendents as well as Barbara Vaudine Carpenter Rankin daughter of Christopher Carpenter and Eunice Green.

The six children of John Carpenter who settled in Northeast Arkansas, were:

Julia born 1862 in Franklin County married Charles Courtney; had four children and died circa 1899, buried at Lake City Cemetery. Her children migrated to California in late 1920s.

John Henry Carpenter born February 12, 1864, died February 8, 1898, married Nancy Slatton had three children, one killed in World War I and two lived around Lake City and Jonesboro; buried at Pine Log as was his son who died in France.

Christopher Columbus born December 24, 1866, died Paragould December 23, 1925. He married first Jennie Hutchins and second Eunice Green. He and Eunice are buried at Langston. His children migrated to California in the 1930s and 1940s.

Joshua E. "Dot" born October 11, 1867, died September 28, 1944, married Emma Hess.

*Cicero Holloway Carpenter and Betty Jane Kay, Galen Richard Key, Ester Joyce Coates - Photo: Fall 1932.*

They are buried at Woods Chapel.

Cicero Holloway Carpenter born March 31, 1877, married first Jane Georgianna Bridges, second Maude Wilson Carpenter, widow of his first cousin, John son of William. Jane Carpenter buried at Langston and Cicero Carpenter at Linwood April 16, 1964. His descendents are around Kansas City, St. Louis, Tulsa, Memphis and Seattle.

Lue Carpenter was born June 29, 1880, in Franklin County and married George Parson. She died May 28, 1970, and she and her husband are buried at Woods Chapel. Most of their descendents have been in California since the 1940s.

My grandfather Cicero Holloway Carpenter farmed until 1918 when the flu epidemic took my grandmother leaving him with four children under 12 years of age. He gathered that crop, sold out and moved to Star City, Arkansas, to be near his Bridges in-laws where he bought into a grocery store as a partner of one the Fist families. About 1920 or so the Bridges removed to California and he sold out and returned to Paragould. Around 1937 he married the widow of his cousin and they farmed and raised a few head of cattle at Bowman.

*Millie Carpenter Knight daughter of William Carpenter Louise Green born Franklin County, Alabama circa 1920.*

Ham Carpenter served in the Confederate Army as a captain in Company B of 11th Alabama Calvary formed out of Company E of Patterson's Command. His nephew Silas Berklin Seay, son of sister Martha Carpenter, was in his command as well as a McGuire cousin and his youngest brother Joshua H. Carpenter born March 14, 1842, in Whitfield County, Georgia, source being the Affidavits of S.B. Seay, Joshua Carpenter, L.P. Seay. John Carpenter served but, we were unable to find a record of his service.

**CARROLL** – Granville Carroll, was born 1830 in Giles County, Tennessee. He was the son of James Carroll born 1787 died 1856 and Nancy Luty born 1804 died about 1878. He was a farmer along side his father. Most of his brothers and sisters lived in close proximity of the James Carroll mansion. Not to be deceived, most farm houses in the 1850s were called mansions.

Granville married Lavina Tyler in 1849 in Giles County. She was the daughter of Thomas Tyler and Sarah. From the marriage of Granville and Lavina were three sons, James T. born 1853, William Gilbert born 1854 and Arelious Granville born 1856 all in Giles County, Tennessee. From the court records of Giles County we learned that Granville and Lavina died within one day of each other in 1856, leaving these three small boys orphans. Two of the boys William Gilbert and Arelius Granville were living with the Thomas Gordon family in the 1860 and 1870 census of Giles County. By 1877 William had moved to Cotton Plant, Missouri. Arelius was reported to still be living in Giles County but nothing was said of James T., except for a record of him receiving a final disbursement of his grandfather, James Carroll Sr.'s, estate. He received one third of Granville Carroll's inheritance.

By 1880 James Carroll was living in Greene County, Arkansas, with his wife Mary Potts-Carroll born 1856, the daughter of George H. Potts born 1830 and Elizabeth Garrett-Potts born 1831. Enumerated in the 1880 census with James and Mary are their first two, of five children: Carol Ann (actually Sally Ann) later to marry J. E. Roberts and an unnamed son later to be named William Thomas "Tom" who marries Florence Trantham.

In the 1900 census we see the other three children enumerated: Giller born July 1882, who married Luther Williams; Buford B. born November 1885, married Eunice Haneline; and Aurelliou G. (Arelious Granville known as "R. G.") born August 1888 first married Alsie "Elsie" Black born July 1893, daughter of Dudley Black and Mary Jane "Mandy" Corbett-Black. His second marriage was to Mattie Stout, the daughter of John Edward Jackson and Armenta Bell Noel. Her first husband was F. A. Stout.

James and Mary Carroll lived in Greene County from 1877-1883. Sometime after the tax roll was taken in 1883 and until after July 1885 they lived in Texas. Her father George H. Potts and stepmother Mary Starnes Potts were enumerated in the 1870 Greene County, Arkansas, census. George and Mary Potts moved to Texas between 1876-1879. Both were reported to have died around the same time in 1883-1884. James and Mary Carroll went to Texas to get her orphan siblings. Buford was their only child to be born in Texas.

**CARROLL** – James Carroll, died in 1891 in Greene County, Arkansas, at the age of 28. He had delivered a wagon load of cotton to the gin and on the way back his horses spooked throwing him from his wagon. He came into the house where Mary was waiting supper for him and told her what had happened. He said he did not feel well and thought he would skip supper and go to bed. Later when Mary retired she did not notice anything unusual. As the night wore on Mary moved closer to her sleeping husband only to find him cold. The accident had broken his neck and he had died shortly after retiring. Mary died in 1935. They are both buried at the Hartsoe Cemetery in Marmaduke, Arkansas.

Arelious Granville "R. G." Carroll was born September 8, 1887, in Greene County, Arkansas. From his marriage to Alsie Black he had five children: James Floise born September 13, 1910, who married Nola Mable Smith; Dudley Bynum born October 30, 1911, who married Nellie Silkwood; Arelious Murrell born April 14, 1915, who married Christine Gaskill; Leonard Leslie born May 14, 1917, who married Esther; and Ettar who married Earnest Smith.

Alsie died January 20, 1919 from the influenza epidemic which ravaged the world. She was buried in Liberty Cemetery in an unmarked grave.

In the marriage of R. G. and Mattie Jackson-Stout were born: Wauldine born September 15, 1923, who married Carman Barnhart; Veola Marcella March 1, 1926, who married Russel Fowler and Kenneth Cowen; Maxine born January 1929 died 1936; and Marlin and Arlin (twins) born July 26, 1936. Marlin married Brenda Peterman and Arlin married Lula Vickroy. From her first marriage were: Nathan born 1914, Edward born 1916, Thelma born 1918 and James born 1920 who married Audrey Grimes.

R. G. Carroll worked for the railroad until around 1928 when the railroad, like so many other companies, reduced their payroll as much as they could. After that, supporting the large family became an all consuming effort. He bought 100 acres of land and put his half grown boys to work doing men's jobs. Almost everyone during that period was working for the railroad indirectly, cutting ties or milling for them. The family remained in Greene County until about 1942 when they moved to Flint, Michigan, to work in the auto plants. By then the only children still living in their household were Veola and the twin boys, Arlin and Marlin. After his death in 1950 he was returned to Greene County where he was buried in Liberty Cemetery.

After being widowed for the second time Mattie Jackson married ? Warwick. She died in 1977 and was buried in Liberty Cemetery, as well.

Arelious Murrell Carroll was born April 14, 1915 died November 25, 1996, in Hanford, Kings County, California. He married Birdy Christine Gaskill on November 17, 1934, in Greene County, Arkansas. Christine was born September 19, 1917. She is the daughter of Henry Oscar Gaskill born 1889 and Gagie Parker-Gaskill born 1892 both born in Greene County. Henry Oscar was the son of Calhoun Conway Gaskill born 1862 and Alwiltie Noel-Gaskill born 1867. Gagie Parker was the daughter of William Parker born 1869 and Nancy Sims born 1875 both born in Greene County. William Parker was the son of Charles G. Parker. Nancy was the daughter of Thomas Marion Sims and Jane Elizabeth Reynolds.

Murrell Carroll and Christine had three children. Charlene born 1934 in Marmaduke; Floreeta M. born 1938; and Mikel born 1940 in Kings County, California.

Murrell was an active farmer in California from 1937 to 1948. His first job was for $ .50 a day, when he could find the work. He was a proud man but not proud of some of the places he was forced to house his family. As the economy got better he was able to get a farming job for $100.00 a month and a house. He was given a bonus at the end of the year. That "bonus" gave him the down payment for his first home with 10 acres in 1948. He was still farming but this time for himself. He was also working as a laborer for Lacey Milling Company. When he retired from Lacey in 1983 he was their flour miller.

From 1983 until 1994 you could find Murrell and Christine on their annual visit to Marmaduke, Arkansas, looking up relatives and old friends. His health would not allow the trip in 1995 or 1996. His sister Ettar Smith is still a resident of Marmaduke.

**CHILDERS** – Joseph Holmes Childers was born May 1, 1862, near Walnut Ridge, descending from an old family of Virginians. His great-grandfather Isom Childers was a veteran of the War of 1812 and an early settler in Arkansas. About 1828 Isom sold his land on Copper Ridge along Clinch River in Virginia, moved with his five sons and two daughters to Lawrence County, settling along Strawberry River where they played an important part in the settlement of the Lower Strawberry Valley. James was prominent in the affairs of the community in Old Walnut Ridge, representing the county in the legislature several terms.

*Joseph Holmes Childers family. Front row left to right: Allen, Joseph Holmes, Eliza Josephine and Olen. Back row left to right: Carl, Hazel Irene and Albert.*

John Morgan Childers was born in 1852 and married Seletha Jane Hardin. He didn't follow his father politically but remained a farmer. Their children were: Ersula, Mary, James, Joseph Holmes, Sarah, John Crockett and Emma. In 1870 John owned 80 acres of land in Cache Township and died a few years later.

Joseph Holmes Childers was a devout Christian and joined the Pleasant Hill Methodist Church in Lorado where he was the Sunday School superintendent and music director for many years. He married Eliza Josephine

Farrar, born November 18,1861, and died January 31, 1916, daughter of Nimrod and Demarius Farrar. To this union seven children were born:

Allen Childers born 1888 married Clifford Gleghonr and had a daughter Jolene.

Olen Childers born 1890 married Zeffie Ellington and their children were Wilgus and Samuel.

Omer Childers born 1892 died young.

Roy Childers born 1894 died infancy.

Hazel Irene Childers born January 26,1897, died January 30, 1993, married Oliver Cook. Their children are Joseph Edward and Juanita.

Albert Childers born 1899, never married, but remained at home to take care of his father. He left an impression of Christian influence on many lives.

Carl Childers born 1901 died young.

When the "cyclone" of 1929 hit Lorado, it destroyed Joseph's house, and blew him into a gully, the cook stove landing on top of him, crippling his leg. Still he was full of life and his granddaughter Juanita thought he was the greatest " horse shoe" pitcher in the world. When he could no longer farm his land, Joseph and his son Albert moved to Bono and operated the "Bono Cafe" which became the favorite eating place of farmers around the area, who would go to Jonesboro on Saturday to shop but come back through Bono for some of Albert's five cent hamburgers. Everyone knew and loved "Uncle Joe" and enjoyed hearing him go to the cafe door and holler "Get 'em while they're hot boys, get' em while they're hot."

He was much respected and his gentle manner is still remembered by those who respect his memory and the impact he made on their lives. He died October 9, 1949, and didn't leave his family a large estate, but a lasting legacy of Christian ideals, honesty and integrity. Funeral services were held in the Lorado Methodist Church that he loved so well. Perhaps even as friends and loved ones mourned their loss he was leading a "Heavenly Choir" in song. He was buried beside Eliza at Pleasant Hill where they rest from their labors and lie in peaceful sleep, awaiting the summons to "come up higher."

**CHUNN** – Omer Talyor (Mose) Chunn, was born in Jackson, Tennessee, on July 17, 1893. He died at Paragould, Arkansas, on April 19, 1974, at the age of 80. He married Amelia Alma Katherine Haberling who came to Paragould from Switzerland with her parents as a child. Amelia was born May 24, 1895, and died September 2, 1979, in Michigan at the age 84.

*Photo of Omer Taylor (Mose) Chunn family. Left to right: Mose Chunn, Amelia Chunn, Fannie Marie (Chunn) Dinwiddie, Mary Louise Chunn and Oma Lee (Chunn) Thomason. Back row: Earl Taylor Chunn, Harry Chunn and Roy William Chunn Sr.*

Omer was a horse cobbler, blacksmith, and built truck beds. Omer and Amelia had six children. They were:

Earl Taylor Chunn was born October 11, 1913, and died September 1989.

Harry Chunn was born March 1, 1919, and died June 16, 1978, at the age of 59.

Roy William Chunn was born May 5, 1921, and resides in Paragould.

Fannie Marie Chunn Dinwood was born September 14, 1924, and resides in Paragould.

Mary Louise Chunn was born January 20, 1927, and died November 19, 1944, at the age of 17.

Oma Lee Chunn Thomason was born March 16, 1936, and resides in Paragould.

**CHUNN** – Samuel Lee Chunn, born December 22, 1865, in Jackson, Tennessee, and died December 5, 1958. He came to Arkansas between 1900 and 1905. He was a blacksmith, farmer, had a sorghum mill and ground corn in the Village Community.

*The Chunn family at the family home on what is now Highway 69 South. Beginning at the front left is Luther "Doc," the family dog, Samuel Lee, Mary Ruth, Fannie and Henry. The rear beginning at the left is Omer Taylor, Dewey and William Bill.*

He and his wife, Fannie Poole Chunn had nine children.

Odra O'Neil Chunn Reed was born October 18, 1887, and died April 4, 1974.

Rosy Lee Chunn was born April 18, 1891, and died January 21, 1949.

Omer Taylor "Mose" "O.T." Chunn was born July 17, 1893, and died April 19, 1974.

Dewey Sampson Chunn was born September 12, 1895, and died June 27, 1937.

William Thomas Chunn was born February 9, 1898, and died December 11, 1963.

Luther "Doc" Chunn was born June 14, 1900, and died September 1, 1968.

John Henry Chunn was born November 17, 1905, and died September 6, 1988.

Mary Ruth Chunn Hester was born February 10, 1909, and died March 4, 1999.

All the children were born in Tennessee except the last two. There was an unnamed child which did not survive. Mr. Chunn built a home at Village Community which is now Highway 69.

**CLARK** – Joe Clark married Mary Thompson. Their sons came to Arkansas from Tennessee. Tom Clark owned land where the Paragould Country Club is now. Wesley Clark settled around Pine Knot. John Clark settled around Campground community and married Martha Hunter. Their sons were William, who died in the Mexican War, Joseph, last heard from at Pea Ridge during the Civil War and John Jarvis Clark.

John Clark (1832) married Mary Smelser (1829). Their children were Betty, Sarah, George Washington, Billie Franklin, Joseph Henry, Victoria, John Crowly, Janie and Martha Elizabeth. Their descendents are as follows:

Betty married Doc Witcher. Children were Mary, Alex, Lou, Onie and Cynthia.

Sarah married J. W. Watson and had no children.

George married Eliza Morris. They had Vinnie and Sally. After Eliza died George married Zera Stury and had Williard and Wade.

Joseph Clark married Zevlia Hall and bore Sylvia and Marvin.

Victoria Clark married Tom Spillman. Their children were Tyler, Onie and Acres.

John Crowly Clark married Rebecca Kennemore and had Ella, Elizabeth, Gilbert and Crowly.

Billie Franklin Clark married Laura Melissa Ginger, whose family owned a farm where Big Lake and Wild Life Refuge are now. They had children named Sarah Anne, John Wesley "Bud", Martha Miranda Victoria "Vickie", Mary (Melissa or Elizabeth), Susie Mae, Lillie Jane "Ginny", Roy McKinley and Henry Clark, who died at 20 months.

**CLARK** – Joseph Gilbert Clark, born September 22, 1914, died March 16, 1999, was the third child of John Crowley and Rebecca Kennemore Clark. After Gilbert's father's death, his grandfather, John Jarvis Clark, helped support the family until Gilbert, his brother, John Crowley, and his sisters, Mary Ella and Martha Elizabeth, were old enough to work.

John Crowley married Hester Mertz. They had one son, Phillip.

Mary Ella married Verlie Tedder. They had one son, Billy.

Martha Elizabeth married Woodrow Futrell. They had two daughters, Patricia Rowe and Melinda Brinkley.

Gilbert attended Commissary and Stanford schools. By age 12, he was doing a grown man's job, driving a team in the construction of Highway 25. Years later, he was employed by the state highway commission under Governor Marion Futrell and also farmed.

On December 31, 1938, Gilbert married Jeffiteen Inez Morrow, born April 4, 1918, the daughter of Jeff and Pearl Goins Morrow. She was born at the home of her grandparents, W.P and Lydia Lafferty Goins. When she was 6 weeks old, her father was sent to France to serve in World War I. Inez attended Evening Shade School through the eighth grade and moved in with her Aunt Mary Goins in Paragould when she was 14. She attended Paragould High School, graduating in 1937. She taught school at Oak Ridge, and after she married, she taught at Stanford.

Gilbert and Inez bought a farm at Evening Star, later moving north of Paragould where they owned another farm. They bought a farm in the Commissary Community and lived there for eight years. While Gilbert farmed, Inez taught school at Pruett, west of Stanford. Between crops Gilbert operated his gravel truck.

*Gilbert and Inez Clark*

They moved to Paragould in 1951 where Gilbert again worked for the highway commission and Inez worked at Eli Walker shirt factory. In 1958, they moved to Center Hill. They owned and operated Clark's Grocery on Highway 412 West from

1965 to 1975 before retiring to 106 Academy Drive. Gilbert is buried in Morrow cemetery.

The couple's three children are:

I. John Joseph born February 22, 1940, married Alma, daughter of Hubert and Mary Lynne Haymore of North Carolina.

A. John Keith born July 16,1962.

1. Married Marcia, daughter of Charlie and Lynette Lambert Blevins

a. Heather Suzanne

2. Married Kimberly Bunch

a. Haylee Briann

b. Hannah MaeAnn

3. Married Cathy, daughter of Bryon and Lola Newcomb Franz

a. Anthony Brown, stepson

b. Aaron Clark, adopted

B. Darrell Ray born January 8, 1964; died June 4, 1976.

C. Mary Ann born March 31, 1965, married Ted, son of Jerry and Sue Riggs Simpson.

D. Gregory Scott born March 29, 1966, married Gina, daughter of Joe and Linda Kissinger Counts.

a. Joseph Counts

II. Jeff Morrow born October 7, 1944, married Patsy, daughter of Ollie and Dorothy Metheny Whitworth. They later divorced.

A. Rebecca Jane born August 5, 1974.

B. Whitney Worth born November 13, 1977, married J.J., son of Phillip Blankenship and Dottie Proctor Blankenship Lloyd.

III. Jimi Nett born July 3, 1948, married Roger, son of Hugh and Nora Riggs Bowman.

A. Katie Clark born July 31, 1984.

**CLARK –** The Clark family history was collected and saved by the late Audie Franklin Morrow, Paragould, Arkansas.

Joseph and Mary (Thompson) Clark, of Tennessee, had sons: Robert Clark, who died in a Memphis hotel fire, Tom Clark, John Clark, a twin born in 1807, and Wesley Clark.

Tom Clark settled in Paragould, Greene County, Arkansas. He once owned land where the country club and golf course are now.

Wesley Clark settled in the Pine Knot area. His descendants were: Mamie Bass, Mattie Bass and Mrs. Walter Hyde.

John Clark, born in 1807, settled around the Campground Community. He married Martha Hunter, born 1810. Their sons were: William, who died in the Mexican War; Joseph, who died at Pea Ridge during the Civil War; and John Jarvis Clark, born January 31, 1832, in Greene County, Arkansas.

John Jarvis Clark married Mary Ann Smelser, born August 1, 1829, daughter of Abraham Smelser. They had nine children: Betty born in 1857; Sarah born December 3, 1859, died April 2, 1908; George Washington Clark born July 17, 1862, died January 1934; Billie Franklin Clark born December 25, 1865, died December 7, 1920; Joseph Henry Clark born August 29, 1867, died February 24, 1958; Victoria born May 24, 1870, died January 8, 1933; John Crowley Clark born June 28, 1873, died 1916; Janie died age 9; and Martha Elizabeth.

Sarah Clark married Rev. J.W. Watson.

George Clark married Eliza Morris. Their children: Vinnie and Sallie. George Clark's second wife was Zera Autry. Their children: Willard and Wade.

Joseph Clark married Zeulia Cordela Hall.

Victoria Clark married Tom Spillman.

Betty Clark married Dock Witcher.

Billie Franklin Clark married Laura Melissa Ginger, daughter of Pete and Melissa Ginger. Their children: Sarah Anne married Jim Bill McDaniel; John Wesley died age 18; Martha Miranda Victoria "Vickie" born March 17, 1892, died March 24, 1931, married Charles "Chink" Edward Stevens; Mary Melissa married Jake Hunter; Susie Mae born October 13, 1895, died 1992, married Arthur Leroy Davis; Mose, died age 3; Lilly Jane "Jenny;" Roy McKinley Clark married Betty Sneel; and Ruby Cline and Henry Clark died age 20 months.

Lilly Jane "Jenny" Clark married Audie Morrow born April 20, 1898, died October 11, 1973. Their children: Idean Page born February 9, 1919; Lou Jean Smith born July 26, 1921; David Morrow born November 22, 1923; Genevieve Speer born May 19, 1926; Alberta Pillow born April 7, 1929; O.D. Morrow born June 17, 1932; Gentry Lee Morrow born November 13, 1934. Lilly Jane Morrow died in 1988. Jenny and Audie are buried in the Morrow Cemetery in Standford, Greene County, Arkansas.

**CLARK –** My grandmother, Zeulia Cordelia Hall Clark, was not only a beautiful person with her dark hair, flashing black eyes, delicate features and form, but she was also highly intelligent with a desire to excel and a humble heart. She was born on November 17, 1878, to Thomas and Lavonia Hall in Greene County, Arkansas, in their homestead on the Cache River. Zeulia's parents had combined their farms; Lavonia's first husband, Jeptha Futrell, had died leaving her with two small sons, Daniel and Marion, and expecting another which was stillborn after Lavonia struggled clearing land they had purchased from the Iron Mountain Railroad. After Thomas and Lavonia married they built their new home on land there. Zeulia grew up fast, at six, she nodded off at dawn making biscuits for the family and then pulled calves away from their mothers in order to milk. She helped care for her two younger brothers, Ira and Arta Hall, and squeezed in her prized schooling.

*Joe and Zeulia Clark and family. Joe Clark, age 43; Zeulia Clark, age 32; Sylvia, age 14; Marvin, age 12; Golvia, age 9; Lillian, age 6; Una, age 3; and Clessa age 3 months. Circa 1911, Springdale, Arkansas*

Eight days before her 17th birthday, Zeulia married another Greene Countian, Joe Clark, 11 years her senior. They started housekeeping in Marion's three-room cabin on Sugar Creek near Crowley's Ridge. When their first child, Sylvia (my mother) was born on August 13, 1896, they moved back in with Zeulia's parents. Before their second child, Marvin, was born January 23, 1899, they had moved nearby. Then came another move and another baby, Golvia on October 7, 1901. This became the pattern of their lives.

Joe bought a share in the old commissary store where Zeulia bore Ruby, November 11, 1903, who died in 12 days. Joe soon wearied of the store and bought a 40-acre farm. Now Zeulia thought he would surely settle down. But as soon as the crops were gathered, he moved again. Their fifth child, Lillian, March 15, 1905, was an infant when they moved to Texas with high hopes. But Texas made no difference in their struggles: more moves, another baby, Una born August 2, 1907.

Joe heard Christians were wanted at Mena, Arkansas, but the climate didn't suit, so he put them on a train headed for Northwest Arkansas. Zeulia protested that she was in labor and didn't think she could make it, but Joe said "you have to." When the train stopped in Springdale, they rushed to the nearest hotel where Clessa was born on December 6, 1910. Within a week Joe hired a covered wagon to move them to Elm Springs, where they farmed a few years before heading toward Greene County, stopping at County Line for about a year.

Zeulia bore two more girls while moving around in Greene County– Lavonia born November 9, 1914, and Lois born December 19, 1918. They tried Texas again, farming cotton, corn, and prize-winning watermelon, and producing their last child, Joe born May 13, 1921. Back in Arkansas by 1929, near Springdale, I remember Grandma Zeulia picking strawberries, beans, and grapes, singing as she worked, and enthusiastically encouraging us to get ready for church to walk over the mountain with her when there were too many for the buggy.

She kept her faith in spite of her trials, like the time her new baby chicks smothered and she collapsed to the floor uttering "that's just hell." Their last big move was to Missouri where Joe suffered with hay fever, so Zeulia did most of the work, and weakened, succumbed to pneumonia January 21, 1936. Her tombstone appropriately reads: "She hath done what she could."

**CLARK/MOSS –** I had no idea I would ever be interested in family background; but thanks to the M&NA Railroad and Francis Bland, I became involved.

I went to the Greene County Library to look at a book on *Short Line Railroads* that I knew was there. I wanted some information on the M&NA Railroad. My dad and I used to catch this train at Harrison and ride it to Kensett to visit with relatives. My dad took care of some business and we would catch the train back home that evening or the next morning. The train stopped at every little community and picked up cream cans and set off baby chickens. I have a lot of memories of that old train. The M&NA ran from Joplin, MO to Helena, AR. It went through Harrison, Pindall, Marshall, Leslie, Edgemont, Heber Springs, Pangburn, Searcy, Kensett, Cotton Plant, Fargo and Helena. Passengers that used the M&NA said the letters meant "May Never Arrive".

*George and Shirley Moss, Sept. 1998.*

The morning I went into the library to gather information on the M&NA Railroad, Francis Bland came to the area where I was and made a profound change in my life. I had known for many years that we were kin through the Clark family. He started showing me Tennessee and Arkansas census indexes with the Clark family listed. He asked me many questions about the Clark family; some I could answer, some I could not. I decided then and there I should know the answers. My mother was a Clark. I knew some about the Clark family, but nothing of my father's family. His father and mother died when he was young. He had no brothers or sisters. An old maid Aunt "Tennessee" Moss, who was a schoolteacher, kept him and sent him to school. This is about all I knew about the Moss family. I decided I should know more.

First Clark family: My mother was Vestle Clark, (July 4, 1902-March 31, 1976). She lived her whole life in Arkansas. Her father was Robert Fleming Clark, born October 7, 1869 in Haywood County, TN, died Jan. 9, 1929, in Paragould, AR. By trade, he was a carpenter. He held many positions in County-City government. He had been a deputy sheriff, police chief, fireman, street commissioner, constable and justice of the peace.

My mother's mother was Nancy Elizabeth Moss Yow, born April 18, 1867 in Haywood County, TN and died July 7, 1958 in Paragould, AR. My grandfather's father was John Clark, born April 25, 1822 in North Carolina, died May 30, 1898 in Greene County, AR. He was a farmer. He homesteaded and bought other land in Greene County, AR. He also owned land in Haywood County, TN. He came to Greene County in 1872. He was the father of 18 children by two wives. He lived on State Highway 49, just south of Greene County High Log Dog Trot House.

My grandfather's mother was Easter Susan Lewis, born May 31, 1844 in Haywood County, TN, died Nov. 3, 1893 in Greene County, AR. Her grandfather was James Lewis, born 1756 in North Carolina, died 1844 in Edgecombe, Colorado. He was a Patriot of the Revolutionary War. He was a supplemental patriot for me.

My grandfather's grandfather (or my great great grandfather) was Joseph Clark, born Dec. 20, 1794 in North Carolina died Sept. 9, 1871 in Greene County, AR. He came to Greene County in the 1850s and homesteaded land. He lived on Old Greensboro Road, three-fourths mile north of the Greene and Craighead county line (State highway 351). He gave the land for Clark's Chapel Cemetery and School. First burials in Clark's Chapel Cemetery were two Union soldiers going home from the Civil War. My great great grandmother was Biddie Ann Permenter, born June 10, 1801 in North Carolina, died Sept 1891 in Greene County, AR.

I knew little about the Moss family. My father was John Louis Moss, born May 18, 1886 at Gaither (Boone County) AR, died July 1967 in Denver, CO. Since there was no 1890 census of Boone County, I got the 1900 microfilm of the Boone County census and since there was no index, started looking at the complete county. I knew my dad would be 14 years old and found him and his mother living with his grandfather, Radford Louis Cone in Crooked Creek Township of Boone County, AR. My grandmother was a Cone. My great grandfather Radford was a Confederate veteran and died in 1923. I sent in for his death certificate and found he was buried at White Church Cemetery in Boone County. I located it through a local funeral home. Shirley and I drove up to this fenced cemetery on top of a mountain at Harrison and before I shut off the ignition she said, "Look, there are some Mosses."

*Submitted by Robert George Moss*

**CLARK/PERMENTER** – Margaret and Michael

*The family of Francis Clark Sr.*

Clark sailed from Southampton England on the Glasgow to Barbados in 1669. Sailing with them and their family was the family of Zachariah Moorman. The Clark family consisted of Micajah, who was married to Ann Moorman, the daughter of Zachariah; Francis; Edward; Roger; William; Thomas; Christopher and David Terrell.

The Moorman family consisted of Thomas, Charles and Sally Ann, who was married to Micajah Clark. Micajah and the Moormans came on to Charleston, SC then to Virginia in 1670.

Michael and Margaret and some of their sons settled on the Island of Barbados where they owned land and slaves. Michael died there in 1679 and was buried on the island. In 1680 Margaret was in Christ Parish in Virginia. Near her was her son, Edward and his wife, Ann (Allison) Clark. Children of Edward were: Christopher, Francis, Allison and John. 1722 Christopher, his wife and family and Francis, his wife, Cordelia Lankford and family moved to Albermarle District in Virginia. They were all Quakers at that time.

In 1752 Christopher, son of Francis married Elizabeth Stone. In 1754 Christopher and family and brother, Francis and family moved to Anson County, NC.

Christopher Clark entered a request for 412 acres on April 26, 1768 from the North Carolina Land Grant Office. The land was on the southwest of the Pee Dee River in Anson County. The land was issued on Dec. 16, 1769.

Christopher also entered a request for 300 acres on the southwest side of the Pee Dee River on Island Creek on Dec. 26, 1768. He was issued the land on April 9, 1770.

Christopher requested a grant of 100 acres on Watery Br. and was issued the land on Oct. 26, 1767.

Francis Clark, Jno. Crawford, Thomas Moorman and Isham Hailey together requested 7.8 acres on Island and Shoal in Pee Dee River on Dec. 21, 1768. They were issued the grant on May 4, 1769.

Francis Clark requested a grant of 50 acres on waters of Solomon's Creek. He was issued the land on May 22, 1772.

In the 1810 Anson County Census there are two Clark families shown: Joseph Clark Sr., with two sons (one under 10 and the other 10 to 16) and five daughters (two under 10; one 10 to 16; two 16-26). His wife was listed as 26-45; Joseph, Sr. was listed as being over 45 in 1800, 1810 and 1820.

The other Clark family was that of Francis Clark. Francis was over 45, with his wife shown as between 16 and 26 years of age. There were four sons (two under 10; one 10-16 and one 16-26) and three daughters (one under 10 and two 10-16).

In the Anson County NC 1820 Census, seven Clark families are listed. Joseph Clark Jr. is shown with a son under 10 and a son 10-16. Joseph was born Dec. 20, 1794 and his wife, Biddy Ann was born June 10, 1801.

Joseph Clark Sr. is listed as 45 and over, his wife as 45 and over, with one female under 10, one female 10-16; one female 16-26 and one female 26-45.

The other five Clark families are James, Christopher, Richard, William and Mary Clark.

Will of John Permenter

(Anson County, North Carolina – Will Book of 1821, pages 111-112.)

In the name of God, Amen, I, John Permenter of the County of Anson and State of North Carolina, do hereby make this my last will and testament.

Item: First, I lend unto my loving wife, Elizabeth, all my stock of every kind also the tract of land whereon I now live with its improvements, with all my household and kitchen furniture, also all my crop on hand, during her widowhood; after her death or marriage, I give the above said land mentioned to my son, Braton Jr. Permenter and his heirs forever.

I will that all the balance of my land be equally divided between my four sons, Vis: Ruffin Permenter, John J. Permenter, Needham K. Permenter and James R. Permenter. I give and bequeath to my daughter, Elizabeth Permenter, one bed and furniture. I also give to my daughter, Maria, $250 and to my daughter, Biddy, $250. (Biddy was the wife of Joseph Clark, who moved to Greene County, AR.)

Lastly, I appoint Littlebury Diggs, Ruffin Permenter, Joseph Clark, J., John F. Auld and Hiram Clark, Executors to this my last will and testament. In witness whereof I hereunto set my hand and seal this 19th day of July in the year of our Lord 1821. Signed, sealed and delivered in the presence of us.

John Permenter

John F. Auld (was a member of the House of Commons, 1783)

James Wall

John Permenter

The 1830 Anson County, NC Census lists eight Clark families. The male heads of their households were Benjamin, William, Christopher, David, John, Thomas, Joseph Clark Sr. and Joseph Clark Jr.

Joseph Sr. between 60 and 70 years of age, had one son, 10-15 years, another son, 30-40 and two daughters: one, 15-20 and the other, 20-30. Joseph Clark Jr., his wife, Biddie Ann and their nine children were also living in Anson County in 1830.

Some time before 1840, Joseph Clark Jr. and his family moved to Gibson County, TN. In the 1840 Gibson County Census they were living next door to the family of Thomas and Mary Laman. In that census he was listed as being between 40 and 50, and Biddy Ann, between 30 and 40. They had three sons and three daughters.

In 1850 they were still in Gibson County. At that time their children were Salina (1831); Christopher (1832); Susan (1835); Elizabeth; Sarah "Sally" (1840); James (1844) and Nancy (1846). Salina was born in North Carolina, but all the other children were born in Tennessee. In that census, Joseph Jr. was living at # 553 house (numbered in the order of visitation by the census taker). The Thomas Laman family was living at # 520.

Thomas Layman, son of Thomas and Mary Laman, was born in 1820 in Tennessee. He married Eliza Bland Jan. 6, 1848 in Gibson County. Eliza was the daughter of John Bland, a Baptist minister, who died in 1856 in Gibson County. He was the great-great grandfather of the Bland family of Paragould.

By 1860 the Joseph Clark family had moved from Gibson County, TN to Greene County, AR and resided in St. Francis Township. By 1870, Joseph and Biddey Clark were living in Cache Township. At that time Tennessee, John and Elihu Clark, orphaned relatives, were living with the family.

By 1880 Biddy Clark, now a widow, was living with her daughter and son-in-law, Ann and Whitfield Boyd, in Poland Township.

Joseph and Biddy Clark are buried in Clark's Chapel Cemetery.

**CLAYTON** – Gregory C. "Guy" Clayton was born in Beech Grove, McLean County, KY 1870-72 to Edward Pierce and Mary Catherine (Clements) Clayton. His grandparents were Charles and Barbara (Hagan) Clayton and great-grandparents are believed to be Joseph and Eleanor Clayton. Joseph was born in the 1750s, probably in Virginia. Charles was born Feb 2, 1800 in Nelson County, Ky. and Barbara was born in 1805-06, also in Nelson County, to "Nancy" Ann (Cissell) and Benjamin Hagan II. Charles and Barbara were married in 1830 in Bardstown, Nelson County, KY and moved to Daviess County in 1837. Edward and Mary were married in Daviess County Jan. 12, 1857. It is believed that Joseph's grandparents came to the United States from England. The Clayton's were devout Catholics and most were farmers, owning land in Kentucky.

Gregory was the fifth of six children born to "Pierce" and Mary Clayton. His siblings were: Georgia Ann (1857); Johnette (1862-63); John Edward (1864); Charles Edward (1866), Mary Julie (1876).

Gregory married Anninsia Nora "Anna" (Mackey), who was born 1872-74 in Beech Grove, KY to native Kentuckians. They married April 3, 1894 at St. Benedict's Catholic Church in Beech Grove. In 1903 they packed their possessions and five children into a covered wagon and traveled to Boydsville, Clay County, AR to join family already settled there, arriving in the spring. Two more children were born to them. Their children were: Asia, Jerome Gilbert, Mary Elizabeth, Carmel Joseph, Dorothy Anna, Magdaline Mary and Aloysia Gertrude. The priest from St. Mary's in Paragould baptized Magdaline and Gertrude. The other children were baptized in Kentucky. The family continued affiliation with St. Mary's throughout the years they lived in the area. Gregory was inducted into the Knights of Columbus at St. Mary's in 1913. He

L-R: Tom; Jerome Clayton in Army uniforms. About 1918

farmed at Boydsville, then moved to Rector in 1906 and worked at a sawmill. His parents had also moved to Arkansas and after Mary died in Dec. 1903, Edward lived with Gregory. Edward died between 1910 and 1920.

In 1918 Gregory moved his family to nearby Paragould, in Greene County and worked at Wrape's Heading Mill. Asia and Mary had already moved away. One by one the other children moved away. In 1924 Gregory and Anna moved to Chicago, IL where some of their children were living, remaining there until they died in the 1960s.

Gregory's son Jerome, called "Red", was the only one of the children to remain in Paragould. He was born in Beech Grove, KY Sept. 30, 1897. He completed six years of school at Rector and when he was 19, enlisted in the army. Honorably discharged as sergeant in July 1919 from Co. L, 153rd Infantry, he served one year in combat in France during WWI. When he was discharged he joined his family in Paragould, where he went to work at Wrape's Mill. He worked there almost 30 years as a saw filer, losing a finger to the saw.

Soon after Jerome joined his family in Paragould, he met a pretty Catholic girl, Catherine Frances Beising. Four years later, on Jan. 10, 1924, they were married at St. Mary's Catholic Church in Paragould.

Catherine "Katie" was born Nov. 26, 1904 in Paragould to Frank Joseph and Iola M. "Flora" Beising. Frank was born in Cincinnati, O in 1856 to German immigrants. Ola was born in 1876 in St. Joseph, MO to John and Martha (Miller) Flora, natives of Missouri and Indian. Catherine's brother, Edward Joseph, was born in Paragould in 1901. He married, had children and later moved away.

Jerome and Catherine's children were: Jerome G. Jr., Mary Catherine, Francis "Frank" Eugene, Robert William, Patricia Ann, James Alan and Sharon Lea, all born at home in Paragould. The family lived in several locations around Paragould before buying a home on Bard Road in 1939 for $350, paying for it with monthly payments of $20.00.

When Wrape's Mill closed, Jerome found a job in Memphis, TN at National Cooperage Company, working there five years, until he died Dec. 24, 1955.

Catherine was a homemaker all her married life. She died in Paragould May 6, 1978. She and Jerome are buried in St. Mary's Catholic Cemetery in Paragould, next to her parents.

*Submitted by Mrs. Betty J. Clayton*

**CLEMENTS** – In the older section of Mt. Zion Cemetery stands a cluster of tombstones bearing the Clements name. Among these are the markers for Rev. Mannen (sic) E. (Emanuel) Clements and his wife, Nancy.

Their Greene County, Arkansas, story begins about 1853 when they moved their family from Tuscaloosa County, Alabama, to a farm in Salem Township, located near Mt. Zion Baptist Church on what is now Highway 141. Somewhat unusual for that time, the family came alone, leaving many relatives in Tuscaloosa County. Their children, all born in Alabama, were:

(1) Sarah A., 1828 - 1869.
(2) A. P., 1830 - 1866.
(3) Samuel M., 1831-1909, married Katie Hutchins.
(4) Liddia, born circa 1834.
(5) William Thomas, 1836 - 1885.
(6) Elizabeth, born circa 1838.
(7) Caroline, born circa 1840.
(8) Mary C., 1844 - 1912.
(9) Clementine, born circa 1844.

(10) Jacob Pryor, 1848 - 1884.
(11) Nancy L., 1851 - 1892.

Nancy married General Butler Blackwood. There were nine children born of this union. After Nancy's death, Butler married Nancy's niece, Elizabeth "Bett" Clements, the daughter of Samuel M. Clements. Butler and Bett were also blessed with nine children. Bett died in 1956.

The families of John Lamb Jr. and Ann Houston and James Lamb and Rebecca Houston had settled in the neighborhood about 1850, arriving from Lauderdale County, Alabama. As often happened, William Clements "sparked" and won Mary Ann Lamb for his bride while David Lamb wooed and wedded Mary Clements. David and Mary are the great-grandparents of Joan Lamb Towery, the compiler of this article. Their son, William "Bid" Clements Lamb, married Lula Mitchell. Then another double marriage occurred. Their son, John, married Nancy Caroline Rhea, and their daughter, Irene Lamb, married Nancy Caroline's brother, Moses Rhea.

Manning pastored Mt. Zion Baptist Church from 1853 until his death in 1858. In his book, *Historical Sketches of the Mt. Zion Baptist Church,* Rev. R. C. Medaris describes Manning: "He was a strong preacher; had a good influence over his churches. He was Moderator of Mt. Zion Association two or three sessions. He died in 1858, loved and respected by all who knew him."

In the Clements section of the cemetery is another tombstone of special interest. It is inscribed: "Tom Clements (colored), 1826 -1916." The epitaph on the back reads: "Let me die the death of the righteous and let my last end be like his. Numbers 23:10." "Uncle" Tom was one of several slaves Manning and Nancy brought with

*"Uncle" Tom Clements, former slave of Rev. Manning Clements and wife, Nancy.*

them from Alabama. When Manning was dying, he asked Tom to take care of Nancy, and to the best of his ability, Tom did.

After the Civil War when Tom became free, Nancy gave him a cabin and some land on Poplar Creek. He was a respected member of Mt. Zion. Rev. Medaris calls him "a man of prayer." One Uncle Tom story illustrates this: "When the church members got into an argument, Tom would stand up and pray quite loud until the argument ceased." Also Tom is reported to have officiated at the funerals of more than 100 white people. Manning Clements' origins have thus far been traced back to the birth of his father, Jacob Hilliard Clements, about 1776 in South Carolina - probably in Cravens County which no longer exists.

Manning's mother was Jane Frances "Fanny" Sims whose first husband, Zachariah Simpson, had left her a young widow with a son, also Zachariah. Jacob and Fanny married before 1797. Their farm was located in the southern part of Laurens County, South Carolina, near the Saluda River. Their nine children were: (1) Sarah (2) Manning E. (3) Amy (4) Rebecca (5) James L. (6) John C. (7) Lidia (8) Thomas B. and (9) Wade Hampton.

By 1805 Jacob had moved his family to Green County, Kentucky, where there were family connections. In 1808 they were living in Tennessee.

It has not been established where. About 1816 they moved on to Alabama, settling in what is now Monroe County. By 1823 the Clements family were living in Tuscaloosa County, Alabama on their farm near Northport and Benion's Creek, north of Tuscaloosa. That year Jacob, Fanny, Manning and Rebecca were received as members of the Baptist Church of Bethel, Falls of Black Warrior River.

The relationship among the Clements, Pryor, Sims, Simpson and Doughty families was a close one. Some had traveled together from South Carolina and their children intermarried. Joseph Pryor, also a Baptist preacher, with eight daughters, had a farm near Jacob. Predictably, Manning Clements married Nancy Pryor, born 1805 Tennessee, in 1824 and his brother, James, married Sarah Pryor.

On February 10, 1845, an order was entered in the Orphans Court of Tuscaloosa (book 3, page 207) authorizing Manning Clements as a Baptist minister to solemnize marriages in the state of Alabama.

Jacob Clements died in 1846 in Tuscaloosa County, Alabama. His children are named in his will. Fanny died in 1856.

After Manning's death in 1858, Nancy continued living on their farm with some of her children and several black servants until she joined her husband in 1885.

At least 27 persons having the name of Clements are buried at Mt. Zion Cemetery.

**CLEVELAND** – John Wesley Cleveland was born Sept. 23, 1872 in Arkansas to Matthew V. and Martha Ann Hicks Ellis Cleveland. The Cleveland's had married in Georgia, and then moved to Alabama where oldest son Russell Reno was born.

*John Wesley and Ola Owens Cleveland with their four oldest children, Fairy (in back), Bertie, Viva and Floy (about 1908).*

After the Civil War ended, Matthew, who had been a Confederate soldier, moved his family to Tennessee where daughters Alta and Mary Artie were born. Later the family moved to Greene County, AR, where son John Wesley was born, followed by sisters Olive A., Rosa Lee and Georgia Cleveland.

Matthew died at age 47 when John was 10 years of age and the youngest child was two. At the time they were living on a farm, raising cotton, corn and sorghum cane. The family continued to reside there for several years.

John met Viola Owens who was born to James W. and Artie Owens on Oct. 14, 1878. They were married on Dec. 26, 1895, by the well-known Methodist Minister, Reverend A. C. Griffin.

The couple lived in Poland Township in 1900 and later moved to the Red Onion, Mo. Community, living just south of the Arkansas-Missouri state line in Craighead County, from about 1911 to 1916. John farmed and cut timber to clear the land near the railroad. Originally, this land was part of a swamp land grant in which the state granted land to a person in return for residence and improvement on the lands. Records indicate that in 1899 cottonwood, ash and cypress trees were to be cut and, after lying for 90 days to dry, they were to be shipped to a mill in Lake City, AR, for 50 cents to one dollar per 1,000 feet. In 1911, the timber contract mentioned red oak and sassafras trees were excluded and not to be cut. This land, at one time, sold for 50 or 60 cents per acre. The Cleveland family eventually bought over 100 acres in the area. After about five years, the family moved to Greene County and operated a small country store for a time. Then they moved to a home on the Paragould-Jonesboro highway, later moving to South Fifth Street.

Children born to John and Ola were: Fairy Evelyn, Charles Wesley who died at age 11 and one-half months, Alberta Rosella, Viva Lorene, John Alvin, Floy Esther, Irma Estelle, Artie Juanita, Alma Bernice and Norma Jeanette Cleveland.

The Clevelands were long-time members of Pruett's Chapel Methodist Church where John was on the Board of Stewards. He and Ola were active in that church and some of their children attended Pruett's Chapel school.

John was a quiet man. He was a strict but loving father who had a special love for animals and raised his children to treat them kindly. John was known to be fair and honest in his business dealings. One son-in-law is quoted as saying the two men he most respected in his lifetime were his own father and John Cleveland, his father-in-law.

Ola always enjoyed being around people and loved to invite relatives to spend the night on Saturday and go to church the next morning. She always had a treat for any child who stopped to visit.

John died on Oct. 9, 1947. His funeral was at Wood's Chapel Methodist Church with burial in the Wood's Chapel Cemetery. Ola died on Aug. 31, 1964 and was buried next to her husband.

*Submitted by Anita Phillips*

**CLEVELAND** – Matthew V. Cleveland was born July 19, 1835, in Georgia and was christened in the Methodist Church.

On Sept. 6, 1854, Matthew married Martha Ann Hicks Ellis in Bartow (Cass County), Georgia. By 1860 they were living in Ashville Township in St. Clair County, AL. He was a farmer and their son Russell Reno was then nine months old.

Matthew was a Confederate soldier who entered the Civil War in 1861 as a private in Company D, 25th Regiment of Alabama Infantry. He was described as having a ruddy complexion, brown hair, and blue eyes and was five feet six inches tall. In June of 1862 he was reported as absent from his company because of illness. On Dec. 31 of that year, he was reported as severely wounded near the first woods during the operations before Murfreesboro, TN as a member of Dea's brigade. On July 14, 1863, he was reported as a deserter from the rebel camp but was recaptured in Louisville, KY, then sent to Camp Chase, O and finally to Fort Delaware. He was released from the prison in Delaware on June 14, 1865.

*Martha A. Cleveland, widow of Matthew V. Cleveland*

Following the end of the Civil War, the Cleveland family moved to Tennessee where two daughters, Alta and Mary Artie, were born. The family then moved to Greene County, AR, where they settled in the St. Francis Township by 1870.

By 1880 the family had moved to Poland township and four more children had been born: John Wesley, Olive A., Rosa Lee and Georgia. According to his granddaughter, Matthew's health was never very good after he returned from the war. Soldiers were forced to live under terrible conditions, eating such food as parched corn and hardtack, which caused many health problems.

Matthew died on July 16, 1882, in Paragould at the age of 47 and was buried in Wood's Chapel Cemetery in Greene County. The couple had two sons and five daughters, the youngest of whom was only two years. At the time of Matthew's death, they were farming, growing corn, cotton and sorghum cane.

Martha eventually lived with her grown daughters in the Greene County area. She applied for and received a Confederate widow's pension from the government in 1901, from which she received $50. a year. By 1909, the amount totaled $62. a year. Martha died on Oct. 21, 1918 and was buried next to her husband in Wood's Chapel Cemetery.

Sources: Cleveland family history compiled by Brenda Forbess Chandler, Herren and Allied Families history by Louella Herren, military records, census records, newspapers

*Submitted by Bernadine Robinson*

**CLIFFORD** – Thomas Jewell Clifford, and Mary Ethel Burgess were married on January 10, 1925. They resided at 901 Rector Road for over 40 years.

Jerry Clifford was born to them in 1928. In 1946 they started a "second family" with Larry and Nancy. Larry lives in the family house with his family at this writing.

Tom was a member of the Paragould Fire Department when the Third Street building was constructed. His name appears on the plaque outside the building.

*Mary Burgess Clifford and Tom J. Clifford (1946) on their 21st wedding anniversary.*

He was a plumber and pipe fitter most of his life, working in Paragould until the 1960s. Early in his career he contracted with the CCC to install plumbing at Crowley's Ridge Park. He also worked at Oak Ridge, Tennessee, where the atomic bomb was developed. He spent the last several years of his life doing pipe fitting work along side his son Jerry in other states including refineries in Baton Rouge, Louisiana, and helping to build the nuclear power plant in Athens, Alabama.

Tom was active in the Greene County Amateur Radio Club (HAM). An attic scientist, he built crystal radios, repaired analog radios and TVs and built his own telescope, walking around a barrel for weeks to grind and polish the lens.

Mary Clifford was well known for the generosity of her kitchen, baking sugar cookies and pies for the sick and those she loved.

Both were charter members of Calvary Baptist Church.

**CLIFTON** – On May 7, 1930, John Earl Clifton was born to John Ayers and Velora (Vines) Clifton on a farm about two miles south of Evening Star. As a boy, he helped his dad farm and is still farming and living on the home place where he grew up.

He married Wanda (Gramling), daughter of Clyde and Cora Gramling, July 15, 1947. He ran a dairy for a while then went back to farming.

Marjorie Taun, their first child, was born June 16, 1948. Then two years later on April 5, 1950, Juanita Lynn was born.

In 1956 they moved to Lake Village in Chicot County and farmed there three years, but there was no place like Greene County, so they came back home. May 9, 1958, Earl Keith was born.

All the children graduated from Stanford High School.

Taun married Albert Louis Orick June 17, 1966. Three children were born to that union. Jonatha Shalon on August 5, 1968; Taunya Lynn, July 19, 1972; and Clifton Louis, August 2, 1979. Taun and Louis farmed until he passed away on September 6, 1988. He was buried at Morrow's Cemetery. On July 1992 she married Jimmy Smith. They live at Stanford.

Jonatha Shalon married Michael Ray Clark July 20, 1991. Michael farms and Jonatha teaches at Delaplaine. They have three children: Jocelyn Rachelle born March 22, 1992; Shealynn Micael born August 15, 1994; and Emily Taun born July 28, 1999.

Taunya Lynn married William Sisco. They are the parents of three children: Beau Louis, born November 27, 1990; Tanya Jo, born October 2, 1991; and five years later on April 24, 1997, Tristin Levi was born. They live in the house her father and mother built which is within a 100 feet of the home place where her great-grandfather John Clifton raised his family.

Clifton Louis graduated from Delaplaine School May 1998 and he farms with his uncle and aunt, Archie and Lynn Henson.

Lynn married Archie Henson November 28, 1968. They live on her grandfather's homeplace south of Evening Star where they have the Henson Flying Service. There were three children born to that union: Shane Ayers, born May 31, 1971; Shannon Lavon, born August 23, 1973; and Shayla Velora born March 7, 1981.

Shane is married to Elizabeth Harralston. They have three sons: Colby Ryan, born September 7, 1986; Colton Ayers, born October 21, 1989; and Cord Shane, born December 30, 1991.

Shane and Shannon farm with their dad. Shayla graduated from Paragould High School May 1999.

Keith married Rebecca Harris on March 17, 1979. They live in the Evening Star Community and have two children: Megan Danielle, born December 1, 1984; and John Keith born July 10, 1986. Both of the children attend Delaplaine School. Keith is in the land leveling business.

**CLIFTON** – The Cliftons of Greene County are descendants of Daniel Clifton born in Salem County, New Jersey, June 18, 1921, and Nancy Ellen (Keith) Clifton.

James Harry Clifton, the fifth of nine children, was born to Daniel and Nancy in Bonapart, Iowa, August 20, 1860. The family moved to Peeksville, Missouri, in Clark County and by 1869 they were living in St. Genevieve, Missouri.

James Harry was married to Clara Ayers in Hickman, Kentucky, on November 12, 1884.

*James Harry and Clara (Ayers) Clifton, circa 1884.*

On September 13, 1885, Mamie Pearl was the first child of James and Clara. Two years later, October 3, 1887, Ella was born followed by John Ayers on January 8, 1889. Daniel was born April 20, 1892. The family moved from Hickman, Kentucky, to Barfield, Arkansas, in Mississippi County. Lillie was born September 11, 1893, followed by James on November 22, 1896. Six weeks later on January 8, 1897, Clara died and was buried in Barfield.

By 1900 James had moved his family to Knoble, Arkansas, and from there to the Evening Star Community, which was called Black Jack at the time. He bought a place just south of Evening Star.

After James' children were grown, he married Melvina Brand. One of his daughters, Lillie, had married Carl Brand, a son of Melvina. Lillie and Carl had eight children. Mamie married Jess Mason and to that union were born five children. They lived in Paragould until the time of Mamie's death. Ella married John Hots. They lived in the Evening Star Community and raised their eight children there. Several of their children still live in Greene County.

Daniel married Emma Wagner and they bought a farm south of Evening Star and raised their two sons, Fermond and Emory. The youngest son, James, married in Texas and there was a son and daughter born to him and Opal.

John the oldest son, married Velora Vines, daughter of William and Alice (Holland) Vines, October 4, 1922. They bought a farm south of Evening Star and lived on that place and raised their family which consisted of four children: Vernon born December 26, 1923; Alma born July 24, 1926; then came Earl along with the Depression on May 7, 1930. On January 16, 1934, Clara was born.

Vernon married L.V. Metheny. Their issues are Dawna, August 26, 1945; Darrell, May 6, 1948; Bonita, November 19, 1949; and Clifford, September 27, 1958.

Alma married Gerald Davis. Issues are: Joan, November 27, 1946; Wesley, November 30, 1948; and Phillip, March 11, 1953.

Earl married Wanda Gramling. Issues are: Taun, June 16, 1948; Lynn, April 5, 1950; and Keith, May 9, 1958.

Clara married Billy Lovelady. No issues.

Besides the 10 grandchildren of John and Velora there are 19 great-grandchildren and 10 great-great-grandchildren.

John died December 3, 1962, at his home and Velora lived until June 19, 1978. They are buried in the Jones Ridge Cemetery.

**CLINE** – George Cline from Alabama had a son, Michael Cline. He in turn had a son, Jacob H. Cline, who fathered Thomas William Cline.

In 1890 Thomas William Cline (1849-1930) and wife Margaret Jane Gilliam (1853-1935) and brother Andy Cline came to Arkansas from Alabama and settle west of Paragould. They lived in a one-room building near a spring until larger living quarters were built. The older people and children came on the train. Bill Yarbrough, Jesse and Jim Rickman, Oscar and Bud Cline (Andy's sons), Joe and Eaf Cline (T.W. Cline's sons) came in covered wagons, bringing farming tools and household goods. Some rode extra horses.

Among their descendants was Joseph "Joe" Calvin Cline, (1883-1974), who married Effie May Treece (1889-1970). They lived on Old Walcott Road (now Greene 707 Road). Joe and Effie's children were: Iva, Ruby, Luther, Vincent, Linley, Norma, Alma and Aubrey Murrel. Ruby, Luther and Norma are still living. The others are buried in Finch Cemetery.

As was common practice in those days, Joe built his house from pine timber cut from his property. In 1922, he hauled the logs by wagon and team to Martin's Sawmill about a mile toward Paragould on Old Walcott Road and had it rough-cut. The finished lumber for the floors, walls and ceilings was later taken to a Paragould sawmill to be sized.

*Effie May Treece Cline and Joseph Calvin Cline on their front porch on Old Walcott Road in 1968*

Lula Cline (1885-1970) married Hiram Higgins (1881-1953). Their children are: Dexter, Opal, Selma, Ledger, Laverene, Inman and Villa. Hiram and Lula are buried in Linwood Cemetery.

Jacob Eaf (1888-1977) married Lillie F. Gramling (1891-1925). They are buried at Warrens Chapel, Walcott. Their children are: Wilma, Lester, Eleanor, George, Ray and Earl

N. I. Zear Cline (1890-1976) married Mabel Ellen Grooms (1894-1977). They are buried at Center Hill Cemetery and had one son, John T. Cline.

Louis B. Cline (1891-1978) married Claudia Pillow (1891-1978) and they had three children. Claudia is buried in Linwood Cemetery.

Galvin A. Cline (1894-1970) married Ella Little (1896-1960). They had two children; Geraldine and Kenneth and are buried at Center Hill Cemetery.

Floy D. Cline (1896-1916) married James Andrew Little (1893-1980). They had a daughter Orintha and are buried at Center Hill.

Several of the Cline descendants still live in Northeast Arkansas.

*Submitted by Ruby Clark*

**COLBATH** – Jeremiah Jones Colbath was born in Farmington, NH on Feb. 16, 1812. In 1833 at the age of 21, he legally changed his name to John Henry Wilson. He learned the trade of shoe making and at the age of 27 owned and operated his own shoe factory.

Shoe making did not interest Wilson as he had acquired a love for politics. In 1840 he was elected to the Massachusetts House of Representatives and later to the State Senate. He ran and held many other offices, but lost a race for Governor. In 1855 he was elected to the United States Senate. During Ulysses Grant's run for a second term as president of the United States, he chose Henry Wilson to be his running mate. Henry Wilson served as vice president from 1873-75. He suffered a stroke in office and died only serving three years of his term.

Wilson helped found the Republican Party. He wrote several books, one being *The History Of The Rise And Fall Of Slave Power In America*. He was strongly opposed to slavery.

Wilson married Harriet Howe in 1840 and to this union was born two children, Clara and Henry. Clara fell in love and eloped with the stable boy, Burdett Mason.

*George T. and Junie Mason Price Family: George T., Junie and children, Mason, Emagene, Betty Sue and Madyleen.*

The Wilson family disowned Clara; she never reunited with her family. Her parents wrote to her years later, but she chose to not open their letters.

Clara and Burdett Mason decided to migrate to Arkansas in 1880, after living in the states of New York, Pennsylvania and Michigan. They made the trip by wagons, floating them across the Mississippi River and settled at Strawberry, AR. They were farmers and lived their entire life in the Strawberry vicinity. They are buried in Mt. Zion Cemetery near Strawberry.

E. V. Mason was the eighth child of the 11 born to the Burdett Masons. E. V. married Emma Williams of Strawberry where they farmed and raised their family of five children: Claude, Floyd, Junie, Cora and Amy.

Junie Mason was the third child of the E. V. Masons. In Oct. 1919 she married George T. Price, son of W. H. and Octavia Sullivan Price of Calamine, AR.

In the mid 1930s the George Price family moved to Beech Grove and eventually to Paragould, AR. To this union was born four children: Mason, Emagene, Betty Sue and Madyleen.

George Price retired as custodian of the National Bank of Commerce in the 1960s. His wife Junie was a housewife and a seamstress.

Of the four Price children, Madyleen is the only one still living in Paragould north of Memorial Gardens Cemetery. The others live in California, Florida and Hope, AR.

Madyleen Price married Gale Holifield, son of L. N. and Bessie Holifield of Camp Ground, in Dec. 1945.

Madyleen and Gale Holifield are retired, having worked for State Farm Insurance for 36 years. They have two sons, Keith and Jeff living Paragould and five grandchildren: Chase, Lucy, Abigail, Drew and Seth.

*Submitted by Madyleen Price Holifield*

**COLE** – Bruce Cole was born May 10, 1930, the son of Luskie Lee and Nellie Mae Cole, in Flint, Michigan. He attended first grade in Flint and then his family moved to Marmaduke, Arkansas, where he attended school until the eighth grade. His family moved to Bragg City, Missouri, where he graduated as valedictorian of his class in 1949. His dad had died in 1945 and his mom and younger brother Terry moved back to Paragould, Arkansas, after Bruce graduated from high school. Bruce entered Arkansas State College in Jonesboro, Arkansas, in May 1949 in a suit given to him and very little money. He worked in the cafeteria and book store for his room and meals. He was in ROTC and Baptist Student Union. He became State B.S.U. President.

*Bruce and Betty (Jordan) Cole, taken May 1986.*

He married Betty Sue Jordan, second daughter of Oral Myron and Annie Mary Jordan of Marmaduke, Arkansas, on February 11, 1951. He graduated from Arkansas State College. Bruce taught school in Parma, Missouri, the summer of 1952 and he and Betty moved back to Jonesboro where their first son, Alan Keith was born September 30, 1952. They moved back to Parma, Missouri, where he taught until May 1953 when he took a teaching position job at Hayti, Missouri, where he stayed until his retirement.

*Bruce and Betty (Jordan) Cole taken on their wedding day, at the First Baptist Church in Marmaduke, Arkansas, February 11, 1951.*

During the summer of 1953 he worked part-time at Dalton Oil Company and Hays in Hayti, to supplement the $2,400.00 he was receiving as a teacher.

*Keith, Brian, Craig and Gary Cole, sons of the late Bruce Cole and Betty Jordan Cole, of Hayti, Missouri, made in September 1998 in Black Mountain, North Carolina.*

Their second son, Steven Craig was born August 18, 1957. Bruce received his masters degree from the University of Missouri. He also attended George Peabody at Nashville, Tennessee. Their third son, Gary Dean was born August 6, 1958. He became a deacon in Hayti First Baptist Church where he served at various times as Sunday school superintendent, B.Y.P.U. director, Sunday school teacher, B.Y.P.U. teacher, treasurer, worked with the R.A.s and was church janitor. He was voted Young Educator of the Year by the Jaycees, served on the board of the Conran Memorial Library, was teaching extension classes from several colleges, taught GED classes and was a part-time instructor at Mississippi County Community College in Blytheville, Arkansas.

*The family of the late Bruce Cole taken July 1999 at Bunker Hill, a teacher's resort, near Mountain View, Missouri. Standing: Craig, Karen, Gary, Sherry, Keith, Katie, Susan, Brain and Betty (bending down). Seating: Travis holding Jesse, Aaron holding fish, Jordan holding Caleb.*

Their fourth son, Brian Lee, was born December 7, 1967. Bruce was honored by the Hayti Chamber of Commerce and given the Distinguished Citizen of the Year award in 1977. Bruce was senior sponsor at school and had charge of the year book.

Bruce was diagnosed with cancer in August 1988, went through chemo and radiation treatments twice and died on February 12, 1990, and is buried at Harvey's Chapel Cemetery near Marmaduke, Arkansas.

Betty lost a good husband, the sons lost a great dad and Hayti and the community lost a great man.

Keith is married to Katie Gardiner; Craig to Karen Atwood, has two sons Jordan and Travis; Gary to Sherry Wilson has two sons, Aaron and Caleb; Brain to Susan Weatherford, has one son Jesse.

**COLE** – John W. Cole, born in Tennessee, came to Arkansas and married Melissa Bell Gilbert in 1904. She was the daughter of Ned Gilbert and Lucinda Lovelace. Lucinda was the daughter of William and Delila Lovelace, all from Indiana. Ned was from Kentucky. Melissa and John W. Cole had three children. The first, Glossie died as a baby. The second child, Dempsey Lee Cole was my father. The third Nellie Bell Cole. Then John Cole died. Melissa then moved to Delaplaine, AR and married Thomas Fletcher Wheeler. They had eight children, half brothers and sisters of my father Dempsey Lee Cole. Dempsey was married once before he married my mother and had one son. Then Dempsey married my mother Ruthie Docey Beatrice Quinn. She was the daughter of Ezra Olin Quinn and Lettie Swafford. Both were born in AR. Ezra was

*Thomas and Melissa Wheeler –1950*

the son of Joseph Ashford Quinn, born in North Carolina and Nancy E. Jones, born in Tennessee. Joseph and Nancy had 11 children. They lived around Brighten, AR. Joseph died and Nancy married J. B. Adams. They had one son. Lettie was the daughter of James W. Swafford, born in Missouri and his wife Mandy Ellen, born in Mississippi. James and Mandy had 10 children. They lived in Arkansas. Ezra and Lettie had seven. My mother was their fourth child. Now my father, Dempsey Lee Cole and my mother, Ruthie Docey Beatrice Quinn had 13 children. They lost their first three as infants and I was their first child to live so I was always the oldest. I had three children by my first marriage: Steve Allen Gilbert, Keith Allon Gilbert, and Rhonda Valrew Gilbert. Steve had four children: Michelle Tony, Faith and Adam. Keith had six children: Keith Jr., Steven, Kimberly, Christian, Nicholas and Kasey. Rhonda had two sons, Tony Morrison and Rickey Daniels. Rhonda and Keith each had one grand child and Steve had six grandchildren. After that marriage I married William Benton Swan. We had three daughters, Ruthie Samantha Swan, Valinda Serena Swan and Leslie Ann Swan. Ruthie has four children: Kris, Crystal, Jason and Sabrina Jones. Serena has two children, Tiffany and Steve Eason and Leslie has two children, Jade and Katie Beck.

*Dempsey and Ruthie Cole-1941*

William Swan was the son of Harold and Edith Swan and the grandson of J. W. and Nora Chase Swan and Nola Morris Clark. It took a lot of people coming in from other states and getting married to form this large family of mine. By now I guess you are wondering who I am. Well I am Ellen Valrew Cole Gilbert Swan and I am married to William Benton Swain since Jan 10, 1965. We mostly are Greene County people.

*Seated L-R: Ezra and Lettie Quinn with son, Arthur Quinn in lap Standing: Arthur Swafford, brother to Lettie Quinn*

*Submitted by Valrew Swan*

**COLE** – Ned Rochelle Cole (1861-1943) was the grandson of Dennis Cole (1800-1878), founder of the Epsaba Community in Greene County. He moved to Greene County from Tennessee with his parents John Thomas and Elizabeth (Stanford) Cole and his siblings Zelphia, John Hamilton, Mary, Martha, Lavisa, and Sarah. A sister, Caldonia, was born after they migrated to Arkansas. Ned Rochelle's birth name was Edward but he always used Ned.

He married Martha Carolyn Owen, daughter of Daniel Owen and Martha High (Gramling) Harris (widow of Dr. Matthew Harris). Ned Rochelle, like his sister Zelphia, was a schoolteacher but supporting his family came from his farming interests. The entire family was highly talented in the field of music. Many recall that in the evenings, you could hear, from the porch of the homestead, the sounds of the musical instruments and singing flowing across the Ridge. This talent has been passed on to grandchildren and great-grandchildren.

*The picture is of Ned Rochelle and Martha Carolyn (Owen) Cole and their 10 children taken in the 1920s. Bottom row from left: Ned R. Cole, Martha C. Cole, Betty, Truly, John, Ruth, Dessie, and Lawrence. Top row from left: Vannie, Anne, Gladys and Chester.*

When Ned Rochelle died his land was divided between his sons. As was customary in those days, the girls were to be provided for by their spouses however they were heirs to great homemaking skills: cooking, gardening, sewing, etc. taught by their mother. World War II started the migration of the close-knit families to the larger cities for employment, mainly connected with the war effort. Most never returned to live back home in Greene County.

The children of Ned Rochelle and Martha Carolyn were:

Martha Elizabeth "Betty" married first George Watkins. George died one week before their daughter Georgia was born. Betty married second James Robert Penny, a widower with two children. (See The James Robert Penny family).

Truly had a blacksmith shop in Beech Grove. He married Enid Williams and they had Osmer and Dorothy Lou. During the 1940s they moved to Michigan. He was a carpenter, specializing in cabinet making.

John Daniel married Rhoda Penny. He was a carpenter and involved in farming. (See The James Robert Penny family)

Ruth married John Roberts. They remained in Greene County and their children were Buena and Burrell.

Dessie married Herman Williams and they made their home in St. Louis. Their children were Delbert, Bueren, Nina, Erma, Hershel, Roella, Vancel (died at birth), Naomi, Eldon and Glenda.

Lawrence married Tressie Spain. He farmed and then moved to St. Louis where he was employed by Lincoln Engineering. Their children were Elvis, Imogene, Lester and Woodrow.

Vannie married Allen Church. They lived in Leachville and later moved to St. Louis. They had two boys A.V. and Gerald.

Anne stayed at home to care for her parents. When they died she and her husband Rube Burroughs moved to Michigan and then to St. Louis. They had no children and retired in Paragould.

Gladys married Otis Eubanks. After living in Leachville, they moved to Michigan and raised four children: Willodean, N.R., Marcella and Carolyn. When Otis died, Gladys returned to Paragould and married Westley Ryals.

Chester became a Baptist minister, pastoring churches in Arkansas and Missouri. He married Beatrice Rogers and they had Dorman and Doris Mae. The Southern Baptist Association sent him to Michigan as a 'church planter.' He remained there until he died.

**COLLAR** – Clifford Harry Collar was born on February 15, 1917, in Caddo County, Oklahoma. He had six brothers and sisters: Grant Harold Collar, Hazel Collar Blucker, Ester Collar Webb, Velma Collar Englert, Oliver Carl Collar and Richard Alvin Collar.

Clifford moved to Greene County in 1936 after his father, Hermann Josef Anton "Jack" Collar, sold the family farm at Saltillo in Faulkner County, Arkansas. The new farm was located one and one-half miles northwest of Walcott. Clifford's father became ill and died before making the move to Greene County. Clifford, his mother Grace, and younger brothers Carl and Richard made their home on the new farm. Eventually all left except Clifford who married Wilma Ednas Noles on July, 24, 1939.

Ednas was the daughter of Lucian Noles, born May 22, 1885, in Benton County, Tennessee, died July 10, 1949, near Walcott, and Mary Frances Pillow, born February 13, 1891, near Walcott, died December 31, 1979, in Paragould.

Clifford began rice farming in 1948, and continues to live across the road from the site of the original family home. Ednas died April 17, 1997. Clifford and Ednas have four daughters. Nell Collar Lyon of Chesterfield, Missouri; Sandra Collar Rogers, Shirley Collar Wilson and Debra Collar Newberry all reside in Greene County at this time. Clifford has nine grandchildren: Jeff Lyon, Michelle Lyon, Mike Rogers, Brian Rogers, Casey Rogers, Kris Boyd, Kelsey Wilson, Eric Newberry and Jeremy Newberry.

*Clifford and Ednas Collar.*

**COLLIER** – Andrew Othello Collier was born July 30, 1886, in Clinton, Kentucky. His father, a Baptist minister, died leaving a family of small children; four boys and two girls. His widow brought the children in a covered wagon, alone, to Greene County and they settled in the Browns Chapel Community. There Andrew became a Baptist minister serving churches across Greene County.

*Back row from left: Freda Margaret Collier, Opal Collier, George H. Collier, Helen Collier, Glen Collier, Geraldine Collier and John Ed Collier. Front row from left: L.T. "Pete" Collier, Rev. Andrew Othello Collier, Hettie Rogers Collier and Claude Franklin Collier.*

On September 21, 1906, Andrew married Hettie Rogers, daughter of Rufus Rogers. They had 10 children : Herman died at age 10, Glen Nelson, Opal Irma, Helen Ruth, Claude Franklin, George Henry, L. T., Nettie Geraldine, John Edward and Freda Margaret.

As the Collier family developed the marriages were as follows: Glen Collier married Irene Hensley; Opal Collier married Tom Roy and later Mack McKelvey; Helen married Raymond Phillips; Claude married Mozelle Holloman; George married Mary Monteith; Geraldine married Harry Coffman and later Marshall Jarrett; John Ed married Hermenia De Luryea; and Freda married Tom Harmon.

Two of the sons Glen Collier and John Ed Collier were also Baptist ministers serving in area churches alongside their father.

During World War II three of the boys were sergeants in the United States Army; Claude Collier, L. T. and John Ed Collier. L. T. was killed in Germany.

Claude was elected for three consecutive terms to the Arkansas House of Representatives where he worked hard for Greene County constituents.

For more than 20 years George Henry served as president of the board of education of Greene County Tech School District during her developmental years. He was also a leader in Greene County agriculture.

Andrew Collier's grandchildren also served. Four granddaughters Janie (Phillips) Williams, Ella (Phillips) Breazeale, Betty (Phillips) Penn, and Raymell (Phillips) Goodwin served as Baptist ministers wives.

Nelson Collier is a career Army service man.

Erma Sue (Roy) Ratton was a graduate registered nurse. Glenda (Roy) Coates was an LPN.

Arkansas State graduate Margaret (Peggy Collier) Jackson is the owner-operator of Simply Delicious Catering. George H. Collier Jr. M. D., was a family practice physician and Jon D. Collier, M. D. is a radiologist.

Larry Coffman is a pharmaceutical representative. Mark Jarrett works with the Arkansas State Highway Department.

Grandson Jerry Harmon is a loan officer with the Alliance Mortgage Company of Memphis, Tennessee. Eddie Harmon is with the United States Postal Service, he also works with the Memphis City Police on a volunteer basis.

Granddaughters Ann Marilyn, Virginia Wilma, Linda, Janene, Patricia, Jackie Francis, Kay and Kathy were all wives and mothers.

Andrew Othello Collier and his children believed so long as we love we serve.

**COLLINS** – John Albert Collins was born in Jonesboro, AR on Aug 21, 1884. He was the son of Rufus L. and Martha Thomas Collins. Rufus served as the Police Chief of Jonesboro and later as sheriff of Craighead County. In 1909 he was elected to the Arkansas House of Representatives, where he served one term. His grandparents, Martin and Eliza Loftus Collins, traveled to Craighead County by wagon train in 1858 from Spartenburg, SC. They married enroute.

John married Margaret Elsie Jones in Memphis, TN in June of 1903. Elsie was born in Green River, WY on Dec. 7, 1884 to Floda H. and Willemina Framer Jones. Willemina had come to this country from Norway. They moved to Jonesboro and later Texarkana, TX where they raised a family of seven children. Floda was an agent for the Cotton Belt Railroad.

John and Elsie had one son, Orris Fenn Collins, born Aug. 9, 1907 in Jonesboro, where

*John A. and Elsie Jones Collins*

John was in the theatre business. From there the family moved to Poplar Bluff, MO and Hope, AR before coming to Paragould in 1921 to operate the Majestic Theatre.

John owned and operated theatres all over northeast Arkansas, including theatres in Paragould, Marmaduke, Rector, Wynne, Marked Tree and Newport. Most of them closed during the Great Depression.

In 1923, John became manager of the newly built Capitol Theatre. A grand opening was held and more than 1000 people attended. His son, Orris, joined him in managing the theatre. In 1935, the Collins family bought the Capitol and it remained in the family until 1986, when it was donated to the Paragould Fine Arts Council.

John and his brother, Eli Whitney Collins, were two of the nine founding members of the Independent Theatre Owners of Arkansas.

John and Elsie were both talented performers. He had a fine voice and Elsie was a pianist and dancer. They were featured in many local and regional stage productions and toured in numerous light opera productions when they lived in Jonesboro.

In later years, John spent most of his time at Collinwood Farm, a 345 acre wooded section of land on Crowley's Ridge. He built a spacious log cabin in the late 1930s. The cabin was built overlooking a man-made lake and was built from logs cut on the property. "The Cabin", as it was affectionately known, was the scene of many family gatherings for many years. John, Elsie, Orris, Frances and their three children, Pat, Joan and John, spent many happy times there.

John died on March 13, 1954 and Elsie died on Jan. 14, 1967. They are buried in Linwood Cemetery.

*Submitted by Pat Fulkerson*

**COLLINS** – Orris Fenn Collins was born on Aug. 9, 1907 in Jonesboro. He was the son of John Albert and Elsie Jones Collins.

He grew up in the theatre business, as his father, John, was a theatre manager when Orris was born. From Jonesboro the family moved to Poplar Bluff, MO and Hope, AR, before coming to Paragould in 1921 to operate the Majestic Theatre on Pruett Street.

He attended Paragould school and married Frances Neely, daughter of Herschel and Eva Neely, in 1924. They had three children, Patricia Ann born June 2, 1931, Joan Carol, born Oct. 17, 1932 and John Neely, born on March 23, 1939.

John Collins was named manager of the newly built Capitol Theatre in 1925, assisted by his son, Orris. The Collins family bought the Capitol in 1935 and opened the Sunset Drive-In in 1950. Many Paragould families have fond memories of the drive-in. It was closed in 1985 when the site was sold for a shopping center.

The Capitol Theatre, which played host to countless movies, stage shows and vaudeville acts, closed in 1986 and was donated to the Fine Arts Council. In 1990, the Collins Theatre Foundation was formed and took over the active management. It was renamed the Collins Theatre, a fitting tribute to two men who devoted their lives to the entertainment of Greene County residents.

Frances was a devoted wife and mother, running the theatres during WWII when Orris served overseas with the army. She was a charter member and past president of the Arkansas Methodist Hospital Auxiliary and a member of the Ladies Golf Association. She was also a member of the Tri-State Motion Picture Theatre Owners. Both were members of First United Methodist Church.

Their daughter, Pat, married Bill Fulkerson on June 24, 1949. They had three sons, William Andrew "Andy" III, born on Jan. 19, 1950, Richard Alan, born on Oct. 27, 1954 and David Collins, born on July 21, 1958. Andy married Sonjia Gatewood in 1977 and they have one son, Jonathan Andrew. Rick married Serena Scott McDaniel in 1990 and David married Patricia Keeling in 2000.

*Orris and Frances Collins, Feb. 1977, Diane and Ed's wedding.*

Joan married Ralph Ratton on June 10, 1951. They have five children: Donna, Diane, Lanie, Carol and Rob. Donna married in 1975 and had one son, Joseph Scott Payne, who died on Oct. 9, 1987. Donna married Preston Bland in 1989. Preston has one son, Robert Preston Bland III. Diane married Ed Gathings and they have Neely Ann and Allison Elizabeth. Lanie married Tim Mangrum and they have Erin Elizabeth and William Scott. Carol married Doug Vail and they have Katherine Carol and Caroline Collins. Rob married Leighann Shepard and they have Abby Elizabeth.

John married Rose Ann Reiskamp in March of 1967. They have no children and live in Chesterfield, MO.

Orris died on Jan. 10, 1967 and Frances died on July 3, 1990. They are buried in Linwood Cemetery.

*Submitted by Pat Fulkerson*

**COOK** – Christopher Columbus Cook, grandson of one of the early settlers in Greene County, Arkansas, was born March 2, 1852, and married Margaret Emily Lamb November 15, 1875, daughter of James and Rebecca Lamb. Christopher died September 22, 1884, when he accidently shot himself while cleaning his shotgun. Margaret, widowed at age 26, remained a widow until her death on March 18, 1930. They are buried in the Lamb Family Cemetery on land once owned by her father, located off of Highway 141 and 358 in Lorado, which is now deeded to the Pleasant Hill Methodist Church. Five children were born, one dying in infancy.

John Thomas born 1876 married Mary Elizabeth Knight, their son John Wavey died in infancy.

James Edward, Fannie Elizabeth born 1881 married Gus Henry Powell, children Christia and Ermon.

Sarah Jane born 1884 married George Franklin Cathey, had one son James Halys.

James Edward "Ed" Cook was born December 6, 1878, and married Leona Adella Burgess October 16, 1900. She was born October 16, 1877, daughter of Hugh and Mary Ann Burgess. Their farm and all belongings was destroyed in the "Cyclone" that hit Lorado in 1929 but Della salvaged enough feathers from their featherbed to make two pillows. Ed and his sons rebuilt their home and part of the land he owned is now covered by Lake Frierson. Their children were Oliver, Anna born 1902 married Henry Metcalf, one daughter Opal. James born 1907 married Roselee McKinney, one daughter Mildred. Cecil born 1909 married Charleslee Gleghorn, one son Harlan. Barney born 1911 married Betty Peters and had Patsy and Billy. Essie born 1914 married Kenneth Darr; their children, Glendale, Kenneth Ray, Jimmy, Scotty, Joan and Jerry. After Della's death Ed married Mildred Morgan and had three sons, Harold, Larry and Chris. Della died in 1936, Ed died in 1969 and both are buried in Mt. Zion Cemetery.

*James Edward and Leona Adella Cook. Children: Anna, Oliver and James Jr.*

Oliver Ralph Cook was born August 11,1901, and married Hazel Irene Childers, daughter of Joseph Holmes and Eliza Josephine Childers. When he was young "singing schools" were held where people were taught to read music and sing by sounding "shaped notes." He attended these schools and learned to read music, later forming a Gospel Quartet consisting of himself, Bob Craft, Dolph Turman and Gee King. Oliver and Hazel were members of the Pleasant Hill Methodist Church. In winter, when going to church he would put straw in the wagon bed and Hazel would warm bricks and put them in to keep their children warm. The 1929 "Cyclone" destroyed their farmhouse but they were not injured. Their children are Joseph Edward born 1922, in the Air Force, World War II. He married Ruby Smotherman and their children are, JoEllen, Janice, Larry and Dennis. Juanita born 1927 and married Harold Stacy. Their five children are Linda Stacy, married Ronald Coffman and they have Connie, Caren, Rowdy and Randy who married Monica and they have Jorden, Curtis and Kasey. Michael Stacy married Patricia Harmon, their daughter Michelle married Dana Dawson, a son Trey. Cheryl Stacy married Jim Davis, their children Staci (who has Alissa, Kelsey and Taylor), Kari and Chad. Cheryl then remarried and has Hillary Rae Henderson. Daryl Stacy married Carol Bruce and has Stefani, Jennifer and Steven. Glenn Stacy married Glenda Deckard and has Anthony, Wade and Aubrey.

Oliver was a man of the soil but became a minister of the gospel in later years dying in 1985 and buried in Belleville, Illinois. Hazel died in 1993 and is buried in the Pleasant Hill Cemetery in Lorado.

**COOPER** – James Jefferson Cooper was born in Holmes County, Mississippi. On June 19, 1847, the son of James West Cooper, born about 1817 in Richmond County, North Carolina, and Sarah Cooper (maiden name unknown but believed to be Covington). Sarah was born in South Carolina about 1824. James Jefferson's siblings were Lucy Ann, Martin T., Samuel N. and William W.

Shortly after the Civil War ended James West moved his family to Greene County, Arkansas. With the exception of Samuel born about 1844 and died July 7, 1863, at Vicksburg, Mississippi, of dysentery, while serving in the Confederate Army. James West apparently died in Greene County, sometime after their arrival.

Lucy Ann born March 29, 1840, married Joel Gulledge McCone in Holmes County and moved from Greene County to Drew County, Arkansas. Sarah Cooper moved with them and died there as the 1880 Mortality Census shows her death in that year.

Joel, Martin and Samuel were all comrades serving together at Vicksburg. Martin was wounded and discharged in the latter part of 1862. His wife Sally B. applied for his pension on the 28th day of February 1907, stating that he had died on March 18, 1879. She received $100.00 and gives Lorado, Greene County as her post office. Her maiden name is not known. The men served in Pemberton's Command, under Captain Wafford, First Mississippi Light Artillery.

Lucy Ann died in Drew County on December 22, 1932, evidently outliving all of her children.

*Group photo of the Lloyd, Cooper and Rogers families of Greene County, circa 1910. Bottom row from left: Jeff Wilcockson, Ollie Phillips, Judson Cooper, Tyler Swindle, Alton Rogers, Alva Burton, Clyde Phillips, Sylvia Swindle Edwards, Ruth Phillips, Mildred Rogers Coe, Clarice Kennedy Armstrong, Rubye Rogers, Alma Burton Smoot, Hettie Swindle Rogers and Estelle Rogers. Second row: John Swindle (seated in chair), Unknown, Cecil Rogers, Ira Swindle, Ed Rogers (holding son), Herschel Rogers, Ray Burton, Mable Burton Holcomb, Edith Phillips McIver, Ludie Cooper Buchanan, Hazle Kennedy Dyer, Cora Rogers Thompson, Ora Cooper Clark, Fred Swindle, Lura Cooper Kennedy, Van Cooper and Edgar Burton (behind Van Cooper). Third row from left: Harold Rogers (head above Ira Swindle), Maurice Burton, Lucy Ann McCone, Joel McCone, Hester Ellen Lloyd Cooper, James J. Cooper, unknown, Nancy Clyne, Dr. Adolphus Clyne, Rev. G.W. Lloyd and unknown. Fourth row from left: Johnny Swindle, unknown, unknown, Mrs. Wilcockson, Alice Burton, Gertie Cooper, Becky Wilcockson, Vester Phillips, Nan Phillips, Ki Lloyd, 11. Julia Cooper Rogers and son Adrian, Wassie Rogers and son Cary, Ella and Opal Nutt Rogers and Mary and Marguerite Swindle. Fifth row from left: James B. Cooper, Sallie Jo Kennedy Thacker, Mr. Wilcockson, Tom Lloyd, unknown, Jeff Swindle and Joe Matthew Rogers.*

Not much of William W. is known. He is shown in the 1880 Census, living in Poland Township, with his wife Ellen, daughters Ann, Sarah J. and son William. He is not named in James Jefferson's obituary so it is possible that he was deceased by that time.

*First row from left: James Jefferson Cooper, Hester Ellen Cooper and her sister Sarah Lloyd Osteen. Back row from left: Claudia, wife of Tom Lloyd; Tom Lloyd; Rev. G.W. Llqyd and wife Fannie Highfill Lloyd.*

James J. Cooper married Hester "Hettie" Ellen Lloyd, daughter of Thomas D. Lloyd and Sarah Ellen Shaver Lloyd. She was born in Poinsett County, Arkansas, on February 2, 1845, and had been married before to a man named Stone. She had one son by this marriage named Edwin. He later took the name of his stepfather. Edwin was a Baptist minister and a student at Thompson's Classic Institute in Paragould. He was ordained in 1895 and pastored at Rock Hill, Center Hill, Fair View, Unity and Browns Chapel. He married Gertie Freeman. Other children of the marriage of James J. and wife Hester were, Sarah Alice (Mrs. Frank Burton), Mary (Mrs. John Swindle), Julia Frances (Mrs. Joe M. Rogers), Samuel who married Alice McLaughlin, Nancy Jane (Mrs. Vester Phillips) and she later married Joe M. Rogers after the deaths of both of their spouses. Lura who married Dr. Tyler Kennedy and after he died from being kicked by a horse, she married Dr. Wylie Hutchins. They lived in Manila, Arkansas. Last of the sons was James Burton Cooper, who married Zena Russell.

James Jefferson and Hester Ellen died within days of each other in 1929 and are buried in Browns Chapel Cemetery.

**COOPER/DAVIS/NOBLE** – About 1852 my Cooper ancestors came to Arkansas from Spartanburg County, South Carolina, in wagons. My great-grandfather William D. Cooper and family came with his brother Richard S. Cooper and family. They settled in Greene County near the present town of Brookland. In 1859 when Craighead County was formed, they lived in its boundary. Their parents were James and Sarah Cooper. Think they had other siblings who continued to live in South Carolina area: brothers Matthew, Lorenzo and maybe some sisters.

William's wife was Elizabeth (unknown). Their children were: Nancy married Frank A. Gregson (son of George and Rachel); Julia married William McEwen; Tolvier Davis married Mary Morris and Laura Bridge; my grandfather Henry Harrison married Sarah Leach (daughter of Abner) and Harriett Adeline Davis (daughter of Benjamin Franklin Davis and Letecia Victoria Adeline Noble); Lorenzo married Nancy Noble (daughter of William A. Noble and Elizabeth (unknown). William and Elizabeth died in the 1870s.

Richard had two wives and about 20 children. Richard died 1892 and second wife Elizabeth (unknown) died 1914. Both are buried at the old Cooper's Cemetery.

*Henry Harrison Cooper's family, taken about 1907-1910, by the home near Clinton School near Brookland, Arkansas. Back row from left: Henry Harrison Cooper, wife Harriett (Davis) Cooper, daughter Sarah "Sally" Cooper, and son Marion Cooper. Front row from left: daughter Bessie Cooper and son Walter Monroe Cooper, born February 9, 1902.*

My grandfather Henry Harrison Cooper born 1851 in South Carolina married first Sarah Leach in 1873. They had one son, William H., who died young. Sarah died 1884 in Tennessee. Henry married second Harriett Adeline Davis in 1885. They had nine children. Rosa married first James Columbus Pounds, married second Adrian Nicholes; Albert Harrison married Annie Morrison; Isaac Thomas died young; baby boy died young; Sarah Jane married George Nathaniel West; Marion Henry married first Margaret Hildreth, married second Annie Cerstvik Borovsky; Bessie married Fred Fears; my father Walter Monroe married Amanda Lee Stalcup (on Christmas day 1924); baby girl died young. Henry died in March 1933.

My grandmother Harriett Adeline Davis was daughter of Benjamin Franklin Davis (served in Civil War - 13th Ark. Reg. of Infantry Company E - May 1861 to May 1865) and Letecia Victoria Adeline Noble. No information on Benjamin after many years of researching. Letecia was daughter of William A. Noble and Elizabeth (unknown). William and Elizabeth's children were: Martin; Isaac T. married Mary Roy; my great-grandmother Letecia married Benjamin F. Davis; Kesiah married first James Sutfin and married second William Gibson; Martha O. married Jasper Sutin; George Washington married Nancy Ann Louy; Winnifred married Reece Jones; Rachel; Nancy married first Lorenzo D. Cooper and married second Tom Griffin. Harriett died in 1944 in Tulsa, Oklahoma. Both Henry and Harriett are buried at Macedonia Cemetery.

William A. and Elizabeth Noble came in late 1840s to Greene County from Tennessee.

**COSSEY** – J. M. and Belma Cossey moved to Greene County in the 1960s coming from Craighead County to the Walcott area. They reared their family of five children: Jannena Marie, Michi Ann, Melinda Kay, Kristie Gail and James Monty while operating a large Holstein Dairy.

Jannena married Randy Allred; their children are Julie Marie and Jimmy. Julie is married to Jody Blankenship. Michi married Phillip McClelland. Phillip and Michi's children are Adam, Nicolas and Mike Eric. Melinda Kay married Kim Reeves; their children are Kevin and Kyle. Kristie married Rodney Head, their children are Holly, Abbie and Katie. Monty married Andrea Baird. All the children live either on the family farm or within a mile.

J. M.'s parents, James Montgomery Cossey Sr. and Bessie Lee Sears Reed, moved from Independence County to Craighead County in the 1930's. His grandparents, Jacob Riley Cossey and Mary Ida Qualls Cossey; Jacobs mother was Elizabeth Qualls. Bessie related she was born of Nathaniel and Melda Sears in a covered wagon in Kansas. They died soon after and she was adopted and reared by the Reed family.

Belma's parents, Beaurell E. Riggs and Ruth R. (Sipes) Riggs, lived in Craighead County all their lives. Beaurell's family (J. E. and Ada Ivy "Condry" Riggs came from the Pocahontas area and Parsons, TN. Ruth's folks, George Washington Sipes and Mary Della (Ashby) Sipes, were early settlers in Craighead and Greene Counties.

All the families attend Walcott Baptist Church, Light Baptist Church and Pleasant Valley Baptist Church. They are involved in church activities as a deacon, teachers, piano players, vacation Bible schools, lay renewal weekends, Christmas caroling, outreach ministries, softball, etc.

*Cossey Family (left to right): Andrea Cossey, Jan Allred, Kyle Reeves, Belma Cossey, J.M. Cossey, Melinda Reeves, Kim Reeves on bottom row. Top row, Kristie Head holding Abbie Head, Rodney Head, Monty Cossey holding Holly Head, Randy Allred, Julie Blankenship, Jody Blankenship, Jimmy Allred, Adam McClelland, Michi McClelland, Phillip McClelland, Kevin Reeves, Mike McClellend and Nicholas McClelland.*

The family takes part in camping, fishing, horseback riding, swimming, softball, showing horses, cattle, etc. at local events and around the state. Family celebrations at holidays and for all birthdays, births and anniversaries are top priority.

Clubs and organizations they have been involved in include Associated Milk Producers, Inc. (Belma is a past state president of the Women's Auxiliary), Business and Professional Women, Greene County Farm Bureau, Riding Clubs, Arkansas and Paragould Realtor's Association, United National Real Estate United Power, Greene County 4-H and others.

J. M. and Monty are involved in raising cattle, farming and remodeling projects. Belma previously worked as an abstractor and with the National Association of Department of Agriculture. She started a real estate business in the early 1980s and maintains a national franchise office in the Old Walcott Bank building in Walcott. Plans are to expand part of the building into a family-type museum.

Jannena teaches kindergarten at Greene County Tech. Randy and Jimmy owns a trucking firm. Phillip works for the Cupp Organization; Michi is a homemaker and 4-H leader. Kim is employed by Greene County; Melinda is a registered nurse at Arkansas Methodist Hospital. Rodney is a master plumber, Kristie a homemaker.

Andrea is a student at Williams Baptist College. The Nutt Valley Farm employs Adam and Nicholas works for the May Family Farm. All others are in school.

*Submitted by Mrs. Belma W. Cossey*

**COTHREN** – Pioneers from South Carolina to Arkansas. In the horse and oxen-drawn wagons was a migration of people related to the Gramlings. The year was 1857 and the Benjamin Crowley family had already settled near what is now Walcott in western Greene County of Arkansas.

In one of the seven wagons led by Rueben G. Gramling, was Sarah R. Gramling who had married Andrew Jackson Cothren. They had five children: William Henry, Rueben, Pressley, Fannie and Mary. William Henry and Mary Magdalene Gregory Cothren had four children: Visor, James Wesley, Nancy and Mack Cothren. After the death of Mary Magdalene, William Henry married his second wife Alice Dearing. Mary Magdalene is buried at Owens Chapel and William Henry and Alice Dearing Cothren are buried at Warrens Chapel. To the union of William Henry and Alice was born George Cothren.

Visor Cothren married Allie Lorrance and they had two sons, James Wesley "Jim" married Virginia "Virgie" Spillman and they had eight children; Nancy married Harvey Spain and they had 10 children, five surviving to adulthood: Maude Lenderman, Carrie Lemmons, Dora Potter, Tom Spain and Jenny Spain who never married. Mack Cothren married Alice Spillman, a cousin of Virgie Cothren. Mack and Alice had seven children: Mollie Shoemaker, Vestal Futrell, Pearl Goins, Jackson Cothren, Bertha Martin Clines, David and Macon Cothren. Their half-brother George Cothren married Irene Harris. George and Irene had three sons.

The eight children of Virgie and Jim Cothren were: Garvin who died at are four or five; Walsie Taylor had two sons; Belle Harris had one daughter; Thelma Harris had six children; Griffen Cothren married Ina Johnson and they had nine children; Opal Bazzell had three sons; Lucille Gwyn had three daughters;

*James Wesley "Jim" Cothren, Virgie Pauline (Spillman) Cothren*

Gene Cothren married Vaudean Hester and they had six children. Gene moved his family to the Texarkana area in the 1950s and most of the children live in that area.

When today's youngsters hear the names Crowley, Gramling, Cothren, Harris or Spillman, they may never know about the hardships of settling a new place in a new state. The spirit of adventure and the courage demanded of such pioneering families was duplicated many times over to populate an area. Even today those hills of Crowley's Ridge echo the names of these families, for there are hundreds of descendents of the Cothren, Gramling, Harris and Spillman families still living in the vicinity. We celebrate this kinship!

*Submitted by Mary Catherine Holden*

**COX** – Christopher Huffman Cox was born in Kentucky on April 7, 1871, to Charles and Lizzie Harrelson Cox who lived in Nebo, KY.

He married Ida Julia Veazey on July 30, 1895 in Nebo. She was the daughter of a wealthy landowner, Andrew Jackson Veazey and his wife, Mary Frances Clements Veazey.

Five children were born to the Cox family in Kentucky: Pearl, Lanoleen, Roy Huffman, William Christopher and Charles Veazey Cox.

In late 1904 during the timber rush, the family left Nebo for Arkansas in a covered wagon.

Assisting the family were Hunter and Martha Young, Ida's sister and brother-in-law. Mr. Young worked as a ferryman, helping people cross the Mississippi River near Cairo, IL. One life-threatening part of his dangerous job was "swimming" the animals across the river.

Everyone made it safely across and the family eventually settled in the Mounds community on a farm at B. Vincent's Corner, east of Marmaduke, AR. Here the following children were born: James Taylor, Robbie Elizabeth, Loyd Jackson, John Ray and Simon Daniel Cox.

Mr. Cox was a farmer and did timber and sawmill work in the area. He died Feb. 3, 1914 and was buried in Woodland Heights Cemetery in Rector, AR.

His death left Mrs. Cox with several children still at home. They eventually moved to the Fritz community, now known as Neighbor's Corner and later to the John Weber farm.

*The Cox Family about 1902 in Madisonville, KY. Seated: Christopher Huffman Cox, Ida Julia Cox; standing Pearl Latta. Front: Roy Cox, William Christopher Cox, Charley V. Cox, Lanoleen Cox*

Mrs. Cox often spoke of her sons as the 'big boys', meaning those born in Kentucky and the "little boys", those born in Arkansas. One of the 'big boys', Charley, was a timber worker, which required long hours from daylight until dark. In the winter, he would arrive home with his clothes and boots frozen. His pay would buy extra food to be put on the table for his mother and the "little" boys to eat.

Ida Cox was a treat church worker and Sunday school teacher at both Mounds and Fritz. Around 1923, when church members used the school building as their place of worship, she let the Sunday school classes meet in her home.

Mrs. Cox was a great lady known by many as "Mother Cox". With her responsibility, understanding, ability, love and prayers her children remained with her until they married and left for the big cities in Michigan and California. Only Roy, Taylor, Jack and their families continued to stay in Greene and Clay counties.

Mrs. Cox left the Weber place in 1935 to live with her children. She died Aug. 15, 1944 in Detroit, MI and was buried in Woodland Heights Cemetery in Rector, AR

*Submitted by Sadie Cox*

**COX** – Henry Donald Cox (1904-1978) was born in Greene County, Arkansas, to Emory Ethel and Pearl Tennison Cox. On March 8, 1925, he married Iva Leigh McDaniel 1908-1969, daughter of Hillary and Wilma Craig McDaniel. Donald and Iva are buried at Brown's Chapel Cemetery beside twins Donald Gene and Doris Jean who died as infants in 1930. Other children born to them were Almeda 1926 and Laveda 1927.

At the time of their marriage Donald was teaching school at Pruett's Chapel. He had been certified to teach by attending one of the Normal Schools in Greene County. W.A. Branch was the teacher. Donald had a horse and buggy and furnished transportation for Mr. Branch in exchange for tuition. He taught school seven years beginning at age 18. Other school positions included Wood's Chapel and Pine Knot.

Donald served at the Greene County Courthouse in the circuit and chancery court clerk's office from 1931 until 1939. He was deputy to Earl Beaton four years subsequently being elected for two terms of his own. Iva was his deputy. His Father E.E. Cox served as Greene County clerk 1916-1921.

His years in business included Cox Service Station and Cox Auto Supply. Both were in partnership with his brother Leland Cox. He and Iva owned "The Little Mint" for a short time.

Donald was named manager of the Paragould Chamber of Commerce in 1954. He was given the title of executive vice president in 1960. In 1966 he served as president of Arkansas Chamber of Commerce Managers. He resigned from the Paragould Chamber of Commerce in 1972 having completed almost 18 years.

Donald and Iva were active in civic affairs throughout their 43 years of marriage. He served as president of Northeast Arkansas Baseball League in 1938 and Greene County Fair Manager for eight years beginning in 1953. He was elected to the City Light Plant Commission three consecutive five year terms, the last eight years as chairman. He was chairman of the Greene Acres Nursing Home building program and was a member of the Rotary Club.

Iva enjoyed working with him during the fair years and the nursing home program. They took great pride the day the elderly were moved from the "Poor Farm" to the Greene Acres Nursing Home. They often talked of the county wide participation in bringing this about. Iva was a member of the Howell Home Demonstration Club and Paragould Garden Club serving as president of both groups. She grew beautiful flowers, iris being a favorite.

Donald's second wife was Mildred Cox Nickols. They were divorced prior to his death.

Almeda married Jim Brewer on December 23, 1951, in Paragould. Their children are Julie Liegh, Karen Anne and Clifton David. Grandchildren are Noah, Skye, Grace, Faith and Jacob.

Laveda married Newell Stedman Bowman on November 11, 1946, in Elkton, Maryland. Their children were Roxane, Donald Duane who is deceased and Aaron Leroy. Grandchildren are Ezra, Ryan and Blaise.

**COX** – James Henry "Jimmy" Cox of Finch married Ella Bobo of Lorado on November 28, 1882, in Greene County. James was born July 6, 1857, in Fort Scott, Kansas, where his parents, Henry and Nancy Loyd Cox stopped while going by wagon from California gold fields to Tennessee. Ella was born March 29, 1866. Her parents were Elisha Madison and Elizabeth Miller Bobo. Her father served as a Confederate lieutenant during the Civil War.

Briefly, James and Ella lived with friends, then lived in his parents' home in Holcomb, Missouri, for two years. In 1885, they bought a 180 acre farm, just south of Liberty Church of Christ on Crowley's Ridge in Greene County. The house they built was modern for 1885, having a freeze-proof cellar dug in hard clay under the house. They built a large cistern, located so they could draw water on their back porch. The roof was of corrugated iron, with gutters and pipes arranged so they could catch water for the cistern when it rained. Mr. Cox used a mule team and a digging "slip" to build stock water ponds in the lot and in each pasture.

On their farm, this couple and their growing family raised all the food for family and livestock. They grew wheat and made their own flour. They made some of their clothing by spinning cotton yarn and knitting socks, stockings and sweaters. They had apple, peach, pear and plum trees, as well as grapes and berries. They had several "cash" crops in addition to cotton. Apple juice, both sweet and tart, was produced using a mill to chop the apples and squeeze the juice, which was easily sold. They raised mule colts, selling them as two year-old, after being trained for riding and harness. They kept and milked several Jersey cows. A mechanical "separator" removed the cream which was sold. The family drank milk, made cottage cheese, with excess milk eaten by chickens and hogs. Eggs and pork, were eaten by the family, with the extra sold or traded. Mr. Cox was an area "crops" reporter for *Progressive Farmer*.

*James Henry "Jimmy" and Ella Bobo Cox. The photo was made on their wedding day, November 28, 1882.*

James and Ella became dedicated members of Liberty Church of Christ. As their children became of age, each one became a member. Mr. Cox served as an Elder and sometimes preached. All of the children attended Clark's Chapel School.

Their children:

Emery Ethel born September 21, 1883; married Pearl Tennison September 13, 1903; eight children; after her death he married Hattie Jordon McGrew; one child; died April 9, 1957.

Henry Osmer born November 27, 1886; married Josie Hyde; eight children; died November 16, 1953.

Elizabeth R. born December 29, 1888; died September 26, 1894.

Amy Victoria born September 3, 1890; married Walter Greenway; four children; died November 23, 1966.

Joseph Louis born September 8, 1899; married Elva Treece December 22, 1918; seven children; died April 19, 1965.

Joel Jefferson born September 8, 1899; married Florence Kenney February 2, 1918; four children; died December 8, 1988.

Robert Ellis born December 25, 1903; married Vera Andrews August 22, 1924; one daughter; died June 14, 1996.

Willie Herbert born August 4, 1905; married Flossie Miller October 1, 1927; two daughters; died April 5, 1954.

Lessie Olive born October 9, 1909; married Kenneth Pack June 22, 1929; two children.

James Cox died February 2, 1912; Ella Cox died January 15, 1951. This family also includes a great many great-grandchildren, plus two following generations.

**COX** – Joseph Louis Cox of Liberty, and Elva Elizabeth Treece of Finch were married at Walcott December 22, 1918, shortly after Louis' November 11, 1918, draft call was cancelled. Louis Cox was a son of James H. and Ella Bobo Cox, and attended Clark's Chapel School. In 1912, when his father died, Louis, age 12, was the oldest child still living at home. His mother said, "Louis, since you are the oldest, you are the man of the family, and in charge of the farm." So he helped raise his four younger siblings. Elva was the youngest child of Robert Wiley and Katherine Cline Treece. Her father died when she was 10 months old. She grew up with her mother, and brother Tellas Treece. She attended Finch School.

For several years Louis and Elva were sharecrop farmers. In 1927, to add to his income, Louis became a shoe salesman for Joseph's on Pruett Street, at first part-time and then as a full-time employee. He worked there until the Depression caused Joseph's to reduce their work force.

Jobs were hard to find, so Louis decided to become an independent salesman of household appliances. Although few people could buy, he did earn some, which along with a cow, chickens, and a large garden, he was able to support his family. One benefit of that job was acquiring appliances for his family at reduced costs. The Louis and Elva Cox family was one of first families in West Paragould to have a washing machine, electric iron, electric sewing machine, radio and refrigerator. For added income, Elva Cox and children did washing and ironing for several other families. For several summers the Cox family did laundry for several members of the Paragould Browns, a professional baseball team.

From 1933 through 1936, he was employed by Arkansas Highway Department. His primary job was to keep accounts on all district equipment, and order parts to keep it in repair.

*Joseph Louis and Elva E. Treece Cox on their wedding anniversary, December 22, 1919.*

In 1937 Louis worked as crew supervisor to build a high fence around Paragould High School football stadium. In May 1937, he was employed by Life and Casualty Insurance Company, a job he held for 25 years, until he retired. He worked in many south Arkansas towns but lived in Little Rock the last nine years. He died April 19, 1965.

Although he had just eight years of formal schooling, it included a strong background in math and spelling. Louis became a very educated person, by reading a newspaper and listening to radio news daily. He easily learned each job that he held.

Children:

Evelyn Christine born October 9, 1922, married Harold Brockett; children Lynn, Diane, Nurse, died March 26, 1949.

Nealia Almeria born April 25, 1925, married Hugh Liddle; children Hugh Jr., Treece, Keith; school teacher.

Jimmy Wiley born March 3, 1928, married Mattie Boone; children Wiley Jr., Llene, Nancy; newspaper production.

Rita Louella born December 5, 1929, married Ray Wilson; children David, Dennis, Dean. Later married Shelby Raynes; nurse; died January 15, 1987.

Elva Mae born June 4, 1939, married Richard Gamma; children Richard and Mark. Later married Bill Gilmore. Office rental management.

Joseph Louis Jr. born January 14, 1945. Apartment rental management.

**COZART** — Charlie Louis Cozart was born in 1916 in Pittsboro, Mississippi, son of Hiram and Ida Cozart. His family moved to Greene County in 1918. It was here that he met and married Willie Thomas Hay in 1938. Together they raised a family of five.

In the early years, Charlie owned a garage at his home in the country and later worked for Stimson Auto Parts in downtown Paragould. From 1959 to 1965 he and Willie owned and operated Cozart's Grocery that had formerly been Bogan Grocery. The Cozarts sold their home on US 49 in 1977 and moved to a newly built home in Paragould on Kennedy Street.

*Back row from left: Beverly Gail and Donna Marlene. Center: Charlie Louis, Willie Hay and Jerry Louis. Front from left: Rita Avis and Judy Aneeta. Circa 1964.*

During the years after they owned the grocery, Charlie worked for two judges in the county as a "go for." He delivered parts to any machinery that was broken down in the county and served as the Civil Defense director until the early 1980s and made many trips to Little Rock to see to the county's needs.

Charlie and Willie were longtime members of the Arkansas Antique Auto Club and were made honorary lifetime members for their support and participation.

Charlie retired at age 65 and although he suffered many medical setbacks, he continued an active and enjoyable life until his untimely death in 1987. That same year in Paragould, the annual Christmas parade was held in Charlie's honor.

The following article from November 30,1987, *Paragould Daily Press* is of note.

"Everyone loves a parade, the saying goes, and no one loved parades more than Charlie Cozart. Cozart was instrumental in organizing the first Paragould Christmas Parade, held November 28, 1972, and played an important role in the event's production for many years, organizers of this years 16th parade note. The theme of the first parade was "Happiness Is," which seems a fitting description of Cozart and his contribution to the parade through the years. For that reason, organizers are dedicating the 1987 Paragould Christmas Parade "in loving memory of Mr. Charlie Cozart."

The children were Jerry Louis, born 1941 and died in an accident in Seattle, Washington, in 1967 after enlistment in the U.S. Air Force.

Beverly Gail, married Jerry Austin in 1968 and had two children, Damon and Sabrina.

Donna Marlene, married first Rick Duhigg, one daughter, Barbara "LeLe," married second, Mike Hyde, one son, Billy.

Rita Avis, married Charles White in 1976, had two children, Kristina and Robert.

Judy Aneeta, married Terry Hinson in 1977, one child Teri Lee.

As of 1999, Willie still lives in Paragould along with Donna, Rita, and Judy and their families.

**COZART** — The earliest Cozart to settle in this area was Hiram Cozart. He was born in Mississippi in 1873 and became a farmer. He married Ida Lee Richberg in 1893. They raised seven children, Hubert born 1895; Huet born 1897; Harvey born 1900; Winnie born 1903; Ruth born 1908; Barney born 1914; and Charlie born 1916.

Economic times inspired Hiram to move his family to Arkansas in the fall of 1918. He first appeared on the tax rolls of Greene County in 1919 which showed him to own one dog, $50.00 in horses, two head of cattle, and two mules. His total assets were $150.00.

Hiram continued to farm until he began working for the McCannon Medical Company. He sold medical supplies from the back of a wagon for money or barter. In a letter sent back to Calhoun County in 1924 he referred to his job and also noted that Paragould lost $400,000 in property to fire. He said that the roads were bad to travel over, but that Crowley's Ridge was "almost a solid gravel pit" and it wouldn't cost much to build roads here. He also said that the crop in 1923 was bad and said "The boll weevil is pretty bad here."

The family continued to grow here with the exception of Huet who died in 1916 in Mississippi.

Of note is Ruth who trained at the Dickson Hospital to become a nurse in 1929. She married Simon Steinberg and spent most of her career and life in the Texas area. She and Sy became very successful at real estate and investment. She lived in Texas until Sy's death, moved back to Arkansas and resides in Paragould as of 1999.

*Hiram Thomas Cozart and Ida Lee Richberg's wedding picture, circa 1893.*

Winnie married Marvin Guinn and moved to Florida where she died in April 1997.

Hubert died in January 1968.

There is no information on Harvey.

Charlie and Barney made frequent trips back to Cozart family reunions in Calhoun County and are still remembered by residents there today. Barney married Edna Davis and spent his life in the area until his death in Blytheville, Arkansas, in 1979. Charlie married Willie Hay and is well known in Paragould and Greene County where he lived until his death in 1987. (See separate family history)

**CRAWFORD-BLALOCK** — Audra Kathleen Crawford Blalock was born June 25, 1886, in Weakley County, Tennessee, to James Y. and Minnie Mae Irvine Crawford. The parent's ancestral lines show soldiers who fought in the Revolutionary War, the War of 1812, and the Civil War, as well as having a Baptist minister and several Methodist Circuit Riders. She grew up in a time when few females attended school, but her parents thought it important for all their children to receive an education, so the Crawford girls went to school along with the boys. Very few women worked outside the home, but Audra and her older sister worked in a woolen factory sewing men's clothing. It was here that she met Leonard Blalock. They married on October 4, 1906, in Fulton, Tennessee.

The newly married couple made their first home just outside Mayfield, Kentucky. Here were born three children, daughter Kathleen, son Rupert, and a daughter Willie Bea, who lived only a short while. Far along into her fourth pregnancy, in December of 1912, Audra and Leonard with their two children moved to Greene County, Arkansas, following in the steps of his parents who had migrated years earlier.

In February of the next year, another daughter, Reba Adell was born. Seven years later, when they were well settled in their home in the Camp Ground Community another son, Warren, was born.

*Audra Kathleen Crawford Blalock.*

Miz Blalock (as her friends and neighbors called her) was well known and liked in her community. Her windows sported lace curtains and neighbors said her floors were so clean one could eat off them. She was the person called to help with a child's birth or when someone was ill. She was relied upon to feed and house the visiting preacher, because she always had plenty of food, even in the hardest of times. She was frugal, but her family was educated; well fed, because she had a large garden, fruit trees, chickens, cattle and pigs; and well dressed, because she knew how to sew, turn collars and cuffs. She was the person in the community to whom one turned to in times of trouble.

After she was widowed in 1935, she continued living on the Camp Ground farm for several years and in the 1940s moved into the town of Paragould where she planted another (not so large) garden, kept a spotless home and still found time to tell her grandchildren about the times of her life. She was the motivating force behind her children's education, temperament and successful lives. Though none of her brothers or sisters ever lived in Arkansas, she made her home here and her husband's family hers in every sense of the word. She survived most of Leonard's brothers and sisters.

**CROCE** – It is not known when Sammuel K. Croce, born 1837 and died 1889, and Susannah Raver Croce, born 1847 and died 1930, moved to Arkansas. They began in Pennsylvania, to Illinois and on to Arkansas. They had originally headed for California but the horses became weary. They are buried at Gainesville Cemetery, Greene County, Arkansas. Their children were:

Ada R. Missouri born in O'Keen, Illinois, and married John Yeargain January 3, 1900.

Bell married John Pierce and died in Illinois.

Nora married Charley Luscher and buried in Linwood Cemetery.

Doscia married George Wilson and buried at Linwood.

Clara married John Rust.

Ruth married Mr. Valaudingham and died in Texas.

Henry married Maggie and died in Florida.

*Sammuel K. Croce.*

The family attended Union Hill school and church.

Clara and John Rust have three grandchildren in Paragould area. John and Ida have a granddaughter. Carolyn in Sikeston, Missouri, and grandson Delbert in Fenton, Missouri.

Sammuel does show on 1890 Greene County Tax list.

Sammuel was the son of Henry and Elizabeth and grandson of Peter and Elizabeth Croce. He was a corporal in the Revolutionary War.

**CROCKETT** – Robert Sterling Lee Crockett was born September 23, 1865, in Mississippi, the son of William Henderson Barnett Crockett born June 10, 1821, in Bedford County, Tennessee, and Sarah Elizabeth Newsom, born July 27, 1833, in Hardeman County, Tennessee. William Henderson Barnett Crockett was the son of Samuel Crockett born 1799, Bedford County, Tennessee, and Mary Ann "Polly" Hamilton. Samuel Crockett moved to Mississippi circa 1839. Samuel Crockett was the son of Samuel Crockett and Sarah (Wilson) Crockett who were born in Pennsylvania and moved to Robertson County, Tennessee, in 1788. This Samuel Crockett was the son of William and Margaret Crockett. Sarah Elizabeth (Newsom) Crockett was the daughter of Sterling Newsom who came to Greene County with his family circa 1854 from Mississippi, born circa 1802/5 in North Carolina and Nancy H. Hamilton(?) born circa 1815 in Tennessee.

*Front row from left: Edwin Crockett, Clarence Crockett, John Crockett, Ivy Crockett Finley, Martha (Miller) Crockett holding Nancy Crockett, and Robert Sterling Lee Crockett holding Marvin Crockett, circa 1905. Two gentlemen in the back ground, unknown. The big picture in front of the fence is suspected to be picture of William Henderson Barnett Crockett, father of Robert Sterling Lee Crockett.*

William Henderson Barnett Crockett and Sarah Elizabeth (Newsom) Crockett were married about 1850 perhaps in Mississippi and had nine children: Thadeus Constantine Napoleon born 1851 married Nancy Jane Newsom; Rebecca A. Cunningham; Elvira Hitchcock; William Barnett born 1855 married Penelope "Neppie" Branch and lived in Texas; Lafayette Columbus Francis Marion born 1858 married Sarah Margarette Rampy and lived in Texas; Musie Dora/Isadora born 1861; Sarah Ann born 1862 died before 1878; Robert Sterling Lee Crockett married Martha Caroline Miller; Samuel Edwin Johnson (twin brother of Robert Sterling Lee) married Holly Johnson and Dora Cadenhead; John B. born 1867 who died before 1878; and Benjamin F. Crockett born 1874 and died circa 1877. According to an article on his life, their son, Judge William Barnett Crockett, states Sarah was the mother of 15 children.

In 1875 William Henderson Barnett Crockett while moving his family from Mississippi to Texas became ill and died near Hot Springs, Arkansas. Sarah Elizabeth (Newsom) Crockett and five children are listed on the 1880 census of Lee County, Arkansas. Sarah Elizabeth died circa 1890 near Walnut Ridge. By 1890 Lee Crockett had moved to Greene County and is listed on the Reconstructed Census from personal property tax records.

On January 25, 1893, in Greene County, Robert Sterling Lee Crockett married Martha Caroline Miller, daughter of Jacob M. and Rebecca Ann Miller. Jacob Miller was born in 1845 in St. Francis County, Arkansas, the son of Robert R. Miller and Permelia C. Carothers/Carruthers both of Virginia. Lee and Martha had nine children: Clarence married Mattlean Layton; Henry died before 1910; John married Delcie Crowley; Ivy married Richard Finley; Marvin Lander married Martha Bennett; Nancy Ann married J.M. Armstead, Gordon Simpson, L.V. VanHorn; William Elmo married Eulene Stairn; Mildred Self married Claude Blevins; and Robert who married Bertha Carmichael and Jestine Doughty.

Robert Staling Lee Crockett died in Greene County on December 19, 1913, and Martha Caroline (Miller) Crockett married Walter B. Finley in 1915 and moved to East St. Louis, Illinois, where she died November 23, 1924.

Many descendants of the Crockett, Miller, and Newsom families still reside in Greene County today.

**CROFT** – In his *History of Greene County,* B. H. Crowley claims Dr. George B. Croft was one of the earliest settlers and probably the first physician to arrive in Greene County. Various sources note that he was an avid hunter, a good doctor, a very religious and generous soul and a Democrat very much involved in the "Southern cause."

His wife, Sarah Harris, was educated in Virginia and shared Dr. Croft's interest in politics and current events. Her family settled in Poinsett County and founded the town of Harrisburg; B. H. Crowley wrote that Dr. Croft's home was the best in Greene County. (See the Harris's of Harrisburg)

He served as a state representative in the fifth and sixth General Assemblies, the first with James Clarke in 1844 and the last with J. M. Mitchell in 1846.

And he allied himself with Henry Rector in the 1860 gubernatorial race, which indicates he opposed the "Johnson family dynasty." Although Greene County voted "Unionist" in Feb. 1861, Dr. Croft worked "for secession."

The Crofts moved to Texas during the war years. It is not clear who managed the property while they were away, but there are records indicating that Lt. Col. Solomon Kitchens camped twice with his regiment on the Croft farm. It was also near the Croft place where Gen. Jeff Thompson rejoined his command in 1863.

George and Sarah Croft returned to Greene County following the war. At that time he gave each of " his oldest and most faithful Negroes 40 acres of land and a mule."

But Dr. Croft became active in one of the several KKK companies in Greene County. B. H. Crowley reported that Dr. Croft and John Clark inducted him into the Klan. However, the Crofts moved to Kentucky during part of the Reconstruction period. Sometime after that, the doctor and his wife returned to his home place with his brothers, Logan and Thomas.

In 1871, he filed the following will: G. B. Croft Last Will, State of Arkansas, and County of Greene

I, George B. Croft of the State and County

aforesaid written, being satisfied of the uncertainty of life and being of sound and disposing mind and after due consideration and calm reflection, have come to the purpose and determination to make this will.

First, I desire that my body be buried or deposited on the hill about 120 yards east of my house and I appropriate $300 for the use of my gravestone.

Secondly, I desire that my wife, Sarah take charge of my entire estate, both real and personal and that no bond security restraint whatever be required of her and that she have the control with out any restraint in accordance with this will.

I request that my friend, R. H. Gardner, act as my executor to dispose of such property as my wife may wish to have sold and to collect such debts as have to be collected by law and all money that she may collect to pay the same over to my wife, Sarah Croft.

I also appoint "Littleboy" Lollick my attorney to see that this will is executed with a fee of $100. and if he makes any collection with 10%.

I appoint Benjamin H. Crowley my wife's attorney at law to aid her attending to the estate outside the executor's business with a fee of $50 and percentage.

I desire my executor to sell such property as my wife may think prudent to dispose of on one or two years credit taking notes with good security be worth the amount of their homesteads and exemptions and when the amount is over $50, take a mortgage on real estate to double the amount.

I also desire for my executor to secure the sale debts owed me by collecting the same, or otherwise have them well secured.

I have no debts to pay for I owe no man anything but goodwill.

I give to my friend, R. H. Gardner; all my books written on divinity except my large Bible and give that to the first Christian preacher that Greene County may produce.

I desire that my homestead, with all other adjoining lands there unto, to writ: The northern half (1/2), S. 22, T.17, R.4E, N.W.S.E. Sec.22, T17, R. 4E; N 1/2, S. E., S. 1/2, N. E, Sec., all in S. 21, T. 17, R.4 E; S _, S. E. Scc. 21, T. 17, R4 E.

After the death of my wife, Sarah Croft, the above lands, including my homestead, I do donate and give for the use and benefit of a Christian College, or Seminary of learning, as called by some Campbellites.

Said institution of learning to be located on said donation and to be under control and management of the Christian Campbellite organization and for the purpose of carrying on said school or institution of learning.

I do grant and give the above described lands with all detainment and all appurtenances thereunto, for the use of said institution of learning and only for the purpose and never to be sold or disposed of but to remain in fee simple in said institution until said institution of learning goes out of operation.

I appoint R. H. Gardner, R. C. Mack and A. J. Lemmons as trustees of said estate; any one or two or all can act, but I prefer for all to act and for them to rent or lease said lands to the best advantage and to be certain always (unclear, line destroyed) and for the good care and management of the land individual thus renting or taking certain to have the place house, orchard and yard well taken care of and after said institution of learning is organized, my trustees can and pay over to the trustees of said school all money in their hands and I desire that once a year a copy of this donation be furnished the *Christian Review and Gospel Advocate* publication providing they will publish it without charge.

No person or persons to exercise any authority over said promises during the life of my wife, Sarah Croft (and) all my other lands, not named or included.

The list above, my wife and the executors may dispose of as they may think best, but not to sell them for less that three dollars per acre.

If my wife, Sarah Croft, should die before I do, I desire my will be carried out in full and that all my estate go to the said institution of learning in the presence of fear of God.

I have made this my last will revoking and sitting aside all wills or whatever or portion either written or verbal and I declare this to be my last and free will made without the fear of God, or hope of reward. But in the fear of my God and hope of honoring his name, I make this my last will on the 8th day of April 1871. G. B. Croft, Witnesses: B. H. Crowley, A. G. Warmick, and James Hide.

Dr. Croft died in 1876. He was born in South Carolina in 1800. Logan R., his brother who was crippled by rheumatism, was born in Kentucky in 1812. Thomas S. was also born in Kentucky in 1841.

Sarah, his widow, died in 1898 at the age of 93. The Croft school was established after her death. Much of the Croft money had been depleted by the time of her death. The sale of produce from the farm was to be used to maintain the school. Mrs. Mueller reports in her history that the farm was not very productive and school's existence was a struggle.

In 1906, the Campbellite denomination split. One group, the Church of Christ, took over the Croft church and school. Among the early teachers were Professor Johns and brothers A. D. and Neely Gardner. The school closed in 1939.

*Submitted by Judy McGee*

**CROWELL** – George Crowell Sr., born July 7, 1747, in Pennsylvania and died October 23, 1837, in Stanly County, North Carolina, was a son of Peter Crowell and Catharine (maiden name unknown). Peter Crowell left a will dated October 1763 in Mecklenburg County, North Carolina, which named four sons: William, Simon, Dietrich and George subject of this article. George married Jemima Sherrin who was born about 1745 in Mecklenburg County, North Carolina, and died date unknown, in Stanly County, North Carolina.

*Crowell Family, 1912. Back row, left to right: Mary Malinda Crowell, Lilly Verna Crowell, Harvey Leander Crowell, James Alexander Crowell. Front: John Avery Crowell holding John Tyler Crowell, Beaulah Benton (Wood) Crowell holding Cora Lois Crowell. Not shown is Harold Edmond Crowell, last child born to this family, 9 May 1916.*

George Crowell Sr. served in the American Revolutionary War, enlisting in Warren County, North Carolina. He applied for pension on October 18, 1833, in Montgomery County, North Carolina, at the age of 86 years. This pension application showed where he fought, that he was married and had four children when he first entered the service; that he had resided in Montgomery County, North Carolina, for nearly 40 years; when and where he was born; that his father came and settled in Mecklenburg County, North Carolina, when the subject was still a young child.

George and Jemima had the following children:

John born about 1771 North Carolina, married Jenette McMackin.

William born about 1777 North Carolina, married first Elizabeth Kimball; second Rebecca ?.

George M. born August 15, 1789, North Carolina, married Nancy Kimball.

Moses born 1784/90, married Elizabeth Reed.

David born February 14, 1798, North Carolina, married Theodosia Biles.

Peter born 1798/1800, married Mary ?.

Katherine married Solomon Miller.

Fannie married John Bullin.

Elizabeth married William Thompson.

Several descendants of George and Jemima eventually settled in Arkansas, one of whom was James Crowell born November 1838 Waverly, Tennessee, died 1911 near Walcott, Greene County, Arkansas. James was a son of John Crowell and Jenette McMackin and grandson of George Crowell Sr. and Jemima Sherrin. James married Rebecca Jane Brown in Humphreys County, Tennessee, and had four children. At some point in time, James, Rebecca and children moved to Greene County, Arkansas. The children are:

Mary Jane born 1870 Humphreys County, Tennessee, died 1889, buried in Jonesboro, Arkansas; married on March 17, 1888, in Greene County to Beverly Allen Martin.

*Harvey Leon Crowell, June 1999.*

James Harvey born June 1872 Humphreys County, died September 2, 1918, Paragould, Greene County; married on September 26, 1897, in Greene County to Florence Wood.

John Avery born September 15, 1875, Fulton County, Kentucky, died June 1, 1960, Paragould, Greene County; married on November 7, 1897, in Greene County to Beaulah Benton Wood.

William H. born September 5, 1886, Fulton County, Kentucky, died December 15, 1949, Jonesboro, Arkansas; married September 3, 1908, in Greene County, Arkansas to Sarah F. Walker.

Harvey Leon Crowell a member of the Greene County Arkansas Historical Society, is the grandson of James Harvey Crowell. His father was Harve Leander Crowell born November 19, 1902, Paragould, Greene County, died June 13, 1892, Paragould, Greene County; buried in Linwood Cemetery, Paragould, Arkansas.

**CROWLEY** – According to the crest of the Crowley Family, the Coat of Arms, the Crowley family descended from Melisius, King of Spain, through the line of Hermon, his eighth son in 350 AD. The founder of the family was Brian, son of

Eocha Mc, a King. This is where the Crowley name originated. In Ireland, O'Cruaolaoic. In English, Crowley, sometimes Crawley, Croley or Crolley.

The next documentation we have of ancestry is:

Sir Ambrose I born about 1610 died 1696 and both he and his wife were buried at Mitchem Parish Church in Stourbridge, England.

Ambrose Crowley I had a son, Ambrose II (1635-1721). He was married to Sarah Morris who had influential family in America, Philadelphia, PA. Ambrose Crowley I had eight other children, but I am only mentioning the lineage of Benjamin Crowley, founder of Crowley's Ridge.

*Marion Gramling on the tractor mowing underbrush between markers in the Crowley Family cemetery located behind Wiley Crowley Home just off Highway 168 across from Warren's Chapel Methodist Church.*

Ambrose Crowley II had a son named Samuel, born 1669. He also had 11 other children. Samuel Crowley went to sea and came to America, where his mother's relations lived in Philadelphia, PA. His mother's relatives, the Morris', were mayors, justices and held other positions.

*Cemetery after it was cleared*

Samuel Crowley later moved to Halifax County VA. He had a son, Jeffery Crowley (March 29, 1702-1762). He was married to Effie Nearne (about 1704 Bedford County, VA-1756).

During Jeffery's lifetime, he held over 1000 acres of Virginia land and was a breeder of and raced fine horses and owned a racetrack called "Crowley's Path".

Among Jeffery's children was Benjamin Crowley Sr. (1735 VA – 1817 Lexington, Oglethorp County, GA). He was married to Sarah Strong (1742 VA) about 1761.

Benjamin Crowley Sr. moved to Oglethorpe, GA in 1784.

Benjamin Crowley Sr. and his brother, Samuel, were both in the Revolutionary War. Samuel was reported to be the first man killed in 1774 at the Battle of Point Pleasant. Benjamin and Samuel were long hunters. They hunted for fur. Due to Samuel's skills in tracking and hunting, it is believed that Samuel was a guide or spy for the American Army when he was killed.

Among Benjamin Crowley I children was Benjamin Crowley II, (1758 Lexington Oglethorpe, GA-1842 Walcott, AR) the founder of Crowley's Ridge was married to Annie Catherine Wiley, who died 1850 in Walcott, AR.

Benjamin Crowley II, his wife and children moved to Kentucky in the late 1700s. He was a professional surveyor of land. He served in the War of 1812. As part pay for services to his country, he had been awarded a land grant in the Louisiana Purchase. At 63 years of age, old enough to settle down if he ever would, he began disposing of as much of his property as possible and prepared to move the remainder to his new home in the spring of 1821, with his wife and five boys: Thomas 25, Samuel 23, John 21, Wiley 18 and Ben Jr. 14; and three girls: Polly 16, Peggy 11, and Sally 9. When they arrived at New Madrid, they found that the New Madrid earthquake had sunk the land grant.

There were three major earthquakes.
(1)  Dec. 16, 1811
(2)  Jan. 23, 1812
(3)  Feb 7, 1812

The Crowley family crossed the muddy Mississippi River at Cape Girardeau, MO and came down into Arkansas on the west side of the Black River, following the only mail route then in the state. They stopped on Spring River near the county line between Lawrence and Randolph Counties. The group made camp and planted a crop in the rich soil. When the crop was in, Benjamin and his five sons started east looking for a better place to settle.

Striking an Indian Trail running east, the male Crowleys crossed the Black River at Old Davidsonville and finally the Cache River. They struck the hill country a little north of where Walcott now is and named the upheaval of land "Crowley's Ridge", a name that remains to this day.

The ridge is about 200 miles in length, from Cape Girardeau, MO to Helena, AR. The width varies from less than a mile to 12 miles. The highest point rises to 550 feet.

When they found several large springs and saw the fine hillsides sloping off to the Cache River Bottoms, Benjamin Crowley said to his sons, "This is good enough," and they made camp. After spending the night at their camp, they returned to the family, located on Spring River. Benjamin Crowley remained to gather his crop, but sent some of his sons back to build houses and to prepare for the coming of the family and livestock.

Christmas day 1821 was celebrated by installing the family and belongings in the new home. At that time they were the only white settlers within a radius of many miles. They settled on a 240-acre tract of land. The home site was near what is now the swimming pool at the State Park. There were still many Indians in the area, but not large villages. Indians living here were farmers, hunters and peaceful people. There were frequent Indian gatherings at the big springs near the home site. Indian hunters were often asked to join on hunting expeditions with the settlers. All sorts of wild animals, including buffaloes, wolves, bears, panthers, wildcats and catamounts roamed over the country, finding food provided by nature. Hunting was very profitable. They would sell the products of a winter hunt at either Memphis or Cape Girardeau. Word got back to Kentucky that the Crowley's had found the happy hunting ground, good cropland, ideal spring water, everything a hardy pioneer might desire. Kentucky friends began to come into the region.

Here on Crowley's Ridge near Walcott, they set out orchards and placed land into cultivation. All of his children settled near him.

Benjamin's fourth son, Wiley Crowley (March 28, 1803-between 1845-1850) married Lucy Capps; part Indian. They built a home about one and one-half miles from his father's home, about 1832. The home stood until around the late 60s or early 70s. The Historical Society tried to get it restored and incorporated in the State Park, but at the time there were no funds available and the house was torn down. Directly behind the house is a family cemetery.

A post office named Crowley was established in 1832 with John Crowley and Benjamin Crowley as postmasters. In

*Family grave markers in the Crowley Family Cemetery*

1846 the post office name was changed to Walcott. It is believed there was a man named Walls who lived on a hill and spent much of his time lying on a cot in his yard watching people go by. People began calling the little town Walcott. It was once called flea town from clouds of fleas attracted by the roaming livestock.

The first court was held in 1833 in the family room of Benjamin Crowley's home, presided over by Judge John T. Jones of the third judicial circuit. The grand jury held its deliberations under the shade of twin oaks nearby. The trees were many years later struck by lightning. All that remains is a very large stump.

Isaac Brookfield was one of the earliest circuit riders in Northeast AR. With the support of Benjamin Crowley and other early settlers on the ridge, Brookfield organized the first church in Greene County in the Crowley home. This was before the formation of the county in 1833. A log church was built on the plantation, which is now within the Crowley's Ridge State Park. Nearby was the first burial place on the Ridge, containing the grave of Benjamin Crowley, marked with a natural stone monument erected when the park was built. Other members of the Crowley family are buried within the cemetery. The church building was destroyed by fire in 1870. When the church was rebuilt, a new site was chosen and renamed Warren's Chapel, honoring D. B. Warren, the circuit rider who assisted in rebuilding the church. The church was built on a five-acre site, which was a gift to the church, by Wiley Crowley's widow, Lucy Capps, Benjamin H. Crowley and Elizabeth J. Crowley dated 1876. Lucy was at that time married to Dr. Mellon. The church is now located on Highway 168, about one and one/half miles from the State Park.

*Wiley Crowley house*

The Crowley's and the Daniel Boone family were related in England when Theodocia Crowley, Jeffery's second cousin, married Charles Boone in 1742 at Kent, England. They came into the Transylvania District in Kentucky in the late 1700s. The Boones in England were Quakers and at least two of the Crowley's were Quakers. The two families were closely associated in America in colonial days.

Alice Hamet wrote, after the Boone family left the Quaker Church, they became affiliated with the Baptist Church in North Carolina and later migrated to Tennessee where both they and the Crowley's were members of the same church.

*Submitted by Julia "Judy" Hughes*

**CROWLEY** – Ben T. Crowley was born to Lucien G. and Emma Crowley. Ben's wife was named Jewell. Ben was a grandson to Captain Benjamin Harrison Crowley and Elizabeth Jane Crowley and second great grandson to Benjamin Crowley, pioneer.

*L-R: granddaughter Judy, Ben, Jewell and grandson, Bobby*

July 1933, Benjamin T. and wife, Jewell E. Crowley, sold approximately 23.6 acres to the State of Arkansas for the use and benefit as a State Park, namely Crowley's Ridge State Park, for $280.00, subject to conditions and limitations that when discontinued as a State Park, will revert back to the grantors.

Ben and Jewell moved their family to California. They had two daughters, Charlotte and Marian.

*Submitted by Judy Gramling*

**CROWLEY** – Benjamin Crowley was born circa 1758 in Bedford County, Virginia, the son of Benjamin Crowley born circa 1740 in Orange County, Virginia, and Sarah Strong, born July 24, 1742, in Virginia. Benjamin Crowley's grandfather was Jeffrey Crowley born in the early years of 1700 in England. Jeffrey Crowley married first a woman named Effie (believed to be short for Affiniah). It is believed Jeffrey Crowley is the son of a Samuel Crowley, son of Ambrose Crowley a well known English iron monger with a long and distinguished English lineage.

*Crowley homestead built circa 1830 by Benjamin Crowley and his son, Wiley Crowley.*

Benjamin Crowley Sr. moved with his family and many friends, neighbors, and relatives from Virginia to Oglethorpe County, Georgia, between 1782 and 1795. The census of 1782 of Virginia shows Benjamin Sr. as a resident; the Oglethorpe County, Georgia, records document the marriage of his son, Benjamin in 1795 to Catherine Wiley. Benjamin and Catherine (Wiley) Crowley left Oglethorpe County, Georgia, some time after their marriage of 1795 and before 1810 when Benjamin Crowley appears on the Christian County, Kentucky, census living next door to Matthew Wiley, brother of Catherine Wiley.

Benjamin Crowley and his brother, Samuel, are listed on the Muster Roll of Scouts and Spies in Georgia in 1795 searching for Indians and providing surveillance information to the frontier settlers of Georgia. Benjamin is also found on a list of Insolvents living within the Indian Boundary of 1797 Grainger County, Tennessee. From early Arkansas tax lists, Benjamin Crowley is listed in 1815 as a taxpayer in Lawrence County, Arkansas. It is therefore assumed that Benjamin Crowley came to the northeast section of Arkansas between his appearance on the 1810 census of Christian County, Kentucky, and the Arkansas Tax List of 1815. Benjamin was approximately 57 years old when he moved his family from Kentucky to establish a new life in Northeast Arkansas.

Catherine "Annie" Wiley was born circa 1771 in Virginia and died in 1850 in Greene County, Arkansas. Annie's father was Peter Wiley born circa 1745 and died circa 1805 in Oglethorpe County, Georgia. Annie's mother was Mary Sharkey born circa 1755, daughter of Patrick Sharkey and Anne Knollys of Virginia. Benjamin and Catherine "Annie" Wiley Crowley had the following children:

Thomas born March 18, 1796, Oglethorpe County, Georgia, died between 1823/29 Lawrence County, married Cynthia Campbell.

Samuel born February 28, 1798, Oglethorpe County, Georgia died March 13, 1837, in Greene County, married Sarah Lamb, married second, Sarah "Sallie" Jane Hutchins.

John born February 28, 1800, died before June 27, 1816, in Lawrence County.

Wiley born March 27, 1803, in Oglethorpe County, Georgia, died circa 1847, married Lucy Capps born 1814 in Tennessee died 1861 Crowley's Ridge.

Polly born April 05, 1805, in Kentucky died circa 1841 in Greene County, married Abraham Pevehouse.

Benjamin III born November 1, 1807, in Greene County, died before 1830.

Margaret "Peggy" born May 15, 1810, in Henderson County?, Kentucky, died before 1860, married first Charles Robertson, second John McDaniel.

Sally "Sarah" born 1812, died before 1840 in Greene County married Thomas Lamb.

Being one of the early settlers of northeast Arkansas, Benjamin Crowley played an important role in the development and establishment of early Greene County history. Benjamin died circa 1842 at about 84 years of age and his wife Annie died circa 1850. There are many descendants of the original Crowley family still living in and around Greene County today, and scattered across the world.

**CROWLEY** – Sally Crowley was born about 1812. She was the daughter of Benjamin and Catherine "Annie" Crowley who were the first settlers in this area. Lawrence County, Arkansas, records show that Thomas "Tom" Lamb married Sally Crowley June 21, 1829. The family is shown in the Lawrence County 1830 census with one female under five. Sally was deceased by 1840 census of Greene County. Tom was left to care for their two daughters Catherine who was 10 and baby Mary C. who was born September 21, 1839.

By 1850 Thomas was married to a young woman named Elender. They had children Samuel and Elender.

Daughters of Sally and Tom were married by 1860.

Catherine married Joseph Austin. Children born to this union were Mary E., M.J., Benjamin Crowley and John S. Catherine Lamb Austin was deceased by 1870.

Mary C. married Jasper McDaniel. Children born to Mary were John, Sarah, Jasper "Jap," Hillary and Sherman. Her half brother Samuel F. Lamb was listed in the McDaniel household in 1860. Mary C. Lamb McDaniel died February 8, 1902. She is buried in Brown's Chapel Cemetery beside her daughter Sarah J.

There was little information on Sally Crowley when my mother Wilma McDaniel Highfill (deceased) began her research on her great-great-grandmother. She traced Sally's children through the above mentioned records to show the relationship to her Grandfather Hillary McDaniel.

**CROWLEY** – Wiley Crowley was born March 27, 1803, in Oglethorpe County, Georgia, the fourth son of Benjamin and Catherine (Wiley) Crowley. The old house that stood on Crowley's Ridge until the 1960s was built by Wiley Crowley and his father, Benjamin, about 1832.

*Samuel Jefferson Crowley and Nancy Jane (Sutfin) Crowley.*

Wiley married Lucy Capps about 1832. Lucy Capps was born circa 1814 in Tennessee according to census records. Her brother Nimrod Capps married Cynthia Mattix.

Wiley and Lucy had the following children:
John Thomas born 1837, said to have died about 1864 during the Civil War.

Elizabeth Jane born July 5, 1838, and in 1858 married her cousin Benjamin Harrison Crowley, son of Samuel Crowley and Sarah Jane Hutchins. Elizabeth Jane died May 19, 1880, and Benjamin Harrison died March 25, 1913.

William born 1839, died 1859.

Cynthia born 1842, died circa 1845.

Samuel Jefferson born September 26, 1846, married circa 1866 to Nancy Jane Sutfin born July 4, 1848, daughter of Jacob "Jake" Sutfin born circa 1809 in Tennessee and Sarah Jane "Sally" Pevehouse born circa 1829 in Arkansas.

Wiley Crowley died about 1847 and was buried at the old Crowley house in Walcott. Lucy (Capps) Crowley died about 1861 and is buried in Warren's Chapel not far from her son, Samuel Jefferson.

Samuel Jefferson Crowley and Nancy Jane (Sutfin) Crowley had the following children:
Benjamin born about 1867.
William Thomas born August 28, 1868, married Cynthia Josephine Gramling.
Wiley Jasper born October 30, 1870, married Viney J. Sims or Myrick.
John Lewis born January 5, 1874, married Missouri Elizabeth Robertson born June 14,

1874, in Vernon, Lamar County, Alabama. Missouri Elizabeth Robertson came to Greene County about 1888 with her father and mother, Joseph B. and Mary Savannah (Williams) Robertson and the rest of her family.

James Benjamin Crowley born 1875 married Emma Phillips.

Lucy Virginia born September 16, 1879, married George A. Gramling.

Sarah Jane Crowley born March 8, 1880, married John Welch Turpin.

Samuel Jefferson Crowley died September 20, 1882, and is buried in Warren's Chapel next to his wife Nancy Jane (Sutfin) who died September 1889.

Many descendants of the Crowley's, Sutfin's, and Robertson's still reside in and around Greene County and throughout the world today.

**CROWLEY** – William Thomas "W.T." Crowley was born in 1868, the son of Samuel Jefferson and Nancy (Suftin) Crowley, son of Wiley and Lucy (Capps) Crowley, son of Benjamin and Annie (Wiley) Crowley, the founder of Crowley's Ridge.

W. T. Crowley married Cynthia (Gramling) Crowley, born in 1871.

W. T. and Cynthia had seven living children: Thomas Crowley, Ruth (Crowley) Cline, Nancy (Crowley) Boozer, Bessie (Crowley) Amorine, Eula (Crowley) Hughes, Thad Crowley and Wiley Crowley.

W. T. Crowley was postmaster for Walcott post office around 1910 or 1912. He also served as Greene County Sheriff, 1933-1936.

W. T. "Billy" and Cynthia built their home on the farm inherited from his dad, a portion of the original Benjamin Crowley plantation located at the junction of Highway 412

*W. T. "Billy" Crowley, Sheriff of Greene County*

and 141. All the children except Wiley were born and lived there until Eula was about six years old.

When W. T. was chosen postmaster, they moved to the Crowley home, south of what is now Crowley's Ridge State Park. That is where Wiley was born.

They farmed the land from the now park, to Highway 141. They watered their horses at a spring under a large tree at the entrance to the present swimming pool of the park. At the upper end of the now pool was an old quagmire. Cows would wade into this and mire up with only their horns sticking out.

They later moved back to their previous home.

W. T. and Cynthia were wonderful Christian parents and grandparents. They were members of Warren's Chapel Methodist Church and were upstanding members of their community.

W. T. "Billy" Crowley died in 1939 and is buried at Warren's Chapel Cemetery. His wife, Cynthia, died in 1942 and is buried at his side. They left a legacy for the family to cherish down through the ages.

*Submitted by Judy Gramling*

**CUNNINGHAM** – John E. Cunningham and Martha Elizabeth Thomas were married February 17, 1879, near Bolivar, Tennessee. They lived just north of Memphis and had two sons, Arthur "Doc" Cunningham born in 1879, and William "Bill" Thomas Cunningham, born in 1881.

*Aunt Mat and Uncle John Cunningham; grandsons James Phillip "J.P." in foreground and Winston in background. Picture taken around 1918.*

The lure of good timber brought "Uncle John," "Aunt Mat" and their two young sons to Arkansas on a train ride by way of Little Rock and finally the couple wound up at O'Kean, Arkansas. With two young sons and no place to go the couple was approached by a man called Preacher Warren who told them of an opportunity to make a crop and live in a home owned by a man named George Walden. This they did for two years on ground owned by Mr. Walden located just south of Oak Grove School.

After two years of farming for Mr. Walden, the couple and their two sons moved to a farm knows as "The Bass farm" located approximately two miles north of the Paragould Landfill. In 1885 the couple purchased 40 acres from a Mr. John Clark which was located just north of Highway 49 North across from the Monroe Plant. Here they built a log cabin, farmed, and lived for 14 years. During this time the following children were born: Mike born in 1885, Belle born in 1887, Ida born in 1890, Eva born in 1893, Walter "Buck" born in 1895, and Roy born in 1897.

In 1899 "Uncle John and Aunt Mat" sold everything and outfitted two teams and wagons and along with their eight children headed to Texas where "Aunt Mat's" cousin lived. While there, Roy their 2 year old son developed pneumonia and died. He was buried in Texas. After three months the family grew homesick and returned to Greene County, Arkansas, where they purchased 80 acres from W.F. Hasty just across the railroad from the Cotton Belt School and due north of the Paragould Landfill.

In 1905, twin sons were born to "Uncle John and Aunt Mat" but the boys only lived for two weeks.

"Uncle John and Aunt Mat" also raised four grandchildren, all children of son William "Bill" and his wife, Willie Woods Cunningham. Their names and dates of birth are: Georgia, 1906; Carl, 1908, Winston, 1911 and James Phillip "J.P.," 1915. Stella, born in 1903, died at the age of 5.

*The Cunningham family, picture taken around 1910. Front row from left: Georgia and Carl. Second row: William "Bill," Willie, John E. (Uncle John) and Martha (Aunt Mat). Third row: Walter "Buck," Bell, Ida and Eva. Fourth row: Arthur "Doc," Mike and Andrew Thomas (brother of Aunt Mat)*

The Cunninghams raised hay, corn, hogs and cattle. They were one of the first families in the Cotton Belt Community to have an automobile. "Uncle John" paid $500.00 cash for a brand new 1926 Chevrolet touring car and it was very common for neighbors to visit the Cunninghams in order to use their battery powered telephone.

"Uncle John" died in 1928 at the age of 70 and "Aunt Mat" died in 1951 at the age of 89. The last surviving child was W.R. "Buck" who died in 1995 at the age of 97. All of the Cunninghams (excluding Roy who was buried in Texas) are buried in New Friendship Cemetery.

James Phillip "J.P." Cunningham is the only surviving grandchild and resides in Paragould with his wife Elaine (Wright) Cunningham.

**CUPP** – The first Cupps to arrive in Greene County, Arkansas, were Warner and Anna who moved from Cobb County, Georgia, and settled in Greene County, Arkansas, sometime after 1840. Their seventh child Henry had been born in Cobb County on January 10, 1839, shortly before the move. Warner and Anna reared a family of nine children: Emily, William "Doc," John, Mary E., Jacob, Nancy, Henry, Eliza and Sarah L.

Henry Cupp served in the Civil War as a Confederate with Company D; Davies' Battalion, Arkansas Cavalry, private. He was taken prisoner of war on May 11, 1865, and paroled at Wittsburg, Arkansas, May 25, 1865. When he enlisted at Greene County, Arkansas, he was 25 years old, had blue eyes, light hair, and a dark complexion, was 5'6" tall, and stated he was born in Cobb County, Georgia.

Margret Dennis was born November 4, 1845, in Arkansas to Robert John and Eleanor Thompson Dennis. Robert had arrived in St. Francis Township in 1837 from Tennessee or Kentucky. On August 3, 1840, Robert and Eleanor Thompson were married. About 1848 the Robert Dennis family moved to Crowley's Ridge where he resided until his death. Margret Dennis married Henry Cupp in 1866 and died on December 17, 1869, when their daughter Sarah Ann was just about 2 years old.

Henry Cupp had grown up on his father's farm and was always a very industrious farmer. He owned a large well-stocked farm, much of which

*L-R: Eula Crowley, Beatrice (Majors) Crowley, Tom Crowley, Cynthia Crowley, W. T. "Billy" Crowley, Wiley Crowley, Pauline, daughter of Ruth Crowley Cline and Noah Cline, Jack, son of Tom and Beatrice, Louie, son of Ruth (Crowley) Cline and Noah Cline*

was under cultivation. He was one of the prominent farmers and stock raisers of the country, had decided political views, and was very interested in progress and development.

Henry Cupp died November 9, 1895. Henry and Margret Dennis Cupp are buried in Mount Zion Cemetery, Walcott, Arkansas, with their infant daughter aged 2 months. Also buried in a row beside them are: Henry's second wife Louisa R. (Stevens) Cupps with her infant daughter and infant son Warner next to wife number three, Nancy Adaline (Smith) Cupp and her children Rake and Pearly.

*Henry Cupp at home in his later years.*

Henry and Louisa called Lucy, had one daughter Emmaline "Emma" J. Cupp who married Joseph A. "Jack" Fielder. Emma had passed away by the time her father died. Henry's last wife, Icyphena Evaline/Emeline Lane Cupp, and her one small daughter, Mary H., are buried behind his monument. Icyphena and Henry had two sons who lived to maturity: Henry J. Cupp born January 10, 1887, and Laborn "Labe" R. Cupp born December 21, 1891.

Henry Cupp had kept an old, beat up trunk whose hinges were missing packed full of money and IOU's. People knew Henry had money and couldn't read so they just scribbled nothing on the IOU'S, which made them no good after he passed away. Henry also would take a roll of bills and put them in knot holes in his barn. Then he'd put a corn cob up there and break it off.

There had been rumors that someone would kill Henry for his money, so as soon as Jim Tyner heard Henry had passed away, he hitched his pack on his back and carried his gun. He found so much money in that trunk that he decided he would have to get it to one of the banks. He started out and walked all the way into Jonesboro, arriving about the time the banks opened the next morning.

Following their father's death, Henry's sons, Henry and Labe Cupp, managed to get their inheritance money before they were of age. They rode trains about the country side to all the big cities, spent all their money like it was water, and soon had spent all their inheritance. The daughter, Sarah Ann, and her husband James McDonald "Jim" Tyner got their start by paying $1,000.00 for Henry Cupp's livestock brand when he died.

For years, succeeding owners plowed up money as they farmed what had been Henry Cupp's land. Everyone would say, "It was probably some of the Cupp money in its day."

**CUPP** – The chronology of the Joe Wesley Cupp family, in Greene County AR, starts about 1845 with Warner and wife Ann Cupp who were from Georgia, residing in St. Francis Township. The 1850 Federal Census lists seven children, the first five being born in Georgia, the last two born in Arkansas. Their known children were: William (1829), John (1830), Jacob (1832), Nancy (1837), Henry (1840), Eliza (1845) and Sarah (1849) (preceding information from George Rowlands, *Fathers of the Ridge*). Jacob's son Warner was the grandfather of the subject of this history.

Joe Wesley Cupp was born Aug. 18, 1926, near Stanford, AR, to Thomas Jefferson "Jeff" and Virginia Belle McClure Cupp. This family later moved to Craighead County, AR where Joe grew up and attended school at Dixie. He enlisted into the US Army in 1944 while still in high school. After his discharge he returned to school, graduating in 1947. Upon graduation Joe enrolled at Arkansas State College, majoring in agriculture. He later transferred to University of Arkansas where he graduated in 1951.

On Jan. 11, 1947 Joe married Dessie Lee Brown of Dixie (see Brown Family by Helen Brown Wood). To this union two children were born, daughter Sherry Ann (1948) and a son Ronald Wayne (1949), both in Greene County. After graduation Joe secured a position with the University of Missouri Extension Service, first in New Madrid County, MO then in Butler County, MO, then finishing his career in Franklin County, MO where he retired in 1984.

While residing in Poplar Bluff three sons were born: Randie Joe (1953), Steven Ray (1955), and Bruce Edward (1958). This family moved to Union, Franklin County, MO in 1959, where they reside today. Joe died in 1994 and is buried in the City cemetery at Union, Dessie works for the Union school system where she plans to retire in 2001.

Sherry Ann Cupp married Carl Rogers and to them was born a son, Carl Kenneth Rogers III. This marriage ended in divorce. Sherry then married David Ginnett and they have a son, Micah Joseph Ronald Ginnett. This family presently lives at Washington, MO. Sherry is employed by East Central College at Union, MO. David is renovations manager for Drury, Inns, Inc.

*Cupp Family about 1963. Front: Joe W. Cupp, Dessie Brown Cupp and Steven Ray Cupp. Rear: Ronnie Cupp, Sherry Ann Cupp and Randie Joe Cupp*

Ronald Wayne "Ronnie" entered the US Army after graduation from high school. Ronnie married Placida Geraldez in 1998 and they are parents to a son, Lee and daughter, Ivy. They presently live in Union, MO.

Upon graduation from the University of Missouri-Columbia, Randie Joe enlisted in the US Navy where he attend Officer Candidate School and graduated as a lieutenant. He served as a supply officer on the USS Flint. He married Terri Remy and they have two children Amanda Lee and Andrew Michael.

Steven Ray entered the US Marine Corps. Steve married Beverly Catsoulis and they have two children Kelly Joann and Joe Wesley II. This marriage ended in divorce. Steve then married Stephanie Sheets and they have one son, Aaron Thomas and they presently reside in Seminole, FL where Steve is employed by Eckerd University. Stephanie is a Registered Nurse.

Bruce Edward was born Aug 17, 1958 and died one day later. He is buried in City Cemetery, Poplar Bluff, MO.

*Submitted by Sherry (Cupp) Ginnett*

**CUPP** – Warner Cupp was born to Henry Cupp of Wilkes and Gwinnett County, Georgia, in 1806. He married Anna about 1825 probably in Gwinnett County. Anna was born in 1810 in South Carolina. They lived in Cobb County, Georgia, for the 1840 Census and were in Greene County, Arkansas, for the 1850 Census. Warner was very successful at farming until his death on February 27, 1871. His wife Anna only lived until January 18, 1872. They are buried in Mt. Zion Cemetery, Walcott, Greene, Arkansas.

Warner and Anna had nine children, the first seven being born in Georgia and the last two being born in Greene County, Arkansas. After their arrival, all the family members remained in Greene County.

Emily Cupp was born March 25, 1827, in Georgia. She married James E. Walldrum about 1846-1847 in Greene County, Arkansas. She is listed on the 1870 Mortality Schedule for Greene County, Arkansas. She died April 19, 1870, in Greene County and was interred in Mt. Zion Cemetery.

William "Doc" Cupp was born about 1828 in Georgia. He married his first wife Mary Jane Shane about 1850 in Greene County. He had a second marriage to a Jane. He is probably the William Cupp who is buried at Cross Roads Cemetery, Greene, Arkansas.

John Cupp was born April 11, 1831, in Georgia. John married an Elizabeth about 1859-1860 in Greene County. His second wife was named Clarinda M. He died on September 7, 1899, in Walcott, and was buried in Fairview Cemetery, Greene County.

Mary E. Cupp was born May 8, 1832, in Georgia. She married William H. Hutchins about 1850 in Greene County. Mary passed away January 15, 1878, in Greene County and was buried in Mt. Zion Cemetery in Walcott.

Jacob Cupp was born February 7, 1833, in Georgia. He married S.A.E. who was born about 1832 in Tennessee. His estate records in 1882 listed his wife as Margaret E. He died February 17, 1882, in Greene County and was buried in Fairview Cemetery, Greene County.

Nancy Cupp was born about 1837 in Georgia.

Henry Cupp was born January 10, 1839, in Cobb County, Georgia. About 1866 he married first Margret Ann Dennis who died on December 17, 1869, when their daughter Sarah Ann was just about 2 years old. Henry married second Louisa R. Stevens, third Nancy Adaline Smith, and fourth Icyphena Evaline/Emeline Lane. Henry and his four wives are buried along with their children who died as infants in Mt. Zion Cemetery, Walcott. Henry died November 9, 1895, in Walcott.

Eliza Cupp was born July 17, 1846, in Greene County, although the tombstone says "1838." She married W.R. Marten and died April 28, 1876, in Greene County.

Sarah L. Cupp was born December 27, 1849, in Greene County, Arkansas. She was blind and never married. She died May 3, 1914, in Greene County, and was buried in Mt. Zion Cemetery in Walcott.

**CUPP/NEWBERRY** – Vance Cupp Sr. married Laura Mae Newberry on May 7, 1922, in Light, Arkansas. They are parents of five children who lived to adulthood; one child, Mayo Cupp died as an infant and is buried in Shiloh Cemetery.

The oldest child, Claribel Cupp Faulkner White was married to Charles Earl Faulkner. From that marriage were born two children Constance Suzanne "Connie" Faulkner Colmer who now lives in Overland Park, Kansas, with her husband Jay and their two children Justin and Courtney Colmer. Justin is attending the University of Iowa as a sophomore and Courtney is a junior in high school. Claribel later married Jack White who is now deceased. Claribel died January 1998. She was a retired teacher, and Jack was a salesman.

Claribel's second child is Ronald "Ronnie" Wayne Faulkner who is a retired Army Lt. Colonel and is married to Helen Barker Faulkner and they live in Sierra Vista, Arizona, with their two sons, David and Andrew. Their sons are attending school in Tucson.

Their second child, Evangeline Cupp Cothren is married to J. C. Cothren and lives in Light. They are retired educators, business persons, and have one son, Jackson David Cothren who is married to Angela Lynn Coy Cothren and they live in Dayton, Ohio. They have one daughter Lauren Ellis "Ellie" Cothren who is not yet in school. Jackson graduated from the Air Force Academy, spent five and one-half years in the Air Force, came back home to work with his father in business, and after three years returned to Columbus, Ohio, to enroll at Ohio State University and has now completed all work for a PhD except his dissertation. Jack also is working under civil service for the Air Force at Wright-Patterson Air Force Base. Angela graduated from University of Mississippi.

Their third child is Vance Cupp Jr. who is married to Virginia Maxine Stone Cupp and they live in Light. They have two children: Jannie Cupp Distretti who is married to Johnny Ray Distretti and they live in Walcott. They have two daughters: Ashley and Casey, who are students at Greene County Tech. Jannie graduated at Arkansas State University is a licensed CPA, and they are farmers in Light and Walcott. Vance Jr., and Maxine's other child is Vance Cupp III who is married to Nancy Carlson Cupp and they live in Paragould with their two children Madeline and Quentin who are not yet in school. Nancy and Vance III graduated from the University of Arkansas, and Vance has degrees from University of Iowa and Indiana University. They both work in the family business. Vance Jr., manages the Vance Cupp and Sons, Inc., a grain and farm land business.

Their fourth child is Claridy Colleen "Pete" Cupp and he is married to Esther Williams Cupp and they live in Light. "Pete" works for the State LP Gas Board and Esther is a former beautician. They have three children: Rebecca Colleen Miller, Jackie Freeman and Jill Elizabeth Cupp. Rebecca "Becky" is married to Jimmy Doyle Miller who works in transportation for Ferrell Gas Company and "Becky" is employed at Emerson Electric. They have three children, Allison, Kristen, and Matthew. Allison is married to Sammy Poe and they live in Paragould. Allison is attending Arkansas State University.

Kristen is attending Black River Vo-Tech, as is Matthew. There is one grandchild, Landon Miller. Jacqueline "Jackie" is married to Breckery Freeman and they live in Paragould. Breck is associate pastor of Southside Baptist Church, and Jackie is a teacher-on leave to be a mother of four children: Seth, Jonathan, Sarah, and Adam all of whom are young. Jill Elizabeth lives in Burke, Virginia, and is an office manager for Fairfax Covenant Church in Fairfax, Virginia. She is a graduate from Arkansas State University with a degree in public relations and she works also as a representative of Mary Kay.

The fifth child is James Michael Cupp and he is married to Mary Lou Pratt Cupp and they live in Light. They are parents of two daughters: Lisa Kaye Cupp Williams Armstrong Hancock and Kellie Ree Cupp Blake. Lisa has two children Michael and Mackenzie Williams. Michael is married to Christie and they have a daughter Brianna and they live at Light. Michael works with industry and Christie works in the family grocery store and station. Mackenzie is attending Williams Baptist College as a freshman. Kellie is married to Allen Blake and they have two sons, Jeffrey and Jordan, and they live in Paragould. Kellie graduated Arkansas State University and works in human resources with Prestolite. Allen works in industry in Jonesboro, and their boys attend Greene County Tech.

Vance Sr., is the son of Charles Jacob Cupp who was born in 1872 and died in the 1930s. He was married to Mary L. Palmer and they are parents of six children. Warner, Patriarch of the Cupp family in Greene County, was born in Cobb County, Georgia, in 1804, and by 1840 he had emigrated to Greene County and was quite successful in farming. Vance farmed in the early years of his life for John Edward Newberry, his father-in-law. Later the Newberry Gin was built at Light and Vance became the manager of the gin from the early 1930s until rice became the main crop in western Greene County closing the cotton gin and was the start of a new business dealing in grain, fertilizer, and chemicals. That business is now the Vance Cupp and Sons, Inc., and is being managed by the oldest son, Vance Cupp Jr. The corporation owns between 1,400 and 1,500 acres of land in the community. Vance Sr. died in 1974, and Laura died in 1983.

*Vance Cupp, Sr. (left) and Vance Cupp, Jr. (right) standing on the cotton gin platform beside the first bales of cotton ginned after rebuilding the old gin that burned down in 1945.*

Laura was the daughter of John Edward Newberry and Rosa Adelaide Biggs, whose parents were Barbara Etta Bell Johnson, daughter of Lt. Col. Benjamin Johnson and Eldo Rado Cado ERC Biggs. His nickname was "Pink." John Edward Newberry is the son of James Franklin and Mary A. Morgan Newberry. He is the grandson of John H. and Nancy Dacus Newberry, and the great-grandson of James S. and Sarah Howell Newberry. Their family came here from North Carolina and Alabama. Rosa died in 1933; John Edward died in 1938. They are buried at Mt. Zion Cemetery.

We share the feeling that Greene County is a "good" place to live and work and rear our families.

**DACUS** — Clarinda Elizabeth Dacus, was born about 1850 in Cherokee County, Alabama. She was the daughter of Pascal L. "Pack" Dacus and Amanda A. O'Dell who settled in Greene County, Arkansas, in 1852. Clarinda Elizabeth Dacus married about 1867 in Greene County, Arkansas, to her first husband, Robert Marshall Lamb. Robert Marshall Lamb, born 1848 in Waterloo, Lauderdale County, Alabama, moved to Greene County, Arkansas, in 1851 with his parents, John Lamb Jr. and Ann Houston. On March 11, 1881, Robert was accidentally beheaded by machinery at the Dacus Gin at Walcott, Greene County which was owned by his father-in-law, Pack Dacus. He is buried in the Lamb Cemetery in Greene County, but his tombstone has been destroyed. At the time of Robert's death, their youngest child, Jones Houston Lamb, was 2 years old, and Clarinda Elizabeth was expecting their sixth child, Robert Marshall Lamb Jr. who wasn't born until May 6, 1881.

Clarinda Elizabeth Dacus Lamb remarried on March 2, 1884, in Greene County to Rubin Al H. Winn who was born about 1835 in Carroll County, Tennessee. Al Winn was the son of Minor M. Winn and Nancy Yarbour. Clarinda Elizabeth Dacus (Lamb) Winn died from tuberculosis about 1886 in Greene County, shortly after giving birth to her second son by Al Winn. She is buried next to her first husband in the Lamb Cemetery, but her tombstone has also been destroyed. Al Winn died from tuberculosis shortly after the death of Clarinda. It is not known where Rubin Al H. Winn is buried.

Clarinda's two youngest Lamb sons, Jones and Robert Jr., went to live with their Dacus grandparents. Pack and Amanda Dacus both died in February of 1895 and Jones and Robert Jr. then went to live with their older sister, Mollie Lamb who had married Emmerson Dod Winn.

Clarinda's two Winn sons were supposedly raised by an unrelated family.

The children of Clarinda Elizabeth Dacus and Robert Marshall Lamb, all born in Greene County were:

Mary Elizabeth "Mollie" Lamb born June 14, 1868, who married Emmerson Dod Winn.

Lucie Annie "Nannie" Lamb born March 27, 1870, who married William A. Edwards.

John Thomas Lamb born April 4, 1873, who married Lillie Minerva Grayson.

California "Callie" Lamb born December 25, 1875, who married Steve D. Edwards.

Jones Houston Lamb, M.D. born February 8, 1879, who married Nora Lee Tyner.

Robert Marshall "Bob" Lamb Jr. born May 6, 1881, who married first to Emma Seay and second to Lillie Bowlin.

The children of Clarinda Elizabeth Dacus and Rubin Al H. Winn, both born in Greene County, were:

James Edward Winn born January 25, 1885, who married Liddie Wade Davis.

Elmer Winn born about 1886 who died single.

Clarinda Elizabeth Dacus has many Lamb and Winn descendants still living in Greene County, Arkansas.

**DACUS** — Lewis Cass Dacus (1855-1910) came from Cherokee County, Alabama (settled in Greensboro settlement) and married Melinda E. Roy (1851-1889). Melinda Roy Dacus' parents were Abel Roy (1807-1870) and Levinda McDaniel (1808-1864). Cass and Melinda had three sons: Andrew Jackson, Theodore and Silas, and two daughters: Charlcie and Alta.

Cass lost his wife in 1889 when the daughters were very young. (The youngest, Alta, was not a year old when she died.) A story told by his granddaughter, Ruth O. Dacus Schisler— the girls received new dresses sewn by some caring neighbor women. One day when Cass and the older brothers were cultivating a cotton field near the home and a younger brother was cooking a meal, the girls playing in the loft decided to cut up the new dresses and make doll clothes for their dolls.

Andrew Jackson married Purcas Addia Cole in 1901. He was a carpenter and built the original or one of the older buildings of Rock Hill Baptist Church. He cut the logs, milled the lumber and built the building. When he finished the building, the church was unable to pay for his labor or for the materials.

We have been told that Abel Roy donated the property to Rock Hill Church and Cemetery.

L. Cass and Melinda Dacus are the great-grandparents of E. Randall Schisler, A. Byron Schisler, Addie Schisler Johnson and Melendia Schisler Bennett.

**DACUS** – According to available census, Nathaniel Dacus was born 1779 in Virginia and settled in South Carolina by 1808. Around 1835 he and his family had moved to Cherokee County, AL where they remained until the mid 1850's. At this point they traveled to Greene and Craighead counties in Arkansas where most descendants still reside.

Nathaniel and Mary Dacus were parents of John, Jerral, Nancy, Paskel L. and J. Robert, all born in South Carolina. John was born 1808. His daughter Purcilla married George W. Nutt who served in the Civil War with Co. H., Missouri Volunteers. His father was Elder William Nutt who organized the Mt. Zion Baptist Church in Greene County, AR.

Nancy (1818) married John H. Newberry, the son of James Swain Newberry and Sarah Howell. John served in the Civil War as a private, Co. G, 3rd Arkansas Calvary. He was killed accidentally during the retreat from Corinth, MS in October 1862. Nancy and John's son Lawrence married Sarah J. O'dell. He was mentioned in Paragould's newspaper, the *Soliphone*, as having attended Bud Ryan's Party for Old Folks, in 1930. His daughter, Florence and her husband Gove Fletcher, owned a store at Finch about 1921.

Jerral J. was born 1820. His sons, Washington Lafayette and Lewis Cass, married sisters, Rebecca and Melinda Roy. Basil Dacus, grandson of Lewis Cass, taught in the Walcott, Stanford and Greene County Tech schools.

Pascal L. (1831) married Amanda A. O'dell. Their children were Clarinda Elizabeth, James Harrison, Sarah, John L., William Thomas and Nancy, all born in Alabama. Pascal served in the Civil War as a corporal in Co. A with Davies Battalion, Arkansas Calvary. He was granted 280 acres in Greene County for his military services.

Clarinda Elizabeth (1849) married Robert Lamb, son of John Pay Lamb and Ann Houston. Clarinda and Robert's grandson, Jones Houston Lamb was elected mayor of Paragould in 1970 and again in 1972.

James Harrison (1848) married Lucinda Elizabeth Heard. Their son, John "Lawrence" was a dedicated businessman who owned a general store in Light, AR. Currency was coined for trade at the store. The coin in my possession is the size of a penny. One-side states, "Five Cents GOOD FOR MERCHANDISE' the other side states, 'DACUS & NEWBERRY GENERAL MERCHANDISE, LIGHT, AR. James Harrison later married Eliza Jane Bobbitt. Their children were James Uphratus, Robert Morris, Alta, Delbert Flossie and Elondris "Lon". Delbert and Lon married sisters, Ruth and Hattie Jones, daughters of Tomas Jasper Jones and Nancy Elizabeth Friar. Lon Dacus operated a rolling store throughout Greene County around 1935. Lon and Hattie were the parents of Ruby, Lawrence, Luchiel, Bill and Max. Max married Patsy Witt, the daughter of Albert Witt and Louise Patillo. Max, although venturing into different businesses, remains loyal to his first love, real estate. Max and Pat are the parents of Darlene, Max Jr. and myself, Carolyn. I am married to Jim Andrews and we have two children. Our son, Captain Jimmy Andrews, is a West Point graduate who is a helicopter pilot in the US Army. He married Tara Millay, a resident of Paragould until their marriage. Pamela Andrews, our daughter, was the chief photographer for KAIT-TV until 1999, when she began teaching television at Greene County Tech.

*Submitted by Carolyn Dacus Andrews*

**DAVENPORT** – James Davenport, great-grandfather of Roy Davenport, left Gwinette County, Georgia, (approximately 1850) and settled at Goobertown just south of Greene County. He later married Mary Boling, Greene County native and four children were born to that union. In addition to farming, James was known to have panned for gold in Oregon. Upon their death they were buried at Wood's Chapel Cemetery in Greene County.

One of the children from that union was Russell Davis Davenport, grandfather of Roy Davenport. He later married Lula Lee Edwards whose father, Robert Lee Edwards, was Craighead County judge. Russell was a farmer and was named as one of the 51 Craighead County pioneers. Russell and Lula spent their lifetime in the Goobertown area and were blessed with eight children. Upon their death they were buried at Pine Log Cemetery in Craighead County.

*The Roy Davenport family. Front from left: Margie Davenport, Fallyn Taylor Davenport and Norma Davenport holding Jenna Brianne Davenport. Back: Roy and Dennis Davenport.*

One of the children from this union was James Curtis Davenport, father of Roy Davenport. He married Lois Levine Adams and they had six children. In their earlier years they resided at Goobertown and in later years moved near Jonesboro on Highway 49 North. Curtis was a farmer/carpenter and Lois retired from General Electric. Curtis and Lois did most of their shopping in Paragould where they traveled by horse and wagon between the railroad tracks from Goobertown to Paragould. They are buried in the Pine Log Cemetery in Craighead County.

Roy Davenport, son of Curtis and Lois, along with his wife, Margie, and son, Dennis, settled in Greene County in 1974 moving to Center Hill from West Memphis. Dennis was 9 years old at the time and enrolled in the fourth grade at Greene County Tech. Roy and Margie opened Davenport's Auto Truckstop which they operated for four years. Since selling the truckstop, some 22 years ago, (as of this writing, January, 2000) Roy has been employed by Dr Pepper Bottling while Margie has been employed as superintendent's secretary at both Greene County Tech School District (17 years) and Paragould School District (5 years). After living in the Center Hill area for 19 years, they moved to the Stafford subdivision six years ago.

Dennis Davenport is now married to Norma Noles of Walcott and they have three daughters: Rebecca Suzanne Davenport (deceased, buried at Mt. Zion Cemetery); Fallyn Taylor Davenport, age 8 and a second grade student at Greene County Tech; and Jenna Brianne Davenport, age 4, who attends PALS. Dennis' family also resides in the Stafford subdivision. Dennis is employed at Dr Pepper Bottling while Norma teaches third grade at Greene County Tech.

Roy has two aunts and uncles who had resided in Greene County for several years prior to his moving to Greene County, Ray and Murleen Davenport and Robert and Merle Davenport. Ray and Robert are brothers to James Curtis Davenport.

Ray and Murleen came to Greene County from Craighead County in 1937 and have remained Greene County residents since that time. Ray, age 90, retired from Independent Tire in 1974 and Murleen, age 87, retired from Dollins Furniture in 1977. They have resided on South Seventh Street for 36 years.

Robert and Merle Davenport came to Greene County from Craighead County in 1969. They resided on West Court Street until 1998 when they moved to Philadelphia, Pennsylvania to be near their only child, a daughter, Micky Davenport Bergey, and her family. Merle retired from Montgomery Ward in Paragould. Robert was self-employed.

**DAVIDSON** – The Martin Van Buren Davidson-Artie Lee Wright family moved to Greene County from Benton County, Tennessee, the town of Camden, in approximately 1901. They moved to a farm near Beech Grove, Arkansas, and raised their family. They remained there until their deaths and are buried in the Beech Grove Cemetery. I don't know if their parents came with them, or before them, or if they remained in Tennessee. Martin Van Buren Davidson married Artie Lee Wright June 6, 1896, in Benton County, Tennessee. Artie's siblings were: Lushion, Viola, Lula and Mag. Lushion went to New York City. Mag went to Trenton, Tennessee, married and raised a family. The others remained in the Southeast Missouri/Arkansas area with their families.

*Artie, Vera, Valla, Martha, Joseph, Una, Virgie, Woodrow and Van Davidson.*

Martin Van Buren's parents were James Davidson, born in 1830 in Humphreys County, Tennessee, and Martha Ann, (I do not know her maiden name), who were married in Humphreys County, Tennessee. Their children were: Nancy, William B., Martin Van Buren, Sarah, James A. and Enos. Artie's parents were S. C. Wright and Sarah Herren (or possibly Herrin). The children of Martin Van Buren "Van" and Artie were: Vera who married Avery Cunningham; Valla Buren "V.B." who married Versa Vee Huckabay; Martha who married William Edwards; Joseph who married Trula ?; Una who married ? Marchbanks; Virgie; and Woodrow Wilson who married Eugenia Stallcup. Vera, Martha and Woodrow stayed in the Beech Grove Community. They were all farmers. Woodrow also owned a store in Beech Grove and in his later years became the sheriff of Greene County. Una and Virgie remained on the home place for much of their lives. Joseph and Trula moved to Flint, Michigan, where he was employed with Chevrolet. Valla and Versa moved to a farm near Malden, Missouri. Valla was a farmer and in his later years also owned a controlling interest in the International Harvester Dealership in Malden.

Valla served in WW I, Abraham was in the Revolutionary War, and at least one family member served in the Civil War.

Martin Van Buren's father, James, born 1830 in Humphreys County, Tennessee, and his grandfather was Samuel H. Davidson, born 1795 in Benton County, Tennessee, married first Nancy Alexander and second Catherine Warrick. His father, Abraham, born 1755 in Guilford, North Carolina, was the one who served in the Revolutionary War in the Virginia Militia out of Pittsylvania, Virginia; his father John Davidson, born 1730 in Bertie, North Carolina, and died 1770, was the first generation born in the United States. He married Hannah Hughson.

A good history of my maternal great-great-grandparents: Presley Huckabay and Mary Bullock and Gilbert W. Stevenson and M.J. "Mattie" Thorp who settled in Greene County is published in *Biography and Historical Memoirs on Northeast Arkansas*.

**DAVIS** -The Charles Arthur Davis family moved to New Friendship community, Greene County, AR about 1943 from Dunklin County MO. This was a farm family who lived around Cockrum and Cardwell mostly raising cotton on 40-acre farm to support a family of nine children. Recollections have it around 1936 they had $25.00 per month to make a crop with and to live on. In the fall of the family would pick cotton for one week to get enough money to buy 100 pounds each of sugar, flour, beans, etc for the winter. Their treat was a box of dried apricots. The children remember the day the family moved from Cockrum to Cardwell, they had to walk several miles home from school.

Sorghum molasses making was a fun time for the grandchildren. Also they enjoyed the peach and fig trees at the New Friendship farm. The well was on the back porch, which was something different too. The house was nice and there was a barn, smoke house and hen house included in the out buildings. This place was possible with the help of a son, L. A. who was in the service and over seas in WWII. Buying a 70-acre farm was definitely a step forward for the Davis's.

Charles Arthur married Oct. 1, 1910 Nannie Elizabeth Shultz at Kennett, MO by H. T. West, justice of peace. "Lizza"(Jan 25, 1890 MO) was the daughter of William "Willie" and Mary E. Bagus Shultz. While "C. A." farmed she was busy with the garden, canning and sewing for her girls. She could cut out a dress without a pattern and sew it up to fit each one. One day she was out back washing tubs of greens to put up when someone taking picture came by and while she was busy with him, Bert their horse, ate all of the greens. Nannie Elizabeth died on her 56th birthday at her home at New Friendship. She was the oldest child of her family, which consisted of four sisters: Martha Jane, Sidney M., Ruth E. and Ina and two brothers, William V. "Bill" and Hezakhi.

*John B. Davis about 1910.*

C. A. and Lizza's nine children are:
1. Mildred Irene (Dec 25, 1911- Apr 2, 1999 Kansas City, MO) married Warren Greenway
2. Raymond J. B. "Bud" (Sept 7, 1913- Oct 1983) married Chole unknown
3. Ruth Marie "Tootsie" (Aug 31, 1915- April 2 1999 Paragould, two hours before her sister Mildred) married Thomas Horrell
4. Langdon Arron (Sept 29 1917- March 26 1992) married Pearl Ellington
5. Hazel Helen Hortense (Oct 17, 1919) married Herman Toombs
6. Billy Gene (Nov 13 1921- May 12 1970) married Joyce Reeks
7. Lola Fayrene (Aug 6 1926) married Bobby Joe Jones
8. Bobbie Joy (May 20 1928) married Jack Mosky
9. Johnny Parker (Nov 25 1930-July 15 1989) married Belva Jean Janes

*Charles Arthur and Nannie Elizabeth Davis about 1945.*

Charles Arthur (Oct 6, 1888 MO) the son of John B. and Nancy A. Davis, remembered only having a sister who died when she was about 12 years old. The 1900 Fifth Civil District, Lake County, TN Census showed Nancy as the mother of six children, one living. These records show John was born Sept 1859 in Illinois, Nancy born May 1860 in Arkansas. Nancy died with TB between June 1900 and 1910. John, a widower was living as a roomer in 1910 at Senath, MO. occupation, barber. As the family remembers, he was living with his sons and his wife where he died shortly after his first granddaughter was born.

Family get togethers were a tradition. The Davis's were Baptist. C. A. and Lizza are both buried at the LuLu Cemetery near Hollywood, MO.

Several descendants are still living in Greene County.

Sources: Census, marriage, deed and family records including much research done by Stacey Jean Terry Flanery, records which have since burned along with her home.

*Submitted by Patsy Toombs Crockett Yates*

**DAVIS** – Susie Mae (Clark) Davis, was born October 13, 1895, the daughter of Billie Franklin and Laura Melissa (Ginger) Clark in Greene County, Arkansas. She was a homemaker and a member of the Seventh and Mueller Church of Christ in Paragould. Susie Davis died in 1992, age 97. She was buried in the Duty Cemetery north of Walnut Ridge.

Susie Clark married Arthur Leroy Davis, born March 10, 1893. Their children: Avis born April 8, 1912, died March 2, 1925; Dora Dorene born November 19, 1914; Miles Leslie born August 18, 1917; Thelma Louise born October 30, 1920; Audrey Faye born March 9, 1923; Charles Edward born February 4, 1925; Richard Dewayne born October 22, 1927; Billie Franklin born August 31, 1930; Carl Samuel born July 6, 1933; Layia Cona Jean "Connie" born July 14, 1937.

Dora Dorene Davis married Deward Miller. They lived at 906 Alice Street in Paragould. Their children: Winsford Lee Miller, Carolyn Houston, Paragould; and Patsy Sollis, Corning, Arkansas. Dora Miller died May 31, 1990, age 75.

Carl Samuel Davis married Vivian Stevens, daughter of Charles Edward and Rosie Katherine Stevens. They live in Paragould. Their children: Samuel, Steven and Tracy.

Leslie Davis lives in Doniphan, Missouri.
Edward Davis lives in North Wilkesboro, North Carolina.
Richard Davis lives in Tulsa, Oklahoma.
Billy Davis lives in Lafe.
Thelma Pillow lives in Paragould.
Faye Wood lives in Harrisonville, Missouri.
Connie Allison lives in Beech Grove, AK.

**DAVIS** – Our branch of the Davis family started when my father William Thomas Davis immigrated to Greene County in 1907 from Tennessee at the age of 16. His older brother Alvin Davis had preceded him there. Working at whatever he could to support himself, he was able to take up farming by renting land and providing a portion of his produce as rental payment. While doing this he met and married my mother Stella (Horne) on July 18, 1915. This union produced 10 children of which there are still six survivors at this date in Oct 2000. My dad spent his entire life farming in the area of Beech Grove, Stanford and lastly Evening Star.

Farming in those days was a hardscrabble existence and they were always at the mercy of weather and bankers. My father was fortunate that he had my Grandfather Horne to help look after him. In 1935 my grandfather Horne bought their first Farmall tractor and in 1936 my dad followed suit with the same make and model. By this time he was farming with three teams of horses and was able to use two teams and their equipment as a trade in for the Farmall F-12 tractor. By 1939 my grandfather Horne had talked Dad into becoming a landowner and had located a farm for him to buy near Evening Star with his backing. This was accomplished and we moved to Evening Star in Jan. 1940. This meant that now we had to switch from the Beech Grove High School to the Delaplaine High School. Some of us were so young that this was of no particular importance, but to my older siblings this was indeed a traumatic move.

During the mid 30s the Methodist church in Beech Grove decided to build a new church. My Grandfather Horne had a reputation as a carpenter and was asked by the trustees to build it. He declined and recommended they hire my Uncle Alvin Davis to build the church and they did. Uncle Alvin would consult almost every night with Grandpa Horne during the construction.

Also during the 30's I remember that my dad ran a one chair barber shop next to the Woodrow Davidson Merchandise store in Beech Grove. He operated this shop only on Saturdays and I often accompanied him. While he cut hair I would play up and down the creek that runs through Beech Grove. The really big thing was that at noon Dad would buy me a bologna and cheese sandwich at Woodrow Davidson's store. Woodrow would always slice the bologna and cheese and it seems in my memory that he cut it at least one half inch thick. It was wonderful because this was something we never got at home. We only had hot biscuits and cornbread three times a day so store-bought white sliced bread was like cake along

*William Thomas Davis laying by corn, Beech Grove 1930.*

with that bologna and cheese. I think the haircut cost a quarter and the sandwich was either a nickel or a dime.

During the depression my dad grew his own wheat. This wheat was cut, shocked and then threshed. I can recall the thresher arriving, pulled by a huge steam tractor. The threshing produced a huge pile of straw and during those days we had mattresses made from that straw. I asked my mother about this and she told me that it took 50 pounds of flour and 20 pounds of cornmeal each week to keep our large family in biscuits and cornbread. All of this on a wood burning cook stove. She also told me that the flour was hidden in the attic, suspended on a platform. I asked her why it was hidden and she said to keep the government from getting it. She didn't know any detail of why, but in researching this I discovered that indeed the United States government did have an anti-hoarding law during the depression and could confiscate your food if they considered it to be in excess. Since most of the food that we consumed was grown on the farm it was always a treat to get anything store bought. Once each year we had cheese and that was during Christmas and once each year we had ice cream and soda pop and that was on July 4th.

I have come to realize over the years that we had a wonderful childhood without radio, electricity and lots of other things we have today. I also realize that the high school education that we received was just about equal to the college educations received by others that I've known over my lifetime. All of my siblings and most all of my classmates moved away from Greene County and excelled in whatever career they chose. I think it was due to the community expectations and the good basic education that we received. We just didn't have the tremendous focus on sports and all the courses that are now the norm.

I left home when I was 16 years of age and with my parents' consent joined the US Army in 1948. I had a wonderful 27-year career, served in Japan and Europe plus the Korean War and the Viet Nam War, retiring in 1975. I retired as a chief warrant officer from the Corps of Engineers and was a nuclear reactor operator and a paratrooper among many other things that I was privileged to be able to do.

*Submitted by Delmer Eugene Davis*

**DAY** – Bertis Edgar Day, born February 28, 1883, in Gibson County, Indiana. He was the son of James Andrew Day and Cassandra Woods. His siblings were: Mahala "Halie," Alzada, Nettie. His brother, David and set of twins sisters died young. After his mother died Bert took care of his father who had suffered a sun stroke. He resumed his schooling later.

*"The Day Girls," Betty, Martha, Nettie and Eva in front of the Day home.*

He married Lovena Francis Bradford, daughter of Samuel Perry Bradford and Susan E. Taylor on September 13, 1907, in White County, Illinois. They had one son, Burtis F. Day, in Illinois (1908) before moving to Greene County in 1909 to the Holly Grove Community.

They lived in the "Bottoms" until Lovena became ill and moved back to Illinois where two daughters, Eva and Nettie were born. Moving back to Greene County in 1914, Lovena said her family told her, "If you ever got your feet wet in Arkansas, you'd always go back."

Bert established his family in the Holly Grove Community and with his carpenter skills built his own home along with several of the homes and stores in the community. They had chosen a homestead location, but when they returned they purchased land closer to the established road and school (Scott Noel and Tom Payne were teachers) that was already at Holly Grove. Bert also cleared timber, worked at the stave mill at Halliday, farmed, and served on the Moring school board for several years. While at the stave mill, he worked with Cull Noel, and also worked together in the Basil Bottoms in lumber snaking logs with Henry Tomlinson who had a team of mules. He supplemented his family's table through farming and his avid interest in fishing and hunting.

On Armistice Day when the whistle blew to announce the end of the war, he and his family were in the field picking cotton and could hear the whistle.

His sister Net (Day) Taylor visited Bert and his family after they had returned to live the second time in Greene County. She was surprised to see the changes in the land. Net thought, "One could just fish from their back porch," from what she had heard about Arkansas.

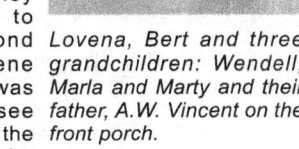

*Lovena, Bert and three grandchildren: Wendell, Marla and Marty and their father, A.W. Vincent on the front porch.*

Their children: Burtis Francis Day, Eva (Day) Dowdy, Nettie (Day) Zollner, Martha (Day) Blackwood, Bradford (died infancy), Ruth Imogene (died 11 years old), Betty (Day) Vincent, and Robert Samuel "Bobby" (died infancy).

Bert died at his home at the age of 82 on the evening of December 24, 1965. He is buried at New Friendship Cemetery. Lovena died at the age of 95 at Arkansas Methodist Hospital on May 26, 1980, and is also buried at New Friendship Cemetery. The youngest daughter, Betty (Day) Vincent, the wife of A.W. Vincent, and three grandsons and their families now reside at the homestead.

**DeBONS** – Jean "John" Benoit DeBons passed on one memory of his trip across the Atlantic from his home in Saviese, Switzerland, as a 4 year old. During the voyage his hat blew off and flew into the ocean. That must have made a real impression because he was travelling from Havre, France, aboard *SS Labrador*, in December 1882. The ship landed in New York on the 28th, and Ben, his five older sisters, one younger sister, and his parents John Germain DeBons and Mary Dubuis DeBons began their life in America. Their destination was Bay City (Linwood), Michigan, where Mary's brother Louis had settled earlier.

The family stayed in Linwood for a time, and Germain learned farming there. Shortly after their arrival in Michigan, son Louis was born April 1883 in Bay City. In 1885 sister Anna was born nearby in Linwood. At that time opportunity existed in Arkansas, near Conway, where many friends of the DeBons family from Switzerland

*Ben and Bertha DeBons with baby Louis Joseph, about 1903.*

had settled. Before 1888 the family moved to Conway to be near their friends, Carl and Veronica Luyet. Their last daughter Dora was born in Conway in 1888. The DeBons home was about six miles east of Conway near Vilonia. Germain apparently had a difficult time learning to farm. He became ill and died on September 30, 1894, and is buried in St. Joseph's Cemetery, Conway.

Sixteen year old Ben became more or less independent after the death of his father. He worked for a time with brother-in-law Adalbert Lachowsky, who married Ben's sister Marie Eugenie in 1895, and operated a hardware store in Conway. Ben later worked for the railroad in Little Rock, learning sheet metal work. He married Bertha Florian of Conway on January 5, 1901. She had been a housekeeper for contractor George Donaghey of Conway, who later became governor of Arkansas and built the Capitol.

Ben and Bertha moved northeast to Newport for a short time where he installed the roof on the courthouse tower. The rising river and flooding in Newport forced him to move Bertha and son Louis, born December 14, 1901, back to Little Rock. They moved farther northeast to Paragould and lived on Fifth between Main and Garland. Louis caught pneumonia and died in Paragould February 18, 1905. He is buried in St. Joseph's, Conway. Their second son, John Benoit Jr., was born on February 1, 1906. The third son, Albert A., was born after they moved to Buttermilk Hill, at 305 East Main Street, on June 29, 1908. Their only daughter, Marie Rosine, September 4, 1910, and Eugene Joseph, March 30, 1913, were born in the new home at East Main and Fifth Avenue.

Ben started DeBons & Company Tinners and Sheet Metal Workers in about 1905. The original shop was on Pruet Street, but by 1908 the shop address was 119 W. Main. Before 1920 the shop moved to 107 W. Highland where it remained next to the ice plant until 1962. The "new shop" was built on N. Third and remained open until 1988. The 1908 Paragould directory has advertisements for DeBons Tinners and for his metal roofing, cornice work, and guttering that never leaks. Ben was in business with another brother-in-law, Ray Sillin, of North Little Rock for a time, and with his own brother Louis until his death in 1929 in North Little Rock. He also opened a tin shop in Jonesboro for a short time.

Ben built his house on 15 acres on Country Club Road in 1917. His children Bennie died of appendicitis at age 15, and Marie passed away at age 23. Son Albert began working in the tin shop in 1921 and continued there until his death in 1988. Youngest son Eugene completed high school in 1932 and joined the company officially. He remained there until 1988 except for a break before the war in the Charleston, South Carolina, shipyard, and for service in the U.S. Navy Seabees in the Pacific Theater. Ben died of a heart attack in Paragould on June 29, 1949, and Bertha lived on in the family home until her death on January 13, 1963.

**DENNIS** – Laurence Thompson Dennis, called "Lar" or "L.T.," was born in St. Francis Township in Greene County, Arkansas, on August 20, 1843, the second of 12 children born to Robert and Elinor (also spelled Eleanor) A. (Thompson) Dennis, early arrivals in Greene County who were wed in Randolph County, August 3, 1840.

Her father, Lawrence Thompson, was the first county clerk of Greene County. He and his wife, Jane (Mattix) Thompson, were married May 15, 1822, in Harrison County, Indiana, before arriving in Arkansas Territory, where Elinor was born in Old Lawrence County, Arkansas Territory, November 19, 1825.

Robert and Elinor moved to Salem Township around 1850, about four miles southwest of Walcott. The Walcott area is where Lar lived his entire life.

He was a successful farmer, a former justice of the peace, and a member of Mount Zion Baptist Church for 72 years, of which he was church treasurer 50 years and secretary of the Sunday school 42 years. He died at home in Walcott from illness due to his advanced age on February 11, 1936, and is buried at Mt. Zion Cemetery.

*Lawrence T. Dennis, Walcott, Arkansas.*

Lar enlisted in and served the Confederacy from 1862-1865, serving in Co. D, 6th Missouri Infantry as well as Co. E, Davies' Battalion, Arkansas Cavalry. Family tradition is supported by a newspaper story that he was the last survivor of 100 men on the Arkansas Ram, which ran the blockade, and was in the siege of Vicksburg at the end of the war.

His first wife was Nancy Ann Newsom, daughter of Sterling and Nancy H. Newsom; Ann and Lar were married in Greene County on February 12, 1865. They had two living children of five born to them: William Pleasant "Will" and Mary Jane "Jennie" Dennis. Ann died in Greene County on December 16, 1874, and is buried at Mount Zion Cemetery.

His second wife, whom he wed April 29, 1875, in Greene County, was Martha Jane Gramling, daughter of Reuben M. and Lucy Ellen (Seay) Gramling Sr. They had 11 children: Lawrence M., who died young; James E; Walter Anderson; twins Leapo Seaton and Gopel Wiley, who died at 2 months of age; Lucy; Thomas J.; Nancy Ann "Nan"; twins Ida, who died at 1 year of age, and Ada, who lived to age 89 and died in 1982; and Laura.

Jane (Gramling) Dennis died July 27, 1915, and is also buried at Mt. Zion.

*Submitted by Patricia (Martin) Dennis*

**DIAL** – Willard Dial, son of Willis Dial and Mary Ann Cullins Dial and Lettie Gibson, daughter of Calvin Gibson and Anna Miller (a twin) Gibson, married and lived in Craighead county and Greene County. They had four daughters: Willadean Dial Fletcher Johnston, Verbadean Dial Ellington, Christeen Dial Sparks and Betty Marie Dial Lyerly. Willard died in 1939 leaving Lettie a young widow with four small girls to raise. She continued to farm with help from friends and neighbors and especially her dad and brother, Henry.

*Seated: Willadean and Lettie, second row: Betty, Verbadean, and Christeen Dial.*

Willadean married Randol "Dutch" Fletcher and has two sons, Willard " Butch" Fletcher and Jim Fletcher. Dutch died in 1992 and Willadean has married Elvis Johnston.

Verbadean married Gordon Ellington and has five children: Judy Carol Reddick; Curtis Ray Ellington; Dennis Gordon Ellington; Danny Edward Ellington and Karen Annette Greene.

Christeen married Murl Sparks and has one son, Ricky Wayne Sparks.

Betty married Harold Lyerly and has three sons: Murray Lyerly, Monty Lyerly and Michael Lyerly.

These grandchildren grew up as a very close family. They got together on all four daughters birthdays, Easter, Mother's Day, Independence Day, Thanksgiving Day, Christmas Day and Mama Lettie's (as we all called her) birthday. They all attended Clark's Chapel Baptist church. They all still live in Greene County.

Willard and Lettie are buried in Clark's Chapel Cemetery. Dutch is buried in Finch Cemetery.

*Submitted by Judy Reddick*

**DIGGS** – On the hutch sits a unique glass bottle. I pick it up, remembering its heritage. As I turn it over and over in my hand, the overhead light reflects the beautiful basket-weave pattern on the clear glass.

There's no stamp or manufacturer's mark of any kind. The glass bottle is empty now, and the small cork has almost been swallowed by the neck. The cork may eventually plop to the bottom, but since the bottle has been in my possession, no one has tried to remove it.

Even though the manufacturer of this bottle is a mystery, it's no mystery as to where the bottle came from or who carried it–a tall, lanky, 17-year-old Tennessee boy, leaving his home in Huntingdon to come to Greene County, Arkansas, to seek his fortune. Before he left, his mother had filled this unique bottle with asafetida and whiskey. This mixture was to be used in the event her boy got sick.

With this one-half-pint whiskey bottle in his hip pocket, he said good-bye to his folks in Tennessee and came to Arkansas, settling two miles east of Walcott on Crowley's Ridge. This boy, James "Jim" Diggs, married Sarah Lamb August 14, 1892, in Paris, Texas. Together, they reared four children: one son, Lawrence Diggs, and three daughters, Edna, Mary, and Ola. Mary married Darrell Willcockson, and they had three children: Goldie, Betty, and yours truly, James. (Our name was subsequently shortened to Willcox, the only explanation being that it was too long to spell and write out).

Most farming on Crowley's Ridge was on a small scale. Grandpa raised sheep, had a cow or two, a flock of chickens, hogs to fatten, and a garden. He grew corn on the best ground, the branch or creek bottoms. Usually cotton was grown on the less fertile land. Lespedeza hay was grown and hauled to the barn for feeding the horses and cows. Grandpa also had geese and picked their breast feathers to stuff the pillows and make feather beds. Peaches and apples were dried on top of the tin roof of the chicken house. Tomatoes, green beans, corn, homemade soup, and blackberries were canned and placed in the root cellar, along with several bushels of Irish and sweet potatoes.

Families grew most everything they needed, except for a few staples, such as sugar, coffee, and tobacco; however, some even grew their tobacco. Many farmers had apple or peach orchards. Grandpa Diggs had a T-Model truck he used to peddle peaches and haul geese to Walcott to sell.

On one trip, he had driven to Walcott to sell some geese. These geese were in a crate in the back of the truck. When he drove up and got out of the truck, a fellow he didn't know came up to him and said, "G- d-- goose." Grandpa thought this man was calling him some bad words until he saw the man was pointing to the geese, and then he repeated what he had said earlier.

Grandpa said this man was a Dutchman and was trying to say, "Got them goose!"

My mother and father, Mary and Darrell Willcox (Willcockson), raised their family in a house located on the west side of Crowley's Ridge. To the east of our house was the ridge, and to the west, flat farming land. We were two miles south of Walcott and one quarter mile north of Mt. Zion Church.

Living this near the church, we were able to hear the church bell ringing, calling us to worship, or if during the week day it began tolling, we knew there was to be a funeral that day. Mother told us the bell tolled once for each year that person had lived.

During a revival, it was customary for visiting preachers and evangelists to stay with a family that lived near the church. One spring our church was having a revival and Brother Bob was the visiting evangelist. After services on Saturday night, Brother Bob came home with us to spend the night.

Now mother had about a dozen white leghorn chickens that were just 2 weeks old. In order to ensure their survival to frying size, they were brought into the house just before dark to save their young innocent souls from Devil Rat and any other lurking demons. We had a double fireplace, one side in the bedroom and the other side in the living room. Surrounding the hearth in the bedroom a little pen was built out of cardboard boxes and a piece of metal sign. The metal sign advertising motor oil was placed over the mouth of the fireplace. This pen was wired, taped and propped in such an engineering feat that had a tornado blown the roof off the house, the chickens' pen would have still been standing. It was in this room that Brother Bob was to sleep.

It was after dark, so the lamp (coal oil, as we called it) had to be lit. After striking a match, lifting the globe, and lighting the lamp, the room was transformed from almost total darkness to such an intense brilliance that one could almost recognize objects in the room. Yes, there 's the cook stove, but, alas, it moved! With relief, I realized that Brother Bob was standing in front of the stove, and it was his shadow that moved. Then mother picked up our sole source of illumination and headed for the bedroom to light the other lamp on the dresser. Like moths drawn to a flame, my sisters and I followed. However, since my sisters were older than I, and also afraid of the dark, I had a difficult time getting to the bedroom first. I think mother was surprised to find me in the bedroom waiting for the second lamp to be lit. My haste was purely with the intention of seeing Brother Bob's reaction when he found out there was a chicken pen in his bedroom!

The extra light illuminated the room to such an extent that only by squinting could one begin to recognize each other. The light also woke the baby chicks. Brother Bob spied the contraption on the hearth from which emanated excited peeps. "What's that you have in there, Mary," Brother Bob asked, pointing to the chicken pen.

"Why, that's my baby chicks. I have to bring them in at night so the rats won't catch them," explained mother, as she moved toward the hearth, holding the lamp high above the pen. Brother Bob followed, bent over the knee-high wall of the pen, picked up a peeping chick. The chick turned his head, studying Brother Bob, contented to be safe in his big hands. Then the axe fell.

"How long will it be before these babies are ready to eat?" he asked.

"Oh! About five more weeks should do it," Mother replied.

There was an audible gasp. An audible gasp that rose from the pen, the house, or from me. As Brother Bob bent over to replace the chick, his shadow fell across the small group of chickens huddled in the corner. The shadow of death. Silence shrouded the room as if some sinister sin had been committed. The seed of fear had been sown in the hearts of these innocent babes and for three days after this horrible night, the chicks were in such an agitated state that they refused to eat.

I have often wondered how Brother Bob began his sermons when he preached in areas far removed from our community. It seems as if I can hear him now as he grasps both sides of the pulpit, and with his deep resonate voice, "Brothers and Sisters! I have slept with the chickens, Yeah! Verily, I have roosted with them!"

Perhaps the cobwebs of time have allowed some embellishment of this tale, but the truth is, Brother Bob did sleep with the chickens.

Mt. Zion Community was a wonderful place in which to be reared.

Most men and boys in this and surrounding communities hunted. Since there were no "NO HUNTING" and "NO TRESPASSING" signs, and no golf courses near by, there was great freedom to be had. There was also an abundance and variety of small game along the edge of pastures, wood lots and crop lands on Crowley's Ridge. Squirrels and quail were held in high esteem and ranked tops as table fare. Rabbits and 'possums were also a boon to the young Captain Nimrod. For a poor country boy, with a dog at his side, had everything he needed for a joyful trek through the countryside. That is, except shells. These were expensive and one was not to be foolish with one's ammunition.

Leaving Lorado traveling west, one leaves the Ridge and begins a gradual descent to rice and bean country. Some of this land is gumbo land and when wet forms a sticky mess; but this level and soil is ideal for growing rice.

During the 1960s and 1970s, some late-maturing varieties of rice weren't ready to harvest until October, and many times weather dictated how long the crop remained in the field. Many fields of rice were harvested just before duck season opened and waste grain left after harvest was a duck magnet. Hordes of migrating ducks from the duck factories of the north descended on these harvested fields to feed. Most of these ducks were mallards.

One farm just west of Lorado and just off Crowley's Ridge is owned and operated by Richard Nutt and his son, Raney. One of their major crops is rice.

Starting in early fall after some of the rice is harvested and stored in giant grain bins, preparation for duck season begins. Anticipation runs high as we cut river cane, and weave it in either chicken wire or hog wire shaped to fit over one of the rice levies. Two or three five-gallon buckets turned upside down serve as a place to sit. Decoys are then checked for strings and weights; boots and hunting coats are inspected.

After all the rice was harvested, the levies were repaired so any rain that fell would flood the fields, giving the ducks an ideal winter habitat.

If one loves to duck hunt, and has a good friend who owns a rice field, one can consider himself fortunate. If that comrade also likes to duck hunt, share the morning sunrise and all the experiences of the hunt, well, what more can anyone ask?

Take the time Raney, Richard's then 10-year-old son, was sharing a wire and cane blind with us. Action had been slow this particular morning, but enormous flocks of blackbirds had streamed overhead continuously. Now rice farmers love blackbirds about as well as icemen love freezing weather, since these birds feed on the rice before its harvest. Therefore, we did some pass shooting. One bird fell behind the blind, crippled and unable to fly.

Raney was asked to give it the coup de grace. As Raney approached the downed bird, bent over to pick it up, the bird became a regular behemoth, wings spread outward, mouth open, malevolent black beady eyes glaring. Raney was so astonished by this unexpected behavior from such a small bird that he stepped backward, his boot making a smacking sound as it came out of the sticky gumbo. He looked at us hesitatingly, buying time.

"Dad, what's he doing?" Raney asked.

"He's going to flog you," Richard replied. "You made him mad!"

After much laughter from the blind and a copious amount of coaxing, Raney finally dispatched the bird.

Raney is now a grown man with a family of his own, but the mere mention of the blackbird attack still stirs up a few laughs.

Years later out blinds became more sophisticated. They were constructed out of plywood, had a top to keep out cold and rain, and also contained a stove for cooking, which was lit on chilly days to help keep us warm. Since we now had a stove in the blind, steak and eggs and hamburgers were often cooked during our duck hunts. It was noted that most of the time our hunting coats weighed more going to our blinds than they did on the return trip. With this setup, no day was considered unsuccessful even if we never killed a duck.

Young duck hunters, like young hunting dogs, sometimes need special training in order to get everything right. This was especially true of Morris.

Morris, Richard's youngest son, soon became an avid duck hunter and enjoyed spending a morning in the blind by himself. He also loved to spend ammunition. He professed he enjoyed being by himself and not having anyone to tell him when to shoot. He loved the independence that grown-ups enjoyed.

One morning Morris was hunting by himself not far from their house. Richard kept hearing a constant barrage of shots from Morris' direction.

"I think I had better go check on Morris," Richard told his wife, Ginny. "He might get over the limit."

As Richard approached, ducks were still circling the decoys spread in front of the blind.

Morris admonished, "Dad, hurry up and get in the blind. You're scaring off the ducks!"

As Richard entered the blind, he noticed several ducks piled up on the floor of the blind. The point system was in effect at that time and Richard saw that Morris had reached the total allotment. "Morris, come on now. You have your limit."

"No, Dad! I want to stay. The ducks are still flying!"

"Now, come on, Morris, you have plenty of ducks," Richard replied.

Richard won this argument and Morris, the young pup, and his dad headed home with a limit of mallards.

Many fond memories are shared in the duck blind. I'll leave it to your imagination to blend sunrise colors, mix in a few clouds, and place the most beautiful colors on the eastern sky as the sun peeps over Crowley's Ridge, illuminating the decoys happily dancing to the sighs of the gentle south wind.

Yes, many days of such wonder and beauty filled our souls, and one seems compelled to declare:

*The Lord certainly wound this day up and turned it loose on us!*

**DIGGS** – Louis Diggs was born in Brookland, AR. His parents were George Mack and Rose Ella Sears Diggs.

Nola was born at Heber Springs, AR. Her parents were Virgil Olonzo and Iva Ladd Eldridge.

Louis and Nola Diggs and daughter, Sherry, moved to Paragould from Cardwell, MO in 1963. Sherry is married to R. Larry Hobbs and they live in Miami, FL.

The Diggs have another daughter, Rosemary Diggs Buck. She is married to Ronald Buck. They moved to Paragould in 1987 from Indianapolis, IN. They have one son, Captain Brian Buck, who is in the US Air Force and is presently stationed in Honolulu, HA. He is married to the former Yvonne Hammick of Cuba, MO. They have one son, Alexandre Buck.

Louis died in Nov 1989 and is buried in Memorial Gardens.

*Submitted by Nola Diggs*

**DIGGS** – Riley Diggs was born in North Carolina on Sept. 3, 1923. He was one of five sons born to Elisha and Elifall Diggs: Thomas, William A., Riley, James M. and Henry.

Elisha moved his family from North Carolina to Henry County, TN, where his uncle, Pleasant Diggs, had settled earlier, southwest of Paris, later known as the Palestine community.

During the move, progress was slow due to dangerous and frequently impassable roads, which had to be cleared of rocks and trees so the covered wagons could proceed. Because the path was so steep at times, someone had to walk on the lower side of the wagons and push to prevent the wagons from overturning. Pine blocks were used to brace the wagon wheels so the horses could rest. Some of these blocks were kept as a remembrance of the difficult journey.

Because of weather conditions this trip was made for the most part in the summer months, sometimes in the evening hours due to extreme heat. Two men led the way, holding lighted pine knots. Cows were tied to the back of the wagons to prevent their escape.

There were provisions for the people and feed for the animals but not all needs could be met so substitutions were made. One such recorded instance was the use of a bread tray as a baby's bassinet.

On Dec. 10, 1846, Riley married Nancy Clark and their daughter Nancy E. Diggs was born on Oct. 13, 1849. On Sept. 10, 1850, Riley's wife died. Riley then married Nancy's sister Sarah Clark. On July 26, 1852, they moved to Weakley County, TN, near McKenzie. Their children born in Tennessee were: Ellen Ora (the only one remaining in Tennessee to marry), Mary Ada, William Henry who died at age 14 months, James Robert, Benjamin Franklin, John Thomas, Josephine Robinson, Myrtie Lee, Harriet Bulah, Charlie Covington and Sara Fessona. The youngest William Warren was born in Arkansas.

*Riley Diggs*

According to an obituary of Riley's daughter, Josephine Thomas, the Diggs' family moved to the Chalk Bluff area in Clay County, AR during the 1870s. About two years later they moved near Rector. During this time, records show that Riley, a Mason in Paris Lodge # 108, Tennessee, visited Wisdom Lodge # 343 in Clayville (now Greenway), AR.

By 1877 the family was living in Greene County in the Bethel community on what was known as the Rose place, later the Melvin place. From there they moved to the Gross place, later the Joe Norton Place.

Riley was a charter member of the first Masonic lodge in Greene County, possibly located at old Bethel, a thriving community at the time. He also served as a justice of the peace in St. Francis Township during the mid- 1870s.

Riley was a Methodist minister, in Tennessee and in Arkansas, where in 1876, he became pastor at New Hope Mission in the Jonesboro District of the White River Conference. As a circuit rider, he traveled many miles on horseback going to his appointments in Clay, Greene and Craighead counties. It is said that Riley also conducted the first revival ever held in Craighead County at Greensboro.

According to family history, Riley had to cross a creek one spring Sunday morning after a heavy rain, became soaked, then preached in his wet clothes. One man present that morning called it a rousing sermon.

Reverend M. M. Smith, a prominent Methodist minister and Reverent T. B. Williamson stopped at Bethel in Dec. 1890, where Riley was to join them for the 100-mile horseback ride to annual conference in Searcy, but Riley was too ill to go. Reverend Smith said that after a short visit and prayer, they shook hands and Riley told them he would see them at the "great annual conference in Heaven." Riley Diggs died a few days later of pneumonia on Dec. 15, 1890. He was buried at Wood's Chapel Cemetery southwest of Paragould.

Sara A. Diggs died on Mar. 6, 1899 and was buried next to her husband.
*Submitted by Ralph Diggs*

**DIGGS/CLARK** – Riley Diggs was born Sept 3, 1823 North Carolina (probably Anson County) son of Elisha and Elifall Diggs. Riley married Dec 10, 1846 Nancy Clark and they had one child, Nancy E. Diggs (Oct 13, 1849 - Feb 3, 1866). Mrs. Nancy Diggs died Sept 10, 1950 and Riley married July 25, 1852 her sister, Sarah Fessona Clark (Sept 18, 1836 NC).

Riley and Sarah Diggs had 11 children while living in Weakley County, TN. They moved to Clay County, AR about 1876 and settled near what is now Rector. The Diggs' family moved to Greene County about 1877. One more child, William Warren Diggs, was born in Arkansas. Other children were:
1. Elen Ora (1854) married George Deck
2. Mary Ader (1856) married J. H. Thomas
3. William Henry (1857)
4. James B. C. (1859)
5. Benjamin Franklin (1861)
6. John T. (1863)
7. Josephine (1865) married J. H. Thomas (her sister's widower)
8. Myrtie (1867) married J. W. Jones
9. Harriett Beulah married J. C. Wood
10. Charlie C. Diggs
11. Sarah Fessona (1874) married M. F. Phillips and
12. William Warren Diggs.

Riley Diggs was a Methodist minister and conducted the first revival ever to be held at Greensboro. He rode on horseback in Clay, Greene and Craighead County on his circuit.

Riley was also a Mason, a charter member of the first Masonic Lodge in Greene County.

Riley Diggs died Dec. 15, 1890 and Sarah Fessona Diggs died March 6, 1899. They are buried in Woods Chapel Cemetery, as well as most of their children, grandchildren and great grandchildren.
*Submitted by Charles Diggs*

**DILLMAN** – The marriage of Dr. James Arl Dillman to Elnita Eileen Justice in 1930 brought together two families with long-time ties to Paragould and Greene County.

Dr. Dillman, born 1895, was the son of Aletha Isabel Dickson Dillman (1870-1938) and Arl Jacob Dillman. His mother, Aletha Dillman, was one of three children of Mary E. Dickson (1847-1932) and James A. Dickson (1845-1892), both of whom were born in Tennessee and moved to Paragould after their marriage. The other two children of this marriage were A. G. Dickson (1867-1909) and Nancy Dickson Thompson. A. G. Dickson studied medicine at Vanderbilt University and in France before returning to Paragould to become one of the town's early physicians.

*Dr. and Mrs. James A. Dillman*

The Dickson family was responsible for the building of the city's first hospital located at the corner of Court and Third Streets. It was first known as The Paragould Sanitarium and later as the Dickson Memorial Hospital. James A. Dickson was also a founding father of the First Methodist Church of Paragould. His daughter, Aletha, founded the woman's group at the church.

After graduating from Paragould High School, Dr. James A. Dillman went to Tulane University to study medicine and served in the U. S. Army medical corps during WWI before returning to Paragould where he joined Dr. Paul Dickson (no relation) in the practice of medicine.

Dr. Dillman married Elnita Eileen Justice soon after she completed her nurses' training at the Mayo Clinic. She worked as a nurse at the Dickson Memorial Hospital until their daughter, Suzanne Elizabeth Dillman Dahling, was born in 1932. Soon thereafter, the Dillmans built a family home at 515 W. Highland Street. Dr. Dillman's medical office was at 114 N. Pruett Street. He was active in civic affairs and was instrumental in planning the construction of the Arkansas Methodist Hospital. He retired in 1946 and moved to California where he lived until his death in 1975.

Eileen Dillman survived her husband, her parents, two brothers and sister, all of whom had moved from Paragould to California. She died in 1993. Her daughter, Suzanne Dillman Dahling, resides in Menlo Park, CA and publishes a technical stock market advisory service.

Mrs. Dillman's parents were the last to move from Paragould to California in 1947. They were Ella Olive Spain Justice (1879-1951) and William Benton Justice (1878-1957). Mrs. Justice ran the Justice Flower Shop at 316 S. Second Street and her husband ran the Justice Monument Shop at 322 S. Second.

The other Justice children were:
1. Bonita (1901-1905)
2. Wayman (1903-1985)
3. Thelma Elizabeth (1908-1982)
4. William Benton Jr. (1913-1989)
5. Jack Thomas (1915-1996)

William Jr. "Bill" was the first to move to California where he became an actor with the screen name of Richard Travis. He starred with Betty Davis in the movie, "*The Man Who Came to Dinner,*" which had its world premier at the Collins Theater in Paragould in 1941.

Mrs. Justice was the daughter of Elizabeth Araminta Barnhill Spain and T. C. Spain, a native of Tennessee. Mrs. Spain was born in Paragould in 1861 and died there in 1881. Mr. Justice's father, Benjamin Franklin Justice (1855-1935) moved to Paragould from Illinois. He established the Paragould Marble Works about 1916, which his son later took over as the Justice Monument Company.

Dr. and Mrs. Dillman's daughter, Suzanne Dahling, who keeps in touch with local friends and regularly attends reunions of her 1950 high school class, has kept the family ties to Paragould.
*Submitted by Suzanne Dahling*

**DODDS** – Allen Dodds was born in Georgia in 1827. His father, James Dodds was born in Virginia. This was disclosed in the 1860 Craighead County Census of Allen Dodds.

James' first marriage was to Sarah Thomason, who lived but a short time after the marriage. James chose for his second wife, Winnie Berden, a Georgian whose Grandfather Penn was an officer in the Revolutionary Army. James Dodds and wives, Sarah and Winnie had 12 children. Allen was one of them. He had five brothers and six sisters. Allen was reared on his father's farm and was educated in the county schools. He married Juliett Saye, who was born in 1826. They began their family in Gwinnett County, GA and had seven children.

The Dodds moved from Gwinnett County to Greene County, AR in 1855. The children born in Georgia were:
1. Rebecca C. (1851)
2. Rhodaphus (1853 GA)
3. Margaret P. (1855 GA)
4. Juliet E. (1859 Craighead County, AR)

In 1859 Craighead County was formed, taking part of Greene County.

The other three children, all being born in Craighead County, were Laura, Alice and Rosa Lee. Juliet, the fourth child, married Edwin G. Barrett on Jan. 20, 1885. Edwin and Juliet E. were the grandparents of Winifred Landrum Bland, who was the great-granddaughter of Allen and Juliet Dodds.

Allen taught school in a log cabin at Philadelphia in the 60s. Uncle Billy Barrett, who attended his school while a lad, told that the pupils would often bar Mr. Dodds out of the building. They would get to school before the teacher arrived and lock the door. When Mr. Dodds came, they refused to let him in until he treated them with ginger cake. Allen also taught at a school near Greensboro.

When Allen and his family came to Greene County, he had been a member of the Baptist Church, while Juliet, his wife, had been a Presbyterian back home in Georgia. Since there were neither of these churches where they settled, they joined a group of residents who were Methodists.

*Allen Dodds*

Allen became a Methodist minister. He gave a part of his land for a church, cemetery and school. The church and cemetery became known as Union Grove.

On June 1, 1861, Arkansas cast its lot with the Confederacy at the beginning of the Civil War. Allen left his family and joined the 13 Arkansas Regiment Company " E" at Harrisburg in Poinsett County right after the first of June 1861. The 13th, under the command of Colonel Tappan, fought their first major engagement at Belmont, Mo. The 13th was the only Confederate Regiment stationed along the Mississippi at Belmont. At the same time that Allen was stationed with the 13th, General Grant was stationed in Cairo, IL with 7500 Union soldiers. His responsibility was to destroy a tremendous steel chain stretched across the Mississippi from Belmont to Columbus, KY where there were high bluffs and the Confederates had constructed heavy embattlements. Grant would not attack Columbus because there were four Confederate regiments and the bluffs on the Columbus side of the river and only one regiment, the 13th, Arkansas, on the Belmont side.

"The enemy came down on the other side of the river (Belmont) at 8:30 today, 7500 strong, landed under cover of gunboats and attacked Colonel Tappan's camp. I sent over three regiments under General Pillow, to his relief. Then at several intervals sent other regiments. It was a hard battle; lasted from 10:30 till 5 this evening. To General Cooper From General A. S. Johnston- Nov 7, 1861."

General Grant was defeated and driven back to Cairo. Second Lieutenant Allen Dodds was wounded by a gunshot and was placed in an old hospital in the town of Columbus. On May 2, 1862, Allen Dodds, Second Lieutenant, was granted a pardon by the Army of the Mississippi by General Beauregard. He traveled back to Craighead County and joined the 4th Arkansas, Cavalry Company "I" under the command of Col. Milton Baber.

On July 4, 1863, Allen fought in the battle at Helena. During the battle a bullet struck him in the left shoulder after glancing off a Bible he carried in a pocket over his heart. He was captured and sent with a group of 725 prisoners to the federal military prison in Alton, IL arriving there July 9, 1863.

Information shown on a Muster and descriptive Roll for Allen Dodds, a private, Company "I", 45th Regiment, Arkansas Cavalry, along with other prisoners of war belonging to the army of the northern sub-district of Arkansas and surrendered on May 14, 1865, by Brigadier General M. Jeff Thompson, C. S. A., commanding said army to Major General G. M. Dodge, U.S.A. commanding, Department of the Missouri. Paroled at Jacksonport, AR June 5, 1865.
*Submitted by Winifred Landrum Bland*

**DOLLINS** – Ed Dollins and Bertha Vera Witt were married on Dec. 24, 1909. To this union three children were born: Bonida Alice (Oct. 29, 1910-Sept. 3, 1946), Chalma May (May 1, 1913-Feb 27, 1980) and J. C. (June 18, 1922-July 1, 1987).

*L-R: Danny, Ed, Jay, Dutch, Lana and Sandra Dollins*

Besides owning Dollins Furniture Company, Ed and Bertha, known locally as Uncle Ed and Aunt Dutch, owned a Shetland pony farm for several years. Ed and his grandchildren rode in Paragould's parades with the ponies hitched to buggies. The pony farm was located on what is now known as Linwood Drive. The Dollins' family was the first family to settle that area. At that time the street was graveled.

Both Ed and Bertha came from large families. They hosted many family reunions at their home on Linwood Drive.

*L-R: Chalma, Sandra, Jimmy, Noma, and Danny Dollins*

Chalma married Noma E. Smith on May 20, 1940. To this union three children were born: Sandra Joe (March 30, 1941), Danny D. (Sept. 4 1943-Jan. 4, 1984) and Jimmy B. (Sept. 29, 1949-May 20, 1964). In 1987 Noma Dollins was crowned Ms. Senior East Arkansas. She then went to the Ms. Sr. Arkansas contest in Harrison, where she placed second runner-up. She won Ms. Congeniality.

Danny was very active in rodeos and was Missouri's Junior Bareback Champion. Danny married Linda Anderson. They helped run Dollins Furniture. People in great need knew Danny for his generosity. Danny and Linda had three children: Jeannie (Nov. 29, 1966), Laura (Oct. 16, 1968) and Cindy (June 14, 1972). They also had two grandkids, Danny (March 29, 1984) and Addison (Oct. 22, 1990).

Sandra Joe married Charles Hollis from Greenway, AR. Four children were born: C. Matt (Jan. 27, 1968), J. David (May 15, 1970), D. Luke (May 5, 1975) and Michael Joseph (Sept 2, 1978). They have five grandchildren.

J. C. married Betty Ross Ratton of Monette, AR. To this union, three children were born: Lana Kay, Jay Chalma and Bonita Ann.
*Submitted by Sandra Dollins Hollis*

**DORTCH** – Harold Roy Dortch was born April 2, 1933, in Clay County, Arkansas. His parents were Roy Albany Dortch and Alice (Wooldridge) Dortch. He graduated from Knobel High School, Knobel, Arkansas, in 1950 and enlisted in the United States Navy. Harold served his country during the Korean conflict until 1954. Upon completing his tenure, he continued his education at the W.R. Moore School of Technology, graduating in 1956.

Mozelle (Lovelady) Dortch was born April 3, 1935, in Clay County, Arkansas. Her parents were Luther and Irmae (Green) Lovelady. She was a graduate of Rector High School, Rector, Arkansas (1953), Draughon's Business College, Memphis, Tennessee (1954), and attended Memphis State University, Memphis, Tennessee from 1954-55. She married Harold Dortch on May 22, 1955. They have two children: Harold Roy "Chip" Dortch Jr. and Kimberley Kaye (Dortch) Varvil. Harold and Mozelle also have four grandsons: Joshua Lynn Noel, Zachary Daniel Noel, Jonathan Cody Noel, and Harold Roy "Trey" Dortch III.

Beginning in 1956, Harold spent two years as a quality assurance technician for Presto, Jackson, Mississippi. He also served as a resident engineer for Thiokol Corporation, Elton, Maryland, (1958-65 and 1965-66) and a liaison engineer for General Electric, Huntsville, Alabama (1965-66).

In February 1972, Harold and Mozelle moved their family to Paragould, Arkansas. That same year, he started his own business, Harold Dortch, Inc. The business was first located in a building on the corner or Highway 412 West and Reynolds Road.

In 1974 Harold and Mozelle purchased two acres on Highway 49 South. They built a home and a new shop building on that land and relocated the corporation. There would be two other additions to the physical premises of Harold Dortch, Inc. to accommodate the growth of the business. Harold sold the corporation in October 1998 and joined Mozelle in retirement. She had retired three years earlier, May 1995, after serving as controller for Farm Credit Services from 1975 to 1995.

Their retirement has been spent working around their new home, traveling, and "spoiling their grandkids."

**DORTCH** – Harold Roy "Chip" Dortch, Jr. was born July 15, 1960, in Huntsville, Alabama. His parents were Harold Roy Dortch and Mozelle (Lovelady) Dortch. Irmae Lovelady, his grandmother, proclaimed upon his birth that he was "a chip off the old block," thus the nickname that would stay with him throughout his life. His family moved to Greene County in 1972. He graduated from Greene County Tech High School in 1978 and received a bachelor's degree in finance from Arkansas State University in 1982. Chip was always proud of the fact that he began working at KHIG radio station when he was 15 years old, worked 55 hours a week to pay for his college education, and completed the task in four years.

Chip met his future bride, Stacy Lynn Clark, during a worship service at First United Methodist Church, Paragould, on August 25, 1991. Three days later, they had their first date at the Candlelight Steak House, followed by the traditional "popcorn night" at her grandparents' home in Jonesboro. Chip proposed to Stacy on October 18, 1991, at the Convocation Center, Jonesboro. The question was "popped" on all four sides of the center score board simultaneously during a Lady Indian volleyball game. That wedding proposal was the first one ever in the history of that building and since that time there have been several more. This seemed as a fitting location since both of them share a love of Arkansas State University athletics, primarily football and basketball. They were married on August 15, 1992.

Stacy was born July 5, 1967, at St. Bernard's Hospital, Jonesboro. Her parents are Rev. Norman Wayne Clark and Doris Linda (McKinney) Clark. She graduated from Rogers High School, Rogers, Arkansas, in 1985, and attended Arkansas State University for two years after that.

December 26, 1995, was the most special day in the couple's life because that was the day that their prayers had been answered with the news of Stacy's pregnancy. On August 18, 1996, Harold Roy "Trey" Dortch III was born at St. Bernard's Hospital, Jonesboro.

Stacy is a multifaceted lady as evidenced by her abilities in the various occupations she has held. She is a licensed dental assistant and beautician, but it is her love of children that has led her to become a teacher's aide at Paragould Junior High School.

Chip spent 16 years in the banking industry before leaving for a sales career in the private sector (as he puts it, "...same profession, different products"). His love and passion comes in playing an active role in Trey's life, as well as becoming more involved with the affairs of his church. Nothing is more important to him than his faith, family, and friends; values he shares with Stacy and that they will try to instill with Trey.

**DOWLER** – Bert Dowler born Oct 6, 1894, Phelps County, MO, the son of Thomas Franklin Dowler and Mary Jane "Judy" Brown McDaniel. On Sept. 22, 1922, Bert married Ruth Mae Wilson (July 4, 1903) in Greene County, AR) the daughter of Charles Wilson and Mary Jane Howder.

Bert died Jan 5, 1946. He was a WWI veteran. Ruth died Jan 23, 1992. They are buried in Linwood Cemetery, Greene County, AR.

Their children were:
1. Marie, married Winston Martin
2. Sena, married Jim Cole
3. Tony married Myrtle Mae Askins
4. Bertha married Vealus Davidson
5. Jack married Wanda
6. Bill married Georgia Gonser
7. Jim
8. Harold married Mary Ida Brasher
9. Robert married Cora Mac White
10. Wayne married Loretta White
11. Jerry married Joyce Fortenberry
12. Gloria Jean married Cloys Lacy
13. Larry married Bettie Scott
14. Cheryl married David Jones

Bert Dowler's father, Thomas Franklin Dowler, was born Nov. 18, 1840 in Knox County, TN. His parents were William Dowler and Susan McCaughen. Thomas moved with his family to Crawford County, MO and was listed on the census for that county in 1850.

On Dec. 27, 1864, Thomas married Nancy Cuthbertson. After Nancy's death, Thomas was married on March 16, 1868 to Mary Hicks. Children from this marriage were:
1. Cora
2. George
3. William
5. Isabelle
6. Rose
7. Samuel.

Mary died in 1885 and Thomas was married on Oct 11, 1890 to Mary E. "Judy" Brown McDaniel. Judy was the daughter of Richard Brown and Martha Jane Glenn. Judy's first husband was killed in a hunting accident and left her with four children: Samuel, Emily, Cora and James.

Thomas and Judy moved to Greene County, AR about 1905 and settled on land between Hooker and Beech Grove. Emily McDaniel (daughter of Judy) died in Greene County and is buried in Meadows Grove Cemetery.

*Bert and Ruth Dowler*

Children of Thomas and Judy were:
1. Jake Dowler (March 29, 1891 Cuba, MO) married Clydie Cole. After her death, Jake married Gertie Mosby Hooker
2. Bert Dowler (Oct 6, 1894 Phelps County, MO) married in Greene County, AR to Ruth Mae Wilson
3. Rhodes David "John" Dowler (Jan 15, 1895 MO) married Fannie Meadows
4. Lewis Dowler (Feb 1898-before 1910).

Judy died April 3, 1925 and is buried at Oak Forrest Cemetery near Bland, MO. Thomas died March 25, 1931 and is buried at Bixby, OK.

Ruth Dowler's father, Charles Jackson Wilson, was born July 5, 1864, in Knox County, IN. He was the son of Thomas B. Wilson and Narcissus Autler. On Jan 19, 1896, in Vincennes, IN, Charles married Mary Jane Howder, born Jan 30, 1875. Mary Jane was the daughter of Christopher Howder and Mary Jane Wilson.

In about 1896, Charles and Mary Jane bought a farm west of Hooker, in Greene County, AR. Around 1900, Charles built a log barn which still stands on the property. In 1903, Charles contracted with Stark Brothers to plant an apple orchard. Stark Brothers supplied the trees and, in return, they received a percentage of the fruit that was harvested.

Later, Charles and Mary Jane moved to Flint, MI and Bert and Ruth became the owners of the farm. Except for about two years when her parents lived in Paragould, Ruth spent her entire life on this farm.

The children of Charles and Mary Jane Wilson were: Roy who married Myrtle Weddington; Ralph who married Louella; Ruth who married Bert Dowler; Robert who married Helen Shannon; Bert who married Jean Smith; and Bertha who married Ewell Williams.

Charles died July 31, 1948. Mary Jane died Sept 14, 1958. They are buried in Linwood Cemetery, Greene County, AR.

This farm has been in the family for over 100 years and is now owned by eight of Bert and Ruth Dowler's children.

*Submitted by Larry Dowler*

**DUNN** – Frank Marion Dunn (1851-1915) and Laura Lee (Jordon) Dunn (1867-1918) came to Greene County in the 1880s from Virginia.

They bought a farm in Gainesville, AR and had a family of 10 children,
1. Frances (Dunn) Wood (1885-1920)
2. Bert (1887-1930)
3. Rosco (1888-1915)
4. Emet (1890-1958)
5. Clarence (1895-1909)
6. Ray (1898-1914)
7. Lemuel (1900-1921)
8. Charlie (1903-unknown)
9. William "Bill" (1906-1989)
10. Lauretta (Dunn) Maberry (1910)

Although they were of the Baptist faith, they attended the Methodist Church, because it was the only church in Gainesville at the time.

After Mr. Dunn died in 1915, the farm home burned. Mrs. Dunn became ill and died in 1918. By then Bert was married and living in Paragould with his wife Georgia and their children Leon, Marie, Martha and Bud. Emet was also married and had moved to El Paso, TX. The remaining children were sent to live with relatives in De Soto, MO. Bill returned to Paragould when he was 15 years old and lived with his brother Bert and his family. He worked at Kirby's Drug Store and graduated from Paragould High School in 1925. That was the first class to graduate from the new school building located at the corner of West Court and Seventh Street. He wrote the dedication to the new building and the class poem.

*Frank Dunn Family, 1911–Gainesville, AR. Seated, far left: Frank Dunn, Laura Dunn holding infant Lauretta (Dunn) Maberry. Seated on ground, far left: William "Bill" Dunn. Back row, second from left: Georgia Dunn, Bert Dunn, Emet Dunn and Frances Dunn.*

Bill married Addie Jean Pemberton on Dec. 23, 1928. Addie Jean was born Jan. 14, 1912 in Poplar Bluff, MO and came to Paragould as an infant.

They had a daughter, Mary Ann, born on March 4, 1931. She married Eldon Stickler on June 9, 1951 and they had three children, Penny (1953-1962), Andy (1956) and Laura (1964). Also three grandchildren, Stacie, Lindsey and Katie Stickler. They still reside in Paragould.

Bill was a pharmacist and worked at City

Drug Store for many years before opening a store of his own, Dunn-Lane Drug Company. He served in the U.S. Navy during WWII.

Lauretta returned to Paragould in 1928 and attended Paragould High School, then married Elmer Maberry of Paragould in Feb. 1930.

Elmer was a decorator for Joseph's, Graber's and later Belk department stores. He painted the advertisement backdrop that still hangs at the Collins (Capitol) Theater. Lauretta opened a dress shop on North Pruett Street in the early 1950s, which bore her name.

A U. S. Army veteran of WWII, Elmer died Dec. 20, 1989. Lauretta now resides a Paragould Nursing Center.

**EAKER** – Jonas Eaker was born July 13, 1813, the son of Christian/Christopher and Jane (Wilson) Eaker in North Carolina.

His family moved to Cape Girardeau County, MO when he was a small boy. On April 24, 1831 he married Nancy Bailey. They had eight children.

On Feb. 9, 1835 the first county court of Stoddard County, MO met at A.B. Bailey's house and Jonas Eaker was the county clerk and in 1855 he was county judge of Stoddard County, MO.

He served in the Confederate Army in 1861 and 1862.

After his wife died he moved to Greene County, AR and married Charity Jane Thomasson born July 4, 1837 in Tennessee, daughter of Arnold and Charity Thomasson. They had seven children:
1. Arnold Lee (Feb 26, 1865)
2. Eleanora A. (Jan. 11, 1867)
3. Cornelia T. (1869)
4. Virginia C. (Nov. 22, 1871)
5. Jonas C. N. (Oct. 27, 1874)
6. Tilden Scott (Dec. 29, 1876)
7. Minnie A. (Jan 1880)

Jonas farmed and also served as justice of the peace for Union Township and a probate judge in Greene County, AR.

Jonas died July 4, 1893 and Charity Jane died Oct. 26, 1908. They are buried at the Eaker Cemetery in the Camp Ground community.

There are several of Jonas and Charity's great-grandchildren and great great grandchildren living in Greene County today.

*Submitted by Sandra Keeling*

**EDRINGTON** – Larry Edward Edrington and Sharon Grace Reddick were united in marriage Dec. 9, 1961. Reverend Wesley Ryles performed the ceremony at the Revival Center Pentecostal Church in Paragould. After the wedding we said our farewells to family and friends and traveled to Sandwich, IL to begin a journey that has lasted almost 39 years thus far.

*Sherry and Larry Edrington*

Larry was born July 12, 1943 to Owen Herschel and Wilma Addie (Faughn) Edrington. He has three brothers, Junior Edgar, Johnny William and Billy Dale. All four children were delivered at home. The family lived on a cotton farm in the Bard community. Larry and his brothers grew up in a loving Christian home. Their mother was a wonderful homemaker and enjoyed gardening. Their father was a sharecropper, later employed by the Greene County Road Department as a gravel truck driver.

Larry realized at an early age the importance of hard work. He chopped and picked cotton for his father as well as others in the community. The money he earned was used for school and other necessities. During the summer he enjoyed fishing. Larry loved to visit his grandparents, John and Janie Edrington. The couple lived beside the Big Slough ditch. He and his grandmother spent many memorable occasions fishing together. She was a special part of Larry's childhood.

As a youngster he liked to hunt during squirrel season. His parents permitted him to own a shotgun at the age of eight. He liked winter the best. His favorite pastime was trapping.

*Josh Edrington, Madelayne Ellis, Shannon Edrington.*

Larry's formal years were spent at Lakeside, Alexander and Greene County Tech Schools. He was an honor student and a member of the Tech Beta Club. Involved in school sports, he played basketball and baseball.

As a teenager the big thing was driving and cruising Paragould with his cousin, Berlin Walker. Larry was 17 when we became engaged and a year later married Sharon, daughter of Marion Carlos and Beaulah Dean (Fox) Reddick, born July 27, 1944 in Royal Oak, MI. She returned to Greene County in 1945.

I was blessed with two sisters, Fretsie Virginia and Donna Lynn and four brothers, Marion Franklin, Carlos Edward, Henry Michael and Phillip Lee.

My mother was a homemaker. She enjoyed quilting and loved visits with her sister, Lula Allen and brother-in-law, Herbert. My father was a WWII veteran. He was an excellent draggling operator.

When I was nine my Grandmother Gertie May Fox lived with my family. She always had long hair worn in a bun. I was of the opinion she needed a new hair do. With scissors in hand I began the task of creating a new look. Grandmother began to laugh with each snip. She was laughing so hard everyone thought she would be sick. Needless to Grandma Fox never wore her hair in a bun again.

I enjoyed visits with my Uncle Milo and Aunt Blondale Stevens. Also, Aunt Dovie Stevens who lived in Puxico, MO.

In summer I spent time with my grandparents, Roosevelt and Artie Reddick. They lived in a log house in the Mounds community. My grandmother always made the best chocolate gravy. I have many delightful memories of their home.

Growing up I worked in the cotton fields with my brothers and sisters. My parents relocated several times in order for my father to find work. My education began in Michigan. I later attended Elmwood and L. W. Baldwin in Paragould. My favorite teacher was Mrs. Beasley who taught sixth grade.

My family moved to the Mounds community. I continued my schooling at Alexander and Greene County Tech High.

I was 16 when Larry and I were engaged. We are thankful to God for our rich inheritance and cherished memories of time past.

*Submitted by Sharon Edrington*

**EDRINGTON** – Our parents Larry and Sharon Edrington were married Dec. 9, 1961. Dad was employed at Emerson Electric Company where he retired after 37 years of service. Dad was an excellent mechanic. He loved racing his 57 Chevy at George Ray's drag strip. Several trophies were won. Our father has always been devoted to his family.

Besides caring for children and our home, our mother was employed as a C.N.A. for the Paragould Nursing Center and Greene County Health Dept. Also employed at Crowley's Ridge College as a cook. Her greatest achievement is being a loving Christian mother and grandmother. Mom and dad love White River and enjoy excursions with Aunt Revonda and Uncle Bill Edrington.

Our oldest brother is Clinton Blake, born July 23, 1964 at former Community Methodist Hospital in Paragould, delivered by Dr. Andrews. Clint loved motorcycles and music. His formal education began at Lakeside elementary. The family moved to Marmaduke in 1971 where he attended grade school and junior high. In 1976 our parents bought a farm in the Stanford community and Clint transferred to Stanford High School. Later he attended Crowley's Ridge College and Arkansas State University. He worked in agriculture and did custom harvesting. Clint married Lorie D. Smith of Jonesboro in 1993. She also attended Crowley's Ridge College and Arkansas State University. They have one son, Joshua Mark Twain Edrington, born May 5, 1994 at St. Bernards Hospital in Jonesboro, AR. Josh is a marvelous child. They reside in Colorado.

*Clint, Lorie and Josh Edrington, Larry and Sharon Edrington, Rickey and Heather Ellis, Chris and Dianna Edrington.*

On Sept. 30, 1968 Christopher Shannon, our second brother, was born. Dr. Asa Crow at Community Methodist Hospital in Paragould delivered him. Chris was very inquisitive and loved taking things apart to see what made them work.

He played rhythm guitar with a young local band called "Gold River" when was 15. His education began at Marmaduke, later transferred to Stanford and completed elementary and high school in 1986. Chris attended Black River VoTech before starting to Arkansas State University where he graduated with a B. S. in Electrical Engineering in 1999. Honors included National Deans list, A.S.U. Presidents list, Deans Lists and a member of Phi Kappa Phi. He presently attends the University of Missouri-Rolla with his Masters Degree in Electrical Engineering in progress. Chris married the former Dianna Lynn Summitt of Paragould July 1, 1988. Dianna also attended Arkansas State, graduated with a B. S. degree in Business Accounting and received her C.P.A. status shortly thereafter.

The have one son, Shannon Garrett, born March 4, 1996 at Arkansas Methodist Hospital in Paragould. Dr. L. L. Shedd delivered him. Shannon is an exceptional boy. They are expecting a second child in Feb 2001.

The family is active in the Baptist church and dedicates their musical talents to the worship of God.

Heather Dawn, the youngest of three children, was born Nov. 23, 1973. Dr. Asa Crow delivered her at Community Methodist Hospital. Heather was a wonderful child. She always enjoyed church, attended Marmaduke Church of Christ when she was small and as a young adult attended Commissary and Seventh and Mueller Church of Christ.

She liked cheerleading and beauty pageants and was a member of Stanford and Greene County Tech bands. Heather attended school at Stanford through the 10th grade, transferred to Greene County Tech and graduated in 1992. She attended the College of Cosmetology and received her beautician's license and was employed at Stacy and Company.

On May 22, 1994 Heather married Ricky Leroy Ellis. They are both employed at Emerson Electric in Paragould. Ricky attended Arkansas State University before their marriage. The couple has one child, Madelayne Grace, born on Feb. 21, 1997 at St. Bernard's Hospital in Jonesboro, AR. She is absolutely charming. The family attends Stanford Baptist Church.

In 1982 our parents became involved in foster care. We have one foster brother, Keith Collier. He resides in Rockford, IL. He is the father of four children.

We are grateful God put us together as a family.

**ELLINGTON** – Chester Ellington was the only son of Ervin Ellington and Lela Davis (a twin) Ellington. Chester had a sister, Eva Ellington Pack, who lived to adulthood and had 10 children, Bessie, who died as a child, and another sister who died in infancy.

Chester married Susan Woolverton of Tennessee and they had four children: Juanita Almajean, Chester Alton, Ervin Daulton "Cotton" and Gordon Gustus. They lived in the Finch community and Chester farmed until the boys served in the armed services and then he drove a bus and worked in maintenance for the Greene County Tech School District.

*Gordon Ellingron, Cotton Ellington, Chester and Susie, Almajean Perry, Alton Ellington.*

Almajean married J. D. Perry and they moved to St. Louis. Alton married Wava Herren and they, too, moved to St. Louis after Alton served in the Navy during WWII. They lived in the same house, Alma jean upstairs and Alton downstairs. J. D. died in 1964 and Wava died in 1974.

Cotton married Emma Dee Rhea and they lived in Craighead County, first Jonesboro and then Brookland. Gordon married Verbaddan Dial of the Finch community and they have lived in Greene County all their lives. Cotton and Gordon both served in Germany with the Army.

Almajean had one daughter, Patricia Joann; Alton had four children: Lola Mae, Rhudonna Louise, Allen Ray and Neva Pagetta.

Cotton had four children: Shelia Nioka, Terria Lisa, Scott Anthony and Christopher Gus. Cotton died in 1999.

Gordon had five children: Judy Carol Ellington Reddick, Curtis Ray, Dennis Gordon, Danny Edward and Karen Annette Ellington Greene. Curt lives in Blytheville and Danny lives in Mountain Home; however, the other three are still in Paragould.

Judy married Barry Dale Reddick and they have three children: Bryan Dale Reddick, April Leigh Reddick Miller and Ashley Dawn Reddick Shelton.

Dennis married Carla Ruth Boyd and they have one daughter, Kersten Ley Ellington.

Karen married David Truett Greene and they have two daughters, Mallory Kathryn and Meredith Karole.

Chester, Susie J. D. and Cotton are buried in Clark's Chapel Cemetery. Wava is buried in Liberty Cemetery.

*Submitted by Judy Reddick*

**EMPFIELD** – The restoration of the Greene County Courthouse is dear to my heart. Lynus J. Empfield, my grandfather, was a pioneer jeweler in Paragould and made the precarious climb to the tower to make adjustments to keep the clock in perfect time for many years.

Lynus J. Empfield, known as " L. J." was born to Henry and Kathrine Johnston Empfield, at Penn's Run, PA in 1866. The parents' ancestors had come to America in the 1700s from the Rhine River Valley.

Henry took his family westward and in Illinois volunteered in the Civil War. He was assigned to Gen. Sherman's command. Following a crippling accident, he was discharged and the family continued to Hannibal, MO where Lynus grew to manhood. He became a bookbinder and was employed in the U. S. Printing Department in Washington D.C.

Returning to Hannibal, he married Jennie Laura Grady, a pretty girl whose family had come to Hannibal from Delmar, MD. Their children were: John Robert, Mary Lemuel, Mildred Marguerite and 10 years later, Harry.

*Mildred Marguerite Empfield and Mary Lemuel Empfield*

*L. Buddy Bevill and Harry Empfield*

Lynus had learned watch making and opened a shop, but soon sought better business opportunities in Paragould in the early 1900s.

He established a home at 310 West Garland Street and opened a jewelry business at 104 West Emerson with a partner, Mr. R. E. Lackner. A later partner was Mr. J. V. Landrum.

He prospered making frequent business trips to St. Louis for supplies and special items for his customers. He also found time for civic activities, serving as a councilman and alderman.

*Jennie Gardy and Lynus Johnston Empfield.*

All went well until his oldest son, John Robert, came back from service in the Spanish-American war. He had volunteered, served three years in Cuba and Alaska, but had contracted tuberculosis. The family was devastated. His father took him to New Mexico, seeking a cure, but he died at age 25 in 1908. To make matters worse, Jennie Laura fell victim to the same disease.

The girls, Mary and Mildred, were sent to Galloway Girls' School in Searcy, but were concerned for their mother and returned home after one term. Their mother died in 1912.

Soon after her death, Mary married Burleigh Bevill, a pro-baseball player from Paragould, later moving to Illinois, where she died at 87 years of age.

*Mildred Marguerite Empfield*

Her surviving children are: John and Richard Bevill and Ruth Purrman near Mulberry Grove, IL. A sister, Mrs. Mary Sherman, lives in California.

Harry, the youngest Empfield, died in Chicago, IL in 1964 and left no children.

My mother, Mildred, married Carl Louis Price, who had been sent to Paragould from Little Rock, by the Iron Mountain R. R. as a locomotive fireman. They soon were transferred back to Little Rock, where I was born in 1914.

My mother was diagnosed and spent a short time at the Booneville Sanatorium, but died in her home in 1915. Lynus Empfield was left lonely and bereft of family. His health soon failed and he disposed of his business to Mr. T. J. Colling. He died in 1916.

Lynus, Jennie Laura, John, Mildred and Harry are buried in Linwood Cemetery.

I was sent to live with my Price grandparents until my father re-married in 1918. My stepmother was Chlora Bryant, a schoolteacher. She was a won-

*John Robert Empfield*

derful stepmother. I always longed to know more of my grandparents' family Ruth Purrman, Mary Bevill Empfields' daughter, helped me in my research.

No one else attended the courthouse clock and it finally stopped at "25 minutes past eight", having run for 35 years.

*Submitted by Mrs. Marguerite P. Gardner*

**EUBANKS** – James Eubanks, January 8, 1800, South Carolina, February 29, 1879, Greene County, Arkansas, married about 1814 Frances Massey, 1810 South Carolina, 1864 Greene County. Their children born Georgia were: William P., 1814; Drewry Alvin, 1827; John Buck, August 19, 1830; Amanda Arantha, December 2, 1832; Frances, 1836; Talitha Jane, 1839; Charles Posey, March 4, 1844; E. Johnson, 1845; and Armina Lavonia, September 11, 1846.

James married second Anne Rowe, widow of H.W. Pitts, and one son Alexander Stephen was born February 28, 1866, Greene County. Anne died; James married third Mrs. Cynthia A. Compton on March 16, 1869, Randolph County. Five of James' children predeceased him.

William married Sarah before 1846 in Georgia. He enlisted with kin in Company "D," Davies Battalion, Arkansas Cavalry. Children born in Georgia: Frances, 1846; John Pickney, 1848; Julus I., 1852; Sonora Sarah, 1854; Joseph Buchanan, December 1857. In Arkansas: Allie Aminta, May 1860; James "Posey," May 1863; Henry Gordon, March 1865; Thomas Lee, June 15, 1869. Probate records found in Books two and three, Greene County.

Alvin mined gold in California, served as sheriff of Greene County and captain of the home guard during the Civil War. He married in Georgia about 1845 to Sarah and died October 1879 Greene County. Children: James, 1846; John C., May 1850; Charles C., October 1857; Manta Buna Bernice, October 1858; Vesta, 1859; Jackson Nebraska, June 16, 1860; William, June 1862; Andrew Marion, 1865.

John enlisted in Company "F," 48th Alabama Infantry, was captured at Gettysburg July 2, 1863; held at Johnson's Island, Ohio; and released on amnesty May 12, 1865. He married first before 1852 in Alabama to Sarah; second to Elizabeth Carolina Hoffer, widow of Jackson Marion Hicks Sr. John died 1909 Bronte, Coke County, Texas. Children of first marriage: James E., January 1853; George William Alfred, February 14, 1855; John Lemuel, 1856; Joel Joseph, March 1862; Mary Nancy Ann, 1866. Second: Alvin L., 1874; Amanda Elizabeth, March 14, 1877; Anderson Mack, November 30, 1879; Charles Alvin, May 26, 1881; Belva C., June 22, 1885.

Amanda married about 1852 in Georgia first Andrew Jackson Moore, died during Civil War; second May 4, 1863, Greene County to Jonathan Futrell (served in Davies Battalion). By 1868 family lived in Lampasas County, Texas, where Amanda died on January 4, 1910. Children: first–James William, September 25, 1853; John Lemuel, October 4, 1855; Frances V., 1859; Charles E., 1862. Second: Jeptha J. 1868.

Talitha married as second wife about 1867 in Georgia to Drury Flurrow Hall. Children: Allie Lavonia, May 1868; Margaret Talitha, April 1870; William F., April 1870; Alvin Lee, May 12, 1874; Alice Longstreet, September 12, 1876. Talitha probably died in Greene County.

Charles Posey enlisted Company "D," second Arkansas; wounded at Shiloh. He married first in Georgia to Margaret C. Morrow (died Lampasas County about 1883); second September 25, 1892, to Dora A. Moss, the widow Brown. Children: first–Ora B., 1867; Frances Delila, May 11, 1870; Georgia S. V., 1877; Mattie Ann, April 7, 1877; Margaret C., 1889. Second: Lonnie Earl, (adopted) January 1893; Carl Carlton, January 26, 1894; Clara Olcie, August 12, 1896; Leedie Lavesta, December 1898; Thomas James, January 24, 1902; L. D., December 18, 1904.

E. Johnson enlisted with brother William. He married Eveline. Children: John William, January 24, 1866; Franklin, April 1870 Randolph County. Johnson's heirs were living in Comanche County, Texas, when his father died in 1879.

Armina married first 1864 in Greene County to Jepetha Futrell; second January 31, 1878, to Thomas Randolph Hall, stepson of Armina's sister Talitha. Armina died January 5, 1910, Paragould. Children: first– James Daniel, February 14, 1866; Junius Marion, August 14, 1870; Jeptha Armina Exea, 1876. Second– Zeulia Cordelia, November 18, 1878; Zahn Zera, July 9, 1881, Ira Ishmel, January 19, 1885; Arta Elza, December 25, 1887.

*Submitted by Patty McGinty*

**EUBANKS** – John Buchanan was the third son of James "Jimmy" Eubanks and Frances Massey. He was born Aug. 19, 1831 in Cherokee County, GA. He married Sarah (unknown). John appeared in the 1860 census of Blount County, AL along with his wife and three sons James, William A. and John. He enlisted in the 48th Alabama Infantry Regt. in 1862 in Auburn, AL. Promoted to Sub-Lieutenant and then 1st Lieutenant. John and the 48th were transferred to General Thomas "Stonewall" Jackson's Division of the Army of Northern Virginia. Their first battle was at Cedar Mountain near Culpeper, VA in 1862 and they were in every campaign until Gettysburg where he was captured July 2, 1863 and sent to Johnson's Island prison camp in Ohio July 18, 1863. He was released in 1865 after oath of Amnesty.

*John Buchanan Eubanks 1831-1909*

After the war he followed his father, James Eubanks and his brother, Drewry Alvin Eubanks, to Greene County. His brother, Drewry, had been sheriff of Greene County from 1862 to 1864. John appeared on the 1870 census with his wife Sarah and children: James B., William A., John L., Joel L. and Nancy A. Sarah died about 1871. John married Elizabeth Carolina Hopper about 1873. They moved to Bronte, Coke County, TX and had six children: Alvin, Belire, Amanda, Anderson, Charles and Belva. Carolina died about 1891 in Bronte, TX. John's granddaughter Averil, aged 81, remembered her grandfather in a letter she wrote in 1986. One day he went rabbit hunting and after a while sat down to rest. He leaned back against a tree and died. When his horse returned without him, Uncle Alex went out and found him. He died in Aug. 1909.

*Flora Elizabeth Green Eubanks*

*Very early photo of Paragould. Ox cart on Pruett looking west on Court. (Court house in background–dirt streets.)*

William A., John Buchanan and Sarah's second son, was born Feb 14, 1855 in Blount County, AL. He married Flora Elizabeth "Betty" Green, born Dec. 22, 1856, in Forsyth County, GA, daughter of John William Green and Rachel Minerva Mooney Green on March 22, 1873. Flora Elizabeth was named for her mother's sister, Flora Elvira Mooney, who married Pleasant Green Light who settled northwest of Walcott. This area was named Light AR after the Light family.

William A. and Flora settled near Beech Grove and had the following children:
1. Sonora Jane "Jennie" (1875-1942)
2. John Lemuel (1876-1954)

*The family of William A. and Flora Elizabeth Green Eubanks–1895. First row: Claudia Mae, Mary Eva, Flora Elizabeth holding Dona Clifford, Frances M., Sonora Jane. Second row: Rufus Clinton, Cora Gertrude, John Lemuel, Alice Asalee, Albert A.*

3. Claudia Mae (1878-1937)
4. Cora Gertrude (1880-1951)
5. Rufus Clinton (1882-1946)
6. Alice Asalee, a twin (1884-1962)
7. Albert A., a twin (1884-1919)
8. Frances M. (1886-1926)
9. Mary Eva (1888-1926)
10. Dona Clifford (1890-1972).

Flora Elizabeth "Betty" Green Eubanks, later known as Grandma Betty, was widowed at age 35, but through her strength and hard work, she kept the farm and her 10 children together. The older children were a source of strength, not only to her but the younger children. The oldest son, John Lemuel, often drove oxen to Gainesville to have the wheat ground into flour. Grandma Betty spent many hours at her spinning wheel making yarn and thread to use for the family. Many descendants of her 10 children are still living in Greene County.

For any who knew Grandma Betty they would remember she always wore long flowing skirts and usually wore a cape instead of a coat. She was truly a pioneer woman, with much strength, perseverance and faith, which were passed on to many in the generations that have followed.

*Submitted by Helen Eubanks Funk*

**EUBANKS** – John Lemuel Eubanks was the son of William "Ap" and Elizabeth (Green) Eubanks. He was the grandson of John William and Rachel (Mooney) Green.

John William Green was honored in 1998 for his heroism in the Civil War. He fought in 27 out of 28 battles as a Confederate soldier.

*Lem and Julia Ellen Eubanks and their first four children: Grace, Gladys, Neal and Beatrice*

Lem was one of 10 children:
1. Sanora married William Garner
2. Claudia married (1) Henry Dehart (2) Daniel Smith
3. Gertie married (1) Benjamin Askins (2) William Belk
4. Rufus married (1) Cole (2) Eva Brekenridge
5. Albert married Brekenridge
6. Alice married (1) Brashears (2) Watson (3) Wilson (4) Fryer
7. Francis married Brecken-ridge
8. Eva married Hick McAntosh
9. Dona ma-rried Arthur Taylor

Lem married Julia Ellen King, the daughter of W. G. and Rachel (Smith) King. Julia had two brothers James H. King and Hayden King. She had one half brother, John Brashers.

Lem was a farmer and raised his family at Beech Grove, AR. They had eight children. Julia died with the birth of their last child, Imogene. Imogene died six weeks later. The remaining children ranged in age from three to 15. Oldest to youngest they are listed:

*Jimmie and Faye*

1. Grace married Prentiss Breckenridge
2. Gladys married Bailey Morrow
3. Neal married Neva Breckenridge
4. Beatrice married Earl Orick
5. Jimmie married Edith Owens
6. Faye married Harvey Williams
7. Gus married Pauline Lloyd

Times were hard and the family survived by the older ones taking care of the younger ones. They all had many stories to tell. A favorite was when Jimmie and Faye were playing horse with rope for reins and knocked all of the family dishes off of the table. Only one pitcher was saved. Lem had to go to town to buy dishes so they could have supper.

Later Lem married Martha Smith Owen, widow of Wash Owen. Martha had one son George Owen.

The second generation moved to Paragould. Neal, Jimmie, Gus and their brother-in-law Bailey Morrow were dairy farmers. They bottled and delivered milk over Paragould for several years.

The Eubanks family was a close family and enjoyed hunting, fishing and family get togethers. Most of them settled in the Greene County area. Sister, Grace, relocated to El Paso, TX. When she would return to Paragould for a visit, the family would get together to visit with her. The family also sought out any reason to get together to fry fish and hushpuppies.

*Baby Gus*

*Submitted by Linda Arnold*

**EUBANKS** – John William Eubanks, January 24, 1866, Greene County, Arkansas, August 18, 1936, Fry, Brown County, Texas, was orphaned as a young man and moved to Comanche County, Texas, to live with his cousins Lavonia and Maggie Hall's family. While hauling freight into Camp Colorado he met and married September 25, 1884, Coleman County, Texas, Betty Ann Daniel Swain, September 1859- October 17, 1933, Grosvenor.

Working together they purchased a home place which had a log cabin on the Brown-Coleman county line establishing a large orchard, tanks with windmills, gardens, and a clapboard home. John added a boardwalk from the house to the kitchen where Betty would not have to walk in mud. John was a master carpenter and did his own blacksmithing. He raised cattle, hogs, and chickens for personal consumption. Planting the crops was by mule team pulling a walking plow with the children helping. After building the new house, the family used the log cabin as a corn crib and built a storm-root cellar for their canned goods and fresh fruits and vegetables. About 1930 John added a new kitchen and dining room to their house and tore down the old kitchen.

Into this family eight children were born:
Maggie Lavonie May 12, 1885, Thrifty, Brown County-October 2, 1885, homeplace, named for her father's cousins.

Alice Pearl July 30, 1886, Thrifty - June 4, 1971, Palestine, Texas, married January 1, 1919, William Henry Smith.

William Franklin January 31, 1888, Burkett, Coleman County-November 30, 1910, Grosvenor, Brown County.

Mattie Van July 18, 1891, Burkett - September 8, 1966, Brownwood, married December 25, 1912, Robert Lee Lewis.

James Henry December 2, 1893-January 23, 1894, Burkett.

Isaac Daniel February 27, 1895, Burkett - September 9, 1961, Temple, Texas.

Joseph Elbert September 1, 1897, homeplace-November 29, 1957, Temple.

Maudie Mae December 23, 1902, homeplace-January 6, 1990, Midland, Texas, married December 17, 1933, Wilburn Wadkins.

John, Betty, William, Mattie, James, and Joseph were buried in the Howe Cemetery, Coleman County about one mile from the homeplace. William died from pneumonia after going swimming on a dare in freezing weather. Maggie, a "premie" was buried in Mud Creek Shore Cemetery at Fry. Pearl was buried in the Land of Memory, Palestine, Texas. Isaac was buried at Bangs. Maudie was buried in Midland.

Pearl and Henry had three children:
Vernie Mae February 7, 1920, Rockwood, Coleman County, married June 21, 1941, Lloyd Jason Bennett.

Riley Myrle June 17, 1924, Buffalo, Coleman County-February 19, 1979, Palestine, married January 26, 1944, Mrs. Dorothy Lee Combs Cherry.

Betty Bell December 25, 1926, Fort McKavett, Texas, married September 4, 1953, Pasadena, Texas, Howard Winston Williams.

Mattie and Lee had five children:
Ellis Clyde November 21, 1913-August 11, 1963, Brown County, married Amanda Ashcraft.

Delmar Earl May 16, 1916-Novmeber 17, 1993, Brown County, married Wilda Kummer July 21, 1948.

Hazel Oleta August 28, 1918-October 30, 1950, Brown County.

Arnold June 22, 1920-July 15, 1924, Brown County.

Thomas Kyle August 23, 1923, Grosvenor-May 20, 1977, Cisco, Texas, married first June 5, 1948, Daulphin County, Pennsylvania, Anna Mae Frank, second Marion Delores Taylor.

Maudie and Wilburn had four children:
Wilburn Jay October 18, 1936, Grosvenor-October 4, 1975, California, married P. ?, Kaye Coffman, and Cheryl Leishman.

Sterling Rayburn February 25, 1938, Ballinger, Texas-June 26, 1950, Midland, Texas.

Harvey May 17, 1942, Brown County, married Vickie ?.

Betty Vivian June 27,1943, Brownwood, married February 14, 1963, Midland to Kenneth R. Farmer.

**EVANS** – It is uncertain when the Evans family first appeared in Tennessee, but David W. born in 1803 and Virginia Jane Evans were living in Perry County, Tennessee, in 1840. They were the parents of eight children, who were Lankford, born 1831; Elirabeth, born 1834; Melinda, born 1815; Martha, born 1837; Allen Leonard, born 1840; George, born 1841; Sarah, born 1845; and David L., born 1849. Lankford G. Evans served in Co. K 42nd Regiment TN Infantry CSA during the Civil War. Enlisting December 28, 1861.

Lankford married first Manerva Jane Dabbs in 1851. They had five children: Richard Allen 1853-1935, Arkansas; Francis Marion 1854-1938 Arkansas; John 1857-1940, Arkansas; Mary 1859-1935, Arkansas; and George 1865-1925, California. After Manerva's death Lankford married Martha Jane Sanford. From this union four children were born: Savana 1873-1970, California; Joseph 1874-1948, Arkansas; Benjamin 1877-1964, Michigan; and Lula 1879-1922. This family moved to Oregon County Missouri, in 1880s with Lankford's sister Martha Sullivan and husband John Allen Tomlin. Later these families moved to Fulton County, Arkansas. When Martha died Lankford lived with his various children until his death in Greene County, Arkansas on October 3, 1923.

*The Charlie Evans family. Left to right, front row: Myrtle Evans (Mother), Velma Taylor, Lara Bea Chaffin. Back row: J.W. "Jack" Evans, Charlie Evans (Father), Parrish, Bob Aaron, Owen, and John.*

Richard Allen Evans married Frances Elnora Little, daughter of Isaac and Elizabeth Roberts Little in 1874. They were the parents of these children: Malessa Josephine 1875-1951, Washington; Martha Elizabeth 1877-1934, Illinois; Robert Wiley 1879-1947, California; John Lee 1881-1903, Arkansas; Ella Jane 1883-1961, Arkansas; Mary Ada 1885-1940, Arkansas; Maudie Belle 1887-1937, Arkansas; Thomas Aaron 1889-1903, Arkansas; Charles Elmer 1891-1963, Arkansas; Nettie Gertrude 1893-1959, Arkansas; Jessie Pearl 1895-1974, Arkansas; and George Homer 1898-1973, California. The first three were born in Tennessee. The other in Arkansas except Ella Jane who was born in Missouri.

Richard Allen, wife and most of his children moved to Greene County, Arkansas, circa 1900, where they resided east of Marmaduke in the Mounds area and are buried in New Liberty Cemetery north of Paragould.

While most large families scatter to other areas many descendants of Richard Allen and Frances still reside in Greene County today.

Charles Elmer Evans, 1892-1963, married Lillie Myrtle Rodgers, 1895-1979. Their children are: Roland Parris Evans, Frances Laurabe, John Ray, Robert Earl, Velma Faye, Alva J.W., Charles Owen, Thomas Aaron and Darrell Wedsel Evans.

Alva J.W. Evans married Edith Lively. Their children are Nita Faye (Evans) Bland, born April 11, 1953; Jackie Lynn, born June 12, 1956; and Michael Bruce, born March 30, 1959.

Charles Owen Evans married Georgia Warren. Children are: Mickey Owen, Rhonda Carol (Evans) Harlan, Mark, and Angelia (Evans) Bradshaw.

*Charles and Myrtle Evans.*

Thomas Aaron Evans married Carmel Hoggard. Children are: Tommy Evans and Tammy Evans, Darrell Evans, born September 24, 1931, and died March 8, 1932.

Roland Parris Evans married Jerome Robinson. Their children: Jimmy Dean, Jerry Pat, Judy Layne Evans (deceased), and Janet Jacque (Evans) Loar.

Frances Laurabe Evans married Elton Ray Chaffin. Their children are: Charles Efton Chaffin, Rayetta Fay (Chaffin) Gardner and Ricky Chaffin.

John Ray Evans married Mavis Grubbs. Their children are: Darrell Wedsel Evans (deceased) and Larry Gene Evans.

Robert Earl Evans married Imogene Valentine. Their children are: Billy Earl and Richard Evans.

Velma Faye Evans married Jack Taylor. Their children are: Susan Carol (Taylor) Corley and Scott Duane Taylor.

There are many teachers and preachers in the Evans family. Greene County is still home to many of the Evans family.

**FAHR** – John M. Fahr (Pic 303), was the son of Mathis Fahr who came to America from Freeburg, Germany, as a stowaway on a freighter at the age of 13 and settled in Illinois in 1847.

John M. was born on May 2, 1860, at Mount Vernon, Illinois. He married Hattie Stout in 1891 where they had one son Joseph. In 1895 he moved his family to Arkansas and settled on the Knight farm three miles east of Paragould. Three years later they bought a 160 acre farm two miles north of Halliday where they were blessed with six more children: John A., William, Louis, Mary, Henry and Kate. Hattie Fahr passed away on May 8, 1909, leaving Mr. Fahr with seven young children. In 1910 he married Etta Kiestler and they were the proud parents of four children: Calvin, Alice, Frank and Robert.

*John M. Fahr's breeding stock in 1915. From left: Frank Fahr, John M. Fahr, Calvin Fahr, Bob Elkins and Louis Fahr.*

After clearing the 160 acre farm north of Halliday of timber, he turned it into a row crop and livestock farm where he grew corn, cotton, wheat and oats. The real pride of his farming operation was his breeding stock. Since horses and mules were the power of the farming operation in that era, he always had horses and mules for sale to other farmers in North Greene County. Mr. Fahr was also known as the Farmers Banker since he bought and sold farms and financed many other farmers in buying their own farm. He also financed many of young men to go on to higher education but along with the loan he always had a piece of advice which was "Son, no matter how much money you make always save a little."

Mr. Fahr retired from farming in 1936 and moved to Makmaduke where he bought a 42 acre farm inside the town of Marmaduke. He took with him his matching pair of Clydesdale mares and steel rim wagon, which he used to go back to the old farm when weather permitted. He used his wagon since it rode more comfortable than his pick up truck. This 42 acre farm is now Marmaduke City Park and Housing section.

Mr. Fahr was elected mayor of Marmaduke in 1937. During his term as mayor the Marmaduke water system and fire department was developed.

John M. Fahr died December 14, 1951, at the age of 91 and was laid to rest in the New Liberty Cemetery near Halliday. He left behind his wife Etta, eight sons, three daughters and 44 grandchildren.

**FARLEY** – Leslie Farley (Jan. 29, 1960 Paragould, AR) son of Larry and Pat Farley was the third of eight children. His brothers include: Larry, Kenneth, Brian and Shawn Farley and his sisters Theresa Lewis, Lisa Taylor and Debbie Ainsworth.

*Rev. Leslie Farley with his father, Larry Farley and mother, Pat Farley.*

Les attended his first three years of school, kindergarten through second grade, in St. Louis, MO moving to Bloomfield, MO for the third and fourth grades. Fifth and sixth grades were spent back in Paragould at St. Mary's Catholic School. He then went to Paragould Middle School for two years and on to Paragould High School where he graduated in 1978.

Les served four years in the US Navy before going to St. Joseph's Seminary in Covington, LA where he received his BA graduating cum lade and then went to Gregorian, the North American College in Rome, Italy. After Rome he studied at St. Mary's Seminary University in Baltimore, MD where he received his master of divinity in May 1993.

Father Les Farley was ordained to the Roman Catholic priesthood Saturday, May 29, 1993 at the Cathedral of St. Andrew in Little Rock, AR by Bishop Andrew J. McDonald, Bishop of Little Rock.

On Sunday, May 30, the Rev. Farley celebrated his first mass in front of family and friends at St. Mary's Catholic Church in Paragould, where he had served often as an altar boy. He was joined at the altar by the Rev. Richard Davis of St. Mary's, the Rev. Vincent McMurray of Baltimore, and the Rev. Warren Harvey of Little Rock and Brian Cool of Baltimore. Father Farley was presented a check for $1500.00 from the parishioners of St. Mary's and following mass; well wishers greeted him at a potluck lunch in the parish hall.

Rev. Farley's first assignment was an Associate Pastor of Immaculate Conception Church in Fort Smith, AR beginning June 5, 1993. On July 28, 1995, he became pastor of both St. John the Baptist Church in Engleberg and the Mission of St. Joseph in Corning and later Immaculate Heart of Mary in Walnut Ridge, where he served three years. On June 12, 1998, he was appointed pastor of St.

Mary's Church in Batesville, St. Cecilia Church in Newport and the mission of St. Mary's in Mountain View. He was given the added responsibility of spiritual director for Cursillo effective Aug. 7, 1998.

As of June 2, 2000 Father Les has served as fulltime vocation director for the Diocese of Little Rock. He is in charge of recruitment as well as being director of seminarians. He still remains spiritual director for Cursillo.

Father Les Farley is the only priest to have ever come from St. Mary's Catholic Church in Paragould. Is it any wonder that the parishioners are extremely proud of him and grateful to him for his dedication?

**FARLEY** – Tony Farley and his wife, Eula (Garner) Farley was each twins and their twin siblings died near birth.

Their residence during most of their life was in the Commissary-Union Grove area of Greene County. Their farm operation of many years ago was hand picked cotton and dairy farm.

*S/N Orman Farley and Corp. Norman Farley, both age 23.*

Tony was also a schoolteacher at several of the old-style, community, one-room schools. He also in those old days taught at Greene County High School located on the highway from Paragould to Jonesboro. He was also one of the first school board members of Stanford High School when it was constructed.

Tony was elected and served as representative of Greene County at the state capitol in Little Rock during the 1940s.

*PFC. Houston Farley, age 19 and PVT. Wilda Mae Farley, age 21.*

Tony and Eula had five children during 1926 through 1932. All the children had experience in chopping and hand picking cotton. Also, the children all started to school in the old-style, one-room community school and later they all graduated from Stanford High School. They later attended college type education.

The oldest child from year 1926 is Sherrell Verneil (Farley) Shock. More young work from her was the Trailblazer Café in Paragould. Later she was a secretary at the state capitol in Little Rock during the terms of two governors and is now a retired senior citizen at Hot Springs Village, AR.

The next two children from year 1928 were twin boys named Norman and Orman Farley. Both served military duty. Norman also has milk production related work and health department work and is now a retired senior citizen in Texas. Orman had years' work for U. S. government and died of cancer in 1986 in Texas.

Next child from 1930 is Wilda Mae (Farley) Harris. She did some hospital work while young when Paragould Methodist Hospital was first constructed, also military duty and owner of a convenience store. She is now a retired senior citizen in Texas.

Last child is Houston Farley of year 1932. Following military duty, government employment and dairy farm owner, he is now retired in Greene County, AR.

Tony and Eula Farley were in a nursing home together during the last years of their lives. They are now both deceased.

*Submitted by Houston Farley*

**FARRAR** – Curtis Farrar, son of W. D. and Carrie M. Simpson Farrar, pioneers to Greene County, AR, was born Feb. 7, 1900. He was the second child of Walter D. Farrar and Carrie M. Simpson, pioneers to Greene County, AR. Curtis became interested in the mercantile business and following in his father's occupation, went into business in Jonesboro in his early manhood. He opened his first store in the 1930s and remained in business until the 1970s. Curtis was 6' 2" tall, sandy red hair and bluish eyes. He was a longtime member of the First Methodist Church. He married Louise Roberts and they had no children. A large and loving family surrounded them. Their niece and nephew, Peggy and Tom Roberts have fond memories of them. Tom mentioned that Curtis had a horse and did some riding.

Curtis died Oct. 12, 1977 and is buried in Woodlawn Cemetery, Jonesboro, AR. Louise never remarried. Louise was 5'2" with black hair and dark eyes. She died April 30, 1999 at the age of 92, in Jonesboro, AR and funeral services were at Blessed Sacrament Catholic Church, with Jack Harris officiating. Burial was at Woodlawn Cemetery, Jonesboro, AR. Pallbearers were James Tate, Gaylon Tate, Steve Cline, V. E. Tate, Wyne Tate, Jessie Tate and Dennis Nix. Mrs. Farrar was the retired owner and operator of Farrar Grocery in Jonesboro. She attended Blessed Sacrament Catholic Church.

*Standing: Curtis and Louise (Roberts) Farrar. Sitting: Ruby (Atkinson), Otis, Jewel (Rice) Farrrar.*

*Submitted by Evelyn Euritha Wagner*

**FARRAR** – Otis Farrar was born Nov. 3, 1903, the third child of W. D. and Carrie Simpson Farrar, early pioneers to Greene County, AR. The store business failed to interest Otis, as he found too many outside activities. He started to high school in Jonesboro and completed college there. Otis married Pearl Williams and they both taught school and went to school intermittently for years. They have one daughter, Sarah Jo, who was born in 1945 and she plans to also follow the teaching profession. At the present time, 1966, Sara Jo is a senior at the University of Arkansas and will graduate in Jan. 1967. Sarah Jo is very much like her mother; talkative, full of fun and always enjoys a good joke or prank. Pearl passed away in 1952 and Otis and his daughter lived together until she was a sophomore in college in 1964, when Otis married Clara Ruth Grimes of Marmaduke. The live and work in Little Rock where Otis has been with the State Department of Education for more than 20 years and Clara Ruth with the Agriculture Extension service about the same length of time. This was written by Grandmother Eddith (Simpson) Snowden's brother John R. Simpson in 1966. I would like to add Otis's obituary notice dated in 1986.

Ottis Farrar, 83, of 1512 Kavanaugh Blvd., former director of the Education Department's Civil Defense Education Program, died Sunday. Farrar had been with the program for 30 years at the time of his retirement. He began teaching in 1929 at Bono and later served

*Otis Farrar, 1903-1986*

as superintendent of the Bay Public Schools. He also taught at Trinity Elementary School and Monette High School. In 1955 he was included in *"Who's Who in American Education."* Farrar received his bachelor's degree from Arkansas State University at Jonesboro and his master's degree from Oklahoma State University at Stillwater, OK. He was a member of Alpha Gamma Rho fraternity, the Arkansas Education Association, the Pulaski Heights Lions Club and Pulaski Heights Presbyterian Church. Funeral will be at 9:30 a. m. Tuesday at Griffin Leggett Healey & Roth by the Revs. George Gunn and Terrell Atkinson. Burial will be in Woodlawn Cemetery, Jonesboro. Memorials may be made to a favorite charity. Survivors are his wife, Mrs. Clara Ruth Grimes Farrar; a daughter, Mrs. Sarah Jo Smith of Memphis, TN and a sister, Mrs. Jewel Rice of Jonesboro.

Otis's mother, Carrie (Simpson) Farrar was the sister of Eddith Simpson, this writer's grandmother. I might add I was mighty proud of Otis. Original story by John R. Simpson.

*Submitted by Evelyn Euritha Wagner*

**FARRAR** – Peter Farrar was born in 1804 and was an early settler in Tennessee where he owned 257 acres of land. He married his wife Polly in 1827 and six children were born. Polly died in 1848 and Peter remarried having eight more children. He died in 1866 leaving a sizeable estate to all his children.

Nimrod Farrar, son of Peter, was born 1838. He married Demarius Jane Yarbrough in 1855 when he was 17 and she was 15 years old. She was the daughter of Joel and Nancy Yarbrough, also early settlers in Tennessee. Nine years after their marriage the Civil War came along. Nimrod enlisted in the 8th Tennessee Confederate Cavalry Co. A Tennessee Marshall Rangers in 1861. When released in 1863 he returned home and in 1870 his occupation is listed as a farmer with a real estate value of $1,000.00 and personal estate of $5,000.00.

Two sisters of Demarius had moved to Arkansas in the 1860s so about 1871 Nimrod moved his family to Greene County where he bought land and began farming near Paragould. He also held credentials with the Methodist Episcopal Church South and became a "Circuit Riding Preacher." His assignment was the "Gainesville Circuit" consisting of Friendship, Hurricane, Harvey's Chapel, Scatter Creek, Beech Grove and Strong's Chapel.

Nimrod and Demarius had nine children:

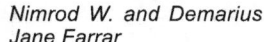
Nimrod W. and Demarius Jane Farrar

Sarah Farrar born 1856 married J.F. Lytle. Their children were Ezra, Mack, Myrtle and George. Sarah then married John Goodwin and had Homer and Leonard.

Nancy Jane Farrar born 1859 married William Little and had Linley and Verda.

Eliza Josephine Farrar born 1861 married Joseph Holmes Childers. Their children were Allen, Olen, Omer, Roy, Hazel Irene, Albert and Carl.

James Knox Polk Farrar born 1866 married Martha Coleman. Their children were Ednis, Elcie, James Stacy, Morris, Mamie, Donnel and Pauline.

Walter Farrar born 1869 married Carrie Simpson. Their children were Ruby, Curtis, Otis, William and Jewell.

Lillian Bell Farrar born 1872 married Edward Dee Hairrell. They had Maude, Clarice, Winnie, Beatrice, Ethel and Monra.

Edward Farrar born 1876 married Mary Emma Willcockson. They had Charley, Mallory. Earl, May and Olene.

Leona Farrar born 1878 married Francis Marion Thomason and had Esther and Mable.

After Demarius died, leaving small children, Nimrod married Rebecca Sipert whose parents had perished in a steamboat fire when moving from Alabama to Arkansas, and she raised the motherless children as her own.

Demarius died January 22, 1881, Nimrod died January 31,1890, and they are buried in the Pleasant Hill Cemetery.

**FARRAR** – Ruby Farrar was born in 1898 and was the first born to the Farrar family. She was always full of fun and taught school during adult life. One story that John R. Simpson loved to tell of Ruby was this one – Ruby, being the oldest one of the girls, began to date some of the boys a little and one sent her a box of candy. Each piece of candy was wrapped in aluminum foil. She was real proud of this candy- too proud to eat it really, so being a big hungry kid, Otis goes in and eats most of the candy, wrapping cotton in the foil and put it back in the box. This proved to be very embarrassing when her date showed up and they decided to have some candy, to find only cotton wrapped in the foil that once contained the luscious candy!

Upon reaching adulthood she married Loy Atkinson soon after Loy's return from overseas duty in WWI, in which he received severe wounds in combat. Their first child was born in May 1925, a boy whose name is Terrell. Terrell was a very quiet young man who followed in his father's footsteps by joining the Marines during WWII and saw active service in the Pacific and China area. After WWII he returned home, entered college and graduated from Hendrix College, as well as S.M.U. in Dallas. He afterwards entered his great-grandfather's profession, as a Methodist minister. He is now, (1966) pastor of Grace Methodist Church in Dallas, TX. Terrell married Grace Richardson of Rust, TX, who was a nurse. They have two boys. Terrell is conducting a tour through the Holy Land in April 1967 and is a very prominent minister in the Texas Conference. In 1926 Ruby and Loy had born to them a daughter, Viola. Viola was much like her mother –full of life and enjoyed the companionship of her father at whatever work he was doing. Viola was at his side if at all possible regardless of what kind of work he was doing, she attended and graduated from college and married Myron Conley. They have two daughters and live at Benton where she is teaching and has been for a number of years. Loy Atkinson died just as his children were grown, about 1949. Ruby never remarried and is living in her home in Jonesboro, AR. (1966)

Ruby died about 1985.

*Submitted by Evelyn Euritha Wagner*

**FARRAR** – John R. Simpson's memories of the Farrar family life in Greene County, AR.

Carrie and Walter had a beautiful life together and they were proud of their children and of Carrie's daughter, Leona. As Leona grew up she became interested in school and education and taught school for a number of years in her younger days and helped support the family. She never married. Carrie's health broke down in a few years after their marriage and most of her life thereafter was in poor health with a stomach ailment. Carrie was short, snappy and left-handed. She worked hard to please the children and her husband with a variety of cooking, such as cake, pie and other good things the family enjoyed. Early in their married life you could see the devotion of Walter and Carrie exemplified. At one time when Carrie exposed a desire to have a rocking chair, Walter proceeded to cut a load of wood and haul it to Jonesboro where he sold it for $.75. Then he went to a second-hand furniture store and bought a rocking chair with the $.75. This was a long journey, which required a full day for the round trip and necessitated Walter's going without his noon meal. However, he considered himself fortunate in obtaining a rocker for his wife. This is just mentioned to show what sacrifices they would make for each other.

*W.D. Farrar and Carrie Simpson Farrar*

Walter heard that Ravenden Springs was a good place for people with stomach trouble, so he sent Carrie there, where she stayed a number of months and showed some improvement. While there she wrote Otis a card, addressing it to him, which was the first piece of mail he ever received and he still has the card and considers it priceless.

At that time the family lived on a farm in the southern part of Greene County, near Lorado and the next summer (1910) three families traveled in two wagons and a hack, to Ravenden Spring and back. On the first day one of the horses stuck a stone in his foot and one of the adult boys took the hack and went back to Lorado; the rest piled in two wagons and journeyed on to Ravenden Springs. They forded Cache River and crossed the Black River on a ferry – it was about a three-day journey. The children of the families had lots of fun sleeping on the ground and in the wagons. Most of our family slept in the wagons, on the ground and under the wagons, but Walter's sister, Kate who was with the family, said she would not sleep under the wagon like a dog. So she fixed her a pallet on the ground near the wagon. During the night the horses got loose and one of them, being blind, made Kate real glad to get under the wagon for fear she might get stomped by the horses. They stayed in Ravenden Springs for a number of weeks and this was one of the highlights of our young years.

There were many things that made this trip very interesting, one of which, to the regret of Otis, his dog Curley went with the group and when they left to come back home he was forgotten-so that ended the story of the boy and his dog.

*Submitted by Evelyn Euritha Wagner.*

**FARRELL** – I moved to Paragould in July of 1971 as a wildlife officer for the Arkansas Game and Fish Commission. I'll never forget the day we received our assignments. Mr. Aubrey Fowler, enforcement chief of the AGFC made the announcement that I would be going to Greene County. I turned to the guy on my left and asked, "Where the heck is Greene County?" He didn't know. And then, AGFC Director Andrew Hulsey announced that I would be living in Paragould. Again, I turned to the guy on my left asking, "where is Paragould?" Same answer, he didn't know. In 1971, Paragould had no US highways running through it and to get to Paragould, you actually had to be going there. You didn't travel "through" Paragould going anywhere.

I worked for the AGFC until March 1973, when I resigned and became a deputy for the Greene County Sheriff's Department under Sheriff James L. Cox. I worked this position until I resigned on Dec. 31, 1973 in order to prepare a campaign for the office of sheriff. In the spring of 1974 I, along with five other candidates, campaigned for this office. I came in second, gaining a runoff spot against Max Higgins. Max won the election, but I ran a pretty good race, at the time having lived in Greene County less than three years.

Before moving to Paragould, I lived my entire 23 years in McGehee, AR. My father's name was Sammy Winfred Farrell. He died in 1982. Dad was in the Navy during WWII and was stationed at Millington, TN for a short time before going off to the South Pacific. It was while stationed at Millington that he met my mother. My mother's name was Dorothy Cousar and she was born and raised in Cotton Plant, MS. Mom was working in Memphis for the C.D. Shy Company when she met my dad.

My mother's father was Robert Thomas Cousar from Cotton Plant, MS. I've traced his descendants back to: my great-grandfather, James Leonadas Cousar (July 7, 1846) and great-great-grandfather, Thomas Cousar (1820 SC). Mom's mother was Trannie Etta Barkley. I've traced these descendants back to: my great-grandfather, Samuel Thomas Barkley and great-great-grandfather, Ben B. Barkley. The Barkley's have thus far been traced to North Carolina.

My father's side of the family has some interesting twists. My dad's father was Winfred

Vetau Farrell, known to me as Papaw Vetau. Vetau was born in Drew County, AR on Sept. 19, 1900. He was the youngest of six kids, five boys and one girl. Vetau was quite an entrepreneur. During WWII, he managed to buy a 1200-acre farm for little more that paying the back taxes on it. During WWII, there were two Japanese internment camps located in southeast Arkansas, one in Rohwer and the other in Jerome. Somehow, soon after WWII, Vetau managed to acquire both these internment camps from the US Government. The barracks at these camps consisted of many buildings 20 feet wide by 120 feet long. Vetau got into the house moving business and started cutting these buildings into thirds, making three 20x40 feet houses. He began buying lots all over McGehee and moving these houses to his vacant lots, thus amassing a huge number of well-built rent houses, most of which are still in use today.

My dad's mother was Helen Gould Parris. Helen was born on Feb 15, 1905 to Samuel Albert and Mary Josephine Parris. Samuel Parris was born in England and came to this country at age three. Samuel's father was a Methodist preacher. Samuel met Mary Josephine Cobb in Clendenin, WV. Samuel and Josephine married in 1900 and rode to Charleston, WV on a freight train in an empty boxcar. Samuel went to work for railroad magnate Jay Gould and soon settled in McGehee, AR, working for the railroad. When daughter Helen was born, she was named after Jay Gould, just as Paragould is named after Jay Gould. Samuel and Josephine had a large, two-story home and she turned it into a boarding house for railroad employees. From what I understand, in the early and mid 20th century, McGehee was a turn-around point for many Paragould railroad employees.

Helen and Vetau married on March 27, 1920 and soon thereafter moved to northeast Arkansas for a while, living and building roads in the Wynne area. My father was born on Feb 3, 1922 and not long after that, Helen and Vetau divorced. Helen remarried to Robert Blair Stobaugh Sr. who was from Humboldt, TN and had relocated to McGehee, AR. Robert owned the City Laundry in McGehee for a number of years.

I am a "baby boomer", having been born on June 8, 1947. I have a brother, Winfred DeWitt Farrell, who was born on April 22, 1960 and is currently living in Austin, TX. We are both single, so I suppose we will put an end to the Farrell family lineage. My father was an only child and none of my uncles produced any male children that lived long enough to reproduce. The Farrell family just wasn't very prolific.

In 1993 I re-entered ASU and completed a BS in Psychology with a minor in music. In 1995 I entered graduate school at ASU and in 1997 completed a masters in rehabilitation counseling. I had numerous lucrative job offers in such states as Wisconsin, Montana, Utah and Wyoming, but at my age, I really didn't want to relocate and start over. I love Paragould. This summer, I will have lived in Paragould for 30 years. I think it is one of the best cities in the United States for raising a family. Should anyone be interested in finding out more about my family, I have established a website at: http://groups.yahoo.com/group/Farrell-Stobaugh-Cousar-family. I am constantly adding information to this site.

Advice I could give to young people today? Yes! Get you education. Get as much as you can, as soon as you can. And finally, learn as much as you can about your family history. Write it down. Interview your parents, aunts and uncles, grandparents, and great-grandparents if at all possible. Ask them questions, wait a few months, then ask them more questions. Genealogy is a fascinating hobby, but the sooner you can get started, the easier it becomes.

*Submitted by Robert Samuel "Ron" Farrell*

**FAULKNER** – John David Jonas Faulkner, 1860 -1954, son of Governor Hill and Frances "Biddy" Marshall Faulkner was born in Sardis, Mississippi. When David was 14 he came with his parents, two aunts–Martha McDonald and Mary Fitzgerald, a cousin James T. Edwards and their families by wagon to Greene County.

David was a Baptist minister, teacher and farmer. He married three times and fathered 14 children outliving all three of his wives and four of his children.

*Raymond, Orman, J.D.J., Mary Rutledge Faulkner, Lona, Ora, Ethel, Naomi, Emma, Mary, Sally, Grace and Jewel.*

His first wife was Emma Thorne, 1862-1882, daughter of Josiah and Martha Ann Blythe Thorne. Both were 20 years of age when they married September 8, 1881. Emma died five months later and is buried in Gainsville Cemetery.

His second wife was Texas Ann Weatherly, 1868-1902, daughter of Samuel H. and Martha Ann Valentine Weatherly. They were married October 29, 1884. Nine children were born to this union. Texie and David's log house was about 20 feet square with one window. A fireplace was on the south end and three beds were on the north end.

His third wife, Mary Angeline Rutledge, 1874-1945, daughter of Robert Marion and Tabitha Jane Thetford Rutledge. They married September 30, 1902. Five children were born to this union. Their first born died at birth in 1903. The original log home was later moved and a new home was built for David and Mary. It had two rooms with a detached kitchen. Additional rooms were added later.

Their son Raymond and his wife Christina returned to Greene County about 1972 and restored the home. Christina still lives there with three of their four children nearby.

Reverend J.D.J. Faulkner followed in his father's footsteps becoming a minister in the Baptist denomination. *The Baptist Ministerial Directory* in 1889 stated that he received his Arkansas license May 1878 (age 18) and was ordained July 25, 1880, at Union Grove Church. At this time he had served churches at Fair View, Gainsville, Providence, Macedonia, Unity, Brown's Chapel, Rock Hill, Rector and Walcott. He attended Mount Pleasant Academy at Barren Fork, Arkansas in the late 1880s. He and Texie buried their third born child, Annie Frances, there. *History Of Arkansas Baptist* 1948 stated that he is well educated and a thoroughly clear and very able expounder of the Word of God in the pulpit of his churches, a wise and truly faithful shepherd of the sheep and always a deeply interested friend of missions and the Baptist denomination.

He died at age 93 having served in the ministry over 70 years. In *The Story Of Epsaba* Darrell Edgar Stone wrote that it was estimated that Reverend J.D.J. Faulkner preached over 14,000 sermons and that he was survived by over 400 descendants. His Masonic funeral service was held at New Friendship Baptist Church. He is buried in the nearby cemetery between his wife of 18 years Texie and his wife of 42 years Mary.

**FELTY** – Bonnie Clifton Felty and Emma Lou Norwood Felty are farmers in the Stanford area. Bonnie just celebrated his 71st birthday, but that hasn't slowed him down much. They work hard and are successful farmers. They farm enough ground to keep the family employed anytime they want to work. Bonnie is the type of farmer who seems to work year round. He is a mechanic when machinery breaks down and spends many winter days getting the machinery ready to go in the spring. Emma Lou is the cook for the family-field workers and hired hands. She, also, has spent many days baby-sitting with grandchildren and great-grandchildren.

It all began when Bonnie and Emma Lou married in 1949. They lived on a 40-acre farm in Greene County, which belonged to Joe Felty, Bonnie's dad. They cleared and farmed this land several years before buying their first 80-acre farm east of Walnut Ridge. However, they continued living in Greene County. They had three children, often described as stair-steps because they were so close in age. Their names are Cathy, Gary and Danny. The kids were taught to work in the fields chopping and picking cotton, picking up chunks to clear the land and driving a tractor to cultivate the ground. The boys also grew up and became farmers, as did the daughter and her husband, Philip Rowe, who recently retired from school teaching to farm full-time. Although they each have their own farm operation, they work together during the busiest times of farming. Bonnie and Emma Lou welcome all the help they can get and occasionally, they get help from grandsons and grandsons-in-law.

*Bonnie and Emma Lou Felty*

Bonnie and Emma Lou seem satisfied with their life. It agrees with them and keeps them young. They still enjoy going and doing the things they have always done. In the winter they try to keep up with basketball games from Tech, Delaplaine, Stanford and Paragould. They enjoy Sunday afternoon drives in the country. They like to discover where unknown roads will wind up. Sometimes, they drop in on a friend or visit the sick. When they are not going to ball games, they enjoy having friends over to play card games, dominoes, or to "pick and grin." Bonnie has been singing with a band that plays at nursing homes and other benefits. He has always loved listening to gospel, country and bluegrass music. For many years he enjoyed singing gospel songs while encouraging his daughter to play the piano. He now, sometimes, leads songs in church. They are members of the Stanford Baptist Church.

Recently at his 52nd high-school reunion, Bonnie expressed how blessed he has been with an occupation he loves, a wife by his side, three children and six grandchildren and four great-grandchildren. He and Emma Lou have many friends and they seem to love people. They have always been willing to help their family and friends when needed. Because of this love and unselfishness, the family likes to get together and celebrate his birthday to express their best wishes for many more years to come, even though, Oct. 18th is always the busiest farming time.

**FELTY** – Joseph "Joe" Felty migrated to Greene County in 1906 at the age of three. His parents, John Lewis and Cally Ida (Howard) Felty brought their family, consisting of nine children, from Beaver Dam, KY. They stopped on a creek south of Marmaduke to rest. A local doctor and landowner stopped and asked the family to stay and farm his land. They stayed two years before moving to the Commissary community about 10 miles west of Paragould. They lived on the creek across the road from the Church of Christ. It was a bad location because the house flooded each time it came a heavy rain. This prompted them to move after the first year to a Cache River farm near O'kean. Here the Felty family bought a 40 acre farm and lived for 20 years before moving to Malvern, AR. By this time their family had increased to 15 children, but only 13 survived to adulthood.

Joe Felty, the seventh child, grew up and married Bessie Allison before his family moved to Malvern. They had nine children during their marriage:
1. Harold
2. Wanda Rogers
3. Billy Joe
4. Bonnie
5. Vernon
6. James M.
7. John
8. Max
9. Mary (May)

In 1929 they moved to Lake Village, AR where he and his brother, Netter and his family rented 200 acres of farm land for one dollar an acre. They made two good crops but the depression hit, then falling prices caused them to move to Holly Grove, AR in debt. They stayed in Holly Grove for four years before moving to Walcott, AR for two years. Afterward, they moved to the Stanford, AR area. After farming the Cupp farm for two years, the family settled on the Woolsey farm across the road and remained there for about 11 years. He gradually gained enough financially so he could afford two tractors, four teams of horses and a 40-acre farm. With the help of his teenage sons and this equipment, he made good crops. Because of the good crops, he was given an opportunity to farm the Bill Gramling farm. He moved to Stanford and lived in a two-story white house for about 14 years. When he retired he moved to his 40-acre farm west of Stanford. He sold his farm equipment to his sons, Bonnie and John, who were already farming for their livelihood. At this time he cared for his wife, Bessie who was disabled from diabetes, until she passed away. Later, he married a nice, widowed woman, Retha Balwin. They had several good years together taking it easy, fishing and going camping with the family. He outlived both wives and three of his sons, Vernon, Harold and John. He died at the age of 96 in 1999.

Joe is best remembered as a faithful Christian deacon of the Baptist faith. He was honest and tried to treat his family and neighbors well. He was a hard worker who provided the necessities for his family. He enjoyed being with his family. The Felty family developed a close relationship with one another, thanks to the many family reunions they had at Joe and Bessie's house.

*Submitted by Cathy L. Rowe*

**FORESYTHE** – The earliest recorded evidence of our Forsyth ancestors in Scotland is from 1296. This date is the oldest recording that provides proof of the existence of the Forsyth name, now spelled as Foresyth, Foresythe or Forsythe. After the English defeated the Scots, the Scots were forced to sign allegiance to Edward I of England by signing the "Ragman Roll". Robert De Fauside was among those to sign his name in 1296.

The Foresythe's were one of 50,000 Scots who emigrated from Scotland to Northern Ireland in the 1600s to avoid war, hunger and religious repression in their native land of Scotland. During the potato famine that ravaged the island in the 1840s over two million of the Scots living in Northern Ireland immigrated to the American colonies in the 18th Century.

The Scottish and Irish ancestors immigrated to the North American continent and settled along the Atlantic seaboard from Nova Scotia to Georgia. The Foresythe's first arrived in the Cape Fear area of North Carolina and settled in places like Granville and Orange County.

The next generation moved to western Tennessee and settled in the counties of Crockett, Dyer, Dickson, Gibson, Lincoln, Madison, McNairy, Shelby, Tipton and Lauderdale. The Foresythe's then relocated to Northeast Arkansas to Greene, Craighead and Mississippi Counties and Southeast Missouri with families settling in Dunklin, Ripley and New Madrid Counties.

Robert F. Foresythe was born in Nov. 1864 in Tennessee. Robert died in 1934 in Monette, AR. He had three brothers. James (1859), John (1865) and William Lee (1869). Robert's first marriage was to Sarah Singleton. They had two children Sylvester and Sedessie. Sarah died giving birth and was buried in Manila, AR.

Robert's next marriage was to Verdie Victoria Summers on Dec. 14, 1904 in Manila, AR. They had three children, Arminta, Leman and Dovie. Verdie was born in Franklin County, Benton, IL on Dec 22, 1891. She was the daughter of James Logan Summers and Cansady Cumi Denham Summers. James and Cansady married Feb 15, 1889 in Franklin County, IL. Cansady's next marriage was to Eli Morgan of Manila, AR.

Robert Leman Foresythe was born Dec 13, 1909 in Manila, AR. Leman died Nov 18, 1985 at the age of 76. He was buried at Linwood cemetery in Paragould, AR. Leman was the youngest son of Robert and Verdie Summers Foresythe.

He married Daisy Dean Smith on June 13, 1929, in Greene County, AR. Daisy was the daughter of George and Synthia Smith of Marmaduke, AR. Daisy was born March 23, 1913 and died on Dec 27, 1959 in Paragould, AR of heart complications that resulted from rheumatic fever contracted as a child. Daisy was 46 years old at the time of her death.

*Robert Leman Foresythe and Daisy Dean Smith Foresythe*

Leman and Daisy had five children:
1. Byron (1930 Marmaduke, AR)
2. Nadgerine (1935 Marmaduke, AR)
3. Edsel (1938 Paragould, AR)
4. Dale (1941 Paragould, AR)
5. Nadine "Deanie"(1943 Memphis, TN)

Leman was a large man (6'1"-240 lb.) with coal black hair and steel blue eyes. He was known for both his mechanical and artistic abilities. He worked in construction and operated a photo studio at the same time. His greatest passion was fishing, which he did as often as he could.

Dale Curtis Forsythe was born Oct 29, 1941 in Paragould, AR. His parents were Robert Leman Foresythe of Manila, AR and Daisy Smith Foresythe of Marmaduke, AR. He is a descendant of Jonathan Howton, born in London, England April 3, 1757 and Robert Forsythe born 1864 in Tennessee.

Dale married Judy Kay Gatlin on Dec. 16, 1961 in Greene County, AR. They had two daughters, Michelle Renee Forsythe born Oct 1, 1962 in Wichita Falls, TX. Stephanie Lea Foresythe was born June 3, 1969 in Bad Axe, MI. Dale married Barbara MacKenzie of Lowell, MA and is currently living in Acton, Ma.

Dale graduated from Paragould High School in May 1959. Dale received an associate's degree from William Rainey Harper Community College in Palatine, IL and then his bachelor's degree in business at Elmhurst College, Elmhurst, IL. Dale later attended executive training courses sponsored by Digital Equipment Corporation in association with Harvard University.

Dale spent four years in the Air Force. After the service, Dale worked for several computer-manufacturing companies-Digital Equipment Corporation, Compaq Corporation and Intel Corporation. During this time he held positions such as US area logistic manager, corporate programs manager and senior operations consultant.

*Submitted by Dale Foresythe*

**FOSTER/STONE** – John Thomas Foster was born in Marmaduke, Greene County, AR Jan. 19, 1880, one of the children of John Anderson Foster and Amanda M. Barton Foster. John Anderson came to Arkansas by covered wagon in 1969 from Cog Hill, near Athens, McMinn County, TN with his wife and three children. He was born in McMinn County May 3, 1843, a son of Perry and Caroline M. Foster. John Anderson's family first settled in the Hurricane Community of Greene County and later moved to a farm nearer Marmaduke. The first three children, Elizabeth

"Lizzie", Mary Jane "Molly" and William Miller were born in Tennessee. Three more children were born in Arkansas, Sarah "Sally," Katherine "Cassie" and John Thomas "Tom."

Tom married Kittie Vyletta Stone, daughter of James Baucher and Frances Orlena "Lena" (Ross) Stone on Dec. 19, 1903. Kittie was born April 22, 1887 in Marmaduke and died Dec 27, 1965. One child, Clarence Bryan "Slim" Foster was born to them. The family lived in Marmaduke until moving to Tallulah, Madison Parish, LA around 1922.

Kittie grew up in the Marmaduke Methodist Church, later joining the Church of Christ and was a dedicated church member. Upon moving to Tallulah and finding no congregation of her denomination there, she set about to start one. At Kittie's death and largely through her early efforts to establish a Church of Christ in her community, her funeral was held in a new sanctuary that could seat 500 people.

*Wedding Day: John Thomas "Tom" and Kittie V. Stone Foster.*

Tom worked in the lumber business in Marmaduke and in Tallulah, LA except for one brief period during WWII when he was employed at Fort Polk, LA with the civilian maintenance division. His knowledge of lumber was so noted that at 80 years of age, Chicago Mill Lumber Company located in Tallulah, called him back to train young men to grade lumber. One of these men said that Mr. Fosters eye for lumber was so good, he could determine with a quick look how many board feet was in a "stack."

Both Tom and Kittie are buried in Silver Cross Cemetery, Tallulah. Bryan died in 1938 and is buried next to his parents.

Though Tom and Kittie only had one child, they have many descendants. Bryan married Sallie Land and they had three children: Sally Jo Gibson of Harrison, AR, Reid Thomas Foster of Alexandria, LA and Eloise Latoof of Marerro, LA.

Sally Jo married J. O. Gibson Jr. They have four children: Janet Diane Minks, Carolyn Ruth Hubbell, James O. Gibson III and Sally Annette Hennard. There are eight grandchildren, Adam and Derek Hubbell, Christy, Mark and Ben Gibson, Allie, Kittie and Montie Hennard.

Reid married Diane Jarvis and they have two children, Steven Jarvis Foster and Robin Marie Dantin. Robin has two daughters, Amber and Sarah.

Eloise married Raymond Latoof. They had three daughters, Bryanna Green (deceased) who had two sons, Austin and Joshua; Cecilia Naquin who has two children, Ian and Ivy and Angela Cagle who has two children, Olivia and James.

*Submitted by Sally J. Gibson*

**FOX** – George Washington Fox was born near Carbondale, IL about 1859. He had at least two brothers, Albert and Elijah. According to census records, his parents were also born in Illinois; however, another source indicates that his father came from Scotland. George was first married to Martha Wright on March 8, 1890. Both were residing in the town of Blairsville, in Williamson County, IL. Martha died on June 10, 1913 and was buried at Harvey's Chapel near Marmaduke, AR.

George, often referred to as "G.W.," married his second wife, Gertie May (Snyder) Stevens, on Oct 7, 1914. Gertie, born in Paw Paw, IL in 1879, was the daughter of Jerome and Anne Elizabeth (Bedford) Snyder. Two daughters, Lula (1915) and Beulah Dean (1920) were born to the union.

George had relatives living in Bernie, MO and Clay County, AR. As a young man, he often steamed from Illinois to Blytheville, AR by riverboat and then traveled overland to visit his relatives. On one occasion, he witnessed the robbery and murder of a man on the boat. The victim was subsequently thrown overboard. Fearing that the killers had seen him, he got off the riverboat at the next stop.

George worked in the logging industry and later is believed to have worked in law enforcement in Illinois. Around the turn of the century, he migrated to the Missouri boot heel and was sheriff of Cardwell, MO for a time. A lumbering town, Cardwell had its share of hooligans. During his tenure there, a black man was accused of raping a young white girl. A vigilante group is said to have dragged the accused to death behind a horse. Sheriff Fox was apparently unable to stop the actions of the mob.

*George W. and Gertie (Snyder) Fox*

George does not appear in the 1910 census of Greene County, AR but was in the county at the time of Martha's death in 1913. Early in the marriage to Gertie, the family was living near Lamb's Chapel in the Alexander Community. George was engaged in farming. In March of 1926, during severe flooding, he developed pneumonia and died. His body was hauled by wagon to Harvey's Chapel for burial. Because of so much groundwater, his body had to be weighted down so the grave could be filled.

Gertie, with her two young daughters, bought a 40 acre farm about a half mile northeast of the Fairview Baptist Church. There, with the help of her son Milo Stevens, the family weathered the disastrous era of the Great Depression. Gertie owned a milk cow, raised chickens and grew most of the family's food. The bank deferred the principle on her mortgage and just collected the interest on the note. Gertie sold eggs and produce in Paragould to raise money for this purpose. It took a year to raise the $19.00 in interest due by the payment date.

Gertie was first married to Kirby Smith in 1895 and had one child, Emuel (1898). Upon Kirby's death, she remarried this time to William S. Stevens. Gertie helped to raise her stepdaughter Florence (1894). To them were born two additional children, Dovie M. (1902) and Milo C. (1904). Gertie died on Dec. 30, 1954 and was buried next to Kirby at Fairview Cemetery. Gertie was a loving and generous person who was a credit to her family, friends and community.

*Submitted by Ryan Reddick*

**FRENCH/McCLURE** – During the early 1890s Cynthia Bell (Bomar) and Thomas Anderson French and their family migrated from their homes in the hills of Carroll and Henry Counties, TN to Greene County. Other members of the Bomar family had migrated to Greene County in the 1860s. The French's traveled 200 miles by wagon and on foot through Murray, KY to Cairo (where they ferried the Mississippi); on to Chalk Bluff to ford the St. Francis River and settled on Crowley's Ridge. At that time the bottomland of Greene County, now recognized as some of the most fertile in Arkansas, was considered worthless because it flooded. With Cynthia and Thomas came nine of their 10 children, all grown and their spouses.

One of the French daughters, Theodosia (Aug 24, 1859 Henry County, TN) had married Riley McClure (Nov 7, 1856)in Hollow Rock, TN, May 18, 1875. Riley was the son of Dice Pace McClure and her McClure husband, whose given name is unknown, but whom the family has affectionately known through the years as "The Wanderer" because of his lifelong habit of wandering! Theodosia and Riley brought their seven children with the French clan; another son and daughter were born after arriving in Greene County. This last son was Virgil D. McClure (Jan 17, 1895).

Virgil D. was in the first Greene County group drafted during WWI; he earned the Purple Heart. After the war, he returned home to farm for the remainder of his life. On July 24, 1921, Virgil D. married Ethel Lee (Sept 21, 1902 Bernie, MO). Ethel's parents were John William Lee (Dec 22, 1863-Nov 13, 1931) and Jana Williams; they had married Aug 18, 1895.

Ethel and Virgil had two children. Willadean Eula born Dec 1, 1922, died from diphtheria Aug 23, 1928. On Sept 30, 1939, Gary Lee was born at his parents' home one-half mile

*McClure/Ray family reunion about 1923. Standing: Thomas Irby McClure and wife, Cullen Vincent and wife Zona (McClure), Virgil D. McClure, Ment Meridith, Marion Ray, Emily Pace, Irene Ray, Miss Sally Ray, Lorene (Ray) Weaver and husband Dee. Seated: Frank Pace and wife, Ethel McClure holding daughter Willidean (in front of husband Virgil D), Lola (McClure) Meridith holding daughter Geniva, Oda (McClure) Ray and husband Henry holding son J. S. and unknown Ray couple and child. Front: Parker McClure (son of Irby) and Henry Ray's hired hand.*

south of the Greene County/Clay County line near the Cotton Belt Railroad; this was less than a mile from his father's birthplace. Except for Gary's college years at Murray State, Murray, KY and three additional years in Kentucky after graduation, he has been a lifelong Greene County resident.

*Theodoshia (French) McClure and family, about 1905. Standing: Virgil D. McClure, Oda (McClure) Ray, Ellen (Johnson) McClure, Theodoshia, Lovie (McClure) Pace holding son Elmer, Lola McClure and Zona McClure. Seated: Marvin McClure, Marion Ray, Henry Ray, Lorene Ray and Frank Pace holding son, Zelma.*

On June 5, 1960, Gary married Marilyn Kay Gordon of Milan, TN. They had four children: Leianne Kaye, Lucinda Gaye, Gordon Michael and Timothy Patrick. Marilyn McClure died Sept 14, 1987. Leianne, married to Mark McGinnis, has two children, Amy Elizabeth and Zackary Gordon. Lucinda's children are William Winston, Melissa Lynn and John Michael Lawson; her husband is Mike Ford. Gordon Michael has one daughter, Lauren Emily.

On May 10, 1997, Gary married Beverly Ann Newsom, originally from Alabama, but at that time living in Memphis. This marriage added another daughter, Ruth Carol (Norris) Baurle, to the McClure family. Ruth and her husband Eric have two sons, Logan Thomas and Ethan Eric.

Beverly and Gary McClure live in the McClure-Highfill Home at 701 West Highland in Paragould. The McClure's have lived in this home since Aug 17, 1969.

*Submitted by Mr. & Mrs. Gary L. McClure*

**FRUCHEY** – Bert Fruchey (1870 Paulding, OH) had three brothers, Walter, Charles and Wilbur. In the early 1900s Bert married a doctor's daughter. The young couple had an argument over a piano and the young couple got a divorce and Bert came to Greene County. Here he met and married Sarah Jane (Pillow) Wiggins in 1921.

Bert and Sarah Jane had three sons: Jack Bert, Donald Lafayette and Wilbur Stanley "Dube". Bert raised one stepdaughter, Estelle Wiggins.

Bert was known for his handle making. He made handles for many farmers in Greene County.

Sarah Jane was an excellent cook and for many years worked for Gertie Frields.

Bert never heard from his family for 40 years, except for a letter edged in black notifying him of mother's death. After 40 years his brother, Walter, visited him in Greene County and the two had a very emotional reunion. His brother was wealthy and owned a washing machine factory in Ohio. After he saw how Bert lived, he came back every year to see that he was doing well.

Jack Bert married Violet Greer. They had one daughter, Jackie Sue. His second wife was named Ann.

Donald Lafay-ette married Betty Morrow. They had two boys and one girl. Rodney Bert, who died at age 12, Roger Jack who married Kotoe Igarishi and had 12 children. Donna Jo married Carey Fortenberry and had two children, Kellie Dawn and Carey Layne. Kellie Dawn married Dr. Tom Alfano and had Emily Addison.

Estelle Wiggins married Clem King and they had no children.

Wilber Stanley "Dube" married Eula Mae Olive and they had two sons and one daughter. Olan Stanley married Sally Scott and they had two sons, Kendall and Chris. Sharon Denise married Danny Andrews and they had two daughters and one son. Cheyenne married Bret Winstead and they have two sons, Payden and Gannon. Danny Jr. married Amber Klingensmith and they have one daughter, Abby Dawn. Sandy Kaye married Scot Havens.

Walter Lynn married Regina and they have two daughters Rachel Elizabeth, Anna Victoria and one son. Luke Alexander.

Bert was found dead among the shavings of his handles in Nov. 1947 and is buried in Pine Knot Cemetery beside his wife, Sarah Jane.

*Submitted by Betty Shrable*

**FULKERSON** – William Andrew Fulkerson was born Feb 22, 1884 in Colt, AR. He was the son of Andrew Jackson Fulkerson and Rebecca Jane Casteel. Lola was born Dec 31, 1889 in Hamlin, AR. She was the daughter of Anna Penelope Robertson and John Lomax Gailey. Lola's grandparents, John and Nancy Sherrill Robertson, migrated to Arkansas in a covered wagon by way of Chattanooga, TN from Georgia. As they reached the top of Lookout Mountain, the Civil War was in progress. John Robertson left his family and went to war. Nancy was left to fend for the seven daughters and one son. Soldiers helped them kill game while they were camped on Lookout Mountain. The family finally came to Cross County.

*William and Lola Fulkerson and son Garland in front of old High School.*

Here is another story concerning the Robertson family. Some travelers stopped by the family farm one day asking for one night's lodging and food and water for them and their horses. The next morning they found a $20.00 payment. They later found out it was Jesse James and his gang.

John Gailey came to Cross County from Tennessee to teach school. Anna was his student. They married in 1881 and opened a general store. They had three children, Lola, Burnice and Lillian. John died Oct 19, 1895 so Anna raised the children alone. She ran the store and became postmistress.

William Andrew Fulkerson married Lola Gailey in 1909. Her mother disapproved of the marriage so Lola had to hide underneath the wagon seat as they drove past her mother's store. When her mother found out about the nuptials, she sent a posse after them, but they weren't found. Anna later changed her mind about Will, as he was called.

Will and Lola had two children before they moved to Paragould in 1926 from Searcy. Garland Gailey was born on Feb. 20, 1911 and Mae was born Oct 1914. Will worked for the Missouri Pacific Railroad as a brakeman. On Oct 19, 1928 William Andrew Fulkerson Jr. was born. Lola died July 29, 1938 of cancer. On June 29 1939, Mae married Dr. Amos Dillon Garner. They moved to Chattanooga, TN.

When WWII started Garland went into the Army as a private and rose to the rank of captain. After the war, Garland was in several business ventures but was mainly a salesman. At the time of his death, he owned a bookstore. He married and divorced twice, having no children. He died July 26, 1987.

Bill Pat Collins June 24, 1949. They have three sons, Andy Rick and David. Bill died July 29, 1993. Mae and Dillon also had three sons, Phil, Mike and Doug. Mike died Nov 17, 1977.

William Sr. married Sallie (Threlkeld) Hickson on Jan. 19, 1954. He died March 29, 1962 and Sallie died in May 1983.

*Submitted by Pat Fulkerson*

**FULKERSON/COLLINS** – William Andrew Fulkerson Jr. "Bill," son of W. A. and Lola Galey Fulkerson was born Oct 19, 1928 in Paragould, AR. His family, including a sister, Mae and a brother, Garland, moved to Paragould in 1926 from Searcy. They were originally from Cross County. The elder Fulkerson came to Paragould to work for the Missouri Pacific Railroad, a job he held until forced to retire at the age of 70. Bill's mother died in 1938 and since his brother and sister were older and had moved away, he had more or less to raise himself since his father was away so much. He went to work delivering *Cinemags* for the Capitol Theatre when he was 12. He later sold popcorn, took tickets and became the projectionist, when the regular one was called to service during WWII.

Patricia Ann "Patsy" Collins was born on June 2, 1931 in Paragould to Orris and Frances Collins. She later had a sister, Joan Carol, born Oct 17, 1932 and a brother, John Neely, born March 23, 1939. Her parents and grandparents owned the Capitol and Majestic Theatres.

Bill and Pat married on June 24, 1949. Their first son, William Andrew Fulkerson III was born on Jan 19, 1951, Richard Alan Fulkerson was born Oct 25, 1954 and David Collins Fulkerson was born July 21, 1958.

Bill worked at the Sunset Drive In when it was built in 1950. He went into flying, becoming a crop duster and flight instructor. He was a civilian flight instructor for the Air Force in Malden, MO for four years. When the Air Base closed in 1960, he started Paragould Flying Service. He was a FAA flight examiner. His flying career ended in 1970 when he had a heart attack. He later went into aircraft sales.

Pat worked at the Sunset Drive In and Capitol Theatre until they closed in 1985 and 1986. She then worked at Linwood Child Care.

Andy married Sonjia Gatewood Jan. 28, 1977. He became an attorney, graduating from the University of Arkansas Law School in 1980. He was Paragould's municipal judge for 14 years. He has his own law practice and he and his wife, Sonjia, own a title company. He is seeking his PHD and is teaching part time at ASU. Andy is very active in Boy Scouts and formed a Law Explorer Post, where he serves as advisor.

Andy and Sonjia have one son, Jonathan Andrew, a student at ASU. Jonathan served a two-year term as National Explorer and Venturing President. He married Donna Gramling in 1998 and they have a daughter, Juli Andrea.

*William Andrew and Pat Collins Fulkerson*

Rick is a graduate of ASU and is employed at Emerson Electric. On July 10, 1995, he married Serena McDaniel Scott. She has four children and five grandchildren.

David received his bachelor and masters degree from ASU and teaches at Delaplaine High School. He married Patricia Keeling March 17, 2000. She has a 12-year-old daughter, Lori.

Bill died July 29, 1993 of heart failure.

*Submitted by Pat Fulkerson*

**FUTRELL** – Governor J. Marion Futrell was born, Aug 14, 1870 at Jones Ridge in northwest Greene County. He was the son of Jeptha and Armenia (Eubanks) Futrell. As a boy he attended the Greene County Common Schools. He was graduated from the University of Arkansas after completing the four-year course prescribed for Bachelor of Science, in three years. He later taught school in the counties of Greene, Independence and Craighead.

He was elected to the Legislature from Greene County in 1897 and re-elected in 1899 and 1901. He was elected circuit clerk of Greene County in 1906 and served four years. He was elected to the Senate in 1912 and served in the sessions of 1913 and 1915. After graduating from the University he applied himself to the study of law during his spare time at home and while teaching. His duties as circuit clerk made him familiar with legal forms and court pleading and procedures. It gave him a more favorable opportunity to make progress in his preparation for the law.

He was married to Miss Tera Ann Smith, Sept 14, 1893. To this union were born the following children: Dr. Byron Futrell, Dan Futrell, Mrs. Grady (Nye) McCall, Mrs. Herbert (Prentiss) Farrell, Mrs. Alfred (Ernie) Maddox and Mrs. C. F. (Venice) Moore.

*Governor J. Marion Futrell*

J. Marion Futrell was elected Governor of Arkansas in 1933. A newspaper item stated that hundreds of Greene County residents took a special train to Little Rock on Jan. 10, 1933 to watch one of their own, J. Marion Futrell sworn in as the 30th Governor of Arkansas.

The crowd that jammed into the House chamber at the Arkansas State Capitol that day was said to have been the largest inaugural assembly ever up to that time. Even the governor-elect's wife and family had trouble making their way through the packed crowd to their front-row seats. The day marked a festive start for what would be an administration of austerity. As an international economic depression worsened into what we now call the Great Depression, the state government of Arkansas faced financial bankruptcy.

Under Futrell's administration, constraints that still limit the General Assembly's authority to tax, spend and issue bonds were put into place. At the end of the Futrell Administration, the state that had been on the brink of bankruptcy just a few years earlier had a surplus in its treasury.

Arkansas' first sales tax of two percent was adopted during Futrell's administration. He supported it only after the federal government cut off its aid to force Arkansas to pay its share of public education and relief cost.

Re-elected to a second two-year term as governor in 1934, Futrell was governor when Arkansas celebrated 100 years of statehood in 1936 with centennial celebrations around the state.

There was no governor's mansion at that time; the Futrell family spent most of his administration in a rented house.

When Futrell left the governor's office in 1937, he stayed in Little Rock to practice law. He later ran unsuccessfully for the Arkansas Supreme Court.

Futrell suffered a stroke in 1948 and was in poor health until he died June 20, 1955. Governor Futrell's remains were borne to his last resting place in Linwood Cemetery at Paragould by six grandsons. They are Bill Farrell, Bob Farrell, Marion Futrell, Wood Futrell, Jimmy Dan Maddox and Andy Moore. Emmett Smith, a close friend and preacher, conducted the funeral service.

A memorial service for Governor Futrell was held in Little Rock and prepared by Lee Miles to the Supreme Court of Arkansas. Lee Miles had been a friend and associate of the Governor since his early days in the long Legislative sessions of 1913. Mr. Miles had enjoyed many hunting trips with Governor Futrell and had become a very close and special friend.

After Governor Futrell's death, Emmett Smith kindly adopted his widow "Aunt Tera", taking her to church and other places. At times Emmett would say, "maybe it was the other way around, maybe Aunt Tera adopted him." Tera Futrell is also buried beside her husband, Governor Futrell in the Linwood Cemetery.

Greene County is very proud to have had a fellow citizens serve as governor of our great state of Arkansas. Many Futrell descendants still reside in Greene County.

*Submitted by Greene County Book Committee*

**GARDNER** – Albert David Gardner, eighth child of Richard Hannibal Gardner and Sarah E. Towles Gardner, was born September 7, 1871, near what is now Lafe, Greene County, Arkansas. His grandfather was Dr. Richard Whitehead Gardner, grandmother was Eliza Harriet Thomas Gardner. His great-grandparents were John and Patience Whitehead Gardner, who died in Weakley County, Tennessee. His mother died when he was 9 years old and for several months he lived with his oldest brother's family. His father remarried and he continued living with his father and stepmother, brothers and sisters. He was studious and ambitious as he grew up and taught school at age 16. He held public offices and was a well-known accountant. He taught in Christian schools from 1905 to 1918 in Missouri and Arkansas. He established Monea College in Rector, Arkansas, in 1911. He coined the name Monea, which stood for Missouri and N.E. Arkansas. He later taught at Croft College (Academy), located 12 miles west of Paragould, near Stanford.

He was prosperous as a young man, dealing in real estate. He served two terms as county clerk, from 1900-1904. Many urged him to seek state office, but in 1905, he changed his priorities to one of helping train young people for lives of service to God and their fellowman. In the spring of 1922, he moved to Santa Rosa, California, to help finance Santa Rosa Academy, where his brother, Oliver Whitehead Gardner, was president. He was aided in all his undertakings by his beloved and faithful wife, Della Dollison Gardner; his first wife, Ada Trice, having died July 12,1901.

The children of Albert David Gardner are as follows:

1. Juanita Cecil, daughter of Ada Parolee Trice Gardner, born November 8, 1897, at Paragould, married Lucian Earl Taylor May 24, 1921, at Memphis, Tennessee. Issue: Mary Parolee "Marilee," born August 18, 1922, married Lloyd Pruitt issue: Barry Lee Pruitt born April 1, 1944, and Barbara Elaine Pruitt, born March 29, 1946.

Ellis Trice Taylor, born August 28, 1930. Cecil died March 18, 1992, and Earl died September 5,1985. Both buried at Croft Cemetery in Taylor section.

2. Ada Gardner, born July 6, 1901, died September 24, 1901. Buried next to her mother in Linwood Cemetery in Trice family lot.

3. Miriam Gladys was the third child and the daughter of Della Dollison Gardner, born August 1, 1904, married W.M. "Bill" Taylor born September 29, 1900, and died December 25, 1985: Issue: Harding Lipscomb, born March 23, 1923, married Joyce Hudgins issue: Cammie and Paul Taylor; William David born June 29, 1925, married Rose Marie Hecht, issue Davy Taylor born May 20, 1949. Second marriage Hilda Negron, issue: George William, born May 17, 1964; James Alfred, born October 27, 1931, married Alice Newman, issue: Stephen, Donald, Mark, Jimmy and Patty; Bonnie Lou born February 11, 1935, married Tony Libhart, issue: Deanna, Emily Dawn and Anthony III; Joe Allen born November 23, 1938, married Joyce Flemon, issue: Tamra Lynn and Alan.

4. Elizabeth, born July 13, 1906, in Rector, Arkansas, died October 5, 1906.

5. Albert David Jr., born October 27, 1907, Odessa, Missouri married Mary Lydia "Marilyd" Colley: issue: Eleanor Joan, Charles Albert, Albert David III, John and Michael.

6. Tolbert Fanning Gardner born September 8, 1909, Odessa, Missouri, married Pearl Cantrell. Issue: Richard Harold married Rosalee Alvina Gailon, issue: Jodi and Lane Scott "Scottie;" Brenda married Thomas Arvin Byron.

7. Lois Dean born April 23, 1912, married Bude H. Little on October 7, 1934, in Paragould. Issue: Mary Elizabeth born October 7, 1936, married James Cook October 15, 1954. Issue: Deborah Ann born March 16,1956; Becky born August 6, 1958; Elouise born February 24,1960; James Daniel born May 13, 1961. Nancy Eleanor born August 6, 1938, married first Hal Price April 1958, issue Juanite "Nite" born June 19, 1959, and Jeffery born December 19,1962; Virginia Beatrice born February 22, 1940, married Eual Higgins January 12,1957, issue: Cindy born December 19,1957, and Phyllis born July 20, 1959; Carl Neal born November 29, 1941, married De Anna Marko August 16, 1961; issue: Richard Little June 25, 1962; Paul Roger born October 11, 1944; Charlotte Lois born May 17, 1947, married Randy Bolding. Issue: son and two girls.

8. Jasper Hannibal Gardner born December

8,1913, married Alta Bea Hillis 1937. Issue: Joel married Renai Gentry, issue: Dean Alan born 1962 and Belinda born 1964. Martha lives in Memphis, Tennessee; James married Sharon Pace. Issue: Eric born 1971; Whitney born 1974 and Rory 1977 Jasper lives in Searcy, Arkansas.

A. D. Gardner died in Jonesboro, Arkansas, on February 13, 1952, of bronchial asthma and complications; buried Croft Cemetery. His grave is very close to grave of Dr. Croft.

**GARDNER** – The Gardner family had migrated from Southampton County, Virginia, to Robertson County, Tennessee, in 1799. In 1825 when the lands west of the Tennessee River were opened for settlement, John and Patience Whitehead Gardner moved to Weakley County, Tennessee. Their grandson, Richard Hannibal Gardner, arrived in Greene County, Arkansas, in 1857 from West Tennessee. He was born on November 18, 1831, in Weakley County, 12 miles south of Dresden, Tennessee. He was the son of Dr. Richard Whitehead Gardner and Eliza Harriet Thomas, the daughter of Major John Thomas Jr., of Weakley County. Major Thomas Jr. was the son of Gen. John Thomas Sr., of South Carolina. Dr. Gardner studied medicine at Louisville Medical College and received a Commission from President James H. Polk, with whom he was personally acquainted, a surgeon in the Mexican War. He served in General Cheatham's Brigade, Tennessee Volunteers. He was in Mexico until the end or the war, then returned to Weakley County. His wife died in September 1847, and while he was in Mexico, developed a chronic case of dysentery, which resulted in an early death for him. He passed away in 1852, while visiting his cousin, Betsy Carr, in Robertson County, and is buried in the Carr family graveyard. Before he died, he gave Richard Hannibal to Tolbert Fanning, a renowned Christian preacher and president of Franklin College, located five miles east of Nashville, Tennessee. He was 11 years old when he went with Tolbert Fanning and stayed at Franklin College until he was 21 years old. In the fall of 1853 he returned to West Tennessee after securing a job as leveler on the Nashville and Northwestern Railroad, of which his uncle, John A. Gardner, was president. He stayed with this railroad until March 19, 1856. On this date he married his college sweetheart, Miss Sarah Eliza Towles, daughter or Joseph and Elizabeth Towles, formerly Elizabeth Massey. They remained in Nashville for one year, then moved back to West Tennessee for a year and removed to Greene County, Arkansas, in October 1857 and sold goods until the fall of 1859.

He ran for assessor of the county, moved to Gainesville, and was appointed deputy clerk, under H. W. Glasscock, which position he held until the breaking out of the Civil War, and in June 1861, assisted Capt. Flavius S. White to make up the first company of volunteers from the county. He was appointed quartermaster until the regiment was organized; was then elected first lieutenant of the company, with Capt. F. S. White. The regiment remained at the Camp Ground three miles south of Gainesville. Col. Cross of Poinsett was the Colonel. He remained with the Company until it was reorganized in June 1862 and was allowed to return home to serve as recruiting officer. He returned home by way of Memphis and only got on the Arkansas side but a few days before the fall of Island 10, and with the Federals becoming in command of the Mississippi River to Vicksburg. He got up the White River as far as Des Arc and found his wife and two children at Hickory Plains, at his Uncle Albert Thomas. After making arrangements for his wife and children to be taken home, he went to St. Francis County and joined Capt. Allen's Calvary Company, which was soon made an infantry company. He was elected captain of the Company, and so remained until peace. He was with the Company in every fight or skirmish and received not a scratch; was never sick; had but one furlough.

*Richard Hannibal Gardner and sons and grandson. Front row: Arthur Cains, grandson Neely Gardner, and R.H. Gardner. Back row: Oliver Whithead, Albert David and Richard Neal Gardner.*

He was elected clerk of the county in 1864, but would not leave his Company, took the Amnesty Oath at Jacksonport in May 1865, and returned home just north of Gainesville to find his wife and children without food, except as his friend, H. W. Glasscock, could spare a portion of his very scanty allowance of very poor beef and some cornmeal, all the variety of vegetables he had.

In July he was of to be in Gainesville the next Saturday to meet Federal troops. He expected another fuss with the Federals, but was pleasantly surprised to learn that he had been selected and recommended as clerk of the county, and was soon commissioned by Gov. Murphy, and held this office until the election of 1866. By that time the state was being run by the notorious Powell Clayton and it was of no use for a Confederate to offer for office.

In 1872 he ran for the office of surveyor and held that position until 1882. That year his friends encouraged him to run against the incumbent David B. Warren, who had held the office of circuit court clerk for 10 years. He was elected after the hottest Canvas ever in the county by a large majority. He remained in the office for the next two terms. In April of 1875, he sold his farm above Gainesville and bought a hotel in Delaplaine on the St. Louis and Iron Mountain Railroad, a then very flourishing and business station. He remained there until the death of his wife in February 1880. He married again in August of the same year to Mrs. Lou G. Batey Harris from West Tennessee. She was the mother of one child, who died at 1 month old. His wife died in October 1881, suddenly, of heart disease.

In the fall of 1882 he was elected clerk of the county and on the 13th of November of that year was married to Mrs. Anne E. Thompson, daughter of James M. Johnson, native of Mississippi. They remained in Gainesville until the county seat was moved to Paragould.

His children by his first wife, Sarah E. Towles, were: Arthur Cains, born April 16, 1857; Fredonia Claypole, born January 24, 1859; Joseph Stapleton, born August 5, 1860; Hannibal Elmore, born December 15, 1862; Flora Gertrude, born August 25, 1865; Ada B., born November 21, 1867; Oliver Whitehead, born August 14, 1869; Albert David, born November 7, 1871; Richard Neely, born July 30,1874; Algernon Sidney, born November 9, 1876. His children by his third wife, Anne E. Johnson Thompson were: Berah Blanch, born September 6, 1883; Kathleen Mavourneen, born August 29, 1886, and Maggie Albertine, born June 1, 1889.

He was the founding member of the Christian Church in Paragould, which was organized September 6, 1885, under the name of the Church of Christ. The first service was held in the old Famous building, which stood next to the railroad behind Joseph's store. In his obituary which appeared in the *Paragould Soliphone* in April 19, 1906, the following was noted: "As a public official he was painstaking, accommodating and efficient. He was a plain man of the people, and the people trusted him. In private life he was as nearly without faults, as it is possible to be and yet be human. He is absolutely clean and was actuated always by the promptings of Christianity in whatever he did. We never knew a man who came nearer living in ideal Christian life." R. H. Gardner died on April 11, 1906, while visiting his two sons, Al and Neal, both professors at Western Bible and Literary College in Odessa, Missouri. His third wife, Anne. E. Johnson Thompson Gardner died in 1929 at the age of 85.

**GARMRATH** – G. Wayne Garmrath, moved to Paragould from Flint, Michigan, in 1962.

Wayne was born and raised in the Stanford Community in 1932. After graduation from Stanford High School, he served in the U.S. Army four years. Wayne died in 1990 and is buried in Greene County Memorial Gardens.

*Garmrath family: Clifton, Geraldine, Wayne and Steve Garmrath made at Harmon Play Field on November 19, 1980.*

Geraldine (Smith) was born in Paragould but lived most of her life in Poplar Bluff, Missouri, where she graduated from Poplar Bluff High School and Bluff City Business College. The couple were both working in Flint, Michigan, when they met, married and had two sons, Clifton and Steve.

In 1997, Geraldine retired from the Greene County Department of Human Services after 32 years of service. Clifton and his son, Matthew; Steve and his family, Lantha (Felty), wife; three sons Tyler, Alex and John Koy all reside in the Paragould area.

**GARMROTH** – This family was raised in the Stanford Community. They were cotton and soybean farmers all the years they resided in the community. All the children attended Stanford School and Stanford Methodist Church during those years.

Martin and Betty had four children: Danny, Cheryl, Patty and Jimmie. They moved to the Marmaduke Community after starting their family. Martin and Betty are deceased and are buried at Cude Cemetery, Marmaduke.

Alma Jean married Roy Arant. They lived in Paragould with a son, Brent. Alma Jean owned and operated a beauty shop most of her life. She

*The family of Harry C. and Dora Garmrath: Lynn, Wayne, Harry "Pet," Joe, Dora, Alma Jean and Bob. In front is Harry Lynn. Martin Carroll "M.C." not pictured. The family gathered for this picture in 1951.*

is deceased and buried in Greene County Memorial Gardens.

Billy Joe married Betty Orick and they had three daughters. Linda, Debbie and Pam. The couple continues to live in the Stanford Community.

George Wayne married Geraldine Smith. They have two sons, Clifton and Steve. The family moved from Flint, Michigan, to Paragould in 1962 where they have continue to reside. Wayne is now deceased and buried in Greene County Memorial Gardens.

Bobby Max married Laura Jean Edwards. The couple have two children, Bryan and Beth. Bob is deceased and is buried in Greene County Memorial Gardens.

Harry Lynn and Veranda Rogers and they have three daughters. They are Carol, Lee Ann and Christy. The couple live in the Clinton, Arkansas, area where Lynn pastors a church.

**GARNER** – The Garners now living in Greene County AR are descendants of pioneers who migrated from North Carolina to McNairy County, TN in the early 1800s and on to Greene County, AR between 1870 and 1890.

The story begins with Margaret "Peggy" Garner and her two sons Calaway and Noah. They left North Carolina prior to 1809, stopped in Eastern Tennessee for a few years and settled in McNairy County near where Finger is today.

*Albert Clyde Garner and wife, Orah Della (Rowe), and children (left to right); Wavaline, Curtis, and Marcella ca. 1929.*

It is not known when the family arrived in West Tennessee but the first record of them is the 1830 McNairy County, TN population census. Calaway is listed has head of household with his mother, Margaret and brother Noah. Nothing is known of the fate of the two sons' father.

Around 1833 the Reubin Queen family paused near Margaret's home on their way west from Carroll County, TN. They had left their home in North Carolina between 1819 and 1827 and had stopped in Carroll County on their way to Texas. Reubin and Mary's daughter Laura (fourth of eight children) met and married Noah. The Queen family continued on west to Texas. In 1850, Noah and Laura Garner owned a $500 farm and could neither read nor write.

Noah and Laura raised 14 children, all born in McNairy County and five made the move to Greene County, AR. However, there is no evidence that Noah and Laura ever left McNairy County. One of their sons, George died in the Civil War.

Laura lived to 58 and Noah died at 75. They, along with Noah's mother, Margaret, are all buried at the Cave Spring Cemetery in Chester County.

Noah and Laura's fifth child, Noah Zachariah married Sarah Clemens in McNairy County around 1862. Sarah was the daughter of James and Elizabeth Clemens/Clement. Sarah's older sister Elizabeth Clemens had married Zach's older brother Calaway a few years earlier. Sarah and Elizabeth are thought to be part Indian (possibly Cherokee). However, no record of this has been found. Zach, like his father, was a farmer. And also like his father, parented a huge family of 11 kids.

After starting their family with eight kids in McNairy County in 1878, Zach moved his family west. They traveled in a wagon pulled by a team of mules, crossed the Mississippi River on a pull ferry and stopped in northeast Arkansas along Crowley's Ridge. Here Zach and Sarah finished their family with three more girls. The first girl they named after their home state, Tennessee.

Zach and Sarah settled in Union Township of Greene County, four miles due east of the settlement that would become Stanford, AR. They selected an area of good bottom farmland with a creek running through it. It was located approximately one-half mile due north of where Mt. Home church is located today. By 1883, Zach's farm had grown to over 200 acres. Today the land is still being farmed but not much remains in Zach's line. It is however still known to many of Zach and Sarah's descendants as "The Ole' Home Place"

*Submitted by Hank Garner*

**GARNER** – Robert S. Garner, the oldest child of George and Melissa Garner, was born Aug 13, 1897 in Greene County, AR. He married Delphia Howard, daughter of Richard and Tennie Howard, also of Greene County. Delphia was born Oct. 16, 1903.

*L-R: Robert Garner, Donna Fears Archer (baby), and Donald Fears*

Their ancestors had come to Arkansas from Tennessee. The Garners were farmers in the Crowley's Ridge section of Greene County. In addition to the regular row crops, they supplemented their income by planting sorghum and operating a sorghum mill for several years.

Six children were born to this union. All six are still living.

Nye Garner Cureton was born Aug 31, 1924. She is married to William Cureton of Cash, AR, who was born Oct. 19, 1919. Nye is a retired teacher and William, a retired farmer.

Ambrose Garner was born Aug 25, 1926. He is married to Margaret Copeland from Jonesboro. Margaret was born April 22, 1932. Ambrose and Margaret have spent their entire married life in Florida where both taught in public schools and colleges.

Elfreda Garner Fears was born July 29, 1928. She is married to Donald Fears of Stanford. Donald was born on March 5, 1926. Elfreda has devoted her time to being a wife and mother. She and Donald have a farming operation in the Stanford community. They have four children:

1. Ronnie Fears (Nov 18, 1952) married Linda Gilliam (March 28, 1954) they have three children: Victoria, Jessica and Deirdre. Linda is a housewife. Ronnie works for Emerson Electric and farms.

2. Cathy Fears Reeves (April 25, 1954) married Johnny Reeves from the South Greene County community. They have one son, Adam. Cathy and Johnny live in Meridian, MS where they have various business interests.

3. Jerry Fears (Dec 24, 1944) married Lenrose Killigrew of Gulfport, MS (Oct 2, 1952). Jerry and Lenrose live in Milton, FL

4. Donna Fears Archer (July 11, 1962) married Mike Archer (Jan 7, 1962). They have two children, Alexander and Erica. Mike is in law enforcement and Donna is a bank employee.

*L-R: Lois Garner Martin, Neal Garner, Ambrose Garner, Nye Garner Cureton, Faye Garner Greene, Delphia Garner. Seated: Elfreda Garner Fears, holding Ronnie Keith Fears*

Faye (Garner) Greene (June 8, 1932) married Charles Greene (Feb 12, 1931-June 12, 1983) of Nelsonville, O. The Greene's lived their married life in St. Louis, MO. Faye is a housewife and Charles was an aerospace engineer. They had two children:

1. Carol Greene Anderson (July 30, 1957) lives in Dallas, TX with her two children, David and Amy.

2. Jeffrey Greene (Nov 29, 1962) lives in St. Louis.

Lois Garner Martin (Nov 29, 1937) married Gene Martin of the Dixie community. They have lived in Germantown, TN for many years where both have worked in the business community.

Neal Garner (Sept 14, 1942) the youngest of the Garner children married Melba Thompson (May 16, 1945) of Paragould. They have lived more than 30 years in the Griffithville community in White County where they are farmers. They have one child, Jamie (Feb 8, 1979).

The Garner family has worked hard and been blessed with good health, prosperity and many happy achievements!

**GARNER/FULKERSON** – Mae Fulkerson (Oct 1, 1914 Heber Springs AR) was the daughter of William and Lola Fulkerson. He was a brakeman for the Missouri Pacific Railroad. She had two brothers, Garland (Feb 20, 1911 Hamlin, AR) and William Andrew Jr. (Oct 19, 1928). Dillon (Sept 22, 1913, Paragould) was the son of Mr. and Mrs. Gilbert Garner. Gilbert Garner was a schoolteacher who became a pharmacist. He owned and operated Garner Drug Store from about 1922 until he sold it in 1953. Dillon had one brother, Houston.

Will Fulkerson moved his wife, Lola and two children, Mae and Garland to Paragould in 1926 from Searcy to work for the railroad. Their youngest child, Bill was born in 1928. Lola died in 1938.

Mae married Dr. Dillon Garner June 29, 1938. Dillon had graduated from the University of Arkansas and Tulane Medical School in 1938. They moved to Chattanooga, TN, where he was a surgical resident. Their first son, Philip, was born Oct 10, 1940. Dillon won a fellowship in surgery at the Cleveland Clinic so the family moved to Cleveland. He entered the army in 1942 as a lieutenant and left the service when the war was over as a major.

*Mae and Dillon Garner, Sept. 1974.*

They moved back to Paragould where Dillon opened his medical practice. Their second son, Michael Andrew, was born Jan 5, 1948. In 1951 they moved to Dallas, TX, where Dillon started his practice specializing in surgery. Their third son, Douglas Gilbert, was born June 30, 1953.

Phil graduated from the University of Texas and married Alice (Anderson) Lindsey "Vicki" in 1962. He served three years in the Navy. Their daughter, Edie, was born Dec 15, 1966 and Jason was born May 30, 1970. Phil works for Baxter Pharmaceuticals in Mountain Home, AR.

Edie married Robert Stewart and they live in Collierville, TN. They have two sons, Matthew and Joshua. Jason and his wife, Heidi, live in Nashville, TN, where he is in the music business. They have one son, Jackson, born in 1999.

Mike graduated from Vanderbilt University. He studied International Business in Canada. He then moved to San Francisco, where he worked for an insurance company. He eventually moved back to Dallas. Mike died Nov 17, 1977, of a heart attack at age 30. His heart had been weakened by polio, which he had as a child.

Doug graduated from Vanderbilt University and married Kathy Hoffman in 1976. They had two sons, Justin (Feb 17, 1981) and Matthew (April 30, 1984). They later divorced. In 1996 he married Jane Allen from Fayetteville, GA. They live in Greenville, S. C. where Doug works for Amoco Oil Company. Justin is a student at the University of Arizona and Matthew is a high school senior.

Dillon retired from the medical field in 1987. They moved to Greenville, S. C. in 1999 to be close to their son.

*Submitted by Pat Fulkerson*

**GERDES** – August P.H. (June 7, 1866-March 20, 1948) came to Greene County from Franklin County, MO about 1887 and purchased land in Union Township in the Ramer's Chapel community. He was the son of Ludwig "Louis" (1841) and Marie (Sickendieck) Gerdes of Missouri. In 1889 he returned to Missouri and on Oct 10, 1899 married Louise Kappelman (March 2, 1870-March 19, 1947), daughter of Fred and Katherina Panhorst Kapelman.

*Louis Gerdes.*

They returned immediately to Greene County and farmed in Union Township until about 1922 when they moved to Lafe. Their children:
1. Louis (June 19, 1891-June 26, 1985)
2. Emma (1893)
3. Lydia (1895)
4. Oswald (1897)
5. Ida (1902)
6. Arthur (1904)
7. Otto (1906)
8. Mary (l908)
9. Helene "Lena" (1911)

Louis, a WWI US Army veteran, married Nov 22, 1922 Ollie Pearl Brown (Dec. 13, 1903-Dec 28, 1977) daughter of Oscar T. (1880) and Dosha (Warren) Brown (1881). They farmed in the Mill Creek community in Clay County on the northern border of Greene County. Their children:
1. Marion (1923)
2. Norman (1926)
3. Edward (1927)
4. Melva Deane (1930)
5. Cloyce (1935)

Edward G. (Dec 20, 1927) was in the USCG 1945-1947; married Aug 20, 1948 Mildred Catherine Stephens (Jan 24, 1927) daughter of James C. and Nancy Belle Stephens. Their children:
1. Randal Keith (1952) RN, married Jan 2, 1971 Charlotte R. Bowers (1952) RN.
2. Mark O. (June 14, 1962), software engineer, married March 15, 1990 Toni L. Barnhill (1969).

**GETSON** – The first rice crop in Greene County was grown on the farm of Jack (1863-1944) and Rachel Getson (1875-1951) in 1911. Jack's father was a captain in the Confederate Army and the family moved from Mississippi to Texas soon after the war. As a young man he was a cowboy and herded cattle to market on the Old Chilsom Trail. He followed the timber industry going from Oregon to Emminence, Missouri, where he met and married Rachel Carr. They came to North East Arkansas around 1890; settling and buying farms in Lawrence, Randolph and Greene Counties.

By the turn of the century he was shipping many car loads of cattle and hogs to St. Louis on the Iron Mountain Line. The family home place is about a half mile southeast of O'Kean in Greene County, and is still owned and farmed by his descendants.

Jack and Rachel were the parents of 10 children of which seven grew to adulthood: Mable, Tom, Cina, Samantha, John, Juanita and Sarah.

Mabel, 1892-1953, married Henry Russell, 1886-1949; merchant. Issues: Amos married Laura Cook and Sylvia married Harry Midgett.

Thomas married first Hazel Fowler and second Opal Gates. Tom was a veteran of WWI and a farmer. Issues: Juanita married first Eulis Phillips and second Cecil Heral; Betty married Shelby Griffin; Doris married Telfair Biggs Jr.; Tommy married Betty Alphin; Jimmy married Pat Smith; Lois married Ralph Steele; and Shirley married Jackie Crabtree.

Cina married Joe B. Like, a farmer. Issues: Verna married first William Roth and second Edward Clement; Joe Jr., 1921-1943; Leveta married first Willis Cribbs and second Arvil Ball; Johnny married Frankie Nunally; Lavaughn married Robert Moore; Ann married E. W. Rooker; Bonnie married first Todis Gates and second Bly Sifford.

*Jack and Rachel Carr Getson, circa 1930*

Samantha married Lee Rice; teacher, mail carrier, landowner. Issue: Wanda Lee married Jim Vaughn-teacher, writer and publisher.

John married Inez McKnelly. In 1955 they were Greene County Farm Family of the Year. Issues: Carolyn married Vondus Elledge; Norma married first Kenneth Roberts and second Larry Mouser; Helen married Dallas Roberts; John Carman married first Judy Ellis and second Jerry Vaughter.

Juanita married Harry Ragsdale, farmer. Issues: Randall, 1932-1940; Marion married Joyce Neece; Nathaniel married Geraldine Gentry; Harelon, 1939-1964, married Nellie Ivy, June, 1941-1958; Ronnie married Debbie Haynes.

Sarah married first Joe Friar, second Rudolph Goldman, and third Grant Ford. She retired from nursing profession. Issues: Larry Friar married first Nancy Givan and second Charlyn Witte; Owen Goldman married first Rosita Henn and second Dr. Helen True; Annetta married first Gale Studebaker and second Dennis Bosque; John Curtis married first LaDonna Adams and second Eva Colley.

Jack and Rachel have many descendants.

**GLENN** – Wayne Glenn came to Paragould in 1986 from Dexter, MO, where he was in the grain bin, irrigation and metal building construction business. He worked for G G Electric until he met Martin Buchman and Bill Lester and they formed a corporation, known as The WAG Company, Inc. Wayne had invented a backhoe that attached to a pick-up truck and The WAG Company manufactured and marketed the product.

Martin Buchman introduced Wayne to Pauletta (Pillow) Killian in Sept. 1986 and a lasting relationship ensued and they married on Oct 7, 1987. This formed the coming together of two families. Wayne, son of Elmer and Noma Glenn, his children, Christopher Charles Glenn and Natalie Nicole Glenn and Pauletta, daughter of Paul and Euna Pillow and her children, Audrey Kay Killian and Cara Lynn Killian.

Pauletta taught social studies and coached volleyball and track at Paragould High School until 1988. At that time they formed a partnership and went into the business of selling and installing garage doors. The name of their company started out as Shamrock Enterprises, but someone else had that name so they changed it to Paragould Overhead Doors. Wayne continued in his manufacturing business and changed its name to Glenncorp, Incorporated in 1994.

Wayne and Pauletta joined First United Methodist Church in 1988. Cara was added to the roll when she was baptized in 1995. Cara attends Paragould High School, Where she is a sophomore and a cheerleader.

After graduating from Ridgecrest High School in 1988, Audrey attended Arkansas State University and worked for them part-time and obtained a degree in finance in 1992. Audrey is employed at Teleflora.

Chris Glenn, after a year at Southwest State in Springfield, MO, came to live with Wayne and Pauletta in 1991. He attended Crowley's Ridge College and worked for Glenncorp part-time and obtained his degree in industrial engineering from Arkansas State University in 1997. He is now employed at Darling Store Fixtures.

Natalie stayed in Dexter and attended Southeast Missouri State in Cape Girardeau, MO, graduating with a degree in political science. She is employed by the registrar's office at Southeast.

In 1991 Audrey married Steven Boggs, son of Roger and Phyllis Phillips and in 1996 Chris married Amy Eubanks, daughter of Wendell and Jennie Eubanks. In March 1997, Audrey and Steven Boggs had a daughter, Kali Tristen Boggs.

Wayne died on July 5, 1999.

*Submitted by Pauletta Glenn*

**GOEBEL** – Since the early 1900s, Greene County has been home to Mary Agnes (Okle) Goebel.

As a young girl, she and her family moved to Paragould from Pine Bluff.

Her father, Charles Frederick Okle, was an engineer for Cotton Belt Railroad in Paragould, while his wife, Minnie Myrtle (Hill) raised three children, Mary Agnes, Charles Joseph and James Francis in a house on South Third Street.

All three children attended elementary school at St. Mary's Catholic Church

Mary Agnes, who was born on Sept 3, 1912 in Pine Bluff, graduated from St. Mary's in 1926 and moved to St. Louis with her father, who was transferred by the railroad. Her brothers were sent to school at Subiaco College (now Academy) in Subiaco, AR.

While in St. Louis, Mary Agnes attended St. Philomena's Technical School, a sewing school for girls. Almost 10 years later, her father was again transferred by the railroad and they moved to Malden, MO., where Mary Agnes would meet her future husband.

On April 10, 1934, Mary Agnes married Leonard Alfonso Goebel at St. Bernard's Catholic Church in Malden. Leonard, who was born on July 16, 1909 in Ridgeway, IL, was the son of Nicholas Theodore and Elizabeth (Conner) Goebel.

One year after their first child, Mary Agnes, was born in 1935, the family moved to Paragould living in a house just across the Arkansas-Missouri state line off of Highway 412. They made two more moves onto property owned by the Abell and Straub families before finally settling into a home that Leonard built in the 1940s in the Oak Grove area.

Over the years, the couple raised 10 children and one nephew, including Mary Agnes, Ida Marie, Ella Josephine, Phyllis Ann, Leonard Lawrence "Larry", Helen Elizabeth, Adrian Gerald, James Leon Maxwell, Margaret Jeanne, Martha Alice and David William.

All but the two youngest children attended St. Mary's school and all but one graduated from Oak Grove High School. Both Larry and Adrian are veterans of the U.S. Army.

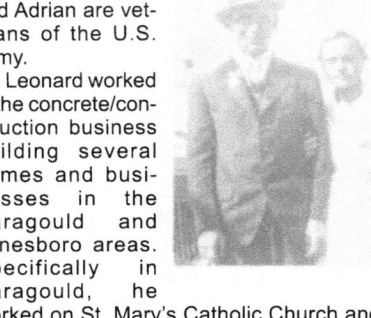

Leonard worked in the concrete/construction business building several homes and businesses in the Paragould and Jonesboro areas. Specifically in Paragould, he worked on St. Mary's Catholic Church and built the first Reynolds Park swimming pool. In Jonesboro, he worked on the bridge still standing on what is now appropriately named Bridge Street.

Mary Agnes was a homemaker and soloist at St. Mary's Catholic Church.

Leonard died on Nov. 30, 1968 and is buried at St. Mary's Cemetery. Mary Agnes currently lives on West McDonald Street in Paragould.

As of July 2000, she has 21 grandchildren, 24 great grandchildren and one great great grandchild.

*Submitted by Jo Lampkins*

**GOINS** – Charles Albert Goins was born November 17, 1881, in Coles County, Illinois. He was the second of William Preston and Lydia Elizabeth Goins' 11 children. The family moved to Greene County, Arkansas, in 1884.

Albert lived in Paragould from 1884 until 1896. His father farmed and raised cattle. In 1895 he opened a meat market in Paragould where Albert was trained in all the work of the meat market.

In 1896 the family moved to a farm in the Cache bottoms that his father got through the Donation Act. Here he farmed, cut fence posts, and fenced the farm. He learned the blacksmith and sawmill trade. Also he learned to run the wheat thrasher which they took all over the county to thrash wheat.

*Charles Albert Goins.*

In March 1901 he married George Ann Morrow, 1880-1937. They were the parents of six children: Ora, 1902-1942; Roy, 1904-1904; Bertha, 1908-1908; Eva, 1911- ; Edna, 1913-1914; Fred, 1915- .

Two of these children had issue. Ora married Ruby Ward and they had Joanna Goins. She married Larry Justice and had a son, Travis, and a daughter, Gwen.

Eva married Check Daughhetee. They had Grady, Alma Dean and Danny Buster. Grady married Mary Joe Henson. They had four sons: Joe, John, Jim and Gaylon.

Alma Dean married Carl Hamlin. They had a son, Phil.

Danny Buster married Pearlie Roberts and had Angie and Danny Lee.

In 1901 Albert and Georgeann moved to Peach Orchard in Clay County. He worked for Abb Brown when he first moved there. Albert had a very interesting and varied career. He had many interest. He had a store, warehouse, and cafe. He bought and sold lumber, logs, animal hides, chickens, eggs, etc. He bought, raised, and sold mules and hogs. He raised plants and sold them at home and all over the county. He had a broom maker and sold brooms. He bought several lots in Peach Orchard and built rental houses on them.

In his early years he would go to picnics all over the county. He would dig a pit, roast a pig, and sell barbecue sandwiches and cold drinks. He had cupid doll stands where people played games and the lucky winner won a cupid doll.

Albert died December 20, 1955, and is buried in Morrow Cemetery in Greene County, Arkansas, between his wife, Georgeann and son, Ora, and close to his mother, father, brother John, and sisters, Mary and Pearl.

Albert has many relatives in Clay and Greene Counties and scattered all over the country. His son, Fred Goins, and daughter, Eva Goins Daughhetee, still live in Peach Orchard on the property their father bought and lived on. They have both retired. They have discontinued raising plants, the broom marketing and other business ventures.

One can still visualize all of these ventures while standing on this property which is all still in the family. Eva's husband, Check Daughhetee, had a large trucking business which his sons carried on after his death. All of Albert's and Georgeann's deceased children and Albert's siblings, except Roscoe, are buried in Greene County.

**GOINS** – Both John and Cora were born in Arkansas, living on farms all their lives. Cora, one of 10 children born to Mary Alice (Burkeen) and Logan Smith, was born in Randolph County in 1910. John, born in 1902 in Greene County, was one of 11 children of Lydia (Lafferty) and William P. Goins. They were married November 23, 1930, in the home of Tillman Prince.

Six girls and one boy were born to Cora and John: Doris (Reeves), Louise (Richardson), Mary (Reilly), Lois (Richardson), Jane (Howard), Lydia (Brown), and David. Three girls, neither triplets, nor twins, share the same birthday, November 1st. Cora earned a degree in education at Arkansas State College and taught school 35 years. Her first teaching experience began in one-room buildings at Grambling and Pruett Schools. She taught junior high several years at Stanford and Lafe Public Schools. Before retirement, she certified to teach in the Stanford elementary grades.

John was in military service stationed at Fort Snelling, Minnesota. He also worked in paper and lathe mills in International Falls, Minnesota, on the Canadian border. It was here that, for the first time at age 18, he met one of his older brothers, Rosco Goins. Life was good here and he enjoyed sharing these experiences with friends and relatives.

With help from Walker and Logan Smith, Jeff Morrow, Charles Wallis and Bill Wallis, John built a house for his family in the "hills" section of their 140 acres. The family settled here in time for their fourth daughter's birth in 1937. It was wonderful having electricity, and later "running" water. Their first clothes' washer, a Maytag, was purchased in 1940. That same year, a floor model radio was bought, bringing friends and relatives on Saturday nights to hear the "Grand Ole Opry" together.

Most of their social life centered around

church and school activities. Both Cora and John were Christians and raised their children likewise. They were active members of The Commissary Church of Christ where John served as an elder for several years. Both taught Bible classes.

*John and Cora Goins.*

Farm life was difficult, yet rewarding. There was always work to be done with the farm, equipment, fields, gardens, orchards, cooking, canning and the animals. With seven children to raise, teaching, farming (plus John drove a school bus several years) and doing community work, time seemed to go by quickly!

In 1937 John traded their farm mules, Buck and Kate (gifts from John's dad), for an F-12, steel-tired tractor which made life a little easier and less stressful. Also, John built a smokehouse and fruit cellar to store the 500 quarts of fruits and vegetables that were canned each year.

John died September 28, 1982, at age 79. Cora died November 18, 1994, at age 84. Both are buried in the Morrow Cemetery between Stanford and Beech Grove near the farm they always gladly called "home."

**GOINS** – Seven children grew up in the John and Cora Goins household between Beech Grove and Stanford, AR. Mom and Dad loved all and we always had plenty of good food to eat, clothes on our backs and shoes on our feet. We were a spiritually united family, not spoiled, but well behaved with a great respect for our parents and grandparents as well. Each of us children had something unique to contribute to our family and later to the community. People trusted us to honest, genuine, face value persons.

To the union of Doris (Goins) Reeves and Junior Reeves (Fairview community) were born five children:
1. Norma Lou Reeves (Beech Grove, AR)
2. Norman Reeves (Paragould, AR)
3. Junetta Becker (Paragould, AR)
4. Raymond Reeves (Clarinda, IA)
5. Charla Kay Reeves (Beech Grove, AR)

Louise, the second daughter, married William Richardson of Cardwell, MO. Together they had one daughter, Sandra Meeker. She is active in city and community affairs.

The third daughter in the family, Mary (Goins) Reilly, met and married Edwin Sidney Reilly of Hope, AR. The children in this marriage are:
1. John Edwin Reilly (Fayetteville, TN)
2. Mary Katherine Roznos (St. Louis, MO)
3. Thomas Allen Reilly (St. Louis, MO)

Kenneth and Karin Lois Richardson, the fourth girl in the family, recently returned to Paragould after living in St. Louis for nearly 40 years. Their children include:
1. Robert Dewayne Richardson (St. Louis, MO)
2. Cynthia Richardson Noblin (Paragould, AR)
3. Jimmy David Richardson (St. Louis, MO)

Jane Elizabeth Howard, fifth daughter, married Jearl F. Howard of Paragould and both have been teachers at Crowley's Ridge Academy for many years. Their children are:
1. Carie Lynn (Howard) Samuel (Springfield, MO)
2. Timothy Howard (Fulton, MS)

Lydia (Goins) Brown, the sixth and last daughter, met and married Orville Brown of Wichita, KS while teaching school in Denver, CO. Their two children are:

Lisa Ann (Brown) Walton (Cedar Rapids, IA)
Phillip O. Brown (Louisville, KY)

David Leon Goins, the only son and the last child in the family, married Judith Marie (Palmer) Goins and together they have five children:
1. Stephan Preston Goins (Beech Grove, AR)
2. Leah Michelle Douglas (Paragould, AR)
3. David Allen Goins (Beech Grove, AR)
4. Beverly Tripp (Paragould, AR)
5. Rebecca Jane Goins (Paragould, AR)

To this point in history, there are 35 great grandchildren in the John and Cora Goins family. We are proud of our history and thank those who had the foresight to publish this wonderful, Greene County Historical Book.

Leonard Alfonso Goebel married Mary Agnes Goebel on April 10, 1934 at St. Bernard's Catholic Church in Malden, MO. Two years later, the couple moved to Paragould and raised 11 children, including a nephew.

**GOINS** – Mary Irene Goins, was born in Paragould, Arkansas, on July 29, 1886, the daughter of William Preston and Lydia Elizabeth "Lafferty" Goins.

The family moved to the farm acquired by her father in 1896 by the Donation Act in what was called Cache River Bottoms. She went to county schools. Then she went to Paragould in 1909 and took nurses' training. This school was on the top floor of the Dixon Memorial Hospital. She graduated from there in 1913 and began a nursing career.

She had a very interesting and varied career. She was the Public Health Nurse during the existence of the pest house or the quarantine house where the highly contagious patients were kept with such diseases as typhoid and yellow fever. She worked with Dr. Scott, who was the county doctor. The pest house existed until approximately 1920. She was also the nurse for the patients from the county poor farm.

She was a nurse at Dixon Memorial Hospital for many years and was supervisor of nurses at one time. Mary Goins was the Metropolitan Insurance nurse from 1933-1938, according to their records in New York, New York. She usually did this work in the morning and private duty at night. At one time she did private nursing for Governor Futrell.

*Mary Irene Goins*

She belonged to the Alumnae Association of the Dixon Memorial Hospital School of Nursing, organized in 1930. Her uniforms were starched and ironed to perfection, and her shoes were always shined. She always looked nice and professional. Some of Mary Goins' uniforms, a white shawl and other items are in The Mark Twain School Museum in Poplar Bluff, Missouri.

She was a member of Seventh and Mueller Church of Christ and taught the Ladies Bible Class.

In 1941 she bought the big house at 602 South Eighth Street that J. E. Landrum's widow, Eula, had built in 1906. She lived there until her death in 1957. She kept this house painted in excellent condition, as it was her pride and joy and some show of accomplishment for her many years of hard work. She also took pride that she nursed so many different people in her nursing career and helped most to regain their health.

She is buried in Morrow Cemetery in Greene County, Arkansas, next to her mother and father and close to her brothers, Albert and John, and her sister, Pearl Goins Morrow.

**GOINS** – William Preston "W.P." Goins was born May 11, 1853, in Hamilton County, Tennessee, to Oscar Claiborne and Nancy Florence "Potter" Goins. He left Tennessee between 1870 and 1878 and went to Clark County, Illinois where he met and married Lydia Elizabeth Lafferty, daughter of Parmenas and Mary Lafferty. In 1884 they moved to Greene County, Arkansas, in three covered wagons.

They had 11 children, eight boys and three girls: Roscoe, Albert, Lewis, Mary, Jimmie, Edna, Chester, Jessie, Pearl, William and John. Five died in infancy. Chester died at 24 with a ruptured appendix.

Roscoe married Syavia Ruter and settled in International Falls, Minnesota. Albert married Georgeann Taylor and settled in Peach Orchard, Arkansas. Mary was a nurse and didn't marry. Pearl married Jeff Morrow. John married Cora Smith and both families settled in Greene County, Arkansas.

In 1884 W.P. bought land on Fairview Road and farmed it. In 1895 he opened a meat market on Court Street and closed it in 1896.

On November 9, 1896, he took the Donation

*John and Cora Goins and seven children (left to right): David Goins, Lydia Goins Brown, Jane Goins Howard, John and Cora Goins, Lois Goins Richardson, Mary Goins Reilly, Louise Goins Richardson, and Doris Goins Reeves.*

211

Act to 160 acres of land in the Cache Bottoms. He built a log cabin, improved and paid taxes on the land. Because it was swampy land, W.P. traveled to Little Rock to obtain help in draining it. After workers helped to clear and drain the land, he hired a dredge boat operator to dredge the ditch now called "Swam Pond."

*William Preston and Lydia Elizabeth Goins.*

He owned a black smith shop and sawmill. He bought, raised and traded cattle, horses and mules. He owned the first threshing machine in Greene County. He bought it in 1912 and traveled throughout the county helping other farmers harvest their crops.

The farm has been in the Goins family and farmed by the Goins family for over 100 years. David Goins, his grandson, farmed this land and was named one of two top farm families in 1997 by the Farm Bureau.

In 1912 W.P. Goins bought the Big Rocks. This 40 acres is still in the Goins family and it is a tradition to go up there on Easter Sunday and have a traditional egg hunt.

W.P. planted large orchards of apples, peaches, apricots and blue concord grapes. He raised bees and sold honey and bees wax. They had a press to press the bees wax. At one time he had 150 stands of bees.

He told many stories of growing up in Tennessee and living through the Civil War there. The Union soldiers camped on their plantation once. They took all their food supply and killed all their hogs, except one old poor sow. They had to tear the boards out of the smoke house floor and boil the dirt and strain it to get salt.

He owned a fiddle. He played for the soldiers one night and when he awoke the next morning the soldiers were gone and so was his fiddle. He followed them. The soldiers were crossing the Tennessee River on logs. He found the one that had his fiddle and went for it. The soldier wasn't going to give the 12 year old boy his fiddle. W.P. was about to drown him so the story goes. The officer saw this and made him give W.P. his fiddle. David Goins, his grandson, has the fiddle 134 years later.

W.P. died in 1950 at 97 and half years old. He is buried in Morrow Cemetery in Greene County, Arkansas, next to his wife Lydia, with John, Mary, Pearl and Albert buried close by. All the other children, except Roscoe are buried in Greene County.

**GOOD** – Harold C. Good (Feb 6, 1913 Blytheville, AR) was the oldest of 12 children of John Lafayette and Sarah Myrtle (Nutt) Good. John L. and S. Myrtle were married March 17, 1912 in Blytheville, AR. They later moved to Big Island (near Dixie community) in Craighead County, AR.

Harold C. Good married B. Lorene Sims, daughter of Herbert and Maude (Byrd) Sims in 1931 at Deason Lake (near Dixie community) in Craighead County, AR. Harold and Lorene moved to Greene County in 1937-38. During WWII, Harold did not serve in the armed services due to a physical impairment (loss of three fingers from right hand). He worked in a defense plant in Detroit where airplane motors were built. They had four living children: Hoyt, Gail, Myrna and Steve, all graduated from Paragould High School during the 1950s.

Harold did some farming, but carpentering was his real interest. The family lived in the farming areas of the county until fall of 1950 when they moved into the city of Paragould. Their home was at 1025 S. Sixth St. until they departed for California. During the 1940s and 1950s, he built several homes in Paragould, as well as remodeling homes. During this period, he also worked on the Norfork Dam, the dam at Paducah, KY and construction at Eaker AFB in Blytheville.

Following the graduation of their youngest son, Steve, in 1958, Harold and Lorene moved to California where he continued in the building and construction trade until his retirement in 1976. He was a life member of the United Brotherhood of Carpenters and Joiners of America.

13 years of retirement were on the Colorado River in California where favorite fishing holes were easily accessible. Sightseeing was an enjoyable past time and many miles were placed on a truck camper as they seized the opportunity to see America from California to Maine and across the northern states to Washington taking in scenic National Parks along the route. There were several return trips to Arkansas to visit family (including daughter, Myrna, who lives in Peach Orchard) as well as a couple of trips to Hawaii (where son, Steve, lives).

*Harold and Lorene Good.*

Harold was a very practical man. For example, in 1991 after living in California for 31 years he decided to return to Paragould. When asked by his daughter, Gail, (who returned to Paragould in 1997) why he was returning to Paragould, he replied, "I'm going home to be close to the graveyard." At that time he was still very active, having just returned from a trip to the northwest to visit grandchildren, great-grandchildren and the burial place of his son, Hoyt, in Eureka, CA. However, he always planned for events that he knew lay ahead. Lorene died in Aug 1995 and Harold died in Jan 2000. Both are buried at Woods Chapel Cemetery among friends and family. They were always active in the Baptist Church and their Christian lives had a positive influence on their children and grandchildren. Immanuel Baptist on Mueller Street was their Paragould church home.

*Submitted by Jim Walker*

**GORDON** – In 1799, John Gordon was born in North Carolina. John and his brother, Frederick (1801), migrated with their parents to Carroll County, TN. In 1861, John's wife, Elizabeth, had died and John and at least three of his sons, Jacob F., John Walker and Erwin T., migrated to Greene County. "Ole" John was buried in Mars Hill Cemetery, which at that time was in Greene County; after the division of Greene in 1873, Mars Hill was in Clay County.

*John Randolph and wife, Hennretta Dodd Gordon*

Jacob F.'s son John Randolph "Buck" (1862) married Hennretta Dodd (1869); their children:
1. Edith married Arnold French
2. Auda married Cleve Hamilton
3. Jewell married Essie Glassgow.

Some of John Randolph's descendents still live in Clay County.

Jacob F.'s son Ernest Simpson (Sept 4, 1876) married Nannie Alma Overton. Their children:
1. James Ford
2. William Claud
3. Janie Pearl
4. Robert
5. John Overton
6. Alma Ruth
7. Richard Jacob

Robert had two children, Michael and Patricia. Patricia married Larry Joe Miller and they live in Greene County.

Ernest Simpson's fifth child, John Overton (June 30, 1916), married Mildred Ester Webb (March 14, 1918). They moved to west Tennessee in 1952. Their children:
1. Marilyn (1941) married Gary Lee McClure (1960-1987)
2. Carol (1942) married Gary Heath
3. Linda (1945-2000) married Robert Cross
4. John Douglas (1954) married Vicki Bray.

Jacob F.'s three sons differed in their religious beliefs. John Randolph was Primitive Baptist and believed the world was square. James A. was Methodist and Ernest Simpson "Tom" was Church of Christ. It was noted that the brothers had 'very hard discussions about religion."

*Ernest Simpson Gordon*

John Walker Gordon's second son, John Walker married Sarah A. before the family left Tennessee in 1859. Their children:
1. Mary Jane (1856)
2. Cordelia (1859)
3. John William (1861).

Later, John Walker married Mary R. and their children:
1. Sarah (1865)
2. George (1873)
3. Florni (1875)
4. Irvin (1877)
5. Ezra (1880).

*John William Gordon*

John William, son of John Walker and Sarah A., married Mary Ellen Johnston. The couple had 14 children; the third of who was Charlie Clayborn (1891) married Linnie Walters (1919-1962). One of Charlie and Linnie's sons was John William Gordon of Piggott (1924). John and his wife Grace's children:
1. John Richard
2. Phillip Earl
3. Joe Robert
4. Tammy Joyce

Two of their sons, Phillip and Joe, live in Greene County.

*James Overton's home in Greenway, AR. Left to right: Mary Roberts Overton (James Overton's second wife), James Harmon Overton, Robert Overton, Minnie Overton, Ella Overton Oliphant and daughter Rowena Elizabeth Oliphant, Nannie Overton Gordon and daughter Pearl Gordon, Ernest Simpson Gordon. Boys: James Ford Gordon and William Claud Gordon (sons of Ernest Simpson and Nannie Overton Gordon).*

Erwin T. Gordon's' third son, Erwin T., (1845) married Mary A. Their children:
1. John
2. James
3. Pleasant
4. Richard
5. Mutibder (f)
6. Mary
7. Morthy (f)

*Submitted by Mr. and Mrs. Gary L. McClure*

**GRADY** – The Grady's now living in Greene County, AR are descendants of pioneers who migrated from Kentucky to Dunklin County, MO and on into Greene County, AR in the 1870s.

The story begins with the William A. and Ruth Eliza Grady family found on the 1880 Greene County, AR census in Cache Township: GRADY, William A. 38 (about 1842) KY; Ruth E. C. 32 (about 1848) MO; Edgar H. 12 (about 1868) MO; Murry 10 (about 1870) MO; William 8 (about 1872) MO; Maggie M. 6 (about 1874) MO; Phillip M. 4 (about 1876) MO; Minnie L. 1.5 (about 1878) MO.

William A. (1842 KY) is said to be the son of William B. Grady and Sarah Jane Puckett, both from Kentucky. William A. Grady's wife was Ruth Eliza (1848 MO). William and Ruth had at least eight children. The six listed above plus two others: Mary Myrtle (1881) and Archidamia (1887).

Edgar Houston married Nettie Sorrell in 1893. Murry married Sudie in 1899. William Doug married and had at least four kids. Phillip married Susie McGehee in 1895. Minnie and Archidamia never married. Mary Myrtle married William Counts in 1906.

William and Ruth Eliza's fourth child, Maggie Mae, was born in Missouri on Nov 5, 1873. In 1890, Maggie lived in extreme northeast Arkansas on the Saint Francis River in a town called Bertig. In May of 1987, my father and I were able to locate the Bertig Cemetery but the town of Bertig had been swallowed up by the St. Francis River. On Christmas day in 1890, at the age of 17, Maggie married William Henry Garner in Greene County, AR.

William Henry was the third son of Noah Zachariah Garner and Sarah Clements/Clement. After their marriage, Henry and Maggie remained on Zach's farm and raised a family of eight or nine including twins, of which only four reached adult.

In 1908 Maggie died at the young age of 33. She was buried alongside other Grady family members at Center Hill Cemetery but her marker has since disappeared.

Today there are literally hundreds of Grady descendants of Henry and Maggie living in and around Greene County and others can be found scattered across many states.

*Submitted by Hank Garner*

**GRAMLING** – Adam, the first Gramling, came to this country in 1734 at the age of five years. He was born in Germany in 1729 and married Elizabeth Gassaway, also from Germany. They settled on the West Bank of Whitford Stage Swamp, about seven miles east of Orangeburg, SC, now known as East Orange. He and his wife are buried there.

The Gramling Family Reunion is held every year on the first week of June at "Four Holes Center" in Orangeburg.

Joseph Richard Gramling was born Feb 14, 1820. On Nov 5, 1841, he married Cynthia Brannon. In 1857 they gathered up their children and possessions and joined a caravan of covered wagons drawn by oxen. They bade farewell to their friends and loved ones. Exactly who the others were in the caravan is unknown to this writer except a widowed sister, Ellen Cothren and her children: William, Fannie, Mary, Pressley and Ruben.

What courage it must have taken to leave the security of a home for an unknown place. They traveled through the wilderness, over the mountains, through the swamps and across treacherous rivers and, finally, after three months, the weary travelers arrived on the western slopes of Crowley's Ridge. It was here they found a place they liked and selected a spot on which to build their home.

The house was on a hillside overlooking the level land of Cache River Valley. There were springs bubbling of white sand. The springs were like miniature fountains of cold clear sparkling water. Water being plentiful, a tan yard was built. Here they tanned the hide of cows into leather. The leather was made into belts and shoes for the family. They also raised sheep and the wool was cured and spun into yarn. This yarn was woven into clothing and knitted into stockings.

There was also a gristmill. Corn was ground for corn pone, bread and grits. Some of the corn was made into hominy. Today, these are still favorite dishes of the South.

Timber was very plentiful and a sawmill was started to cut lumber into planks and hewn logs. Their home was made from this timber and it stood for almost 100 years. Their house overlooked fields of wheat, corn, oats and vegetables. Cotton, with help of slaves, was also grown. The slaves stayed with the family until they were freed.

A flourmill and cotton gin were later added to the farm. The first mills were called treadmills. Oxen furnished the power to operate until the invention of the steam engine. The couple of pioneers had 11 children. The oldest, Martha married William Blackwood; Henry C. Gramling married Sally Hally; Joseph Gramling, Jr. married Mary Blackwood; Joseph Gramling, Jr.'s second wife was Mary Austin; Josephine Gramling married unknown Irving; Andrew G. Gramling married Lucy Peevy House; John H. Gramling married Ell Hutchins; Ben Martin and Ruben S. died during infancy.

Many more Gramling families came to Arkansas from South Carolina a few years later. Adam and Elizabeth Gramling (Methodist Minister) and their children:
1. Martin Luther, Methodist minister
2. Conrad Luther
3. Adam Jr.
4. Christian
5. Michael
6. Elizabeth, twin
7. Israel, twin, was a school teacher
8. Richard, twin, died as an infant
9. Katie, twin died as an infant
10. William C. killed in Civil War
11. John, Methodist minister

Second generation: Martin Luther and Mary H. Gramling, Ruben and Elizabeth, Margaret, Henry.

Third generation: Ruben and Martha R. Gramling, Ruben's second wife Elizabeth "Betsy", Ruben's third wife, Cindy Bollinger, Ruben's fourth wife, Lucy Ellen Seay. Ruben, Martha and their children are buried in Owens Chapel.

Fourth Generation: Sara "Sallie" Gramling married Andrew Jackson Cothren. Their children: William Henry, Presley Mack, Rubin, Fannie, and Mary Sara.

Also from South Carolina came Tom Gramling, father of Hem and Doom. Martin Gramling, father of Dave and Ben, along with daughter, Sara E. (Gramling) Spillman. Many other Greene Countians can trace their ancestry back to Joseph and Cynthia (Brannon) Gramling. This family had an important part in development of churches, schools and agriculture in Greene County.

**GRAMLING** – George Andrew "G. A." Gramling (Nov 16, 1859 Greene County-Aug 20, 1921) married Lucy Jane "Lou" (Pevehouse) Gramling in 1882. Lou Pevehouse (April 22, 1864 Walnut Ridge, AR-Oct 26, 1938) a daughter of Wiley and unknown (Bowman) Pevehouse.

Their children:
1. Tommie
2. Bertie
3. Johnnie "J. B."
4. Lillie (Gramling) Cline
5. Claudie
6. Albert
7. Cyntha (Gramling) Cothren.

Johnnie, Lillie and Cyntha lived to be adults. George, Lou and their seven children are buried in Warren's Chapel Cemetery, located on highway 168 near Walcott.

George and Lou were successful farmers. They built a seven-room house with three porches and three fireplaces. The lumber for the house was from the sawmill owned by George's father, J. R. The house was insured for $700.00; the smokehouse and contents were insured for $500.00. They also built a barn and silo made of lumber.

J. R. died in 1882. George and a younger brother, John Harrison Gramling, bought his farmland from the other heirs.

George and Lou grew corn, cotton and hay. They hand-milked a herd of 25 cows and pastured cattle on the open range. Lou was a storyteller and told her grandchildren how life was in the "olden days" and bits of family history. She owned a dish that made the long oxen-drawn covered wagon trip from Spartanburg, S. C., to Florida and then to Greene County.

*Family of George and Lucy "Lou" (Pevehouse) Gramling, Daughters Lillie and Claudie-Son, John "J.B." standing, Nephew W.C. "Bill"Gramling seated, center*

George's mother, Syntha, spent her last few years of life in the home of George and Lou. They also took in a 13-year-old, nephew, William Camp Gramling, "W. C." "Uncle Bill". He lived with them until he married at age 23. When Bill married he was paid for his work with a deed to 40 acres, a team of mules, a farm wagon and equipment necessary for farming in those days.

Bill was several years older that George's son, Johnnie, but they were much like brothers, including arguing. They argued about many things, their favorite subject being over the best beef cattle to grow. Bill grew Blank Angus registered cattle and Johnnie grew registered Hereford.

*Submitted by Lottie Gramling Hooton*

**GRAMLING** – Johnnie Bandy Gramling (Feb 28, 1889 - June 15, 1953 Greene County) was the son of Andrew George and Lucy Jane (Pevehouse) Gramling. He married Hattie Myrtle (Mangrum) Gramling (Oct 29, 1901 Augusta, AR - Jan 26, 1990) on Nov 25, 1921. She was the daughter of Y. C. and Margaret (Amorine) Mangrum. John, Myrtle and their two sons Bob and Bill, are buried in Warren's Chapel Cemetery.

*Myrtle (Mangrum) Gramling*

Their children are:
1. Lottie (Gramling) Hooton (Oct 19,1922)
2. George Gramling (Sept 10, 1924)
3. Margaret (Gramling) Moon Tatum (April 22, 1926-Nov 27, 1986)
4. Lewis Gramling (Sept 22, 1927)
5. Lindy Gramling (Sept 15, 1929)
6. Johnnie Lou (Gramling) Norman (May 13, 1931-April 25, 1987)
7. Winnie Sue (Gramling) Greenway (Jan 18, 1933- Nov 3, 1994)
8. Marion Gramling (Aug 4, 1934)
9. Robert "Bob" Gramling (April 22, 1937-Nov 4, 1995)
10. William "Bill" Gramling (Aug 26, 1946-Dec 25, 1950).

John and Myrtle were farmers, as were five generations of Gramlings before them. They bought the George and Lucy (Pevehouse) Gramling farm from the heirs and in addition bought a number of acres adjacent to the land they owned. They grew corn, cotton, wheat hay, registered Herfords, hogs and sheep. They also had a few acres in a peach orchard.

John Gramling was a great grandson of Ruben Martin and Martha (Rey) Gramling. All Gramlings in this area are descendants of Ruben and one of his four wives.

*Submitted by Lottie (Gramling) Hooton*

**GRAMLING** – "J. R." "Uncle Dick", a son of Ruben Martin and his first wife, Martha (Rey) Gramling, was born Feb. 14, 1820 in Spartanburg, S. C. and died Oct. 31, 1883. He married Syntha (Brannon) Gramling Nov 25, 1841. They were the parents of 11 children. Two died in infancy. A son, Private William Capers Gramling, was killed in the Civil War. He was a Union soldier. J. R., Syntha and their two infants are buried in Owen's Chapel Cemetery about eight miles west of Paragould.

*Joseph Richard and Syntha (Brannon) Gramling*

Historians place the date that J. R.'s family settled on Crowley's Ridge as 1856. Some of his descendants believe it was earlier and believe the family left Spartanburg, traveled to Florida and came to Crowley's Ridge. It is a known fact that several Gramlings left South Carolina in the mid-1840s, settling in Georgia, Missouri and Florida.

A ledger belonging to J. R. leads one to believe he was well established in business in 1856. The ledger covers business transactions from 1856 to 1864. By this time he was making household furniture, farm wagons, operating a sawmill, gristmill, tanning yard, slaughterhouse and general store.

The following are entries made by "J. R.":
1. Oct. 20, 1856 to Gramling cash lent $10. Dec. cash $10. Coffee, sugar $2.00. Paid on account $14.92 in meat.
2. Nov 20, 1856 – Sterling Gregory cash $20, Dec 29 Cash $5, July 27, 1857, account settled.
3. July 1, 1860 – Thompson 10 bu. Corn $10.50.
4. Dec. 18, 1861 –purchased corn sheller $20, hand saw $3.50
5. Dec 21, 1860 – Thurran Blackwood – 2 boxes pills, 50 cents, June 27, 1861 – 4 boxes pills, Dec 15, 1861 – 4 boxes pills $1.00.
6. Nov. 18, 1864 – B. M. Gramling – 1 cupboard to be paid in good money (meaning Union or Confederate?)
7. Sept 9, 1864 – government due me for iron to be paid by P. R. Lester Co. The ledger served as an address book: Sarah Seay, Spartanburg or Boiling Springs; Rev. John Gramling, Hamburg, Flurrida (Florada); Henery Gramling, Malin, Masura (Malden, Missouri); Alexander M. Moore, German Town, Shelby County, Tenn.; Mr. Hester – Organ County, Masura (Oregon County, Missouri).

*Submitted by Lottie Gramling Hooton*

**GRAMLING** – Marion Frank Gramling (Aug 4, 1934) son of John Bandy and Myrtle (Mangrum) Gramling, Stanford community. He was the eighth of 10 children and a descendant of Reuben Gramling who settled in Greene County in the 1950s.

*Heritage Trail Walk 1986; Spinning Wheel: Eula (Crowley) Hughes; Churn: Vickey (Gramling) Brents; Behind chair: Judy (Hughes) Gramling*

October 27, 1954, he married Julia "Judy" Hughes (April 21, 1937) daughter of Acton F. and Eula M. (Crowley) Hughes of the Walcott community. She is the third great granddaughter of Benjamin Crowley, founder of Crowley's Ridge, in 1821. They have two children: Vickey Dean (Gramling) Brents and Marion Clinton Gramling, one grandchild, Nathan Clinton Gramling.

Vickey is married to Timothy L. Brents, son of Coy and Kathryn (Hunt) Brents. Vickey is a Spanish teacher and sang with the Golden Tones gospel group for a period of time. Clint is employed at Monroe Auto and played bass guitar for the Golden Tones. Clint was married to Ann Travis in 1986 and divorced in 1991. They had one son, Nathan, who is a student at Greene County Tech Junior High School. Nathan also plays basketball for Tech.

Marion was a farmer by trade and had worked at Arkansas Highway Department, Emerson Electric at St.Louis and Paragould, Singer plant at Truman and Borden's Milk Company in Jonesboro before surrendering to the ministry in 1965, while farming at Shell Lake, AR. He pastored Second Baptist Church in Forrest City from l965 to 1972. He baptized over 350 people during that seven years and ranked in the top 10 in baptisms in the Arkansas Baptist State Convention one of those years. He pastored Temple Baptist Church in Demott, AR from 1972 to 1975, Mt.Zion Baptist from 1975 to 1985, Rosewood Baptist from 1985 to 1996 and Stanford Baptist Church from 1996 to the present.

Judy (Hughes) Gramling attended Walcott Elementary and Junior High Schools. She played basketball at Walcott and Greene County Tech, which won the district championship for years 1953 and 1954, then pressed on to the semi-finals in the State tournament. Judy sang in the Tech Girl's Trio, along with Peggy

*Front: Vickey; Row 2, L-R: Tim, Clint; Row 3, L-R: Judy, Nathan, Marion*

(Ryan) Dunn and Martha (Lindley) Brown. She was Miss Greene County for 1953-54. She worked at Grabers Department Store, Paragould, Forrest City Public School, Dermott Public School, Greene County Tech School and instructor at R & M Beauty School, later called Vogue and Pat Goin's Beauty College.

*Miss Greene County 1953-Judy Hughes*

The family participated, along with other family members, in the Heritage Trail Walk at Crowley's Ridge State Park, May 10, 1986, The Episode Benjamin Crowley Pioneer; the Crowley's Ridge Story in 1990 in which Judy portrayed Annie Crowley, Benjamin's wife (the others were pioneers), and the Crowley's Ridge Story in 1995, in which they all portrayed Indians in the scene, "The Red Man".

Marion and Judy live on a portion of the John Gramling family farm and own and farm a portion of the original Crowley Plantation she inherited from her parents.

*Submitted by Julia "Judy" Gramling*

**GRAY** – Daniel Gray was born September 15, 1815, in Tennessee and moved to Lawrence County, Arkansas, in the 1830s. This part of Lawrence County was later formed into Greene County.

Daniel did not stay in one location very long at a time. He was married three times. He had 17 children by three wives. Jane Rowe was his third wife, whom he married in Arkansas and then moved to Texas in about 1875. Jane was the mother of seven of his children. The youngest child named Madella later married John Welch from an early Greene County pioneering family. Of Jane and Daniel's children only Louisa and Madella lived to be grown.

*John William Welch and Madella Welch and their son, Marion Charles Welch about 1900.*

Daniel lived in different parts of Arkansas, then he moved to Texas. He owned property in both states. His oldest son, Roy, was given the land in western Arkansas. His youngest daughter, Madella, obtained the property in Jack County, Texas. It still belongs to her heirs.

Madella was born in a log house near Jacksboro, Texas. The house is still standing today (1999); however, it has been restored recently by Madella's grandsons.

Daniel's first home, after getting married the first time, was in Greene County, Arkansas. He and his third wife, Jane Rowe, lived there for a time before their move to Texas. After the deaths of two of his children and his wife, he decided to move back to Greene County, Arkansas. Daniel hired a couple with a wagon, to accompany them. He needed a woman to look after the children and to do the cooking and laundry.

All his possessions and the family were loaded into two mule-drawn wagons. Daniel's son, Marion, drove one wagon. They went north through sections of Oklahoma, turning off about where Ft. Smith is now. They traveled down into the Arkansas River Valley and then up into the northeast corner of the state. It took six weeks to get to Greene County.

Madella was about 4 or 5 years old. She remembered seeing some Indians near the Red River, where the wagons crossed. They cooked over campfires and slept in their wagons. About once a week they would camp for a day, and the lady would wash all their clothes. Daniel Gray lived to be 84 years old and died at the home of his youngest daughter, Madella, Mrs. John Welch.

For more history about Daniel Gray read *Greene County Historical Quarterly,* Vol. Four, Winter 1968, Page 23, and also *History of Greene County* by H.B. Crowley (written 1906).

**GREEN** – John William Green, son of Roger Green of Forsyth and Hall County, GA. His wife, Rachel Manerva (Mooney), great-great-great-granddaughter of William Moleneaux, one of the "Mohawks" who dumped the tea in the Boston Harbor in 1773.

Six months and one day after the firing of Fort Sumter, S. C., Green, along with his father-in-law and two brothers-in-law enlisted in the 38th Infantry Regiment. The 38th was under the command of General Robert E. Lee. He served in Company L and M as 2nd sergeant. His mustering papers referred to him as a stable sergeant because he was responsible for the horses and mules.

With the men away from home, women not only cared for their families and did household chores but also raised crops and managed farms. Rachel not only saw her husband but her father, father-in-law, brother and brother-in-law go off to war. Her father, Robert Mooney, died in the cruel Union Camp Chase prison in Columbus, OH.

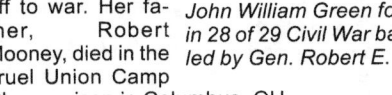

*John William Green fought in 28 of 29 Civil War battles led by Gen. Robert E. Lee.*

Union soldiers captured Green at Fort Steadman, VA on March 25, 1865. Seven days later Lee surrendered. After being a prisoner for three months, Green was released on June 27, 1865. He walked from Point Lookout, MD, to Flowery Branch, GA. He traveled at night and slept during the day. To survive, he killed animals and stole food. Arriving home, he found his wife and their five children living in a land devastated by the war.

In 1868, four families, the Green's Mooney's, Light's and McDonald's left Forsyth, GA and headed for Arkansas in a wagon train. Crossing the Mississippi River near Helena, they turned north up Crowley's Ridge where they joined relatives who had preceded them. Settling in Greene County, Green purchased 80 acres of land near Beech Grove. He died in Nov 1880 but his wife did not receive a pension until 1913. The Green's had nine children:

1. Sonoro
2. Rufus Decater married Mary Marie J. Griffith
3. Flora Elizabeth married William Alfred "App" Eubanks
4. William C. never married
5. Montivia Caroline married Joseph Joel Eubanks
6. Augustus G. married Ludie Gipson
7. Robert Hamilton married Della Margaret Kennemore
8. Albert J. married Mollie Fryar
9. John William "Doc" Jr. married Alice Roberts

The descendants, the Sons of Confederate Veterans organization and the Arkansas Battery Artillery of the Confederate States of America, honored Green on May 23, 1999 at the Beech Grove Cemetery by unveiling a marble Civil War headstone furnished by the United States of America, performing a 21 gun salute and firing a cannon in the soldier's honor. His service was performed 138 years ago but his country and his descendants have not forgotten.

*Submitted by Lucille (Green) Robinson*

**GREEN** – Nathaniel M. Green born March 7, 1813, in Wilson County, Tennessee, died August 20, 1889, and was a Baptist minister. He was my great-great-grandfather. He married Jane Robertson July 19, 1834. She was born July 31, 1814, and died February 16, 1854. Their third son was my grandfather, Martin Luther Green, born June 3, 1848, in Wilson County, Tennessee, died April 25, 1902. He was a carpenter and was buried in Linwood Cemetery, Paragould. He married Margaret Josephine Bomar. She was born December 24, 1847, and died November 3, 1924; burial Linwood Cemetery.

Margaret was my grandmother. They had four sons: Marcus A. Green born December 20, 1868-died October 17, 1907, in Paragould; Thomas M. Green; Robert S. Green; and my father, Don H. Green. All were born in Wilson County. My father was born October 28, 1879, in Wilford, Wilson County and died December 29, 1956. He was buried in Linwood Cemetery.

He married Mary Lelia Bell Webb in 1912. She was born May 29, 1883, in Bethel, Arkansas, and died November 20, 1970, in Paragould and is buried in Linwood. My grandfather and family moved from Tennessee to Gainsville in Greene County. The Green family moved to Paragould when the county seat was moved from Gainesville. My parents had two sons, Donald Webb Green, born September 8, 1913, and lives at 720 West Main, Paragould. Their other son, Robert Euclid Green, was born June 1, 1915.

Webb married Allie Holt on September 11, 1938, in Atlanta, Georgia. They have two sons, Donald Webb Green II and Gordon Ray Green.

*Robert E. Green, Jr. (left), his mother and father on board Air Florida DC-10, July 14, 1982, at Dallas-Ft. Worth Airport boarding non-stop flight to London, England, for eight days.*

Robert Euclid Green married Mary Hazeldine Layl on April 16, 1944, at the First Methodist Church, Paragould, Arkansas. They live at 3 Gwendine Dr., Paragould. They had one son, Robert Euclid Greene Jr., born August 19, 1948, in Paragould, Arkansas, and died September 12, 1982, in Dallas, Texas, and was known by family and friends as "Reg." He was our pride and joy. After graduating from the Paragould school system he graduated from A.S.U. with a B.S.E. degree in 1970. He was a life member of Sigma Phi Epsilon and had served as a Page for Rep. E. C. " Took" Gathings and toured Europe for 59 days with a group from S.M.U. in Dallas. In December 1982 Hazeldine and I established, through the First Methodist Church in Paragould, the "Reg" Green Memorial Scholarship Fund for deserving students from Greene County, Arkansas, high schools, currently $2,000.00 per year is granted and may be renewed each year with a 2.5 maintained grade point.

My mother's family moved from Mississippi through Tennessee and finally settled in the Bethel Community where my grandfather was postmaster and constable. He owned several 100 acres and farmed it with cotton, corn and soy beans. James W. Webb had married Mollie Webb and they had five children (an infant died) and a son, James Andrew Webb died as a youth. My mother was born May 29,1883, and died November 20, 1970. My grandmother, Mollie Wood Webb, died before I was born.

**GREGORY/THURMAN** – Horatious Gamewell Gregory (Oct 5, 1869 Greene County-March 1943) was the son of William Riley Gregory (Feb 16, 1826-Feb 20, 1888) and Sarah Elizabeth Houston (July 16, 1832-Nov 18, 1901) Horatious had a brother, Sterling Mack Gregory (Dec 1873) who married Radie Spillman in 1901.

William Riley served in the Civil War, ran a store in Gainesville and Mack Gregory ran a store at Crossroads.

Horatious was married (1) Lou E. Spillman (Jan 17, 1876-March 6, 1893 in childbirth), the child a son, William Riley Gregory, lived five years.

Horatious went to Poplar Bluff, MO, to work in a sawmill and there he met and married (2) Artie Agnes Thurman (March 11, 1878-1966) in 1902. They had four daughters:
1. Cora (1903-1907)
2. Flora (1905-1910)
3. Ethel Mae (Feb 29, 1908- June 4, 1997)
4. Mabel Roberta (Nov 10, 1911- May 5, 1996).

The girls were born and lived on the southeast corner of the intersection of Highway 412 and the Old Jacksonport Military Road. Mabel and Ethel went to school at Crossroads. H. G. ran a store at Commissary on the banks of Sugar Creek. When Mabel was seven years old they moved to Stanford. John Blair who ran a store at Stanford and H. G. swapped stores. The store set right in front of the current home of Steven Powers, next to a 'big old tree'. They lived next to the store on the west. According to Mabel, everyone went to church at Owen's Chapel, which was non-denominational. It was one of the largest churches around in the early 1900s.

Artie Thurman was born in Butler County, Mo to Robert Huston Thurman (June 7, 1850) and Nancy C. Patty (1858-1887) Artie's mother died when she was nine years old and her father married again to a young girl not much older than Artie. Artie raised the six younger children until she married at the age of 24.

Ethel Mae Gregory married, Dec 16, 1933, George Elonzo Hunt (March 24, 1910-Feb 14, 1994). He was the son of Oliver Carroll Hunt and Mary Elizabeth Pillow. George was a farmer and worked for the Missouri Pacific Railroad. Ethel retired as a second grade teacher at Stanford School. Their children:
1. George Edwin Hunt (June 12, 1937) married Norma Faye Mann. They had one child, Timothy Edwin Hunt
2. Brenda Ruth Hunt (April 22, 1941) married Bill Welsh Logan and lives in Lake Jackson, TX. They have two daughters, Sarah Suzanne and Lori (Hunt) Logan.

*Front middle: Artie Agnes Thurman Gregory, on left, her daughter, Ethel and in back her daughter, Mabel. Also in picture are children, grandchildren and spouses.*

Mabel married Robert Earl Grambling (June 17, 1910-1985). Earl was the son of William Camp Gramling and Mary Crawford. Earl owned the Stanford Gin and was on the board of directors of Security Bank. Mabel and Earl had four children:
1. Glen Earl
2. Jerry Merle
3. Joy Ann
4. Judy Maureen Gramling.

Glen married Mildred "Mick" Hyde and they have three children: Richard Glen, Robert Scott and Kelly O'Neal.

Jerry married Norma Lee Owens and they have five children:
1. Pamela Diane
2. Patricia Nanette
3. Jerry Michael
4. Martin Gregory
5. Rebecca Lee

Joy married Clifton Haley Powers. They were later divorced. They had three children, Steven Clifton, Elizabeth Ann and Christopher Earl.

Judy married Donnie Franklin Rowland. They have three children, Angela Suzanne, Todd Franklin and Matthew Alan.

Glen, Joy and Judy and families live in Greene County. Jerry and family live in the Little Rock area.

*Submitted by Tim Hunt*

**GROSS** – Donald Lee Gross Senior was born July 27, 1936, in Saint Louis, Missouri. He was a son of Robert Noah and Elinore Aschenbach Gross.

As a young man he moved to Paragould, Arkansas, on July 3, 1954. He married Myrma Acuff in Kennett, Missouri.

Their children were Donald Junior born September 25, 1956; Robert born July 1, 1957; Patty born February 22, 1959; Tony born October 22, 1960; and Kimberly Sue born October 22, 1960. Kimberly Sue died soon after she was born.

On January 22, 1977, Donald Gross Sr. married Debby Casteel. To this union was born Tammy Dawn.

Children of Tammy Dawn are: Dawn Renee born October 29, 1995; Andy born February 3, 1997; and Hunter born January 24, 1999.

*Donald Lee Gross Sr. family. Front row: Tony. Back row from left: Robert, Donald Jr., Patty, Myrna and Donald Sr.*

Children of Robert Gross are: Craig born March 31, 1980; Myranda born February 10, 1985; and Katie born April 28, 1997.

**HAGOOD** – Marion Francis Hagood was born in Giles County, TN in 1859. He married Amanda Boston in 1901. They had five children:
1. Noble
2. William, twin
3. Winfred, twin
4. Minnie
5. Oma

They moved to Greene County in the 1890s and settled on a farm in the New Friendship area. His mother, Phebea and younger sister, Etta moved with them, maybe also a younger brother, George. William used to tell us that he and Winfred walked across the Mississippi River on ice when they moved here. Amanda died in Jan 1902.

Within a few months Marion Francis remarried, to a widow with five or six children.

Noble married Nola Anderson in 1908. They had two sons, Burrell and Earl. They farmed in the New Friendship area until 1943, when they moved to California.

*First row, left to right: Fern Hagood Baker, Willa Hagood Congleton; back row: Thomas Winford Hagood, Kenneth Dean Hagood, Marion Riley Hagood*

Minnie married Albert Dollins and lived in Paragould. They had no children. She died in 1941.

Winfred married Mamie Howard. They had three children: Adrian, Darrel and Zelma. They lived in Paragould for a few years and then moved to Florence, AL. Winfred died in 1965.

William farmed and served in the Army during WWII. He married Verdie Sheffield in 1923. They had seven children:
1. Willa M (Dec 1, 1923)
2. Jimmy Verellie (Jan 12, 1927-Jan 1955) died in a car accident.
3. Vernay died as an infant
4. Thomas Winfred (Jan 5, 1931)
5. Marion Riley (March 26, 1933) named after grandpa
6. Glenda Fern (March 10, 1939)
7. Dean (Sept 3, 1944)

William worked at Hasty's and Wrape's Mill when it was running and did odd jobs when it shut down. He always had large gardens in the spring and summer. All four sons served in the army. William Died in 1967.

Oma Hagood married Sherman Skaggs. They lived in Memphis, TN and had two daughters. Oma died in 1986.

Willa M. married David Congleton. They had four children: Dale, Don Terry and Jeff. They all lived in Missouri except Jeff, who lives in Texas.

*William Thomas and Verdie Sheffield Hagood*

Thomas moved to St. Louis after his discharge. He married Effie White and moved to Paragould a couple of years later. He has worked at Samuel's Salvage for many years. They have three children: Tina, Thomas Jr. and Todd. They also raised a grandson, Eric. Thomas Jr. and Todd live in Paragould and Tina lives Illinois.

Marion married Jane Crossno while in the army. They had a son, Rickey and were divorced in 1955. He moved to St. Louis after his discharge and then moved to Paragould. He married Elizabeth Russom in 1957. They had four children: Sharon, Roger and twins, Lesley and Shane, who died as an infant. They both worked at Elder for many years. Both Sharon and Lesley live in Paragould. Roger lives in South Carolina. Marion died Oct 1, 1999.

Glenda Fern married Clarence Baker. They had four children: Buddy, Barb, Ken and Crystal. They all live in Missouri except Ken, who lives in Florida.

Dean married Bronda Casteel. They had two daughters, Kellie and Micki. They all live in Tennessee.

The Hagoods have lived in Greene County for over 100 years.

*Submitted by Elizabeth Hagood*

**HALL** – I began life as a baby on December 25, 1887, in Greene County, Arkansas. Like Abraham Lincoln, I was born in a log cabin. There the similarity ends. I was free born; there was no hospital or doctor expenses. While quite young I suffered an accident that impaired my vision. I have had poor vision ever since.

My mother taught me at home before I was old enough to go to school. She taught me from the Bible; my parents were Christians. My father died when I was 10; I was 21 when my mother passed away. There were five children in the family and I am the only one left.

The schools were poor. The first one I attended had no desk - just long benches. We did, however, have a central heating system, a big wood-burning box stove that sat in the center of the building. In cold weather its was red hot. Those who were near roasted, while those farther away froze. There was no juvenile delinquency, at least none that the parents could not handle. There were no child labor laws either. We were put to work quite young, and our hours were regulated by the sun. There were no unions except for the Western Union and the Union Pacific.

I taught school a number of years. The attendance was poor; the children were kept at home when needed in the fields. There was some freedom, however; you could read your Bible or offer a prayer without being arrested. I attended Freed Hardeman for a short time. I also took a business course at San Angelo, Texas. I was postmaster when a two-cent stamp would carry your letter as far as an eight-cent one will today. I was a justice of the peace for six years, but had to move out of the precinct to get rid of the job. I was a fuel supervisor for three years for the Arkansas Highway Department.

*Arta E. Hall*

We moved to California in 1937. I worked for Kiser Cement Company for over 16 years. I met my wife, Jeanette, at school. We were married on February 14, 1911, and have been married ever since. I was baptized by R. N. Garner when I was 16. My wife was baptized after we were married, in 1916. I am here by the grace of God. My faith has preserved me all the hard years. The future of this country is doomed. "Unless they repent they shall likewise perish." The wicked will be turned into hell with all the nations that forget God.

My mother's maiden name was Armina Levona Eubanks. She was born September 1846 in Georgia. She married Jeptha Futrell before she married my father. My father was born in Georgia, probably in 1851. He had been married before he married mother. He had one son by this marriage. His Aunt Martha Moore took him to Texas when he was 18 months old. My father never saw him again. His name was Drury Flurnoy. My parents had four children: Zeulia Cordelia, November 18, 1879; a son Zahn who died at 18 months; Ira Ishmael, January 19, 1884; and Arta Elza December 25, 1887. My children are: Clevie Pauline, March 12, 1912; Louie Travis, June 5, 1914; Helen Gertrude April 28, 1916; Tom Randol November 8, 1918; Bryce Cardigan October 25, 1920; Rupert Lee September 23, 1922; Dan Ira May 2, 1927; and Donald, July 20, 1932. Deaths: Bryce burned to death March 27, 1926. Clevie died of cancer September 2, 1971. Tom died of cancer April 1973. All of the above was written by Arta Elza Hall in February 1978.

To finish Uncle Arta's story, I will add this postscript. Aunt Jeanette died in November 1979. Uncle Arta married Katie Bozzard in January 1980. He was 92 and Katie 73. They had 15 years together in his home on Laurie Avenue, San Jose, California. Uncle Arta died in January after his 107th birthday. He was alert and witty until shortly before his death.

*Submitted by Tomazine Morrow Reeves, November 10, 1999.*

**HALL** – Greenup Hall was born about 1797 in Rowan County, NC, son of Joseph and Katherine Wilson Hall. In 1813, while still in Rowan County, NC, Greenup was under the guardianship of Francis Neely to learn a trade.

When his father's estate was probated in 1818 in Rowan County, NC, Greenup was in Marion County, AL with his older sister, Jincy Hall Harris, brother-in-law, Nicholas Harris and older brother, Richmond Hall. Refer to articles on Nicholas Harris and Richmond Hall elsewhere in this book.

Greenup was counted on the 1829 Sheriff's Census for Lawrence County, AR. He was living in Spring River Township, over 21 years old, unmarried. On the 1830 Lawrence County, AR census, he was shown to be 30 to 40 years old. A female, age 10 to 15, was also counted.

Greenup paid Lawrence County, AR territorial taxes for 1830 through 1832 in Cache Township. For 1832 and 1833, he paid personal taxes in Cache and Languil Townships in Lawrence County, AR.

From the Territorial Papers of the United States, Greenup Hall was a magistrate for Lawrence County, AR, commissioned Nov 12, 1833. Greenup paid territorial tax in Greene County, AR in 1834. He was commissioned a county surveyor for Greene County, AR on Jan 13, 1834 and Aug 7, 1835.

No other records have been found for Greenup Hall. On the 1850 Greene County, AR census, in the household for his brother-in-law, Nicholas Harris and sister, Jincy Hall Harris, there is a 17 year-old boy, John F. Hall, born in Arkansas, living with them. Backing up to the 1840 Greene County, AR census for Nicholas Harris, there is a boy, born 1830/1835, living with them, who would fit the age of John on the 1850 census. Could John F. Hall be the son of Greenup?

*Submitted by Loyce Renfroe Kelso*

**HALL** – Richmond Hall (Dec 4, 1794 Rowan County, NC-1863), was the son of Joseph and Katherine (Wilson) Hall. In 1813, while still in Rowan County, NC, Richmond was under the guardianship of Francis Neely to learn a trade.

When his father's estate was probated in 1818 in Rowan County, NC, Richmond was in Marion County, AL with his older sister, Jincy (Hall) Harris, brother-in-law, Nicholas Harris and younger brother, Greenup Hall. See articles on Nicholas Harris and Greenup Hall elsewhere in this book. While in Monroe County, MS, he purchased land near present day Amory, MS. He was also a Methodist minister for the county. His first marriage was to Mary Cook. He was counted on the 1820 and 1825 Monroe County, MS censuses.

After leaving Mississippi, he and his family are next found in Lawrence County, AR on the 1829 Sheriff's Census living in Spring River Township. He was commissioned a magistrate on Nov 20, 1829 and Nov 5, 1831 for that county. He performed a number of marriages and one of them was for his niece, Lemerles Katharine (Wilson) Harris on Dec 30, 1832, to Thomas Stanford. See article on Thomas Stanford elsewhere in this book.

He paid Lawrence County, AR taxes in 1830 and 1831 in Cache Township. He paid Lawrence County, AR taxes in Cache and Languil Townships for 1832 through 1834. He paid Greene County, AR taxes for 1834 through 1837. He paid non-resident Greene County, AR taxes in 1857.

Richmond and his first wife had a total of eight children, names for five are known: Matilda, Richmond, Greenup, Anderson and Wilson H. Hall.

After his first wife died, he married Mary F. about 1848 probably in Poinsett County, AR. They had one son, William, age 4/12 on the 1850 Poinsett County, AR census. On the 1860 Poinsett County, AR census, only Richmon Hawl, age 65 and wife, Mary, age 42, are shown. More on this family can be found in the *Poinsett County, Arkansas History and Families Book* published in 1998 written by same author/researcher.

*Submitted by Loyce Renfroe Kelso*

**HALL** – Wilson Moses Hall was born to Paul "Dad" Hall and Ruth (Sims) Hall on Dec 6, 1915 in Greene County, Paragould, AR. His paternal grandparents were Alec Hall and Nancy (Brown) Hall. His maternal grandparents were Johnny Sims and Susie (Casey) Sims. Growing up, Wilson enjoyed hunting. He attended Paragould High School located at the corner of Court and Seventh Street. As a young man, he worked with the Works Progress Administration and the Civilian Conservation Corps, helping to construct Crowley's Ridge State Park.

*Wilson M. Hall*

*Sgt. Wilson M. Hall*

In 1938, Wilson served the US Army 31st Infantry and later served the 134th Airborne division stationed in the Philippines. He was captured and died in a Japanese POW camp in Manchuria on Jan 2, 1943. He was in the "Death March on Bataan." Several years after the war had ended, Sgt. Wilson M. Hall was the first Greene County soldier returned home for burial. Services were held at East Side Baptist Mission (currently Third Avenue Baptist Church) on Third Ave. and Locust Street, the same street as his childhood home. The Adams-Jackson Post 17 funeral party of the American Legion was used for the first time. The funeral party consisted of a firing squad of eight and a commander, six pall bearers, four color guards and a chaplain. He is buried in the Center Hill Cemetery alongside his maternal grandparents.

Wilson had two sisters, Mozell Vowell and Susie Pippins and five brothers (four in the armed services), Norris, Army WWII; John Alec, Navy WWII and Korean; Harold "Dooger", Navy WWII; Billy Joe and Carl "Candy Man", Marine Corps Korean. His name appears on the WWII memorial at the 1888 courthouse. And his memory will live on through family photographs, stories, letters and honors received during his military service. He will always be in our "HALL" of fame.

**HAMPTON** – Manoah "Noah" Bostick Hampton, was born in 1841 in Lincoln County, Tennessee. He was the fourth of 12 children born to James Matison and Malissa Owen Hampton. He and later Martin Hampton, his brother, migrated to Union Township, Greene County, Arkansas.

At the outset of the Civil War, while still residing in Lincoln County, Tennessee, Manoah had joined Turney's Regiment which was transferred to the Army of Northern Virginia. In time his regiment was incorporated into Archer's Brigade.

Following the war he married Mary C. "Mollie" Stevenson of Giles County, Tennessee, and joined his parents in Shelby County, Tennessee, in the late 1860s.

Before moving from Shelby County they had two daughters, Martha M. "Mattie" Hampton born in 1869, and Sallie Nola, born in 1872.

In the Greene County 1880 census, both daughters, 10 and 8 years of age, were living in the household along with James R. Miller. James Miller helped Noah Hampton with farming and was 24 years of age at the time. In the 1880 census Manoah 's mother, Mary Malissa, and his brother Pinkney, were enumerated. Mary Malissa and Pinkney were also reported in Shelby County, Tennessee, that year. James Stevenson, Mollie's younger brother was boarding with the Hamptons in Union Township in 1880.

Noah Hampton was a farmer in Greene County. He had 100 acres under the tiller in 1889. He and his family were members of the Oak Grove Methodist Church. He died in Greene County on November 4, 1894, and was buried in the Gainesville Cemetery. Noah's son-in-law, James R. Miller, petitioned the court in Greene County to administer the remainder of Noah's estate on January 22, 1896. The estate consisted of $300.00 cash and personal property yet to be inventoried. No real estate was mentioned in the proceedings.

(See photograph with James Robert Miller biography.)

**HAMPTON** – Martha M. "Mattie" Hampton, was born on December 21, 1869. She was the oldest daughter of Manoah and Mollie Hampton. Mattie and James R. Miller were married on December 26, 1883. Mattie and James had three daughters: Minnie Mae (1887-1974), Lillie (1888-1974), and Lala V. (1892-1894), and six sons: Roy Hampton (1893-1983), Ray (1896-1898), Elbert (1898-1918), Robert (1900), Herbert (1903-1904), and Homer (1906-1988). Five of their children reached adulthood and married. Lala and Ray died at age 2, Herbert, at age 1, and Elbert died at age 20. The family attended the Oak Grove Methodist Church.

Minnie Mae married James Alfred Walden and they had two children: Clifton and Orine.

Lillie married twice, first to R.S. Stutes. After the death of her first husband, Lillie married Bob Gardner, who was a ward of James and Mattie Miller during the 1920s. Following her marriage to Bob Gardner, Lillie died in childbirth on January 18, 1924. She was buried next to her first husband in New Friendship Cemetery.

Roy Hampton Miller married Willie Ellen Pannell (l895-1981). Willie Ellen was the daughter of L. G. "Dot" Pannell and Alice Pendergrass. They had six children: Francis Juanita (1916-), Mary Louise (1918), Roy Milton (1921-1996), Reba Elizabeth (l923-), William Lilbourn (1924-), and Fairy May (1929-1998). Reba E. Miller married her third cousin, William O. Hampton Jr. great-grandson of Manoah Hampton's brother, Martin Hampton.

Following the death of her husband, James Miller, Mattie moved in with her daughter Minnie Mae and her son-in-law James A. Walden.

Mattie Miller died at age 81 on March 29, 1951. She was buried in Gainesville Cemetery.

(See photograph with James Robert Miller biography.)

**HAMPTON** – The youngest daughter of Manoah and Mollie, Sallie Nola Hampton, married in Greene County, Arkansas, on March 20, 1892. Her husband was Will F. McKelvey. Will McKelvey, was born in 1864 and died in 1941; Nola died in 1943. There were at least six children born to this marriage: Helen, Mary, Leonard, Thomas R., Earl and Shirley.

(See photograph with James Robert Miller biography.)

**HARMS** – Henry C. Harms, the great grandfather of Lydia Lueker Tritch, boarded a ship from Hamstedt, Germany for America in 1829. His parents were not happy to see him leave. In those days it was very dangerous to sail the seas. His parents' prayers and love was with him as he was sailing out to sea. As he was sailing, he noticed his homeland getting smaller and smaller until he could see it no longer. He thought, would he ever see his father and mother again, but he trusted in God's loving care.

One night after he was on the sea for a week, his ship was wrecked and they were all thrown into the sea. He noticed a hatch cover with a ringbolt floating around. He grabbed a little girl and told her to put her arms around his neck and hold on tight. He reached for the ringbolt on the hatch cover and put his arm through it and began to float.

On the second day the little girl could not hold on and he lost the little girl. It was so lonely and scary on the sea, especially since a big wave came and wrenched the little girl away. Then on the third day an English ship captain noticed him floating on the piece of wood with a ring and took him aboard. He was nearly dead and blinded by the seawater. He was taken to the hospital in England. In the hospital, he was given a big black stovepipe hat to put by his bed for donations. Many put money and many took money out. He finally got well after several weeks and went to some folks in Cole Camp, MO.

Henry C. Harms later went back to Germany and married his childhood sweetheart Catherine Trina Meyer. They had five children:
1. Henry B.
2. Peter
3. Charles Henry
4. Johann (Lydia's grandfather)
5. Margaret

Johann married Adelhied Ficken. They again travel to America to Cole Camp, MO. Then Johann, Adelhield, their family (which included Louise Caroline Harms) and also a good friend Johann Hink traveled to Augsburg, AR. They traveled with covered wagons and horses for several days around 300 miles. Many robbers and bushwackers traveled the country. Jessie James had been killed only two weeks prior to their departure from Cole Camp, MO. Often they had to use two teams of horses for each wagon to pull them over the mountains. They finally arrived at Augsburg, AR.

The Harms family loved singing folk songs and telling folk tales that were handed down from generation to generation. They were strong in the Lutheran Church and their faith. Great grandfather Henry (the one found at sea) was also strong in with his faith in the Lord and handed this down through his children. His favorite Bible verse was "For surely I know the plans I have for you, says the Lord, plans for you and not for harm, to give you a future of hope." Jeremiah 29:11.

Great grandfather's middle name was "Sea" because of his travel to sea. He went to his heavenly home Nov 22, 1897. He prayed for all his children to have a rich heritage in the Lord. Henry " Sea" Harms was the grandfather of Louise Caroline (Harms) Lueker and great grandfather of Lydia Lueker Tritch both of Greene County.
*Submitted by Kerry Reddick*

**HARRIS** – My mother, Clara Jeffery Hanks Harris, one of 14 children born to Roland Hansel Hanks and Hula June "Jennie" Jeffery Hanks. They were married August 17, 1877, in Ozark County, Missouri.

Her father was a highly respected citizen in Mount Olive, Isard County, Arkansas, located on the White River. Notes from the family diary reveals, her father was employed as a farm manager for the Perrin Brothers, 1891-1897, during

*Clara Jeffery Hanks Harris.*

part of the time the journal was kept up to date. The usual rate of pay was $1.00 per day for white males, 75 cents for blacks, (former slaves) and 50 cents a day for kids. Most of the work was with cedar timber, raising and killing hogs, hay, corn, spreading manure, making coffins for deceased persons, planting crops, hauling firewood, killing and preserving meat. He was also appointed a U.S. Marshal and was postmaster at Livingston, Arkansas. He was an early advocate of improved road systems in Isard County and served as road commissioner.

The early life of my mother, Clara Jeffery Hanks Harris, is recorded in the history of my father Robert Virgil Harris.

My mother was well known as a excellent and expert seamstress having been trained from childhood in needlecraft, and the use of the sewing machine, the making of thread with the spinning wheel, and the weaving of cloth. Being one of eight sisters and six brothers these duties were the most important responsibilities a person could be trained to do, as she did in everything that was important to her.

**HARRIS** – James P. Harris was born 1811 in Rowan County, NC, son of Nicholas and Jincy (Hall) Harris. See article on Nicholas Harris in this book. Before 1830 he married Mary J. unknown. They had about nine children, names for seven are known and all were born in Greene County, AR.:

1. Lemerles E. (1840)
2. Jincy/Jinsey (1842)
3. Letha A. (1844)
4. Zelicia/Zillah E. (1846)
5. Amanda J. (1847) Thomas Paul John (1849)
6. James P. Harris, Jr. (1859)

James is found paying personal taxes for 1834 in Lawrence County, AR. From 1834 through 1836 he paid Greene County AR territorial taxes. From Greene County, AR tax records, he paid taxes for 1838, 1840, 1842, 1843, 1851, 1852, 1854, 1855, 1857, 1861 and 1862. In 1868, J. P. Harris is shown deceased. It has not been determined whether he fought in the Civil War or not.

"*On Original Entries of Lands for Greene County, AR*" James P. Harris bought a total of 360-acres from period 1839 to 1860. He had a total of 120 acres from Arkansas Land Patents for 1844 and 1857. President James B. Buchanan signed the land patent for 40 acres, dated Oct 30, 1857. On the 1857 taxes, he paid for 400 acres of land valued at $2000. For 1861 taxes, he paid for 800 acres of land valued at $4000. Per tax records for 1862, James P. Harris had 1,120 acres valued at $4360.00.

Based on the *Goodspeed Biographical Historical Memoirs for Greene County, AR,* James was a surveyor from 1862 to 1864.

This family was counted on the 1840 through 1870 censuses, all in Greene County, AR. In 1840 the family lived in Cache Township. They lived in Powell Township in 1850 and in Salem Township in 1860. In 1870 widow, Mary J. Harris and family still lived in Salem Township. The first annual settlement of his estate wasn't available due to courthouse fires. The administrator, B. H. Crowley, filed the second and third annual settlement of estate. To settle his debts, the administrator sold real estate belonging to J. P. Harris's estate on April 22, 1876 at the old Salem Camp Ground. There were two purchasers, A. M. Knight and Edward L. Bobbitt. This Harris family was one of the early pioneer families for Greene County, AR.

*Submitted by Loyce Renfroe Kelso*

**HARRIS** – Jeffery Hanks Harris (June 6, 1926) was the third son of Robert Virgil Harris and Clara "Jeffie" (Hanks) Harris. On June 28, 1943, he married Gladys May Masters, the daughter of Jacob C. and Gertrude Masters. Born to them were Janet Ann (April 17, 1945), Glenda Kay (June 5, 1947) and Cathy Joan (June 22, 1954).

Janet married Fred Welshans and born to them was Freddie Welshans Jr. and Jeff Welshans. Janet now lives in Bossier City, LA.

Glenda married Mike Spain June 6, 1965 and born to them was Michelle Rene Spain Carvell who now lives in Memphis, TN and Michael Glen Spain who married Krystal Neal. Born to Michael and Krystal are Michael Neal, Drake and Mallory. They live in Walnut Ridge, AR.

*Jeff and Gladys Harris*

Cathy has three children: Jacob Clinton Kersey (Aug 3, 1977), Gregory Aaron Wilkin (Nov 6, 1983) and Anna Catherine Wilkin (July 23, 1986).

Jacob married Darenda Kerley and they now live in Dexter, MO. Aaron married Andrea Whitley and they now live in Paragould. Cathy and Anna Live in Paragould.

Janet Welshans has four grandchildren: Freddie Welshans III, age 16; Deanna Welshans, age 8; Brittney Ann, age 7 and Sam, age 3.

Glenda Spain has three grandchildren: Michael Neal Spain, age 9; Drake, age 2 and Mallory, age 1.

*Submitted by Jeff Harris*

**HARRIS** – Jincy Elvira Harris was born Sept 8, 1830, probably in Lawrence County, AR. She was the daughter of Nicholas and Jincy Hall Harris, granddaughter of paternal grandparents, James and Hannah Stapleton Harris and maternal grandparents, Joseph and Katherine Wilson Hall. Jincy had many siblings, but the names of only two are known. Her older brother, James P. Harris, was an early pioneer of Lawrence County and Greene County AR. Her older sister, Lemerles Katherine Wilson Harris, was married to Thomas Stanford Dec 30, 1832 in Lawrence County, AR by her uncle, Richmond Hall.

On the 1850 Washington County AR census, Jincy is found visiting her sister, Lemerles Katherine Wilson (Harris) Stanford. She returned to Greene County AR and married James Monroe Renfroe on Dec 30, 1856. James, the son of Samuel Pinkney Renfroe, had been living in Greene County since about 1851, migrating from Pickens County, AL.

Jincy and James had six children; the first three died young. Bible records reveal the following names for her children:

1. Thomas Hicks (July 13, 1858-July 14, 1858)
2. James Samuel P. (July 11, 1859-Oct 14, 1859)
3. John William (Jan 28, 1861-Aug 7, 1867)
4. Sarah "Sally" Caroline (Feb 11, 1864-May 25, 1932)
5. Nicholas Harris (Feb 10, 1868-Feb 9, 1940)
6. Quixy Ann Renfroe (Oct 10, 1870-unknown)

They were all born in Greene County. Both Sally and Nicholas named their first-born girl after their mother. The Jincy, Elvira or the combination of both names has been passed down to her other descendants.

Her father deeded her 80 acres. Since the courthouse has burned numerous times, this transaction cannot be confirmed. However, reviewing "*Original Land Entries for Greene County, AR*", Nicholas Harris bought 40 acres in 1836 and "*Arkansas Land Patents*" show he bought 40 acres on Aug 16, 1838.

Before the family moved to Stone County, AR, Jincy sold the 80 acres to William Cupp, Sept 2, 1874 (found in Book 51, page 20). The property was in Salem Township, somewhere near present-day Lorado. Jincy appears for the last time in the 1880 Stone County Arkansas census. She died Jan 11, 1884. It is unknown whether she died in that county or on their move or in Carroll County, AR.

The Renfroe family came to Stone County, AR after 1874. Sally Renfroe married Wiley Redmon Risner in Stone County on Sept 5, 1880. Their first daughter, Jincy Elvira Risner was named for her mother and called "Ella". She was born Nov 4, 1883, a few months before her namesake died.

Jincy was a pioneer of Greene County, for this Harris family was in said county at its formation. See related articles on Nicholas Harris, James Monroe Renfroe and Richard Hall elsewhere in this book.

*Submitted by Marty Green Wallace and Loyce Renfroe Kelso*

**HARRIS** – Nicholas Harris was born 1785 in Rowan County, North Carolina, the son of James Harris and Hannah Stapleton. On July 24, 1810, in Rowan County, North Carolina, he married Jincy Hall, born about 1788 in North Carolina, daughter of Joseph Hall and Katherine Wilson. They had about seven children, names of three are known;

(1) James P. Harris, born 1811 in Rowan County, North Carolina, married Mary J. before 1830 and died in Greene County, Arkansas, before 1870.

(2) Lemerles Katherine Wilson Harris, born November 4, 1815, Lincoln County, Tennessee, married Rev. Thomas Stanford on December 30, 1832 in Lawrence County, Arkansas; marriage performed by her uncle, Richmond Hall.

(3) Jincy Elvira Harris, born September 8, 1830 in Arkansas, married James Monroe Renfroe December 30, 1856, in Greene County, Arkansas. See the article on James Monroe Renfroe elsewhere in this book.

Nicholas Harris sold his plantation he inherited from his father to his older brother John and left Rowan County, North Carolina, after September 1812. A daughter was born in Lincoln County, Tennessee in 1815. By September 1818, Nicholas Harris and family, with two brother-in-laws, Richmond and Greenup Hall, were living in Marion County, Alabama. On January 4, 1820, Nicholas Harris and Richmond Hall bought land in Monroe County, Mississippi, not far from present day Amory, Mississippi. I'm not sure if the Nicholas Harris found on the 1830 Ruther-

219

ford County, Tennessee, census is my great-great-grandfather. Earliest record found on Nicholas Harris in Arkansas is where he was paying taxes in 1831 in Lawrence County, Arkansas. (Taxes for 1830 were due in 1831.) His youngest daughter, Jincy, consistently shows she was born in Arkansas on census records. His two brother-in-laws, Richmond and Greenup Hall, were listed on a sheriff's census for Lawrence County, Arkansas, in 1829. Nicholas Harris was a magistrate for Lawrence County, Arkansas and was commissioned November 12, 1833. By 1834, Nicholas Harris, Richmond and Greenup Hall were paying territorial taxes in Greene County, Arkansas. Nicholas Harris was commissioned a magistrate for Greene County, Arkansas, October 27, 1835.

Nicholas and Jincy Harris are found on the 1840 Greene County, Arkansas census living in Union Township. On the 1850 Greene County, Arkansas, census, they are living in Big Creek Township. The 1857 Greene County, Arkansas, taxes reveal Jincy Harris was a widow. On the 1860 Greene County, Arkansas, census, Jincy Harris is living in Salem Township. She is found on the 1870 Mortality Schedule, dying of old age in Greene County, Arkansas.

Nicholas and Jincy Hall Harris were some of the earliest pioneers in Greene County, Arkansas. Original Entries of Land for Greene County, Arkansas, shows dates as early as 1836 to 1854. Per Arkansas Land Patents for Greene County, Arkansas, dates range from 1838 to 1856.

*Submitted by Loyce Renfroe Kelso*

**HARRIS** – Theron Lee Harris was the second son of Robert Virgil Harris and Clara "Jeffie" Harris. He was born March 3, 1921, at 736 North Pruett St. He served in the Navy on a destroyer in the North Atlantic during WWII and he graduated form the University of Arkansas in Fayetteville in 1950. His wife, Vivian, is a native of Chicago, IL. Born to them is a son, Willard, two daughters, Debbie Letterman and Cheryl Johnson. They live in Crown Point, IL.

*Robert Hansil, Clara Jeffie Harris (mother), Jeffery Hanks Harris, Theron Lee Harris*

Theron Lee Harris passed from this life April 30, 1986. Vivian Harris now lives in Crown Point, IL.

*Submitted by Gladys Harris*

**HARRIS** – William H. Harris (May 21 1770 to 1703-March 3, 1844) was the son of Mathew of Nelson/Amherst County,VA and Elizabeth Tate, (daughter of Henry Tate (Revolutionary War, VA) and Sarah, daughter of Robert Netherland). Mathew (Revolutionary War, VA) was the son of William Harris and Mary, daughter of John and Sarah Netherland of Albemarle County, VA. William's parents were Mathew Harris (died 1727 and son of Robert) and Elizabeth, daughter of William Lee of York County, VA. William Lee was the son of Dr. Henry Lee and Alice Davis and grandson of Mr. Henry Lee, Burgess of Virginia in 1652 and Marah Adkins of York County, VA.

William Harris married Susanna Roberts, daughter of Elliott and Elizabeth Phillips of Nelson County, VA, on Nov 22, 1792 in Amherst County, VA. He was a surveyor, magistrate of Greene County, AR and a planter. When Poinsett was formed from Greene County, William became its first magistrate. He presided over the first court of Poinsett County in his home until a courthouse could be built at Bolivar. He served until 1840.

William brought his family to the area before 1830. William Henry, John and Benjamin were the only surviving sons that accompanied the family. Daughters Mary and Frances came, but did not marry. Elizabeth "Betty" married William Newsom and may have come to Arkansas. James, her son, is in census records after 1844. Sarah married Dr. George Croft and died in 1898 in Greene County. Sophia married Caleb T. Harris, a lawyer in Madison County, TN and probably died in DeSoto County, MS, after the 1850 census. Some of Sophia's children show up in records of Greene County later. Sophia, Betty, William Henry, John and Benjamin were the only children of William and Susanna Harris who left descendants.

When William began surveying the Military Lands across the Mississippi River after the 1811-1812 New Madrid earthquakes, Memphis was just a tent city and settlers ferried the Mississippi. Susanna remembered seeing lumps of coal thrown up by the quakes. William Henry remembered that the area was a 'troubling' wilderness with an occasional shanty. The people raised mostly corn and livestock. They had to be careful of bear, panthers, wolves, rattlers and wild cats. Crows and blackbirds destroyed grain and bear stole pigs from pens. Settlers used wooden mortars to grind grain, as there were no mills in the area. People lived near creeks and ate game until they could clear land and erect homes.

Indians were in the area when the Harris's arrived, but they weren't a threat, mostly Cherokees who escaped the Trail of Tears migration. William's will showed he built a mill and left property jointly to his children. William Henry's children and grandchildren stated that the three brothers donated land for the courthouse and Methodist church in 1856 and the town was named in honor of their father.

William and Susanna Harris other children who left no issue and died prior to the move to Arkansas: Mathew (1793-1825); Schuyler (1812-1815) and Ann born and died 1803.

*Submitted by Annette P. Williams*

**HART** – James Hafford Hart was a boilermaker for the Missouri Pacific Railroad. He worked at the roundhouse in Paragould. He was born in Paris, Tennessee, on June 7, 1883, and died on August 29, 1938. He married Mary Eva Hayley in 1906. She was born September 25, 1887, in Hickory Plains, Arkansas.

They moved to Paragould in the 1920s and lived in a house at the corner of Court and North 3 1/2 Streets. The family attended the First Baptist Church of which Mary Eva Hart was a member until her death in July 1986.

They later moved to 1038 West Kingshighway. That particular part of Kingshighway, west of Seventh Street, was a gravel road at the time.

Hafford Hart and his wife Eva had four children: Pauline, Amon, James, and Richard.

James married Mary Louise Miller of the Oak Grove Community.

(See the photograph with James Robert Miller biography.)

**HARVEY** – In 1888 George Richard Harvey and his wife, Bessie Aplin, were living in Somerset County, England. George's florist business brought him to Northeast Arkansas on two different occasions. After the second trip he returned to England and convinced his wife, Bessie, to get the children ready, "we are moving to Arkansas."

George was the son of Thomas Crossman and Ellen Elizabeth Harvey. The father was a prominent land owner with property located in Ashcott, Pedwell and Shapwick, England. Thomas died August 13, 1909, and Ellen, on May 4, 1919, aged 83 years. They were buried in the churchyard in Shapwick, England.

George was born in Ashcott, Somerset County, England, on November 6, 1858. He was a well educated person, being in the banking and florist business in England. He was a small man in stature standing 5 feet 5 inches, weighing 105 pounds, and almost always wore a suit with vest. Bessie, born June 22, 1860, in Dormoth, England, was, also, a small woman being 5 feet 3 inches in height and weighing 103 pounds.

George and Bessie arrived in the United States with their two children, Alice and Richard, landing at Otis Canby Boat Dock in New York. They arrived in Gainesville by train and traveled to Paragould staying at the McHaney House. Later, moving to the Joe Knight place, located near the intersection of present day Highways 412 and 135, better known as Twin Oaks. Circa 1895, they moved to Craighead County, Arkansas, settling on Newton Island. While he operated a sawmill and farmed land in the Big Island Community, she would give birth to six children: Nellie, born October 1888 (soon after their arrival in the Arkansas), Eva, Nora, Arthur, Tom and Roy (the author's father).

It is difficult to imagine what Grandma Bessie would have thought when she came to the swamp lands of Northeast Arkansas. Leaving the rolling hills of southwestern England for the mosquito infested swamps of Arkansas must have been dreadful for her. Soon after their arrival on Newton Island, her eldest daughter, Alice, would succumb to the mosquito born disease, malaria, on July 8, 1895, at age 10. She was buried in a cemetery on the Carpenter place southeast of the Dixie Community, in Craighead County.

Grandma Bessie was a very sweet person who cared for other people. Every day she would have hot tea with her homemade bread and butter. She brought a Tennyson birthday book with her from England and made entries of the family's birthdays and special events. The book is now in the possession of the author of this sketch.

Grandma Bessie died January 3, 1946, followed by George on September 11, 1946. They are buried in the Woods Chapel Cemetery, Greene County, Arkansas.

**HARVEY** – Roy Harvey, the youngest child of George Richard and Bessie Aplin Harvey, was born January 25, 1901, at Cross Cypress, in Craighead County, Arkansas. He married Mary Bean, born in White County, Illinois, on November 7, 1903, whom he had met after her family moved to Paragould. Roy was a lifetime farmer and gin operator in the Dixie Community, Craighead County. They had eleven children: Lillian, Helen, Ruby, a baby girl (died in infancy), Norman, Wava, Arthur, Eugene, Wilma Jean (died in infancy), Linda and Roy Lee. Mary died April 20, 1981 followed by Roy on June 18, 1983. They are buried in the Memorial Gardens in Paragould.

I, Arthur Harvey, the sixth child born to

Roy and Mary Harvey, was born February 8, 1937 in the Dixie Community. Soon after graduating from the Dixie High School, I worked at the *Paragould Daily Press* for five years. In 1957 I was assigned to Company C, 327th Anti-Aircraft Battalion, Arkansas National Guard. The unit was placed under federal control by President Eisenhower, and ordered to report to Central High School in Little Rock, during the civil rights integration movement of the school. The unit members patrolled the school grounds with bayonet tipped M-I Carbine rifles until the civil unrest subsided. After leaving the *Daily Press* I gained employment at the Emerson Electric Company, Paragould plant. After spending 36 years with the company, I retired in 1996 as a supervisor.

*Standing from left: Michael and Todd. Seated from left: Arthur, Clara and Charitti Harvey*

By my first marriage I have a daughter named Cynthia Joan, currently living in Memphis, Tennessee.

Clara Ann Hester and I were married on January 26, 1963, in Paragould. We have three children: Michael Blane, married Mary Goehring; Arthur Todd, married Michelle Castle; and Charitti Ann, married Micky Don Sullinger. We have five grandchildren: Lacresia Nicole, Lashea Annette, Arthur Joshua Todd, Lauren Emily Harvey and Jakob Bradley Sullinger. They all reside in Greene County, Arkansas.

**HARVILL** – Thomas and wife Sarah McFall were married in Savannah, TN. They decided to move west with two young children. They farmed near Forrest City and Blytheville before settling at Epsaba in Greene County. The names of the children are:
1. Homer
2. Mamie
3. Maudie
4. Claud
5. Mary
6. Floyd
7. Amos
8. Glen

Thomas sold the farm and the family moved to Beech Grove. They also lived at Bluff Springs, Big Rocks and Commissary before moving back to Beech Grove.

As the older children married, they all rented land and farmed together. The Stedman farm at Commissary was the last tract they farmed together.

Homer and Eula lived at Beech Grove a few years and then moved to Flint, MI. Their children are:
1. Willakay
2. Betty
3. Marion
4. Genevieve
5. Lonnie

Mamie married Roy Williams. They lived and farmed north of Beech Grove. Roy was driving a team of horses that got spooked and ran into a farm, giving Roy a broken jaw. Roy survived.

He and Mamie moved to Manila. They lived there a few years before moving to Missouri in 1949. The names of their children are:
1. Imogene
2. Edward
3. Delbert
4. Marie
5. Ellsworth
6. Dwight
7. Letty
8. Charles
9. Patsy
10. Mickey
11. Darrell
12. Joseph
13. Judy

Maudie married Jim Nelson. Their daughter, Jeweline, married J. W. Cole. Maudie ran a store on Lake Street for many years.

Claud wed Mamie Dacus. They had a daughter, Wanda Jean. Wanda died of a tumor at the age of 32.

Claud owned and farmed 40 acres west of Stanford until they retired. They moved to Festus, MO to be near the grandchildren, Jeranette and Jeff.

*Thomas and Sarah Harvill*

Mary wed Cephus Elmer Myrick. They lived and farmed near Stanford and Beech Grove. Their children are:
1. Thelma
2. Ida
3. Tommy
4. Virginia
5. Larry
6. Janie
7. Janice.

Floyd married Mildred Garner. Most of their life was spent near Big Rocks. Names of the children are Mary Jo, twins Glenda and Linda and Charles Floyd.

Amos married Sylvia Taylor. They had three children: Charles Ray, Glenda and Rita. They lived and farmed at Stanford.

Glen died in infancy in 1921.

*Submitted by Pat Myrick*

**HAWKINS** – Samuel Burton Hawkins, son of Drewry Haywood Hawkins and Mary Eveline (Burton) Hawkins, was born February 1868 at Supply, Randolph County, Arkansas. On August 27, 1887, in Randolph County, Arkansas, he married Susan Arbell Robinson. Susan was born February 1882 in Randolph County, Arkansas. She was the daughter of William S. Robinson and Mahala W. Bruce.

Samuel had 11 brothers and sisters and one step brother:
1. James Henry Hawkins, born October 2, 1853, who married Sarah Meeks, Sarah Ann Robinson, Sarah Virginia White and Florence A. Riley.
2. Drewry Haywood Hawkins Jr., born October 17, 1856, who married Lucinda Adaline Redwine.
3. Isaac Hawkins, born about 1860.
4. Tilford Austin Hawkins, born November 2, 1862, who married Josephine Johnson, Luvinia E. Davis, and Minnie California Ford.
5. Willis L. Hawkins, born June 1871 who married Lurina Sue Graham.
6. Thomas Ephraim Hawkins, born October 27, 1873.
7. Lydia J. Hawkins, born about 1855 who married Pleasant Branchflower Hatley.
8. Nancy D. Hawkins, born about 1858.
9. Permelia Elizabeth Hawkins, born February 9, 1861, who married James Madison Jackson.
10. Mary F. Hawkins, born August 30, 1864, who married Thomas Jesse Redwine.
11. Martha Farley Hawkins, born about 1870, who married Pleasant S. Davis.

His stepbrother was:
12. John Larkin Hawkins, born about 1849, who married Virginia Ann Robbins.

Susan Robinson Hawkins had four sisters and two brothers:
1. Sarah A. Robinson, born about 1865.
2. Angolia F. Robinson, born about 1873.
3. Charlotte A. Robinson, born about 1876.
4. Rennie Robinson, born November 27, 1880, who married James Ranson Brooks.

Samuel and Susan had five children:
1. Dovie Mozella Hawkins, born March 14, 1891, who married Cater Dement and William Henry Robinson.
2. Troy Dale Hawkins, born August 1893, who married Alice Starling.
3. Elvis Bryan Hawkins, born September 12, 1897, who married Maudie Ethel Jacobs.
4. Noah Hawkins, born October 16, 1900, who married Josie Fear.
5. Infant that died in birth.

*Hawkins family. Bottom row from left: Noah, Samuel, Susan and Elvis. Top row: Mozzella (Hawkins) Robinson, William Robinson and Troy, taken about 1905.*

Samuel and Susan moved to Clay County about 1920. He was a justice of the peace and held court in the front yard of his home. His hobby was bookkeeping and he was nicknamed Sam B. Bo Bunkem the beehiver. Susan died February 6, 1925, and was buried at Hitt Cemetery in Success, Clay County, Arkansas. After Susan died, Samuel lived with his son Elvis and family in Success for a couple of years and then later moved to Corning, Clay County, Arkansas, to live with his daughter, Mozella Dement and family.

Samuel Burton Hawkins died July 7, 1838, and was buried under a tree close to his wife at Hitt Cemetery in Success, Arkansas.

**HAY** – Samuel B. (1817 GA) and Julia A. (unknown) Hay (1817 GA) were in the 1850 Forthye County, GA Census and the 1860 Gwinnett County, GA Census. They had five known children:

1. William B. (1839 GA)
2. Nancy M. (1843 GA)
3. George T. (1846 GA)
4. Sarah J. (1848)
5. Luranda (1853 GA)

George Thomas Hay (Dec 12, 1846 TN) married Louisa C. Edwards (Sept 10, 1849 GA) and lived in Craighead County before moving to Greene County around 1900. George Thomas Hay was a member of the Masonic Lodge at Brookland, AR in 1883, which was the former Greensboro Masonic Lodge. George Thomas and Louisa Hay had two known children: Charlie Oscar Hay (Jan 26, 1874 AR) married in 1903 Greene County Maggie Cuba Barfield (Dec 10, 1879 AR), daughter of Lorenzo D. and Nancy M. (McDaniel) Barfield. They had four known children: Eunice (1905 AR); Albert "Alford" (1905 AR) married Mattie A. Powers in 1928; George Tillman (1910 AR) married Vauddean Stuart (March 13, 1913) in 1934, the daughter of William W. and Lizzie Stuart. George and Vauddean had twin daughters, Maggie (Sept 28, 1936 -Sept 28, 1936) and Mary (Sept 28, 1936-Oct 1-1936), Polly and Patrick Wayne Hay.

Willie Hay (1918) daughter, in 1938 married Charlie Cozart. Willie T. Hay (Nov 1881), daughter in 1905 married Albert Baine.

George Thomas Hay died Jan 3, 1911 and Louisa died Aug 1, 1923. They are buried at Pine Log Cemetery in Craighead County, AR. Charlie Oscar Hay died April 8, 1958; Maggie Cuba Hay died March 10, 1965; Vauddean Hay died Aug 18, 1965 and they are buried at Woods Chapel Cemetery near Paragould, Greene County, AR.

*Submitted by Patrick W. Hay*

**HEATH** – Verlyn G. "Butch" Heath was a mere two years old when his family moved from Marked Tree to Paragould in 1945. His father, Verlyn L. Heath and mother, Helen Graves Heath, started Heath Funeral Home that same year. His family first lived on West Emerson Street and in 1946 bought a home at 314 West Main Street, where his mother still lives today. Butch grew up in the family business and at the age of 13 began to work both after school and on weekends. Besides his parents Butch has a sister, Lynda (Heath) Bryant, who still resides in Paragould.

Jan (Schwamb) Heath was born in Paragould in 1951 to Russell and Jean Jenkins Schwamb, but moved to California when she was five. Jan's grandfather, Fuller Jenkins, worked for Mr. Heath from the time he started the funeral business in Paragould. Her grandmother, Mary Shearer Jenkins, would baby sit Butch and his sister from time to time when they were young. So it was inevitable that eventually Butch and Jan would meet. Jan has two older brothers, Stephen Wayne Schwamb, who lives in California and Philip Alan Schwamb, who lives in Idaho.

*Clockwise, from left: Jan, Butch, Zachary, Jeremy, and Whitney.*

A couple of months after his discharge from the military, Butch and Jan officially met in the spring of 1970. They had known of each other through their families, but until that time they had not had a chance to get to truly know each other. They were married Aug 20, 1972 in Paragould.

Butch is currently president of both Heath Funeral Home of Paragould and Heath Funeral Home of Hardy, which he and Jan established in 1993. He is also founder of the Greene County Rescue Squad, which he started in 1983. Jan operated a dance studio the first few years of their marriage, is a licensed funeral director and has worked in the family business.

On Aug 10, 1976, their first son, Zachary, was born. Zac is a graduate of Arkansas State University in Jonesboro, with a degree in Theater Arts. He is a Licensed Funeral Director, but is currently working as an actor in Christian Theater in Pennsylvania.

On Jan. 1, 1979 their second son, Jeremy, was born. Jeremy is currently a senior attending Arkansas State University, majoring in Business Management. He is also a licensed Funeral Director and plans to enter the family business in the near future. He also works part time as a deputy for the Greene County Sheriff's Department.

On Jan. 19, 1981, their daughter, Whitney, was born. Whitney is currently a sophomore at Arkansas State University, majoring in Exercise Science. She plans to graduate within two years and then further her education at another university.

Butch and Jan are still living in Paragould and reside at 617 West Main Street.

**HEATH** – Verlyn Leon Heath was born in Nettleton, Craighead County, AR on Feb 25, 1914 at 4:30 A.M., the seventh child of Isaac Newton and Mollie Florence (Benham) Heath. At the age of two years, he moved with his family to Lake City, AR. When Verlyn was nine years old his mother died after being ill for about four years. That same year his father lost his drug store business due to the malaria outbreak and so many customers inability to pay.

Early in 1924, Verlyn, his father and his sister, Constance moved back to Nettleton. I. N. did odd jobs and Verlyn, age 10, delivered newspapers. He rode his bicycle from the Nettleton School to the newspaper office in Jonesboro. His route covered the houses from Jonesboro to Nettleton and the houses in Nettleton. In 1928, I. N. was elected Tax Assessor of Craighead County. The family moved into Jonesboro so he could walk to work at the courthouse.

Verlyn entered funeral service in 1930 at the age of 16 when he went to work for Gregg Funeral home in Jonesboro. He worked at Kroger on Saturdays. He participated in all high school athletics and was a Jonesboro High School basketball star. He was selected Mr. Jonesboro High School in 1930 and was an Honor Student. He was an active member of the DeMolays and a member of the First Methodist Church Drama Club.

When Verlyn was 17 and a sophomore in high school, his father died leaving him with $500.00. Edward O. Cherry was appointed his guardian. Verlyn moved into the apartment at the funeral home. He worked and finished school. He was graduated from Jonesboro High School in May 1933.

In 1934, Verlyn took his $500.00 and enrolled in Worsham College of Embalming in Chicago. He waited tables in a nursing home for his meals and worked at Postlewait Funeral Home in Chicago at night for a place to sleep. When he was graduated from Worsham College, in 1935, he was the youngest licensed embalmer in the United States. He returned to Gregg in Jonesboro.

On Dec 1, 1936, Verlyn and Helen Elizabeth Graves were married. They lived in the funeral home apartment.

Verlyn worked with Gregg Funeral Home until 1938. On October 20th of that year he assumed managership of Hancock Funeral Home in Marked Tree, Poinsett County, AR. The Heath family made their home in Marked Tree for seven years. It was during this time that their two children were born. Lynda Kathryn Heath was born Feb. 10, 1941 and Verlyn Graves "Butch" Heath was born March 20, 1943.

Verlyn and Helen founded the Heath Funeral Home and the Verlyn L. Heath Burial Association in Paragould, Greene County, AR on Aug. 1, 1945 when they purchased the Irby Funeral Home. In 1952 they bought the A. J. Emerson Funeral Home in Paragould, which they merged with their firm.

Verlyn was very active in professional, civic and religious affairs throughout his career.

He served as president of the Arkansas Club of Burial Associations, Northeast Arkansas Funeral Directors Club, Arkansas Funeral Directors Association and the Arkansas State Board of Embalmers and Funeral Directors. Verlyn served every office in the Arkansas Funeral Directors Association and was secretary/treasurer for 13 years. Governor Dale Bumpers appointed him to the Arkansas Burial Board in 1972. In the fall of 1973, he was elected and installed as a District Governor of the National Funeral Directors Association at the annual convention in Cincinnati. His district included five states: Arkansas, Louisiana, Mississippi, Oklahoma and Texas. He served for four years. In 1954 and again in 1982, Verlyn was named the Arkansas Funeral Director of the Year. To date he has been the only person in Arkansas to receive this distinguished Mortician of the Southwest Award more than once.

*Verlyn and Helen Heath.*

During his career he was licensed in three states: Arkansas, Missouri and Illinois. As a young man, he turned down an offer to play professional baseball and became one of the most successful funeral directors in the state of Arkansas.

Verlyn was quite a dedicated Rotarian. During his 55 and a half consecutive years of weekly perfect attendance, he served in many official capacities including that of District Governor in l1954. He served as president and as secretary of the Marked Tree and Paragould clubs, vice president in Paragould and eight consecutive terms on the Paragould Board of Directors. He attended meetings in 50 state capitols and Mexico and Canada, met with at least one Rotary Club in a city for each letter of the alphabet. Each city on the list is also from a different state. When he learned that there was only one "X" city in the United States that had Rotary charter, off to Xenia, OH he traveled. He also met with at least one club chartered in every year from 1905 when Rotary was organized in Chicago, IL to 1990. The Paragould Rotary Club honored him by making him the club's first Paul Harris Fellow. When he joined the Marked Tree Rotary Club in 1938 he never dreamed that he would set and accomplish all of these goals in his lifetime.

Some of his other activities included:
1. President of the Junior Chamber of Commerce in Marked Tree in 1941
2. Chairman of Greene County Red Cross Fund Drive

3. County Chairman of Red Cross in Poinsett and Greene County
4. Secretary of Paragould Young Men's Civic Club
5. Served as Board member for Paragould Chamber of Commerce
6. Treasurer and president of Memorial Insurance Company of America
7. Member of the Board of Stewards of First United Methodist Church- five years in Marked Tree and then 30 years in Paragould
8. Treasurer of Paragould Methodist District Fund
9. Treasurer, chairman of ushers, secretary of Men's Bible Class of First United Methodist Church of Paragould
10. Member of the Board of Directors for the Hospital for Crippled Adults in Memphis, TN for 25 years.

Helen Elizabeth Graves was born March 31, 1917 in Jonesboro, Craighead County, AR the only child of Polk Laffoon and Kittie (Woodward) Graves.

As a child, Helen attended Blessed Sacrament School. She went to Holy Angels Academy in grades nine through 12, where she was graduated in May of 1935. She attended Arkansas State College (now Arkansas State University) for the school year of 1935-36.

Helen took piano lessons for 12 years and still has the Baldwin Baby Grand she received for her birthday at age 12. She also enjoyed dancing lessons for several years. At the age of 18 years she was an entrant in the Miss Jonesboro Contest held at the Strand Theater, April 23, 1935.

Sigma Phi Gamma was her sorority. She held several offices including president. Tennis was one of her favorite activities as a young girl. She loved to go to dances. Later she enjoyed Bridge, Garden Club and helping with various charities including the March of Dimes. Helen has served as treasurer of "21 Club" (a couples supper club) since 1946. She is a member of St. Mary's Catholic Church.

Helen is part owner of Heath Funeral Home and president of the Verlyn L. Heath Burial Association. She holds an Arkansas Funeral Directors License. For many years she handled all the bookwork at the funeral home. Helen worked right along side her husband and at one time she even helped with the ambulance work.

Verlyn and Helen retired in 1984 turning the management of Heath Funeral Home over to their son, Verlyn G. "Butch" Heath and their daughter, Lynda (Heath) Bryant.

Lynda married Jimmy Ray Bryant. They have three daughters, Kimberly Ann Bryant, Tanya Lynn Ellington and Melanie Heath Bryant. Tanya and Scott Ellington have three children, Jordan Lee McBride, Bradley Heath McBride and Jack Ellington. Verlyn G. "Butch" married Janet Dawn Schwamb. They have two sons, Zachary Justin Heath and Jeremy Ryan Heath and a daughter, Whitney Allison Heath.

Verlyn suffered from poor health the last several years of his life. He died Jan 6, 1995 at the age of 80. He is buried in St. Mary's Cemetery in Paragould.

Verlyn taught his children that you never know how your actions and words might influence another person's life, no matter what age they are. He acknowledged that he had started considering the funeral profession as a child as the result of the kindness shown to him by the funeral director, Mr. Langford, at the time of his mother's death. Whether he was known as Daddy, Granddaddy, Mr. Heath, Mr. Funeral Service, Mr. Rotary, or Verlyn, he definitely touched and influenced the life of many people.

**HENDRIX** – Dewey Anderson Hendrix was born in Blossom, Texas, on August 15, 1902, to Levi Jefferson and Alice Arlene Hart Hendrix. They moved to Montgomery County, Arkansas, when he was a young man. On November 29, 1922, he married Dona Ardena Brown. They traveled to Hot Springs, Arkansas, by wagon to get married at the courthouse. It was about 30-40 miles, but it took them most of the day.

Children were soon to follow, in August of 1923 they became parents. Levi David "L.D." was born first. Their other children were Bueford, Arlene, Vernie, and another son born dead, then Donie, and Junior were born in Montgomery County. A black lady, who lived nearby, delivered all these children and was loved dearly by the family. A small 7-year-old boy, Dena's nephew, John D. Hicks, came one fall afternoon in 1925, wanting to work for them and live there, since his dad had died, and his mother had remarried. From that day on he was raised as their own son, and until his death he was a member of the family and like a brother to the other Hendrix children.

Dewey was a rancher and a farmer of corn and cotton, with the help of the children as they were old enough to work. Dena was a housewife and mother, washing lots of clothes on the rubboard, and helping in the field or taking meals to the fields. In the summer they ran their cattle on the open range. In 1938 word came that a lake would be over the farm. Today, the fields where they had farmed corn and cotton is covered with water from Lake Ouchita. The walls of the old cistern are still standing at the site of the old homeplace on the banks of the lake.

L.D. Hendrix, about 1939-1940, Hendrix homeplace.

Dewey heard of land in Greene County and traveled here to see. He inquired of neighbors about farmland, that he had heard of thru the Federal Land Bank and bought 40 acres with a large house on it. The family was excited about moving here to a new, larger house. When the banks were going broke in Montgomery County, Dewey hid his money in the corncrib, which helped him get started in Greene County. They arrived in Hooker, Arkansas, January 9, 1939 late in the night and their new residence, to a cold house, with no electricity at that time. With the lanterns the girls tried to see what their new home was like. Electricity would not come until the early 1940s.

Dewey's father had died before they left Montgomery County, so his mother moved here soon after, living to the age of 91 years. He also had a brother William Clinton Hendrix to move to Greene County shortly afterward. In Greene County they farmed cattle, hogs, corn and cotton. Dena and the girls raised a large vegetable garden and canned hundreds of quarts of fruit and vegetables each year. They raised most of what they ate.

In 1944 they had another daughter, Shirley born at the Lafe Hospital, in Lafe, Arkansas, delivered by Dr. Frank W. Lloyd. The children all married in Greene County. John Hicks married Juanita Williams; L.D. married Dorothy Mosley; Bueford married Ellen Williams; Arlene married Jerry McBee; Vernie married Jack Hill and later married Warren Wilcox; Donie married Doyle Hahn; Junior married Vearl Smith; and Shirley married Paul Smith.

Dena and Dewey Hendrix, about 1949 or 1950.

In 1952 gravel was found on the property and tons have been hauled from there, which is known as the Hendrix Gravel Pit.

Dewey passed away October 9, 1969, and at the time of his death he owned 1,000 acres of land in Greene County, and he and his sons were cattle farmers, and farmers of rice, soybeans and milo. Dena died January 26, 1977 leaving only the children, and grandchildren. Since her death L.D died in 1977; Vernie in 1982; Donie in 1986; Bueford in 1989; and John "J.D." Hicks in 1994. Arlene is still living in Point Blank, Texas; Shirley in Paragould; and Junior at Lafe.

In the 1940s when electricity came to that area, Dewey purchased a large radio, and many came to hear the Grand Old Opry on Saturday nights. The old home place where many fun times, and friends and neighbors gathered to share food, fellowship, and farm talk is still there, it was sold in 1997. Shirley lived there until 1996. Junior and one of L.D.'s sons, Rick, still farm the old Hendrix farm. Dewey and his family worked hard and long hours and Greene County was truly good for the Hendrix family and John Hicks and they loved living here, with many good times had by all the family over the years. Dewey was a person who was always willing to help anyone who was in need of help, trying to make Greene County a better place than he found it.

**HERAL** – William Edward Heral was born June 8, 1893, in Siebert, Kit Carson County, Colorado, to William Sherman and Rosina Maud Chamberlin Heral. Their other children were: Mary August "Gussie" (1895-1971) married Frederick Oglesby; Carrie Emma (1897-?) married Arden Bolton; Charles Franklin (1899-1903); Arthur Raymond (1901-1982) never married; Dacie Ruth (1903-?) married Charles Baremore; Rosie Alice "Dollie" (1907-1992) never married; Grace Marie, born Lawrence County Arkansas near Murta Junction (1909-1970) never married.

Most of W. E.'s life was spent in and around O'Kean but just outside O'Kean lies both Greene and Lawrence Counties. From Greene County he entered the Army during World War I where he served in France as a military policeman, honorably discharged at Camp Pike, Little Rock, Arkansas, on July 31, 1919.

W. E. first married Ila Mae Holder. She and their baby both died. After he returned from the war, he married Dora McKnelly. Their son Edward Delbert was born in 1922. Dora died February 24, 1923, when Delbert was only 4 months old. He was reared by his grandparents Thomas and Edith Mann McKnelly. Delbert married Emma Rothe then Margie Rogers.

On September 21, 1925, at Walnut Ridge, W. E. married Willie Felicia Rickey, daughter of Thomas William and Mary Lavena Hicks Rickey. They first lived in Greene County where was born to them: Wanda Louise (1926-1983) married Charles Bode; Viola Maxine (1927) married Albert Lance; and Albert Ray (1928) married Margaret Boozer. They moved to Lawrence County where their last four children were born: Cecil James (1930-1987) married Juanita Getson; Rose Mary (1931-) married Bill Hibbard;

Alice Lillian (1933-) married Howard "Joe" Snow; and Arthur Glen (1934-) married Lucille.

Their grandchildren: Edward "Jr.," Mildred, Joann, Thomas, Dean, Jean (twins), Patricia, Bob, Kenny, Sue, Gary, Deborah, Eugene, Lanny, Darlene, Tammy, William, Albert Ray (1972-1993), Jim, Wayne, William K., Gaye, Rebecca Faye (stillborn), Marilyn (1951-1996), Tim, Jon and Thomas.

*William Edward Heral in World War I uniform.*

In early life, timber work was his occupation. The family remembers him hewing railroad ties with a broad ax. Later he farmed. In 1936 the family moved to Randolph County, one mile from O'Kean, where they lived until 1956 when they moved into O'Kean. He served as mayor of O'Kean from 1959 to 1961.

Willie died December 31, 1958, of cancer as did Wanda in 1983, both age 56. W. E. died October 16, 1970. Of the surviving five children, all but Glen live in same county or adjoining county of their birth.

**HERGET** – Alfred G. Herget Jr. (March 30, 1920) and Virginia L. Wood Herget (March 30, 1926) were both born Paragould, Arkansas.

His parents are Alfred G. Herget Sr., Pekin, Illinois, (July 18, 1887 to June 20, 1947) and Mabel Jackson (Herget) born Gainesville, Arkansas (February 1, 1889 to January 25, 1977). Paternal grandparents: Phillip Herget, born Hergenhausen, Germany and Sophia Becker (Herget) Indiana; their families moved to Pekin, Illinois. Maternal grandparents: Richard Jackson, Stoddard County, Missouri, and Jennet Stedman (Jackson), Asheville County, North Carolina. Jacksons originally from near Nashville, Tennessee moved to Stoddard County and because sympathetic with South during Civil War moved to Gainesville, Arkansas as did Stedmans.

Virginia's parents are William Franklin Wood, (January 3, 1900 to July 11, 1975) and Hettie L. Cruse (Wood) (January 11, 1902 to March 26, 1972). Paternal grandparents: John Frank Wood and Naomi McDaniel (Wood). Maternal grandparents: Thomas Vess Cruse (December 22, 1875 to January 11, 1955) and Susanna E. Stuart (November 28, 1883 to January 29, 1967) all from pioneer Greene County families.

Alfred's siblings: Richard Phillip Herget, Mary Herget (Cochrane) and Ann Herget (Kelly). Virginia's sisters: Beatrice Wood (Craver) deceased, Beauton Wood (Simpson) deceased, Mary Wood (Brinton) and Martha Wood (Morgan) (twins).

Alfred G. Herget graduated from Paragould High School in 1938 and Virginia in 1944. Alfred, voted most outstanding athlete, and on third all-state football team. Graduated from Texas A&M 1942, (Agri Eco) and in World War II four years as Radar Technician; was on island of Kwajalien, South Pacific and later on board ship invasion of Japan but war ended before reaching Japan. Virginia loved all sports especially basketball, and was homecoming queen and won many other honors. Worked for FBI, Washington, DC and father's store. After World War II Alfred and Virginia returned to Paragould, met and later married on August 21, 1948, at the First United Methodist Church in Paragould. Alfred entered the insurance business, Ford and Herget Insurance, and retired 1988.

Alfred and Virginia have three daughters: Janet (December 19, 1949), Susan (April 10, 1952) and Sarah Louise (August 21, 1964) all born Paragould and graduates of Paragould High.

Janet attended Hendrix College two years and graduated from U of Arkansas; married to Benjamin R. Hyneman, three children, Benjamin Brian, Matthew Rowan and Lindsey Ann. They live in Jonesboro, Arkansas.

Susan, U of Arkansas two years; married George Smith; two children Virginia Louise and Andrew Ryan. They live in Oxford, Mississippi.

Sarah graduated U of Arkansas; married Todd Franke; one child Jackson Thomas. They live in Rogers, Arkansas.

Religion -All methodists and most of deceased are buried in Linwood Cemetery and some Woods and McDaniels in Woods Chapel Cemetery. Great-grandparents Stedmans in Hartsoe Cemetery near Marmaduke and Jacksons in Stoddard County.

Alfred G. Herget served as president of the Paragould Chamber of Commerce, Rotary Club, Fox Hills Golf Club and is the founder of Paragould Country Club (history of Fox Hills and PCC in Lipscomb Room of library). Virginia active in Arkansas Methodist Hospital Auxiliary for many years and serves as volunteer coordinator for Critical Care Unit. She is adored by her husband, children and family.

Grandfather Richard Jackson was a merchant and land agent for the Iron Mountain Railroad and very strong believer in education, leaving a trust to educate all of his grandchildren as he did his own children. Mabel Jackson graduated from Ward-Belmont, Nashville, Tennessee, and her sister Frances Jackson (Donaldson) was the first girl to graduate from Vanderbilt.

**HESTER** – Homer Edmond Hester, the son of William and Tilman Ann Hester, was born in the Finch community on Sept 26, 1892. He received the rudiments of public education by attending the Finch school.

In his early youth Homer worked with his father in construction, often working two oxen that were frequently paid more that he. Homer said that he could pick a fly off the oxen ears with a bullwhip without touching the oxen.

On July 1, 1916 he married Nealie Wood, the daughter of Oscar and Jessie McNeil Wood. Moving to Memphis, Homer was employed as a streetcar conductor. When they learned Nealia had a terminal kidney disease, they returned home. She died in 1920 and was buried in the Finch Cemetery beside her two infant children, Delium and Jessie.

Homer met Margaret "Mandie L." Jameson, the daughter of Daniel Douglas and Clara Stroughmatt Jameson, at a square dance in the Alexander community. During their courtship, Homer would not enter the sloughs where she lived, but would leave her at the end of the lane. She would walk home alone through the "sunk lands". Agreeing to be married, they drove to Bard and were married on July 25, 1925 by a JP while sitting in his father's Model-T Ford automobile. To this union were born:

*Homer and Margaret Hester*

1. Wanda Fonzine
2. Bobby Gene
3. Billy Gurnade
4. Daniel Ashley
5. Clara Ann

Homer periodically engaged in sharecropping, peddling groceries and ice door to door and other business ventures. During this period he acquired the skills of a barber and returned to that profession when his other endeavors no longer proved satisfying. He worked on and off in various barbers shops on Wall Street and in Marmaduke for over two decades. Around 1946, developing essential tremors in his right hand, he discontinued barbering. For the next several years, he owned gravel dump trucks, sharecropped and was a public school custodian.

Around 1953 Homer gained employment as a taxi driver for the 200 Cab Company. In 1962 he and Margaret started their own taxi company, City Cab Company, initially working out of their home at 430 East Main Street. Laboring through many hours of hard, frustrating work, they ultimately purchased his former employer's taxi company and a competing taxi service, thus becoming the only taxi service in Paragould for many years. He drove the taxi every day, working into his 80s, while Margaret managed the telephone and two-way radios.

Inheriting his father's love of music, Homer was commonly seen with a music book in his hand. First, singing with the Finch Quartet and later, the Hester Quartet, consisting of his two sons, Bob-tenor; Bill-bass; a nephew, Mack-soprano and Homer-second tenor, the quartets performed at numerous social and religious functions throughout the region and periodically had a regular Sunday morning program on radio station KDRS from the 1920s to 1949.

Home died on April 28, 1976 and Margaret on June 8, 1995. They are buried in the Finch Cemetery.

*Submitted by Daniel A. Hester*

**HESTER** – James D. Hester was born 1799 in the Ragland District, Granville County, NC, the son of Michael and Joanna Melton Hester. James moved with his parents to Polk District, Rutherford County, NC, about 1808.

*James D. and Cynthia Lancaster Hester, c. 1857.*

Cynthia Lancaster, according to family lore, was the daughter of an American Indian (name and tribe unknown, probably Cherokee) and Thomas Lancaster. She was born circa 1809 in Spartanburg County, SC.

Cynthia's children were: Joseph Mack Hester, born 1853, in SC, married Alice Bell Ward; William Decator Hester, born 1849 in NC, married Tilman Ann Webb; James Tom Hester, born 1848, in N. C, married Sarah A. Woodson; Martha M. Hester, born 1847 in North Carolina, married Francis M. Hutson: Sarah Ann Hester, born 1844, in North Carolina, married William Leander Wood; Charles C. Lancaster, born 1831, in North Carolina, married Mary F. Wood.

Heeding the call to Crowley's Ridge, James and Cynthia left the Rutherford County, NC area, along with the Bobo, Gramling, Seay and other Carolina families, during the winter of 1857. They presumably started the long journey after the crops were gathered in order to reach Arkansas in time for spring planting. Apparently, they crossed the Mississippi River at Thebes, IL, entering Missouri at Grays Point and traveled the Military Road (Osage Trail) southward toward Greene County. It was soon after crossing the river, into Missouri, that James came down with a fever, while the family camped at a schoolhouse. There he died and was buried in a nearby church cemetery. His burial site is unknown.

Cynthia, along with her six children, continued the trek to Arkansas. Census and tax records indicate that the family settled in Cache Township.

While Charles Lancaster was serving in Company D. 5th Arkansas Infantry Regiment, during the War for Southern Independence, Cynthia died about 1863-64. She was buried in the Old Shiloh Church Cemetery, which today is located in Crowley's Ridge State Park. The young surviving Hester children were farmed out to different families in the area who cared for them until Charles returned home from the war, a cripple.

*Submitted by Daniel A. Hester*

**HESTER** – William Decator "Bill" Hester (Sept 12, 1849 Rutherford County, NC) was the son of James D. and Cynthia Lancaster Hester.

The earliest family lore concerning Bill occurred during the Civil War. His mother learned a Yankee patrol was in the Walcott area foraging. She sent Bill, along with a trusted Negro man, to take the family's cows into a hollow and hide them until the patrol departed. After awhile, they heard the patrol approaching their hiding place. While lying close to the ground to escape detection, an ant crawled into Bill's ear and started kicking. The commotion caused quite a bit of discomfort and Bill started to give their position away. The Negro told him to hold still while he spat chewing tobacco juice into the ear to kill the ant. The strong juice did the trick.

Upon Cynthia's death, about 1863-64, her children were farmed out to different families to raise, their older half brother, Charles, was away fighting in the war. After the surrender, Charles returned home and started looking for his family. He located Bill and the youngest brother, Joseph Mack, in what is now Clay County. He found them lying in a corncrib deathly ill from typhoid fever. Carrying them back to their home in the Walcott area, on his back, Charles nursed them back to health.

Bill married Mary Jane Newsom Thompson about 1872, the daughter of Sterling and Nancy Newsom. She, the widow of Edward Thompson, had three children when she married Bill: Joseph, Nancy and Addison. To this union three additional children were born: Ida, Tom Jeff and Lucy. Mary Jane died June 29, 1880 and was buried in the Finch Cemetery.

While Mary Jane was ill, her niece, 17-year-old Tilman Ann Webb, helped Bill by nursing Mary Jane and taking care of the young ones. It is apparent that Bill and Tilman Ann took a liking to each other after Mary Jane's death.

They wanted to get married; however, her mother and stepfather were much opposed to the marriage. Regardless, love prevailed. They chose a way to get around the predicament. During a Sunday church service in the Finch Baptist Church, while her stepfather was praying on bent knees and with eyes closed, Tilman Ann crawled through an open church window onto the back of a horse ridden by her fiancé, Bill. They galloped off at a high rate of speed and headed to the nearest JP. They were married on Oct 2, 1881. The much-opposed marriage resulted in 12 children:

1. David
2. Izora
3. Lawrence
4. Minnie
5. Thurmond
6. Homer
7. Edgar
8. Bessie
9. Callie
10. Lorene
11. Sade
12. Clyde

Engaging in farming, bridge construction and "rolling" houses, Bill was also elected County Assessor from 1892-96. However, his main interest was singing and conducting shaped-note singing schools.

Trading their Finch farmland for a Ford T-model, in 1925, Bill and Tilman Ann spent the remainder of their lives in the Alexander community.

*Submitted by Daniel A. Hester*

**HILL** – Lenora Stevens Hill, was born December 30, 1920, the fourth of 12 children, daughter of Chink and Vickie Clark Stevens. On June 15, 1938, Lenora Stevens married Charles Woodrow Hill, son of Jerry Morris and Drille Hill. They were married in Delaplaine, at the home of her father. Their first home was on the Doctor Hutcherson place. Woodrow worked for the WPA and helped build the Delaplaine school house.

A special person, who treats everyone fairly, she has a basic goodness and love for her family. She is a devoted mother, grandmother, sister, aunt and member of the Delaplaine Church of Christ. Her favorite pass time is needle work, quilting and embroidery.

The Hill home is a calm quiet house. A favorite aunt to her niece's and nephew's, they make her feel special. In the summer, she kept her nephews, who enjoyed visiting the Hill home. She is like a second mother to many of them. One niece tells her "you are unique."

Lenora and Woodrow Hill raised five children: Jerry, Janie Neal, Danny, Rickey and Rita Kay Stormes.

After Woodrow Hill died, Lenora was employed at Delaplaine School, eight years as a janitor and five years in the lunch room.

Lenora was close to her younger sister, Wanda. People thought they were twins. For years, they were the same size. Their mother always dressed them alike.

When she started to school, she would come home and make Wanda do all the things she did that day. Wanda graduated from Delaplaine High School in 1942.

Lenora took care of Lillie, 8 years younger, while her mother worked in the garden, and one fall while their mother picked cotton. Lillie was only 2 when Vickie Stevens died, March 24, 1931.

Lenora remembers her older sister, Imogene, had to learn to sew and cut hair at a very young age. Lenora says "I always thought she was smart. She has a lot of talent and a creative mind. She is the one I talk to when I need to talk to someone."

*Lenora Stevens Hill, age 78, taken spring 1999.*

Her brother, Woodie, would slip off to the tomato patch. He was about 4. He would come back wiping his face, with tomato seeds all down the front of his shirt, and say "you can't see anything on my shirt can you?"

The family always ate at the table. Lenora remembers her brother, Paul, always stood by their father while they ate. He would stand for awhile, then he would say "Daddy can I sit on your knee?" His father would always let him sit on his knee.

Paul stayed with Lenora off and on the last 25 years of his life. He stayed with Lillie the last five months of his life, after he got too sick to be very far from the hospital. He died of leukemia September 6, 1983.

"I am happy to be part of this family. I don't know anyone that I would trade places with," Lenora has said.

**HILL** – Thomas Hill, was born circa 1845-46 in Tennessee to unknown parents who came to Tennessee from North Carolina. Little is known of his childhood. He may have had a brother J. W. Hill who married Sarah C. Baskins. In 1860 at age 14, he lived with the aged farmer James Daulton, and his wife Polly, in Tipton County, Tennessee, where he worked as a farm laborer. Family tradition indicates some involvement in the Civil War, but no official record of his service has been found. On March 24, 1870, he married Amanda J. Johnson in Tipton County. He arrived in Arkansas sometime between 1872-1879, settling in Union Township, Greene County, with his wife, Amanda, and their two young children: Sarah E. "Sallie" (Hill) Brinkley and David E. Hill. In less than a year their small family was struck by tragedy. Amanda died of pleurisy during the summer-early fall of 1880 and their young son David also appears to have died about this time. With one or two small children, Thomas remarried almost immediately to a young woman nearly half his age. On October 21, 1880, he married Anna Mary Angeline Jackson, daughter of Henry James and Michael (Harris) Jackson. They had 10 children: Tular Vistina (Hill) Fortson, Gertie

*Family of William Decator and Tillman Ann Hester. Back, left to right: Ida, Minnie, Thurman, Bess, Sade, Lorene. Sitting: Edgar, Clyde, William D., Tillman Ann, Lucy. Front: Homer and Callie, c. 1925.*

*Thomas Hill family. Standing from left: Ruby Hill, Cleveland "Lola" Hill, Gertie Hill, Florinda Hill and Thomas A. Hill. Seated from left: Thomas Hill, Charles "Hershel" Hill, Anna Mary Angeline (Jackson) Hill and Anna's mother Michael (Harris) Jackson. Photo circa 1906-1907.*

Victoria (Hill) Wintz, Cleveland "Lola" Hill, Thomas A. Hill, William H. Hill, Ruby Michael (Hill) Eubanks, Florinda Jane Hill, Luis Cleophis Hill, Charles "Hershel" Hill, their last child, unnamed, was stillborn.

Thomas, a farmer, always rented his home and moved frequently within Greene County living near the communities of Beech Grove, Gainesville, and on Brushy Ridge near Mounds in Blue Cane Township. Though his wife Ann Mary was a very religious person, attending the Providence Baptist Church near Gainesville, Thomas never went to church. According to his son, Hershel, when asked why he wouldn't go to church he would reply "I've killed too many people and I know I'm a goin' to hell"-alluding to the Civil War. Thomas was quite a character. When ask about his father, Hershel told how the neighbor used to have goats. Every time his father would get a crop up the goats would come and eat it. So when the goats would come, his dad would shoot'em. He was "rough as a cob" Hershel said, "but he was always good to my mother and me."

As Thomas got up in years he developed health problems. A granddaughter remembers visiting as a little girl and described him as an elderly man who had difficulty breathing. After washing his face for breakfast on the morning of January 12, 1923, he fell with a heart attack while drying his face in the hallway porch and died. Thomas died in Greene County and is buried at the Providence Cemetery.

He was survived by his wife Ann Mary who spent her final years at the home of their daughter, Gertie Wintz, in Thompsonville, Franklin County, Illinois. She died in Thompsonville, June 17, 1946, and is buried there at Mt. Zion Cemetery.

**HOADLEY** – Joel Hume "Joe" Hoadley and his twin, James Strickland, were born Oct 26, 1858 in Gibson County, IN. They were the last of eight children born to Isaac and Ann (Penny) Hoadley. Their parents emigrated from England in 1848, settling first in Spencer County and later moving on to Gibson County. There is no known record of Isaac's death. Ann died of typhoid fever in 1879.

*Joel Hoadley*

In 1886 Joe moved to Indian township, White County, IL and it was there he met Susan Virginia "Jenny" Mayberry. Jenny, born Aug 1, 1863, was the daughter of Michael and Susan (Mann) Mayberry of Mayberry Township, Hamilton County, IL. They were married Feb 20, 1887.

Following their marriage they moved to a farm near Norris City, IL. Five children were born during the years they spent there:
1. Lennie (1887)
2. Jessie (1889)
3. Lecter Ann (1892)
4. Lucy (1894)
5. Ernestine (1898).

In 1901 Joe decided to move the family to Arkansas. With the help of his brother-in-law, Chester Carpenter Mayberry, they loaded all their possessions into wagons and moved to Gainesville, AR. From a "Widow" Wise they rented a house and land located across the road from the old Gainesville Cemetery. They were living there when the tornado struck the area in the early years of 1900. Disappointed in the crop yield and learning money could be earned hauling wood to the mills in Paragould, they moved to the outskirts of town where they farmed during the summer and cut and hauled wood in the winter.

In 1907 Chester Mayberry, who made his home with the family, was critically injured when he fell beneath the wheels of a loaded log wagon. He died soon after and was buried at Brown's Chapel Cemetery. At this time the family was living on land adjoining the present day Rogers Nursery. Their neighbor was the Reverend Chapel Rogers, pastor of Rock Hill Baptist Church. The family was close friends with him and his wife, Wassie.

On Oct 18, 1908 their oldest daughter, Lennie, married John Garland. Lecter Ann married Sam Lloyd on Nov 18,1910.

By 1911 the family had moved to the Finch community. The last three children were married during the time they were living there. Jesse married Juliettie Lemmon on Aug 20, 1913; Ernestine married James Woodson on Nov 1, 1913; Lucy married Shelly Lynn on April 8, 1920.

In the late 1920s Joe's health began to fail and they had to give up farming. They moved to the caretaker's house at the rear of Rock Hill church. Joe died there on Dec 12, 1935. Jenny lived with her children until her death on Oct 19, 1958. They were buried at Brown's Chapel Cemetery. Their friend and pastor, Reverend Chapel Rogers, officiated at both services.

*Submitted by Gwendolyn Y. Sutowski*

**HOELSCHER/KEISKER** – Ernest Hoelscher and Lena Keisker both came from Germany to the United States with their families about 1870 and settled near New Haven, Franklin County, MO.

Lena Keisker was first married to a Mr. Mueller. To them were born two sons, Fred and Henry Mueller. After Mr. Mueller's death Lena was married to a Mr. Karmeier and had one daughter, Ida. After Mr. Karmeier died she was married a third time to Mr. Ernest Hoelscher. To this union was born three children: Gus, Herman and Emily. In 1890, the Hoelschers and the six children moved to Loulyma (Lafe), after reading an advertisement placed in the *Germania* by Mr. Herman Toelken.

Fred Mueller married Louisa Hammon and later moved to Springfield, MO. Henry Mueller married Augusta Wegner and remained in Lafe until his death in 1947. His wife died in 1948 and both are buried in St. John's Cemetery.

Ida Karlmeier married Carl Panhorst and had two sons, Arthur and Martin.

Herman Hoelscher first married Freda Goedecke and they had one daughter, Bertha. His second marriage was to Anna Lauchstaedt and they had five children: Ella, Freda, Marie, Ruth and Ervin.

Emilie Hoelscher died in 1906 at age six and is buried in St. John's Cemetery.

Gus Hoelscher married Louis Wegner in 1903 and they had four children, Ernest (1905), Lena (1908), Emma (1913), and Ida (1914). In 1919 the family moved to Cheyenne, WY where Mr. Hoelscher worked for the Union Pacific Railway Co.

In early 1922 Mrs. Hoelscher became quite ill and the family moved back to Lafe where she died May 24, 1922. In 1927 Mr. Hoelscher married Mrs. Helen Meyer of Shobonier, IL. Their children were Lorene (1928) and Raymond (1933).

Ernest Hoelscher was first married to Alma Lueker and second to Mary (Brown) Lee. Lena was first married to Herman Leder then second to Albert Schutt. Emma was married to Norman Schlake. Lorene was married to Vernon Stephens.

**HOFLINGER** – The record compiled by Msgr. Joseph Hoflinger during 41 years as pastor of St. Mary's church in Paragould is an enviable one. His accomplishments are many. The proper beginning of his story was in the "old country" where he was born May 31, 1875.

He first visited the United States in 1890 and returned to Germany to study for the priesthood. He was ordained a priest in Moedling (near Vienna), Austria, on Feb 24, 1906.

In that year, he returned to the United States and was assigned to work in Techny, IL. In 1910, he came to Little Rock and was given the unique assignment of soliciting funds to construct desperately needed facilities for a crowded, inadequate Negro church called St. Bartholomew's.

On Jan 6, 1915 he came to Paragould. At that time, St. Mary's showed indebtedness in excess of $10,000.00, but Father Hoflinger immediately set out to liquidate that debt. Six years later that goal was accomplished.

Father was completely dedicated to the future of his parish. His dream and that of his congregation, was to build a new and permanent church to give glory to God and to be an ornament to our city.

Next on the agenda was a Building Fund. With the Bishop's sanction, he began placing savings in various building and loan associations. In 1929, however, the depression disrupted those plans. Banks and loan associations closed and the outlook was glum. There seemed little hope that Monsignor's dream would be realized, since the "papers" he held were almost worthless. He

*Msgr. Joseph M. Hoflinger*

received offers to sell the "papers" at 10 cents on the dollar, but he rejected those offers and waited for better times. And the better times came, enabling Father to redeem his "papers" at 100 cents on the dollar-full value. In 1935 construction began on the new church. The white frame church had served the parish since 1890. The present red brick church cost $50,000.00. It is of Italian renaissance architecture, with stained glass windows and a rear bell tower. Father Hoflinger was proud of his beautiful little church and made a point of calling attention to the organ, from which the church chimes could be controlled.

While that certainly is a major achievement, it is by no means his lone accomplishment. In 1953, a residence at the corner of Third and Highland was purchased at a cost of $15,000.00 and converted into a new convent for the Sisters. The old convent was torn down to provide a playground for the school. Also, to his credit is the mission church of St. Henry at Rector.

Father Hoflinger came to be a familiar figure in Paragould with his short rotund figure and thick German accent. He had less than a cautious way with an automobile and an inordinate trust in divine providence, especially after missing a country bridge and upending his car " safely" in a creek bed. In the early days of his pastorate in Paragould there was prejudice and attempts were made to terrorize him. He displayed a hat with bullet holes showing where he had escaped a bullet. He made many friends outside of his congregation. Although he was elevated to "Monsignor" in 1944, he remained "Father Hoflinger" to his large number of friends of all faiths throughout Northeast Arkansas.

Pastor of St. Mary's, pastor of St. Henry's mission, superintendent of St. Mary's School – yes, those were his official titles indicating his position. But more than these things, Monsignor had become an institution in this section of the state, loved and respected by all who knew him.

On April 18, 1956, the Pastor, Very Rev. Msgr. Joseph M. Hoflinger, celebrated his Golden Jubilee (50 years) in the sacred priesthood. The Jubilarian in a downtown theater several blocks from the Church celebrated a solemn High Mass. A large procession walked from the church to the theater and returned. On this same day, in the afternoon, the site was blessed and ground was broken for a new school. Sunday, Feb 10, 1957, the Most Reverend Albert L. Fletcher, Bishop of Little Rock, blessed the new school "Hoflinger Hall".

Monsignor Hoflinger retired on Sept 5, 1956 and spent the last few years of his retirement as a Resident Chaplain at St. Bernard's Hospital in Jonesboro.

Monsignor Hoflinger died on Jan 19, 1959, leaving to his beloved parishioners the legacy of four fine buildings, church, convent, and school and rectory, along with four acres of land reserved for the parish cemetery. It was in St., Mary's Cemetery where his body was laid to rest.

*Submitted by Lynda Heath Bryant*

**HOLIFIELD** – About 1912 Ernest Holifield left his western Kentucky home and headed west by train. He had no definite destination. The train had a layover in Paragould, AR and he decided to take a walk down Pruett Street. He found the people and store keepers very friendly and thought this just might be a good place to live and raise a family.

He started looking for work as a farmer, which he soon found. He was a sharecropper for a man named Madox. There was a house on the farm, so Ernest fixed and furnished it and in one year went back to Kentucky and married his sweetheart, Alva Guier. They returned to Greene County and worked for Madox for about three years. Then he found and bought 80 acres northwest of Paragould in Camp Ground community. A Methodist church was there and still is to this day. It was the home church of the entire Holifield family until 1954 when Alva died. Ernest remained on the home place for several years. Later, because of poor health, he sold it and moved to town where he died in 1969.

*L-R bottom: Ernest Holifield, Alva Holifield, Graynell Gladish, Genella Wood, and Hobert Holifield*

Ernest and Alva had three children:
1. Hobert Holifield married Marie Hart. They had four children: Gay, Betty, Patricia and Alton.
2. Genella married Carl Wood. They had three children: Clifford, Doris and Francis.
3. Barbara Graynell married Cecil Gladish. They had three children: Cecil Douglas, Diana and Donald Ernest.

Hobert Holifield lived most of his life in Greene County. He was a carpenter until he lost his eyesight when he was in his early 50s because of diabetes. This tragic condition did not get him down. He went to rehab in Little Rock, AR and learned how to be independent in most ways. He came from rehab determined to be worth something in life. He never gave up, nor allowed his disability to cause him not to do for others. His best talent was to be an upbeat encouraging person. He was an uplifting influence to all around him, until he died Feb. 11, 1993 at the age of 79. His wife Marie is still living.

Their oldest daughter, Gay, married Louis Holland, Jr. They had five children: Lena, Judy, Suzey, James and Eric, They have five grandchildren.

Their second daughter, Betty, married Vernal Huffman. They have three sons, Steve, Mike and Keith and three grandchildren.

Their third daughter, Patricia married Wayne Southerd. They have four Children: Laura Patrick, Bryan and Kelly.

Their son, Alton, married Linda Walton. They have two daughters, Angela, Terra and a son, Chris and four grandchildren.

Genella Holifield Wood lived most of her life in Greene County. She and her husband, Carl Wood owned and operated Wood's Roller Rink in north Paragould until his death in 1968. Genella continued to operate the rink for several years. She was known for her honesty and was a true Christian. She died April 8, 1989.

They had one son, Clifford, who died at the age of 18. A daughter, Doris married James Hoggard. They had three children, Lafawn, Randy and Penny.

A daughter, Frances, married Ralph Huffman. They had a daughter, Nalily, who has three children and a son, Rodney, who has two children.

Barbara Graynell married Cecil Gladish and moved to Flint, MI where they spent 30 years, retired from General Motors and moved back to Arkansas. They had three children. A son, Cecil Douglas, married Pearline Davis. They have three children: Cecil Alan, Barbara Lynn and Jeffery. Cecil died June 1985.

Diana married Charles Premo. They have one daughter, Katie and a son, Bradley.

Son, Donald, married Patty Ryley They have one son, Robert Donald.

*Submitted by Barbara Gladish Guthrie*

**HOLLAND** – Leslie Ted Holland was born in Montauk, MO and came to Greene County in 1924. His father, Jimmy Holland and family came from Tennessee through northeast Arkansas in the late 1800's; and settled in Missouri.

After his father died, Ted came back to Greene County. He was welcomed into the home of his aunt, Alice Holland Vines. Alice and Babe Vines were living on a farm near the Evening Star community. Ted went to work helping with the farming and cutting timber. They would cut trees with a crosscut saw, using a wedge, then a broad axe to hew the ties. Then ties were hauled to Delaplaine and Paragould to sell to the railroad company.

Ted met and married Martha Addie Matthew, daughter of Marion Matthew and Ellen Stevens Matthew, in 1927.

*Ted and Addie Holland and their son Herman*

In those days you could buy property if you could pay the taxes. Ted bought 40 acres and began clearing the land, getting it ready to farm. He built a sawmill and began sawing lumber and ties. With the help of his neighbors, he built a small three-room house and a small barn. He bought some farm animals and began farming on a small scale. In the fall after the cotton and corn were harvested he would start the sawmill business. During the depression, families had to work at different jobs each season to make ends meet. This was a way of life during the late 20s and early 30s. A son, Herman Ray Holland, was born on March 19, 1929 and on Feb 20, 1931, a daughter, Dorothy Gerlene, was born to Ted and Addie.

In those days entertainment was mostly of your own creation. Ted played the guitar and violin. Neighbors would gather on the weekends to listen to the Grand Ole Opry, Amos and Andy and the news on the radio. On Saturdays Ted would cut the boys' hair. This would always be a good time to share the happenings in the community and sometimes to organize a rodeo for the next weekend.

After WWII the sawmill business grew bigger as the demand for ties and lumber to build new houses and other new building projects started. Ted and Addie bought property and a grocery store west of Paragould at the intersection of highways 412 and 141. The property is still in the family. Ms. Addie's and Rick's Auto Country are now located there and is operated by Ted and Addie's grandson, Rickey and Kathy

Jackson. He is the son of Gerlene and the late Albert E. Jackson.

Albert and Gerlene married Dec 7, 1948. Albert farmed, drove a transport truck hauling cars for a few years and then began selling cars. Gerlene attended ASU and received her BSE and MSE degrees there. She taught School and was guidance counselor for 30 years at Greene County Tech. Kathy and Rickey have a daughter and two sons; Juli Nicole, Jeremiah and Joshua. Jeremiah died of leukemia May 23, 1998.

*Leslie Ted Holland, age 17*

Albert and Gerlene have one daughter, Deborah Jackson Fleischer. Deborah was Greene County Municipal Judge in the late 70s. She and her husband, Richard Fleischer, live in Somerville, NJ and have three children: Jennifer, 21, Carrie, 20 and David, 19. They are all enrolled at Rutgers University.

In 1954 Ted quit the sawmill business and bought property in Randolph County. He and his son, Herman, began a farming operation. Herman and wife, Patsy Underwood Holland, have three sons: Ted and Fred, now 50 and Bob, 48, lives in Reno, AR. Ted and wife, Susie live in Maynard, AR. Fred and his wife, Wanda Wesson Holland, live in Urbana, MO. They have two sons and one daughter.

Mark Holland and his wife, Layla live in Louisiana. Shane and wife, Amber live in Springfield. Kristy Holland Olsen lives in Urbana, MO.

In 1964 Leslie Ted Holland died of a massive heart attack. After a short time, Addie "Miss Addie's" moved back to Greene County and lived to be 88 years old. She died July 10, 1998.

**HOLMES-BLACK** – Around the turn of the century Oglesby Holmes of Alton, Missouri, wanted to get a new start so he left for the railroad town of Paragould, Arkansas, seeking work. He met Rosa Ann Joiner (Joyner) and they married March 17, 1902. Two children were born of this union, William Alexander Holmes, March 9, 1903, and Daisy Pearl Holmes, February 19, 1905. Oglesby died December 10, 1905.

*Seated from left: Peter Silas Black and Rosa Joyner Holmes Black. Standing from left: Peter Silas Black Jr., Gladys Lorene Black, Dorothy Black, Daisy Holmes and William Holmes.*

On July 21, 1907, Rosa married Peter Silas Black, who was a widower with two children: Robert Black and Dorothy Black. She and Peter had two children: Gladys Lorene Black, August 9, 1908, and Peter Silas Black Jr., November 22, 1921. They raised these children as our children. Robert lived to be only 9 years old.

Peter Silas Black lived to be 102 years old. He was born in Corydon, Indiana, and lived in Greene County since 1888. He was a farmer, sawmill operator and timber man. He aided in building the first bridge over the St. Francis River. The family lived in Big Island Community and he was a good friend and neighbor. He couldn't turn anyone away who wanted to borrow something whether it was money or some other item.

William Alexander Holmes married Ola Bernice Morgan October 6, 1934. Ola Bernice Morgan was the daughter of Thomas Aaron Jefferson and Gerogia Ethel Peebles Morgan. They married December 2, 1903, in Paragould, Arkansas. Ola's brother and sister are Lola Marie Morgan and R.B. Morgan. Thomas Aaron Jefferson Morgan's parents are Anthony P. and Sallie A. Raleigh Morgan. Georgia Ethel Peebles Morgan's parents were George W. and Sarah J. Bolin Peebles. They married December 2, 1880, in Paragould, Arkansas.

Three children were born to William and Ola: Anna Rose Holmes, William Alexander Holmes Jr., and Mary Lou Holmes. They raised a nephew, William Gene Nipper.

William Holmes began his career with MFA Insurance Company on December 20, 1951. MFA changed their name to Shelter Insurance Company July 1, 1981. William Alexander Jr. and Kaye Holmes now operate the Shelter Insurance Agency almost in the same location on West Kingshighway since the 1950s. William Alexander "Bill" and Kaye have three children: Stephen Brian Holmes, Michelle Diana Holmes and William Mardis Holmes. Stephen's three daughters are Nicole Holmes, and twins Kara Holmes and Kala Holmes.

Michelle is married to Tim Guinn and their daughter is Emily Kaye Guinn. William Mardis is married to Julie Ann Mitchell Holmes.

**HOOTON** – Lottie (Gramling) Hooton was born Oct 19, 1922 near Walcott, a daughter of John and Myrtle (Mangrum) Gramling. She graduated from Walcott in 1940 and married Glyn Bowers Hooten Sept 9, 1942. She received a BSE and MSE from Arkansas State College and taught school at Stanford, Nettleton, Jonesboro and Lovington, NM. She retired in 1979 after teaching a total of 29 years. She was a member of Delta Kappa Gamma Society.

Glyn Bowers Hooton was born in Altus, OK June 6, 1922 and graduated from Pocahontas High School. He attended Arkansas State College and University of St. Louis. He joined the CCCS in Jonesboro in 1940 and worked as a clerk in the office of Soil Conservation division and attended Arkansas State part time. The camp disbanded Nov 1941. Glen moved to Jonesboro and became a clerk in the Jonesboro post office and continued attending Arkansas State part time.

Glyn served during WWII in the U. S. Coast Guard National Headquarter located in St. Louis from Aug 8, 1942 to Nov 7, 1945. He was transferred to Alameda, CA and was sent to St.Louis for discharge from the Coast Guard Nov 7, 1945.

He returned to his pre-war employment as a clerk in the Jonesboro post office. He was a rural mail carrier out of Bay, AR 1953 to 1962.

Glyn and family moved from Jonesboro to Lovington, NM July 1962. He continued working for the postal service and retired July 1972 with 32 years service. After retiring he was an office machine and supply salesman for six years, for four years was a golf pro and manager of Lovington Country Club. He completely retired in 1982.

Glyn and Lottie Hooton's children are: Jane Hooton, born in St. Louis March 15, 1944, graduated Jonesboro High School, 1962. She has a bachelor's degree from University of North Texas and is a retired teacher with 25 years service. She married Jim Cullen in 1963 (now divorced). Their children are Todd Culley, born in Denton, TX May 14, 1960s and Brent Culley, born March 30, 1968.

Gaye Hooton, born in St. Louis March 29, 1945, graduated high school with honors from Lovington, NM, 1963. She has a bachelor's degree from Anchorage Methodist University, graduated cum laude. She has a master's degree from University of North Texas, graduated cum laude. She is an instructor

*Glyn and Lottie Gramling Hooton*

of Intensive English Language at University of North Texas. She married William Childress, Aug 13, 1966 (divorced) and has one child, Amy Childress, born in Anchorage, AK Feb 18, 1971.

Brig. Gen. Vance Hooton, born April 4, 1948 in Jonesboro, graduated from Lovington, NM, 10=966. He has a bachelor's degree from University of New Mexico, Albuquerque and is retired from the National Guard with 20 service years.

Vance and Barbara Howell married May 23, 1970. Barbara was born in Las Cruces, NM March 20, 1948, and graduated high school from Lovington, New Mexico. She has a bachelor's and masters from University of New Mexico. She is a retired teacher. Their children are: Sarah Hooton, Born Jan 15, 1975 and Casey Hooton born Jan 25, 1980.

*Submitted by Lottie Gramling*

**HORNE** – Irvin Simpson Horne, the son of Richard and Sarah (Clark) Horne, was born on July 24, 1872 near the Campground community in Greene County, AR. His parents, Richard who was born on May 3, 1836 in Tennessee and Sarah who was born on July 13, 1840 in Arkansas, were married in 1859. 11 of their 12 children were:

1. Henry
2. Frances
3. Dora
4. Mary
5. Alice
6. James
7. Mack
8. Irvin
9. Alonzo
10. Noah
11. George

When Irvin Horne was a young man, he lived with his sister Alice and her husband Tom Smith to help with the farming. They lived near Lorado and Mt. Zion. While there, Irvin met his future wife, Nancy Catherine Hutchins. Many years later, "Nan" (Hutchins) Horne told about meeting Irvin. She said, "Several of us went to see the flooding on Poplar Creek. Everybody was walking a log across the creek. When it was my turn, I got about half way across and my head started 'swimming' and I fell in. The water was swift and it was carrying me down the creek but Irvin jumped in and saved me." They were married on June 11, 1893.

Nancy Catherine Hutchins, born on Sept 17,

1873, was the daughter of Zachariah and Emeline (Clements) Hutchins. Their children were:
1. Mary "Molly" (Hutchins) Swindle
2. Louainne (Hutchins) Tyner
3. Victoria
4. Nancy Catherine (Hutchins) Horne
5. Wiley
6. Ellis
7. Jacob

*Irvin and Nan (Hutchins) Horne with some of their children; Front: Elva, Jones and Thelma; Back: Bertha*

Nancy Catherine's maternal grandparents, Wiley and Charlotta (Pearce) Hutchins, were early 1831 Greene County, AR settlers and charter members of the Mt. Zion Baptist Church where Wiley was a deacon. Prior to the church being built, the congregation often met in their home. Nancy Catherine Hutchins' paternal grandparents were Manen and Nancy (Pryor) Clements who moved to Greene County, AR from Tuscaloosa County, AL in 1853. Manen Clements was a pastor of the Mt. Zion Baptist Church.

*The home of Irvin and Nan Horne at Beech Grove, AR*

Irvin and Nan Horne's children were:
1. Bertha Edna Horne who married Barney Crowley Lloyd
2. Arley Richard Horne who died when he was 10 years old.
3. Elva Eula Horne who married Hubert Grooms
4. Jones Simpson Horne who married (1) Nadgerine Tinsley (2) Ruth Largent
5. Thelma Bernell Horne who married (1)Andy Olson (2) Sanford Parks
6. Barney Allen Horne who married Jean Nooner.

Irvin and Nan Horne had eight grandchildren:
1. Pauline (Lloyd) Eubanks
2. Meldon Simpson Lloyd
3. Lodema (Lloyd) Penney DeVoll
4. B. C. Lloyd
5. Mildred (Lloyd) Ellington
6. Marian (Lloyd) Pierceall
7. Velma Jean (Lloyd) Miller
8. James Hubert "Jimmy" Grooms

The Hornes loved their grandchildren and Irvin always took them candy when he went for a visit.

Irvin Horne was a successful farmer and cattleman. He hired his brother, Jim Horne, to build a two-story house for he and his family at Beech Grove, AR. Later Irvin and his family moved to Paragould where he became Greene County Treasurer from 1930 until 1934.

Irvin Horne died on April 17, 1945. "Nan" (Hutchins) Horne died when she was 93 years old on Oct 29, 1966. Both are buried in Mt.Zion Cemetery.

*Submitted by Lodema DeVoll*

**HOSKINS** – Thomas C. Hoskins was born in Virginia, probably to William and Dolly Hoskins. He died about 1839 and is buried in Rutherford County, Tennessee, south of Murfreesboro, where he owned considerable acreage. He was married August 4, 1790, to Betsy E. Marshall. They had 12 children who lived to adulthood. The five eldest sons were William, Thomas Jr., John, Daniel and Spill C. who was born in 1797 in Virginia. Before 1830 the family had migrated from Virginia into Tennessee and on September 28, 1860, Spill bought land from the state of Arkansas, Original Entry Deed Book I, page 188. In Book Nine there is also a land grant. Spill and his wife Elizabeth were the parents of William C., Thomas C., Jonathan Brooks, Susan, James, Mary, Martha, Rhoda and Sarah, called Sallie. Sallie married William S. Ford and had a son, Coleman "Coley" who was raised by Spill and Elizabeth since Sallie had died shortly after his birth. They also provided a home for another young boy, James Bramlett.

Jonathan Brooks Hoskins was born October 2, 1833, in Tennessee. His wife, Mary Jane Draper, usually called Mollie was born on July 25, 1840, also in Tennessee to Philip White Draper and Elizabeth Pate. Mollie and Brooks were married in Gibson County, Tennessee, on August 8, 1960. Their first child, Mary Edna was born in Tennessee in 1862 and they came to Arkansas almost immediately afterward. Their other children were James, Jonathan R., Fannie LuElla, Susan Etta, William H., and Robert Lee who was usually called by his middle name of Lee. Mary Edna married John Wesley Patten. Brooks died in 1886 and Mollie died in 1900. Both are buried in the Gainesville Cemetery.

*From left: Edward Brooks "Buddy" Stimson, James Edward "Jim" Stimson, Earvie Stimson Swindle, Susan Etta Hoskins Stimson and William Luster Stimson.*

Susan who has been referred to under the Stimson family, was very young when she married. She often told me that she fell immediately in love with Jim and saw no point in wasting time "courting with" anyone else. She was 13 when they married on January 5, 1884, and their first child, Rachel was born on October 3, of that year. Rachel was the "apple of her father's eye." When she was not quite 5, she was suddenly ill and died within a week. Jim was hunting with other men in the community away from Greene County and when he returned Rachel had already been buried. Two years earlier their oldest son, Isaac Clement had died at the age of 1 year. Other children born to this marriage were Edward Brooks, William Luther and Earvie who all lived to marry and have children of their own.

Fannie LuElla who married Jim's brother Wes also buried their eldest child at an early age. Their other children Hubert and Repsie died while in their teens. Thomas Cannon "Buck," Iva and Gaither lived to have families of their own. These young children and the four parents are buried in the Fairview Cemetery.

**HOWTON** – There are several Greene County families that can trace their line back to Jonathan Howton of London, England. Three are Daisy Smith Foresythe, Dott Curtis Smith and Raymond C. Gibson.

The earliest record of the Howton family starts with Jonathan Howton. Jonathan was born on April 3, 1757 in London, England. Jonathan first appeared in a land grand Certificate #2047 issued in Aug 1804 in Christian County, KY. He next appeared in the 1820 Census, Hopkins County, KY as head of household with three females under 10 living in the house.

*Howton Family Descendants, left to right: Dott Curtis Smith, Harry Smilth, John Smith, Raymond Curtis Gibson, Leman Foresythe (husband of Daisy Smith) holding Byron Foresythe and young Smith boy.*

Jonathan died after July 29, 1826 in Hopkins County, KY. He is buried in Lynn Cemetery, Hell's Half Acre, Hopkins County, KY. He is buried near a blazed tree with a sandstone rock inscribed with the initial "J" made backwards. Hopkins County Deed Book 5, page 72, indicated that this land was deeded to his son, Joseph Howton on July 29, 1826.

Jonathan was married to Ann E. Trover, parents unknown, about 1788 in Pennsylvania, Colonial America. Ann E. Trover was born in 1770 in Prussia. She died in 1830 in Hopkins County, KY and was buried in Ausenbaugh Cemetery, Caldwell County, KY. Little is known about Ann Trover except that her parents emigrated from Prussia, once the largest state in the German Empire. Jonathon and Ann had 11 children. Records of Jonathan Howton were found in Bucks County, PA at the time of his second marriage to Anne Trover.

The following is the story of the Howton's arrival in American as passed down by family members: "Howton's came to the colonies because the oldest son was disinherited due to his wife having Jewish blood. He did a tour of duty in the colonies for the British then returned later with his wife and children. The land at the foot of Tower Bridge in London was supposed to be sold by the Houghton and Howton brothers. One of the family members changed the spelling to read Howton and a deed was found in London with both spellings signed on the same deed."

In around 1857-58, the Howton's left Hopkins County, KY by covered wagon drawn by a team of oxen for Greene County, AR. Jesse Howton, His wife Elizabeth, with their son Joshua Curtis Howton and one free black man by the name of Joe started new life in Arkansas.

In 1862 Joshua Curtis Howton filed a claim under the U.S. Homestead Act for 80 acres. They started to clear the timber, built a cabin and set up a blacksmith shop. Soon after the Civil War, Jesse and his son, Joshua, were doing a booming business in their blacksmith shop. Joshua gained a reputation of being one of the best blacksmiths in Arkansas. Joshua passed this trade on to his children who gained a wide reputation of being excellent blacksmiths and horse trainers.

In 1879, Joshua bought the 40 acres that is still in the family today. Joshua married Eliza from Arkansas around 1857 and had nine children, from 1858-1878. Joshua died about 1882. His wife, Eliza died Jan 21 1878 at age 35. They are both buried in the Starnes Cemetery west of Marmaduke, AR. Eliza's gravesite still has the original headstone.

The sixth child of Joshua and Eliza was, Synthia/Cynthia Ann Howton (Oct 14, 1870) married George Newton Smith in 1888, when he was 26 and she was 18. For a wedding present they received the 40 acres Joshua purchased in 1879. George Smith was from Missouri, as was his father. His mother was born in Germany and only spoke broken English.

George and Synthia Smith had 15 children, which included three sets of twins, first stillborn:
1. Maud
2. Claud
3. Josephine
4. Clyde
5. Charlie
6. Dott
7. John
8. Harry
9. Clarry
10. Lillian
11. Rose
12. Jefferson
13. Violet
14. Daisy
15. Raymond Gibson.

Out of 15 children, only seven lived to see age 18. George died in 1934 and Synthia died in July 1948 and are buried at New Friendship Cemetery.

Dott Curtis Smith was the seventh child of the Smith's and grew up on the Howton farm. He was born Feb 14, 1897 and died March 3, 1978. He purchased the farmstead from his parents whose health was failing. Dott married Irene Sauer and had one daughter, Vickie Jean Smith.

Daisy Dean Smith was the youngest child of George and Synthia Howton Smith. She was born on the farm on March 23, 1914 and died Dec 27, 1959. Daisy married Leman Foresythe in Paragould, AR. They had five children:
1. Byron
2. Nadgerine
3. Edsel
4. Dale
5. Nadine

Raymond Curtis Gibson was born Dec 24, 1912. George and Synthia raised him after their daughter, Maude died. Raymond and Maxine Gibson live in Marmaduke, AR and had 10 children:
1. John R.
2. Jimmy
3. Jeff
4. Max
5. Harry
6. Anna
7. Glen
8. Tony
9. Howard
10. Philip

The Howton farm is still in the family 143 years after being purchased. Dott and Irene's daughter, Vickie Smith Thomas still lives and works the old Howton farm. Raymond Gibson and several of his sons and daughter still live only a few miles from the Howton homestead.

*Submitted by Stephanie Foresythe Sword*

**HUGHES** – Some of the things I remember about Walcott, AR in the early 1900s:

Walcott was then a thriving village. There were three doctors: Dr. Thad Cothern, Dr. Wm. Majors, who was the stepfather of Tom Crowley's wife, Beatrice and a Dr. Hutchins.

The Baptist church, a one-room building, was then just south of the James hill, a very spiritual congregation, preaching services one Saturday night, Sunday and Sunday night a month; one revival a year, two weeks, morning and night services.

*Cynthia Crowley at spinning wheel at park opening. Clara Kuykendall cording cotton 1936 Centennial Year.*

There were two front doors and no back door. One afternoon we were having children's service and a drunken man rode his horse in the front door. We children were jumping out windows everywhere. The town constable soon apprehended him.

Mr. Alonzo Jones owned a gristmill and blacksmith shop across the road north of the church. He ground corn into meal for the people, taking toll for pay. They also sharpened farming tools and shod horses.

I remember hominy grits were unheard of here. My dad and family having lived a year in Florida, learned to like them as a cooked cereal. He shelled corn and taught Mr. Jones how to grind them to the right texture for hominy grits.

The Walcott post office, a two-story building, was across the road. Dr. Cothern's office was on the second floor and the post office, drug store, school supplies, candies and soda fountain on the first floor. My brother hauled the ice from Paragould on Friday nights in a wagon for Dad to sell soda fountain drinks on Saturday.

Walcott had two mail routes and one from Paragould, AR. The two story post office burned.

In this picture in front of the new post office is my Dad, W. T. "Billy" Crowley, postmaster, in black suit, Mr. Sy Barrow and Mrs. Ann Dennis, Walcott mail carriers and a Mr. Bryant, the mail carrier from Paragould. Routes were run either in buggies or on horseback. On down the road Walcott also had a bank. The brick building is still standing. Mr. Carroll Willcockson and Mrs. Flora (Light) Seay ran the bank.

In front of the bank was Dr. Major's home. His office adjoined his house. He owned the first automobile in town. Many a horse has been scared into a runaway by seeing this car.

Walcott was the gathering place on Saturday afternoon for people miles around, visiting, selling their produce. Horses with buggies and wagons were hitched all around.

Mrs. Majors bought the first player piano any of us had ever seen. So we kids would gather on her front porch Saturday evenings to hear it play. We could hardly believe what we saw and heard.

On the north side of the bank, Mrs. J. L. Dacus owned the Mercantile General Store, selling clothes, yard goods, hardware, groceries, anything needed, also bought chickens and eggs from the ladies. Mr. Sol Steinberg ran the next store, a branch of the Paragould Bertig store. He sold furniture, stoves, etc. Next, Mr. Dacus owned the cotton gin. Cotton was the main money crop.

Believe it or not, the next store was owned by a man, you wouldn't call him an undertaker, but he sold coffins, they were called then and now caskets. It was told that he made his rounds to the doctors every morning to see if anyone had died, so he could sell his coffins. We kids shied around his place.

Next in line was the telephone switchboard, run by Mr. Lee Speer and daughters. For about a five-mile radius we had telephones, the kind on the wall with a crank. Everyone had a certain number of rings; ours was one long and three shorts.

There was a calaboose, small jail, behind the gins, where drunks would be kept. It was made of wood and was purposefully burned down by one of its frequent occupants.

The business part of the town was on the west side of the road and some beautiful homes were on the east side.

The one-room church was moved to where the new Baptist church now stands. The big bell that now sits behind the church was moved too. This was rung for church services, also funerals and a call for help. A tabernacle was built behind the church for summertime services. The church was later torn down.

*Walcott Post Office about 1910. L-R: Postmaster W. T. Crowley and his mail carriers, W. A. Dennis, Will Bryant and C. E. Barrow. The umbrella in the background was used to shade the rural carrier when he delivered mail from the horse drawn buggy. The post office at Walcott was successor to Crowley, the county's first post office that was established in 1832 on the family's farm near what became Walcott.*

There was a two-teacher schoolhouse just west of the church. It was a two-story building. The upper story was used for a lodge hall, Woodsmen of the World. The first floor was a two-room schoolhouse. Another room was built on later.

There was a one-room, one-teacher school one and a half miles north of Walcott on my dad's farm before it consolidated with Walcott School.

The Woodsmen Lodge had a charged mechanical goat. The ones being initiated into the lodge had to ride. One day some teenage schoolboys broke into the room and were trying to ride the goat when caught by the teacher. They never tried it again. Bessie Tyner, Nannie Crowley, George Rogers and Edgar Seay were some of the area teachers.

Every fall a circus would come to town. An elephant, trained dogs, clowns and side shows, maybe a two-headed calf and once a spider woman. She was beautiful; her web was rope. A hot air balloon was sent up once. Medicine shows frequented our village. One medicine cured all.

Here is a picture of my mother at the spinning wheel and Mrs. Clara Kuykendall using the cotton bats to be used to spin the thread on the spinning wheel.

This was at the celebration of the formal opening of Crowley' Ridge State Park. The CCC boys were a wonderful group of young men who contributed a lot to the building of Crowley's Ridge State Park. Some of the area girls married these boys, who have made good citizens for our community.

Yes, Acton, my husband and I with my brother Wiley and wife, Winnie and dad boarded the special train headed for Gov. Marion Futrel's inauguration at Hot Springs, AR. It was Acton's and my honeymoon. We had a lot of fun and were happy to have a governor from our hometown, Paragould, AR.

*Submitted by Eula (Crowley) Hughes*

**HUGHES** – Rev. J.H. Hughes was born June 3, 1878. His wife, Myrtle Brentie (Wall) Hughes was born April 2, 1879.

They had four children:
1. Julian Hughes,
2. Georgia Hughes
3. J. D. Hughes
4. Acton Hughes.

Georgia (Hughes) Crick died during the flu epidemic and her infant daughter, Ravanell, was raised as a daughter by her grandparents, Rev. J. H. and Myrtle Hughes.

Bro. Hughes surrendered his life to the ministry and became a Baptist preacher. He moved his family from Graves County, KY to Greene County in 1926 to become the first Greene County Baptist Associational missionary.

Rev. J. H. Hughes was a beloved pastor of many churches in Greene County and some in Craighead County. Bro and Mrs. Hughes were loved and admired by their children, grandchildren and all who knew them. They were truly role models.

Rev. J. H. Hughes died Sept 14, 1951 and is buried in Center Hill Cemetery in Paragould. Mrs. Myrtle died Dec 24, 1956 and is buried by his side.

*Rev. J. H. Hughes Family. Adults: Rev. Jesse Holden Hughes and wife, Myrtle; smallest child: Acton Hughes; left: J.D. Hughes; back: Julian Hughes and Georgia Hughes*

**HUGHES/CROWLEY** – Acton F. Hughes was born May 9, 1911 in Mayfield, KY to Jesse Holden Hughes and Myrtle Brentie (Wall) Hughes. They came to Greene County in 1926.

Acton married Eula M. Crowley in 1932. Eula was born in 1906 to William Thomas "Billy" and Cynthia (Gramling) Crowley in the Walcott community. Benjamin Crowley, founder of Crowley's Ridge was Eula's second great-grandfather. Wiley Crowley was her great grandfather and Samuel Crowley was her grandfather.

*Crowley's reunion at Crowley's Ridge State Park, 1949 or 50. Parents: Acton and Eula (Crowley) Hughes. Boys: Bob and Dewey. Standing: Janie. Seated: Judy.*

Acton and Eula had four children:
1. Jane Ann (Hughes) Reeves Turnbow
2. Julia Dean "Judy" (Hughes) Gramling
3. Jesse Dewey Hughes
4. Robert Gordon "Bob" Hughes

They raised their children in the Walcott community on a portion of the original Benjamin Crowley plantation, located on Highway 412 and 141, some of which was inherited from Eula's father and some they purchased from her siblings. Acton and Eula resided there from 1932 to 1986. They brought their children up in the Walcott Baptist Church where all the family was active members.

Acton Hughes attended school at Walcott, AR, where he was a member of the Walcott School basketball team that won the first basketball championship in Greene County. Acton was a farmer. He served on the county board of education for 24 years, 1949-1973 and as trustee of Walcott Baptist church for 20 years. He was also a member of Woodman of the World and was a Gideon. In his teen years, Acton was a member of the Crusader's String Band, organized in 1925. They appeared throughout the state and other states, broadcast over many radio stations including WMC, Memphis, TN, KBTM Paragould/Jonesboro and Osceola, AR. In later years, Acton and his two daughters, Janie and Judy, played and sang along with others in a band, which broadcast over KDRS, Paragould, AR.

*1930 – First Basketball Tournament Championship. Walcott school won first place against Marmaduke. Back row, left to right: Luther Cline, Acton Hughes and Mervel Rushing; seated: Jeff Blackwood and Marcus Blackwood.*

Eula (Crowley) Hughes graduated from Paragould High School in 1928 and Draughn's Business College in Memphis, TN. She taught school at Walcott, Stanford and substituted at Greene County Tech.

Acton Hughes died Nov 18, 1986. His wife, Eula died Nov 1, 1989. They are buried side by side at Warren's Chapel Cemetery on Highway 168.

*Submitted by Vickey (Gramling) Brents*

**HUGHES/CROWLEY** - Eula was a beloved wife to Acton Hughes, homemaker, mother, grandmother, schoolteacher and friend to all who knew her. She worked in the fields along the side of her husband.

Eula was well loved by all her students. One of her students, Willie Heath, came to her house periodically on her birthday as long as she lived and brought her flowers. She had a way of making all her students feel special and loved.

Another of her students, Viva Farley, commented on her generosity. Mrs. Viva said when she was in primary school, Mrs. Eula invited her and another girl to spend the night with her and Mr. Acton. After supper, Mr. Acton got his guitar and violin out and played music while she and her friend danced. Also, Mrs. Eula would gather the school children around her during recess and tell them stories. On special occasions, she would write poems to them about remembering their teacher in the primary room. Mrs. Viva reminisced about Mrs. Eula being so pretty and the way she dressed. They thought she was a movie star.

Eula also had a humorous side to her. Mrs. Pearl (Newberry) Hamilton furnished this recollection. On one occasion, the last day of school, Mrs. Eula brought a large pan of chocolate fudge for her class. They could hardly wait for the end of the day. When it finally arrived, they all bit into their candy and to their surprise,

*Eula Crowley Hughes Graduation at Paragould High School in 1928*

what they thought were nuts in the candy were chopped up corncobs instead. Mrs. Eula laughed and laughed, but the children didn't think it was very funny. Finally she uncovered another large pan of fudge for them to all enjoy.

Acton and Eula Hughes were not prone to put themselves out front, but were always encouraging and supporting their children and others to achieve. They were the force behind our success, however small or great. Their home was always open to their children's friends. Eula would have supper ready when we got home from school and iron basketball suits for all of us so we could catch the bus to the games on time. If the ballgames were home games, they would be there. If they were too far away, they would wait up for us. If we won, they rejoiced with us. If we lost, they were a comfort and encouragement to us.

Eula participated in the Heritage Trail Walk at Crowley's Ridge State Park in 1986. The episode was Benjamin Crowley pioneer.

Where she sat at the spinning wheel along with other family members, her mother Cynthia (Gramling) Crowley, also worked at a spinning wheel to help celebrate Greene County's pioneer heritage when the park opened in 1936, Arkansas' centennial year.

Everything wasn't always fun and games. We all worked hard together on the family farm to earn a living. My mother and father, Acton and

Eula Hughes, would pay us for our work, so we could buy our own school clothes instead of their buying them for us. If we had any left over, we could spend it on other things we enjoyed. That arrangement gave us an incentive to work.

I thank God for my parents who taught us to work and instilled in us Christian values.

*Submitted by Julia "Judy" (Hughes) Gramling*

**HUNT** – Jason Carroll Hunt purchased 160 acres of land March 4, 1871, in what is now the community of Stanford. He and Sarah Elizabeth Peck had been married in Harrisburg, Arkansas, in 1860. At that time he was a widower with six children ages 3-18 years. Oliver Carroll was born in 1862, the first of eight children born of this union.

J.C. sold part of his land to Carroll in 1885 and when he died in 1889 Carroll purchased the remainder from the other heirs, keeping the farm intact. J.C. was a Methodist and gave the land on which the Stanford Methodist Church and parsonage were built. His son, Carroll donated the land on which the Stanford School still stands.

Carroll was married to Lottie Bowlin in 1886. Lottie died soon after giving birth to their second child, Thomas who also died the following year. He then married Mary Elizabeth Pillow in 1893 and they had a large family of nine children. In addition to his own children he also cared for his youngest brother and sister who were twins and very young children at the time of their parents deaths. Other children came to live with the family for various lengths of time. Most were nieces or nephews but Maynard Jetton, his half-sister's grandson lived with them until his death in 1936 at age 17.

With such a large family it was necessary to do more than grow crops to provide an income. He dug wells and baled hay for people in the area. He also planted an orchard and sold apples and cider. Part of the land he kept in woods to provide firewood and lumber. When their house burned in 1938 trees from his woods provided the lumber for the new house. Although there was never enough money, there was no lack of food nor hospitality.

When the house was being rebuilt men came from miles around to give a days work or a small contribution to the effort.

As he grew older, his daughter Ada and her husband Hayes A. Triplett came to live with him and farm the land. His son, George followed and when Carroll died in 1943, George bought the land. George's son, Edwin and his grandson Doctor Tim Hunt now operate the farm.

Hayes and Ada Triplett purchased a farm northwest of Marmaduke. During WWII they bought a home in Paragould where Hayes was employed by the Missouri Pacific Railroad and Ada operated Ada's Beauty Shoppe. Hayes served as representative in the State Legislature in 1953-1955. He was a Mason, both were active in Eastern Star and Amaranth. They moved back to their farm where Hayes died in 1981 and Ada in 1998.

Their only child Joy married W.C. O'Connor in 1945. They met while serving in the Army during WWII and lived in California where they raised four children. In 1970 they purchased a farm in Greene County and moved here in 1977 to be near her parents.

*Submitted by Joy O'Conner*

**HUTCHINS** – William H. Hutchins (Jan 26, 1829) at Hardeman County, TN) was the son of Wiley Hutchins (1801 GA-1879 AR) and Charlotte Pearce (1804 NC-1877 AR); and the grandson of Zachariah Hutchins (1774-1843 AR) and Charity Shephard (1778 NC-1858 AR). Zachariah served in the War of 1812 in Captain Beverly Wilson's Company, Second Regiment of Tennessee Mounted Volunteer, and under Brigadier John Coffee.

*1865 at Greene County, AR. L: William H. Hutchins; R: Zachariah Hutchins*

The Hutchins' families moved westward across the Mississippi River into Arkansas Territory about 1831. They settled along Crowley's Ridge on Big Creek in what is now Greene County.

Mary Cupp (May 8, 1832 in Cobb County, GA) was the daughter of Warner Cupp (1804 GA-1871 AR) and Anna Ligon (1810 SC-1872 AR). Mary Cupp and William Hutchins were married in 1850 at Greene County. They were members of Mt. Zion Baptist Church where Wiley Hutchins was a charter member when it was founded in 1840.

William, his brothers, Zachariah and Joseph all served in the Confederate States Army (CSA) in the Civil War. William was in S. G. Kitchens Regiment. William and Zachariah survived the war, but Joseph was killed.

William H. Hutchins died on Dec 10, 1877 at 48 years of age and Mary (Cupp) Hutchins died on Jan 15, 1878 at Greene County at 45 years of age. They are buried at Mt. Zion Cemetery with their parents and many members of their families.

The six children of William and Mary (Cupp) Hutchins were born in Greene County:
1. John Wiley Hutchins (1853 AR-1889 AR) married Sidney Grantham (1859 TN-1889) Jan 22, 1877 at Greene County. Sidney died first in 1889 and was buried on a rainy day in May; John Wiley caught pneumonia and died a few days later. Both are buried in unmarked graves at Mt. Zion Cemetery. Their five children were Andrew married Lucy Moss; Robert; Henry; Essie Victoria married Sam Sears; Alice Ada married Chester David Hooker.
2. Mary L. Hutchins (1856 AR-1900 AR) married John Morgan Bowlin (1854 Walker County, GA- April 14, 1935 Greene County, AR) on Nov 10, 1874 at Greene County. Their four children were Cora B. Bowlin, married John Lawrence Dacus; William Robert "Bob" Bowlin, married (1) Ollie Esther Ross (2) Vera White; Lilie M. and Lewis died as infants. All are buried at Mt. Zion Cemetery.
3. Warner C. Hutchins (1859 AR)
4. Nancy E. Hutchins (1863 AR-1891 AR) buried in an unmarked grave at Mt. Zion Cemetery; married John T. Adams on Sept 29, 1878 at Greene County.
5. Josie Elsberry Hutchins (1867 AR-1936 AR) married John H. Gramling in 1882 at Greene County. Both buried at Warren's Chapel Cemetery.
6. Lotsey Ann Hutchins (1869 AR-1890 AR) buried at Mt. Zion Cemetery; Married Oliver C. Hunt in 1885 at Greene County.

*Submitted by Wanda Bowlin Davis*

**HUTCHINS** – Zachariah H. Hutchins (Dec 25, 1835 Greene County, AR) was the son of Wiley (Nov 14, 1801 GA - July 17, 1879) and Charlotta (Pearce) Hutchins (July 11, 1804 NC - Aug 24, 1877) who were married on Jan 11, 1821 in Monroe County, MS. They were buried at Mt. Zion Cemetery in Greene County. The children of Wiley and Charlotta Hutchins included:
1. Elizabeth
2. Martha
3. William
4. Joseph
5. Charity
6. Amanda Catherine
7. Zachariah
8. Mary A.
9. Minerva
10. Esther
11. Emily

Zachariah H. Hutchins was named for his paternal, Irish grandfather Zachariah Hutchins SR. (May 29 1774- Aug 3 1843 Greene County, AR) He was also in a war like grandfather, Zachariah Sr. who fought with Andrew Jackson in the War of 1812. Zachariah H. and his two older brothers were Confederate Soldiers during the Civil War. He was in the 5th Arkansas Regiment, Govans Brigade, and Cleaborn's Division. His brother, Joseph Hutchins was killed during the war. After Zachariah Hutchins fought in the bloody Battle of Missionary Ridge near Chattanooga, TN, he left the Confederate Army after voluntarily serving for two years and five months.

When Zachariah returned home to Greene County, AR, he married Emeline "Emily" Clements (March 10, 1840 AL) the daughter of Manen and Nancy (Pryor) Clements. She was one of 12 children:
1. Rebecca
2. Sarah Ann
3. Abraham F.
4. Samuel M.
5. Lidia Jane
6. William T.
7. Elizabeth
8. Emeline
9. Mary
10. Clementine

*The children of O.C. and Mary Elizabeth Pillow Hunt. Left to right: Ollie Rickman, Everlieu Greer, Dora Garmroth, Etta Sheffield, Frank Hunt, Ada Triplett, George Hunt, Marjorie Bonner, and Ruby Sonnenberg.*

11. Jacob P.
12. Nancy

Like her maternal grandfather, Jacob Pryor, Emeline's father was also a Baptist minister. After the Clements moved from Tuscaloosa County, AL in 1853 to Greene County, AR, Manen Clements was the minister at Mt. Zion Baptist Church until his death in 1858. Zachariah's father, Wiley Hutchins, was a charter member and deacon at Mt.Zion. In the early days, the congregation met in his home.

*Zachariah H. Hutchins*

In 1870 Zachariah H. and Emeline purchased 20 acres of land in Cache Township for $40 from his father, Wiley Hutchins. Later they added another 160 acres to the farm where they raised their children:
1. Marcy C. "Molly" married Jonathan Lee Swindle
2. Louainne married Janeral LafayetteTyner
3. Victoria Hutchins
4. Nancy Catherine married Irvin Simpson Horne
5. Wiley Paramore Hutchins, M. D.
6. Ellis Hutchins
7. Jacob Hutchins

Zachariah H. Hutchins died when he was 45 years old on April 3, 1881. Emeline (Clements) Hutchins died on Jan 12, 1901. Both of them were buried near other family members at Mt. Zion Cemetery in Greene County, AR. One of Zachariah's older sisters was the first person buried at Mt. Zion.

*Submitted by Sandra Penney Sharpe*

**HYDE** – Both James and Sarah (and their parents) were born in South Carolina and they were married August 20, 1844, in Greenville County, South Carolina. Sarah, a full-blooded Cherokee Indian was born August 23,1822, and died July 19, 1905. James was born in 1822 and died August 23, 1882. Both died in Greene County, Arkansas, and were buried in the old Pine Knott Cemetery just west and a little north of the new existing cemetery next to the Church of Christ (1999). My father, Arthur Pillow, their grandson, would have been 15 years old at the time of Sarah's death, and my mother, Ruth Bass, would have been 11 years old. So, both of them would have known her. Ruth was living with Sarah's daughter and son-in-law, Hester and Joe Higgins.

James was a gospel preacher and farmer. He preached at Pine Knott Church when it had only a dirt floor. It was said that he was sometimes barefoot while preaching.

Their first child, Charles F. was born in South Carolina in 1845 or 1846. Second child, B.W. was also born in South Carolina, in 1848. By 1850, they moved to Georgia because their third son, Ara A., was born there in 1850 or 1851. They moved to Cherokee County, Alabama, where their fourth child Asa (Ava or Aray) was born August 23, 1852. They then moved with the Higgins family to Greene County, Arkansas, where the rest of their children were born. M.J. (Bertha) born 1854; Thomas J. (F.) born 1856; Hester A. born 1858; Charlcey Elizabeth born January 9, 1861, died June 24, 1929, and buried at Pine Knott. Charlcey married John William Pillow on July 22, 1881. On June 17, 1880, in District 101, Jones Township, the census listed James Hyde, wife Sarah Hyde and daughter, C. Elizabeth, Hirum Gilum, James Smith and Mary Treadway (boarders) as living in the same house. Charlcey and John Pillow's children were: L. Nora married Lon Roswell; Rosalee married Henry Elmer Earnheart; Oscar died while young; Mollie Christina married Ernest B. Mangrum; Arthur (NMI) married Ruth Abigail Bass; James Claiborne married Estie Ellen Williams; Claudia married Louis Cline (first) and A. D. Washington (second); Pearl married John Frank Morrow; William Joseph married Dona Daniels; and Carrie "Dump" married Rupert Batey. Nora, Oscar, Arthur, James C., Pearl, William and Carrie are buried at Pine Knott. Rosalee, Mollie and Claudia were buried at Linwood Cemetery in Paragould, Arkansas.

**ISHMAEL** – James Pleasant "Pleas" Ishmael and Mrs. Margaret E. Turner were married in 1880 in Greene County, AR. This was his second wife. According to the 1880 Census, Salem Township, living in the household were Pleasant age 32; Margaret age 32; son James age 9; daughter Silvada age 7; daughter Jane E. age 5; stepson James French age 6; stepson John French age 4; R. C. Henry age 32 overseer on the farm; George Wilson age 23 a boarder; William Wyatt age 19 a boarder; Aaron Lewis age 19 a boarder and Anne Ishmael age 25 a boarder.

James P. and Mrs. M. G. Edwards were married in 1897 in Craighead County, AR. This was his third wife. Pleas and M. G. were both 49 years of age. No children were torn to this marriage.

*James P. Ishmael*

James P. and Mattie Brock were married in 1940 in Craighead County, AR. This was his fourth wife. Pleas was 58 years of age and Mattie was 34 years. Children born of this marriage were: Howard L. born 1908, George Clinton born 1910 and Mary Jane born 1912. All three children along with James P. and Mattie are buried at Philadelphia Cemetery in Craighead County.

Howard Ishmael and Miss Linnie Gambill were married in 1940 in Craighead County, AR. No children were born to this marriage. Howard and Linnie were active members of Philadelphia Baptist Church. Howard was Sunday school superintendent for many years and also a deacon. Linnie was an excellent children and nursery teacher. Howard graduated from A & M College in Jonesboro. H was also a schoolteacher. They are buried at Philadelphia Cemetery.

George Ishmael and Miss Pearl Louise Albright were married in 1935 in Craighead County. Nine children were born of this marriage:
1. James Richard (1936)
2. Ronald (1938) twin
3. Donald (1938 twin
4. Gladys (1940) died as an infant
5. Linda Jane (1944)
6. George N. L. (1946)
7. David Phillip (1949)
8. Susan Rebecca (1952)
9. Martha Gale (1955).

Mr. Ishmael, baby Gladys and Donald are buried at Philadelphia Cemetery. Ronald Ishmael is buried at Grandview Cemetery at Grandview, TX. George was a farmer and then a carpenter. Pearl is a retired Licensed Practical Nurse and now living north of Jonesboro.

Mary Jane Ishmael never married. She attended A & M College at Jonesboro. She lived all her life in Craighead County. She worked at Craighead Electric Cooperative. She died in 1912 and is buried at Philadelphia Cemetery.

James "Pleas's" father was John G. Ishmael and his wife was Jane Wyatt. John G. was born about 1808 and Jane was born about 1813 in Tennessee. All of their children were born in Arkansas:
1. Mary (about 1836)
2. John G. Jr. (about 1841)
3. William R. Pinkney (about 1844)
4. James Pleasant (Oct 1847)
5. Fanny (about 1849)
6. Henry C. (about 1851)
7. Ann E. J. (about 1852)
8. Sophia (about 1855)
9. Sidney N. "Sid" (about 1858)
10. Hiram (about 1862).

John G. Ishmael Sr.'s father, Benjamin R. Ishamel Sr. died in Territory of Arkansas, Lawrence County in Feb 1835 on his way from Wayne County, IL. They settled his estate in Lawrence County, the son John G. Ishmael Sr. being the eldest. In 1836, three brothers, John, Benjamin and Caswell Ishmael were on the list of Personal Estate in Greene County, AR.

Benjamin R. Ishmael Sr. and wife (unknown) had 10 children born in Greene and Giles County, TN.
1. John G. (about 1808)
2. Ann (about 1810)
3. Benjamin R. (about 1814)
4. Charles Caswell "Cass" (about 1816)
5. James Pleasant (about 1817)
6. Thomas (May 1818)
7. Henry Campbell (May 1819)
8. Shade Shadrack (about 1823)
9. Viney (about 1827)
10. William R. Pinkney (about 1829).

"Ole" Benjamin, their ancestor, enlisted in the Revolutionary War in 1776 in the state of Pennsylvania. According to the war records, Benjamin was allowed a pension in Oct 1818 while a resident of Nicholas County, KY at the age of 82. Benjamin died in 1822; at that time his wife was 50 years old.

*Submitted by Donna (Robinson) Ishmael*

**ISOM** – The Isaac Guess Isom family of Greene County, AR received its historical beginning east of Brookland. Isaac met and married Clara Bell (Bryant) Wilson at Burnt Hill on the Warsh Wilson Farm. Isaac and Clara Bell moved to West Plains, MO where three children were born: Paul, Roy and Mary. About 1934 or 1935 Isaac and Clara moved by horse and wagon back to Burnt Hill. Shortly after their return to Arkansas, Clara Bell left to live in California. Isaac moved to south Greene County, in the Finch area.

Isaac remained in the Finch area until 1969 when he died at the age of almost 101. The Roy B. Isom family and the community laid Isaac Guess Isom's body to rest around Clark's Chapel Baptist Church. Isaac and his son, Paul are buried at the Clark's Chapel Cemetery.

Mr. Isom fathered several children, starting at the age of 16, probably about 1884. It was said Isaac was married nine times. His ninth wife was Annie Drittles Reinhart from Lafe, AR. Annie stayed with and cared for Mr. Isom until his death. She died in the 1970s and was buried in the Lutheran Cemetery at Lafe.

Roy Benjamin Isom was married to Georgia McMains from New Mexico on Aug 23, 1943. Georgia died Jan 13, 1995 and was buried on the south end of the old Gainesville Cemetery.

Roy B. and Georgia were married more than 51 years. In 1960, after many years of travel, Roy and Georgia settled down with 10 children in the Finch community, southwest of Paragould. Roy B. was a jack-of-all-trades and Georgia was the best mom and grandmom anyone could have.

*Roy and Georgia Isom Family*

The children of Roy and Georgia still are closely related to Paragould and consider Greene County as their home.

In 1965 the Isom family moved from Finch to the Lafe and Oak Grove area. Soon the Isoms were well implanted in that area.

By 1965 the two oldest children were married. Benjamin L. Isom (Aug 11, 1944) and Lois Ann (Brown) Isom have five children:
1. Lesley
2. Paul died as an infant
3. Benny
4. Barbara
5. Sam

Elizabeth "Liz" Isom Haynes (Feb 18, 1949) married Bill Haynes and has four girls and a boy:
1. Margaret
2. Evie
3. Tabitha
4. Charity
5. John

Earnest Isom was born (April 9, 1950) in a "shot gun" house one-fourth mile west of the old Gainesville area. It was an Easter Sunday morning. Earnest married Betty Tracy in 1966, to whom four children were born:
1. Chesley
2. Juanita
3. Edward
4. Tracy.

Everett was born in 1951 in Monette, AR. He married Peggy Sue Hill in 1969. To that union five children were born:
1. Everett Presley Jr.
2. Wesley Kieth, deceased
3. Christopher Neal, deceased
4. April Luetta
5. Charley B.

Luetta Isom was born June 30, 1952 in Auburn, CA. She is married to Buddy Neal and they have two children, Georgia and Kimberly. Iola Christine "Tina" (Dec 23, 1954 NM-July 3,1997) married Bobby Hadley and had three children: Ben, Joe and Iris "Sissy".

Flavia Isom was born Mar 23, 1955 in Finch, AR. She married Arthur Davis and had three children: Harvey, Kevin and Christy. Roy Jess Isom (July 4, 1956 in Sanandreas, CA) is married to Theresa Huffine and they have three children: Rebecca, Jamie and Cindy. Nellie Isom (July 30, 1957 Auburn, CA) is married to Joe Dorth and they have four children:
Anthony
Audra
Glen
Bruce

Clara Isom (Aug 11, 1958 Sanandrais, CA), the baby of the family, was born 14 years to the day from Roy B. and Georgia's first child, Benjamin. Her children are Jeannie, Charles and Lila Mae.

Roy Benjamin Isom died Oct 23, 1000 and is buried next to Georgia Isom at the old Gainesville Cemetery in Gainesville, AR. The third and fourth generations of the descendants of Isaac Guess Isom now proudly take their place in the schools, homes, churches and factories here in Greene County, AR, the place we call home.

*Submitted by Nellie Dortch*

**JACKSON** – Bertha Lee Diggs (Sept 6, 1899),was one of four children born to Charlie Covington Diggs and Sallie Ann McDaniel Diggs. The other children were: Adrian Holmes Diggs (June 23 1896), Edna Mae (Diggs) Shields (Dec 14, 1897) and William Luther Diggs (April 10, 1901).

Bertha's father moved to Arkansas from Weakley County, TN and was a farmer and for a time was owner and operator of a dairy. The family lived in the Wood's Chapel Community in Greene County. Their farm was indeed a family farm because everything had to be done by hand and all the family members worked.

About 1910, the Diggs family raised the first crop of soybeans raised in the area. The county agent gave them the seed and told them it would be good for the land. Charlie Diggs prepared the ground and Bertha Lee dropped the beans by hand.

Bertha attended a one-room school at Old Bethel School. Her last year was in 1916.

The family lived in a four-room house that Charlie Diggs built. He cut the logs himself, hauled them to Paragould and had them planed and "tongue and grooved."

*Bertha Lee Diggs Jackson at Woods Chapel Church, May 1976*

The family went to Paragould twice a year. They went every winter to purchase coats and winter shoes as well as staple grocery items. They went again in the spring for hats and summer slippers. Paragould was called "The Crossing" at that time, because a small community had sprung up where the two railroads crossed.

The Charlie Diggs family hauled their family organ and other musical instruments from their home and entertained at area schools or churches. It was at one of these "ice cream socials" that Bertha Diggs met R. D. Jackson. They kept up a correspondence all through WWI while he was working in Illinois. They were married April 6, 1919, at Wood's Chapel. To this union was born seven children:
1. Charlene (Aug 21, 1920-July 01, 1985)
2. Geraldine (April 27, 1926-Oct 12, 1927) died of diphtheria as a toddler
3. Buren (Sept 30, 1928)
4. Paul (March 12, 1930-Aug 15, 1991)
5. Marlin Dale (Dec 3, 1934- Dec 15, 1998)
6. David (June 10, 1936)
7. Tommy (Nov 1, 1941)

Mrs. Jackson, as were many who lived in depression times, was adept at canning and preserving food to feed her family during winter months. She tended her chickens for eggs and fresh meat, milked cows for fresh milk, butter and sold what extra they could spare in order to have a little "pocket money." She raised a big garden as long as her health would permit. Her married children, grandchildren and neighbors never left her home with hauling away fresh produce in season or jars of canned food, or fresh milk still warm from the cow.

She was also adept at quilt making. Her children and grandchildren cherish quilts made by her. Bertha Jackson had an exceptional vocabulary and could accurately spell almost any word with which she was challenged.

*Submitted by Tom Jackson*

**JACKSON** – Marlin Dale Jackson (Dec. 3, 1934) was the fifth child of Ruel Dewey Jackson and Bertha Lee (Diggs) Jackson. Marlin was born during the depression years while the family was living at Bertha's mother's farm in Greene County. The family lived there from 1931 through 1935. Marlin and his brothers grew up working long hours on the farm and helping his mother with a large garden.

*Marlin D. Jackson (Dec. 3, 1934-Dec. 15, 1998)*

He graduated valedictorian from Dixie High School and received a BSA and BSE from Arkansas State University. At ASU he was recognized for being first in his class and selected as a student of distinction for the college. He was an honor graduate of the School of Advanced Management at Harvard Graduate School of Business and a graduate of Stonier Graduate School of Banking, Rutgers University.

Early work experiences included work in cotton gins, various industries, wheat harvest, corn canning factory, automobile manufacturing, etc., managing the college poultry farm and also employment as a part-time law enforcement officer.

He began his career as a vocational agri teacher at Monette School where he taught four years. On July 1, 1961 he began his banking career at Citizens Bank of Jonesboro as a farm service officer and insect scout. He worked two years in this capacity and was transferred to Farm Loan Representative where he worked two years before he was promoted to vice president in charge of the credit division of the bank. He held this position for the next five years. When he left Citizens Bank, he was divisional chairman for the credit division and vice chairman of the executive committee.

Marlin joined Security Bank of Paragould in Aug 1969. Jan 12, 1971, he became president of Security bank, a capacity he continued to serve until April 15, 1983 when he was appointed by Governor Bill Clinton to serve as Arkansas State Bank Commissioner. He and his family moved to Little Rock where they lived for Approximately five years. The family left Little Rock to move to Conway, AR where they were living at the time of his death in 1998.

As banking commissioner, Marlin had supervisory and regulatory oversight of state-chartered banks, trust companies and industrial loan institutions in Arkansas.

In 1987, he joined First State Bank & Trust Co., Conway, AR as chairman and chief executive officer and after that bank sold to Boatmen's and Nations, he accepted a position at Union Planters Bank of Jonesboro as chairman and ceo.

As a banker, he served on the faculty of various prestigious banking schools such as The Stonier Graduate School of Banking; Rutgers, The University; School of Banking of the South, LSU; Mid-South School of Banking, Memphis State and National Agricultural Bank Management School, Iowa State University. Teaching and agriculture continued to be a part of his life.

He was active in the American Bankers Association; served as chairman of the agricultural division of the ABA; served on the administrative committee and government relations' council of the ABA and was active in the State Banking Association.

He was sought for speaking engagements throughout the United States with major emphasis placed on agriculture and banking issues.

Arkansas State University named him outstanding alumni of 1985; Jaycee Outstanding Man of the Year in 1969; Methodist Lay Speaker of the Year in his district in 1966 and in 1974, was named Man of the Year by Beta Sigma Phi. He also received many other recognitions and awards.

He worked diligently for the community wherever he lived. He served five years on the Greene County Industrial Development Commission, President of the Paragould Area Chamber of Commerce, President of ASU Alumni Association and served 10 years on the board of higher education. Education continued to hold a place of importance with Marlin. He funded scholarships for agriculture majors at ASU, as well as scholarships for other deserving students.

Marlin married Betty Jane Nunn Sept 6, 1958. They have four children, Roy Dewey Jackson, Janet Carol Criswell Jackson, Samuel Dewey Jackson and Marla Jane Jackson.
*Submitted by Betty Jackson*

**JACKSON** – Ruel Dewey Jackson (Nov 29, 1898 near Broten, IL) was one of seven children born to Thomas Walrab Jackson and Louise Jackson. He had five sisters and a brother:
1. Marie (July 23, 1897)
2. Jessie (Aug 24, 1903)
3. Gladys (March 25, 1907)
4. Zelma (April 27, 1911)
5. Lois (Dec 23, 1915) twin
6. Thomas (Dec 23, 1915) twin

R. D.'s grandfathers, George Jackson and David Jennings fought in the Civil War on the side of the North.

In 1907 Thomas and Louise Jackson m moved their family from Illinois to Missouri and lived and worked on the Crites farm near Puxico, Dexter, and Bloomfield, MO. Then around 1911 the family moved from Missouri to Arkansas. Louise and her three little girls rode the train to Arkansas. The household furniture, hay and corn were sent to Arkansas in a special train car chartered by the Jacksons and a man named Hedger and Rube Dooley.

*Ruel Dewey Jackson*

R. D. and his father came to Arkansas in a covered wagon pulled by a team of mares. They drove the cattle, hogs, mules and hauled the chickens and enough feed to feed the livestock on the journey. They traveled during the day and camped out at night. Upon arriving in Arkansas, they settled near Brookland and made their first crop in 1912 on the "Peachy" Johnson place.

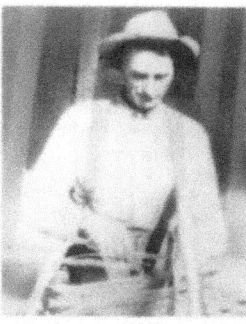
*Thomas Walrab Jackson, "caning a chair"*

Being from Illinois, this was their first experience with growing cotton. Their first cotton crop was about seven acres, or what they thought they could tend and harvest "by hand."

At that time, Brookland was a thriving, prosperous railroad town. It had a couple of doctors, blacksmith, post office, bank, two dry good stores, a number of grocery stores, grist mill, school, church and train depot located in the community.

R. D. attended a one-room school in Greene County at Wood's Chapel. After he grew up, he taught school the winter of 1916-1917 at Greensboro, then the Craighead County seat. After teaching one school year, he went to work in Illinois for Rock Island Railroad as a weight master and bookkeeper. He

*Mary Louise Jackson, feeding her chickens*

worked for the railroad during WWI. He was called up for service in the war, but before he left, the Armistice was signed. In Nov 1918, he came back to Arkansas to stay and married Bertha Lee Diggs on April 6, 1919 at Woods Chapel Church. He was 20 years old and she was 19. After they married, they resided for one crop season in a two-room house just north of the Craighead-Greene County line. He made a living at whatever work he could find. He sharecropped, cut timber, split rails, etc. His workday began at 3:30 a. m. in the summer and 4:30 a. m. in the winter, but despite the long workday, he reserved time to study the Bible with his family. R. D. & Bertha bought their first farmland in 1960. They were married 65 years and raised seven children:
1. Charlene (Aug 21, 1920-July 01, 1985)
2. Geraldine (April 27, 1926-Oct 12, 1927) died of diphtheria as a toddler
3. Buren (Sept 30, 1928)
4. Paul (March 12, 1930-Aug 15, 1991)
5. Marlin Dale (Dec 3, 1934- Dec 15, 1998)
6. David (June 10, 1936)
7. Tommy (Nov 1, 1941)

The Jackson children are fifth generation Methodist. Tommy, David and Marlin followed their father as lay speakers for the Methodist Church, speaking frequently at Methodist churches in Greene and Craighead Counties.
*Submitted by Buren Jackson*

**JACKSON** – Wallace Hoke Jackson and Laura Francis Walker were married on Sept 4, 1948. Wallace served during WWII in the 124th Calvary Division of the U. S. Army, from 1944-1946, spending time in China, Burma and India (CBI Theater). After marrying, they lived in Dyersburg where he was in the shoe business.

Wallace and Laura moved to Paragould, AR in May 1957. They opened Family Shoe Store on Pruett Street on May 4, 1957 and have remained in business for 43 years. They are members of First United Methodist Church in Paragould.

*Wallace and Laura Jackson*

*Wallace and Laura Jackson with their three sons and their families.*

They have three sons, Jim, Davey Joe and Stan. Davey Joe and Jim both reside with their families in Paragould. Stan and his family are stationed at Sembach Air Force Base in Germany. Jim is married to the former Guyla Clark. Their children are Amy, Audri, Morgan, Emily and Steven. Davey Joe is married to the former Rena Ford. They have one son, Kyle. Stan is married to the former Teresa Jones. They have two children, Lincoln and Lane.
*Submitted by Rena Jackson*

**JACKSON/WALTERS** – Julia Bruce Walters (July 15, 1904 Paducah, KY) married Charles Edward Jackson on Aug 12, 1922. They had two children: daughter, Mary Evelyn "Buster" (Aug 19, 1923) and a son Robert E. Jackson (Feb 7, 1936).

Mary Evelyn married Milton Miller, Dec 22, 1946. Milton Miller died June 1996. They had three children: Robert Milton Miller married Sandy and they had two children, Chris and Sandy; Kathy Lee (Miller) Tipton married Jearle, had three boys Clay, Ryan and Chase; Mary Ann (Miller) married (1) Yarnell and had two children Kali and Douglas, (2) Rooney.

*Jessie and Lottie Walters and daughters, Flora, Pansy, Willie and Julia, ca. 1913.*

235

Robert Edward Jackson married Brenda James of Hayti, MO 1961. They had a daughter Kimberly Ann (Dec 26, 1963). Robert and Brenda divorced 1964. Later Robert married Bonnie Usery of Senath, MO. They had a son Matthew E. Jackson (March 20, 1977). Robert died Jan 11, 1983 while coaching basketball in Rockledge, FL. He is buried in Rockledge, FL. He served two years in service in Germany.

Kimberly married Donnie Storey July 1983. They had a daughter, Jennifer (March 20, 1986). Kimberly and Donnie divorced in 1989 and she married Eric Jespersen June 1999.

Robert and Bonnie's son, Matthew married Christine Denice Yoder June 13, 1999. He is now in a church seminary in Fort Worth, TX.

Charles Jackson's father was Albert Davis Jackson (Jan 20, 1865 in Union TWP, MO- Oct 25, 1950). He is buried in Linwood Cemetery, Paragould. He married Nancy Melvina Cammon (Aug 5, 1877-Oct 11, 1943). She is buried Linwood Cemetery. They had nine children:
1. Virgil (1899-July 1900)
2. Charles E. (Oct 1901-March 16, 1981) buried Memorial Gardens, Paragould, AR.
3. Richard W. (Oct 12, 1903- April 21, 1940) buried Linwood Cemetery, Paragould, AR
4. George L. (Oct 1905-July 1983) buried in Clearwater, FL
5. Harry G. (1907-1914) buried in Fairview or Gainesville Cemetery.
6. John Robert (Oct 13, 1910-1953) buried in Linwood
7. Albert Davis (1917-1955) buried in Linwood
8. Lewis (March 1, 1914-July 1963) buried in Linwood
9. Leonard H. (1912-July 1912) lived only two weeks

Julia Bruce (Walters) Jackson's mother was Lottie Ann Houston (Aug 19, 1883 KY- July 28, 1930) buried Linwood Cemetery. She married Jessie Edward Walters (April 15, 1881-April 28,1969) buried Linwood Cemetery, Paragould, AR. Lottie Ann and Jessie Edward were married 1901 in Paducah, KY. Moved from Kentucky to DeValls Bluff, AR, later to DesArc, AR where he had a dairy farm. Moved to Paragould, AR in 1911. They had four daughters:

*Robert E. Jackson, Julia Bruce Walters Jackson, Charles Edward Jackson and Mary Evelyn Jackson Miller, 1979.*

1. Willie Mae (July 10, 1903-June 12 1977) married Roy Gott of Paragould in 1921. They had a daughter Wilma Jane (Dec 22, 1923). Willie and Roy divorced in 1925-26. Years later she married Bill Ollerman. Bill died about 1975 –76 and is buried in St. Louis with Willie.
2. Julia Bruce (Walters) Jackson (July 15, 1904)
3. Pansy Irene (Jan 20, 1906-Jan 11, 1990) buried Linwood Cemetery. She married Tom McKelvey and their daughter died at birth.
4. Flora Bell (March 25, 1907-1996) married Hershel Elrod. They had a daughter, Virginia (July 20, 1925). Flora died on Easter Sunday and is buried in St. Louis.

Jessie Walters (April 15, 1881 KY- April 28, 1969) father of Julia Bruce Jackson buried Linwood Cemetery. His father was James Walters, died 1942, buried in St. Louis, MO. Jessie's mother died 1892. There were four boys born to this marriage:
1. Flavis
2. Roy
3. Jessie
4. Clyde

All are dead. Their father married again to Ada Williams or Lawrence. To this marriage was born five sons and twin daughters:
1. Cyrus
2. Alvin
3. Roscoe
4. Frank
5. Thurman
6. Lola, twin
7. Lee Ann, twin

All the boys are dead and I feel sure the two girls are dead also. Their mother, Ada, died Nov 25, 1923 and is buried Linwood Cemetery.
*Submitted by Julia Jackson*

**JAMESON** – Daniel Douglas Jameson (Feb 14, 1866 White County, IL) was the son of Byrd and Amanda M. Taylor Jameson/Jamerson. Dan's father died five weeks after he was born because of war injuries, sustained near Natchez, MS, while serving as First Sergeant, Company B, 29th Illinois Infantry, the unit Byrd's father had organized in Aug 1862.

While Dan was working in the fields his mother perished, on July 30 1884, from burns sustained while pouring kerosene on a rusty stove hinge. After her death, Dan traveled to Seattle, WA where he worked in the timber industry. Returning home he furthered his education by attending Southern Illinois College.

When the lumber mills opened in southeast Missouri, he and a brother, James Henry moved to Neelyville, MO. Dan met and married Mary Maud Jackson, of Harville, June 13, 1896. Tragically, Mary and their three infant children succumbed to the diseases prevalent in the swamps.

After 1900, Dan and James went to the Ring community, Clay County. While cutting logs for L. L. Woods, near Hickoria, James died on Dec 2, 1904 after a week's illness. Dan buried his brother in a nearby ditch bank.

Leaving Ring, Dan arrived in Greene County at Bethel Station. After gaining employment on the Iron Mountain and Cotton Belt Railroad he returned to Corning, AR, for Clara Pearl Strawmatt, a housekeeper for Judge Hopson. They were married on June 4, 1906 in Paragould.

Moving to Brighton, they operated Ed Ross' hotel. Also, Clara cared for her daughter, Hazel and newborn Margaret.

Dan subsequently obtained employment with the PS&E railroad. He would walk the St. Francis River trestle, often at night with a lantern, on the lookout for sparks from passing steam engines that could ignite the trestle.

Around 1910, Dan claimed a Homestead Patent, number 012485, for 107.37 acres of land located north of Brighton. In addition to clearing the homestead, he worked in the timber by cutting the virgin trees, toggling the logs together and poling them to the mills in Brighton.

On the homestead he planted 25 fruit trees and built a two-room house of lumber from buildings of the closed National Box Company. He moved the family's possessions to the homestead, by barge, up the Roaring River Ditch. Located in the St. Francis Sunk Lands, the homestead was prone to flooding and pockmarked by "blow holes" from the 1812 earthquake. The fertile land would produce 50 bushels of corn and 1800 pounds of cotton per acre. Here, three more children were born: Lucille, died in infancy, Warren and Roosevelt.

*Daniel Douglas Jameson*

Dan encumbered the homestead frequently. In Feb 1927 a mortgage for $850 was given to the Joseph Company. About this time Clara learned she had uterine cancer. Unable to pay the mortgage, due to the doctor bills in Memphis, Dan lost the homestead in April 1929. On May 5, 1929 Clara passed away and Dan followed on Nov 5, 1952. They were buried in The Finch Cemetery.
*Submitted by Daniel A. Hester*

**JERNIGAN** – Ray Jernigan moved, with the Corps of Engineers, to Paragould in 1967. He was born in Marianna, Lee County, Arkansas, March 15, 1933, to Augustus Marvin, son of John Dye and Bettie Byrd Jernigan, and Mary Elizabeth Taylor Jernigan, daughter of Methodist minister Leonard Franklin and Cora Magdalene "Maggie" Webb Taylor.

He graduated from Marianna High School in 1951 and went on to attend Vanderbilt University and Arkansas State.

He is a member of the First United Methodist Church. He is also an avid golfer and bowler.

He became the Greene County Land Surveyor in 1969 and has retained that position into five decades.

Children from his first marriage are Rita Jernigan, a teacher in the Little Rock School System; Ron Jernigan, married to the former Kathy Johnson, is a systems analyst with ALLTEL in Little Rock; Russell Jernigan, who died in 1996; and Randell Jernigan, who, with his wife Robin, own a security system company in Jonesboro.

*Marvin Ray Jernigan*

Ray and his present wife, Gretta Stimson Jernigan, are the parents of Pharmacist Kerry Jernigan Jewison, who is married to Rev. Greg Jewison, and lives in Beaver Dam, Wisconsin; Jocelyn Jernigan Noel, employed at Emerson Electric, married to Rick Noel, and lives in Paragould; Michele Jernigan French, married to John French, is a Federal Probation Officer, and lives in North Little Rock; and Edward Jernigan, an FBI agent, is married to the former Becky Clifton, and lives near Paragould.

The attached picture shows Ray Jernigan standing near a monument at the junction of Phillips, Monroe, and Lee counties. "It marks the base established November 10, 1815, from which the lands of the Louisiana Purchase were surveyed by the United States Engineers. The first survey from this point was made to satisfy the claims of the soldiers of the War of 1812 with land bounties." The monument was erected by the L'Anguilie Chapter of the DAR.

*Bryant-Jetton Family, from left, Mildred (Jetton) Bryant, Ella Varner, Keith Bryant, Brenda Walker, Leland Bryant, Laura Loveall, Ronnie Bryant, Milton Bryant, Moud Malichi "Chicken" Bryant; decendants from Alvie Bryant and Della Emorine and Carol Jetton and Mary Battenfield.*

**JETTON/BRYANT** – Laura Fay (Bryant) Loveall, was the oldest of seven children born to Moud Malichi "Chicken" Bryant and Mildred Marie (Jetton) Bryant. Laura has had Hair Spectrum in Paragould since 1987. Prior to that she was in the RV business in Missouri and real estate in Missouri and Arkansas.

Her siblings were all born in and still live in or near Greene County. Leland and Janet Bryant, Paragould; Hulen and Ella Sue Varner, Delaplaine; Charles and Brenda Walker, Light; Ronnie and Debbie Bryant, Maynard and Keith and Milton Bryant, Beech Grove, AR.

The Bryants are descendants of my great-grandparents, the late Robert Bryant and Louvene Markum Bryant. Our grandparents are the late Jake Alvie Bryant and Della Dora Emorine Bryant.

Our Jetton ancestors are my great-grandparents, the late George Warren Jetton and Anna Belle Marrow Jetton, the late William Battenfield and the late Nancy Hall Battenfield. Grandparents are the late Carroll Aslo Jetton and Mary Opal Battenfield.

*Laura Loveall*

My ancestors were farmers. My grandparents and their children cleared land to farm to make a living. The women helped with anything they could do and mostly kept the family and home comfortable.

My Dad farmed a small parcel of land and then became the country mechanic. His wages were not much but the favors he did were many.

Dad' siblings are:
1. Vernon Bryant, Michigan
2. Morris Bryant, deceased, Walcott
3. Dorothy Bryant Ivie, Paragould
4. Bob Bryant, deceased, Florida

Mom's siblings are:
1. Weldon Jetton
2. Bob Jetton
3. Peggy (Jetton) Miller

All of Paragould.

My parents were Malachi Bryant (June 9, 1924) and Mildred (Jetton) Bryant (March 26, 1929). Laura (Bryant) Loveall, their oldest child was born Oct 5, 1945.

*Submitted by Laura Loveall*

**JOHNS** – Father Clennie C. Johns was born in 1886, in Tennessee and died in Greene County, Arkansas, in 1967. Our mother Judson Frances Faulkner Johns was born in Arkansas and died in Greene County, 1977.

J.W. Johns our grandfather was born in Tennessee. Our grandmother was Nancy Jane Johns. Our maternal grandparents were Joe G. Faulkner born in Mississippi and Carrie (Spillman) Faulkner.

The Johns came from Tennessee to Greene County in early 1900s. Dr. George Croft, an early settler to Greene County; also a physician had invited the Johns family to come to Greene County. He needed help at the Croft School near Stanford. The Greene County area was a good settlement for many people. The Johns family being very interested in education, saw a great opportunity in this county.

*Edrington family in 1975, back row: Betty Bo, Cloyce, William J., Frances Ann, Daphine and Dorothy.*

The J.W. Johns family consisted of six children, including our father Clennie; who became a progressive teacher in Greene County schools. He taught at Crossroads, a one-room school and became well known in the education field. Our mother, Judson Faulkner was a upper grade student taught by Clennie Johns at Crossroads. Teacher Johns and student Judson Faulkner got to be sweethearts and married. Soon after their marriage he was elected Greene County Representative and they moved to Little Rock. Later the Johns family returned to Greene County to make their home.

Joe G. and Carrie Faulkner owned a successful grocery store in the county at this time.

The Clennie Johns family was a happy family, with six children being born to Clennie and Judson. These are: Daphine (Johns) Edrington, Cloyce Johns, Dorothy (Johns) Starling, William J. Johns, Betty Bo (Johns) Medsker, and Frances Ann (Johns) Gay. All six children attended Harding College and Arkansas State University. This family produced teachers, church workers, medical field and farmers.

Daphine Johns, a local Greene County teacher for many years married Maurice Edrington. The Edringtons were residents of Center Hill area, where Edringtons have resided for many, many, years and Maurice hopes to make it his home for the rest of his life. They have one son, Max; who has eight years of college. The Max Edrington family live in the Gulf Coast, Mississippi, area. Their daughter-in-law is a nurse specialist.

Greene County has been good to the Johns family. They have seen so many advancements in the education and farming fields.

**JOHNSON** – Benjamin A. Johnson was the son of Granville M. Johnson and Neureusa (Gardner) Johnson of Tennessee. Ben was the fifth child of 10 children. He was born in Tennessee in 1834 and married Sarah E. Fielder born in 1837. They also had 10 children, the youngest born in 1877 and the oldest in 1856. Shortly after Ben and Sarah married, they moved to Missouri in Wayne County and bought a farm. They continued farming until the war broke out, when he raised a company of Missouri State Guards, of which he was elected first lieutenant. He soon resigned this position and enlisted as a private in the Confederate army, being elected first lieutenant and was soon sent east of the Mississippi and was in the battles of Memphis, Corinth, Iuka, Jacinto and others. He then was transferred to the western department of Arkansas and was made a lieutenant colonel over a regiment. During this time, his family moved to Clay County in Arkansas; Ben joined them for a time. After three years they moved to Cache Township in Greene County. He purchased 160 acres of land and began farming corn and cotton. It was said that he was an active politician, a supporter of churches and schools and a great student of current affairs.

H. B. Crowley wrote in an article published in 1906 by the *Paragould Soliphone* that he appeared satisfied to spend the rest of his days on Sugar Creek, surrounded by his children, grandchildren and great grandchildren, drinking the finest water in the world, eating big red apples and smoking home-made tobacco. Mr. Crowley said he was living with his third wife at this time. His first wife, Sarah, died in 1891. Ben died in 1916.

Ben and Sarah's children were:
1. John W. Johnson (1856)
2. William G. Johnson (1858
3. Barbara Etta Bell Johnson (1860 – 1905) married Eldo Rado Cato "E. R. C." Biggs, also known as "Pink" Biggs in 1878. Barbara is buried at Owens Chapel Cemetery. She was the mother of: Clairdy Edward "Buddy" Biggs (1883-1959), Rosa Adelaide Biggs (1881-1933) married John E. Newberry, parents of:
 a. Laura married Vance Cupp
 b. John Mack Biggs (1885-1973)
 c. Argie Biggs (1886-1905)
 d. Salie May (1890-1909)
 e. Grover C. Biggs (1892-1966)
 f. Lucien Earl Biggs (born 1903-1975)
4. Robert E. Lee Johnson (1863-1864)
5. Adelaide Johnson (1865) married P. Eubanks
6. Samantha C. Johnson (1867) married John Jones
7. Victoria R. Johnson (1869) married James Light
8. Sarah N. Johnson (1871) married James Johnson Bone, parents of Elizabeth "Lizzie" (Bone) Cadenhead
9. Benjamin O. Johnson (1874)
10. Lizzie B. Johnson (1877

**JOHNSON** – In 1850, 1860 and 1870 the Johnson and Edwards families were living in Gwinnet County, GA. In 1865, a troop of Georgian Confederate Soldiers were pushing their way through the fields of Northeast Arkansas. They were George T. Hay, George Anderson Johnson, his brother Will Johnson and Hosea Hopkins. These four soldiers liked the farmland and decided to return to Arkansas after the Civil War. Mr. Thomas Matthews Esq. married George Anderson Johnson and Mary Jane Edwards in Gwinnett County, GA in 1869. The couple and young son, David William arrived at Goodbertown, AR about 1871. Their first child David died in Sept of 1871 and is buried at Pine Log Cemetery.

Not long afterwards the rest of the Edwards family, following the example of the three Edwards sisters and their husbands, also came from Georgia, traveling by train as far as Forrest City then buying teams of horses and wagons to strike out through the wilderness.

In 1880, the Johnson family was in Powell

L-R back Row: Virgil, wife Betsy, Mrs. Mary Janes (Edwards) Johnson, Frank, Ella, Edwin "ED"; children front row: Beechie, Bertha, Ollie and Robert Johnson

Township, AR. On Nov 22, 1884 Frank Hatton, postmaster general of the United States of America, appointed George Anderson Johnson postmaster of Goobertown, AR.

George died in 1891 leaving wife, Mary Jane and nine children. Son, Robert Savage Johnson married Clara Staley in 1896. In 1951 Robert was 78 years old when he died. He had lived 36 years in Paragould operating a grocery store on W. Kingshighway. He and Clara are buried at Linwood Cemetery.

Virgil married Miss Betty "Betsy" Adams in 1895. Virgil died in 1929; he and Betsy are buried at Linwood Cemetery along with a daughter.

Ella married Dr. Russel Roberts in 1897. Dr. Roberts died in 1912, and then Ella married Ernest D. King. Ella died in 1844 and they are buried at Pine Log Cemetery near Brookland, AR.

Frank married Hattie Horn in 1904. He lived in Lake City, AR. Frank died in 1951.

Mary Alice Johnson born in 1881 and died at 10 years of age. She is buried at Pine Log Cemetery.

Edwin married Beulah Cobb in 1906. Edwin died in 1936, and then Beulah married Ernest King. Beulah died in 1977, all are buried at Pine Log Cemetery.

Olive "Ollie" married Marion Sims in 1905. Marion died in 1942 at the age of 61. He is buried at Linwood Cemetery. Ollie then married William Toll; they lived near Oakland, CA. Ollie died in 1970 and is buried at Linwood Cemetery next to her fist husband Marion.

Beechie married William Tom Robinson in 1907. Beechie died two years later in 1909. She is buried at Pine Log Cemetery next to Tom Robinson and his second wife Mary Lou.

Bertha Jane married Oscar Lee Robinson in 1910. They lived at Goobertown all their life. They had six children. Howard, Lola, Gene, twins Norine, Orine and Calla Mae. Bertha and Oscar and all the children, except Gene Robinson are buried at Pine Log Cemetery. Gene being the last descendant of this pioneer family is still living.

*Submitted by Donna Ishmael*

**JOHNSON** – I am Javene (Moore) Johnson and was born Sept 1, 1925 in Beech Grove, AR. My father was Jay Church Moore and my mother was Mary Evelyn "Mollie" (Williams) Moore. We moved to Walcott, AR and lived in the old Crowley house, which is now the location of Crowley's Ridge State Park. Mother died Jan 1, 1930 and left dad with five children, Mildred Evelyn, Joel Clinton, James Earl and Virgil Harold. After mom's death we moved back to Beech and stayed with dad's mother, Clara and stepfather W. C. Owen. I lived with several different relatives until Mildred was old enough to take care of me. At this time we moved into a small house in Beech. Virgil stayed with Aunt Edith and Uncle Jimmy Eubanks and Joel stayed with Uncle Joe and Aunt Viva Williams to help on their farms. Earl passed away at 19 due to a heart problem. Joel married Stella Walters and had a son Robert and daughter Sue. When Grandpa Owen died dad and I moved in with Gramma Owen. Dad worked with the WPA and was gone a lot. Virgil worked for the CCC. When Gramma died, dad and I moved to Paragould where Mildred worked at Mrs. Frields Café. Joel then moved to Flint, MI and died there in 1946. Virgil joined the army. Dad moved to Pine Bluff to work at the arsenal where he met and married Lillian Crowder and moved to Oak Ridge, TN. He then moved to Paragould and

*Back: Jay Church Moore and Mollie Moore; middle: Earl and Joel Moore; front: Mildred, Javene and Virgil.*

opened a grocery store. They sold the store and moved to Pine Bluff and opened another store. Mildred moved to Michigan and had three daughters, Phyllis, June and Jane. Mildred died while visiting me in 1995. Virgil met Willie Lee Heller thru letters she wrote while in the Army, they married in 1946 and had four children, Gary, Barbara, Carla and Marsha. Virgil passed away in 1985 in Paragould. I met and married Alton Johnson while he was stationed in Pine Bluff and had two daughters, Evelyn and Sherry and later adopted Tony and Telesha. Dad died in 1965. I will always call Greene County home.

*Submitted by Javene Johnson*

**JOHNSON** – Mary Charlene Rainwater was born October 13, 1939, the daughter of Elmer Lawrence and Imogene (Stevens) Rainwater in Delaplaine. Charlene graduated from Delaplaine High School, Greene County, Arkansas, May 13, 1957.

On June 24, 1960, Charlene Rainwater married Vance Hoback Johnson, October 13, 1932, in Lemay, Missouri. They had four daughters: Catherine Lorranie born March 2, 1961, and married Joseph Lynn Nation; Kimberly Diann born October 4, 1962, and married Alan Dale Arnold; Debra Beth born November 25, 1970, and married Dennis Reed Cox; and Vicki Kristine Johnson born December 28, 1971.

Catherine and Joseph Nation have three children: Desha Lynn born July 29, 1977; Stephanie Ann born June 10, 1986; and Cobie Matthew born April 15, 1991.

Kimberly and Alan Arnold have three children: Mark Allen born September 30, 1982; Alpha Diann born June 1, 1985; and Alana Dale born February 5, 1989.

Debra Beth and Dennis Cox have two sons: Dennis Reed Cox II born November 17, 1989; and Nathaniel Ryan Cox born December 31, 1992.

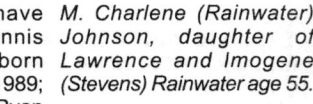

*M. Charlene (Rainwater) Johnson, daughter of Lawrence and Imogene (Stevens) Rainwater age 55.*

**JOHNSON** – Robert Savage Johnson was born Sept 2, 1872 in Goobertown, AR. His mother was Mary Jane Edwards, whose parents were William Edward and Elizabeth Harris. His father, George Anderson Johnson, born May 2, 1844, was the son of William Johnson and Mary Jane Edwards, born Aug 20, 1847. They were both born in Georgia and came to Arkansas in 1870 form Duluth, Guinnet County, GA.

These early settlers established residence, clearing land and building their home, church, school and the first general store in the community. They planted many acres of peanuts, since the plant had been the native crop back in their home state.

George Anderson Johnson's application for a postmaster's commission in 1884 indicated that he was to 'select a short name for the proposed office, which when written will not resemble any post office in the United States". From there it was a natural succession for the name "Goobertown". The post office was located in the grocery store, where they stocked items ranging from nails in kegs to sugar in barrels. George Anderson Johnson remained postmaster until his death, Jan 14, 1891.

*Robert Savage Johnson and Clara Staley Johnson, about 1930.*

Albert Baine, a cousin, was the first schoolmaster. Albert was later associated with the Paragould Post Office.

There were 10 children born to Mary Jane Edwards and George Anderson Johnson:
1. William died at an early age
2. Robert Savage Johnson
3. Virgil Hammet
4. Ella Elizabeth
5. Frank Anderson
6. Edwin Dillon
7. Olive Lee
8. Beechie
9. Bertha Jane
10. Mary Alice

Mary Jane Johnson continued to operate the store and post office until her death, Oct 18, 1918.

Robert Savage Johnson and Clara Staley were married Dec 30, 1872. Clara was born in Rice, Wayne County, WV on Nov 7, 1874. She was the daughter of Anne Gardner (Dec 16, 1835

Lawrence County, OH - Oct 22, 1895) and Stephen Staley (May 28, 1824- Jan 23, 1906 Wayne County, WV).

Four children were born to Robert S. and Clara S. Johnson, all in Goobertown and all attended school there at an early age. The family moved to Paragould in 1914 and established Johnson Grocery at 901 West Kingshighway, where they continued business for over 40 years, until the death of Robert S. Johnson, Jan 13, 1951. The four children graduated from the Paragould schools. Clara Staley Johnson died Dec 6, 1959.

Robert Clyde Johnson (Oct 4, 1897- Oct 2, 1986) married Gladys Brune of Paragould. Their two children are Charles Robert Johnson and Roberta Jeanne Coleman.

Marion Floyd Johnson (Jan 24, 1899- March 10, 1998) married Lora Nettles; they had no children.

Clella Johnson (Feb 12, 1904- April 14, 1998) married Henry N. Bleier and they had one daughter, Henri Etta.

Ellis Anderson Johnson (Feb 17,1907-Dec 23, 1987) married Essie Mildred Little. Essie Mildred, the daughter of James Henry and Addie Carolyn Little of the Center Hill community, died Nov 17, 1964. Their two daughters are Jacqueline Jane (Johnson) Beane and Dorothy Gwendolyn (Johnson) Knowles.

Clyde and Floyd were both in the business office of the Paragould Post Office for many years. Ellis was associated with Stedman Hardware Store and served as staff sergeant in the Army during WWII. He later joined his brothers in the Paragould Post Office, where they worked together for many years. All members of this family were lifelong, faithful members of First Baptist church, Paragould. All the senior members of this family are buried in Linwood Cemetery, Paragould.

*Submitted by Mrs. John Colmore Beane Jr.*

**JOHNSON** – William C. Johnson (Dec 2, 1821 Knox County, TN-Jan 1895) was a son of Pleasant M. Johnson and Eleanor Thomson Johnson. Pleasant served in the Creek War during the War of 1812. Eleanor's father was a Revolutionary War veteran having fought at Eutaw Springs and King's Mountain. William married Amanda Caroline Sanders (Aug 22, 1828 Lincoln County, TN – Aug 14, 1889) in Madison County, TN on Dec 11, 1842. She was the daughter of Samuel Sanders and Malinda Looney Sanders. William and Caroline moved their young family to Lawrence County, AR in 1854 and then to Greene County in 1856 where William was a farmer and stock dealer. William was ordained a Missionary Baptist minister in 1874. William and Amanda were the parents of 13 children and all are buried near their parents in new Friendship Cemetery.

Albert Jefferson Johnson (March 21, 1863 Greene County- Feb 16, 1941) was a son of William and Amanda Johnson. He was born in the midst of the Civil War. Albert married Willie Mae Parhm (unk-May 21, 1951) on Nov 8, 1873 in Greene County. She was a daughter of Thomas Edward Parhm and Eliza May Newberry Parhm. Albert and Willie were the parents of 10 children:
1. Ennis
2. Mamie
3. Clyde
4. Eliza
5. Dennis
6. Ernest
7. Bufie
8. Louis
9. Dawsie
10. Eunice

Mamie (Sept 16, 1893 New Friendship Township- Feb 28, 1928) married Lucilious " Lewis" McGraw (May 12, 1890- May 17, 1936) on May 5, 1912 in Greene County. He was a son of Lucilious Ruben McGraw and Martha E. Morrow McGraw. Lewis and Mamie were the parents of six children:
1. Orene
2. Mildred
3. Lloyd
4. Alberteen
5. Laverna
6. Izetta

After Mamie's death, Lewis moved his family several times while sharecropping.

Orene (June 21, 1913 near Halliday) married Paul Edward Moore on Oct 13, 1933 in Success, Clay County, AR. They were the parents of four children, John, Donna, Paul and Alma.

*Submitted by Daniel E. Moore*

**JOHNSTON** – Floyd Charles Johnston was born in Greene County near Shugtown on Highway 135 South on June 17, 1930. His parents, Charles Sutfin Johnston and Lena Rowe Johnston, are both deceased. His paternal great-grandparents, James H. Johnston and Sarah Graffish came to Arkansas from Alabama in the early 1800s. His paternal grandparents were George Thomas Johnston and Caroline Sutfin. His maternal great grandparents, Henry Adam Rowe and Mary Ann Molly Johnson lived near Fulton, TN. His maternal grandparents, Charles Robert Rowe and Ida Louellen Nanney came to Arkansas in 1913 from Hardin, KY. His parents were married in Paragould, AR in 1916.

The youngest of four boys, brothers Eldon, Elvis and George, he started school at the Goobertown two-room school in 1936, one year before the famous flood of 1937. The family had relocated to higher ground by then to the Sweet Moments community before the big flood came but was flooded with relatives from the flooded Shugtown, Dixie Wilson and Nodena areas who were not so fortunate. Upon completion of the fifth grade he changed schools to the then Greene County High School through the 11th grade. The new Greene County Tech High School was under construction and he was a member of the first graduating class at the new school in 1948. He was editor of the schools first newspaper, *"The Tech Eagle"* and a member of the basketball team.

Floyd received a reward for submitting the winning entry in selecting the "Eagle" as the school mascot and for selecting Green and Gold as the school colors. He and Carolyn Brandon Highfill composed the Alma Mater, all of which the school proudly honors.

Following high school, Floyd enrolled in Draughon's Business College in Little Rock and completed the two-year required courses for a business degree. Draughon's later merged with what is now University of Arkansas at Little Rock.

*Floyd Charles Johnston*

By this time the Korean War was in full swing. He spent four years in the US Navy in San Diego, CA, after which he began his career with Exxon Corporation in Memphis, TN. After retiring, he completed another successful career in real estate in the Memphis area. He has been married to Charla Eason of Memphis for 48 plus years and they have three children: Sandra, Karen and Terry. Also five grandchildren: Melissa, Michael, Matthew, Emily and Tyler

He is now proud to be back home in Paragould. He does a lot of volunteer work with the Senior BEES organization. He was recently appointed to serve on the Senior BEES Board of Director. He also serves on the advisory board of the North East Arkansas Regional Recovery Center for alcohol and substance abuse, a state supported organization. He is a member of Seventh and Mueller Church of Christ.

**JONES** – Jonathon Shelby Jones (Oct 23, 1818 GA-Feb 7, 1901), son of Jonathon and Epasdilla (Jones) Jones, married in Bibb County, Georgia Dec 1, 1840 Bethany Williams (about 1820 AL- July 24, 1885), daughter of Joseph Williams. Jonathon Jones and family came to Greene County by 1860 and settled in the St. Francis Township. Jonathon Jones had two kilns, one in Brown's Chapel community and one on Court Street in Paragould. He sold the bricks for the old courthouse building in 1888 and many other buildings in Paragould. Jonathon Shelby Jones also gave the land for the Browns Chapel Church and Cemetery.

Jonathon and Bethany Jones had eight known children:
1. Epsy Jane Jones (Oct 9, 1841 AL) married Caswell Hall Barnhill as his second wife.
2. Margaret Rebecca Jones (May 7, 1843 AL- Sept 3, 1860) married Tillman A. Webb. Margaret died in childbirth and was the first person to buried in Brown's Chapel Cemetery.
3. Joseph Nathan Jones (May 17, 1845 AL) married a lady by the name of Sally (April 15, 1845).
4. Jonathon Shelby Jones III (Sept 30, 1848 AL) married his first cousin Lorena Paratine Jones (1852) daughter of David Jasper and Elizabeth (Atchison) Jones. Divorced. Married (2) Mattie Slatton.
5. Bethaney Angie Jones (May 1850 AL) married John O'Steen (April 27, 1845 Panola County, MS) son of Harvey and Mary Elizabeth (True) O'Steen.
6. John Quincy Jones (1853 AL)
7. Henry Clay Jones (Oct 17, 1854 AL- Feb 2, 1873)
8. Millard Filmore Jones (Aug 10, 1856 AL) married Mary E. Peterson (about 1857 NC)

Jonathon married (2) Mrs. Mattie Jones, a widow. After divorcing, he married (3) Mrs. Paralee J. Norris.

Jonathon Shelby Jones and Bethany Jones are buried at Brown's Chapel Cemetery.

*Submitted by Jacqueline Mundreon*

**JONES** – William Arthur Jones (June 19, 1888 Gallatin County, IL- June 10, 1980) was the son of John William and Elizabeth Catherine Todd Jones who married on July 27, 1876. Their first two children, born in Posey County, IN, were Stella and an infant daughter who died when she was eight weeks old.

The family moved to Gallatin County, IL, where the following children were born:
1. Charles Milton
2. Thomas Claud
3. William Arthur
4. Ralph Beaumont
5. Mary Ada Jones.

The family then came to Greene County around 1900, intending to buy land around Schugtown, which, according to some sources, was selling for fifty cents an acre. When they arrived, however, they discovered there had been a flood and since there were no ditches for drainage, everything was still underwater.

The family came to Paragould and settled on land southwest of town. The farm was located on Pruett's Chapel Road, with the south boundary at

Finch Road. This area is now the site of the Paragould Country Club. John, or "J. W." as he was known, farmed and raised dairy cattle there.

*Standing L-R: Myrtle Lee Diggs Jones, Ralph B. Jones, Marie Jones Gilbert, Loly B. Rogers, William Arthur Jones, Eileen Jones Keller, Wanda Diane Keller Levaux, Eula Ellen Diggs Jones, Harriet Patterson Rogers and Everett Rogers. Seated: Stella Jones Rogers. Children L-R: Margaret Gail Keller, Robert Jones Keller, Donna Jean Keller, Everett Irving Rogers.*

On Aug 22, 1915, William Arthur married Eula Ellen Diggs. They moved to what is now known as Jones Road where Arthur farmed and raised registered hogs and cattle.

Their children were:
1. Margarette Eileen
2. John Diggs
3. Martha Ellen Jones.

Eula Ellen Jones died on Jan 6, 1974 and is buried in Linwood Cemetery next to her husband Arthur Jones.

Sources: Jones family history.
*Submitted by Eileen Keller*

**JORDAN** – Oral Myron Jordan was born in Marmaduke, Arkansas, the son of Robert Tildon Jordan and Mary Agatha Melton Jordan, July 13, 1908. Annie Mary Huckabay was born in Marmaduke, Arkansas, the daughter of Henry Henderson Huckabay and Mary Emma Boone Huckabay, January 21, 1908.

*Oral Myron "Bus" Jordan and Annie Mary Huckabay Jordan were parents of four children: Mary Agnes, Betty Sue, Robert Eugene and Jerry DeWayne pictured in their parents home in Marmaduke, Arkansas.*

Myron and Annie were married February 25, 1928. Myron worked on the railroad was a farmer, worked as a ginner at Delta Coop Gin, Marmaduke for many years until his retirement. Annie was a homemaker, devoted wife and mother.

Myron and Annie had four children: Mary Agnes born August 8, 1929, Betty Sue born September 11, 1931, Robert Eugene born July 30, 1933, and Jerry DeWayne born February 2, 1945.

Myron went through the eight grade twice. Annie got a third grade education and had to quit school to help take care of the younger children at home.

Myron and Annie were baptized August 20, 1939, in Jones Pond out from Marmaduke, into the Marmaduke First Baptist Church. Myron and Annie were very faithful members of the church until their death. Myron served as a deacon, Sunday school teacher, treasurer, training union teacher and also served in many other positions in the church. Annie served as a Sunday school teacher, training union teacher and was very active in many other ways in the church.

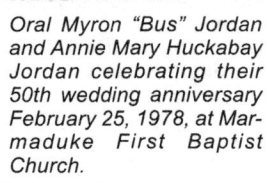

*Oral Myron "Bus" Jordan and Annie Mary Huckabay Jordan celebrating their 50th wedding anniversary February 25, 1978, at Marmaduke First Baptist Church.*

Annie died December 29, 1993, in Arkansas Methodist Hospital in Paragould, Arkansas. Myron died June 20, 1996, in Greene Acres Nursing Home, Paragould, Arkansas, and both are buried in Memorial Gardens, Paragould, Arkansas.

**JOSEPH/SAMUEL** – Early in 1880, S. L. Joseph, a German immigrant, came to Gainesville and opened a store in partnership with Isaac Less. After three years he sold his interest and went home to Germany for a visit. He spent some time abroad, returning through Kansas and finally locating in Paragould in 1885. He formed a mercantile business here as a partner in the Hirsch and Joseph Store. With immediate success, they moved the store into a larger building, the Clyde Mack building.

Mr. Joseph bought the interest of Mr. Hirsch in the spring of 1889, renaming the firm S. L. Joseph Mercantile Company. This very successful business moved into a new two-story building on the southeast corner of the Pruett and Court Streets intersection (now called the old Belk building). That same year (1889) Mr. Joseph married Setta Goldman. They had no children.

Under Joseph's management, the company grew into one of the larger department stores in Northeast Arkansas. Mr. Joseph became friends with a traveling salesman named Joseph Wolf, finally offering him a job with the company, which the latter accepted. In a few years Mr. Wolf was a partner in the Joseph Company.

Meanwhile, Joe Wolf met and married Mr. Joseph's sister-in-law, Ida Goldman in 1893.

As time passed, they opened a store in Rector and named it the Joseph Wolf Company. The Wolf family moved there to manage the business. Their family now consisted of a son, Irwin and three daughters, Beatrice, Lenore and Carolyn.

*Alvin Samuel Gin, about 1940, Second and Garland Streets*

About 1900 Alvin Samuel, 14-year-old nephew of Mrs. Joseph, came from Germany to live with the Joseph family. He received his education in Paragould and worked alongside his aunt and uncle in the business. Mr. Joseph's sudden death in 1909 brought Joseph Wolf and family back to Paragould, after his election to president of the company. At that time Alvin Samuel went to Rector to manage that business for several years.

As the stores were growing, a cotton gin and land interest added to the company holdings. At the time of his death, Mr. Joseph had an interest in a chain of six other stores in east Arkansas and Missouri.

*S. L. Joseph Company, about 1900, southeast corner of Pruett and Court Streets (Old Belk Building)*

Family members, along with Alvin Samuel, purchased the Joseph Plantation Company farm in 1916 and they decided to incorporate. In 1938, Alvin Samuel was able to purchase the cotton gin from S. L. Joseph Mercantile Company.

In 1928 Mr. Samuel married Jessie M. Barksdale, whose family had moved here from west Tennessee. He remained active in the cotton gin and farm related business until his death in 1963. Mrs. Samuel also died the same year.

The couple had one son, Alvin B. Samuel, who had joined his father in managing the cotton gin and other farm interests. He married Carolyn Holiman of Lepanto, AR in 1957. They had four daughters
1. Cynthia Samuel, deceased
2. Angela (Samuel) Buchholz
3. Marion Samuel
4. Courtney (Samuel) Vandiver

Alvin B. Samuel continues to carry on the business tradition and heritage of his ancestors today.
*Submitted by Carolyn Samuel*

**JUSTICE** – Charles Brooks Justice (1863 OH - 1938) married Mary Olivia Brown (1871 IL-1941). Both are buried in Linwood Cemetery in Paragould.

They came to Greene County and bought about 60 acres in the Camp Ground community. They farmed the land and during those years both C. B. and Mary Olivia were schoolteachers in several one-room schools. Both his father and mother taught my father, Eugene.

They had six sons:
1. Wayne
2. Asa
3. Eugene Charles
4. Maurice Brooks
5. Winnette
6. Hayward Connerd

After selling the Camp Ground property, C. B. bought a strip of land at the crossroad of Jonesboro Highway and West Kingshighway. C. B. and sons built, by hand, a large two-story house, complete with a full basement, which accommodated a woodworking shop, wine cellar, food storage and clothes washing facilities. The house was on top

*Greene County, 1906: Mary Olivia Justice and her students; boy in front row, fifth from right, is her son, Eugene Charles.*

of the hill and faced Linwood Cemetery to the east. The place was a virtual "Garden of Eden", with every inch of land producing vegetables, arbors of grapes and many fruit trees.

C. B and Mary Olivia "Ollie" were very intelligent and highly diversified in incredible talents. They were leaders in the community. "Granny" nursed the sick and tutored her grandchildren and other children.

The six sons were allowed to develop their many talents and interests. All were musically gifted, playing piano, violin, and guitar as well as being singers. Their interests ranged from clock making to diesel engines. They were ingenious in intricate woodworking and art projects, with complicated craftsmanship abilities. They hunted with hand-carved bows, developed their own photography and made furniture.

C. B. and sons started the first "chair factory" in Greene County there on the property. They produced wooden chairs from scratch, straight chairs and rockers, with cane-woven seats.

C. B. "Big Daddy" was a tall man and owned a pet wolf. When Highway 25 was built to Walcott, it split his precious property in half. He was infuriated and posted himself, armed with shotgun and his wolf tied at his side, in a vain attempt to stop the engineers from coming through. But, come through they did. (This part of West Kingshighway is now lined with businesses to Sunset Hills and the old Wal-Mart Center). By this time my father, Eugene and our family were living in a second house on the property, just to the north of the main house. Father and sons had also built it.

I have a vague childhood memory of my brother, Harold and I watching out the window as our house was moved back on huge rollers, pulled by teams of horses.

During this same period, my father, Eugene, served in the C.C.C.'s and helped build Crowley's Ridge State Park. My father was married to Pearl Wallace, from Illinois. She had the most beautiful singing voice this side of heaven.

The children born to them were:
1. James Wilburn (1920-1987)
2. Ruth Eileen (1923)
3. Billie Gene (1928-1934)
4. Mary Evelyn (1930)
5. Harold Edwin (1933)

What a happy childhood on "The Hill!"
*Submitted by Mary Justice Swafford*

**KEASLER** – Lawrence Keasler (Nov 27, 1920 Greene County, AR) the son of Jim and Ida (Thaxton) Keasler, married Mary Dover on April 12, 1941. She was the daughter of Griffin and Goldie (Brookbank) Dover. They have lived all their lives in Greene County.

Lawrence grew up working with his father in the family business, Keasler Body Company. He purchased the business from his father in 1952 and continued operating it until he retired in 1985 and sold the business to Haley and Becky (Keasler) Rieck and Gene Parkinson.

For many years Lawrence and Mary were active in Antique Automobile Clubs, but sold their antique automobiles because of failing health.

They have three daughters: Mikie Lou married Jerry Fielder; Martha married Mike Tedder and Becky married Haley Rieck. They have five grandchildren: Lawrence and Brian Fielder, Tommy Parkinson and Mandy and Sydney Rieck.

They also have six great-grandchildren: Ethan, Jeremiah and Brandon Fielder, Cayla Taylor and Tyler and Taylor Parkinson.

Lawrence had two sisters, Irene Higgins who is deceased and Lorene Grooms of St. Louis, MO. He also had two brothers, Louis, who is deceased and Leland who lives in Paragould.

Mary had two sisters, Betty Hughes who is deceased and Gracie Mitchell of Spartanburg, SC.

Lawrence and Mary live in the house they built in 1965 and attend Shiloh United Methodist Church.

"Here! This will help her stay warm," Aunt Grace said as she scurried away from the kitchen to the bedside. Her wrinkled arms were held aloft with a towel swaddled around something. Could you keep a dying person warm? I was puzzled, as most any six-year old would be, but not scared. Was THIS what it was like? Throughout the house numerous family members waited, all solemn, all related by spirit as well as blood, all here with love and reverence because SHE was leaving us.

It hadn't seemed that long ago since all of us had been in the same house, where Granny, her only daughter Grace and Grace's husband William (Bill), lived comfortably, but it was also where her children had brought their children and grandchildren. I was one of the latter. Was it only last summer or the summer before that the whole family had been here? It looked and smelled like June. Sweet peas bloomed along the fencerow next to the cotton field to the east. Butterflies and bees circled and whirled around the flowers. At noon Aunt Grace and Mam-ma Goldie brought out enough food "to feed Cox's army," Aunt Grace said. (Even if this family did not seem to be racially prejudiced, as years passed, I figured out that Cox must surely have been a Confederate.)

Everyone who wasn't from out of state brought dishes laden with food that probably tasted the same as it had when they were children. Had any of those recipes traveled with the Dovers right after the Civil War to White Hall In Poinsett County before Bailey Appleton Dover, his wife Martha and their children Caroline Melinda Phillips, Andrew L., John B., William Franklin,

*William Frankllin and Martha Ellen (Poindexter) Dover were married 50 years, Oct. 29, 1929.*

James M. and Georgia Ann settled in Greene county? Or did Granny's proud Poindexters in Tennessee once serve these dishes? Probably, like our physical appearance, our food was a mixture of our heritage.

Granny's massive oak table with claw and ball feet was stretched its entire length in the big dining room as the sons-in-law flanked Martha Ellen (Poindexter) Dover, our matriarch. Food graced every square inch of table space and the sideboard, temporarily replacing Granny's crystal cups and punch bowl as well as the demitasse cups and saucers. It was a southern custom that the men and any women honored with true age, were seated first. Children were often fed out on the porch, picnic style if we wanted, or in the "little dining room" at a table that had been made years before by William Franklin, Martha Ellen's deceased husband. Daughters and wives willingly took care of their families' needs before they sat down to eat, probably the first leisurely moments of the day for the women. No complaints were heard.

We came from town, on the hills of Crowley's Ridge that streaked down the Delta from Missouri to Mississippi. Some came from Texas and Oklahoma and others from Wyoming. Our roots stretched from Georgia, Alabama, Tennessee and Virginia, among other places, to the sandy soil in the Greene County "bottoms," less than five miles from the St. Francis River that separated Arkansas and Missouri. This farm had been home for several years to the Dovers and this was where the sons of William Franklin and Martha Ellen brought their descendants to honor their heritage.

Although Bailey had been a farmer in Alabama, a Greene County census listed his occupation as "tanner". He apparently bought several acres in Greene County and at least two of his brothers and his son, William Franklin, operated a sawmill near Eight Mile Creek south of Wal-mart. William Franklin could then walk south to Pruett's Chapel Road to the two-story house where his family lived. The children, Mino, John, George, Harry, Rufus, Grace and Griffin, my grandfather, walked to Pruett's Chapel to school at that time. Later they would line "in town" where the children could continue higher education.

After dinner, the noon meal, being the largest of the day, Aunt Grace benevolently assisted her mother to the porch. Aunt Grace was less that five feet tall in the wedge heels she always wore; her mother seemed almost a foot taller. Granny, at 90 and arthritic, accepted her daughter's guidance to a porch rocker, one with the back low enough not to press the fatty tumor that had been growing high on her spine for years. (These fatty tumors are supposedly inherited. My mother has one and I have had one.) "All right, Mama, we've got your rocker so you can see and hear all of the boys." Missing was my grandfather, who died from pneumonia soon after WWI, leaving my grandmother to farm and raise three little girls: Betty Jean, Mary Margaret and Grace Ellen.

Wrapping around the living room, the porch had three sections: the west, where children usually played and went in and out of the house; the north, with the swing where a couple of men sat with just enough room left for one not-too-big child who usually remained no more than seven or eight minutes and the porch rockers occupied by those paying homage to the matriarch for the time being; and the east side, where more children played and adults entered and exited through the living room.

As Granny settled into her chair, she said, "Mary Margaret, get me a twist from that tree." The "twist" was a tiny twig twisted from a small branch, the twisted end fraying and resembling a toothbrush. Granny used the twig to dip her snuff, fascinating everyone under the age of 10. And there she sat, imperial like, holding court with devoted subjects as she gently waved her palm fan.

Even by the time she had reached 90, Granny's mostly gray hair, pulled into a neat little bun, still had a few dark strands that perhaps hinted at a part of her linage. Even more evident of that heritage were her cheeks; she proudly said to her children and grandchildren: "See your high cheek bones; we have these because of our Indian blood." With the soft Delta breeze blowing, Granny brushed a few wisps of hair away from her face as she listened to her sons swapping stories.

I always thought my younger sister, named in honor of Granny, must have been a replica of Granny' s young face: perfectly symmetrical features in an oval bone structure made moon shaped by good eating, high cheek bones, of course, a slight widow's peak and sable colored hair. And what seemed to be fair skin when she was young became Indian brown as my sister Martha Sue became older. When people remarked about my sister's lovely tan when I was along, I simply said, "She got ALL the Indian blood in this branch of the family." Of course, I wasn't envious, just jealous! And I could blame it all on Granny, for the Dovers were fair skinned with light eyes.

Neither squeals of glee, peals of laughter, nor raucous stories from her sons ever disturbed Granny's rocker's rhythm. Uncle George, second to the oldest son, had a laundry in Wyoming and nothing from Cody ever lacked his witty descriptions of persons or deeds. Long sleeves were rolled to just below his elbows and with his left hand he removed his cigarette from what had to be the widest smile west of the Mississippi. Smoothing his silky graying hair straight back from his forehead with his right hand, he took center porch. After a story about "how the bear got away unharmed while the old fella practiced the mountain mile!" Uncle George received his fair share of chuckles.

Not to be outdone, Uncle Harry began a tale about an Indian he knew in Oklahoma. Of all Granny's sons Uncle Harry, who had dark eyes and dark skin from working outside, might possibly have looked the most like one of our Indian ancestors. Granny laughed and shook her head gently with an "I'm glad my boys (all of whom were over 50) have never changed" look on her face.

Uncle Mino, who worked at Clyde Mack's and was the oldest and perhaps the most businesslike and serious Dover son, wore the same expression as his mother. It was Uncle Mino's family that accepted Betty, then Mary and then Grace Ellen, after they finished the eighth grade at Coffman, into their home in town in the winter so his brother's daughters could have high school educations. Aunt Grace and Uncle Bill and Granny and Grandpa Dover also helped raise and educate them, but it was Mino who lived in town at the time.

"If that stock market hadn't crashed, how much do you think Mama's gold would be worth?" one of the sons wondered aloud. Martha Ellen and William Franklin were married 50 years Oct 29, 1929. Their children had presented their parents with gold pieces, which were promptly put in a local bank, never to be retrieved. William Franklin died the following June.

W. F.'s grandfather John was supposedly deaf and William Franklin became deaf. His granddaughter Betty began losing her hearing as a young woman, as did great-granddaughter Martha Sue. Both Betty and Martha Sue had surgery to remove calcium deposits and their hearing, probably worth gold to them, was restored.

Seemingly rooted in her rocker, Granny enjoyed the stories of each son until the wives finished tidying the dining rooms and kitchen. Uncle Rufus, the youngest living son, perhaps ranking only next to Uncle Harry as wearing an almost continuous smile, slapped his hands together and asked, "Are we ready for a little music?" (Does the Delta have cotton?) Like numerous brooks converging, Dovers seemed to swell into a river flowing around the old upright piano in the living room, continuing to flood the porches. We children tried to find unoccupied spots to look into the living room through the windows or screen door. Uncle John, educated, like all his siblings, in the classics, including Latin, would lapse into down-home homilies for effect: "Such goin'on!" as though story telling and music was foreign to Dovers. I never saw Uncle John play the fiddle/violin, but Aunt Grace said he did. She gave me his bow because she said no one else had wanted it.

*Children of William Franklin and Martha Ellen (Poindexter) Dover are, back row, left to right: John B., George M., and Rufus; middle: Mino, Grace Ellen, and Harry; front: Griffin.*

While the family overflow sat with legs cascading over the edge of the porch, we kept time to the music and savored the breezes that swept over the cotton fields. To hear "On a Bicycle Built for Two" was wondrous for us children, but to see the dark, upright piano come to life under uncle Rufus' dancing hands seemed a miracle. As I grew older, Uncle Rufus' talent seemed even more amazing, because I learned he did not read music. He played "by ear." His niece, Betty Jean, could also do this and so can my youngest sister, Becky. Uncle Rufus' daughter, Sarah had a voice the mockingbirds must have envied. As her grandfather accompanied her, everyone justly praised her innate musical talent springing from the depths of generations through her grandfather's veins to her.

And then, regardless of the lack of musical talent that diluted the Dover genes, we all joined in singing. Taking turns as if we were vaudeville acts, others would share the limelight. Aunt Grace then played the piano so Uncle Rufus and Aunt Diva could dance. In four square feet of available living room space they would dance, dance, dance, until finally most of us would be exhausted from watching. However, children would continue to beg for "one more dance," or "one more song" until our parents exclaimed, "You're wearing them out!" We capitulated and went off to do what children did while adults visited.

Now that we had dined, played and sung together, we girls began seriously evaluating each other while the male cousins went back to the huge barn to either play in the loft or taunt the king snake in the corncrib. "Where did you get red hair?" someone asked Uncle Mino's granddaughter Martha Frances. With her brown eyes and flaming hair, it was easy to see that she was going to be a beauty. The oldest of three girls, Martha Frances could have been smug about her looks, but the lack of self-centeredness endeared her to all of us. Joyce, Martha Frances' beautiful younger sister, also had brown eyes, but her hair looked as dark as Granny's must have been when she was young. Janet, Martha Frances' youngest sister, was a perky, pretty blonde. No doubt Dover "beauty" genes had not been diluted in that particular branch of the family tree. But there were others equally beautiful and talented. We perched in the lower limbs of the mulberry trees and chatted away, not realizing that moments like that would not continue forever as age and distance intervened, but the day was not yet over.

Granny continued to rest, doze and bask royally in the presence of four generations around her feet, all of whom had continued to gather at least annually. As evening gently rolled in, Granny introduced a few great-grandchildren to something new, catching fireflies. Because the farm area had been cleared for cotton, it seemed that a blinking carpet stretched beyond the many miles the eye could see in any direction. "If you'll ask your mothers to get you jars and punch holes in the lids, you can put in a little clover and all the fireflies you can catch," Granny said. After chasing and catching numerous fireflies, we retreated to the back yard where we once more ascended the mulberry branches. But this time we had soft twinkling lights overhead and phosphoresce lights blinking in our hands. Sarah began to sing acappella and the sound in the soft night air was almost sacred. We wanted that moment to last forever. It didn't.

We soon had to leave. Parting wasn't "sweet sorrow." I railed about having to leave, but nothing compared to my cousin, Francis Ann! We weren't old enough to understand that although there would be numerous visits to the Dover farm, that particular moment in time, it could not have been ONLY a day.

In hushed tones I heard the words: "Her legs are almost purple to her knees." Another whispered, "Her hands are almost black. It won't be long now." Would Granny hurt if they spoke aloud or didn't tip toe? I looked at all those faces as they paid the final homage to the life within what had been a formidable frame and a soul that seemed too large even for that body. Her almost 91 years still did not mean any of the entourage surrounding the white wrought iron bed was ready for this night, "almost morning," someone spoke softly. And then, although we did not release her willingly from our grasps, we released her lovingly. That was why we were present, to usher her from this life with all the love we had.

Would the stories and music, the mulberry branches or fireflies ever be the same again? Not quite, but the Dover and Poindexter genes possessed a spirit that continues to infuse new descendents with whom we share these and other memories.

*Submitted by Lawrence and Mary Keasler*

**KEELOR/WALKER/WOOD** – Thomas Keelor, a Revolutionary War soldier in the New Jersey Continental Line, was born in 1763 in New Jersey; died in Hamilton County, OH, the year is unknown. Wife's name is unknown, but he fathered at least two children: Howell and Urias. Howell was born in New Jersey April 3, 1803, married Oct 5, 1822 in Warren County, OH to Susannah (McNeal), who was born Aug 1, 1802 in Pennsylvania. They had eight children, all born in Highland County, OH:

1. Edwin (1825)
1. Prissilla (1833)
2. Joseph (1834)
3. Thomas (1835)
4. Urias (1839)

5. David (1843)
6. Hiram H. (1844)
7. Rebecca E. (1845)

Howell was a carpenter.

Thomas, son of Howell, was born in Highland County, OH Oct 1835; married about 1857 to Louise Wilson. Their children were Joseph and Lizzie. Thomas married a second time, to Mary E (Noland) Lawson, April 18, 1872 in Clay County, IN. Mary was born in Kentucky in 1846. Thomas died Sept 18, 1905 and Mary died about 1896; both died in Greene County, AR and are buried in unmarked graves in New Friendship Cemetery. They had four children, all born in Indiana:

*The Keelor Family 1891. L-R, standing: John Prince, Susan (Keelor) Prince, Laura B. (Keelor) Prince, Hershel Keeler, Edward Prince. Front: child: Ida Pillott, Elizabeth Pillott, Thomas Keelor, Mary Keelor, child in lap: Ollie Keelor, baby in lap: Clarence Prince.*

1. Susan M. (FEB 2, 1873-Feb 15, 1873 Greene Co.) married John H. Prince in 1890 and had five children:
   a. Clarence
   b. Gertie
   c. Grace
   d. Herbert, twin
   e. Hubert, twin
2. Laura Bell (Sept 1875) married Edward Prince in 1890 and had two children:
   a. Hallie
   b. Lela
3. Herschel (Sept 29, 1880-Sept 28, 1954 Greene Co) married Ollie (Hopper)and had seven children:
   a. Lucille
   b. Vaudine
   c. Alberta
   d. Laura Lee
   e. Ben
   f. Thomas Jr.
   g. Imogene
4. Ollie (March 16, 1886-Nov 29, 1968 Forrest City) married John Millard Walker Aug 2, 1905 in Greene County.

Thomas served in the Civil War as a Union soldier with Co "G" 11th Regiment of Ohio Volunteer Calvary at Fort Laramie, fighting Indians out west. He was a "scout", hunting for food for his Regiment. Thomas left Terre Haute and traveled by train to Brookland, AR, arriving about 1889. He unloaded his cattle from the cattle car and walked with them to Greene County, settling in Clarke Township, which today is the northern part of Paragould in the original Industrial Park. He brought the first Jersey cow into Arkansas.

Ollie, daughter of Thomas and her husband John had nine children, all born in Greene County:
1. Elsie (Walker) Davis
2. R. D.
3. Orbron
4. Ernest
5. Violet (Walker) Wood
6. Louis
7. Earl
8. Ralph
9. Inez

John Walker (Nov 23, 1881 in Greene County – Dec 27, 1944 Forest City, AR) was the son of Richard Addison and Mary Ellen (Winn) Walker. When Ollie was 10 years old her mother died, leaving Thomas to raise the children. Ollie's childhood was shortened since she then had to do all the cooking and cleaning.

Violet Walker, daughter of Ollie, was born May 29, 1915 in Brighton, Greene County, AR and married George Wood on Dec 30, 1933 in Greene County. George, the son of William Henry and Maude (Fletcher) Wood, was born in Brighton Feb 8, 1910. Violet and George had four children, all born in Greene County:
1. Louis Gene (Nov 25, 1934)
2. Ted (Dec 12, 1936)
3. Anna Mae (Wood) Brymer (April 27, 1939)
4. Kathy (Wood) Jarrett (Nov 18, 1951)

Violet died March 29, 2000 and George died May 9, 1990, both in Greene County. When George was nine years old he and his eight-year-old sister put in a farm crop. He loved to work and was always a hard worker.

Ted Wood, son of Violet, was born Dec 12, 1936 in Paragould, Greene County, AR. He married Patsy Sue (Fletcher) in Paragould April 25, 1955. Patsy was born March 13, 1939 in Paragould to Vernon and Clara (Smith) Fletcher in an old moldy house. When she was 10 days old lightening struck the house, breaking out 34 windows; she cried all night. Ted and Pat had four sons, all born in Greene County:
1. Danny Lynn (Sept 10, 1955-1975)
2. Steve (June 14, 1956)
3. Timothy Allen (Nov 22, 1957)
4. Harlon Wayne (Jan 18, 1961)

Steve was born two months premature and the doctor sent him home with his mother, saying Steve would not live; he is still knocking about today. Ted loved horses and for a few years operated a rodeo arena he built. He worked for the Paragould Light Plant. Pat's favorite saying to express her philosophy of life is "got to keep on keeping on". Ted died in a Memphis, TN hospital Aug 24, 1971. Pat is living in Paragould today.

*Submitted by Steve Wood*

**KENNEMORE** – John Clarence Kennemore was born Sept 1, 1889 in Greene County, AR. His father was Lowery "Larry" Winfield Kennemore, who migrated here from Georgia after the south had been devastated by the Civil War, 1861-1865. After the close of the war many families chose the road westward and many from Georgia migrated to Arkansas. The Kennemores were among them. John's mother was Beulah Nancy Chandler born Feb 26, 1869 in Macon, GA. She was the daughter of Arvis Chandler and Sallie Aderholdt.

After Clarence's father died in 1893, Beulah Nancy married Albert Sidney Snowden, a widower, who had a son Malachi "Mack" Snowden, on Dec 9, 1900.

The family set up housekeeping and soon Clarence and Mack welcomed in three sisters and a brother:
1. Wilma Totsie (Oct 9, 1901)
2. Reba L. (Aug 13, 1906)
3. Mary (March 30, 1909)
4. Albert Wilburn "Bill" (Sept 30, 1971).

Clarence met and married Verna Cole Sept 7, 1945. They had one daughter, Carol, Mrs. Donald Darr; one granddaughter, Carrie Robin Darr (Jan 25, 1967).

*John Clarence Kennemore, 1889-1975.*

Clarence was a native and lifetime resident of Greene County, he was a long time active member of Immanuel Baptist Church, a WWI veteran and former employee of Garner's Drug Company.

Those who knew him told me he was one of the nicest and kindest men that they knew.

John Clarence Kennemore died March 30, 1975. He is buried In Linwood Cemetery.

*Submitted by Evelyn Euritha Wagner*

**KENNETT** – John Kennett was born in Leachville, AR on Nov 18, 1950 to Edna and Everett Kennett. He is the younger brother of Dan Kennett. John developed a love of photography at a young age and began photographing his journeys while building fiberglass coolers. While on a job in Plaquimine, LA, he met Dot Launcy. They married on Sept 25, 1974. For a brief time Dot and John returned to Arkansas, living in Newark. John was working at Kodak and doing photography as a hobby. His hobby turned into a desire for a career in photography and he thought the US Army was the place for him to acquire a good education, thus the journey to Texas. After John completed basic training At Fort Leonardwood, MO, he and Dot moved to Killeen, TX. John was stationed at FT. Hood. Lori Anne Kennett was born to Dot and John on Sept 25, 1979.

After three years in the military, John was discharged. He bid on the photography studio at Ft. Hood and was awarded the contract for several years. Bob DeBolt owned a studio in Killeen and fast became a very important person in helping John to achieve his dreams of having a photography studio of his own. Matthew Paul Kennett joined the family on June 22, 1983. While in Killeen, John kept in contact with Bill Hunter from Paragould, AR. Bill owned Child Art Studio and this was where John always wanted to come home to. So, when Mr. Hunter was ready to retire, John bought the studio and fulfilled his dream. Dot and John moved their family to Paragould. Dot decided to go to college to become an educator and fulfill her dream. She attended Arkansas State University in Jonesboro and graduated in May 1993. She was fortunate to be hired at Woodrow Wilson Elementary and is teaching second grade. Lori is a sophomore at ASU and pursuing a degree in secondary education. Matthew is a senior at Paragould High School and plans to attend Hendrix College and pursue a degree in music and computers. The Kennetts are living in Paragould at 420 West Court Street.

*Submitted by John Kennett*

**KIMBROUGH** – The beginning of the Kimbrough presence in Paragould, Greene County, Arkansas, began in 1909 with the arrival of William N. Kimbrough, his wife Lela Willis Kimbrough and their 18 month daughter, Marguerite. The family had moved from Dyersburg, Tennessee, where William had been in business and associated with his brothers. Because of economic conditions in the Dyersburg area William determined that it would not be possible for him to support his family and thus planned a new start in Paragould, Arkansas. Paragould was a young, upcoming town in the Northeast Arkansas area and William felt it would be a wonderful place to start a new life.

Shortly after moving to Paragould, William built four buildings. He rented three of these buildings and open his own business in the fourth…Kimbrough's Dry Goods. This store flourished and grew along with Paragould which became the county seat.

William and Lela had three more children (Louise, Bill and Paul) after getting settled in Paragould and building a home for their new family at 719 West Court. This home is still standing and in the family.

Mr. Kimbrough became a very successful business man and an important player in the growth of Paragould. During the Depression of 1928/1930, Kimbrough's Dry Goods was one if not the only dry goods store in Northeast Arkansas that would give government workers full value for their pay checks. These pay checks came in the from of script form the government and this script could be turned in to the government by businesses for cash. Most businesses felt that they would never get the full value of the script from the government because of the hard times that had fallen on the country and the state of Arkansas. Mr. Kimbrough decided that he would give full face value for this script which was a major decision on his part. He could have lost much money or even gone out of business if the script was not honored. On the other hand the people he dealt with would lose if he did not fully honor his script. His choice to take a chance on the government and help the people was the right business decision for everyone involved. Families came from all over Northeast Arkansas to do business at Kimbrough's Dry Goods. Some of these families taking a full day, traveling by wagon to do business with Mr. Kimbrough. The store became a corner stone of the business community and Mr. Kimbrough a pillar of distinction. Kimbrough's Dry Goods remained in business until the late 1960s when the store building and stock was sold by the four family children. The reason was Marguerite, Louise, Bill and Paul and their children had chosen another life other than the dry good business and moved from the Paragould area.

Marguerite returned to Paragould and now lives in the family home on West Court Street. Marguerite had no children. Paul lives with his son in the Benton, Arkansas, area. Paul had one son, Paul Jr. Louise passed away in 1995 and had one daughter, Ann (McKelvey), now living in Knoxville, Tennessee. Bill passed away in August 1999 and had one son, Bill Jr., now living in Golden, Colorado.

For further information you can contact Bill Kimbrough Jr. at wxprof@aol.com.

**KIRK** – Earl was born to Joseph F. Kirk and Flora Tennessee Kirk on Nov 2, 1914 at Pollard, AR. He lived in the Clay County area until he went to college at Arkansas State College in Jonesboro. He was first educated at Cummings Chapel grade school, Pollard Junior High and Piggott High School.

Matilene Freda Seal was born to Ollie Thomas Seal and Bertie Belle Braden on Jan 12, 1918. After she graduated from Piggott High School, she went on to Arkansas State College. Earl received his degree from ASC in 1937 and married Matilene on April 17, 1937. They then spent three months at Ford's Trade School in Dearborn, MI. It was a good three months for a honeymoon. He was a member of the National Guard, worked at the dairy barn, took up cleaning and pressing, kept house for one of the professors, drove for the captain of the Guard and anything else he could find to do. He spent the next 12 months at the University of Missouri. The following year he got a job teaching Vocational Agriculture at Norman, AR. It was a wonderful place, but he had the opportunity to come to Paragould in 1939.

While he was teaching school, he also worked for the Meriwethers, managed Winston Mack's farm and built the first frozen food locker in Paragould. Needless to say, his Ag boys won many awards at the state and national levels.

In 1945, Earl bought half interest in the Meriwether's business, started selling Butler grain bins (which later became Earl Kirk Construction Company) and got his pilot's license. He served, as Rotary president, Chamber of Commerce president, was a member of the Young Men's Civic Club, belonged to the Elk's Club, was named chairman of the Board of Stewards of the First Methodist Church and was president of the Mid South Farm Equipment Association. It was during his time in office at the Chamber of Commerce that the citizens of Paragould decided we needed more industry. He worked tirelessly to bring industry to Paragould for many years. He was also chairman of the Airport Commission for many years. In 1986, the airport was named for him. He was chosen Citizen of the Year in 1960 and again in 1976. Earl died on July 14, 1986.

*People to People Tour in Tokoyo, Japan, 1978, Earl and Matilene Kirk*

*Mother's Day, May 9, 1977. L-R: Earl, Sara, Tommy, Gloria. Seated: Matilene, Donna*

The Kirk's have four children, ten grandchildren and at last count, 11 great-grandchildren. There are:
1. Gloria (Kirk) Merrill, husband is Clint
2. Donna (Kirk) Brazil, husband is Charles
3. Thomas Joseph Kirk, wife is Theresa
4. Sara (Kirk) Donaldson, husband is Chris

Earl Kirk was a great advocate of good homes, good schools, good churches and good roads. When he was five years old, he came to Paragould on the passenger train to see one of his uncles. When he got off the train, he saw this huge sign hanging across the road that read, "You will like Paragould," and he always did!

After Earl's death in 1986, Matilene Kirk has remained the matriarch of the family. Her home is always a safe haven and a great place to eat!

*Submitted by Matilene F. Kirk*

**KIRSCH** – William F. Kirsch was born Feb 12, 1886, in Belleville, IL to Wilhelm and Elisabeth Kirsch. Kirsch died in Paragould, AR, Oct 10, 1967. He came to Paragould in 1910, fresh out of Washington University Law School, where he had graduated at the top of his class. After coming to Paragould, he practiced law as a partner of J. D. Block, until Block's death in 1929.

A leading citizen in all areas of the community, Kirsch was elected to the Arkansas State Senate for the First Senatorial district, then composed of Greene, Clay and Craighead counties. He served from 1923-1927. He was a founder of the Paragould Rotary Club and was elected its first president. In the financial world, he was part owner of the former Lipscomb Motor Company and became a director of the former National Bank of Commerce in 1917. He was its president from 1929 to 1950 and was still a director at the time of his death.

In the field of law, he was a recognized lawyer throughout the state and served on the Arkansas Board of Law Examiners. Kirsch was a member of Phi Delta Phi legal fraternity and was a member of the order of the Coif. He maintained an active law practice until his illness and was senior partner of Kirsch, Cathey and Brown law firm.

One of his proudest achievements was serving as attorney for the St. Francis Drainage District, which was instrumental in procuring government participation in building levees and dams to channel the St. Francis River, thus releasing hundreds of acres of flood land for farming.

*William F. Kirsch*

Kirsch enjoyed farming and was a considerable landowner in Craighead, Greene County, AR and Dunklin County, MO. His farm manager was Robert Sparks; an innovative farmer from Cardwell, MO. Sparks is the father of Bettye (Sparks) Busby, member of the Greene County History and Family book committee.

In 1916 Kirsch married Jessica Gordon Lipscomb of King William county, VA. She was the daughter of Charles W. and Mary C. Lipscomb. The Lipscombs left Virginia and moved to Marmaduke, AR. The Kirsches were parents of two children, a daughter, Mary Elizabeth (Kirsch) Brenneisen and as son, William F. Kirsch Jr., who practiced law in Memphis, TN.

William F. Kirsch and his brother-in-law, Samuel Scott Lipscomb, have contributed much to Greene County by the establishment of the Lipscomb-Kirsch Charitable Foundation, providing funds that helped build the new Greene County Courthouse and the S.S. Lipscomb History Room at the Greene County Library.

*Submitted by Mary E. Brenneise*

**LACEY** – The Lacey family arrived in Greene County about 1905 coming from Cumberland County, Illinois. This family consisted of Elias LeRoy, and wife Margaret Mabel Housman Lacey, with children Lydia Mariah, age 8, and Ernest Elias, age 4. They settled on land about two miles west of Delaplaine. The children attended school at the Denman Community School.

Lydia married Jim Lee and moved to the vicinity of Water Valley, Mississippi, where they raised their family.

Ernest married Mabel Helen Bracken, December 7, 1928. She was the daughter of Samuel Warren Bracken and Hannah Theodocia Leturno Bracken. The Brackens came to Arkansas from Alexander County, Illinois. After a short stay in Flint, Michigan, where Ernest worked at Buick Fisher Body, a division of General Motors, he and Mabel settled in Delaplaine. There Ernest farmed, worked in timber, did carpentry, and Mabel taught school in the surrounding area until 1941 when she acquired a position in the Delaplaine school system and remained there until she retired after 46 total years in that profession.

One child, Vernon Leon Lacey, was born to this union on February 17, 1930 at Delaplaine. Vernon was married on September 20, 1950, to Ellen Rose Craig born February 10, 1933. Vernon served in the United States Army from 1950 until 1979 when he retired and they moved to their current residence in Paragould. Ellen accompanied him on all assignments during his 29 plus years military service except when he was in Korea and Vietnam.

Ellen and Vernon have two children: Pamela Sue, who is a human resources specialist in San Antonio, Texas, and Dennis Vernon, who is an attorney in Wichita, Kansas.

Ellen's ancestors, Alfred Taylor Craig and Martha Brown Craig, first came to Greene County about 1875 from Hardeman County, Tennessee, settling in the Beech Grove area. This couple had 16 children and raised 14 to adulthood.

One of the 14, William Charles Craig, Ellen's grandfather, married Letitia Ellen Woodard in Gainsville. The Woodards came to Greene County from Henderson County, Tennessee. William Charles and Letitia Ellen had four children: Vertis, Ellen's father, was born January 28, 1901, and was married on January 27, 1924, to Cecil Mae Baugh. She was born February 20, 1908, to Charles Baugh and Minnie Ada Cole Baugh. This couple had five children of which Ellen was the youngest. Ellen had four siblings: Mattie Jane, Vertis, Charles Harry and Joseph Leland.

**LADY** – H. E. Lady came to Paragould, Arkansas, from the area known as the "Land Between the Lakes" near Kuttawa, Kentucky, in 1907. When he first arrived in Paragould he was employed in a local lumber mill. For 23 years he operated a meat market on Pruett Street. Mr. Lady had the first electrical refrigeration equipment in Paragould.

*John Campbell Lady*

Mr. Lady and his wife, Alice Campbell Lady, had one son, John Campbell Lady and two daughters, Billie Lady Kiersky, and Sarah Maude Lady Whitten.

Billie and her husband Louis Kiersky had two children, David and Caroline. David married Julia Ann Anderson and they had a son David and a daughter Tina. Caroline married Dr. George Thompson and they have a son Dr. Mark Thompson, and a daughter named Sarah Ellen Thompson Vardeman.

John Campbell Lady married Edith O. Davis and they had three children, William Lady, Sarah Lady Franks, and Joann Lady Miller. Joann married Joe Miller and they have one son, Scott Miller. Sarah married Dale Franks and they have a son Bryan Franks and a daughter Gaye Smith. William married Patty Lee and they have a son Billy Holtzclaw and a daughter Amy Lady.

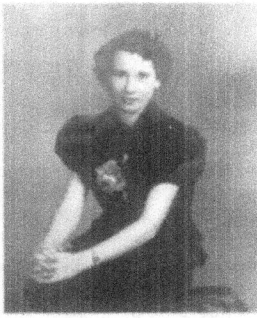
*Edith Lady*

**LAFFOON** – Leonard and Guy Laffoon married sisters, Vivian and Mary Berry and their families were the first Laffoons to live in Greene County as far as records show. They were sons of Edgar and Annie Laffoon of Pope County. They had a brother, Glen and two sisters, Lois and Jewel.

Leonard and Guy went to Mississippi County to pick cotton in the early 1930s when they met the Berry sisters. Leonard and Vivian married Dec 7, 1933; Guy and Mary married Jan 18, 1935.

They all farmed in Mississippi County until 1940 when they bought adjoining farms east of Halliday across from the old Mooring School.

During the time they were in the Leachville area, Leonard and Vivian had three children:
1. Billie Ann
2. Betty Jean
3. Bobby Lee

Guy and Mary had one son, Lowell Edgar after the move to Greene County. Guy and Mary had another son, Larry Dale, who died at age 14 from Lympho Sarcoma.

Leonard and Vivian's oldest daughter, Billie Ann, married Roland Mullins. They live in Jonesboro and have two sons: Joel,who married Risa Hill; they have two daughters, Amy and Katie and live in North Little Rock; Gary who married Gayla Jones; they have a daughter Riley and a son Tyler and live in Mammoth Spring.

Their son Bobby married Marilyn Hughes of Walcott. They live in Hattiesburg, MS and have a daughter and son: Valerie, her husband and two children live in Hattiesburg, also. David married and divorced and has a daughter and lives in Mobile, Al.

Betty, the third child of Leonard and Vivian, married Arlen Ferguson and later divorced. They had a daughter Jo Ann and a son Danny. They all live in the Jonesboro area.

Guy and Mary's son Lowell married Brenda McDonald. They have three sons. Scott, the oldest, is a medical doctor at Jonesboro and lives in Monette. He married Lisa Blankenship in 1984. They had three children: Jeffrey, Lauren and Kyle. They divorced and the children live with their mother in the Dallas, TX area. Scott later married Sherry Uthoff.

Gregory Alan, the second son, married Leanna Rainbolt and divorced. He later married Kim Simpson. They have a son, Trace. Greg is a surgeon and lives in Hot Springs.

The third son, Christopher Bryan, married Catherine Underwood. They have a son, Alexander Christopher. They live in Paragould where he is in business with his father at the Red Goose Deli and Florists' Interlink.

Glen, the youngest of the Laffoon brothers, married Noyes Mickler of Opelika, AL. They lived in California several years when their two sons, Neil and Kelvin, were born. In 1972 they moved to Paragould. Neil married Rhonda Baker from Louisiana and lives in Paragould. Kelvin married Suzanne Lemmons. They live in Jonesboro.

All of the Laffoon offspring have graduated from Oak Grove High School, until it consolidated with Paragould. Chris graduated from Paragould.

As far as I know at this time (year 2000) there are 10 Laffoons living in Greene County, all chipped off the same block!
*Submitted by Mary Laffoon*

**LAM** – James Alexander Lam was born in Hernando, MS on March 15, 1882, to Squire Nicholas and Susan Parthena Davis Lam. Their children were:
1. Ferrell
2. James
3. George
4. Maria
5. Lonnie died in the late 1890s or early 1900s.
6. William, twin
7. Twin to William died at birth

In 1890, finding it difficult to make ends meet on a farm laborer's wages, the family boarded a boxcar, traveling after midnight and came to southeast Arkansas. Later they arrived in Greene County settling north of Paragould. It is said that Squire Nicholas farmed and worked as a carpenter for the railroad.

*Squire Nicholas and Susan Lam family about 1890s or early 1900s. Top: Ferrell, James. Front: William "Eb", Maria, George Lam*

Susan died in 1891 at age 34. Later, James said his most vivid memory of his father was at Clark's Cemetery when his mother, Susan, was buried. Seated under a tree with tears streaming down his face, Squire held two year old William with the other five children gathered around him.

The family moved to Bard where Squire married Mrs. W. J. Harris on May 7, 1895. It is said she was good to the children. Squire Nicholas died during the winter of 1899 and his wife, unable to support the children, allowed them to be raised by different families. James lived in various homes, working for room and board only. He often went hungry and had very few clothes. One man promised if Jim would work through crop planting and harvesting, he would buy Jim a pair of new overalls, shirt and shoes and permit him to go to school. The man did not honor the agreement, denying Jim the chance to go to school. Only after he was married and the father of two, did he have the opportunity to go to school. His brother-in-law, George Bridges, later

*H.E. Lady Meat Market. H.E. Lady on left. Man on right unidentified.*

a physician here, taught at Barr Camp where Jim went long enough to learn to read and write.

Jim met Lela Bridges in 1903 and they married on Aug 20, 1904, in Main Shore Township. Their children were:
1. Estel Pearl died in infancy
2. Sadie May
3. Dorothy died at age two and a half, resulting from smallpox and pneumonia.
4. Drucilla
5. Estie, twin
6. Hester (male) twin

Sadie remembers playing with sister Dorothy in the sand under the corner of their house before Dorothy contracted smallpox. James was unaware he had been exposed to the disease but quickly recovered.

James and Lela lived in the Alexander community where he was a school director. Later they bought 40 acres on Brushy Ridge in the Mounds community, clearing 20 acres of woods and building a three-room house with front and back porches and a split shingle roof.

In 1907 the first school there was taught during the summer in a tent. Later that year, a school building was erected. This was also Mound Union Church where James was a Sunday school director.

*James Alexander Lam family 1957. Top: Chester Owens, Estie (Lam) Owens, Lucille (Crowell) Lam, Hester H. Lam, Robert Inman, Drucilla (Lam) Inman, Sadie (Lam) Cox, Lloyd "Jack." Middle: Derinda (1959) Lam, Jack E. Cox, James L. Lam, Lela (Bridges) Lam, Dreda Owens. Front: Chris H. Cox, Bobby H.Lam, Rena Mae Lam, Dewayne Owens, Thelynn "Buddy" Owens*

James was a farmer, woodcutter and sawmill worker. At age 40, he began a 25-year career as machinist for Missouri Pacific Railroad. He and Lela were active in the church and community where he served several years as constable.

In Dec 1916 the family moved two and one half miles south of Paragould to a 60-acre farm adjoining the Missouri Pacific Railroad where they engaged in farming, registered Holstein dairy work and grew vegetables and fruit. Today the intersection of roads by that farm is known as Lam's Crossing.

James helped organize a non-denominational church at Village, two miles south of Paragould on Pekin Road. He was a director of the one-room school there, grades one through eight. Eventually a curtain was hung down the center as a divider before a larger two-room school was built just a few yards north. This later became Village Baptist Church.

Jim was instrumental in the consolidation of Village, New Hope, Pruett's Chapel, Old Bethel and Wood's Chapel, all one and two-room schools, into the Greene County School on Highway 49 South. He served a total of 24 years as school director in various districts.

Jim died on March 21, 1961 and was buried at Brown's Chapel Cemetery. Lela Lam died April 30, 1971 and was buried next to her husband.

*Submitted by Sadie Cox*

**LAMB** – Alfred Enoch Lamb was born in Wynne, Arkansas, March 3, 1900. His father was Charles Michael Lamb born 1875 either in Alabama or Louisiana. He was a carpenter and taught dad the trade also. But dad learned to be a black smith.

He first married a woman by the name of Birdie Campbell. They had three sons and a daughter. Samuel died as a small child, the rest lived. Birdie died around 1939. I don't know where they married. She is buried at Pine Knot.

He married the second time to a woman by the name of Frankie. They had a son. He came home from work and found her with another man, so they divorced.

Then he married Eva Mae Pigg Wells. Her father was Clarence Oscar Pigg. She was born in Mt. Vernon, Illinois, on December 5, 1905. She also had been married before and had three daughters and a son. One daughter has died, the rest are alive and well. After they married; they had two daughters, I am the youngest one.

They both sold their property and bought a house on Fourth Avenue which had been torn down by a tornado. It was a two story house. Then dad tore it down and built the house and the shop that was there for 33 years. That is the only house I remember living in. I never moved until I married. They moved into it when my sister was 6 months old. I was born the following December 1947. It has been torn down and a parking lot is there now.

For a long time he was the only blacksmith around. Then another came to town. But there was work enough for both. He shoed horses and made their shoes when he couldn't buy them. He shoed the big Clydesdale horses one year when they came down from St. Louis for the Christmas parade. I never saw such big horses feet before. They were beautiful animals. He shod small ponies and riding horses. He made plows and sharpened them. He had wood working saws and machines. He built picture frames and shelves to put them on. He could do just about anything you needed done. Every one knew him for miles around. He went to farms to shoe horses or fix something for them. I remember mother making a picnic lunch when he went out in the country to work. We loved to go with him and have a picnic.

A lot of times on Sunday after Sunday school, we would go riding around through the country. Sometimes we would stop and wade in a stream, or fish, or go hickory nut hunting. Mom would plant a garden every year.

He was also a very Godly man. They both were ministers of the Gospel. He played the guitar and mom played the French Harp. Then my sister and I learned the piano and organ and accordion. We loved to make music together.

**LAMB** – A lonely and neglected graveyard is in the middle of a cow pasture off of Highway 141 and Road 358 in Lorado. It is the "Lamb Family Cemetery," situated on land once owned by James Lamb in the 1850s. Here lie many members of the James Lamb family, once a prosperous and highly respected citizen of the Lorado Community.

At times the wind howls through the branches of the huge cedar tree which is in the center of the cemetery and rises high above the once new and perfect tombstones, but now are broken and scattered by the cattle roaming through the pasture, some trampled and buried under the thick grass growing around them. If these broken pieces of stone could speak they would tell the story of the beginning of the family in Greene County.

They would tell how James Lamb descended from the Lamb's of Pennsylvania and whose parents were John and Cloey Lamb. They were early settlers of Alabama, where James was born on July 22, 1821, and married Rebecca Houston in 1841. Rebecca was born in 1818 to Ross and Mary Houston.

The stones would tell the reason James left Alabama. According to Alabama Land Deeds his land was situated near the banks of the Tennessee River and in 1847 there was a "great flood" which nearly wiped out the Waterloo area. Possibly the "flood" and the dreaded "Yellow fever" epidemic prompted James' decision to leave. He sold his land 1850 and arrived in Arkansas in early 1851 with his wife and children, his mother-in-law Mary, and his brother John Lamb Jr. and his wife Ann, sister of Rebecca.

*Seated: Mary Jane Lamb. Standing from left: Rebecca Ann Lamb and Margaret Emily Lamb, daughters of James and Rebecca Lamb.*

The stones would tell how James located on land along Big Creek, Salem Township. He began to improve his land and soon had a prosperous and productive farm, but in a few years the horrors of the Civil War were upon the countryside. In 1861 James enlisted in the Confederate Army and served until 1863 when he returned to his farm. His military record describes him as 5 feet 10 inches high, light complexion, blue eyes, and light hair.

The stones would tell of the 11 children born to James and Rebecca. An infant born and died 1842; David Ross, born 1848, died infancy; Sarah Louise, born 1850, died infancy; all left in graves in Alabama. How the remaining children grew to adulthood and began to marry and start families of their own. James Peulis, born 1843, married Lou Ellen Drummond; Rebecca Ann, born 1845, married first James Bobbitt and then Joe McDaniel; Mary Jane, born 1847, married Sam Welch; Maranda, born 1852, died young; William Morgan, born 1854, married first Sarah Grayson and then Fannie Shelton; John Thomas, born 1856, married Rebecca Ann Smith; Margaret Emily, born 1858 married Christopher Columbus Cook; and Rhoda Abigail, born 1860, married William Swindle.

Rebecca Lamb died October 20, 1881; James Lamb died August 23, 1896, and were buried next to each other in the Lamb Family Cemetery. On James' tombstone the inscription reads "Ex-Confederate Soldier." Rebecca's tombstone reads "Jesus Loves the Pure in Heart." The passing of time, the elements and neglect have all but destroyed this once loved resting place of the Lamb family, but now forlorn and forgotten under the shadowy branches of the huge cedar tree.

If the stones could speak they would ask "why."

**LAMB** – John Lamb Jr. was born in 1816 in Williamson County, Tennessee. He was the son of John Lamb Sr. and Cloey who settled in Lauderdale County, Alabama, about 1821. John Lamb Jr., married on November 1, 1838, in Waterloo, Lauderdale County, Alabama, to Ann Houston born 1816 in Newberry County, South Carolina, who was the daughter of Ross Houston Sr. and Mary Ann. In 1851 John Lamb Jr., and several of his siblings moved their families to Greene County, Arkansas: sister-in-law, Rhoda Hardin Lamb, widow of Morgan Lamb; James Lamb and wife Rebecca Houston; Mary Lamb who later married John Wilson Willcockson/Wilcoxson; brother-in-law, Reuben Adams and wife Sarah Lamb; and possibly others.

John and Ann Houston Lamb had five children, all born in Lauderdale County, Alabama: James Houston Lamb born August 10, 1839; Mary Ann Lamb born April 25, 1842; John Jones Lamb born December 10, 1843; David L. Lamb born December 25, 1846, who married Mary Clements; and Robert Marshall Lamb born 1848 who married Clarinda Elizabeth Dacus, daughter of Pascal L. Dacus and Amanda A. O'Dell. Ann Houston Lamb died in Greene County, Arkansas, about 1871 and was buried in the Lamb Cemetery. Her grave is not marked as her tombstone was destroyed.

John Lamb Jr., remarried between 1872 and 1873 in Greene County, Arkansas, to Rebecca Cardwell, the widow of Henry Cook Jr. They had three daughters as follows: Della Lamb born about 1873; Susan Lamb born December 10, 1874; and Ruth Ann Lamb born about 1876. Rebecca Cardwell (Cook) Lamb died about 1876 shortly after the birth of Ruth.

John then married a third time to Elizabeth A. Travis on December 28, 1878, in Craighead County, Arkansas. There were no children from this third marriage.

John Lamb Jr., owned a farm between Finch and Lorado where he lived and worked for over 30 years until his death in January of 1885. He was buried in the Lamb Cemetery on the family farm but his tombstone was destroyed. When John died, he left three minors: Della, Susan and Ruth Lamb. Since his widow, Elizabeth, was not the mother of his children, it is understandable that she might not have wanted to be responsible for them. David Lamb son of John Lamb Jr., and half brother to these three little girls, was appointed their guardian on February 4, 1885. All three young daughters lived to adulthood, married and left descendants in Greene County, Arkansas. Of the five children of John and Ann Houston Lamb, James Houston Lamb and John Jones Lamb moved their families to Coos County, Oregon, while Mary Ann Lamb, wife of William Thomas Clements, David L. Lamb and Robert Marshall Lamb remained in Greene County, Arkansas. Many of their descendants still live in Greene County, Arkansas, today.

The Lamb Cemetery is located on a reserved one acre plot in the NW/4 NE/4 of Section 30-16N-4E, in Greene County, Arkansas, known as the old Ellis Wall farm which was later sold to Paul Arnold. The 40 acres of land where the cemetery is located was originally purchased by John Lamb (Jr.) as a United States Patent dated March 1, 1856. During John's lifetime he conveyed this same tract of land to his brother, James Lamb.

**LANDRUM** – John Vincent Landrum came to Paragould in 1883 from Carroll County, TN and became a partner with his brother James Monroe Landrum in the mercantile business. He married Ella Margaret Stalcup the next year, 1884.

John Vincent Landrum's second son was Charles Vincent Landrum, born April 17, 1887, in Paragould. Charles married Ima Ervy/Irvie Cashon Pewitt, daughter of William Harve and Almorah Cynthelia Milner Cashon, of Mayfield, KY, on Nov 29, 1916. They had five children, all born in Paragould.

Charles Frederick was born Sept 16, 1919. He married Margaret Carolyn Ford Oct 19, 1947 and they had two daughters, Mary Jean and Nancy Ross. He died April 6, 1986, in Paragould.

The second child and only daughter, Emma Jeanne, was born Aug 20, 1924. On Aug 11, 1946, she married Billy Bob Layl, from Pocahontas, AR. They had one daughter, Charlotte Jean.

Billy Monroe, the third child, was born Nov 3, 1926. He married Glenda Lee Jones; they had two children, William Harold and Megan Sue.

Next son, Joseph Cashon Landrum, born June 11, 1931, married Mary Jean Emrich, from Tyronza, AR. They had five children: Joseph Emrich, Michael Vincent, Robert Andrew, Wallace Hill and Jill Suzanne.

Youngest son, Robert Eric, was born Sept 9, 1936. He married Dorothy Jane Porting, from Axtel, Ks and they also had five children:
1. Allison Ann
2. Mark Eric
3. John David
4. Jeffrey Porting
5. Jason Patrick

Charles Vincent received his education in the schools of Greene County, AR and graduated from Professor Thompson's Institute, a local business school. He entered the insurance business with his father, a partnership that continued until his father's death in 1938. Charles continued the business and it prospered to warrant a later partnership.

Charles was a member of the Masonic Lodge in Paragould as long as a family member can remember. He and his entire family were faithful and loyal members of First Methodist Church in Paragould, as were his parents before him.

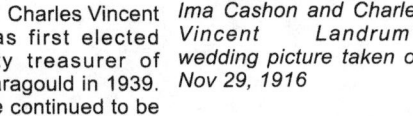
*Ima Cashon and Charles Vincent Landrum's wedding picture taken on Nov 29, 1916*

Charles Vincent was first elected city treasurer of Paragould in 1939. He continued to be re-elected for many terms, serving a total of 27 years and eight months. His tenure in office is believed to be the longest in the history of Greene County. In an interview with the press at his retirement in 1966 as city treasurer, he jokingly said that "they couldn't beat me, so they just abolished the position."

Charles Vincent Landrum died Aug 23, 1969, at age 82. Ima died Feb 5, 1987, in Piggott, AR. They are buried in Memorial Gardens in Paragould, AR. In some families, their history lies in buildings, money or fame or other accomplishments. In Charles Vincent's family, it was relationships. His was a close family, whose surviving members remains in-touch and close with each other.

**LANDRUM** – Horace Milton Landrum was born Dec 31, 1885, a baker by trade. He married Margaret, daughter of Edwin Gilbert and Juliette (Dodds) Barrett, originally from Craighead County, AR, on May 19, 1912. Their children were: H. Milton, born Dec 6, 1914, in Paragould, died Sept 22, 1994, in TX; Winfred, born in Blytheville, AR and married Francis Bland. Their children are listed in the Bland sketch.

*Margaret Barrett and Horace Landrum*

**LANDRUM** – John B. Landrum, the sixth child of John Vincent and Ella Margaret Stalcup Landrum, was born on May 9, 1896, in Paragould, Arkansas. He attended local schools and went on to attend the University of Arkansas where he majored in music and became an accomplished clarinetist.

John enlisted in the U.S. Army on May 28, 1917, as a Musician 1st Class, serving in the Infantry Band on the 89th Div. He was stationed at Camp Beauregard in Louisiana for a year and then sailed with the A.E.F. for France. He served for a year and returned to Camp Pike, Arkansas, where he was discharged on August 19, 1919.

While stationed at Camp Beauregard, John met Grace D. Butler, daughter of entrepreneur Jesse Butler and Dewetta Grace Whatley Butler of Natchitoches, Louisiana. Grace was a college student at Lake Charles, Louisiana, majoring in horticulture. When John returned from military service in 1919, they were married and settled in Lake Charles where John owned a small oil company. Their first child was born during their residence there and died in early childhood. Two years later, they moved to the Little Rock area where John was hired as a machinist by the Missouri-Pacific Railroad. Three children were born during their time in the Little Rock area.

At the urging of his parents, John moved his family to Paragould in 1931 during the early years of the Great Depression. Their fifth child was born in Paragould in 1933. John had difficulty finding permanent, full-time employment in Paragould due to the Depression. He and Grace traded their house for a farm about five miles outside the town where he and their son, Edwin, implemented new farming techniques recommended by the U.S. Department of Agriculture. They were among the first farmers in the area to plant soybeans, peanuts and alfalfa. In addition to the usual crops of cotton and corn, they also planted a small orchard and a field of strawberries, which was the envy of farmers nearby. The farm also yielded many arrowheads and artifacts left behind by Native Americans who had inhabited the area many years ago.

To improve his family's economic situation, John sought full-time employment. He was hired as a machinist by the U.S. Navy Department in 1938 and moved his family to Washington, D.C. He retired from that position after 20 years.

Subsequently John was hired as a master machinist by a firm that pioneered in making cameras for satellites and space vehicles. During his tenure there he received many accolades and awards. He retired at the age of 83 to be with Grace, who had cancer. She died in March 1981.

John died December 23, 1991, at the age of 94. He is buried in National Memorial Cemetery in Falls Church, Virginia, alongside Grace, his beloved wife of 61 years.

John was a member of the Masonic Blue Lodge. Both he and Grace were active members of the Order of the Eastern Star in Washington, D.C., and were active in their Methodist church in Falls Church, Virginia.

**LANDRUM** – Three Landrum brothers came to Greene County, Arkansas, from Weakley County, Tennessee, during the last century. They were from a long-line of Landrums that came to this country from Scotland in 1688. The two brothers, James and John, settled in Essex County, Virginia. Their families then migrated to Halifax County by way of Chesterfield and Buckingham Counties in Virginia. From Halifax they found their way to Weakley in 1827. Our line is traced to James with allied families Hawkins, Hart, Clark, Covington, Young, Mosley, Browne, Lucas and Brusner.

"Six hundred dollars will buy a lot and put up a tolerable fair house" in Parmley (later named Paragould) claimed James Monroe Landrum in a July 22, 1882, letter addressed to his younger brother, John Vincent of Weakley County, Tennessee. However, John Vincent did not follow his brother's suggestion. He moved to Carroll County, Tennessee, and went into the mill business instead of coming to Greene County.

*Children of John Vincent Landrum and Ella Margaret Stalcup. Top row from left: Horace Milton, Charles Vincent, Robert Edgar and John Bennett. Bottom row from left: Lillian Eva, Vivian Ella and James Samuel. The picture made late 1918 or early 1919, while John Bennett was serving in the Army during World War I.*

Records indicated E.D. "Ed" Landrum moved to Greene County in 1865, James Monroe came to Greene county after 1876. Their brother John Vincent followed in 1883. John Vincent was born in 1853, son of James and Emerline (Anderson) Landrum. He was educated in the common schools of Weakley County, Tennessee. He taught school in Gibson County for three years and then moved to Carroll County. Coming to Paragould in 1883, he became a partner in James Monroe's mercantile business, one of the first merchants in Paragould.

He married Ella Margaret Stalcup in 1884. She was the daughter of Charles Thaddeus and Nancy Aletha (Hyatt) Stalcup. Records of the First Methodist Church reveal that Charles Stalcup started the Sunday School when the church was located on property that is now the First National Bank parking lot.

In 1885 John Vincent sold his interest in the East Court Street store to James Monroe and went into partnership with his father-in-law in a grocery/general store business. That partnership was dissolved four years later and John Vincent operated the store until he sold it to A.J. Tetrick of Cape Girardeau, Missouri, in 1891. He managed the store for Tetrick for a short time then went into the insurance business. He continued in this business until he died in 1938. He served as city treasurer 14 years on the school board nine years and second ward alderman for two terms.

John Vincent and Ella had eight children.

(1) Horace Milton married to Margaret E. Barrett, owned a bakery known as the Highland Pastry Shop.

(2) Charles Vincent Landrum married to Ima Cashon, was associated in the insurance business with his father.

(3) Robert Edgar "Boots" Landrum married to Verna Sumpter became a jeweler and operated the Paragould Jewelry Company with his partner, Frazier Hammond.

(4) Lillian married to Walter Waddy lived in Blytheville.

(5) The next child died at birth.

(6) John Bennett married to Grace Butler, lived in Falls Church, Virginia and worked at the U.S. Navy shipyard in the Washington, D.C. area.

(7) Vivian, married to Joseph Dunavant worked for the *Paragould Daily Press*.

(8) James Samuel, married to Helen Sigman, the youngest child in the family, was a linotype operator with the *Courier News* in Blytheville for 50 years until his retirement.

**LANE** – John Cole Lane was born in 1861, the son of Jacob and Harriett Lane, and a grandson of Randolph and Biddy Lane. In 1884 he married Margaret Elizabeth Martin, the daughter of William and Angeline Martin. (Angeline was a Cherokee woman) The Martins were born in Alabama, while their daughter was born in Randolph County, Arkansas. At the age of 15, Margaret bore their first child, Sarah Harriett Angeline Lane. Four years later, Thomas Reynold Lane was born to them, called "Rannell" (thought to be a corruption of Randolph). Four years later, in 1893, came Ella Catherine Lane. John Cole and Margaret made their home in Ravenden Springs where John carried on the tradition of his father as a blacksmith, a trade he passed on to his son, Reynold. For reasons unknown to us, Margaret passed away in 1894 at the age of 24.

*From left: Ella, Helen, Arval, Carson, Arthur, Billie, John Cole and Mary Lane.*

John remarried soon after to Mary Ellen Beck, the daughter of Oliver and Eliza Beck. Mollie, as she was called, was also a Ravenden Springs native. There were eight children born to them; Arthur in 1897, Arval in 1899, Johnnie (who changed her name to Helen) in 1905, Willie Opal, (who changed her name to Billie) in 1908, Kennard in 1911, Howard in 1913 and Bernard in 1916. Sadly, Howard died in 1917 of a bowel obstruction. In 1927 John Cole died, leaving Mollie to raise the remainder of her children alone. She spent the rest of her life living with her various children and was a positive fixture in her grandchildren's lives, till her death in 1955.

Her stepchildren called her Aunt Mollie, and she brought them up as her own, as well as her own large brood. John Cole, Margaret and Mollie are all buried in Janes Cemetery in Ravenden Springs.

**LANE** – Thomas Reynold Lane was born in Ravenden Springs on February 15, 1889, to John Cole and Margaret Lane. He was a good baseball player, who was sought after for the major leagues, but as baseball wasn't considered a respectable living at the turn of the 20th century, he became a blacksmith like his father and grandfather. In 1910 Reynold married 19 year old Virgie Ann Rogers, the oldest child of Walker and Mac Rogers, also of Ravenden Springs. In 1911 Verma Inez was born to them, and in 1913 Mary Eileen, who sadly passed away six months later. William Leslie was born in 1918, and Lowanda McAda surprised and completed the family in 1930. Reynold and Virgie moved around a lot, for various reasons, so Eileen was born and died in Walnut Ridge, Leslie born in Gatewood, Missouri, and Lowanda was born in Ravenden Springs. During her young childhood, the Lane family lived on a steep hill overlooking the Spring. While Lowanda was growing up, her beloved big sister was already a wife and mother, and Lowanda's nephew, Keith Dodd, born in 1933, was a playmate. In 1936, Reynold, Virgie, Les and Lowanda moved to Ann Arbor Michigan, where Reynold continued as a blacksmith.

Virgie died in 1938 of a cerebral hemorrhage, leaving a grieving family behind. The stable which housed the horses of the Sealtest Dairy, for which Reynold was blacksmith, was below the house the family lived in, and unfortunately, burned down, killing all of the horses. Reynold was badly kicked trying to save them. The dairy company replaced the horses with trucks, and Reynold became a truck mechanic till his retirement in the 1950s.

In 1952, Leslie married Miss Vernie Hampton, and Lowanda married Stanley Wylie in 1954. Reynold lived out his remaining years with Les and Vernie on a farm in Ann Arbor, where he was much adored by his grandchildren. (Lowanda bore four children, who were equally loved by Les and Vernie, who remained childless.)

*Reynold and Virgie Lane circa 1910.*

Reynold died of injuries sustained in a car crash in 1966. He is as missed today as he was back then, and many happy memories are shared by members of the Lane and Rogers families. Reynold and Virgie are buried in Janes Cemetery in Ravenden Springs.

**LAWRENCE** – Gersham Avery Lawrence was born 1866 in Hickman County, KY, the eldest son of William L. and Nancy Sarah Simmons Lawrence. He came with his father in 1885 to Greene County. He died April 15, 1931 in Brookland, AR. He married Martha Elizabeth Shearer 1890 in Paragould, AR, daughter of Van Shearer and Clarissa Thompson. She was born 1867 in Craighead County, AR and died Aug 13, 1937 in Brookland, AR.

Everyone knew Gersham as "G. A." or "G. Avery". He was farmer in the Brookland area.

G. Avery and Liz raised nine children, most of whom stayed in the area:

1. Mamie Lena married Mach Heard
2. Clarence married Geneva Wilkerson
3. Morris Ellis married (1) Etta McCracken and after her death (2) Estelle Reese
4. Mary Susan married Andrew Lewis Camp
5. Commodore Dewey married (1) Vaudine Parker (2) Selma Leach
6. Kate married Mack Barringer
7. Halli Bob married Gaines Wood
8. Melvin married Winnie Stuart.
9. Davis Addison "Ad" married Vera Qualls.

*Gersham Avery Lawrence and wife, Martha Elizabeth Shearer.*

Many of the descendants of G. A. and Liz are still living in the area.
*Submitted by Dee Burr*

**LAWRENCE** – William L. Lawrence was born 1844 in Ballard County, KY and died 1904 in Paragould, Greene County, AR. He married Nancy Sarah Simmons 1865 in Hickman County, KY, daughter of Jesse Simmons and Sarah Roberts. She was born 1847 in Fulton County, KY and died 1933 in Paragould, Greene County, AR.

William L. Lawrence served in the Confederate army from 1861 until 1865. He served in Company E, 12th Tennessee Infantry until the middle of the Battle of Corinth. When Gen. Sydney Johnston was killed, the Army of Tennessee regiments were re-organized. He was then transferred to Company L, Third Kentucky Infantry. He was captured Sept 25, 1864 near Athens, Al and was transferred to Louisville Military Prison in Kentucky. He was to be transferred to the prison in Camp Chase, OH but escaped enroute. After he escaped he rejoined his unit. He fought until the end of the war, riding with Gen. Bedford Forrest in the defense of Selma, Al.

William Lawrence died at the age of 55 at his home. He had been active in the Ancient Order of United Workmen. Nancy lived to be 86, living out her years on Pruett Street in Paragould, AR. He and Nancy are buried in Linwood Cemetery, Paragould.

William and Nancy were the parents of 10 children, seven living to adulthood. William Alva, Emma D. and Clinton Olin all died young.

Gersham Avery, known as G. A., was born in Kentucky and lived his adult life around the Brookland, AR area. G. A. married Martha Elizabeth Shearer, daughter of Van Buren Shearer and Clarissa Thompson.

Ivy Jess Lawrence was also born in Kentucky. He married Virginia Shearer, sister to Martha Elizabeth. He also lived in the Brookland area.

John Wesley Lawrence, born in Kentucky died as a young man in 1900. His wife, Mollie Johnson, had died shortly after giving birth to their only child, Anna Mae in 1894. Anna lived with her grandparents until her death in 1928.

Luther Lewis Lawrence was born 1875 in Kentucky and died 1958 in Paragould, AR. He married Eva Smith, 1901. She was born 1883 and died April 18, 1912. He then married Rosa Elmira Norton in 1913. She was born 1888 and died 1969 in Paragould.

William James Lawrence, born in 1877 in Kentucky, married Ila Caston in 1903. William died in 1913. The writer knows nothing more of this family.

Julia Barzilla Lawrence was born 1883 in KY and died Oct 13, 1927 in Paragould. She married George Hermann Kingston in 1903. He was born 1882 and died 1961 in Paragould, Greene County, AR.

Numerous descendants of William and Nancy still reside in Greene and Craighead Counties. A Lawrence reunion is held bi-annually on even years. All Lawrence descendants are welcome.
*Submitted by Dee Burr, great great granddaughter*

**LAWSON/JOHNSON** – Nina Louise "Jill" Lawson-Rockwood was born on September 21, 1923, in Little Rock, Arkansas, the daughter of John Francis Lawson and Lou Evie Johnson, both of Paragould and the stepdaughter of John Rockwood. On June 5, 1941, she married Eugene Sanford Browning, son of Eugene Rutledge Browning and Bessie Lee Sanford of Paragould, in Atlanta, Georgia. They had two children: Robert Eugene born November 2, 1943, in Emory, Georgia, and Elizabeth Louise born January 3, 1947, in Richmond, Virginia. Jill died on October 2, 1993, in Chesterfield, Missouri; Robert died on February 4, 1994, in Glendale, Missouri; and Eugene died on February 2, 2000, in Bridgeton, Missouri. They are all buried in the Linwood Cemetery in Paragould, Arkansas. Elizabeth resides in Glendale, Missouri.

*From left: John Francis Lawson and Edmonia Ellen (Lawson) Perkins. Bottom: James Edward Lawson Sr., Herschel Dixon Lawson and Mrs. Divernon "Divie" (Clark) Lawson.*

Jill's parents were married on April 12, 1920, in Jonesboro, Arkansas. Their oldest child was James Franklyn "Jack" Lawson born on August 21, 1921, in Paragould and died on June 2, 1987, in Atlanta, Georgia. Jack is buried in the Marietta National Cemetery in Marietta, Georgia. He served in the Navy during World War II and was present at sea during the signing of the treaty with Japan. Jack married Sarah Landrum and had three children, James Franklyn Jr. "Frank," born December 15, 1949, Ronald and Donald twins born January 26, 1951. Don died on September 9, 1995, in Fort Worth, Texas. Jack and Jill's mother, Lou Evie, was born on August 29, 1901, in Paragould, the daughter of Dr. Frank Cheatham Johnson and Lou Evie Lay. She died on January 7, 1989, in Sarasota, Florida. Her ashes were scattered in the Gulf of Mexico. She and John Rockwood have a memorial stone in the Linwood Cemetery. Lou Evie married her second husband, John Rockwood, on February 7, 1937, in Washington, D.C.

Jack and Jill's father, John Francis Lawson, was born on May 18, 1894, in Paragould, Arkansas, the son of James Edward Lawson and Divernon "Divie" Clark. He died on June 26, 1941, in Detroit, Michigan, and is buried in the Linwood Cemetery in Paragould. He served in France during World War I as a Sergeant, 14 Co. Trans. Corps. and started with Fisher Body in 1924 working in the Fleetwood Metal Department. He had four siblings: Edmonia Ellen born August 3, 1896, and died September 8, 1990, who married Ray H. Perkins; Cecil Julious born August 26, 1900, and died February 10, 1901; James Edward Jr. born April 25, 1916, and died December 2, 1972, who married Mrs. Margaret Panisko Szabo; and Herschel Dickson "Dick" born August 9, 1907, and died May 29, 1975, who married Adaline Knox. Edmonia had one daughter, Susan, and Herschel had two children, Dick Jr. and Alice Ann. James Jr. had two step-children, Albert William and Margaret (deceased) Szabo.

Lou Evie Johnson's mother was born on October 29, 1869, in Vildo near Whiteville, Tennessee, the daughter of James Asbury Lay and Georgianna C. Andrews. She died in Jonesboro, Arkansas, on July 16, 1954. The earliest known Lay ancestor in this country was Abraham Lay born about 1700 in England. He married Sarah Grimes of Fairfield County, Virginia. The earliest known Andrews ancestors are Henry and Lucy Andrews of Sussex County, Virginia. Lou Evie's father was Dr. Frank Cheatham Johnson born on May 14, 1862, near Jackson, Tennessee, and died December 11, 1937, in Paragould. Her parents married on October 28, 1888, in Crockett County, Tennessee. Dr. Johnson's parents were William Paschal Johnson and Mary Eugenia Wood. The earliest known Johnson ancestor in this country was William Johnson born about 1720 in England who married Mariah Rebecca Larkin. Dr. Johnson was one of the first dentists in Northeast Arkansas and Mrs. Johnson learned the trade from her husband. The Johnson's other children were: Ethel Louise born April 20, 1890, and died September 4, 1975, who married Clarence "Jack" Shreve and then Norman Donaldson Jr.; William Paschal born October 5, 1898, and died in infancy; Mary Ann born March 30, 1893, and died January 10, 1980, who married Newton L. Eudaly; and Dr. Frank Cecil born August 14, 1995, and died October 30, 1964, who married Martha Noel. Ethel and Jack Shreve had two children, Billy (who died young) and Francis. Mary had one daughter, Florence "Pat,"

*Dr. Frank Cheatham Johnson and Mrs. Lou Evie (Lay) Johnson.*

*From left: James Franklyn "Jack" Lawson-Rockwood, Lou Evie (Johnson) Lawson Rockwood and Nina Louise "Jill" (Lawson-Rockwood) Browning.*

and Frank had two daughters, Nannie and Noel. The Johnsons were related to the late Dr. James W. Johnson of Paragould and his half-brother, Judge Robert Edward Lee Johnson. Some of surnames connected to Dr. Johnson's line include: Tweedy, Miller, Faison, Kilbey, Dixon, Lewis, Lawson, Love, Smith, Flood, Hill, Plouvier, O'Brissell, Kuykendall, McFarland, Branch and Finch. Some other surnames connected to Mrs. Johnson's line are: Fouche, Scofield, Donaldson, Loftin, Cooper, Barham, Newsom, Harrup, Holt, Rawlings, Gilliam, Crawford, Carter, Sheppard, Collier, Henshaw, Briggs, Norwood, Ingram, Jordon, Stuard, Ligon, Clarke, Flake, Ridley, Filmer, Lather, Carter, Spenser, Sperry, Lightfoot, Judkins, Argall, Sherbourne, Bychett, Atesbury and Wall. Mr. and Mrs. Johnson are both buried in the Linwood Cemetery.

From left: Dr. Frank Cecil Johnson, Ethel Louise (Johnson) Shreve Donaldson, Mrs. Lou Evie (Lay) Johnson, Mary Ann (Johnson) Eudaly and Lou Evie (Johnson) Lawson Rockwood.

John Francis Lawson's father, James Edward Lawson, was born on July 27, 1867, in Blackford, Kentucky. He was the sheriff of Greene County from 1910 to 1912. He was the constable of Clark Township and also served as a member of the police force of which he was chief prior to becoming a peace officer. He worked as a foreman on the hub mill and operated a cafe in Paragould before becoming a peace officer. He also worked for several years at the Joplin Missouri Power Plant and for the Fisher Body Company in Detroit, Michigan. He died on May 10, 1948, in Paragould and is buried in the Linwood Cemetery. His earliest known Lawson ancestor was Mason Leason Lawson who married Nelly Smallwood. The Lawson family is originally believed to have come from Virginia. Nelly's family descends from the Smallwoods of Maryland. His father was John Francis Lawson who married Mary Elizabeth Calvert. His father's twin brother was James W. Lawson who also moved to Paragould. Mary descends from the Calverts of Maryland. His mother's parents were Francis Ruffin Clark and Susan Ann Lewis. Francis was a well digger and the son of Francis R. Clark Sr. and Mary E. Mydgett. The parents of Francis Sr. were Joseph Clark and Biddie A. Permenter. The Clarks are believed to descend from Sir Thomas Clarke in the 1500s in England. The parents of Susan Ann Lewis were William A. Lewis and Sarah Eleanor Spann. Susan was born on November 6, 1852, in Haywood County, Tennessee, and died on October 5, 1933, in Paragould. Francis was born on May 4, 1849, in Haywood County, Tennessee, and died on December 12, 1929, in Paragould. Susan and Francis are both buried in the Linwood Cemetery. William's parents were Gabriel Lewis and Tabitha Ivy. Some other surnames connected to the Lawson family are: Bland, Reynolds, Vaughn, Brooks, Farrow, Hinton, Etheridge, Kirkland, Doyne, Stone, Brent, Cotton, Herron, Perkins, Karcher and Scott.

**LIGHT** – George O. Light, born April 27, 1872, one of the foremost citizens of Paragould and Greene County, enjoyed an extensive acquaintance in the community. Since early in his career he had been prominently identified with public affairs, having served as circuit court clerk for several years, followed by serving the county in the state legislature. During the latter years he was associated with local banks, the Security Bank as cashier and with Paragould Trust Company.

For several years Mr. Light was secretary of the Paragould School Board. He was instrumental with others from the Paragould First Baptist Church in organizing the Second Baptist Church in 1912. He was the men's Bible teacher of the church.

Mr. Light was a noted orator and was called upon to speak to many clubs, businesses and social gatherings. He married Mary Dow Faulkner, daughter of G.H. Faulkner, well-known and well-loved Baptist minister of Greene County. They are the parents of 10 children: Cullen Chloe, who died in childhood; Lurline Henry; Frances Hammond; Otis Lamar Light; Agnes Marie; George Clinton Light; Jane Ophelia Wadley; Amelia Weatherly; Charles Doris Light; and Anna Lee Mickey.

Mr. Light died at the age of 51. During the afternoon the city paid their respects with the closing of the banks, schools and many businesses.

R.S. Thompson Classical Institute, circa 1895. Standing: Alvey Otey, Frank Dickinson, L. Steveson, Dr. Hammett, Frank Weatherly and Ben Walker. Sitting: Will Barnhill, Harvey Forsythe, George Otis Light, Tom Jackman, Jason Light and T. Breckinridge, grandson of John Russell Light. George Otis Light and Jason Light were the sons of Pleasant Green and Flora E. Mooney Light.

**LIPSCOMB** – Samuel Scott Lipscomb was born in King William County, VA, Feb 17, 1890 and died in Paragould, AR on April 24, 1969. He was the youngest child of Charles Wiley and Mary C. Lipscomb. The Lipscombs, with three sons and two daughters, moved to Marmaduke when Sam was a child. Lipscomb was married twice, first to Vada Allen and after her death to her Aunt, Eva Allen.

While living in Marmaduke he was owner of the Lipscomb Livestock Barn and The Farmers' Mercantile Company. Also Lipscomb owned many acres of farmland in the Marmaduke area. Moving to Paragould, he obtained more land holdings, Lipscomb and several associates built the Lipscomb Ford Motor Building on West Kingshighway, which was operated from 1940 to mid 1950s.

Samuel Scott Lipscomb

Lipscomb was a director of the First National Bank of Paragould and was instrumental in raising funds to build the main exhibit building at the Greene County fairground.

The Lipscombs had no children of their own. Three nieces and four nephews held a special place in their hearts.

The S. S. Lipscomb Research Room of the Greene County Library was made possible by the generosity of Samuel Scott Lipscomb. The new Greene County courthouse also benefited from the Lipscomb-Kirsch Charitable Foundation.

*Submitted by Mary Elizabeth Brenneisen*

**LITTLE** – James Henry Little was born in St. Francis Township, Greene County, AR in 1863. His parents were John W. Little, born in North Carolina in 1832 and Elizabeth, born in North Carolina in 1836. The family came to Greene County in about 1855 and settled in St. Francis Township. Their known children were:
1. William W. (1857)
2. John A. (1859)
3. James Henry (1863)

James Henry married Addaline "Addie" Carolyn McIntosh on Jan 8, 1887. Addie was the only child of Nancy Carolyn Clark McIntosh. James Henry owned and operated a general store, blacksmith shop and dairy in the Center Hill Community, where the family home still stands, southwest of Crowley's Ridge Academy. They grew Cotton and raised cattle. They were lifelong faithful members of Center Hill Baptist Church. James H. died May 27, 1928. Addie Carolyn died April 19, 1936. Both are buried in Center Hill Cemetery.

Their children: Jessie married Ira Titus Russell, son of W. M. Russell and their children were Bert, Sherrel and Robert. Ira T. and Jessie lived and farmed near Shiloh Church for many years.

James Andrew "Andy" married Floy Cline, sister to Galvin Cline and daughter of W. L. Cline. They had one daughter, Orenta. Floy died while Andy was serving in France during WWI. Andy later married Elsie Gay, daughter of Silas Gay, who came to Greene County from Illinois. Andy and Elsie operated a general merchandise store and service station for many years just west of Center Hill Church. Andy and Elsie were the parents of three children Elwanda, Louisine and James.

Kelly married Dorothy Hurst from St. Louis and their two sons are Gerald and Kelly Gene. Ella married Galvin Cline, brother of Floy, whose father was W. L. Cline. They had two children, Geraldine and Kenneth.

Idella married Wiley Walters and they had one daughter, Maxine. Essie Mildred married Ellis Anderson Johnson, son of Robert S. and Clara

*James Henry Little, ca. 1925.*

Johnson. Their two daughters are Jacqueline Jane and Dorothy Gwendolyn.

Elwyn married Juanita Dacus from Fayetteville and they had one son, Kenny. Elwyn and Juanita taught school in Greene County for many years. Elwyn later became the Greene County School superintendent. He was also instrumental in the consolidation of the Greene County Technical School District.

Beatrice Carolyn married Gene Coffman of the Coffman community, whose father built and owned the first movie house in Paragould. They did not have children. Beatrice Carolyn also taught school in the Greene County Schools.

Many of the members of the James Henry and Addie Little family are buried in Center Hill Cemetery.

*Submitted by Mrs. John Colmore Beane, Jr.*

**LLOYD** – Bertha Edna Horne was born on Feb 21, 1898 near Beech Grove, AR. In later years, she would often laugh and say that she was one day older that George Washington who was born on Feb 22. Bertha was the oldest child of Irvin Simpson and Nancy Catherine (Hutchins) Horne.

On March 28, 1915, Bertha married Barney Crowley Lloyd who was the son of John M. and Sarah Jane (Halley) Gramling Lloyd. Sarah Jane was the half sister of Benjamin Crowley, grandson of the first settler in the Greene County area.

*Barney Crowley Lloyd and Bertha Edna Horne with their two oldest children Pauline and Meldon Simpson about 1919.*

When Bertha's father, Irvin Horne, became Greene County treasurer in 1930 and moved to Paragould, she and Barney bought her parents' two-story house at Beech Grove and raised their family there. Bertha and Barney Lloyd had seven children:
1. Pauline married Gus Eubanks
2. Meldon married Marie Castleberry
3. Lodema married (1) Lionell Penney and after his death, (2) Bill DeVoll
4. B. C. married Dorothy Austin
5. Mildred married Kenneth Ellington
6. Marian married Gene Pierceall
7. Velma Jean married Gussie Miller

Bertha Lloyd and her older children worked the farm at Beech Grove while Barney Lloyd traded in cattle, sold insurance and worked for the Drivers License Bureau. He was a school board member and also the song leader for the Baptist church in Beech Grove. He was a lifelong Democrat. Barney Crowley Lloyd established B. C. Lloyd Real Estate in Paragould. Years later, his son B. C. Lloyd joined him in selling real estate and business continued for over 50 years.

Bertha (Horne) Lloyd was a charter member of Calvary Baptist Church in Paragould. She loved to quilt and during her lifetime, she made over 100 quilts. Her grandchildren received quilts as gifts for special events such as, graduations, marriages and births. Bertha and Barney Lloyd had 17 grandchildren:
1. Wendell Eubanks
2. Dan Eubanks
3. Margaret Lloyd
4. Sharran (Lloyd) McCullar
5. Sandra (Penney) Sharpe
6. Barry Lloyd
7. Patsy (Ellington) Humphrey
8. Brenda (Ellington) Johnson
9. Pam (Miller) Dickey
10. Cathy (Pierceall) Cook
11. Phil Eubanks
12. Bill Miller
13. Tim Miller
14. Debbie (Pierceall) Jennings
15. Mark Miller
16. Stan Lloyd
17. Kenny Ellington

Barney Lloyd died on Oct 23, 1969. Bertha (Horne) Lloyd died when she was 94 years old on May 12, 1992, the day after Mother's Day. Although she was the oldest, she outlived all of her siblings and two of her children. Barney and Bertha Lloyd are buried at Memorial Gardens in Paragould.

*Submitted by Bill Miller*

**LLOYD** – Thomas D. Lloyd was born May 30, 1805, in Livingston County, Kentucky. He was the son of Frethias Lloyd and Elizabeth Gable Lloyd. Frethias and Elizabeth were married in Greene County, Tennessee, on January 28, 1796. Frethias was from New Jersey and Elizabeth was from Pennsylvania. Elizabeth died a short time after Thomas was born and Frethias returned to Greene County, Tennessee, and married Elizabeth Carter on January 28, 1806. Thomas left home at an early age and came to Arkansas when it was still a territory and there is some evidence that some of his brothers came with him. The Territorial Papers of Arkansas, Vol. 19, page 172, state that Thomas was appointed a magistrate in St. Francis County in the year 1835. It was about this time that he married Sarah Ellen Shaver, daughter of Joseph Shaver and Mary Ann Corzine. Sarah or Sally as she was called by her family, was said to be half Cherokee Indian, although there is no record of her Indian descent on any rolls. A typewritten statement by Ki Lloyd of his recollections and history of Sarah Shaver Lloyd said she had long black hair and sat in a low rocker and smoked a corn cob pipe. She was said to have been born at Pocahontas, Arkansas Territory. Ki Lloyd was a grandson.

Thomas became a Baptist preacher and was ordained at a meeting of Mt. Zion Association at Lebanon Church near what is now Hydrick in 1859. He was a pioneer organizer of Mt. Zion Church in Greene County and at Macedonia Church in Craighead County. He moved his family to Greene County about this time and settled on Village Creek. His family of sons and daughters are as follows:

Edith born 1835 and died at an early age.

R.W. "Bob" Lloyd born 1838 and died in the Civil War fought for the Confederacy.

Ellen born 1839 and died at an early age.

Wiley H. born 1843 and died in the Civil War; captured and died in a northern prison.

Hester Ellen born February 21, 1845, married James Jefferson Cooper in Greene County (see sketch on the Cooper family).

Nancy born October 1848 married Daniel J. Elliott and after his death in 1875, she married Doctor Adolphus G. Clyne. Dr. Clyne was a well-known doctor in Greene County and his gravestone in Browns Chapel declares him to be an "old time country doctor."

*First row from left: Cora Rogers, Winston Rogers, Joe M. Rogers, Byron Rogers and Julia Rogers. Second row from left: Joe Alton Rogers, Adrian Rogers, Cecil Rogers, Dwight Rogers and Harold Rogers.*

George W. Lloyd "Cap" as he was called, was a Methodist preacher and was one of the first ministers to serve at Woods Chapel in Greene County. He married Frances "Fanny" Highfill daughter of Rev. Hezekiah Highfill.

Thomas R. born August 22, 1858, married Claudia (maiden name unknown).

Sarah J. born 1853 married Samuel Osteen.

James H. born February 1859 married "Tennie" her maiden name is unknown.

Thomas D. died on September 11, 1887, and Sarah "Sally" died November 12, 1901, and their grave is marked with a tall spire in Browns Chapel Cemetery.

Accompanying picture is of the Cooper, Lloyd and Rogers family. List is attached of all the people that could be identified. The original photo was damaged in mailing years ago and the copy made as is.

**LLOYD/WOODS** – Uncle Cap Lloyd and Aunt Fanny (Woods) lived on a farm on what is now Wirt Street. He was a preacher at Woods Chapel. They had five children:
1. Della
2. Charlie
3. Tempa
4. KI
5. Emma

Della married Will Fligor. He cleared the land located at Sixth Street and West Kingshighway, where the Dodge Store is now located. He built their house and his cabinet shop on the lot. Will Fligor was foreman of the CCC camp when Crowley's Ridge State Park was built. Will and Della had two children:
1. Ruth married Fred Whipple and they had one child:
a. Willene who married Alan Phelps and they had four children:
I. Georgia Anne married Bob Gisiner and they had one child, Gwendolyn Margaret who is single and attends Tulane University.
II. Cora Lee married Mike Hailey and they have no children.
III. Lloyd Alan married Rita Johnson and they had two children, Charity and TJ. T. J. lives in Virginia and is single. Charity lives in New York State and has four children: Cassandra, Michael, Dillon and Hunter.
IV. Richard Steven, never married.
2. Lloyd married Grettie Miller and they had no children.

*Submitted by Willene Glover*

**LOCKWOOD** – William Riley Lockwood, seeking a warmer climate, moved south from Tomah, WI in 1902. The family of four, William, his wife Anna and their children Edith and Fred, located in Warren County, TN for 10 years. The family then relocated to Greene County, AR in 1912, buying a 79-acre farm in the Center Hill community.

While in Tennessee, Fred met and married Myrtle Willie Cooper Jan 17, 1908 and George William was born to them on July 11, 1909. After moving to Arkansas, a daughter, Winnie Ruth, was born to Fred and Myrtle on Aug 14, 1913. William Riley's health was not strengthened by the move south and family members remembered that he heard the ringing of the church bells signaling the end of WWI and he died later that day.

Fred changed the farm to a dairy business. Homemade ice cream was a family favorite in the summer months.

George married Mira Irene Weaver in 1930. They had two daughters; Alfreda Nadine and Virginia Ann. Winnie Ruth married Wiley Crowley in 1933. Two children were born to them, Frances Marion and Billy Ray.

*Standing: Fred Lockwood and Edith Lockwood; seated: Anna Lockwood and William Riley Lockwood.*

George worked for Mid-West Dairy until Sept 1943, when he became an employee of the New First National Bank (now the First National Bank of Paragould). His employment continued until retirement in Feb 1975. Mira Irene worked at Joseph's/Burr's/Belk's Department Store for over 25 years, retiring Dec 31, 1972. After Wiley Crowley's death, Winnie worked with her father in the dairy business.

*Center Hill home of William Riley and Anna Lockwood (destroyed by fire in the 1940s)*

Shiloh United Methodist Church and Griffin Memorial United Methodist Church are communities of faith that blessed our family through joys and sorrows.

For the grandchild and great-grandchildren of William Riley and Anna Lockwood still remaining to re-live family memories, Greene County will be remembered as our home where love and family ties warmed our hearts.

*Submitted by Alfreda Lockwood Spence*

**LOVELADY** – Joseph and Deborah (Harris) Lovelady emigrated to Greene County in 1852, where he was given 200 acres of land as a compensation for service rendered in the Florida War. Before coming to Greene County they lived in Hamilton County, Tennessee. Joseph was the son of John, born in Tennessee in 1787, and Mary also of Tennessee in 1789. The 1890 census shows Mary living with her son, John, in Greene County, Arkansas.

Three of Joseph's five children were born in Tennessee: John, Robert and Mariah, who later married William Spain. Joseph Jr., and Sevier were both born in Greene County. Joseph Sr. died April 12, 1861. Their son Robert became a prominent physician in Greene County, and according to Goodspeed's *History of Greene County*, he was the second resident of Crowley's Ridge to graduate in any profession.

Sevier married Josephine Kaminer Boyd on November 2, 1882. They were the parents of the following children: Ada, Nora, Paralee, Lillie, Clara, Claude, Carl, Henry, Luther and Bertha.

Ada married Calvin Green and they were living in Clay County at the time of their deaths. They had three boys: Cleo, Byran and Al and four girls: Annie Croffard, Olene Speers, Skeet Roof and Dean Simmons. Skeet and Dean are living in Rector and others have passed away.

Nora married Emery Butler and to that union were born three girls: Weda Williams, Reba Boyd and Rada Owens. Reba is living in Paragould. Weda and Rada have passed away.

Lillie first married Charlie Strait. Then she married a Carr. They had three children: Thomas, Carl James and Geneva.

*Sevier and Josephine Lovelady.*

Clara married Adolph Lee. They had three girls and a boy. Carl married Lorine Blalock and they were the parents of three children: Wayne, Louise and Kenneth. They were living in Piggott at the time of their deaths. They have a grandson, Carl, now living in Greenway.

Henry was married to Esther Miles who was a sister to Fred Miles that had married Bertha Lovelady. Bertha and Fred had one daughter, Alleen.

Luther married Irmae Green and they had three children: Lawrence Allen, who has passed away. Billy Max and Mozelle who is married to Harold Dortch. They have two children: Chip and Kim and four grandchildren.

Claude married Nellie Jackson, the daughter of Alvin and Rebecca (Hatly) Jackson. They had five children: Randall, Rachel, Bobby, Billy and Jimmy.

Randall married Betty Denbow and their issues are: Ronnie, Diane, Gary and Donna. They live in St. Louis, Missouri. Rachel married Billy Zolman and they also live in St. Louis. Bobby married Glenda Robinette and they live in Memphis, Tennessee. Their issues are: Kenneth, Glenda, Donna and Steven. Jimmy was married to Wanda Burkett to which three children were born: Debbie, Terry and Tammy. Billy married Clara Clifton and they live on the Lovelady home place near Beech Grove. They are the only Loveladys that live in Greene County that are descendants of Joseph and Deborah Lovelady; however, there are other descendants living in the county.

**LUEKER** – Charles Henry Lueker was born in Mt. Olive, IL in 1873. Mt. Olive was near Lutchfield, IL. Later, his brother, Fred Lueker and sister, Sophia moved to Augsburg, AR with his father Gottliep Lueker. Augsburg, AR is where Charles Henry Lueker married my mother, Louise Harms, Dec 15, 1906. They were blessed with eight children. Alma Lueker married Ernest Hoelscher. Ruda Lueker married Bill Panhorst. They had three children: Billy, Charles and Bobby. Pauline Lueker married Herman Gerdes and was blessed with five children:

1. Constance "Connie" Gerdes
2. Doris Jean
3. Joann
4. Marilyn
5. Carolyn Gerdes.

Herman Gerdes died when he was 32 years of age. Pauline, eight years later, married James Wallis. Erwin Lueker married Anna Marie Scheck. They had four children:

1. Erwin Jr.
2. Lizette
3. George
4. Jonathan

Anna died and Erwin married Margret Rymon. Benard married Mabel Tritch and they had five children:

1. Benny
2. Gloria Jean
3. Robert
4. Richard
5. Mark

Carl Lueker married Minnie Gerdes and they had four children:

1. Carl, Jr.
2. Karon
3. Ester
4. Lois

Louise Lueker married Harlan Welch. Lydia Lueker married Marvin Tritch and they had four children. Ronald Tritch married Donna Wooldridge and they have two children: Jason and Stacy. Stacy married Chrystal McCandless. Orin Tritch married Ann Bolick and they have two children: Kevin and Gretta. Kerry Tritch married Baker Miles and later married Kevin Reddick and they have two children: Tiffany Lenee (Reddick) Miles and Aaron Reddick. Kim Tritch, the fourth child, is living Route 2, Paragould, AR.

*Old Mill at Lafe, AR.*

Charles "Henry" Lueker and Louise "Harms" Lueker moved to Lafe, Greene County, AR in 1924. Five railroad boxcars were used to make the move. Farm equipment, chickens, hogs, cattle, four teams of horses, furniture, household goods and clothing were all moved. My father, Charles, rode the boxcar filled with equipment. The boxcars were stopped at Lafe. They settled on a 118-acre farm south of Lafe. At 9:00 a. m. and 4:00 p. m. lunches were carried to the field for the workers. At noon dinner bells were heard all over the countryside. Horses were brought in to water at the creek and then put in the barn. Men washed their hands, faces and feet before they ate lunch. Because of walking, men had to have a 30-minute rest before returning to the fields. Later, Fred Lueker bought a riding cultivator with two rows being plowed at once, which was a lot easier.

Lafe, AR had five grocery stores, a flourmill, blacksmith shop, post office, school, three doctors, a clinic, bank, and four gas stations. We would take corn and wheat to the mill to exchange for flour and cornmeal. We had our own chickens, eggs, pork and beef. We also raised our own vegetables in the garden.

My father always made sure we went to church and Sunday school. We had to milk several cows before we went to church. My father's favorite Bible verse was "Blessed are dead which die in the Lord for they shall rest from their burdens and their works do follow them." Revelations 14:13.

Charles Henry Lueker was born at Mt. Olive, IL in 1873. Louise Caroline Lueker was born at Cole Camp, Mo in 1889. Both spent their last days at Lafe, AR. Charles Henry Lueker died Nov 15, 1947 and his wife Louise died Feb 26, 1968.

*Submitted by Ronnie Tritch*

**LUEKER** – Gottlieb and Catherine (Tiermann) Lueker were married in Mt. Olive, IL. Three children were born to them while living there: Sophia, who later married Will Harms in Pope County, AR; Fred, born in 1871 and Carl, born 1873. The family moved to Pope County, AR about 1900.

Fred Lueker married Bertha Hempel from Saxony, Germany. In 1909, they moved back to Litchfield, IL. In 1911 they moved to Lafe, AR. Three children were born while they lived in Pope County, AR: Agnes (1900); Martin (1903) and Erna (1905). Another child, Frances, was born in Lafe in 1917.

Agnes married Oscar Scheer; Martin married Millie Rupp; Erna married Arthur Gerdes and Frances married (1) Dwight Cooper (2) Walter Braasch.

Charlie Lueker married Louise Harms. To them were born eight children:
1. Alma married Ernest Hoelscher
2. Ruda married Bill Panhorst
3. Pauline married (1) Herman Gerdes (2) James Wallis
4. Ervin married Annie Schick
5. Bernhard married Mabel Tritch
6. Louise married (1) David Williams (2) Harlan Welch
7. Lydia married Marvin Tritch.

**MADDOX** – Charles Berry Maddox, Sr. came to Paragould in the late 1800s. He and three brothers bought 160 acres of swampland, cleared and built a cabin from timber on the land, which was eventually called Pekin Road. He cut small timbers and laid them for a roadbed. He worked as a cook at a café, which years later were called "Corner Café," to help buy the land.

Charles met Margret White from Alamo, TN and they were married in Dec 1903. She came here and lived with her sister, Ella (White) Riggsbee and was a milliner. They moved to the farm and lived in the cabin until they built a large two-story house in the spring of 1912. To their union was born four children:
1. Charline Maddox married Millard Jones, who had Bill and Charles.
2. Martha Maddox married Jack Thomas and their children were Jackie and Martha
3. C.B. Maddox Jr. married Dorothy Davis from Brosley, MO and they had four children:
   a. Mary
   a. Mildred
   b. James

*Left to right: Edward Maddox, James Maddox, C. B. Maddox Jr., Mary Maddox, Dorothy Maddox, Mildred Maddox; center: Dorothy Maddox "Dot".*

   c. Edward
   d. Dorothy Jane
4. Helen Maddox married Clarence digs and they had Louise and Stanley Diggs.

*Left to right: C. B. Jr., Charles Berry Maddox Sr., Charline Maddox, Helen Maddox, Margaret Maddox, Martha Maddox.*

C. B. and Dorothy married in 1933. He worked at Johnson-Cloyce Hardware store for two years. They then moved to the farm in 1935, in the original house, which had been moved down the lane from the big house. He farmed with his dad until his death in 1946. In 1948 C. B. and Dorothy built a house on the original cabin plot, which is now Highway 69 and Second Avenue. He eventually bought the entire original farm except 40 acres. He and all his children were born and raised on this farm. His widow, Dorothy, still lives on and maintains the farm.

*Submitted by Millie Fleeman*

**MAHAN** – Todd Benjamin Mahan was born June 11, 1870, at Harrisburg, Poinsett County, Arkansas to Francis L. and Mary Frances (Harris) Mahan. He was the youngest of their four children. Two older sisters born in Memphis Tennessee, during the Civil War, both died there as small children. His older brother Alfred lived to be 84 years old. Both Alfred and Todd farmed south of Harrisburg for many years. Todd's father died when he was about 4 months old. His mother later married Daniel P. Barber and they had a daughter Fannie Daniel Barber who later married James Buchanan Molder and her family lived most of their lives in the Harrisburg area. Mr. Barber later died and Mary Frances married Robert Johnson, a native of Mississippi and a Confederate Army Veteran. They had no children.

As Todd was growing up his mother's brothers served as father figures for him. He seemed to be close to Uncle John M. and Uncle Chester A. Harris. The town of Harrisburg is named after Todd's great-grandfather William H. Harris.

Todd later met a young lady who was living with his uncle and aunt, Hosea and Sue (Harris) McGee. Sarah Lavenia Butler was an orphan whose mother, Mary E. (McKeown) Butler, died in Mississippi when she was a very young girl and her father Byron "Bee" Butler died when she was 12 years old. Sarah was born February 22, 1872, in Chickasaw County, Mississippi. After her father's death she lived with her stepmother Mary (McKinney) Butler and her younger brother Thomas Byron and her half-sisters Edina and Ethel and her half-brother James Harvey Butler. Her stepmother later married Webb Walker and they had several children. During that time Sarah had gone to live with "Aunt Sue" McGee. A romance developed between Todd and Sarah and they were married September 10, 1890, when she was 18 and he was 20. The newlyweds sharecropped their first year. On February 8, 1891, Todd purchased from his uncle Chester A. Harris 20 acres south of Harrisburg for $125.00. He continued to share crop additional land raising cotton and corn for sale and raised cattle, hogs and chickens and had a garden for family needs. The farm was about two miles south of Harrisburg and was reached by traveling along O'Possum Hollow Road which curved following along the top of the ridge away from town. He later bought 50 more adjoining acres from the estate of his cousin Ruth Harris. On the farm seven children were born to Todd and Sarah and are as follows:

Mary Frances "May" born July 28, 1892, died August 24, 1970, married December 10, 1910, in Harrisburg to James F. Hills (1884-1962), both buried Chapel Hill Memorial Gardens, Wyandotte County, Kansas. Parents of Lena Maude, Rena Irene, Edith Mae and Dorothy Lavenia.

Minnie Cora, born October 16, 1893, died at age of 1 year and 11 months, buried on family farm-no marker visible now.

*50th wedding anniversary, September 10, 1940, in the front yard of family home near Harrisburg, Arkansas. Front: Todd Benjamin and Sarah Lavenia (Butler) Mahan. Back from left: Sue Mahan Peck, Bess Mahan Jacob, Ollie "Bud" Mahan, Maude Mahan Mitchell, Trudie Mahan Beard and May Mahan Hills.*

Gertrude Melvernia "Trudie" born August 27, 1896, died April 20, 1951, married December 27, 1915, in Harrisburg to Robert Leo Beard (1895-1969). Trudie buried Roselawn Cemetery, Little Rock, Arkansas. Leo willed his body to The University of Arkansas Medical School. Parents of Mary Thelma, Helen Imogene and Wilma Pauline.

Ollie William "Bud" born October 8, 1898, died May 4, 1972, buried Lone Tree Cemetery, Stuttgart, Arkansas. Married several times, but the mother of his children was second wife, Mary Ann Rogers (1902-1975) buried Monette Cemetery, Monette, Arkansas. Parents of Gladys Juanita, Thomas Benjamin and Virgie Geneva.

Ora Sue born August 22, 1901, died March 30, 1997, married November 16, 1921 in Harrisburg to George Dewey Peck (1889-1955); both buried Memorial Cemetery, Fremont, Nebraska. Parents of Ruby Doris and George Robert.

Bessie Fay "Bess" born August 28, 1903, died August 18, 1988, married June 11, 1922, in Harrisburg to Eugene Ellis "Jake" Jacob (1902-1980) both buried Linwood Cemetery, Paragould. They had no children and adopted a son Kim.

Maude born May 29, 1906, died October 6, 1992, married December 24, 1932, in Harrisburg to Alvie Murl Mitchell (1904-1981); both buried Linwood Cemetery, Paragould. Parents of Benjamin Eugene and Thomas Murl.

Todd and Sarah Mahan continued to live on the farm south of Harrisburg until 1949 when they sold it and moved to Paragould at 907 Wirt Street near their daughter Maude. Todd Mahan died February 16, 1960, and is buried in Linwood Cemetery in Paragould.

Sarah lived to be almost 99 years old dying November 7, 1970, at Community Methodist Hospital in Paragould of pneumonia-the only time she was ever a patient in a hospital. Her body was laid to rest beside her husband Todd.

**MANN** – Buddy Lee Mann was born April 15, 1925 at Red Onion, near Cardwell, MO. the second child of Melvin and Iona Bryson Mann, he has lived in Greene County his whole life and attended Lakeside School.

Buddy was drafted into the army in 1943 at the age of 18. After basic training at Fort Hood, TX, Fort Lewis, WA and Fort Bragg, NC, he was shipped to England, then to the Alsace-Lorraine region of France. His battalion fought all across Germany and at the end of WWII, he was near Munich, Germany. He saw the Dachau and Buchenwald concentration camps. After the war ended, Buddy was assigned to defusing bomb and artillery duds in Germany. While in Germany, he saw his brother, Duane, for the first time in three or four years. Buddy was discharged in 1946.

He and his sweetheart, Ida Florine Swafford (Jan 22, 1928) were married Nov 14, 1946.

In 1949 Buddy joined the Marine Reserves. He was called to active duty in 1950. After a six-week refresher course, he was shipped to Korea. He was in the First Marine Division, initially assigned to B Company, 1st Battalion, 7th Regiment and then to B Company 1st Motor Transport Battalion as a fuel truck driver and later as company dispatcher. He rotated back to the states in 1951 and was discharged in 1952.

One highlight of Buddy's life occurred in Sept 1994. Touring Washington, D. C. with the Senior Bees, he and three other veterans were chosen from the group to place a wreath at the Tomb of the Unknown Soldier.

*Buddy Lee and Ida Florine Swafford Mann and children, Martha Jean and Richard Lee*

Buddy worked for Partain's Furniture and was one of the original employees of Emerson Electric. He retired from the Paragould Post Office in 1990 with 30 years of Federal service.

Gospel music has always played a big part in Buddy's life. He was a member of the Gospelaires from 1950 to 1967 and of the Songsmen Quartet from 1967 to 1985.

Buddy played baseball all his life and played in the softball league until age 60. He was a certified baseball umpire for the Babe Ruth League in the 60s and 70s and was on the football Chain Gang for PHS in the 70s and 80s.

Ida Florine Swafford, raised by her mother, Ethel Daily Langley and stepfather Curtis Langley, never knew her father Ed Swafford. Her parents had divorced when she was a baby.

Ethel Pearl Daily (1909-1994) was born in Greene County, the daughter of Josephine Smith (1879-1954) of Hamburg, IL. Josephine's parents were Jasper and Elizabeth Smith. Ethel's father was Perry Elvis Peterson (1859) of Hartford, IN. The Daily family had adopted him.

Florine has a half-brother, Elmer Gene Langley (1936) of Colorado Spring, CO. He is a PHS and ASU graduate. A retired elementary school principal, he is currently involved in real estate.

Florine graduated from PHS in 1946. Her first job was at Potter's Shoe Store. She also worked at the Shirt Factory. She began working at Belk's in 1960 and retired in 1984.

She and Buddy have been active members of the Assembly of God Church for over 50 years.

They have two children, five grandchildren and two great-grandchildren.

Their daughter, Martha Jean Trotter (Dec 18, 1947) graduated from PHS in 1965. She is a lab technician for City Light and Water in Paragould. She married Tom Gurley in 1965. They had two sons, Michael Gurley (Aug 26, 1966) and Jason Gurley (Nov 10, 1970). They divorced and she married Don Trotter (March 6, 1944) on Oct 21, 1974. They have two sons, Mitchell Trotter (Jan 10, 1976) and Brian Trotter (Sept 19, 1977).

Richard Lee Mann (Sept 30, 1952) is a 1970 PHS valedictorian and graduate of Arkansas State University. He is supervisor of customer services at the Paragould Post Office. He married Brenda Kay Reynolds (Sept 24, 1950) on May 19, 1972.

Their daughter, Katrina Marie (Jan 21, 1976), a graduate of RHS and ASU, married Paul Prince in 1999.

*Submitted by Buddy Mann*

**MANN** – Melvin Duane Mann born January 19, 1923, and died April 23, 1994, the first born of Melvin Dured Mann and Hattie Iona Bryson, married Velda Alice Collier of Craighead County on February 29, 1949, in Paragould at the home of his parents.

Duane joined the Civilian Conservation Corps when he was 18.

He volunteered for the Army on April 9, 1943. With Company A, 65th Signal Battalion, he served 18 months in Europe. He participated in the Rhineland and Central Europe Campaigns. He was discharged March 29, 1946. He joined the Army Reserves February 7, 1949, and was called to active duty October 8, 1950.

*Melvin Duane Mann and Velda Alice Collier Mann, April 1949*

He went straight to Korea after only a few days at Fort Hood, Texas. He was with the 2nd Battalion, 35th Infantry Regiment, 25th Infantry Division. He rotated out of Korea September 23, 1951, and was discharged January 30, 1953.

He said he ran through the streets of Seoul, Korea four times, twice he was chasing the Chinese and twice they were chasing him. Duane said that winters in Korea were as bad as the enemy! One time they were trying to take a hill, but it was so slick that they kept sliding back to the bottom of the hill. They would laugh about this to keep from cracking up. He talked about trying to sleep in the pup tents in sub-zero weather, two men to a tent. A pup tent was five feet long. Duane was six feet two inches tall. No matter what he did, one end was always sticking out!

Velda Alice Collier was born November 2, 1928, in the Hackberry Community, south of Caraway, Arkansas, in Craighead County, the sixth of nine children born to Thomas Andrew Collier born January 5, 1900, and Vertie Mae Bogard born October 19, 1905. Her father, Thomas was born in Pope County, Illinois, the third son of James and Margaret Collier. Her mother was born near Owensboro, Kentucky, to Loyd Bogard and Magnolia Cox. They married December 23, 1918, in Ancell, Scott County, Missouri. Margrett, the oldest child, was born in 1919 in Missouri. The family then moved to Golconda, Pope County, Illinois, where Claire, Vivian and Zenobia were born. In February 1925 they moved near Caraway, Arkansas, where Zella, Velda, Bud, Tommy and Faye were born.

Melvin met Velda at Caraway while his family was farming at Milligan Ridge, a small community between Caraway and Manila. They remained in Paragould after they were married. Melvin and Velda worked at whatever they could to make a living, especially picking cotton. Melvin worked for the railroad for a while and temporarily for City Light and Water.

When he returned from Korea, he worked for ARKLA Gas laying pipelines for the city of Paragould. He went to work for CL and W April 4, 1953, and retired February 1, 1985, after 32 years. He was outside foreman. He retired in 1991 as a Paragould volunteer fireman with 20 years.

Velda was busy at home caring for four children; but when they were older, she worked at the Ely and Walker Shirt Factory for 13 years and then worked briefly at the Home for the Golden Years until her poor health forced her retirement. She has been a member of First Assembly of God since July 28, 1957.

All of their children are Paragould High School graduates.

Patricia Ann born October 26, 1950, while her Dad was in Korea, married Barry Dale Letson on December 10, 1968. She has been employed at M. F. Block Insurance, Inc. for 31 years. Barry works at the AHTD. They live in Paragould and attend Victory General Baptist Church in Jonesboro. They have two daughters: Beth (Mrs. Greg) Beeler who has two daughters and Tina (Mrs. Keith) Jackson.

Melvin Dwight born March 12, 1953, meat market manager for Farmers Market in Leachville, married Patricia Lynn Tucker on May 8, 1987. She works for Arlees in Leachville. They have six children: Michael, Kevin, Melanie, Misty, Matthew and Tiffany and six grandchildren.

Brenda Sue and Linda Lou were born December 20, 1954. They are both employees of the U.S. Postal Service–Brenda in Paragould and Linda in Jonesboro.

Brenda married Charles Alan Vangilder May 7, 1977. They have two sons, Jason and Daniel. Alan is manager at Hogland's.

Linda married Robert Dale Forrest January 1, 1983. They have three children: Robby, Heather and Andrea. Bob works for the USDA.

**MANN** – Melvin Dured Mann (1902-1983) and Hattie Iona Bryson (1904-1975) were married April 7, 1922, in Paragould, Arkansas. Melvin's grandparents, John and Fannie Hall were in Paragould as early as the 1880s. They ran a hotel near the intersection of Pruett and Main Streets.

Melvin's parents, Terry Abraham Mann and Ida Mae Nall were married in Ripley County, Missouri. His father deserted the family when he was 6 months old. His mother moved to Paragould in the early 1900s and later married Edward Otho Acuff. They had four children: Nolen, Cecil, Edna Mae and Alfred.

*Melvin Dured Mann and Hattie Iona Bryson Mann and their children: back row: Thomas Terry Mann and Melvin Duane Mann. Front row: Norma Faye, Buddy Lee and Merle Glenn. Picture taken shortly after World War II.*

Iona's family, John Pinkney and Martha Jane Austin Bryson came to Arkansas from Benton County, Tennessee, in 1900 and settled near Gainesville. Iona was orphaned as a teenager, her education over at the eighth grade. She went to live with her older sister, Laura Jackman, in the Village Creek Community south of Paragould.

After Melvin's mother remarried he didn't get along with his stepfather, so at the tender age of 11 he ran away from his home in Paragould. His formal education ended in the fifth grade, but his real education was just beginning. He traveled on trains and lived alongside the railroad tracks with hobos for the next several years. He talked of sitting around the campfires at night, eating out of tin cans. At one point in time he worked for Kelloggs in Michigan.

He eventually returned to Paragould and married at the age of 19. Iona was 17. They began married life with a skillet and a quilt. He went to work for Wrapes Heading Mill and she worked as a domestic on "the other side of the tracks."

Often in the fall of the year they would take their family and a "batching outfit" and go pick cotton in the Bootheel of Missouri. Her sister's family, W. H. and Eula McCord would generally pick with them. Occasionally they would try sharecropping, but would go broke and come back to Paragould and the Mill. They talked of going to square dances in the 1920s and dancing all night. They were excellent dancers and won many contests.

In the late 1930s Melvin worked with the W.P.A. and helped construct several roads and schools in Greene County, including Highway 141 thru Stanford and also the school there.

Although he was raised Primitive Baptist and she Methodist, they began attending the Assembly of God Church on Lake Street in the early 1930s at their oldest son's insistence. They became active members and workers in the church for many years. Both Melvin and Iona loved to sing and in the 1930s they sang gospel music on the radio, sometimes as a duet, or as a trio with Richard Pickney. Melvin sang lead or tenor and Iona sang a beautiful natural alto. Their descendants are still active in that same church which is now located on Fairview Road.

In the 1940s Melvin worked as a section foreman for the Missouri Pacific Railroad. He was also an excellent carpenter and barber. During the Depression he cut hair for the whole neighborhood for free. Iona took in "washin' and ironin'" for folks on the West side of town. Her boys would use a little wagon to pick up and deliver the clothes.

They had five children: Melvin Duane (1923-1994), Buddy Lee (born 1925), Thomas Terry (1928-1995), Merle Glenn (born 1931) and Norma Faye (born 1939). All but Merle Glenn lived, married and raised families in Paragould. Merle and his family live in Texas.

While growing up, the boys worked at various jobs such as a cook at the Corner Cafe, Wrapes Heading Mill, and picking cotton.

Duane Buddy served in the Army during World War II in Europe. Duane and Merle served in the Army and Buddy and Tommy in the Marines in the Korean War. They were all four in Korea at the same time. Merle served in Vietnam.

Duane, Buddy and Tommy attended V.A. School at night to get their G.E.D.s. Merle obtained his while in the military.

The four brothers were inducted into the Veteran's Hall of Fame at Greene County Tech High School in 1996.

**MANN** – Merle (Mug-gen) Glen Mann (Hottie) born March 14, 1931, is the youngest son of Melvin Dured and Hattie Iona (Bryson) Mann. He attended schools in Greene and Mississippi County. He was a pitcher for the American Legion Team in Manila.

Merle enlisted in the Army shortly after he turned 17, on June 19, 1948. He retired July 1, 1968, with the grade of E6 as a Senior Emergency Medical Instructor. He served in both the Korean and Vietnam War. He served two tours of duty in Korea, one in Vietnam, two in Germany and one in Hawaii. Stateside he was stationed at Fort Meyers, Virginia; Fort Ricker, Alabama; Ford Hood, Texas and others.

All four brothers were on the front line in Korea at the same time and during some of the fiercest fighting of the war. Merle went to see Duane just before Duane rotated home. He went to see Tommy, but got there about eight hours after Tommy rotated out.

While in the service Merle was active in all sports and was a pitcher for the Division Trains Baseball Team.

On December 10, 1953, Merle married his childhood sweetheart, Margaret Ellen Keeling, of Milligan Ridge, Arkansas. They were married at Black Oak, Arkansas, by Justice of Peace Johnson.

Ellen, born March 18, 1934, in Roseland, Arkansas, near Manila and the Little River was the fifth of 11 children of Finis Andrew Keeling born November 3, 1901, died September 18, 1975, married September 1, 1923, and Luva LaVada Littleton born July 17, 1907, died November 18, 1983. Ellen's father Finis was born at Russelville to John Tildon Keeling and Sarah Marlene. The Keelings migrated from Germany in the 1700s. Ellen's mother, LaVada, was born at Atkins, Arkansas, to William Oscar Littleton and Mattie Ellen Banks. Ellen's first four siblings Ruth, J.W., Ruby and Ethelene were born at Pottsville, Arkansas. The sixth and seventh babies, Charlene and Joan were born on Little River near Lost Cane in Mississippi County. Number eight and nine, Janelle and Connie were born near the Friendship Community in Greene County. The two youngest, Barbara and Ronnie, were born at Milligan Ridge in Mississippi County. Three of Ellen's siblings, J.W., Barbara and Ruby currently reside in Greene County.

*Merle G. Mann Sr. and Margaret Ellen (Keeling) Mann and daughter Carolyn Ann, 1957, by the Tomb of the Unknown Soldier.*

Merle and Ellen were boyfriend and girlfriend since he was 13 and she was 10. Once Ellen was folding clothes in the bedroom and Merle grabbed Ellen and kissed her. About that time her dad, Finis, walked by, so Merle jumped behind the door. Well, her dad stopped and started talking to Ellen and the longer he talked, the more he leaned on the door. He finally leaned on it so hard that Merle had to groan. Mr. Keeling then pulled open the door and said "Boy, what are you doing behind the door?" When they were in their teens, they would smooch behind the doors. Always, Ellen's little brothers and sisters would run tell their dad. Not long after Merle joined the Army, Ellen and Ruby went to Michigan to live with their married sister Ethelene and to find work. After several years in the Army, Merle looked Ellen up, and they were married.

Ellen attended school in Mississippi County. Merle and Ellen are retired and live near Fort Hood, Texas. They have four children and eight grandchildren, all who live in the same area.

**MANN** – Norma Faye Mann, daughter of Melvin and Iona Mann, was born in Greene County on August 24, 1939. She attended schools in Greene and Mississippi Counties, and received her G.E.D. in 1963. She has since attended ASU., N.W. Mississippi Junior College and Cornell University.

As a child, Norma spent a great deal of time chopping, picking and pulling cotton in Arkansas and Arizona. She and her family also picked fruit in Michigan. At the age of 14, she quit school and went to work as a housekeeper for a family who owned a grocery store in Paragould. The hours were 7:00 a.m. until 6:00 p.m, six days a week. The salary was $15.00 a week. Her parents kept half of that for room and board.

At the age of 15, she went to work for Hollowell's Cafe as a waitress, cook, and dishwasher. The hours were 7:00 a.m. to 4:00 p.m., six days a week, the salary was $17.00 per week. After one year, she got a raise to $19.00 a week.

When she was 18 years old Norma went to work for Kroger. It was August 26, 1957. The salary was $1.00 an hour. Men made 5 cents more per hour. Norma thought she was rich. Her Dad was making 75 cents an hour at Wrapes Heading Mill. For the most part she worked at Kroger and Big Star for the next 25 years and resigned March 1, 1983, as co-manager at Kroger to stay at home and raise her daughter, Kristin.

Norma was married January 26, 1960, to George Edwin Hunt born June 12, 1937, son of George Elonzo and Ethel Mae (Gregory) Hunt of Stanford. From this marriage she has one son, Timothy Edwin Hunt born January 16, 1961. The marriage ended in divorce.

Tim Hunt was an honor graduate from

Stanford High School in 1979. He graduated from the University of Arkansas in 1983, and was an honor graduate from the University of Tennessee Dental School in Memphis in 1987.

Dr. Tim Hunt has a dental practice in Paragould. He was married June 27, 1987, to Carla Lyan Hughes born February 19, 1959, of Memphis. Carla's parents, Dr. Walter and Jeanette Skinner Hughes are both Tennessee natives. Carla is a graduate of Memphis State University, and Arkansas State University. She is a kindergarten teacher at L. W. Baldwin School. They have two children, Amanda Bryson Hunt and Collin Hughes Hunt.

*John and Norma Mann Addison and family. John's daughter Kathy (back); Norma's father Melvin Mann Sr., and Norma's son, Tim Hunt and John and Norma's daughter, Kristin, in front, 1982.*

Norma was remarried July 24, 1977, to John Wiley Addison born June 16, 1937, of Jonesboro. John is the son of Wiley Oliver Addison and Lillie Mae Richardson. John is retired from the United States Air Force, and is currently a captain with the Paragould Police Department. He was selected Law Officer of the Year in 1989. He is a graduate of Arkansas State University with a degree in criminology. He has four children from a previous marriage.

John Addison's children are:

Lily Margarete Addison, a graduate of Nettleton High School and ASU. She is a lab technologist for Baptist Hospital in Little Rock.

Lawrence Wiley Addison, graduate of Nettleton High School, is a body shop manager in Jonesboro. He is married to Robin Hoke.

Bruce Eugene Addison, graduate of Nettleton High School, is married to Vickie Ring of Cave City, an ASU graduate. They are both employees of the Jonesboro School District. They have two children, Danielle Nicole and Matthew Oliver. Bruce has one daughter by a previous marriage, Ashley Marie of Boise, Idaho.

Kathryn Renee Addison, a 1982 graduate of Paragould High School lives in Boise, Idaho, with her daughter, Storie Rene` Hall. Kathy is an assistant equipment buyer for Albertson's in Boise.

John and Norma have one daughter, Kristin Johanna Addison born December 11, 1980. Kristin was the valedictorian of her 1999 graduation class of Greene County Tech High School. She is currently attending Harding University in Searcy, Arkansas.

The Addison's attend church at Seventh and Mueller Church of Christ where they are involved in several ministries.

Norma has been or is currently in the Greene County Historical and Genealogical Society, 4-H Leader, GCT Band Booster Officer, Greene County Fair Superintendent, and Master Gardener. She and John have also been foster parents.

They currently live on 29 acres, south of Paragould in the Old Village Creek Community, where they garden, raise animals and enjoy nature and wildlife.

**MANN** – Thomas Terry Mann was born March 4, 1928, and died November 11, 1995, in Greene County, the middle child of Melvin and Iona Mann. He attended Lakeside School and worked at the Corner Cafe and Wrapes Heading Mill in addition to picking cotton. He joined the Marine Reserves February 15, 1949, along with his brother Buddy. He was ordered to active duty June 5, 1951. He received basic training at Camp Pendleton, California. He was sent to Korea and was with the First Marine Division. He made corporal November 23, 1951. He left Korea April 10, 1952, and was discharged October 8, 1952. He was in Korea during some of the fiercest fighting. Once a hand grenade landed at his feet. It was a dud. Another time his company was trying to take a hill, and the enemy was attacking them from the top of the hill, and the U.S. Navy was firing heavy artillery at them from the coast. Tommy and his brothers, Duane and Buddy, served as Color Guard for several years at parades, ballgames, and other ceremonies.

Tommy retired from City Light and Water in March 1990 with 30 years of service. He was a construction supervisor. Tommy enjoyed working in yards and loved flowers. At one time, after his retirement, he was taking care of 40 or more lawns.

On August 1, 1953, he married Eva Dean Snyder born April 3, 1933. Eva is the daughter of James Carl (William) Snyder born September 1, 1905, and died February 12, 1995. William was born in Stanford, the son of Walter Jerome and Lilly Belle Snyder. Eva's mother is Margaret Alice Patton born April 25, 1912, and died April 13, 1987, born in Missouri, her parents were Alvin and May Patton. Eva was the second of 11 children. Her siblings: Dorothy, Lois, Lily Mae, Billy Gene, Anna Faye, Diane, Michael and Cathy were all born in Greene County. Eva, Juanita and F.A. were born in Craighead County.

*Thomas Terry Mann and Eva Snyder Mann at Walcott State Park.*

In 1951 Eva graduated from Dixie High School. Eva worked at several places in Paragould including Ed White Shoe Factory, Home for Golden Years, Big Star Bakery and Paragould Laundry. She and Tommy attended the Assembly of God Church.

Tommy (Terry) and Eva have two daughters, both Greene County Tech graduates.

Beverly Kay Mann, born February 3, 1956, graduated in 1974, married Terry Scott born December 4, 1976. They have one son, Phillip Dean Scott born December 10, 1978. They moved to Humble, Texas, in 1983 and own Scott's Janitorial Service.

Terry Lynn Mann born June 24, 1961, honor graduate 1979, married Gene Smith born May 30, 1964, on November 3, 1984. She is employed at Northeast Arkansas Obstetrics and Gynecology, P.A. and Gene is employed at Darling Store Fixtures.

**MARSHALL** – Hoyt B. Marshall (Feb 1, 1903) son of John and Emma Marshall was born in Craighead County. He married Louisy C. Atchison, daughter of Elbert and Lucy (Holt) Atchison, on Dec 15, 1923.

Hoyt B. and Louisy had two children, Martha Ann and Hoyt E. who married Maxine Ferguson. Martha Ann married (1) Burrell A. Thompson, who died Sept 2, 1986 (2) James R. Chiles on Nov 28, 1993.

Hoyt B. had two brothers, Russell Marshall and Leonard Robertson and three sisters. His sister, Alma married Charlie West, Erna married Brewer Glenn and Clara married Ed Mesche.

The Marshalls were active in community and political affairs in Greene County. Hoyt was a businessman and raised registered white face Hereford cattle. He was a member of First United Methodist Church.

*Hoyt Marshall*

Hoyt B. died June 26, 1967 and Louisy died March 12, 1960. They are buried in Linwood Cemetery. They left a legacy for their family to cherish down through the ages.

*Submitted by Martha Chiles*

**MARTIN** – Alois Martin came to the United States twice during the 1880s from his birthplace in Moersch, Baden, Germany. Born September 5, 1854, he married Christiana Kastner, also of Moersch, on February 3, 1880. Florian, his first son, was born in Moersch, now known as Rheinstetten, on November 19, 1880. Alois and family arrived in New York aboard *SS Herder* on March 16, 1881, and settled in Fort Wayne, Indiana. His first daughter Anna was born there in 1882. Before his second daughter Sophia was born in December 1883, he had moved back to Germany to settle some affairs with his brothers. Ludwig, 1886, and Rosa, 1888, were born in Moersch before Alois moved his family to America for the second time. The family arrived in New York on October 29, 1888, aboard *SS La Bretagne*, and in June 1889 Charles was born in Indiana.

*1930 reunion of the Martin family for the 50th anniversary of Alois and Christiana. Front from left: Sophia, Alois, Christiana and Anna. Back from left: Louis, Charles, Florian, Rosa, Otto and Frank.*

Alois and Christiana's last six children were born in Paragould: Louisia, 1892; Katherina, 1894; Karolina, 1897; Frank, 1898; Otto, 1900; and Helena, 1906. The family spent some time in Pocahontas before moving. Alois bought a lot in Paragould (Lot 3, Block 2, in the Cardwell Addition) from J. F. Cardwell on July 22, 1892, paying $45.00. His home, still standing, was on Pekin Road, a block south of 149.

Alois' first three Paragould daughters died young: Louisia, age 4, in 1897; Katherina, age 11 months, in 1895; and Karolina, 1 month, in 1897. They are buried in Linwood Cemetery in a single grave with the inscription, "Hier ruhen imfrieden drei geschwester, Katherina, Karolina and Louisia Martin." (Here rest in peace three sisters...) Daughter Helena, Alois' favorite, died of blood poisoning in 1915 at age 9, and is buried in St. Mary's Cemetery.

Alois worked as a laborer at Pekin Cooperage Company, but spent much time tending his grapes and his garden. He was also an early and active member of St. Mary's Catholic Church in Paragould. Alois and Christiana celebrated their 50th wedding anniversary in Paragould in 1930, and their eight adult children returned home for the event.

The Martin children proved to be independent, moving to various parts of the country. Florian remained closest, settling in Cardwell, Missouri. Anna (Welling) moved to Texline, Texas, in the Panhandle. Sophia (Kolb) settled in Edmond, Oklahoma. Ludwig (Louis) moved to St. Louis, as did Otto and Rosa (Desmond). Charles settled in Appalachin, New York, and Frank in Baraboo, WS.

Christiana died of a heart attack in the family home on August 1, 1935, at age 75, and Alois, grief-stricken, fell ill and died at Alexian Brothers Hospital, St. Louis, on January 17, 1936, at age 81. Alois and Christiana had been residents of Paragould for 44 years. Both are buried in St. Mary's Cemetery.

Alois came from a long line of Martins who were linen weavers in Moersch, near Karlsruhe. Johann married there in 1743; son Lorenz, born 1767 and Franz, Alois' father, born 1807. Many Martin cousins still live in Rheinstetten. Until they died in the 1960s, Florian and Sophia continued to write to their German cousins, and several descendants have visited since then

**MARTIN** – Evered Meade Martin was born Dec 25, 1835 in Shelby County, KY to Mansfield and Susan (Cox) Martin. Evered was in the Union army, White County, IL, Company G, 87th Infantry. He married Miss Elizabeth Hedges, daughter of John Hedges and Lucinda Stallings on Oct 24, 1853. They had nine children:
1. Lavassa L. (male?) (1855 KY- unknown)
2. William Henry (1856 KY- unknown)
3. John M. (1858 KY)
4. Franklin "Eugene" (March 18, 1861 KY)
5. Sarah "Sallie" Elizabeth (April 29, 1867 IL)
6. George W. (1869 IL)
7. Charlie E. Aug 19, 1872 IL)
8. Mary J. (1876 AR)
9. Georgia Ann (1881 AR)

This birthplace information is from the 1880 Greene County, AR Census.

Evered and Elizabeth brought their family to Greene County, AR prior to Nov 1876, as Mary J. Martin was born here then. E. M. Martin purchased property in Greene County in 1878. Elizabeth (Hedges) Martin died Sept 6, 1889 and Evered died April 3, 1891. He accidentally shot himself crossing a fence with a loaded shotgun. Both are buried at Pruett's Chapel Cemetery. In the 1880 census his occupation was listed as "farmer". Three of his children, Charlie E. Martin, Sarah Elizabeth (Martin) Woods Benner and Georgia Ann (Martin) Branch are buried at Pruett's Chapel.

Franklin "Eugene" Martin married Harriett Ann Nichols/Nockols, daughter of John Nichols/Nickols, Sept 24, 1882 in Greene County, AR. They had at least five children:
1. John Everett (Sept 10, 1884- Jan 21, 1970) is buried at Finch Cemetery
2. Thomas Jewell (Sept 12, 1886 –1902/4) of pneumonia, burial place unknown
3. Mary Louanne (Martin) Vannoy (July 28, 1889- Aug 8, 1971) buried at Shiloh Cemetery
4. Two unnamed infants buried beside Harriett (Nichols) Martin at Browns Chapel Cemetery.

Harriett (Nichols) Martin died about 1893. Eugene married Mrs. Mollie Nix, Sept 17, 1894. They moved to Boone County, AR and had two more daughters: Mary Frances (headstone reads Frances M. Sneeringer), Aug 16, 1895, married William Z. Bates Sept 1, 1912 in Boone County, AR.

*Elizabeth (Hedges) Martin with Mary J. and Georgia Ann about 1888/89.*

Frances (Martin) Bates Sneeringer died Nov 10, 1972 and is buried at Maplewood Cemetery, Harrison, AR and Maggie (about 1899) married Johnny B. Carpenter Nov 1, 1916 in Paragould. Maggie Carpenter died in 1918 in the Great Flu Epidemic at Paragould, place of burial unknown. It is believed Eugene Martin married a third time to Mrs. Jane Gaither. It is not known when or where Eugene died or is buried.

John Everett Martin married Ora Effie Wilkins, daughter of Joseph Jefferson and Sarah Jane (Griffin) Wilkins in Capps, Boone County, AR, Dec 19, 1906. They were the parents of eight children
1. Clara Ella (1907)
2. Zola Corneli (1909)
3. Joseph Eugene (1911- 1972)
4. Ralph Ernest (1914-1916)
5. Edna Marie (1917- 1938)
6. Minnie Juanita   (Oct 19, 1920)
7. John Porter (1923)
8. Effie "Grace" (1930-1999)

John Everett Martin had various occupations, including: railroad worker, minister, newspaper editor, justice of the peace and custodian of the First Church of God in Paragould.

Juanita Martin had seven children:
1. Harold Dean Morris, twin (1937-1937)
2. Willie Gene Morris, twin (1937-1937)
3. Seva Aldene Morris (1938)
4. Charlene Futrell (1942)
5. Claudene Futrell (1943)
6. Christine Laverne Futrell (1946)
7. Chester "Wayne " Seats (1952)

Some information and photo given by: Catherine Holt of Paragould, granddaughter of Sarah Elizabeth (Martin) Woods Benner. Additional Information given by: Mary Stanley of Owensboro, KY.

*Submitted by Charlene (Futrell) Peel*

**MARTIN** – John Raymond "Jack" Martin was born December 29, 1905, in Calhoun County, Iowa to Mary Caroline (Trullinger) and Harvey Benjamin Martin; the youngest of two children.

Jack was interested in electronics as a boy, receiving his first amateur radio license at the age of 16. When he moved to Arkansas as an adult, his assigned call letters were W5HFP. Upon graduation from Rockwell City High School in Iowa in 1926, Jack entered Gulf Radio School in New Orleans, Louisiana, where he became an instructor after completing the course. He held several jobs installing or operating radio stations, the last being in Little Rock, Arkansas, at KGJF, which later became KARK. It was there he met Edna Earle Haggard, the seventh of eight children born to Addie (Whitworth) and Hiram Charles Haggard; born April 5, 1910, in Louisiana (we think). She graduated from St. Vincent's School of Nursing in Little Rock, June 1929.

Jack and Edna were married in Benton, Arkansas, on July 5, 1929, and moved to Paragould, Arkansas in March 1930. Their first child, Patricia, was born August 6, 1930. Jack worked for W. J. Beard installing Radio Station KBTM, continuing as station engineer for one year and 10 months. Due to the Depression, Mr. Beard could not pay wages to Jack, so he quit, returning to Iowa to work for his father in his plumbing business.

In December 1932 Jack and family moved to Hot Springs, Arkansas, where he worked at Sam Stone Music Box repairing radios. In December 1933 Jack was summoned back to Paragould by Mr. Beard to help move KBTM to Jonesboro. Here they would stay the remainder of their lives. Edna worked at Dr. McClure's Clinic, Dickson Memorial Hospital and private-duty nursing for several years, then joined Jack in running his business.

*Edna (Haggard) and John "Jack" Martin, 1974.*

Jack established Martin Radio Repair Shop in 1935 on North Pruett, later moving to 220 South Pruett, next to Clyde Mack Company. Son John Jr., was born January 31, 1935, and Betty Jo was born August 28, 1937.

In 1941 Jack built a home at 1207 West Kingshighway for his family, including his father, Harvey, who was living with them. Harvey married Calada Webb December 25 that year and moved to her home on South Fourth Street.

A fire destroyed the Radio Shop in 1948. Jack proceeded to fulfill his dream, along with Edna, establishing Martin Wholesale Radio Supply in a building behind their home. That business flourished and supported three generations of the family. Changes in the industry resulted in closing the business May 30, 1989.

Jack's retirement years were busy socially and he was active with his "Ham" radio hobby. He lived with Betty the last two years of his life. Edna died September 11, 1977, in Paragould and Jack died June 19, 1990, in Paragould. Both are buried in Linwood Cemetery in Paragould. Survivors were Patricia, husband Stanley Dennis, and five children; John Jr., wife Martha (Dover), and three children; Betty (widow of Robert Clayton) and four children.

**MASTERSON** – Norman James Masterson was born in Dexter, MO on April 28, 1917 to Harley and Ethel Durham Masterson. In 1922, the family moved to Craighead County.

On Friday the 13th day of Sept 1940, he sat in a recruiter's office in Little Rock, AR. With him were, Henry Norris Cathey of Paragould, Garrett King of El Dorado, Wallace Adams of Lake City and a Mr. Timberlake. The recruiter told the men he had three openings – Panama, Puerto Rico and the Philippines. The group looked at Norman and he replied "the Philippines".

After a two-week stay at Ft. McDowell, CA, the group boarded the USA T. Grant, headed for Manila Bay. Norman had been on the island of Corregidor for 13 months when Japan bombed Pearl Harbor followed by the Philippines the following day. General McArthur sent orders that Corregidor be defended to the last man, however on May 6, 1942, General Wainwright walked right past Norman carrying the white flag of surrender. By this time, there no trees left standing on the island.

The first six months of internment was at Camp Cabanatuan on the Philippines. Norman survived solely on rice with worms in it. For the next three years, home would be Camp Mukden in Manchuria, China. Temperatures plummeted to –40 degrees at night. During the first winter, 500 of the 1500 prisoners died.

*Norman James Masterson aboard the USA T. Grant in 1940.*

Here they ate fish heads, milo, dog and iguana. Russian soldiers liberated the camp after the atomic bombs were dropped on Hiroshima and Nagasaki. Norman later found out plans had been made to march the officers to another location and execute the enlisted men. Before this could be done, the United States parachuted four officers (three American and one Chinese) into the camp to inform the captors that Japan was going to surrender at noon that day.

The first leg of Norman's journey home was aboard a B24 bomber flying from Okinawa to the Philippines. In talking to the co-pilot, he found out the pilot was from Jonesboro, AR. The co-pilot told him to sit in his seat while he napped. Norman laughs about being the co-pilot on the first plane he ever flew on. At the Philippines, he boarded a ship for the return to San Francisco. Only three of the five sitting in the recruiter's office on that Friday the 13th came home.

On Norman's first day back in Jonesboro, he met Hazel Dean Pearce at the Armistice parade. They were married soon and had three children: Gary Norman, Charlotte Ann and Judy Kay. The family moved to Paragould in 1963 and Hazel died on April 23, 1989. Norman worked as a tractor mechanic for Bridger Farm Supply in Jonesboro and Curtis Cruse Equipment in Paragould before retiring after 32 years. In 1993, he was elected to the Greene County Tech Veterans Hall of Fame sporting a POW medal, bronze star, eight campaign ribbons and three presidential citations.

**MAY** – William Thomas May was born December 28, 1855, close to Hollow Rock, Carroll County, Tennessee. His father was Green B. May (second) who was born in Tennessee in 1835. Green B. May (second) was shot down in his own front yard in 1864 by a roving band of bushwhackers. Green was about 29 or 30 years old. He was not a soldier. Researchers found that four brothers of the surname May settled around Amelia County, Virginia, in the early 1700s. They were Thomas, John, Benjamin and William. It is believed they were English because in 1750-51 in King and Queen counties of Virginia, there was an account book belonging to a merchant that listed various charges to William May Jr., Benjamin May, James May, Thomas May and Juda May. These are all names that have continued on thru our family line in Bute County (later Franklin County), North Carolina.

William Thomas May is a direct descendant of William May, who is believed to be the son of one of the four May brothers. William Thomas May married Narcissus Adaline Hollingsworth on April 7, 1878, in Hollow Rock, Carroll County, Tennessee. Narcissus was the daughter of Robert Hollingsworth and Mary Willett. They reared nine children and eight of them were born in Carroll and Benton Counties, in Tennessee and the ninth child was born in Paragould, Arkansas.

Their children were: Leona, Julia, Margaret, Henry Elmer, William Edgar, John Calvin, Robert L., Clara Estele and Myrtle. The May family like so many others came to Arkansas searching for a brighter tomorrow. They had come to Greene County around 1900.

The four boys attended Oak Grove School, north of Paragould. Henry Elmer often talked about having to carry water from a spring up to the school. A picture of the Oak Grove School, with teacher and students was made in 1902. The exact location of the school at that time is not known. Stories have it located east of Highway 135 there in the Oak Grove Community, possibly moving later to a location in the general vicinity of the present Oak Grove Baptist Church.

*Top row: Calvin May, Addie May Davidson Thompson, Elmer May, Laura Jane Smith May, Maggie May Hampton Ford and Ed May. Middle row: James B. Reed holding William Reed, Della May Reed holding Eunice Reed, Vera Pearl Davidson, William T. May holding Myrtle May, Robert May, Narcissus Hollingsworth May holding Fred Thompson, Lela Boudy a boarder and school teacher. Two girls in front: Lillie Davidson and Clara May.*

William Thomas May was a farmer and stave mill worker. Times were hard back in those days and William had many mouths to feed. I'm sure William Thomas had given much thought and consideration of moving his family to this area, being prime timber country was probably at the top of his list. The logging/timber industry provided a lot of work to many people. William and Narcissus moved their family to several locations in Greene County over the years and as the children grew up they were soon married and went about raising their own families. Although most of them lived in Greene County, Robert L. May moved to Iowa. Calvin and Robert both served in the armed forces during World War I.

They, like so many others helped to establish communities, some even becoming towns, later cities. Their "westward ho" move to Arkansas brought about May families that are still growing. Many pass on, many are born, and there's no end.

William and Narcissus reared a large family, and their children reared large families. Many of the offspring have served in the U.S. Armed Forces, some lost their lives fighting for our country.

William and Narcissus were pioneers in their own rights, it wasn't an easy task, but they did it. William and Narcissus are buried in New Friendship Cemetery, Greene County, Arkansas.

**MAYNARD** – Samuel Benton and Thomas Washington Maynard were the sons of William H. and Mariah Jane Atteberry. Both Samuel and Thomas settled in Greene County, AR in the early 1900s

Samuel was born in Arkansas on June 26, 1876. He met and married Eva Victoria Foshee on Sept. 21, 1902 in Ripley County; MO. Eva was the daughter of Phillip Benton and Susan A. (Patterson) Foshee. Samuel and Eva had nine children:

1. Willie Benton (1903- Aug 26, 1903)
3. Lehman (Sept 1, 1906 – Oct 5, 1972)
4. Lela Abby (March 1, 1908- Feb 14, 1978)
5. Ruth (May 17, 1911- May 3-1999)
6. Tommy (1913 – April 19, 1914)
7. Victoria E. "Vic" (Aug 4, 1915- June 13-1986)
8. Leoria (June 24, 1909)
9. George (1921 – Aug 1921)
10. Susan "Susie" (Feb 8, 1922)

Lehman, the oldest son of Samuel and Eva, had the responsibility of helping his mother to support and raise his sisters after the death of Samuel. Lehman married Hilda Reid on Nov 30, 1929. Lehman and Hilda had two children Eldon and Florence. Hilda died in 1932 and about 1938 he married Birdie Pasisatte. They didn't have any children. Birdie died in a fire in 1968 and in 1970 Leman married Daisy Micenhaammer.

Lela Abby, the third child married Brantley Sigel "Sig" Young in 1927. Lela and Sig had five children:

1. Hazel Aileen
2. Carl Lavaughn
3. Evalene
4. Floyd
5. Patsy

Lela and Sig separated when the youngest, Patsy, was four years old. The oldest daughter, Hazel and Lela worked very hard to make a living and keep food on the table. They cut cordwood with a crosscut saw, picked and chopped cotton, share cropped, whatever it took. Even Evalene, Floyd and Patsy helped pick or chop cotton, as they got old enough. When Floyd was 11 he was drawing adult wages of $3 to $4 a day for eight to 10 hour days. It was hard work! Some time after Sig passed away in 1953, Lela married Ben Wagner. Lela is buried in Memorial Gardens Cemetery in Paragould.

*Samuel Benton Maynard's family: L-R: Wife Eva Victoria, daughters Susie, Leoria, Vick, Ruth, Lela and son Lehman 1940s*

When Ruth, the fourth child, was a young girl their family lived down the road from Alvin Young's family. Alvin had a son named Melvin Wesley. Every time Ruth and her family visited, Alvin would tease Ruth and tell her he was giv-

ing Melvin to her. On Feb 6, 1909 Ruth, 17, and Melvin 21, married. They had 11 children:
1. Geneva
2. Juanita
3. Paul
4. Earl
5. Neddy "Ray"
6. Gerald
7. Clarence
8. Donald
9. Herbert
10. Cloyce
11. Glenda

Ruth and Melvin grew a very large garden to help feed their family and Ruth always had the most beautiful flower gardens.

Victoria married (1) James Stacey and they had one child, James Earl Stacey. (2) Roy Clark and they had six children
1. Robert "Bobby"
2. Helen, twin
3. Ellen, twin
4. Betty
5. Tom
6. Roger

Vic and Roy moved to Rockford, IL and raised their family.

Leoria married Dolph Crouch on July 19, 1934. Leoria and Dolph had five children:
1. Leon
2. Marlene
3. Ronald
4. Lavern
5. Jan

Leoria is now 82, even though she doesn't look it and maintains a beautiful yard and flowerbeds.

Susie married Pharus Forrester on Dec 23, 1944. They had three children: Danny Lee, Larry James and Linda Sue. Susie's mother, Eva, stayed with the Forrester's much of the time until her death in 1962. Susie retired from G. E.

Thomas Washington Maynard (Feb 20, 1881 Ripley County, MO) married (1) Lora Smotherman, died sometime before the 1910 census.

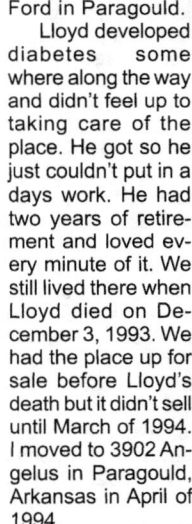
*Samuel Benton Maynard and wife, Eva Victoria (Foshee) Maynard and two of their children Lehman and Lela Abby 1908.*

There were three children born to this marriage:
a. Clayburn (1906-1969) married Daisy
b. Augusta E. "Gusty" (1908-1976) married (1) Walter Cox (2) Joe Prevo
c. Hughus L. (1910) is believed to have died as a child.

(2) Clara Bell Starling of Peach Orchard on Oct 10, 1911. There were no children to this marriage. (3) Mattie Eller Story in 1916. Mattie had two children, Welza and Wesley Gray. There were 11 children born to this union:
a. Mary Eva (1919-1947) married Durell Pratt
b. Samuel Irvin (1921- 1983) married Edith Page
c. James Clarence "P J" (1925-1987) married Avaline Cates
d. William "Jack" (1927-1997) married Martha Lookdoo
e. Oleda "Lorene" (1931), twin married Paul Ainley
f. Bonnie Oweida "Irene" (1931) twin, married Charles Russom
g. Mattie Fay (1933) twin, married Alvin King
h. Thomas Ray (1933) twin, married Barbara Williams
i. Charles (1938) married Sharon
j. Nancy Marie (1923-1989) married Artie Page.

Thomas owned 120 acres in Delaplaine and was a farmer and raised a few cows and pigs.

Samuel Maynard died Oct 5, 1926; his wife Eva died July 7, 1962. Thomas Maynard died Sept 24, 1956 and his third wife, Mattie died Nov t, 1965. All are buried at Smithwick-Allen Cemetery in Knobel. Many of their descendants are still living in or around the Greene County area.

*Submitted by Patsy Boyd*

**McCLELLAND** – Lloyd Earl McClelland, and myself, Jo Margaret LaRue McClelland, with four children, Carol Suzanne "Suzie," Sherri Lynette, Cynthia Ann "Cindi" and Steve Lloyd McClelland moved to Greene County on July 31, 1970. Lloyd and I bought 280 acres in section seven and eight township 17 range five, at 2971 Greene 624 Road.

Lloyd had a dream of raising cattle. He spent his weekends trying to build up the farm and at one point we had 52 head of cattle. During this time Lloyd worked at McCarty Motor Company in Jonesboro and drove back and forth for 14 years. He left McCarty Motor Company and went to O'Neal Ford in Jonesboro and then to Pannell Ford in Paragould.

*Spence and LeAnn Hamilton, children of Suzanne.*

Lloyd developed diabetes some where along the way and didn't feel up to taking care of the place. He got so he just couldn't put in a days work. He had two years of retirement and loved every minute of it. We still lived there when Lloyd died on December 3, 1993. We had the place up for sale before Lloyd's death but it didn't sell until March of 1994. I moved to 3902 Angelus in Paragould, Arkansas in April of 1994.

*Bobby and Matthew Kelly.*

Suzie, our oldest, is teaching third grade in Conway, Arkansas. She has two children, Spencer and LeAnn Hamilton and two stepchildren, Bobby and Matthew Kelly. Her husband, Bob Kelly has left his district manager position at Frito-Lay and started a new business, Hubcap Master in Little Rock.

*Skyler Drake McFarland four and one-half years old. Jeffrey London Word, six months old, April 5, 1997. (Children of Chandra and Jeff Word)*

*Steve and Susie (Huffine) McClelland.*

Sherri married Art Namors and they have three daughters, Charidy, Chandra and Charell. Art is a supervisor at Emerson Electric where he has worked for 26 years. Sherri is teaching first grade at Greene County Tech. Charidy works at Dillards in Jonesboro and continues to go to college. Chandra graduated from Arkansas State University, (ASU) in 1998 with a radiology degree. She is continuing her education and will graduate with a radiation therapy degree in 1999. Chandra married Jeff Word. They have three sons, Skyler, London, and Cade. Jeff works for Frito-Lay. Charell is going to college and manages Sun-tanz in Paragould and Walnut Ridge.

*Jo Margaret LaRue McClelland, Charell Namors, Charidy Namors, Chandra Namors McFarland Word, Jeff Word, Sherri McClelland Namors, Minnie Kersey Namors Brown, Art Namors. (Jeff Word and Chandras wedding.)*

Cindi is married to Ken Parker. They have two children, Jenifer Christal and Scott Justin Parker. Ken has worked at Southwestern Bell for 23 years. Cindi is attending ASU, and guess what she wants to do, teach! Jenifer is a manicurist, specializing in artificial nails at Phyllis' Beauty Salon. Scott works at Wellsco (a computer place) in Paragould.

*Lloyd and Jo Margaret LaRue McClelland's children Steve, Cindi, Suzie and Sherri, 1983.*

Steve married Susie Huffine. He works for Adversiting Express and has worked in the printing business for 20 years. Susie works for Human Services in Jonesboro. Susie parents are A.D. and Rosa Huffine.

Lloyd was raised at Monette Arkansas. His parents were Robert Lee McClelland and Donna Davidson McClelland. I was raised around Bassett, Wilson, and Dyess, Arkansas. We moved to Michigan in September 1950 because we were told there was plenty of work in Michi-

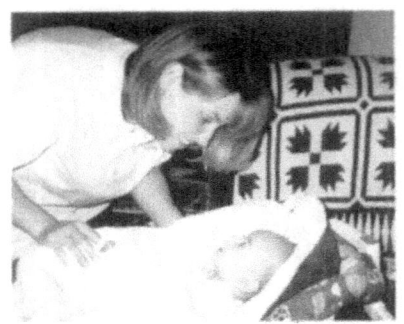

*Chandra and Cade Word at Grandma Jo's house, May 1999.*

gan. All of Lloyd's mother's family, (except his mother) had moved there. Some of Lloyd's dad's family has moved there too. Lloyd always said he was going back to Arkansas when he retired. So I said, "If you are planning on going back, we're going back now." Our parents were aging and I hated those rushed trips. So we moved back to this part of the country and I have never regretted that decision. Lloyd had his farm (cattle dreams) and I could go see my mother, Mae LaRue. I could go visit her and be back home in time to cook supper. My mother died February 21, 1992. I'm thankful for the time I got to spend with her. My dad, W.C. LaRue, died May 6, 1954, while we were living in Michigan. That was one of those "rushed trips" that I hated so. We were the last ones to get there and I never forgot it.

*Back: Ken Parker and Scott Parker; front: Cindi Parker, Jenifer Parker and Jo Margaret McClelland*

*Lloyd and Jo Margaret, Christmas 1981.*

I'm happy and content here at 3902 Angelus. We've seen Paragould grow a lot and it is a good place to live. I'm selfish enough to hope my children and grandchildren stay here. I wish my Suzie was here too - at least she is only 155 miles away. Susie's husband Bob has been good to come and bring her and the kids home quite often.

**McCLURE** – Four letters found in an old trunk in the attic of a Greene County farmhouse revealed the Civil War experiences of my great-great-grandparents, Hankins and Malvina McClure. In the first letter to his wife, dated September 1862 from "Camp Hope," Arkansas, Hankins described the hardships of Confederate camp life–lack of food and warm clothing and said that he "had a chill and coff bad every night."

In the second letter, dated October 12, 1862, from Conway County, he asked that his gloves be sent, said that he had received the clothing and potatoes, and that he would "send her some money if he ever drew any, that he couldn't get anything for the people in this country are on starvation." He said that they were on the march toward Springfield or the northern part of Arkansas.

The next letter, written April 26, 1863, came from a comrade in his company, who told Malvina how her husband died and where he was buried. He died of typhoid fever on November 22, 1862, in a military hospital where his regiment had camped along the Mulberry River in Crawford County, Arkansas. He was buried in his "warring clothes" in a cemetery nearby, and that "they buried more than 200 soldiers at that place." He was only 27 years old.

The fourth letter, dated August 8, 1865, from Illinois was from Robert McClure, who expressed his sorrow at hearing of his brother's death, and said that this was the first word he had received from his family since the war began.

In the summer of 1860, Hankins and Malvina had moved from Carroll County, Tennessee, to Greene County with their young sons and her parents, Thomas and Elizabeth Patton. Thomas Patton bought land on the Finch Road, with D.H. McClure as a witness.

Hankins enlisted in the 30th Arkansas Infantry, which was organized in June 1862, under the command of Colonel A.J. MacNeill of Oak Bluff, a community then a part of Greene County. This regiment was assigned to Brigadier General Dandridge McRae's Brigade, but didn't engage in any major battle until the Battle of Prairie Grove in December 1862.

After the war, Malvina married Benjamin Cobb, a Confederate veteran, and had five children; only two, Rosalie and Faulkner, lived to adulthood. Malvina died in childbirth in 1877. Henry, Hankins and Malvina's third son, died at 21 years old in 1879.

Hankins and Malvina McClure had four sons: Lafayette, Isaac Joseph, William Henry and Thomas Hankins. Lafayette married Margaret Deason and lived near Cardwell, Missouri. Isaac married Nancy Victoria Herren, the daughter of James and Rebecca Higgins Herren, early settlers in the county and long-time members of the Pine Knot Church of Christ. Isaac and Victoria had four sons: Elmer Orestus "Res", Edmund, Arthur, and a son who died at birth with his mother in February 1886. The two are buried in the Crossroads Schoolhouse Cemetery in Lorado.

In October 1886, Isaac married Mary Ann Newsom and the couple had 12 children. He farmed in the Poland Township area and in the Cache River bottoms. Two of his sons, Edmund and Hosea were soldiers in World War I. Edmund was killed in 1918, and Hosea was gassed in the trenches in France.

Isaac's oldest son, Res, married Bertha Atchison, the daughter of Samuel and Arabella Randall Atchison, on January 19, 1902. Res and Bertha were members of the Pine Knot Church and are buried in the cemetery along with many family members and other relatives. The couple had seven children: Flossie, Wilbert, Albert, Agnes, J.C., Glen and Gladys.

Thomas the youngest son of Hankins and Malvina married Mary Ann Honey and lived in Greene County until his death in 1911. The couple had six children: Gilbert, Arlen, Malvina, Irene, Effie and Jeff. They are buried in the Liberty Church Cemetery.

**McCORMICK** – William L. McCormick was born September 15, 1909, in Henderson County, Tennessee. At the age of 12, he and his parents, Jonothan David McCormick and Cora Isabell Gilliam, moved to Arbyrd, Missouri, where he met Ruthy Mae Champ. Her parents were Grover C. Champ and Mahala Mizell. Ruth and W. L. were married August 16, 1928, in Arbyrd, Missouri.

On September 8, 1929, their first child was born, Joy Wayne McCormick. Joy grew up in Paragould, Arkansas, and married William Henry Thomas. W. L. and Ruth's second child was a boy. His name is Donald Ray McCormick. The third was Mavis Sue McCormick (Clark). The fourth, Lizabeth June McCormick (Miller) and the fifth was Janey Lee McCormick (Clark). The sixth child was a boy, Tim Coy McCormick and the seventh was Tex Leroy McCormick. The eighth and ninth were, Barbara Joan McCormick (Hayes) and Brenda Diane McCormick (Sharp, Vaughn). Brenda married Coy Sharp in 1967 in Paragould, Arkansas.

*Back row: William Loidy McCormick holding Janey Lee (baby), Ruth Mae Champ and Joy Wayne. Front row: Donald Ray, Mavis Sue and Lizabeth June. This picture was taken in Cardwell, Missouri.*

William L. loved westerns and he named his first child after John Wayne and the second after Don Red Berry. He named the third one after his sister Mavis who died in a car accident in 1934. Lizabeth June and Janey were named after a radio show called Judy and Janie. Tim and Tex were named after Tim McCoy and Tex Ritter.

William L. McCormick was a farmer as his fore fathers before him. He was also trucker, logger, horse trainer, factory worker and a bar owner. As a farmer, he raised cotton. Ruth, his wife, worked in the field with him. Often she would take her small child to the field with her. The child would lie on the cotton sack and Ruth would pull it behind her as she picked the rows of cotton. They chopped and picked cotton and William would then load cotton and take it to the cotton gin. William's father had a truck farm and he and his brothers would haul soy beans, cotton and watermelons to Cardwell and St. Louis and other towns and cities. When he worked as a logger they cut the trees down and used a team of horses to pull logs out of the forest. The logs were loaded onto the truck and hauled to the sawmills. During 1930 to 1940 he was one of the best horse trainers around Southeast Missouri.

William and his family moved to Greene County, Arkansas, in 1940. They lived at Bard, Brighton and then moved to Dick Keuters place by the big slough ditch. He farmed there for several years and the children attended the Lakeside School in Paragould.

It was getting tough to make a living for nine children so William L. and his family moved to Aurora, Illinois, about 1951. He got a job at a factory and started to save money, however tragedy struck the family. Tex Leroy died in 1952 of a ruptured appendix and was brought back to

Paragould, Arkansas. He was buried in Linwood Cemetery. He was only 7 years old.

William L. returned to Illinois and threw himself into his work He got a part time job hauling trash. Soon he purchased a house in Aurora, located on Mountain Street. One day the factory that William L. had been working for closed down, so he decided to buy a tavern. He purchased one in 1968, located on River Street in Aurora and called it MC's.

Although William L. lived in Illinois, he still returned often to visit his parents in Cardwell, Missouri, and his daughter Joy and his sister Thelma McCormick (Killian, Lovelace) who lived in Paragould, Arkansas.

October 1970, William lost another son, Tim Coy McCormick in a motorcycle accident. His last remaining son, Donald Ray had gotten a job offer to move to Florida in 1969. Donald and his family had been living there for more that a year. William L. went for a visit with them and bought some land in Panama City Beach.

In 1971 William decided to move to Florida. His daughter Mavis Sue and her husband also moved there. They purchased a tavern and called it MC's. It was located on Thomas Drive in Panama City Beach. During his ownership, there was a young man making music with his guitar. William L. walked over to him and said. "Boy, that's what the jukebox is for." Years later that young man was heard on most jukeboxes all over the country. His name was Don Williams.

In 1975 W. L. retired from business and died of stomach cancer November 2, 1976. William Loidy and Ruth were good people, who worked hard and lived through the Depression of 1929, two World Wars, an assassination of President Kennedy and saw a man walk on the moon. They were the average Americans of the 20th century who believed in God, the Flag and Country and the people of the United States.

**McCULLOCH** – James McCulloch was born 1825 in Tennessee. On June 7, 1849, he married Elizabeth Turner in Henry County, Tennessee. Together they had four children: George W., born 1850; Martha J., born 1854; John Thomas born April 18, 1857; and Mary Ann born 1863. James and Elizabeth came to Greene County with their family in the early 1870s settling first in Clark Township. Elizabeth died between 1880 and 1900.

George W. was married after 1870, his wife died after 1874. They had one child, Callie born in 1874. Callie married John T. McHaney in Greene County July 12, 1893. Callie and John had six children: Ira, Walter, George, Clyde, Clay and Leonard.

John Thomas married Amanda Caroline Thompson, born June 11, 1867, daughter of James W. Thompson and Virginia (Miller) Thompson of Greene County. John and Amanda had at least 15 children: Victoria married William Wilkerson; Nathanial, Sam married Lula Greenway; Iva married Carl Hart; Robert; Joseph A. married Clara L. Daniel daughter of Thomas Daniel and Addie (Adams) Daniel of Craighead County; William C.; Myrtle married A.D. Smith; Virginia Mae married Glen Webster; John; Esco married Fred Donavan; Arden; Vera; Elizabeth; and Irene. Sam died January 16, 1913, less than a year after he and Lula were married. John Thomas died August 10, 1910. Amanda died December 7, 1945, in Missouri. They are both buried in Fairview Cemetery in Greene County.

Mary Ann married Jesse S. Nettles November 3, 1881, in Greene County.

**McDANIEL** – Hillary McDaniel was born to Jasper and Mary Lamb McDaniel August 31, 1869. Both parents were descendants of Greene County's earliest settlers. He married Wilma Craig March 19, 1891. She was born in Hardeman County, Tennessee, December 6, 1871, to James Lawrence and Elizabeth "Betty" Cox Craig. Betty was a widow when the family moved to Greene County.

Children born to Hillary and Wilma were Robert Samuel who married Effie Leigh Brooks; James Arthur who married Carlene Jones; Mary Elizabeth; William Thomas who married Marguerite Gourley; David Cline who married Mae Crockett; Ezra Hillary; Iva Leigh married Donald Cox who compiled Hillary and Wilma's family sheet; and Pearl Lena who married J. Clifford Diggs. Her second husband was Osmer T. Fletcher. All children and spouses are deceased except Marguerite who resides in a nursing home in California at this time.

Grandchildren of Hillary and Wilma were Shirley Gwyndolyn, Robert Samuel Jr., who were called Jill and Jack; LaRue; Arthur Gaines; Garnet Craig; Wilma Laverne; Thomas Wilbert; Nellie Louise; Joe Walden; Dale; Arlene Almeda; Pearl Laveda; twins Doris Jean and Donald Gene; and Billy Gene. Mary died at age 2 when she fell into the fireplace suffocating before anyone could rescue her. Ezra died from influenza in 1918 at age 14. Nellie died when she was a child. Twins Doris Jean and Donald Gene died within a few days of birth. Grandchildren who have died in adulthood are Jack, Joe, Wilma, T.W. and Billy Gene.

All children of Hillary and Wilma remained in Greene County except Sam and Dave who moved to Michigan. Sam and Arthur served in the United States Army during World War I. They were in France at the same time.

The McDaniel farm of about 80 acres was located off the Jonesboro Highway on what is now McDaniel Road. It is about five miles from the corner of Linwood Cemetery in Paragould to the farm. Most of the original farm is presently owned by their son Arthur's children. A part of the old house still stands. Family members remembered that the kitchen chairs had cane bottoms and that stairs in the kitchen led to an unfinished attic that was used for storage. Shelves were built under the stairs. The family ate summer time meals on a screened porch along one side of the house.

Like most of the farm families at that time they planted large gardens. Out buildings included a cow barn, chicken house, hog houses, feed storage and stalls, cellar, smokehouse, well/bath house and an out-door privy. The garden was located near the back of the house. At sorghum making time Hillary and the boys made sorghum at nearby farms for a share of the molasses. The family prepared meat for the coming year on hog killing days.

The family attended church at Brown's Chapel Baptist Church. Wilma Craig McDaniel died February 25, 1918. Hillary McDaniel died October 1, 1931, from Bright's disease. They are buried at Brown's Chapel Cemetery.

**McFALL** – Arthur McFall was born January 5,1891, to George W. McFall and Litisha (Ragsdale) McFall in Gainesville, Arkansas.

On August 27,1911, he married Bessie Gordon, daughter of John Edgar and Bula (Mitchell) Gordon at the home of Mr. and Mrs. Pres Hammond in Gainesville. They had 10 children: Adrian McFall Mildred (McFall) Smith, Vaudene (McFall) Hammon, Ramond McFall, Imogene (McFall) Willey, Murlene (McFall) Dial, Reba (McFall) Cunningham, Cecil McFall, Wayne McFall, Ellen (McFall) Forrest.

Arthur farmed most of his life in Greene County, with a team of horses and a team of mules he farmed 40 acres, growing cotton, corn and hay. The cotton crop provided money to live on until the next fall. We had milk cows, chicken, and hogs for meat. Mother canned vegetables and fruit in the summer. We made our own lard from the hog fat, so we had plenty of food to eat.

*Picture of McFall family (Vaudene is missing), from left: Wayne, Arthur, Bessie and Ellen. Second row: Cecil, Imogene, Murlene, Reba and Mildred. Back row: Adrian, Ramond.*

Brought up on a farm we were taught to work at an early age, and to take pride in all we did. The older children went to school in a two room school house, the little room were grades primer through fourth, big room had fifth through eighth. The school house also used for church on Sunday's. September we started picking cotton we were paid for picking, we bought our school clothes with our money. We would ride to town on a wagon load of cotton on Saturday and spend the day shopping. We each got 25 cents to spend however we wanted to. We could buy a hamburger, a soda, or an ice cream for five cents each. To go to the movies with friends, that cost 10 cents. It was our choice to spend it all or save some.

Christmas was always a time to enjoy. Mother and Mildred would start baking pies and cakes two days before Christmas. The house smelled so good. We didn't get many toys, we got fresh fruit, candy and nuts. Santa always put a coconut under each bed for us. As we grew up things changed, the older ones married, Ramond was drafted into service in 1943, he served three years in the Marines.

We were leaving home one by one now. Arthur sold his farm equipment and moved to St. Louis for awhile then came back, bought a home on East Court Street in Paragould and lived there until his death, December 28, 1969. Bessie died February 1, 1980. They were laid to rest in Memorial Gardens in Paragould.

Ramond died March 19, 1977, Mildred died February 1, 1993, and Vaudene died May 27, 1997.

**McGRAW** – Lucilious Ruben McGraw (May 15, 1862 Gibson County, TN - Nov 4, 1947) was the son of John Ruben McGraw and Catherine Wallace. He married Martha E. Morrow in 1888 and they moved to southeast Missouri in the late 1880s and to Greene County, AR about 1905. They were farmers in the area around Old Liberty Church. They were the parents of eight children:

1. Shirley
2. Lucilious
3. Amelia
4. Harry
5. Leonard
6. Albert
7. Malvin
8. Vertis

Martha died on Oct 8, 1933 and Lucilious married her sister Margaret Morrow in 1934. Lucilious and Martha are buried in Old Liberty Cemetery.

Lucilious "Lewis" McGraw (May 12, 1890) married Mamie Clara Johnson May 5, 1912 in Greene County, AR. They were the parents of six children:
1. Orene
2. Mildred
3. Lloyd
4. Alberteen
5. Laverna
6. Izetta

They were farmers and sharecropped in various places in Greene County, Clay County and in southeast Missouri. She died in 1928 and is buried in New Friendship Cemetery and he died in 1936 and buried in Pope Chapel Cemetery, Ripley County, MO.

*Submitted by Daniel E. Moore*

**McINTOSH** – Many years ago the "Mackintosh" clan originated in Scotland. From this clan, our family began.

Charles McIntosh and Charles' brother George worked on a ship to get to America sometime in the early 1800s. They landed in South Carolina. Charles met and married Sarah Carter on Jan 17, 1834. They farmed in South Carolina and then migrated to Indiana. While in Indiana they had one son, Jeffrey Spencer McIntosh, Sr. who was born Oct 25, 1834. Charles died shortly after the birth of Jeffrey, sometime in 1835. Sarah and Jeffrey then moved to Illinois.

Jeffrey Sr. grew up in Illinois and met and married Electran Ann White. They homesteaded land in the Mill Shoals area that later became known as the McIntosh Bottoms. They had a successful farming operation and raised 13 children. One of which was Jeffery Spencer McIntosh, Jr. born April 21, 1870.

Jeffrey, Jr. helped his father on the farm now known as the McIntosh Settlement. Jeffrey, Jr. married Sarah Melissa Chapman and they had two children, Orville Bryan and Helen Madge. Jeffrey Jr. and Melissa moved to Colorado in 1902. Jeffrey became involved in a sugar beet refinery.

In 1906 they moved to Pineville, AR, just outside of Calico Rock. They began a pickling cannery with Jeffrey's brother, James Oscar, who had joined them from Illinois. James and Jeffrey's mother, Electran, who was still in Illinois became very sick in 1911. They were asked to come back to Illinois by their brother William. James Oscar made it back to Illinois but Jeffrey and Melissa stopped in the Hopewell community just outside of Marmaduke. Jeffrey and Melissa then bought Alhf Market in the Hopewell area. They had another child, Pearl, who died at an early age. Helen Madge married Marvin Ahlf, a long time Methodist minister from the area. Orville married Ethel Hopper of the Rector area.

Jeffrey, Jr. and Melissa sold their market and started a farming operation. After several years, Orville and Ethel took over the farming operation. Orville helped lay bricks for the first paved streets in Rector. The had three children:
1. Rheda Aline married Gene Gogue of Rector.
2. Jeffrey Carson joined the military and passed away in 1978.
3. Wendell Augustus (June 1, 1919) married Lela Lucille Robertson in 1939. He worked on the farm with his father until Orville passed away. Wendell and Lucille had two children:
    a. Jerry Don (July 17, 1945) married Pamela Ruth Day of Marmaduke in 1965. They continue to live in Marmaduke and have three children. Lorie Don (Nov 21, 1967) Reesa Paige (Jan 30, 1970) and Nichole Rae "Nikki"(Jan. 24, 1972). Lorie married Chuck Long of Paragould and they have two children, Bethany Ashton (Dec 7, 1993) and Hannah Autry (Jan 5, 1996). They reside in Marmaduke. Reesa married Bryan Cain of Jonesboro and they have two children, Erica Taylor (Oct 11, 1991) and Morgan Alexis (Sept 3, 1992). They reside in Jonesboro. Nikki resides in Marmaduke.
    b. Donnie Ray (Aug 6, 1947) married Carolyn Ruth Clark of Pine Bluff, AR in 1972 and resides in Rogers, AR. They have one son, Mark McIntosh (Aug 4, 1976).

Wendell moved his family into Marmaduke in 1963. He eventually retired from farming and bought and ran McIntosh Grocery in Marmaduke.

*Submitted by Jerry D. McIntosh*

**McLERKIN/WHITNEY** – Ralph Paul McLerkin (June 10, 1890 Brighton, TN.- Jan 16, 1971) was seven years old when he moved to Arkansas with his parents and his three brothers, Ross, Roy and Harvey. The McLerkins settled in the Brown's Chapel Community. Paul, as he was called, later married Maggie Ann Wood, who lived in the Wood's Chapel community. Maggie (June 22, 1894-April 15, 1974) had five brothers, Charles, Alex, Frank, Clyde and Roy. Paul and Maggie had one child, a daughter, Ann Naomi (June 28, 1931).

Paul McLerkin taught school in Greene County and at one time was the principal of Elmwood School. He was also a bookkeeper and worked for the Bertig Company. In 1939 he was elected to the office of Greene County Circuit Clerk, after serving as deputy clerk under Donald Cox. After his four-year term of office, his deputy, Curtis Curse, was elected to the office. Curtis was soon drafted in the army and Paul served most of Curtis' term while he was away. Paul served as deputy in the same office years later under Russell Phillips.

*Ralph Paul McLerkin, Greene County Circuit Court Clerk 1939-1942*

*Ralph Paul and Maggie Ann (Wood) McLerkin*

Paul McLerkin was a lover of horses and he and his daughter, Ann, were charter members of one of the first organized saddle clubs in Greene County. He attended First United Methodist Church and was a member of the Men's Bible Class, serving as their secretary for many years.

Maggie McLerkin was a homemaker and was active in the West Paragould Home Demonstration Club. She won several honors with her sewing ability and always brought home many prize ribbons from both the county and district fairs. She taught Sunday school at First United Methodist Church for many years and was a member of the Women's Society of Christian Service.

*Ann (McLerkin) and family: L-R: James Edward Whitney and Ann (McLerkin) Whitney. Children: Paula Ann and Ross Edward*

Ann McLerkin married James Edward Whitney Jr. after a courtship of many years, which began when Ann was elected as homecoming queen at Paragould High School by the football team, which won the state championship in 1948. James was captain of the team and their first date was for the homecoming dance following the game. They have two children, Paul Ann and Ross Edward. James died on March 20, 1974.

Ann Whitney has earned degrees from Arkansas State University and has studied at other educational institutions. She taught school in Greene County from 1950 until 1960. She and her husband, James, owned and operated a Walgreen agency Drug Store in Paragould for many years. She taught in the College of Business at Arkansas State University for seven years and was the supervisor of instruction for the Cotton Boll Technical Institute for 10 years before her retirement in 1999. She taught Sunday school at the First Methodist Church for 11 years and is still active with children's activities as they concern her grandchildren.

*Submitted by Ann Whitney*

**McSPADDEN** – Roy O. McSpadden (March 22, 1889 Ft. Payne, AL- April 29, 1990) migrated from Alabama to Paragould, Greene County, AR. Roy was a corporal in the US Army in WWI. He met and married Reba Snowden, daughter of Albert Snowden and Beulah Chandler Kennemore Snowden.

Roy was a member of the Masonic Lodge, American Legion, Methodist Church, veteran of WWI, retired employee of Paragould Country Club. Roy and Reba have two sons.
1. Roy Albert McSpadden (Sept 12, 1935) married Linda Fletcher June 13, 1954 and they have four children:
    a. Roy W. McSpadden married TroyLynn and their son is Roy Edmond McSpadden.
    b. Vickie L. McSpadden married Richard Shelby and their children are Brooke Shelby, Blake Shelby and Sam Shelby.
    c. David P. McSpadden married Kathy and their children are Christy McSpadden and Whitney McSpadden.
    d. Christopher Lee McSpadden married Stacey.
3. Jerry McSpadden (Aug 30,1939) married Judy Wrape June 1962. Jerry and Judy's children are:
    a. Leah McSpadden
    b. Jennifer McSpadden

*Roy O. McSpadden*

Roy A. McSpadden, son of Roy O. and Reba, was appointed to the Arkansas Methodist Hospital Executive Board of Trustees in 1984. He is presently serving on the AMH Finance Committee, the Land Acquisition Committee and the Nursing School Committee. Mr. McSpadden is an active businessman in Paragould. He district manager of Turner Dairies, Inc of Paragould and has received the president's award for manager of the year for the dairy division of Turner Dairies, Inc. He is past president of the Paragould Exchange Club and the Paragould Area Chamber of Commerce. He is a member of the Paragould Rotary Club, the Paragould School District Board and the First National Bank Board. He is presently Secretary/Treasurer of the Paragould High School Booster Club. He and Linda are members of the First Baptist Church of Paragould. Roy said he is looking forward to retirement and hitting the golf links!

Reba Snowden McSpadden died Jan 4, 2000. Roy and Reba are buried with her parents in Linwood Cemetery, Paragould, AR.

*Submitted by Evelyn Euritha Wagner*

**MEREDITH** – James B. Meredith was one of the early settlers of Greene County, Arkansas, having arrived sometime in the 1840s from Wayne County, Tennessee. He was born in 1802. His state of birth is not known with certainty since some records indicate that it was Kentucky while other records show that it was Tennessee. His wife Rebecca was born in North Carolina in 1803.

In 1850 James B. and Rebecca Meredith were living in St. Francis Township, Greene County, Arkansas. Their children at home at this time were: Mary, 1832; Elizabeth, 1835; Jane, 1838; James F., 1840; and Thomas E., 1842.

*James Fitzgerald Meredith and his wife Martha Ann Jane Nettles Meredith. James Fitzgerald Meredith was the son of James B. and Rebecca Meredith.*

In 1880 James B. and Rebecca Meredith were living in Union Township, Greene County, Arkansas, with their son Thomas and daughters Mary and Jane. James B. was 77 years old and Rebecca was 76 years old. Thomas later married Cordelia Barr on August 10, 1885. Mary and Jane never married. A daughter Elizabeth wasn't listed, she was already married to E.S. Ragsdale. A son James F. was already married and listed next to James B. as head of household in the census.

James Fitzgerald Meredith, son of James B. and Rebecca Meredith was born in October 1841 in Tennessee. He married Martha Ann Jane Nettles in 1865 in Greene County, Arkansas. Martha was born May 23, 1848, probably in Piggott, Arkansas, the daughter of John Nettles and Nancy Beacher. To this union were born nine children: Mary M.I., John W., Minnie Alice, William L., George Louella, Nancy "Lora," James F., Pearl Mae and Rosie. All of their children were born in Greene County, Arkansas.

Mary M.I. "Belle" Meredith was born in 1868. She married Thomas Riley Shepherd on January 20, 1886, in Greene County, Arkansas. Their only daughter Leona was born December 14, 1886, in the Fairview Community, Paragould, Arkansas. Belle died with the measles when Leona was 2 years old in 1888 or 1889. Belle had a son that died when it was only 6 weeks old. The other version of the story is that Belle died when Leona was 2 years old, but she died in childbirth as did the boy baby. She was buried in Fairview Cemetery, Paragould, Arkansas, an unmarked grave. Thomas Riley Shepherd remarried and moved the family to Harrisburg, Arkansas, in 1903. On October 9, 1904, Leona married Eli Alonza McGee in Harrisburg, Arkansas. (See Thomas Riley Shepherd family history.)

John W. Meredith was born in 1870 and died in 1917 or 1918 of pneumonia. He married Mary Fannie ?. They had three sons: Owen, Euel and Elden. John died at Beech Grove near Paragould and was buried at Fairview Cemetery, an unmarked grave.

Minnie Alice Meredith was born April 10, 1872, and died January 15, 1941. She married John Hays Shepherd (November 3, 1867-1920?) on April 21, 1889, in Greene County, Arkansas. Minnie's sister Belle married John's brother Thomas Riley Shepherd. Minnie and John had six children: Noxie Lee, John Winn, Iris Jewel, Ruby Lee, Alden Opal and Ira Bill. Minnie died at the home of her son Opal near Cardwell, Missouri. John and Minnie were buried at Fariew Cemetery, an unmarked grave.

William L. "Will" Meredith was born November 1, 1872, and died August 16, 1917. He married Ola Agee on December 20, 1896, in Greene County. An infant son was born and died January 31, 1898. Will had a fruit and confectionery business on Court Street in Paragould. He died of typhoid and was buried at Linwood Cemetery in Paragould.

George Louella Meredith was born in November 1874 and died in 1817 or 1918 of the flu. She married Joe H. Jeter on December 30, 1894, in Greene County. They had six children: Jesse L., Joseph Marion, Wilma, Otto T., Anna and George R. Three of the children died in the flu epidemic of 1917. Louella is probably buried near her four children at Fairview Cemetery, an unmarked grave.

Nancy "Lora" Meredith was born in 1877 and died in 1940. She married Lon Horn on November 29, 1899, in Greene County. They had one son Arthur. Lora later married Callie Duncan. Lora was buried at Fairview Cemetery.

James F. "Jim" Meredith was born in 1879. He married Dollie Fry. They had two daughters Buell and Jewell. Jim was deputy sheriff at Cardwell, Missouri, for awhile. He later moved his family to Flint, Michigan.

Pearl Mae Meredith was born August 18, 1884, and died May 31, 1928. She married David Vernie Thomason (January 10, 1877-October 6, 1911) on December 29, 1901, in Greene County. They had four children: Essie Lee, Wilma Ovene, Vernie Everett and Virginia Irene. Pearl died of tuberculosis at her home in Lake City, Arkansas. Pearl and David were buried at Fairview Cemetery.

Rosie Meredith was born in August 1885 and died in childbirth. Rosie was already dead when her brother Will died on August 16, 1917, and wasn't listed in his obituary. She married John Tom Smith on August 3, 1904, in Greene County. They had one son Arby. Rosie was buried next to her sister Belle but neither have monuments.

James F. Meredith died February 24, 1908, and was buried at Fairview Cemetery. James F. served as a soldier in the army of the Confederate States being a member of Company H, 5th Regiment of Infantry from the State of Arkansas. After his death Martha received a pension. Martha later married W.E. "Will" Ford on January 19, 1913, in Greene County. The pension stopped after Martha remarried. When Martha and Will couldn't take care of themselves they went to live with their own children. Once again Martha started receiving her pension. Martha Meredith Ford died Sunday night, February 17, 1924, at the home of her daughter, Mrs. Pearl Thomason near Fairview Baptist Church and was buried by her husband James in Fairview Cemetery.

**MERIDETH** – Jasper Newton Merideth, 1845-1936, was orphaned at about 2 years of age. He was raised by a Mr. and Mrs. W. D. Reynolds. Mrs. Reynolds is believed to be an aunt, but no one knows if she was his mother or father's sister. It is said Newt Merideth married first to a Sally (unknown) or Sarah (unknown) for six months. She died from a gun shot to the foot or leg when a gun propped in the corner fell and discharged.

Newt Merideth's second wife was Orlena M. Freeman. They had 17 children: Henry, 1872-1969, married Anna; Georg, 1874-?, married Dora; Frank, 1878-? married Callie Patten; Osmer, ?- 1922; Jim (unknown) married Vera; Tom, 1882-1962, married Ada Patten, a sister to Callie; Minton (unknown) married Lola McClure; Neely, Thaddus, Obbie, Ovid (all unknown), Anne (unknown) married Ernest Thorne; Eva (unknown) married Jim Kennedy; Nancy (unknown) married Will Jackson. There also was a set of twins and another baby, whose name is unknown. No one seems to know much about Newt Merideth. In the 1860 census he was living in the Reynolds' home at 12 years of age. No one seems to know how he accumulated his property holdings, but in 1900 he donated property for the Merideth school house. He also donated land for the Tokio church and had one of the sorghum mills in Greene County. He educated all 14 of their living children.

Orlena Freeman was the daughter of Presley Freeman, and she was said to have owned some property also.

**MERIWETHER** – William Winston Meriwether, 1833-1893, was the sixth generation descendant of Nicholas Meriwether, who had emigrated from England to Virginia around 1650. "Wint" was a resident of Lake County, Tennessee, in 1861 when he married Sarah Ellen Tippett, 1839-1897, the daughter of a Methodist minister. Meriwether served as a captain in the Confederate Army during the Civil War. Their first child, Robert Winston, 1862-1950, was born near Marianna, Arkansas, where "Sally" had fled as a war refugee. Back in Tennessee after the war, Wint farmed and operated a ferry on the Mississippi River. In 1883 Captain Meriwether, his wife and their two children Bob and Ida Mae, 1866-1962, moved to the railroad crossing of Paragould and the two men established a retail store, W.W. Meriwether & Son Hardware Company. After a short time on West Main Street, the store was relocated to 212 South Pruett, where it was operated by three generations of the family until 1962.

After the death of her parents, the Meriwether home at 324 West Garland was occupied by Ida and her husband William Woodford Bandy, 1860-1949. Bandy was a member of the first graduating class from Vanderbilt University School of Law, and during his long career as an attorney in Paragould also served terms as prosecuting attorney and circuit judge.

In 1890 Bob Meriwether married Kate B. Hays, 1869-1952, a daughter of Alfred Birchum and Annetta Spillman Hays. "Squire" Hays was a member of the famous Orphan Brigade of Kentucky troops during the Civil War, and when he died in 1932 was buried in a Confederate uniform. He served a term as mayor of Paragould and was a long-time justice of the peace who held court on his front porch. The Hays home at 611 West Court is still standing. Among the Hays grandchildren raised in Paragould was Orine Porter (Gardner), well known as a Latin teacher and later principal of Paragould High School. His brother, Albert Hays Porter, served in the fledgling U.S. Army Air Corps in France during World War I, and was a long-time associate of Meriwether Hardware.

*Bob and Kate Meriwether and their sons (from left) Ray, Bill and Lilbourn. Circa 1914.*

Bob and Kate Meriwether had at 305 West Garland a home that was later moved around the corner to 312 South Third. The couple had three sons who reached maturity.

Lilbourn Hays Meriwether, 1892-1972, was a graduate of the University of Arkansas. In 1920 he married Alma Hickson, 1891-1994, whose father John and brother Fred operated Hickson-Rogers Lumber Company in Paragould. Lilbourn and Alma lived in Denver, Colorado, where he was a wholesale representative of Graybar Electric. Their daughter Elizabeth Ann, born 1930, and her husband, retired U.S. Army Colonel Timothy H. Donovan, born 1929, live in Columbia, Missouri. They have a daughter Kathleen born 1954, a son John born 1957, and three grandchildren.

Robert Ray Meriwether, 1896-1972, was a sergeant-major in the Army during World War I. After the war he joined his father in Meriwether Hardware. In 1928 he married Marie Thompson, 1906-1966, of Marked Tree, who became well known in Paragould for her beautiful singing voice. Ray and Marie lived at 306 South Third with their two children, Jane Marie born 1932 and John Thompson "Jack" born 1933. Jane is married to John Henry Johnson, born 1921. The couple, who live in Rochester, New York, have three daughters: twins Lynne Meriwether and Ellen Loring born 1960 and Anne Barrington born 1965; and two grandchildren. Jack Meriwether born 1933 has been city manager of Texarkana and Little Rock and an administrator with the *Arkansas Gazette* and the University of Arkansas System. He married Peggy Crane, 1937-1983, of Fort Smith, and the couple had two sons, Daniel Crane born 1961 and John Thompson Jr., "Thom," 1962-1980. Jack, Peggy and their sons lived in Paragould in 1973-75 while he was a vice president of the First National Bank of Commerce. Jack currently resides in Little Rock.

William Winston "Bill" Meriwether, 1904-1966, graduated from Hendrix College before joining his father and older brother in Meriwether Hardware. In 1927 he married Rosalie Diffey, 1906-1988, of Cotton Plant and the couple lived at 309 West Garland. Bill was on active duty with the U.S. Army in World War II and the Korean War, achieving the rank of lieutenant colonel. Their son Robert Winston "Bob," born 1928, was a teacher and then principal at Paragould Senior High School before teaching at Hendrix College for 34 years. He married Sylvia Kuraner, born 1928, of San Antonio, and the couple have three sons: William, born 1953; David, born 1955; and Nicholas, born 1957; a daughter Sarah Kate, born 1965; and nine grandchildren. Bob and Sylvia live in Conway. Bill and Rosalie's daughter Rosemary, born 1929, married Eugene G. Rapley, born 1929, of Fort Smith, where the couple now live. They have a daughter Nancy, born 1953, a son "Gil," born 1955 and four grandchildren.

**METHENY** – Alfred Moses Metheny and twin brother, Wilfred Aaron, were born January 17, 1925, just below the state line in Arkansas. However, because the country doctor was not expecting twins, in his excitement, he recorded their birthplace as Cardwell, Missouri. They had two older sisters, Ludia Elizabeth "Polly" and L.V., and a half-brother, Arlie Metheny. Later another sister, Ruby Mae, and a brother, William Chester, completed the family. They were an average farm family until their home burned a short time before Christmas 1930. Their mother died in June 1931 of leukemia.

The nation's economy made life hard at best, but being a farmer without a wife and with seven children to provide for, made life exceptionally hard for this family. The children were scattered among family and friends while their dad tried to farm. When they met for church services was the only

*Alfred and Golvia Metheny.*

time all of them could be together, and they continuously begged their dad to let them all come home. Finally he did bring all but Chester, who was still not 2 years old, to live with him. Polly was 10 and L.V. was 8 and they tried to do the cooking. Their dad was both mother and father to them. At night he would gather the kids together and teach them music; therefore, Alfred learned his do-re-mi's by the time he learned his ABCs. The family would sing at funerals from the time Alfred and Wilfred were 8 years old. They developed a deep love for singing. Both sang tenor and later Alfred sang high tenor in some men's quartets. After moving to Alabama, Alfred conducted several singing schools.

When they reached high school age, the boys would take turns going to school while the other would stay home and help their dad make a crop.

In 1942 the family moved near Evening Star, in Greene County, where Alfred went to Delaplaine School. In 1944 they moved near Stanford. Alfred married Golvia Elizabeth Morrow, daughter of Jeff and Pearl Goins Morrow. They both graduated from Stanford High School in 1944. Alfred and Wilfred left for the Navy on June 5th and served on a floating dry dock in the South Pacific until getting out of service in February 1946.

Alfred farmed in Greene County from 1946 through 1950. Moved to Paragould 1951 where their children were born. They moved to Albertville, Alabama, in 1963 where he sold poultry equipment until retiring. They were members of the Church of Christ.

Their first born: Alfred Daniel, born 1944, married Doris Jane Dillin, born 1947, their children: Stephen Daniel, born 1970; and Tara Brooks, born 1978.

Second child: Stephen Bryance, born 1946, married Barbara Elaine Moore; their children: Kristin Bryance, born 1970, married Wendy Stokes, born 1969, had children Jordan Irene, born 1995, Jewel Eileen, born 1999; Jeffery Scott, born 1972; and Stephen Shane, born 1975.

Third child: Golvia Damara, born 1951, married Jerry Lynn Landers, born 1952; their children: Jarrod Marlin, born 1974; Nick Morrow, born 1976.

Fourth child: Hilda Gayle, born 1953, married Roger Hard, divorced; their children: Lewis Preston, born 1974, married Femia Marie Hatcher Parker, born 1979: their children: Delisa Parker, born 1994; Jada Elizabeth, born 1999; Eric Roger, born 1978.

Fifth child: Dwight Julian, born 1956, married Trena Denise Lemaster, born 1957, divorced; their children: Amanda Elizabeth, born 1979; Dwight Julian, born 1980. Third marriage to Judith Dodd Hatcher, born 1947.

**METHENY** – William Marion Metheny, called "Bill" was born June 12, 1891, near Peach Orchard, Arkansas. His parents were Alfred Waters and Ellen Elizabeth Allison Metheny. They were born near Lexington, Kentucky, but their nine children were born in Arkansas. Alfred became ill with the flu and died February 17, 1906, Etta died two weeks later from it on March 5. They are buried in Wise Cemetery, near Peach Orchard.

Their oldest child Menona 16, and Bill 15 wanted to keep the family together by farming their land. However this was not allowed, so the children were scattered. Five lived with a paternal aunt, two being twins. The youngest, twin boys lived with a neighbor, while Bill and Orval 13, hired out for their room and board.

In 1908 Bill went to Indiana and worked for a coal mining company for two years. He came back to Dunklin County, Missouri, where he and a sister Etta set up house keeping while Bill sharecropped a farm. Etta married in 1912 and Bill batched until he and Susie Wallace married in 1914. The twins Leonard and Glen went to live with them in 1915. After the birth of two children and death of the oldest, Bill and Susie had saved enough money to but a farm near Beech Grove. Before they could move Susie and the twins took the flu, resulting in Susie's death, February 2, 1920. Bill left Arlie with in-laws while he, Glen and Leonard worked the farm that year, then sold it and moved back to Mississippi County, Arkansas.

On December 20, 1920, he married Rose Etta Julian, daughter of Daniel and Lou Gill Julian. Bill brought Arlie home to live. To this union were born six children: Ludia Elizabeth "Polly," L.V., twins Alfred and Wilfred, Ruby Mae and William Chester.

While Chester was a baby their house burned destroying everything. In March of the next year Etta developed osteomyelitis and died June 27, 1931. History repeated itself and Bill's children were scattered among family and friends. After a year all of them but Chester came home. He lived with the Julians until he started to school. Having seven children and no wife made for a hard life. However Bill was a man of deep faith and strong determination, a characteristic he passed on to his children.

He moved his family near Evening Star in 1942, Polly had married Fred Patterson in 1939 and Arlie joined the Marines, leaving five children at home. In 1943 L.V. married Vernon Clifton. In 1944 Alfred married Golvia Morrow. Bill moved near Stanford. In January 1945 he sold out and moved to California. In July 1946 after his three sons and two sons-in-law were discharged, Ruby married Walter Newell of Massachusetts and he came back to Arkansas. He married Pearl Kinder Rogers. He died January 8, 1949. He, Susie and Etta are buried in the Silverdale, Missouri Cemetery.

**MILLER** – Clifton Miller brought his family from Kentucky. They lived and logged on Cache River before moving to Randolph County, AR. At this time their children were
1. Abraham
2. James C.
3. Clifton
4. Feeby (later spelled Phoebe)
5. Stedman

His wife, Feeby and sister, Mary Bell Tomes came along. Feeby died.

Clifton married Dora Howard of Lima, AR in 1883. They had two sons, John Morgan and Palestine. After Dora died, Clifton gave the homestead to his sister and came back to Cache River. He bought land in Greene County. The family put logs on a tram train that went to Sedgwick. Clifton died April 1900. The heirs sold the land to W. L. Gage.

Abraham and Stedman moved to Perry County and son, Clifton, moved to Newport, AR.

Phoebe married W. Stringer. She died of pneumonia a few years later. Abraham's family got sick. He came back to Light to live near James C.

James C. wed Mary C. Alford. They were called "Jim" and "Kate". They raised their family north of Light. Their children were:

*Clifton Miller*

1. James
2. Mary
3. Sally
4. Nellie
5. Joe
6. Artie
7. Bessie
8. Homer

Kate's mother, Mary Jane Wilson, lived with her.

James C., John and Palestine made their homes near Light, AR.

Palestine married Sarah Parker. They lived near Cache River.

A son, Monroe, died at ages four.

Son, Woodrow, was killed in 1945 while serving in the army.

Roscoe lived across the road from his parents. Roscoe's wife, Letha and daughter, Catherine, still live there.

John Morgan married Elizabeth "Lizzie" Nelson Brashears. They lived and farmed near Faulknerville, north of Light, AR.

**MILLER** – James Robert Miller, husband of Mattie Hampton, had come from Gordon County, Georgia, where he was born on April 8, 1856. Before coming to Greene County in 1819, he had farmed and had been a school teacher in Georgia. His parents were W. W. and Amelia Erwin Miller of South Carolina and Georgia. In 1889 Amelia Miller was living with Mattie and James in Greene County. In the obituary of James R. Miller he was reputed to have taught school in Greene County a short time after his arrival. James later became a deputy clerk in Greene County for four years. About 1894 he commenced serving one term as county and circuit clerk for Greene County. Following that James Miller served 20 years as justice of the peace. He was formerly a member of the Oak Grove School Board and an active member of the Oak Grove Methodist Church for more than 40 years. During later years he was engaged in farming. James R. Miller died at his home in Oak Grove on December 25, 1 932, at 76 years of age following a bought with pneumonia. He was buried in the Gainesville Cemetery.

*Front row from left: James R. Miller (seated), Clifton Walden (Minnie Mae's son), Martha "Mattie" Miller, Juanita Miller (Roy H. and Willie Miller's daughter) and Mary C. "Mollie" Hampton. Second row from left: Homer Miller (son of Mattie and James), Robert "Bob" Gardner (ward of J.R. and Mattie Miller), James Alfred Walden (husband of Minnie Mae), Minnie Mae Miller Walden (daughter of J.R. and Mattie), Robert Miller (son of J.R. and Mattie), R.S. Stutes (husband of Lillie), Elbert Miller, Roy Hampton Miller (son of J.R. and Mattie) and Willie Pannell Miller (wife of Roy).*

**MILLER** – John Morgan Miller took Elizabeth "Lizzie" Nelson Brashears to be his wife. They had a large orchard. They raised fiber to make brooms. John made shingles. They raised chickens, guineas, ducks, geese, hogs, cows and mules.

Lizzie planted hollyhocks along the fence so the chickens could hide from the hawks. Their children are:
1. William "Bill"
2. Ruth
3. Marvin
4. Nelsie
5. Ellen
6. Lucille
7. Leslie
8. J. N.
9. Milburn
10. Lavelle
11. Dora
12. Alvin
13. Nora

Bill served in the army. He married Arzinia Evans late in life. He died in 1981.

Ruth wed Lawrence Dulaney and they had:
1. J. C.
2. Kay
3. Goldie
4. Shirley
5. Wanda
6. Larry

Ruth lives west of Light.

Marvin married Mattie Ward and they had one daughter, Janet. They lived several years in California before returning to the Stanford community, where Marvin suffered a fatal heart attack in 1954.

Nelsie married Earl Bailey. She lived one-fourth mile from her parents. Their children are:
1. J. C.
2. Carl
3. Boyd
4. Patricia
5. William "Billy"
6. Jerry
7. Beverly
8. Marilyn

Ellen and husband, Pierce Bryant made California their home. They have a son, Lynn and a daughter, Cynthia.

Lucille wed Jim Muska and she has a daughter, Evangeline Culp. They live in Fenton, MO.

Leslie served in the army. He married Anita Simpson. Their children:
1. Leslie Jr.
2. Beverly
3. Stacey
4. Danielle, adopted

J. N. joined the navy and made a career or it. His wife is Satako. He is retired and lives in Florida.

*John Morgan Miller and Elizabeth Nelson Brashers Miller.*

Milburn married Geraldine Lenderman. He taught school at Pumpkin Center. They moved to Cahokia, IL. Their children:
1. Shelia
2. Michael
3. Paula
4. David
5. Dennis

Lavelle, nicknamed "Bob", married Pearline Walton. He served in the army. Their children are:
1. Georgia
2. Kevin
3. Melba
4. Teresa
5. Timmy
6. Robin

They live in Cahokia, IL. Bob retired from McDonald Douglas of St. Louis, MO.

Dora attended college, and then chose St. Louis as her home. She married Doug Doggett. Her children are:
1. Steve
2. Susan
3. Kim
4. Patty.

**MILLER** – Milo and Virginia Miller of Marmaduke, Arkansas, had two children. Larry Joe was born in 1940 and Rita four years later. Both graduated from Marmaduke and Arkansas State University. Larry Joe played basketball on Marmaduke's State Champion teams in 1957 and 1958. Rita also played basketball and was a cheerleader at Marmaduke. After high school, she married Danny Dortch and they live east of Marmaduke.

Larry married Patricia Lynne Gordon of Rector on August 10, 1962. Pat is the daughter of Robert and Loretta Gordon of Rector, Arkansas. Pat has a brother Michael, who resides in Oakdale, California. Pat was a top cheerleader for the Rector Blackcats when she graduated in 1960. She attended Arkansas State and Draughton's Business College until their marriage in 1962.

After moving to Paragould in 1963, Pat and Larry had two sons. Steve was born in 1964 and Scott in 1966. Both sons graduated from Oak Grove High School and Arkansas State University. Steve also graduated from the University of Arkansas School of Law and is an attorney in Springdale, Arkansas. Steve married Kim Jones of Siloam Springs, Arkansas. They presently reside in Siloam Springs and have three children: Ellis, Karagin and Kenzie. Scott lives in Paragould and has been working in real estate and insurance sales since college. Scott married Aimee King of Paragould and they have one daughter, Emily.

Larry's first jobs were as an accountant at Ellington Ford Sales, assistant office manager at Foremost Dairies, and finally as traffic manager at Darling Store Fixtures for 28 years. Pat was a receptionist at the Doctors Building for Doctor Bradsher and McGaughey, and later as a telephone operator during the time that Southwestern Bell had an office in Paragould.

In 1965 Larry took a part time job at the Sunset Drive-In Theatre and over the next few years developed a friendship with Mr. Durward Moore, who was the projectionist during that time. In 1971 Larry, Pat and Durward formed a partnership to build a twin cinema theatre in Paragould. In June, 1972 they opened the Plaza Twin Cinema. Durward retired in 1985 leaving Pat, Larry, Steve and Scott to continue the operation until it was sold in September 1998. The theatre was good for us in three main ways: It kept the family close because we were always working together; over the years we met and became acquainted with almost everyone in and around Paragould; and we saw a lot of movies. During the 27 years we employed many high school students and it is always a pleasure seeing them working in many areas in Paragould now with children about the same age they were when working for us. My only regret is that I didn't keep a diary of all the funny, strange and unusual incidents that happened at the theatre over the 27 years. I'm sure the teenagers during this era will remember "Flash Light Freddie."

**MITCHELL** – In a sharecropper's farmhouse in the Black Jack Community in northwest Greene County, Arkansas, on October 25, 1904, Alvie Murl Mitchell was born. He was the son of Edward William and Viola Marie (Mick) Mitchell both natives of Saline County, Illinois. Edd and Viola moved to Greene County between 1900 and 1902. Their daughter Stella Marie, born in Saline County in 1896, came with them. They had lost three other children in Illinois. In all they were the parents of 10 children with only five reaching adulthood.

Alvie grew up on the farm with his parents and siblings and attended the Black Jack School. He only finished the fourth grade as his father didn't see the need for an education to work on a farm. In the fall of 1928 the family moved to Harrisburg in Poinsett County and continued to farm. Alvie also worked at other jobs including carpentry and hired out as a railroad brakeman with the Missouri Pacific Railroad on February 14, 1929. When the Great Depression hit he was laid off from the railroad.

After moving to Harrisburg he met Maude Mahan, the daughter of Todd Benjamin and Sarah Lavinia (Butler) Mahan. They were married on Christmas Eve 1932. Times were hard and they were very poor. They lived in a house owned by Maude's father and Alvie worked at whatever he could get like many men in that day and time. The author has heard his parents speak of the times that he cleared "new ground" for as little as 50 cents a day digging up stumps of trees that had been cut.

Not too long after this Maude and Alvie moved to Kansas City, Missouri, where three of Maude's sisters and their husbands had moved from Harrisburg to find jobs. Alvie got on with a railroad bridge gang crew that maintained the bridges for the Missouri Pacific in the Kansas City area. Maude worked for a time with Montgomery Ward in Kansas City. On September 3, 1939, their first child, Benjamin Eugene was born at Bethany Hospital in Kansas City, Kansas. He was named after his grandfather Todd Benjamin Mahan and a maternal uncle Eugene Ellis Jacob.

*Front from left: Alvie and Maude (Mahan) Mitchell, back row from left: Tom and Bennie Mitchell.*

When Bennie was two Alvie received a call from Ralph Martin, a railroader with the Mo Pac in Paragould, that they were hiring trainmen. Though Maude liked living in Kansas City near her sisters and their families, Alvie wanted to return to Arkansas.

Upon moving to Paragould they first lived in a rent house on the northwest corner of Third and West Kingshighway that was owned by Mr. William F. Kirsch an attorney. Next they bought a house at 905 W. Emerson from Mr. William A. Branch. It was while living here that Bennie started to school right across the street at Woodrow Wilson. Their second child Thomas Murl was born July 12, 1944, at Dickson Memorial Hospital in Paragould. They next bought six lots from Mr. Hiram Higgins on Wirt Street in the Howell Addition and built a new home there and moved in during the summer of 1947. Bennie and later Tom both attended L.W. Baldwin Elementary School and went on to graduate from Paragould High School, Bennie in 1957 and Tom in 1962. Alvie was promoted to conductor on June 7, 1942, and continued to work for the railroad until the middle 1960s when his health began to fail and he had to retire. At that time they had "pulled" most of the trains off that ran through Paragould to McGehee (his usual run) and they moved to Memphis while Tom was still in college. Tom continued to live at home and finished his degree in business management at Memphis State University, married a Memphis girl, Shirley Ann Smith and started on a career with Sears from which he retired in November 1999 in Atlanta, Georgia. Both Bennie and Tom took part in athletics in junior and senior high school and Alvie took a great deal of interest in following his sons' athletic careers and later his first grandson Lance's career at Paragould High School.

Alvie had several health problems including colon cancer, a heart attack and for several years battled crippling rheumatoid arthritis. His last years were mostly spent in a wheelchair watching television since he couldn't use his hands to do carpentry work to build things like he enjoyed doing. He died at Arkansas Methodist Hospital in Paragould on November 20, 1981. His widow Maude lived the rest of her life at their home at 800 Wirt Street in Paragould and died October 6, 1992, at Arkansas Methodist Hospital. They are buried at Linwood Cemetery next to Maude's parents, Todd and Sarah Mahan.

Alvie was an extremely hard working, Christian man who overcame a lack of formal education and made a good living for his wife and two sons. However, he did appreciate the need for an education and was very proud that his sons were both college graduates.

**MITCHELL** – September 3, 1939, was a very important date in history. On that date Great Britain and France declared war on Nazi Germany and WWII got cranked up in earnest. It was also a very memorable date to the author for on that day at Bethany Hospital in Kansas City, Kansas, Benjamin Eugene Mitchell was born. His parents were Alvie Murl and Maude (Mahan) Mitchell both natives of northeast Arkansas. Alvie being born at Black Jack in Greene County and Maude at Harrisburg in Poinsett County. They had moved to Kansas City, Missouri, from Harrisburg to seek work during the Depression after they married in 1932. In the summer of 1941 just before Bennie's second birthday, they moved to Paragould where Alvie started to work as a brakeman (and later as a conductor) for the Missouri Pacific Railroad.

Bennie started his education at Woodrow Wilson Elementary School right across the street from his home at 905 W. Emerson. He went the first two years there before the family moved to 804 Wirt Street in the Howell Addition. He attended L. W. Baldwin Elementary School for grades third though fifth and then the United Sixth and Seventh School before going to the eighth grade at the old Paragould High School at Seventh and Court Streets. He graduated from PHS in May 1957.

Sports were very important to Bennie as he went through his school years and he played football, basketball and ran track as well as playing Little League, Babe Ruth League and American Legion Baseball. He had the unique distinction of being the only player to play on the very first Little League Championship team-Lions Club in 1951 and then the very first Babe Ruth League Champion-Easy Pay Tire Store in 1954. Both teams were coached by Noel "Dobe" Stuart. The 880 yard relay team that he was a member of in 1957 still holds the school record for that event as the team won the district track title and finished second in the state meet that year. The 1956 Bulldogs football team was also district champions.

*Front from left: Carolyn Rose (Pannell) Mitchell and Benjamin Eugene Mitchell. Back from left: Kristin Michele Mitchell and Gregory Lance Mitchell.*

Growing up in Paragould in the 1950s Mitchell had numerous jobs from paper boy, to grocery sacker at Kelley's Grocery to soda jerk at Hiway Sundries. It was while working at the latter, which put in a pharmacy in the spring of 1957, that he became interested in the idea of being a pharmacist. He enrolled at Hendrix College in Conway to start his pre-pharmacy studies in September 1957. He ran track on the AIC Championship varsity track team in the spring of 1958. He transferred to Arkansas State that summer and completed his pre-pharmacy work there while again running on the track team in the spring of 1959.

In the fall of 1959 he enrolled at the University of Tennessee's College of Pharmacy in Memphis and graduated with a B.S. in pharmacy in June 1962.

In the summer of 1960 while working at Hiway Pharmacy after his first year in pharmacy school he met Carolyn Rose Pannell who had just moved to Paragould from Leachville for her dad Doy Pannell to take the Bulldog's basketball coaching position. Carolyn and Bennie had both been students at ASU during the 1958-59 year but had never met. Their romance moved along rather quickly and they were married April 1, 1961, at East Side Baptist Church in Paragould. They lived in Memphis for the next 15 months while Bennie finished pharmacy school with Carolyn working for a pediatric oncologist as a secretary at The University of Tennessee.

In June 1962 they loaded all their belongings in a small U-Haul trailer and moved to Paragould where Bennie took a position as registered pharmacist at City Drug where he remained until August 1970. On St. Patrick's Day 1963 their first child was born, Gregory Lance Mitchell at Community Methodist Hospital in Paragould. And on September 22, 1968, their second child, Kristin Michele Mitchell was also born at Community Methodist Hospital. In August 1970 Bennie left City Drug and worked as a hospital pharmacist at the hospital. At this time after much thought and prayer and with his wife's blessing he decided to return to medical school, a dream he had for several years. In the fall of 1971 he enrolled in graduate school in the Department of Pharmacology at U.A.M.S. in Little Rock and over the next five years earned a master of science degree in pharmacology and a doctor of medicine degree. After doing a flexible internship in Little Rock the next year he entered private practice in family medicine with Dr. Sam Watson at 901 W. Kingshighway where he has spent the last 22 and one-half years (as of this writing) with the last 12 and one-half years solo after Dr. Watson retired. This is the same building where he worked as a pharmacist at City Drug for eight years.

After returning from Little Rock, Carolyn became active in the family business Pannell Ford Mercury Inc. which she runs along with their son Lance after the death of her father in November 1999.

Lance graduated with honors from Paragould High School where he participated in football, basketball and track as well as baseball in the summer. He attended Vanderbilt University and ASU before starting work full time at the auto dealership. In 1984 he married Kimberly Dawn Poe daughter of Sam and Mary (Diggs) Poe and they have three children Lindsey, David and Landon. Kristin graduated from Crowley's Ridge Academy where she was an honor student and was homecoming queen her senior year. She graduated from Hendrix College with a B.A. degree in business and economics and worked a year as a staff accountant in Little Rock before deciding to go back to school to become a pharmacist. She then attended ASU for two years to finish the required pre-pharmacy courses and enrolled in the College of Pharmacy at U.A.M.S. in Little Rock and graduated with a Doctor of Pharmacy degree in June 1997. While in pharmacy school she met Gary Frankowski a medical student and son of Gary and Susan (Finke) Frankowski of Oakland, Marion County, Arkansas. They were married in November 1994 and have two children Sara Rose and Ryan Paul. At this writing Gary is finishing his residency in anesthesiology at the University of Missouri at Columbia where Kristin works as a staff pharmacist at the University Hospital.

At this writing the Mitchells are looking forward to retirement in a few years to enjoy traveling, gardening and watching the grandchildren grow up. They have been Southern Baptists for a number of years and are members of First Baptist Church in Paragould. Bennie says that if he could sum up his life in one word it would be BLESSED.

**MITCHELL** – Colonel John M. Mitchell, with his wife, Elizabeth Drane, and their children are listed in the 1840 Greene County census as living near Gainesville, then a village just becoming the county seat. The census lists the birth place of daughter, Sarah, as Illinois, 1840, so it is likely they had only recently arrived.

The household included: Mary, 1835 Illinois; Alexander, 1838 Illinois; Sarah, 1840 Illinois; and John Luther Kuykendall, 1828 Illinois.

It has yet to be determined where in Illinois the Mitchell family had been living. The census lists John as a farmer born in Tennessee in 1810. Elizabeth was born in Kentucky in 1814. Considering the age of Mary, their marriage would probably have taken place before 1835.

Two more children were born to them in Arkansas: Silas W., 1844 and James Drane, 1849.

James Drane Mitchell was the great-grandfather of the compiler of this article, Joan Lamb Towery.

Living with the Mitchell family was a young man, John Luther Kuykendall. The 1850 census identifies him as a merchant while the 1860 census describes him as a farmer. John L. was among those "splendid soldiers of Greene County serving in the Mexican War." On his return he married Sarah, the daughter of John Mitchell. They are buried in the Gainesville Cemetery.

John and Elizabeth Mitchell apparently died sometime after 1850. In the 1860 census Silas and James were living with their sister, Sarah, and her family. John Mitchell was a skilled carpenter. He contracted to build Greene County's first frame courthouse in Gainesville. It consisted of three floors: offices on the first floor; courtroom on the second; and a Masonic Hall on the third. The construction was supervised mostly by James Crowley-Mitchell, a slave John bought from the estate of the widow of "Old Ben" Crowley. Also at Gainesville, John erected the first cotton gin in Greene County and he had a mill there.

In 1849 John Mitchell was elected to the Greene County Internal Improvement Commission, serving as treasurer.

James Drane Mitchell left Gainesville early and settled in the neighborhood of Old Herndon. Following in his father's footsteps, he also became a builder. About 1871 he married Dove (Dovey) R. Grayson, the daughter of Christopher Columbus Grayson and Mary Rhea. Mary's parents were Obediah Rhea and Elizabeth Littlepage who settled in Greene County in 1836.

James and Dove Mitchell had eight children:
John P., 1872-1901, married Flora Schisler;
Lula "Lou," 1874-1936, married William Clements "Bid" Lamb;
Mary Ona, 1875, married Alfonse Carr,
Altha, 1878-1883;
Lillie. 1879-1884;
Alexander, 1882, married first Lena; second Grace;
Ethel Anna, 1885-1920, married Eugene Boucher; and
Willie, 1888, married Otto Fink.

Lula Mitchell and "Bid" Lamb were grandparents of Joan Lamb Towery. Their two children who lived were:
Irene, 1898-1990, married Moses M. Rhea and
John P., 1902-1989, married Nancy Caroline Rhea.

Dove Mitchell died in 1894. She, Altha, and Lillie are buried at Pleasant Hill Cemetery.

James D. did much of his work away from home, building mills and gins. He earned $2.00 a day while the common wage was $.75, and was able to afford a surrey. Mary Ona and "Alf" Carr moved into the house to care for the younger children. While working at Sedgwick in Lawrence County, James took a fancy to his boarding house landlady, a young widow named Savannah Kidwell. Granddaughter, Tommy Cook, tells about their courtship: "He soon began to write notes and leave them where she could find them, and she answered them." They married in 1900. Three daughters were born to them: Jemma, Grace Drane and Olleta.

James sold his home at Cross Roads and built a big two level home in Walcott where there was a high school. "Vannie" Mitchell again kept boarders. This house burned about 1916 and they moved to Jonesboro where James worked for the JLC&E Railroad. He was foreman for constructing boxcars.

James Drane Mitchell died in 1939 and is buried by Savannah at Trinity Cemetery in Craighead County.

**MITCHELL** – The R. L. Mitchell family's roots were in middle Tennessee in the community of New Friendship. R. L. Mitchell, Sr. migrated from

267

New Friendship to Greene County, AR, sometime during the year of 1903, settling in the Paragould area where he farmed for a number of years. He and his wife, Clara Sloan, had four sons and two daughters:
1. Reuben
2. Conley
3. Randal L. Jr.
4. Cecil
5. Olive
6. Lenola

Randal L. Mitchell, Jr. graduated from Paragould High School and worked for a while at the Wrape Heading Mill. During this period of time he completed a correspondence course in funeral directing and embalming and obtained his license in that field. He went to work at Trice Bros. Furniture and Embalming Company, as manager of their store, and continued with them for several years. Later, he left Trice Bros. and opened his own furniture and embalming business, but the business eventually failed. He and his brothers-in-law, Jack and Willie Wyatt, decided to go into business together and opened Mitchell and Wyatt Undertaking Company, buying out Trice Bros. undertaking interests. After a while Randal Mitchell bought property at 120 N. Pruett Street in Paragould and established Mitchell Funeral Home there. The business continued in that location from 1923 until 1968, at which time Richard M. Mitchell built a new facility on West Kingshighway, where Mitchell Funeral Home continues today.

After graduating from Paragould High School, Richard M. Mitchell attended St. Louis Mortuary College and received his license in 1941. He returned home and joined his dad in business.

Richards's two sons, Dick and Bobby Mitchell, studied at Dallas Institute of Mortuary Science following their high school graduations and joined Mitchell Funeral Home as licensed funeral directors and embalmers in 1969. Later their two sisters, Caroline and Suzanne, also obtained funeral director licenses and have worked in the family business to a minor extent. Mitchell Funeral Home of Paragould and Rector has proudly served Greene and Clay counties for more than 75 years and continues into the 21st century.

*Submitted by C. Mims*

**MONTGOMRY** – Fanny Simpson Montgomry is the seventh child of Dr. Vincent B. and Sarah Simpson, whose families migrated to Greene County, AR from Kentucky. Fanny's children are:
1. Mae (Montgomry) Sigler who has two children
   a. Nadine (Sigler) Horner
   b. Marlin Sigler
2. George Montgomry and his children:
   a. James Montgomry
   b. Leah Montgomry
   c. Betty Jo (Montgomry) Fuller
3. O. B. Montgomry has two children
   a. Ruth M. Schlersemerfer
   b. George Montgomery
4. Ida (Montgomry) Wood's child is Travis Wood
5. Sam Montgomry whose daughter and son are;
   a. Elsena
   b. Joe Montgomry has a son, Paul Montgomry.

*Submitted by Evelyn Euritha Wagner*

**MOORE** – Andrew Jackson Moore was born in Tennessee circa 1830. He married Amanda Arantha "Allye" (pronounced "Allie") Eubanks, the daughter of James Eubanks and Frances Massey. The marriage must have taken place in Georgia after 1850 for Amanda can be found with her family in the 1850 Murray County, Georgia, census. By the time the 1860 census was taken, A.J. and Amanda were in Greene County, Arkansas. They were a part of the large movement of Murray/Gordan County, Georgia, families who left Georgia in 1859. Page 47 of that census lists A.J. Moore, age 30, born in Tennessee; wife Amanda, age 28, born in Georgia; J.W., age 6, born Georgia; John, age 5, born in Georgia and Francis, age 1, born in Arkansas.

According to A.J.'s nephew Arta Hall, A.J. was called "Jackson." Jackson was a schoolteacher. He taught James Eubank's younger children in Georgia. Arta Hall also said that Jackson was not a hearty man. He had "lung problems." However, he was conscripted into the Confederate Army. In *The Eubanks Family* as told to his daughter Golvia Lewis by J.H. Clark, is recorded a sad story that has been passed down in several lines of the family. "Amanda (Eubanks) married Jackson Moore, perhaps in Georgia–lived on the place that we know as the old Sherwood Batey place–but the Moores likely were the original owners. ...Jackson died of some illness contracted while in the Confederate Army. He was brought home in a wagon. His family knew of his illness–perhaps someone in Greene County had gone out to bring him home after it was known that he was sick. When the wagon approached, the boys went out to meet it, and to see their father who had been away from home for what, at least to two young boys, was a very long time, only to find their father had died on the way home–that he did not live to make the trip–but his body was in the wagon."

In a letter to his grandsons, James William Moore, the son of Jackson wrote: "Altho" My Father was a school teacher, his life was sacrificed (sic), in the Confederate Army for the slaves owners. So I and my brothers and sister had to go into life without the necessary preperation (sic) as my father died from hardships in about three months, after he was forced to go into the Army." [Quoted as written.]

By the 1870 census, Amanda was remarried to Jonathan Futrell. They are found in Cache Township in household #57. They are listed as: Jonathan Futrell, 36, born Kentucky; Larmandy, 35, born Georgia; John D. Futrell, 11, born Arkansas; Jeptha J. Futrell, 2, born Arkansas; James Moore, 17, born Georgia; John Moore, 15, born Georgia and Charles E. Moore, 8, born Arkansas. By this time, the child Frances must have died and the Moores had another son. No further information on Charles has been discovered. On Amanda's Texas Confederate Pension Application #14080, Amanda states that she and "John" Futrell were married May 4, 1863, in Greene County, Arkansas. Jont died November 4, 1877. He served in Price's Regiment.

Amanda and her new husband and family went to Comanche County, Texas where Jont was killed in a gin fire. Amanda made her home at the end of her life with her son James William in Lampasas, Texas. Amanda was born December 2, 1832, and died January 4, 1910, in Lampasas. She is buried in the Oak Hill Cemetery.

**MOORE** – David Littleton Moore was born April 18, 1874, in Greene County, Arkansas. He was the son of William J. Moore and Martha J. Duffel. William J. and Martha had six other children: Ella N.E. "Eastep," born 1870; William Henry, born 1876; Matilda A.B., born 1878; Arthur M., born 1880; George A., born 1881; and Lucy J., born 1884. Lucy "Josie" died at 17 years old in 1901. William J. Moore was born 1848 in Tennessee. He was the oldest of seven children of Arthur M. and Elizabeth (?) Moore. Martha J. Duffel was born 1851 in Osceola, Mississippi County, Arkansas.

David L. Moore married Margaret Paralee Wright in 1894 and they had nine children. Hattie J. (Vaughn), born 1895; Eva Lee, born 1897; Floyd E., born 1899; Straud W. "Wes," born 1902; Charles C., born 1904; Clyde, born 1905, Beulah E. "Elsie" (Retherford), born 1910; Lucy H. (Belanger), born 1912 and Audie M. (Guest), born 1915. Eva Lee was stillborn and Charles died at 3 years old. Margaret P. died in 1921 at 43 years old. Margaret is buried at Wright Cemetery near Marmaduke. David and Margaret had lived in the Marmaduke area all their lives, raising all their children there. When grandma Margaret died, that left my mother Beulah E. to take over the household chores, because she was the oldest living daughter, while grandpa and the boys worked the fields. Hattie had died in 1919, leaving her husband Clarence with their small son Luther D. Luther died a short time after his mother. They are also buried at the Wright Cemetery with Charles and Eva Lee.

Beulah E. married William Erva Retherford August 1, 1931, and together they raised five children. (see Retherford family biography).

David L. moved to Flint, Michigan, in the early 1940s and lived the rest of his life there. He died in February 1955.

**MORGAN** – Wilford Bice Morgan, farmer and salesman, was born August 5, 1859, in Kentucky, and died November 24, 1946, age 87 in Paragould, and was buried at the New Friendship Cemetery. He died at one o'clock Sunday afternoon at his home, 100 East Baldwin Street, following an illness of four weeks due to heart disease. He was the son of John M. Morgan, a master tailor, born 1833 in New York, and Louisa A. Russell, a homemaker, born December 1832 in Tennessee. Wilford married Martha Luidie Elkins on October 10, 1882, in Obion County, Tennessee. Martha was born April 2, 1864, in Tennessee and died August 14, 1924, age 60 at the local hospital following an illness of more than two weeks and was buried at New Friendship Cemetery. Martha was the daughter

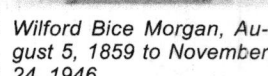

*Wilford Bice Morgan, August 5, 1859 to November 24, 1946.*

*June 1977, at the funeral of Lottie Mae Byrd Morgan, Lottie's family. Back row: Harry Edwin Morgan, Glenn E. Morgan, Wendell E. Morgan and Jack Byrd. Front row: Harriett Charlene Morgan Seachord, Virginia Dalton and Mary Sellars.*

of Ezekiel Elkins, farmer, born 1818 in Tennessee and Sarah Elkins, homemaker, born 1830 in Tennessee. Wilford moved his family to Paragould in 1901 by covered wagon. Wilford and Martha had sons, John Robert, Jessie A., Charley R., Ernest M., Burrel A., Alford B. and daughter Elva A.

*Harriett Charlene Morgan Seachord family: Stephen Cleo Jr., Melissa Francine, Donna Maria, Harriett Charlene and Stephen Cleo.*

John Robert "Bob" Morgan, farmer and driver for Dr. Pepper Company, was born November 21, 1889, in Obion County, Tennessee, and died March 22, 1974, in Sutter County, California. John married Lillie Mae Smith on October 2, 1910, in Paragould. Lillie, a homemaker, was born September 11, 1887, in Illinois and died December 18, 1937, age 50 in Paragould and was buried at Linwood Cemetery. Lillie died at 1:00 p.m. in the afternoon at her home, 753 North Pruet, following an illness of three years due to a complication of diseases. Lillie was the daughter of Charles Henry Smith, farmer and a carpenter, born June 7, 1861, in Hamilton County, Illinois, and died October 8, 1925, in Paragould and Mary Dollar, a homemaker, was born February 18, 1856, in Jefferson County, Illinois, and died February 10, 1931, in Paragould. Charles and Mary are buried at the Linwood Cemetery. John and Lillie had sons: Harry Edwin, Herman Robert, Kenneth Winston, Charles Wilford and a daughter Hazel.

Harry Edwin Morgan, a truck driver, was born July 7, 1912, in Paragould. Harry married Lottie Mae Byrd June 25, 1932, in Paragould. Lottie was born December 19, 1912, in Ponset County, Arkansas and died June 13, 1977, age 64 in Fort Smith and was buried at Linwood Cemetery. She was the daughter of Jasper Byrd born September 30, 1889, in Arkansas and died December 23, 1968, in Paragould and Isabel Whitworth born May 1895 in Arkansas and died May 1913. Harry and Lottie had sons: Wendell Edward, Glen Earl and daughters Harriett Charlene, Shirley E., Mary Carolyn and Virginia Lee.

*John Robert "Bob" Morgan, November 21, 1889 to March 22, 1974.*

Harriett Charlene Morgan was born September 13, 1946, in Yuba City, California. She married Stephen Cleo Simoneau Seachord on September 30, 1967, in Marysville, California. Stephen was born February 10, 1945, in Hastings, Nebraska. They had a son Stephen Cleo Jr., and daughters Melissa Francine and Donna Marie.

**MORRIS** – Robert Marion Morris was born in Parkin, Cross County, AR on Feb 13, 1935, son of Robert Walter and Bernice Ann (Ligon) Morris. He served four years in the U. S. Air Force. On July 30, 1956, in Dixon, Lee County, AR, Robert Marion married Frances Ann Morris (Sept 19,1935 Foreman, Little River County, AR) daughter of John James and Frances Charline (Culbertson) Morris.

Robert and Frances Morris lived six years in Rockford, IL, where Robert worked for Woodward Governor Plant, Inc. before moving to Greene County in Feb 1962. They bought a 120-acre farm in St. Francis Township. Robert Marion then went to work at A. D. T. factory in Jonesboro for six years before going into the dairy business. After three years in the dairy business, Robert sold out and went to work for Atlas Asphalt, Inc. in Jonesboro, from which he retired in Jan 1999.

Robert and Frances Morris had three children. First-born was Sharon Kay "Casey" Morris (Sept 17, 1957 Rockford, IL) married in Broussard, LA on Dec 15, 1985 to Mark Rolland Fisher (May 15, 1956 Albuquerque, NM- May 15, 1991) the son of Rolland Edward Fisher and Jean Ellen Shaw Fisher. Sharon Kay " Casey" and Mark Fisher had one son, Nicholas Mark Fisher (Dec 10,1986 Lafayette, LA). Sharon still resides in Lafayette and runs her own business, Ranger Aviation, located in Lafayette.

The second child, Teressa Gale Morris (April 23, 1960 Rockford, Winnabago County, IL) married June 25, 1982 in Paragould, AR to Brian Steen Duncan (July 23, 1959 Jonesboro, AR) the son of Billy Steen and Barbara Ann (Witt) Duncan. Teressa and Brian have two sons: Brady Steen Duncan (March 8, 1986 Jonesboro, AR) and Tanner Ryan Duncan (Jan 20, 1991 Jonesboro, AR). Brian and Teressa Duncan moved to Greene County in 1994. Brian works for Craighead Electric Co-op as Key Account Manager and Barton's of Paragould employs Teressa in the carpet and cabinet sales division.

The last child born to Robert and Frances Morris was Robert Marion "Robbie" Morris Jr. (June 23, 1963 Paragould, Greene County, AR- May 2, 1998 Clay County, AR) who died in an automobile accident. He had one daughter; Jennifer Machele Morris (Feb 13, 1985 Paragould) Jennifer Machele is a freshman at Greene County Tech School this year (2000-01).

*Submitted by Frances Morris*

**MORRIS** – Captain William W. T. Morris and Sarah M. Jackson were married on Feb 7, 1850. The names of their nine children were:
1. Mary F.
2. Minnie Bell
3. Alfred Thomas
4. William Jack
5. Dixey J.
6. Susan E.
7. Lottie W.
8. Sarah C.
9. John W.

Captain Morris did not serve in the War Between the States, but he was a man of great influence and his friends automatically gave him the title of captain and for 30 years he was known as Captain Morris.

In Dec 1871, Captain Morris with his wife and nine children started in wagons from Newbern, TN, to Scatterville, AR. On Dec 23, they reached Point Pleasant on the Mississippi River. The river was frozen, the wind was high and it was raining and they couldn't cross the river. The owner of the ferryboat gave Captain Morris permission to move his family into the boat.

On Christmas Eve night, while the owner of the boat was attending a Christmas ball at his nearby plantation, a severe storm came up and the cable ropes were broken and the boat went floating down the Mississippi River, with no one to pilot or guide it.

On Christmas day, men in small boats rescued the five daughters, but the captain, his wife and four sons were all left on the boat still floating downstream.

After being on the boat almost a week, supplies of food and wood were exhausted and the children became hungry and cold.

*Grandpa Jack and Grandma Mollie Morris. Grandpa's 81st birthday, Mar. 23, 1942.*

When an island was seen in the distance, Captain Morris decided he would try to get to the island by walking on the ice and then bring the children and Mrs. Morris across on the ice to the island.

While his family was watching from the boat, they saw the ice break and the captain go down. But it so happened the water was shallow and he escaped and reached the island safely, then brought the family over.

After hearing cries of distress from Captain Morris, some men came to his rescue and he learned that he was on an island near Osceola, AR. After reviving themselves, they took passage on the first steamboat, coming north and reached Point Pleasant safely. When they arrived, they found their daughters, who had been taken care of by the generous people who lived in that area.

After crossing the Mississippi, they then crossed the Negro Wool Swamp on the Old Pole Road and reached the first settlement at Clarkton, MO.

They crossed the St. Francis River at Chalk Bluff and came to Scatterville, where they stopped at the home of John Bearden.

On Jan 26, 1872, Captain Morris and his family moved to Blue Cane and settle on 320 acres where his son Jack Morris resided until his death on July 3, 1943.

Uncle Jack Morris and Aunt Mollie Purett were married on Oct 9, 1884 and the had 11 children:
1. Minnie A.
2. Connie J
3. Ida Amacey
4. W. J.
5. Ruthie L.
6. Bertha M.
7. Dixie
8. Beulah E.
9. Floyd J.
10. Claudie C.
11. Raymond Parrish.

Raymond Parrish Morris and Jewell Lee German were married on March 31, 1929. They bought an 80-acre farm north of Marmaduke in Dec of 1947. Raymond and Jewell lived on the farm until their deaths, his on July 15, 1955 and hers on Oct 11, 1994. They had one son Aaron Lageral Morris.

Aaron Lageral Morris and Emma Mae Wright were married on July 8, 1950. In 1951, they bought 40 acres adjoining Raymond and Jewell's property. They lived on the farm until the early 1960s when they moved to Marmaduke. Aaron and Emma's children:

269

1. Shirley
2. Dianne
3. Linda Kaye
4. Pamela Raye
5. Randy Lee

Shirley Dianne Morris married Timothy Holcomb and their children:
1. Misty Dianne married Shannon May
2. Timothy Jason

Linda Kaye Morris married Rickey Alan Dickinson and their children:
1. Lisa Michelle married Billy Martin and their three children:
   a. Lauren Brenn
   b. Alexander Caughley
   c. Chandler Reece
2. Chris Alan

Pamela Ray Morris who is now married to Dean Keith Lackey has one son Quincy Luke Roberts, whose father was Stephen Dale "Luke" Roberts. She also has two stepchildren, Caci Dawn and Levi George Lackey.

Randy Lee Morris has on son Aaron Lee. Aaron's mother is Diana Lynn Ogg. Aaron will have the honor of carrying on the "Morris Family" name.

*Submitted by Randy L. Morris*

**MORROW** – Cecil Morrow was born February 20, 1897, to James Berry and Pamelia (Breckenridge) Morrow. In 1918 he joined the Army, but was discharged in 1919 due to injuries he received. On October 24, 1924, he married Belvia DeHart who was born December 14, 1904, to John Henry and Claudia (Eubanks) DeHart. Cecil and Belvia lived on the 60 acre bottom farm, where they raised sugar cane. All the children and cousins (Alvin's children) cut and stripped the cane, then it was taken to the mill where it was made into sorghum molasses. It was a happy day when the work was finished. The children watched the sorghum being made. It was so much fun taking the cane stick and putting it into the hot sorghum, then eating it. The families kept all they needed for winter and some was sold for profit. It was used to eat with butter and sop with a hot biscuit. Also to make popcorn balls, sorghum candy and cookies, cakes and many more delicious treats.

Cecil and Belvia later moved to the home place, where they continued to live and care for Cecil's dad until his dad's death in 1957. Cecil and Belvia then tore down the old home place and built a new home. Their son Jerry and wife Doris built a home across the road from the home place. They cared for Jerry's parents (Cecil and Belvia) until their deaths. Jerry and Doris's son Keith moved into the home place and is still there (1999). Five generations have lived on the Morrow farm. Cecil and Belvia had five children:

*Cecil Berry Morrow, born February 20, 1897, and Belea DeHart Morrow, born December 14, 1905. They married October 5, 1924. This is a wedding picture.*

(1) Inetha Morrow born June 18, 1925.
(2) Juanitha Morrow born June 23, 1928.
(3) Joy Morrow born December 1930.
(4) Bobby Morrow born December 14, 1933.
(5) Jerry Morrow born August 15, 1939.

**MORROW** – James Berry Morrow was born March 31, 1865, to William Franklin and Mildred Anders (or Andrews) in Beech Grove, Arkansas. James Berry married Pamelia J. Breckenridge on October 14, 1886. She was born on March 8, 1868, and her parents were David and Elizabeth Breckenridge. Elizabeth's father was Jessie Williams. She first married John Lovelady and had two sons, John and Jessie. Elizabeth and David had six children. Pamelia was the fourth child. They had four boys and one girl. They were Wayon Daniel, Telfer Alvin, Jasper Neal, Cecil Berry and Vadie (Navada) Alberta. Pamelia died October 9, 1898, and James Berry died on June 20, 1958.

James Berry then married Minnie Campbell who was born on March 8, 1883, and died March 5, 1905. Together they had two children, Marion and Dinky. He found himself with small children to raise and no mother to help.

He then met and married Ellen Chadwick and together they had no children. James and Ellen raised the children together with lots of love for each other and the children. She is buried at the Morrow Cemetery. James Berry is buried, along with his first two wives, in the Owens Chapel Cemetery.

Mr. Morrow was known throughout the community as '"Uncle Jim" and was quite a character. He lived to be 94 years old. James Berry could jump any gully on the farm at 90 years old. He attended Commissary Church of Christ. He always had a bottle of whisky with him. He would put hard candy in the whisky and use it for medicinal purposes. During church services he would start coughing and take out his bottle and take a big drink, right in the amen corner. The ladies of the church had a field day with this, but it never stopped Uncle Jim from drinking his cough medicine. James Berry had several interesting tales told about his life. One of the few I have been told is that he walked to Beech Grove to see the first match struck in this area.

*Back row standing: Parthenia Morrow. Second row from left: James Berry Morrow and Pamelia Breckenridge Morrow. Front row from left: Waymon, Alvin and Vadie.*

He owned 60 acres of bottom land near Cache River. He acquired 80 acres of hill land while working for the railroad company. The railroad was established around 1885. It was a branch line of the Cache Valley Railroad and was the first line built through Craighead County. This line was named The Kansas City, Fort Scott and Memphis Railroad. One branch of the railroad went to Jackson's Commissary, another to Johnson's Sawmill on the Daniel Futrell farm, and the other went south of the big rocks to a gravel pit. The Jim Morrow home place is just above the big rocks. It is a farm that was never bought and sold. This is where James Berry raised his family. Most of his children stayed on the farm to care for their father at different times. Cecil his youngest son, stayed the longest and took care of him until he died. The farm is still in the family. Cecil's youngest son, Jerry, and his wife Doris, built a home across the road from the home place and there they raised their children. They still live there and many memories are brought to life each time the family visits.

**MORROW** – Jasper "Jap" Morrow was born September 22, 1877, Giles County, Tennessee, to Thomas James Morrow and Nancy (Ball) Morrow. In past histories written about the Morrows coming to Greene County, Arkansas, we learn that William Franklin Morrow, a brother to Thomas James Morrow left Tennessee at the age of 20. Reasons given for him leaving his family was that his father had died, his mother remarried and he didn't get along with his stepfather. William Franklin married Louisa Wilcockson, daughter of Samuel Wilcockson after arriving in Greene County and settled in the Walcott area. After the death of Louisa, William Franklin married Mary Mildred Anders, daughter of Philip Anders and Rebecca Smelser Anders.

After William Franklin left his home in Tennessee he had no contact with his family for over 30 years. During this time, unknown to him, two of his brothers, John D. and Thomas James came to Arkansas from Tennessee by wagon train, crossing the river at Memphis, settled around Forrest City, Arkansas, and later moved to Wynne. It was here in 1882 that by chance they met a man who knew William Franklin and gave them his address in Greene County. They wrote William telling him that they would like to move to Greene County. When William Franklin got to Wynne to visit his brothers, John D. was sick with yellow fever. William went back to Greene County to get his ox-wagon to move his brothers. When he returned to Wynne, however, John D. was dead and Thomas was ill with the fever. William loaded John D.'s wife (Margaret Ann Ball Morrow) and children, brought them to Greene County and then returned for Thomas and his family. Thomas had died also. He loaded up Thomas' wife (Nancy Ball Morrow) and children to move to Greene County.

William homesteaded 193 acres east of Walcott, where he supported his own family, plus his brother's families. It is told at times there were 21 people around the table for meals at William Franklin Morrow's home. One of these children was Jasper "Jap" Morrow, son of Thomas James Morrow and Nancy Ball Morrow.

Jasper married Malinda Lynn Burkeen December 21, 1900, in Greene County. She died October 10, 1916, and is buried in the Morrow Cemetery. Their children were:

James Gordon Morrow born October 17, 1901, married Gertie Mae Fears.

Thelma Irene Morrow born July 8, 1906, married Calvin Busby.

Jessie T. Morrow born May 5, 1906, married Lois Morrow (distant cousin).

Junious Darrell Morrow born March 8, 1916, married Lucy Stevens.

Listed below are the grandchildren of Jasper Morrow:

Children of James Gordon and Gertie Morrow: Hughey Leon Morrow, born September 19, 1922, married Mildred Downs. Dorothy Violet Morrow, born April 12, 1927, married Freeman Ragsdell.

*Jasper "Jap" Morrow, father of Thelma, Gordon, Darrell and Jessie.*

Children of Thelma Morrow Busby and Calvin Busby: 1. Newell Eugene Busby, born September 2, 1924, married Maxine Campbell. 2. Trudy Wilheim Mae Jewell Busby, born May 7, 1926, died May 10, 1926. Warren Henry Busby born April 29, 1927, married Deanie Waddell and second Roberta Floyd. Elmon Leo Busby born September 30, 1929, married Alene Gladish. Ethan Cleo Busby born May 22, 1931, married first Norma Greer and second Bettye Sparks Overbay Busby. Lindy Lee Busby born April 28, 1933, married Nicole Scherf. Wilda Mae Busby born February 8, 1937, died at one month. Billy Gene Busby born April 25, 1938, married Winnia Lou Bullington died September 17, 1990. John Calvin Busby born October 5, 1941, died December 31, 1949.

**MORROW** – Jeff Luther Morrow, 1895-1964, the second son of John Louis, 1858-1901, and Emma (Smith) Taylor Morrow, 1870-1903, was born west of the Big Rocks that are located between Stanford and Beech Grove. Jeff was about 5 years old when his father died and about 7 years old when his mother died. He and his brother John went to live with their Uncle Samuel and Aunt Parthenia (Breckenridge) Morrow. Their sister Iva went to live with their Uncle Dave and Aunt Ethel (Smith) Morrow. Their Aunt Ethel was their mother's sister. They also had another uncle, Jefferson Nelson Morrow, who married their mother's other sister Minnie.

When Jeff was 13 years old, he and his brother moved with the Sam Morrow family to Five-Mile Springs in Randolph County, Arkansas. While living there, Jeff had measles and was sick for a long time. Later, they moved back to Greene County, close to Walcott, and then to Stanford where Sam ran a store. Eventually the family moved to the Evening Shade Community.

Jeff lived with his Uncle Sam until he was 21 years old. When he left, his uncle gave him a horse, and then he moved in with a cousin, Champ Futrell and his family, and in the spring of 1917, raised a crop there.

Also in 1917, Jeff married Alma Pearl Goins, 1898-1972, daughter of William Preston and Lydia Elizabeth (Lafferty) Goins, and they lived with the Futrell family until the crop was gathered. Then he and Pearl set up housekeeping at his father's homeplace after his Uncle Dave Morrow moved from there.

Jeff was inducted into the Army on July 22, 1918, and sailed to the Allied European Forces in France on September 1, 1918. Pearl and their first child returned to live with her parents while Jeff was gone. Jeff always said that he got within hearing distance of the gunfire but never had to experience any fighting because the war ended. He was discharged with an honorable discharge on November 30, 1918, because of U.S. demobilization. He returned to the United States on April 3, 1919.

Jeff and Pearl bought a house and land close to Pearl's parents and lived there approximately three years. After living other places for short periods of time, they moved to the homeplace of Pearl's parents when her parents retired to a smaller house. Pearl was born and lived on this farm that her father had acquired by accepting the Donation Act in 1896. They also reared their family of seven children there who are as follows:

*Jeff and Pearl Morrow.*

Jeffiteen Inez, born 1918, married Joseph Gilbert Clark, 1914-1999, whose children are John Joseph, born 1940, Jeff Morrow, born 1944, and Jimi Nett, born 1948.

Mary Janice, born 1921, married Warren Mock, 1921-1998, whose only child is Michael, born 1941.

Louis Preston, 1923-1928.

Golvia Elizabeth, born 1926, married Alfred Metheny, born 1925, whose children are Alfred Daniel, born 1944; Stephen Bryance, born 1946; Golvia Demara, born 1951; Hilda Gayle, born 1953; and Dwight Julian, born 1956.

June Carolyn, born 1932, married Lawrence Anthony Rizzotto, born 1933, whose children are Rebecca Anne, born 1958; Leah Susan, born 1962; and Anthony Samuel, born 1966.

John Dwight, born 1935, married patsy King, born 1937, whose children are Mark Dwight, born 1957; Lisa Renee, born 1963; and Timothy Louis, born 1965.

Leah Kate, born 1939, married Jimmy Leon Smith, born 1940, whose only child is Jimmy Leon Jr., born 1963.

Letha Fay, born 1941-died 1941.

Pearl was a homemaker and an active member of the Stanford Home Demonstration Club for years. She raised a large garden every year and did much canning and freezing of garden produce. She also loved flowers and gardening was her hobby. She and Jeff raised cotton, corn, wheat, soybeans, hogs, cattle and chickens. They sold eggs and cream.

Since Jeff suffered from severe asthma attacks, they were forced to move from the farm into Paragould in order to get out of the dust raised by farming. While living there Pearl became an active member of the Greene County Historical Society and enjoyed working on articles about the county as well as on the genealogy of some of the families living in the county. She researched her own family as well as both sides of Jeff's family and was able to obtain information about several generations past.

After Jeff's death Pearl managed to stay active for a number of years. She did of cancer in 1972.

Jeff and Pearl were members of the Church of Christ and Pearl loved to sing in church. She and Jeff lived active lives by enjoying their family and many friends and living life to the fullest. They are buried in the Morrow Cemetery.

**MORROW** – John Frank Morrow (1893-1965), the first son of John Louis Morrow (1858-1901) and Emma "Smith" Taylor (1870-1903) was born west of the Big Rocks, located between Stanford and Beech Grove.

John was about seven years old when his father died and about nine when his mother died. He and his brother Jeff went to live with their Uncle Samuel and Aunt Parthenia (Breckenridge) Morrow. Their sister, Iva, went to live with their Uncle Dave and Aunt Ethel (Smith) Morrow. Their Aunt Ethel was their mother's sister. They also had another uncle, Jefferson Nelson Morrow, who married their mother's other sister, Minnie.

When John was 15 he and his brother, Jeff moved with their Uncle Samuel's family to Five Mile Springs in Randolph County, AR. While living there John was on the river, where they were floating some trees they had cut to the sawmill and broke his arm. Later they moved back to

*John Frank and Pearl Pillow Morrow*

Greene County near Walcott and then to Stanford where Uncle Samuel ran a store. Eventually the family moved to Evening Shade community.

John lived with his Uncle Sam until he was about 18 years old, when his mother and dad's estate was settled. He then lived with Daniel and Liza Jane (Morrow) Futrell. Liza Jane was his dad's sister.

In 1919 John married Pearl Ester Pillow (1900-1978). They lived at Stanford by the Sugar Creek on Cooper's place and then moved to East Bottoms on Uncle Bill Pillow's place. Then John and Pearl exchanged places with Uncle Bill and moved to the old home place, which was great-grandfather Claborne Pillow's place, near Pine Knot community in Poland Township. They bought the place, raised cotton, corn, sorghum, peanuts and sweet potatoes and had a big orchard. They lived there the rest of their lives.

John and Pearl (Pillow) Morrow had nine children:
1. Samuel Eugene (1921-1998) married Dorothy Sandlin. Their children:
   a. Danny Jean (1943
   b. John Frank (1958)
   c. Brenda Jean (1961)
2. James Albert (1923-1941) came down with rheumatic fever and damaged his heart. He passed away at age 18.
3. Erma Lucile (1925) married Emmit Noel Pogue (1920-1982). Their children:
   a. George Wayne (1942)
   b. John Lee (1945)
   c. Thomas Ray (1947)
   d. Linda Kay (1949)
   e. Ted Joe (1951)
   f. Beth Ann (1961)
4. Ellis Arvie (1927) married Hettie May Hale (1927). Their children:
   a. Jack Dale (1948)
   b. Donna Jean (1950)
   c. Sherry Lynn (1962)
5. Exah Deanna (1928) married Thomas Edward McMenamin (1925-1996). Their children:
   a. Thomas Edward (1947-1976)
   b. Margaret Ann (1954)
   c. Elizabeth Marie (1958)
6. Eldred Sonny (1930-1997) married Francis Hoyer (1931-1996). Their children:
   a. John Eldred (1959-1988)
   b. James Frank (1962)
   c. Shirley (1948) stepdaughter
   d. Patricia (1952) stepdaughter
7. Harrald John (1932-1993) married Virginia Sims (1934-1999). Their children:
   a. Stepiha May (1956)
   b. Cynthia Ann (1958)
   c. Carol Jean (1960)
   d. Remonia Jane (1962-1999)
   e. Douglas Harold (1964)
8. Billy Joe (1934) married (1) Louise Butler (2) Patricia Jorden. Children of Billy Joe and Louise:
   f. Larry Joe (1951)
   g. Debra Sue (1954)
   h. Sylvia (1958-1964) Harold Wayne (1966)
9. Shelba Jean (1937-1937)

**MORROW** – John Louis Morrow, 1858-1901, son of William Franklin, 1830-1899, and Mary Mildred (Anders) Morrow, 1833-date unknown, was born in Greene County, Arkansas, between Stanford and Beech Grove.

On November 27, 1879, he married Adeline Taylor, 1860-date unknown. Their children were as follows:

George Ann, 1880-1937, married Albert Goins, 1881-1955, and their children who lived to be grown were Ora, 1902-1942, who married

Ruby Ward, 1910-1996, and had one child, Jo Anna, born 1929, who married Laurence Justice, born 1921.

Eva born 1911, married Chester Daughhetee, 1909-1995, and had three children who are Grady, born 1928 who married Mary Jo Henson, 1932-1996, Alma Dean, born 1933 who married Carl Hamblin Jr., born 1934, and Danny Buster, born 1944 who married Pearlie Roberts born 1949. Fred born 1915, married Alice Ray, birth date unknown and died in 1997 and had no issue.

Their second child, Bell, 1882-1920, married George Jetton, 1871-1956, and their children were Carrol, born 1903 who married Mary Battenfield, 1908-1979; Earl, 1904-1992, who married Cora Shewmaker, 1902-1986; William, 1907-1999, who married Vertie Barr born 1912; Frank, 1914-1981, who married Opal Morrow, born 1915; Annie May, 1917-1998, who married Houston Davis born 1916; and Maynard, 1919-1936.

Their third child, Mary Jane, 1887-1908, married George Wheeler, 1882-1961. Their only son was Clennie, 1907-1987, who married Ida Thurman, born 1907.

After Adeline's death, John Louis married Anna (Robinson) Smith, 1854-death date unknown, in 1889, who was the daughter of G. N. and Elizabeth Robinson and the widow of William C. Smith. Anna's former husband was injured when a horse fell on him during a battle of the Civil War after which he was brought home a cripple. John and Anna had no children.

John Louis' third marriage was to Emma (Smith) Taylor, 1870-1903, on January 7, 1892. She was the daughter of Anna (Robinson) Smith and William Smith. Emma had two sisters, Ethel and Minnie, who married two of John Louis' brothers, David Franklin and Jeff Nelson. John Louis and Emma had three children: John Franklin, 1893-1966, who married Victoria Cupp with no issue, and then to Pearl Pillow, 1900-1978, and their children were Samuel Eugene, 1921-1998, who married Dorothy Sanders; James Albert, 1923-1941; Lucille born 1925 who married Emmet Pogue, 1917-1982; Ellis Orville, born 1927, who married Hattie Hale born 1926; Exah, born 1928, who married Thomas McMenamin born 1930; Eldred, 1930-1995, who married Lena Torrence; Harold, 1932-1993, who married Virginia Sims; Billy Joe, born 1934, who married Louise Butler; and Shelby Jean, 1937-1937.

John Louis and Emma's second child was Jeff Luther, 1895-1964, who married Alma Pearl Goins, 1898-1972, and their children were Jeffiteen Inez, born 1918, who married Gilbert Clark, 1914-1999; Mary Janice, born 1921, who married Warren Mock,, 1921-1998; Louis Preston, 1923-1928; Golvia Elizabeth, born 1926, who married Alfred Metheny, born 1925; June Carolyn, born 1932, who married Lawrence Rizzotto, born 1933; John Dwight, born 1935, who married Patsy King, born 1937; and Leah Kate, born 1939, who married Jimmy Leon Smith, born 1940.

John Louis and Emma's third child was Iva Louis, 1902-1984, who married George Brown, 1904-1948, and had one child Arra Virginia, born 1924.

John Louis and Emma were farmers and lived near the Jackson Commissary area and are buried in Owens Chapel Cemetery.

**MORROW** – Phillip Bailey Morrow (Sept 11, 1898-Nov 2, 1990) was the sixth child born to Phillip Samuel and Parthenia Breckenridge Morrow. They were married in Greene County, Sept 16, 1886. Their early years were spent in the Beech Grove and Evening Shade area. Bailey married Gladys Eubanks Oct 3, 1920 and they had one daughter Earline (Jan 15, 1922).

Bailey, Gladys and Earline came with his parents to the Fourth Street house, which his parents occupied until their deaths. Shortly thereafter, Bailey started his successful and long-standing dairy on rented land across Eight Mile Creek.

In 1926 he purchased a house and 80 acres from the Purcell family at the corner of the Old Mill Road and Highway 1-W. That parcel of land became known as the P. B. Morrow Dairy Farm.

A familiar sight on the streets of Paragould was the P. B. Morrow Dairy truck. Rain or shine, sick or well, he delivered milk door to door every day. He continued to do this nearly 40 years and lived on the original site until his death at 92. Gladys preceded Bailey in death by eight years. Both are buried in the Morrow Plot in the Center Hill Cemetery. They were a devout Christian family and were members of the Church of Christ at Seventh and Mueller.

*Bailey Morrow–A Collage Photo: His dairy used the same type bottle cap as shown for 40 years. 1948–Bailey with his dairy truck and milk in carrier. 1952–Bailey preparing for cow feeding time. This was a newspaper ad for Purina Feed Co. that ran frequently in the local newspaper. 2000–Madeline Aswad, first great-great granddaughter, wearing overalls and his trademark Purina Cow-Chow cap.*

Bailey and Gladys' daughter, Earline, served during WWII as a second lieutenant in the Army Nurse Corp. She married Robert Zatlin, an Army Air Corp Captain in 1946. They have two daughters, Jane (1948) and Mary (1950). They established a home and raised their daughters in Wellesley, MA. Jane married Peter Knights in 1969 and produced five great grandchildren for Bailey and Gladys:
1. Cynthia
2. Rebecca
3. Robert
4. Matthew Bailey
5. Elizabeth

Mary married Michael Stroud in 1973 and produced two more great grandchildren: Jennifer Lee and Lesley Jane. Jeffrey Morrow Stroud was deceased as an infant. All these grandchildren and great grandchildren were their pride and joy in their later years.

Now the great grands are producing the great, great grands! As shown in the collage photo, wearing Bailey's trademark overalls and his Purina Cow-Chow cap, is their first great great granddaughter Madeline Elisabeth Aswad (March 23, 2000), the first born of Cynthia Knights Aswad and Dr. Paul Aswad. On Sept 7, 2000, Rebecca Knights Krechting and husband Christopher Krechting became parents of Victoria Lynne, a second great great granddaughter!! All currently reside in Needham, MA. right next to Wellesley, where they grew up. The close family ties that were important and upheld by Bailey and Gladys were instilled in all of us, to be valued and kept alive by frequent contact and caring for each other. We remember how much and how well they loved us all. Paragould is still a second home. A legacy was left.

**MORROW** – Men melted at the sight of Sylvia's big soft black eyes and shy smile. Girls envied her tiny waist and perfect bosom. But everyone admired her inward beauty of quiet, Christian spirit.

She was the first child of Joe and Zeulia Clark, born August 13, 1896, near Crowley's Ridge in Greene County, Arkansas. By six, she was scolded into responsibility for her siblings and by nine, she chopped and picked cotton in Texas. Studious and bright, she filled her fourth grade composition book with weighty, romantic poems. Once at 14, she was whipped with a rope by her farther who mistakenly thought she had given a boy her Arbuckle coffee coupon ring.

When 16, she sobbed at leaving her first beau as the family made one of its countless moves. More suitors appeared, but her truest love was learning. When public school ended at eighth grade, she studied another year with her teacher, but Papa said "No" to her plea for college and moved them back to Paragould. There the handsome, auburn-haired, blue-eyed Tom Morrow became smitten by her. Tom, son of hard working Sam and Parthenia of Walcot, repeatedly proposed. Finally, after a year, she abandoned her dream of college and accepted.

Tom's brother Marcus attended a normal school for teachers and invited Sylvia. She passed the teaching certification exam but the ink was barely dry before she became pregnant with Durward, January 8, 1916; soon after, Douglas, November 17, 1917; and then Tomazine, August 20, 1919, an infant when the family took the train to Texas.

*Tom and Sylvia Morrow and children. Front row: Joy, Carmyn, Graydon, Thomazine, Douglas and Durward. Back row: Una May, Sylvia, Thurston, Tom, and Sula Jo. This photo was made in August 1940.*

Times were restless and so was Tom. After several moves and Graydon, September 13, 1921; Carmyn, August 2, 1923; and Joy, April 22, 1925, they moved to a place called "Troubles End" in Springdale, Arkansas. But their troubles didn't end. Tom found no work. So after the seventh child, Una May, May 14, 1928, they tried cotton picking in Texas. Back in Arkansas, the Depression devastated the heartland and left them so poor that Sylvia had her next baby, Sula Jo, January 2, 1932, without a doctor.

Sylvia wanted more education for her children, so they ended up at Huntsville where Durward and Douglas could go to a vocational-technical school. But measles swept through the family and they returned to Paragould where Tom was hired by the state highway department–his first job with a paycheck. Thurston arrived on October 25, 1935, to complete the family. Soon after, Sylvia lost her best friend, her mother, and a part of her died. And the moves began again, back to Northwest Arkansas, from place to place until they fulfilled Sylvia's life dream and bought their own property.

Douglas and Graydon left to fight in World War II, Tomazine married, and Carmyn became Sylvia's first child to attend college. With so many of the older children gone and anxious over the welfare of her sons, Sylvia gave up on working the farm. Soon the Korean War arrived and Douglas was killed. The lessons learned from Zeulia had helped Sylvia manage moves and lean years, but nothing had prepared her for this. She barely ate or slept for over a year. Two years later, Tom died of cancer. Trying to focus on the lives that remained, Sylvia buried her heartache. Within a few years, her eyesight failed. She courageously coped another two decades in diminishing health.

Sylvia treasured her 44 grandchildren and knew several of her almost 100 great-grandchildren before she lapsed into semiconsciousness. She died April 25, 1985, at the age of 88, but her dream had been that if she could only reach 104, she would have touched three centuries.

**MORROW** – Thomas Orlan Morrow was born August 13,1931, in Southeast Missouri in a little place called Paulding. There was one school and store. His parents were Tilfer Alvin Morrow and Tilda Caroline (Kinnie) Ridge Morrow. There were nine children born of this union. Three sisters, Odean Leonard Barger, Estalean Harber Jett, Betty Jean Fruchey Southard Shrable and five brothers, James Harold, J.H. Eugene, Donald Lee, Billy Wayne and Alva Leland. Billy Wayne died at 3 months; and Alva Leland died at 18 months. The family moved to Paragould when Tom was 4 years old.

Tom graduated from Greene County Tech in 1951 and received his barber licenses in 1952. He worked for Emerson Electric and retired after 33 years. During this time, Tom ran for 3rd Ward Alderman and held that position for eight years. Tom was the first to carry all three wards. He

*Thomas Orlan Morrow*

helped to change alderman being elected by all wards, to only being elected by the ward they were to represent. He was instrumental in the development of the Paragould Mini Rise, Paragould Community Center and Pecan Grove Housing, and the Water Company being run by private individuals of the Water District, to being owned by the City of Paragould. Supported the annexation of Center Hill into Paragould. Tom served as a board member for the Greene County Fair, Greene Acres Nursing Home, and chairman of the Parks and Recreation. While in office he helped with the revision of the City of Paragould's Code of Ordinance. Served on the Greene County Quorum Court. Member of the Greene County Historical Society, Paragould Jaycee's, where he served as president for one term, ran the Paragould Jaycee BINGO, and was a member of the Jaycee Rodeo Board. Was active with the Little League Baseball program. After Tom retired, he became an active member of the Arkansas Methodist Hospital Auxiliary. He attends Paragould Christian Church where he teaches Sunday school. Tom was married to Mary Louise Maddox. They had four children, three girls, Marsha Arlean, Debra Darlean Stevens Parten, Tommie Jo Kathryn Whitby, and one son, Barry Steven. Daughter Marsha was stillborn.

He is now married to Gracelin Roberta Williams White, with whom he raised two sons, John Christopher White and Curtis Don White. Tom has seven grandchildren: Steven Lee Stevens, Jennie Suzanne Whitby, Amy Elizabeth Stevens, Jennifer Marie Morrow Shelton, Samantha Yvonne Morrow, Keith Tanner White and Emily Grace White, and two great-grandchildren, Christian Dale Lee Stevens and Katriona Michelle Pansy Shelton.

**MORROW** – William Franklin Morrow, 1830-1899, son of Thomas and Eliza Ann Morrow, was born in Maury County, Tennessee, and later moved to Giles County, Tennessee. He left home when he was 20 years old with the family of Samuel Willcockson after marrying Samuel's daughter, Louisa, on October 7, 1850. They arrived in Greene County, Arkansas, and settled near Walcott, becoming some of the earliest settlers of the area. They had one son, Isaac, who lived to be 8 years old, and Louisa died shortly after his birth.

William Franklin, called Frank, married Mary Mildred Anders born 1833 in 1855. She was the daughter of Phillip and Rebecca (Smelser) Anders. Their children were John Louis, 1858-1901; William Riley born 1860; Phillip Samuel, 1863-1947; James Berry, born 1865; Jefferson Nelson, born 1867; Eliza Jane, born 1869; and David Franklin, born 1872.

*William Franklin Morrow and Mary Mildred Anders (Andrews), circa 1858 in Greene County.*

After Mary Mildred's death, Frank married Hannah (Parker) Greer Taylor in about 1878, who had three children of her own: Moses, Carroll and George Taylor. The Greene County Census for the year of 1880 shows Frank's six children and Hannah's three, plus her granddaughter, Hannah Greer, living in the household.

After Frank left his home in Giles County, Tennessee, he had no contact with any members of his family for over 30 years. During this time, and unknown to him, two of his brothers, John D. and Thomas, came to Arkansas from Tennessee by wagon train, crossing the river at Memphis. They originally settled around Forrest City, Arkansas, and later moved near Wynne, Arkansas. It was here in 1882 that they, by chance, met a man who knew Frank and gave them his address in Greene County. They immediately wrote to him, telling him that they also wanted to move to Greene County. Frank saddled his horse and went to Cross County to get them. When he arrived, they were all elated to be reunited after 30 years. The reunion was marred somewhat because John D. was sick with yellow fever. Frank went home to get his ox wagon to move all of them. When he returned, John D. had died and Thomas was sick with the fever. Frank loaded up John D.'s wife, Margaret Ann Ball, and children, brought them back to Greene County and then returned for Thomas and his family. By that time, however, Thomas had died also. Frank then loaded up Thomas' wife, Nancy Ball, sister of Margaret Ann, and children and brought them to Greene County also. This made 21 faces to feed around the table, and the meals were cooked on an open fireplace.

Frank homesteaded 193 acres of land, two or three miles east of Walcott and worked at other jobs also. It has been said that he was loved and honored by all who knew him, and that he was a useful citizen, a splendid neighbor and an upright and faithful Christian gentleman. He died in Greene County and is buried in Owen's Chapel Cemetery, as is his second wife, Mary Mildred. Many of his descendants still live in this area today.

**MORTON** – Shelburn Hendrix "S.H." Morton born August 1, 1873, in Wells County, Indiana, was my great-grandfather. He moved to Poplar Bluff, Missouri, in 1880 and lived with his mother, Abbie Morton (maiden name not known). His father is not known, but the census stated that his father was born in Kentucky.

In 1920 census S.H. was living in the Mainshore Community of Greene County, and was farming with his wife, Edith Ann (Lambert) Morton, born February 14, 1883, in Wells, Indiana. Her father was John Lambert, born about 1813 in Ireland.

Children listed: Lawrence V., son, 15; Lewelin, daughter, 13; Georgia, daughter, 10; Barney, son, and Burney 6 (twins); and Ceava E., son, 4 and a half. There were other children born later: Edith, Edna, Geraldine and Eugene (twins). Edith married Raymond Cox and died when she was 21 with tuberculosis.

My grandfather, Barney Irwin Morton, married Helen Bernita Gladish, born February 8, 1940, in Dunklin County, Missouri. Her children were Jimmy, July 14, 1940; Catherine Ann, October 5, 1943; and Barney Otto, April 5, 1945. Jimmy died in 1943 of pneumonia and is buried at Pine Knott with my grandparents. Catherine "Cathy" married Donald Strope, December 24, 1959, in Greene County, and their children were Helen, Donnie and John. Otto Barney Morton, who is my father, married Mattie L. Reddick, June 6, 1964, of Mounds, Arkansas. My mother is the great-great-granddaughter of Humphrey Reddick and Mary Alice from *Fathers of the Ridge*. Their children were Pamela, Tina, Teddie and Kathleen.

In 1919 S.H. and Edith bought 20 acres from G.M. Tennison. In 1920 they purchased 60 acres from W.C. Batey, land originally from Bertig Land Company. In 1923 they purchased 39 and one-half acres from J.H. Cozart.

S.H. Morton lived at Village in 1931, which was around Old Pekin Road in Paragould. At that time the whole family helped farm and raise the crops. Then they moved to what used to be called Bailey Trading Post on the St. Francis River, almost on the Craighead County line.

My Grandpa Barney would tell about having to get up long before daylight and travel by boat and lanterns to Childers, Arkansas, by way of the river to trade their goods and come back home later in the night. In 1935 they moved across the Eight-Mile, right on the Craighead line to what to this day is the Morton homeplace where my parents still live. When they first moved there it was nothing but swamps and cypress trees. They cleared the land and worked the ground, using the lumber to build their homes. My sisters and I grew up in the original house that they built in 1935. My dad and grandpa moved the house up the road to higher ground, about a quarter mile from where it was built. They set the house on logs and slowly rolled it to where it now sets, up near the Eight-Mile ditch, pulling it with teams of horses. My parents still live there today and farm the Morton land, raising soybeans and winter wheat.

**MOSS/LEE** – Shirley Lee was born in Paragould, Arkansas. She married George Moss in 1959. George was born in Harrison, Arkansas. They have one daughter Marian who married Andy Peeler of Jonesboro, Arkansas. They have two children, Eric and Logan.

My father was Frank Lee, who was born in Paragould, Arkansas, in 1904. He was employed by Cotton Belt Railroad. His father was John Lee who was born in Illinois. He was a carpenter. His father was William Lee enlisted in the First Arkansas during the Civil War. He lived in Stranger's Home and enlisted at Lauratown in Lawrence County. He died very early in the war and is buried in the Black Rock area. His wife was Minerva Brown who returned to Illinois.

Frank's mother was Evelyn Weaver. She was born in Lawrenceburg, Tennessee. Her father was David Weaver, born in Winchester, Tennessee. Peter Weaver was his father, his mother was an Eastep. David Weaver came to Greene County about 1890. He was a blacksmith, and at the time of his death was Paragould's oldest citizen. He was a Civil War veteran, serving in the third Kentucky Cavalry. David married Nancy Jane Carter, September 20, 1855, in Lawrenceburg, Tennessee. David and Nancy Jane Carter Weaver are buried in Linwood Cemetery in Paragould, Arkansas. John and Evelyn Weaver Lee are buried in New Friendship Cemetery in Greene County, Arkansas.

My mother was Mattie Houston. She was born in McCracken County, Kentucky. Her father was James Houston, born in Vienna, Illinois. His parents were Samuel Houston born in 1805 in Virginia. His mother was Celia Mathis, born in North Carolina about 1825. Both are buried in McCracken County, Kentucky.

James Houston married Hannah Martin, born in Saltillo, Tennessee. Her father, Benjamin Martin was in the Civil War. He served in the Union Army, enlisting at Bethel, Tennessee. He was injured in the battle of Helena, July 4, 1864. He married Charlotte Vickrey on November 30, 1865, in Hardin County, Tennessee. This family is in McCracken County, Kentucky by 1870.

The Houston's came to Greene County from Prarie County, Arkansas, moving to the Center Hill Community. James Houston was a farmer. He and Hannah Martin Houston are buried in Center Hill Cemetery.

Benjamin Martin is buried in Oak Grove Cemetery, in Paducah, Kentucky.

Frank and Mattie Houston Lee are buried in Linwood Cemetery in Paragould, Arkansas.

**MOTHERSHED** – John Wesley Mothershed (Feb 1867 MS) son of William and Ana Elizabeth (Pierce) Mothershed, was listed on the 1870 Census of Greene County, AR. John W. Mothershed's grandparents, Thomas and Charity (Swindle) Mothershed left Tennessee for Arkansas in the 1850s. It is not known why they left Tennessee. Since the Mothersheds were blacksmiths and a railroad company was putting a bridge across the Tennessee River during the 1850s, it is possible the bridge was completed and the family decided to leave, or the impending political friction concerning slavery was heating up and may have caused them to seek a more stable political state, or it could have been because of a land grant by the government for Thomas' father John Jett Mothershed's service in the War of 1812. Thomas Mothershed died enroute to Greene County, AR and is buried in an unmarked grave in Fairview Cemetery near his sister Lucy (Mothershed) Cole.

*Alvie L. and Venita Mothershed 1966.*

Thomas and Charity Mothershed's oldest son, William Mothershed, married Ana Elizabeth Pierce on June 15, 1856 in Benton County, TN. They left Tennessee with his father's brother named William Mothershed and settled in Marshall County, MS. It was here that their second child, John Wesley Mothershed, was born in 1867. Soon afterwards he joined his mother and other siblings in Greene County, AR.

John W. Mothershed married Mary Ellen (maiden name unknown). Together they had 11 children recorded. For some unknown reason they lost land by tax default *Deores Book 40* page 307, sec. 5, t/s 18, range 7, Sept 28, 1901. The land was deeded to C. K. Anderson on Jan 25, 1909, who paid taxes on said property for nine years. They later sold to S. P. McHaney, 160 acres of land on Locust Creek, Oct 25, 1915 for $500.00.

On Feb 15, 1915 my grandfather, Alvie Lee Mothershed, Sr. was the last child born. His parents died soon after he was born. His older siblings helped raise him until his teens. On Oct 4, 1937, he married Venita Irene Huffine (Oct 13, 1917 MO) at the Greene County Courthouse. Their children:

*John Wesley and Mary Ellen Mothershed 1900.*

1. Mary Jewell Mothershed (Aug 29, 1938).
2. Jo Ann Mothershed (July 19, 1940)
3. Alvie Lee Mothershed, Jr. (Dec 19, 1946)

During their marriage they survived the Great Depression, suffered through WWII and experienced three burnouts losing everything but their children and the clothes on their backs. Living mainly around the Dixie and Schugtown area, the children attended Dixie Schools where both daughters graduated. Mary married Robert M. Rudder from Lake City and moved to Chicago. Children:

1. Robin Ann
2. Mary Lee
3. Jacqueline Venita Rae
4. Charles Franklin
5. George Douglas Rudder

Jo Ann married Charles D. Mayne from Claysville, PA and moved there with him. Children:

1. Kimberly Delores (Mayne) Cross married Clay Hoenshell and now resides in Mansfield, TX. They have one daughter, Brittney Noel Hoenshell.
2. Charles Robert Mayne lives in Texas.

Alvie Lee Mothershed Jr. married Lavonda Jean Porter Hendrix of Paragould, AR. Children:

1. Michael Lee Mothershed married Karen Sue Woodall of Jonesboro, AR. They have one daughter Madison Ellen Mothershed.

They lived and died in Greene County and were married for 59 years. Alvie, Sr. died on Jan 16, 1997. Venita later died on May 6, 1999 and is buried beside her husband in Pine Log Cemetery. Their descendants still live in Greene County and the Mothershed name has been in Greene County for around 130 years.

*Submitted by Michael Mothershed*

**MUELLER** – Louis Frederick Mueller (Nov 22, 1863 Lyon, Franklin County, MO- May 10, 1945), the son of Benjamin and Mary Gerdes Mueller. His father had come to the United States as a stowaway on a cattle ship from Holland. On arriving at Ellis Island, he signed up as a cook's helper with a caravan of gold seekers headed for California. However, he stopped in Franklin County, MO, married a local girl and established his home there. His wife was the former Anna Sophia Stolte. They were married at Beaufort, Mo on Sept 18, 1890. They came immediately after their marriage to Arkansas and settled on a farm approximately three and one-half miles northeast of Loulama (Lafe). They lived on the same farm until the early 1920s when they built a home and lived in Lafe. Anna S. Mueller died April 22, 1957 and is buried with L. F. in Linwood Cemetery, Paragould, AR.

**MYRICK** – Daniel Myrick and Margrett VanCleve Myrick came to the United States from Ireland. They lived in Tennessee. Their children:

1. Steven Franklin (March 9, 1872 TN- March 25, 1924 MO), known as "Frank" or "Buster" is buried at Mountain Home Cemetery. He married Ida Lou Wheeler on Nov 3, 1896.
2. Ella married John Tom Wheeler
3. Emma
4. John Robert

Buster and Ella came to Arkansas about 1894. No information is known of John. Emma married a Baker and lived in Tennessee.

Buster was a sharecropper, who lived around the Commissary community.

*This house and store were on our corner across the bridge.*

1. The oldest son, Luther, lived only six moths and is buried at Mountain Home Cemetery

2. Bertha married James William Harris and ran a dairy on Bard Road for several years. Their Children:
   a. Reginald
   b. Imalee
   c. Douglas
   d. Joan
   e. Bert
3. Audie wed Dolphe Shearer, moved to Illinois and after retirement they came back to Greene County, AR and lived in Paragould. Their children:
   a. Junior
   b. Betty
   c. Bobby
4. Elmer married Mary Harvill. He farmed and worked in Greene County. They had seven children.
   a. Thelma married Charles Norman. They had a daughter, Kathy. Thelma died of cancer in May 1961.
   b. Ida wed David Wideman and they have Pam who lives at Potosi, MO.
   c. Tommy married Patricia Bailey. Tommy lives at Commissary where both his grandfathers lived and farmed during their lifetime. Tommy and Pat have farmed along Sugar Creek for 40 years with the help of their children, Tim, Dan, Latricia and Karrie.

Picture of "Buster" Myrick taken in 1922.

   d. Virginia married Charles Davis. Their children are Vicky, Mellenee and Chuckie. Virginia died July 1995.
   e. Larry married Shirley Irwin. They had Farrah and Matthew. Larry resides at Delaplaine.
   f. Janie wed Ronnie Vines. Their three girls are Kim, Lisa and Crystal. Janie lives near Evening Star.
   g. Janice married Jerry Cross. No children were born and they divorced. Janice lives at Elizabeth, AR.
   Elmer died of cancer Oct 3, 1960.
5. Earle married Opal Like. He took his wife and son, Cleatus Weldon, to Michigan to live. Earle died of a heart attack in April 1961.
6. Mozelle married Melvin Rowland. Their children:
   a. Kenneth married Ozella Freeman. They had Steve and Leslie.
   b. Kay married Charles Harvill. Their girls are Randi and Charla.
   Ida died of milk fever when Mozelle was born and Aunt Mag Hyde raised Mozelle.

**NEELY** – Herschel Neely (Jan 6, 1870 Carroll County, TN) was the son of Christopher Columbus Neely (1834) and Solonia M. Brown. Eva Gertrude Potter (April 1873) the daughter of Lorenzo Ruggles Potter, from Luzerne County, Pa.
Christopher Columbus and Solonia Neely had six children:
   1. Frank
   2. Herschel
   3. Hardy
   4. Lilly
   5. Christopher C.
   6. Andrew
They moved from Carroll County, TN in the spring of 1883, reaching Clay County, AR on April 19, 1883. They moved to a small farm two miles north of Rector. In 1888, they moved to Rector. Christopher was appointed postmaster at Rector in 1889. He died in Feb 1899 and his wife, Solonia died on Dec 12, 1912. Both are buried at St. Mary's Cemetery in Rector.

Eva Gertrude Potter was born in 1873 and moved from Illinois to Paragould in the early 1890s. Her family was in the hotel business. She had four siblings, Walter, Bert, Dell and Cora.

Herschel Neely moved to Paragould in 1904 and he and Eva were married. The Neely family owned and operated Neely Brothers, a mercantile store. In 1922, he was appointed postmaster of Paragould.

Herschel and Eva had three children, Frances Lavan (Feb 8, 1906), Ralph (1908) and Mary Alice (June 6, 1911). Ralph died in 1910 with the measles.

Frances married Orris Collins on July 8, 1924. They had three children, Patricia Ann (June 2, 1931), Joan Carol (Oct 17, 1932) and John Neely (March 23, 1939).

Mary Alice married E. Vernon Wills. They had three sons, Vernon Whitney (Aug 22, 1931) Scott Neely (Nov 26, 1932) and Keith Clark (Feb 13, 1934). Mary Alice and Vernon divorced in 1939 and he was killed in an automobile accident in 1944. Mary Alice married John Richard Parkhurst in 1945 and they were divorced in 1951.

Eva Potter Neely and Hershel Neely

Herschel Neely died in April 1931, just a few weeks before the birth of his first granddaughter, Pat. Eva went to live with her daughters, dividing her time between Frances and Mary Alice and to help care for their children. Eva or "Ev" as she was called, died in Sept 1941.
Frances died on July 3, 1990 and Mary Alice died on May 3, 1994.
*Submitted by Pat Fulkerson*

**NEELY** – John and Polly Neely, who were born in the late 1700s, had one son, Andrew Neely (Sept 4, 1804-Aug 20, 1886). Polly died Sept 7, 1840 and John died March 17, 1822.
Andrew Neely married Comfort Hunter Neely (Feb 29, 1805-June 17, 1846) on Feb 5, 1828. They had seven children:
1. Francis Marian Neely (March 20, 1830-Feb 3, 1869)
2. Mary Adaline Neely (June 10, 1832- Oct 25, 1886)
3. Christopher Columbus Neely (Feb 28, 1834- Feb 1899)
4. Lavina Jane Neely (June 1, 1836-1915)
5. John Wesley Crockett Neely (April 24, 1838- Feb 24, 1863)
6. Sarah Harrison Neely (June 2,1840-June 11, 1863)

Descendants of Hardy and Emma Hugh Neely which include their children and families: Frank Harold Neely, Almeria Neely Willcockson, Reba Neely, Howard Neely, Geraldine Neely Harrington.

7. Martha Emily Neely (Jan 30, 1843- Oct 6, 1886).
Andrew Neely had a second marriage to Martha M. Blair (Sept 22, 1819-Aug 19, 1901). Their marriage resulted in four children:
1. George Washington Neely (Dec 11, 1848- Aug 24, 1886)
2. Roxanna Evelena Neely (Nov 10, 1850- unknown)
3. Haywood Blair Neely (Oct 1854-Sept 5, 1881)
4. Hiram Abiff Neely (July 16, 1859-April 3, 1863).
Christopher Columbus Neely married Solona M. Brown in 1865. The children of that marriage:
1. Frank Neely (April 1868- Jan 30, 1899)
2. Hershel Neely (Jan 6, 1870-1931)
3. Milton Hardy Neely (April 25, 1872- Sept 16, 1964)
4. Lilly M. Neely (March 12, 1875- Jan 5, 1913)
5. Christopher Columbus Neely, Jr. (April 19, 1877- Dec 12, 1905)
6. Andrew Clyde Neely (April 19, 1880- Nov 23, 1957)
Hershel Neely married Eva Gertrude Potter and had three children:
   a. Francis, who married Orris Collins and had three children; Patricia Ann, Joan Carol and John
   b. Mary Alice, who married Vernon Wills and had three sons: Vernon Whitney, Scott Neely and Keith Clark
   c. Ralph died in infancy
See additional info on Neely family included in history book.
Milton Hardy Neely married Emma Vaughn (May 13, 1876- March 30, 1949) on Jan 2, 1898. They had five children:
   a. Frank Harold Neely
   b. Almeria Neely
   c. Lois Reba Neely
   d. Howard Neely
   e. Geraldine Neely
Frank Harold Neely (Oct 22, unknown) died at the age of 90 plus years. He married Caroline and had two children:
   a. Caroline Ann married David Williams and had eight children, one dying at childbirth. Caroline (Jan 10, 1936) presently lives in Lafayette, LA.
   b. Frank, Jr. (July 16, 1938) married Caroline and had two daughters. They live in the Dallas area.
Almeria Neely (Sept 5, 1903- May 26, 1990) married Ike Willcockson (Dec 29, 1895- Nov 12, 1971) had three daughters:
   a. Martha Jeanne (March 28, 1932)
   b. Emma Jann (Feb 10, 1938)

c. June Ann (June 19, 1948)

Jeanne and Jann live in Paragould, AR and June Ann lives in Little Rock.

Reba Neely (Mar. 13, 1907 – May 28, 1996) never married. She was a long time employee of Security Bank in Paragould.

Howard Neely (June 28, 1909) married Margaret McCullough and they had two daughters:
  a. Nina Hugh
  b. Nancy

They presently live in Lake Charles, LA. Howard celebrated his 90th birthday in 1999.

Geraldine Neely (Jan 28, 1913- May 26, 2000) married Haywood Eugene Harrington. They had three children:
  a. Sandra Ann
  b. Eugenia Kay
  c. Jack

Sandra married Frank Smith and had five children. She is presently married to Bill Clark. Eugenia married Alex Hopkins and had three children. Jack and Becky Harrington had two children. Sandra and Jack live in Jonesboro, AR and Eugenia lives in Charles Town, WV.

*Hardy Neely and Emma Vaughn Neely*

**NEWBERRY** – John H. Newberry, was born January 13, 1820, in Washington County, North Carolina and moved to Cherokee County, Alabama, with his parents, James S. and Sarah Howell Newberry about 1839. James Newberry was the father of 19 children, of whom seven sons died serving the Confederacy in the War Between the States. John Newberry moved to Craighead County in 1854 with a group of other families from Alabama that came in a caravan and moved to the Greensboro settlement. He moved to Salem Township, Greene County by 1860, where he farmed 480 acres and served as a justice of the peace. He enlisted in Company G of the 1st Regiment, Arkansas Mounted Volunteers which became the 3rd Regiment, Arkansas Cavalry, CSA, in October 1861. This regiment was in the Corinth Campaign in the summer of 1862 and the Battle of Corinth, October 3-4, 1862.

John Newberry was killed in a bizarre accident on the retreat from Corinth. He was killed by a falling tree as the regiment downed trees across the road to impede the Union Army pursuit. He died on October 21, 1862.

John married Nancy Dacus, daughter of Nathaniel Dacus and Mary Cannon, in 1842 in Centre, Cherokee County, Alabama. Nancy Dacus was born about 1818 in South Carolina and died in 1883.

The *Greene County Citizen* newspaper published a story in 1939 about Nancy Newberry. It seems that she was a strong woman and continued to farm after her sons left home. She produced a bumper crop in 1874 and stored it in two barns. When a drought hit in 1875 she sold it for $1.00 per bushel. Word got around that she stashed the money in her house. A man named Conroy got a job working as a hand for Mrs. Newberry and heard about her corn money. While working in the field with other hands he slipped away, went to her house and robbed the 69 year old woman of her money. He shot her and left her for dead. She was shot in the hip, but recovered to live to be 76. Conroy was caught by a posse and jailed at Gainesville. The story does not report on his fate.

John H. Newberry and Nancy Dacus had the following children:

James Franklin "Jim" Newberry was born June 18, 1843, in Cherokee County, Alabama. He served in Company D, 5th Regiment, Arkansas Infantry, CSA from June 13, 1861, to March 7, 1865. He was wounded at Murfreesboro and served in the siege of Chattanooga. He was captured and was a POW before being exchanged just before the end of the war. He died on December 27, 1892, and was buried in Mt. Zion Cemetery. Jim Newberry married Mary A. Morgan, daughter of John B. Morgan and Caroline Simmons, about 1866 in Arkansas. Mary A. Morgan was born on April 22, 1849, in Alabama and died December 13, 1879, in Greene County. Jim and Mary Newberry lived near Gainesville. Their children were: Martha Elizabeth, Frances, William, Martha, Sarah Francis "Sally," Robert, John Edward and Isabella. Jim Newberry married Charity Ross in 1880 and they had the following children: Laura Ellen, James Jefferson, Eugene Bedford, Myrtle Grover, Ora Holland and Betty Selma.

Other children of John and Nancy Newberry were:

John Ervin Newberry was born June 14, 1851, in Cherokee County, Alabama, and died November 26, 1933. He married Martha Elizabeth "Mattie" Morgan on August 25, 1872.

Lawrence Leventon Newberry was born June 18, 1854, in Mississippi and died February 5, 1937, in Greene County.

Thomas Washington Newberry was born on March 30, 1857, and died on January 29, 1942.

**NEWSOM** – The oldest male offspring of Starling/Sterling and Nancy (Hamilton) Newsom, Obe became a leading and prominent citizen of the Finch community. He was born Dec 12, 1835, in Tippah County, MS and came to Greene County with his parents in 1855, settling in St. Francis Township.

During his trips to Old Greensboro, he met and married his first wife, Mary Ann McDaniel, around 1860. She was born in 1839 in Shelby County, TN and was the daughter of John and Sarah Margaret McDaniel. Before the Civil War interrupted their life, they had two children: Nancy Jane (1860) and John Sterling (March 18, 1861). Obe and his brother T. H. Newsom, surrendered to the Federals at Wittsburg, AR on May 25, 1865 and was paroled, along with the remnants of the Confederate forces still left in Arkansas. His parole documents shows that he was 29 years old, blue eyes, light hair, fair complexion, 5'6" and was born Dec 12, 1835, in Tippah County, MS.

*O. S. Newson and John Newsom.*

Returning home, Obe went about the business of raising and caring for his family. He and Mary Ann had another son, James Edward (Feb 19, 1866) and a daughter, Mary Ann (April 23, 1866). Following the death of Mary Ann, his wife, on April 20, 1867, Obe married Catherine Cook. From this union, they had Martha (1871) and Pernicy "Necy" (Dec 3, 1872). Upon the death of Catherine (Dec 1872) Obe married Margaret C. Arnold, the daughter of Absolom and Mary (Coble/Cobb) Arnold. From this marriage, they had the following children:
1. Aurora E. (Sept. 27, 1874)
2. Ezra White (Feb 16, 1876)
3. Francis (Dec 12, 1877)
4. William U. "Willie" (April 15, 1880).

In 1880 he was to become the second postmaster for the Finch post office and also served as a justice of the peace. Obe was a surveyor for Greene County, AR from 1882-1888 and 1900-1902. In 1894, he helped survey the town of Cardwell, MO for the Cardwell Land Company.

When Margaret, his third wife, died on Feb 18, 1893, Obe married Julia A. Elmore, on June 11, 1896. Julia was a widow from Alabama and they had no children. Due to advancing age and inability to perform manual labor, Obe was granted a pension of $100.00 from the state of Arkansas, on Aug 9, 1912, for his Civil War service. He would die, nearly three years later, on March 25, 1915. It is stated on his death certificate that he was buried with his family in Newsom Cemetery, now called Finch Cemetery.
*Submitted by Roger D. Newsom*

**NEWSOM** – Sterling Newsom (Oct 24, 1802 NC) married Nancy H. (1815 TN) about Sept 1832. They were the parents of:
1. Sarah Elizabeth (1833 Hardeman County, TN)
2. Obadiah Sterling (1835 MS)
3. Mary Jane (1838 MS)
4. Theophilus H. (1838 MS)
5. John (1840 AR)
6. Hester Lucy (1843 MS)
7. Nancy Ann (1845 MS).

With the signing of the Treaty of Pontotoc, in 1834, the Chickasaw Nation allowed the purchase of their former lands by white settlers. Taking advantage of the treaty, Sterling moved from Hardeman County, TN and purchased the NW one-fourth, Section 20, Township 1, Range 1E, in Tippah County, MS (now Benton County).

In 1840 Sterling was enumerated in the census records for Mitchell Township, Poinsett County, AR (annexed to Cross County in 1862). Along with his family, two female slaves were also listed, one-under 10 years of age and the other between 10 and 24.

While living in Mitchell Township, Sterling, his wife and family traveled north along Crowley's Ridge to Walcott, a distance of approximately 60 miles, to attend the closest Baptist worship services in the area. Along with other northeast Arkansas pioneers they were among the charter members of Mt. Zion Baptist Church.

For some reason, Sterling moved his family back to Tippah County around 1843. The family was counted in the 1850 census residing in the 3rd Division.

Returning to Greene County, AR, in 1855, this time to stay, Sterling obtained a land patent, certificate number 5981, for 80 acres near the Finch community. The patent conveyed the ownership of land located in Section 24, Township 16, Range 4E, presently owned by the Herschel McMillon family.

In the mid 1860s, Sterling's wife, Nancy died and supposedly she was buried in the Mt. Zion Cemetery. After her death Sterling married Rhoda E. Ward Tatum, a widow with two infants, about 1867. To this union were born:
1. Woodsie (1868)
2. Willie (1872)
3. Sterling Orestes (1876).

Sterling owned and operated the second cotton gin ever established in Greene County. The apparatus was located near his residence, which was located adjacent to the present site of the Finch Baptist Church. The gin was a treadmill design, propelled by four mules or oxen and later converted to steam power.

Mt. Zion being the nearest Baptist church and together with bad roads and creeks to ford during high water, traveling to Sunday worship was very difficult at times. It was decided by several citizens of the Finch community to establish their own church. In Aug 1872, 13 local Finch residents held their Sunday worship service under Sterling Newsom's gin shed. Out of this humble beginning sprang the present day Finch Baptist Church. A marker stands approximately 300 yards east of the present church building denoting the site.

Sterling Newsom died on Feb 16, 1877. He was the second person buried in the Finch Cemetery.

*Submitted by Daniel A. Hester*

**NOEL** – Alice Mariah Noel was born February 13, 1869, at Halliday, the fourth child of John W. Noel and his wife Martha Thompson and died Christmas morning, December 25, 1910, at Lutesville, Missouri, while on a visit to her brother-in-law Addison Key. My father loved Christmas but was always in a pensive mood after the presents were opened and while breakfast was being prepared. I was about 14 when I learned the reason for the sadness as he measured time since death had taken her. She was 41 years old and left eight surviving children, two sisters, one brother and her second husband, my grandfather, Thomas W. Key. She was described as being tall, red-haired and as being "fleshy." There was a fire at the home of her daughter Eva Angeline Baker (Becker) Hoyer and no picture of Alice Noel Key exist today.

*Christmas 1956, 352 No. Whitter Street, St. Louis, Missouri. Front from left: Richard Key, Frank S. Key and Della Carpenter Key. Back from left: Jason E. Key, Phillip Key and Betty Key.*

John W. Noel was born in 1839 in Gibson County, Tennessee, and removed to Greene County, Arkansas, after his release from a military prison Camp Randall, Wisconsin, in 1862. John and Henry Noel were in Company D 55th Brown's Tennessee Infantry on Island 10 in 1861. He married Martha Thompson the daughter of John W. Thompson, deceased and his wife Lucy Mealer Thompson, out of Giles County into Greene County by 1852. John and Martha became the parents of seven children, i.e. Stephen Henry Noel born January 7, 1867; Alice Mariah born February 13, 1869; and Mary Elizabeth born November 24, 1878, the only three to live to maturity. Henry married Mary Belle Dodd and has descendents living in Clay County, Dunklin County, Missouri, and California. He died at Holcomb, Missouri, in 1908 and is buried at Pine City Cemetery. Alice married, first Washington Baker (Becker) and had four children: Rozellen, Robert E. Lee, Eva Angelina and Jim. On October 27, 1897, she married Tom Key at Clarkton, Missouri, as his second wife. She has descendants in Greene County, St. Louis, Kansas City, Little Rock and Memphis.

*Rhine Building, Paragould, Arkansas, 1952: Stuart Mueller, architect, unidentified, L.V. Rhine, Mike Rhine, unidentified and Frank Key, builder.*

She is buried at Union Hill Cemetery in Ballinger County, Missouri. Mary Elizabeth married Joe McConkey and has descendents in Greene County. She died June 22, 1922, and is buried at Linwood.

*July 19, 1972, Dan Noel's funeral, Modesto, California. Back row from left: L.T. Noel, Elmer, Alvin, Henry and John Wesley Noel. Front row: Louella (Cowell) Noel and Pauline Noel.*

By 1880 John and Martha Noel were living at Boydsville, Arkansas, and Henry Noel and his family together with Mary Noel Reece and husband Charley had moved to Halliday from their homes in Gibson County, Tennessee. One of Henry's descendents is in possession of a 67 acre tract of land that Martha inherited from Lucy Thompson.

Frank Sevier Key born July 7, 1898, at Clarkton, Missouri, to Tom and Alice Key was a builder of some of some distinction. From 1919 to 1924 he was associated with Bechtel and traveled to Mexico, Central America, Havana and Canada with that firm. They were in Mexico City in August 1923 when Warren G. Harding died at the Cow Palace in San Francisco. Mr. Bechtel Sr. had just arrived in Mexico City and he told daddy and Steve Bechtel to return to San Francisco and make some repairs to the family home. They did and checked into the presidential suite at the Cow Palace and partied until Mr. Bechtel returned and sent them to the Bechtel home to live. Steve Bechtel developed this organization into a mammoth private corporation.

*Swope Park, Kansas City, July 4, 1927. Frank S. Key and Betty.*

My father generally worked in northeast Arkansas building churches, schools, commercial properties, etc. During the second World War he was in Kansas, Illinois and Kentucky. He retired from Huttig Sash and Door in 1964 and worked for a time registering Social Security recipients for Medicare benefits. In 1966 he was called in by Huttig and sent to Fulton, Missouri, to assist in the final preparation for dedication of the London Church of St. Mary Altermanbury Chapel on Campus Westminister College. The construction company could not fit the windows into the church built in the 12th century destroyed, reconstructed by Sir Christopher Wrenn in 1677, gutted during World War II and removed to Fulton as a gift of the United Kingdom, dedicated March 3, 1966, to commemorate the visit of Sr. Winston Churchill. Daddy made a point of observing those festivities.

*Fellowship Hall of Beech Grove Baptist Church, Dyer, Tennessee. From left: Bertha Ann Noel Fahr, Myrtle Noel Johnson and Betty Key, descendents of John W. Noel and David Henry Noel of Gibson County, Tennessee.*

The genealogy of the Noels goes back to Ardenne, France and the Netherlands. John W. Noel was son of Liberty Anderson Noel and his wife Elizabeth Grissom. He was the son of Thomas Noel born 1794 in Washington County, Kentucky, and his wife Nancy Ann. This Thomas was the son of Muscoe Noel and his wife Elizabeth Smith of Mercer County, Kentucky; he was the son of Thomas Noel out of Cumberland County, Virginia, through Halifax County, who with his wife Drucilla was in Mercer by 1789. This Thomas was the son John Noel and Ann Garnett and he was the son of James Noel and Elizabeth Evans. He was the son Cornelius Noel and wife Elizabeth Page. Cornelius was naturalized in 1686.

**NORMAN** – Ralph Columbus Norman (Dec 11, 1897 Beech Grove, Greene County, AR) was the son of John William Norman. His family was fairly new to the area as his father and grandfather, John Columbus had moved down from Scott County, MO in 1887. The Normans had arrived in Cape Girardeau in 1805 when Rueben Norman settled there. Rueben had been born about 1760, possibly in Virginia. He was a cooper by trade.

*Ralph and Vestal Norman.*

John William married Martha "Mattie" Garner, the daughter of Callaway Branson and Elizabeth Clement Garner. On Oct 15, 1918, at the age of 45, John William died of pneumonia, leaving Mattie a widow with six children and carrying a seventh. Mattie continued to work their farm of 80 acres north and west of Beech Grove. She did not die until June 17, 1964. A great deal of the responsibility for the family fell to Ralph, especially as his older sister Cora died the year before. His younger siblings were:

1. Flora,
2. Charlie,
3. Nancy,
4. Evia
5. Vera.

On July 27, 1919, Ralph married Vestal Horne, the daughter of Jim and Janie Horne, also of Beech Grove. Jim Horne operated a small grocery west of Beech Grove. Ralph and Vestal had six children:

1. Berlas
2. Javene
3. Genoal
4. Maxine
5. Wendell
6. Laverna Kay

They farmed mostly in the Beech Grove community, but did live briefly at Stonewall and Greenway. Ralph bought the Meadows place in 1931. The Meadows Grove Cemetery is just to the south. This farm was on present Highway 141, about two miles north of Beech Grove. In 1944 the family moved to Michigan but returned in 1946. Ralph later bought the Clyde Mack farm, about one and one half miles farther north on Highway 141. Berlas, the only child to farm, worked this farm until 1972 when Ralph and Vestal sold out and moved to Paragould. Ralph died in 1982 and Vestal in 1983. Ralph's son, James Berlas married Marjorie Jovene Williams, the daughter of Joe and viva Williams in Sept 1941. They had four sons:

1. James Weldon
2. Larry Winston
3. Mitchell Duane
4. Ronald Norris

Ralph distinguished himself in the community with his carpentry skills, a trade he had learned from his father-in-law. He was widely respected as a craftsman and many houses stand today, which were built with his hammer and saw. Ralph had been brought up with broadaxe and crosscut saw. In the winter months, he used this skill to cut ties for the railroad. Both Ralph and Vestal were active in the Nazarene church all their lives. They were a pair, he as particular about his tools as she was about her kitchen. Ralph and Vestal are still alive today in the minds of us who knew them. They had an impact upon their children and grandchildren who made all of us better people.

*Submitted by Norris Norman*

**NORWOOD** – Gus Norwood was a small farmer in the Stanford and Beech Grove areas. He married Gladys Webb on Sept 30, 1930. They had five daughters and two sons:

1. Loretta Burner
2. Emma Lou Felty
3. Shirley Morgan
4. Genola died of tetanus April 21 and buried on her 12th birthday
5. Reba Smith
6. Wendell "Gus"
7. Donald

All of the children presently live in the Paragould or Jonesboro areas.

Some of the things Gus and Gladys enjoyed were fishing, attending auctions, playing pitch and board games and receiving visits from family and friends. Both of them were members of the Church of Christ and attended churches at the Commissary, the Mountain Home and the Evening Star communities. Many friends remember Gus and Gladys for their unique talents and the way they shared these to help their friends. Gus was a good mechanic. He worked on many people's tractors and sometimes got paid $25 for a complete overhaul job, but most of his work was done as a favor. He also liked working on small appliances, watches and clocks. Gladys was a good seamstress and enjoyed making quilts and crafts. She cut patterns from newspaper and sewed dresses for one dollar. Many people still recall her sewing for them. She is also remembered for her cooking skills, especially her homemade rolls. Gus and Gladys had a warm, friendly house. They always welcomed company. Gus and Gladys are deceased now, but they taught their children these trades. Gus died in Feb 1984 and Gladys died May 18,1984.

The earliest Norwood ancestors in Greene County were John B. Norwood and his wife Aquilla. They had a son, Albert and a daughter, Etta Lee. John Norwood was a carpenter in Paragould. J. A. "Albert" married Emma Palmer in 1902. They moved to Texas shortly afterward. Gus came to this area as a young boy about eight years old in 1916. His mother, Emma, Brought her three children to Paragould on a train from Texas. She was sick and died a few weeks later. Charlie and Willie Welch of Paragould received the family. They may have been related. Emma was buried in the Moore Cemetery in an unmarked grave near Stanford. Her husband, Albert Norwood, had left the family in Texas to find work as a carpenter. Years later, Gus received word from Albert's second wife that he had passed away. No further contact between the families was ever made. After Emma's death, her children Paul, Gus and Gwendola remained in this area. Gus and Paul grew up in foster homes, but baby Gwendola was raised by Deli and John Welch.

Gus had a difficult life. He stayed with different foster families; among them were John Gramling, Will or Jess Raglan and Lee Burris. He developed a close relationship with the childless couple, Ella Russell Burris and Lee Burris. In later years Mr. Burris spent weeks at a time living with Gus and his family. They called him "Grandpa". Gus raised his family during the depression without much financial security. He had poor health. Chronic earaches as a child resulted in much hearing loss as an adult. He had a sore leg and had it amputated after many years of suffering with it. Nevertheless, he continued, determined to live the best life that he could under the circumstances.

*Gus and Gladys Norwood, 1980.*

**NOWELL** – A Baptist minister, James Thomas, known as "Tom" was born 1859 in Carroll County, Tennessee. He was the son of James G., born 1827, and Mary Jane Nunnery Nowell; the grandson of Cullen and Patsy Pearce Nowell; the great-grandson of James, Wake County, North Carolina; and the great-great-grandson of John and Mara Nowell of Johnston County, North Carolina. His brother was J.G. Jr., and sister, Callie Nowell Morris. Half brothers and sisters were Sarah J.P., John Cullen, John Allen, Willis Jackson, David Qulin, Isabell, Henry, Martin Hawkins, Alanzo, Allen and Lelia.

"Tom" first married Eliza P. Todd and had a son, Obed. Eliza died at an early age and so did Obed. Nancy K. Rainey was the second wife who came with him in the early 1900s to Arkansas in a covered wagon driven by oxen. They crossed the Mississippi at Cottonwood Point. Sister-in-law, Dert and children Ebron, Esther, Jeanie, Callie and Effie. Calista died at an early age.

January 1, 1905, "Tom" married Nancy Annies Williams in Greene County, Arkansas. Their living children were John born 1911 and Sallie born 1908. Deceased children were Jesse, Jimmy, Willy and Bettie.

*James Thomas and Nancy Annies, (William) Nowell, November 1942, in front of Nowell homeplace.*

James Thomas last remembered his mother offering to get him an apple from a tree. He was too short to reach. He ran from her as he had not seen her in a long time. Grandpa Nat Nunnery received a letter from Mary Jane in 1889 while she was living in Orange County, California. Tom lived a long, fruitful life and was instrumental in organizing the New Home Missionary Baptist Church. A granddaughter, Verneal Hamilton, still attends today. Many couples in the Marmaduke area were married by Tom. This service was $1.00.

Farming was his occupation in addition to spreading the gospel.

Grandchildren still living are: Carolyn Nowell Cox of Sikeston; Delbert of Fenton, Missouri; Hershell of California; Verneal Hamilton of Rector, Arkansas; Ola Dickerson of Hot Springs, Arkansas; Merl Brewer of Jonesboro, Arkansas; Iva Jean Walpole, Dexter, Missouri; Kathleen Wright of Wasco, California; Betty Colou Sparks of Elizabethtown, Kentucky; and Sue Farley of Knoxville, Tennessee.

This writer remembers sleeping in the south room of the old homeplace, which was very cold. Two beds were in the main room by the fireplace. The old green and ivory wood stove kept the chill out of the big kitchen. The big kitchen table was surrounded by the water bucket stand, flour barrels and two kitchen safes. It was a treat to receive a piece of candy from a tin ordered through the mail and kept in the safe.

Spice jar salt and pepper shakers dated 1874 were found in the rubble a few years ago by a granddaughter.

**NUTT** – When I was small growing up on Crowley's Ridge in Northeast Arkansas, I remember many stories told by my grandparents about how and why we were living in the area.

My paternal Nutt heritage began in this country when William and Elizabeth Nutt began a family in the early 1700s in Augusta County, Virginia. He purchased one large water gristmill and built many others on 831 acres. (While on a trip with my mother, Mrs. Gordon Nutt, we visited the area and saw the old mill building.) His direct descendants also operated gristmills: Robert M. Nutt (my great-grandfather), and his son Robert W. Nutt (my grandfather) in late 1800s, and Gordon Nutt (my father) in the 1940s.

Some of the Nutt descendants migrated to North Carolina near Andrew Jackson on Waxhaw Creek where William Nutt and sons obtained a title to over 600 acres. This move was due, in part to forays with Indians who had killed many of the Virginia settlers and stolen their horses. Many families (Hoods, McCowans, Ellis, Spears, Rays, Scotts, Campbells, McCains) traveled together and some families intermarried (brothers marrying sisters, etc.). Later, some followed the Tennessee River to Wilson and Giles County and then to Shelby County, Tennessee. Some families moved to Alabama and Texas.

From Shelby County, my forebears moved to Howell County, Missouri, and on to Northeast Arkansas near Gainesville, then to the Lorado/New Herndon area. I was told that my great-great-grandfather rode by horseback, crossed on ferries to start/help start Missionary Baptist Churches. Some of his grand and great-grandchildren also became preachers.

I left the area to marry and assist my husband in obtaining graduates degrees in Florida and then helped start three junior colleges. We had five children who have migrated back to the SW/SC area:

Deborah (Al) French, loan officer, Mercantile Bank, North Little Rock (who named her daughter Elisabeth); Emily Wilson-Godinet, radar instructor with FAA, Oklahoma City, Oklahoma (daughter Kira); Valerie (Neal) Keating, Cabot Elementary School teacher (son Bradley); John B. Wilson Jr., landscaping assistant; and Scott Wilson, insurance agent, who live in Clarksville, Tennessee.

I moved back to Northeast Arkansas in 1971 with four of my five children to start a new life and enrolled in Arkansas State University in Nursing. A required speech class sent me into heart palpitations and resulted in an EKG and cardiac prescription. As I prepared my first speech, I came across material on my great-great-grandfather William Henry Nutt. The material indicated that he had helped start the first Missionary Baptist Church in five counties. He was buried beside one of the churches, located at Knob, Arkansas. I then presented all this information in a speech which was well received (made an A) and cured me of my palpitations! While on another trip with my mother in 1978, we toured Nova Scotia in Canada. Brochures listing places of interest had a museum and a display of paintings by Elizabeth Nutt. She had been an instructor and painter held in high esteem in that area. When she became ill she returned to her native England so she could be buried in her family plot when she expired. The brochure contained her picture, and she displayed some of the same features (mouth/lips) as my grandfather, R. W. Nutt. My mother was quite taken aback to see the portrait which resembled her departed father-in-law!

On vacation in September 1999, with my daughter, Deborah French, we toured London, England.

While at Windsor Castle, we saw St. George's Chapel (the castle grounds) which is used by the Royalty and Eaton villagers. In a hallway off the choir room, a glass-enclosed case displayed a large open book. There were architectural drawings of vaults and coffins. (Many of the chapels/cathedrals have vaults in the floors that contain the remains of the Royalty and well-known people.) There was a paper beneath the book that stated "A.Y. Nutt, Surveyor (architect) of the coffins and vaults, for the quire (choir) in the late 19th century."

When I was a young girl, my grandmother used to tell us there was some connection to the royal family of England. We thought it was just stories made up to entertain us and we joked about the royal connection! Needless to say, Deborah and I were impressed by the connection to the royal family, no matter how small. We did discover several families in England with the Nutt surname.

These experiences have reminded me that our past can be linked to our present and serve to entertain and enlighten us as we discover these links.

Bob Nutt

**NUTT** – Richard Morris Nutt was born October 3, 1936, the second child of Gordon and Sophronia Scott Nutt. His sister is LaVerne Nutt Wilson. Their grandparents were Sidney and Mattie Pratt Scott of the Fontaine Community in southwest Greene County and Robert Washington and Elsie Schisler Nutt. Uncle Bob and Aunt Elsie lived off Nutt Lane, named for Gordon Nutt who donated the land to build the road. That road is now Greene Road 326.

Bob Nutt's grandfather, William, started several Baptist churches up and down Crowley's Ridge. Elsie Nutt's father, Henry Schisler, owned several businesses in the area where she and Bob settled when they were married in 1898. The settlement was called Old Herndon and was located in the area of what is now Lake Frierson. The land was purchased from the Nutt family estate after Uncle Bob and Aunt Elsie died.

Gordon and Sophronia Nutt were farmers and business people. They owned a grocery store at Slabtown, across from North Hills Golf Course, on Highway 141 North. Richard and LaVerne lived in the log house with their parents, next door to the store. They had a show building across from the store. Gordon showed movies there and also traveled the countryside showing them. Richard has many fond memories of these trips with his dad.

Picking cotton on Sidney Scott's farm. Left to right: Sidney Scott, Oliver Scott (son), Mr. Moore, Mattie Ree (Pratt) Scott, Sophronia Scott Nutt (wife of James Gordon Nutt, daughter of Sidney and Mattie Scott), Mrs. Moore, son of the Moore's, Richard Robert Scott (son).

Gordon and Sophronia began putting their farm operation together in the Great Depression buying a 40 acres here and there until at Gordon's death, 1966 at 63 years of age, they had purchased the 1,200 acre farm in the Lorado-Fontaine Community. They moved to the farm in 1950 when Richard was 14 years old.

**NUTT** – Richard is married to Virginia "Ginny" Patterson. They still live in the house that was built shortly after their marriage on Highway 168 in the Lorado-Fontaine Community.

Richard managed the family farm three years for his mother after his Dad's death and then started renting it from her plus tilling land belonging to himself. Richard and Ginny have two sons, Richard Raney and Morris Gordon.

Raney married Jayne Finch and they have a farm operation in the Fontaine Community of approximately 2,500 acres. Jayne is a certified public accountant. She and Raney graduated from Arkansas State University. They have two children: Tyler, 1990 and Mackensie, born 1995. They were named Greene County Farm Family in 1994.

Morris, also a graduate of ASU, married Kelly Lynch, a math instructor and she is taking time off to be with their son, Kevin Lawson Nutt, born 1998. Morris is an investment broker with Edward Jones in Cordova, Tennessee. He and Raney also have farm interests together.

Cotton was the main crop on the Nutt farms until the 1970s but insects and low yields forced an end to it. Today rice, corn, soybeans, wheat and sometimes grain sorghum are grown.

In the fall months, the colors of timber on Crowley's Ridge are breathtaking from the farm; and in winter, it is common to see the fields flooded for duck hunting.

Agriculture has had some tough times, but it has been a happy life for the Nutt family.

**NUTT/KNOTT** – William Nutt (1st) 1705-1758 DAR National # 636743, and wife Elanor, of Augusta County Virginia, and descendants. The children of this marriage were: 1. Andrew, wife Margaret; 2. William Jr. (2); John; Eleanor; ( possibly others). He moved to an area four miles south of present day Staunton, Virginia. This is the first recorded transaction whereby he purchased land. On May 24, 1750, Dennis Dyer, and Abigail deeded back to William Nutt, miller, in Beverly Manor approximately 181 acres. On November 4, 1741, William Nutt, and others, appraised the estate of John Campbell. William Nutt (1st) and Eleanor, appear in the *Tinkling Spring: Headwater Of Freedom,* by Howard M. Wilson, ThD. Pub/ 1954. He states that "when the Reverend James Anderson preached at the home of John Lewis, in 1738 only eleven people in the entire settlement had procured title for their lands. Among those there were the William Nutt family. From this date the Nutt family's name appeared on many deeds, one whereby William Nutt's land cornered on Andrew Nutt's land.

William Nutt Jr., (2nd), was born about 1730-35. We know that the Nutt family moved to Anson County North Carolina, as they purchased 600 acres of land by petition on September 21, 1751. It was indicated William (2), was married when he enlisted under Captain Andrew Pickens in 1755. Most likely he was married three times, for in land transactions in the Carolinas we find the names of two wives on separate deeds. Received a land patent on April 5, 1753. Among those receiving land grants in Anson County and locating in and near Waxhaw settlement were: John Hood, William Hood, Andrew McCowan, Alexander McCawan and Hugh McCain.

William Nutt (3rd), the only son of William and Agnes Hood, we have evidence of, was born between 1761-1770 while they were living on the Waxhaw Creek in then Mecklenburg County, North Carolina, later upper Lancaster County, South Carolina. William (3rd) married Mary McCowan who had been born in 1760-1770, she died the latter part of 1853 in Dallas County, Arkansas. The Children of William (3rd) and Mary

McCown, as known and indicated are: 1. Elizabeth Nutt, 2. Nancy Nutt, 3. William Henry Nutt, 4. Sampson McCown Nutt, (great-great-great-grandfather of Houston Dale Nutt ) 5. Robert Washington Nutt, John Nutt, Thomas Nutt, James Nutt, Walter Nutt, Pleasant Nutt, Josiah Nutt.

William Henry Nutt, (4th), was born in 1800, either in Chester or Lancaster County, South Carolina, and he died in 1845, and is buried near the Old Bethlehem Missionary Baptist Church in Clay County, Arkansas. He married Elizabeth Spears who had been born in Kentucky between 1800-1805, she died before 1850 and is buried beside her husband at Bethlehem Missionary Baptist Church, near Knob, in Clay County, Arkansas. *The History Of Arkansas Baptist,* by Rogers, tells us that he had been preaching up and down Crowley's Ridge for four years by 1842. In 1999 he still has descendants that are preachers. One Todd Fox Missionary Baptist in Montana, and Telfar S. Rhea Jr. a Missionary Baptist preacher, at Newport, Arkansas and Robert Walter Nutt, Missionary Baptist preacher in Northeast Arkansas.

Before 1836, William Henry married Elizabeth Speers, born 1800-05, died 1853, along with members of the William Spear/Speer family, and the James McCown family appear in records in and around the Wolf Creek, Shelby County near Memphis, Tennessee, as road commissioners and overseers. These families emigrated to Arkansas beginning in 1836, to a rise in the ground near present day Crowley's Ridge State Park. (Grady Nutt Jr. ). William Henry's brothers traveled in opposite directions, one to Alabama (Sampson) and one to Texas, William Henry was married three times, one marriage produced a son Robert McCowan Nutt, born June 1828, died March 16, 1913, Robert Washington Nutt, born Howell County, Missouri, on January 28, 1875.

R.W. Nutt was the father of James Gordon Nutt, born March 1903, the father of Richard Morris Nutt, born October 3, 1936. Richard still lives in the same area where his grandfather and great-grandfather settled earlier. Richard Morris Nutt, like his ancestors is a farmer, along with one son Raney Nutt, born October 2, 1963, in the Lorado/Fontaine part of Greene County. He and Raney more than 1,500 acres. Crowley's Ridge State Park.

The Speers/Spears, Nutt's, McCowan/McCown, Rhea families along with other familiar names are listed together, from Virginia south through North Carolina, South Carolina, Alabama, Tennessee, then into Arkansas.

(The compiler is James Sidney Scott Sr., grandson of Sarah Ann (Nutt) Rhea. The submitter-editor Elsie LaVerne (Nutt) Wilson. Their great-grandfather was Robert McCowan Nutt.) We wish to thank Irene E. Amato for her contribution to the Nutt genealogy.

**ODOM** – Joe and Sarah Odom, with daughters Laura and Angela, moved to Greene County in 1984 from Marion, AR. Joe works for the Union Pacific Railroad as a trainman and were transferred to this area. The family settled in Paragould.

Sarah is the daughter of Floyd Staten and Elsie (McIntosh) of West Memphis, AR who was originally from Halcomb and Bradley, MS. Floyd lost both parents during the Flu Epidemic in 1918.

Joe is the son of Joe H. Odom, Sr. and Thelma (Tolleson) of Barnes, MS. Joe Sr. was originally from Attala County, MS. He served with the 3rd Armored Division in Europe during WWII.

Laura attended ASU and graduated from Black River Vo-Tech. She lives with husband Stan Hovis and son Tyler Cribbs in Paragould.

Angela graduated from ASU and CARTI Radiation Therapy College. She and her husband, Glenn Hamasaki live in Tucson, AZ.

Sarah's sisters and their families, after visiting Greene County, decided this was a good place to live and moved to Paragould after their retirement.

Becky and Perry Jarman with family, Doug and Cindy moved from Apple Valley, CA in 1987. Perry is retired from the Santa Fe Railroad. Doug and his family returned to California and Cindy with husband Andy Booth and son A. J. live in Paragould.

Perry's sister Nina and husband Robert Smith, moved here in 1996. Nina died in 1997 and Robert moved to West Memphis, AR.

Margie and Don Fuller, with sons Dona A and Jerry moved to Paragould in 1992. Don is retired from the USAF (SAC) and Margie is a retired nurse. Don A. is an officer in the Army National Guard and teaches Military Science at ASU. Jerry married Penelope (Cash) in 1997 and with daughter Mackenzie Allison and son, Mason live in Paragould.

*Submitted by Joe Odom*

**ORICK** – The Orick family came to Greene County, AR, in early 1902. They were avid hunters and had heard that the hunting was very good in Arkansas. They came from Flora, IL in Clay County.

Stillman and Emma Orick and their children, a nephew, his father John and mother Nancy, a brother Ira, a sister Elizabeth moved to Arkansas. A sister, Lillie was married to Elija Justes, stayed in Illinois.

Ira was married to Mytrle Clark, they moved to Stuttgart, AR. They were buried there.

*Ira and Maxine Orick. Taken Aug. 21, 1979.*

Elizabeth married Howard Ellis and lived in Greene County. They are buried in Morrow Cemetery.

Emma's father Abram McHenry came a little later, her mother Margaret had died and was buried in Illinois.

They all settled in the Sugar Creek and Commissary communities near Stanford and Blackjack (now Evening Star). They were farmers.

My uncles, Earl and Roy and my dad Ira played baseball in their younger days.

*Front row: Grandma Emma holding Roy, Allie, and Alma. Back row: Earl, Hazel, Goldie, and Mable, 1910.*

None of them stopped hunting and fishing till the day they died. They are all buried in Morrow Cemetery. They passed on the love of these sports to their descendents. All through the years grandsons and granddaughters have been playing these sports. Some have added tennis and golf. Gender did not make a difference. The girls fish and play ball as well as the boys.

Today Jonatha Clark, a great-granddaughter of Stillman and Emma, is a coach at Delaplaine High School. Her sister Taunya Sisco helps coach the girl's peewee teams there also. My dad, Ira married Maxine Beauchamp daughter of Albert and Maudie "Merts" Beauchamp on Oct 1, 1938. They had nine children.
1. Ira Ray who died in 1972
2. Albert Louis who died in 1988
3. Riley Mac who died in 1966
4. Kenny Joe
5. Darrell Glenn
6. Katey
7. Bonnie
8. Sadie Rose
9. Emma Lee

Katey, Kenny and I still live in Greene County, AR. They had 15 grandchildren and 16 great grandchildren. Ira died in 1985, Maxine died in 1999. They are buried in Morrow Cemetery.

*Ira Ray holding Lou Shipman, Granddad Beauchamp, Grandma Beauchamp, Louis holding Darrell, Emma Lee Shipman, Judy Overshine (a cousin), Rily Mac. In front: Katey, Bonnie, Kenny, and David Shipman. Very front: Sadie.*

My name is Emma Lee (Orick) Shipman, and I married James F. Shipman on Oct 5, 1957, in Warren's Chapel Methodist Church, where we are members and attend regularly. We have a son, David, daughter-in-law Lynda and a daughter Louise "Lou". We have six grandchildren:
1. D. J.
2. Geoffrey
3. Jordan
4. Tiffany
5. Jacob
6. Taylor

We also have two step-grandchildren, Christy and Drew.

*A birthday party for our mom, Maxine Orick. She was 80 years old. It was Oct 11, 1998; her birthdate is Oct. 14, 1918. Others in picture: Darrell, Emma, Katey, Bonnie, Sadie, and Kenny.*

Our branch of the family has been living and farming in the Evening Star area all my life. James and I have been farming since 1963. Our son David farms with our grandsons and us on the farm. They are avid hunters just like their grandfather before them.

*Submitted by Emma Shipman*

**ORR** – James Hamilton Orr was born in Tennessee circa 1840. He married Mary E. Harley and lived in Henry County, Tennessee, during the 1870 census. James was listed as a physician by occupation. By the 1880 census James had moved his wife Mary E. and their children to Greene County. By the 1890 census (Greene County Reconstructed census) James was "gone." James died in Mayflower, Arkansas, (Pencer Funeral Home records) in 1896.

James married second, Amanda Stephens of Greene County, Arkansas. James had two children by Amanda. They were Cortez Orr and Otto Orr. Otto Orr married Lillie Abigail Breckenridge daughter of Rufus Walker Breckenridge and Cordelia Brackenridge/Breckenridge Whitlock of Greene County in 1916. Other children of James and Mary E. Orr were: William (not listed in Greene County census and buried at Pine Knot Cemetery); Mary K who married George Dodd in Riply County, Missouri; Lura who married Matthew Biggs in Greene County, Arkansas; James H. who first married Dove C. Grayson in Riply County, Missouri, and second Mrs. Lucy Craig Williams in Greene County, Arkansas; and Afonzo Orr who married Hattie Dodd, in Riply County, Missouri, and second married Minnie Bonds in Greene County, Arkansas.

Otto Orr and Lillie Abigail Breckenridge were married February 22, 1916, in Greene County, Arkansas. Their children are Maurice Cortis Orr, Amanda Janice Orr, Geneva Orr, Valaska Edith Orr, Houston Bresee Orr, Peggy Sue Orr, Connie Walker Orr and Ronnie Willie Orr. Otto's and Lillie's children were reared in Greene County.

Houston Bresee Orr and Wilma Jean Gladish were married January 19, 1951, in Paragould, Greene County, Arkansas. Houston graduated from high school in Beech Grove. Their children are Linda Jean Orr and Houston William Otto Orr. Houston Bresee Orr owned and operated Oak Grove Lumber Company and later owned Rector Lumber Company and Wilma Orr taught school in Oak Grove. Houston and Wilma Orr still reside in Greene County. Their children, Linda and Houston "Bill" Graduate went to school at Oak Grove. Bill still resides in Greene County while Linda now lives in North Little Rock, Arkansas.

Orr's buried in Greene County, Arkansas are:
James H. Orr, son of James H. and Mary E. Orr, buried at Beech Grove Cemetery.
Afonzo Orr, son of James H, and Mary E. Orr, buried at Jones Cemetery.
Cortez Orr, son of James H. and Mary E. Orr, possibly buried at Pine Knot Cemetery.
William Orr, son of James H. and Mary E. Orr, buried at Pine Knot Cemetery.
Ronnie Willie Orr, son of Otto and Lillie Breckenridge Orr, buried at Beech Grove Cemetery.
Christopher Bruce Higgins, son of Bruce and Linda Orr Higgins, buried at Memorial Gardens Cemetery.
Jonathan Michael Bruce Higgins, son of Bruce and Linda Orr Higgins, buried at Memorial Gardens Cemetery.
Brent Wayne Orr, son of Houston William Otto and Judy Orr, buried at Memorial Gardens Cemetery.
Maurice Cortis Orr, son of Otto and Lillie Breckenridge Orr, buried at Memorial Gardens Cemetery.

**O'STEEN** – John O'Steen (April 27, 1845 Panola County, MS) son of Harvey and Mary Elizabeth (True) O'Steen, ran away to war at the age of 15 and enlisted in Captain Adair's company at Jonesboro. In 1870, he married Bethany Angie Jones (May 1850 Bibb County, AL) daughter of Jonathaon Shelby and Bethaby (Williams) Jones.

John O'Steen's family moved to Craighead County, AR in 1859 and settled in Greensboro. His father was a gunsmith by trade and John learned the trade before enlisting in the war. Upon his marriage, John O'Steen moved to Greene County where he continued his trade until 1888, when he sold out and engaged in the mercantile business. He was elected Probate and County Judge in 1882 serving six successive years. Prior to his election, Mr. O'Steen served four years as justice of the peace and one term as constable.

John O'Steen owned 160 acres of which some 40 acres was under cultivation. He was a Mason and a member of the I.O.O.F. John and Bethany O'Steen had a total of five children:
1. Mary A. (1873)
2. Infant daughter (1874-1874)
3. Infant daughter (1877-1877)
4. Samuel H. O'Steen (1881-1882)
5. Angeline P. O'Steen (1883-1884)
6. Nora Inez O'Steen (Jan 1885) married George McCracken had at least two children: O'Steen and Wren, before moving to Glendale, CA.

John O'Steen died Aug 12,1908 and is buried at Brown's Chapel Cemetery in Greene County. Bethany died after 1920, probably in Glendale, CA as she is on census with her daughter and family in 1920.

**OVERBAY** – The Overbury "Overbay" family were English, with segments of the family residing in the English Shires of Cloucester, Middlesex and Warwick.

Our first ancestor coming to America was Nicholas Overbury, settling in Dinwiddle County, Virginia, around 1663. Later migrating to Georgia and Tennessee.

Daniel Byrd Overbay was born in Georgia in 1853, died in Greene County, Arkansas, October 2, 1885, and is buried in the Nellie Moore Cemetery. He married Elizabeth Caroline Massengill, who was born January 12, 1841, in Greene County. She was the daughter of Leroy Massengill and Catherine Thompson. Their children were, Jeremiah born July 8, 1880, Obediah Dan born April 20, 1883, Lola Amanda Adele born February 1885, and Daniel born 1887. Daniel Byrd Overbay served in the Civil War and later taught school in this area.

*Obediah "Obe" Overbay*

Obediah Dan Overbay married Anna Lela Snow, daughter of Mardis Woodrow Snow and Francis Wamble. Their children were: Clarence Henry Overbay born December 7, 1909, in Lawrence County, Arkansas and married Iva Barnes.
Opal Marie born June 24, 1915, and married Arch Wilborn; Mardis Woodrow born January 3, 1918, and married Mary Myrtle Edgin; Dairl born February 18, 1921, died March 31, 1922; twins Bernas Loyd and Mildred Bernice born April 11, 1926.

Clarence Henry Overbay Sr. and Iva Barnes were married May 16, 1931, in Lawrence County, Arkansas. They were the parents of Clarence Henry Overbay Jr. born February 20, 1933, and married Bettye Jean Sparks, daughter of Robert Sparks and Myrtie Johnson Sparks. Wilma Dean married Lindell Chilton, Shelby married first Terrell Sando, second Daniel Walsh; Shirley married Milton Kirkendall; Carolyn Sue born April 5, 1943, married Donald Eugene Master; Omer David born July 9, 1939, and died in an auto accident December 31, 1959.

Clarence Henry Overbay Jr. the first child of Clarence Overbay Sr. and Iva Barnes Overbay married Bettye Jean Sparks. Their children are: Clarence Overbay III born April 29, 1954; Omer David Overbay II born August 13, 1960; and Lea Ann (Overbay) Vanaman born June 29, 1962. Clarence attended the University of Tennessee, Martin, Tennessee and graduated with a law degree from the University of Missouri in January 1960. He and his family moved to Kennett, Missouri, where he associated in law practice with Tom B. Mobley and was elected prosecuting attorney of Dunklin County, Missouri, in August 1960. He was serving in this office at the time of his untimely death on October 19, 1962, from an accidental gunshot wound. Omer David Overbay II married Paula Austin and lives in Greene County; Lea Ann married Charles Vanaman, divorced and also lives in Greene County; Clarence Overbay is a Lt. Colonel in the Arkansas National Guard and lives in Jonesboro, Arkansas, with his family. His daughter, Laura Overbay resides in Greene County.

Bettye Overbay, widow of Clarence Overbay Jr., remarried Ethan Busby and lives in Greene County.

Other Overbay descendants still living in Greene County are Kay (Overbay) Holmes. Kay married Bill Holmes and they are the parents of three children: Stephen, Michelle and Marty.

**OWENS** – William C. Owens married Elizabeth Blythe and had three children:
1. Mary Adelaide married a Roberts
2. James R.
3. William Lee Owens.

Ezekial Church married Sarah Charlotte Owen and had six daughters:
1. Laura Bell married (1) White (2) Cass Baird
2. Sarah "Sadie" Eliza
3. Emmarantha Luiza
4. Ida Charlotte
5. Minnie Elba
6. Clara Edwin married (1)Jay Moore (2) Robert Marchbanks (3) William Lee Owens

*William Lee and Clara Owens*

Ezekial rode the circuit as a Methodist preacher. He also fought for the Confederate side in the Civil War. He returned home unharmed to release his slaves and to resume farming. He continued to preach and lived around the Evening Star area.

William Lee Owens married Clara Edwin Church in 1909 in Greene County. They had two children:
1. William Cleo married Rada Butler
2. Clara Edith married Jimmie Eubanks

Since times were hard and these two were determined survivors, they each brought children to blend in to their home. William Lee brought his daughter Nellie and Clara brought her sons Jay Moore and Garland Marchbanks. Nellie married Charlie Boyd.

In 1895 tragedy came to Clara's life. In November she lost her mother Sarah Charlotte Church, her sister Ida Moore, her brother-in-law Robert Moore and her husband Jay Moore. In one week's time an epidemic influenza claimed their lives.

Clara Marchbanks worked as the postmistress for BlackJack (Evening Star). Clara was working for the postal service when she met William Lee Owens. They married and relocated to Beech Grove where they ran a General Merchandise Store. They provided supplies and groceries to farmers until the depression forced them to close the store. After the depression he continued to farm and work as a carpenter.

*Cleo Owens and Edith (Owens) Eubanks*

Clara and William continued to farm cattle. Daughter Edith Eubanks lived nearby. They would send cattle to pasture in the morning and they would return to be milked. Mom and daughter would send notes to each other in the cow's bell when the green beans needed canning or if they needed to borrow something.

*Submitted by Linda Arnold*

**PANNELL** – Doy Mack Pannell was born at Turkey in Marion County, Arkansas, on December 31, 1919. He was the son of Moses Reeder "Mose" and Jessie Lee (Brown) Pannell. He was born at his Grandpa Wasden Brown's house as his mother and dad were living with her father, a widower, at the time. Doy was the oldest of six children, three boys and three girls born to Mose and Jessie. Doy grew up on the family farm and attended school at Eros, Pyatt and Bruno graduating from Pyatt in 1938. On December 7, 1939, he married his high school sweetheart Vera Rose a graduate of Bruno High School. Vera was the daughter of Ira and Eula (King) Rose and was born and raised in the Eros Community. Doy attended Arkansas Tech College at Russellville for a year, worked for a couple of years then entered the Army. He served with Company H, 108th Infantry Regiment and attained the rank of sergeant while serving in motor transportation. He took part in the Southern Philippines Campaign and when the war ended was stationed in Korea and Japan as part of the Army of Occupation. He was discharged from the service on May 14, 1946, at Camp Chaffee Arkansas.

After leaving the Army he started his teaching and coaching career as junior high coach at Pyatt. He coached the senior high team the next two years. He then moved to Bruno where he coached the next four years before moving to Bergman in Boone County. He coached both girls and boys teams at Bergman for a year. In 1954 he moved his family to Leachville in Mississippi County where he taught and coached for six years. He had several outstanding teams at Leachville including a junior boys state champion in 1958 and topped it off with the AA-AAA senior boys championship in 1960.

*From left: Vera (Rose) Pannell, Carolyn Rose Pannell and Doy Mack Pannell (1945).*

In the summer of 1960 he accepted the senior boys basketball coaching job at Paragould, a school more noted for it's football and track programs than for basketball. He took the Bulldogs to the state tournament each year he coached there. In 1963 the Bulldogs won their only state title in basketball, to date, winning the AA-AAA crown.

During his early coaching career he earned his BSE from Arkansas State Teachers College in Conway by attending night classes and summer school commuting from Marion and Boone counties to Conway to accomplish this. He also obtained his MSE from Arkansas State University after moving to northeast Arkansas.

*Front: Vera (Rose) Pannell and Doy Mack Pannell. Back: Marilyn Kay Pannell (1968).*

He was also high school principal at PHS for one year. He retired from teaching and coaching in 1972. He sold insurance for a few months then bought the Chrysler, Plymouth and Dodge automobile dealership in Paragould and ran it as Pannell Motor Company, Inc. until March 1982 when he sold it. He acquired ownership of the Ford and Mercury franchise in January 1982 and ran it as Pannell Ford Mercury, Inc. from then until his death on November 21, 1999. Doy and Vera were very big on family and family values. They were both Southern Baptists and lived their lives by Christian principles. They had two daughters, Carolyn Rose was born January 25, 1941, in Eros in Marion County at the home of her maternal grandparents. Marilyn Kay was born October 20, 1952, in Harrison, Boone County, Arkansas. No doubt the biggest heartache to the Pannells was the death of Kay in an auto accident on New Year's Eve 1979. The irony of the date was that it was the 90th wedding anniversary of Kay and her husband James Berry Rogers and Doy's 60th birthday. Kay was a registered nurse and the mother of a 3 year old daughter Angela Kay.

After Doy's death Pannell Ford Mercury continues on as a family business managed by his daughter Carolyn Mitchell and his grandson Lance Mitchell.

**PARTLOW** – Thomas Allen Partlow (Sept 5, 1825), chairman of the Wilson County Court received his education in the Gladesville School and remained with his parents until he was 22 years old. On May 19, 1847 he married Margaret Williamson, a native of Wilson County (Aug 1825) the daughter of Thomas Williamson. After their marriage they located near his old home and followed agricultural pursuits. Thomas and Margaret had one child, Cloe. On Jan 20, 1859 Margaret died and in 1863 Thomas A. married May Ann Robins, who lived only 18 months after their marriage.

Hayward Riddle was one of four children born to Thomas Allen and his third wife, Martha E. Ray (April 2, 1836), a native of Wilson County, TN, the daughter of William Ray. Their children were:
1. William A.
2. James R.
3. Natalie M.
4. Haywood who came to Paragould in 1907.

In 1840 he learned the tanner and currier's trade, which he carried on for some years. In 1861 he enlisted in Company G, State Guard. He took an active part in battles at Lexington, Oak Hill and Springfield. In 1865 Thomas Allen came home and in the fall of the same year enlisted again and was with General Morgan until he made his famous raid through Kentucky, Indiana and Ohio after which he returned home. After the birth of Haywood in 1865, his dad moved to the 22nd district in Wilson County.

Thomas Allen is the son of Thomas and Cloe (Hooker) Partlow. The father was of French descent, born in 1796 in South Carolina and was a farmer by occupation. At one time he owned 513 acres. He was a soldier in the War of 1812 and fought in the Battle of "Horse Shoe Bend". His mother, of German descent, was born in North Carolina.

Haywood R. Partlow (Feb 18, 1876 Wilson County, TN) came to Paragould in 1907 as superintendent of schools and served in that capacity until 1912. He was the first county supervisor of education in Greene County, serving six years. He also served two terms as Paragould city attorney around 1915. He was a member of First Baptist Church and taught Sunday school for over 20 years.

*Charles Partlow*

For a short time, he lived in Florida and while there he authorized a textbook on Florida land titles, which was used by the University of Florida Law School. When Woodrow Wilson School was built he took an active part in its planning and construction. The building was used for a high school until a school was built on West Court and Seventh Street. It housed grades seven through 12 and Woodrow Wilson housed classes through the sixth grade when the high school moved to the new building.

Haywood Partlow returned to Wilson County, TN and enrolled in Cumberland University and completed a three-year law course in one year. He subsequently was admitted to the bar, after which he was associated in legal and abstract business in Paragould with Cecil Shane and later with L.V. Rhine. Haywood Partlow, his wife, Alice and their son, James K. Partlow, were the only members of the Partlow family who came to Greene County from Wilson County.

In 1939 Haywood Riddle Partlow had his law office in rooms five and six of the Crowley Building in downtown Paragould. He and his wife lived on Route Five. James K., their son, established an abstract business. He and his son, Charles were partners in this company for many years. Charles was mayor of Center Hill during the time that it became an incorporated town and was mayor of Paragould for many years. James K.'s other son, James K. Jr. "Buster," was associated with the Cotton Belt Railroad for many years until his retirement.

Haywood Partlow died in Paragould Jan 14, 1956.

**PAYNE** – Jesse Eppi Payne (1807/1808 SC- Jan 15, 1870 Greene County, AR) married Feb 25,1832 in Shelby County, TN, Louisa McDaniel (1814 KY-died in Greene County, AR) the daughter of Stacy and Sally (Lamb) McDaniel. Jesse and Louisa had 12 known children:
1. Francis (1833), male?
2. Harriett (1836)
3. Mary Jane (1838)
4. Susannah (1839)
5. Milton (1842)
6. Eliza (1843)
7. John (1846)
8. James C. (1848)
9. Emily (1850)
10. Paralee (1851)
11. Columbos (1853)
12. Elias Conway Payne (1856).

Eliza Payne married Isaac W. Willcockson and had six known children:
1. William H.
2. Louis
3. John Toliver
4. Lura
5. Paralee
6. Julie Willcockson

Elias Conway Payne married his cousin, Emily Elmira McDaniel, daughter of James D. and Sarah (Hall) McDaniel. They had five known children:
1. Sam (1885)
2. Louis (1887)
3. Tranum (1889
4. Millie (1890)
5. Eura Payne (1892).

James C. Payne (1848 Greene County, AR) married Alsadora Ward, daughter of Gideon and Mary Ward. They had three children:
1. Jesse Hill (March 19, 1871)
2. Orastus Hubbard Payne (Aug 29, 1872)
3. Flora Alice Payne (Oct 6, 1876).

James C. Payne died before 1878 and Alsadora remarried Dec 27, 1876 Reuben W. Fletcher. Flora Alice married Jan 15, 1890 J.F. Smith. They had 12 children:
1. Jake
2. Hill
3. Jack
4. A. P.
5. John L.
6. Earl
7. Woodrow
8. Dolly
9. Medola
10. Leona
11. Princess Mary
12. Della Nete Smith.

Orastus Hubbard "Hub" Payne married in 1890 Nancy Caroline Pegg. They had nine children:
1. Calley
2. Martha Alice
3. James Marcus
4. Perlie
5. Paralee
6. Carroll Crawford
7. Almarie
8. Princess
9. Caraway Payne.

Jesse Hill Payne (March 19, 1871- Feb 23, 1903/1904) married Delaney Conzory Willcockson (Aug 24, 1874). They had five children:
1. Joseph Moss
2. Burl Franklin
3. William G.
4. Josie L.
5. Dora Payne.

Jesse Hill remarried two more times: (2) Frances York Nov 12, 1903, she died 1918. (3) Mrs. Dora E. Henson, March 21, 1922. At least five more children were born:
1. Tennie
2. Odell
3. Thomas
4. Estell
5. J.J. Payne.

Joseph Moss Payne (Sept 12,1894) married Bessie Gertrude Newberry, daughter of Lawrence Newberry. They had four children:
1. Dolford Franklin
2. Richard Paul Payne
3. Olive Lucille
4. Canna Jodina Payne.

*Submitted by Janollah Diggs Payne*

**PENNEY** – Marvin Fleetwood Penney (March 4, 1888),was the son of Thomas Jefferson "T.J." and Liddia (Cox) Penney. His parents, T. J. (Feb 12, 1890) and Liddia were married on April 3, 1881 in Greene County, AR. Children born to this union:

*Marvin and Stella (Corbin) Penney with their children. Front: Lowell and Lionell. Back: Winston and Imogene 1939*

1. Charles
2. William Albert
3. Pearl
4. Marvin Fleetwood

After Liddia's death, T. J. later married Laura Mobley, their children:
1. Mamie
2. Maynard
3. Rufus Emery
4. Henry Leslie
5. Myrtle Odean
6. Lillian Gladys
7. Mary Penney.

Marvin Penney was over six feet tall with blue eyes. He met his future wife, Stella, at a party given by his sister in Gainesville, AR. On Nov 28, 1917, Marvin Fleetwood Penney married Bessie Estella "Stella" Corbin at her sister, Della (Corbin) McLendon's house. Marvin wore a dark suit and Stella wore a light brown dress.

Bessie Estella "Stella" Corbin (Oct 20, 1897) was the daughter of Francis Marion and Viola Elizabeth (Yates) Corbin.

During WWI, Marvin was in the army. After the war, Marvin and Stella Penney returned to Greene County, AR where they purchased a farm.

Marvin and Stella Penney had five children:
1. Marvin Lionell Penney
2. Inez Penney who died when she was nine years old
3. Winston Marion Penney
4. Imogene Penney
5. Lowell Winfred Penney

They had five grandchildren:
a. Linda Jean (Gillespie) Kyzer Shook Bird
b. Stanley Gillespie
c. Sandra (Penney) Sharpe
d. Phyllis (Penney) Bell
e. Bethany (Penney) Smith.

Marvin Penney died on June 22, 1967. Stella (Corbin) Penney was 91 years old when she died on May 6, 1989. She had outlived all of her children except Imogene (Penney) Higgins. Marvin and Stella Penney are buried at Gainesville Cemetery in Greene County.

*Submitted by Linda (Gillespie) Bird*

**PENNY** – Caleb Penny (1823-1872) with his siblings and parents, William and Sally Penny, moved from Johnston County, North Carolina, to Gibson County, Tennessee, between 1830 and 1840. Caleb married Martha Gentry in 1850. Seven children: William, Molly, John, Thomas, Lee, Emily and James Robert were born to this couple in Weakley County before they migrated to Greene County, Arkansas, about 1869.

James Robert "Bob" Penny was born October 22, 1868, and died December 15, 1945. As a young man he left home and returned to Tennessee where he married Frances Agnes "Grace" Dawson. They had two children Rhoda and Hoyt. When Grace died, Bob returned to Greene County where he met and married Martha Elizabeth "Betty" (Cole) Watkins, young widow of George Watkins, who had a daughter Georgia. (See the Ned Rochelle Cole family). Bob and Betty had children: Albertine, Rochelle, Caleb, Amogia, Gehronda and Ned. All of the children are remembered throughout the area for their musical abilities. They preformed individually, as a family and with groups, both instrumentally and vocally.

*Top row from left: Caleb Penny, Rochelle Penny, Amogia Penny, Gehronda Penny and Ned Penny, Middle row from left: Rhoda Penny, James Robert Penny, Martha Elizabeth (Cole) Watkins Penny and Hoyt Penny. Bottom row from left: Albertine Penny and Georgia Watkins.*

Bob was a merchant in Gainesville and a stockholder in the bank there when Gainesville was still an active community. Later he worked at Wrape's Heading Mill, was a timberman and farmed. In World War I he worked in Little Rock for the War Department. Five of his children served in World War II.

Rhoda married John Daniel Cole. They lived in Blytheville during the building of the Air Force base. Later they moved to Indiana and to St. Louis where Rhoda was employed by Missouri Baptist Hospital. Born to this couple were Fernand, Olivrene and Jay. (See The Ned Rochelle Cole family).

Hoyt married Fannie Swindle and they had two children: Bill, who died in infancy, and Carolyn. He worked for the Missouri Pacific Railroad and lived at Oak Grove. Even as a young man Hoyt assumed the position of patriarch of the family and was highly respected by all that knew him. Albertine married Rev. Russell Lee. Most of their lives were spent in Indiana and Missouri. Albertine used her musical talents in connection with their ministry. Their children Jim and Penny.

Rochelle married Betty Baldridge. They had Karen, Stanley and Cheryl. In 1935 Rochelle joined the CCC's and later joined the Army where he served in Alaska, Africa and Italy during WWII. He was wounded in Italy and received the Purple Heart and an individual citation. After the war Rochelle went into business in St. Louis. Upon retirement he returned to Paragould.

Caleb served in the Army during WWII in France and Germany. He married Alberta Ladigo and after the war was employed by the Chrysler Corporation in Indianapolis, Indiana. Their children were Sherwin, Lonnie, Bob and Jacqueline.

Amogia, after attending Arkansas State, taught school at Oak Grove. While serving in the WAVES during WWII she met and married Mitchell Osadchuk, director of the Army Band in Washington D.C. After the war they lived in Michigan where they were in the field of education. Amogia received her master's degree from the University of Michigan. They had one son, Michael.

Gehronda worked in a defense plant in Jacksonville, Arkansas, at the beginning of WWII and later joined the WAVES. She married Don Ferguson and they made their home in Minneapolis, Minnesota, with their children: Don, Jan, Jim and Richard. Later they moved to Texas.

Ned served in the Pacific Theatre during WWII. After the war he attended ASU where he received bachelor and master's degrees and an Army Officer's commission. After a second tour of military duty during the Korean War, he continued in reserves and National Guard and retired with 27 years service. As an educator he worked in music, counseling and administration in Missouri and Arkansas schools. He married Patsy White and they had two children, Ned Jr. and Cecilia.

**PERKEY** – Many people in the Paragould area are familiar with the name Don Perkey. Don and his wife, Loree', have owned a local shoe business for almost 43 years.

The son of Alvis and Ruthel Crow Perkey, Don Perkey (Dec 7, 1927) graduated from Cave City High School and from the Dallas Mortuary College in Dallas, TX. He is a licensed embalmer and funeral director. A veteran, who served in the US Navy during WWII, Don Perkey served aboard the battleship *New Jersey*.

Loree' (Campbell) Perkey (Jan 6, 1931), the daughter of Othar and Oletta Campbell, is a graduate of Delaplaine High School and Capital City Business College in Little Rock. She later attended Harding College in Searcy.

Don and Loree' Perkey were married July 15, 1949 in Little Rock and have been married almost 52 years. The couple spent their 50th wedding anniversary at the White House at the invitation of President Bill Clinton. They stayed in the Lincoln Bedroom, which was quite the honor.

The couple has two daughters, Donna and Patti. Donna Perkey (July 21, 1953) is a graduate of Crowley's Ridge Academy, Crowley's Ridge College and Harding College. She married Robert Helvering and the couple has been married for the past 27 years. They have two sons, Doug, 24, Daniel 21. The Helverings reside in Omaha, NE.

*Don and Loree' Perkey*

Patti Perkey married Don Ernest. They have been married for 22 years and have three children:
1. Kristin 17
2. Katie 14
3. Jonathan 10.

They reside in Reston, Virginia.

Don and Loree' Perkey worked with the Smith Mortuary in Charleston for three years before moving to Jonesboro, where he was employed with Gregg Funeral Home from 1953-1958. In 1958, the Perkey's embarked on a new phase of their lives. They moved to Greene County and decided to open a new business. In May 1958 the doors of Sample Shoe Store were opened at 219 South Pruett Street. Don and Loree' were the proud new owners. In 1983 they moved to their current location and changed the name to Don Perkey's Shoes Inc.

Don and Loree' have been members of the Seventh and Mueller Church of Christ since 1958. Don has always played an active role in the community, serving on the Paragould City Council for 25 years. He is a past president and board member of the local Chamber of Commerce. He has perfect attendance with the Paragould Kiwanis Club for the past 42 years.

Loree' Perkey is a member of the local Chamber of Commerce and is on the Ambassador Committee. She is also a member of the Paragould Business and Professional Women.

*Submitted by Don Perkey*

**PEVEHOUSE** – William Pevehouse, born April 7, 1826, is said to be the first white child born in Greene County, Arkansas.

He was the son of Abraham and Polly "Crowley" Pevehouse. He was the oldest child of their four known children; then Wiley, Margaret and Lucy.

Abraham and Polly Pevehouse both died in 1835 and Ben Crowley's son Samuel and his wife Sarah "Hutchins" Crowley took William to raise. Ben and Annie Crowley raised the others.

Samuel Crowley died and Sarah married Robert Henry Halley and they raised William.

William Pevehouse owned a large lot of stock and kept them on the range and stayed at the home of the Halley's.

Haley and William Pevehouse spent a lot of time bear hunting as bear was plentiful in Greene County and was used for meat bacon (for frying like hog lard was used) and lard. They kept 10 or 12 well trained dogs. Their main trail dog being a large black hound with yellow mouth and nose they called Watch. He was a valuable dog and treed many bears. Then the other dogs would take over and do the fighting as the owner's didn't want Watch mauled. Often the hunters would have to pin in the fight with the bear and more than once Halley would put the breach of his gun in the animal's mouth while Pevehouse would slay the bear with his long hunting knife.

William Pevehouse's name appears prominently on the church books of the early Methodist congregations of the county as secretary in other official capacities.

He married Altamirah Ferguson and moved to Washington County, Arkansas. He died during the Civil War and was buried in Clarksville "Johnson County," Arkansas.

His widow Emily Altamirah "Alta" drew a pension after the war for his Civil War services.

**PHILLIPS** – Caroline Melinda Dover (July 25, 1842 Montgomery County, Al) was the daughter of Bailey Appleton and Martha Ann "Patsy" Fielding Dover. Her siblings were
1. Elizabeth
2. Andrew
3. Martha
4. James M.
5. William Franklin
6. Marcus J.
7. Georgia A.

Caroline married John Perry Phillips on Oct 4, 1866, in Blount County, AL. He was born on Aug 6, 1837 in Montgomery County, AL. At the time of his marriage to Caroline, he had one son, Daniel Carter, age 10 and a daughter Sarah R., age 8 from a first marriage. A daughter, Melvina Palestine was born to John and Caroline in Alabama.

The family moved to Poinsett County in Arkansas in 1868, settling in the Farm Hill area, where John was a farmer. The children born to the couple there were:
1. Oralee Anna
2. Vester Appleton
3. Enoch D.
4. Major Franklin
5. Ludie Lain
6. Elrod Vasteen

John and Caroline were members of the Farm Hill Methodist Church, south of Harrisburg, AR, where he was a trustee.

John Perry died on March 9, 1883 and was buried in the Farm Hill cemetery in Poinsett County, AR.

After her husband's death, Caroline decided to move her family to Greene County. Her parents, Bailey A. and Martha A. Dover and her brothers, Andrew, James and William Franklin Dover were among the early settlers of the Center Hill community. Moving with the children, household goods, poultry and livestock and traveling on foot proved to be quite difficult. When they became exhausted and could to no further. Caroline sent someone to tell her family in Greene County they needed assistance. Eventually, help arrived and they were able to continue their journey.

*Caroline Melinda Dover Phillips*

The family moved to the Pruett's Chapel community, where, by 1900 three children, Major, Ludie and Elrod were still living at home. Caroline's daughter, Melvina Bridges, a widow, lived nearby with her four children.

Caroline, a Methodist from her youth, was a member of the Pruett's Chapel Methodist Church.

Caroline died of pneumonia on Feb 15, 1907.

All seven of her children were with her at her death. Reverend A. C. Griffin, well-known Methodist minister, presided at her funeral. Another Methodist minister, Reverend T. T. Williamson, wrote a memorial to Caroline in which he described her as "an earnest and consecrated Christian, as affectionate mother, a true friend and a good neighbor" who would truly be missed. Caroline was buried at Pruett's Chapel Cemetery with Dover family members.

*Bailey Appleton Dover, father of Caroline Phillips and early settler in the Center Hill community*

*Submitted by Anita Phillips*

**PHILLIPS** — Major Franklin Phillips (Aug 9,1876 Poinsett County, AR) was the son of John Perry and Carline Melinda Dover Phillips. The family was living in the Farm Hill community where John Perry farmed. They attended the Farm Hill Methodist Church where John was a trustee.

John and Caroline had a daughter, Melvina Palestine, born in Alabama. Children born in Arkansas were:

1. Orahlee Anna
2. Vester Appleton
3. Enoch D.
4. Major Franklin
5. Ludie Lain
6. Elrod Vasteen

A son, Daniel Carter Phillips and a daughter, Sarah R. Phillips, were born to John Perry and his first wife in Alabama.

*Seated: Major Franklin and Sally Diggs Phillips; Standing between parents (back): William Irvin Phillips; Standing: Letha, Russell Everett, Marlan Holmes Phillips; Front: Bonita and, in lap, Franklin Diggs Phillips*

After John's death on March 9, 1883, the family moved to Greene County where Caroline's parents Bailey A. and Martha A. Dover had been living. They settled in the Pruett's Chapel community and became members of the Pruett's chapel Methodist Church.

On Dec 8, 1901, Major married Sarah Fessona Diggs, daughter of Riley Diggs, a Methodist circuit rider and his wife, Sarah Clark Diggs. Their family moved from Tennessee to Arkansas during the 1880s. Major and Sally were married in Greene County by the well-known Methodist minister, Reverend A. C. Griffin.

The children born to the couple were:

1. William Irvin
2. Letha
3. Russell Everett
4. Marlan Holmes
5. Bonita
6. Franklin Diggs Phillips.

The family was active at Pruett's Chapel Methodist Church where Major was a Sunday school superintendent, on the Board of Stewards and a trustee of the church.

The family moved to the eastern part of Greene County for a short time where they cleared land and farmed. Their health deteriorated due to the swampy conditions, so they moved then to a home at the foot of "Gravel Pit Hill" on the Paragould-Jonesboro Highway, now Highway 49 South.

*Adult Children: Standing: Irvin, Letha. Seated: Russell, Bonita, Marlan*

Major developed complications following an appendectomy and died of pneumonia on Feb 28, 1923. He was buried in Linwood Cemetery.

Sally eventually moved to North Sixth Street and became active in the First United Methodist Church. She died in 1950 and was buried next to her husband.

*Submitted by Anita Phillips*

**PHILLIPS** – Gerald Everett Phillips was born in Paragould on Sept 26, 1932, to Russell and Veva Sims Phillips. He had one older brother, Alfred Eugene Phillips, who was born April 23, 1931 and died Aug 13, 1995.

Gerald attended Paragould schools and graduated in 1953. In 1951, his National Guard unit was called into active service when he was a senior in high school He returned to graduate in 1953.

On Jan 9, 1960, Gerald married Vivian Hanemann, daughter of Edgar and Elaine Hanemann, of New Orleans, LA. They had two children: Russell Hays Phillips and Julie Marie (Phillips) Hill. Granddaughter is Ashley Leilani Phillips.

Gerald was deputy Circuit Court Clerk from 1955-1958, the same years that his father, Russell, was Circuit Court Clerk. Gerald was elected Circuit court Clerk from 1963-1972 and Greene County judge from 1973-1976. He and his father were the first father and son to hold the same office in Greene County.

*Gerald Everett Phillips*

Gerald, who was member of the First Baptist Church, died on Aug 13, 1992 and is buried in Linwood Cemetery.

*Submitted by Vivian Phillips*

**PHILLIPS** – Marlan Holmes Phillips Sr. was born on Nov 6, 1908, two miles southwest of Paragould to Major Franklin and Sarah Fessona Diggs Phillips. He was one of six children:

1. William Irvin
2. Letha
3. Russell Everett
4. Marlan Holmes
5. Bonita
6. Franklin Diggs Phillips.

Paternal grandparents were John Perry and Caroline Melinda Dover Phillips. Maternal grandparents were Riley and Sarah Clark Diggs.

After attending Pruett's Chapel School for five years, Marlan went to school in Paragould, graduating in 1927. He then attended Paragould Business College for a year.

Marlan worked at Security Bank from Aug 1929 until Dec 1930. On Jan 9, 1931, he began working for the Paragould Water Company as bookkeeper and collector. He became superintendent of the Water Works in March 1934 and held that position for a record 43 years until his retirement in 1973.

While there, he modernized the billing and bookkeeping department, organized a new tax book for all Improvement Districts, handled collection of taxes and retirement of bonds against those districts and supervised extended water services in the city.

Marlan was the first customer to hook up to City Light and Power on Jan 17, 1939 and later was the first City cable customer in 1980.

In 1941 Marlan also accepted the responsibility of operating the Sewer Department. In 1959 he was the first Water Works manager to be selected by the United States Department of Commerce as a regional member of the National Defense Executive Reserve in the water and sewer utilities division. He was also a member of the American Association and Trustee from Arkansas on the Board of the Southwestern Water Works Association, serving on various committees. In addition, he was the first secretary of the Northeast Arkansas Water Works Association and chairman of that organization.

*Marlan Holmes Phillips Sr.*

In 1964 major improvements in water and sewer facilities were begun. Marlan spent many hours with contractors, engineers and others supervising these improvements. Following the completion of the project, a letter was received from one federal agency stating: "We also feel that special commendation should be given Mr. Phillips for his part in coordinating the project. His extreme diligence in the preparation and keeping of project records has been stated as being the best ever seen by this office and the project auditors".

In 1964 the American Water Works Association recognized Marlan by presenting him with a lifetime membership. He was also very honored to be named Arkansas Water Works Manager of the Year in 1969.

Marlan was also quite active in community organizations. He was a member of the Rotary Club, serving as secretary for two years and he sponsored over 100 persons from this area to the hospital for crippled adults in Memphis, TN. He was on the board of directors at Community Methodist Hospital, served eight years on the Paragould Planning Commission and was a director of the Chamber of Commerce. At one time Marlan was a director of the Paragould Baseball Club, a member of the old Northeast Arkansas Class D League. He also was a member of the swimming pool committee and roll call chairman for the Greene County Red Cross chapter.

Marlan married Inez Catherine Barker, daughter of Edgar and Grace Utz Barker on Oct 10, 1936. They had two sons: Marlan Holmes Phillips Jr. of West Memphis, AR and Thomas Melton Phillips of San Luis Obispo, CA. Holmes and his wife Darlene Wince Phillips had two daughters, Deborah Lynn Griggs and Pamelia Sue Phillips. Melton and Rona Rhine Phillips had one son, Scott, who married Hope Elliott of Auburn, AL. They now live in Columbus, GA. Marlan's two great-grandchildren are Danielle and Phillip Griggs.

*Inez and Marlan Phillips at Mid-South Senior Olympics in Poplar Bluff, MO*

When he retired in Dec 1973, Marlan said he wanted to spend time in his vegetable garden and do a lot of fishing. He also became quite active in the Senior Citizens Olympics. In May 24, 1990, he won gold medals in the following events:

Shot put, football field goal kicking, javelin, football accuracy throw, softball accuracy throw and set a new record of 114 feet, seven inches in the Frisbee throw. His silver medals that year were in softball distance throw and football distance throw, in the age 80 plus category.

Marlan was a member of the First United Methodist Church and on the Board of Stewards for 14 years, serving as secretary for 12 years. He was a lay speaker at Camp Ground, Pine Log, Pruett's Chapel, and Warren's Chapel and Wood's Chapel Methodist churches and taught Sunday school for over 25 years.

Marlan died on Feb 3, 2000 and was buried in Linwood Cemetery. He was blessed with good health, a wonderful memory and his many "chums" can attest to his great sense of humor.

Throughout his life, Marlan was a loyal and devoted member of the Methodist Church. He was always willing to share his faith and knowledge of the Bible. Because of his special interest in children, the Pruett's Chapel United Methodist Church dedicated their new playground equipment on May 23, 2000, in "loving memory of Marlan Phillips."

*Submitted by the Marlan Phillips family*

**PHILLIPS** – Russell Everett Phillips (Nov 5, 1906) was the son of Major Franklin and Sally Diggs Phillips, one of six children:
1. William Irvin
2. Letha
3. Russell Everett
4. Marlan Holmes
5. Bonita
6. Franklin Diggs Phillips

Russell attended Pruett's Chapel and Paragould schools.

He married Veva Jewel Sims (Dec 12, 1909) on July 13, 1930, the daughter of Foster and Lecie Sims. The couple had two children: Alfred Eugene (April 23, 1931- Aug 13, 1995) and Gerald Everett "Jerry" Phillips (Sept 26, 1932- Aug 13, 1992). Both are buried in Linwood Cemetery.

Grandchildren are Russell Hays Phillips and Julie Marie (Phillips) Hill. Great-granddaughter is Ashley Leilani Phillips.

Russell worked for Clyde Mack Company for 22 years before becoming a salesman for Belk Simpson.

*Russell Everett Phillips*

He was elected Greene County Circuit Court Clerk from 1955-1958. His son, Gerald, was deputy Circuit Court Clerk during this time. Gerald then was elected Circuit Court Clerk from 1963-1972 and Greene County Judge from 1973-1976. This was the first father and son to hold the same office in Greene County history.

Russell was a member of the First Methodist Church and especially enjoyed attending the Men's Sunday School Class there. His hobbies were hunting and farming. He and Veva owned and sold the land where Arkla Plant was built now owned by Sunlite Casual Furniture. They also owned the land where American Railcar is located. Russell was always anxious to get to his farm and work in the garden during his spare time.

Russell died on Dec 16, 1965 and is buried in Linwood Cemetery. Veva Phillips died on Nov 24, 1994 and is buried there as well.

*Submitted by Russell Everett Phillips*

**PILLOW** – Arthur was born January 30, 1890, at his parents' house on Martin Lane west of Pine Knott Church of Christ. He died June 22, 1952, at Paragould Hospital and was buried at Pine Knott as was his wife, Ruth, who was born March 26, 1894, at her parents' house on Pine Knott Road, and died August 24, 1974. They were married January 11, 1913, by John Higgins, Elder and minister of the Pine Knott church. Monroe Greenway, cousin of Arthur's, was best man. Ruth Bass was attired in a light blue satin dress she had made and black high top button shoes. Those who attended were: Hester and Joe Higgins (foster parents of Ruth), Sabie and Audie Higgins, and Beulah Pillow. They bought the house Ruth was born in near her grandfather, Asa Herren. It was east and just around the corner from the church. When Arthur was young, he had a disease in his right hip which made his right leg shorter than the left, so he had to walk on his toes and was unable to farm. He always wore black leather hightop shoes. He went to a normal school to qualify to teach, which he did for several years. Many of his students told me they loved him as a teacher. A plane flew over one day, so he let school out so they could see the plane. One of his school contracts was dated July 21, 1919, and stated that he was hired for $60.00 a month for two and one half months. It was to be kept open for eight hours each day, and he was to be the janitor. It was signed by J.J. Woodson, J.W. Hyde and W.R. Greenway.

On November 2, 1920, he was elected justice of the peace of Poland Township. Later, he got a job with Hurt Grocery Company in Paragould as janitor and Barnsdall Oil Company. In 1927, he was hired as a jobber for Barnsdall Oil Company, and worked until 1935 when he was elected Greene County judge for two terms, which ended in December 1938. He returned to the oil company. He and Randal Mitchell bought out Barnsdall Oil Company, in this county and named it Greene County Oil Company. He worked there until his death in 1952. His daughter, Dora, and one son, Douglas, worked for him for awhile. Douglas bought Lion Oil Company after that.

Arthur had blonde hair and blue eyes. Ruth had auburn hair and grey eyes. He loved people and was very outgoing, and Ruth was reserved and shy. They were both members of the Church of Christ as was each of their ancestors for four generations back. Arthur always had a lot of foxhounds at his house at 1216 West Main Street, because he loved fox hunting. Ruth loved keeping house and just being at home.

*Arthur Pillow and Ruth (Bass) Pillow*

They had eight children, with the first two (a boy and girl) who passed away at birth. Nina was the oldest and married Florian Martin. Douglas married Theda Wiseman. Gay married John L. Watson. Dora married Glen Hunter, and Melba married Robert Abney. All lived in Paragould, except Melba, who lived in Searcy then, moved in 1999 to Leesburg, Georgia.

**PILLOW** – Claibourne was born in Tennessee April 14, 1826, and was listed as a laborer in the 1850 Giles County, Tennessee Census. Emily Ginger was born in Tennessee on August 22, 1826. They married, possibly in Tennessee, January 27, 1848. They moved to Greene County, Missouri, before 1857 because one of their sons, John William was born there October 23, 1857. They then moved on to Greene County, Arkansas, before 1850 because Claibourne served in the Kitchens Infantry during the Civil War. Claibourne died in Greene County, Arkansas, June 19, 1895, and Emily died in 1911 after having lived with her son John William and family for 17 years. Both are buried in the Pine Knott Cemetery having been members of that congregation. He was a farmer and she was a housekeeper.

Their children were:

James Milton David born January 5, 1849, in Tennessee; was killed in a sawmill accident. He married Mary Lucy High;

Sara Martha Matilda born June 3, 1852, married G. W. Hyde;

Clabourne "Bud" born April 14, 1854, married Mary Jane Herren;

John William born October 23, 1857, in Nixa, Greene County, Missouri, married Charlcey Elizabeth Hyde;

Steven Nimrod born January 30, 1864, married Susan Elizabeth Burns;

Susan born 1859 married Jack Hyde.

Claibourne's brother, Levi, moved to Greene County before his brother. Levi married Elisabeth Willcockson. They had two daughters, Anna and Matilda, and a son, Isaac Henderson. Their descendants live in the Bard Community.

Claibourne and Levi's parents were James and Martha Ferrell of Giles County, Tennessee.

Narcissus married Thomas Cott Honey and they were parents of several children, including John Honey, who was a Greene County judge. Another brother, Stephen and wife, Martha Jane Castleberry Pillow, moved to Greene County for a while, but returned to Harrison, Boone County, Arkansas, to live. They were all members of the Church of Christ.

**POE** – Dr. Fielding A. Poe came to Paragould with his wife and three sons in 1940 to set up a general medical practice in northeast Arkansas. Dr. Poe was born in Stoddard County, MO on Aug 10, 1899, the third son of Reverend William D. and Molly Poe. During WWI, the young Poe served for a time in the U.S. Marine Corps. He was discharged honorably shortly after the war ended in Europe.

Life was not easy in those days for any boy fresh from the farm, but Poe did manage to work, save and put himself through medical school in St. Louis, MO, obtaining his medical degree in 1924. Poe courted and wooed Glenna "Billie" Burke of Warrensburg, MO who was teaching school in the St. Louis Suburb of University. They were married in 1925. Through the course of their marriage they were blessed with three sons:
1. Fielding Jr. (1926)
2. James David (1929)
3. Glen Edward (1939)

The Poe family was not unfamiliar with Arkansas life. In 1930 Dr. Poe moved his family to Gillett, AR to set up his fledgling medical practice. Gillett was in many ways typical of colorful existence in the depression era. The Poes returned to St. Louis in 1934 where he and his brother, Dr. Arthur Poe shared offices, until 1940 when Dr. Poe, a small town boy at heart, desired to practice medicine in a smaller locale.

As the depression was still in existence and times were hard, Dr. Poe maintained two offices to cover expenses. One office was in Paragould and the other in Lafe. Described by many as a typical country doctor, it was not uncommon for Dr. Poe to travel the countryside making house calls. He would travel typically to three of more calls each day, often traveling 20 miles or more into the surrounding country.

While Dr. Poe considered himself a general practitioner, he specialized somewhat in obstetrics. Many of his house calls were out in the country at all hours to deliver a baby at a farmhouse. Paved roads were the exception at that time rather than the rule and the gravel roads of Greene County were well known by Dr. Poe. Even though it was contrary to the intended plan, Dr. Poe even delivered his own grandson at the Poe Clinic on a hot summer night in 1952.

Dr. and Mrs. Poe were active in civic affairs in Paragould. Dr. Poe was president of the Kiwanis Club and served as the governor of the Mo-Kan-Ark 15th district of Kiwanis International. Dr. Poe was also an avid supporter of Boy Scouts and he was active in the Paragould Masonic Lodge. He was active in the American Legion as well as other civic and charitable causes. The Poes were active in the First Methodist Church and Dr. Poe served on the Board of Stewards, as well as serving as a lay leader. The Poes seldom missed a church service or function. Glenna Poe belonged to numerous organizations and she served as local P.T.A. president and was president of the Arkansas P.T.A. for two years in the 1950s.

Their children progressed through the Paragould education system and went on to respected professions. Fielding, Jr. and Glen Poe were school administrators and James D. Poe retired from government civil service. James D. Poe has returned to Paragould, proving that you can go home.

Glenna Poe died on Dec 23, 1966 and Dr. Poe followed her death on May 11, 1968.

**POPPE** – Our Poppe family consists of the descendents of the three Poppe brothers and their wives, who emigrated from Germany many years ago. These brothers were Angelus Poppe and his wife Anna Marie Tomhafe; Henry Poppe and his wife Katherine Schlacerman; and John Poppe and his wife Adeiaide Groty.

Angelus Poppe and Anna Marie (my great-grandparents) were the first relatives who came from Germany to the state of Ohio in the winter of 1856 The second of the two brothers, Henry Poppe and Katherine came over to Ohio in 1858. The third of the brothers, John Poppe and his wife Adelaide came from Wense in Germany to Ohio in 1875.

*Poppe Sawmill*

Angelus and Anna Marie's first child, Elizabeth, was born in Germany on September 1854. Their second child was our grandfather, Henry, born January 15, 1857 near New Knoxville, Ohio. His wife, our grandmother, was Sarah M. Katterhenry born in 1866. They were married April 12,1883. It was in 1905 Henry and Sarah, with six of their nine children, then living in Kettlersville, Shelby County, Ohio, moved to Greene County, Arkansas. Grandfather Henry had purchased a 40 acre farm in the Hibner Church Community northeast of Marmaduke, Arkansas, from a land agent peddling his wares in Ohio.

Our grandmother, Sarah M. (Katterhenry) Poppe, born in 1866 was a relative of Neil Armstrong, the astronaut and first to land on the moon. Neil Alden Armstrong's fifth great-grandparents were Diderich KotterHenrich and wife born before 1708. They were the fourth great-grandparents of our grandmother Sarah M. (Katterhenry) Poppe.

It was in 1905 that my grandfather, Henry J. Poppe, came to Greene County, Arkansas. He and my grandmother, Sarah Katterhenry Poppe , and six of their nine children, then living in Kettlersville, Shelby County, Ohio, moved to a farm in the Hibner Church Community northeast of Marmaduke. While living in Ohio they purchased a 40 acre plot in this Arkansas community. It was at this same time that the Elsass family, from a neighboring town in Ohio, purchased land in Clay County, Arkansas, about 10 miles north of my grandfather's land.

Henry Poppe had owned a small sawmill in Kettlersville. When he began the move to Arkansas he rented a railroad box car and shipped the mill, together with his live stock, furniture, clothing, and other belongings by rail to Rector, Arkansas. His three oldest sons rode in the boxcar to care for the livestock on the 600 plus miles trip. Henry, Sarah, and the six other children made the trip on a passenger train. On arriving in Rector, their first night was spent in a hotel. The next day they traveled by buggy or hack to their new home.

Sometime later the three oldest boys, William, Edward and Emil returned to their homes in Ohio. They lived the remainder of their lives in close proximity to their original home in Shelby County, Ohio.

The six other children: Rheinard, August, Alvina, Mathilda, Julius and Ruth remained with their parents on the farm in Greene County.

Children and grandchildren of Henry and Sarah Poppe:

William Poppe married Hermina Althoff on October 15, 1908; children Myra, Paul and Naomi.

Edward Poppe married Arminta Althoff on Marvh 12, 1912.

Emil Poppe married Nellie Henrietta Dickman on March 12,1912; children: Esther and Donald.

August Poppe married Rosa Leirer- on August 19, 1914; children: Verman, Raymond and Glenda Fay.

Rhinehart Poppe married Leona French on April 4, 1920; children: Mabel, Victor, Mary Zula and Wandalee.

Alvina Poppe married Herbert Bland on October 16, 1916; children: Francis, Mary Lou and Robert "Bob."

Matilda Poppe married Jessie H. French on March 25,1926; child-Mary Jess French.

Julius Poppe married Edna Bills on November 24, 1923; children: Christine J., D-B-G.

Ruth Poppe never married.

**PRANGER** – Fred Charles Pranger, came to Greene in 1887 as young man, married Willie Reeder in 1894. They had nine children, seven of which became adults. Carl Meldoren, Merle G. Pranger, Viola (Robbins), Willie Marie (Shoultz), Elanora (Prince), Mary Lucille (McGowan), Nina Mable (Davies) Pragner, also raised a baby, Bob Dortch. All deceased. Eight of the Prangers children are buried in Greene County. Seven in Linwood Cemetery, Carl is in Memorial Gardens, Merle is buried in Fresno, California, with his family members.

*Standing: Carl Pranger. Fred and Willie Pranger, Merle Pranger, Viola Pranger Robbins, Lucille Pranger McGowan, baby Elonora Pranger Prince.*

Fred had a grocery store in north end of town, now known as Rector Road. Many people stopped in wagons to buy supplies. In early years, he owned the Old Corner Cafe. He also was a commercial fisherman. He moved to Old Bard Road and lived with Carl and Rena (Burgess) Pranger till his death in 1955. He had 19 grandchildren, three of these still live in Greene County: Alton McGowan, Gerald Robbins and Donald Pranger.

Donald and his wife Devona live next to the old home of Fred Pranger, at this time is being torn down.

Fred had accident as very young boy and chopped knee cap and was crippled, but manage to raise the large family.

He has 62 grandchildren, 84 great-grandchildren, 20 great-great-grandchildren.

Fred Charles Pranger's father and three uncles came to the United States by boat from Germany about 1847 and settled in Ohio. The elder Mr. Pranger came to Arkansas in a wagon.

**PRINCE** – After the 1880 census of Hamilton County, IL, at least four sons and three daughters of Henry and Rebecca (Bright) Prince came to Greene County, AR. The mother of the Prince children came with them. Rebecca (Bright) Prince (1840 IN – Dec 26, 1897 Greene County, AR) married Henry W. Prince (1829 IL) May 25, 1857 in Hamilton County, IL. The death of Henry W. Prince is unknown. Rebecca is buried at Clark Cemetery.

At least nine children are known to be have been born to Henry W. and Rebecca Prince:
1. Joseph R. Prince (1858) married Ada Key
2. John H. Prince (1862) married (1) Susan M. Keelor (2) Mrs. Mary L. Wilson
3. J. Edward Prince (1866) married Lara B. Keelor (sister to Susan)
4. Louisa Catherine Prince (1868) married George Washington Haygood
5. Margaret Lucretia "Creasy" Prince (1871) married Robert F. Riley
6. Samuel R. M. Prince (1874) married Mertie Bracken
7. Thomas E. Prince (1876) married Ada Hopper
8. Charlie Prince (1879)
9. Jannie (1881) married W. A. Johnson.

Most of the Prince family and their spouses are buried at New Friendship Cemetery except for Rebecca Prince.
*Submitted by Bob and Francis Morris*

**PRINCE** – Henry William Prince and his wife, Rebecca Bright, moved to Paragould from Hamilton County, IL in the 1880s. They had five sons and three daughters:
1. John Henry
2. Edward
3. Samuel
4. Joseph
5. Charlie
6. Lucreatia
7. Janie
8. Kathryn

John Henry and Edward married sisters, Susan M. and Laura Bell Keeker, in a double wedding ceremony in Paragould, June 18, 1890.

John and Susan settled on North Second Street. John was employed at Wrape Stave Company for many years. Their children:
1. Clarence
2. Gertie
3. Grace
4. Herbert, twin
5. Hubert, twin
6. Ersilee
7. Ralph

Their son, Clarence, was a farmer in eastern Greene County and in St. Francis County. He married Ethel Oma Edwards, March 24, 1917. They had three children: Maurice E., Elsie and Sudie.

M. E. Prince served in WWII in Europe, 1943-1945, built houses in St. Francis County, Paragould and Greene County for 50 years and preached in rural churches for over 40 years. He pastured Baptist churches including Eight Mile, Pleasant Valley, Big Creek, Nutt's Chapel, Delaplaine, Walcott, Vine's Chapel and Lafe.

He married Lucy Cupp in Paragould, May 16, 1942. They had four children. Clarence Eugene married Betty Blankenship, served in Europe and in Vietnam and retired from the army. Sharon married David Murphy who has worked as an engineer in the Oak Ridge, TN area for most of his career. Kay, a nurse, married Terry Brinkley, a hospital comptroller. Gary, whose wife is Debra Garmroth, is a Paragould city fireman and a building contractor. Nina, a medical secretary, married Frank Curtis who works for Paragould City Light and Water.

*Prince Family – Front row: Ollie Keeler Walker, Elizabeth Keeler Pilot, Thomas Keeler holding Ida Pilot, Mary Knowland Keeler holding Clarence Prince. Back row: John Henry Prince, Susan Keeler Prince, Laura Bell Keller Prince, Hershal Keeler, and Edward Prince.*

After Lucy's death, M. E. married Wanda Culp Monroe, a Paragould High School teacher. She has two sons. Dr. Lance Monroe, a Paragould Medical Clinic family practice physician and is in the Naval Reserves. His wife is Kathy Pratton. George Monroe was City Parks and Recreation director for 19 years and is a rural carrier for the post office. His wife is Jan Sanders.

Elsie Prince married William Wood, Feb 16, 1942, at Wynne. They left their farm at Finch in 1955, moving to St. Louis. Bill worked at McDonald-Douglas for 27 years. They returned to Paragould in 1982 after he retired. Their daughter, Judy is married to Tim Ashby who works in construction. Their son, Terry, married Theresa Loftin. He is known in the area as the "Weatherman" on KAIT News.

Sudie Prince married Leonard Pruett, June 5, 1946, at Forrest City. They moved to California in 1951. Leonard worked at the Long Beach Naval Shipyards and Sudie was employed at Northrop Aircraft. They returned to Paragould when they retired in 1992. They have three daughters. Trina lives near Louisville, KY and is married to Tim Gossett, who is employed by the Borden Company. Yuvonne is a medical receptionist in Paragould. Sandie married Robert Case who retired from the navy. They live in Washington.
*Submitted by M. E. Prince*

**PRITCHETT** – In 1891 Charles and Lucy Jane (Lewis) Bland moved with their three children, Lenora, May and Herbert from Crockett County, Tennessee, to Greene County, Arkansas to join Lucy Jane's older sister Susan Anne Clark.

Susan Anne and her husband Frances had moved to Greene County in 1880 when Frances purchased property in the Fairview Community, northwest of Paragould, from Captain Joel Anderson.

In 1892 Charles and Lucy Jane also became Greene County landowners when they purchased property in the 300 block on Hunt Street in Paragould.

When Charles died in the latter part of 1892, he was buried in the Bramlet Cemetery on Fairview Road. Also, at this location are the graves of the three young children of Francis and Susan Clark.

In 1895 Lucy Jane married E.R. Reynolds, who lived near the Fairview Baptist Church. The three children from this union were the twins Arvin and Marvin and a younger son Lewis. Lucy Jane died on December 28, 1898, and was buried in the Fairview Cemetery.

On October 17, 1898, the 16 year old Lenora Bland married John Hardy Pritchett, the tall, dark haired, 22 year old son of Benjamin Franklin and Mollie (Burns) Pritchett from Fulton County, Kentucky.

Their three children were Loys Bland, May 5, 1902-July 1, 1988; John Harold, August 2, 1907-October 29, 1986; and Dorothy Lucille Pritchett Walker Rogers, January 24, 1914-September 22, 1971. Loys had no children. Dorothy Lucille had one son, William Rogers.

John Harold "J.H." Pritchett had seven children: one daughter, Johnnie Patricia Pritchett Painter, with his first wife, Christine Cowden Nelson Pritchett Reid. Patricia married Ben F. Painter and had one child, Gerald "Jerry" Keith Painter.

With his second wife Bessie "Betty" Imogene Ballinger Layne Pritchett, J.H. had one stepdaughter, Jean Carmein Layne Vlaco. Carmein and her husband Nicholas Vlaco had two daughters, Michelle Vlaco Whitson and Renae Vlaco Campbell.

The other children of J.H. and Betty were: Betty Lou (Mrs. Ted Conrad) Pritchett, who had two children, daughter, Tracy and son, Jason. Becky Sue (Mrs. Bucky Jones) Pritchett, who had two children, daughter, McKinley and son, Kenneth. Charlotte Ann (Mrs. Gerald Haynes) Pritchett, who had two daughters, Sheila and Angie. John Harold Pritchett Jr who had two daughters, Shannon and Ashley. And Don Micheal "Rusty" Pritchett who died at 8 years of age.

*John Hardy Pritchett as the first fire chief of Paragould, Arkansas.*

**PRUET** – The Pruet family was from Roane County, TN. Willis and Polly (Williams) Pruet had 15 children, nine of whom lived. Willis Pruet died 1851 in Memphis, TN and Polly Pruet died 1860 in Greene County, AR.

*W. S. Pruett home.*

By 1860, three of their sons were living in Greene County: Robert W. (1826-1909), Charles D. (1828-1887) and Willis S. (1829-1907) and at least two of their daughters: Susan M. Bandy (A. L.) and Mary Ann Shrite/Srite (Henry).

All three sons served in the Civil War. Charles and Robert Pruet had a partnership in a mercantile store on Charles' farm until they moved it to town in 1882 and operated it until Charles' death in 1887. Charles also had a cotton gin and engaged in stock production. Charles and his first wife Caroline M. Nelson did not have any children when she died in 1873. Charles remarried to Irene McElwee, also no issue. In 1879 Charles and Robert Pruet deeded one acre for Pruet's Chapel Methodist Church in St. Francis Township. Robert and his wife gave the pulpit furniture.

Robert also purchased 160 acres in St. Francis Township.

Robert Pruet married (1) about 1851 in Tennessee to Eliza J. Stuart, (2) Fannie A. Owens, Nov 1, 1876 in Greene County, AR.

Willis S. Pruet married, Dec 18, 1851 Shelby County, TN, Elizabeth Tucker, with whom he had three children: Julia, Sarah and Theresa. After the Civil War, Willis bought 271 acres along the railroad, which included much of the site that Paragould now stands. Willis S. Pruet owned about 600 acres in the vicinity of Paragould.

*Willis S. Pruett.*

Willis S. Pruet yielded a tract of land for downtown Paragould, the courthouse square (to help secure the county seat) and the land for the First Methodist Church. When Paragould began to expand and reached North Third Street, Willis S. Pruet refused to yield any more land and merchants began building on Pruet Street, thus making it the main downtown.

The Pruet families are buried at Pruet's Chapel Cemetery and Linwood Cemetery.

**PUCKETT** – Deal Puckett (June 23, 1914) was the fifth of seven children of Webster and Susie Puckett in Sharp County.

As a young man teaching school at Calamine, Deal became interested in a young girl by the name of Lanell Price, but in Jan 1935 the Price's moved to Greene County to operate a farm for Mr. Jack Rowe near New Home.

Deal Puckett's introduction to Greene County was a dramatic and memorable one. He and a friend soon drove over to visit the Prices. Prior to this time there had been a bank robbery at Strawberry, AR and it was suspected that the robbers were hiding in the hills near the Jack Rowe farm. Puckett and his friend had barely arrived when 17 officers from Paragould and the area also arrived. Armed with rifles, they surrounded the house and barn and ordered Puckett and his friend out for questioning. The roads were blocked for hour and it seemed inevitable that they would be unjustly incarcerated, but because they were able to provide good solid references they were finally allowed to go free.

Deal Puckett and Lanell Price were married in June of 1935, and returned to Sharp County where Deal was employed as a teacher.

In 1950, Deal with his wife, Lanell and daughter, Carolyn moved to Greene County, where Deal was employed by the Greene County Tech School Board as principal, coach and teacher of Beech Grove Junior High School.

A daughter, Charlotte was born in 1951.

In 1955, the Puckett's moved to Lafe where Mr. Puckett served as superintendent of the Lafe School for 16 years. As a result of his leadership they provided a conducive learning environment and graduated many qualified students, as well as boast the highest paying teacher's salary schedule in the county.

In 1971, the Puckett family moved to Oak Grove where Mr. Puckett again became school superintendent. A building program was in progress most of this time. During his eight-year tenure student enrollment increased from 750 students to approximately 1150.

Both Mr. and Mrs. Puckett worked hard to supplement his teaching income. He did bookkeeping at the cotton gin, worked on a delivery milk truck route, picked cotton and clerked at the general store. For years the Pucketts kept a milk cow and raised productive gardens. Mrs. Puckett worked as a substitute teacher, sewed almost all of the clothes for herself and her daughters, pieced and quilted quilts, raised and cared for chickens and gathered, cooked, canned and froze garden produce. In addition, her yard also boasted the most lovely, showy flowers in the neighborhood.

*L-R: seated: Lanell and Deal Puckett, standing: daughters, Carolyn Puckett and Charlotte Slinker.*

Devout members of the Woodland Hills Church of the Nazarene, Deal and Lanell are wonderful Christian examples. They have been happily married for 65 years. Their older daughter, Carolyn is a retired teacher who taught 40 years in the Lafe and Oak Grove Elementary Schools. Their younger daughter, Charlotte is married to Glen Slinker and teaches in Fort Gibson, OK. They have two sons, Jason and Keith.

*Submitted by Carolyn Puckett*

**PURCELL** – John E. Purcell was born in 1862. He took over the operation of the family farm upon the death of his father, William P. Purcell, in 1898. In 1899 he married Lyda M. Jeter, the daughter of James H. and Sue U. Jeter. The Jeters had come to Greene County from Millington, Tennessee, in 1886. James Jeter was a Confederate veteran who served in the 14th Tennessee Cavalry under Forrest.

John E. and Lyda Purcell had three children: a daughter, Lillian, who died in infancy in 1901, and two sons, John J. Purcell who was born in 1902, and William H. Purcell who was born in 1907. John J. Purcell was the quarterback on the 1921 Paragould High School football team that went undefeated and was recognized as the Class B State Champions.

In addition to the farm, John E. Purcell operated a sawmill for several years, and was instrumental in opening several roads. He, William McDonald, and another landowner acquired and donated land to open what is now East Kingshighway from Second Street to the Highway 135 intersection. He donated the right-of-way and opened what is now Purcell Road, and Fairview Road from Highway 135 to Purcell Road. In 1912 he and William McDonald opened a road directly into Paragould connecting Purcell Road to North 4th Street.

John E. Purcell turned the operation of the farm over to his sons in 1930.

Lyda died on December 18, 1945, and he died on August 28, 1949.

His oldest son, John J. Purcell, married Anna E. Lorenz in 1935. They had two sons, John E. and Donald G. Purcell, who still reside on the family farm. William H. Purcell never married. John J. died on July 18, 1966, and William H. Purcell died on October 15, 1994.

**PURCELL** – An independent arrives from Independence County, told in first person by Lee McKnight Purcell.

Around 1933 and possibly the month of November, I arrived in Paragould from Batesville, AR. I was brought here in the company of my parents, Gus and Shelley Ginn McKnight. We brought with us the history of the Ginn and the McKnight families. My name was Ollie Lee McKnight. The Ollie was for my maternal grandmother, Ollie Green Hinkle Ginn. The Lee was for Viola Lee Suddath McKnight, my paternal grandmother.

*Christmas Morning 1998 (West Main) – L-R: Brock, Don Tyler, Paige, Phillip, and Berkli Wooldridge.*

My Grandmother Ginn's parents were Luvy Jane (Ross) Hinkle and Joshua William Cass Hinkle, who married in 1877- my great-grandparents. Her parents were James J. and Mary A. (Wren) Ross. She was a Cherokee Indian. Lucy Jane was born Oct 1856, Fulton County, AR. Joshua who was the son of John D. and Arena (Beckham) Hinkle, was born July 18, 1948, Wayne County, TN. He was a medical doctor and died July 14, 1929. He was 82 years old and still practicing medicine when he delivered me.

Their children were:
1. Ollie Green Hinkle, my grandmother
2. Shelby Boone Hinkle, my great uncle
3. Scudder Hinkle, great uncle
4. John A. Hinkle, great uncle.

My grandmother, Ollie Green Hinkle, first child of Dr. Josh Hinkle and Lucy Jane, married Robert Erving Ginn, son of Barrett Ginn. Their children were:
1. James Ginn
2. Shelly Ethelyne Ginn, my mother
3. Jack Ginn, still living in Texas
4. Lindley Ginn
5. Bill Ginn
6. Boone Ginn, living in California.

*74th Birthday at Purcell's.*

My mother married Gus H. McKnight, one of 11 children. His father was Bryan Augustus McKnight, a Methodist minister. My mother and father met in Mountain View, AR. His father was the minister of the Methodist Church in Mountain View. I am the only child of their union. I was born in Mountain View. When I was two months old we moved to Batesville. When I was eight years old we moved to Paragould and I was so sad to leave Batesville. I was in the third grade and my teacher was Merle Stuart. Other teachers included Mrs. Eubanks, then Monra Cathey (Emmy Witt's sister) and Mr. B. G. Hope. I later learned to love Paragould more that any place on earth. I graduated from Paragould High School at age 17 and attended the University of Arkansas. At age 20, I married Frank D. Williams. Lee Jr. Purcell was born at Cherry Point, N. C. Her father was killed in a plane crash when she was 10 weeks old. Donald Irving Purcell, Ollie Lee McKnight Williams' second husband, later adopted Lee Jr.

The children of Donald Irving are Lee Jr. and Augusta Paige Purcell. Paige was born April 1, 1952 in Paragould, AR.

Lee Jr. Purcell married Gary Lowe and they had one child, Dylan Purcell Lowe (May 10, 1983 Los Angeles). Lee Jr. became an actress and has received two Emmy nominations. Lee and Gary later separated.

Paige married Phillip Wooldridge (March 9, 1949). Their children:
1. Berkli Paige (Oct 11, 1975)
2. Brock Purcell (March 27, 1979)
3. Don Tyler (Oct 2, 1983) born on Don and Lee's wedding anniversary. We never forget it!

*Christmas 1999: Lee Jr. and son with Bobby Dahlquist and Don Purcell.*

I met my husband, Donald I. Purcell, when we were freshmen at the University of Arkansas. He was from Rector, Clay County, just 24 miles from Paragould. He always says I scared him to death when we first met. He's not scared now though. We celebrated our 50th Wedding Anniversary in Oct 1999.

Don's mother was Gurtha Elizabeth Randleman, who married Elmer Marion Purcell on Sept 16, 1916. Gurtha's parents (Don's grandparents) were Cora Malissa Franklin, from Rector, AR and Walter Randleman, who married Dec 18, 1867. Gurtha had two sisters and a brother who reached adulthood. Gurtha's cousin, Lillian Randleman, was a long-time Clay County librarian. We were privileged to have a part in their 50th Anniversary. He was born Aug 3, 1894 and died at Rector, AR. where he was a long time druggist. He and Gurtha had two sons: Elmer Marion, Jr. and Donald I., born Dec 6, 1926 in Rector, AR. Don was educated at University of Arkansas and University of Louisville, U of A Medical School and was a U.S. Navy Lt. Occupation's Radiologist. Their home address is 1800 Barnhill Road, Paragould.

Lee and Don belong to First United Methodist Church. We sit on the third row on the right in the back. I can say I've sat there for 64 years; that's how long I've been a member. Another interesting note: My library card is # 57. We've both read a lot of books.

Don wants you to know that Agnes Hinkle Ayers was co-star with Rudolph Valentino in the "*Sheik*". She was Frank Randleman's stepdaughter and a silent film star. Agnes came from California in her own private railroad car to visit Fay Randleman's daughters.

Addendum! We are proud to live in Paragould. We've loved every minute of it!

Some More: An interesting note: "Hinkle Lake" in Waldron, AR is named for my great uncle, Scudder Hinkle, my Grandmother Ginn's brother. Also, my husbands' grandfather, John Purcell, gave the land for Purcell Cemetery in Clay County, AR. Guess that's all.

And not only that, but my Grandmother Ginn was the first postmistress in Stone.

One more thing! Believe it? I graduated from Paragould High School as did my daughters, Lee and Paige; Paige's three children, Berkli, Brock and Don Tyler. Don Tyler will graduate in two years. Berkli and Brock actually graduated from Ridgecrest before it became Paragould High School again. I love you! Lee M. Purcell.

**PURCELL** – William P. Purcell was born in 1825 in Wilson County Tennessee, the son of James P. and Margaret Purcell. His parents were born in Virginia and North Carolina. His mother died soon after his birth, and in 1828 his father moved the family to Western Tennessee, just south of Dyersburg. James Purcell died about 1836.

About 1844, William P. moved to Arkansas, settling southwest of Lake City. He married Sarah Clark in 1845. Sarah was the daughter of James and Abigail Clark, who had settled in Greene County (directly east of the present location of the Purcell farm), in the fall of 1846. William P. and Sarah had a son who died in infancy, and three daughters, Jane (Purcell) Jackson, Ann (Purcell) Hopkins, and Margaret (Purcell) Fisher. Another son, John E. Purcell, was born in 1862.

William P. Purcell and James K. Norsworthy jointly owned a store in Gainesville prior to the War for Southern Independence. In the late summer of 1864 William P. joined the 7th Missouri Cavalry CSA and saw combat during Price's Raid in Missouri. He was a farmer for the majority of his life until his death in December 1898.

**RAINES** – William Raines (Jan 1869 Henry County, TN) married Martha J. Elizabeth "Betty" Denning (Nov 1869 TN).

The Raines family moved to Clay County, AR and is shown on the 1900 census of Clay County. Two of their children were born in Tennessee. They are Elizabeth Edna (Sept 1891) and Florence B. (Feb 1897). After arriving in Clay County, AR, two more children were born: Dora and Joe Andrew Leland (Mar 17, 1911-July 2, 1978).

*L-R Front: Verda Raines and daughter in law Beverly Raines. Back row: Joe, Johnny and Edward Raines.*

Joe married Verda Powers in Greene County Sept 14, 1939. To this union were born two sons: Edward William (Nov 26, 1941) and Johnny Carlee (Nov 17, 1943). Joe was a fireman for Missouri-Pacific railroad from Nov 1942 until 1952. He later was employed by Arkansas State University in Jonesboro and retired from the maintenance department in 1959.

Edward William attended the Paragould School and served as drum major with the Paragould High School band. While attending A.S.U. he met and married a fellow student Velma Lanay Watson from Swifton, AR Jan 10, 1970. The Raines taught school in Osceola, AR, Luxora, AR, Sullivan, MO and Poplar Bluff, MO. In 1977 they moved to Alaska. In 1991 they came back to their hometown and taught school at Oak Grove and Knobel. Ed passed away May 9, 1997 while running track in the Missouri Senior Olympics in Poplar Bluff, MO.

Ed and Lanay's children are:
1. Jennifer Lanay (Aug 17, 1970)
2. Carrie Elizabeth (Jan 8, 1973)
3. Dennis Edward (March 30, 1974)

Johnny Carlee married Beverly Price in Miami, FL May 15, 1970. He entered the U.S. Air Force in March 1961 and served until retirement in Dec 1981. Johnny served in Viet Nam as well as many other bases in Germany, Texas and Arizonia. He is business manager for FN Manufacturing Company located in Charleston, SC.

Johnny and Beverly's children are Pamelia Gail (Oct 29, 1972) and Michael Edward (Aug 17, 1974).

After Joe's death Verda Raines married Woodrow Futrell, a long time resident of Greene County. The Futrell Family history appears elsewhere in this book.

*Submitted by Verda Raines Futrell*

**RAINWATER** – Elmer Lawrence Rainwater, was born June 28, 1907, the son of Martin Amzier and Clara Viola (Hamilton) Rainwater in Denton, Lawrence County, Arkansas. Lawrence Rainwater died November 5, 1997, in Paragould, and was buried in Greene County Memorial Gardens.

Lawrence, a friendly, hard working man, and his brother, Earl Rainwater, farmed together. The farm was located in the hills, out past Five Mile Spring, Randolph County, Arkansas. Lawrence hired himself out as a day laborer to area grain and cotton farmers. He also worked in timber, making cord wood and railroad ties.

He hired himself out as a farm hand to Charles "Chink" Edward Stevens, Delaplaine. He met the oldest daughter and courted her for several months.

On April 16, 1938, in Delaplaine, Lawrence Rainwater married Imogene Stevens, daughter of Chink and Vickie (Clark) Stevens. They had 10 children: Mary Charlene, Linda Jean, Karen, Larry Allen, Shirley Ann, Gary Kenneth, (twins) Reggie Duane, Peggy Diane, (twins) Kevin Dee and Keith Lee.

Lawrence Rainwater left his pig operation in August 1938 to pick cotton. He went back to Randolph County to gather in the crop that fall. He turned his pig operation over to his brother, Earl, and moved to Delaplaine. He farmed and worked in timber for many years. He began working on the Missouri Pacific Railroad, as a section hand in April 1945. He retired in 1965.

*Lawrence Rainwater, 1930, age 23.*

Lawrence was devoted to caring for his family, and raised grandson, Keith Lee Rainwater

Jr. Throughout his life he enjoyed gardening. His grandchildren remember, he was always the first person out the door to greet his guests.

**RAINWATER** – The story of a Delaplaine woman, is from an essay written by granddaughter, Kimberly Johnson in 1976.

When grandmother was 11 years old, her mother died. She took charge of the house, and assumed responsibility for six younger sisters and brothers.

Grandmother was committed to her family and home. Because her father got up at 4:00 A.M. everyday of his life, she also got out of bed, to fix breakfast and prepare for the day.

There wasn't any electricity or gas in farm homes back then. Grandmother cooked on an old wood burning stove with a dutch oven rising from the back and level with her eyes, where biscuits and cooked meat were stored. There was a reservoir on the left side for heating water. The old heavy irons for ironing clothes always sat on the back.

*Imogene Stevens Rainwater, age 57, and Lawrence Rainwater, age 69. Photo taken November 1976, Child Art Studio, Paragould, Arkansas.*

Grandmother worked hard all her life. She worked in the fields on her father's farm, hoeing cotton, corn, peas and gathering in the corn.

Water was pumped by hand and carried into the house in buckets. On wash day, a lot of water had to be carried. Grandmother did the wash in a tub on a washboard. The clothes were scrubbed piece by piece, and then hung outside on the line to dry. In the summer the clothes dried fast, but in the cold winter months, the clothes froze stiff in grandmother's hands.

Grandmother started sewing early, as all farm girls had to do back then. She still remembers asking for her father to bring home some cloth, when he went to the small village to buy supplies. This was shortly after her mother died, and she still remembers how surprised she was, when he came home with material for a dress. All dresses were cut free-hand, and all on the same style. Grandmother never darned socks, but she did patch blue jeans and overalls for her father and brothers.

Grandmother quilted, using many bright colors, left over from her sewing, and used several patterns, from patch, old fashioned girl, dutch girls, double wedding ring to butterflies.

Imogene Stevens was born in Greene County, Arkansas, on July 12, 1919, daughter of Charles Edward "Chink" and Vickie (Clark) Stevens.

**RAINWATER** – Karen Rainwater, was born in Greene County, April 3, 1942, daughter of Elmer Lawrence and Imogene Stevens Rainwater. She is a devoted daughter, sister and aunt.

She started school in a two-room school house in O'Kean, and later attended Delaplaine School. Karen graduated from high school while the family was living in Bradford.

A beautician, Karen worked in St. Louis, Missouri; Phoenix, Arizona; and Pocahontas, Arkansas. For several years she owned the "Headdress" in Delaplaine. She is presently employed with the Delaplaine school district.

Karen has helped raise many of her nieces and nephews, driving them to swimming and ballet lessons, sports events and to McDonalds.

A talented seamstress, Karen made formal wear for her nieces— prom dresses, beauty contestant dresses and dancing costumes. She helped with the care of her father in his declining years, closing her shop as the need arose.

Reading is a favorite pass time, and she loves being around the family and doing things for the children.

*Karen Rainwater, September 1967, age 25.*

**RAINWATER** – Keith Lee Rainwater, son of Elmer Lawrence and Imogene (Stevens) Rainwater, was born October 25, 1955, in Jonesboro, Arkansas, the youngest of a second set of twins. The family lived in O'Kean, Randolph County. Keith Rainwater died July 25, 1985, in a motorcycle accident, near Beech Grove, in Greene County. He had worked the late shift at the Dana Corporation in Paragould, and was almost home. He lived with his parents in Delaplaine. He was buried in Greene County Memorial Gardens.

Keith was an upbeat, positive person, efficient and personable. He always looked for the good in people. He was very helpful, and had a lively sense of humor.

Keith attended Delaplaine School. The coach saw him out run his best runner and talked him into going out for track. He was always willing to go the extra mile. He had a big heart. Keith won many ribbons in relay track for 100 yard dash, 440 yard relay, 880 yard relay, half mile relay, mile relay, shot put and high jump.

Keith was expert in swimming and diving. He enjoyed diving off a bridge banister into the Black River at Greenville, Missouri. He and his twin brother, Kevin, spent many days skinny dipping in rice canals.

Keith worked in construction for many years, around Imboden, Arkansas; Greenville, Missouri; and Paragould, Arkansas. For a time he worked for GTE and climbed telephone poles with ease. He and his brother, Reggie, had a lot of fun working together at the Dana Corporation. Keith was fast. He always gave one hundred percent.

Keith married at 17 to Connie Jean Diles born December 3, 1955, died June 25, 1977. They had one child: Keith Lee Rainwater Jr., born March 10, 1973. He is employed with Sears in Jonesboro and attends Arkansas State University.

**RALEY** – Howard Thomas Raley, born in Kentucky in 1888, and Anna Straub, born in Pocahontas, Arkansas, in 1891, were married at St. Mary's Catholic Church in Paragould on April 8, 1913. They had nine children: Pauline Elizabeth, Anna Loretta, Louis Adrian (married Vaudine Couch; had three sons, Louis, Michael and Patrick; died in 1965); Frances (married Lewis Hayden; had one son, Charles Lindel); Mary Virginia (married Rudolph Ephrussi; had four daughters and two sons); Marcella (Sister Anne Michele, St. Scholastica's Convent, Ft. Smith, Arkansas); Howard Thomas Jr. (married Joyce Clements; had three sons and a daughter); James Jefferson "John" (married Elnore Lane; had two daughters, Laura and Carol, and a son, Brian); and Joseph Ronald.

The Raley family came to Paragould in December 1905 and the Straubs in the early 1890s. The Raleys were originally from Great Britain and the Straubs from Germany.

**RAMER** – The Ramer family arrived in Greene County from McNairy County, TN in the early 1870s and consisted of John Wesley and Sarah E. Ramer and their children:
1. Thomas Jefferson (1857-1929)
2. John R. (1854)
3. Elijah A. (1861-1952)
4. Wesley G. (1870)
5. William T. (1849-1930)
6. George W. (1859-1942).
7. James T. evidently died as a child.

They settled in northern Greene County in what is now known as the Ramer's Chapel community where they farmed for many years.

John Wesley and Sarah E. are buried in Starnes Cemetery.

Thomas Jefferson Ramer homesteaded what is now known as the McDowell place. He gave the land to establish the Ramer's Chapel Methodist Church and Cemetery and the land to establish the Ramer's School. He married (1) Rachel Eastep and they had one child, Cornelius (1876-1957). (2) Martha Fannie Starnes Dec 24, 1880 and they had the following children:
1. Jim (1883-1884)
2. Robert Lonzo (1886-1966)
3. Ader (1890-1890) died in childbirth
4. Martha F (1890-1890) died in childbirth
(3) Sarah Josephus Starnes Aug 7, 1890, the niece of Martha F. and their children:
1. Jewel Agnes (1893-1945)
2. Vadie (1895)
3. William Pinkney (1896)
4. Ella (1899-1908)
5. Lena (1899)
6. Meadie (1901)
7. George (1904)
8. Della (1906-1979)

He moved to Cleburn County, AR before 1910 where Sarah died in 1915 and he died in 1929. Both are buried at Quitman, AR.

Elijah Ramer married Druscilla Stephens (1856-1913) and both are buried at Ramer's Chapel Cemetery. They had the following Children:
1. Morgan (1885)
2. John W. "Wes" (1886-19970)
3. Louiza E. (1888-1969)
4. Luther E. (1890)
5. Frank M. (1893-1952)
6. James Herbert (1894)
7. Flora F. (1896-1979)

William T. "Bill" Ramer married Elizabeth Reynolds and they had the following children:
1. John W. (1868
2. Nancy A. (1873)
3. Amanda W. (1879)
4. Luther (1879)
5. Luda E. (1880)
6. Ida (1884-1974)

The lived in the Camp Ground community and Bill, Elizabeth and Ida are buried in Fairview Cemetery.

George W. Ramer married Ann Hamilton (1861-1943) and they had the following children:
1. Sarah (1886-1961)
2. Lillie (1889)
3. Emily (1893-1970)
4. Matilda (1898-1979)
5. Joseph (1896)
6. Joel

**RATTON** – Ralph Robert Ratton II (Sept 26, 1929 Paragould, AR) is the son of Ralph Robert and Isis Mary Coffman Ratton. Ralph I (Jan 17, 1902

Newark), was the son of Robert Redman and Lucy Beard Arnold Ratton. Ralph has one sister, Betty Ross Hyde (July 22, 1924) and one brother, Michael Coffman Ratton (Feb 14, 1933). Isis Mary Coffman (Sept 27, 1908), was the daughter of Michael Ross and Cora Allison Coffman.

Joan Carol Collins (Oct 17, 1932 Paragould) was born to Orris F. (Aug 9, 1907 Jonesboro) and Frances Neely Collins (Feb 8, 1906 Paragould). She has one sister, Patricia Collins Fulkerson (June 2, 1931) and one brother, John Neely Collins (March 23, 1939).

Joan and Ralph Ratton, Dec. 1994.

Ralph is a 1947 graduate of Paragould High, the University of Arkansas and the University of Missouri at Kansas City School of Dentistry. He grew up in Paragould, living for a time in Monette, where his father was in the gin business. He practiced dentistry in Corning, AR.

Joan Collins graduated from Paragould High in 1950 and attended Gulf Park College and Arkansas State University. The Collins' were in the theatre business.

Ralph Ratton and Joan Collins married June 10, 1951 at the First Methodist Church. They had five children:
1. Donna Frances (July 23, 1952)
2. Diane Elizabeth (July 23, 1952)
3. Patricia Elaine (July 17, 1956)
4. Joan Carol (Oct 13, 1958)
5. Ralph Robert III (Feb 1, 1969)

Donna married and had one son, Joseph Scott Payne (April 17, 1975). Scott died on Oct 9, 1987 and is buried at Linwood Cemetery. Donna married Preston Bland on July 29, 1989. Preston has one son, Robert Preston Bland III of Nashville, TN. Preston is a partner in the Dr. Pepper-7-UP Bottling Company.

Diane married Ed Gathings on Feb 19, 1977. They have:
1. Neely Ann (Jan 29, 1978)
2. Allison Elizabeth (Aug 30, 1985)

Diane graduated from ASU's School of Nursing and received her Registered Nurse Practitioner degree from the University of Arkansas School for Medical Sciences. Ed graduated from ASU and is the owner of Countryside Package Store.

Lanie married Tim Mangrum on June 12, 1982. They have:
1. Erin Elizabeth (Jan 2, 1985)
2. William Scott (Feb 2, 1988)
3. Joan Carol (Feb 9, 1986-Feb 9, 1986) twin,
4. Mary Frances (Feb 9, 1986- Feb 9, 1986) twin

The twins are buried in Linwood Cemetery. Lanie is the owner of Linwood Child Care and Anton and Associates employ Tim.

Carol married Doug Vail of Stuttgart on July 30, 1983. They have:
1. Katherine Carol (May 16, 1991)
2. Caroline Collins (Aug 29, 1995)

The live in Brownsburg, IN; where Doug is employed by Dow-Elanco. They are University of Arkansas graduates, Carol with a nursing degree and Doug with a degree in agriculture economics.

Rob married Leighann Shepard and they have Abby Elizabeth (Aug 5, 1996). Rob is a graduate of the University of Arkansas and the University of Arkansas School of Law. They live in Newport where Rob is with the law firm of Thaxton, Hout and Howard.

**REDDICK** – Joe Bertig Reddick and Florence Whiteside were married and had 11 children:
1. Imogene (Reddick) McCartney
2. Billy Reddick
3. Glenivee (Reddick) Beaver
4. Vernon Dale Reddick
5. Joe Harold Reddick, deceased
6. Kenneth Reddick
7. Randal Reddick
8. Jimmy Don Reddick
9. Teddy V. Reddick
10. Freddie Reddick, died in infancy
11. Gaylon "Gabby" Reddick

They farmed in the Alexander community.

Most of the family went to St. Louis as they reached adulthood. Billy and Vernon came back to Greene County. Billy is married to Almeria Waldrum and has two children: Joan Gail Morten and Jerry Lynn deceased. Vernon married Merveena Smith and has two sons, Barry and Kevin. Jimmy Don and Teddy later came back to Greene County. Jimmy Don is married to Donna Vangilder and has one daughter, Janet Clayton; and Teddy is married to Beatrice Coffel and has two sons, Timothy and Mark.

Front row: Imogene McCartney, Glenivee Beaver. Second row: Vernon, Gabby, Kent, Randal, Joby, Teddy, Billy, Jimmy Don Reddick.

Joan Gail married Gerald McPherson and has two sons, Stacey and Steven. Jerry Lynn married Rita Cothren and had two daughters, Wendy (Reddick) Harvey and Michelle (Reddick) Darr.

Barry married Judy Ellington and has three children: Bryan Reddick, April (Reddick) Miller and Ashley (Reddick) Shelton. Kevin married Kerry Tritch Miles, daughter of Tiffany Miles and has one son: Aaron Michael.

Janet Reddick married Larry Thompson and has one daughter, Cassie

Timothy married Faith Hayes and they have two daughters, Charity Hope and Laken McKenzie. Mark married Nicole Beasley and they have two children, Wesley Duane and Reagan Lindsey.

Joe and Florence are buried in Reddick Cemetery.

This is just one branch of the Reddick family tree. Every Reddick in Greene County is related to the other.

Of special note: three Reddick siblings married three Whiteside siblings:
Joe Reddick and Florence Whiteside
Ray Whiteside and Lura Reddick
Willie Reddick and Maggie Whiteside.
*Submitted by Judy Reddick*

**REDDICK** – Marion Carlos Reddick (March 4, 1922 Mounds, Greene County, AR- Jan 21, 1976 Paragould, AR) born to Theodore Roosevelt and Lillie Grace (Rippy) Reddick, is buried in the Fairview Cemetery.

Marion is said to have been a very handsome child with dark skin and wavy black hair. Many profess that he looked like his mother. He began his formal education at the Reddick School, a one-room schoolhouse, which was built on land donated by his grandfather, Humphrey Columbus Reddick. Marion learned to read, write and cipher math. Not a serious student, he ended his education upon completing the fourth grade.

Marion C. and Beulah D. (Fox) Reddick

For the most part, Marion lived a normal childhood until the death of his mother in 1932. Her death fractured the family unit. His father was not prepared to raise his two young sons alone. For several years, Marion sought refuge with friends and other relatives. Often, he slept in barns and did farm chores for his keep. During his teenage years, he worked primarily as a farm laborer.

With the world at war, Marion was drafted into the U. S. Army. He took his oath in Little Rock, AR on Oct 15, 1942 and shipped immediately to Camp Adair, OR for training. He qualified with the pistol and certified as a mortar gunner. While occupying a foxhole during maneuvers, he suffered a crushed ankle when a tank rolled a large stone into the hole. After a lengthy hospital stay, he was discharged from the army on Oct 8, 1943.

While on convalescent leave in June of 1943, Marion met and married Beulah Dean Fox, daughter of George Washington Fox and Gertie May (Snyder) Stevens. During the early years of the war, Beulah worked in a war factory in Joplin, MO making first aid kits. Resulting from the marriage were seven Reddick children:
1. Sharon Grace
2. Marion Franklin
3. Fretsie Virginia
4. Carlos Edward
5. Henry Michael
6. Phillip Lee
7. Donna Lynn

Beulah, faithful mother and loving housewife, labored until her death in 1995.

Early in the marriage, the family bought a pair of mules and tried their hand at sharecropping. The work was hard and the profits were few, so Marion and Beulah migrated to Detroit, MI. There, Marion took a job as a foundry worker for a large steel company. The family economics were good until Dwight Eisenhower was elected president. During the ensuing recession, Marion lost his job. Returning to Paragould, he went to work for Paragould City Light and Water.

Marion is probably best remembered by those who knew him as one of the finest heavy equipment operators in the state. He worked pushing timber with a dozer and later became a skilled dragline operator, having worked on such projects as the floodway ditches in Missouri and the Obion River project in Kentucky. For a time, he worked in Michigan hanging glass in tall buildings with a crane.

*Submitted by Carlos Reddick*

**REDDICK** – Marion Franklin Reddick (1945 Mounds, AR) was born to Marion C. and Beulah D. (Fox) Reddick. He was married in 1968 to Marsha Diann Acuff of Paragould, daughter of Alfred and Martha (Edmiston) Acuff. The marriage produced two children, Melissa and Ryan.

Frank's family migrated to Michigan when Frank was about four years old. He began his formal education at the Middle Belt School in Plymouth, MI. Frank completed kindergarten through second grade before the family moved back to Paragould where he attended Elmwood Elementary School. While in third grade, he got his first paddling from Mrs. Mabel Fitzgerald. The family moved out near the Greene/Craighead County line to operate a dairy farm. Frank went to school at Greene County for a year and a half or so. He confessed that Mrs. Warren slapped his hand with a ruler on many occasions for not having a ready answer to a question. Her general punishment for noncompliance was the assignment, of what seemed like thousands, of math problems. Frank met her years later, relating that he was a math teacher. She instantly took credit for providing him the right kind of punishment. After moving back into town, Frank attended school at Baldwin Elementary. He had Ms. Geraldine Dover in fifth and sixth grades. She was the epitome of a great teacher, one who always nurtured her students by structuring success for each one. Frank considers her the best teacher that he ever had. After sixth grade, Frank attended school in the county and graduated from Greene County Tech.

*Frank Reddick, Diann, Melissa, Ryan*

Diann was not as eager to go to school. On her first day of school at Woodrow Wilson, she threw a tantrum, refusing to attend class. Her mother took her home that day. After a good spanking, she was made to sit on her bed all day. Returning to school the next day, she remained in class this time. Diann's family moved to the east of town and she enrolled at Lakeside for a while. Returning to Paragould, she attended Baldwin Elementary. Afterwards, she went on to Paragould Junior High and Paragould High School.

Following high school, Frank enlisted in the army and completed basic training at Fort Polk, LA. That was followed by AIT at Redstone Arsenal in Huntsville, Al. Following a short leave, he was ordered to the 510th Ordinance Detachment in Chunchon, South Korea. Frank served for 13 months as an acquisition and track radar technician in the HAWK missile system. His prominent memories include the winter cold, the spring monsoon rains and the smell of human fertilizer in May. Frank returned to Huntsville and taught systems electronics at the missile school for the rest of his army tour.

Frank and Diann met while he was home for a weekend. Diann was working at the Pizza Drive In as a "car hop". The relationship quickly developed and they were married about a year later. The marriage has now lasted for 32 years.

Frank worked at Emerson Electric while attending college at Crowley's Ridge and Arkansas State University. He graduated with a BSE in 1971 and an MSE in 1973. Diann worked at One Hour Cleaners as a counter clerk and later at Montgomery Ward as a salesclerk. She started her college career at Crowley's Ridge. Transferring to Arkansas State University, she graduated with a BSE in 1981 and attained her Master's Degree in 1987. Choosing careers in education, Frank is currently completing his 30th year at Jonesboro High School while Diann is in her 19th year of teaching in the Paragould School District. She is presently employed at Baldwin Elementary in second grade.

Frank also served for 23 years in the Arkansas National Guard. He rose to the rank of first sergeant with B Company, 875th Engineer Battalion (Combat Mech) and retired in Sept 2000.

Frank and Diann attend the Seventh and Mueller Church of Christ. Frank is a deacon and teaches Bible classes. Diann has worked as a department supervisor and teacher. Both are active in the works of the church.

Their daughter, Melissa, married Spencer Furby of Fredericktown, MO. Melissa completed the BSE and MSE degrees as ASU and taught school for four years before becoming a stay at home mom. Spencer received his bachelor's degree from Freed-Hardeman University and has completed two Master's Degree programs at Harding Bible College in Memphis. The proud parents of Noah Hunter Furby (1998) they reside in Kennett, MO, where Spencer preaches.

Ryan Heath Reddick married Amanda Gandy of Jonesboro. Ryan has completed three years of school at ASU and currently works at Hytrol in Jonesboro. Amanda works as a teller for American State Bank.

*Submitted by Melissa Furby*

**REDDICK** – Theodore Roosevelt Reddick (Oct 27, 1901 Mounds, Greene County, AR- June 29, 1971 Paragould) was born to Humphrey Columbus and Mary Alice (Livesay) Reddick.

Often called Roosevelt or "T.R.", he was married in 1919 to Lillie Grace Rippy, the daughter of William H. and Rebecca E. Rippy. Grace was a beautiful young woman of Indian and Irish lineage. The marriage bore two children: Marion Carlos Reddick (1922) and Dallas Edward Reddick (1929). The marriage was cut short when Grace died in 1932. In her third pregnancy, she succumbed to the labors of childbirth. Grace was buried in the Reddick Cemetery with the baby.

Roosevelt was devastated with the loss of Grace. After a time of emotional healing, he married Artie (Smith) Lam the daughter of James Alex and Margaret (Davis) Smith in 1935. This union produced six more Reddick children:
1. Theodore Wesley (1936)
2. Gerald Porter (1938)
3. Lawrence Austin (1940)
4. Alice Cordelia (1942)
5. Mattie Lorett (1945)
6. Harold Lee (1947).

In 1908 Roosevelt's father died, followed by his mother in 1909. He was taken in by his older half brother Humphrey. This relationship only lasted for a few years. One spring day, the family was said to have been chopping cotton in a nearby field when a tornado appeared not far off. During the excitement, Roosevelt threw down his hoe and ran away, never to return as a resident of his brothers home. For some time he lodged with two men who hid him when persons searching for him would come by. According to Edgar "Uncle Jake" Reddick, Roosevelt was later taken in and raised through much of his teenage years by the Marion Evans family.

*Theodore Roosevelt and Lillie G. (Rippy) Reddick*

As a young man, Roosevelt began making his own way by clearing land. He later helped to clear the right-of-way for the Big Slough and Mayo Ditch drainage projects near Mounds.

The recipient of little formal schooling, Roosevelt was basically self-taught. During the late 1930s, he migrated to St. Louis. For a time, he operated a street trolley for the city. Unhappy with city life, he returned to his humble beginnings in Greene County. Although a man of modest means, he esteemed himself in the community through his work. Having gained good skills in math, he worked as a surveyor, income tax preparer and bookkeeper for the local gin. He also operated an 80-acre farm on which he grew cotton. Additionally, Roosevelt served as a polling place worker in the local voting ward for many years. A resourceful man, he cut hair on Sunday afternoons at his home for the price of 25 cents.

Roosevelt enjoyed telling about the primitive times around Mounds. On one occasion, he told of taking the milk bucket and heading out to milk the cow. Suddenly, he came fact to face with a black panther lying across the path. Afraid of being attacked, he remained still, for what seemed an eternity, until the panther moved on.

*Submitted by Mattie Morton*

**REED** – Elizabeth Chunn (May 28, 1919 Paragould, Greene County, AR) was born to William "Bill" and Beatrice (Treece) Chunn.

Elizabeth attended Village School and graduated from Greene County High School in May 1939. She married J. P. Reed (May 13, 1914) April, 9,1939, the son of Lawrence Ollie and Dee (Overall) Reed.

*J. P. and Elizabeth Reed.*

The Reeds were successful farmers in the New Hope community and moved from rural Greene County in the early 1960s. Elizabeth started her business career with the Agricultural Department U.S.D.A. Services in 1953 and retired from that same occupation in 1974. J. P. worked many years as a real estate broker, two terms as Greene County Court Clerk, Employment Security Division, and four terms as Greene County Judge. J. P. died June 14, 1995.

J. P. and Elizabeth have provided The J. P. and Elizabeth Reed Foundation for the purpose of establishing scholarships for graduates from Greene County schools. It was established in 1999 and first funding in 2000. It is to be used for ministerial, medical and other student desires.

*Submitted by Geraldine Garmrath*

**RENFROE** – James Monroe Renfroe, nicknamed Squire, was born December 10, 1831, in Washington County, Georgia, son of Samuel Pinkney Renfroe and Eliza. (See elsewhere in this book.)

On December 30, 1856, he married Jincy Elvira Harris, daughter of Nicholas Harris and Jincy Hall in Greene County, Arkansas. Were it not for Bible records, I would not have his marriage date due to the courthouse fires in Greene County, Arkansas.

During the Civil War, he was a private in the Missouri 10th Cavalry, Co. B, the same outfit his younger brother, Samuel, served in.

He was a justice of the peace for Greene County, Arkansas. He saved a marriage license of a wedding he performed in his home in Salem Township in Greene County, Arkansas on August 23, 1874. The couple he married was John W. T. Lamb, age 25, to Eady E. Cook, age 19, both of Greene County, Arkansas. On this marriage license, it states he was a duly authorized justice of the peace for said county.

Bible records show they had two sons born and died before the 1860 census was taken. On the 1860 Greene County, Arkansas Census, Salem Township, no children were shown. They had another son born in 1861 who died in 1867. In the Bible and on the 1870 Greene County, Arkansas Census, Salem Township, Sarah "Sally" Caroline Renfroe, born February 11, 1864, and my grandfather, Nicholas Harris Renfroe, born February 10, 1868, were shown. Since the 1870 census was taken on June 14, the last child, Quixy Ann Renfroe, was not shown since she was born October 10, 1870.

In 1850 James M. Renfroe was living with his parents and siblings in Pickens County, Alabama. On the Greene County, Arkansas Original Entries of lands, he bought 40 acres in 1851 at 25¢ an acre. He paid taxes in 1857; both of these dates earlier than when his parents arrived in Greene County, Arkansas.

James and Jincy sold 200 acres to William Cupp for $900.00 on September 2, 1874, prior to their removal to Stone County, Arkansas. On that same date William Cupp bought another 80 acres for $600.00 from Jincy Elvira Renfroe.

On February 3, 1896, R. A. Isom of Greene County, Arkansas, wanted to perfect the title to J. M. Renfroe's homestead located in Lorado area of Greene County, Arkansas.

**RENFROE** – Samuel Pinkney Renfroe was born May 7, 1802, probably in Warren County, Georgia, the son of Enoch Renfroe Jr. and Elizabeth Hall. He married about 1820 in Washington County, Georgia, to Eliza born about 1808 in Georgia. They had at least 11 children, names for five are definitely known: my great-grandfather, James Monroe Renfroe (see elsewhere in this book); Elafare Renfroe, born 1834 in Georgia; Samuel Pinkney Renfroe Jr., born 1838 in Georgia; Cornelia F. Renfroe, born 1847 in Alabama; and Zachariah Taylor Renfroe, born January 15, 1851, in Alabama. The name for another daughter could possibly be Matilda Renfroe, married to Jacob C. Swindle. This family was living next door to Jincy Harris on the 1860 Greene County, Arkansas Census. Refer to the article for Nicholas Harris for connection to the Renfroe family. One of their girls was named Eliza J. Swindle. On the 1870 Greene County, Arkansas Census, E. J. Swindle, female, age 16, was living with James Monroe Renfroe and family. Could Eliza J. Swindle be a granddaughter of Samuel?

Samuel was found living in Washington County, Georgia, on the 1830 census. He was living in Muscogee County, Georgia, on the 1840 census and living in Pickens County, Alabama, on the 1850 census.

He is next found living in Greene County, Arkansas, Salem Township on the 1860 census. Arkansas Land Patents shows he bought 120 acres in Craighead County, Arkansas, in 1860. From Original Entries of Lands he purchased 120 acres in Greene County, Arkansas, in 1861. In tax year 1868 commencing November 22, 1869, and ending December 6, 1869, a total of 80 acres were sold to A. F. Wood for nonpayment of taxes.

We do not know whether he fought in the Civil War or not. His son, Samuel Pinkney Renfroe Jr., was captured by the Union Forces on November 2, 1863, about eight miles southwest of Bloomfield, Stoddard County, Missouri, on his way to surrender. On November 16, 1863 in Cape Girardeau, Missouri, he was questioned. In his confession he said he was 26 years old of Greene County, Arkansas, a second sergeant of the Missouri 10th Cavalry, Co. B, enlisted March 22, 1863. He was transferred to Gratiot Prison in St. Louis, Missouri, where he died Christmas Day 1863 from lung inflammation.

Before 1868, Samuel died in Greene County, Arkansas. His widow, Eliza, was found living with their married daughter, Cornelia Fraziar, in Salem Township on the 1870 Greene County, Arkansas Census.

**RETHERFORD** – James Wilbur Retherford and Mary Elizabeth Rightnowar were married April 25, 1903, in Paragould, Greene County, Arkansas. They had moved there from Mt. Vernon, Jefferson County, Illinois. James W., born 1879 in Illinois, was the son of Jesse F. Rutherford, born 1835 in Tennessee and Mary Eva "Mahala" Wilfong, born 1842 in Illinois. Mary Elizabeth Rightnowar, born 1884 in Illinois, was the daughter of Shadric Jefferson Rightnowar, born 1853 in Illinois and Maria Smith, born 1857 in Illinois.

James W. and Mary E. had four children:
George Wilbur, born March 13, 1904;
Rosa Anna, born between 1904 and 1908. She died very young and is buried at Lansing Cox Cemetery, South East of Paragould.
James and Mary's third child was my father William Erva, born June 23, 1908;
Raymond Marion, born January 25, 1912.

James W. died in 1911, at 32 years of age just a short time before Raymond M. was born. Mary Elizabeth married a second time to a man named Charles Farthing, also from Illinois.

Mary and Charles had one daughter, Opal Marie (Wood), born January 15, 1924. Opal died December 26, 1996, and is buried at Brown's Chapel. Opal and her husband Dewie had two boys.

Mary Elizabeth died July 12, 1941. She was 57 years old and is buried at Lansing Cox Cemetery with James W. and daughter Rosa Anna.

William E. married Beulah Elsie Moore, August 1, 1931, in Cardwell, Dunklin County, Missouri. They had five children, J.W., born 1932; William R., born 1933; Betty L. (Hopkins), born 1936 (me); David E., born 1939; and Margaret D. (Bair), born 1943. We were all born in Paragould. While living in Paragould, dad worked for the railroad and mother worked at the shirt factory. We moved to Flint, Michigan in 1945 and dad went to work at General Motors. Mother also worked for General Motors after a few years. They both had to retire for health reasons.

Dad moved back to Paragould about 1970 and stayed until his death, December 28, 1988. He was 80 years old.

Mother remained in Flint until her death, October 14, 1991. She was 81 years old.

I married Richard J. Hopkins in Flint in 1956 and we raised five children: Vickie L. (Potter) born 1957; Daren J., born 1959; Scott J., born 1961; Mary C. (Reed) born 1964 and Stacey L. (Peck) born 1973. We adopted Stacey after the death of my sister Margaret in 1982.

I can recall when my Uncle Raymond came home at the end of WWII after serving in the Army. He had previously married a woman named Ollie Spears and they had three children. Joyce (Newsom), Linda (Ritter) and William Raymond "Billy Ray." They also moved to Flint. Raymond also worked for General Motors, and after he retired, he moved back to Paragould.

George Wilbur "Red" stayed in Paragould and with his wife Sadie (Jackson) raised five children. James; Genevieve (Holloway); Jack; Leonard; and Gladys (Edminston). George W. and Sadie; William E., and Raymond are all buried at Brown's Chapel. George and Raymond's children all still live in Paragould.

**REYNOLDS** – My grandfather, William Thomas Reynolds (1871-1914), his brother Don (1873-1923), mother Kathrine (Cathrine) and possibly father (name unknown) came to Arkansas from Tennessee in the late 1800s and settled in probably Paragould or Rector. In 1895 my grandfather married Dollie Hitchcock (1880-1914). They had two children, my father Donald Omer (1898-1973) and my Aunt Thalia E. (1906-1970). Dad married Helen G. Ward (1899-1969) in 1919, and my sister Helen Yvonne was born in 1920, and I, John T. "Sonny," in 1933. We lived at numerous addresses on the south side when living in Paragould, as well as residing in various other states. My sister had five children with her husband, Howard Hollis (deceased), between 1938 and 1955. I have one child with my wife Jean (married 1959), John Jr. born in 1960, my wife having three children when we married.

My dad was in WWI, and I retired from the service (1953-1973), including a tour in Vietnam. My son served for 11 years, including serving in Desert Storm. For God and Country, I hope we helped.

Mom died in 1969, and when Dad married Mary Amanda Byrd in 1970 they resided at 912 W. Howell, a home I visited in 1971, and again when dad died in 1973. I found it to be a very warm and loving home. I did not return to Paragould again until 1991 and I have visited many times since. Mary's niece's husband had a hobby of cleaning up old railroad spikes and putting various information on them. He made one for me in 1971, and I found out recently he made one for dad in 1972. When my wife and I visited Paragould during the Christmas holidays in 1999-2000 we went to the City Clerks office to get information regarding the family burial plot. During that visit we met Goldie Wise, and when we explained who we were, and what information we needed, she showed us a railroad spike with "D.O. SCOBY REYNOLDS, 1972" on it. MY FATHER! She related how a young man, James Tritch, residing in my fathers last residence on Howell, had called and then brought in the spike and asked her to try and find its owner. The young man's 10 year old son Tyler "T.J." had found it and showed it to his Dad. The spike had been found in a storage room that had been cleaned numerous times, but had never surfaced until now. I was fortunate to have been able to meet with this man and his son, to thank them, and hopefully made a lasting friendship. Something like this could only happened with God's help.

My wife and I have been contemplating returning to live in Paragould, and if this miracle is not a major factor in that decision, nothing else could be.

**REYNOLDS/BLAND** – I, Francis Bland, am preparing the following information to explain our family's relationship with the Reynolds family. My grandmother, Louisa Jane Lewis Bland, came with her husband, John Charles Bland and their three children, Lenora Mae and my father, Herbert Francis Bland Sr. from Crockett County, TN to Paragould, AR in 1891.

The family purchased a home in the 500 block of North Third Street in the summer of 1892. John Charles, my grandfather, died before Christmas of 1892. He was buried in the Bramlett Cemetery that was located in the country, about five miles from downtown Paragould. The reason for his burial in Bramlett is that three of the children of Francis and Susan Clark (sister of my grandmother, Louisa Jane), who had moved from Tennessee about 1880, were buried in Bramlett Cemetery.

*L-R: Herbert Bland, Peck Ritter, Marvin Reynolds, Mr. Thompson and Louis Reynolds*

Elisha Rufus Reynolds (1835 McNairy County, TN) with his second wife, Laura Ann and daughter, Sybillia Reynolds, had moved to Greene County where he had homesteaded 800 acres of land near the Fairview Baptist Church. Laura Ann died Feb 6, 1894.

My grandmother married Mr. Reynolds in 1895 and they had Rufus Arvin and John Marvin, twins, and a baby brother, Louis. My grandmother died about three months after Louis was born. Aunt Lenora had married John Pritchett about six months before her mother died. At the death of her mother, she took her brother, Herbert Bland and her sister, Mae to live at her home on North Second Street in Paragould.

Elisha Rufus Reynolds remarried twice and kept Uncles Arvin, Marvin and Louis at his home in the Fairview community until his death in 1915. My father, Herbert Bland and Alvina Poppe married in 1916. Uncle Marvin told me that on Sunday three weeks after my parents married, they told the Reynolds' brothers that they wanted Arvin, Marvin and Louis to come and live with them. So Uncles Arvin, Marvin and Louis came to live with us and be a part of our family.

The three brothers began to work for Peck Ritter, who owned a bottling and ice cream manufacturing company. At the time of his graduation from Paragould High School in 1921, Uncle Louis left Peck Ritter for St. Louis, MO, where he attended Washington University for one year. He then returned to Paragould and took back his job with Mr. Ritter.

Uncle Marvin had opened a restaurant, called Duroc's Chili Parlor. On the night of Aug 26, 1922, one day after my fourth birthday, Uncle Marvin and Uncle Louis had closed the restaurant and along with Dutch Reynolds were on their way to our house at 11 o'clock. They ran into two criminals who had attempted to rob Mr. Lady, a butcher and Mr. McDonald, but they were scared off and hid behind a big tree on the lot just north of the Catholic Church. As my uncles were later walking to our home about two and one-half blocks north of the church, the two criminals, Walter Harrison and Roy Boone, stepped out from behind the tree and shot Uncle Louis in the chest. He was carried to a house about a half block north of the church on Second Street, but died about midnight.

After his brother's death, Arvin left for St. Louis and went to work for the St. Louis Street Car Company, where he worked for about three years. During this time he met and married Lottie Williams.

In the latter part of 1925, Uncle Marvin and my dad, Herbert, decided to start a bottling plant in Paragould. Arvin returned from St. Louis and the tree brothers opened Mellow Moon Bottling Company in April 1926. In Aug 1929 they secured the Dr Pepper franchise and to this date in 1999 the plant is still known as the Dr Pepper Bottling Company of Paragould. The brothers were active in the company until their deaths, Herbert in 1955, Arvin in 1963 and Marvin in 1970. The grandchildren of Herbert Bland now operate the Dr Pepper Bottling Company.

*Submitted by Francis Bland*

**RHEA** – James McCowan Rhea, born 1870, on the West bank of the Cash River in Lawrence County, to Moses Boling Rhea, b. 1822, a son of Obediah Rhea, born 1790, died 1855, one of the first settlers in Northeast Arkansas, proceeded only by his brother John Rhea, who came to Lawrence County in 1833.

James McCowan Rhea was the son of the third wife, Mary Slavins, born 1840, died 1871, of Moses Boling Rhea. James received a good education for the time period, since his father owned the ferry across Cash River, and later the bridge over Cash River. His father owned the race track at Walnut Ridge, and other members of this family owned a hotel where James got married to Sara Ann Nutt, is also, where the enfair breakfast was held. His uncle owned the freighting business in the area, with lines to Cape Giraudo, Missouri, and Batesville, Arkansas.

After James McCowan and Sarah were married they moved to Crowley's Ridge, just south of Lorado, Greene County, Arkansas. James was learned in the law and wrote deeds, bought and sold land, was an insurance agent, traveled to and over nearby counties selling fire insurance, Stark fruit trees, and was a horse trader. James was also on the school board at Crossroads, and a road commissioner. Sarah was a housewife and the mother of nine children.

Their children were: Rutha Rhea, died 14 months; Mart Rhea, died young; Jane Victoria Rhea Goodman, born January 1, 1895; Mose McCowan Rhea, born 1896; Dovie Rebecca Rhea Dennis Ivie, born September 17, 1900; Nancy Caroline Rhea Lamb; Sallie Edith Rhea Scott, born April 2, 1906, died January 30, 1998; Telfar Sherman Rhea Sr., who was named after a banker in Paragould, Telfar Sherman Stedman; and still living is Chriatian Elizabeth Rhea Adams, called "Chrissie." All of their children were born on Nutt Lane, which runs by Crossroads Cemetery and the used to be Crossroads School, with grades one through eight.

Their son Mose McCowan Rhea was the sergeant major of the U. S. Army during WWI, and distinguished himself in service. Jane married Elmer Goodman a farmer in Greene County. They had two girls, and one son. Dovie married first Loy Dennis, they had one son Rhea Dennis, second Earl Ivie, with whom she had one daughter, Joyce Virginia Ivie. Nancy "Callie" had one son, Mitchell Lamb, and two daughters, Jean Lamb Cornish, and Joan Lamb Towery. Sallie married Richard Robert Scott, of Fontaine, Greene County, Arkansas. They had one son, James Sidney Scott Sr., and one daughter Nina Florence Scott Swicegood. Telfar Sherman Rhea Sr. married Cleve Blackwood, they had one son who died about 4 years of age, two daughters, Carolyn Rhea Frierson, and Marilyn Rhea Willhite. "Chrissie" Rhea married Buel Gage Adams and had two daughters and one son, Lyle Gage Adams, Beverly Ann Adams, married Charles Adams of Conway, and Sarah Lou Adams, married Roland Morris, whom she met at Baylor University.

**RHEA/RAY/RAE/WRAY** – The farthermost we have proved ancestry is to Reverend John M. Ray, a Baptist preacher, born about 1739 in Virginia, died February 16, 1813, aged 74, buried Ray Cemetery in Van Buren County, Tennessee, at age 74. Married February 7, 1763, to Mary Gray, born about 1743, died February 12, 1814, buried in Ray Cemetery in Van Buren Tennessee. The Rae Cemetery is located 10 miles from McMinnville, Tennessee. There is family history pointing to an ancestor, Joseph Rhea in Fahn Ireland, pastor to a Presbyterian church, has not yet been proved. Land grant No. 6795 conveyed 100 acres to John Rea, he served as a chaplain during the Revolutionary War. As for proof that the was the father, land records found by Mrs. Jack R. "Mary" Marks now confirms that he was.

Moses Rhea born 1767, died 1830; married Hannah Ritter. Served as executor, of John Rea deceased Page 232 Warren County, Tennessee, minutes, April 8, 1816. Mose's will on March 19, 1830, stated he knows that he is in poor health makes a will dividing his land between family members. He left to Hanna Ritter his beloved wife the mansion house and kitchen together with all furniture goods and chattels etc. He divides land into four parts between daughter Polly Hubbert, to Joseph Rea lot #3 to daughter Elizabeth Gibbs Lot #2, and to my son, Obediah Rea also the balance of a 500 acre tract. Also dividing land between two daughters Jane Campbell and Susannah Sims. He also divides moneys and furniture to sons James, John T., William and Alford.

Obediah Rhea, born 1790, died 1855; married Emma Elizabeth Littlepage, born 1799, died 1871. Obediah immigrated to Arkansas in 1836, following his brother John, who had already settled in what later became Randolph County. Obediah and other Rheas left Madison County, Tennessee, which in the 1830 census shows it to be northeast of Memphis, Shelby County, and settled in what finally became Greene County, Arkansas, in about 1835 and planted a crops and then went back to Tennessee and got his family and settled about 10 miles of what finally became Jonesboro, Craighead County, Arkansas. He rode his horse to Batesville, Arkansas, land office and filed on 200 acres in SE SE 21, R 4E -40 acres, E-1/2 SW21, T16N, R4E 80 acres, W1/2 SE 31 T16N R4E 80 acres. The oldest son John did not migrate to Arkansas, he had a young child and the mother didn't want to move, so she hid out the child, and John just decided not to go move.

The 1850 Census of Greene County, Arkansas, Powell Township, gives the following information: Dwelling 324/ Ray (Rhea), Obadiah as 60m, a farmer, born in Virginia, (1790), Elizabeth 51f, born in Kentucky, 1799, with three daughters at home. Other children, Moses Boling Rhea, b. Warren County, Tennessee, June 6, 1822, settled in Arkansas about 1835 age 13. Moses Boling Rhea lived in Greene County until he was 23 years old, then settled on his farm seven miles east of Walnut Ridge, Arkansas (Lawrence County, across Cashe river, where he is buried, on his old farm. He was a freighter to Cape Girardeau, Memphis, Powhatan,

295

Jacksonport, Forest City and other ports. He operated a ferry across Cache River, when it was much wider than today, and was quiet an obstacle to pioneer crossing. He built the road bed between Walnut Ridge and Paragould, he later owned the toll bridge at Cache River.

As per Goodspeed he married Sarah C. Lamb February 8, 1844 and was married four other times. Moses Bolling was in C.S.A. with Price's invasion of Missouri in 1854. Children of Moses Bolling Rhea were James Moses Rhea, William Paul Rhea, John Rhea, Flavious Rhea, Ob Rhea, William Rhea and Aunt Sis Rhea. There is a picture taken at Walnut Ridge showing two sons and four sisters, namely Emma Rhea Pierce, Nancy Rhea Edwards, Mose Bolling Rhea, Thomas D. Rhea, Elizabeth Rhea Rutherford and Mary Rhea Grayson.

Elizabeth Rhea Rutherford married Dr. Rutherford who was on the committee to pick a place for the city of Jonesboro, Craighead County, Arkansas.

**RHINE** — Lyle V. Rhine (Nov 29, 1894, Bloomfield, NE) the son of Fred A. and Nettie (Cooper) Rhine attended the elementary school of Olathe, KS and graduated from high school at Columbus, KS. Mr. Rhine received the B.S. degree from Kansas State Apicultural College, Manhattan, KS in 1917, specializing in agriculture and horticulture. He was State Apiarist of Kansas for two years, 1919 and 1920.

On Aug 7, 1920, L. V. Rhine married Miss Julia Gordon of Columbia, MO, daughter of Carey H. and Julia (Long) Gordon. Her grandfather, John D. Gordon donated the land on which the University of Missouri was built and her uncle, Boyle G. Gordon was the first Dean of the Law School of the University on Missouri.

Mr. and Mrs. Rhine taught school for one year at Stockton, KS and two years at Hartford, IA. He received his law degree from Cumberland University, Lebanon, TN in May 1927. In September of the same year they came to Paragould. Mr. Rhine was principal of Paragould High School for three years and Mrs. Rhine was Home Economics teacher during that time.

In 1930, L. V. Rhine entered law partnership with H. R. Partlow in the Rhine building. He bought several sets of abstract books, which have developed into the Greene County Abstract Company. L. V. Rhine owned Greene County Abstract until his death in 1984. Upon his death Robert Young, local attorney and Ethan Busby, purchased the business. Several years later Busby sold his interest to Young.

*L. V. Rhine*

The Rhines never had any children but gave much love and affection to neighbor kids and children of employees at the Rhine Building. After Mrs. Rhine's death, Rhine married Olga Hooper.

Rhine was president of the Chamber of Commerce for two years and was influential in obtaining Crowley's Ridge State Park. He was a 32nd degree Mason and Shriner.

L. V. Rhine passed away in 1984 but is still remembered by many Greene county residents for his contributions to the county.

*Submitted by Lindell Hooper*

**RICE** — Noah (1870-1948) and Susan (1874-1947) Rice became residents of Greene County in the Delaplaine area in 1914. Prior to this time the interrelated families of the Rices, Stubblefields and Looneys were among the first settlers in Northeast Arkansas, coming to what is now Randolph County in 1802 from Hawkins County, Tennessee.

After coming to Greene County they lived two miles west of Delaplaine farming and raising livestock. There were six children: Lee, Rex, Harry, Mary, Martha and Byrdie.

Lee (1895-1979) married Samantha Getson (1908-1985). They were both teachers. In 1930 Lee became mail carrier and landowner. He was a veteran of World War I. Both worked diligently for the consolidation of Delaplaine School District. Issue: Wanda Lee married Jim Vaughn both retired teachers. She wrote and directed historical dramas and he wrote and published educational material for schools.

Rex (1908-1949) married Mable Gunter (1909-1985). He was a farmer and worked in timber making and hauling ties. Issues: Howard married Wanda Lea Huckabee and is involved in manufacturing. Beulah (1934-1939).

Billy Joe married Glenda Herring and is retired from Cinch Manufacturing Company. Ralph married first Caroline Sharrock and second Joyce Cartwright and involved with manufacturing and trucking industries.

Harry (1901-1993) married Nina Thomas (1911-1990). He and brother Rex went to Michigan and worked in the automotive industry and returned to Greene County and farmed. Issues: Thomas Alvin (1932-1985) married Gaye Penny. Retired as a Lt. Colonel, and was one of the most decorated soldiers from Greene County; Korean and Vietnam Wars. Doris Jean married Rupert White. She taught school for 30 years in the Delaplaine schools. Following a coaching career Rupert became a farmer.

*Noah and Susan Dalton Rice*

Mary (1906-1949) was a school teacher. She and husband Chacy Eveland (1901-1967) owned land and managed a mercantile business. Issues: Chacy R. married first Nona Voight and second Marsha Walsh. He retired from the military as a Lt. Colonel; served in Korea and Vietnam. Darlene married first Charles Dean and second Steven Paulsen. An artist and teacher, has an art school in Little Rock. Phyllis married William Wilkinson; both retired teachers. She as grade school principal and he as Superintendent of Delaplaine schools. Solomon married Brenda Hightower and retired from Cinch Manufacturing Company. Randy married Linda Tyler and operates a Farrier business; very active in Civil War reenactments.

Martha (1909-1980) worked with her husband Percy Thomen (1904-1984) operating their farm and mercantile business. Issues: Bernice married Thomas Bone; retired teachers. H.P. Jr., married first Elsa Graham and second Linda Henderson. He is a business man with multiple manufacturing interests in several states. Donald married first Frances Taylor; second Peggy Stanley; and third Evelyn Jones. He was affiliated with the trucking industry.

Byrdie (1916-1989) was married to first Ivan Shrader and second William Hartwick. She retired as a telegrapher and office manager of Cotton Belt Railroad.

Noah and Susan have many great and great-great-grandchildren.

**RIPPY** — William H. Rippy (1867 NC) and Rebecca (1870 IN) are listed in the 1900 census living in the Vigo Township of Knox County, IN at the time.

William H. and Rebecca brought their family to Greene County, AR about 1905. Born in Indiana, the first seven children were:
1. James "Ben" (1889)
2. Claud (1894)
3. Oscar (1896)
4. William "Bill" (1898)
5. Golda (1899)
6. Francis L. (1902)
7. Lily Grace (1904)

After settling in Arkansas, two more children were born. These were:
8. Lote (1904)
9. Martha J. (1908)

The 1910 census also shows William's brother Grover living with the family.

According to Edgar Reddick, husband of Martha "Janie' (Rippy) Reddick, the Rippy home was located near the Mounds community on the land later bought by Marion Evans. Edgar indicated that a Rippy forged a deed to the property of William H. and sold the land. John Rippy, another brother, came out against the plot. After William's death, it was said Marion Evans came around getting signatures from the children in an effort to clear the title to the property.

William and Rebecca took the kids and moved down near Brinkley, AR settling in the Morton community. The farm on which they settled had no clear title to it. As with many homes of that primitive era, their house had dirt floors and was very hard to heat. Rebecca soon developed pneumonia. At the same time, Oscar contracted diphtheria. An elderly lady told of Oscar crying for his mother as she lay dying. The winter of 1911 saw the death of Rebecca. As winter faded, William left the children with friends and returned to Indiana to find work and a place to move his remaining family. He fell ill, died and was buried in Indiana.

Upon William's death, the older Rippy children took in part of the kids. Walter Evans and his wife took in and provided for Martha, Lily Grace and Lote. Jim Lamb helped to raise some of the boys. As the children entered the age of majority, they went various directions. William "Bill" entered the army and served his country in the trenches of France during WWI. He developed severe respiratory problems from breathing German mustard gas. After the war and a broken marriage with Ruby Walls in 1920, he went to Michigan and later retired to Canada. Claud also migrated to Canada and died near Prince Albert. Golda married Artie Potter in 1923 and moved west where he became an instructor in a California college. Lotie married Nora Moore in 1925 and also spent some time in California. Frances married Violet Reddick in 1927 and moved to Michigan. James married Nettie Evans in 1910 and farmed near Marmaduke. Lillie Grace married Roosevelt Reddick in 1919 and lived in the Mounds area. Martha married Edgar Reddick in 1926 and also farmed near Marmaduke. Upon retirement, most who had left the area returned to their roots in Greene County, died and were buried here.

*Submitted by Phillip Reddick*

**RITCHEY** – Mary Bernadette Payne Furgerson Ritchey, born March 27, 1881, in Geneva, Henderson County, Kentucky, to Henry Elmore Shelby Payne, and Amanda Elizabeth "Betty" Mattingly. Mary's father was rarely home so Betty made a garden every year for their food.

Mary could make biscuits that melted in your mouth and she would say, "I know I washed my hands last week," as she stirred the biscuits with her finger to make sure the dough felt just right.

Noah Alonzo "Lonnie" Furgerson, and his sister, Maude, married Mary, and her half-brother, William "Bill" Downs. The ladies wore lovely blue capes they had made, and the double wedding took place in St. Vincent's Catholic Church, in Waverly, Union County, Kentucky, on November 12, 1901, by Father Haggarty.

*Mary and John Ritchey.*

Lonnie and Mary traveled and lived in a tent moving from place-to-place without even time to plant a garden. They had four children: Mary Agnes, Mable Elizabeth, Thomas Alonzo, and James Edward. Lonnie Furgerson passed on May 9, 1916, and was buried somewhere in Missouri. Lon's parents were John Furgerson and Eliza Purdue. His entire family grieved over his tragic end.

Mary moved back to Arkansas and helped to care for her mother, Betty, who passed away after a lengthy illness on January 12, 1923. Soon after this Mary met John Ritchey, a woodcutter and farmer, in Paragould, Arkansas. They lived in Greene County all of their married lives and raised their daughters. Their daughters were Pauline, Margaret, Aileen, and Iva Lee from a previous marriage of John. They all had happy childhoods and enjoyed the quiet farm life that they shared. Mary and John lived at Gainesville, Greene County, Arkansas, when her husband, John passed away May 14, 1970, and he was buried at St. Mary's Catholic Cemetery, Paragould, Arkansas.

When Mary was 86 years young she was still fairly active. Some years before she had been president of the Center Hill Quilting Club. Mary remembers seeing the Northern Lights as they shone here in Arkansas when she was a young woman, and she thought this a most awe-inspiring event. If she bent from the waist, she could still milk a cow with her slightly crippled hand. Mary loved yellow roses the best, but she grew many kinds and colors in her yard. She also enjoyed morning glories, peonies, and violets. She liked her faithful banty hen best because she was so good to care for her baby chicks. In the twilight of a summer's eve to the chorus of the whippoorwill and the eerie beauty of fireflies flitting about, Mary awakens from her nap. She thinks it is morning for only an instant before she notices that the sun is going down in the west. Mary was laid to rest alongside her beloved, John, as she passed away on January 28, 1976. She is fondly remembered by all whose lives she touched.

**ROBESON** – Enoch Terrell Robeson (June 17, 1861 Cairn Rock Hardin County, IL) married Norah Winborn Phillips (May 23, 1863 Crittendon County, KY) on Dec 9, 1880 at Marion, KY. To this union were born seven children all near Marion KY:
1. Henry Orville (Oct 12, 1881- May 30, 1939) married Effie Hughes in 1899. Effie died in 1959. Children:
   a. Bonita Hazel (1903 Las Vegas, NM)
   b. Christopher Hughes (1913 Harrisburg, IL)
2. Ethel (Robeson) Lynn (Feb 11, 1884- May 21, 1961) twin, married Tom Lynn in 1919. There were no children.
3. Edith (Robeson) Moore (Feb 11, 1884- Feb 19, 1974 AR) twin, married Bailey Moore, March 8, 1902. Their children:
   a. Claude Leo (1903 Corona, CA)
   b. Jean Paul (1905 Harrisburg, IL)
   Edith resided at Lafe, AR until her death.
4. Levada (Robeson) Schramm (April 4, 1886- Feb 3, 1977 Strongsville, OH) married William A. Schramm in 1908. They had no children. Will died in 1956.
5. Lola Terrel (Robeson) Howard (Nov 14, 1888- Feb 24, 1988) married Raymond Jess Howard in 1908. They had no children. Ray died in 1963 and Lola resided in Hooker community, AR until her death.
6. Ruth Robeson (April 15, 1892-April 24, 1892)
7. Irvin DeWitt Robeson (July 31, 1893- 1967 Hooker community, AR) married Mary Elizabeth Holbert May 25, 1893. Mary died in 1959 in the Hooker community. They had eight children:
   a. Paul DeWitt, Hooker community
   b. Floyd Dexter died in 1944
   c. Hazel Levada Wright, Florida
   d. Ruth Lucille Maerker, Virginia
   e. Henry Ray, Hooker community
   f. Claude Carlos, WWII casualty 1944
   g. John Franklin died 1979
   h. Dorothy Ann Tucker, St. Louis, MO.

In 1907 Enoch Robeson migrated from Harrisburg, IL to Blytheville, AR to buy and sell horses. Norah and the children followed in 1908 and established their home where they lived until 1917, when they bought a farm at Lafe, AR (the present Lum Thomas farm). In 1935 Irvin and Mary moved their family from Blytheville to Lafe and later to the Hooker community where they lived until their deaths.

Enoch acquired other parcels of property during the years and died at home in 1943. Norah followed him in death in 1946.

*Submitted by Miriam N. Robeson*

**ROBINSON** – Gene Robinson (1914 Greene County, AR) grew up in Powell Township. Gene attended Antioch School at Goobertown and helped the family with the farming work. He graduated in 1933 from A & M College in Jonesboro, AR.
Gene married Miss Charlsie Mabry in 1936. They moved to Washington, D.C. where he had a government job. Two children were born while they were living in Washington, D.C.: Robert Charles, born in 1938 and Donna

*Gene and Charlsie Robinson 1997*

Jean, born in 1939. They moved back to the farm for a while, and then moved to Memphis, TN where the third child William Lee was born in 1942. While in Memphis, Gene was employed at a machine shop. After Gene and family moved back to Jonesboro, He was employed at H. A. Field Machine Shop.

The Robinsons moved to Michigan and lived there for approximately seven years. Gene worked for General Motors, Turnstead plant in Flint MI. The family moved back to Arkansas in the summer of 1957.

Gene retired from Colson Caster Company of Jonesboro. He continued to be active and busy on the 'farm' for many years. They have 10 grandchildren:
1. James Ishmael
2. Barbara Ishmael
3. Rhonda Robinson
4. Rudy Robinson
5. Rob Robinson
6. Rachelle Robinson
7. Rachel Robinson
8. Mark Robinson
9. David Robinson
10. Sam Robinson
11. William Lee Robinson Jr. died in 1964 and is buried at Pine Log Cemetery.

Gene and Charlsie have 12 great grand children. Many children and grandchildren are living in the Brookland and Goobertown area of Arkansas. Several of Robert's children and grandchildren are living in Fort Smith, AR.

*Submitted by Donna (Robinson) Ishmael*

**ROBINSON** – Oscar Lee Robinson (1888 Powell Township, Greene County, AR) lived most of his life in that area except when he attended Business College. Oscar married Miss Bertha Jane Johnson in 1910. They had six children:
1. Howard (1911)
2. Lola (1912)
3. Gene (1914)
4. Norine (1917) twin
5. Orine (1917-1925) twin
6. Calla Mae (1921)

Oscar was a farmer, cattleman, businessman and secretary-treasurer of Craighead Electric Cooperative for many years. He is listed in Arkansas Who's Who. He and his wife Bertha were members of the New Antioch Baptist Church. Bertha was one of the original pioneer charter members. She played the piano for many years and taught Sunday school; she was also church treasurer for many years.

Bertha (1889 Goobertown) was a lifelong resident of that community.

All of Oscar and Bertha's children are buried at Pine Log Cemetery near Brookland, AR, except Gene Robinson. He is the last living of this pioneer family. Gene is retired and living near Goobertown with his wife Charlsie (Mabry).

Howard Robinson married Helen Montgomery. They had no children and were divorced. Howard later married Martha. They had no children.

Lola Robinson married C. L. Caldwell; they lived in Centerville, VA. They had no children. Lola was employed with the U. S. Government for many years. C. L. Caldwell was a retired military man.

Norine Robinson married Vince Stevens and lived in Alexander, VA. They had no children. Norine also retired from the U. S. Government.

Calla Mae Robinson married Bert Cruse. They had one son, Michael Lee Cruse. Calla Mae divorced and the married Charlie G. Johnston about 1949. Calla Mae and Charlie lived in Jonesboro for several years then moved to Little Rock, AR.

Grandson, Mike Cruse married Susan and lived all their married life in Little Rock, AR area. Mike is a retired attorney for the State of Arkansas. They have a daughter Beth and a son Brad.

L-R, standing back row: Howard, Lola, her husband C. L. Caldwell, Calla Mae, her husband Charlie G. Johnston, Norine and Gene Robinson. Front row: Donna Jean Robinson, William Lee Robinson, Mike Cruse, Robert Charles Robinson, Oscar Robinson about 1950.

Oscar's parents were James Robert "Bob" Robinson and Mary Ann Johnston. Bob Robinson was about 25 years old when he died in 1899. At that time, Oscar was only six months old. Anna then married Joseph Sims. Mary Anna Johnston's parents were Samuel Johnston (1836) and Rebecca F. Boozer. They married in 1854 and came from Alabama.

Oscar's grandfather, James Harvey Robinson, one of the oldest settlers of the county resided at Goobertown. James Harvey came to this country in 1844 and died on the same place where he settled with his father. They came from North Carolina. James Harvey Robinson married Cassandra "Jane" Armstrong in 1856. Her family came from Virginia. James Harvey died at the age of 80 odd years in 1915. During his time, Harvey Robinson was a splendid man and was held in high esteem by all who knew him. He is buried at Pine Log Cemetery near Brookland.

The Goobertown area is still populated with many generations of this old pioneer family.

*Submitted by Donna Ishmael*

**ROGERS –** James Thomas "Tom" Rogers, was born June 17, 1849, in Graves County, Kentucky, the son of Sterling Rogers and Nancy Childers. He married Martha Ann Sawyer, born August 5, 1854, the daughter of Jones Madison Sawyer and Nancy Anderson Chapman, on March 17, 1870, in Graves County. The family moved to Carlisle County, Kentucky, and then came to Greene County in 1888. The trip to Arkansas took two weeks with one horse team and one oxen team carrying the entire family. Some descendents claim they were on the way to the Ozark Mountains, but were convinced to stop and settle in Greene County. The family slept in the wagons until cabins were built. Littleberry and Rufus Rogers, brothers of Tom Rogers, also moved from Graves County to Arkansas. James Thomas lived and farmed in Greene County for the remainder of his life. Mattie Rogers died April 15, 1911, and Tom Rogers married Mrs. Susan Neely in 1912. He died on October 24, 1926, and is buried at Brown's Chapel Baptist Church.

Children of Tom and Mattie Rogers:

James Sterling Rogers born on March 3, 1871, in Graves County, Kentucky and died in 1963 in Conway, Arkansas. He was executive secretary of the Arkansas Baptist Convention for 16 years and was a superintendent of Arkansas Baptist Hospital, Little Rock and author of the book *A History of Arkansas Baptists*. He was married to Sally McDaniel in 1894.

Joseph Matthew Rogers was born September 21, 1872, in Graves County and died on March 13, 1956. He married Julia Cooper on December 19, 1894.

John Luther Rogers was born on August 28, 1874, and died August 19, 1955, in Greene County, Arkansas. He married Rosa Lee Cleveland.

Holly A. Rogers was born August 30, 1877, and died December 3, 1961. He married Georgia F. Cleveland in 1899.

Robert Chapel Rogers Sr. was born February 3, 1880, in Graves County and died on November 15, 1970, in Greene County. He married to Wassietella Bentley on January 23, 1901.

Brothers, from left: John Matthew Rogers, Little Berry Rogers, Rufus Rogers and James Thomas Rogers.

Loly Berry Rogers was born July 19, 1881, and died June 2, 1971. He married Stella Jones.

Ethel Zola Rogers was born May 5, 1887, in Arlington, Kentucky, and died June 6, 1967, in Memphis, Tennessee. She was married to Doctor Martin Luther Bearden in 1905.

Effie L. Rogers was born October 10, 1889, in Greene County and died December 4, 1912. She married William Taylor.

Minnie F. Rogers was born March 7, 1892, and died on July 13, 1990. She married Ed Scott November 27, 1910.

Nancy O. Rogers was born in January 1898 and died in the 1920s in a car-train wreck in Mississippi.

Another son, Willie Rogers died in infancy.

**ROGERS –** Joe Matthew Rogers of Greene County, Arkansas, was born in Graves County, Kentucky, on September 21, 1872, the son of James Thomas Rogers and Martha Ann Sawyer Rogers. The family moved to Arkansas about 1884 with five brothers and three sisters. James Thomas had originally set out for the Ozark Mountains in Northwest Arkansas but when they arrived in Greene County, a good friend persuaded them to stay. Joe Matthew married Julia Frances Cooper on December 19, 1894, with Elder W. J. Bearden officiating the ceremony. They established a home in the Browns Chapel Community. Their home sat on top of a hill with a wrought iron picket fence surrounding the front yard. The Rogers family had raised tobacco in Graves County, Kentucky, and Joe continued the tradition, building a barn to smoke and cure the tobacco. He made it into twists and would sell it from a cart on the steps of the bank on Court Street every Saturday for years. He was named a justice of the peace for the county in 1902. He farmed for many years until moving into Paragould around 1939.

Joe and Julia raised seven sons and one daughter. One son named Norman passed away at an early age.

Their daughter, Cora born September 4, 1896, married Lehman Thompson and after his death, married Mr. Scott and upon his death married Mr. Merrill Rice and resided with him in Sturgis, Michigan, until his death. She moved to Little Rock, where she passed away in 1982. She was a beloved teacher and principal in schools in Paragould including Baldwin and Paragould High.

Cecil Rogers, the oldest son, married Marion Ellis of Cape Girardeau, Missouri, and upon their divorce in 1930, married Dora Gravatt Mims. She passed away in 1942 and he then married Inez Keeney of Brookland, Arkansas. Cecil operated a grocery store for several years before going to work for Hurt Grocery Company and Bertig Gin Company. He passed away in Pahokee, Florida, on June 3, 1987.

Thomas H. Rogers married Hazel Sparks and moved to Knoxville, Tennessee, and passed away there on April 24, 1946.

Joe Alton Rogers married Ruby Hopkins and passed away on July 24, 1937, in Paragould.

The rest of the sons moved away to Detroit during the Depression years to work in the auto factories as did many young men from Greene County.

Adrian Rogers married Ruth Barron and died in West Palm Beach, Florida, November 21, 1980.

Dwight Rogers born April 21, 1911, married Helen McKelvey and resided in Pontiac, Michigan. The date of his death is not known.

Winston Rogers born August 28, 1912, married Theda Pruitt. He resided in Pontiac, Michigan, and passed away in Phoenix, Arizona, on July 6, 1965.

Byron Rogers born July 23, 1916, married Norma Harrington and resided in Pontiac. He passed away in Brooksville, Florida, in 1983.

Joe M. Rogers died March 15, 1956, and is buried in Browns Chapel Cemetery. Julia passed away November 8, 1941.

**ROGERS –** Paul Everett Rogers, was born September 15, 1903, the son of Loly Berry Rogers and Stella Jones Rogers in Greene County, Arkansas. He had six brothers and sisters: Ted Rogers, Fred Rogers, J.T. Rogers, Gladys Rogers (Mrs. Earl) Garner, Martha Rogers (Mrs. John) Lee and Elnora Rogers (Mrs. C.J.) Acuff. Everett graduated from Paragould High School, where he played on the 1920 champion high school football team. He grew up on the family farm located on Pruetts Chapel Road just west of Paragould. The farm produced milk from a Jersey dairy, registered Duroc hogs and field crops such as cotton, soybeans and feed grains and forages for the livestock. He worked as a teller for the First National Bank when it was located at the corner of Court Street and Pruett Street in Paragould. Following that, he owned an insurance agency for the Metropolitan Insurance Company. He served as Greene County Assessor from 1945-1948 where he met his future wife, Harriet Elizabeth Patterson. Harriet was the County Home Demonstration Agent for the Cooperative Extension Service and both of their offices were in the old courthouse. Everett and Harriet were married December 14, 1947, in Forrest City, Arkansas.

Following Everett and Harriet's marriage they moved to Forrest City, Arkansas, to operate a soft drink bottling company started by Harriet's parents, Irving Cook Patterson and Anna Elizabeth Gwinner Patterson. They had one child, Everett Irving Rogers who was born December 11, 1948, in Memphis, Tennessee.

In 1953 the family moved back to the Paragould area to resume the family farming operation. Upon moving back to Paragould, the

Rogers family operated the Hill Home Polled Hereford farm, where they raised registered Polled Herford cattle. Everett was always studying better ways of farming and was named as an Arkansas "Farm Family of the Year." He was also recognized as a "Pioneer Breeder" by the American Polled Hereford Association. Everett served for many years as secretary of the Arkansas Polled Hereford Association. He served on the Greene County Fair Board for several years and on the board of directors of Craighead Electric Cooperative. The Hill home farm cattle operation is documented in the book *Cattle on a Thousand Hills*, by C.J. Brown (1996 University of Arkansas Press) along with other Greene County livestock producers. He was a very careful steward of the land. He did everything he could to preserve the land and leave it in better condition than when he got it. He always used the manure waste from the cattle on the farm to improve its fertility and organic content. He was very careful to place the highly erodible land in grass and only use the flat creek bottoms for cultivation. It upset him greatly to see hill land eroded due to improper cultivation when it should have been used for pastures or forests. His dream of seeing more of Crowley's Ridge preserved for grassland and forest use rather than be eroded by cultivation was fulfilled. Everett felt very strongly that the young people were our future and he was always eager to help young people in any way that he could. He often sold calves to 4-H and FFA members at lower than regular prices to help in their projects. He also worked to see that the junior's club calves had buyers at the premium sales following their junior livestock shows.

Everett died August 19, 1973, and is buried in Linwood Cemetery, Paragould, Arkansas.

Harriet Elizabeth Patterson was born October 10, 1906, in Missouri and was an only child. She attended Stephens College in Columbia, Missouri, and Iowa State University. She majored in home economics and was employed by the Cooperative Extension Service as a home demonstration agent. She resigned from the extension service in 1974, following her marriage to Paul Everett Rogers and they moved to Forrest City. Upon their return to Greene County, she began teaching home economics in the Greene County Tech School District for many years, until her retirement. She was a faithful worshiper at the Pruetts Chapel Methodist Church where she served as pianist until her eyesight and arthritis forced her to stop playing. She was always a strong supporter of school and youth activities and spent many hours and miles taking youth to various activities.

*Everett and Harriett Rogers, December 1947.*

Everett and Harriet had one child, a son, Everett Irving Rogers born December 11, 1948. He was active in 4-H and FFA activities while in school. He graduated from Greene County Tech High School in 1967 and received a bachelor of science of agriculture degree from the University of Arkansas, Fayetteville in 1971. He was accepted into the professional program of the University of Missouri, Columbia where he received his doctor of veterinary medicine degree in 1975. He returned to Paragould and opened the Rogers Animal Clinic which he operated for 20 years. In 1995 he sold the clinic and began doing contract veterinary relief work for various veterinarians in Arkansas and Missouri.

Everett I. married Sandra Gayle Collar on June 11, 1971, at Walcott Baptist Church in Walcott, Arkansas. Sandra is the daughter of Clifford Harry Collar, a pioneer Greene County rice farmer and Wilma Ednas Noles Collar and was born June 12, 1949. She has three sisters, Nell Collar Lyon, Shirley Collar Wilson and Debra Collar Newberry. Sandra attended Greene County Tech High School and graduated in 1967. She received her bachelors degree in elementary education-library science from Arkansas State University in 1971. She served as the intermediate school librarian for the Greene County Tech School District until 1998 at which time she was hired as the Greene County public librarian.

Everett I. and Sandra Rogers have three sons. Michael Everett Rogers was born September 19, 1974, in Columbia, Missouri. He attended Greene County Tech High School and graduated in 1992 and received his bachelors degree from the University of Arkansas, Fayetteville in 1996. He is currently (1999) the circulation manager for the *Paragould Daily Press*. Brian Jared Rogers was born May 15, 1979, in Paragould, Arkansas. He attended Greene County Tech High School and graduated in 1997. He is currently (1999) enrolled in the University of Arkansas, Fayetteville majoring in mathematics. Casey Wade Rogers was born August 17, 1981, in Paragould, Arkansas. He is currently (1999) a senior at Greene County Tech High School.

**ROGERS** – Robert Chapel Rogers Sr. was born February 3, 1880, in Graves County, Kentucky, and moved to Greene County in 1888 with his family. Reportedly he wanted to live in the Ozarks, where his father was headed when they moved from Kentucky, but his parents decided to settle in Greene County. He attended Ouachita College and farmed on family land south of Paragould for many years. He was a pastor for many churches in and around Greene County. He also held many revivals, including some back in Graves County. Reverend Rogers died on November 15, 1970, in Greene County, Arkansas.

He married Wassietella Bentley, daughter of Benjamin Dudley Bentley and Martha Louise Catherine "Kittie" Brannon, on January 23, 1901. Wassietella Bentley was born April 19, 1884, in Greene County. Her father was a horse trader from Alabama and she became an accomplished horsewoman. Wassie Bentley's mother was born in Western Arkansas just before the Civil War. Her grandfather, James Brannon, served in both the Confederate and Union Armies. Her grandmother, Elizabeth Ford Brannon, lost her father, John Ford, to "bushwhackers" in Missouri during the war. Jim Brannon moved the family to Randolph County after the war and eventually settled in Greene County. Wassie Rogers died June 22, 1964.

Robert Chapel Rogers Sr. and Wassietella Bentley had the following children:

Mildred Rogers was born June 11, 1902, in Greene County and died on October 13, 1987, in Longview, Texas.

Rubye Rogers was born June 26, 1904, in Greene County. She lived for many years in Memphis, Tennessee, and died September 8, 1991, in Greene County.

Joe Rogers was born and died April 6, 1906.

William Carey Rogers was born on July 31, 1908, and died September 11, 1983, in Maryland.

Colletia "Letty" Rogers was born on October 7, 1910. She married Donald McHaney and lived for many years in Flint, Michigan. She died January 9, 1988, in Greene County.

Robert Maurice Rogers was born April 2, 1917, and died on January 25, 1998, in Texas. He married Beechie Barron and lived for many years in the Memphis area. They had one son, Phillip.

Robert Chapel Rogers Jr. was born June 5, 1920, in Boone County, Arkansas. He married Bernita Rowe June 17, 1950, in Paragould. Their children are Carey Wayne of Nashville, Tennessee; Patrick and Kathleen of Columbia, Missouri.

James Carral Rogers was born January 22, 1927, and died July 24, 1981, in Greene County. He married Wanda Felty and served as a rural mail carrier and proprietor of a local nursery. Their children are Michael, June, Chris and Susan. Michael died November 23, 1974. June, Chris and Susan live in Paragould.

*Robert Chapel Rogers and Wassietella Bentley Rogers*

**ROGERS** – Rufus Van Rogers was born November 20, 1926, in Greene County, Arkansas, to William Matthew Rogers (1895-1975) and Sibyl Morten Rogers. William Matthew Rogers was a son of Rufus William Rogers (1852-1937) and Sarah Davis Rogers.

Four Rogers brothers, Rufus William, James Thomas, L. Berry, and John Matthew, the sons of James Sterling Rogers came to Greene County, Arkansas, from Graves County, Kentucky, in the late 1800s. The Rogers family had lived in Martin County, North Carolina, before living in Kentucky.

As a young man, R.V. Rogers helped work the farm of his maternal grandfather, Noble Van Morten which was located near Marmaduke, Arkansas. After high school at Paragould, in 1945 he enlisted in the U.S. Army and served at the end of World War II. After returning from service, he worked for Hurt Grocer Company in Paragould and later got a job at the local Kroger store in Paragould. Kroger sent him to work in their store at Pocahontas, Arkansas, in the late 1940s.

*Left to right: R.V. Rogers, W.H. "Scott" Rogers and Joan Rogers in 1968 Pocahontas, Arkansas.*

It was in Pocahontas that he met and married Joan (pronounced JoAnn) Holobaugh, a daughter of Jim and Irene Holobaugh. Jim asked R.V. if he would be interested in being a barber. He said he would, so R.V. and Joan moved to Little Rock while he attended barber college. R.V.

Rogers graduated from Eaton Barber College in 1950. He and Joan moved back to Pocahontas where he began barbering at the Sanitary Barber Shop.

R.V. and Joan had two sons: James Van Rogers (1954-1954), and William Holobaugh "Scott" Rogers (the writer of this sketch).

We lived on Church Street in Pocahontas and had excellent neighbors. People seemed closer back in the 50s and 60s. One neighbor and his wife ran the local theater, and the others included a newspaper publisher, a building contractor, a radio announcer, a railroad man, a postman, a missionary, and a mechanic. All of these people are well known to the people of Pocahontas. They were all very good to my family and myself over the years.

R.V. Rogers barbered for nearly 20 years in Pocahontas. He had kidney problems and had the first successful kidney transplant in the state of Arkansas in 1964. He continued to barber after the transplant and lived his life to the fullest, graduating from Southern Baptist College, and attending Arkansas State College before his death. He died of heart failure on Sunday, October 19, 1969, in Pocahontas. He was the best father a person could have, and is greatly missed today.

In 1973, Joan Holobaugh Rogers married Hugh Hightower, whose family had come to Pocahontas from Fulton County, Arkansas. Hugh and Joan are retired Pocahontas school teachers. Hugh had a total of 30 years in the field of education, most of which was in the Pocahontas Public School System. Joan had 22 years of service to Arkansas education, most of which was with Pocahontas Public Schools.

Hugh and Joan are active in the First Baptist Church. He is also a District Deputy Grand Master in Arkansas Freemasonry and she is active in the Order of the Eastern Star.

W.H. "Scott" Rogers lives in Jonesboro, Arkansas, and works in pharmaceutical distribution.

**ROGERS** – Rufus William Rogers (1852-1937) was born near Mayfield, Graves County, Kentucky, to James Sterling Rogers and Nancy Childers Rogers. James Sterling Rogers had lived in Martin County, North Carolina, before locating in Kentucky.

James Sterling and Nancy were the parents of Sarah, John Matthew, L. Berry, James Thomas and Rufus William Rogers. The four Rogers brothers moved from Graves County, Kentucky, to Greene County, Arkansas, in the late 1800s. Three stayed and raised families in and around Paragould, and the fourth returned to Kentucky.

Rufus William Rogers first married Nettie Jones and after her death, married Sarah Davis. The children were: Nealy, Sally, George Henry, Eddie Newton, Lela Ursery, Lilly, Chester "Buck," Hettie Erma, Rufus Cline, William Matthew, Dewey Washington, Della Vivian, Nettie Etta, Adolphus Gustavius, Lee and Clyde Rogers.

The R.W. Rogers family lived on the old family farm near the present day Brown's Chapel Church.

Most all of this particular branch of the Rogers family are of the Baptist faith. Many were ministers, and one was a high official in the Baptist convention in years past. There is also at least one member of the family currently serving God as a Baptist minister in the state of Arkansas.

R.W. Rogers was a well-known farmer and lived in the Marmaduke area in his later years.

Our Rogers line came to Greene County, Arkansas, from Martin County, North Carolina, through Graves County, Kentucky. In the very early days the family lived in the state of Virginia. Over many years of research, there is even a hint of distant kinship to the famous Will Rogers of Oklahoma.

Information from long ago indicates that the Rogers family operated a brick kiln at Arlington, Kentucky, near Mayfield, before moving to Arkansas.

Rufus W. Rogers died August 1, 1937, in Greene County, Arkansas. He had reached the age of 85.

*Rufus William Rogers, 1852-1937*

**ROGERS** – William Walker and Mary McAda Elkins were married October 3, 1889. In 1893 they moved from Sharp County to Randolph County, and settled in Ravenden Springs. Together they had eight children; two, Violet and Clifford, dying in early childhood. When their oldest daughter (to reach adulthood) was 3 years old, they moved their family to Ravenden Springs. There they spent the next 56 years together, raising their children Virgie, Claude, Verlie, Coda, Vasta and Ivora, as well as often hosting their abundant grandchildren.

*From left: Claud, Virgie, Sara Louiaiana Virlie, Mary Macada, Vasta and Coda William Walker Rogers.*

Walker was a carpenter, and when work was scarce, he ran a concession stand in Ravenden Springs. Both were of Cherokee and English-Irish decent, and had black hair and blue eyes. Walker was a superintendent of the Sunday School at the Methodist Church for 30 years, while Mac was a staunch Baptist.

Mac was a talented seamstress, who made hats and dresses in Ravenden Springs, and many of her grandchildren still cherish her hand crocheted doilies. She also taught Sunday School for 25 years at the Baptist church. A loving couple who cherished their family, Walker and Mac Rogers brought up a fine family who to this day carry on the tradition of love of family and worship, and are sorely missed by those that remember them and those who were born after they passed away; Walker in 1950 and Mac in 1958. They were my great-grandparents, and even though I was born after their passing, I cherish their memory.

**ROONEY** – Ronald Kelley Rooney, along with his wife, Lois and their four children: Ryan, Aaron, Tara and Kevin moved to Paragould in August 1988 when he accepted the position as president and CEO of Arkansas Methodist Hospital. Ron became active in community as well as state affairs having served as president of the Paragould Greene County Chamber of Commerce board, chairman of the Arkansas Hospital Association board, member of the Collins Theatre Foundation board, and member of Paragould Rotary.

In 1998, Ron received the A. Allen Weintraub Award, the highest honor given by the Arkansas Hospital Association. Born August 10, 1944, in Nyack, New York, Ron now calls Paragould his home having built the family house on McDaniel Road which they affectionately refer to as *Merry Acres*.

*Ron and Lois Rooney, 1999*

**ROSS** – Caleb and Alifal Hutcherson Ross migrated from Maryland to Paducah, KY where Thomas Tedford Ross was born in 1825. He married Martha Otey and they were the parents of two children Charles Henry and Susan. Martha died at the young age of 23 and he married Martha's sister, Elizabeth. They were the parents of:

*Thomas Tedford Ross*

1. Warren
2. Frances Orlena
3. Margaret A. Ross.

In 1873 at the age of 48 "T.T." moved his family on a farm two miles north of the settlement of Marmaduke where he farmed for five years.

In 1878 he sold his farm and built the first store in Marmaduke. It was a two-story structure with living quarters on the second floor. The store was located east of where the railroad is now located. The railroad was not surveyed out until 1882. T.T. lived to the ripe old age, for the era, of 75 and was one of the first to be buried in Harvey's Chapel Cemetery.

Charles Henry married Mary Agnes "Aunt Sukie" Stone and they were the parents of:
1. William Thomas
2. Allie
3. Charles Ira.

Charles Henry was a veterinarian and like his father Charles Ira took up the family trade. Both were licensed by the State of Arkansas. William Thomas married Dovie Perry and had five children. Allie married Zack T. Hansbrough and had two children. Charles Ira married Mayme Smith and had three children:
1. Charles Odell
2. Edwin Hale
3. Robert Houston.

Z.T. and Allie Hansbrough had a son that died at the age of two and a daughter Iola. William Thomas and Dovie Ross had three daughters and two sons:
1. Mavernene, died young
2. Agnes
3. Jane
4. W. T. Jr.
5. Wesley H.

*Submitted by Charles Ross*

**ROSS** – Edward Grady Ross (April 26, 1908 Savanna, TN) was the son of John Ross and

Florence Gertrude Hinkle Ross. They moved to White County, AR when he was three years old.

Marion Martel Ross (Dec. 4, 1920) was born to Thurston S. Daniel and Caroline Virginia Reynolds Daniel.

Martel and Ed married on July 29, 1939 in Little Rock, AR.

Our first son, Edward Grady Ross, Jr. was born Sept. 28, 1941 in Dr. Hawkins' hospital, Searcy AR).

We moved to Paragould in Nov. 1941, a few weeks before Pearl Harbor and lived in a large furnished upstairs apartment in the home of Mr. and Mrs. Marvin Reynolds. Later we moved to a furnished house on North Second Street. When I became pregnant with our second son, we moved back to a rented house, unfurnished, on North Second Street.

Our second son, Daniel Franklin Ross, was born Dec. 27, 1944, in the old Dickson Memorial Hospital.

Our youngest son, William Robert Ross was born Nov. 19, 1946, in the Dickson Hospital as well.

On Oct 31., 1948, we moved into our first new home, having to leave some of our possessions outside and they were not bothered.

On July 12, 1952, our only daughter, Cynthia Gwynne, was born in the new Arkansas Methodist Hospital.

On June 6, 1968, our son Edward married Annie Edmonds. They had two sons, Stephen Edward Ross (April 10, 1971 Ironton, MO) and Michael James (Nov. 7, 1974 Little Rock, AR). Later Edward married Linda Mitchell in Little Rock, AR.

Our second son, Daniel married Carol Ann Galloway on June 3, 1967 in Jonesboro, AR. They have two sons: Brian Daniel (Nov. 26, 1974 Jonesboro, AR) and Phillip Andrew (Feb. 28, 1978 Jonesboro, AR).

Our youngest son, William Robert married Mary Margaret Stack on Dec. 27, 1971 in Kennett, MO.

Our only daughter, Cynthia Gwynne married Henry Frank Buehling on Sept. 9, 1978 in Paragould AR at First United Methodist Church. They have one child: Louis Ross Buehling (June 14, 1984, Traverse MI).

We moved to Paragould because my husband had a job waiting for him with the Farm Security Administration. He liked this kind of work as he grew up on a farm and he enjoyed helping the farmers.

After that job, he became supervisor of the G. I. Bill of Rights (education), helping veterans get into college. He put his heart and soul in this work, even tutoring some in college math at our home. His last job, and favorite one, was selling insurance for Ford and Company over about seven counties to farmers, so he was back around farmers again. Russell Ford hired him. Russell and his wife were good friends also.

In 1965, we built our new home at 1500 Linwood Drive where I still live. Husband, father and grandfather died March 4, 1982. Such a sadness for all of us and he is still missed.

**ROSS** – Lewis W. Ross was born in 1855 and died in 1879 at age 24. He is believed to have died in Greene County.

He married Charity Elizabeth Dennis on March 17, 1878, at Greene County. Charity was born on June 13, 1860, at Greene County.

She was the daughter of Robert Dennis, 1818 Tennessee -1867 Greene County, and Elinor Thompson, 1825 Lawrence County, Arkansas Territory-1888 Greene County. Robert came to Arkansas about 1837. He and Elinor were married on August 3, 1840, at Randolph County, Arkansas. They were charter members of Mt. Zion Baptist Church. Charity was the 10th of 12 children born to this union. Robert, Elinor and many of their descendants are buried at Mt. Zion Cemetery.

Lewis W. Ross and Charity E. (Dennis) Ross had one child, Ollie Esther Ross, born April 13, 1879, at Greene County. Ollie Esther married William Robert "Bob" Bowlin on April 12, 1896, at Greene County. They had eight children; all born in Greene County
1. Mary (1897-1898)
2. Sudy Gladys (1898-1991) married Edwin E. Stewart
3. Elsie Lu (1900-1995) married John T. Cochran
4. Edith Marie (1902-1977) married first Francis E. Taylor, married second Lorenzo Goff
5. Orlean (1905-1976) married Clifford Smith
6. Willie Luther "Bill" Bowlin (1908-1966) married Elma Goff
7. Irene (1910-1911)
8. Laura Allene (1912-1996) married Gwyndolyn Dacus.

Ollie Esther died of pneumonia on April 7, 1913, at age 33. Bob married second, Vera White. Ollie, Bob and Vera are buried at Mt Zion.

Charity E. (Dennis) Ross, married James Franklin Newberry, as his second wife on June 22, 1880, at Greene County. They had six children, of whom three died young.

**ROWE** – The Rowes now living in Greene County, AR are descendants of pioneers who migrated from South Carolina to Cass County, GA in the early 1800s and on to Greene County, AR in the 1850s.

The story begins with Joseph and Jamiah Rowe. They were both born in South Carolina but bore their family in Georgia. It is in Georgia they are found on the 1850 Cass County (now Bartow County) Census:

Rowe, Joseph, 48 (about 1802 SC); Jemima, 38 (about 1812 SC); Ann, 18 (about 1832 GA); Jane, 16 (about 1834 GA); James H., 12 (1837 GA); John W., 10 (about 1840 GA); William S., 8 (about 1842 GA); Sena (f), 6 (about 1844 GA); David, 4 (about 1846 GA); Martha, 1(about 1849 GA).

Around 1853, Joseph and Jamiah had one more child, Rosey. Between 1853 and 1860 Joseph moved the family west. They settled in northeast Arkansas along Crowley's Ridge in Cache Township of Greene County. It is not known exactly when Joseph and Jamiah arrived in Greene County with their nine kids but the first record found of the family in Arkansas is the 1860 Greene County population census.

In 1860, Joseph and Jamiah's farm was valued at $1000 and their personal property at $1000. This was a tremendous sum of money in 1860.

The Rowes had at least nine children. All nine were born in Georgia and all nine migrated west with their parents. By the 1870 census, all but one girl, Martha, had left the household. She and Joseph lived alone as Jamiah had probably passed on by 1870. Joseph was gone by the 1880 census.

The lineage before 1850 has not been proven. It is thought Joseph may have been in Kershaw County, SC in 1840 and possibly in Early County, GA in 1830.

Joseph and Jamiah's third child, James, is listed as a 12 year old on the 1850 Cass County, GA Census. Around 1860, James married Rebecca and by the 1870 Greene County AR Census, they had two sons, Joseph N. and James H. (1863 AR). The 1880 Greene County Census listed James with his second wife, Martha.

The Rowe descendants that live in Greene County, AR today are mostly descended from James and Rebecca's second son James H. In 1886, James H. married Beulah Muse and in 1895, he married Clara Morrow.
*Submitted by Hank Garner*

**ROWE** – Robert Lee Rowe, was born April 7, 1893, in Randolph County, Arkansas, the son of Gilbert Rowe and Sarah Newberry. The Rowe (an anglicized spelling of the German Routh or Rough) came to Arkansas from Catawba County, North Carolina, after a short stay in Bollinger County, Missouri. Robert married Cleo Casey on September 25, 1915, in Light. The family originally lived in the "Cache Bottoms" near Light but moved to Center Hill about 1933. Bob Rowe worked as a timber purchaser as a young man and later worked for the State Department of Revenue. He died on October 1, 1946, at the age of 53 and is buried in Center Hill Cemetery.

*Robert Lee Rowe, Cleo Casey Rowe and son Robert Wayne Rowe.*

Cleo Casey, daughter of Sidney Albert Johnston Casey and Margaret Elizabeth Creel, was born November 2, 1897, in Greene County. She always told grandchildren that her birthplace was "a sharecropper's shack on a sand hill in Light, Arkansas." Both her paternal grandfather (Hiram Casey) and maternal grandfather (Bill Creel) were Confederate veterans. She grew up helping to raise, hoe and pick cotton. She was a lifelong Baptist and member of the Center Hill Baptist Church and later, the East Side Baptist Church of Paragould. She was loyal "yellow dog Democrat," a trait shared by many of her descendants. She died April 24, 1984, in Paragould.

Robert and Cleo Rowe had the following children: Helen Rowe was born September 1, 1917, and is a current resident of Paragould. Sidney Rowe was born January 21, 1921. Cyrus Lee Rowe was born on October 7, 1922. Both brothers joined the Navy at the outset of World War II and died March 1, 1942, in the sinking of the *U.S.S. Pecos* in the Pacific Ocean. Bernita Rowe was born January 8, 1925, and married R.C. Rogers and is a current resident of Greene County. Their children are Carey, Patrick and Kathleen. Robert Wayne Rowe was born on January 17, 1938, and currently resides in Texas. He is the father of Lilah and Lee Rowe.

**ROWLAND** – Bill Gene Rowland (May 4, 1930 Beech Grove, AR) attended the Beech Grove High School and after leaving school enlisted in the U. S. Army on Nov 28, 1949. He received his basic and advanced infantry training at Fort Riley, KS.

Upon completion of his infantry training, in March 1950, Bill was stationed on the northern Japanese island of Hokkaido, arriving there on May 11, 1950. He was assigned to Company I, 3rd Battalion, 31st Infantry Regiment; the regiment had never served in the Continental United States, always being stationed in the Far East.

Less than a month after his arrival in Japan, the Communist North Koreans crossed the 38th parallel and invaded South Korea.

Bill's unit landed at Inchon, Korea, on D-day plus one, as a part of General MacArthur's historic invasion to cut off the communist forces in the south. His unit fought the communist forces, forcing them across the Yalu River into communist Manchuria.

Forbidden to cross into Manchuria to pursue the enemy, his unit dug in along the east side of a place called the Chosin Reservoir.

Then, on Nov 27, 1950, the Communist Chinese hoards crossed the Yalu River and attacked the defending U. S. forces. After being under attack for virtually 80 straight hours by waves of Chinese forces, the U. S. forces were staggering with mental and physical fatigue, the results of constant attacks, sub-zero weather and a shortage of supplies. At dawn, Dec 1, 1950, the U. S. forces were ordered to attempt a break out to the south, to escape the encircling Chinese troops. After reaching safety on Dec 12, 1950, of the original 190 members of Bill's company, only 11 were still walking, Bill was one of the 11.

For his actions during the Battle of Chosin Reservoir, 20-year-old Sgt. Bill Rowland was awarded the Silver Star, on Christmas Eve 1950, personally by Major General Almond, the 10th Corps Commanding General.

In addition, during the Communist Chinese forces spring offensive campaign, in June 1951, Bill's platoon, he being the platoon sergeant, was committed to attack and secure commanding terrain stubbornly defended by a numerically superior hostile force emplaced in well-fortified positions near Hwach'on-Myon, Korea. After Bill's platoon took their initial objective, the platoon was ordered to continue the advance. After advancing half way toward the final objective the Communist Chinese forces counter attacked, en mass. During this attack Bill sustained a wound by small arms fire. As a result of the wound he was awarded the Purple Heart.

Bill was honorably discharged from the U. S. Army on Aug 30, 1956. Returning to Greene County, Bill married Mary Elizabeth Hester. They have two children: Mark and Elaine. He is retired from Yellow Freight Transportation Company.
*Submitted by Daniel A. Hester*

**RUDI** – Albert Rudi and Dorothy McPherson were married Feb 5, 1956 at the Morning Star Methodist Church near Paragould in Greene County.

We have two children Michael "Mike" and Deborah (Rudi) Ness. Mike is married to the former Cyndi Foster and they have one son Dustin Rudi that attends Greene County Tech. Debbie is married to Norman Ness and have two sons and one daughter: Joe, James and Jeannie Ness. Joe Ness is married to the former Angie Mock. James and Jeanine attend Greene County Tech.

*L-R: Debbie, Dorothy, Albert and Mike Rudi*

Albert is the son of Karl and Lydia Rudi who was born and raised Germany. They came to America and to Greene County in the 1920s and were married in the St. John's Lutheran Church in Lafe, AR.

Albert is the middle son of five children, Erna Rudi, Henry Rudi, Albert Rudi, Karl Rudi and Robert Rudi. He was raised on a farm. He attended Morning Star, Light, and Lakeside and graduated from Greene CountyTech High School in 1949 and lived in the Morning Star Community throughout his education. In 1952 Albert entered the U. S. Army and was stationed in Anchorage, AK. After serving two years he was discharged in 1954.

After that he stated working for Breznik Motor Company, a Studebaker Dealer. In later years it was the Chrysler dealership. He worked for them 22 years with several different owners.

Dorothy is the daughter of Wallace and Reba Powell McPherson, who came to Greene County in 1938. The middle daughter of five children, Hester Wooldridge, Arlon McPherson, Dorothy Rudi, Oather and Delmer Ray. Dorothy was raised on a farm and graduated from Greene County Tech High School in 1953. She was an at home mom until 1971 when she stared working at L. A. Darling Store Fixtures.

On Oct 1, 1976, Albert, Dorothy and Mike opened the family owned business, "Rudi's Auto Repair" on Ward Lane, just south of the Greene County Fairgrounds. In 1981 Mike added a 24-hour wrecker service to the business. Thanks to all of our good customers we have had a very successful business for 24 years that is now continuing with Mike running the auto repair and wrecker service and his son Dustin hopes to continue the business in his future.
*Submitted by Albert Rudi*

**RUSSELL** – Jefferson J. Russell (1825 KY) married Betsy Jane (1825 KY) and in 1850 Jefferson and Betsy were living in Hopkins County, KY and their children were:
1. John J.C.Russell (1846)
2. Ann Mary (1849)

Nancy Russell 45 years of age was also living with them and I believe Nancy is Jefferson's mother.

In 1860 census: J.J. Russell 36yrs. is a farmer. E. J. "Betsy Jane" Russell, 35, John C. 14, Ann Mary 11, Joseph (James?) 6 and William M. 11 months old.

In 1867 Ann Mary Russell eloped with William F. Simpson. They settled down and promptly started their own family.

The Civil War had wiped out all the southern families and the Russell and the Simpson families had read about the inexpensive good land west of the Mississippi River. It was in Arkansas. Well, in covered wagons they all left Kentucky and came to Greene County, AR around 1880.

Shortly after arriving on Dec 27, 1883, William M. Russell married Avery "Ava" Ann McHaney, daughter of Lafayette and Nancy C. McHaney. In 1900 William M. and Avery Russell were living in Spring Grove Township and their children were:
1. Cleveland (1885)
2. Ira Titus (1887)
3. James L. (1890)
4. Zena L. (1892)
5. Fanny M. (1896)
6. Carlis (a son) (1898).

Ira T. Russell married Jessie Little, daughter of James H. and Addie McIntosh Little. Their children are:
1. Bert
2. Sherrell
3. Robert

Bert was a resident of Paragould.
William M. Russell died in 1938 and was buried at the Center Hill Cemetery and his wife, Avery Ann died in 1944 and was buried at the same place.

Ira T. and Jessie Russell operated a farm near Shiloh Church for many years. Ira T. died in 1966 and was buried at the center Hill Cemetery. Jessie died in 1976 and was buried at the same place.
*Submitted by Evelyn Euritha Wagner*

**RUSSELL** – T. C. "Hub"Russell (Dec 8, 1884 near Gainesville-March 24, 1968) married Minnie Gooch (Nov 5, 1887-Jan 14, 1964).

His grandfather, Jefferson J. Russell was a justice of the peace in Gainesville where he maintained an office. His father was William M. Russell and his mother was Avery "Ava" Ann McHaney. T. C. Russell lived in Paragould for 30 years, although at various times had lived in other parts of the United States. He owned B & B Cleaners and until later years was actively engaged in business.

Mr. Russell was a dapper and charming man and up until the last months before his death, he was faithful in attending Historical Society meetings. He was always willing to talk about early days at Gainesville when it was a thriving town. Although only a child of seven, he recalled vividly the fire that nearly destroyed Gainesville in 1891 and wrote his recollection of the event for the *Quarterly* and was helpful in creating the map of Old Gainesville which was published in one of the early issues of the *Quarterly*.

One of the last times he attended a Historical Society meeting, he spoke sadly of a visit he had made to the site of Old Gainesville two years ago and said that the site of his hometown was only a series of gullies and one might find a few nails or a fragment or two of crockery to mark the location.
*Submitted by Evelyn Euritha Wagner*

**RUSSELL** – T. C. Russell's account of the fire that nearly destroyed Gainesville.

The original business section of old Gainesville was almost entirely destroyed by fire about 1891, recalled t. C. Russell of Paragould.

As a boy of seven, Mr. Russell, lived with his parents on a farm about a mile south of Gainesville. He saw the whole conflagration from the first flame until the business section was almost entirely destroyed.

It was a cold fall morning in either the year 1890 or 1891 and Russell was on his way to school, which was located in the town of Gainesville. He was accompanied by his father William M. Russell and his Grandfather Jefferson J. Russell. So good is his memory, he remembers that both men were riding grey horses.

The little boy was riding behind his father on that particular day. Usually, he recalls, he made the trip each day to school riding behind his grandfather who was justice of the peace and went to his office every day. The grandfather would wait until school was out and give the small grandson a ride home.

On this day, Mr. Russell's father had accompanied the older man on a business errand in town. Just as the party crossed the bridge over the stream at the southern edge of the town, they saw flames shoot through the roof of the post office. Will Russell immediately cried "Fire," to rouse the citizens, for it was still before business hours.

The men sent the small boy on to school and they raced toward the center of the town to assist in fighting the flames. No one came to school that day and from the school ground he watched the flames progress down Main Street whipped by a chilly wind. The men had only pumps and buckets to fight the fire and when it had advanced to the end of the block, the wind suddenly changed and carried the flames to the building across the street. It was noon before the flames were brought under control and only two stores had been saved, Dick Jackson's Store and the Frank Scott Mercantile Company.

It was revealed that an overheated stove had started the fire in the post office that had spread to the whole business section. Postmaster Webb had gone down to his office in the early morning started a fire in the stove, so the place would be warm by opening time, and then returned home for breakfast.

T. C. Russell told this account to Myrl Rhine Mueller, writer and editor of *"A History of Greene County Arkansas"*. Myrl Rhine Mueller has since died and the book is out of print.

*Submitted by Evelyn Euritha Wagner, great great granddaughter of Jefferson J. Russell*

**RUTLEDGE** – James M. "Jim" Rutledge was born April 28, 1826, in Rutherford County, Tennessee. He was the son of David and Angeline Williamson Rutledge. He moved with his family to Gibson County, Tennessee, around 1830. He was one of 15 children (13 lived to adulthood) born to his parents.

Jim Rutledge married Mary Ann Taylor, daughter of James and Mary Mullins Taylor, in Gibson County, Tennessee, August 13, 1851. Jim and Mary Ann were the parents of nine children born between 1853 and 1870.

On May 30, 1861, in Jackson, Tennessee, Jim Rutledge volunteered for duty with Company I, 12th Regiment, Tennessee Volunteers for service in the War Between the States. Upon his discharge he returned to his family in Gibson County, Tennessee. He remained there running his family farm until around 1890 when he and his wife, Mary Ann, moved westward to Greene County, Arkansas.

He had a brother, Robert Marion "Bob" Rutledge who had moved to Greene County with his wife Tabitha several years earlier. Several of Jim's and Mary Ann's children also relocated to Greene County near the same time.

Mary Ann Taylor Rutledge died September 21, 1898, and James M. "Jim" Rutledge died May 24, 1904, in Greene County, Arkansas. They are buried in Providence Cemetery in Greene County.

**RUTLEDGE** – Robert Marion "Bob" Rutledge, was born March 12, 1835, in Gibson County, Tennessee. He was one of 15 children born to David and Angeline Williamson Rutledge. The family moved from Rutherford County, Tennessee, to Gibson County, Tennessee, after the 1840 census. Angelines's brother Beverly Williamson had settled there in 1839.

*Robert M. and Tabitha J. Thetford Rutledge*

Bob married Tabitha Jane Thetford January 28, 1858. Born January 1, 1842, she was the daughter of William and Mary "Polly" Williams Thetford. It is believed that they moved to Greene County, Arkansas, in the early 1860s. From 1862 until 1864 he served in Company "H," Fifth Regiment, Infantry of Arkansas of the Confederate Army. His wife Tabitha and his brother David's wife Martha shared a home during the war.

Tabitha and Bob's 11 children: David E., married Emma L. VanArdsdale; William Robert lived only 4 months; Elizabeth died at age 16; John Henry married Lilly Wright and Lucinda Ambrosia Hancock Blalock; George Washington married Mary J. Haislip and Mary Butler; Thomas M. died age 8; Mary Angeline married Reverend J.D.J. Faulkner; Augusta Virginia married Arthur H. Livesay; Fannie Belle married John E. Butler; Willis T. married Myrtle Livesay; and Prudence who only lived one year. The 1910 Greene County census shows that six of their children were deceased.

Her parents and Mary's sister Jennie lived in a log cabin that was the former Faulkner home. It had been moved nearby when a new one was built for J.D.J. and Mary.

Bob's bother David returned to Tennessee. A brother James moved to Greene County after 1870. All of Tabitha's siblings settled in Greene County. Her mother was there by 1880.

Descendents of Bob and Tabitha remember that in their last years Grandma was blind and Grandpa was deaf. "They were a loving couple that was married 53 years." They were my great-great-grandparents.

She died December 10, 1911. He died February 20, 1912, just three months after her death. They are buried in Hartsoe Cemetery near Marmaduke.

**RYAN** – My great-great grandfather, W. Z. Ryan was born 1818 in Mississippi and sometime later moved his family to Phillips County, AR. I know they were there in 1850, but could not determine when they actually moved from Mississippi to Arkansas. Obviously, they crossed the Mississippi into Arkansas somewhere around Helena. But I am sure my great grandfather G. W.'s (1848) birthplace was Arkansas.

*A group of people standing on the porch of Ryan Brothers Hotel, later known as Cole's Hotel on East Main. Mary Ida Ryan on the right rubbing her head.*

By 1860 the Ryan family had moved to Greene County and settled in Salem Township (the Walcott area). My great grandfather, George W. married his wife Mary in 1870. I am sure that is why my mother was named Mary. My grandfather named her after his mother. My grandfather, W. G. "Uncle Bud" Ryan was born in 1875 and his brother W. David Ryan "Uncle Warren" was born in 1878. My favorite uncle, John Alonzo "Uncle Lon" was born on Christmas day in 1882. There were two other siblings that I don't remember: Ader C., a sister, born in 1880 and James Edward born in 1886.

My grandfather married my grandmother, Kate Thornton of Harrisburg on March 10, 1910. They had two children: Mary Ida Ryan, my mother and Woodrow Wilson Ryan. I don't know exactly when they moved to Paragould, but he established and operated several restaurants in the 20s, 30s 40s and 50s, maybe even earlier that the 20s. Older citizens probably remember his location at 125 W. Court Street, later to be Bill Corder's Grocery store and Ima's Fashions in the 60s.

But I can remember other locations as a very young kid, one being on Second Street across from what used to be Easy Pay Tire Store. Max Brengard used the same building when he put in a tire retreading manufacturing operation. He also had a restaurant on Highland Street. I can remember going into that restaurant when I was four or five and talking to one of my favorite friends, Mr. W. J. Beard. My mother used to sing on his radio station, KBTM. Mr. Beard would eat in our restaurant because he knew my granddad and they were probably close to the same age. My grandfather also operated a grocery store for a short time on Hunt Street between Pruett and Second Streets.

*Right: My mother, Mary Ida Ryan with a friend in front of my granddad's restaurant on W. Court Street in the early 30s.*

My mother married Maurice H. King in Jan 1945. My Uncle Woodrow married Alma McNeil, daughter of Mr. and Mrs. Hal McNeil, a short time later. They had six children, four daughters and two sons. One son, William G. died one day after birth. The other, William Haley, died in July of 1969. My mother had only one child.

My grandfather, his brothers, except Uncle Warren who is buried in Linwood Cemetery, his sister and his two children are buried in Mt. Zion Cemetery.

Most people will always remember my grandfather as a restaurant owner. But he was also a very generous man. He made it and gave it away. One example was published in the Greene County Historical Society *Quarterly*. He provided a free chicken dinner to everyone who was 75 years or older. That group included 137 citizens who took advantage of his generosity. The story was published in the May 1, 1930 edition of the *Daily Press*. My mother registered each guest and those names also appeared in the *Quarterly*.

I appreciate the contribution and hard work of my very dear friend, Francis Bland, another very generous man, who did all of the research on the Ryan family. A book should be written about him and all he has done and given to the people of Greene County, especially the youth. His help and effort allowed me to write this brief history of my family coming to Arkansas and Greene County.

*Submitted by Buddy King*

**SANDERS** – Douglas Sanders (Jan 11, 1860) was the son of Lindsey Westwood Sanders and Sarah Francis (McGuire) Sanders, who moved to Greene County in 1878 from McNairy County, TN. They bought farmland in the Oak Grove Community. Douglas had two sisters, Sarah and Leona, four brothers Joel Alfred, William, Commodore Perry and Ulysses.

Douglas married Cora Minnis on Dec 12, 1892 in Greene County. They had three children: Fannie, who died young, Lindsey/Linsey (Oct.1895) and Thomas Bell (May 31, 1898). Cora left Douglas and he and their boys moved home with his parents. His parents died between 1904 and 1906 and are buried at the New Friendship Cemetery, but without a marker.

In 1907 Douglas married Kate Wallace from Pennsylvania. They farmed the home place until their death. He died on Feb. 24, 1934. Kate died Feb. 1943. Lindsey and Thomas Bell survived them.

Lindsey never married and died about 1957-1958.l He was a wanderer and did not keep in close touch with his family. The family was later informed that he was very ill in the Paragould Hospital during this time. He was never heard from again.

Thomas Bell Sanders married Jennie Martha Sheppard in 1932. They had one son, Lovoy Bell (Jan 23, 1936). They purchased additional land on the north side of the original farm. They attended church at the New Friendship Baptist Church. Thomas Bell died Feb 15, 1943, two weeks after his stepmother. His death was caused from being kicked in the stomach by a young colt. He was buried at the New Friendship Cemetery. Jennie was ill with double pneumonia and Lovoy was only seven years old at the time of Bell's sudden death. She continued to farm by hiring a relative to share the work.

Jennie died in 1978 and was buried at the New Friendship Cemetery beside her husband Bell. She and Lovoy were members of the Church of Christ, attending at Gainesville, Second and Walnut and Seventh and Mueller churches.

On Sept 6, 1959 Lovoy married his next-door neighbor, Erie Cook. After a short residence in Flint, MI they returned to Oak Grove. Lovoy began farming the land in 1961. They also purchased additional land on the south and west sides of the farm from Erie's parents. They have one son, Terry Robert Sanders (July 16, 1960). Lovoy loves woodworking and has built several pieces of furniture, but he is most famous for his beautiful grandfather clocks.

Terry married Debra Ann Hollis of Paragould on June 6, 1981. They have three children: Chad Matthew (Oct 4, 1985), Todd Andrew (Dec 2, 1988) and Megan Rebecca (July 31, 1993). Terry and his family live in Oak Grove Heights on land that joins the Sanders' farm that he purchased from his grandfather Cook.

Lovoy and Erie and Terry and his family are members of the Center Hill church of Christ where Terry serves as a deacon. The children attend Crowley's Ridge Academy. Terry and Debra are graduates of the Academy and Terry is currently serving on the Academy board.

*Submitted by Lovoy Sanders*

**SANDERS** – Though born in Mt. Olive, IL, Fred and Faye Sanders lived the majority of their married life in Greene County, AR and reared their family there. Fred Sherman Sanders (Jan 8, 1875) and Minta "Minnie" Faye Sisk (March 24, 1875) were married Sept 16, 1896 in Gallatin County, IL. Two sons, Fern Haward and Herbert Charles and a daughter, Lucy Adeline, were born in IL. They then moved to southern Missouri where two more daughters, Lena Clara and Lila Belle, were born. The family settled in Greene County in the Cotton Belt community in about 1911-12. There, their last two daughters, Hattie Este Lee and Naomi Faye were born.

A farm family, the Sanders relocated to the Friendship community in 1928 and later settled in the Unity community. It was a custom among neighbors to gather to assist each other with lumber cutting, hog killing and sorghum making. The Sanders attended Baptist churches during their more than a half century as residents of Greene County.

The oldest son, Fern Sanders (1897-1983) married Lucy Green in 1922 and lived in Friendship before moving to Washington State and later returned to farm in Arkansas. They had three children.

Herbert Sanders (1900-1983) wed Florence Brecher and farmed in the Cotton Belt community before moving to California. They reared six children. Herbert was a veteran of WWI.

Lucy Sanders (1902-1962) married Albert Campbell and they had five children. They too had farmed but later owned a grocery and feed store on North Pruett Street in Paragould during the 1940s.

Lena Sanders (1905-1946) married Charles "Pat" Roy in 1923 and had six children. They lived in Cotton Belt, but moved to Paragould where Pat was a meat cutter. After Lena's death Pat and the children continued to live in Paragould, but Pat later moved to Pekin, IL and remarried.

Lila Sanders (1909) married Benonia Rutledge in 1925 and they became the parents of four children. They too lived in Cotton Belt before moving to California, later returning to Greene County to the Fairview community. "B" did construction and carpentry.

*Fred and Faye Sanders*

Este Lee Sanders (1912-1995) and Orval Hawley married in 1929. They settled in Halliday near Orval's parents and reared four children. They farmed several acres, primarily cotton. As the children became adults and married, they built homes on the property where some still live.

Naomi Sanders (1915) married Bennie Brashears in 1932. They lived in Paragould where Bennie was a barber and had three children. Bennie died in 1951 and Naomi married Homer Pratt whose family had strong ties in Greene County.

Fred Sanders retired from farming in the early 1940s and bought a house on East Lake Street in Paragould where Fred and Faye spent their latter years.

Faye died on Nov 5, 1966 at age 91 and Fred followed a few months later on March 4, 1967 at age 92. They are buried at Linwood Cemetery in Paragould.

The Sanders Family holds a bi-annual reunion.

*Submitted by Naomi (Sanders) Pratt*

**SCHEER** – August Henry and his wife, the former Louise Sudmeyer, were natives of Washington, MO. They first moved to Kansas then Russellville, AR, then to Lafe in the 1880s. They traveled in a covered wagon with their two oldest sons, August F. and Henry, herding their cattle. They were interested in settling near a Lutheran Church and school. Many Germans had already settled near Lafe and the land was very cheap. Mr. Scheer purchased quite a large tract of land there, most of it from Peter Mueller,

father of "Lafe" Mueller. In addition to August F. and Henry, the Scheers had four other sons:
1. Edward "Ed"
2. Alfred
3. Oscar
4. Ben

August F. Scheer married Mary Kapplemann and had three children:
1. Leona, married Martin Panhorst
2. Deno married Edna
3. Martin married Willodean

Henry Scheer married Annie Dammann, their children included:
1. Henry August
2. Emil died as a young man
3. Martha
4. Clarence married Lena Gerdes
5. Dora married Carl Meyers
6. Louis married Mildred McAbee
7. Elmer died young

Edward Scheer married August Doerful in 1910. Their children included:
1. Clara married Harold Braun
2. Louis Paul married Glenda Gale
3. Alice married Rual Horton
4. Gladys married Joe Bill

Alfred Scheer married Esther Tritch and moved to California. Their children included:
1. Louise
2. Melvin
3. Earl
4. Willis
5. Allen
6. Leroy.

Oscar Scheer married Agnes Lueker. They were the parents of Ralph, who married Gladys Panhorst and Ray, who married Mona Watson.

Ben Scheer married Lydia Spitzer. Their children included:
1. Robert Henry
2. Pauline married Jimmy Tritch
3. Marvin
4. Betty married Bob Svoboda.

**SCHISLER** – Henry Richard Schisler (1849-1911) was born near Lorada, Arkansas. He married Mary Emily Dollar (1815-1873). Henry was a prominent businessman who owned and operated several stores and mills (commissary, grist mill, saw mill, and a casket factory) in South Greene County. He built a stately home which is still standing in Greene County west of Frierson water-shed Lake. The property where the lake is located at one time belonged to the Schisler family. The family has a photo where a photographer was taking the family photograph in front of the old home. Henry refused to have his picture taken, so the photographer lined the family where it would include Henry sitting in his rocking chair on the front porch.

Walter A. Schisler (1869-1962), son of Henry and Emily, married Dovie Nutt (1872-1952), February 11, 1891. The following children were born: Laura Schisler Smith, Mary Lee Schisler Bauers, George E. Schisler, Flora (Floy) Schisler Lindley, and Quincy A. Schisler. Walter was a travelling salesman and in the later years of his life operated a grocery store in Jonesboro, Arkansas. The store building is still standing on the corner of Burke Street and Culberhouse Street. When Walter and Dovie lived near Lorado, Dovie told a humorous story concerning one of their neighbors who was moving. When they passed the Schisler home with their belongings in a wagon, the lady waved to Dovie and said "Good bye good ole Arkansas, we are moving to Lake City." Walter and Dovie were devoted Christians and long time members of Huntington Avenue Methodist Church now known as the Cornerstone Methodist Church.

George E. Schisler (1901-1997), older son of Walter and Dovie, married Ruth O. Dacus (1902-1992), daughter of Andrew Jackson and Purcas Dacus, on June 20, 1923. George and Ruth were married 69 years. George would always tell you the following story as to when he fell in love with Ruth. Ruth was teaching a Sunday School class for the young adults at the Lorado Baptist Church, Lorado, Arkansas, and he was visiting the class. When Ruth finished the Bible story, she asked if there were any comments. George stated "He had learned the first lesson." Ruth asked "What was that?" He said "I have fallen in love with the teacher." George said "she pulled her class book in front of her face to hid her blushing face." Both George and Ruth were born near Lorado. They had four children: E. Randall Schisler, M. Melendia Schisler Bennett, A. Byron Schisler, and Addie Lee Schisler Johnson.

**SCHREIT** – Frank Joseph Schreit, was born September 2, 1896, in St. Louis, Missouri. His parents were Frank George Srajt, an organ builder, and Bertha Svaloda Srajt, a homemaker, both having families who immigrated to the United States from Austria in the 1800s. The Slavic spelling of the surname Srajt, was later changed to the Germanic spelling, Schreit, for convenience in spelling and pronunciation. Frankie, as he came to be called, grew up in a very strong Slavic family orientated neighborhood, where his leisure hours were spent at the nearby lodge. There, he learned to box, play the mandolin and share many meaningful times with family and friends. He had an older sister Josie, and a younger brother William.

In 1911, at the age of 14, Frankie found summer employment at the Ely and Walker Dry Goods Company, working as a doorman and errand boy. He became so interested in manufacturing that he decided, with his parents approval, to work full time and complete his education at night school. At that time he received $6.00 a week for 49 and one-half hours of work.

By 1918, he had been promoted to foreman of the cutting room. His career was interrupted for a short time by World War I, when he entered military service, and served as a corporal in the U.S. Army. After he was honorable discharged in December 1918, he returned to St. Louis where he resumed a friendship he had shared with Anna Haba, a salesperson and model for the Famous and Barr Company. Her family and relatives arrived in the United States from Vizovice, Moravia in the early 1900s. Together, Frank and Anna enjoyed picnics, swimming, music, dancing and playing card games. They were married April 28, 1919, and became the parents of two children, Jane born in 1921 and Frank Joseph born in 1924, while living in St. Louis.

In 1924, Frank and his family moved to Festus, Missouri, where he was named manager of the local Ely and Walker plant. He oversaw the manufacturing of shirts, robes, and other apparel. During his 13 years in Festus, Frank continued to enjoy fishing, camping and bowling. A daughter, Patricia, was born in 1933.

Frank Joseph Schreit, age 60, in 1956. Manager of Ely and Walker Dry Goods Company in Paragould.

Opening of Ely and Walker Dry Good Company in Paragould, Arkansas. Frank J. Schreit, manager is shown with parents Mr. and Mrs. George Srajt, St. Louis, Missouri.

During this time in Paragould, Arkansas, the local civic leader became aware of the need for gainful employment for its women. Through the hard work of Maurice Block, Ray Meriwether, Russell Mack and William Kirsch, a contract was secured with the Ely and Walker Corporation to bring the first modern, textile manufacturing industry to Paragould and Greene County. Building the plant was a community project from start to finish. With the help of the Chamber of Commerce and the two local railroads, construction on the 270 x 300 feet facility was started in December 1936, and completed in August 1937, at a cost of $82,000. Frank Schreit was selected by Ely and Walker to be the first plant manager, and the family moved into their new home on the corner of Sixth and Poplar Street. Before the machinery was installed, two benefit dances were held in the building to allow the community to see the results of their efforts.

The Ely and Walker Dry Good Company, East Park Street Paragould, Arkansas, the first textile manufacturing plant to be built in Greene County.

Under Schreit's management the plant prospered with 400 employees, 90 percent of whom were women. Normal operations were stopped during World War II when "Uncle Sam" took over as boss. The entire plant was converted to make Army and Navy shirts. Over 19 government contracts were fulfilled despite trying to maintain a steady work force depleted by the loss of women employees leaving to join their husbands in service, or to stay home with children. A vacant field next to the plant was divided into plots for use by any employee who wanted to plant a Victory garden.

Frank Schreit saw many changes in the shirt manufacturing industry during his 55 years with the company including specialization, better and faster sewing techniques, and the creation of permanent press fabrics. His strong work ethic, honesty, and family devotion earned him the nickname of "Pop," and he was called that by all his friends. He served as chairman of the Chamber of Commerce Industrial Committee, and was a member, for many years, of the Rotary Club, Greene County Wildlife Club, Ducks Unlimited, and the First United Methodist Church. He became an avid duck hunter and St. Louis Cardinal baseball fan.

His retirement in 1966 gave him time to do some extensive traveling with his wife Anna. He especially enjoyed the company of his children; Jane and John Willis McKenzie, Frank and Mary Ann Atkins Schreit of Paragould, and Pat and Joe Tannehill of Panama City, Florida.

Paragould's Ely and Walker plant continued to operate, under three different owners until 1985, when it was permanently closed. The building is presently occupied by the Emerson Electric Company, headquartered in St. Louis, Missouri.

After a lengthy illness, Frank "Pop" Schreit died on December 27, 1967, in Paragould, and was buried in the Memorial Gardens Cemetery. He was survived by his wife Anna who died in 1997 at the age of 98.

**SCHUESSLER/SCHISLER** – Nicholaus Schuessler/Schisler (1811-1863) was born in Hersfeld, Hesse, Germany, became an artisan tanner in his youth, left the port of Bremerhaven on August 25, 1837, and arrived in America about one month later. He married Mary Louisa Anderson, born in Tennessee (1818-1881) in 1848. Two children died young, but four sons survived, Henry Richard (1849-1911), James Calvin (1856-1924), John Thomas Humbolt (1859-1890) and William Ranslor (1862-1939).

The original Nicholaus Schisler home place was located about one-half mile northeast of the old "56" school house (school district #56) on 240 acres atop Crowley's Ridge in Greene County. The home site was a pleasant wooded area near a running spring among a grove of birch trees.

Nicholaus carried on his tanning trade from this site. Old family records list his sale of shoe leather in the 1850s to other local pioneers of that community: Lane, Tyler, Bradley, Self and others. Nicholaus formally patented the homestead in 1859 before his death on Christmas day, 1863. (Vol. AR0670.435, Land Ofc. Batesville, July 1, 1859, Doc# 12157.) Craighead County was formed in 1859 from a portion of Greene, Poinsett and Mississippi Counties, placing the Schisler home one-half mile south of the Greene County line in North Central Craighead County. His grave is one of about a dozen in the old original Trinity Cemetery about one-half mile south on a hill behind the home site.

After Nicholaus' death the sons worked hard helping their widowed mother maintain the home place. They farmed, raised garden vegetables, sold chickens and eggs to neighbors. The sons bought better land about three-quarters of a mile further west of the home place down in the "bottoms" where they cleared new ground for large farm crops, orchards and new homes. The three younger sons lived out their lives in the "56" Community and raised large families. Henry went to California about 1870 where he died in Pomona in 1911.

The youngest son, William Ranslor, my grandfather, was highly respected and widely known as "Uncle Ranny" in the "56" Community, nearby Bono and Jonesboro. He married Margaret Omelia Roxanna Risner who was known as "Aunt Roxie." He was active in community, church and school affairs, and deeded land to the school district for the "56" school house which doubled for Methodist church services for many years.

"Ranny" and his brother, James Calvin, married Risner sisters which gave the large families many "double cousins" that promoted a family community closeness. "Ranny" and "Roxie" had nine children: John Quincy, 1885-1967; Willie, died young; William Richard, 1889-1971; Mary Louise, 1891-1920; James Ernest, 1894-1980; Harry Griffin, 1896-1956; Jack, 1898-1989; Sophia Gertrude, 1902-1978; Mattie Lena, 1904-1987.

The youngest, my mother, Mattie Lena, married James Leroy Williams, and I am the eldest of their children. Having lived in the "56" Community in boyhood, I personally knew many of the second generation, and all of the third, therefore I can attest to the accuracy of this family data. All of the above named are now deceased.

**SCHUG** – The Schug Family came from Bamberg, Baveria, Germany. Andrew, the husband of Aunt Annie, came to this country in June 1881, soon after his father's death. His five brothers came to the United States at other times. Uncle Andy, as he was called, said that all each one had when he arrived was a feather pillow, made by their mother and given to them with her blessings, to bring to the new country because she was certain to never see them again. Uncle Andy was buried with his head resting on this same pillow. The Schug boys left behind at least four sisters. The oldest sister named Mary, born before 1850, was never wed. There was a sister Ruth and another sister Elizabeth. The fourth sister was a Catholic nun named M. Maria Schug who lived and worked at the English Institute, Tafelhof Street #3, Nurnberg.

Uncle Andy and his five brothers Andreas Kasper, Pete, Mike, Charles, and John (Johann) made their way to St. Louis, where they worked for a short time. Andreas Kasper lived the remainder of his life in St. Louis. He and his wife, Mary Dupler, had the following children: Irwin, Edward, Lawrine, and Andrew. Andreas Kasper was involved in an accident in 1907, as a result of which he died and is buried in St. Louis. According to the *St. Louis Post Dispatch*, at the time of his death, Andreas lived at 264 Lemay Ferry Road, St. Louis, and died from a concussion to the brain.

Pete Schug, born 1867, moved to Judsonia, Arkansas, and was a successful farmer in truck patching. He married Alice Walters and had one son, Roy Schug, who married Annie I. McDaniel, daughter of Henry and Hattie McDaniel of Schugtown. They had one daughter, Martina Schug. He died in 1925 and was buried in Evergeen Cemetery at Judsonia, Arkansas, which is in White County.

After arriving in the United States in 1886, Charles Schug, born March 16, 1865, also moved to Judsonia, Arkansas, and farmed in truck patching. He and his wife, Mary E. Walters had the following children: Phillip, Charlie George, Mary and Elizabeth. After his death on December 16, 1927, Charles was buried in Evergreen Cemetery at Judsonia, Arkansas.

Mike Schug was born July 5, 1850, and died June 11, 1911. He came to the United States in April 1882. He married Emma Pauline Celensky, who was born June 29, 1867, and died August 4, 1902. They were married April 16, 1887. Their children were: Frank, born February 26, 1889, died August 19, 1891; Andrew, born April 13, 1891, died September 21, 1961; Martha, born 1893; and Lawrence, born 1898, and died 1964. Mike and Emma Pauline Schug, are buried in the Coffman Cemetery five miles southeast of Paragould.

John (Johann) Schug, born about 1866, came to the United States in June 1885. He came to Greene County, Arkansas, and applied for citizenship on October 17, 1889. He shortly thereafter returned to Bamberg, Germany and lived the rest of his life there. He married a woman named Anna and at his death had a daughter 15 years of age, a son 13, and another daughter 8. He died June 24, 1909.

Andrew Schug, born June 5, 1857, died January 13, 1941, entered the United States in June 1881. He married Anna Lee Nixon, daughter of John Nixon and Sarah "Sallie" Robertson, who was a granddaughter of Benjamin Crowley, first settler on Crowley's Ridge. Andy and Anna's children were: Clara, born July 13, 1887, died September 5, 1907; Fritz, born January 26, 1889, died March 4, 1974; Will born February 9, 1891, died July 29, 1893; John, born April 4, 1893, died May 26, 1968; Joe Frank, born April 4, 1896, died January 11, 1897; Infant, born and died November 14, 1897; Wiley Albert, born June 17, 1898, died January 11, 1960; and Selma, born June 15, 1904, died April 25, 1906.

Andrew Schug, the pioneer who gave the Schugtown Community its name, started his career in St. Louis. This job brought him to Paragould in 1883, the year Paragould was chartered and named after two railroad executives, J. W. Paramore and Jay Gould. After arriving in Paragould, Andrew Schug and his partner Fritz Grumb, began the task of cutting white oak timber into stave bolts on a large tract of land. These were hauled by oxen and carts to a stave mill in Paragould where they were made into kegs and shipped to St. Louis.

*Andrew and Anna Schug April 18, 1936, 50th anniversary, three sons standing left to right: Wiley, John and Fritz.*

Being conservative people, as most Europeans, Schug and Grumb hewed the treetops into cross ties and sold them to the railroads. The ties were hauled by oxen to Old Bethel. The round trip required more than a day and Andrew would spend the night at Old Bethel, where he met Anna Lee Nixon, an employee there.

After a short courtship Andrew and Anna Lee were married April 18, 1886, and moved to the St. Francis River bottoms where they lived in one of the crude log structures built by Andrew and his friend, Fritz Grumb. At this time they were pretty much to themselves except for another half-dozen families, a million mosquitoes, and a lot of water. Being industrious, Andrew shortly built a better home and finally a nice home on the Greene-Craighead County line. There they reared four of eight children born to them The old Schugtown Community was one-half mile east of where Schugtown is today on the old Lake Road that turned east on the old Joe Norton farm, south between the three Indian mounds, and on to Lake City. It consisted of the Schug home, grocery store, sawmill, cotton gin, and a Methodist church.

After the cotton gin burned and the Lake City-Paragould Highway was rebuilt to miss old Schugtown, a new gin was built on the new highway. The grocery store and sawmill were moved. The relocation of these facilities put them one-half mile further west of the St. Francis River bottoms which, at that time, came within a quarter of a mile of the Schug home. Boats were tied out there for year-round traveling. As (Fritz, John, and Wiley) the Schug brothers' business expanded, a gin was built three miles south of Schugtown and the three brothers honored their father by giving him the privilege of naming the new community. He called it "Dixie." Also, they gave the land for the new consolidated school system of Dixie. This school was in operation from 1938 until it closed in 1978.

**SCHUG** – Lawrence Schug was born August 6, 1898, in Greene County. The youngest son of Michael and Emma Schug, who were immigrants from Bamburg, Bovaria, with Michael arriving in Greene County in April 1882. Lawrence was orphaned at the age of 9 and continued to live with relatives at Schugtown.

On October 21, 1923, he married Eula McDaniel, daughter of Otho and Vina Nixon McDaniel. They moved to Paragould in 1925 and raised three children: Emma Schug Townsend, Norris Schug and Jane Schug Honen.

Lawrence worked for the Missouri Pacific Railroad for 35 years at the Round House. Eula worked for Faustenia's Dress Shop for 25 years and did alterations at home.

On February 13, 1964, Lawrence died and is buried at Memorial Gardens. Eula died on July 9, 1998, and is buried at Memorial Gardens.

*Lawrence Schug and Eula McDaniel October 21, 1923, on their wedding day.*

**SCHWAMB** – David Nelson Schwamb son of Otto and Roxie Crews Schwamb (Aug 14, 1925 Greene County) lived on a farm between Stanford and Beech Grove in a house his father and grandfather Theodore Karl Schwamb built from timber grown on the farm, and then sawed at the mill across the road, that Theodore ran. He was the youngest of four children, Gerturde, Carlos and Telpher J. Schwamb.

He lived there until his teen years then moved near Paragould finishing high school at Oak Grove in 1942. He then served in the Army until 1946. After being discharged he returned to Paragould for a short time before seeking greener pastures in California. There he met and married Mary Sedessia Baker (July 10, 1924 Grady County, OK) daughter of James William and Nancy Rosetta Bean Baker. To this union five children:

1. Nelson Clifford Schwamb (July 25, 1953) married July 5, 1974 to Shannon Lee Kriste (July 12, 1956). Their children were:
   a. Scott Anthony (Oct 5, 1978) married Virginia McPherson Powers in Oct 1999. Their children:
      I. Trenton Powers (Oct 1998)
      II. Anthony John Schwamb (March 24, 2000).
   b. Christina Lynn Schwamb (April 27, 1981)
2. Michael Allen Schwamb (April 19, 1955) married May 17, 1975 to Kathleen Ann Bise (July 27, 1953). Their children:
   a. Allen Michael Schwamb (June 2, 1978)
   b. Robin Kay Schwamb (April 27, 1981)

3. Danell Marie Schwamb (Feb 13, 1958) married July 16, 1977 to Leslie Allen Love. Divorced. Their son: Joshua Love (Feb 22, 1988)

4. Lorna Kay Schwamb (Jan 23, 1959) married April 8, 1978 to Paul James Field (April 20, 1958). Sons:
 a. Adam David Field (July 28, 1984)
 b. Jason Paul Field (Dec 6, 1987)

5. Melodee Lynn Schwamb (May 10, 1961)

David spent sometime in southern California then settled in Selma, the San Joaquin valley. We worked many years as a troubleman with the Pacific Gas and Electric Company. He and his family are of the Assemblies of God faith, with one son being a minister and the rest of the family very active in its work and mission. They are a very musically talented family.

**SCOTT** – James Sidney Scott, born May 21, 1881, at Fontaine, Greene County, Arkansas, died May 9, 1946; married Mattie Pratt, born February 12, 1879, died June 26, 1954, at Paragould. They are buried at Lorado Baptist Cemetery. Mattie's mother was a widow in the Walnut Corner Community, she died in childbirth, of a son, Virtus Birmingham. Mattie was 2 years older than Sidney when they got married.

Sidney and Mattie lived in and around Fontaine, but Sidney had health problems, and they moved seeking a better climate for Sidney, to Hot Springs, Arkansas, and operated a boarding house for awhile, then moved out to Chickasaw, Oklahoma, then back to Crowley's Ridge, near where Lake Frierson is now located, just across the line from Greene County. Later they moved to a farm three miles northeast of Fontaine and lived there until Sidney died May 9, 1946. Sidney had a heart attack while clearing 80 acres of wood west of his farm. He died in the hospital at Jonesboro. Mattie died in the home of her son James Oliver Scott, at Paragould.

*James Sidney Scott Sr. and Lou Scott.*

3. Leonard Scott, no data on birth date or death date.

4. Sarah Scott, born July 30, 1886, married Andrew Bass, born February 27, 1905; had 11 children. Sidney was a son of Richard Robert Scott, known generally around the Fontaine Community as "Dick" Scott, and his wife Tielitha Easter. "Dick Scott and second wife are buried in the Methodist Cemetery at Lorado, Arkansas.

5. Thomas C. Scott, possibly born as Colonel Cleveland Scott. born January 4, 1889, married Mary E. Simpson; had 12 children.

6. William Scott (possibly named Ransom Beagles Scott), known as "Bill," born January 4, 1891; married October 20, 1912; married Maude Lee Williams, born February 25, 1894; had seven children.

7. Jess Scott, born 1893, died 1907.

8. Benjamin Scott, born September 1, 1904, died April 19, 1963; married Maude Lee Cook, born January 27, 1902; had three children.

9. "Ben" Scott, was a manager for W. C. Sloan Sr. farms at Fontaine, he accumulated a larger acreage in and around Fontaine and was a successful farmer.

Gus Scott, born April 20, 1908; married Mary Bobbit, October 20, 1910; had six children. Gus and Mary owned and operated a general store at Fontaine, in their early life.

Sidney and Mattie Scott's children are: Richard Robert Scott (2nd) born September 8, 1902, died April 17, 1955. Sallie Edith Rhea born April 2, 1906, died January 30, 1998. They are buried at Rest Hill Cemetery, Sherwood, Arkansas, James Oliver Scott, Sophronia Scott Nutt. Richard worked in lumber yards at Jonesboro, Paragould, Nashville and Conway. He retired in 1954. James Oliver and wife Olene, were farmers in the Fontaine area, then in WWII they worked in defense factories in Detroit, Michigan, then moved back to the Paragould area. Gordon Nutt and Sophronia Scott Nutt, were farmers, owned a general store on the road to Jonesboro, then owned and operated nice 1,500 acre farm, and were very successful, between Fontaine and Lorado.

Richard Robert Scott and Sallie's Children are, James Sidney Scott Sr. born September 13, 1924, and Nina Florence Scott Swicegood. James Sidney Scott Sr. married Betty Lou McKeithen at Clarksville, Arkansas, on August 20, 1950. Their Children are: James Sidney Scott Jr. JD., born May 20, 1954, Richard McKeithen Scott, MSCE, born September 29, 1956. Richard is a computer systems engineer with Verio, Inc., at Dallas Texas, Susan Elizabeth Scott Clark, Jr., CS, her husband is, Paul James Clark, Jr., CG born February 28, 1959, one daughter Kathryn Leigh Clark, a second grader, age 7. Paul is a professional real estate appraiser, with an office in North Little Rock, Arkansas. Susan is computer specialist with Arkansas Children's Hospital.

*Richard Robert Scott.*

James Sidney Scott Jr. married first Judith Billingsley R.N., no children. Married second Teresa Maxwell, MD of Jonesboro; one child, James Sidney Scott III, born December 5, 1991. "Sidney" is a second grader. Married third Jane Forsyth Mier Scott, MD, one daughter, Elizabeth Grace Scott, born February 4, 1998. All of Richard Robert Scott's (1st) children lived near Fontaine in Greene County and were farmers, he enjoyed being near his children and grandchildren. Richard Robert Scott, (II), son of Sidney and Mattie Scott, born 1902, worked in retail lumber yards in Jonesboro, Paragould, Nashville and Conway, Arkansas. Richard Robert Scott and wife Sallie E. Rhea Scott, are buried at Rest Hills Cemetery in Sherwood, Arkansas.

James Sidney Scott Sr. owned two lumber yards, in North Little Rock, and Little Rock, later he became a professional real estate appraiser being awarded the professional designations of SRA, SRPA, MAI.

James "Jay" Sidney Scott Jr. J.D. is an attorney, in North Little Rock, and is a major in the Arkansas National Guard. His wife is a pediatrician in practice with Baptist Memorial Hospital in North Little Rock. James Sidney Scott III, age 7, is a second grader at Pike View Elementary School in North Little Rock, Arkansas. Jay and Jane have one daughter, Elizabeth Grace Scott. Jane has two sons, Collier Mier and John Mier

Look for a Scott family record book in the Greene County Public Library, Genealogy Room.

**SCOTT** – Richard Scott, (1st) was born in North Carolina, on June 9, 1791, and died February 14, 1857. His father has been identified as William Scott, whose place of birth and death hasn't been identified. Richard enlisted as soldier in the War of 1812, from Cumberland County, Kentucky. He married Jane Beaty, born October 11, 1796, they married in Overton County, Kentucky, on September 26, 1816. Research shows that Overton County is actually in Tennessee. The boundary line between Kentucky and Tennessee was not finally decided until 1958.

A Johnson County, Missouri, copy of Goodspeed quotes them as saying that Richard Scott's parents were from Scotland and that Jane Beaty was from Irish stock. Richard being a soldier in the War of 1812, he served for six months and then one extra month, his packet is in the National Archives in Washington, D. C.

Richard received two parcels of bounty land, the first in November 1850 and the second on April 16, 1855, in Johnson County, Missouri. When Richard and Jane moved to Rose Hill Community in Johnson County within six months time they purchased 1,200 acres of land. They described the area as having both elk and bear nearby. Both Richard and Jane Scott are buried on their farm in the Rose Hill Community, near Warrensburg, Johnson, Missouri. Three of their children are buried there with them. (Had nine children; five sons and four daughters.)

Their children were:

1. Sarah B. Scott, born November 13, 1817, in Kentucky.

2. Dr. Leonard A. Scott, born Saline County, Missouri, on March 5, 1820, died Grayson County, Texas, on April 7, 1904.

3. Sidney A.S. Scott, born Howard County, Missouri, on September 4, 1823, died in Missouri October 26, 1864. Married first Susan Jackson of near Holden, Missouri, and married second Sophronia Baker, born August 2, 1837, died October 5, 1904. Sidney and Sophronia were married October 23, 1855.

4. Francis Marion Scott, born December 16, 1827, died as a captain in the Confederate Army during the Civil War.

5. Louisa Marian Scott, born August 21, 1830, died March 6, 1891; married first to Nathaniel H. Baker, born in New Jersey about 1823, died 1836. Lousia remarried second William E. Baker, born May 8, 1841. Nathaniel and Louisa were buried in a private burial plot on the Scott Farm at Rose Hill, Johnson County, Missouri.

6. Joseph B. Scott, born September 1, 1833, died of wounds and exposure during the Civil War. It is believed that he wasn't married.

7. William W. Scott, born February 23, 1833. He was hanged after the Civil War by Union sympathizers, to an apple tree at Rose Hill Community, Johnson County, Missouri, buried in private plot on the Scott Farm.

8. Emily J. Scott, born June 5, 1840, Rose Hill, Johnson County, Missouri. Had two children; died in St. Louis, Missouri.

9. Mary Ann Scott, born October 31, 1842; married first to Payne E. Reed; married second Samuel Jackson Reed.

Sidney A.S. Scott, had three children of first marriage and six of second marriage to Sophronia. After Sidney died Sophronia married Ransome Hale Beagles, and they had three children.

Richard Robert Scott, known as "Dick Scott." His middle name was not generally known until his obituary was read as his funeral. (My mother, Sallie E. Rhea Scott, married to Richard Robert Scott, was handed the obituary at the funeral, it was written on a regular paper pad.) Richard was born October 8, 1856, in Johnson County, Missouri. Died April 16, 1939, at Fontaine, Greene County, Arkansas. He married first Tileitha Easter, born January 1, 1856, died September 22, 1898.

Family history relates how Richard, being a 21 year old man in his stepfather's home, left Missouri after having a disagreement with his stepfather, tearing up some furniture. He joined another man, who had a wagon and Richard a team, they started out southward, then wound up working on a railroad dump at Sedgwick, Arkansas, between Hoxie and Jonesboro. One morning Richard woke up, and the team and wagon were gone. Somehow Richard got a job and ran his luck into a general store and cotton gin at Fontaine, Greene County, along with several hundred acres of land. Richard Robert Scott and Tileitha Easter had seven children, and two of the second marriage.

Their children were:

Anna Violet Scott, born November 18, 1878; married December 10, 1896 to Alex Lee born April 4,1870, died September 17, 1949.

Sidney Scott, born May 21, 1881, died May 9, 1946; married Mattie Pratt, born February 12, 1879, died June 26, 1954.

Leonard Scott, died young.

Sarah Scott, born July 30, 1886; married February 27, 1905 to Andrew Bass, born October 3, 1886 at Iris, Arkansas; had 11 children.

Thomas C. Scott, born January 4, 1889, died October 1, 1962; married Mary Elizabeth Simpson, born December 5,1893; 12 children.

William "Bill" Scott, born January 4, 1891, at Lorado, Arkansas; married October 20, 1912, possibly named Colonel Cleveland Scott, lived on a nice farm one and one-half miles northeast of Fontaine, Arkansas, to Maude Lee Williams, born February 25, 1894; had 7 children.

Jess Scott, born 1893, died 1907.

By second marriage Benjamin Richard Scott, September 1, 1902, married Maude Lee Cook, born January 27, 1900.

Gus Scott, born May 20, 1908, married Mary Bobbit, born October 20, 1910.

**SCOTT** – William Dewitt Scott (March 15, 1912 Montgomery County, AR) was the son of Robert Lee Scott and Sarah Virginia Keown. On Nov 22, 1935 Dewitt married Ilene Carrier (Nov 24, 1916 Montgomery County, AR), the daughter of Elbert Milton Carrier and Martha Elizabeth Wilhite.

Martha Wilhite Carrier (March 19, 1896 in Oden, AR- Jan 24, 1996 Paragould, AR) lived the later years of her life in Paragould, AR. She and Bert are buried in Lee County, AR. Their children:
1. Ilene
2. Chester
3. Glenn
4. Roy
5. Wilton Carrier.

Even though they were both born in Montgomery County, Dewitt and Ilene did not meet until after their families moved near Marianna, Lee County, AR, in the late 1920s.

After their marriage, the couple continued to live in the Marianna area until 1958, where Dewitt farmed and operated a sawmill. The family also opened a neighborhood grocery at Holub's Crossing. While living in Lee County, the couple had two children:
1. Donald Dewitt Scott (April 28, 1942)
2. Bettie Ilene (Sept 8, 1944).

*Dewitt and Ilene Scott.*

In the fall of 1958, Dewitt and Ilene bought a section of timber and farmland near Lafe in Greene County, AR. In 1961, they sold this property and purchased Light's Grocery Store on Lake Street and the family moved to Paragould. Dewitt and Ilene continued to operate their grocery until they retired.

In 1963, Donald married Loretta Randles. Their children are:
1. Lora married Rodney McClelland
2. Lisa
3. Leslie married Whitney Edwards

Also in 1963, Bettie married Larry Dowler. Their children:
1. Trent married Jana Stallings
2. Robin married James Norman

William Dewitt Scott died June 22, 1992 and is buried at Memorial Gardens in Paragould. Ilene Carrier Scott continues to make her home in Paragould.

*Submitted by Bettie Dowler*

**SEARS** – Aaron Athel "Otis, wife Sadie Mae Albin, daughters Gladys, Mildred, Irene and Mable" Sears appear in Marmaduke, Arkansas area 1920. They had moved from Crawford County, Missouri, where Otis was working as a miner of both coal and "hard rock."

Otis Sears was born March 11, 1883, Illinois and died June 10, 1967, Florida; married June 17, 1905, in Columbus, Kansas, Sadie Mae Albin born February 25, 1889, Kansas and died April 30, 1971, Florida, daughter of William and Susan Baker Albin. This marriage produced five children, the above four daughters and a son William Charles who died March 25, 1911, and is buried at Davisville, Missouri, all children born Missouri.

*Aaron A. Sears family, circa 1930. Front from left: Aaron A., Sadie Mae and Lela Juanita. Back from left: Clara Irene, Gladys Lillian, Mildred and Mable Iona.*

For health reasons Otis was forced to give up his career as a miner. Being acquainted with the Futrell family Otis decided to move to Greene County and try farming. First settling in the Hickory Grove area west of Marmaduke then later in the Post Oak Community where daughter Jaunita was born. After living here several years the family moved to Flint, Michigan, where daughter Mildred had gone after her marriage.

Eldest daughter Gladys married Albert Bradsher, son of James and Flora Bradsher of Hurricane Township, and they had two children, Harold and Doris. Albert 1898-1931 and Gladys 1909-1932 both died from tuberculosis and are buried in Harveys Chapel Cemetery.

Second daughter Mildred married Euin "E.L." Wood (see E.L. Wood family) and moved to Flint, Michigan, later returning to Greene County.

Clara Irene, third daughter, born April 12, 1913, and died November 24, 1938, married Grady Earl Nettles, son of Eugene and Lucinda Slaw Nettles of Paragould, and they became parents to five children Dorothy, Marion, Donald, Cecil and a stillborn son.

Mable Iona, fourth daughter, born October 7, 1916, presently lives in Florida, married first Soloman Rutter and second Clayton Godfrey 1917-1992. Daughter Kim Godfrey Capton and family live in Grand Blanc, Michigan.

Lastly Lela Juanita born August 6, 1923, Greene County, Arkansas, died July 20, 1981, Michigan married Grant L. Weeks September 27, 1941. Their children are Judith, Grant L. Jr. and Timothy.

Aaron Athel Sears was born in Fayett County, Illinois, son of Thomas M. and Sarah Greenwood Sears. His immigrant ancestor is Richard Sears who first appears in Maine (Plymouth Colony) 1633. His lineage is as follows: 1. Richard 1590 England-1676 Maine, 2. Paul 1637-1707 Maine, 3. Samuel 1663-1741 Maine, 4. Judah 1699-1766 Maine, 5. Alden (second great grandson of John and Prisilla Mullins Alden, pilgrims) 1738 Maine-1803 New York, 6. Edward 1778 Maine-1831 Ohio, 7. Ashel Parker 1816 New York-1874 Illinois, 8. Thomas Melville 1849 Ohio-1928 Illinois.

This Sears family followed the typical westward migration pattern, starting in Maine to New York to Cincinnati, Ohio on to Illinois, ending up in the Missouri/Kansas area before Otis broke the pattern and moved to Arkansas then Michigan.

Otis retired from General Motors in 1955 and he and wife Sadie moved to Florida, where they built a house and remained until their deaths. Both are buried in Genesee County, Michigan.

**SELF** – Dr. George Simpson Self was the son of Noble J. Self and Jane (Miller) Self and was born October 1, 1876. He was the youngest of 10 children. George S. grew to manhood in Craighead County. Orphaned at an early age he worked hard and acquired the education necessary to obtain a teaching license. Teaching school allowed him to earn enough money to enter medical college at St. Louis, Missouri, and Louisville, Kentucky. After graduating from medical school he moved to Stanford where he established a medical practice that he maintained for 44 years. George S. married Danielle Selma Boyd on July 19, 1903. This marriage produced two daughters, Mildred Sunshine (Self) Tatum and Vivian Lucille (Self) Robb.

While working in his medical practice George S. was also engaged in farming and livestock trading. He proved to be a very good businessman and in the following years became very prosperous. He also entered politics and was elected to two terms as county judge of Greene County, serving from 1938 to 1941. George S. died on March 18, 1945, at the age of 68 years. Selma died June 18, 1970, at the age of 86 years.

George's oldest daughter, Mildred Sunshine Self, married Earl Tatum and lived in the Stanford Community where Earl was a farmer and store owner. They had two children, Martha, who died at birth, and Regina, who married Charles Penry of Paragould.

Charles and Regina were both educators with Regina being a classroom teacher and Charles a high school science teacher and later a long-time principal at Paragould Middle School. Charles and Regina had one daughter, Tracey.

George's youngest daughter, Vivian Lucille Self, married Brodie A. Robb of Stanford on December 23, 1932. This union produced one child George M. Robb. Brodie was a farmer and cotton gin owner in the Stanford Community. Lucille attended college at Conway, Arkansas, in the late 1920s and early 1930s and taught school at Light, Rice, and Stanford. Brodie died July 2, 1984, and Lucille died November 2, 1990.

*Dr. George S. Self preparing for a house call.*

George M. Robb graduated from Stanford High School in 1951 and married Glenda F. Harvill on August 14, 1954. They both earned masters degrees from Arkansas State University in Jonesboro. George M. entered the Army as a Second Lt. in 1955 and completed flight training to become an Army aviator. He served four years active duty in the United States and Germany.

After separating from the Army George M. was employed as a teacher, basketball coach and principal at Stanford while Glenda worked as an elementary teacher. In 1971-72 they both accepted positions in the Paragould School District where George M. held positions as teacher, basketball coach, middle school assistant principal, district federal coordinator, and assistant superintendent. Glenda was an elementary teacher, gifted and talented facilitator, and elementary and middle school counselor. George M. retired in 1990 and Glenda retired in 1995.

While working in education George M. maintained his military relationship as a fixed wing and helicopter pilot in the Arkansas National Guard and retired with the rank of Major in 1978.

George M. and Glenda were blessed with two daughters, Kim Denise (Robb) Jackson and Robin Ann (Robb) Yates. Kim chose a career with the Department of Defense and Robin became a high school business teacher. While working for the DOD in England, Kim married Danny L. Jackson on February 17, 1983. This marriage produced two children, Danny L. Jackson Jr. and David Allen Jackson.

Robin married Phillip Yates of the Oak Grove Community on December 7, 1979, and they have two children Madison Ann and Caleb Wayne.

**SHANE** – Grandma Shane, as she was known, outlived her brothers and sisters, her husband, many of her children and several grandchildren. Clara Ann Day was born January 18, 1843, in Madison County, Tennessee, to Lemuel and Mary Senter Day. Mary was the daughter of William Senter, born about 1765, and his wife Jenny Ann. Lemuel was the son of Elizabeth and John Day, born about 1770, who resided mainly in Eastern Tennessee. Clara met and later married J. John Shane September 5, 1866, in Madison County. John was the second son of William and Louna E. Lyons Shane. He was born in 1840 in Tennessee. William was one of seven sons born to Robert and Elizabeth Shane who ventured to America from County Down, Ireland about 1800 via Alabama, journeyed North to Tennessee and settled in Medina, Tennessee, in 1801. Robert and Elizabeth died in 1847 and 1852 respectively and are buried on land they donated for the Mt. Zion Church and Cemetery, Gibson County, Tennessee.

After serving in the Confederate Tennessee Infantry, John moved his wife Clara, and their children, Thomas and Mary Lou, to Greene County and settled on acreage on the north side of what was called the Unity Road, just off Highway 135 North, south of Oak Grove. After moving they had several other children: Sarah (who died as an infant); Christopher (who married Leno Steele. They are buried in Linwood Cemetery); Josephus Ed (who married Carrie Steele, moved to California and is buried there); Fannie (who married a Weatherly and after his death a McKelvey); Annie (who married Tom J. Bentley, by whom she had a daughter, Mackey. They are all buried in Linwood Cemetery.); Sam M. (who married Artie Thompson. They are buried in Linwood Cemetery.); William (who is buried at Friendship Cemetery); and John Cecil (who married Pauline Bushand is buried in the Elmwood Cemetery, Blytheville, Arkansas.)

Mary Lou Shane married Sam M. Stutes in Greene County on March 14, 1885. She was 16; he was 30. Their children were John F. "Bun" Stutes who married Leatha J. Adams. He is buried at Friendship Cemetery. R.S. Stutes, their second son was born in 1888. He married Lillie Miller and died in 1919, having had no children. He is buried at Friendship Cemetery also. Clara Rebecca Stutes, named after her two grandmothers, was born on August 27, 1891. Married Edward Brooks Stimson on December 7, 1908, in Greene County. She died June 21, 1927, and is buried in the Bentley plot in Linwood Cemetery.

When Sam died in April 1892, Mary Lou was left with three small children; the oldest just under six and the youngest, Clara, less than 1 year. Mary Lou immediately merged her household into that of her mother's and they made their home together until 1917 when Mary Lou died. Mary Lou and Sam's graves are in the Friendship Cemetery.

Clara Day Shane saw some of her brothers destroyed by the Civil War; her husband's brothers served in the same war; buried four of her children and her husband predeceased her by 45 years. She also saw two of her sons become prominent businessmen, one son become a lawyer and another an architect. She lived a long and well-fulfilled life. Clara and John are buried in the Friendship Cemetery in Greene County.

*Standing from left: Mary Lou Shane Stutes and Clara Rebecca Stutes Stimson. Seated: Clara Ann Day Shane, Ruth Mildred Stimson Holsombeck and at their feet the dog.*

**SHEPHERD** – John Shepherd married Margaret Catherine Reed in Walker County, Alabama. The date is unknown since the courthouse burned but they probably married in 1863 or 1864. Margaret Catherine Reed was born March 5, 1843, in Walker County, the daughter of Thomas L. Reed and Minerva Jones of Jasper, Alabama. Thomas was born in 1813 probably in South Carolina, although one census states Tennessee. Minerva was born on February 14, 1810, in South Carolina, the daughter of Wallace Jones Jr. and Susan Beavert. Minerva was married to ? Whitney and had children. After his death she married Thomas L. Reed and had a family including Margaret Catherine. Minerva died February 9, 1895, and was buried at Cemetery on Key Hill, Antioch, Alabama, northwest of Oakman in Walker County.

Little is known about John Shepherd. In census records his children state that their father was born in Alabama. According to his wife's obituary they married in Walker County, probably in 1863 or 1864. In 1864 a son was born in Leighton, Colbert County, Alabama. It was this son that told family members that his father's name was John and that his father was an orphan. We cannot find the family in the 1870 census. In the June 15, 1880, Lawrence County, Alabama Census, his wife Margaret Catherine, age 36, is a widow living with her parents and children. John Shepherd was dead by this date. The family was probably living in Leighton, Alabama, which is right next to the Lawrence County line.

The family then moved to Paragould, Greene County, Arkansas, in 1883. On May 20, 1885, Margaret Catherine Shepherd married John Monroe Minton in Greene County. Margaret Catherine and her daughter probably didn't stay in Arkansas very long, but at some point they moved back to Alabama. John Monroe must have died. It is not known if Margaret Catherine returned to Walker County, her mother died there in 1895. She did live with her daughter in Newtonville, Alabama, and they moved to Fayette in the early part of the century, both are in Fayette County. Margaret Catherine died there on December 13, 1932, and was buried at the Fayette City Cemetery.

John Shepherd and Margaret Catherine Reed were the parents of three children: Thomas Riley, John Hays and Jane Paralee Shepherd.

Thomas Riley Shepherd was born December 15, 1864, in Leighton, Colbert County, Alabama, and died April 6, 1948, in Blytheville, Mississippi County, Arkansas. Thomas Riley said that his father John was an orphan and that he died when he was 16 or 17 years old. According to census records John was dead, having died before June 15, 1880, and Thomas Riley was only 15 years old. His father probably had just recently died. Thomas Riley eventually settled in Arkansas, married, had a family and became a Baptist minister. (See Rev. Thomas Riley Shepherd history.)

John Hays Shepherd was born November 3, 1867, in Alabama. He married Minnie Alice Meredith on April 21, 1889, in Greene County. She was born April 10, 1872, and was the sister of Belle Meredith, the wife of his brother Thomas Riley Shepherd. John and Minnie were the parents of six children: Noxie Lee, John Winn, Iris Jewel, Alden Opal, Ruby Lee and Ira Bill. Noxie Lee (May 1891-?) married Tom Smith, John Winn (October 22, 1893-June 17, 1924) married Eva L. Smith on November 12, 1913, Iris Jewel (September 1899-?) married Walter Edwards on December 31, 1919, Alden Opal (1903-?) married Bobbie Weatherly on November 7, 1920, Ruby Lee (May 1, 1904-June 5, 1988) married M.D. Hooks on August 26, 1902, and Ira Bill (1910-?) married Lou Etta Hyde.

*From left: Jane Paralee Shepherd Whitney, John Hays Shepherd and his wife Minnie Meredith Shepherd.*

John Hays Shepherd was a diabetic and died around 1920. His wife Minnie Meredith died January 15, 1941. They are buried at Fairview Cemetery, Paragould, Arkansas, and have unmarked graves.

Jane Paralee Shepherd was born April 17, 1870, in Walker County, Alabama, and died March 4, 1952, in Fayette, Fayette County, Alabama. She was the wife of Richard Graves Whitney (1857-1940), and helped run the Whitney Hotel in Fayette. Paralee was burning papers in an open fire and received serious burns and died. They were the parents of two children, Ruby and Aubrey. Ruby married Charlie Trammel and had two daughters Frances and Jeane. Frances resides in Metarie, Louisiana. Jeane married Lecial Lockart and lived in Orange, Texas, but died several years ago. Aubrey married Wilma ? and had a daughter Anna Faye Whitney. Aubrey's second marriage was to Nauflett Shirley and they had a son Ronald Whitney who lives in San Francisco.

Paralee and Richard Whitney and their children Ruby and Aubrey are all buried at the Fayette City Cemetery, Fayette County, Alabama.

**SHEPHERD** – Thomas Riley Shepherd was born December 15, 1864, in Leighton, Colbert County, Alabama. He was the son of John Shepherd and Margaret Catherine Reed. (See John Shepherd family history.) His father John died sometime before the June 15, 1880, census. The family they moved to the Fairview Community, Paragould, Arkansas, when Thomas Riley was 19 years old in 1883. His mother's brother Polk Reed was already living in Paragould. On May 20, 1885, Margaret Catherine married John Monroe Minton in Greene County.

*From left: Jane Paralee Shepherd Whitney, sister of Thomas Riley Shepherd; Jane Ragsdale Shepherd, wife of Thomas Riley Shepherd; and Thomas Riley Shepherd.*

Thomas Riley Shepherd married Mary M.I. "Belle" Meredith on January 20, 1886, in Greene County. Belle was born in 1868, the daughter of James Fitzgerald Meredith and Martha Ann Jane Nettles. (See James B. Meredith family history.)

Thomas Riley and Belle were the parents of a daughter, Leona, who was born December 14, 1886, in the Fairview Community. Belle died in 1888 or 1889 and was buried in the Fairview Cemetery, an unmarked grave.

Leona grew to womanhood and married Eli Alonza McGee on October 9, 1904, in Harrisburg, Poinsett County, Arkansas. Eli and Leona were the parents of eight children: Winnie Dill, Earnest Glenn, Luther Vernal, Harry Robert, Woodrow Wilson, Carlton Russel, Tommy Elcanah and William Harlan McGee. Leona died August 19, 1963, and Eli died July 10, 1964, and are buried at Farm Hill Cemetery in Harrisburg. (See the McGee family history in the book *Poinsett County, Arkansas History and Families* published in 1998 by Turner Publishing Company)

After his first wife died, Thomas Riley married Jane Ragsdale on January 2, 1890, in Greene County. Jane was born March 4, 1867, in Arkansas. They were the parents of three children: Otis, Bonnie and Leslie Thomas Shepherd.

Otis Shepherd was born in 1892 and died in 1949. He married Aurine Cothren on February 21, 1914, in Greene County. After his first wife died, Otis married Herma Lancaster. Their only child Wynette married Worth D. Holden. Otis worked for the railroad and later owned a grocery store. He died of a heart attack and was buried at Elmwood Cemetery in Blytheville, Arkansas.

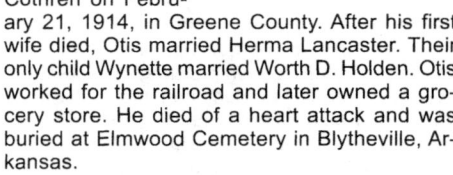

*Mary M.I. "Belle" Meredith Shepherd, wife of Thomas Riley Shepherd.*

Bonnie Shepherd was born March 16, 1898, and died in 1970. She married William "Bill" Jeremiah Rodgers on November 23, 1929, in Blytheville, Arkansas. Bonnie and Bill both worked at the post office there. They had one daughter, Billie R. Mills. Bonnie and Bill are buried at Elmwood Cemetery in Blytheville.

Leslie Thomas Shepherd was born in 1908 and died in 1980. He married Clarice Rodgers on March 28, 1929, in Blytheville. During the war he worked at a military base at Columbus, Georgia, and stayed. They had a daughter named Beverly and adopted a son and named him Tommy. Leslie was living in Columbus, Georgia, at the time of his death.

Around 1892, Thomas Riley Shepherd and family left Paragould and were living in Clarksville, Texas. Leona was a child of 6 and remembered crossing the Red River on a ferry. The family eventually moved back to Paragould.

Thomas Riley and family moved to Harrisburg, Poinsett County, Arkansas, in 1903. They loaded up the mules and wagon and household goods on the train at Paragould and came to Harrisburg. Thomas Riley and Jane and their daughter Leona joined the Bethel Baptist Church in 1904. Thomas Riley farmed and studied for the ministry. He was ordained the 1st Lord's Day in July of 1907 at Bethel Baptist Church, located two miles south of Harrisburg. In 1908 he was the church pastor.

Thomas Riley served as pastor of numerous rural churches in Poinsett and Craighead counties before moving to Blytheville in 1910. He continued serving rural churches while he worked as a engineer for the Creamery Package Company in Blytheville.

Thomas Riley had visited his mother in Fayette, Alabama, during her last illness. Margaret Reed Shepherd Minton died of pneumonia at the home of her daughter Paralee Whitney, Whitney Hotel at 10:30 Tuesday morning, December 13, 1932. Funeral services were held in the home and burial was in the Fayette City Cemetery.

*Leona Shepherd McGee, daughter of Thomas Riley Shepherd and wife of Eli Alonza McGee.*

Thomas Riley retired from the ministry in 1936.

Jane Ragsdale, wife of Thomas Riley Shepherd, died at her home Monday night, March 24, 1947. Services were held Wednesday at First Baptist Church, Blytheville. Burial was in Elmwood Cemetery.

Thomas Riley Shepherd died at Blytheville Hospital at four Tuesday afternoon, April 6, 1948, following a illness of two days. Services were held Wednesday afternoon at four at First Baptist Church, Blytheville. He was buried by his wife in Elmwood Cemetery.

Additional family histories can be found in the book *Poinsett County, Arkansas History and Families* published in 1998 by Turner Publishing Company.

**SHIPP** – Cora Cordelia (Caldwell) Shipp (April 26, 1897 Glenwood, AR) arrived on a cold, snowy day to Joseph and Cordelia Alice (Keith) Caldwell. On a 100-acre farm in Montgomery County in Glenwood, AR, her parents Joe and Cordelia raised 10 children, 7 boys and three girls:

1. Oristes
2. Zora
3. Ellis
4. Dottie
5. Della
6. Clifford
7. Elizah
8. Cora
9. Winford
10. Hershell

Cora was the granddaughter of Irish immigrants. Her maternal grandparents, Jim and Sarah Keith, traveled by ship from Dublin, Ireland and settled on a 160-acre farm in Montgomery County in Glenwood, AR.

Cora was raised on the 100-acre farm in a spacious, seven-room house with two fireplaces.

*Cora Cordelia (Caldwell) Shipp age 12.*

The family burned oil lamps and cooked on a wood stove. Cora was 12 years old before she saw an automobile. She walked a mile each day to and from school and she was a very good student. One of her favorite subjects was geography. On Sunday, Cora's favorite day of the week, her family traveled to church by horse and wagon. Cora loved attending Sunday school and church.

The Caldwell family enjoyed living in the

*Charles Frank Shipp and Joyce Velema Shipp.*

country and working together on the farm. For fun during the winter, the children would sled up and down the snowy hills and in the summer, Cora loved to tag-a-long with her brothers and go fishing. For personal entertainment, Cora played the organ. One of her favorite songs was "Pat, Pat, On My Back."

Christmas was a very special time for the family. Her mother would bake sorghum molasses cookies and cakes and Santa filled their stockings with stick candy, apples, and oranges. The children would shoot firecrackers, roman candles and burn sparklers. Also they would place red, hot fire coals on a shovel and shoot them through the air. Even though the family did not have a Christmas tree at home, Cora always enjoyed and was excited about helping decorate the Christmas tree at school.

Cora's formal education was completed when she finished the eighth grade, as there was no high school in Glenwood. She continued to live and work at home until she was 25 years old. Then she traveled to Hot Springs, AR and worked on Bath House Row for two years. Next it was on to an oil-boom town in Oklahoma where she met her future husband, Charles Frank Shipp (July 5, 1876). Charles worked for the Rock Island Railroad Company. Cora married Charles at the age of 30 at the courthouse in Walnut Ridge, AR. A justice of the peace performed the ceremony. A two-week honeymoon was enjoyed at a clubhouse on the Black River. The newlyweds bought an 80-acre farm in Noland, AR and began farming their land. Their children:

1. Joyce Velema Shipp (Aug 18, 1928)
2. Charles Harry Shipp (April 23, 1932)

Several years later, Cora and Charles moved to Walnut Ridge, AR and purchased a tavern/restaurant. However, following WWII, due to an unstable economy, the family fell upon hard times and had to sell their business. After living nine years in or around Walnut Ridge, the family moved to Paragould, AR in 1946 and purchased a home on 416 East Main and Cora would reside there through her 100th birthday. Charles worked for the Missouri Pacific Railroad and Cora purchased another tavern/restaurant near Highway 412. After a short period of time, Charles developed health problems and Cora sold the restaurant. Due to poor health, Charles was forced to retire from the Railroad Company. Cora went to work for Holden's Bakery on Pruett Street. Their daughter, Joyce, a senior in high school, had to drop out of school and take care of her convalescent father. Charles Frank Shipp died on March 7, 1947.

Cora's daughter, Joyce Shipp, married James Edward Brooks Dec 24, 1947. Ed worked for Wrapes Heading Mill and Hurt Grocery. Joyce worked for Emerson Electric 30 years before retiring due to health problems. Cora's son-in-law and daughter preceded her in death. James Edward Brooks died June 10, 1981 and Joyce Velema Brooks died Sept 19, 1993.

Joyce and Ed had two children, David Jerome Brooks (Jan 12, 1950) and Glen Allen Brooks (Dec 17, 1952). Ed and Joyce's first son, David, graduated from Paragould High School in 1970. Immediately following high school he joined the U. S. Army. He married Sue Radatz, a 1971 Paragould High School graduate, on June 27, 1975. Presently, they live in Jonesboro, AR. Frito-Lay Manufacturing Company employs David and Sue works in the medical field as a medical record technician.

Upon graduating from Paragould High School in 1971, Glen Allen Brooks, the second son of Joyce and Ed, was employed by Emerson Electric. He presently serves as quality supervisor for the company and has completed his 29th year of service at Emerson. Glen married Donna Adams, originally from Leachville, AR, a 1972 Paragould High School graduate on Oct 20, 1973. Donna is presently employed a manager of Adams Florist.

Cora's son, Charles Harry Shipp, joined the U. S. Army Dec 8, 1952. He served 18 months in the Korean War. Charles married Fayrene Roswell Dec 19, 1959. She had two infant sons. Charles worked for N.E.ARK. Sign Company for 20 years and then established his own business, Shipp Siding and Remodeling Company and was self-employed for 20 years. His wife, Fayrene, worked for several years at the Vandervoot Hotel and the local shoe and shirt factories. The couple raised their two children, David Wayne Remagan (Jan 30, 1952) and Charles Christopher "Chuck" Remagan (Sept 30, 1953 Paragould). David and Chuck attended school at Oak Grove. David presently lives in Paragould and is employed by D&G Trucking. Chuck lives in Little Rock, AR and is employed by Weaver Bailey Construction Company.

*Front: Joyce Velema Shipp and Charles Harry Shipp. Back: Cora Cordelia (Caldwell) Shipp.*

Cora Shipp's traditional values were rooted in a strong work ethic love of her family. A widow at the age of 50, Cora sought to provide for herself and her family. Never having learned to drive, she bought her first car, a 1949 Chevy, for $100. She passed her drivers test and continued to work for the public. In 1956 she worked at the old Panama Café for Jeff Kelly. Later she worked four years at the Vandervoort Hotel where the First National Bank is presently located. She worked at the Alex Fletcher Grocery store and for Jones Lamb at Lamb's Cafeteria on Pruett St. She spent her last seven years of employment as a waitress for C. B. Smith at the Ember-Glo Restaurant on North End Avenue. Cora retired at the age of 75. Following retirement she continued to be active. She sat with the Howell sisters and attended to their needs until they passed away. Cora stopped driving her car when she was 90 years old. She was a member of the First Baptist Church. She lived independently in her home, located at 416 East Main, through her 100th birthday. Cora Cordelia (Caldwell) Shipp died at the age of 100 years at the years at the Paragould Nursing Center on Sept 9, 1997.

This article was composed from the handwritten memoirs that Cora wrote when she was 86 years old. Cora believed in a strong work ethic. A member of the working class, she exemplifies the many hard working people of Greene County that has made this area a modern and progressive community. Her "zest for life" and love of family remains in the hearts of family and friends that knew her and loved her: "Blest be the Ties that Bind."

*Submitted by Glen Brooks*

**SIMPSON** – Betty Simpson, the second child of Vincent B. and Sarah Simpson whose families migrated from Kentucky to Greene County, AR.

Betty Simpson lived with her husband, Manse McChesney in Marion, also in Crittenden County. Manse was in the grocery business. John loved his Aunt Betty; she was quite a character and a staunch Democrat. She called the Republicans "them hateful old Republicans." They had four children, but John only met two, Harry and Harley. Harry and family lived in Frankfort, the capital city of Kentucky. He was State Commissioner of Education and later ran for governor on the Democratic ticket, but at that time, "them old Republicans" were too strong in Kentucky and he was defeated by the Republican nominee. John liked Harry. He was a big friendly handshaking fellow and just to know him was to admire and to respect him. His wife was a fine, well-educated person and a wonderful mother. They had a son, Harry McChesney Jr. and a daughter Ann McChesney

Harley, the second boy, lived in Paducah and he too was in the grocery business. John liked Harley alright; he was nice and seemed to enjoy talking to John about Arkansas and the people; but his wife and two high school kids, Ruth who later married a Bockman, and a son John did know his name.

John just said, phooey! They were snobs and had no time whatsoever for a country rube from the backwoods of Arkansas. John really thought their attitude toward him hurt Harley more that it did him. One night after supper he took John to town. They went first to Harley's grocery store and he showed him all around and talked to him about his business. He really was doing a big business. He then said he had to go to a club meeting and that he wanted John to go with him, as his guest. That was just getting too deep for a country boy, thought John, so he thanked him and told him he would just walk around and see some of the town. After walking around looking and window shopping, John stopped on a corner and just stood there looking at the bright lights. A man walked up and in a very friendly manner began talking to him. He said, "You are a stranger here ain't you?" John told him he was. He talked on, asked where John was from and how long he intended to stay. John was beginning to get a little suspicious of him. He took John by the arm and "Come on, I'll take you around and show you a good time." John was a country boy, but had enough good old horse sense not to fall into a trap like that. He jerked his arm loose and said, "I am expecting a friend any minute and I don't think you would like to meet him". He walked away and immediately a policeman walked up and said, "I listened to your conversation, you did the wise thing." That guy is the worst kind of a crook. Pretty soon Harley came up and Harley and John went home. John never mentioned his experience to Harley at all. The next morning John left early.

Betty had two daughters: Sallie married a Wooldridge and had two sons Keith and Manse Woolridge. Annie married Bill Cox; they had two sons, Bill Jr. and Paul Cox.

*Submitted by Evelyn Euritha Wagner*

**SIMPSON** – George Simpson, the first born to William F. Simpson and Ann Mary Russell, never seemed the least interested in school until he was 22 or 23 years old. He had acquired about a sixth grade level. But suddenly he became deeply interested in getting an education. He first went to country schools for two or three short terms, then attended Thomson's Classical Institute here in Paragould. He married a Paragould girl, Della, in 1896. He taught in rural schools of Greene County

for a while and farmed in between terms. Later he bought a hill farm and made some money buying and selling cattle and hogs. When the children were ready for high school they decided to move to Paragould. Only three of their children were living when they came to Paragould: Harold, Bera and Edgar. Edgar died a few years later, Harold became an invalid and he is now almost totally paralyzed. Bera married and is now living in Bay Town, TX. Her parents have been dead for several years. George died in 1938. John R. Simpson wrote this in 1966.
*Submitted by Evelyn Euritha Wagner*

**SIMPSON** – Georgeann was the oldest child of Dr. Vincent B. and Sarah Simpson, whose family migrated from Kentucky to Greene County, AR.

She married a man named Ewell Travis. They had no children. When John Simpson visited in 1901, they were living in Weston, Crittenden County, KY; a picturesque little town nestling in a sort of cove on the banks of the Ohio River. He owned a drug store. I think the highlight of John's visit there was watching the steamboats as they came in to unload and take on freight.
*Submitted by Evelyn Euritha Wagner*

**SIMPSON** – Jimmie Simpson was the second son of William F. and Ann Mary Simpson, he was born in 1872 and died in infancy.
*Submitted by Evelyn Euritha Wagner*

**SIMPSON** – John Simpson was the fifth child of Dr. Vincent B. and Sarah Simpson who migrated to Greene County, AR from Kentucky. John's children are:
1. Hayden Simpson, his children:
   a. Ethel (Simpson) Taylor
   b. Thelma (Simpson) Shepherd
   c. Victor Simpson
2. F. C. "Edd" Simpson, his children:
   a. Howard Simpson
   b. Levine (Simpson) Ford
   c. Berna Lee (Simpson) Brently
3. Lucy (Simpson) Haynes, her child:
   a. Mildred (Haynes) Terry
4. W. M. "Will" Simpson, his child:
   a. Camille (Simpson) Valentine
5. J. W. "Walter" Simpson, his children:
   a. Hughie E. Simpson
   b. J. Frank Simpson.
*Submitted by Evelyn Euritha Wagner*

**SIMPSON** – John R. Simpson (Sept 19, 1882 Paragould, Greene County, AR) was the youngest son of William F. and Ann Mary Russell. His parents, along with his brothers and sisters:
1. George
2. Carrie
3. Tom
4. Eddith

migrated here from Kentucky along with his mother's family, the Jefferson J. Russell's. John lived all his life here, except for a time, when he taught in Japan. I came across a small manuscript he had written about his life and life in Greene County. You will find many stories that I have submitted on his behalf. I know now why I was fortunate enough to inherit it. It was to share with all of Greene County, AR.

John followed many of the Simpson family line into the teaching profession.

He married Zera A. Thompson, also a teacher, and the daughter of Rev. James Thomas Thompson. They started a family:
1. Elaine (1913)
2. Donald (1915)

Elaine met Mr. Yoneshige when her father was in Japan and whom she later married. Elaine Yoneshige went on to become a consultant for the city library system of New York City, 1965.

Francis Bland, "Mr. Dr Pepper" of Paragould, told me this story of his sixth grade teacher at Woodrow Wilson Elementary School. John started a contest between his students in math. It went over so big that it was adopted countywide. Francis won the math contest for the whole county; this had been a great victory for Francis, as there was a girl, Mary Elizabeth Kirsch, who always won. He finally beat her!

*Walter Carl Wagner and Evelyn Euritha Wagner (John R. Simpson's great niece).*

Francis also remembers visiting John shortly before he died. He took him a box of cigars in the nursing home. That was treat for John.

John went on to become principal of Woodrow Wilson School. He also served two terms as Greene County Clerk.

Zera A. Simpson died Nov 16, 1969 and John R. Simpson died Dec 22, 1973 at the Home for the Golden Years; he was 91. They are both buried in Linwood Cemetery, Paragould, AR.

John was the youngest brother of my grandmother Eddith (Simpson) Snowden. I was proud he was my great uncle.
*Submitted by Evelyn Euritha Wagner*

**SIMPSON** – John R. Simpson tales of a permanent home at last! Life on the Old Henry Smelser Home. John R. Simpson was born in Paragould, Greene County, AR. He was the son of the early pioneers, William F. Simpson and Ann Mary Russell. He taught at Woodrow Wilson Elementary School.

In Oct 1900, believe it or not, Dad finally decided to buy a home. He and Tom went in together and bought the old Henry Smelser Home at Cross Roads. The house was old but in pretty good repair. There were 90 acres in the tract, 25 or 30 acres of woodland and the balance in cultivation. It was in the midst of a thickly settled community with a school just across the road and three churches within easy reach, two Methodist and one Baptist. We had our church memberships transferred to Owens Chapel, the Methodist church nearest our home.

We were delighted with our new home. It gave us a feeling of security. We felt that we belonged, that we had at last begun to take root and become stabilized. It gave us an incentive to work harder and try to improve our home. We even held a deeper interest and concern for the welfare of the community at large because we were now a permanent part of it and not just sojourners. Our first home! As I sit at my typewriter just 66 years later, (1966), I am forced to pause and ponder the past change and growth in every phase of human endeavor that has been wrought. Back then the average farmer's tools were a turning plow, a one-horse shovel, hoe and a horse drawn barrow and a homemade cotton planter. It took a day for us to slog through the mud to Paragould and back. In the home we had no electric lights, no telephone, no refrigerator, no radio, no television, nor other conveniences that we now consider necessities. This is where John R. Simpson's manuscript ends. I only wished I had got to meet my great uncle, he was my kind of guy!
*Submitted by Evelyn Euritha Wagner*

**SIMPSON** – John R. Simpson tales of the possum hunt on the old McDonald farm. John R. Simpson is the youngest son of William F. Simpson and Ann Mary Russell, pioneer families to Greene County, AR. He lived almost all his life here in Greene County, AR.

The Simpson family had moved to the Old Bob McDonald farm and again the family settled into farm life. It's 1897 and John says: "'We had no close neighbors and at first it was kindly lonesome for Tom and Eddith, Tom was then 23 and Eddith 20. They enjoyed, of course, being with other young people and having a good time. Will Jennings, the young man boarding with us, knew everybody for miles around and through him they soon became acquainted and active participants in the social activities of the community.

The widow Maxwell was our closest neighbor. She had seven boys and they all had a sister apiece, that was what they would always say when asked about the size of the family. The three youngest boys were somewhere near my age. We enjoyed possum hunting. One night we had been out for some time trapping through the woods and hadn't jumped a thing. Suddenly the dogs opened up. We tore out through the woods just as hard as we could go. When we got to them we found they had treed something in a little old hollow tree. Well, we were sure that it was just a rabbit but I decided to twist him out any way. So I cut a long stick with split end, rammed it up the hollow tree and began to twist. When I got a good grip on him I eased him down until I could get hold of a hind leg and yanked him out. The scene that immediately followed cannot be described with mere words. The little creature that I yanked out of the hollow tree was black with a white stripe down his back and had a bushy tail. With that tail he sprayed boys and dogs alike with the most sickening unbearable odor that I have ever experienced. The dogs lay down on the ground and rolled and whined. That ended the hunt but it didn't end the smell. We finally decided before we reached home to strip off our clothes and hand them up in the woods. We then went to the creek scrubbed our bodies thoroughly and slipped in home to dream about polecats".
*Submitted by Evelyn Euritha Wagner*

**SIMPSON** – John R. Simpson tales of life on the Bob McDonald farm. John R. Simpson is the son of William F. Simpson and Ann Mary Russell, early pioneers to Greene County, AR from Kentucky. John taught the sixth grade and became principal of Woodrow Wilson School.

With all the moving that William F. Simpson did, they kept within six miles of Old Gainesville up until 1897. In the fall of that year we moved to the Bob McDonald farm about 10 miles northwest of Paragould. That was a good move. Mr. McDonald had planned it for his country home but decided later to move to Paragould. It was a nice home with six large rooms and stood right square on top of Crowley's ridge. On the east were a fine apple orchard and some peaches and grapes too. To the south stood the barn on a lot that opened out to a large pasture in which was a stock pond. But I want to tell you a little about this barn. It faced the west with the ground sloping sharply downward to the east. There were double doors that opened into a wide hall that ran the full length of the building. On the north side of this hall was a harness room and corncrib with a row of stalls on the floor and a row of stalls down below the floor level. There was a narrow hallway that extended all around so you could feed the stock without having to enter the stalls at all. There were two big cisterns, one on either side of the hall at the east

end. Overhead was a great loft that would hold tons of hay. I think I can safely say it was the finest, most modern and most convenient stock barn in northeast Arkansas. You could go in to feed or water all your stock without coming in contact with any of them. Mr. McDonald always kept some stock out there. Besides horses and cattle, he had a big flock of white angora goats. He kept a young man out there all the time to look after the stock and the farm too. We furnished him room and board; of course he paid us for that.
*Submitted by Evelyn Euritha Wagner*

**SIMPSON** – John R. Simpson tales of life on the Henry Wood Farm. John R. Simpson is the son of William F. Simpson and Ann Mary Russell, early pioneers to Greene County, AR from Kentucky.

My father William F. Simpson was a good, honest, hardworking man but he was a very poor manager. He didn't seem to possess that forward outlook; that urge to achieve or to plan for a future day. He lived too much in the present. When they first came to Arkansas he could have bought good land at a very very low price. But we continued to rent and to move from place to place.

After four years at the Judge Mack place we moved to the Henry Wood farm, three miles east of Gainesville. It was good creek bottomland but the house was something awful. It was an old long house with two rooms and a big attic overhead. Mother almost cried her eyes out. Mr. Wood told her if we would stay on he would build us a new house. By early spring our new house was ready to move into and we were happy again. The land was good and our neighbors wonderful. We had just about everything we needed except money. This was about the time of the great panic of 1893 that swept the entire country. Thousands of banks and business houses could not pay their debts and many thousands of people were thrown out of work and wages for those who had jobs were reduced to a mere pittance. The bottom had dropped out of all farm products. We had bales of cotton lying in the front yard. Our cribs were piled full of corn, but $25 was about as much as we could get for a bale of cotton and corn in the shuck was selling for as little as 25 cents a bushel. We sold a good milk cow for $8.

But, so runs the inevitable tides of life, sometimes low and sometimes high, as slowly onward grinds the relentless wheels of time.
*Submitted by Evelyn Euritha Wagner*

**SIMPSON** – John R. remembers his childhood memories in early life in Paragould, Greene County, AR. Winter, with all its gaiety, had a way of passing; and spring, with its log rolling and the planting of crops to follow. There are very few living today that ever attended an old time log rolling. It is a memory that I would regret very much to have erased.

During the winter months we cleared new land, cutting the underbrush and piling it in heaps to be burned. Then, with cross cut saws, cut down the trees, trim them and cut the body into logs 10 to 12 feet in length. Then, when spring came, log rolling began. The men, with their long hand sticks on their shoulders and the women, with cooking utensils and baskets of food, would gather at their neighbors' home and the day would begin. The men would pair off, somewhat according to size and strength, with five or six couples to a large log. They would shove their sticks under a log and at the signal each man would grab his end of the stick and all come up together kidding and bantering each other as they walked toward the heap. This went on till they heard the old farm bell chime out the hour. This all sounds serious and very solemn, but not so; these hardy men, with jokes, pranks and banter, turned this day of backbreaking toil into a day of fun and feasting. When they gathered around the long table heaped and piled with every good thing to eat, which their women had so bountifully prepared for them, they humbly bowed their heads and gave thanks to God for their many blessings.

At the age of eight I was a regular hand in the field. Dad traded for a little old sorrel mule. He was smallish but strong and tough as they make them. We called him Jack; well Jack was my plow mule. Contrary! That mule was so doggone contrary if you said "gee" he would be sure to turn haw. Back then the land was new and had lots of stumps. Jack absolutely refused to go near a stump. He would just simply circle around it while I hung onto the plow handle with one hand and tugged on the line with the other till I got him back on the right row. I was too young then to make any definite decision as to what my future vocation should be, but that old contrary mule was a definite factor in my decision as to what I would not be.
*Submitted by Evelyn Euritha Wagner*

**SIMPSON** – Mariah Sue Simpson is the sixth child of Dr. Vincent B. and Sarah Simpson, whose families immigrated to Greene County, AR from Kentucky. Mariah Sue married a Givens and their children are:
1. George Givins and his child is:
   a. Parl Givens
2. Tom Givins
3. Sallie (Givens) Devers, whose daughter is Gretus Devers.

*Submitted by Evelyn Euritha Wagner*

**SIMPSON** – Tom Simpson was the fourth child of Dr. Vincent B. and Sarah Simpson, whose families migrated to Greene County, AR from Kentucky.

His children were:
1. Nonnie (Simpson) Daughtrey's children were:
   a. Willard Daughtrey
   b. Irene (Daughtrey) Gillett
   c. Charles A. Daughtrey.
2. Grace (Simpson) Curry's children were:
   a. Eugene Curry
   b. Lacy Curry
   c. Russell Curry
   d. Willie (Curry) England
   e. Freda (Curry) Battle
   f. Verda (Curry) Neal
3. Elle (Simpson) Cox
4. Bertha (Simpson) Perdew's children were:
   a. Deane Perdew
   b. Herman Perdew
   c. Grace (Perdew) Evans
5. Bill Simpson's children were:
   a. Adeline (Simpson) Marshall
   b. Tom Simpson
   c. Charles Simpson
   d. Bettie (Simpson) Rowe
   e. Velda Simpson
6. Deane Simpson's children are:
   a. Murl Simpson
   b. Earl Simpson
   c. Esther (Simpson) Trow

*Submitted by Evelyn Euritha Wagner*

**SIMPSON** – Tom Simpson (1874) was the third son of William F. and Ann Mary Simpson, early pioneers to Greene County, AR. He was the runt of the family and must have been 17 or 18 before he weighed 100 pounds. He began to grow rapidly until he was an average size man.

Tom was a good boy but he had an awfully high temper. He was little but strong for his size and hard as nails. When the family moved out here from Kentucky and Tom started to school at Gainesville he had a fight almost every day. Being a new boy from another state the kids tried to bully him. But they soon learned that the little wasp from Kentucky was plenty able and willing to take care of himself. He had a nickname "Bub" that he bore until he was a grown man. I don't know how he came by it, but I was a good-sized boy before I knew what his real name was. Everybody called him Bub.

Bub made a farmer, a good one. With the exception of about two years at Wrape's Heading factory in Paragould, he spent his entire life, up to the day of retirement on the farm. When John was eight years old, he was 16, just twice John's age. He remembered they had quite an argument about this. John maintained that if he were twice my age then he would always be twice as old. He tried to explain it to me but I just couldn't see it that way. Tom died in 1953.
*Submitted by Evelyn Euritha Wagner*

**SIMPSON** – Dr. V. B. and Sarah Simpson were early pioneers to Kentucky. Some of the children of V. B. and Sarah were among the early pioneers to Greene County, AR. Kentucky was originally a portion of Fincastle County, VA, a wilderness inhabited by the Cherokee Indians. In 1775, Daniel Boone planted a settlement and named it Boonesborough. By treaty the land was purchased from the Indians. After a long hard struggle, Congress, in 1791, agreed to admit Kentucky in the Union.

It is evident from what John Simpson gathered by mouth, that V. Simpson was among the hardy pioneers that opened up and settled a wilderness that finally became one of the great states of the Union.

John had no definite knowledge concerning the ancestors of V. Simpson, John Simpson's great grandfather, nor where they came from, but through the similarity of names, he was led to believe that they originally came from England and perhaps Scotland. From an encyclopedia published in 1900 John found that the early Christian names of the Simpson's of those countries were very similar, such as George, William, John, etc.

The only thing John ever learned about the life of his great grandfather was the story of his death from his father, Dr. V. B. Simpson. In those days family feuds were not uncommon. It was such a family feud that brought about the death of John's and this writer's great-great-great-grandfather. He and his wife, one Sunday afternoon, were riding along a road that paralleled the Ohio River when suddenly a gun fired from an open window and Vincent Simpson fell from his horse, mortally wounded; the name of the assassin, Henry C. Shouse. Shortly after this, Shouse was killed. They tried to pin his murder on John's grandfather but he denied it and they were unable to prove that he did it. In 1901-1902, John visited his relatives out there for the first time and found this story to be a well-known legend among the older people there.

Grandfather Simpson was a country doctor. In addition to his medical practice he owned and operated a small plantation. Prior to the Civil War he had a few slaves that cultivated the land, tobacco being the principal money crop at that time.

It is difficult for us to even imagine the hardships and suffering the people of the South and some of the Border States endured at the time and for a long time after the war ended. Every man that was able to carry a gun had been drafted into the army, leaving their wives and children to the cruel ravaging of such merciless gangs as the bushwhackers that roamed the country, plundering and burning as they went. Before the war John's Grandfather Russell was considered a wealthy man, after the war, nothing! His slaves had been set free, his business destroyed, he was a tobacco merchant, bought the farmers' tobacco and shipped it in hogsheads to the factories to be finally processed.

*Submitted by Evelyn Euritha Wagner; original story by John R. Simpson*

**SIMPSON** – William F. Simpson (March 3, 1846), the third child of Vincent B. and Sarah Simpson, came to Greene County, AR as pioneers from Kentucky, along with the Jefferson J. Russell family.

In Crittenden County, KY, his early life was pretty much the same as that of any country boy of that day and time. In the closing months of the Civil War he enlisted in the Confederate Army but was never engaged in any major battles. John Simpson recalled an amusing little episode that his father related to him as a boy. His squad was swimming their horses across the Tennessee River when a Federal gunboat, steaming up the river, began firing on them. His father had just reached the shore when a man in front of him plopped down, stuck up his foot and yelled, "Help me get this d—boot off Simpson, it's full of water". My father yelled back "To hell with your boot, get up from there and ride or you will soon be full of lead."

*Raymond Wilfred Snowden with his mules – 1931. Grandson of William F. Simpson and Ann Mary Russell.*

After the war was over and things had begun to settle down, the dashing young Bill Simpson happened to meet a charming young lady by the name of Ann Mary Russell. What at first appeared to be only a passing friendship soon developed into a romance, which culminated in marriage. Ann Mary's father, Jefferson J. Russell, was bitterly opposed to the match and swore that he would never permit his daughter to marry that upstart rebel soldier; the old squire was a Federalist. So Bill and Ann Mary carefully laid their plans to elope. The night had come. Young Simpson, with two horses groomed and saddled, was nervously waiting near the home: Inside the house in her room Ann Mary sat anxiously watching the clock as it slowly ticked the minutes away. The hour had arrived. Ann Mary slipped quietly out the back way; they mounted their horses and quickly galloped away. The next morning Jefferson J. Russell with his two oldest sons road out early in pursuit of the elopers but they were much too late. The lovebirds had already reached the Ohio River, secured a skiff and rowed across the river into Illinois where they were united in holy wedlock, 1867.

After the honeymoon, Bill and Ann Mary settled down in their new home near Dawson Springs and began the serious business of raising and providing for a family. Jefferson J. Russell had become reconciled and was even a little proud of his son in law.

*Submitted by Evelyn Euritha Wagner*

**SIMPSON/FARRAR** – Carrie, after a long time as a young widow, finally met a young man by the name of Walter D. Farrar, who had come with his family from Tennessee. Walter's father was a pioneer Methodist minister. Through this friendship, Carrie and Walter married on April 11, 1897. Walter owned a farm near Lorado, a little country village in southern part of Greene County. Leona didn't quite know what to do because she had lived with her grandparents practically all of her young life. She was told that she could go with her mother and stepfather, or stay with her grandparents. She decided to stay with her grandparents but cried because she was afraid she had made the wrong decision. But soon after the honeymoon she joined her mother and new father and was delighted with her new home situation.

*Breckinridge Mercantile Company, opened April 20, 1907. Owners: W. D. Farrar and Carrie Simpson Farrar.*

Walter and Carrie had four children:
1. Ruby
2. Curtis
3. Otis
4. Jewel

As the Farrar family grew and developed they were a jolly, enjoyable group of youngsters and seemed to enjoy each other very much. Walter was an avid sports fan. He knew most of the professional baseball players by name, their salaries and what position they played. In Otis's early career in the school he coached boys' athletics. When Walter attended a game he would always tease Otis about the game. Otis would try and defend his team in saying they played a good game and Walter would smile and say it didn't do much good unless it "goes through the hoop".

Walter and Carrie spent their adult life as active members of the Methodist church. Walter was on the official board and was superintendent of Sunday school for a number of years. They were very punctual in attending most activities of the Methodist Church.

After the children were grown and married, one Monday evening in 1938, Walter dropped dead in the store in which he had spent the biggest part of his adult life. Three weeks from that date Carrie passed away and thus closed this chapter of the Simpson family. Otis was the first of the W. F. Simpson branch of the Simpson line to earn a bachelor's degree. We are all proud of his achievement and I expect others, in the not too distant future, to reach that goal.

*Submitted by Evelyn Euritha Wagner*

**SIMPSON/RUSSELL** – Bill and Ann Mary Russell's children:

1. George (1868)
2. Carrie
3. Jimmie died in infancy
4. Tom
5. Eddith

As time went by they began to read about a new country west of the mighty Mississippi where land was cheap and game plentiful. So, early in 1881 the Russells and the Simpsons with three covered wagons loaded to capacity with furnishings and supplies, started on their long trek to Arkansas, the land of promise. It was a long, tiresome journey but a very exciting one, especially for the young folk. Eddith, then four years old, would sit up on the front seat with her daddy and sing, "going away to the wild goose country."

They finally arrived and settled just one mile south of Gainesville, Greene County, AR. It was the county seat and metropolis of northeast Arkansas. It boasted a population of near 200 souls, two churches, Presbyterian, and Methodist, a two room school house, a frame building used as a court house, a post office, two general merchandise stores, cotton gin, grist mill and saw mill all combined, also a blacksmith shop together with a few other little shops.

On Sept 19, 1882, a new member was added to the family, a baby boy they named John R. Simpson.

In the early 80s two railroads were built through Greene County and they crossed at a point 10 miles south Gainesville, It was at this point that the little settlement was incorporated and named Paragould. About 1883 or 1884 the county seat was moved from Gainesville to Paragould. Soon after this Judge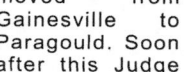

*Ann Mary Russell Simpson.*

Mack moved from his country home one and one half miles southwest of Gainesville to Paragould and we moved into his old home. A very wide hallway separated the four front rooms with two rooms on each side with an ell running back forming the dining room and kitchen. There was a big fireplace in each of these two rooms, also a fireplace in each of the two front rooms.

The Simpson's were a happy family in their new home. George and Carrie, the two oldest children had grown up and our place became the center for the young people of the community to gather for their play parties and candy breakings. Bill and Ann Mary enjoyed the frolics as much as the youngsters, but in a different way. Bill would join in and promenade to the lusty singing of *Old Dan Tucker, Skip to My Lou and Shoot the Buffalo.* John said he could see and hear them now, in his imagination, as they sang "and we'll shoot the buffalo, yes we'll shoot the buffalo and we'll rally through the cane breaks and shoot the buffalo." Ann Mary didn't take an active part, but heartily enjoyed watching the others.

**SIMPSON/THOMASON** – Carrie, the second child of William F. Simpson and Ann Mary Russell, was 11 years old when they came to Arkansas. She was a vivacious girl, active and full of fun. She and her brother, George, grew up together and was very close. They were popular with the young folks of the community and enjoyed life to the fullest. She married at the age of 17, some ten years before George. Her first husbands' name was John Thomason. He was a fine young man and they were a very happy young couple. But their happiness together was short-lived. John died about two years after marriage leaving Carrie a very young widow with a little girl baby, named Leona. I have lived 76 years since his death but his passing is quite vivid to me still. It must have been around midnight. He said to Carrie "Light the lamp honey, I can't see." Then he pointed to the upper corner of the room as a smile played across his face and said: "I see them, there they come" and he was gone. John was only eight or nine years old but made a deep and lasting impression on him. "What would I not give to know what he saw, or thought he saw?" said John R. Simpson.

After the death of her first husband Carrie with her baby Leona went to live with her parents, Bill and Ann Mary Simpson. They made their home there for the next six or seven years.

*Submitted by Evelyn Euritha Wagner*

**SIMS** – Marion and Miss Ollie Johnson were married in Greene County, AR in 1905. Ollie was the daughter of pioneer couple George Anderson and Mary Jane (Edwards) Johnson of Goobertown, AR.

Marion was tax assessor for Paragould, AR. Marion and Ollie lived in Paragould for many years.

*Marion and Ollie Sims, 1900s.*

Marion died and is buried at Linwood Cemetery.

Ollie Sims then married Mr. Will Toll. They lived in California. Ollie died and is buried at Linwood Cemetery in Paragould next to her first husband.

*Submitted by Donna (Robinson) Ishmael*

**SIMS/ROBINSON** – Anna (Johnston) was married to James Robert "Bob" Robinson. Oscar was about six months old when his father Bob died in 1889. Bob Robinson is thought to be buried at the Sims Cemetery in the Goobertown area.

*L-R: Anna (Johnston) Robinson Sims, son Oscar Robinson, grandson Gene Robinson and great grandson Robert Charles Robinson age 6 months. About December 1938.*

Anna then married Joseph Sims. They were listed in the 1900 Brookland, Craighead County, AR Census. At that time children in the household were a daughter Blanche; a son Clifford; a daughter Claudie; a son Wesley and a son Earnest.

Anna Robinson Sims died in 1950 and is buried at Pine Log Cemetery near Brookland, AR.

Anna's father, Samuel Johnston (1836 – 1870), married Rebecca F. Boozer in 1854. They came to Arkansas from Alabama.

*Submitted by Donna (Robinson) Ishamael*

**SLOAN** – William C. Sloan Jr. and LaVerne Scott Sloan made their home at Fontaine from 1952-1982. W.C. Jr. and his brother Frank farmed with their father, W.C., who was owner of the "company farm." W.C. and his wife Elizabeth Fuller also had two daughters, Barbara and Betsy.

LaVerne was the daughter of Ben R. and Maude Lee Cook Scott, who originally lived at Fontaine. Ben was a landowner there. The Scotts had two other daughters, Sophia and Doris, and one son, John R.

W.C. Jr. and LaVerne raised their children, William C. Sloan III and Phoebe Sloan at Fontaine. Later the Sloans moved to Jonesboro. Phoebe married Donald D. Crocker and moved to Little Rock. The Crockers have one daughter, Katherine Elizabeth. W.C. III lives in Jonesboro.

W.C. and LaVerne currently reside in Jonesboro.

**SMELSER** – Abraham Smelser came to Greene County, Arkansas May 6, 1836, and settled on a tract of wild land located in Cache Township. He opened up 100 acres. Abraham and his wife, reared a large family of children. They both died of smallpox in 1863.

John W. Smelser, their oldest child, was born in Kentucky. He married Nancy Clark, born in Tennessee. He settled with his parents in Greene County, Arkansas. In 1864, he joined Price in his raid through Missouri. After the war, he gave his attention to farming and merchandising at Crowley. He and his wife were members of the Methodist Episcopal Church. They had seven children. Joseph P. Smelser, their fifth child, married Margaret Adams.

Mary Ann Smelser, daughter of Abraham, married John Jarvis Clark, son of John and Martha (Hunter) Clark, Campground Community. John Jarvis Clark was born January 31, 1832. Mary Ann Smelser was born August 1, 1829. They had nine children: Betty, Sarah, George Washington, Billie Franklin, Joseph Henry, Victoria, John Crowley, Janie and Martha Elizabeth.

Billie Franklin Clark married Laura Melissa Ginger, daughter of Pete and Melissa Ginger. They had nine children: Sarah Anne, John Wesley, Martha Miranda Victoria "Vickie," Mary Melissa, Susie Mae, Mose, Lilly Jane "Jenny," Roy McKinley and Henry Clark.

The Ginger family owned a farm where Big Lake and the wild life refuge is now. They had one son, Louis Ginger, who moved to Chicago, and three daughters. Ginger "Ginny" Ginger married Jim Tucker. Miranda born April 26, 1870, died December 23, 1904, married Robert L. Watson. Their children: Moss Watson, John Watson, Ed Watson and Chris Watson.

**SMELSER** – James Abraham "Abe" Smelser (Nov 28, 1861, Greene County) the son of William P. and Margaret Smelser married four times, twice widowed and once divorced. He fathered 21 children, many of who died in infancy or early childhood.

His first wife, Leanna Taylor (April 14, 1857-February 1888 Greene County); they were married in 1881 and had three surviving children:
1. Viola (Smelser) Scobey
2. Margaret (Smelser) Clark
3. Willie Smelser.

Leanna's tombstone in Beech Grove Cemetery is inscribed "Leeoner J." which is apparently how her name was commonly pronounced.

Abe and his second wife, Judith "Judy" P. Roberts (May 31, 1863 Carroll County, TN- Sept 21, 1891 Greene County); were married on Jan 22, 1889. Their first child was born Sept 15, 1889 and died the following day. Their third child was born and died on Sept 15, 1891. Judy died six days later, leaving her second child, James Ernest (Nov 15, 1890) without a mother.

He and his third wife, Anna Bell Boaz Croft, were married in 1892. Anna had been married before and had a son, George Croft and a daughter Lee Croft. Abe and Anna had eight children with only one surviving infancy, Ollie Bulah (Smelser) Jones. Abe and Anna divorced due in part to religious differences.

Abe's fourth wife was Zona Belle Willis and they were married on Nov 24, 1909 in Greene County. She was 26 and he was 48. Called by the familiar "Zone" by friends and family, she preferred Zona. Abe and Zona had six children. They were:
1. Mildred Ruth Smelser (1911-1912)
2. Margarette (Smelser) Conklin
3. James Smelser
4. Dale Smelser, twin (1918-1920)
5. Paul Smelser, twin (1918-1920)
6. Fay Smelser (1916-1917)

Abe was 57 when his last child was born.

He worked for Henry Breckenridge as a clerk and assistant postmaster in Henry's store in Beech Grove. Henry was married to Mary Eliza Roberts, Judy Roberts' sister. Henry was postmaster of Beech Grove and Abe was appointed acting postmaster for approximately one year when Henry fell seriously ill. Abe later opened a store of his own in Beech Grove that he operated until his death. Henry Breckenridge's daughter, Myrtle (Breckenridge) Hammond, remembers her Uncle Abe Smelser very well. She describes him as a tall man, over six feet, well built, who stood very erect and was always well groomed. He had dark brown hair with a reddish cast, very dark eyes and wore a moustache that he kept neatly trimmed.

Abe died Feb 22, 1921 in Greene County of pneumonia, leaving Zona a widow with three young children. He is buried at the Beech Grove Cemetery.

He was the great-great grandson of Paulser Smelser who died in Bedford County VA about 1778. One of Paulser's sons also named Paulser migrated to Kentucky after 1787. Migrating to Greene County with their families in the late 1830s was three of the younger Paulser's sons and one daughter:

*James Abraham "Abe" Smelser*

1. William G.
2. Abraham
3. Stephen
4. Rebecca Andrews.

Abe's father was William G.'s eldest son, William P. He and wife Margaret had two sons, Jesse (1859) and James Abraham "Abe" (1861). According to the 1860 census, they were living in Cache Township and their post office was Crowley. William P. died between 1861 and 1867. Although he was in his 20s during the Civil War no record of service has been discovered. He most likely died in 1863 of disease because he lived next door to his uncle and aunt, Abraham and Nancy Smelser, both of whom died of smallpox in 1863 according to *The Goodspeed Biographical and Historical Memoirs of Northeast Arkansas*.

*Submitted by Brian Smelser*

**SMELSER/DICKERSON** – James Ernest Smelser (Nov 15, 1890 Greene County, AR) the son of James Abraham "Abe" and Judith "Judy" P. (Roberts) Smelser, was the only child of their three children surviving infancy. After Judy's death in 1891, Ernest lived with his maternal grandmother, Elizabeth Anne "Annie" (Parish) Roberts and maternal uncle, S. T. Roberts.

On July 31, 1909, Ernest married Ella May Dickerson, daughter of Thomas "Tom" Robert and Frances "Fanny" Pearilee (Summers) Dickerson. Tom was born in Obion County, TN about 1855 and married his first wife, Francis Julia Dollins, in Greene County in 1879. Following her death, he married Ella's mother, Frances Summers on Aug 3, 1881. Both of Tom's wives were named Francis/Frances and both were called by the familiar "Fanny." Tom and his first wife had one daughter, Minnie. He and his second wife had six children. Ella was born in Greene County on May 18, 1891.

Center: Elizabeth Anne "Annie" (Parish) Roberts. Left: Nellie (Owens) Boyd. Right: James Ernest Smelser, about 1896

Ernest and Ella (pronounced Eller) had 13 children:
1. Eula (Smelser) Ford (1910)
2. Bulah Olean Smelser died in infancy
3. Earlon Woodrow Smelser died in infancy
4. Erie (Smelser) Green
5. Bruce Smelser
6. Bert Smelser
7. Maxine (Smelser) Cummings Martin
8. Thomas Smelser
9. Etha Zuline (Smelser) Hooker
10. Mary Ruth Smelser
11. Marie (Smelser) McGarraugh
12. Faye (Smelser) Partlow (1933) twin
13. Willie J. Smelser (1933) twin

They have a total of 30 grandchildren and were affectionately called Poppy and Mommy by their children and grandchildren.

After their marriage they bought a 50-acre farm on Overcup Slough located north of Beech Grove in the Cache River bottoms, where they lived for about 15 years. Three houses were located on the farm that were part of a former lumber camp and one of the houses served as their living quarters and the others were occasionally rented. The area was low and marshy and plagued with flies and mosquitoes. Taxes were levied on the land to dig ditches to drain the area. The land was not suited for the crops Ernest raised and he eventually let his land go for taxes. His maternal uncle, S. T. Roberts, called Uncle Thomas by the family, later purchased the land.

Ernest and Ella moved their family frequently over the next several years, renting farms that had a house in which the family could live. This was not uncommon in the late 20s and 30s. The customary rents of the time were a one-quarter share of the cotton crop and a one third share of the hay and corn crops. Some rents were paid in cash but most were paid in shares.

In 1928 they moved to an 80-acre farm about a mile east of Beech Grove known as the Roy Breckenridge place. In 1930 they moved to the Pres Williams place, which was one and one half miles south of Beech. Around 1932 or 1933 they moved to the Gramling place which was also south of Beech. In 1936 they moved to the Mack place located on what is now Highway 141 between Hooker and Beech Grove. They lived there until 1946. Russell and Winston Mack owned the farm.

Ernest's Uncle Thomas owned a farm about two miles west of the Mack place where Highway 141 turns south toward Beech Grove. By 1946 Uncle Thomas's wife, Erie had passed away and he was seriously ill. Ernest and Ella moved into the house with Uncle Thomas and cared for him until his death in 1948. On his uncle's death Ernest inherited part of his uncle's land and the house in which he lived.

Ernest and Ella lived on the S.T. Roberts place until Ernest retired from farming in 1963 and sold the farm. They bought a large house on North Third Street in Paragould. Ella insisted on a house with enough room for her children and grandchildren to stay with them on their annual visits from Flint, MI. Typical of families of their generation, many of their children had left Arkansas for jobs outside the state. Ella also insisted on a large front porch, spanning the front of the house and spent most late afternoons in her rocking chair on the porch.

James Ernest Smelser, about 1905

Their home was always the gathering place for the family when they lived on the farm and after they moved into town. There was always a house full of children and grandchildren on every holiday. Visits by their children living in Michigan were a special event. Brothers and sisters living in Arkansas would flock to their house for a visit. The women always prepared a large meal and the house was filled with wonderful aromas, laughter and much happiness.

As a young man, Ernest was at least five inches shorter than his father's height of six feet. He was slender and muscular and worked long hard days. Like his father, he was well groomed and dressed neatly. His favorite attire was Duck Head brand bib overalls with a blue work shirt, or a dress shirt for trips into town or to the doctor. He appeared serious most of the time but loved to tell funny stories and would laugh until he cried.

Rheumatoid arthritis and a heart ailment led to his retirement from farming. The arthritis caused his hands and feet to become drawn and swollen and he became stooped. In spite of this he walked the five blocks to downtown Paragould every day to meet and visit with old friends that were also retired. He died on Nov 16, 1965 one day after his 75th birthday in the Community Methodist Hospital in Paragould.

James Ernest and Ella (Dickerson) Smelser, 50th Wedding Anniversary, July 31, 1959

Ernest was known for his honesty. On his death, Woodrow Davidson, a former storeowner in Beech Grove and a former sheriff of Greene County, remarked, "That man there, his word was worth more than most men's signature."

Ella continued to live in the house on North Third Street with one of her daughters, Mary Ruth, for several years after Ernest's death. The house became too much to care for and they moved into a smaller house on West Thompson Street in the early 70s. She died at home on Sept 13, 1978 outliving her husband by nearly 13 years. She is buried at Ernest's side in Memorial Gardens located north of Paragould.

*Submitted by Smelser*

**SMITH** – Charles Henry Smith, farmer and a carpenter, born June 7, 1861, in Hamilton County, Illinois and died October 8, 1925, in Paragould age 64. Charles was buried at the Linwood Cemetery. Charles died at 9:30 p.m. on Thursday following an illness of several months, was confined in his room only about 90 days. Charles was survived by his wife, Mary Smith, three sons, Lawrence Smith of Truman, Arkansas, R.L. Smith and Earl Smith, Paragould, three daughters, Lillie Morgan and Laura May of Route 2, and Ida Cline of Paragould. One brother, John Smith of Whittinton, Illinois, one sister, Susan Hunt of McLeansboro, Illinois.

Charles was the son of Robert George Smith, farmer, born January 14, 1819, in Tennessee and died May 13, 1879, in Illinois and Mary J. "Polly" Cox, a homemaker, born May 1, 1825, in Tennessee and died December 10, 1885, in Illinois. Robert and Mary were married June 15, 1844, in Tennessee.

Charles married Mary Marguerite Dollar, February 19, 1880, at Hamilton County, Illinois. Mary Dollar, a homemaker, was born February 18, 1856, in Jefferson County, Illinois, and died February 10, 1931, in Paragould aged 67. Mary died at 12:35 a.m. in the morning at the home of her daughter, Ida Cline, of Paragould, east of the Eight Mile Creek bridge. Her death followed a three weeks illness due to complication of diseases. Mary is buried at the Linwood Cemetery. Mary was survived by three daughters, Laura May and Lillie Morgan, of Route 2, Ida Cline of Paragould, three sons, Lawrence Smith, of Melville, Louisiana, Robert Smith of Paragould and Earl Smith, near Paragould; 24 grandchildren and 16 great-grandchildren.

Charles Henry Smith, June 7, 1861 to October 8, 1925.

Mary is the daughter of Ivy R. Dollar, farmer, born 1816 in South Carolina and died January 21, 1899, in Montgomery County, Ohio, aged 83 and Margaret B. Ashford, homemaker, born February 4, 1819, in Alabama and died 1870 in Hamilton County, Illinois, aged 51. Ivy and Margaret were married June 30, 1841, at Itawamba County, Mississippi.

Charles and Mary had sons Lawrence Nelson born January 12, 18??; Robert Smith born March 2, 1883; Roy Smith born December 28, 1891; Earl Smith born January 20, 1899 and daughters Lillie Mae Smith born September 11, 1887, who married John Robert Morgan on October 2, 1910; Laura Smith born August 18, 1885, who married Henry May on December 10, 1905; Blanche Ida Smith born September 15, 1895, who married Noeh Albert Cline.

Charles took his daughter, Laura, to cook for him when they made the first trip to locate a place to live in Greene County. Charles moved his and his brothers family from Hamilton County, Illinois, to Greene County, by wagon in 1899. They stopped to work on farms as they traveled to earn money for their trip. In 1905 when Laura married Henry May, Charles was so mad at her that he hung all of her clothes on a fence. He depended on her to take care of all the younger children.

*Lillie May Smith Morgan, September 11, 1887 to December 18, 1937.*

**SMITH** – David Alexander Smith, was born July 8, 1826, in Rutherford County, Tennessee. He was the oldest child of Stanford and Margaret "Tassey" Smith's 12 children. This Smith family came from Cork County, Ireland in the 1700s and settled in Wake County, North Carolina, before moving to Rutherford County, Tennessee. Then on to Greene County, Arkansas, in about 1850.

David was educated in schools in Tennessee and learned the building trade of his father.

David first bought 160 acres of Sugar Creek. He built buildings cleared the land and set out an orchard. After living here for 15 years he bought 225 acres of land between 412 West and Stanford known later as the Shewmaker place. The community of Stanford was named for his father Stanford Smith. As he opened the first cotton gin and general store. When David opened the first post office there the name was official.

David was active in politics. He served as bailiff of Greene County. He was a patron of education and director of his school district.

David built most of the better homes in Greene County with the help of Dr. Croft's slaves. These homes included Ben Crowley's and Mrs. Boyd's.

*David Alexander Smith and Margaret Pevehouse Smith.*

In January he married Margaret Pevehouse, daughter of Abraham and Polly (Crowley) Pevehouse.

They were the parents of six children:
William 1858-1893,
Sara Ann 1860-1880,
Mary Elizabeth 1862-1863,
Susan Cansada 1868-March 29, 1940,
Logan H. Roots 1870-May 31, 1939 and
James Alexander 1875-June 9, 1937.

Susan Cansada, Logan and James all had issue. Susan married G.B. Harris. Logan married Mary Alice Burkeen and James married Nancy Smith.

David's wife died in 1879 and was buried in old Shiloh Cemetery in Crowley's Ridge State Park with two of his children, Sara and Mary and the early pioneers of the county.

After 1879 when the Log Church house burned at old Shiloh they went two miles north and built their church Warren's Chapel and started a cemetery there.

After Margaret's death David married Fannie Cothern. There were no children to this marriage. David, Fannie and William are buried side by side at Warren's Chapel. Cannie Harris is there also.

Logan and James are buried in Morrow Cemetery.

Good Speed wrote about David in his *History of Greene County, Arkansas* published 1888 as he was a prominent man for the times.

David died in 1901. He has many descendants scattered all over the county. All proud to be of his heritage.

Susan Cansada had six children; three lived to be adults. Logan had 10 children, seven lived to be adults. James Alexander had one son, Macon.

**SMITH** – David "Bill" Conred Smith, the youngest of 10 children of Logan H. Roots Smith and Mary Alice Burkeen Smith, was born on March 24, 1916, in Greene County, Arkansas. He died March 16, 1985, in Corpus Christi, Texas, and was buried at Morrow Cemetery in Greene County, Arkansas. He married Lillian Ella Hots on September 30, 1942, and had three children, all born in Paragould. They were Barbara Elouise born on September 5, 1943; Doyle Wayne born on October 19, 1944; and Rebecca Kaye born on November 19, 1947. David was an educator and a Christian. These two areas were the dominant things in his life.

He began his education in Greene County while living near Sugar Creek on the Futtrell's place. He later quit school to help support the family remaining out of school for three years. Mr. Albert Buchanan volunteered to pick him up and take him to school if he would return. He took him up on his offer. He attended a country church school where Mr. Buchanan taught geometry and Brother Starling taught Bible. He then attended the 11th grade at Beech Grove and graduated from Evening Shade as valedictorian. In 1942 he began his teaching career. His first job was in a one-room school with eight grades and 65 students. He taught at Cotton Belt School, Stanford, Greene County, Lakeside, Swifton, Maila, Tuckerman and then he moved to Corpus Christi, Texas, where he taught math at Sundeen Junior High and High School and finally at Mary Carroll High School. He was at Carroll High School for 22 years, retiring in 1981. He obtained his bachelor's degree from Arkansas State University in Jonesboro, and his master's degree from Memphis State University. Both of these were earned by taking classes at night, on Saturdays and during the summer because he was teaching full-time. After moving to Corpus Christi he applied for a job with an oil company that would have greatly increased his income. He was rejected because of his age. At the time, it was a disappointment. Near his retirement time, he stated how thankful he was that the job was not available to him because teaching was the most rewarding job he could imagine. Upon his retirement from teaching, he began to work full-time for the Windsor Park Church of Christ.

Working full time for the Church of Christ was

*David Conred Smith and Mary Alice Smith (mother).*

very natural for David Smith. While still living in Arkansas, he had preached at some of the small churches in the Paragould area. His first preaching was at Pine Knot. While preaching at Bethel, he baptized his first person, Mr. Colman Lemons. In the Swifton area, he and Mr. Bill Wheeler preached at small area churches. They would rotate preaching in the morning and evening. When he moved to Corpus Christi, his preaching days slowed down but he became an elder in a new congregation, the Windsor Park Church of Christ, in October 1956. He remained an elder there until his death.

**SMITH** – Emmett Floyd Smith, Jr. (March 14, 1920 Weldon AR) was the third son of 10 children of Hester (Grady) Smith and Emmett Floyd Smith. Their other children:
1. Omar
2. J. C.
3. Emmett
4. Metta Moore
5. Bill
6. Charles
7. Jessie Lou Fondren
8. Keith
9. D. R.
10. Marilyn Smith.

He graduated from Beedeville High School in 1940 and entered Harding College, now Harding University, that fall. In 1942 he went to Campbell, MO to preach for the Church of Christ. That same year he married Emma Geer of Cowen, TN. In 1944 he went back to Harding to complete his degree in English. In 1946 he graduated along with his brother, Bill and his sister, Metta. Three siblings graduating together set a record at Harding, which has not been broken. The return of service men and women at the end of WWII caused a teacher shortage. Dr. Benson, president of Harding, asked Emmett to come back and teach English. He taught for one year.

Emmett always thought of himself as an educator. Because of the influence of R. N. Gardener, his high school superintendent, and others, he dreamed of starting a K-12 school where the Bible would be taught every day. To prepare for such an undertaking he went to Peabody College in Nashville and completed a master's degree in education and administration. With the encouragement of several families in Greene County he moved to Paragould in 1948. He preached for the new church at Seventh and Mueller Streets and started making plans for the school. Crowley's Ridge Academy opened in 1953. Seeing the need for a junior college, Crowley's Ridge College opened in 1964 on a 120-acre tract of land west of Paragould on Highway 25, the former country place of Dr. R. J. Haley. Emmett served as president of CRA and CRC until 1970. He was president of CRC until 1973. He returned as Chancellor in 1975-1979. During this time he preached for the Seventh and Mueller church for nearly 18 years.

In 1955 Emmett and Emma had a son, Emmett Floyd Smith III. In 1960 a daughter, Emma Lou was born. Three daughters were born to Emmett Floyd and his wife, Jeanina, Emily Katie and Claire. Emma Lou and her husband, Tad Danner have two children, Andrew and Allison.

After Emmett's wife's death in 1986, he married Nita Brinkley, widow of Arlin Brinkley. The Brinkley's had five sons:
1. Larry
2. Terry
3. Phillip
4. Randy
5. Danny

In retirement, Emmett was able to realize another dream, doing mission work in Europe. He and Nita made three trips to Bucharest and Brasov, Romania, teaching English and the Bible. In 1994 they taught in Donetsk, Ukraine.

Emmett helped to pioneer educational TV in Arkansas and was appointed to the board of the Arkansas Educational TV Commission by four Arkansas governors. At the time of his death he was the only charter member of East Arkansas Planning and Development Council. In recognition of his work in the community and in education, he was given the U. S. Congressman's Medal of Merit. March 21, 1997 the State of Arkansas awarded him the Arkansas Certificate of Merit for outstanding service to the community and state.

Emmett Smith

Harding University conferred upon Emmett the honorary Doctor of Laws degree in 1970 and Distinguished Alumnus Award in 1977.

Emmett Floyd Smith Jr. died Nov 23, 1997 and is buried in Pine Knot Cemetery near Paragould, AR.

*Submitted by Mrs. Emmett F. Smith*

**SMITH** – Frank S. Smith, son of John Smith and Elizabeth "Crickett" Brogden Smith married Norma Moore, Daughter of Alfred Moore and Emma A. Barton Moore and they had four children:
1. D. C.
2. A. J. died in infancy
3. Farrell "Shorty" deceased
4. Merveena

After Frank's death, Norma married Rollie Fox.

D. C. Smith married Garnetta Vinson and they have one son, Keith. Keith has never married.

Shorty married Vernelia Braden and they have two children, Ronald Smith and Gayla Brady Davis. Ronald is not married. Gayla married Richard Brady and has three children: Chris, Angela and Richie. Gayla has now remarried.

*Aug. 4, 1968 – Grandma Fox and Grandma Moore.*

Merveena married Vernon Reddick and they have two sons, Barry and Kevin. Barry married Judy Ellington and they have three children:
1. Bryan Reddick
2. April (Reddick) Miller
3. Ashley (Reddick) Shelton

Kevin married Kerry Tritch Miles (Tiffany Miles' daughter) and they have one son: Aaron Michael Reddick.

Norma, Frank and Rollie are buried in Harvey's Chapel Cemetery.

Shorty is buried in Woodland Heights Cemetery at Rector, AR.

**SMITH** – James Smith first settled at Glaze-Kenon Creek, Lawrence County, Arkansas in 1814. His son, James M. Smith, and wife, Rebecca Sharp, had nine children. He was a confederate soldier in Robert Shaver's Company, 35th Regiment Arkansas Volunteers. He served from 1862-June 1865. James Solomon Smith, born February 25, 1852, son of James M., had three children. He came to Greene County around 1900 and died February 9, 1909, and is buried at Fairview Cemetery. William Rufus Smith, born April 1, 1879, son of James Solomon, had seven children and died March 15, 1931, buried at Fairview Cemetery. William Ephraim Smith, born April 16, 1921, was the son of William Rufus and Loretta (Braswell) Fields. On December 17, 1938, he married Dorothy Stanfill. They had three children: Shirley, Billy and Jimmy. He died March 28, 1989, and is buried at Shiloh Cemetery. Jimmy Wayne Smith, born 1945, son of William Ephraim, married Brenda Rogers. They had three children: Jeffery, Shelia Carter and Lesa Brengard.

Solomon Eli Rogers, born October 1862 in Illinois, came from Iowa to Perry County, Arkansas, around 1900, with his wife Laura Bell Barnes. They had seven children. He died in Van Buren County. Louie Amos Rogers, born March 1889 in Iowa, son of Solomon Eli, married Della Ward. In 1922 he moved to around Manila to help build a highway. Della ran a boarding house for the men who worked on the highway. They had six children: Thelma, Carl, Bennie, Emily, Albert and Amos. He died in a field while farming on Goldsmith Road June 25, 1930, and is buried at the Mountain Home Cemetery. Bennie Solomon Rogers, born in Van-Buren County in December 1920, was the son of Louie Amos. In 1942 he married Alma Lowanda Burmingham, born 1927 in Greene County. They had five children: Eugene, Brenda Smith, Eddie, Joyce and Judy Orr.

*The family of Louie Rogers: Back: Nancy Idella "Della" and Louie Amos Rogers. Front: Thelma L. and Carol Lee Rogers, two of six children, taken around 1920.*

Ethan Ruff Burmingham, born 1841 in Tennessee. He married Mrs. Elizabeth (Leatherwood) Pratt on May 16, 1886, and lived at Fontaine, Arkansas. They had three children: Etta Mae, George Washington and Andrew Jackson. George Washington Burmingham, born 1890 in Greene County, married Mary Etta Jane Easter on September 18, 1913. They had 13 children: Effie, Edith, Earl, Edward, Cecil, Ethel, Lowanda, Aubrey, Ray, Grady and twin girls. He died in 1939 and is buried at Pleasant Hill Cemetery.

Rubin Easter, born 1855 in Missouri. He, his brothers and sisters, came to Arkansas from Illinois with an uncle who was a prize fighter around 1880. He married Jane Burrow January 3, 1884, and lived near Fontaine. They had five children: Richard, Sidney, Maryetta Jane, Ezra and Pearlie. Rubin died around 1909 after being kicked in the head by a horse. His son Richard, served in WWI and died in 1919 aboard ship from food poisoning. His name is listed on the Statute of Liberty at the Greene County Courthouse.

**SMITH** – James A. "Bud" Smith (1848 NC) married Nancy Lenora "Dolly" Anderson in 1878 by Mr. W. M. Sims, Justice of Peace. They had nine children. James Smith died in 1900 and Nancy "Dolly" died in 1927. They had an infant girl, who died young and is buried at Pine Log Cemetery near James and Nancy.

*L-R: Etta, Belle, Mary (Scrap), Stanley and Lee Smith*

The other children of James and Nancy were
1. Stanley Smith married Maud Anne Mills
2. Mary Scrap married Ben Stewart
3. Anderson M. Smith married Mabel Smith
4. Irvin M. Smith married (1) Lela Williams (2) Jewel Moore
5. Belle Smith married Claud Mabry
6. Ida "Lee" Smith married William "Harvey" Robinson
7. Charles Benjamin "C.B." Smith married Samantha Gatlin
8. Etta Smith married (1) Hallie Bowles and divorced (2) Archie Hobgood.

Nancy's father was William Jeptha Anderson (1823 GA) married Sophia Pitts in 1845. William Jeptha was a Confederate soldier.

James Smith's father, Allen Smith (1811 NC), moved to Gwinnett County, GA when his son was four years old. They were listed on the 1850 Census of Gwinnett, GA. Allen Smith married Rebecca Lockridge in 1838.

Many descendants of the Smith family are still living in the Brookland area.

*Submitted by Donna (Robinson) Ishmael*

**SMITH** – James Arthur Smith was born June 3, 1899, in Seymour, Indiana to Arthur Lycurtis Smith and Annie Francis Cole Smith. He was from a family of five girls and seven boys. Three of the children died at an early age. His family was farmers in Indiana of hay, cattle, sheep, hogs, corn and turkeys.

*The Hendrix family. Back row from left: Arlene, Dena, John Hicks, Bueford (in back), Dewey and Vernie. Front: Junior and Donie.*

Arthur Lycurtis had been to Greene County when he was about 17 years old to visit relatives here, which was the Hooker family from near Hooker Switch (which is today known as Hooker). Evidently he saw something in Greene County that he liked, so on February 6, 1910, with five children and a wife they boarded a train in Brownstown, Indiana, for Greene County. They brought their cattle, sheep, hogs, farming equipment and household goods with them. They put all this in one train car and one of Annie Francis' brothers rode in the car with them. Young Arthur had a dog named Pedro that he wanted to bring with him, but the only way the dog could come was to ride in the car with the cattle. He didn't want to be separated from his dog so he rode in the cattle car also all the way from Indiana.

On February 7, 1910, at 8:00 a.m. the Smith family arrived at their destination, Hooker Switch, Arkansas. The switch track was very near to the Big Creek Baptist Church, and part of the old railroad dump is still there being used for a county road today. They departed the train with their belongings and began life in Greene County. They moved in a house about one mile west of Lafe, Arkansas, when they first settled here to what is now known as the O.T. Reinhart place and lived there two years. At that time they bought 40 acres of land with a house and timber on it, near Gainesville, Arkansas. Arthur Lycurtis and his sons cut the timber off the 40 acres with a cross-cut saw.

Arthur chopped and picked cotton, after they had cut the timber, and then he stated working for Mr. Mack Rowe at his sorghum mill near the Blue Hill Cemetery. When winter came he worked for Mr. Rowe in the timber business. When he was 13 years old he went to work for Mr. Charlie Hooker who lived near to where they had gotten off the train. He worked for them year around, so he lived with them. He was paid $5.00 a month and his room and board, just enough to buy his clothes and a few extras. In his spare time he hunted rabbits and squirrels, and he had a love for hunting his whole life.

*Dena and Dewey Hendrix at their home at Hooker, Arkansas, with their new Studebaker car, about 1951 model.*

*Standing from left: L.D. Hendrix, Dewey Hendrix, Shirley (Hendrix) Smith, Junior Hendrix and Bueford Hendrix. Front from left: Vernie (Hendrix) Hill-Wilcox, Dena Hendrix, Arlene (Hendrix) McBee and Donie (Hendrix) Hahn. Photo circa 1955.*

While working for Mr. Rowe Arthur had met one of his daughters, Ruthie Erder Rowe, and he fell in love with her. They were married on September 28, 1919, at the home of Mr. and Mrs. Mack Rowe by a Preacher Williams, who was pastor of the Scatter Creek Methodist Church. He gave the preacher $2.00, which was all the money he had, for the ceremony. They lived with the Rowes until they could get them a house built on the Rowe's place. They built one room about 15x15 and a small side room. When they married they had a #8 cookstove, three cane bottom chairs, a small rocking chair, and one iron bedstead with a feather bed. Arthur made them a table out of rough lumber, and Erder made a dresser out of some boxes and a lard stand and sat a mirror on it. They lived in the little house and farmed for a year and their first child, a daughter, Fannie Mable was born June 11, 1920. Farming was bad that year so Arthur went to work on the walking dredge boat that was dredging Cache River. A few years later he went back to farming and also he worked at the Chevrolet plant in Michigan. He later worked for the Henry Wrape Stave Mill as a timber buyer for about 25 years.

During this time other children were born. Racheal October 28, 1922, she only lived 4 months, dying of pneumonia; Bertha June 25, 1924; Margaret October 20, 1926, died December 17, 1926; Nellie January 19, 1928; Charles Arthur September 11, 1930; Harold June 29, 1933; Ruthie September 23, 1935; and Vearl June 19, 1937. Last of the children was Paul born August 22, 1940. Mable died in September 1997.

In the fall of 1931 Arthur moved his family to Clay County (the Cache Lake Community). Erder died April 23, 1968, and Arthur lived until August 4, 1988, to the age of 89 years. He was an avid hunter and fisherman.

Greene County had given the Smith family a good start and they always loved Greene County.

**SMITH** – James Oliver Smith (1879-1969) married Joycie Carolyn Wyatt (1882-1981) in Greene County and made their home in the Ramer's Chapel community. Both are buried in the Ramer's Chapel Cemetery.

He was the son of Thomas Jefferson (1848-unknown) and Elsa Jane Moore Smith (about 1855-unknown) and she was the daughter of John Mitchell (1856-unknown) and Margaretta Abigail Dortch (1861-unknown) Wyatt.

Their children were as follows:
1. Thomas Jefferson "Tommie" Smith (Dec 12, 1903-May 19, 1981)
2. Ruby Bell (1913-unknown)
3. Johnnie
4. Mary
5. Bessie
6. Delores
7. Lizzie Beth
8. James
9. Eugene.

Thomas Jefferson married Aug 6, 1927 Lea Onnie Ramer (1927-unknown) daughter of Robert and Minnie Brewer Ramer. They had the following children:
1. Gerald D. Smith (1929)
2. Cleatis Adrian (1932)
3. Naomi Melvina (1935)
4. Infant Smith died at birth.

Gerald D. Smith married Feb 10, 1955 Velma Inez Stephens and they had the following children:
1. Becky Jalan (1957)
2. Lisa Dawn (1966).

Cleatis Adrian married Nov 28, 1955 Ruth Whitt and they had the following child: Carl David (1966).

Naomi married May 27, 1961 Carlos Bradford and they had the following children:
1. Tammy Loraine
2. Joyce Ann

**SMITH** – John C. And Pauline Smith celebrated their 50th anniversary on October 6, 1984. Included in the picture are their three children, Weldon, Geraldine and Donald.

John Calvin was born January 20, 1911, at Piggott, Arkansas. He was the son of George Washington and Martha (Gowen) Smith. He served in the U.S. Army from 1927 to 1932. He deceased 1990 and is buried in Brown's Chapel Cemetery. John returned to Paragould and met Pauline Chunn. Pauline was born July 11, 1918, to Dewey and Mary Chunn in Greene County, Arkansas.

Weldon married Betty Jo Key. Prior to Weldon's death September 1995, he served as the coordinator at Outreach Mission. He is buried in Greene County Memorial Gardens.

Geraldine married Wayne Garmrath. She was a service representative for the Greene County Department of Human Services and retired after 32 years of service.

*John C. and Pauline Smith celebrating their 50th anniversary with their children Weldon, Geraldine and Donald. Made at East Side Baptist Church.*

Donald married Bettie Taunton and resides in Alexander City, Alabama. He owns and operates his own painting and metal finishing garage.

The family moved from Paragould in 1945 to Poplar Bluff, Missouri. In 1955 the family moved to Flint, Michigan. Employment took him and his family to this booming town of Flint, Michigan, where he worked for General Motors until he retired in 1972. Pauline owned and operated a ceramic shop in Flint. When they retired, they moved back to Paragould and the ceramic shop moved with them to Tech and Walcott Road.

Pauline's Ceramic was a family business from 1972 until 1996 when she sold the business. After 40 years of teaching and working in ceramics, the desire and love for it is still a part of her life.

**SMITH** – Johnathan Smith was born July 20, 1852, in Benton County, Tennessee. His wife Sarah Elender Kee was born February 16, 1866, in Benton County, Tennessee. They were married June 2, 1887, and had four children while living in Tennessee; Fannie, Addie Belle, Lillar and Lester.

They moved to Greene County in the Campground Community sometime between 1901 and 1906. They had two more children: Vestal and Chester. They were hard working farmers. Not much was known about their lives.

Sarah once had a vision that the clouds were parting and two angels being there. She prayed to God instantly to spare her life until she had her children raised. Her youngest was 17 when she died.

*Johnathan Smith and Sarah Smith.*

Johnathan liked to sit his grandkids on his lap and sing religious songs to them while twirling his handlebar moustache. Sarah once made a dark brown print dress for church. She got axle grease on it from the wagon while going to church.

Johnathan lived with his son and daughter-in-law, Chester and Pearl Smith at Bard Community. When he got weak and unable to care for himself, he went to live with his daughter and son-in-law, Addie and Johnny Pegg in the Alexander Community. He didn't want to be a burden to Chester and Pearl because they had small children and his daughter's children were bigger.

Johnathan died November 16, 1935, and was buried at Fairview next to his wife. At the grave, his daughter Vestal fainted. Some men went across the road to get her a drink of water. The people refused to give them water. The raised six children and have many ancestors here in Greene County.

**SMITH** – Mr. E. M. Robinson, Justice of the Peace, married Lee Smith and William Harvey Robinson in January 1912 in Craighead County, AR. Harvey was a railroad worker. They had one daughter named Orma. They lived all their married life in Paragould, AR. Harvey, a retired employee of the Missouri Pacific Railroad, died in 1954 of a heart attack at his home in Paragould at the age of 63. Mrs. Lee Robinson died at her home at the age of 80 years in Dec 1954. Lee was a longtime resident of Paragould. She was a homemaker and had seven great grandchildren at the time of her death.

Orma Robinson married Arlie Martin. They lived in Paragould and had a daughter named Marlene and a son named R. H. Martin. Orma died in 1976 and her husband, Arlie died later. They are buried at Linwood Cemetery.

Marlene Martin lived and worked in Paragould. She had a couple of husbands. She had children but I don't know how many or their names. I do know, that at one time, Marlene was married to a man by the name of Saurheaver. I am assuming that Marlene is buried at Linwood Cemetery also. Her brother R. H. Martin lived in Paragould, Jonesboro and Searcy, AR. I do not know anything else about him. A great grandchild of Harvey and Lee Robinson is living in the 'home place' in Paragould.

Belle Smith and Claud Mabry were married in 1916 in Craighead County, AR by Mr. R. L. Akers, Justice of the Peace. They lived all their married life in the Brookland, Powell Township, AR. They had two daughters: Charlsie (1919) and Mary "Josie" (1921). Claud Mabry died in 1965. He was a farmer, veterinarian and a deputy sheriff of Brookland at one time. Belle died at the age of 84 years in 1974 at the home of her daughter, Charlsie in Jonesboro, AR. I remember Belle (Smith) Mabry as being a kind, caring person who always loved having company. She always made the best homemade soup and oatmeal cookies. I never heard my grandma say an unkind or ugly remark about anyone. She was a hard worker and always had a good garden with lots of fresh vegetables in the summertime.

L-R: Belle Smith and Lee Smith, 1900's.

*Submitted by Donna (Robinson) Ishmael*

**SMITH** – Logan H. Roots Smith was born December 14, 1870, in Greene County, Arkansas. He was the son of David Alexander Smith and Margaret (Pevehouse) Smith.

On January 31, 1895, he married Mary Alice Burkeen, daughter of Jessie and Eliza Burkeen. They had 10 children: Sudie (1895-1957), Jessie (1897-1969), Hettie (1899-1969), Nettie (1902-1994), Walker (1904-1936), James (1907-1925), Cora (1910-1994), Rebecca (1912-1923), Clinnie (1915-1915) and David (1916-1985).

Logan, named after a famous man of the South, was a farmer and timber worker. He cut and hewed logs for railroad ties and made shingles and clapboards to cover houses. He was a hard-working Christian man. He died May 31, 1939, and is buried in Morrow Cemetery next to his wife, Mary Alice, and eight of his children. He has many descendants, all proud to be of his rich heritage.

*Logan H. Roots Smith age 32 years old, Mary Alice Smith age 27 years old, Sudie Eliza Smith, Jessie Alexander Smith, Hettie IsaBelle Smith and Nettie Lauerlin Smith (baby).*

Sudie married Jim Wheeler and had one son, Marlin; then she married Henry Hutchins. There were no children to this marriage.

Jessie married Susan Pillow. They had G.L., Jessie Lou, James, L.R., Alice and Earl.

Hettie married Melvin Busby. They had Roxie Charlie, Mary Alice, Margie and Hester.

Nettie married Clarence Jones. They had Dillman, Clarice, Almeda, Jewel, Ben and Athen.

Jim died at age 17 from a snake bite.

Walker married Lillie Henson, had one son, Bynum Stanley.

Cora married John Goins. They had Davis, Louise, Mary Demonra, Lois Jane, Lydia and David.

Rebecca died at 11 years old with epilepsy.

Clinnie died at 3 moths old with pneumonia.

David married Lillian Hots. They had Barbara, Doyle Wayne and Rebecca Kay.

Mary Alice (Burkeen) Smith (August 22, 1875- November 17, 1951) was a hard-working Christian woman. She raised 10 children of her own through the Depression, plus she raised Adaline Smelser, a girl whose mother had burned in a house fire.

Mary Alice raised a garden, canned vegetables, raised chickens and cows for eggs and milk to help Logan feed their family. She pieced and quilted beautiful quilts and sewed most of the clothes for their family.

She was very religious and could tell you where anything was found in the Bible. She entertained her grandchildren by telling them stories. Many were about her growing up in the Boston Mountains in Arkansas, Big Piney and Little Piney Mountains, also ghost stories. She would mold bowls, people and animals from clay. She could make shadows of animals on the wall and flip her fingers to make them look like they were moving.

She made Jacob's Ladders from twine, and spool necklaces from empty spools of thread. She taught them to sew and to quilt. If their stitches were too big they had to take them out and make smaller ones. She gave the girls thimbles for Christmas.

**SMITH** – Macon Ogustus Smith (August 22, 1914-January 1, 1986) was the son of James Alexander (November 28, 1876-June 19, 1937) and Nancy Ann (Burkeen) Morrow Langham Smith (October 20, 1882-February 9, 1961). He was the grandson of David A. (July 8, 1826-November 24, 1901) and Margaret (Pevehouse) Smith (January 6, 1855-May 30, 1879) and the great-great-grandson of Stantford (1812-1876) and Margaret (Tassey) Smith (1819-1874).

The early settlement of Stanford was named for his great-great grandfather Stantford, and in usage, down through the years, the second "t" in the name became lost. Macon lived in or relatively near this community most of his life.

When Macon was 21 years old, his father was returning to his home from a pasture where he had taken his team. As he crossed the road in front of his house, he was struck by a truck. Being slightly deaf and apparently failing to see the truck, his father became confused when the driver sounded his horn, and as he stepped backwards, stepped into a rut and fell down in front of the truck, the wheels of which crushed his chest, killing him almost instantly. This traumatic experience left Macon as the head of the family and with the care of his mother, Nancy.

On September 26, 1937, Macon married Reba Eldora Taylor (February 9, 1921-March 29, 1997) who was the eldest child of William Carroll (February 9, 1894-July 9, 1982) and Pearl Elnora (McElrath) Taylor (September 16, 1900-May 3, 1994). They had three children: Jimmy Leon, who married Leah Kate Morrow; Glenna Pearline, who married Ronald Ryles; and Shirley Ann, who married Michael L. Harmon. They have three grandchildren: Jimmy Leon Smith Jr., Vanessa Leigh (Ryles) Harris and Andrea Lynn (Harmon) McCarter. They have two great-grandchildren: Keely Ann McCarter and Jacob Talon Harris, and a step-great-grandchild, Savannah Dawn Harris.

Macon and Reba farmed in the Stanford Community before owning and operating a small grocery and restaurant combination, and Macon's mother lived with them until her death on February 9, 1961.

After leaving the store business, Macon worked for Brewer Brothers Oil and Gas, and Reba worked in the cafeterias of the Stanford and Greene County Technical Schools. Macon had one brother, Charley (September 16, 1918- November 7, 1918), and two half-brothers: Ezra Morrow (1904-1915), who died at age 11, and Oran Langham (January 30, 1908-February 12, 1986) who married Sybel Harvey (July 21, 1914-March 25, 1979). Reba had four sisters and two brothers: Pauline, Monzell, Ruth, Inez, William Carroll Jr. and R.V.

*Macon and Reba Smith.*

Macon enjoyed hunting and fishing when he was younger, and he gave many of his friends their bi-monthly haircuts. Reba enjoyed raising flowers, and she always raised a garden every year and preserved the food from it. Although Macon had heart surgery and suffered from heart trouble which eventually caused his retirement, he and Reba managed to enjoy their family and friends and life in general, and Reba continued working until Macon's illness and heart trouble caused his death.

After Macon's death, Reba moved her mother into her home and cared for her until her mother's death in 1994 from cancer. Although Reba also suffered from cancer at the time of her mother's death, she managed to live for three more years. She lived an active life and always put her family, church work and friends before herself.

Macon and Reba were loved and respected not only by their families but also by their many friends throughout the county.

**SMITH** – Thomas Turner Smith (Sept 9, 1830 TN), son of Stanford Smith and Margaret Tassey had blue eyes, light hair and complexion and when grown was five feet, 10 inches tall. In the 1850 census he lived with his father in Cannon County, TN. Thomas married Locinda Jane Tennyson, daughter of Abraham Tennyson and Parmelia Carrigan, Aug 7, 1856 probably in Tennessee. Both Smith families had moved to Cache, Greene County, AR by the census of 1860.

Thomas enlisted in the Civil War in Greene County and served in the 13th Arkansas Infantry. He was severely wounded at the battle of Shiloh, having a head wound and losing part of his hand. According to family history, the hospital in Memphis, TN to which he was sent for treatment was full so he returned home to recover

*Thomas Turner Smith and granddaughter, Emily Jane Linesay.*

from his wounds. He was hidden by his family from the Federals and from recruiting officers of the Confederate Army, who were forcing any "able-bodied" men back into service. The family was troubled as well by marauding renegades from Missouri and Arkansas. It is said they had to bury hams and food under the smokehouse to save them from being stolen. Subsequently Thomas completed his service with Co. D, Davie's Battalion, Arkansas Cavalry and was mustered out at Wittsburg, AR, May 25, 1865 at the age of 36.

Locinda Jane Smith's granddaughter, Alma Kay, in an interview in 1967 stated: "Locinda, with her husband Thomas Turner Smith, was one of the party of Arkansas men (most of them ex-Confederate officers) and their families who left Arkansas in early 1870s for Oregon." It can be assumed that the men took the well-worn Oregon Trail, which has been called the world's longest graveyard, with one body, on average, buried every 80 yards. People lost their lives to influenza, cholera, severe dysentery or accidents. They were crushed by wagon wheels, stepped on by oxen or killed when a simple cut turned into a gangrenous infection. Nearly 35,000 people made the trip from 1843 to the mid 1860s when stagecoach lines and then railroads replaced the trail as the main overland route. One out of 10 died along the way. Drownings were common. Many women gave birth along the way. On average it took about 160 days to make the 2,000-mile trip. In a good day, pioneers could make 20 miles. Fortunately the women from this group were able to come by train, which was, in those days, an arduous trip but not one as severe as traveling overland would have been. They went first to Oregon City, Clackamas County, in the northern part of the state and lived there approximately 14 years. They then joined her brother Hiram Franklin Tennyson's family on the lower Coquille River at Randolph and helped him mine for gold at Cut Creek. Thomas later turned to farming. He died in Coquille Feb 3, 1913.

*Submitted by Loanne Linesay Rebuck*

**SNOWDEN** – Albert Sidney (April 11, 1871 Black Oak, AR) was the first-born child of Malachi C. Snowden and Kate Elizabeth Young. He spent nearly his entire life in Greene County, AR.

Albert first married Miss Cole, who died in childbirth with their son Malachi "Mack" (Sept 22, 1896). After his first wife's death he met and married a widow, Beulah Nancy (Chandler) Kennemore on Dec 9, 1900. She also had a son John Clarence Kennemore (Sept 1, 1889). They started life with a ready-made family. Soon these children were added to the family:

1. Wilma Totsie (Oct 9, 1901)
2. Albert "Bill" Wilburn (May 18, 1904)
3. Reba L. (Aug 13, 1906)
4. Mary Snowden (March 30, 1909)

Albert Sidney was an active member of the community. In 1904 Albert was given a certificate signed by Jeff Davis, Governor of Arkansas for Tax Collector on Oct 31, 1904, this with a certificate signed by Franklin D. Roosevelt for the term of four years as postmaster of Paragould, AR hang on the bedroom wall of his oldest daughter, Totsie Burroughs now 98 years old and still living in Paragould. Albert served as postmaster from 1917-1922 and 1935-1950. He also served as deputy sheriff of the county. Albert ran for sheriff and lost, but after that there was to be a hanging and Albert said "I would have had to resign," as he couldn't have hung the man.

He had been a member of the Paragould Masonic Lodge # 368 for approximately 55 years. Sidney and Beulah Nancy had been life long members of the First Baptist Church. In 1916 he was president of Greene and Lawrence Counties Drainage Districts.

After Albert retired he opened "Snowden Café". He just retired from one job to another.

Beulah Nancy was a busy homemaker and was active in church activities. Beulah died April 18, 1953; she was 84 years old and is buried in Linwood Cemetery. Dr. Thomas McSpadden, pastor of the North Paragould Presbyterian Church, officiated at her funeral, along with her minister, Rev. Lewis D. Ferrell, pastor of First Baptist Church.

Albert died May 6, 1959 at the age of 88. His survivors: Mrs. L. B. Burroughs SR, Mrs. R. O. McSpadden, Mrs. Mary Huntsman, one stepdaughter, Mrs. Blanche Light, two sons, Albert Wilburn and Mack Snowden and one stepson J. C. Kennemore; a stepsister Miss Ethel Mae Rowe.

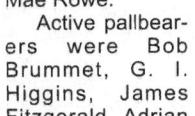

*Albert Sidney Snowden Family – Picture taken Jan. 1902. Beulah, Albert holding Totsie; back: Clarence Kennamore and Mack Snowden.*

Active pallbearers were Bob Brummet, G. I. Higgins, James Fitzgerald, Adrian Raley, Luther Ray Cline, Hancel Yopp and Cecil Emmert.

Honorary pallbearers were Clyde Johnson, Jim Fitzgerald, Cecil Mitchell, Clarence Dover, Frank Hyde, Maurice Miller, Cecil Farley, Fred Johnson, Ellis Johnson, Ott Johnson, Roy Bradford, Hardy Neely, Sam Shane, Jones Horne, Al Grooms, Will Raglin, Leonard Looney, Jap Edwards, Guy McSpadden, Charles Sims, Charles Austin, Ed Roleson Jr. and present and past Greene County office holders.

*Submitted by Evelyn Euritha Wagner*

**SNOWDEN** – Alice Amelia Snowden married Charlie Hill Faulkner, the second child of G. H. and Francis Faulkner. He was born May 17, 1864 and came with his parents to Greene County. He lived a full and busy life. In his early 20s he was a mail carrier and carried the mail from Greensboro in Craighead County to Gainesville, Greene County seat.

He married Alice Amelia Snowden in 1890, the second child of Malachi C. Snowden and Kate Elizabeth (Young) Snowden.

Charlie was a farmer; also drilled wells, owning a well auger and also a sorghum mill. He kept a hired hand to help cultivate the crops and hired the cotton picked for in those days it was picked entirely by hand.

Charlie Hill was also a builder and carpenter owning a complete set of carpenter's tools. He helped to build a house for his father and he built two houses for his own family.

In early 1900 he lost his well auger in a well cave-in. He also sold his sorghum mill. From 1904 to 1906 he again carried the mail, this time from the old Crowley post office to Stanford and Rice, a few miles west of Stanford. In 1907 he rented his farm and moved to Paragould. He kept books for the Farmers Union Gin and was overseer for the farm of G. O. Light.

*1989 – Nieces of Alice A. Snowden. Wilma Totsie Burroughs (left) and Mary Snowden Huffman, sisters.*

Later he became night watchman for Joseph's Gin during the ginning season and then for Joseph's Store (now Belks) and Bertig's Store (later Grabers) until his health failed in 1939. He was a night watchman for over 20 years and passed away April 9, 1950. He was a great reader, particularly the Bible. He would read himself to sleep with reading the Bible and his children would tease him about reading the Bible in the daytime and carrying a gun at night. He was converted at the age of 17 and was a member of the Union Grove Baptist Church, which he joined in his early manhood.

Charles Hill and Alice (Snowden) Faulkner and seven children:

1. Lillian married Johnnie Swindel
2. Earl Faulkner
3. Irene married Mr. Brogden
4. Martha married Cone Murphy
5. Jerry Faulkner
6. Snowden F. Faulkner, who at the time of his death in 1963 was with the J. W. Burns Detective Agency

7. Charles Faulkner died in infancy.

Alice was the sister of Albert Sidney Snowden, Samuel Issac Snowden and half sister to Ethel Rowe.

*Submitted by Evelyn Euritha Wagner*

**SNOWDEN** – Eugene Lyle Snowden (July 27, 1905) the second child born to Samuel Isaac Snowden and Eddith Simpson Snowden, early pioneers to Greene County, AR.

The Snowden family moved to Jonesboro, AR. Growing up with five brothers and one sister:
1. Raymond Wilfred
2. Samuel Maurice
3. William Malachi
4. Wayne Wilson
5. Weldon
6. Isaac Junior
7. Zelma

Pearl Brust was a neighbor of Lyle's. One day when he saw her riding her horse with her hair blowing in the wind, he said, " I have to have her". And so he did. They were married May 3, 1928. Disappointing many a young man in Jonesboro who also had their eye on the lovely Pearl, this was told to me by their son, Eugene Russell Snowden. According to their daughter, Doris, Lyle's sister, Thelma was instrumental in fixing her brother Lyle up with her good friend Pearl.

*1937 – Eugene Lyle Snowden and Pearl Brust Snowden and children (L-R): Donald, Doris, and Janette.*

They moved to an area of Detroit called "Hill Billy Heaven", known for the southerners that came north for jobs with the auto industry. There Lyle went to work for Packard Motor Company, learned enough skills to later go to work for General Motors Company with a good paying job. He stayed there till he retired.

They raised a large family:
1. Clyde Eugene (May 13, 1929 - Nov 10, 1929)
2. Janette (Sept 2, 1930)
   a. Eugene Russell (June 9, 1950), later adopted by Lyle and Pearl, married Jeanie Rachubka Feb 19, 1972, their children:
      I. Eugene Russell Snowden Jr.
      II. Janet Pamela Snowden
   Janette Snowden later married Joe Mohmmad. Their children are:
   a. Joey Mohmmad, an air line pilot for Northwest airlines
   b. Jamie Mohammad who is an R. N.
   c. Mark Mohmmad who is a supervisor Air Traffic Controller
   d. Miriam Mohmmad whose husband is a contractor
   e. David Mohmmad died in 1990
   f. Rose Mohammad owns a beauty salon in Virginia.
3. Doris Ella Snowden married John Carl Bowling on March 31, 1950 and their children are:
a. Gale Lynne Bowling married Rex Bricka July 14, 1973 and their children are:
   I. Wyatt Sean
   II. Mathew Alan
   III. Holly Renee Bricka
b. Vicky Bowing married Paul Maxwell and their children are:
   I. Allison
   II. William Russell
   III. Katie Maxwell
   IV. Vincent Bowling is unmarried and in partnership with his father of B and G Areo Space Metals.
4. Donald Lyle married Roxanne and their children are:
   a. Mike
   b. Tim
   c. Shawn
   d. Patrick Shannon
   e. Heather Snowden.
5. Priscilla Ann Snowden (Sept 29, 1941) married Melvin Barnes and their children are:
   a. Christopher
   b. Melody Barnes.
6. Sharon Louise Snowden (Oct 28, 1943) married Douglas Ross and their children are:
   a. Laura
   b. Brian Ross.
7. Linda Snowden (Oct 22, 1948) married Roy Barlow and their children are:
   a. Jamie
   b. Shannon

*Submitted by Evelyn Euritha Wagner*

**SNOWDEN** – Isaac Junior Snowden was Lt. Isaac "I. J." Snowden, WWII Naval Fighter Pilot. His grandparents were early pioneers to Greene County, AR. He was the youngest son of Samuel Isaac and Eddith Simpson Snowden. He had six brothers and one sister:
1. Wilfred
2. Lyle
3. Maurice
4. Bill
5. Wayne
6. Weldon
7. Zelma

I. J. Snowden married Marty Hellman in 1940.

At Patriots Point in Charleston, SC there is a US Navy ship museum. They have the USS Yorktown aircraft carrier on display along with other ships you can go on and explore. There also is the WWII Navy Hellcat F6F fighter on display; this is the same plane I. J. Flew in WWII.

*Isaac Junior Snowden with his wife, Marty Hellman Snowden, 1940.*

There are two bronze plaques with I. J.'s name on them. They read: Lt. Isaac J. Snowden was on the light aircraft carrier the Belleau Wood (CVL-24) in the 24th wing that was part of the 58th battle group in the Pacific campaign. He joined the 24th air wing as soon as it was formed in Sept 1942 and flew almost daily combat missions for two years until he was killed June 18, 1944 at the age of 24. His many missions included dogfights and bombing runs of land and sea targets while avoiding intense AA Fire in the process.

On Sunday, June 18, 1944 eight Hellcats took off from the Belleau Wood to bomb the beaches at Guam to soften it up for a landing of US Marines. On the way to the target, 14 Zeros jumped them and a big dogfight took place with seven Zeros shot down and no Hellcat losses. The eight planes then continued from there to the bomb run on Guam and proceeded to bomb and strafe the beaches. After dropping his bombs I. J.'s plane got hit with ground bases AA. His wingman looked over and told I. J. that his plane was on fire so I. J. bailed out and safely landed in the harbor at Guam. A Jap boat picked him up before the Americans could rescue him and took him prisoner. His body was never recovered. There is a headstone in the Oaklawn cemetery in Jonesboro, AR with his name on it but the grave is empty.

Lt. Isaac J. Snowden's awards include 11 battle stars and a presidential citation for extreme courage in the face of hostile enemy fire.

This memorial was discovered by I. J.'s nephew, Eugene Russell Snowden and shared with the rest of the Snowden family.

Another nephew, Jason Ballard, discovered a book, "Paddles" by author John A. Harper. The book has this account of I. J.s last day.

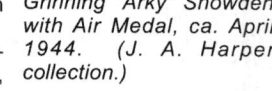
*Grinning "Arky" Snowden with Air Medal, ca. April 1944. (J. A. Harper collection.)*

"So what happened to Arky? He bailed out about two miles off shore. Yeah. He was in his raft when we left. Not five minutes later a submarine surfaced right next to Arky's life raft. Looked like Arky had it made. But just then the big shore battery bracketed the sub with big geysers of water. The sub just disappeared in a big white splash. I couldn't see Arky in all the white water. We went over and made a couple of strafing runs on the shore battery. When we got back, the sub had her periscope up and looking for Arky. But Arky wasn't in his boat any more. I guess he must've gotten bounced out of his boat by the water bursts from the shore battery. He never did put out any dye marker and he never waved at us. I think he was wounded pretty badly when he got hit and really couldn't do much for himself. Gone, huh? Arky's gone."

There are lots of stories of "Arky" as his fellow shipmates called him. I. J. was one of many men who fought and died for their country. I was proud he was my uncle.

*Submitted by Evelyn Euritha Wagner*

**SNOWDEN** – Malachi C. Snowden (1840 Memphis, Shelby County, TN) was an early pioneer to Greene County, AR. His parents were Nathan and Sarah (Gregory) Snowden.

After the death of Malachi's parents, Nathan and Sarah in 1841 and 1847, Malachi and his brothers were scattered.

Enoch, Malachi's oldest half brother returned to North Carolina and married a local girl, Georgiana. They had one son, Edward (1859). I suspect that his mother's side of the family and possibly Enoch's were still in North Carolina.

Francis was living with the William Wash family in

*Albert Sidney Snowden (1871-1959), oldest son of Malachi C. Snowden.*

1850. He was 21 years old. He was still in Memphis, TN in 1870.

Samuel, in 1850, was living with G. W. Davis family and was 18 years old. Samuel married M. J. and they have Rufus (1857), Freeman (1861) and Alvin (1864).

Isaac and Malachi, in 1850 were living with Jared Edwards' (the executor of their father's will, which left Isaac and Malachi enough money to cover their future schooling expenses and ownership to some slaves) family. Isaac was 12 years old and Malachi was 10 years old.

Isaac married Martha and they had Joseph (1861), Alice (1863), Eugene (1866) and Frank (1869).

In 1860 Malachi was 21 years old and an overseer for Samuel Bond, a physician on a plantation in Tennessee. It had to be a really large plantation, as the value of real estate lists it for $154,000 and personal property at $135,000.

On Aug 14, 1861 Malachi joined Capt. R. W. Pitman's Company 13 Regiment Tennessee Vols in the Confederate Army. My cousin, Eugene Russell Snowden, says that when visiting the battlegrounds of Shiloh, that he came upon some information that our Great Grandfather Malachi was part of that battle. His regiment was considered heroes during that battle. Malachi mustered out May 6, 1865. It states in his service records that he was of fair complexion, light hair, blue eyes and 5'9" tall.

In 1869 Malachi met Kate Elizabeth Young and they married. Their children: Albert Sidney (April 11, 1871 Black Oak, AR), Alice Amelia (May 13, 1875), and Samuel Isaac (Feb 11, 1879 Madison, AR). Before Samuel Isaac's birth, his father died of yellow fever, in Forrest City, St. Francis County, AR. The 1880 census lists all the children, but also Alfonso Dunn, as a brother, but I'm convinced that Alfonso Dunn was a boarder. Katie seemed to always, at one time or another have boarders. I am thinking that he was there to help with the farm. Kate needed all her time to care for her young children. Katie Elizabeth Young Snowden returned to Greene County, AR.

*Submitted by Evelyn Euritha Wagner*

**SNOWDEN** – Malachi "Mack" Snowden (Sept 22, 1896) was the son of Albert Sidney Snowden and his first wife, Miss Cole. His mother died in childbirth, it is thought. After his mother's death, Mack and Albert went to live with his grandmother, Katie Young Snowden.

Mack left home and joined the army at the age of 16 years old. He lost three fingers during this time. He lived in Indianapolis, IN.

*Malachi "Mack" Snowden, ca. 1888.*

Mack met and married Miss Elizabeth Snowball. They had a daughter, Ruth Snowden (Jan 29, 1920). She married a Mr. Delk.

He later worked as a painter at the Art Gallery. It was thought in Washington, D.C.

Mack died Oct 19, 1976 and Elizabeth died Dec 28, 1971.

*Submitted by Evelyn Euritha Wagner*

**SNOWDEN** – Mary Snowden was the youngest child of Albert Sidney Snowden and Beulah Nancy Kennemore Chandler. Mary was born March 30, 1909 in Paragould, Greene County, AR. She had blond hair, blue eyes and stood about 5'3" tall and was very pretty. Mary taught at Welch schoolhouse; then moved to St. Louis from 1930 to 1946. Perhaps drawn there by her brother Bill, as he owned and operated a drive-in restaurant there. Mary was employed as a nurse for Dr. Brady; a pediatrician in St. Louis, MO. Mary married William Huffman. They had one daughter, Mary Nancy Huffman (April 24, 1942 St. Louis, MO). In 1946 the family returned to Paragould and Mary went to work for Dr. Baker in Paragould.

Mary Nancy married Bob Fredrick and they had two daughters, Melissa Fredrick (Jan 19, 1968 Pine Bluff, AR) and Chrissy Fredrick (Aug 8, 1971 Pine Bluff, AR). Mary Nancy later married William Huntsman and they had one son, Rob Huntsman Jr. (Feb 17, 1974 Greenville, MS). This writer thinks Rob looks better that any male model dreams of looking.

*Wilma Totsie Snowden and Mary Snowden.*

Mary Nancy now resides in Memphis, TN and is married to David Chappel. She teaches school there.

Mary Snowden Huffman was living with her sister, Totsie Burroughs of Paragould until recently and now lives in Greene Acres Nursing Home located in Paragould.

*Submitted by Evelyn Euritha Wagner*

**SNOWDEN** – In 1830 Nathan and Sarah (Gregory) Snowden were living in Currituck County, NC. In the census, it shows two sons, Enoch (a son by a previous marriage) and Francis. Nathan is listed as between 30-40 years and Sarah as between 20-30 years of age. Enoch F. Snowden (1826) and Francis Snowden (1829). Sarah was the daughter of Samuel and Betsey Gregory.

Samuel and Betsey (Savillo) Gregory, besides Sarah, also had a son named Malachi and Mary, and Emily who married Samuel Sturges. There was a large number of Snowden and Gregory's living in North Carolina at this time.

The families moved to Memphis, Shelby County, TN by 1840. After Nathan and Sarah came to Shelby County, three more sons were added to the family, Samuel (1832), Isaac (1838), Malachi C. (1840). Sarah died between 1840-1841. Nathan married Mary Gregory (Betsy's sister) March 17, 1841. Nathan died just before 1847. Our Malachi (this writer's great grandfather) was but seven years.

*Submitted by Evelyn Euritha Wagner*

**SNOWDEN** – Raymond Wilfred Snowden (Feb 20, 1904) was the first born to Samuel Isaac and Eddith Simpson Snowden. Their families were early pioneers to Greene County, AR.

He followed his parents into farming. He met and married May Irene Harvey. He farmed in Truman, AR. Jimmy Moon remembers him to be a hard working man. He was a good farmer. Jimmy also remembers him having the first battery-operated radio in Truman, AR. He remembers all the young people would gather in Wilfred's front yard just to listen to the country music. Wilfred would turn up the volume for them. That radio or one that's much like it is in the possession of Brian Minyard, Wilfred's grandson. Wilfred and Irene had six daughters.

Irma Lou (June 7, 1931) married Gilbert Len Brewington, they had one son, Wilford Lynn Brewington Beasley who married Carol Lynn Smith; children are Lori Allison and Crissy Lynne Beasley. Wilford Lynn later married Susan Kathleen Felkins and their son is Scott Lynn Beasley. Irma Lou later married Earnest Warner Beasley and their children are: William James Beasley, who married Lee Mahan and their children are: George Warner, William James, Paige Beasley and Lisa Nichole Beasley.

Nelletta June Snowden (June 30, 1933) married Harold Gene Terry. They have three children Harold Gene, Peggy June and Raymond Stanley who married Sherie Lynn Merriet; their son is Raymond Wayne Terry.

Winfred Louise Snowden (Feb 27, 1938) married Ray Minyard and their children are: Timothy Ray, who died at the age of five years of leukemia. Stephanie Regina and Brian Eugene Minyard. Ray Minyard died Jan 6, 1971 due to a tragic truck accident. He drove for Kroger Grocery Markets.

Sandra Sue Snowden (April 12, 1942) married Richard Wayne Flora. Their children are: Claire Lorraine who married Patrick James Conner and their son Alexander Conner (Feb 27, 1998), Rebecca Elizabeth Flora married Todd Ogden.

Rosalyn Regina Snowden married Billy Ray Ballard. Their children are: Jason Kyle who married Jacqueline

*Raymond Wilfred Snowden and Irene Harvey Snowden, Aug. 1930, Truman, AR.*

Arlene and their children are a daughter, Jordan Alexandra Ballard and a son, Grayson Kyle (Dec 12, 1999); Charisse Ballard who married Darren Ray Findley and their son is Derek Ray Findley.

Patricia Ann Snowden married Donald C. Hutchins, their daughter Melanie Donette Hutchins married Timothy Lee Sumpter, and their daughter is Brittany Nicole Sumpter. Melanie Donette Hutchins later married Jimmy Lee Benskin, their son Hayden Rhys Benskin. Patricia and Donald had a daughter, Sheila Caroline Hutchins (July 10, 1970).

*Submitted by Evelyn Euritha Wagner*

**SNOWDEN** – Reba L. Snowden (Aug 13, 1906 Paragould, Greene County, AR) was the second daughter born to Albert Sidney and Beulah Nancy (Chandler- Kennemore) Snowden. Growing up, Reba was very pretty and popular with all the young people. She was a member of the First Baptist Church.

Reba went to St. Louis and started work at Rexall Drug Company, in the box-manufacturing department, where she met Roy O. "Mac" McSpadden. They were married Dec 24, 1930.

Reba and Mac returned to Paragould. Reba's father had opened the "Snowden Café" and she and Mac went into partnership with him in 1944. Reba was well known for her culinary skills. Business was booming. Reba and Mac had their first son, Roy Albert McSpadden (Sept 12, 1936) Jerry McSpadden was born Aug 30, 1939.

Reba was a member of the Eastern Star and Roy was member of the Masonic Lodge. Roy was also a member of the American Legion, member of the Methodist Church, veteran of WWI, retired employee of Paragould Country Club.

Mac (March 22, 1898 Ft. Payne, AL- April 29,

1990) died when he was 92 years old. He left behind, Reba L. McSpadden, his wife and two sons, Roy A. McSpadden and his wife Lynda Fletcher; Jerry McSpadden and his wife Judy Wrape.

*Roy O. "Mack" McSpadden and Reba Snowden McSpadden.*

Reba died 10 years after Mac on Jan 4, 2000. She was 93 years old. Together they had two sons, six grandchildren and nine great-grandchildren. Roy A. says that one more great-grandchild is expected in Sept 2000. Also surviving Reba are her sisters Totsie Burroughs and Mary Huffman both of Paragould.

*Submitted by Evelyn Euritha Wagner*

**SNOWDEN** – Samuel Isaac Snowden was the son of Malachi C. Snowden who was from Shelby County, TN. Malachi was a sergeant in Captain R. W. Pitman's Company, 13th Regiment, Tennessee Infantry during the Civil War. Samuel's mother was Katie Elizabeth Young. She came to Greene County, AR when she was seven years old. Malachi died of yellow fever in Forrest City, AR before Samuel was born.

*Samuel Isaac Snowden and wife, Eddith Simpson Snowden, 1934.*

Eddith was the daughter of William F. Simpson and Ann Mary Russell. The Russells and Simpsons were pioneers from Kentucky and were very prominent in the Methodist Church.

Samuel Isaac and Eddith were married Dec 25, 1902, in Paragould, AR. "Ike" farmed and Eddith took care of the home. They moved a lot, but Eddith was used to that as her parents moved from farm to farm also. She was experienced in moving a lot. They started a family of eight children, seven boys and one girl:

1. Raymond Wilford (Feb 20, 1904) married May Irene Harvy Aug 20,1930.
2. Eugene Lyle Snowden (July 27, 1905) married Pearl Brust May 19, 1928.
3. Samuel Maurice Snowden (Nov 26, 1906) married (1) Margert Stevens in 1927; Margert died Dec 27, 1939 (2) Winnie Bell Free Oct 3, 1940.
4. Zelma Snowden (Jan 28, 1910) married Les Esper July 25, 1936.
5. William Malachi Snowden (Dec 3, 1911) married Winfred "Babe" King Sept 8, 1937.
6. Wayne Wilson Snowden (Jan 16, 1914) married (1) Jennie Mae Stephens Dec 3, 1933 (2) Helen Nora Johnson in 1941.
7. Weldon Simpson Snowden (Nov 25, 1915) married Hilda Mae Hockell July 21, 1940.
8. Isaac Junior "L. J." Snowden (May 29, 1920) married Marty Hellman in 1942. I. J. was a Naval fighter pilot on the Belleau Wood Carrier Squadron # 24; he was shot down on Gram Island, June 12, 1944. Samuel Isaac and Eddith never recovered from his death.

Ike and Eddith later moved to Jonesboro. Eddith was thrilled with their new home, as it was the very first to have indoor plumbing and electric lights. They perished in a fire at their 212 Arlington Court, Jonesboro, home Sept 18, 1956, at 1:00 P.M.

*Submitted by Evelyn Euritha Wagner*

**SNOWDEN** – Samuel Maurice "Morris" Snowden (Nov 26, 1906) was the third child of Samuel Isaac and Eddith Simpson Snowden, early pioneer family to Greene County, AR.

In 1927 Morris married Margert Stevens. They had three children: Billy died in infancy, Jacquelyn Arlene (Oct 10, 1929) and Harry Gerald Snowden (Dec 3, 1934). Margert died Dec 7, 1939 in Michigan and is buried in Brookland, AR.

Jacquelyn "Jackie" met and married Robert L. Niemann Sept 1, 1956. Robert distinguished himself as a humanitarian and an author of *Out of Their Darkness*, which describes their ordeals while on assignment in Japan as a writer for the U. S. Army Broadcasting. A humanitarian campaign to restore the sight of needlessly blind Japanese children was initiated by Niemann. In the final five months of his tour of duty, his group sponsored 315 sightless persons for medical treatment. At that time there were no eye banks in Japan for corneal transplants. Through his endeavors, a foundation was created to offer sight to those who were correctably blind and a drive was started to establish nationwide eye banks. Because of the results of his labors, the U. S. Secretary of the Army and the Order of the Rising Sun by Japan decorated Niemann with the Meritorious Civilian Service Award. He and his wife, Jackie were honored in 1971 by a 45 minute official audience and tea at Tohgu Palace with Crown Prince Akihito and Princess Michiko. He was a member of the Los Angeles Press Club, Pacific Pioneer Broadcasters, UCLA Alumni Association and a past member of the Writer's Guild of America. Robert died Dec 19, 1986; the loss is still felt by his loving wife and widow, Jackie.

Jackie and Robert have two children, Gregg Lawrence and Dana Arlene. Gregg married Melissa; they have one daughter, Ashley Nichole. Dana Arlene married Thomas Chestnut. They have two sons, Shane and Nathan Chestnut.

*Samuel Maurice Snowden and wife, Margert Stevens, 1927.*

Harry Gerald Snowden (Dec 3, 1934) married Norma Jean Merriman Feb 23, 1955. Harry spent three years in the Paratroopers, 11th Airborne Division and mustered out in 1956. He was an auto mechanic in North Little Rock, AR after the service. He was a construction subdivider and land developer. He opened the first public swimming pool in Greenbrier, AR. He owned two Exxon Stations, Dairy Dinner and the first Auto Parts Store in Greenbrier. He became a State Highway Patrol Officer in 1972 and retired Oct 1998. He is a member of the Masonic Lodge # 290 of Greenbrier. He and Norma Jean are long time members of Greenbrier Baptist Church. They have two children, Jerry Lynn (April 2, 1956) married Marsha Kay Goodman and they have two children, Brandy and Branden Jeremiah. Jerry Lynn Snowden just retired as Conway, AR's police chief at the age of 44. Terry Diane Snowden (Dec 8, 1958) married Doug Harmon and they have one daughter, Rachel Lee Harmon.

*Submitted by Evelyn Euritha Wagner*

**SNOWDEN** – Samuel Maurice (Nov 26, 1906 Walcott, AR) was the third son of Samuel Isaac Snowden and Eddith Simpson Snowden, who were pioneers to Greene County, AR. It's now early 1940 when Maurice, a widower from Arkansas, meets Winnie Bell Free on a blind date. They doubled with Maurice's brother Isaac Junior and Nadine Brown, a friend. They were engaged and Winnie was asked to join Maurice in Michigan at Bill and Babe Snowden's house. Three months later they married in Nepollean, OH, Oct 3, 1940. Lyle, Pearl and five years old Donald Snowden were driving back from Toledo, OH with the newlyweds in the back seat. Donald kept turning around and saying "they're at it again" (Kissing). Winnie inherited a ready-made family, Jackie, nine years and Harry, five years.

They rented an apartment for about six months; bought three lots in Royal Oak, MI and built their first home and added their first child, Carole (Dec 22, 1941). What a Christmas gift! Jackie and Harry had a baby sister. Daniel Harvey and Samuel Isaac Snowden were born June 29, 1945 and their family was complete.

Carole Snowden married Ronnie Mobbs Dec 22, 1958. Their children are:
1. Ronda Carol Mobbs married Clarence Keith Woodrome; their children:
   a. Jessica Nicole
   b. Mitchel Woodrome
2. Bryan Laron Mobbs married and had:
   a. Ashley Nicole Mobbs
3. Chris Fredrick Mobbs married Faith Annette Raish; their children:
   a. Michael Mason
   b. Charity Mobbs.

Ronnie is retired from the Fire Department.

Dan Harvey Snowden married Maydean Cardin, their four children are:
1. Steve Allen Snowden (March 3, 1963) married Cindy Lee Graham; their children:
   a. Kylie Danielle
   b. Griffen Allen Snowden.
2. Timothy Wayne Snowden married Elisha Dawn Dicky; their children:
   a. Kayla Cheynne
   b. Ashton Leigh
   c. Timothy Scott Snowden
3. Robbie Dean Snowden married Melissa Ann Rowlette: their daughter:
   a. Shelby Grace Snowden.
4. Daniel Harvey Snowden Jr. married Melissa Ann Reid; their daughter:
   a. Taylor Brooke Snowden

Dan Harvey Snowden later married Sheila Marie Cronan; their sons are Jason Andrew and Jonathon David Snowden. Dan Harvey is in the land developing and cattle business, he owns outlet and antique stores.

Samuel Isaac Snowden married and his children are:
1. Samalita Elizabeth Snowden married Gerald Lynn Martin

a. Brody Lee
b. Sady Free Martin
2. Thad Maurice Snowden married Shelly Scott.

Samuel Isaac Snowden later married Jackie Lynn Mobbs. He is a fire chief for the Fire Department in Little Rock. He refinishes and collets antique furniture.

Samuel Maurice is known to break out with a song at any given moment. He also teaches Sunday school up to this day. When encouraged will give a sermon on the scriptures any time. He has a real love of the Lord in his heart and enjoys sharing it with all. Aunt Winnie Bell is known far and wide as being the best cook anywhere! Her children, grandchildren and great grandchildren are the delight and love of her life.

Maurice and Winnie Bell Free Snowden, 1941.

*Submitted by Evelyn Euritha Wagner*

**SNOWDEN** – Wayne Wilson Snowden (Jan 16, 1914) was the sixth child of Samuel Isaac Snowden and Eddith Simpson Snowden. Their parents were pioneers to Greene County, AR. He first married Jennie Mae Stephens Dec 3, 1933. They had two children, Evelyn Euritha Snowden and Thomas Clark

*Wayne Wilson Snowden, 1914-1988.*

Snowden who died in infancy. Wayne later married Helen Nora Johnson in 1941. They had five children:
1. Bill W. Snowden (June 19, 1942) married Jeanine Spencer, June 27, 1969; their sons:
   a. James Anthony Wayne Snowden died young, May 31, 1991.
   b. Christopher Spencer Snowden married Cherriee Hydas March 3, 1994; their sons:
      I. Justin James
      II. Joshua Andrew
      III. Joseph Snowden.
2. Shirley Snowden married Hugh Daryl Conway Jr. in 1961; their sons:
   a. Daryl Wayne married Blacna Julia Flores
   b. Robert Hugh Conway married Carolyn Saunders in 1984; their children:
      I. Amber Renee
      II. Nicole Brittany
      III. Trent Levi Conway.
3. Darlene Snowden and Richard Marchi's son, Guy Richard Marchi Sproles is Darlene's oldest son. Darlene married Robert Kyle Sproles Jr. in 1968; their children:
   a. Shelley Louise married (1) Richard Resendez Jr.; their son: Nicholas Richard Resendez (March 6, 1990). (2) James Levi Ellis Jr. and their daughter: Kylee Nicole Ellis (July 11, 1997). Shelley, James, Nicholas and Kylie live in San Bernardino, CA.
   b. Klayton Kyle Sproles married Melandie Ossen in 1985; their daughters:
      I. Ashley Meagan (June 18, 1995)
      II. Kylie Ann (June 6, 1997).
4. Leon "Rick" Snowden (May 3, 1959) married (1) Evelyn; their child: Christy Snowden (about 1981) married and had two sons. (2) Denise; their children: Ashley (about 1987) and Colton Snowden (about 1993).
   a. Timmy Lee Snowden (Aug 29, 1959) youngest child of Wayne and Helen married (1) Donna Louise Piersson July 30, 1977; their children: Timmy Lee Snowden Jr. (Feb 17, 1978) married (1) Karen Diane Harrison; their children: Taylor James (May 15, 1998) and Amber Marie (Feb 5, 2000), (2) Bonnie Elizabeth Evans on March 19, 1994. On April 1, 1999, Tim adopted Bonnie's daughter, Rebecca "Becky" Snowden (April 26, 1983).
   b. Jeremy Jay Snowden (Dec 28, 1979)
   c. Chandra Dawn Snowden (Oct 11, 1984)
   d. Janil Elizabeth Snowden (May 31, 1998).

Wayne Wilson Snowden died Feb 17, 1988.
*Submitted by Evelyn Euritha Wagner*

**SNOWDEN** – Weldon Snowden (Nov 25, 1916 Lorado, AR) the seventh child born to Samuel Isaac Snowden and Eddith Simpson Snowden grew up in a large farming family. Seven brothers, Raymond Wilfred, Eugene Lyle, Samuel Maurice, William Malachi, Wayne Wilson and Isaac Junior Snowden and one sister, Zelma Snowden. He worked on the farm, enjoyed playing baseball with the brothers and attended church socials and barn dances.

He attended Thorn and Stephens Schools in Truman, AR.

He met Hilda Hockell and they married July 21, 1940 in Jonesboro, AR.

They made St. Louis, Mo their home and had one daughter, Patricia Ann Snowden (May 9, 1941). Patricia Ann teaches school in St. Louis, MO.

Weldon worked in real estate and did very well. He made a good deal of money in real estate.

*Weldon Snowden, 1916-1999.*

Weldon died Feb 1999 of Parkinson disease. He was 83 years old. He willed his body to science and perhaps scientists will be able to learn enough to help others.

People who knew him said he was always kind, gentle and thoughtful of others. He was the kind of person you would want to be friends with.
*Submitted by Evelyn Euritha Wagner*

**SNOWDEN** – Wilburn Albert Dewitt "Bill" Snowden (May 4, 1904 Paragould, Greene County, AR) the second child born to Albert Sidney Snowden and Beulah Nancy Chandler-Kennemore entered the world with two brothers, Malachi "Mack" Snowden and John Clarence Kennemore and one sister, Wilma "Totsie" Snowden.

*Bill and Waltie Snowden.*

I know not a lot of Bill, except that everyone that knew him liked him. He was a little restless. He had brown hair and light eyes, was over six feet tall and went to California when he was young. According to his sister, Totsie Burroughs (who at this writing is 98 years young), he was a guard at a Ford motor plant in St. Louis, MO. He came back home during the depression. He was there when F.D.R. was elected president in 1932. Then left for St.Louis again. This time he met and married Waltie Grandstaff on Valentines Day but do not know the year. He opened a drive in restaurant and was very successful. He and Waltie retired and went to Elden, FL. I guess they just couldn't stay retired, as they opened another drive-in restaurant. He died Oct 31, 1971 at 68 years of age. It is thought that Waltie stayed in Florida or went back to St. Louis.
*Submitted by Evelyn Euritha Wagner*

**SNOWDEN** – William Malachi "Bill" Snowden (Dec 3, 1911) was the son of Samuel Isaac Snowden and Eddith Simpson Snowden. Their families were pioneers to Greene County, AR. He had seven brothers, Raymond Wilfred, Eugene Lyle, Samuel Maurice, Isaac Junior, Wayne Wilson and Weldon Snowden and one sister, Zelma Snowden.

*1937 – William Malachi Snowden with wife, Winfred "Babe" King Snowden, married Sept. 8, 1936.*

Bill grew up on the farm and attended school in Arkansas. But he heard of jobs in Detroit, MI. His brothers Morris and Lyle were there working. Their brother I. J. also came up. Bill got a job with General Motors. He met Winifred " Babe" King when he and his brothers were boarding with her family in the early 1930s. They started dating. One of their favorite places to go was "East Wood Gardens". He was fun to be with and a kinda jovial guy. Besides being a really good looking guy! One night Bill said, "Hey Babe, you wanta get married?" They were married Sept 8, 1936. They set up housekeeping with her parents in Highland Park, MI.

Their first daughter Donna Jean (June 26, 1937) was in the choir, on the debating team and a cheerleader. Donna married Robert Negus and they had Robert Charles and Debbie Ann Negus. Donna had developed a bad cough while pregnant with Debbie. She was treated with antibiotics but they didn't do any good. After Debbie was born and tests were made it was discovered that she had breast cancer and Hodgkin's disease. While Donna was ill, she knew things were getting bad in Highland Park and wanted to move. She found Livonia about 15 or 20 miles out of Highland Park. Her parents built in Livonia, after Donna's death April 3, 1956, Bill and Babe adopted Robbie and Debbie. There was a grade school on one end of the road and high school on the other end.

Babe told me all the girls after they were born were baptized at the Free Will Baptist Church near their home. They were regular attendees.

Karen Lee Snowden (Oct 25, 1939) was in the Glee Club and won the sixth grade spelling bee, even though she was shy in school. She met James Braham. He was in the Navy. They

were married June 19, 1957. They have four children:
1. Russell James (July 23, 1959) married Tina Schefsler in 1985; they have one son, David James Braham (Sept 3, 1986).
2. Shelly Lee (July 26, 1960) married Patrick Lowry their children: Ryan Patrick Lowry (June 26, 1986) and Amber Lea Lowry (Feb 12, 1991).
3. Kimberly Ann Braham (July 28, 1962)
4. Jason William Braham (July 9, 1969).

Judy Ann (Nov 4, 1944) was homecoming princess throughout high school and as a senior made Homecoming Queen. She and Carl Volk went to school together and later married; their children:
1. Paul Volk
2. Carl Volk
3. Kristen Marie Volk
4. Derek Volk (Nov 10, 1973)

Bill died Feb 6, 1988 after a long bout with Parkinson disease.

*Submitted by Evelyn Euritha Wagner*

**SNOWDEN** – Wilma Totsie Snowden (Oct 9, 1901 Paragould, AR) the first-born daughter of Albert Sidney Snowden and Beulah Nancy Chandler (Kennemore) Snowden had two older brothers, Malachi "Mack" Snowden and John Clarence Kennemore. Her brother Albert Wilburn Snowden (May 18, 1904), Reba Snowden (Aug 13, 1906) and Mary Snowden (March 30, 1909). She is a life long member of the Immanuel Baptist church. Totsie was an energetic and busy teenage. She was a take-charge person always independent and devoted to her parents and family.

A young man moved to town, his name was Leonard Bryan Burroughs, in 1919 and caught Totsie's eye. It wasn't long before they found they cared for each other. They were married Sept 7, 1921. Their only son Leonard B. Burroughs Jr. was born May 12, 1923 in Paragould, AR.

Leonard B. Burroughs was a native of McKenzie, TN, prior to moving to Paragould, AR. He was a retired head of the Paragould Sanitation Department and a member of the Masonic Lodge.

Leonard died Nov 18, 1971 in Paragould, AR. He was 71 years of age and is buried in Linwood Cemetery, Paragould, AR.

Totsie who is 98 years young is still living at the family home at 305 South 14th Street, Paragould, AR. She still does her own cooking, house cleaning, and laundry. She is also very fortunate to have her daughter-in-law, Betty Sue Burroughs living next door. She even washed her own windows and baked me a poor man's apple pie, which I nearly ate all of, when I went to visit with her at the end of April 2000.

*1904 – Wilma Totsie Snowden, four years old.*

*Submitted by Evelyn Euritha Wagner*

**SNOWDEN** – Zelma (Jan 28, 1910 Greene County, AR) the only daughter of Samuel Isaac and Eddith Simpson Snowden would grow up among seven brothers, Raymond Wilfred, Eugene Lyle, Samuel Maurice, William Malachi, Wayne Wilson, Weldon and Isaac Junior Snowden. I heard she was spoiled and she loved it. Pearl Snowden, Eugene Lyle's wife, said this of her sister-in-law. "When Zelma needed a new dress for a square dance party, her dad would give her only enough money to buy the cheapest dress, then Wilford and Lyle, feeling sorry for her would dig deep in their pockets and give her more money for a dress. The evening of the dance, Zelma would show up in the prettiest ready-made dress there. I was so jealous as I stood there in my plain, homemade dress!" Another story from Maurice Snowden: "If it wasn't for Margaret Snowden, Maurice's first wife, Zelma and Les wouldn't have met. Margaret was out walking on Grand Circus Park and got to talking to a strange woman who was also from the south (Dallas, TX) and got friendly. That woman was Winona Coffey. Soon Margaret and Maurice and the Coffeys got to visiting with each other and became close friends. Zelma moved up from Truman, AR. Les was working at the Free Press and John Coffey was his foreman. Zelma boarded with the Coffeys and John decided he wanted Les to meet Zelma. Les was invited out and fixed up with Zelma and the rest is history." Zelma and Les Esper were married July 25, 1936 in Detroit, Mi.

*The Les Esper Family (L-R): Les, Celeste, Eugene, Annette, and Zelma Snowden Esper.*

They had three children: Eugene Isaac Esper married Judy Schully in 1960, Celeste Susan Esper married Joseph Caleel and Annette Eddith married a young man named Walter.

Jackie Niemann wrote this about her Uncle Les. She couldn't recall whether it was 1938 or 1939 but she was living in Arkansas with her grandparents while her mother was in a TB sanitarium in Detroit. During the summer she was sent to spend it with her father and to visit her mother at the sanitarium, even though it meant talking from the outside grounds up to her window.

One weekend during this time Aunt Zelma and Uncle Les took her with them out to "THE COTTAGE", an old vacation spot that was owned by Les's parents. It was a wonderful time and it passed too quickly. So, Zelma and the kids stayed on for the remainder of the week while Les went back to work in Detroit. And, for some reason that escaped her, she had to go back with him, left her disappointed because she was having such fun with all the family. After a while Les pulled over and sent her into an ice cream parlor for a triple-decker and told her he understood her disappointment. It was an act of kindness she never forgot.

Zelma Snowden Esper died Jan 4, 1997 in Detroit, MI.

*Submitted by Evelyn Euritha Wagner*

**SNYDER** – Jerome Snyder was born in 1835 in Pennsylvania. Census records indicate that his parents were born in New Jersey. He married Anne Elizabeth Bedford (date unknown). Although census records give her birth in Pennsylvania, family tradition holds that she was born in England.

According to Gertie Snyder, daughter of Jerome and Elizabeth, the Bedford family was quite prosperous. With visions of adventure and the promise of prosperity, they left their estate in England and sailed for America. During the passage to the new world, Elizabeth's sister became ill and died. Her body was buried at sea. The port of arrival is uncertain at this time.

As a boy, Jerome was raised in Pennsylvania. From information passed down by family members, he served in the Union Army during the Civil War. He is said to have fought in numerous engagements and was wounded on six different occasions.

*Jerome Snyder*

Jerome's marriage to Elizabeth began a life on constant movement across the country. Experiencing health problems, Elizabeth was advised by her doctor to travel to promote better health. With their first known child Walter (1875), they began their migration. They traveled to Michigan where William was born in 1876. From there, the family moved west to Lee County, IL where Gertie was born at Paw Paw Grove in 1879. By the time Emma Lora was born in 1884, the family was residing in Cedar County, NE. Somewhere along the way, two other daughters, Hattie and Mary were born. In time, the family loaded their covered wagon again and moved on. During this leg of the journey, Elizabeth delivered another daughter (name unknown). Ill from the complications of giving birth, she died and was buried along the dusty Nebraska trail. As providence would have it, Jerome found a nursing mother at a nearby farmhouse. The woman agreed to keep and nurse Elizabeth's newborn. Jerome traveled back to Nebraska and visited the child on a couple of occasions.

By the 1900 census, the family was settled in Greene County, AR. Prior to their arrival, Hattie went crazy and was committed to an asylum, where she later died. Mary, at about the age of 16, was thrown from her favorite pony and impaled on a stick protruding from the ground. She was killed almost instantly.

The 1900 Greene County Census found Jerome living with his daughter Emma in the Union Township. The other children had married and started their own families in the Greene and Craighead County areas. Jerome was defined as a laborer in the census. He died sometime after 1900 and the site of his burial is somewhat in question. The foregoing accounts are believed to be accurate but are certainly open to scrutiny.

*Submitted by Frank Reddick*

**SONGER** – Evan D. Songer Sr. was born September 2, 1883, in Randolph County, Arkansas, the son of Benjamin R. and Mary Jane Lomax Songer. He moved to Greene County in the early 1900s to seek employment and worked on several farms as a laborer and also cleared land in and around the Big Island Community.

On September 1, 1907, he married Annie White Songer, who was a native of Gainesville, Arkansas. She was living with her aunt and uncle Tom and Van Evett in the Brighton Community.

They raised seven children, Mildred Songer Wilkerson, Frances Songer Williams, Evelyn Songer Watson, Lawson Songer, Emma Jean Songer Cole, Princess Doyle Songer Riley, and E.D. Songer Jr. They lived on Giles Island south of Big Island, until about 1913 they bought a farm in the Coffman Community (one mile west of the old Coffman School). They raised various crops, and raised chickens and sold eggs and cream. While living in the Coffman Community, he served as road overseer in the Mainshore Township. He was the county committeeman for the Agricultural Adjustment Administration (a cotton allotment program). He served on the school board of the Coffman School and later on as a board member of the Oak Grove School. They moved to the Oak Grove Community in 1936, where he ran a dairy farm and sold milk to the old Midwest Dairy. He also served as a member of the county FHA committee for loans available for the first time for farm improvements, such as pastures, drilling wells, for irrigation.

He was a devout Christian and would drive for miles in a wagon, before the automobiles became available, to attend the Church of Christ. He knew the scriptures and could back up his belief whenever necessary. He served on the grand jury anytime he was asked to do so.

In 1950 he sold his Oak Grove farm and moved to a small acreage on Fairview Road, there he grew truck patches, and raised chickens for laying hens. He took pride in the eggs he sold and his new pullets had just begun to lay in August 1955.

On August 15, 1955, he was delivering eggs to the Vandervoot Hotel in Paragould, which was located where the First National Bank now stands. Most delivery men used the east side entrance of the building where the freight elevator was used as an entrance to the kitchen. On that day some of the employees had taken the elevator upstairs, and had left the door open. He

*Wedding picture of Evan D. Songer and Annie White Songer; married at Brighton, Arkansas, on September 1, 1907.*

stepped into the entrance and fell to the basement, and was badly injured. He was taken to St. Bernards Hospital in Jonesboro. On August 17, 1955, he passed away in Jonesboro and is buried in Linwood Cemetery in Paragould.

**SPENCE** – Our family descends from Britton Spence, father of Allie Britton Spence. Allie Britton Spence is buried in Shiloh Cemetery next to his wife Mattie Sue Dean. Allie passed away in December 1948 with his wife preceding him August 1947. Allie and Mattie had Clyde, Ray, Aubrey, Cecil, Ruth and a baby boy not named who died (buried at Fairview Cemetery in Greene County).

Ray Lafayette Spence was my grandfather. He was born August 25, 1899, in Poinsett County and died June 19, 1979, in Jonesboro, Craighead County; buried in Paragould at Linwood Cemetery. Ray Spence was a teacher/principal for 46 years. He married Mabel Lorene Huston on August 12,1928, in Paragould. (Her parents were John Milligan Huston and Hallie Bernam Corgan Huston; buried at Linwood with death dates 1929 and 1944.)

Mabel was a teacher also with 40 years of service upon her retirement. She was born in Illinois on December 24, 1906, and passed away December 21, 1993. She is buried alongside Ray at Linwood Cemetery. They were the parents of Ray Loren Spence and John Huston Spence born November 10, 1932, and October 17, 1935.

Ray Loren Spence married Alfreda Lockwood (daughter of George W. and Mira I. Weaver Lockwood) on December 28, 1951, at Griffin Memorial United Methodist Church on East Court Street in Paragould. They had four children: Pamela Karen, Patricia Darlene "Patty," Virginia Lorene "Lori" (deceased), and George Ray born in Paragould, Arkansas, Lawton, Oklahoma, Germany, and Fort Sill, Oklahoma, respectively. Lori is buried at Center Hill Cemetery.

My uncle, John Huston Spence is married to Barbara Simmons of Kentucky. They reside in Oak Ridge, Tennessee, near their three children and their families. They have sons Kyle Ray, Terry Barton, and daughter Karla Renee.

Both Ray Loren Spence and his wife Freda enjoy being grandparents to Jennifer Karen and Jeffery Warren Spence Cowan (children of Richard and Pamela Spence Cowan). They have their daughter Patty who resides with them in their home. George is in private practice as an attorney in Northwest Arkansas, and lives with his wife Linda, a court reporter.

Also, John Huston Spence and his wife Barbara are enjoying being grandparents to their grandchild Khari (daughter of Kyle). Kyle and his wife, Cindy, are accountants. Terry, a police officer, is married to Melanie. Karla is married to the Reverend Billy Kurtz.

**STALLCUP** – Charles Thaddeus Stallcup (1836 NC) the son of Nancy Evaline Young and Jesse Richerson Hyatt Stallcup. He married Nancy Aletha Hyatt in 1860. She was born in Cherokee County, NC in 1840, the daughter of Jesse and Jane McTaggart Hyatt. Nancy and C. T. were parents of five daughters, four living to adulthood. Nancy died in White Pine, TN in 1877. C. T.'s second wife was Susan Cluck. The family followed Susan's sister, Mattie Hammond, wife of Dr. Hammond, to Paragould in 1882 or 1883.

One of Charles Thaddeus' daughters was my grandmother Ella Margaret, who married John V. Landrum Nov 6, 1884. John Landrum, my grandfather and Charles Thaddeus were partners in a mercantile firm on East Court Street for several years until he left Paragould in 1889. He moved back to Tennessee, where he died in Russellville, TN in 1919.

Family stories tell that he would not live in a town that had no Sabbath school for his daughters to attend. He took it upon himself to establish one in the Methodist Church.

The Stallcup family history in America begins with Jan Andriesson of Sweden. He embarked on a Swedish ship, "Key of Kalmar" as a cook. He wore a woolen cape, which he frequently used for a towel. It became soiled, greasy and glossy, giving the appearance of polished steel. For this reason the sailors nicknamed him "Steel Cape" which in Swedish was "Stalkofta" or in Dutch was "Stalkappe".

After landing in Delaware he retained the nickname and became John Anderson Stalcop. Land was granted to him in 1671 composed of 600 acres, which is now occupied by the City of Wilmington, DE. He gave the land where "Old Swedes Church" and cemetery are located. By the time of John Anderson Stalcop's death he and his children were known as Stallcop, or some variations such at Stalcop, Stalkop, Staalkopp, Stallcup, Staulcup. So it is said all Stallcups in the United States are related.

*Submitted by Winifred Landrum Bland*

**STALLCUP** – John Wesley Stallcup (1853 Weakley County, TN) was a direct descendent of John Anderson Stallcup who came from Sweden to the Swedish Settlement on the Delaware River in 1641. His forbearers later migrated in about 1765 to Orange County, NC, on to Gibson County, TN and later to Weakley County, TN. He married Liza Newberry in 1873. He had a stepdaughter, Willie Parham (Johnson) and a daughter, Tempest Stallcup (1874). They came to Greene County, AR and located in the Haliday Community where he worked at a sawmill and did some farming to support his family. The family soon increased to include:

1. Effie (1881)
2. Edward R. (1883)
3. Osmer (1886)
4. Pearl (1887 or 1888)
5. Woodford (1892)
6. Dennis died young

The family moved to Beech Grove about 1897. The children attended Beech Grove School. After renting land from others such as the "old Roswell place", John bought 160 acres of land from S. T. Roberts. It joined the Roberts' homestead, one of the oldest farms in the community. The farm had oak and pine timber to provide lumber or cross ties. The Lee Eaker sawmill was about two miles from the farm. A large spring furnished an adequate supply of water and there was good creek bottomland to grow cotton, corn and vegetables.

In 1897, John's wife, Liza died. John returned to his home in Weakley County, TN in 1898 and again in 1899. He married Laura Hawks on Oct 25, 1899. To this second marriage were born:

1. Elsie (1901)
2. Fay (1904)
3. Bryan (1906)
4. Herbert (1908)
5. Payola (1910)
6. Elvis (1912)
7. Buford (1914)

John Wesley enjoyed hunting and fishing. The family usually kept two or three black and tan hounds to hunt raccoon, opossum, rabbits and squirrel. Quail were plentiful near cultivated fields. Cache River and various sloughs and ponds were roosting and feeding areas for wood ducks. Spring rains brought on fish runs in the Cache River and tributaries.

*Front row, L-R: Hugh Stalcup, Shade (Shadrack) Stalcup, Ham (James Hamilton) Stalcup, George Stalcup, Thad (Charles Thaddus) Stalcup. Back row, L-R: Lou Stalcup (Hugh's wife), Laura Stalcup (John's wife), Sue Stalcup (Thad's wife), Naomi Stalcup Robinson (sister).*

*John Wesley Stallcup, 76 years old, taken in Bud Ryan's Cafe, Paragould, May 1, 1930 at a dinner for persons in Greene County 75 years of age or older.*

One of the most enjoyable times in the lives of his children, grandchildren, other kinfolks and friends was a Sunday afternoon or holiday visit to the Stallcup home. The Stallcups were known as honest, hard working people. They were also noted for jovial hospitality and good will. The Stallcups were known as very religious people in general. Some member of the family was usually asked to say the blessing before each meal.

The family lived close to each other until the 1920s when some members of the family moved to Rector, Caraway and other areas for farming. Some relocated to St. Louis, Mo and Flint and Detroit, MI. The Great Depression of the 1930s resulted in further movement out of Greene County.

John Wesley Stallcup died in 1936 at the age of 84 years and was buried in the Beech Grove Cemetery beside his wife, Laura and near many of his friends and kinfolks. Reverend Chappel Rogers who had known John from his earlier years in Greene County conducted the memorial service.

*Submitted by Alice Davidson*

**STALLCUP** – Woodford Stallcup was born April 29, 1892, in the New Friendship Community near Halliday, Arkansas, in Greene County. His parents were John Wesley Stallcup and Liza Newberry, who were both born in Weakley County, Tennessee, and moved to Greene County, Arkansas, about 1880. John was a farmer and sawmill worker.

*Woodford Stallcup and Lissie Cunningham Stallcup soon after they were married. They were married on January 15, 1916.*

After living near Halliday for a few years the family moved to Beech Grove, Arkansas. One of the places where they lived was on the old Roswell place located on the old hill road between Beech Grove and Meadows Grove. Woodford attended school at Beech Grove. One of his early teachers was Ike Wilcockson. Woodford's father purchased 160 acre tract of land from S.T. Roberts in 1904. One of Woodford's early jobs was helping his father build a house. They cut pine logs. One of the first chores that he did by himself was hauling logs to a sawmill owned by Lee Eaker.

Woodford married Lissie Cunningham on January 15, 1916. Lissie was the daughter of Robert Franklin Cunningham and Erie Puckett Cunningham. Woodford and Lissie had two sons: Robert Allen Stallcup born February 18, 1917, and Odie Talmadge Stallcup born December 2, 1918. Allen and Talmadge attended grade school at Jackson College School and graduated from Beech Grove High School in 1935.

Woodford Stallcup was active in providing better educational activities for young people. He served on the school board of Beech Grove Consolidated Schools for eight years.

Woodford was very active in the Beech Grove Church of Nazarene. He was a teacher and superintendent of the Bible School at that church for over 30 years.

Woodford Stallcup died on December 24, 1964, at 72 years of age. His wife, Lissie died on February 27, 1983. They were both buried in Greene County Memorial Gardens.

**STANFORD** – In 1827, George Stanford and George's sister Jinnett Stanford, whose husband was Isaac Lamb, emigrated from Marion County, AL to Arkansas. They first settled near Newman Spring, on the east flank of Crowley's Ridge and about five miles across the ridge from the future site of Harrisburg. At that time, the Newman Spring area was in Lawrence County. The George Stanford and Isaac Lamb families became citizens of Greene County by operation of law in 1833 when that county was organized. Their residences near Newman Spring were included within the boundaries of the new county.

George Stanford was a native of South Carolina, having been born there Jan 28, 1785. His wife Jemima Farrar was born in North Carolina about 1798. While still young, they came to Tennessee with their respective parents. They married in 1812 and lived in Lincoln County, TN. In 1819 they moved to Marion County, AL.

About 1839 the George Stanford's and Isaac Lamb or his widow Jinnet, as well as several grown children of those families, left the Newman's Spring area and relocated further north on Crowley's Ridge. On Oct. 1, 1839, George Stanford received a patent for 40 acres of land just northwest of the modern town of Lorado. Nicholas Harris was a close neighbor. His wife was Jincy Hall, a sister of Judge Richmond Hall and Greenup Hall. On Dec 30, 1832, George Stanford's son, Thomas had married Nicholas Harris' daughter, Lemerles Katheryn Wilson Harris.

In the U. S. Census for 1840, on the same page, two lines apart, the George Stanford and Nicholas Harris families were enumerated as residents of Greene County, AR, Thomas Stanford, Booze Stanford and William Stanford, married sons of George Stanford and Jemima, were also shown to be householders in Greene County, as was Jinnet Lamb, the widow of Isaac Lamb.

The Stanford's were farmers, but they were also Methodist preachers. George Stanford had become a class leader and local preacher in Tennessee when he was a young man. He continued to preach at every opportunity in Tennessee, in Alabama and after he moved to Crowley's Ridge in 1827.

At that time there were no real towns on the ridge, only small settlements consisting of a few cabins. Nor were there any organized churches with buildings and grounds of the type with which we are familiar today. At rare intervals a pioneering circuit riding preacher would travel through the country and hold services, wherever he could draw a crowd. Between such visits people of faith gathered in private homes or other available preaching places to hear the gospel proclaimed by a "local" preacher, someone who already lived in the community or somewhere not too far away.

It was not until 1839 that the Methodists established a formal organization in Greene County. It was called the "Greene Mission." It was not a church or congregation in the modern sense but rather a gathering of the local preachers of Methodist persuasion who lived up and down Crowley's Ridge. Greene Mission meetings or conferences were held quarterly under the chairmanship of a presiding elder who was a full time ordained Methodist minister, assigned to perform that duty by the bishop of the Arkansas Methodist Conference.

A microfilm copy of the "Steward's Book" containing the minutes of the Greene Mission Quarterly Conference is on file at the Arkansas History Commission in Little Rock. The first meeting was held on Jan 12, 1839. The next meeting, on April 13, 1839 was held in George Stanford's home. Only he and two other preachers were present. Regular quarterly meetings of the Greene Mission continued to be held through the 1840s, usually in the home of one of the conference members, but occasionally at some other site. For example, the meeting of July 25, 1840 was held at the Stanford campground, presumably near George Stanford's residence. Over the years there was a steady increase in the number of local preachers attending the Greene Mission conference, including several sons of George Stanford.

In Oct 1839 the Greene Mission meeting recommended that George Stanford be ordained as a deacon and given an appointment as a "traveling" Methodist preacher. That recommendation received favorable action at the ensuing November meeting of the Arkansas Annual Conference. His first assignment, for the year 1939-40, was to travel the Madison Circuit.

George Stanford's conference appointment as a full time Methodist minister no doubt represented the fulfillment of a lifelong dream and ambition. Sadly, he did not live long enough to enjoy it very long. He died Dec 17, 1840. The place of his death and burial is not known.

George Stanford's son Thomas followed him into the Methodist ministry. On recommendation by the Greene Mission, he was ordained at the Arkansas Annual Conference in 1842. He was appointed to the Greene Mission as pastor in 1844 and went on to become a popular preacher in other parts of Arkansas and in Texas. Booze A. Stanford and William Stanford, also sons of George Stanford, were active in the Greene Mission as local preachers during the 1840s. John B. Stanford was also a local preacher in the Greene Mission before he was ordained as Methodist minister in 1844. He likely was a relative of George Stanford, but evidence establishing such a connection has not been found.

Most of the Greene County Stanford's had died or gone further west by 1850. The only Stanford surname residents of the county as shown by census returns for that year were Lucinda Stanford age 11 and Thomas Stanford age seven. They were children of William Stanford, a son of George Stanford and Matilda Hall, the daughter of Judge Richmond Hall. William Stanford had died and his widow was remarried to L. B. Futrel. She and her children were living in the Futrel household.

*Submitted by E. R. Stanford*

**STARNES** – Moses Starnes was the 10th child born to Marshall and Paralee (Johnson) Starnes. He was born Jan 9, 1866 in Lauderdale County, TN. At the age of five he came with his family to Greene County and settled northwest of Marmaduke in the Starne's Chapel, New Home, Ramer's Chapel community. He was married Dec 4, 1890 to Nancy Belle Staires, daughter of Bill and Martha Jane (Eastep) Staires. She was born June 1, 1872 in the same community. They remained in that general vicinity throughout their lives, as did all of their children.

He was a lifelong farmer and both he and Belle were Methodists. They attended church at

Starne's Chapel until it was dismantled, then Ramer's Chapel Church.

Moses died Dec 5, 1929 from pneumonia; Belle died May 28, 1954. Both are buried at Starnes Cemetery.

They were the parents of 11 children of which six survived to adulthood:
1. Unnamed infant daughter
2. Flossie Pearl (May 28, 1894-Feb 28, 1919) married William H. Hampton
3. Bertha Ann (May 28, 1895-July 5, 1978) married Nathan May
4. Arlie Earl (Aug 12, 1897) married Benjamin Franklin Brewer
5. James Buel (Oct 3, 1901-July 12, 1980) married Bessie Ruth McDowell
6. Ethel (1902)
7. Vera (1904)
8. Cleophie Beulah "Offie" (Sept 22, 1906-Feb 17, 1982) married Arvin Pemilton Bradsher
9. Nora Belle (Nov 24, 1908) married Buren Francis Arnold
10. Grace (1912)
11. Verneal (Oct 1, 1916) married Earl Thompson.

**STARNES/JOHNSON** – Marshall Starnes (1818-1897) and Paralee Johnson (about 1836-1911) were married May 28, 1851 in Lauderdale County, TN and became the parents of 12 children, all born in Lauderdale County. Three of those died as infants and were not named. The others were:
1. Mary Jane (1852)
2. William (1855)
3. Clinton (1857)
4. Henry (1858)
5. Jurita (1859)
6. Martha Fannie (1861)
7. Moses (1866)
8. Nancy Paralee (1868)
9. James (1871).

In 1871, Marshall and Paralee moved their large family from Tennessee to Greene County, AR and settled near Marmaduke. They bought their first farm from M. M. Wright. It was located about one and one-half miles northwest of Marmaduke. On a hill located on the property was a small plot of greaves. Soon a small building was built near the graves. It was used as both a church and school and was named Starne's Chapel. It was dismantled in the early 1890s and Thomas Jefferson Ramer built a church about three-fourths miles north on property he donated. This church was named Ramer's Chapel and a school, which was named Ramer's School, was built about a half-mile north of this church.

Marshall died in 1897 and Paralee died in 1911. Both are buried in Starne's Cemetery.

Nancy Paralee "Nanny" was the 11th child born to Marshall and Paralee and was only three years old when they moved to Greene County. She married James "Jim" Wright Beaton Jan 6, 1884. He was the son of Collin and Susannah French Beaton from Benton County, TN. After their marriage, they remained in the New Home-Ramer's Chapel community and farmed for many years. They were charter members of Ramer's Chapel Methodist Church.

They later moved to a farm east of Marmaduke in the White Oak community where Jim died Dec 16, 1926 and Nannie died Sept 8, 1934. Both are buried in Ramer's Chapel Cemetery.

James and Nancy were the parents of seven children. All survived to adulthood, married and raised large families; they were:
1. Emma married Charlie Williams
2. Annie married David House
3. Nancy Belle married James C. "Jim" Stephens
4. Hettie married (1) Enoch Fisk (2) Earl Keller
5. Walter married Leona Myers
6. Berlie married (1) Pearl Midkiff (2) Nellie Willard
7. Wesley married Velma Benson.

**STEPHENS** – James Clayborne "Jim" Stephens was born in Greene County near Marmaduke Aug 11, 1886 and died April 26, 1966.

His parents were Spencer Jeff and Lillie Belle Trantham Stephens.

He married Nancy Belle Beaton July 16, 1913. Nancy Belle was born in Greene County, Jan 13, 1894 to James Wright and Nancy Paralee Starnes Beaton.

Nancy Belle died Oct 25, 1970. She and Jim are both buried in Ramers Chapel Cemetery.

They spent almost all of their life as farmers in the Ramer's Chapel community where they reared their 11 children, namely:

*Back row, L-R: Eugene, Wanda, Velma, Loretta, Catherine, Thelbert; front row: Alma, Iva, "Ras."*

1. Arlene (May 7, 1914-Dec 9, 1965) married Thomas Ragle May 19, 1932. Both are buried in Osceola, IN
2. Iva Lee (May 7, 1915) married July 26, 1934 to Charles Chesterfield "Chester" Jamison
3. Alma (Aug 12, 1917) married Loyd White Dec 25, 1933
4. James Carl "Ras" born July 27, 1919 married Gladys Milburn Feb 28, 1955
5. Vernon (March 20, 1921-Oct 11, 1988) married Lorene Hoelscher Aug 8, 1947. Vernon is buried in St. Johns Cemetery at Lafe, AR
6. Thelbert Spencer (Jan 21, 1923) married Viola Williams Dec 21, 1947
7. Burl Eugene (Jan 4, 1925) married Peggy Winchester
8. Mildred Catherine (Jan 24, 1927) married Edward Grayson Gerdes Aug 20, 1948
9. Wanda Lee (Dec 21, 1928) married (1) Harvel Gatewood, Sept 15, 1949. Harvel died April 16, 1996 and is buried in Gravel Hill Cemetery in Clay County. (2) George C. Hardin, Oct 15, 1999
10. Velma (Feb 9, 1931) married Gerald Smith Feb 10, 1955
11. Loretta (Dec 2, 1933 married Charles "Buddy" Smith Dec 24, 1952.

Eight of the nine remaining children currently live in Greene County. The other lives next door in Craighead County, AR.

**STEPHENS** – Spencer P. Stephens was born in Wake County, North Carolina, probably around 1819-1820. The Hayward County, Tennessee, census of 1850 indicates that he was still single. By 1860 he had married Elizabeth and they had four children: John L. (1857), Ellen (1858), Spencer Jefferson (June 20, 1862-Dec. 30, 1906), and Sarah Elizabeth "Betty" (1867).

*Spencer Jeferson Stephens (son of Spencer P. Stephens) and wife, Lillie Belle (Trantham) Stephens.*

Elizabeth died about 1868 and Spencer married Sarah J. Moore of Dyersburg, Tennessee. Their children were George W. (about 1870), Cora (Sep. 24, 1874), Reavus (1879), Isaac (1880) and probably one other child.

The Stephens came to Greene County around 1872 and settled around Gainesville and the Hurricane Community. S.P. and his wife are both probably buried around Hartsoe Cemetery.

Spencer Jefferson (May 20, 1862 - died December 30, 1906), child of Spencer P. and Elizabeth, married Lillie Belle Trantham (March 29, 1864 - June 5, 1908), daughter of Needham J. Trantham and Martha J. Grills, on October 11, 1882. Their children were: Ella Bular (1884), James Claybourne (1886), Ollie B. (1889), Charles (1892), Clarence Edward (1894), Erah Florence (1895), Linnie Ralph (1898), Emry Hawkins (1901), and Albert Thomas (1902).

James Claybourne (August 11, 1886-April 26, 1966) married Nancy Belle Beaton, (Jan. 13, 1894-Oct. 25, 1970) and both are buried at Ramer's Chapel Cemetery. Their children were: Arlene Hester (1914), Iva Lee (1915), Alma Ester (1917), James Carl (1919), Vernon Doyle (1921), Thelbert Spencer (1923), Burl Eugene (1925), Mildred Catherine (1927), Ruby Wanda Lee (1928), Velma Inez (1931), and Loretta Mae (1933).

Mildred Catherine, born January 2, 1927, married Edward G. Gerdes born December 20, 1927, on August 20, 1948, and is a retired school teacher. Edward is a retired National Guard technician. Their two children are Randal Keith, born July 4, 1952, and Mark Owen, born July 14, 1962. Mark is a software engineer. Randal married Charlotte Rose Bowers, born August 9, 1952, on January 22, 1971, and Mark married Toni Lorraine Barnhill, born March 5, 1969, on March 15, 1990. Both Randal and Charlotte are registered nurses. All of the early Stephens were farmers.

**STEVENS** – Charles "Chink" Edward Stevens was born February 15, 1890, the son of James "Jim" Edward and Susa Ann "Susanna" (Foster) Stevens in Elizabethtown, Hardin County, Illinois. For 50 years, he was a farmer in Delaplaine. He died October 30, 1961, in Paragould, and is buried in Jonesridge Cemetery, Delaplaine.

Chink Stevens was an upright citizen, an honest hard working man, well liked and respected in the community. He was a member of Delaplaine Church of Christ.

Chink Stevens married Victoria Jetton. She died in 1912. They had one child: James Robert "Bob" Stevens, July 7, 1910, June 8, 1970, married Maudie Meredith.

On April 5, 1917, Chink Stevens married Martha Miranda Victoria "Vickie" Clark, daughter of Billie Franklin and Laura Melissa (Ginger) Clark, Paragould. They had nine children:

Goldie Irene, January 20, 1918-January 1920 (diphtheria); Imogene, July 12, 1919, married April

16, 1938, Elmer Lawrence Rainwater; Leorna, December 30, 1920, married Charles Woodrow Hill; Wanda, April 4, 1922, married Alfred Eugene Fox; Venita, November 27, 1923, married Earl Rollin Amick; Paul Edward, October 19, 1925-September 6, 1983 (leukemia), buried in Jonesridge Cemetery, married Evelyn Grooms; Arzella, June 29, 1927, married Jewell Edgar and Kenneth Svaglic; Lillie Mae, March 16, 1929-June 18, 1992 (mycosis fungoid), married William Junior Jordan; and Charles Woodrow "Woodie," January 10, 1931, married Clara Mae Pitcher.

Vickie (Clark) Stevens was born March 17, 1892, Paragould. She died March 14, 1931, (pneumonia) and is buried in Beech Grove Cemetery.

On April 16, 1932, Chink Stevens married Rosie Katherine Holloway, April 14, 1900-July 24, 1974, the daughter of John and Berthenia (Golden) Holloway. They had two daughters: Frances, February 24, 1933, married Cleo Pitcher; and Vivian, July 3, 1935, married Carl Samuel Davis.

Rosie Stevens was a very busy wife, mother and grandmother. She earned a special place in the hearts of her stepchildren. They had great respect for her. When the grandchildren came, she was ready to love each one.

James "Jim" Edward Stevens was born April 1862, the son of Dr. George William and Mary Elizabeth (Lipscomb) Stevens in Kentucky. On February 12, 1882, Jim Stevens married Susa Ann "Susanna" Foster, daughter of Rev. Horace and Elizabeth "Betsy" Ann (Hobbs) Foster, Elizabethtown, Hardin County, Illinois. They had 10 children: Mary Ann born April 1883-1919, married Clay Robinson; Delores Isabelle born 1884-died 1894; Lillie Mae born September 1885-died 1928, married Joseph James McGarraugh; George Horace born February 24, 1887-died January 25, 1953; Charles Edward born February 15, 1890-died October 30, 1961; John Robert born 1892-died 1904; Etta Margaret born January 1894-April 1929, married Moss Watson; Austin Willard born December 21, 1896-March 22, 1919; Fred Woodrow born June 1898-died 1904; Edna Cordelia born April 1902-died 1920, married Fred Rice.

*Charles "Chink" Edward Stevens.*

Jim Stevens married Jane Jetton. She died in 1926. The justice of peace and farmer, died in Greene County, January 1919. Susa Ann (Foster) Stevens, February 12, 1864-April 25, 1902, is buried in Beech Grove Cemetery beside Jim Stevens.

**STEVENS** – Martha Miranda Victoria (Clark) Stevens was born March 17, 1992, the daughter of Billie Franklin and Laura Melissa (Ginger) Clark, Paragould.

Charles "Chink" Edward Stevens, Delaplaine, courted "Vickie" Clark, when she was 17. He ask her to marry him. Vickie did not want to get married. She said she would not marry until her 21st birthday.

Chink Stevens married another, Victoria Jetton. They had a son, James Robert "Bob" Stevens. Vick Stevens died a year and a half later.

After Vick died, Chink Stevens again courted Vickie Clark. She said "yes" the third time he asked for her hand in marriage. They were married April 1917. Vickie was 25. They had nine children: Goldie Irene, died age 2 of diptheria; Imogene; Lenora; Wanda; Venita; Paul Edward; Arzella; Lillie Mae; and Charles Woodrow.

Chink said Vickie was so quiet he never heard her get out of bed in the morning or heard her walking around the house. In the kitchen she never banged pots and pans together. Chink said he depended on his nose to tell him when she was in the kitchen.

Imogene Rainwater, Delaplaine, recalls her mother laying apples out in the sun, on a table to dry. The dried apples were stored in clean white cloth bags and hung in the smokehouse.

Vickie Stevens died March 24, 1931, when the youngest, Woodie, was only 6 weeks old. On her death bed, Vickie ask her sister, Jenny Morrow, to take the baby, for she knew she was going to die, and her husband could not take care of a baby, because he had to work. The oldest, Imogene, was 11 years old.

Lenora Hill, Delaplaine, remembers when they brought Woodie home. Uncle Roy Clark, Vickie's brother, was living with his sister, Aunt Jenny. He told the Stevens girls if they didn't take good care of Woodie, he would come and get him, and take Woodie back to Aunt Jenny. They believed him.

Chink Stevens was a farmer and worked close to home. The children stayed in the house by themselves, after Vickie's death. If they went outside to play, they were afraid to go back inside, until their father came in from the fields.

Bob Stevens always teased his sisters a lot. He would read to them.

*Vickie Clark Stevens, 1915, age 23.*

When they worked in the fields, he would tell jokes and sing to them. They thought he was the greatest brother in the world. His sister, Lenora, remembers how hard he worked.

**STEVENSON** – Mary C. "Mollie" Stevenson was born September 20, 1848. She married Manoah Hampton on September 20, 1866. She was the daughter of Thomas Coleman Stevenson and Martha Bennett Stevenson of Giles County, Tennessee. She was very active in the Oak Grove Methodist Church. According to the *Arkansas Methodist Newspaper*, she taught the primary beginners or the "card class" for 50 years.

Following the death of her husband Manoah in 1894, Mollie lived with her daughter and son-in-law, Mattie and James R. Miller.

Mary C. "Mollie" Stevenson applied for Manoah's C.S.A. veterans pension benefit on August 15, 1927. Mollie died on May 2, 1930, and was buried next to her husband in the Gainesville Cemetery.

(See photo with James Robert Miller biography.)

**STEYER** – The family of Rev. Franz Steyer came to Lafe from Wisconsin in 1887. Rev. Steyer served as pastor of the St. Peter's and St. John's churches from 1894 to 1918. Several children were born to the Steyers, including Henry August Steyer (Apr 2, 1884).

Henry August "H.A." was married to Marie J. Braun and to them were born six children:
1. Martin died at age two
2. Carl Conrad
3. Edward
4. Theodore "Ted"
5. Elizabeth married Mel Doering
6. Ernst married Mary A. Fox

Mrs. Marie J. Steyer died March 17, 1962; her husband, Mr. H. A. Steyer died Dec 17, 1971. Both are buried in St. John's Cemetery at Lafe, AR.

In the early 1900s the family of Rev. F. Steyer all agreed to deed the home place to the youngest child, H. A. with the agreement that he take care of the old folks as long as they lived.

This same tradition was continued with the later generation when the youngest, Ernst was given the deed with the same care giving agreement. As a result, there has been at least one Steyer family living on the same property for over 100 years.

**STICKLER** – Eldon "Honkey" Stickler (Aug 7, 1931 Paragould, AR) attended Woodrow Wilson School and graduated from Paragould High School in 1949 and was a member of the 1948 State Championship football team. He attended the University of Arkansas for one year before leaving for the U. S. Marine Corp in San Diego, CA.

On Jun 9, 1951 he married Mary Ann Dunn in Oceanside, CA. Mary Ann (March 4, 1931 Paragould) was the daughter of Bill and Addie Jean (Pemberton) Dunn. She was also a 1949 P.H.S. graduate.

Eldon served in Korea from July 1951 to May 1952. When he returned from service, he enrolled at Arkansas State University and graduated with a B. S. degree in business in 1955.

He accepted a position with the new Emerson Electric plant in Paragould in July 1956 and retired in 1993 as production superintendent. He was an avid golfer, duck hunter and Razorback fan. He passed away Feb 6, 2000.

*Eldon and Mary Ann Stickler, June 9, 1951.*

As long time family members of the First United Methodist Church, Mary Ann is active in Starrshine Circle, the U.M.W. and served as a former Sunday school teacher for many years.

Eldon and Mary Ann had three children, Penny Lynn (1953-1962), William Andrew "Andy" (Aug 2, 1956) and Laura Ann (Sept 19, 1964). They were all born at Arkansas Methodist Hospital in Paragould.

Andy graduated from Paragould High School in 1974 and from Arkansas State University in 1982 with a degree in biology. He is presently the manager of Safety and Environmental Compliance with Darling Manufacturing.

On June 24, 1978, he married Cheryl Starrett (Oct 29, 1959 in Sturgis, MI.) and they have three daughters, Stacie (May 25, 1981), Lindsey (June

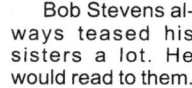

*Laura Ann Stickler.*

8, 1988) and Katie (April 14, 1992). Cheryl's parents, Elmer and Margaret Starrett, came to Greene County in 1971.

Andy and Cheryl are members of St. Mary's Church and the children attended St. Mary's School. Stacie is a sophomore at Arkansas State University, majoring in Elementary Education.

*Andy and Cheryl Stickler, Stacie, Katie and Lindsey Stickler.*

They are active in church and school activities, as both currently serve the positions of president and vice-president of the school board and P.T.C. for St. Mary's Schools.

Laura graduated with honors from Paragould High School in 1982 and Arkansas State University in 1987 with a B.S.E. degree and certifications in science, physical education, health and coaching. She was among the first class to graduate from the new Convocation Center. She teaches science, coaches volleyball and track at Douglas MacArthur Jr. High in Jonesboro, AR. She was selected "Teacher of the Year" from MacArthur in 1996 and has served as chairman of the Science department many years.

**STICKLER** – Jean Stickler (May 26, 1903 Jackson, MO) was the son of Andy and Carrie (Burford) Stickler.

On Sept 7, 1921 he married Hazel Virginia (Snider) Stickler (Oct 21, 1902) of Lutesville, MO, daughter of Albert and Bertha (Proffer) Snider.

His grandfather and grandmother were Holland Dutch and both came to America from Holland when they were children.

Jean and Virginia had two children Patsy Jean (June 15, 1926 Campbell, MO) and Eldon "Honkey" Stickler (Aug 7, 1931 Paragould, AR). They moved to Paragould, AR in 1930.

They were members of First Methodist Church. Virginia was active in church and garden club activities and was a homemaker and loving mother to her children.

*Eldon "Honkey" Stickler, Jean Stickler, Virginia Stickler, and Patsy Jean Stickler.*

Jean was affiliated with Goodwin Poultry Company and later acquired the Buick, Plymouth dealership known as Stickler Motor Company. He was a very active Ham Radio operator and built his own radio. During the flood of 1937, he worked day and night helping direct rescue efforts and relaying messages to families. He served in the U. S. Air Corps during WWII. He also sent and received many messages between service men and their families from all over the world. His call letters were W5DZK. Jean also played semi-pro baseball in Paragould and Campbell, MO during the 1930s. Jean died Nov 29, 1989 and Virginia died Aug 20, 1990. They are buried in Memorial Gardens Cemetery in Paragould.

Patsy graduated from Paragould High School in 1944 and Lindenwood College in St. Charles, Mo in 1947. She worked at the Pentagon in Washington D.C. for several months after graduation. She was married to Col. Mack Blevins from 1947 to 1959 and lived in Germany for three years. During this time, Col. Blevins flew missions for the Berlin Airlift.

Then she returned to Paragould and graduated from Arkansas State University with a degree in nursing. That was the first R.N. class to graduate from A.S.U. She opened the first Coronary Care Unit at Arkansas Methodist Hospital in 1971 and retired as coordinator of the Intensive Care Unit after 20 years of service.

**STIMSON** – Edward Cannon Stimson traveled in a caravan with his parents Isaac and Rachel Tucker Stimson, and several brothers and sisters, from Pittsylvania County, Virginia, through Trigg County, Kentucky, where Edward married his wife Mary Elizabeth Luten, born in 1825. The clan resided in Kentucky for several years before departing again for Texas, which was their original destination. This was not the first time the Stimson clan had moved together as a group. Edward's great-great-grandfather, Solomon Stimson had owned hundreds of acres in Rock Creek Parish, where he was a planter. Today his land is part of the District of Columbia and Prince George's County, Maryland. Solomon and his wife Elizabeth died there, but their son, Jeremiah, who served in the Maryland Colonial Militia, moved with his brothers and sisters and their families to southern Virginia. They settled in Halifax and Pittsylvania Counties.

*One of the Stimson clan; thought to be Edward C. Stimson.*

It was in Pittsylvania County that Jeremiah and Rachel's son Erasmus Sr. and his wife Lucy Wilson raised their family near Sandy Creek, and here that Isaac was born and married Rachel O. Tucker on November 13, 1817, and where their eldest child, Edward was born on October 22, 1819. During the trek to Texas, the families journeyed through Arkansas and Edward and wife Elizabeth decided to stay. Several of their children had been born in Virginia and more were born in Kentucky. Several died before reaching adulthood and were buried in Kentucky.

C.H., Rachel, Isaac and John Wesley traveled with Edward and Elizabeth to Arkansas where two more sons were born, James Edward and Thomas Cannon, called Buck, after the rest of the Stimson clan had continued their journey to Texas. The family lived in Fulton and Izard counties before returning to Greene County where they lived in both Clark and Union townships, finally settling just South of the Oak Grove Community.

After returning from serving as a Confederate corporal in the Civil War, Elizabeth died and Edward remarried Augusta Draffen by whom he had two more sons, Robert and Lafayette, who was called Lafe.

James Edward, known as Jim, was born January 1, 1862. Jim met, and later married Susan Etta Hoskins on January 5, 1884. That same year, on November 23, Jim's brother, John Wesley, married Fannie LuElla Hoskins, Susan's older sister. During their married life the two families had a very close relationship. When Fannie died in 1900, her daughter lived with Susan and Jim for a long period of time. Jim and Susan's or Sudie as he often called her, had Rachel and Isaac Clement. Both died as children and are buried at Fairview Cemetery as are Jim and Susan. They also had Edward Brooks, usually called Bud, William Luster and Earvie.

Edward Brooks, my grandfather, married Clara Rebecca Stutes, December 1908. They made their home in the Unity Community where he farmed. To this marriage was born Ruth Mildred who married Audice Holsombeck and had two daughters, and John D. Edward Stimson who married Reba Adell Blalock and had one daughter, Gretta, who is the last Stimson living in Greene County.

**STRICKLIN/REYNOLDS** – On a crisp, bright Sunday morning, Nov 10, 1889, two Greene County pioneer families were joined with the marriage of Robert Edward Lee Stricklin and Sybillia Ann Reynolds. The setting for the wedding was Fairview Baptist church, in the Fairview community. The ceremony took place following the regular Sunday morning worship service.

Sybillia Ann Reynolds was the daughter of Elisha Rufus and Layra Ann Horn/Horne McEntyre Reynolds, who had migrated to Arkansas from McNairy County, TN. The year was probably 1873 and the journey was arduous and dangerous. Once Mr. Reynolds killed a bear about to attack them, with one shot from his musket while his wife and small children cowered inside the covered wagon. One of those children was Sybillia Ann.

Reynolds homesteaded a large tract of land west of what is now Paragould. He set about clearing the land, building a house and barns. Later he built a cotton gin.

Col. William Lott Stricklin and his wife Almira Moss Stricklin and their small children made the trek from McNairy County, TN at about the same point in time as the Reynolds family. They, too, settled in Fairview community and homesteaded nearby. Col. Stricklin built his home atop a high hill, which today is still known as "Stricklin Hill." Thus, in time the merging of these two adventurous families came about with the marriage of "Bob" Stricklin and Sybillia Ann Reynolds. The newly-weds did not leave their home community, but began a life of farming on the Reynolds land, which they eventually purchased from the other heirs.

Eleven children were born to the couple, five survived to adulthood. Ultimately the children began to reach high school age and there were no school buses then, to transport them to Paragould. Because the parents desired an education for their children they sold the farm, at a sacrifice, to move nearer to town. A five-acre plot was purchased northwest of the city as the site of the family's new home. Trees were cut from the farm and lumber was made to build the house. With the help of his two young sons Mr. Stricklin built their new home and the family moved in at Christmas time, 1917. All of the five children graduated from high school and college. They were:

1. Fred, the oldest, married Sally Martin of Conway, AR
2. Ruby married Granville Cook of Conway, AR
3. Sadie married James Baker of Warren, AR
4. Paul Married Margaret O'Brien of Rector, AR
5. Mary Lou married Henley Smith of Pocahontas, AR

As of July 2000 Margaret (O'Brien) Stricklin is the only survivor and is the owner and resident of Stricklin Place.

*Submitted by Margaret Stricklin*

**STUTES** – John Stutes was born in 1820 in Ohio. His mother, Leah, was born in New York in 1784. Leah and her husband had five sons after they moved to the state of Ohio. John was the second son. The others were Joseph, David, Henry and James. On August 26, 1841, John married Rebecca Davidson in Morgan County, Ohio. John and Rebecca also had five sons: Joseph born in 1846; John in March 1848; James in 1851; Manassa in 1852; and Sam M., born January 7, 1853, all in Morgan County, Ohio. John served in the Civil War. The men in the Stutes family had been loggers by trade for many years. When the Civil War ended, John and his younger brother Samuel came to Arkansas to apply the trade they knew best. At that time, Greene County had a vast supply of timberland and work was plentiful.

*Photograph was taken in the Oak Grove Community. Top row: Lee Hampton, Bessie Blalock, "Bun" Stutes, Amy Simmons, Tom Winder and Lilie Miller Stutes Gardner. Middle row: ?, Charlie Pannels, ?, Alfred Walden, Lucy Blalock Walden, Jake Lacewell and Josie Blalock Lacewell. Bottom row: ?, ? Walden, Mae Miller Walden, R.S. Stutes, Tula Burton Childress, Roy Walden, Clara Stutes Stimson, Harry Walden and Zula Burton Stimson.*

Sam met and later married Mary Lou Shane on March 14, 1885. He was nearly twice her age, and died before their youngest child was a year old. Together they had three children: John F., born in August 1886 and named for the brother of his father. John, mostly known as "Bun," would later marry Leatha Adams and have a son, Thad; R.S., born October 17, 1888, and who died at the age of 21, leaving a young widow, Lilie Miller Stutes; and Clara Rebecca who was born August 27, 1891. She later married Edward Brooks Stimson and they had a daughter, Ruth and a son John D. Edward. Clara, like her brother, R.S., died at an early age in 1927. She was only 35.

Thad was the only child to carry the Stutes name. He moved to Santa Barbara, California, and his only son was killed in the Vietnam War. Today, the only descendants carrying the Stutes name are living in Morgan County, Ohio.

**SWINDLE** – Eula Jean, J. S. Fred and Mack Swindle were children of Ira C. and Mary E. (McDaniel) Swindle.

Our oldest known ancestors lived in North Carolina and spelled their name Swindall. With time and generations it changed to Swindell, then Swindel and Swindle.

The 1790 North Carolina Census listed Samuel Swindall living in the Wilmington District with two males over 16 years and two males under 16 and two females.

Samuel's wife was named Mary. Samuel, our oldest known ancestor, died in 1808.

James Swindell, youngest of Samuel's sons, married Mary Howe, daughter of Job Howe Jr. It is believed that James and Mary Swindell joined a migration of family and friends moving to Humphreys County, TN, which became Benton County around 1836.

Our great-great-grandfather, William E. Swindle (May 19, 1810 NC), was a son of James and Mary Swindle. He probably moved to Tennessee about the same time as his parents. He is known to have lived in Benton County, TN in 1840. He married Catherine Anderson, daughter of John and Elizabeth Anderson.

William E. and Catherine moved to Greene County in 1868. He was 58 years old at that time. Catherine died the next year. They were the oldest of our ancestors to come to Greene County. It is believed they lived in Spring Grove Community, on a farm about one mile west of Rocking Chair Road on what is now Pruett's Chapel Road. Five generations of our family lived and farmed in this area.

William E. Swindle died Aug 11, 1877 and is buried in Fairview Cemetery so he lived in Greene County about nine years.

When great-great-grandfather William E. Swindle moved to Greene County, his second child, John H. Swindle, at age 35, came with him along with his family. John H. Swindle married Isabella Box, daughter of Charles and Catherine Box on April 23, 1863.

Great-grandfather John H. and Great-grandmother Isabella are both buried in Fairview Cemetery also.

Grandfather John Christopher Swindle (1869) the fourth child of John H. and Catherine Swindle was born about one year after his parents and grandparents moved to Greene County. John Christopher married Mary A. Cooper, our grandmother, on Feb 15, 1891. Mary is the daughter of James J. and Heddie Lloyd Cooper.

John C. died May 24, 1952; Mary A. died Aug 23, 1959 and both are buried in Brown's Chapel Cemetery. John C. and Mary A. had the following children:
1. Fred A.
2. Jefferson Wade
3. John L.
4. Ira C. (our father)
5. Silvia
6. Hettie
7. Tyler
8. Onie
9. Margariet

Our father, Ira C. Swindle (Oct. 31, 1897) married our mother, Mary Emma Lee McDaniel, on Dec 10, 1923. Ira and Mary owned a 120-acre farm on Pruett's Chapel Road, west of Rocking Chair Road. This is where we lived and attended Greene County High School and Greene County Tech.

Ira lived to be 97 and died Dec 7, 1994. Mary lived to be 78 and died Aug 10, 1979. Both are buried in Brown's Chapel Church churchyard.

All of our ancestors that we know about were religious people. They were of the Baptist belief.

**SWINDLE** – The history of the Swindle Family has been researched back to William E. Swindle (1810 NC) and his wife, Catherine (1811 TN). In 1850 this family lived in Benton County, TN. Their children at the time were:
1. Caroline (1831)
2. John (1833)
3. Martha (1837)
4. Henry Clay (1839)
5. James (1841)
6. William (1844)

John Swindle, son of William, married Isabell Box (1836) in 1863, the daughter of Charles and Catherine Box, who were residents of Humphreys County, TN in 1850.

In 1880 John and Isabell Box Swindle lived in Greene County, AR. Their children at home at the time were:
1. Roena (1864)
2. Charlie (1866)
3. William (1867)
4. John (1869)
5. Wade (1871)
6. James (1878).

John Christopher Swindle (March 11, 1869-May 24, 1952) married Mary Ann Cooper (Oct 30, 1871-Aug 23, 1959) on Feb 15, 1891. They had nine children:
1. Fred (1891)
2. Jeff (Oct 1893)
3. John L. (Jan 1896)
4. Ira C. (1897)
5. Silva (1901)
6. Hettie (1904)
7. Tyler (1905)
8. Onie (1908
9. Margarite (1910.

Ira C. Swindle (Oct 31, 1897-Dec 7, 1994) married Mary E. McDaniel (Feb 16, 1901-Aug 10, 1979) in 1923. They had four children:
1. Eula Jean (Oct 17, 1924) married Willard Davenport in 1941; they had one daughter, Linda.
2. J. S. (Jan 10, 1927) married Vangie Thomason; they had:
 a. David
 b. Pam
 c. Jerry
 d. Nadine
3. James Fred (Sept 24, 1929) married Martha Jean White Aug 16, 1967; they had one daughter, Gena Lynn (Aug 21, 1968). She married Christopher L. James June 1, 1996 and had a son, Ryan Lee James (May 30, 1999).
4. Mack C. Swindle (Oct 5, 1931) married Emma Jean Roberts in 1954, their children: Edwin, Steven and Rhonda.

**TAYLOR** – George Washington Taylor (1812 TN), Pvt. Co. D Greene County, Confederate Army, and prisoner paroled Wittsburg, AR 1865. Wife, Hanna Grier Parker (1832-1912 TN) George is buried in Beech Grove and Hanna in Croft Cemetery. His children:
1. George W.
2. Carroll
3. John
4. Mose
5. Noma.

Hanna later married Wm. Frank Morrow in 1878. The 1800 Census shows stepsons George, James Carroll and Mose in their home.

George W. (1865-1920), wife Sarah Doughty (1872-1915); children:
1. Ralph
2. Carrol
3. Selma
4. Tera

Also Bertha, Radie, Garrett and Ernest, all died very young.

Ralph (1890-1974) taught in six Greene County schools, two twice. His wife was Lela Roberts (1896-1959); their children:

*L-R: Lesha Taylor, Ralph Taylor; back: Lela Taylor and Lorene Taylor.*

1. Champ (1913-1994) married Mary Julia Cooper (1915-1986); their children:
   a. Ray
   b. Ruth Boring
   c. Dwight
   d. Deceased infant
2. Chester (1915-1935), Southpaw, county baseball
3. Lucille (1916), teacher and clerical retiree
4. Vestle Starnes (1918), retired beautician; children:
   a. Jackie (1941-1945
   b. Jane Allen (1943) sons: Scott and Ronnie
   c. Rebecca Daniels (1946) sons: Danny and Brice
   d. Gregory (1957), wife Leah, son: Reed
5. Odis (1920) Lieutenant Colonel Retired USAF, WWII; wife, Vera Bernal, children: Kenneth (1951), Rory Karen (1954) and Kathleen (1957)
6. Lorene (1922-1974) buried in Paragould
7. Robert 1925-1997), private; children: Eric (1958) wife, Barrie; children: Sydny, Connor; Mauritta (1960) teacher in Alaska.
8. Imogene Hyzdu (1927) retired travel agent
9. George (1929-1993) sergeant, Marine, Korea and oil biologist; daughters: Laura and Kerry
10. James (1932) A1/c Korean War, retired biologist, State of Louisiana, wife; Pamela Woodbridge, children: Julie (1970), Paul (1973) and Vickie Blakewood (1975).

*Evening Shade School, 1913. Ralph Taylor, teacher.*

11. Virginia Lowe (1934) bookkeeper, children:
    a. Elizabeth (1956-1956)
    b. Christopher (1960) wife, Angela Keith, children: Carter, Kendall, Anna, Jenna, Caleb
    c. Richard (1962) wife, Lesa; children: Nicholas and Kristen.
12. Martha Jane (1939-2000) nurse, daughter: Leshia Brock Osborne, children: Richard and Mindy Brock, Crystal Taylor, Russell and Angie Osborne.
13. David (1938) A 2/c, after Vietnam, retired biologist, State of Louisiana, wife, Sandy Burgess; children:
    a. Mary (1964); Tanya, one child Wm. Bruce (1965) wife Melanie, children: Megan and a baby son.
    b. Angela Jackson (1968) children: Heath, Hanna and Sarah
    c. Donna Woodward (1970) children: Tyler and Caitlin

Carroll (1894-1982), U. S. Army WWI, wife Pearl McElwrath, children:
1. Reba Smith deceased
2. Pauline Dearin
3. Monzell Clifton
4. Ruth Miller
5. Inez Denmon deceased

W. C. wife, Wanda; six children.
R. V. wife Mae Rita; two children.

*George W. Taylor and Sarah L. Taylor.*

Selma Johnson (1902-1984) daughters: Alyene Case, Willodean Mandrell, Lt. Col. Bonnie Johnson (1932-2000) ret, USAF nurse.

Tera Arnold (1904-1976), children:
1. A. L. "Jake"
2. Marcella Wells
3. Gray
4. Melba Doris Hyde
5. Betty Balterria, deceased
6. Dorothy Hyde
7. Sue Minto
8. Barbara Collins
9. Janice Car, deceased
10. Larry Arnold.

James Carroll (1867) deceased, wife Emma Smith, child: Dweler

Arthur (1889-1978) wife, Dona, children: Fondell Fletcher, Lester and Jack. Fondell's children: Jo Ann, Bud, James and David.

Lester's children: Michael, deceased infant.

Jack, wife Velma Evans, children: Susan Corby and Scott.

Mose (1869-1935), wife Mary Smelser, children: Earl, Arphia, Ellis, Bill, John, Coe, Joe, Sylvia and Marie. All are deceased except Joe.

John, wife Lillie Grooms, children: Drew, Amber, Daisy, Sylvia, Bill, Vira, Vesta and Kindrell.

Naomi Howell, children: Lizzie Grooms, Noah, Lillie McKenzie and Andrew.

*Submitted by Lucille L. Taylor*

**TAYLOR** – William Mose Taylor was the third son of George Washington Taylor and Hannah Parker Greer Taylor Morrow. The Taylor family had emigrated from Ireland and settled in South Carolina near Spartenburg. Hannah Parker's family had come from Alabama and settled on the Little Duck River in Hickman County, Tennessee. Hannah has a brother named Ben Parker and a sister named Rody. Hannah's first marriage to Willie Green was bitterly opposed by her parents, so she eloped with him. They had a son named Dan Greer. Her next marriage was to George Washington Taylor and they had three sons; George Jr., James Carroll and William Mose Taylor. They had a half-brother named John, by his father's earlier marriage. Mose was born at Beech Grove, Arkansas, on February 26, 1869. His mother, Hannah Parker Taylor, was born March 20, 1832, and died at the home of Mose on August 22, 1912, and buried at Croft Cemetery. After G. W. died, she married Frank Morrow, but did not have any children by him. George Washington Taylor and his brother, Plese, were in the Confederate Army during the Civil War and were captured by the Federals and kept in a prison camp in South Carolina until the war ended. They were given horses to ride home, but the northern soldiers took them away from them—compelling them to walk back to Greene County, Arkansas, which took many weeks.

Mose Taylor married Mary Ellen Smelser, born January 20, 1877, on November 9, 1893, at Stanford, Arkansas. She was the daughter of John Abraham and Sarah M. Gramling Smelser. She had one brother, Willie Smelser, who lived in Stephens, Arkansas. Sarah's father was T. J. Gramling, probably stood for Thomas Jefferson, and had come from Spartenburg, South Carolina. Sarah was a sister to Mem and Doom Gramling. Johnny Smelser had three brothers. One brother was Pink (Pinkney) and the other one was Henry.

Mose and Mary Taylor had a good farm located on the road between Croft Academy and the Commissary, near Sugar Creek, on what we called Taylor's Hill. They had nine children: Lucian Earl, Arpha Sarah, Ellis George, William Mose Jr., John Clennie, Joe Ichabod, Asa Coe, Sylvia E. and Mary Marie.

1. Lucian Earl Taylor, born March 4, 1895, married Cecil Gardner, May 24, 1921. He died September 5, 1985, and she died March 18, 1992. Both are buried at Croft Cemetery. Issue: Marilee Taylor born August 18, 1922, married Lloyd Pruitt; issue: Barry Lee Pruitt married Billie Suddeth: issue Michael Joe, Casey Lee, Matthew Lloyd and Taylor Davis Pruitt. Barbara Elaine Pruitt, born March 29, 1946, married Dr. Ray Hall Jr., issue: Heather Eilene, Holly Kathleen and Colin A. Hall. Ellis Trice Taylor, D.D.S, born August 28, 1930.

2. Arpha Sarah Taylor married Eugene Wilson. Issue: Buena Wilson married Aubrey Shewmaker; Woodrow and Mose Wilson.

3. Ellis George Taylor married Zelma Owens. No children. Died August 30, 1921.

4. William Mose Taylor married Miriam Gladys Gardner, born September 29, 1900, died December 25, 1985, buried in Croft Cemetery. Issue: Harding Lipscomb married Joyce Hudgins, issue: Camille and Paul Taylor; William David married first Rosemarie Hecht; issue: Davy Taylor married second, Hilda Negron, issue: George William. James Alfred married Alice Neyman, issue: Stephen, Donald, Mark, Jimmy and Pattie. Bonnie Lou married Tony Libhart, issue: Deana, Emily and Anthony III. Joe Allen married Joyce Flemon, issue: Tamra Lynn and Allan.

5. John Clennie married Laura White; issue: Lillian, Bonita, Lynn, Carolyn, Mary Alice and Larry Don. He died May 6, 1994. Laura died September 14, 1993. He married second Hazel Barker.

6. Joe Ichabod Taylor married Lucille Autry. He was born May 6, 1908. Issue: Betty Jane married Earl B. Fears; Kay married Herren James Greenway.

7. Asa Coe Taylor married Viva Morrow December 3, 1933. He was born July 12, 1912. Issue: Patsy married first Billie Nix, issue: Kelly Gene Nix and Sheldon Craig Nix; married second Emory Clifton—no children by the marriage; Jerry Dee Taylor born May 24, 1937, married

Jerry Dee Taylor born May 24, 1937, married Shirley Ann Barry; issue: Steven DeWayne born February 7, 1963. Brenda Sue Taylor married Gaylon Ortcutter, issue: Lana and Jana, born March 11, 1977. Billy Edwin married Diane Hyde, issue-Julie and

8. Sylvia Ester Taylor, born January 28, 1916, married Amos Harvill. She died March 14, 1996, and he died December 3, 1995. Buried at Croft Cemetery. Issue: Glenda Faye married George Robb; Charles Ray married June Welch; Rita Joyce married Alan Carter.

9. Mary Marie Taylor, born May 30, 1918, married Thurman Chance. Issue: Diana Lynn born August 7, 1947, married first Ben Jerry Landers, December 2, 1966. Issue: Stephen Kelly Landers, Erin Colleen Landers and Jeremy Brian Landers. Divorced 1978. Married second Ronald Eugene Cushman, July 21, 1984. Issue: Frederick Lawrence Cushman and William Edward Cushman, born January 31, 1987. Frederick born May 2, 1985. Terry Allen Chance born June 13, 1949, married Patricia Ann Jones. Issue: Patricia Ann, Terry Allen and Christopher Chance.

The Taylor family were profound members of the Church of Christ, as were all their children and most of their grandchildren. They were honest, hard working and God-fearing people and held in highest esteem by all that knew them.

**TEAGUE** – It is not exactly known when the Teague family moved to Gainesville, Arkansas. It is known they resided in Monroe City, Indiana, from before their marriage on June 11, 1863. They appeared in the Knox County, Indiana Census for 1870. At that time they showed two children: John Frank, age 3, and Sara E. age 1. The Greene County, Arkansas Census for 1880 shows them in Gainesville. The youngest child, however, was 3 years old and is stated to have been born in Indiana. So the earliest they could have moved was 1877, which was the year they bought their first piece of property in Greene County.

On January 20, 1877, they purchased 120 acres one mile south of what is now Providence Landmark Missionary Baptist Church. Elijah and Samantha were members of that church and Elijah felt called to preach the Gospel. While pastoring that church, the Missionary Baptist Churches held a conference and ordained Elijah to preach on March 27, 1881. It is not known how long he pastored because all church records have been destroyed by fire. When they observed their 50th wedding anniversary on June 11, 1913, (see photograph) another pastor is standing with them and it was only a year before Elijah died.

*Elijah and Samantha Teague at their 50th wedding anniversary held at the Providence Landmark Missionary Baptist Church on June 11, 1913. Minister is unknown.*

Elijah and Samantha were some of the largest landowners in the Gainesville area. On October 26, 1887, they purchased four lots (64, 65, 70, and 71) in the township of Gainesville from H.C. and Elizabeth Oxley and turned right around and sold them to their son, J. Frank Teague. On January 25, 1888, Elijah bought another piece of property in Gainesville form W.R. Clark.

On June 1, 1891, Samantha, my great-great-aunt bought a piece of property that I don't understand at all. A large piece of property in Gainesville, owned by Jacob G. and Catherine Souers, (my great-grandfather and great-grandmother and Samantha's brother and sister-in-law). The puzzle being that the Souers were from Illinois and my family has no record of their ever being in Greene County. The Notary Public, W.C. Blair, however, speaks in the deed, of Catherine Souers being well known by him personally. On September 1, 1895, Elijah bought another lot in Gainesville (Lot #8). On November 4, 1901, Samantha bought a piece of property in the town of Marmaduke and on January 1, 1903, Elijah Teague bought lots 10, 11, 12 in Block 12 in A.H. Moore's first addition to the town of Marmaduke.

When Rev. Elijah and Samantha Teague moved to Greene County, they brought his father and mother with them. There is no record of where they lived but most probably in one of the above locations. J. Frank graduated from school in Gainesville most probably in the Class of '84. He farmed for a few years and then went off to St. Louis and joined the St. Louis Police Department. After a few years with the SLPD he took a job with the Southern Railway as a yard detective. There had been a lot of thefts from boxcar thieves. On the night of February 6, 1911, the thieves lay in wait for Frank. He was later found in an East St. Louis ravine, dying from wounds he received when the thieves crushed his head in. He was brought back to Paragould and laid to rest in Linwood Cemetery.

A year after Elijah and Samantha's 50th wedding anniversary, on December 3, 1914, Elijah passed away and was buried in the Providence Cemetery where he conducted so many funerals himself. Also buried there are his father and mother Frances and Martha Teague.

After the passing of Elijah, Samantha moved to Rector and died at age 96 on November 6, 1941.

With all the property they purchased, it is not listed anywhere that they got rid of any of it.

**TEDDER** – The Tedder family's journey to Greene County, Arkansas actually began with the birth of James Tedder about 1773 in Wake County, North Carolina. This is where he married Nancy Barnes on September 1, 1798. From here James and several other family members next show up in the 1800 Chatham County, North Carolina census and here is where they lived and farmed for the next 30 years. James served with a Chatman County Regiment during the War of 1812. James owned several large tracts of land during these years and fathered five sons to help him with the work: William (born 1799); Hinton (born 1801); John (born 1806); Joel (born 1807); and Elisha (born 1815).

About 1837 the Tedder family made another journey. This time James and sons Joel and Elisha came to Benton County, Tennessee, settling near Camden. William and John stayed in North Carolina. Hinton showed up in Tennessee later. The Tedders settled here and lived for the next 50 years. James died in the fall of 1847. Elisha died young around 1852. This left Joel as the patriarch of the family. Joel and wife Lucinda had daughters Elizabeth Ann, Martha, Anne Mariah and son Edwin M., born May 17, 1839.

During this time Joel may have been a member of the clergy as well as farming as he shows up in a few documents as a representative for Mt. Moriah Presbyterian Church at council of churches in 1849. Edwin married Molinda Yeates on January 3, 1861 and began raising a family: Horace, born about 1862; Cornelius, about 1864; Thomas, August 12, 1866; Cordus T., born May 1868; Victoria, born January 1870; Lillian, born about 1872; and Lucian P., born May 1873. Late in 1883 Edwin packed his family up and made the final journey to Greene County, Arkansas, settling in the Cache Community.

It isn't known what brought the Tedder family to Greene County. Surely the rich, hilly farmland was similar to the terrain back in Tennessee. Whatever it was the family finally found home and there have been Tedders in Greene County for over 100 years. Horace married Martha Langley in Tennessee and brought her to Arkansas. Sadly he had a brain hemorrhage and died one Saturday in 1895 in downtown Paragould. He left children: John, born January 1882; Etta, born September 1884; Marshall, born October 1886; Ada, born November 1888; Lenard born September 1891; and Mary, born May 1895. Very little is known of Cornelius, Victoria and Lillian. Cord married Emma Gregory Wood in 1885 and their children were Lucinda, born January 1884; Corbet, born October 1895; Edward Alexander, born January 1898; Arthur Mack, born July 1900; and Zelma, born February 1903.

Thomas and wife Emma (known to family as Emmer) were married in 1894 and had daughters Dora L., born August 1895; Flora P., born October 1897; George E., born February 1901; Verlie, born May 1905; Mack, born November 1909; and Gradie, born September 1912. Thomas' family resided in the community of Light. Lucian and wife Nancy raised daughters Elsie, born August 1897; Ida, born March 1900; and Eva born 1901.

Molinda Yeates Tedder died September 21, 1901, and is buried at Mt. Zion Cemetery. Edwin lived his last years with son Cord in the Walcott Community, and was living with grandson Ed when he died April 28, 1921. It is believed he is buried next to Molinda, though there is no marker.

*Edwin M. Tedder*

Lucian Tedder died in 1927 and is buried at Mt. Zion by his wife Nancy who died in 1946. Tom Tedder died August 10, 1948, and is buried in Morrow Cemetery along side Emmer who died October 5, 1963. Cord Tedder died September 12, 1943, and is buried at Warren's Chapel with Emma who died November 13, 1953.

Though there are still several Tedder families in Greene County the family has branched coast to coast. There is still a strong family pride in the men and women who settled here over a 100 years ago. They all live on in all of our hearts today.

**TENNISON** – Abraham "Abe" Tennison was born about 1801 in Rowan County, North Carolina. On March 17, 1824, he married Mildred (Parmelia) Caraghan in Rutherford County, Tennessee. They were parents of nine children. The family lived in Lawrence County, Tennessee, until they moved to Greene County, Arkansas, in 1851. He was a farmer and stock raiser dealing extensively in mules. They were members of the Methodist church. He was a Mason.

They lived in the Walcott area. He died November 20, 1858. She died sometime after the 1870 census. Both are buried in the Old Shiloh Cemetery located at Crowley's Ridge State Park.

Their eldest child James S., called Jimmy by the family, was born in Warren County, Tennessee, on March 29, 1826. He had blue eyes, blonde hair and was described as being small, wiry and tough. He was a stagecoach driver in Tennessee. The tales are legendary for his handling a team of four horses. He married Elizabeth Louisa Curry December 28, 1848, in Lawrence County. She was called Betty. They moved to Greene County with his parents in Poland Township. He traded a mule for 40 acres and built a log house. He acquired additional acreage over the years. They were parents of 10 children. As each child married he gave a gift of 40 acres.

James S. Tennison was a Mason who served in offices from Warden to Worshipful Master. As a justice of the peace of Salem Township he performed many marriages for the county. The family were members of the Methodist church.

He died October 28,1900. Betty died May 3, 1904. Both are buried in Old Bethel Cemetery.

*James S. and Elizabeth Curry Tennison.*

George McDonald "Mac" Tennison was born to Jimmy and Betty on March 12, 1865. His hair was blond and he favored his dad. He was a very jolly person.

He married Sallie Jones on September 13, 1865, in Greene County. She was the daughter of John and Sophronia Victoria Hyatt Jones. They were the parents of 10 children. It was difficult to make a living on the 40 acres his father gave him. He sold the farm to his brother Albert and moved to Panther Island where the soil was rich. He raised melons that he brought to his brother "Abb" to swap for apples. To visit his parents he rode the "Bull Moose" train to Bard. The Tennisons continued their love of horses and mules and raised them on their farms.

George McDonald Tennison died March 3, 1937. Sallie died June 30, 1910. They are buried in Clark's Chapel Cemetery. Mac's second and third wives were Hattie Pegg and "Jeffy" Adams.

Mac and Sallie's daughter Pearl Canzada was born September 24, 1886. She married Emery Ethel Cox son of Jimmie and Ella Bobo Cox on September 13, 1903. They were married on the front porch of his parent's home in the Finch Community. He traded a black filly to his father for 80 acres. Six of their eight children were born while living there in a "dogtrot" style house. They attended church at Liberty Church of Christ. The family moved to Paragould in December 1913 when Ethel was elected to serve as county clerk of Greene County. Ethel died April 9, 1957. Pearl died May 12, 1930. They are buried in Linwood Cemetery. His second wife was Hattie Jordan McGrew.

**TERRY** – James Washington "J. W." Terry (Oct 15, 1857 Lincoln County, MO) the son of James Washington and Darthuly Ann (Williams) Terry married Cynthia Ann Monroe Dec 28, 1876 in Lincoln County, MO. They had two children: Luther (about 1878 MO-1891 MO), Alfred Terry (1879 MO-1957 CA) Alfred married Nora Ann Thomas 1902 in Randolph County, AR.

After Cynthia's death, James married Sarah J. Lynn (about 1857 MO-April 12, 1893 Howell County, MO) on Oct 22, 1882 the daughter of John Watson and Louisiana (Callaway) Lynn. They had four children:
1. Louise Edna Terry (1886 MO-1935 Randolph County, AR) married Patrick H. Schunk 1907 in Randolph County, AR.
2. Grover Cleveland Terry (1887 MO-1942 Randolph County, AR) married Ida Lee Milam 1911 in Randolph County, AR
3. Claud Washington Terry (1890 MO-1962 Greene County, AR) married (1) Edna P. "Eda" Gschwend 1911 in Randolph County, AR (2) Amanda Belle Simmons 1942 in Greene County, AR.
4. August Edward "Gus" Terry (March 6, 1892 Howell County, MO- Aug 29, 1975 Greene County, AR) married Hattie Mae Dowdy (Feb 7, 1898-Oct 13, 1993) Sept 19, 1915 in Randolph County, AR daughter of George Washington and Rena (Wolford) Dowdy. Gus and Hattie had 10 children:

*James Washington "J. W." Terry*

a. Baby boy (stillborn)
b. Rosie Mae
c. Josephine
d. Eula Dean
e. George Washington
f. Virgil Eugene "Gene"
g. Alvin Cleveland died at age one
h. Melvin August
i. David Allen
j. Jerry Dewayne

Mrs. Lucy J. Newton (1860 KY-1904 Randolph County, AR) was James's third wife. They were married July 30, 1893 in Howell County, MO. Lucy Jane (1894 Howell County, MO- 1925 Greene County, AR) was their only child, and she married Edgar Lee "Ed" Dowdy 1913 Randolph County, AR.

Mrs. Millie Presley (1860-1920 Greene County, AR) widow of John Presley was James' fourth wife. They married Aug 20, 1906 Randolph County, AR. James and Millie came to Greene county about 1917.

James died as the result of a freak accident. He was a passenger on a bus that ran from Pocahontas to Jonesboro. He had his arm hanging out over a window and a Chevrolet Coupe, driven by D. H. Osborn of Walnut Ridge, scraped the side of the bus, crushing his arm between the two vehicles. Mr. Osborn took him back to Walnut Ridge where he received medical attention and later was moved to Jonesboro where the arm was amputated. He lived for eight days after the amputation and died in St. Bernard's Hospital Oct 14, 1924. The newspaper article of the accident says he was visiting his son, but the family says he was on his way to get married to a Mrs. Danford.

James was Catholic. He was a farmer and owned a farm near Halliday. James and Millie are buried in the New Liberty Cemetery.

*Submitted by Faye Hufford*

**THOLEN/TOELKEN** – Herman Tholen/Toelken (Jan 11, 1851 Germany) lived in Chapin IL where he married Friedalina Sophia "Lena" Ommen (Jan 24, 1955) on Oct 4, 1872. In 1886 Herman left his family in Illinois and rode a train to Gainsville, AR with 35 cents and an ax. There is a story recorded in a quarterly at the Greene County Library. In this account it states that Herman came from New Haven, MO. The 1900 Census shows that he was born in Germany and his wife in Illinois. Edith Fishel From Rushville, IL, who is a great-granddaughter of Frederick Tholen, Herman's brother, who went to Arkansas, has given corroborating information. Herman cut and sold railroad ties to the railroad until he had $40 for 40 acres of hill land about one and a half miles east of Lafe. He built a little log home and sent for his family. The Louis Holland Jr. and Jeff Harmon families now own this land. Remnants of the original home are still there. The Fricke family also previously owned the land. The St. Peter's Cemetery and old lead mine are not far from there, accessible by foot. The Toelken's were neighbors to Fred and Anna Tritch, who lived on the big hill south known as "Tritch Hill".

Herman was a witness to the Tritch will in 1910 and also attended St. Peter's Church with the Tritch, Wegner, Welti, Nething, Frock and other families.

Herman advertised in the "Germania" for German Lutherans to come to the community. He was successful in persuading many families to come.

On March 3, 1887, Kathrena Toelken, infant daughter, died and was the first person to be buried in the Toelken Cemetery. In the same year a child of Fred and Anna Tritch died and was buried there. There were eight Toelken children; three lived to reach adulthood, Fredreika L. Toelken married Henry J. Haller and later died at the age of 21, Earnest Henry Toelken died at the age of 23 and Jake Toelken died in Missouri some years ago. Henry J. Haller later married Clara Ann Kauble who is also buried at the Toelken Cemetery. Mr. and Mrs. Frock are buried at the cemetery, more than likely they are Michael Frock and Margareth (Barker) from St. Peter's, St. Johns Baptismal records. They had three children, Daniel, Sadie and Albert, the youngest, born Aug 20, 1893. Herman Toelken adopted Albert Frock according to 1900 census record.

*The original Toelken home Dec 25, 1999. Note the gun porthole on the left.*

The first physician in Lafe, 1904 to 1905, Dr. Frank Malone, boarded with the Toelkens.

Herman Toelken was installed as Lafe postmaster on May 4, 1905.

Herman died on Oct 25, 1917. The remaining Herman Toelken family has died, Lena being the last on July 15, 1942. This family needs to be remembered as important cornerstone members of Greene County history, as they were instrumental in bringing many good people to the Greene County area.

*Submitted by Loretta J. House*

**THOMASON** – Jack Thomason (April 11, 1905) married Vestal Smith (Jan 12, 1906) on Dec 22, 1922 in Greene County and lived in Camp Ground community. Jack farmed with mules, raising cotton and had a truck patch. He sold vegetables in town and bought staples that he was unable to grow. In the winter he sold wild game such as rabbit, squirrel, quail, opossum, raccoon and fish. He was an outstanding hunter and fisherman. He once shot 17 quail in one shot! How? While walking down a fencerow after the ground had refrozen during the night, a covey of quail feet were frozen to the ground. One shot, none of them flew. What a surprise to him!

Jack and Vestal left Greene County twice and lived in St. Louis. They did not like the city life and returned to Arkansas each time. They once lived in a house they thought was haunted. Every night the door would fly open, no matter how it was secured. Jack and Vestal's brother, Chester Smith, would run around the house in opposite directions with loaded guns, but never saw anyone. Vestal wanted to move because she thought something was going to happen. Two weeks after moving, the house burned. Vestal said that it had been a warning from God to move.

On Nov 1, 1925 during a snowstorm, Jack had to walk to find a midwife for the birth of their first child, Margie. Five boys followed: James, Hugh, Jackie and twins, Bobby and Billie who died at birth, Nov 30, 1933. Solomon Obediah, Jack's father, made them a little pine coffin and they are buried at Fairview Cemetery. There was snow on the ground and the women stayed with Vestal while the men buried the twins. They were buried together, wrapped in a blanket.

*Vestal and Jack Thomason, 1925.*

After five boys, came Elizabeth Ann, Herbert, Ray and the last was Bonnie. When Bonnie was born, Dr. Ellington came early on March 6, 1947. It was a difficult labor and Bonnie was born prematurely. Vestal was going to be loaded into the back of a wagon and taken to a hospital, but Bonnie was born before they left.

When Vestal was expecting, she hid the baby clothes so the other children would not get suspicious. The kids were sent to relatives or neighbors when it was time for the baby. Jack and Vestal were very hard workers. Vestal insisted that Sunday was a day of rest and went to church. Jack and Vestal taught their children to be God fearing, hardworking and honest children. Times were not easy. The children remember sleeping under so much cover in the winter that they could barely turn over in bed. They could sometimes find snow in their bed in the morning. The water bucket was kept in the refrigerator to keep the water from freezing. Today, all the children will say that they would not take anything away from their childhood. It made them strong, ambitious, wanting to do more for their children and being the best citizens they could be.

*Submitted by Gerald F. Scott Jr.*

**THOMASON** – James Wilbour Thomason was born January 3, 1930, in Greene County. He is the son of Jack and Vestel Thomason and grandson of S. O. and Bessie Thomason and Johnathan and Sara Smith of Greene County.

On September 5, 1953, he married Oma Lee Chunn. They have two sons, Vence and Victor Thomason, two grandsons, Ryan and Jordan Thomason.

*James' barber shop, Paragould, Arkansas, September 1999.*

James attended Oak Grove High School and was a Marine during the Korean War. He attended barber college in St. Louis, Missouri, in 1956 and worked in North St. Louis two years before moving back to Paragould in 1958. He opened his barber shop on South Second Avenue (Wall Street) and has been there at that location for 42 years.

He was the fifth barber shop in that block area at that time. The price of a hair cut was 75 cents in 1958.

**THOMASON** – Thomas Jefferson Thomason (Dec 1843 Benton County, TN) moved to Greene County, AR in 1854 with his parents, George and Anna (Cole) Thomason and his brother and sisters.

On Sept 18, 1861 when he was 18, he enlisted as a private in CSA in Gainesville. He was in Company H, Arkansas 5th Infantry.

*Thomas Jefferson Thomason in his Confederate uniform.*

During combat he was hit in the leg with a cannon ball with chains, which caused a lifelong limp. He was taken prisoner in Vicksburg, MS during his tour of duty. He also spent from Sept 20, 1862 until Jan 1863 in the hospital at Munfordville or Harrisburg, KY.

He returned to Gainesville in 1863 and in 1864 he was in Company K Kitchen Regiment Missouri Cavalry; also, Missouri Eight Cavalry. After the war was over the family believes Thomas Jefferson received 600 acres of land, some of which he donated to the Palestine School.

He married Eliza Jane Kent in 1865 in Greene County, AR. They had 10 children:
1. Margaret Emmoline "Emma"
2. Mary A.
3. Eugenia Forrest
4. James William
5. Colombus W.
6. Virginia E.
7. Walter G.
8. Isaac Isaiah
9. Cleve
10. Victoria Lee

He died Aug 5, 1913 and is buried at Fairview Cemetery.

*Submitted by Gerald F. Scott*

**THOMPSON** – James Thomas (1833 near Jackson, TN) was the son of James Thompson of North Carolina and Lydia Terrell Thompson of Tennessee.

Mr. Thompson enlisted in the 21st Company of Tennessee Regiment, CSA, at Jackson in 1861. He saw Confederate service in Alabama, Mississippi and Tennessee. When his regiment was captured at Fort Donaldson he made his escape on a steamboat up the Tennessee River. His regiment was reorganized at Corinth, MS in March 1861. In May of the same year he was sent home on a sick furlough. By Aug 1861 he was sufficiently recovered to enlist in the 14th Tennessee Calvary commanded by General Forrest. As a member of this organization he was active until 1865.

In 1870 Mr. Thompson moved from Tennessee to Arkansas, settling on a farm two miles west of what is now Marmaduke.

In 1878 Mr. Thompson was ordained a deacon in the Methodist Episcopal Church South. Bishop David L. Daggett officiated at the ordination. In his capacity as a minister Rev. Thompson served as what was then known as "local" minister, officiating at funerals, weddings and performing whatever duties were usually done by a "circuit rider".

In 1888 Mr. Thompson bought a drug store from the firm of Huckaby and Moore. The store was located in Marmaduke. He became a licensed pharmacist in 1891. This license and that for minister are well preserved and are in keeping of his daughter, Mrs. Dot Skaggs.

Mr. Thompson first married Mary J. Worrell. They were parents of eight children, none of who are now (1965) living.

For his second wife Mr. Thomas chose Mrs. Martha Ross Brand, a widow. They had five children that became adults:
1. Robert Lee deceased
2. Rosa B. deceased
3. Buena Chole "Dot" / Mrs. W. L. Skaggs
4. Charles C.
5. Zera / Mrs. John R. Simpson died Nov 16, 1969.

Grandchildren are:
1. Mrs. Lillie Vanderbilt
2. Arvel Thompson
3. Mrs. Zelma Hooper
4. Mrs. Chloe Blackford
5. Rev. Marvin Thompson
6. Mrs. Maude Reedy
7. Mrs. Beryl Wynne
8. J. Q. Bachar
9. James H. Bachar
10. Mrs. Helen Thomason
11. Mrs. Robbie Skelton
12. Mrs. Mozelle Grimmett
13. Morris Thompson
14. Donald Simpson
15. Elaine Simpson Yoneshige, consultant for the city library system of New York City (1965).

Two other descendants who have distinguished themselves in their chosen fields are Dr. Dorothy Magallon, practicing physician, Louisville, KY and Miss Betty Jo Rasberry, professor of psychology at Ouachita College, Arkadelphia, AR, (Information last updated in 1965).

*Submitted by Evelyn Euritha Wagner*

**THOMPSON** – John Edward Thompson (Jan 20, 1886 Finch) the son of Joe A. and Rebecca (Willcockson) Thompson married Mattie Miller, daughter of George and Sally (Tennison) Miller.

J. Ed had three children; Cleetis, married Ester Arnold, Irene married Leroy Walden and Mack married Alean Lively.

Active in Baptist church, superintendent of Sunday school at Clarks Chapel Church over 60 years.

Community and politics, held several township offices, state representative six years; state senator four and county judge six years, country merchant at Finch and Walcott, rural mail carrier and a farmer.

Started Greene Acres Nursing Home while judge.

Joe A.'s parents were Edward Laurence Thompson and Jane Newsom.

Edward's parents were Laurence Thompson and Jane Mattix, they came to Arkansas from Indiana in 1823 to Davidsonville, then to near Goobertown, in 1831, was first county clerk of Greene County 1833, third county judge in 1838-1840.

*J. Ed Thompson*

Son of Laurence Thompson (1755); Jane Mattix, the daughter of Edward Mattix, came to Lawrence County from Indiana 1823.

J. Ed's mother, Rebecca Willcockson, daughter of John Willcockson and Mary Lamb.

John was the son of Samuel Willcockson and Francis Gibson, who came to Arkansas in 1851 from Tennessee.

Samuel served two terms in the state legislation, one at old Washington during the Civil War.

J. Ed had three brothers, Jim, Mack and Sam; three sisters, Ollie married Bob Elmore, Ruth married Alex Arnold and Velma married Obe Lovelace, after his death M. Maurice Walden.

The Thompsons were active in the community and political affairs in Greene County.

Laurence, the first to come to Arkansas was first county clerk in 1833, third county judge, and schoolteacher. Joe A., grandson, justice of peace, sheriff, state representative. J. Ed, great grandson, rural mail carrier, merchant, state representative senator and county judge. J. Sam, great grandson, county clerk 100 years after Laurence. Mack A., great great grandson, state representative. Several others held township offices and taught school.

J. Ed was on a number of boards, including: Greene Acres Nursing Home, Williams College, Soil Conservation, moderator of Greene County, Baptist Assn. and several positions with the state Baptist Convention.

Late in his life, when asked 'Of all that you have been involved in, other than church, what are the proudest of?' his reply 'Greene Acres Nursing Home'.

*Submitted by Mack Thompson*

**THOMPSON** – Laurence Thompson (Jan 16, 1799 KY) moved to Indiana where he met and married Jane Mattix, daughter of Edward and Elizabeth Bond Mattix on May 14, 1822. About 1823/24 Laurence, along with the Mattix family, moved to Davidsonville, Lawrence County, AR on to near Goobertown after 1829. When Greene County was formed in 1833, Laurence was the first county clerk.

Laurence and Jane Thompson had four children:
1. Elenor (1825) married L. Dennis
2. Elizabeth (1828) married N. Bobbitt
3. Charity Jane (1834-1835)
4. Edward Laurence (1836) married Mary Jane Newsom.

Jane Thompson died Dec 23, 1836 and Laurence married Mahala Suftin. They had three children: Clarrisa M. (1842) married Van Sheare; Americus Vespusius (1844-1851), James Addison (1849) married Susan Edwards. It is assumed that Laurence in 1856 and is buried at Sweet Moments near Goobertown.

Edward Laurence Thompson married Nov 17, 1859 to Mary Jane Newsom, daughter of Sterling Newsom and they had four children:
1. Joseph Adam (1861)
2. Nancy Ellen (1864) married David Edwards
3. Laurence Thompson (1866-1874).

Edward Laurence in 1870 and Mary Jane married Bill Hester and had three more children.

Joseph Adam Thompson married Rebecca Willcockson, daughter of John W. and Jane Lamb Willcockson, Dec 12, 1881. Joseph Adam died Feb 1928 and Rebecca in March 1928. They are buried at Finch Cemetery. They had 11 children:
1. Ollie (1882) married Robert Elmore
2. Sally (1883-1884)
3. John Edward (1886) married Mattie Miller
4. Hattie (1886-1888)
5. James Sterling (1890) married Ethel Pillow
6. Little Ruth (1894) married Alex Arnold
7. Carroll Mack (1896) married Johnnie Lou Coffee
8. Maggie (1897-1900)
9. Joseph Samuel (1899) married Anna Lee Blackwood
10. Velma (1901) twin, married (1) Obe Lovelace (2) M. D. Walden
11. Elmer (1901-1902) twin.

John Edward and Mattie Thompson had three children: Cletis (1910) married Esther Arnold; Irene (1917) married Leroy Walden and Mack (1922) married Alleen Lively.

James Sterling and Ethel Thompson had 11 children:
1. Inez (1912) married Norman Harrison
2. Ralph (1914) married Velma West
3. Sterline (1918) married L. W. Greenway
4. Arlen (1920-1922)
5. James E. (1922) married Pauline Mouser
6. Norris A. (1924) married Joyce Newboles
7. V. Bernell (1926) married J. C. Wells
8. Betty J. (1928) married Everett Vaughn
9. Glenn Maxwell (1930-1931)
10. Joe A. married Earline Jones
11. Ted J. (1934) married Peggy L. Bayless

Carroll Mack and Johnnie Lou Thompson had two children, a stillborn son in 1931 and Carol Lou.

Joseph Samuel and Anna Lee Thompson had 10 children:
1. Merle (1918) married Virginia Isom
2. Reba (1920) married A. W. Shively
3. Tomazien married J. Ernest Howell
4. J. W. (1925) married Eugenia Nettles
5. Rebecca (1927) married R. B. Childress
6. Anna Lee (1930) married W. C. Hudgins
7. Sammy Ruth (1932) married Bob Diamond
8. Maurice E. (1935) married Barbara Dodson
9. Martha Ellen (1939) married Tommy Jumper
10. Homer E. Thompson (1941) married Henrietta Mangrum.

*Submitted by Mack Thompson*

**THOMPSON** – Robert Faires "Bob" Thompson Jr. (June 14, 1942 Dermott, AR) the son of Robert Faires Thompson and Alice Buell (Stuart) Thompson was raised in McGehee, AR and Enid, OK. Bob attended Texas A&M University and the University of Arkansas School of Law. He was admitted to practice law in Arkansas in 1967.

Charlotte Ann Barkley (Aug 2, 1942 Jonesboro, AR) the daughter of Carl Beresford Barkley and Beulah (Tucker) Barkley was raised in Jonesboro. Charlotte attended Arkansas State University and received a master's degree in English from the University of Arkansas.

Bob Thompson and Charlotte Barkley were married on July 13, 1968, in Jonesboro. In 1969 they moved to Paragould and Bob began practicing law with attorney Robert B. Branch.

Bob and Charlotte Thompson have four children:
1. Robert Faires Thompson III (June 19, 1971)
2. Barkley Stuart Thompson (Nov 17, 1972)
3. Andrew Carl Thompson (March 14, 1976)
4. Charlotte Ann Thompson (Aug 3, 1977).

All four children attended Paragould schools and went on to attend Hendrix College in Conway, AR.

Robert Thompson III also attended the University of St. Andrews in Scotland and the University of Arkansas School of Law. He was admitted to practice law in Arkansas in 1997. Robert married Victoria Ann "Tori" Gibson of Osceola, AR on Aug 9, 1997. In late 2000 Robert and Tori were living in Paragould and expecting their first child in March 2001.

*L-R: Robert F. Thompson, Jr., Charlotte Ann Thompson, Robert F. Thompson III, Andrew Carl Thompson, Barkley Stuart Thompson, Charlotte Barkley Thompson.*

Barkley Thompson also attended the University of Chicago, where he received a master's degree in religious studies and the Episcopal Theological Seminary of the Southwest in Austin, TX. He married Jill Paulette Benson of Little Rock on June 10, 1995. On July 8, 2000, Jill gave birth to Griffin Killough Thompson, Barkley and Jill's first child and Bob and Charlotte's first grandchild. In late 2000 Barkley and Jill were living in Austin.

Andrew Thompson also attended Vanderbilt University in Nashville, TN, where he will receive a Master of Divinity degree. In late 2000, Andrew was living in Nashville.

Charlotte Ann Thompson married Andrew Thomas "Andy" Grumbles of Dermott, AR on July 10, 1999. In late 2000, Charlotte and Andy were living in Conway, AR and building a new home in nearby Maumelle.

Bob Thompson has practiced law at the firm of Branch, Thompson, Philhours & Warmath since 1969. He served as Greene County's delegate to the state Constitutional Convention of 1979-80, as Paragould City Attorney for 20 years and as Greene County's deputy prosecuting attorney for eight years. Bob represented Paragould in the development of the city's cable system and was instrumental in structuring the financial mechanism that allowed for the construction of the new Greene County Courthouse in 1996. Charlotte has taught for many years in the Paragould School System, first teaching high school English and then serving as the librarian for Paragould Junior High School. They have been active members of the First United Methodist Church of Paragould for over 30 years.

**TOELKEN** – It is generally agreed that the Herman Toelken family was the first permanent white settlers in the Lafe area. However, records of other families indicate that many of the well-known and well-established families followed within the next one or two years. For instance, Mr. Toelken came to the area in 1886 and church records indicate that church services were first held by a small band of Lutherans as early as Nov 1886, with the Reverend A. Frederking serving as minister.

It is not known just where Mr. Toelken and his family came from but many of those who followed him came for Indiana, Illinois, Ohio and Missouri.

Whether or not Mr. Toelken was an ordained minister of the church is not mentioned in the church records, but the records state that two of his children were actually baptized by him.

The Toelkens had several children, including:
1. Jake
2. Mollie
3. Ricke
4. Ernest
5. Paulina
6. Heinrich
7. Kathrina
8. Frederick.

Only four grew to adulthood: Jake Mollie, Ricke and Ernest. Jake married Martha Nething; Mollie married Will Gerdes; Fredrika "Ricke" married Henry Haller; Ernest died at the age of 23 unmarried.

**TOOMBS** – Herman Winford Toombs (Sept 3, 1918 Buffalo Township, Dunklin County, MO) the fourth child and son of Luther, a farmer and Vina McClure Toombs, a housewife. Luther was listed as a farm laborer in the 1900 Census at age 10. Herman grew up on a farm south of Cardwell where he lived across the road from Hazel Helen Hortense Davis, the girl he married in 1937 in Greene County. Hazel (Oct 17, 1919 Salem Township, Dunklin County, Senath, MO) was one of nine children of Charles Arthur and Nannie Elizabeth Shultz Davis.

Herman and Hazel's three children, all girls are: Patsy Joann (May 2, 1938 Cardwell, Dunklin, MO), Linda Jean (Nov 3, 1939 Cardwell, Dunklin, MO) and Karen Louise (April 22, 1947 Leonard, Clay County, AR). The family had moved to Clay County Jan 25, 1946. Hazel's mom died that day. Other than the two years they lived in Clay County, the girls attended Lakeside Grade School and Greene County Tech, from which they graduated.

Patsy married (1) Floyd "Dobe" Crockett (Feb 5, 1932) in Lorado, Greene County, AR, the son of John and Delcie Jane Crowley Crockett, in 1956. Their three children, all born in Paragould, AR are the great great great great grandchildren of Benjamin Crowley, the early settler of Crowley's Ridge and Greene County. They are: Steven Floyd (June 16, 1957) married Tabbie Rose Hale and have two children: Maxy Steven Winford (June 4, 1986) and Morgan Joann (March 14, 1997) Patsy's little two pound nine ounce namesake. Clinton Scott (Nov 20, 1959) married Rebecca Jane Martin and has one daughter, Misty Nicole (March 11, 1982). Kim Alicia (April 14, 1961) married Tom Papachriston. They have one son, Nicholas (Sept 14, 1993)

Patsy and Floyd's marriage ended in divorce in 1988. In Craighead County on Oct 1, 1992, Patsy married (2) John Dortch "J.D."Yates (May 29, 1935 Sharp County, AR), the son of Samuel Dortch and Leona Hill Yates. They live in Jonesboro.

Linda married April 26, 1963 Jerry Dewayne Terry (Jan 10, 1941) the son of A. E. and Hattie Dowdy Terry. Their two children are a daughter, Stacey Jean (March 31, 1965 Paragould, AR) married Wayne Flanery and Danita Carroll (May 28, 1970) married Dewayne Gibson.

*Herman and Hazel Toombs, 1987.*

Karen married Jan 10, 1970 Jerry "Butch" Daniels (Sept 7, 1947), the son of Leroy Daniels and Hattie Covington Daniels (now Rickman). Their son is Jarrod Grayson (July 10, 1974 Paragould).

Herman grew up in a farm family and started out being a farm-laborer, sharecropper, renting his first farm in Marmaduke about 1943 for one year before renting Round Island from the L. G. Staub family. Herman purchased his first tractor, a Farmall F-12 with iron wheels, in the mid 1940's and later a new B Farmall from M. A. West, who carried the notes in his shirt pocket. He rented more land from Staub's. All of this land has remained being farmed by Herman and/or his son-in-law. Herman became a successful farmer and bought his first 160 acres near Schugtown in the late 1950s where he and Hazel moved on Jan 25, 1960 and still make their home there.

Cotton and corn were the earlier crops raised with the harvesting all done by hand. The mechanical cotton picker came into operation after his two oldest daughters were grown. Herman also had a milk cow and some hogs, plus Hazel raised chickens. Later, soybeans, wheat, rice and milo were some crops grown.

Herman enjoyed fishing and carpentry in what little spare time he had. Hazel sewed most of her daughters' clothes, made a big garden and canned many jars of tomato juice, green beans, purple hull peas, peaches, etc. The family enjoyed Sunday dinners together. They are members and attend Christ United Methodist Church.

See related article for Herman's family and ancestors.
*Submitted by Patsy (Toombs) Crockett Yates*

**TOOMBS** – William Luther (Aug 25, 1889 Pollard, Clay County, AR- March 10, 1939 Cardwell, Dunklin County, MO) and Vinnie Ellen McClure Toombs (Oct 5, 1891 MO-Sept 13, 1936 Cardwell) were parents of Greene County residents, Herman W. and Norman Wesley "Perry" Toombs. Luther, the

*William Luther and Vinnie Ellen McClure Toombs, ca.1909.*

son of Charles Wesley and Sarah Sally T. Mallard, married about 1909. Vinnie was the daughter of Lafayette (1852-1935) and Margaret McClure. Lafayette the son of Jonathan (about 1825 TN) married Nov 14, 1844, to Elizabeth Hart McClure. Both Luther, a farmer, and Vinnie are buried at the Cardwell Cemetery.

Luther and Vinnie's six children are:
1. William Earnest (July 26, 1910-Dec 19, 1979) married Viola "Odie" Drope. They had one child, Frances Ellen.
2. Edra Arline (July 14, 1913-July 7, 1993 CA) married DeWitt Pruett. Two children: Dallas Wayne and Marian Joy.
3. Edna Eugenia (March 20, 1916-Sept 29, 1990 VA) married James Lawson Harper. Three children: Doris Virginia, Hayward Eugene and Norma Joan.
4. Herman Winfred (Sept 3, 1918) married Hazel Davis. Three daughters: Patsy, Linda and Karen.
5. Alice Thelma (Nov 17, 1920) married Gerald "Dee"Munsey. Three children: Larry Dee, Kaye Ellen and Gerald Robert
6. Norman"Perry"(Aug 28, 1924) married Marcella Hoyer. Three children: Jerry Lynn, Thomas Keith and Charlotte Annette.

Tradition has that once while they were picking cotton, Norman, the baby was put in a diaper and hung on the cotton scales to be weighed. His sister, Alice, cried when she thought they planned to sell him. Another job the children remember as "being the hottest" was picking peas, which were planted in the corn skips.

Luther's siblings:
1. Lonnie married Mary Ollis
2. Ida Belle (Dec 9, 1895-April 12, 1977) married Luther Edison Holcomb. A granddaughter, Karen Holcomb Beliew, lives in Paragould.
3. Fannie Lee Ann (Feb 4, 1895-June 7, 1987) married Robert Joseph Jackson.

The story is told that Charlie, the father of Luther, with his wife Sally moved his family from Pollard, AR across the St. Francis River in a wagon to Dunklin County, MO probably shortly after his father, Owen T. died and never went back, His wife, who was born Oct 28, 1870, died Oct 8, 1908. Charles Wesley (Jan 7, 1856 TN-March 1, 1928), after having lived alone in a tent with lumber all around it near his daughter, Ida, then later lived with Luther. He cursed the mosquitoes and slept with a net over his bed. He must have had a terrible life, as he is remembered as being "cranky".

We trace this Toombs' family back as far as Jan 6, 1811 in Virginia (maybe Charlotte or Gloucester County where the famous Robert Toombs of Georgia's family originated), when Owen T., the father of Charles Wesley, was born. Owen married Feb 28, 1835 in Gibson County, TN; Lucinda Glasscock

*Lafayette McClure, ca.1930.*

(Sept 17, 1813 NC) daughter of Peter and Polly Glasscock. Owen was listed as farmer in Tennessee 1860 Census and grocer retail with real estate value of $5,000 in 1870 in Dyer Station TN. He and Lucinda and most of their children moved from Gibson County in the mid 1870s to Pollard, Clay County, AR, only a few years before Lucinda died Feb 12, 1880. She was buried there on their farm, which started the Toombs

Cemetery. Owen died March 15, 1898 and at least four of the children are buried there also.

Owen and Lucinda Toombs' eight children were:
1. William Elonzo Griffith
2. Owen Peter Thomas
3. Theresa S. M. Emma married Ben Battles
4. Gabriel James Monroe
5. Melchisidic ("idiot" according to census records; also provisions were made for him in Owen's will)
6. Henry Clay
7. Millard Fillmore
8. Charles Wesley.

Owen P. T. "Uncle Tom" also has descendants in Greene County. Three of his sons were Steve T., William O. and James Owen, who lived in Greene County, married Mary Jane Dalton March 17, 1904. A son, Earl "E.L." (Feb 7, 1909) still lives in Greene County; also his children: Faye Toombs Williams, William Mack and Gary. One son, Earl Wayne lives in Michigan. One son and a daughter are deceased. Other children of James Owen were Claude, James and Alma Jean.

The Toombs's heritage goes on.

Source: Census, will, marriage, deed, tax and family records, including extensive research done by Stacey Jean Terry Flanery.

*Submitted by Patsy Toombs Crockett Yates*

**TRANTHAM** – Needham J. (about 1828-1869) married in Tennessee Martha Ellen Grills (about 1829) daughter of Thomas Jefferson (1803) and Harriet W. Smith Grills (1807-Aug 1856). They came from Weakley County, TN to Greene County about 1857 and bought land in the Gainesville area.

Needham's father, Robert Floyd Trantham (about 1800 in Kershaw County, SC) was living with them at the time.

Needham died of pneumonia in 1869, leaving Martha with the following children:
1. Isaac Hawkins
2. Octavia
3. Caldonia T.
4. Philadelphia
5. Thomas J.
6. Charles F.
7. Lillie Belle

Martha died before April 1877. Both Needham and Martha are buried in unmarked graves in Hartsoe Cemetery.

Lillie Belle married Oct 11, 1882 Spencer J. Stephens also of the Hurricane community.

**TREADWAY** – Lawrence Nelson Treadway (March 24, 1914), son of Louis and Susan (Adams) Treadway, and Mariam Inas Williams (January 9, 1920), daughter of Lester Lee and Anna Mae (Lenderman), were married on November 21, 1936, at the home of Jack and Audie Burton. Four children were born of this marriage: George Edward Treadway (August 17, 1937), Nadine (Treadway) Jamison (December 17, 1938), James Earl Treadway (January 29, 1940) and Tommy Ray Treadway (October 10, 1944). Lawrence and Inas are faithful members of the Pine Knott Church of Christ where he was the song leader for over 60 years. Much of his song leading ability can be attributed to Mr. Early Johns who held singing schools in many churches of Christ in this area, usually a two week school was held at Pine Knott, Commissary, Mountain Home, Mulberry and the Liberty Churches during the winter months. Lawrence never missed a night, making sure his children all knew the rudiments of music and his tradition is carried on by George and Tommy who are song leaders at the congregations they attend.

Lawrence and Inas are both retirees of Emerson Electric Company.

George graduated from Crowley's Ridge Academy in 1956, Harding University in 1960 and began teaching math at Carlisle High School in the fall of 1960, where he taught for 34 years. He is presently employed by the Secretary of State in Little Rock.

*Lawrence and Inas Treadway's 50th wedding anniversary. Front: Lawrence, Inas and Nadine. Back: George, Jim and Tommy.*

Nadine graduated from Paragould High School in 1956 and worked at various jobs in Greene County before being elected as Greene County Clerk in 1978, where she served for 18 years before retiring on December 31, 1996. She is presently selling real estate in Greene County.

Jim graduated from Crowley's Ridge Academy in 1958, where he was voted Mr. CRA. He enlisted in the Army in the fall of 1958, making a career until he was given a medical discharge after suffering a brain aneurysm in 1971. Jim died on April 6, 1988.

Tommy graduated from Crowley's Ridge Academy in 1960 and the Memphis Business School in 1961. He is employed in retail sales and management in Berry, Alabama, where he has lived for the past 20 years.

George Edward Treadway married Melba Stepp and they have two daughters: Sheila (Treadway) Lea and Tonya Treadway.

Nadine Treadway married Jacksie Gene Jamison and they have two sons: Jacksie Dean Jamison married Melissa Henderson and they have four sons: Jarred Dean, Blake Andrew, Tyler Lee and Jordan Alexander. Darron Gene Jamison has one daughter, Jade Darrian Jamison.

James Earl Treadway had two daughters: Anita Marie Treadway and Linda Treadway.

Tommy Ray Treadway married Sue Keith, they have one son: Thomas Russell Treadway.

**TRICE** – According to family legend, during the last days of the reign or Queen Elizabeth I, a Scottish nobleman made a visit to the royal court of England. There he fell in love with Mary Dunbar, the Queen's second maid of honor and asked the Queen to release her to marry him. The Queen refused the young man, so Albert Beatrice joined his cousin, James, and sailed to America. Before leaving they decided to shorten the family name from Beatrice to Trice, and in doing this lost their inheritance in Scotland. The young men settled in Virginia and Albert wrote Mary Dunbar regularly. Finally the Queen consented to the marriage and prepared a splendid trousseau for Mary and arranged for her passage to America. They were married when she arrived in Virginia and named a daughter Elizabeth and a son Benjamin Albert, whose initials would be B.A. Trice. In nearly every generation there have been the names of Elizabeth, Albert, Benjamin and James. All the Trices were born and stayed in Virginia until John left for Tennessee in the early 1800s and are descendents of the cousins Albert and James.

One of John's sons was Samuel Thompson Trice. He and his wife, Sarah Smith Trice, were born in Bedford County, Tennessee. They moved to Arkansas about 1852 and settled on a farm eight miles north of Jonesboro, around the old Shiloh Church in the community of Greensboro in Craighead County. In Harry Lee Williams's *History Of Craighead County*, Sam Trice was listed as one of the chain bearers when the county was created and Jonesboro laid out in 1859. He was a justice of the peace for many years and died while serving his first- term as county judge in 1861. He was the second county judge for the county. Their children were: Joe, Thomas Newton, Andrew Jackson, John T. (died single), Sarah T. and Henry Samuel.

Henry Samuel Trice, born November 9, 1853; married Margaret Ann Gambill, daughter of Aaron Gambill, on February 18, 1873, when he was 19 and she 18. She was born October 1, 1854; in Bedford County, Tennessee, and died on March 18, 1928, and buried in the Trice section of Linwood Cemetery. His second wife was Jennie Smith. H.S. Trice died on August 12, 1941, and is buried next to his first wife in the Trice section of Linwood Cemetery. The children of Henry Samuel and Margaret Ann Trice were: Ada Paralee (Mrs. A.D. Gardner); William Francis, Joseph Thompson, Mary Elizabeth (Mrs. J.M. Lowe), Sarah Viola (Mrs. G.L. Adams) and Cecil, who passed away at 2 years old.

*H. S. Trice home corner of Court and 3 1/2 street.*

H.S. Trice moved to Paragould in 1885 from Craighead County and started an undertaking and furniture business. He was the first licensed embalmer in Northeast Arkansas. He was treasurer of Greene County for four years from 1886 to 1890. He was always a generous contributor to good causes in Paragould. He and his family were profound Methodists and he and M.H. Glasscock gave the lots to build the elegant brick second First Methodist Church, then located on Third and Emerson Streets. He used to laughingly say he had been a member of the Board of Stewards of the Methodist Church since he was 14 years old and was still listed as a member of the Board, Emeritus, of the First Methodist Church when he died at age 87 years. He was president of First National Bank for 12 years prior to his death. His sons Will and Joe were associated with him in business for many years. In Goodspeed's early *History of Greene County*, he was listed as a member of the Knights of Pythias.

Issue: 1. Ada Paralee Trice married Albert David Gardner; Issue: Cecil Gardner married Lucian Earl Taylor; Issue: Marilee Taylor married Lloyd Pruitt; Issue: Barry Lee Pruitt married Billie Sudduth; Barbara Elaine Pruitt married Dr. Ray Hall Jr.; Issue: Heather Eilene Hall married Eric Coleman, Holly Kathleen Hall, and Colin Andrew Hall. Ellie Trice Taylor, D.D.S.

2. William Francis Trice married first Carrie Hunter, second Gertie Helwig. Issue: Henry Harlan Trice married Lillian Green; William Hunter Trice married Lucille Goalby; Issue: William Hunter Trice Jr. married first Davene Candida Olivares, divorced; second Linda Jane Stapleton. Issue: Tiffany Lee Trice married first Thomas Gary David, second married Craig Bates; Issue: Christin Lori David, Kyle Matthew Bates, Nacie Marie Bates. William Hunter Trice, III.

David Lawrance Lee Trice married Nancy Jean Sigler, second Lonna Evey, third Nancy Nadua Issue: Jasmine Nadua Trice, Christopher Harlan Trice, Laurance Lee Trice married first Sharon Lee Hildreth, second Jeanette Kenman- Issue: Shannan Lee Trice, Laurance Lee Trice. Frances Elizabeth "Sis" Trice married William A. Johnson. Issue: Mary Frances Johnson married Edward Allen Partain at West Point Chapel, graduated West Point, who rose to rank of Lt. General in U.S. Army, the highest rank achieved by any military man from Greene County. Issue: Lisa Partain married first Steven F. Westfall. Issue: Christopher Partain Westfall, Katherine Elizabeth Westfall, Thomas S. Westfall, divorced; second Howard Sanger, divorced; third Charles Nelson Roberts. Issue: twins Jessica Pearl Roberts and Patrick Wyatt Roberts. John David Partain married Claire Elizabeth Hawes at St. Nicholas Church, Manea, Great Britain; Issue: David Hunter Partain. William A. Johnson Jr., married Carole Jeanne O'Daniel. Issue: Trice Hunter Johnson, William O'Daniel "Will" Johnson, Frances Mabry "Fran" Johnson married Billy Harold Thomas, Issue: William Clayton Thomas. Joseph Thompson Trice married first Anna Hayes, divorced; second Martha "Mattie" Whitsett, no issue.

4. Mary Elizabeth Trice married John Manning Lowe. Issue: Margaret Marie Lowe married Franklin E. Wilbourn. Issue: James Lowe Wilbourn married Mildred Taylor; Issue: Alan Taylor Wilbourn married Amy Marr; issue: Josephine Taylor Wilbourn, Peyton C. Wilbourn. James Daniel Wilbourn married Mary Beth Hays; Issue: Ryan Wilbourn and Allie Elizabeth Wilbourn; Elizabeth Merrick Wilbourn, born 1963. Sarah Manning Wilbourn married William McCandish; Issue: Margaret Marie McCandish married Kelly Rose; issue: Margaret Anne; Vernon Lowe McCandish married Pat Henrie; Ann Manning McCandish married Daryl Miller; Issue: triplets, Stephen Manning Miller, Courtney Ann Miller and Alexander John Miller.

5. Sarah Viola Trice married Guy LeRoy Adams; Issue: Elizabeth Jane Adams married Walter L. Beall; Issue: John Walter Beall married Marilyn Beal Patricia Martha "Tiffy" Beall married James Pollock; issue: Janet Lynette Pollock; married second William Barnett, divorced; Janet Lisabeth Beall, not married.

6. Cecil Trice, died at 2 years old of whooping cough.

The Trice family first lived in a large house on the corner of North Highland and 6th Streets, where the Dillman house is today. This house burned and in 1904 a beautiful brick home was built on the corner of Court and 3 1/2 Streets. This house was demolished to make room for the new court house, which occupied the entire block.

**TRITCH** – Ervin August Oswald (Feb 19, 1919 Lafe, AR) the son of Arthur and Emma Tritch. He was the grandson of Fred and Ann Tritch and August Peter Henry and Louise (Kappelman) Gerdes. The Tritch family moved to the upper Lafe area in 1886 from Kendallville, IN. Before that they came from Germany, as did the Gerdes and Kappelman families.

*Front: Opal, Gilbert, Arthur Tritch, Nadine, Emma (Gerdes) Tritch, Winston and Lucille. Back: Mabel, Marvin, Ruth, Ervin, Irene and Leo*

When Mr. Tritch was a teen, he left Greene County. He rode trains a lot and went to many places, such as California, St. Louis and Illinois. In Illinois, he married Lola Lowman on June 26, 1953, who was born in Platteville, CO. Ervin and Lola had seven children:
1. Loretta
2. Wilbert
3. Marlene
4. Diane
5. Donna
6. Ivan
7. James

In 1972 they moved to Paragould. Loretta stayed in Illinois until 1974, then moved to Paragould. She married Larry House and they have four children:
1. Hailey Bowser
2. Valerie Bowser
3. Anna Bowser
4. Thomas House

The House family had a new addition, Carson Bowser, on Nov 20, 1999, son of Hailey Bowser.

*Front: Donna, Ervin, James, Lola and Ivan. Back: Marlene, Wilbert, Loretta and Diane*

Wilbert lived in Jacksonville Beach, FL with his wife Pamela and sons, Brent and Kyle. In 1998 they moved to Bethel, OH. Marlene married Randy Waddel. They live in Paragould with two sons, Rance Vincent and David Waddel. They also have a grandson, Kyle Vincent. Diane married Jimmy Traywick and they have two daughters, Jasmine and Misty and they live in Paragould. Ivan married Melissa Allen. They live in Bono, AR and have five boys:
1. Matthew
2. James
3. Lucas
4. Tyler
5. Chance.

James Tritch lives in Paragould and has two sons, Steven and Tyler and a daughter, Linda Danielle. Lola Tritch now lives in Jonesboro, AR.

Mr. Tritch had a heart for his home in Lafe, AR. He was a member of St. John's Lutheran Church. He told many funny stories about his growing-up years, his mom and pop, his brothers and sisters and the wonderful people he knew. He had a hard life, like many others who lived in the early 1900s, but he will always be remembered as a kind and loving man, especially by his 22 grandchildren and the countless lives he touched. Ervin spent his last years in Greene Acres Nursing Home. The residents who lived there, along with the staff who cared for him, treasured him. He was a pleasant man to be with. He could make you laugh, even when he wasn't feeling good. He especially enjoyed making the nurses and staff laugh and he never complained. Mr. Tritch wasn't real important as some would be, as far as contributing to the building of communities or investing services or financing, but as a Christian man, he made a difference in many people's lives, as did his family before him.

*Ervin August Tritch 1995*

Ervin Tritch went to be with his Lord on March 7, 1999. He is buried at St. John's Cemetery. His sisters and brothers are:
1. Irene Lewis
2. Mabel Lueker
3. Ruth Lange
4. Opal Spellmeyer
5. Lucille Brasher
6. Nadine Green
7. Marvin
8. Leo Winston
9. Gilbert.

**TRITCH** – Frederick Tritch (Jan 4, 1862 OH) son of Frederick Tritsch (May 23, 1823 Frankish Crumach (Crooked Creek), Odenwald, Germany) and his mother was also born in Germany. The census records from 1870 show them both born in Darmstadt, Germany, as was a child, George (1852). An article about Royal Tritch in the Noble County, IN History book states that they were married in Germany and that they had 10 children, Fred being the fifth.

They came to New York between 1852 and 1857. Children:
1. George (about 1852)
2. Adam (April 7, 1857 OH) married Mary Shade
3. Maria (Dec 11, 1858 OH-Feb 11, 1866)
4. John (Oct 1859 OH) married Dora Wright
5. William (Nov 27, 1863 IN-March 31, 1934) married Sarah L. Mertz
6. Jacob (Dec 19, 1865 IN-Feb 7, 1866)

Information on the other children has not bee acquired yet. They lived in Allen County near Fort Wayne, where in 1863 their sixth child, William was born. In 1864 they moved to Salem Center-Hudson area in Steuben County. His parents lived there until their death, Frederich Tritsch in 1881 in Indiana, Margaret in 1888 in Ohio. Frederick is buried in the Zion Luther Church Cemetery, West Fairfield, Corunna, IN.

Frederick Tritch married Anna Marie Bechler from Wayne Township, in Noble County, IN on Oct 14, 1886. She was the older of two daughters of Jacob Bechler and Savannah Martz. They also had a daughter, Katie, who was married to Jacob C. Beck in Noble County on Dec 29th the previous year. Both couples found their way to the Upper Lafe area in Greene County, AR in 1886. They were among some of the first settlers to the area. It is likely that they heard of the land through advertising in the *Germania* by

Herman Toelken, who was instrumental in getting German Lutherans to come to the area.

The earliest baptismal records of St. John's and St. Peter's show both families recorded a child born in 1887.

*Front to back: Alvin, Nora, Hilda, Arthur, Fred, Anna, Charles, Oswald, Esther, and Cecilla.*

Fred Tritch was a hard working farmer. He and Anna had many children:
1. Ada (1887) is buried at the Toelken Cemetery in Upper Lafe. The marker only has "Tritch" etched in it and is still readable.
2. Cecilla (Nov 25, 1887) married Charles Bogner
3. Altha Mary Katherine (Feb 14, 1889). There is a copy of her baptismal record, showing Fred and Anna as her parents. According to Greene County cemetery records, she is buried at St. Johns with no marker.
4. Arthur George, the father of:
a. Ervin
b. Winston
c. Leo
d. Marvin
e. Gilbert
f. Irene
g. Mable
h. Ruth
i. Lucille
j. Opal
k. Nadine
5. Carl William "Charles" ((April 10, 1892) married Marie L. Scheer.
6. Oswald (April 21, 1896-March 21, 1972) married Martha Fricke in 1921.
7. A "stilborn" child buried at St. Peter's Cemetery (according to Greene County Library records).
8. Elmer Fred Louis (May 9, 1898) was the eighth child according to the church records. He is buried at St. Peter's Cemetery.
9. Alvin (Jan 6, 1902) was married to Sylvia Mifflin in 1923. She is still living in California.
10. Walter (1902) is buried at St. Peter's.
11. Hilda (July 6, 1903) married (1) Tom Wahl (2) Henry Kinon.
12. Martha Eleanor "Nora" (May 21, 1905) married Otto Fricke.

Fred Tritch passed away in 1910, after a long bout with tuberculosis. Anna continued to work hard, along with her children. She sold canned cream and shipped most of it by train to St. Louis. Many remembered her as an excellent quilter.

The Tritch family continues to grow and every year around the Fourth of July there is an annual family reunion held at the Marvin Tritch farm, with hundreds attending. The family continues to remember how God has blessed them, as well as remembering the ones who started the family in Greene County, AR.

*Submitted by Loretta House*

**TRITCH/LUEKER** – Marvin William Fredrick Tritch and Lydia Caroline Bertina Lueker were married on Nov 15, 1947 at St. John's Lutheran Church in Lafe, AR. They lived one mile south of Lafe for one year and then bought a farm of their own near Lafe.

Marvin was a farmer and in 1950 boll weevils hit the cotton and Marvin went to Flint, MI to work at General Motors Company. He worked three months and anxiously returned to farming. Besides farming, Marvin loved to build barns and other buildings on their place. He bought a sawmill and cut a lot of lumber for people to build houses and planned to build one of his own, but never did. In 1952 Marvin and Lydia won Farm Family of the Year.

In 1955 Lydia was severely burned on 65% of her body. She had 10 skin grafts and 54 pints of blood that year. She stayed in St. Bernard's Hospital in Jonesboro for one year. In 1956 Marvin broke his ankle and Lydia was in a wheelchair. Farming and the dairy were difficult, but in 1957 they got back on their feet once again. They purchased more land to farm and had a larger house. They were happy on the farm and enjoyed their work.

*Marvin Tritch family, 1969.*

Marvin and Lydia have four children:
1. Ronald Arthur Charles (Nov 1948 Lafe) married Donna Woolridge of Lafe. They live north of Lafe, between Hooker and Beech Grove. They have two children: Jason Dean (June 14, 1975) and Stacy Marvin (Aug 28, 1979) married Chrystal Candless from Pocahontas on June 30, 2000.
2. Orin Keith (June 14, 1950 Lafe) married Ann Bolick of Stonewall and they also live between Hooker and Beech Grove. They have two children: Kevin Douglas (Dec 17, 1974) and Gretta Suzanne (Nov 22, 1980).
3. Kerry Donnela (Aug 31, 1957 Paragould) married (1) DaRoy Baker Miles for two years (2) Kevin Reddick of Marmaduke. They likewise live between Hooker and Beech Grove. Their children: Tiffany Lene'e (Nov 26, 1981) and Aaron Michael (Oct 28, 1987).
4. Kim Marvin (March 17, 1966) also lives between Hooker and Beech Grove.

Ronnie joined the U. S. Air Force in 1969 during the Vietnam War and was in the Air Force for four years. Orin joined the National Guard for two years.

Marvin was devoted to his Lord. He went to his Heavenly Home on Nov 22, 1976 and is buried at St. John's Lutheran Church Cemetery in Lafe. His favorite Bible verse was "Seek ye first the kingdom of God and all these things shall be added to you." He was a witness of the Lord and stressed regular Bible study and church. Lydia's favorite Bible verse is "I can do all things through Christ who gives me strength."

*Submitted by Lydia Tritch*

**TURNBOW** – My name is Jane Ann (Hughes) Turnbow. I am a third great granddaughter of Benjamin H. Crowley.

My mother and father were Acton F. and Eula (Crowley) Hughes. My maternal grandparents were William T. and Cynthia (Gramling) Crowley. I was born on Court Street in my Grandma and Grandpa Crowley's home. I was raised at Walcott, attended Walcott School and graduated from Greene County Tech in 1952. I played basketball, was a member of the Tech trio and mixed chorus and was in the top four of my class. God gave me a musical talent. I have sung and played the piano since I was six years old. I am now pianist for Rosewood Baptist Church. I played the piano and sang with the "Golden Tones" for 20 years.

I married Carl Reeves on June 29, 1952. Our first son, Carl Randal Reeves (April 12, 1953) graduated from Tech in 1971. He joined the Army and was in the Special Forces called the "Rangers". He married Denita Hester and they have one daughter, Kari Kay Reeves. She starts college this year at A.S.U.

Randy is now working at Monroe and supervisor over the night crew. He is now married to Darlene Sapp.

Our second son, Robin Keith Reeves (Dec 26, 1955) graduated from Tech in 1973. He also played basketball. He joined the National Guard and has made a career of it. He is now a Lieutenant Colonel and is stationed at Ft. Chaffee in Ft. Smith.

Our daughter, Andre Gale Reeves (Oct 4, 1957) graduated from Tech, where she was a cheerleader. She married Tom Harrison and they have five children and one grandchild.
1. Ashleigh Morgan resides with her husband, Will and daughter, Alexis, in Muldrow, OK.
2. Seth Crowley Harrison 15 is a 10th grader at Southside in Ft. Smith.
3. Acton Wiley Harrison 14 is in the ninth grade
4. June Ellen Harrison 10
5. Cynthia Marie Harrison 7

*Seated: Grandpa Billy Crowley, Grandma Cynthia (Gramling) Crowley, baby Tom Crowley. Standing: Nannie (Crowley) Boozer, Ruth (Crowley) Cline.*

Our third son, Ronald Glen Reeves (June 4, 1961) graduated from Tech, played basketball, worked at Monroe, then the Lord called him to preach. His is married to Marianna Walden. They have two children: Kathryn Emmaleigh Reeves 15, attends Paragould School, plays basketball and is a straight "A" student. Carl Ronald Reeves 12 starts to Junior High at Paragould this year, plays baseball, football and basketball.

Carl and I divorced in 1970. I married Jarrett Don Turnbow in 1980. Our address is 417 Cindy Drive, Paragould 72450.

*Submitted by Jane Ann (Hughes) Turnbow*

**TYNER** – James McDonald Tyner, known as "Jim," was born to John Wiley and Lucinda Barnes Tyner on November 15, 1861, in Benton County, Tennessee, the seventh of 10 children. Jim's mother, Lucinda Barnes, was born on July 27, 1824, in Tennessee to Dennis and Amy

Barnes of Stewart County and McNairy County, Tennessee.

On November 7, 1861, just eight days before Jim's birth, his father, John Wiley Tyner, had enlisted in the Confederate Army in Benton County, Tennessee. He served in Conf T-49 Tennessee Pvt. Co. I, 49th Reg. John and Lucinda moved their family from Benton County, Tennessee, about 1870-1871.

The family was very poor and Jim got his first pair of shoes at the age of 9. He walked a railing fence and was so excited he ripped the soles off of them shortly after he got them. So he was barefoot again.

James McDonald Tyner, known as Jim, and Sarah Ann Cupp were married on May 14, 1882, in Lorado Township, Greene County, Arkansas, when she was about 14 years old. Sarah Ann Cupp had been born on October 15, 1867, in Greene County, Arkansas, to Henry and Margret Dennis Cupp. Margret Dennis was born November 4, 1845, in Arkansas to Robert John and Eleanor Thompson Dennis. Margret married Henry in 1866 and died on December 17, 1869, when Sarah Ann was just about 2 years old.

Jim and Sarah Ann Cupp Tyner raised their family near Walcott with all of their children being born there in Greene County. Three of their sons died in infancy: John Franklin born December 18, 1888, and died February 19, 1890; James William born March 6, 1894, and died March 26, 1894; and an infant who died on his birth day on February 5, 1899.

Their son Henry Virgil was born on February 2, 1885, in Walcott and married Carrie Hannah Robb on March 6, 1904, in Walcott. He graduated from Louisville University of Medicine and practiced in Lorado and Spring Grove; Clinton, Oklahoma; Carlsbad, New Mexico; and Paragould. He died in Paragould at the age of 33 years on January 14, 1918.

There were five girls born to Jim and Sarah Ann. Lucinda Adeline, their firstborn, was born on August 6, 1883, and died September 7, 1883. Four of the daughters grew to adulthood.

Nora Lee was born December 16, 1886; she married Jones Houston Lamb on July 3, 1904, in Walcott.

Maggie Mae was born September 27, 1891; she married Thomas Clayborn Potter on December 18, 1910.

Bessie Jane was born April 30, 1895; she married William Fletcher on July 23, 1918.

Viva Demetra was born January 29, 1904; she married first William Leonard Wilcoxson on July 31, 1923, and second John Marshall Nutt on August 10, 1941.

*James McDonald Tyner and wife Sarah Ann Cupp Tyner.*

When Sarah Ann Cupp Tyner's father, Henry Cupp, died in 1895, Jim got his start by paying $1,000 for Henry Cupp's livestock brand. Jim then herded the unbranded cattle and the pigs that had been roaming around and breeding for years in the "bottoms." Jim and his men caught all they could to brand but couldn't stay any longer. There was water down there that came way up over the horses' hooves.

Most of the writing in the Tyner family Bible was in the hand of James McDonald Tyner. The children never saw their mother's handwriting. Once Sarah Ann taught her husband Jim how to write, she stopped writing, saying she was tired of writing. Jim went on to be the president of two banks, one of them the Walcott bank.

An article from the Jonesboro, Arkansas, newspaper when James McDonald Tyner moved to Jonesboro. Mrs. Tyner was 80 years old then and they were celebrating their 65th wedding anniversary. "Mr. Tyner is a retired general merchant. He has extensive farm interests and is a member of the Fisher Street Baptist Church as is Mrs. Tyner."

Sarah Ann died March 20, 1952, in Jonesboro. Jim Tyner died August 16, 1955, in Jonesboro, Craighead County, Arkansas. They are buried together at Oaklawn Cemetery.

**TYNER** – John Wiley Tyner was born in Tennessee on April 2, 1827, the son of William H. Tyner Sr., of McNairy County, Tennessee, in the 1830 Census and of Tishomingo County, Mississippi. Lucinda Barnes was born on July 27, 1824, in Tennessee to Dennis and Amy Barnes of Stewart County, Tennessee, in the 1820 Census and McNairy County, Tennessee in the 1830 Census.

John Wiley Tyner and Lucinda Barnes were married on December 8, 1847, in Benton County, Tennessee. In the 1860 Census of Benton County, Tennessee, we find their children: Davis age 11, Ann age 8, William age 6, Henry age 4 and John W., age 1.

John Wiley Tyner enlisted in the Confederate Army in Benton County, Tennessee, on November 7, 1861, just eight days before the birth of his son Jim. He served in Conf T-49 Tennessee Pvt. Co. I, 49th Reg. John was taken prisoner at Ft. Donelson on February 16, 1862, and was a prisoner of war at Camp Douglas. On September 17, 1862, he was exchanged at Vicksburg. Some of the Tyners and Barnes in Benton County, Tennessee, served in the Confederacy and some in the Union Army and this created much trouble in the family and probably contributed to their moves.

Mary Jane was born February 27, 1864, Janeral Lafeyette on October 4, 1868, and Witt was born in Tennessee and was 3 months old when the 1870 Census was taken in Benton County, Tennessee.

John Wiley and Lucinda Tyner moved their family by ox cart from Benton County, Tennessee, to the northeast corner of Arkansas sometime during 1870. Family tradition had stated that the family moved to Arkansas when their son Jim was 7 years old. A newspaper article on Jim when he was 86 years old stated that he moved "with his parents in an ox wagon at the age of 7 through Cape Girardeau, Missouri." That would be about 1868-1869. It's possible they went then and returned to Benton County because some of the Barnes families made trips back and forth between Arkansas and Tennessee.

If so, he had to move again after the age of 9 following the 1870 Benton County, Tennessee Census. Two routes are recorded which makes it more likely that there were two moves: One story says they moved to "Cape Girardeau, Missouri, then to Pocahontas, Arkansas, and then to Fairview." Another family story says they "crossed the Mississippi River at Birch Point Landing. They stayed one year at Pemiscot Bayou (where Steele, Missouri, is today). They then went to Greene County, Arkansas."

Along their final move typhoid fever took probably Davis, Henry, Witt, Mary Jane and Angeline who may have been a wife of Davis rather than a child of John and Lucinda. The Greene County, Arkansas Census for 1880 lists the family of John and Lucinda with Anne, John W., James and Lafayette. Two of their children now grown, William C. "Doc" Tyner and John W. Tyner Jr., had moved to Farmersville, Texas.

The children of the John Wiley and Lucinda Barnes Tyner family as listed in their family Bible were:

(1) Annie was born April 15, 1851, in Benton County, Tennessee, married first a Mr. George and second a Mr. Howe.

(2) William Clark "Doc" born December 25, 1853, in Benton County, Tennessee and died June 14, 1904, in Farmersville, Collins, Texas. Doc married Nancy Jane Cox on September 27, 1877, in Clark Township, Greene, Arkansas.

(3) John Wiley Jr., born October 5, 1859, in Benton County, Tennessee, and died February 7, 1944, in Strawn, Palo Pinto, Texas. John married Sally King in 1901 in Farmersville, Collins, Texas

(4) James McDonald, known as "Jim," born November 15, 1861, in Camden, Benton, Tennessee, and died August 16, 1955, in Jonesboro, Craighead, Arkansas. Jim married Sarah Ann Cupp on May 14, 1882, in Lorado Township, Walcott, Greene Arkansas.

(5) Janeral Lafayette "Fate," born October 4, 1868, in McNairy County, Tennessee, and died May 1, 1935, in Walcott, Greene Arkansas. Fate married Louanne Hutchins on January 10, 1889, in Greene County, Arkansas.

**VARVIL** – Gerald Wayne Varvil was born November 25, 1965, in Paragould, Arkansas. His parents are Johnny Gerald Varvil and Marcella Mae (Thompson) Rogers. He graduated from Oak Grove High School, Paragould, Arkansas, in 1983. Gerald began working after graduation and is currently an employee of Quality Foods out of Little Rock, Arkansas.

Kimberley Kaye (Dortch) Varvil was born on June 18, 1963, in Houston, Texas. Her parents are Harold Roy Dortch and Mozelle (Lovelady) Dortch. She graduated from Greene County Tech High School, Paragould, Arkansas, in 1981. Kim is currently an employee of HDI CNC Machining, Inc. (formerly Harold Dortch, Inc.), a business her parents started in 1972. They have three sons: Joshua Lynn Noel, Zachary Daniel Noel, and Jonathan Cody Noel.

Gerald and Kim were married on March 10, 1995, and they spend most of their time attending their son's activities and Nascar Winston Cup Races (as often as possible). During the winter months, Gerald, Josh, Zach and Cody are up at Black River either duck hunting or getting ready to go duck hunting.

Joshua Lynn Noel was born in Portsmouth, Virginia, on December 1, 1983. He is currently a student at Paragould High School, where he is on the high school baseball team. His favorite pastime is duck hunting at Black River and going fishing with his grandfather (Harold Dortch) and two brothers.

Zachary Daniel Noel was born in Virginia Beach, Virginia, on November 12, 1985. He is currently a student at Paragoold Junior High School, where he is very active in all sports. He also enjoys duck hunting and fishing, if it doesn't conflict with his sporting events (football, basketball, baseball and track).

Jonathan Cody Noel was born in Dale City, Virginia, on September 30, 1988. He is currently a student at Oak Grove Middle School (Paragould School District), where he plays basketball. His favorite past time is duck hunting at Black River and going fishing with his grandfather (Harold Dortch) and two brothers.

**VARVIL** – Howard Varvil (June 3, 1915) son of Otto and Myrtle Rooker Varvil married Odean Griggry, daughter of John and Elsie Green

Griggry, in 1938. They, together with their children, Doris, Karon, Johnny and Mike ran a dairy farm just outside of Paragould from 1945 until his death in 1966. They milked 26 Jersey and Holstein cows and farmed their 120-acre homestead, growing silage, corn and putting up their own silage with the help of neighboring dairymen.

Mr. Varvil was one of the pioneers in a successful feeding program, called Corno Feeding Program, with Willis Maxwell, of the Maxwell Feed and Supply Company. This program was the first to offer a work-free feed mill on wheels that goes to the farm where it can process more than a ton of grain and then pipe the finished feed directly to the farmer's overhead storage bins or self-feeders-all within 10 or 12 minutes.

*Odean and Howard Varvil*

Mr. Varvil and his wife took pride in knowing their milk was delivered to the families and store in Paragould, later selling their milk to Foremost Dairies. Their milk production was running at about 200 pounds a day, twice a day.

The Varvils survived many tragedies, losing their barn in a fire, with injuries to him; also their house burned a few years later. Determined to hold everything together took work and courage, plus plenty of family fun in the nearby swimming hole and eating watermelon with their neighbors.

Mr. Varvil was active in Oak Grove School where he served on the school board for approximately six years in the early 1950s.

Mr. Varvil died in a car accident in 1966 and is buried at Memorial Gardens Cemetery. His wife now lives in Paragould where she worked 10 years at Emerson Electric. Their son, Johnny, also works at Emerson Electric Company. Their two daughters both live in Missouri. Mike, their youngest son, died in 1981 from a kidney disease and is buried in Memorial Gardens.

*Submitted by Doris Duff*

**VINES** – Judge Waldrum married Paul and Pansy Vines May 8, 1943 in Paragould, AR. They live near Stanford. They had three children: Rudy Mack, Teddy Joe and Jodene.

Rudy Mack married Carolyn Fitzgerald and they live in Oklahoma City, OK. Rudy has worked 30 years in the executive branch at the Mega-Center National Defense at Tinker Air Force Base in Oklahoma City.

Teddy Joe, middle child, farmed for 21 years with his parents. He left the farm to work in an industrial plant in Paragould. Teddy Joe married Vicky Watson and they had on daughter, Melissa. They divorced and he later married Debbie Carpenter. They had one daughter, Tiffany and later adopted a daughter, Ginger.

*Paul and Pansy Vines.*

Jodene, the youngest, is a hairdresser at Center Hill Hair Styling. She has worked in hair styling for 30 years. Jodene married Mike Ellis and they had one daughter, Paige Leigh, who is attending college.

Paul's parents were Tom Vines, son of Babe and Alice Holland Vines and Maudie Vines, daughter of Mr. and Mrs. Frank Holifield. Tom and Maudie had five boys and five girls:
1. Herman
2. Arel "Buddy"
3. Jackie
4. Doris "Bubby"
5. Donald
6. Rosie
7. Nellie Mae (deceased)
8. Margie (Vines) Robb lives in Paragould
9. Imogene (Vines) Brown lives in Pueblo, CO
10. Deloris (Vines) Smith lives in Beech Grove, AR.

*Paul, Pansy and children.*

Arel was killed in WWII in April 1945. He was in the Army Infantry Division in Mindinile Islands, where he was laid to rest. Jackie and Doris live in a nursing home in Paragould. Donald and Josie live in Little Rock most of the time and at Evening Star part time.

Pansy's parents were Otto and Myrtle Rooker Varvill and later a stepfather, Tom Smith. Otto and Myrtle had four sons and two daughters:
1. Howard
2. Ruben
3. Jewell
4. Gerald Varvill
5. Oletta (Varvill) Campbell
6. Orvetta Varvill

*Family Group.*

Myrtle and Tom Smith had two sons: Billy Joe and Bobby Lee Smith. Pansy had four stepbrothers, Ottis, T.A. and twins, Troy and Voy Smith. Paternal grandparents were Phillip Edward and Martha Varvill. Maternal grandparents were William and Clara Brand Rooker. Pansy's step grandmother was Millie Rooker.

**VINES** – William "Babe" Vines was born May 7, 1861. He was the son of Mary (Davis) Vines born 1844, in the state of Mississippi, and thought to be a Civil War widow. They were living in Little Rock at the time of the war.

Around 1865, Mary, along with her son Babe, her sister and brother-in-law, Mitchell and Elizabeth Grooms, two other sisters and their children left Little Rock and moved to Missouri for a while. In 1867 they left Missouri and came back to Arkansas. They moved to Center Hill.

Mary married a Mr. Haggard and had one daughter, Amanda. She was widowed again. Around 1870 she married Lock Rowland. They had two children: Josie Ann, 1872, and Frank, 1874.

Babe married Almeda "Alice" Holland, May 14, 1894. Alice was the daughter of William and Martha (Harris) Holland. She was born August 22, 1869, in Tennessee.

They lived in Center Hill where four of their children were born: Thomas, March 7, 1895; Joseph, October 24, 1896; Lula, March 7, 1898; Velora, May 6, 1899. Roy was born March 30, 1905, just south of Black Jack (which is now Evening Star) where Babe bought a 160 acre farm and lived most of the remainder of his life. He died February 7, 1935, and was laid to rest at Jones Ridge Cemetery next to his wife, Alice, who had died September 1, 1932.

Thomas married Maudie Hollifield and to that union were born 11 children, seven of whom are still living. Paul, born 1923; Margie, born 1926; Imogene, born 1927; Jackie, born 1928; Donald, born 1933; Deloris and Doris, born 1935.

Joe married Etta (Dutch) Potter. They had two daughters. Ola, born 1918, and Vertie, born 1923 (deceased).

Lula married Frank Devore. They had two children: Essie Mae, born 1919 and Hermon, born 1921. (deceased)

*William "Babe" and Alice Vines.*

Roy married Gertie Brooms. To that union two children were born: Floyd, 1924, (deceased) and Margie Mae, 1931.

Velora married John Ayers Clifton, son of James Harry Clifton, who was also an early settler of Greene County.

John and Velora Clifton Family
1. Vernon, born December 26, 1923, married L. V. Metheny (four children) A. Dawna, born August 26, 1945, married Rodney Whitehead (two children) I. Beth and John
B. Darrell, born May 6, 1948, married Janet Key (two children)
I. Jeff and Richard
C. Bonita, born November 19, 1949, married (1) Joe Cannon (two children) Danny and Dawn. (2) Mike Herrington. D. Clifford, born September 27, 1958, married (1) Ann (2) Lanta
2. Alma, born July 26, 1926, married Gerald Davis (three children)
A. Joan, born November 27, 1946, married Steve Scott (two children) Christopher and Karie
B. Wesley, November 30, 1948, married Marilyn Counts (one child) I. Ashley
C. Phillip, born March 11, 1953, married Diane Archer (two children)
I. Lorna and Demetra
3. Earl, born May 7, 1930, married Wanda Gramling (three children)

A. Marjorie, born June 16, 1948, married (1) Louis Orick (deceased) (three children)
1. Jonatha, Taunya and Clifton. (2) Jimmy Smith.
B. Lynn, April 5, 1950, married Archie Henson (three children) Shane, Shannon and Shayla
C. Keith, born May 7, 1958, married Becky Harris (two children) 1. Megan and John
4. Clara, born January 16, 1934, married Billy Lovelady.

**WAGNER** – In 1988 Mr. and Mrs. Clair C. Wagner came to Greene County, Arkansas, leaving the winter cold of North Iowa. Clair, 1913-1994, son of D.A. and Vera (Smith) Wagner, was born in Indiana and grew up in Michigan. D.A.'s grandfather was Barney Wagner (Waggoner), immigrant ancestor from Germany. After some study at Wheaton College, Illinois, and Moody Bible Institute, Illinois, Clair earned a Th.B. at Northern Baptist Theological Seminary, Illinois and was ordained to the ministry. He served American Baptist Convention churches several years in Illinois, Nebraska and Iowa. Having also electronics experience and training he acquired a service and sales store for radio and television in Fayette, Iowa, but also continued some interim and supply ministry.

Mildred Irene Van Syoc, born 1913, whom Clair married in 1939, was born in Iowa to Perl R. and Ada (Mason) Van Syoc. Immigrant ancestors included Cornelis Aertson Van Schaick, born circa 1610, Netherlands; Henry Sater, born 1690, England; and William Mason, I.A. of 1788. Mildred, sfter some study at Iowa Wesleyan College, earned an M.R.E. at Northern Baptist Theological Seminary.

The four children are: Wendell Barnard Wagner, Dike, Iowa; Mrs. Emmet (Lynne Darlene) Beetner, Glen Carbon, Illinois; Mrs. Robert (Ruth Irene) Cload Jr., Cincinnati, Ohio; and David Clair Wagner, Cedar Rapids, Iowa.

**WAGNER** – Evelyn Euritha Wagner is the great-great-great- granddaughter of the Rev. Isaac Brookfield and Nancy Campbell. My great-great-grandmother was their youngest daughter Cynthia Jane Brookfield who married Rev. Samuel Clark, a pioneer Methodist minister. Rev. Samuel Clark was from Ohio; he worked closely with Rev. Brookfield prior to Rev. Brookfield's death.

1999 – The g-g-g-g-great grandchildren of the Rev. Isaac Brookfield and Nancy Campbell; Evelyn Euritha Wagner's grandchildren. From left: John Sharkey, Jarod Sharkey, Chris Gray, Jeff Davies, Ryan Serrano (on Jeff's lap), Austin Serrano, Stormy Serrano holding Garrett Sharkey, Alex Gray; on the floor, Jennifer Sharkey holding Eric Serrano.

My great grandfather was Isaac Wilbur Clark who married Tabitha Jane Magers. My grandmother was Essie Aurelia Clark who married Joseph Lawrence Stephens. My parents were Wayne Wilson Snowden and Jennie Mae Stephens. My mother later remarried George Charles Stursa who later adopted me.

I married George Norman Sharkey June 24, 1955 in Long Beach, CA. We have four children:
1. Jack Douglas Sharkey married Patricia Grierson. They have two children: Jennifer M. Sharkey and John David Sharkey.
2. Jill C. Sharkey married (1) Richard W. Davies. They had one son Jeffrey R. Davies (2) Dennis Gray and they have two sons, Alex D. Gray and Christopher R. Gray.
3. Jay K. Sharkey married Robyn S. Radcliffe and they have two sons, Jarrod Robert Sharkey and Garrett Russell Sharkey.
4. Jan M. Sharkey married Thomas Serrano. Their children are Stormy Nicole, Austin James, Ryan Jacob and Eric Taylor Serrano.

Before George died he said his greatest joy had been his children.

Walter Carl Wagner and I were married on June 28, 1971. We all live in southern California.
*Submitted by Evelyn Euritha Wagner*

**WALKER** – Elbert Earl (Oct 16, 1889) son of Thomas Richard Walker and Virginia Clementine Norville married Hettie Ophelia Riddick (Jan. 2, 1895), child of Thomas W. Riddick and Minnie Alice McFarland, in 1911. Both the Walker and the Riddick families had come from North Carolina, settling first in Crockett County, TN and later in Paragould.

Eight children were born to Earl and Hettie:
1. Farris died in infancy
2. Maurice Richard
3. Virginia Earline
4. James Ernest
5. Martha Sue
6. Mary Ellen
7. Emily Eloise
8. Claire Ann

All of the children graduated from Paragould High School. The boys settled in Tacoma WA (where for a time they had been stationed during WWII) and the girls settled in nearby states. Mary and Claire, the only surviving family members, continue to live in Paragould.

Earl was a brick mason and helped construct many of the buildings in and around Paragould, including his home at the corner of 12th and Main Streets. A time sheet notes that he worked 45 hours at 10 cents an hour the week of March 5, 1904 (age 14 years, six months). The foreman for that week was paid 20 cents an hour, with other salaries ranging from five to 15 cents. Earl died in 1950 and Hettie in 1979.

**WALKER** – The Lee Roy Walker family arrived in Greene County in 1932 and established roots so deep that they never left. Lee was born February 7, 1892, in Indiana. He was the son of James M. (1859, Tennessee) and Sarah J. (1869, Indiana) Walker. Lee was the second of six children. He married Mary Magdeline "Maggie" Evett on February 9, 1918, in Manila, Arkansas. Maggie was the daughter of Samuel Evett (1854, Texas) and Mary Elizabeth "Molly" McClarin (1875, Texas) and was the youngest of six children.

In July 1918 Lee entered the Army, serving in World War I for about a year. He returned to the states in 1919 where he and Maggie lived and farmed first in Leachville and then in the Eight-Mile Community near Paragould. The first five of their six children were born in Leachville; the youngest in Eight-Mile Community: Roy Luther (1918), Henry Cleveland (1921), Della Mae (1923), Opal Geraldine (1925), Barbara Lee (1931) and Helen Pearline (1934).

Roy lives in Paragould. His wife, Clara Swink Walker, died in 1995. Henry married Lois Maxine Edrington in 1941 and they reside in the Halliday Community near Paragould. Della lives in Paragould, the widow of Douglas Wilson Smith. Geraldine "Gerry" died in 1997. She lived in Paragould and was the widow of Paul Boyd. Barbara "Bobbie" lives in Paragould with her husband of 50 years, Willis "W.T." Gibson. Pearline lives in Paragould with her husband of 47 years, Billy Ray Wood.

**WASHINGTON** – Thomas Jefferson Washington moved his family from Union County, KY in 1906. They had six children:
1. Dorris (1886)
2. Stella (1888)
3. Roy (1895) my grandfather
4. William Gobel (1899)
5. Robert (1902-1916) died as a boy is buried Pineknot Cemetery
6. Alton Parker (1904)

Thomas' wife was named Mary Elizabeth Melton.

Thomas was a farmer and carpenter, a talent which he passed on to at least two of his sons, Alton and Roy.

Roy was raised on a farm near the old Alexander School. He married Sussie Reddick in 1915. They had seven children:
1. Clifford
2. Morene
3. James
4. Lavern
5. Jessie Mae
6. Larue
7. LouTrichia

Roy died in 1949 and Sussie died in 1965. They are buried in Linwood Cemetery, Paragould.

Lavern "Babe" Washington (1921 now the Alexander Community) son of Roy and Sussie (Reddick) Washington along with three sisters and a brother were raised in the Alexander community on a farm.

With the outbreak of WWII, he and his brother, James was both drafted. His brother James was drafted first and was later wounded in the Philippines. Babe was drafted in Nov 1942.

*"Babe" Washington.*

He served in the Army Air Corp aboard a B17 Bomber as "The Tail Gunner" with numerous medals awarded for his service over France and Germany.

In Sept 1944 on a 30-day leave from England, he married Ethel L. Sampson of the Mounds community. She was the daughter of Claude and Grace Sampson.

Upon his discharge Babe farmed in the Coffman community from 1945 to 1957 when The Great Flood destroyed his crops. He worked at Emerson for two

*Lavern "Babe" Washington and Ethel Washington.*

years while continuing to farm, he then quit Emerson and resumed full time farming at Alexander.

He continued to farm until 1992 when a stroke forced him to retire and move to Paragould. He died in 1998 and is buried in the Reddick Cemetery. His wife, Ethel, one son, Billy V. Washington, two daughters Sandra Vangilder and Vicki Largent, all of Greene County, survived him. One son, Roy Gene Washington and one daughter, Kerry Lynn Washington who are also buried in the Reddick Cemetery, preceded him in death.

*Submitted by Bill Washington*

**WATSON** – John Thomas Watson (1857 Greenville, TN) married Lousetta Pentecost.

*Watson's General Store in Marmaduke, AR about 1887. John Thomas Watson is on the left.*

Mr. Watson was a Greene County farmer, who owned 400 acres. He also owned one of the few steam engine threshing machines, raising mostly wheat. The Watsons made their home one and one half miles east of Halliday. They had five sons and one daughter:
1. Tom
2. Gent
3. Henry
4. Luther
5. Earby
6. Fannie (Watson) Houston.

John Thomas died in 1918 and Lousetta died in 1927.

**WEATHERFORD** – Stephen F. Weatherford (Jan 5, 1832 Gibson County, TN-May 3, 1887 Greene County, AR) was the son of Willis and Martha Fuqua Weatherford. They lived and died in Crocket County, TN. Willis (1793 VA – Oct 25, 1846 Gibson County, TN) and Martha (April 17, 1801 VA-Nov 12, 1857 Gibson County, TN). After Willis served in the War of 1812 he moved to Tennessee in Williamson County, where he met Martha Fuqua and they were married Feb 16, 1827. By 1832 he and Martha had moved to Gibson County where Stephen F. was born. The Willis Weatherford farm was a neighbor to the Luke Sollis farm. Stephen married Luke's daughter, Harriet, Nov 22, 1852 in Gibson County, TN. Harriet (1833 NC-Nov 26, 1909 Greene County, AR) and Stephen are buried at Clark Chapel Cemetery in Greene County, AR. Willis and Martha were buried near Gadsden, TN at Center Cemetery.

In 1872 Stephen and Harriet moved to Greene County, AR with their children:
1. William R.
2. Martha A.
3. Marion F.
4. George
5. Mary L.
6. Thomas N.

In 1874 their last child Henry Alvie was born.

In 1880, I found Stephen F. Weatherford family on a small farm in Polland Township, Greene County near Clarks Chapel Cemetery.

Stephen's eldest son, William R. Weatherford (1855 TN), moved back to Tennessee in 1875 where he met and married Augusta A. McLaughlin, the daughter of William B. and Narcissus McLaughlin in 1877. They had four children:
1. Arvell B. (1881)
2. Walter S. (1883)
3. Amos L. (1893)
4. Ruth M. (1896)

William R. was my great grandfather; he died in 1900 and is buried at Salem Cemetery near Gadsden, TN next to his in-laws, the McLaughlin's, who died in 1904. Prior to William R.'s death he owned and operated a butcher shop in Gadsden. After his death, August and her family moved to Greene County in 1904 and lived there until her death on Feb 3, 1920. She is buried at Cochrum Cemetery near Red Onion, MO.

Walter S. Weatherford, my grandfather, married Annie E. Henson in 1911 in Greene County. Annie (Dec 1891-Jan 12, 1919) was the daughter of Thomas and Lula Mothershed Henson. Walter died Sept 4, 1941 and is buried with Annie at Lansing and Cox Cemetery near Shug, AR. Walter and Annie had three children: Arlie D. (April 14, 1912-July 7, 1983) my father, Irene G. (Sept 14, 1915-Feb 1, 1970) and Lorene M. (Jan 6, 1918-Sept 12, 1988).

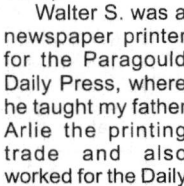

*Harriet Weatherford, 1833-1909.*

Walter S. was a newspaper printer for the Paragould Daily Press, where he taught my father Arlie the printing trade and also worked for the Daily Press. Arlie D. Weatherford married Ada E. Hendrix Dec 19, 1931 in Greene County, AR. Ada (Feb 28, 1916 Brookland, AR-Oct 19, 1990), the daughter of John and Lillie Hendrix, was living near Goobertown, AR at the time of her death and is buried at Woods Chapel Cemetery. Arlie and Ada had four children:
1. Harold D. (May 30, 1935-Sept 9, 1997)
2. Darold Gene (Feb 11, 1938)
3. Donald H. (Aug 25, 1939)
4. Marion E. (Dec 24, 1941-Jan 24, 1943)

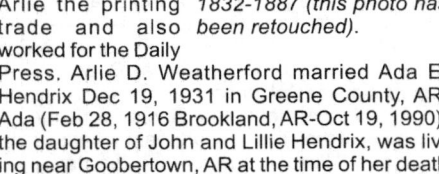

*Stephen F. Weatherford, 1832-1887 (this photo has been retouched).*

Other children of Arlie's with Betty L. Osborn are:
1. Terry Osborn, stepson, deceased
2. Eddie Osborn
3. Benny L.
4. Neal
5. Jeffrey
6. Linda L.

Betty passed away May 25, 1993. Arlie's sister Irene married Hershel Biggs Nov 22, 1930 and had three children: Bobby G., Shirley Fay and Betty. His younger sister Lorene M. married Virgel Dunlap Jan 8, 1934 and they had five children:

1. Helen
2. Ed J.
3. Nancy L.
4. Randy E.
5. Peggy.

Arlie had a half brother; Howard D. Weatherford (1921) married Allison Campbell in 1943. They moved to California.

Walter's brothers' and sisters' marriages:
1. Arvell married Rossie Wilson 1918 Craighead County, AR
2. Amos L. married Hattie Rawls 1919 Greene County, AR
3. Mattie Ruth married Luther Dodge 1920 Greene County, AR

Arvell and Rossie raised Rossie's son James "Buck" Weatherford. Amos and Hattie had one son, Junior Weatherford. Ruth and Luther Dodge had one son, Wilburn.

*Submitted by Gene Weatherford*

**WEBB** – Tilman A. Webb (1835 Hardeman County, TN) the son of James and Monnima (Crisp) Webb. The father followed farming on an extensive scale and was a soldier in the War of 1812, being with Andrew Jackson at the battle of New Orleans.

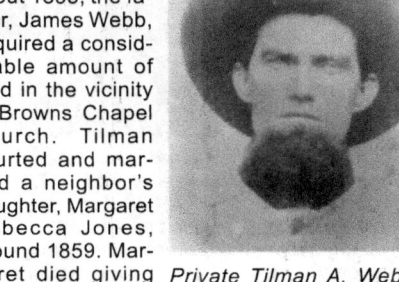

*Private Tilman A. Webb, Jones' First Arkansas Infantry Battalion, CSA.*

Coming to Greene County, AR about 1858, the father, James Webb, acquired a considerable amount of land in the vicinity of Browns Chapel Church. Tilman courted and married a neighbor's daughter, Margaret Rebecca Jones, around 1859. Margaret died giving birth to their only child, a daughter named Margaret J. on Sept 3, 1860. After the death of Margaret Rebecca, Tilman married Hester Lucy Newsom, the daughter of Sterling and Nancy H. Newsom.

Tilman entered the Confederate Army at Pocahontas, AR in March 1862 being assigned to Jones' First Arkansas Infantry Battalion. One month later, arriving in Memphis, TN, too late to participate in the battle at Shiloh, Tilman's unit was diverted to Fort Pillow, TN to bolster the 20,000-man garrison. On April 27, 1962, his unit received orders to proceed to Corinth, MS. There his unit fought in the battle of Farmington on May 9, 1862, during the siege of Corinth.

Known as "The Great Bugout" the Confederate Army evacuated Corinth the night of May 25, 1862. The southern army marched southward from the Tuscumbia River to Rienz and Boonville, then to Baldwyn, stopping finally, in the vicinity of Tupelo, MS. The southern army was strung out for miles along the Mobile and Ohio railroad. It was while the First Arkansas Battalion was camped at Verona, MS five miles south of Tupelo, Private Tilman A. Webb died. It is assumed he perished as a result of one of the many deadly diseases that plagued the southern army since there was no major fighting occurring between the armies during that period.

On Aug 12, 1862, the Confederate States government authorized payment of $5.00 to Dr. T. J. Montgomery, of Verona, to furnish a coffin for the remains of Private Tilman A. Webb. He lies today in an unknown and unmarked grave in or near that place.

On Nov 7, 1862, approximately eight months

after Tilman left Greene County, his widow gave birth to their only child, a daughter named Tilman Ann Webb, the author's grandmother.

*Submitted by Daniel A. Hester*

**WELCH** – William (Dock) Welch, was born in Randolph County, Arkansas, in 1833. When asked when he moved to Greene County, he replied, "I did not move, we just came." He and his wife, Margaret, arrived spending their first night sleeping underneath a black walnut tree.

He was believed by his family to have been one-fourth or one-half Cherokee Indian. During this period the northern part of the Arkansas River Valley was inhabited by Cherokee Indian tribes. They had moved west before more tribes were forced to move into Oklahoma in the operation called the "Trail of Tears".

Dock, as he was called, was a Confederate soldier in the Davis Battalion of Kitchen's Regiment stationed at Marmaduke, Arkansas, during most of the Civil War.

He and Margaret Brashears, who was born in 1841 of Irish descent, were married in 1860 in Poinsett County, Arkansas. Soon afterward they came to Greene County, Arkansas, carrying their possessions to a place about two and one-half miles northwest of where Stanford is located.

They resided in an old log cabin already on the property. Margaret said that her kitchen equipment consisted of: an iron pot, a hunting knife, forks, and plates whittled out of wood by her husband. She had been given a small feather bed and a few bed clothes by her mother.

*Seated: Dock Welch and Margaret Welch. The two older ladies are Mr. Welch's half sisters Sarah Gunnels and Becky Ann Palmer; their maiden surname was Lewellen. The young lady is Viola Palmer Stringer. Ca. 1905.*

The couple had walked to their new home, where they later built a two-story log house. Finally, it was torn down and replaced with a rent house built with sawed lumber in 1920.

*1912 – The Welch School Building on the farm. Later the location was moved and a larger building was built.*

William (Dock) Welch was listed in the 1967 issue of the Greene County Historical Quarterly. After serving in the Civil War, he returned to his wife and family becoming a successful farmer and stockman. They reared a family of six children. Their names were Victoria Johnston, Della Gray Jane Amorine, John Welch, Alice Nugent Lenderman and Charley Welch. They were all married and had children who were born and reared in Greene County.

**WELLS** – The exact date in which Abel S. Wells and his family entered Greene County from Massac County, IL is not known. The earliest records known to date are two Cash Entry Land Patents, dated July 1, 1859 for 40 and 160 acres and the 1860 Federal Census for Chalk Bluff Post Office, Bradshaw Township, Greene County, AR, enumerated on Sept 28, 1860.

Abel (about 1816 KY) married Sarah "Sally" Dunning (about 1824 KY) in Caldwell County, KY on Sept 22, 1840. To this union were born:
1. James
2. Henry
3. John
4. Maranda
5. Samuel
6. William
7. George
8. Abel S.

James died at Camp Butler, IL while serving in the Civil War and his remains are buried in the Armstrong Cemetery near Metropolis, Massac County, IL.

All of Abel and Sally's children were born in Illinois with the exception of their last child, Abel S., who was born in Arkansas and is listed as six months old in the above named 1860 Federal Census.

Sally's date or place of death is not known. But by Aug 29, 1869, Abel has returned to Illinois in Pope County and married Mary Jane Nutty. Abel owns several hundred acres in both Massac and Pope Counties and farms there until his death May 6, 1889. Able is believed to have been buried in Harris Cemetery at Bay City, Pope County, IL. The 1880 Federal Census for Benton Precinct, Massac County, IL lists the place of birth for both Abel's father and mother as Tennessee. The 1812-1814 tax lists for Caldwell County, KY records a John Wells and Samuel Wells, one possibly being the father of Abel Stobuck. However, family historian, Marlin G. Wells has been unable to verify this lineage.

At the time of Abel's death, his son, John was living in Nesbit, Dunklin County, MO, his son, Samuel was living in Myrtle, Oregon County, MO and his only daughter, Maranda Dunning was living in Baxter Springs, Cherokee County, KS. His sons, James and Henry and his second wife, Mary Jane had preceded him in death and his other sons, William, George and Abel were living in Pope County, IL as recorded in the Probate Court Records located at Pope County Courthouse in Golconda.

Abel's sons, John and Samuel continued to live most of their lives in northeast Arkansas and southeast Missouri and married the daughters of M. Henry and Isabela R. (Bray) Williams. John married Leanna Margaret and Samuel married Mary. After Mary's death, Samuel married another daughter of Henry and Isabela's, Magnolia "Maggie".

*Submitted by Marlin G. Wells*

**WELLS** – Chesley Harrison Wells (1885-1972) and Victoria Lee (Thomason) Wells (1888-1974) lived in Greene County, AR from the time of their marriage, Nov 3, 1907 until their deaths in the early 1970s except for a one-year unsuccessful farming experience in Hornersville, Mo. When they moved back, they never left Greene County again.

Conflicting records show that Chesley H. Wells was born either in Dade County, MO or in Lincoln County, KS, Nov 1, 1885. The family had lived in both places, but they moved in 1904 from Kansas to Crowley's Ridge, where they bought a farm about five miles west of Paragould, AR. (Previous owners of this farm were the sister of Chesley's father, Mary L. "Aunt Mollie" and her husband, Uncle Doc Graham. Uncle Doc was a country doctor practicing out of Paragould.) In 1911, when the family moved back to Kansas, Chesley stayed in Arkansas. He had already met and married Victoria Lee Thomason, with whom he raised 11 children:
1. Leland
2. Eunice
3. Bernice
4. Mary Lois
5. Hazel
6. Inez
7. Lucille
8. Edward
9. Harold
10. Martha Jane
11. Eugene.
12. Kenneth, born after Inez and before Lucille, died in early childhood of an undetermined cause, thought probably a spider bite. All 11 children lived to be adults, married, with children of their own, except Hazel, who remained childless. Lucille, Edward and Martha Jane still survive at this writing.

*Chesley Harrison and Victoria Lee (Thomason) Wells.*

The Wells family were farmers, raising most of their own food. Chesley was also a long time schoolteacher. He had had a leg injury that left him with a serious limp through most of his adult life. While the family farmed, he gave all the help he could, but he was rarely home except weekends. His entire teaching experience took place in the historical one and/or two room schoolhouse. When his school was near enough, he commuted by horseback. When his school was too far from home, he stayed in the home of a school patron during the week. This practice was called "boarding" as he had to pay for bed and meals. It was never made clear if he had to pay also for "boarding" his horse, but he probably did.

Some of the schools where C. H. Wells taught are Pine Knot located near today's Pine Knot Cemetery; Palestine, this building, though converted into a dwelling house, still stands at the intersection of Greene County roads 626 and 628; Corner, located a short distance west and north of today's Mountain Home Cemetery and Church of Christ building; and Eight Mile, east of Paragould near Coffman community.

Among some of his many students were:
1. Norman Cole
2. Earline (Weaver) Napier
3. Weldon and Leland Hyde
4. Chester, Macon, Victor, Joe and Alfred Rowe
5. Wilborn and Dean Farley
6. Noel Jetton
7. Doyle Hyde
8. Bud Stevenson
9. Maurice Barr
10. Leon Weaver

11. "Doc" Medsker
12. Earl Fitzgerald.

No records were found in either teacher retirement or Social Security showing when Chesley became eligible to receive either kind of financial assistance. However, he was receiving a small sum (maybe $50 or so per month) when he died Jan 16, 1972. Lee Wells, his wife of just over 64 years, followed him in death two years later.

*Submitted by Thelma P. Wells*

**WELLS** – Eugene S. Wells (1928-1999) was the youngest of 12 children born to Chesley Harrison and Victoria Lee (Thomason) Wells. Except for one year, he lived his entire life within a few miles of his birthplace in the Owen's Chapel-Union Grove community west of Paragould.

His early school years were spent in several one-room schools. He walked to school in the sweltering heat of mid-summer or the ice and ankle-deep snows of winter. Classrooms had no air conditioning and heating was by a wood or coal-burning stove, where those nearest the stove baked; those farthest away shivered. Country schools operated on a "split-term" system, so called because they dismissed part of the year during spring planting, cultivating season, reopened during mid-summer and dismissed again for several weeks during harvest season before resuming in late fall. In 1941, widespread consolidation landed Gene in the newly constructed Stanford High School, in fifth grade, where grades one through 12 were taught under one roof. But the "split-term" and the old-time heating and cooling system remained unchanged for years. With consolidation, distance made busing necessary. For a while, riding a school bus or a pick up truck rigged as a school bus with seats and a protective top was a novelty. Even with a split season, Gene, like several others, had to miss some additional school days to help work on the family farm. He graduated from Stanford with a class of 21 students in 1948.

By that time, small farms were already having difficulty surviving. But Gene was a farmer at heart and did not give it up easily. In the early 1950s he worked at almost any available job that would allow him to continue farming and maybe sometimes have a little spending money.

*Eugene S. Wells and Thelma P. (Burgess) Wells*

After Christmas 1951, Gene went home with his brother and family who were "back home" from California for a visit. Farming was "big" in California. Gene enjoyed the farm work and made money at it; a two-week visit ran into two months. He returned to Arkansas with more that $100 in his pocket and still had money left when he married his high school sweetheart, Thelma Pauline Burgess, in March. He had been working part-time for the Raymond Cox Sawmill and Lumber Company even during high school days. As a family man, he made it a full time job. When the "wage and hour" law first started, Gene's family became rich almost overnight. His wages jumped to about $.75 an hour, and his wife's salary jumped from $15 to $30 a week.

In the logging business, there was no overtime and his days sometimes ended about 7:00 to 9:00 p. m. whenever they got back from the logging woods. There was no insurance, even when one logger put a deep gash in his thigh with a chain saw. Gene's job was using a tractor to drag, stack and load logs to be hauled to the sawmill. Occasionally, he jumped from a tractor that was turning over, or dodged a tree that was being felled when the noise of his tractor drowned out the warning call. He left the logging woods forever, in 1972, when he was hired by Monroe Auto Equipment Company, working nights in maintenance. He had already given up farming when he had to pay more to get the crop ready for harvest than it brought in and after finishing her workday in town his wife had to work alone in fields almost one fourth mile from the house to finish the harvest.

In 1973, Gene and his widowed sister, Hazel (Wells) Jackson started another farming venture. She provided the down payment and Gene got financing from Federal Land Bank to buy the 133-acre farm of the Artemis Fitzgerald estate, co-owned by Walter, Carlton, Donald, Beatrice and Earl Fitzgerald. When Hazel decided to remarry, she gave Gene her interest in the farm. He had repaid more than half of this before she died. One farmer could not afford all the equipment necessary for farming, so Gene and his farm neighbors solved this problem by forming their own voluntary labor co-op. They went from one farm to another, putting in and harvesting their crops. Ill health forced Harold and Walter to limit and finally quit their labor contribution. Then, in 1983, Gene sold his farm to another neighbor, Charles Rowe, who still owns the farm at this writing.

Gene was still at Monroe, but had switched to days, still exercising his love for farming by helping neighbors. Ill health forced him to retire from Monroe in early 1993, but he still helped neighbors farm when he could. Eventually, deteriorating health made him unable to do any farm work other than gardening. In 1997 he made his last garden in spite of suffering in the final stages of emphysema. The following March, a "big heart" finally could take no more. Eugene died on March 9, 1998, of congestive heart failure.

*Submitted by Thelma P. Wells*

**WELLS** – John Wells came to Greene County as a teenager with his father, Abel Stobuck Wells, from Massac County, IL. Abel had purchased two Cash Entry Land Patents, dated July 1, 1859 and his family was enumerated on Sept 28,1860 in the Federal Census for Chalk Bluff Post Office, Bradshaw Township, Greene County, AR listing John as 15 year of age.

John, son of Abel Stobuck and Sarah "Sally" (Dunning) Wells was born in the state of Illinois, probably in Massac County, August 1845. He married Leanna Margaret Williams (March 1855 IL), daughter of M. Henry and Isabela R. (Bray) Williams in 1869. The exact date and place of John and Margaret's marriage is not known, but is believed to be Dunklin County, Missouri, since both John and Margaret are listed with Margaret's parents on the 1870 Federal Census for West Prairie Post Office, Union Township, Dunklin County, Missouri, enumerated of August 17, 1870.

John and Margaret had the following children:
1. Mary M.
2. Flora
3. Alice
4. Henry
5. Sam
6. Randolph
7. Maranda
8. George
9. Francis

George was a veteran of WWI and went by the nickname of "Little George". He is buried at Cardwell Cemetery in an unmarked grave.

The date and place of John and Margaret's death is not known. We do know that they are listed with their family on the 1900 Federal Census for Washington Township, Ripley County, Missouri, enumerated on June 15, 1900. Per this census, they had been married 31 years and had 11 children of which nine were still living.

John's family and his brother Sam's family were very close, due in part to their marrying sisters. Their descendants have remained close through the years; recently, holding a Wells reunion in Paragould in 1997. John lived most of his life in northeast Arkansas and southeast Missouri.

*Submitted by Marlin Glenn Wells*

**WELLS** – Sam Wells (April 18, 1881 Massac County, IL), son of John and Leanna Margaret (Williams) Wells, spent some of his early boyhood days in southern Illinois in Massac and Pope Counties areas where his father was raised and where his grandfather, Abel Stobuck Wells died, May 6, 1889.

*Sam and Maggie Lee (Fuqua) Wells, 1914.*

Sam spent most of his adult life in northeast Arkansas and southeast Missouri and made his living working in timber and farming.

Sam married Ida Elizabeth Broughton, twin daughter of Dr. William Samuel Hayes and Octavia (Quesenberry) Broughton, May 10, 1902. At the time of their marriage, both were residing in Paulding, MO near Leachville, AR.

Sam and Ida had the following children:
1. Sada "Sudie"
2. Pansy Iona
3. Opal
4. Evelyn "Evie"

Ida died July 25, 1912 soon after the birth of her fourth child Evie, and is buried at Cude Cemetery near Senath, MO. Sudie and Evie died in childhood.

*Sam and Maggie Lee (Fuqua) Wells, ca. 1952.*

Following his first wife's death, Sam married Maggie Lee Fuqua, March 19, 1914. Both were residents of Boynton, AR, near Leachville.

*Sam Wells' family – May 3, 1952. Sitting, L-R: Dorothy, Margaret, Alfred, Maggie, Alvin, Mary Jo, and Opal. Standing: Bob, Bernal, Henry, Gary, Calvin "J. C.", Marvin, Orville, and Pansy.*

Maggie (Dec 13, 1894 Buckville/Cedar Glades, Montgomery County, AR) was the only child of David G. and Mary Jane (Boone) Fuqua. To this union were born:

1. Orville David
2. Marvin Samuel
3. Bernal Paul Herman Billy
4. Dorothy Louise
5. Margaret Shirley
6. John Henry
7. Jewel Calvin "J.C."
8. Bobby Joe
9. Mary Jo
10. Gary Eugene
11. Alvin Donald
12. Alfred Earl.

Sam died at his home near Paragould, April 28, 1952 at the age of 71 years and 10 days. Maggie died Dec 26, 1979 at the age of 85 years and 13 days. Both Sam and Maggie are buried at Cardwell cemetery, Cardwell, MO.

Several descendants of Sam continue to reside in Greene County, AR.

*Submitted by Marlin G. Wells*

**WHITE** – One of the oldest established families in this area was that of Mr. and Mrs. Andrew Jackson White. He and his wife, Marcella Thedford White, first came to this area in a covered wagon from Gibson County, TN in 1871. However, they went back to Tennessee for a short while in 1874. When they returned they settled in the Providence Community and members of the family have remained in the area ever since that time. Six children were born to Mr. and Mrs. White:

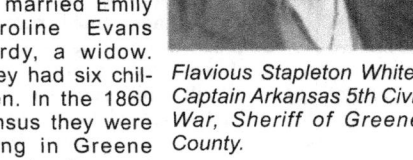

*R.E. Lee White, Effie Lee Potts White and Ollie White.*

1. Stonewall "Stoney"
2. Clinton
3. Monroe
4. Robert E. Lee
5. Lizzie
6. Alice.

Robert E. Lee White grew up on the farm and later owned 120 acres of farmland. He spent much of his time in timberwork and was also a Baptist preacher. He first married Alice Shewmaker who died while giving birth to twins. His second marriage was to Effie Lee Potts and to them were born 12 children:

1. Ollie died at 14 months
2. Arlie married Clarence Cooper
3. Leland married Pearl Graves
4. Lora married Elvis Wright
5. Charley married Ada Arnold
6. Earl died at age of three weeks
7. Edna married Shelly Cooper
8. Alvin married Bobbie Wyatt
9. Lloyd married Alma Stephens
10. Alfred married (1) Elbertine Penney (2) Winnifred Mandrell Johnson
11. Leoma married (1) Leonard Wright (2) John T. Vangilder
12. Geneva married Ralph Wood
13. Elbridge married Audie Lee Richardson
14. Eltee married Anna Bee Richardson

One other son, also names Alvin, was born early in the marriage and also died as an infant.

**WHITE** – Flavious Stapleton White was born February 8, 1824, in Tazewell, Claybom County, Tennessee. His father was James White. The family has no record of a middle name or initial for James, He was a Bostonian by birth. There is no record of the date he arrived in Tazewell, Clayborn County, Tennessee, though he died in the summer of 1842, is buried in what is known as Zacheriah McCubbin's graveyard near Tazewell. Margaret Halton White was F. S. White's mother. Margaret died February 1, 1872, at Greene County, Arkansas, age 71. James and Margaret had nine children, six sons and three daughters. Flavious Stapleton was the eldest child.

There is a Bible record of F. S. White's three wives and 19 children - births, deaths and marriages.

August 3, 1843, Flavious married Emily Jane Warnicutt. They had one child, Amanda Louise, born August 3, 1850, in Tazewell. Emily J. died March 10, 1851.

June 22, 1851, he married Emily Caroline Evans Hardy, a widow. They had six children. In the 1860 census they were living in Greene County, Concord Township, Arkansas. Flavious is shown as Sheriff. Emily C. died July 10, 1865, the same date the sixth child was born.

*Flavious Stapleton White, Captain Arkansas 5th Civil War, Sheriff of Greene County.*

August 10, 1865, Flavious married Sarah Frances Middleton. She was the daughter of B. F. and Jane Middleton, born in North Carolina and Virginia in 1801 and 1806 respectively. In 1850 B. F. and Jane Middleton lived in Gibson County, Tennessee. To this third marriage was born 12 children. The youngest, my grandfather, Charles Hugh White, August 5, 1880. The 1870 census shows the couple living in Gainesville, Arkansas. His occupation is a lawyer, she as housekeeper. 1880 Greene County census has Flavious and Sarah Francis living in Union Township. He is sheriff and she a housekeeper. Ages 56 and 42.

F. S. White is listed in Goodspeed's History as Sheriff of Greene County for three terms between 1858 and 1880. According to other histories it appears that during that period there were two occasions when he served though not elected, completing a term for one Sheriff who died in office. The second was an appointment to the office by Unionist Governor Isaac Murphy, after returning from the war. Following this appointment he was elected in 1866 and 1878 to the same post.

*Sarah Middleton White, wife of Flavious Stapleton White.*

One of his responsibilities as Sheriff was accepting the funds paid in taxes and delivering them to the Auditors in Little Rock. One receipt, of which I have a copy, shows he accepted the funds on June 20, 1867, and the Auditor's office signed as funds received July 19, 1867. The trip was made on horseback and required great caution I am sure in carrying a total of $6,384.23, possibly in cash.

It is indicated in the History of The Methodist Church in Arkansas that F. S. White was on the Board of Trustees in 1857 and that he was recorder for that particular quarterly conference. The book of original minutes from quarterly conferences 1839 to 1884 remain in the possession of the Rev. J. W. Williamson Watson family.

F. S. White organized the second company raised in Greene County at the beginning of the Civil War. It was designated Company E, 5th Arkansas Infantry Regiment. He was elected Captain of the Company and served with distinction at Perryville. November 13, 1862, he was listed as absent without leave; however, was appointed again as Captain by Confederate President Jefferson Davis on June 5, 1863. Captain White continued to fight with the Arkansas 5th through Chickamauga, Missionary Ridge, Ringgold Gap, and the Atlanta Campaign He was wounded near Atlanta July 22, 1864, and was hospitalized in Barnsville, Georgia. He received his discharge, or parole, at Jacksonport, Arkansas June 5, 1865.

F. S. White died March 5, 1896, at age 72 years, and is buried at Gainesville Cemetery. The funeral was under the direction of the Gainesville Lodge Ancient Free Accepted Masons. The Rev. P. B. Wallace conducted the religious portion of the service, according to F. S. White's Methodist beliefs.

Sarah Middleton White died March 18, 1928, at Charles Hugh White's home, 806 West Park Street, Paragould. She is buried in Linwood Cemetery, Paragould, Arkansas. Many of F. S. White's descendants remain in the Paragould area, as well as other parts of Arkansas and throughout the country.

**WHITTEN** – The Whitten family migrated from Germany to England in the ninth century. In the early 17th century, they came to this country, settling first in Virginia and the Carolinas and later in Wayne County, Tennessee. From Wayne County, members of the family moved to Arkansas and other Western States.

In the Whittens Chapel Cemetery, there are five generations of the family buried in Wayne County.

Eli Keasley Whitten was born May 19, 1879. He married Johnnie Essie Boyd, who was born on March 9, 1886, on June 5, 1905. Their children are Jessie Lee, Mary Beatrice, Roy Vernon, Elsie Evelyn, Buford Randolph, Sarah Mable, and Betty Joyce.

*Sarah Lady Whitten.*

The family moved to Craighead County, Arkansas in 1918, settling first in Bay and then in Jonesboro. Roy attended public school in Bay and Jonesboro. He left Jonesboro and attended college at the University of California in Berkeley. He served in the United States Navy during World War II. He spent his working years in public education in California. He married Sarah Lady in San Francisco. Sarah was born in Kuttawa, Kentucky and moved with her family to Paragould in 1907. She was the daughter of H. E. and Alice Campbell Lady. She had one brother, John Campbell, and one sister, Billie.

John Campbell had two daughters and a son. Daughter Sarah married Dale Franks and they reside in Paragould, Arkansas.

Upon retirement in 1974, Roy and Sarah moved to Paragould.

Roy moved his membership into First Baptist Church, the Masonic Lodge, the Scottish Rite, the American Legion, and the Lions Club. He continued his interest and involvement in community betterment efforts. He continues to serve on a number of local organization boards.

Sarah died May 12, 1989 and is buried in Oaklawn Cemetery in Jonesboro.

**WILLCOCKSON** – Isaac W. Willcockson (1838) married Eliza Payne (1843); their children:
1. William H. "Uncle Billie" Willcockson (1864)
2. Louis Willcockson (1867)
3. John Toliver "Uncle Tol" Willcockson (Jan 12, 1869-Feb 17, 1958)
4. Lura Willcockson
5. Paralee Willcockson
6. Julie Willcockson went to California.

William H. Willcockson married Kate Bowlin; their children:
1. Maude married Jim Cleaveland – six children
2. Ruth married Doc Barron – seven children
3. Edna married Curt Atcheson – one child
4. Mary Jane married Elgin McDaniel - 13 children
5. Grace married Ezra Coburn – seven children
   a. Winford married Thelma Cobbs- two children
      I. Carolyn married Bob Childress – one son, Bil and a daughter, Sumer.
      II. Winford Jr. married Carla Woodsmall
   b. Marsella
   c. Playfair married Frank Marret
   d. Joyce married Gerald Pitts
   e. Graham married Juanice Smith
   f. Marion Dean married Billy Tracer
   g. Patsy died in infancy.
6. Stirl married "Dave" Milender – six children:
   a. Horace married Hazel Jones
   b. Reba married George Huffman
   c. Harold married Jane Talbert
   d. Mimah married Charles Whitney
   e. Rex
   f. Lavetta married Johnny Townsley
7. Lucille married Ed Metts – one child, Eddie married Paul Whistle
8. Madge married Jack Crane – one child, Norma Lee
9. Effie married Marlie Emerson – one child, Ann Carolyn
10. Holland married Snowden Faulkner
11. Hayes married Clobell Bush - one child, Brenda
12. Delbert died young.

John Toliver "Uncle Tol" Willcockson (Jan 12, 1869-Feb 17, 1958) married Martha Webster (Nov 27, 1873- July 21, 1947). They spent their entire married life in Greene County and Paragould, AR. Family: Gertrude married Al Gilbert and spent most of their married life in Memphis where they raised one daughter, Faustina who married Walter Edwards and had two sons: Walter Lee and Gil. Faustina late married George Moore. She lives in Memphis.

Isaac Thomas, "Ike" (Dec 29, 1895-Nov 12, 1971) married Almeria Neely on April 19, 1931. Almeria (Sept 5, 1903-May 26, 1990) was the daughter of Hardy and Emma Hugh Neely. They spent their lives in Paragould and Greene County.

"Ike" taught school in his early years in a "one room" school, Pruett's Chapel School, and was in the army in WWI. He served as tax collector in 1926-30. In the 1940s he had the Red Onion Gin and was in the cotton business for a number of years. He served the City of Paragould as mayor in 1949 thru 1951, after which he became associated with the Mid-South Gas Co, (later, Ark-La Gas). He retired from there.

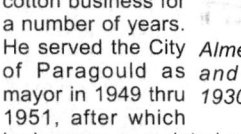
*Almeria Neely Willcockson and Ike Willcockson, 1930s.*

*Ike Willcockson and US Senator J. William Fulbright.*

Almeria and "Ike" had three daughters: Martha Jeanne (March 28, 1932) is retired from Emerson Electric Co. and lives in Paragould. Emma Jann Willcockson (Feb 19, 1938) also lives in Paragould. June Ann (Willcockson) Flye (June 19, 1948) lives and works in Little Rock for the State of Arkansas, Adoptions Section.

Ida (June 1, 1898-Feb 26, 1987) married Wally Ruehle and spent most of their life in Miami, FL, no children.

Doris Etta (Feb 1, 1901-Feb 8, 1995) married Grady Norvell. Moved to California in 1955 where Doris worked at Edwards Air Force Base and Grady at a pharmacy in Palmdale. Grady died in California and Doris returned to Paragould in 1980, no children.

Hallie (June 28, 1905-March 20, 1962) married Sol Steinberg, no children.

Mildred (Nov 28, 1907-March 12, 1990) married Harold Waggoner, no children.

Alfreda (Aug 9, 1910-May 1, 1995) married Cecil Snow and spent most of their life together in Memphis. They had two children: Jane (Snow) Wisenfels had two daughters and John Snow had two sons and one daughter.

Lambert married Amy and lived in Little Rock where he died in the early 1990s.

*Submitted by Jeanne Willcockson*

**WILLCOCKSON** – Thomas Riley Willcockson, (T.R.), whose ancestry goes back to England, and is a descendent of John and Sarah (Boone-sister of pioneer Daniel Boone) Willcockson, was born in Giles County, Tennessee, August 10, 1848. He was the eighth child born to Samuel and Frances W. (Gibson) Willcockson, who arrived in Greene County, Arkansas, from Tennessee about 1851. Samuel and Frances resided in the county almost 20 years before moving to Newton County, Arkansas, about 1870. T.R. stayed in Greene County.

He enlisted and served in the Confederacy as a Private in Co. D, Davies' Battalion, Arkansas Cavalry. In 1868, on December 16 in Greene County, he married Mary Jane Bowlin, daughter of John and Lucinda (Hogan) Bowlin. They had 10 children: Callie, who wed Sterling P. Rousseau; Lucy, who married William P. "Will" Dennis--son of Lawrence T. and Ann (Newsom) Dennisane whose children, Ernest and Mildred, T.R. and Mary Jane reared following Lucy's death; Dena, who wed E.G.H. Tankersley; Mack, who wed Clara Reiser; Idalla, Charley and Myrtle, who died young; Sudie, who married Minton McHaney; Nan, who wed Edward W. Stanley and reared three of Ernest's eight children after the death of Rose and Ernest; and Holland, who married first John Dover and second Telfair Stedman.

*T.R. Willcockson family on Third Street, Paragould circa 1886. Left to right: Mack, Callie, Mary Jane (Bowlin), Sudie, T. R., Lucy and Dena. (Nan and Holland had not been born yet.)*

T. R. and his family lived in the county, where he owned land and farmed; he served as Sheriff and Collector from 1880-1884. He was appointed postmaster in 1884 and was re-elected Sheriff in 1886, at which time he moved his family into the town of Paragould, where they lived on Third Street. He served as Sheriff until 1890 and after that operated a gin at Hornersville, Missouri, and one at Manila, Arkansas.

T. R. died on July 5, 1925, and Mary Jane, who lived with daughter Holland in Paragould during her final years, died December 14, 1938. Both T.R. and Mary Jane are buried in Linwood Cemetery, Paragould, Arkansas.

**WILLIAMS** – Jacob Williams (1829 Cumberland County, TN) came to Craighead County, AR and located on Buffalo Island in 1867. He married Mary Smith of Virginia and owned a 100-acre farm. Dr. Joseph M. Williams, son of Jacob and Mary Williams, was one of the first graduate physicians to practice in eastern Craighead. He served as county medical examiner and as a member of the County Board of Health and was postmaster of Lake City when its name was changed from Oldtown to Lake City. His children were: Alvin C. married Mabel Johnson, daughter of Henry Johnson and died in 1918.

Dr. Jacob M. Williams was the great grandson of Lt. Col. A. D. Grayson.

In May 1861, Lt. Col. Grayson went to Harrisburg to help Col. Tappan organize the 13th Infantry Regiment. Grayson had farmed a vast area near Lester in Craighead County at the time of his enlistment.

Belmont was the 13th first major engagement. It was at Belmont-Columbus on the Mississippi River that the Confederates had constructed heavy embattlements on the east side of the river and had stretched an enormous chain across the river to Belmont. It is about six miles up river from Belmont to Cairo and Union General Grant brought his army, 7500 strong down the river. The Union Army defeated the 13th, which was alone on the west side of the river. In Tappan's report it was made that several of the Confederate forces were called from the Columbus side to help drive Grant off to Cairo. Tappan listed his losses as 12 men killed, 45 wounded and 25 missing. Allen Dodds, Mrs. Francis Bland's great grandfather, was one of the 45 wounded. A. D. Grayson was not wounded.

After the victory at Belmont, the men of the 13th spent the winter at the isolated old west Kentucky town of Columbus. In the spring of 1862, Col Tappan's 13th Arkansas regiment marched to Henderson, TN, then on to Corinth, MS. On July 5th they approached Shiloh where they again would encounter Gen. Grant's Union Forces.

On the morning of April 6, 1862 Colonel Tappan being absent, Lt. Col A. D. Grayson in command, the 13th marched into battle. During the action he fell mortally wounded. The 13th Arkansas went into the fight with 306 men and had 25 killed, 72 wounded and three missing. Standing on the principal driveway and in one of the most historic places in Shiloh National Military Park stands a monument. On one side of the monument and under the seal of the State of Arkansas is a list of the names of five field officers who were killed in the battle. The first listed was Col. A. D.

Dr. Jacob M. Williams, a dentist, living in Monette, AR, married Maud Esther Tapp, daughter of Adra Tapp of Kentucky. They had a son, Jacob Mahlon Williams who graduated from the University of Tennessee Medical School in Memphis, TN. In March of 1942 he married Mary Lou Bland (1921) the second child of Herbert and Alvina Bland. Jake, as most know him, was active in the European theater of WWII. He was in the headquarters of General Bradley during 1943. He was issued five Battle Stars for his wartime service. At war's end after additional schooling in Memphis, TN he and Mary Lou along with their first child, Jacob Mahlon Jr, moved to Paragould where they live today. They had five children:

1. Mahlon married Leslie Skokos and they had three children, Jacob, King, and Jenniebette. Mahlon was a pathologist and he died of Hodgkin's disease at 37 years.
2. Sue married George Cook and they had four children
   a. Becky married Michael Langley and they have a daughter, Tapp
   b. John Jacob married Carrie Waters and they have a child, Jacob
   c. Luke married Jame Pratt
   d. Rachel
3. Janet married Tom Tate and they have a daughter, Maud who married Chris King.
4. Joe married to Noreen Ness and they have two sons: Caleb and Seth.
5. Nanette married Harold Diggs. They have three daughters, Emily, Alison and Elisa.

**WILLIAMS** – According to *Greene County, Arkansas History* and *Fathers Of The Ridge*, among the first settlers in the Beech Grove community was the Jesse Williams family who came from Hamilton County, Tennessee in the 1840s. Other Beech Grove families coming from Hamilton County about the same time included the Loveladys, Friars and Taylors. Another early Beech Grove family, the Breckenridges, also arrived in the 1840s from South Carolina and Tennessee via Missouri. The Williams, Lovelady and Breckenridge families would be neighbors in Greene County for many generations, and over the decades intermarriages would spawn many family lines that would trace their roots to these early pioneers. The families were also charter members of the Beech Grove Methodist Church.

Jesse Williams was the youngest child of George Washington Williams who moved to Hamilton County, Tennessee about 1824 and secured many valuable tracts of land in the area of Ross' Landing (now Chattanooga) on the Tennessee River within the Cherokee Nation. The early white settlers in the area were there in anticipation of the day when they might secure title to the Indian land. Williams was among 53 families who would later be called the "first citizens of Chattanooga;" he was elected one of the six first commissioners. A large island in Chattanooga is still called Williams Island and there is a well-known private school how occupying the old Williams land across from the island.

*Son, George Washington Williams, early 1900s.*

*Grandson, Pleasant (Ples) Williams with his second wife, Amelia Jane Breckenridge, about 1900.*

One of George's four sons, Samuel, would become the first white merchant after the departure of the Indians, and is called, "the Father of Chattanooga." Samuel Williams was named for his grandfather, Captain Samuel Williams, a Revolutionary War veteran. Captain Williams was under the command of Colonel John Sevier at the Battle of King's Mountains, South Carolina. He was one of the "overmountain men" who came from Eastern Tennessee to help rout the British from the Carolinas. Captain Williams rode with Sevier (who would later become the first governor of Tennessee) in many Indian skirmishes; Williams eventually was killed in a skirmish on the Nolichucky River in 1788. That year was "one of the bloodiest, hottest, and hardest of all the years of Indian fighting," according to John Sevier in his later journals.

*Great grandson, William Marion (Bill) Williams, about 1915.*

The Williams family in the early days were from Halifax and Edgecombe Counties, North Carolina, and prior to that from Isle of Wight County, Virginia, going back to the 1600s. One of Captain Williams' uncles was Sampson Williams, a very early settler in middle Tennessee, near Nashborough (Nashville). Sampson served in the Tennessee State Senate from Sumner County in 1799, and was also a well known Indian fighter. According to *Ramsay's Annals*, in June, 1789, "Indians made a bold attack on Robertson's Station. Captain Sampson Williams was assigned the duty of pursuing the enemy. With 60 or 70 men, Williams with his men (one was Andrew Jackson), pursued, finally made a forced march, found the Indians on the side of Duck River, lay in wait til morning when they attacked. Killed one, wounded five or six and left the victors 16 guns, 19 shot pouches, and all their baggage of blankets, moccasins, and leggins." A first cousin of Captain Samuel Williams also was the only man who served both in the Revolutionary War, and the Texas War for Independence in 1836 (when he was 75 years old). He also fought in the War of 1812 as a citizen of Louisiana. There is a monument to Stephen Williams' memory in Austin, Texas.

*Great great grandson, Alfred Williams in 1942.*

Some of the grandchildren of Captain Samuel, and children of George, migrated to Arkansas. "Young Jesse," according to Hamilton County, Tennessee records "went West with the Indians." He had a sister, Hannah Edwards, who settled with her husband in Crawford County, Arkansas, across the river from Indian Territory (Oklahoma). Jesse found his place in Greene County along with other Hamilton County families.

Jesse Williams was born in Paint Rock, Jackson County, Alabama (then Tennessee) in 1815; he married Elizabeth Taylor in Tennessee. They had the following children:

Elizabeth born 1840 in Tennessee, married 1) Lovelady and 2) D. I. E. Breckenridge.

Ann born 1845 in Arkansas.

George Washington born 1845 in Arkansas, married Mary Ann Lovelady.

Samuel born 1851 in Arkansas.

Tennessee born 1853 in Arkansas.

Nancy Caroline born 1855 in Arkansas.

Jesse was a widower in the 1860 Greene County census. By 1870, he had died and had children living with the David I. E. Breckenridge family. In the census, Jesse was a farmer and had real estate valued at $1,200 and personal estate worth $5,000. He was a slave holder.

George Washington Williams, Jesse's eldest son, was born October 20, 1845, in Greene County and died April 1, 1915, in Greene County. He married Mary Ann (Polly) Lovelady, daughter of Henry and Sarah Lovelady. George, a farmer, died in Jones Township at the age of 70 (article picture). He and Mary Ann are buried in an old family cemetery called Wyse, which was on, or very near, the family farm. It is near Brookings on Lake Ashbaugh between Delaplaine and Peach Orchard. George and Mary Ann had nine children, including Samuel and Pleasant ((Ples). Ples Williams ran the family farm until his death in 1926. His widow, Amelia Breckenridge Williams (daughter of Frank and granddaughter of Jim Breckenridge), moved to Peach Orchard where she lived until her death in 1956 at age 84.

The writer of this article is the great granddaughter of Ples and Amelia Williams, granddaughter of Bill Williams and Amy Page Williams, and the daughter of Alfred Williams and Raye Smith Williams. Living grandchildren of Ples Williams are Iva Williams Palmer of Doniphan, Missouri and Velma Williams Palmer of Peach Orchard, Arkansas. A descendent of Samuel Williams (brother of Ples) is Fred Vellance, Cabot, Arkansas.

**WILLIAMS** – Jessie Blanton Williams was a descendant of Ezekiel and Mary Jane Williams. Their family had always lived at Beech Grove, AR, which is a community about 14 miles northwest of Paragould. The Williams' name could be found often in this small rural area, as many extended family members lived and farmed side by side.

In 1917, Jesse married Mattie Frances Robinson. Jessie and Mattie lived in a modest white-boarded farmhouse where they raised eight children, including from oldest to youngest my father, Vernon Ezekiel who married Lorene Branch and had one child, Vern Ann (Williams) Shotts:

*Poppy in his cotton field.*

1. Vernon Ezekiel
2. Ethelene
3. Lola Mae
4. Yuba
5. Ezra
6. Mexine
7. Lula Belle
8. Billy

All the children and later the grandchildren affectionately called them Poppy and Mommie. Jessie inherited 40 acres and at some point was able to purchase 60 more. The family farmed cotton, soybeans and corn and raised sorghum to make molasses. They raised and killed hogs, cattle, turkeys and chickens. It is said that Poppy was the best around at slaughtering hogs and he acted as a veterinarian for the Beech Grove community. Peach and apple orchards supplied fruit for their large family and half of the neighbor's families. In the backyard was a smokehouse for curing meat, a well with a well porch, and an outhouse. The work on the farm was endless and everyone was busy from sunrise to sunset. Jessie was a devout Methodist and on Sundays when there was a day of rest, men in the neighborhood would stop by before church to "argue the Bible." This ritual became very tedious for all the family except Poppy.

*Jessie, daughter Mexine, and Mattie Williams.*

Although the family did not want for anything, money was scarce and everything the family ate was raised on the farm. Stories are told of how Mommie would take some farm eggs and whatever else she had in the kitchen and cook something wonderful. Mattie was famous for her ribbon cake, which Lola learned to make, too. This cake was made from home dried apples, cooking them into a soft apple mixture which was alternated with a thin cake layer resulting in about a dozen or so unbelievably delicious mouth-watering layers altogether. She made banana nut cakes before anyone else knew how and her plain cake with caramel icing was a family favorite. Besides her superb cooking, canning and housekeeping, Mommie quilted and sewed clothes for the family and wrote letters for anyone in the community desiring her assistance. A loving wife and mother, the children all but worshipped her. She died at home in 1957.

Sometime after Mattie died, the old home place was torn down and a new brick home was built in its place. Around 1960 Jessie married Iva Roberts from Rector, AR, formerly of Beech Grove.

*Lola, Ethelene, Vernon, and Yuba Williams.*

Jesse was hard on the children, strict and stern. His children were at least somewhat fearful of him. Poppy had a temper and red hair to go with it. As he grew older and more gray, he had his girls who were beauticians to tint his hair red and keep it that way. My doctor friends like to remind me of the times Jessie fired his doctors when he was hospitalized at Community Methodist Hospital. He did this with some regularity, especially when the doctor told him to quit smoking. He could be very difficult and headstrong. When Jessie was in his 70s, Vernon, my dad, owned three Big Star Grocery Stores in Paragould and Dad put Poppy to work at the Second and Main Streets store barbecuing. This gave Jessie something useful to do, while the shoppers got some tasty barbecue to take home. I can still picture him in his white cooking smock walking around the store. Poppy died in 1973 while I was away in medical school.

The sisters all became great cooks making pies and cakes fit for a king's table. My dad worked in a food-related business all his life, initially as a butcher and later as a grocer and caterer. Dad and Ezra, who was the meat market manager at Big Star, had a real appreciation for a beautiful cut of meat and many customers came to them for special requests. Their training came primarily from those early years on the farm. The Williams' could be accurately described as a hard-working, close knit Christian farm family who loved and cared for one another.

*Submitted by Vern Ann (Williams) Shotts*

**WILLIAMS** – Joe Williams (Jan 25, 1901) was the son of Jesse and Lucy (Craig) Williams. His ancestor, Jesse Williams is believed to have been the first settler in the area, which became known as Beech Grove. Joe would grow up on land received from the federal government in 1856.

*Joe and Viva Williams.*

After Joe's father died on Feb 24, 1906, his mother remarried to James Hampton Orr, a sickly man who died in 1915. His sibling included:

1. Dolly
2. Ezra
3. Callie
4. Bessie
5. Essie

Joe was born after Ezra. Jim Orr died March 21, 1915 and Lucy Orr died on Nov 19, 1963.

His growing up was hard, though common for the time. With needs at home, Joe and Ezra missed most of their education to keep the family. There were crops to raise, stock to tend and wood to cut. They were boys with the responsibility of men.

Viva (June 19, 1902) was the daughter of Wiley and Ada (Kee) Hicks. The family had come from near Camden, TN by wagon in 1905. When Viva was nine her mother died and when she was 10, her father died. The names of the children, who lived to adulthood, were:

1. Sara Belle
2. Enlo
3. Jake
4. Cecil
5. Coleman
6. Viva
7. Audie
8. Milburn.

The three youngest were shifted among the older ones until they were old enough to be married.

In 1918, marriage marked a coming of age for Joe and Viva. Together they would live for 76 years. With the exception of one year of sharecropping at Black Oak in Mississippi County, Joe and Viva lived their entire life in the Beech Grove community. They were lifelong members of the Beech Grove United Methodist Church. Their children who lived to adulthood were:
1. Loraine
2. Marjorie
3. Glenna
4. Manae
5. Adrian
6. Mae Rita

Sharing marked their life. Experiences such as church, guests, friends, work, children and recreation were shared in some manner. Joe loved to hunt and fish and Viva accompanied him to many a camp. It was said that she could cook better over two logs than many other women could cook over an electric range. She did get lots of practice.

The lived on little and made do for themselves, taking most of their food from the land. They raised big gardens, butchered their own hogs and chickens and always found time for neighbors and church. Many today would call them poor, though some saw them as rich. Their richness was in what they gave away and the friends who treasured them. No one went to their home without being fed or given something from the garden to take home. Dying five days apart, Joe died on Dec 6, 1994 and Viva on Dec 10, 1994, their marriage ended as it began, together.

Marjorie married James Berlas Norman in September of 1941. They had four sons:
1. Weldon
2. Larry
3. Mitchell
4. Norris

*Submitted by Norris Norman*

**WILLIAMS** – Levi Thomas Williams, son of Thomas M. Williams and Nancy Bussick and Martichia Ray of Carroll County, TN were married on March 1, 1868 and were the parents of James Thomas Williams. James Thomas (March 1, 1869 TN) was born on their first anniversary. As a young man, James came to Greene County, AR, met and married Mattie Pearl Jackson (Jan 16, 1874 IN) on Jan 4, 1890. They settled in Gainesville and raised nine children:
1. Mabel Martichia
2. Connie Frank
3. Jeoffrey Heath
4. Herman Earl
5. Enid Cleo
6. Eunice Opal
7. Rupert Belvadare
8. Hershel Delmar
9. Effie Agnes

Tom and Mattie farmed their land and also had a little store stocked with groceries on their property. Neighbors from all around would come to buy groceries from Tom and Mattie so they wouldn't have to walk all the way to Gainesville, about a three-mile walk. Tom said he made about five cents on the dollar on his groceries. Every Saturday he would go into the town of Gainesville and sell eggs, chickens and cream and then buy more groceries. Tom loved country music and owned a radio. The radio was only used on Saturday nights to listen the "Grand Ole Opry". Tom died April 27, 1947 and Mattie died in October 1951 and both were buried in Gainesville Cemetery. Tom and Mattie's son, Connie Frank Williams (Feb 8, 1894) married Alcie Elizabeth Brewer (July 10, 1899). Connie met Alcie while she was living with and working for sharecroppers. Connie was hired to pick cotton for the same couple. Connie Frank and Alcie were married Jan 28, 1920 after Connie returned from the war. They had a cotton farm in the Lafe area and raised eight children:
1. Margret Gearlene
2. Wilburn Connie
3. Jewel Udetta
4. Donald Edward
5. Reba Jean
6. Velma Lois
7. Barbara Faye, twin
8. Bobby Ray, twin

Connie Frank served in the Army, Company "L", 38th Infantry, during WWI and was sent to Germany and France. He was an excellent checkers player and played many games at the store in Lafe. He also loved to hunt and fish. Connie always wore bib overalls. On Sunday, he was supposed to dress up for church, so he would put on a white shirt under the overalls!

*Back row L-R: James Thomas Williams, Mattie Pearl (Jackson) Williams, Mabel Williams, Connie Frank Williams. Front row L-R Enid, Effie, Eunice, Hershel, Herman and Rupert Williams. 1912*

Connie had brown eyes and black hair, but while in the army his hair turned snow white at the age of 22 and stayed that way the rest of his life! Alcie was very religious and made sure all her children attended the Missionary Baptist Church every Sunday morning and evening and also on Wednesday evening.

Connie and Alcie's first farm was right by the railroad tracks, then just before WWII he built a new house and farmed the land on the highway down the road from Lafe. Later he moved into the town of Lafe and cared for his wife, Alcie until his death June 12, 1970. Alcie died Sept 12, 1970.

**WILLIAMS** – Mannie and Ruth Williams lived most of their married life in the Hooker community near Lafe. Mannie (Oct 11, 1896 McCrory, AR) was the son of Dixie Walter and Emma Emmaline (Hudgens) Williams. Ruth (Dec 9, 1895 Rector, AR) was the daughter of James Franklin and Ellen Agatha (Yancey) Miller. Mannie's family later moved to Rector. Here he met Ruth and they were married in Rector on Dec 31, 1916. They lived near Rector for the first couple years of their marriage. Here their first son Donald was born in 1918. After moving to a farm in the Hooker community their second son, James Walter, was born in 1921. James died in 1923 and is buried at Providence Cemetery near Lafe. After this Mannie and Ruth had six daughters between 1923 and 1937:
1. Flora
2. Juanita
3. Ellen
4. Viola
5. Martha
6. Delorice

All seven children graduated from Lafe High School. They all eventually married. Donald to Louise Texter, Flora to Leo Merchant, Juanita to John D. Hicks, Ellen to Bueford Hendrix and after his passing to J. R. Edwards, Viola to Thelbert Stephens, Martha to Edward Chambers, Delorice to Gene Stewart.

The family was raised on a farm near Hooker. They raised corn, cattle, cotton, vegetables and soybeans. All the family worked the land and while all times were not easy remained a close family. All the family attended and were members of the Hooker Baptist Church. The home place was still the property of a family member until early 1999. The farm was sold a few years ago.

*Mannie and Ruth Williams, 1917.*

As the years passed the children of Mannie and Ruth had children of their own. Donald and Louise never had children but were greatly loved by several of their nieces and nephews who have enjoyed visiting with them through the years. Flora and Leo Merchant had a son Donnie and a daughter Mary Ellen. Juanita and John Hicks had a son Bobby Charles. Ellen and Bueford Hendrix, a daughter Marsha Diane. Viola and Thelbert Stephens had a son, James Melvin. Martha and Edward Chambers, a son Edward and two daughters Regina and Debbie. Delorice and Gene Stewart had a son Brett and two daughters Donna and Penny. With the exception of Flora and Delorice who live in Wisconsin and Florida respectively the children have gravitated back to the Greene County area. Donald was the only one who never left Greene County. The grandchildren live all across the United States: Alaska, Wisconsin, Indiana, Florida and Arkansas.

Ruth passed away April 13, 1966 at their home near Hooker. Mannie passed away Oct 26, 1983 at Community Methodist Hospital in Paragould. Both are buried at Greene County Memorial Gardens. All of the children and grandchildren of Mannie and Ruth are still living as of October 2000. However, some of the son-in-laws have passed away. They were dear to the family. They are Leo Merchant, Bueford Hendrix, John Hicks and Gene Stewart. Bueford and John are also buried at Greene County Memorial Gardens.

Mannie and Ruth left a trail of lessons and memories for the children and grandchildren. They range from happiness over Santa bringing a new toothbrush to the smell of Ruth's cooking. They include a brother who loved to tease and lessons on the proper way to clean muddy shoes. Mannie and Ruth are gone but the lessons and memories continue.

*Submitted by Marsha D. Ruth*

**WILLIAMS** – Vernon Ezekiel Williams (April 13, 1919) was the oldest of Mattie and Jessie Williams' eight children. Lorene Branch (Dec 13, 1911) was the oldest of nine children of Beulah and William Andrew "W.A." Branch. Vernon grew up on a farm at Beech Grove, AR. Lorene's family lived on a farm for awhile but later moved into Paragould in a small white house at 600 South Seventh Street and then to a large two story rock house at 635 West Garland Street.

When growing up, Mom was expected to take care of her younger siblings. Washing dishes was her household chore, but her sister Frances told that Mom would walk off and leave the pots and pans unwashed. After graduating from high school, Mom immediately got a teaching certificate and began a 10-year career as a typing and English teacher at Oak Grove School. During the war when many of the men were away, by necessity she became the basketball coach despite the fact that she knew very little about the game. During harvest season when there was a school break, Mom rode in a buggy with her dad to weigh-in cotton at Red Onion.

My parents met while taking classes at Arkansas State College, now Arkansas State University in Jonesboro. Dad realized Mom was a whiz at typing and he enlisted her help with his work. On April 7, 1942, they were married and the marriage lasted until my father's death 38 years later. Their only child, Vern Ann Williams, was born Nov 24, 1950.

During this time, Dad worked at the ice plant delivering blocks of ice to people's homes. I've been told that Dad didn't charge people who were sick or who had hardships. He continued to demonstrate generosity and kindness all his life. Whenever a friend or acquaintance died, Dad was known for being at the home of the bereaved with a freshly baked ham, bread and sodas.

*Vernon and Lorene Williams about 1942.*

When Dad was called to war, Mom went with him as far as Langley Field, VA where he shipped out to sea with Germany his destination. Mom worked in the shipyard until Dad returned. They moved back to Paragould and lived at 315 South Seventh Street. In the post-war years, Daddy Branch, my maternal grandfather, was postmaster and Mom went to work as a postal clerk, a job that she kept for 32 years. Dad also took the civil service exam and worked as a substitute mail carrier for a short time.

Dad soon found his niche in the grocery "bidness". He started as a butcher at a downtown grocery store called Corder's, located on the corner of Second and West Court Streets. This was the beginning of a life-long, fulfilling career doing what he loved. After Corder's, Dad worked for Mayrose Meat Packing Company of St. Louis traveling a certain territory selling meat. He arose at four o'clock a.m. to start his daily route. He was a champion salesman and Mom got a new watch every year from Dad's prizes. In the late 1950s, Dad went to work for Gene Stimson as his right hand man. There were two Stimson Big Star Stores in Paragould, one on North Pruett Street and one at Second and Main Streets. Gene Stimson and my Dad had a heyday opening 11 stores in the mid-south, including the super store of the era called Dixiemart in Memphis, TN. Although the money was good, Dad's absence was hard on Mom and me, so he gave up his job for the sake of the family. For a brief time, Dad worked for Turner Dairy as head of the ice cream department, but in the early 1960s, Dad convinced Gene Stimson to sell him the two Big Star Stores in Paragould, which became Vern Williams' Big Star Stores. Over the next 10 years, the Pruett Street store was closed, and new stores were opened on East Kingshighway and at the Paragould Plaza, which are still open today. These stores were truly Dad's forte. They were his work, his hobby and his entertainment all wrapped into one. Many of the county's teenagers got their spending money by being checkers and package boys for Dad where he taught them not only about the grocery business but about having a zest for living a good and honest life.

Dad was like no other businessman I've ever known. He loved talking to his customers, treating each and every one very special. Often he stood at the automatic door waiting to shake hands, give a pat on the back, hug and kiss the more familiar and spoil the children with free candy. He actually walked miles everyday up and down the grocery aisles assisting shoppers in locating goods and visiting with them. Because of Dad, people loved grocery shopping at Big Star. Dad was a fantastic butcher and cook, too. He had a stove put in the meat market and he and his brother Ezra started cooking and catering. At Christmas they catered every factory's party in town as well as many smaller jobs. Talented in every aspect of the business, Dad had a special knack for catching shoplifters. After one such episode, the guilty party complimented Dad by saying, "Mr. Williams, I wouldn't think of shopping anywhere else."

*Vernon and Lorene Williams about 1978*

Dad gave to his community through service in many areas. He was a Kiwanian, a former president of the chamber of commerce and chairman of the board of Arkansas Methodist Hospital. My parents were both active members of First United Methodist Church.

*Drs. Mack and Vern Ann Shotts, Zeke and Mauri, 2000*

Besides Dad's extreme devotion to his grocery stores, he truly loved working with Marlin Jackson at Security Bank. Back when the bank wasn't worth much, they bought the bank from Herbert McAdams. Dad became chairman of the board, a job that he thoroughly enjoyed.

Dad's two other hobbies were fishing and watching the St.Louis Cardinals play baseball. He loved going to Lake Norfork for a two day fishing trip and he went to several World Series games. Looking back at candid photographs and old home movies, Dad was always the one out of a group with the biggest smile seeming to have the most fun.

Dad was sick with heart disease for the last 18 months of his life. He sold the three Big Star Stores to Lynn Greene of Jonesboro prior to his death Sept 16, 1980, at age 60 years.

After Dad died, Mom tried being a lady of leisure for a few months, but that lifestyle didn't suit her. Marlin Jackson offered her a job at Security Bank, which she readily accepted. She described that as the best job in town. She jokingly referred to her position as key personnel, which meant she let customers in their lock boxes and she carried a batch of keys. Mom worked at the bank until her eyesight became so poor that she was forced to quit. She gave up driving long before that and her brother Ed Branch graciously chauffeured her anywhere and at anytime she pleased.

Mom could have been a stand up comedienne, as she made everyone around her have a good time and a good laugh. My friend Cissy Lieblong recalled that the first time she ever saw Mom was at the Paragould Country Club dining room where she slid down in her chair so that Cissy could only see the whites of her eyes.

Fortunately, Mom lived to know her two grandchildren Ezekiel "Zeke" Elliott Shotts (July 31, 1982) and his sister Mauri Branch Shotts (March 20, 1989). They both were such joys to mom. She died June 13, 1992 at age 80.

Even though years have passed since my parents were alive, hardly a week goes by that someone doesn't tell me what fine people they were, recalling some random act of kindness performed by them. This surely is a testament to their characters. My parents gave me the most wonderful upbringing that anyone could have and their lives were blessings to many.

*Submitted by Vern Ann Williams Shotts*

**WILLIAMS** – W.W. Williams was born 1825 in Alabama and was the son of W.W. (born 1775) and Christen (born 1785) Williams according to the Williams family Bible belonging to Carolyn Nowell Cox, a great-granddaughter. W.W. Williams first married Sarah Prudence Thetford in Tennessee. Daughter, Rebecca Jane, married Chesterfield Jamison, and daughter Sarah married Newton Crocker.

W.W. Williams second married Sarah Arnold in Gibson County, Tennessee. Son Andrew married Elizabeth Rutledge in Greene County, Arkansas. Daughter Susan is buried at Hartsoe Cemetery. Son, James Emsey married Maggie Hampton, daughters Roena and Frankie Elizabeth never married, Nancy Annis married Tom Nowell, John Leo died young and is buried at Hartsoe. Millie Bell married Eaton Knight. Many family members buried at Providence Cemetery.

*W.W. Williams, born 1825.*

There are many great, great and grandchildren in Greene County and many surrounding states.

Farming was the occupation. All lived in the Marmaduke - Greene County area.

**WILLIAMS** – Wilburn Williams (Sept 7, 1924, Lake City) and Mertis Javene Norman (Aug 17, 1924 Beech Grove) were born in Greene County, AR. Wilburn's parents were Connie Frank and Alcie Elizabeth (Brewer) Williams. He grew up in Lafe with seven siblings on a cotton farm. Javene's parents were Ralph Columbus and Vestal (Horne) Norman and she grew up with five siblings on a farm. Wilburn and Javene went to school together at Lafe, but never dated until the week before graduation. After graduation Wilburn went into the Marines and fought in WWII. He fought in Saipan, Tinian Island, and Okinawa and was sent into Nagasaki two weeks after the atomic bomb attack, He was wounded in the leg during the fighting in Saipan and recuperated in Hawaii

*Javene and Wilburn Williams*

receiving a Purple Heart. After the war he married Javene. While Wilburn was serving in the Marines, Javene had moved to St. Louis to work in an ammunition plant and then later she and her family moved to Detroit and Javene worked for Dodge. Wilburn also got a job at Dodge and rented a room in the house next-door to Javene and her family. They were married May 29, 1946 at a small ceremony in Greene County. After their marriage they moved to Flint, MI and Wilburn got a job with Chevrolet Manufacturing. After about two years Wilburn decided he wanted a better job and he and Javene and their daughter, Sandra Kay (Feb 26, 1947) moved to California and Wilburn attended airplane mechanic school. After graduation they moved to St. Louis and Wilburn worked as a mechanic for American Airlines. There was a big housing shortage and after a few months Wilburn and Javene decided to move back to Flint. He returned to his old job at Chevrolet but later was apprenticed as a tool and die welder. They stayed in Flint and raised their family. They had two more children, Michael Jerome (Nov 21, 1950) and Gary Wayne (July 16, 1956). Wilburn will never forget growing up in Lafe, picking cotton, trapping rabbits, he got 10 cents for each rabbit, sharing a bed with his two brothers, newspaper wallpaper, the breaking plow pulled by two mules, cutting wood for the wood burning stove, taking "Groves Chill Tonic" when he got sick and playing basketball and baseball at school and also participating on the track team. Javene remembers chopping and picking cotton, icicles in the iced tea, the cistern for storing water, Saturday night baths, church revivals, hog killing day, making paper flowers for Decoration Day and going to church in a horse drawn wagon. Wilburn and Javene still live in the Flint area and are now enjoying retirement and their grandchildren:

1. Stacy
2. Toby
3. Matt
4. Randy
5. Jason
6. Katie
7. Bonnie
8. Travis

And their first great granddaughter, Gracie.
*Submitted by Gary Williams*

**WILLIAMS** – William Thomas (Tom) Williams was born October 30, 1841, in Gibson County, Tennessee. His parents were Charles W. and Clara Clarissa Young Williams. Their farm was located at Bradford and settted there when the area was still a wilderness. By 1850 the Charles W. family was in Des Moines County, Iowa. His sisters Nancy Connell, Polly Thetford, his brother James and their father William Williams lived nearby. It is not known why they made the move to Iowa but all families except James were back in Gibson County by 1860. William may have died in Iowa. James and his family became members of The Church of the Latter Day Saints and settled in Illinois.

Tom served with the Confederate Army from 1863 until 1865. He married Arbella Emaline Hays daughter of Jesse J. and Epsegill M. Butler Hays on October 16, 1872, in Gibson County. She was called Belle. It is believed that Tom and Belle traveled with several Brewer families from Gibson to Greene County, Arkansas in 1884. They were my great great grandparents. His Aunt Polly Thetford who was a widow had earlier moved to Greene County to be near her children. Tom's Mother Clarissa also moved to Greene County sometime after her husband died in Bradford in 1881.

*Family of William Thomas and Arbella E. Hays Williams.*

The Williams home was located near Marmaduke. Descendants of Tom spoke of him as being a kind gentle person. Tom and Belle's children: Thomas Sidney married Bobby Belieu, L.A. died at age two and is buried in the Cumberland Presbyterian Church Cemetery in Gibson County, Emma married Jim F. Brewer, Cora manied Charlie Liddell, twin sister Ora married George Brewer brother of Jim, Jesse Gilbert(Gid) married Della Bradsher, Charles E. married Nora Cloreth Cudd. Arthur Buell married Maty Crews.

Tom died October 6, 1922. Belle died December 11, 1913. Both are buried in Hartsoe Cemetery near Marmaduke. His mother Clara and Aunt Mary Thetford are also buried in Hartsoe.

**WILLIAMS/WINN** – The Williams and Winn families migrated from Tennessee and were among some of the earliest settlers to come to Greene County.

They settled in a beautiful part of the county and named it Beech Grove. It was named for the beautiful groves of Beech Trees that surrounded it. There were lots of hills and running streams everywhere. One stream of water ran through the town and continued on for miles. Three bridges were built across it.

They were a people of courage and ambition. They had faith in God and lived by the Golden Rule.

The records show the first Methodist Church was built in 1850.

The ground was fertile and the people began to make a good living, by farming and establishing businesses.

Ezekiel Williams married Mary Jane Breckenridge. They had three sons: Ellis, Press and Jess and three daughters: Lula, Allie and Lillian.

Ellis married Myrtle Potter. They had three sons: Nolen, Tyler and Dwight.

Ellis and Myrtle made a good living with their business. They farmed, raised cattle, hogs and horses. They had a general store and sold groceries, dry goods, shoes, boots, overalls and men's shirts. They sold all kinds of farm implements and wagons. They ordered everything by carloads. It was shipped to the county seat at Gainesville, AR by train. The boys hauled it to their store by teams of horses and wagons.

One year Ellis ordered a carload of dolls. He couldn't sell all of them so gave every child he could find in Greene County a doll for Christmas. The second floor of the store was filled with caskets to sell.

He had a gristmill to grind corn into meal, a sorghum mill for molasses, a shop to shoe horses and fix farming tools and a sawmill and lots of timber to build houses.

Ellis and Myrtle took a trip west to the Gold Rush. When they returned, they put in a battery operated Delco System so that they could have electric lights and a refrigerator for ice.

Jim Winn married Liddy Davis. They had three children: Clifford, Reba and Hettie. They made a good living with their businesses; they owned a cotton gin, a general merchandise store and a gas station and restaurant. They farmed and raised cattle and hogs. They had tractors to farm with. Their first automobile was a T-Model Ford. Next they bought a Studebaker, later they bought a Durant. Soon they could buy Chevrolets. They had a battery-operated radio that brought in the Grand Old Opry and World Series.

Hettie Winn married Tyler Williams. They had two children: Jane and Franklin. When they married, Tyler was working for the State Highway Department. He helped to build the first blacktop, Highway # 34, to Beech Grove. We received the R.E.A. electricity in our home for Jane's first Christmas and had our first Christmas tree with electric lights. The year Franklin was born we bought our first black and white television.

Tyler's dad and my dad had retired. We went into business. We had a general merchandise store, a gas station and a restaurant. We served lunches for the school kids, farmers, airport workers, the Texas pipeline workers and the highway workers. We farmed and had cattle, hogs and horses. We had a movie theater and showed western films on Friday and Saturday night. We had a cotton gin.

Beech Grove was a lively place. We had four churches. Each had a two-week revival in the summer. We had four stores; three shops, two cotton gins, consolidated school number three, a post office with a 100 mile route, a govern-

*Williams Family Reunion*

ment owned cotton mattress factory, a government owned canning factory, where the farmers could take their vegetables and have them canned in tin cans. We had a good airport.

I like to think of our families as being industrious, noble and wise.

*Submitted by Hettie Williams*

**WINN** – Among the early settlers of Greene County were the families of Minor M. Winn and John D. G. Winn formerly of Carroll County, TN. Minor (1821) was the second known son of John Winn (1796 SC) and Sarah Gardner (1798 ND). John D. G. (1823) was their third son. Samuel C. Winn (1819) was the eldest son and he too migrated to Greene County, along with sister, Amanda (1833), but not until after 1870. Other children of John and Sarah Winn were Robert Allen Winn (1829) and Thomas M. (1835). Early census records reveal that other daughters were born to John and Sarah but their identities remain a mystery.

In 1846 Minor Winn married Nancy Yarbory/Yarbrough of Gibson County, TN. Land records in Carroll County show that Minor sold his farm there in 1857. By 1860, he and brother John were neighbors in St. Francis Township of Greene County. In Nov 1860 a land patent for 40 acres was issued to John in the Southwest Quarter of Section 36, Township 16 North, Range 4 East and in March 1861, a patent for 120 acres in the same section was issued to Minor.

In an interview with the late Floyd Barnhill, Emma Winn Powers, who were Mr. Barnhill's mother in law and the granddaughter of Samuel C. Winn, reported that she remembered her "Uncle Minor" well. She recalled that he had a large yard full of flowers and fruit trees and beehives. She liked to visit him and she and her mother, Annie Rutherford Winn, always visited him on his birthday and that they always had a big dinner. She distinctly remembered the last birthday that she attended. It was after "Aunt Nancy had died and Uncle Minor had married the widow Yarbrough." Emma would have been about eight at the time. Along with her mother and father, Millard Lafayette Winn, Emma walked to Minor's house expecting a big birthday dinner. To their disappointment, there was no special dinner. This was her last visit to celebrate her great uncle's birthday. She remembered Minor as a man of medium or less stature, white headed with black eyes. The "widow Yarbrough" to whom Emma Powers referred was the widow of William H. Yarbrough, thought to be the brother of Nancy Yarbrough Winn.

Minor and Nancy lived in the Finch community where Minor farmed and lived until his death in 1902. Their children were:
1.   William Frank Winn (1850) married Mary Ellen Rutherford
2.   Rubin Alvin H. Winn (1853) married (1) Kisie A. Thompson (2) Clarinda Elizabeth Dacus Lamb
3.   James Wilkerson Winn (1856) married Sarah Elizabeth McMillon
4.   Minor Monroe Winn (1859-Aug 1860)
5.   Emerson Ethredge C. B. Winn (1861) married (1) Virginia Slatton (2) Laura Potter
6.   Samuel Joe Winn (1863) married Mary Mell Zenia Pegg
7.   Edward G. Winn (1867)
8.   Nancy Emily Winn (1872-Sept 1887)

Both Minor and Nancy and most of their children are buried at Clark's Chapel Cemetery in southern Greene County.

No military records have been found for Minor, but brother John served with Co. A of Davies Battalion of the Arkansas Cavalry. Others with connections to the Winn family assigned to Co. A with a Greensboro entry, were Neal McMillon, father of Sarah Elizabeth McMillion and William H. Yarbrough. The entry from the parole records describe John as 43 years old, blue eyes, light hair, fair complexion and five feet eight inches tall. After the war, John lived in Powell Township in Craighead County and died sometime after 1870.

John was first married to Mahala White in Carroll County, TN, who presumably died shortly after 1850. Their children were:
1.   Elizabeth (1842)
2.   Samuel G. (1843)
3.   Newton M. (1845)
4.   Mary Ellen (1849) married Richard Addison Walker.

In 1853 John married Susan Vaughn of Gibson County, TN. Their children were:
1.   John (1854)
2.   Lucinda (1856) married (1)Henry C. Ishmael (2) William John Burton
3.   Luna A. (1857) married Aaron Gambill

The 1870 Census showed another son, John B. (1868) but this child's relationship to John and Susan is questioned. He might have been a child born to them and name for their first-born son who, perhaps, died young, or he may have been a grandson.

Samuel C. Winn, the eldest child of this family, remained in Carroll County, TN until after 1870. Samuel was probably the best educated of his family. Records show that he assisted in the improvement of roads, he served as an election judge in the Fifth District of Carroll County and in 1870, and Samuel listed his occupation as teacher and farmer. The land records of Carroll County reflect that he bought and sold land many times and his name appeared as a witness on many other deeds.

The exact date of Samuel's departure from Carroll County is not known, but he and wife, Catherine Jane "Cassie" Carlton and their family were living in Poland Township of Greene County in 1880 and in June 1882, a patent was issued to Samuel for 120 acres in the Southwest Quarter of Section 34, Township 16 North, Range 4 East. Floyd Barnhill's research reports that the Old Winn Cemetery is located on the land that Samuel homesteaded and that Samuel, Cassie and many of their children are buried there, but no grave markers survive.

The children of Samuel and Cassie were:
1.   Alva E. (1847) married M. Emma Jernigan
2.   Yancy Y. (1848- before 1860)
3.   Millard Lafayette (1855) married Martha Annie Rutherford
4.   Emerson Dodd (1857) married Mary Elizabeth Lamb
5.   Alice A.E. (1860) married Jacob P. Rowe
6.   Mary J. (1862) married James R. Hicks
7.   William E. (1864- 1931)
8.   Louisa Adaline (1867) married James Davis Rutherford.

By 1880, Amanda A. Winn Foster, widow of David W. C. Foster, had arrived with her children in Greene County where she lived in Poland Township not far from Samuel and Cassie Winn. The children of David and Amanda Foster were:
1.   James B. (1858)
2.   Martha Elizabeth (1861)
3.   John L. (1862) married Mollie F. Osborn
4.   Robert A. (1865) married Martha Sullivan
5.   Mary A. (1867) married Jess Tyner

Wesley D. Foster, son of John and Mollie Foster, was the first Greene County native to die in WWI. After being hospitalized for injuries sustained in August 1918, Wesley was returned to the front where he was killed in action in October 1918.

Also living with Amanda in 1880 was her father, John Winn, then 84 years old and a widower. Sarah Gardner Winn died in Carroll County between 1860 and 1870. John Winn undoubtedly witnessed many events during his long life, including the Civil War, which claimed his fourth son, Robert Allen, who served with the 7th TN Cav. USA and who died at the Confederate prison in Andersonville, GA, while his third son, John D.G. served with a Confederate unit from Greene County. It is presumed that the youngest son, Thomas M., had died before 1880 as nothing about him has been found subsequent to the 1870 Carroll County census.

In 1868 the widow of Robert Allen Winn, Martha Elizabeth Foster, married Francis Williams of Carroll County. In 1870, Francis and Martha Williams, along with Martha's children, moved to Clay County, AR where Frances Williams was a successful farmer. The children of Robert and Martha Winn were
1.   Rebecca Ann (1855)
2.   Thomas Allen (1857) married (1) Lucinda (2) Emma Gertrude Obediance Sale
3.   Bailey Paten
4.   Bland

Between 1857 and 1860, Thomas M. Winn married Margaret Elizabeth Carlton Carter, widow of J.D.D.K. Carter and the sister of Catherine Jane Carlton, wife of Samuel C. Winn. Sometime after 1880, Margaret and her five Carter children and five Winn children made their way to Clay County, AR where she died about 1894. Children of Thomas M. and Margaret Winn were:
1.   James W. (1860)
2.   George Washington (1862) married (1) Cynthia B. French (2) Sophia Huckaby
3.   Sarah Matalena (1864) never married and inherited her mother's real estate
4.   Robert (1867)
5.   Emma L. (1869) married James Vangilder.

Circumstantial evidence suggests that John Winn, the patriarch of this family, was the son of Minor Hampton Winn who, in turn, was the son of William Winn, one of three brothers who founded Winnsborough, S.C. and who attained the rank of first lieutenant in the Revolutionary War. If so, then members of this family have served in every major war of America's history, some making the ultimate sacrifice.

*Submitted by Debra Winn Walker*

**WISE** – Goldie Jean Dulaney (Nov 3, 1938) was the daughter of Lawrence T. and Ruth (Miller) Dulaney, in rural western Greene County, known as the Light community, Greene County, AR.

She attended several rural schools in the western part of the county and graduated from Greene County Tech in May 1957. She married Gary Evans Wise Feb 25, 1959.

Gary E. Wise (Dec 16, 1936) was the son of J. C. Wise and Mable (Green) Wise, in the Walcott community, Greene County, AR. He served in the U. S. Army during the Berlin crisis in Germany from 1959-1961. When Gary returned from the military service, he began his employment with selling men's clothing at Clyde Mack's. Later he changed his line of interest to selling farm implement equipment. Gary has other interests, such as horses and selling real estate.

Goldie's business career started with being employed with the Cooperative Extension Service, Jan 1, 1958. The office was located on the second floor of Greene County Courthouse. This employment ended Dec 31, 1982. She ran for public office in 1982, winning the race for Paragould City Clerk and took office Jan 1, 1983. Goldie was elected to a second, third, fourth and fifth term of office, unopposed.

*Gary and Goldie Wise, Feb. 21, 1999.*

The couple has two sons, Gary Don and Greg Evans Wise. Gary Don (Nov 1, 1963) is married to Ronnette (Lepley) Wise and they have two sons, Garrett Lee Wise (Nov 6, 1991) and Grant Alan Wise (Jan 14, 1995). Both boys attend Saint Mary's School. Gary Don is employed at City Light and Water/City Cable as a lineman in the electric department and Ronette is with Cardiology Associates of Northeast Arkansas as registered nurse practitioner. These two families live in Paragould.

Greg Evans (April 18, 1974) married Brandi (Brown) Wise. They have a daughter, Delaney Kathryn Wise (Oct 27, 1999). Greg is employed with J. B. Hunt Transport as senior project manager and Brandi is with Rector High School, teaching Chemistry and Physics. The family lives in Maumelle, AR.

**WOOD** – Billy Ray Wood is the third of six children born to Euin Lee "E.L." Wood and Mildred Sears Wood. While this account contains recent history, the Wood family roots in Greene County date back for about a century. Bill was born July 14, 1933, at Eight-Mile Community, southeast of Paragould. While attending high school at Green County Tech in Paragould, Bill met Helen Pearline Walker. They married April 4, 1953, shortly before Pearline graduated and two years after Bill graduated.

Bill was soon called to military duty and served in Europe during the Korean War. He returned home in May 1955 at which time he and Pearline moved to Flint, Michigan, for a year. After returning to Paragould Bill worked for International Harvester and Pearline worked in a local beauty shop until the birth of their children.

In 1958 their daughter Sherry was born, followed the next year by their son David. Both children graduated from Greene County Tech, just as their parents did: Sherry 25 years after Bill and David 15 years after Pearline. Both children also graduated from Harding University in Searcy, Arkansas.

David married Cindy Cooper in 1983 in Paragould. They have four sons: Kyle (1985), Jason (1987), Ryan (1990) and Tyler (1996). David and Cindy are both employed by and help in the work of The Children's Homes of Paragould.

Sherry married Michael Keck in 1987 in Little Rock. Their children are Jeremy (1991) and Adrienne (1994). Michael is employed with St. Vincent Hospital and also serves as a City Director on the Board of Directors of Little Rock. Sherry is a homemaker.

In December 1998 Bill retired from Baker Implement Company after more than 40 years of service.

Bill and Pearline have been members at Seventh and Mueller Church of Christ in Paragould for 35 years. Bill serves as a deacon and has faithfully driven a Joy Bus to pick up children in the community to bring them to Bible class every Sunday morning for the past 25 years.

**WOOD** – Charles And Helen Wood have resided in Greene County a relatively short time but have roots that are rather deep.

Charles Lee Wood born 1928, Flint, Michigan to E.L. and Mildred Sears Wood grew up and attended school in Greene County graduating from Lakeside (East Elementary). Sarah Helen Brown Wood born 1931, Lake City, Arkansas (Dixie Community), to R.C. and Bertha Randal Brown grew up in Craighead County and graduated from the Dixie Consolidated School. Bertha lived in Paragould after R.C. died in 1947.

Charles and Helen were married 1951 and soon afterward moved to Flint where his Sears grandparents lived. Charles secured a job with a company that transported new automobiles to the dealers and Helen soon became a full time mother.

While living in Flint a daughter Phyllis Rae was born February 4, 1952. Soon afterward a house was purchased in Mt. Morris, north of Flint, where a son Charles Michael arrived September 26, 1955, and then Richard Kendell, another son was born August 19, 1961.

*Charles/Helen Wood Family November 1993. Front row left to right: Brenda DuFord; Helen and Charles Wood; Phyllis and Garrett Meier. Middle row: Mitchall Alen and Donald Lee Wood. Back row left to right: Aaron, Michael, Richard and Lisa Curry Wood; James and Sarah Meier.*

Phyllis graduated from the Mt. Morris School system as an honor student. Upon graduation she enrolled at ASU in Jonesboro, where she graduated in 1974, with a degree in Physical Education. After graduation Phyllis taught in the Blytheville and Oak Grove Districts (latter now consolidated with Paragould). She later returned to ASU and received an MS degree in Special Education and presently teaches in the Paragould school system. In 1977 Phyllis married James Meier, son of Joseph and Marie Arnett Meier, and they have two children, Sarah born 1981 and Garrett born 1986, both are students in the Paragould Schools.

Charles Michael attended school in the Mt. Morris schools and graduated in 1973. After graduation he enrolled at Western Michigan University studying Manuel Arts. He then attended UM Flint and Mott Community College until he earned a degree as a Machinist and presently has his own business. In 1974 Mike married Brenda DuFord, daughter of Don and Gerry Coggins DuFord, of Mt. Morris. Brenda is a graduate of University of Michigan Flint and is a CPA. They have three children: Aaron Michael born 1977 graduate of GMI with Computer Engineering Degree; Donald Lee born 1980, a special child, works for his father and attends school; Mitchell Alan born 1983 presently attends Mt. Morris high school.

Richard upon graduation in 1979 enrolled in Baker Junior College studying for a business degree. Durr Automation, Inc. of Wixom, Michigan presently employs him as a Controls Designer. Richard and Lisa Curry were married in 1992 and have a son Lucas born 1999. Lisa is the daughter of Charles and Jacquelyn McComb Curry of Flint, Michgain.

Upon retirement and return to Greene County, being amateur genealogists, Charles and Helen became involved with the Greene County Library in a project to catalogue the county cemeteries. This project led to assisting in the organization of the Greene County Historical and Genealogical Society and adding to the material in the library's Lipscomb room. They have been involved in the compilation of eight books of these records.

**WOOD** – Euin Lee "E.I." Wood The family of Euin Lee "E.L." Wood arrived in Greene County circa 1910 and settled in the Marmaduke area where they farmed near his grandparents Richard Allen and Francis Elnora Little Evans who preceded them. This family contained Ira, Ella Jane and sons E.L. and Everett. They lived in both the Walnut Ridge school district (#69) and Post Oak school district (#61), near Mounds, where he and his brother Everett attended school.

While living in the Post Oak area E.L. met a young lady, Mildred Sears, who was the daughter of A.A. "Otis" Sears and Sadie Mae Albin Sears. The Sears family had moved to this area from Crawford County, Missouri. Shortly after meeting Mildred E.L., and family moved to Flint, Michigan, where he secured a job.

After getting established in Flint E.L. returned to Greene County where he and Mildred were married November 14, 1927. While living in Michigan they had two children, Charles born 1928 and Bonnie born 1930. After living here until 1933 they decided to return to Greene County when the "Great Depression" hit.

Upon returning to Greene County they purchased a farm that was located southeast to Paragould in the Eight-Mile community. While living here their family increased by four more children, Bill R. born 1933, Doyle W. born 1936, James O. born 1938 and Linda Carolyn born 1941.

*This photo of the E.L. Wood family was taken August 1977. Left to right: James O., Doyle W., Linda Carolyn Stewart, Bonnie Robinson Mildred, E.L., Charles and Bill Wood.*

This land is located on what is now Greene 911 Road, three fourth a mile east of State Highway 135. We now refer to it as the "Swamp" because the road ended at our house, as there was a slough/swamp that made the road impassable most of the time. The nearby Eight-Mile ditch, which was nearby, flooding didn't help either.

In 1951, after another wet spring, they decided to sell and get away from these problems. That fall the farm was sold and "The Old Crowley Farm" near Walcott was purchased. They lived here until their deaths, E.L. from a farm accident April 14, 1990, and Mildred October 15, 1991, from a bad heart helped by E.L.'s untimely accident. Everett, E.L.'s brother, who never married and lived with them, died July 25, 1993, from the result of a series of strokes.

E.L. and Mildred helped establish the Walcott Church of Christ and were very active members. Mildred was active in the Crowleys Ridge Development Council and was a member of the board of directors for over 20 years. They managed to see the three youngest children graduate from Harding University.

Charles married Helen Brown then moved to Michigan, after retiring they now live in Paragould. Bonnie married Garland Robinson; now retired they live on the farm at Walcott. Bill married Pearline Walker and lives in Paragould. Doyle who married Reba Wayland is a retired school superintendent living in Thayer, Missouri. Jim married Sheila Robertson, lives in Overland Park, Kansas, works as an auditor for the state of Kansas and Carolyn, who married Jack Stewart, teaches school at the Crowley Ridge Academy, lives at Walcott.

**WOOD** – I find my Wood family in Logan County, KY in 1799 buying 200 acres of land. In his will dated Sept 4, 1802, James Wood leaves his wife Luccia and children Brewer, Peter, William and Janney the family possessions. My great-great-great-great-grandfather Peter is there at least until 1812. His family shows up in Hickman in 1850. He is listed as being born in North Carolina dies sometime after 1850 census and his wife Elizabeth "Betsey" born North Carolina and dies after 1860.

Clark's Chapel School, 1905, Henry Wood teacher. There are nine men standing behind, Henry Wood is the third from left. Fifth, sixth and seventh are three doctors - Dr. Majors, Dr. Walter Ellington and Dr. Boyd. Standing in front of Dr. Ellington is Finis Ward; he was blacksmith for many years in Paragould. The grown lady in the front is Sarah Elizabeth (McMillon) Winn and two of her children, Etta Winn and Joe Winn.

James (1811 Logan County, KY) married Mille Wood (1813 KY) and they lived in Hickman County, TN where they had four sons and four daughters:
1. Thomas J.
2. Peter A.
3. Leander
4. James C. Wood
5. Nancy
6. Melissa
7. Francis M.
8. Mary F.

They were in Hickman County in 1850 and 1860 census. By 1870 they had moved and settled here in Greene County where the family has been since that time.

William L. Wood, Sarah Ann Wood; sons Benjamin Wood, Henery Wood; daughter Millie Ann.

James Tom Hester (1799 Granville County, NC) married Cynthia Lancaster (1808) a Cherokee Indian from North Carolina and they had three children, Charles Lancaster, James T. and Sarah. They followed Ben Crowley to this region and on the way James Sr. died, but Cynthia and the children continued on. After arriving here, Cynthia died and was buried at Crowley's Ridge State Park because she was an Indian could not be buried in a white man's cemetery.

Fletcher family, 1913. Reuben and Alice Dora, Bill Hester, George Wood on Uncle Bill's lap and Taylor Fletcher (with book). Standing from left: Myrtle and Harmon Fletcher, Mattie Bell (Fletcher) Elmore, Maude and Henery Wood, LaNette Kennedy Kirchoff, and Bill and Aarney Elmore. Eva Rouseau is standing on the porch. Children are: Willodean Fletcher, Alberteen Fletcher, Alex Fletcher and Juanita Wood.

William Leander Wood married Sarah Hester in Greene County and had four children:
1. Villey
2. Benjamin
3. Millie (Wood) Jackson
4. William Henry Wood

William Leander was a charter member and first preacher of Liberty Church of Christ located in the Finch community, where his great grandson, Gene Wood is the minister there today.

William Henry Wood married Maude Fletcher Wood, daughter of Reuben Jr. and Alsadora Ward Fletcher. Reuben Sr. (1811 Granville County, NC) married Elizabeth Basinger Fletcher in Gipson County, TN in 1831 and they had nine children while living in Tennessee. They also follow Ben Crowley to this region and Reuben Sr. died on the way and Elizabeth and her children continued on. Alsadora Ward Fletcher was the daughter of Gideon and Mary Kilkreece Ward from Tennessee. Mary Kilkreece Ward was also an Indian. They moved to this area in 1850 and became charter members of Finch Baptist Church. Henry was a schoolteacher in Greene County and taught at Pine Knot, Finch and Clark's Chapel. At the Clark's Chapel School he had at least three students who eventually became doctors. Henry also served as bookkeeper for several prominent businesses in Greene County.

Henry and Maude had six children. They were:
1. Juanita Wood Turpin
2. George Wood
3. Ruby Wood Nettles
4. William Wood
5. Tom, twin
6. Tomazien Wood Chesser, twin

At one time, the Wood family lived in a little house papered with newspaper. Henry noticed the crossword puzzles on the wall and cut them out to work them. Not long afterwards, he had cutouts all over the walls. Henry Wood lived in Greene County until his death at the age of 72, Maude died in Greene County at the age of 103. They have three children, Jaunita, George and Tomazine who are deceased and three children, Ruby, William and Tom still living. There are 15 grandchildren still living, four deceased grandchildren, 32 great grandchildren and several great great grandchildren.

**WOOD** – James Ira Wood The family of James Ira Wood, born 1877 Sharp County, Arkansas, moved to Greene County from Fulton County, Arkansas after 1910. This family, included Ella Jane (Evans) and sons E.L. and Everett, settled east of Marmaduke and later moved to the Mounds area.

Ira's parents were Thomas, born 1839 Mississippi, and Charlotte Baker Wood, born 1849 Mississippi, who were married 1868 in Monroe County, Mississippi. In 1871 they with young son John, migrated to Arkansas and settled in Sharp County, near Strawberry, where Ira was born. This family later moved to Fulton County, Arkansas where they lived until their deaths. While in Sharp County the family grew to nine children, two dying young.

The parents of Thomas were James Wood born 1798 South Carolina and Isabelle (Morrow?) born 1815 South Carolina who came to Mississippi circa 1837. They were the parents of 10 children, six sons and four daughters all of which reached maturity. The first two were born in South Carolina, third in Alabama and the other seven in Monroe County, Mississippi. Thomas along with brothers William, James and Andrew served in the CSA and all returned home.

Photo from McHaney's Studio Paragould, Arkansas circa 1915. Standing left to right: James Ira and Ella Jane Wood. Seated left to right: Everett and Euin Lee "E.L." Wood.

Ira's family farmed in the Marmaduke/Mounds area until 1925 when they went to Flint, Michigan where Ira, E.L. and Everett worked for General Motors. Ira worked for Chevrolet until his retirement in 1942 at which time he returned to Greene County, where E.L. and Everett had purchased a farm upon their return earlier. This farm, was located south of Paragould, in the Eight-Mile Community in what we called the "Swamp." The family remained here until 1951 when they sold this land and purchased the "Old Crowley Farm" near Walcott.

James Ira died August 7, 1977, near 100 years old, is buried west of Paragould in Shiloh

Cemetery, beside his wife of 58 years, Ella Jane Evans who died December 12, 1961. Only a younger sister born in 1882 outlived him. Ira was a charter member of the Walcott Church of Christ, which he attended as long as he was able. In later years he was unable to see because of cataracts. By the time he had them removed he had lost most of his physical strength. While he was weak in body his mind was still sharp; he never lost the ability to communicate.

Ira Wood and Ella Jane Evans were married January 21, 1903, in Fulton County, Arkansas. They had two sons Euin Lee "E.L." born 1904 and William Everett born 1906. E.L. married Mildred Sears in Greene County and they had six children. Everett never married.

These two brothers formed a partnership and farmed together for over 50 years until they retired and sold the equipment in 1985. Their farm still lives today as The Wood Family Farm, Inc. The six children of E.L. and Mildred inherited the farm, at Everett's death, and kept it as a memorial to these dearly loved ancestors.

Ira's older brother John and wife Ada also moved to Greene County and settled in the Lafe area where they had two sons Cecil and Herschel Lee. John and Ada are buried at New Liberty Cemetery near Halliday. Cecil lives in California and Herschel and wife live in Mountain Home, Arkansas. Sarah Isabella Banks, older sister of Ira, also lived in Greene County and is buried at New Liberty Cemetery.

**WOOD** – William Andrew Wood (Jan 1, 1870 Greene County) was the second son of William A. J. and Loucinda Emeline (Webb) Wood, grandson of William H. and Eliza (Anthony) Wood and great grandson of James Ray Wood Sr. By age 10, William Andrew Wood had adopted the name of "Ed" and the name remained with him.

In 1897, Ed's parents gave him a parcel of land for $1.00. He took up the life of a respectable Nettleton citizen, became a barber and owned his own shop. Because he was rather rebellious against his parent's standards and loved the outdoors, Ed soon grew weary of "normal" life. He sold his land to a cousin, James Whitmell and Mary Rosanna (Wood) Webb in 1899 for $300.00 and much to his parents' dismay, sold his business, too. He used a portion of his proceeds to purchase a home on Fourth Street for his parents, tucked the remainder into his pockets and headed off to work in timber. Whether it was lumberjack, railroad roust about, field hand, or sharecropper, Ed did not care what his work was just as long as he was outside breathing the riches of God's earth.

*Wm. Andrew Wood and Lee Allen Wood.*

On Jan 14, 1906, Ed Wood married Elizabeth Sarah Yearta in Nettleton, Craighead County. To this union, seven children were born:
1. Virdie May (1906-1906)
2. Paul Edward (1907-1984)
3. Hershel (1910-1910)
4. Orene Elnora (1911-1998)
5. Delmas Lemar (1914-1928)
6. Stanley Claude (1918-1995)
7. Earlene Rubye (1922)

All of the children were born in Nettleton except the last. Two children died in infancy and one died of meningitis. Before the birth of their last child, the Ed Wood family moved to Greene County.

For many years, the family lived in several places around Greene County and Ed continued his carefree existence. The children attended country schools and learned to love and appreciate simple pleasures. Ed had been raised a staunch Methodist, but religious training fell into the hands of their mother. According to daughter, Earlene, "Mom was Baptist and Pop was Methodist. Now that was an interesting situation! Don't remember the Methodist ever winning out in that battle!" After joining the CCC, Ed's youngest son, Stanley, purchased a home for his parents on Main Street. Once they moved to town, the youngest child attended Sunday school at the Baptist church, was baptized and took an active role in the youth activities.

Ed Wood and Betty's mother both died on Dec 15, 1943. When recounting the day, Earlene (Wood) Farmer shared that the family went to one funeral in the morning and other that afternoon. Ed, Betty and four children are buried in Wood's Chapel along with brother, Lee Allen and Mary Ellen (Farrell) Wood, sister, Sarah Elnora Howard; uncle and aunt, Thomas and Elizabeth (Powell) Wood, aunt and uncle Sarah and William Stuart; parents William and Loucinda Wood; grandparents William H. Wood and Andrew and Winifred (Coburn) Webb; great aunt Nancy (Boggan) Wood and numerous other aunts, uncles and cousins.

**WOOD** – William Franklin Wood (Jan 3, 1900 Greene County, AR) married Hettie L. Cruse on Oct 26, 1919. Hettie (June 11, 1902 Craighead County, AR) and Frank were active members of the First Methodist Church in which they both enjoyed singing in the choir.

Frank's grandfather, William Wood and Hettie's grandfather, James Wilse Stuart, helped acquire the land on which Woods Chapel Church and cemetery sets.

Frank and Hettie had five daughters:
1. Beatrice
2. Beauton
3. Virginia
4. Martha, twin
5. Mary, twin

Frank's parents were John Francis Wood and Mary Naomi McDaniel Wood. Frank had one sister and four brothers:
1. Maggie
2. Charlie
3. Alex
4. Clyde
5. Roy.

Frank's mother died when he was seven

*Front L-R: Frank, Hettie, Beatrice, Mary, Virginia, Martha, Beauton, Homer Craver, Burk Brinton, Alfred Herget, Harold Morgan and Jim Simpson*

years old so his sister Maggie then 13 years old helped her father raise the family, after their mother died.

Thomas V. Cruse and Susanna Stuart Cruse were Hettie's parents. Hettie had two sisters, Velma and Emma, and also a half sister and brother, Julia and Harold.

Frank moved from the family farm in about 1925 to manage a dry goods store called "Freeman Sample Store", owned by a Mr. Freeman from St. Louis. His brother Clyde worked there also.

Freeman Sample Store was located at 207 Pruett Street in downtown Paragould. After working for Mr. Freeman for several years, Mr. Freeman gave Frank a bonus, which gave Frank a chance to open up his own dry goods store in about 1931 called "Woods Cash Store". Hettie and all five daughters helped during all those years in which the store was open.

After 20 years Frank sold "Woods Cash Store" to his brother Clyde and his wife Lela. Frank bought a small furniture store from Donald Boozer, which he called "Paragould Furniture Store" in about 1951 located at 213 Pruett St. After a few years, he sold the furniture store to his sister in law and brother in law, Velma and Donald Stevenson.

Frank became a real estate broker, which he thoroughly enjoyed until he retired in about 1972.

Frank and Hettie enjoyed having nine grandchildren, five boys and four girls.

**WOOD** – William H. Wood (1812 NC) the second child of four sons and one daughter born to James Ray Wood Sr. and his first wife. William Wood was a farmer, landowner and charter member and trustee of the Methodist Episcopal Church South. As recorded in the Greene County courthouse, a Deed of Conveyance between William H. Wood and the church was executed on July 24, 1861, for land for a church and cemetery. Not until 1864, did Wood's Chapel Cemetery receive its first death, William's sister in law, Jane Bogan, wife of James R. Wood Jr. Since then, however, many Wood descendants and other family members have been buried there.

After his mother's death, William's father mar-

*Woods Chapel Cemetery.*

ried again in 1824. James Sr. and Susan had seven children. By 1832, Williams' older brother had moved to the southern part of Alabama and acquired property. Whether William traveled with him or followed later is not known, but it was in Montgomery County, AL that William met and married on July 1, 1838, Eliza, daughter of James Anthony.

With Susan's death around 1839, William's father was again widowed. Around 1843, James Sr. moved his second family, five daughters and two sons and joined his third son, James R. Jr. in Mississippi. It was there Sr. met and married Martha D. Shelton in 1846.

By 1840, William and Eliza had one son.

From Montgomery, William moved his family to Cherokee County, AL. Eliza's two sisters, Jane Anthony and Mary, wife of William Huggans, accompanied them. By 1850, William's first son had died and three more children had been added: Thomas Jefferson (1841-1892), Sarah Drusilla (1845-1915) and William A. J. (1847-1905). These children would ultimately reside in Greene County, marry, raise families and be buried in Wood's Chapel.

Prior to Jan 4, 1856, William moved his family to Mississippi to help work his father's farm. By then, James R. Sr. had three more children with one on the way. After his father's death on Jan 29, 1856, William helped manage the farm for Martha until the estate closed four years later. Around 1859, as seen in the land grants, William, along with his brother, James and brother in law, William Huggans, acquired land in Greene County and established a homestead. It is not known whether it was childbirth, the hardship of the times, or the travel from Arkansas to Mississippi that proved to be too much for Eliza, but in late 1860 or early 1861, Eliza died. Where Eliza was buried is not known. But it is believed she was interred somewhere on the Wood farm. The search for her grave still goes on by some descendants today.

On Dec 12, 1861, William H. Wood married Sarah Ann, daughter of Hezekiah H. Highfill. To this union, four more children were born.

William H. Wood died on Oct 22, 1871 at age 59 and was buried at Wood's Chapel. Of his eight children, seven lived to adulthood to continue the proud Wood heritage.

**WOOLDRIDGE** – Thomas Harley Wooldridge (June 16, 1926 Cotton Plant, AR) son of Chester and Grace Wooldridge. After serving the army, he came to Greene County in 1947 when his parents bought a farm in eastern Greene County.

He met neighbor Hester McPherson and mar-

*Hester, Harley, Kathy, Rick, and Randy Wooldridge.*

ried on Dec 8, 1948. At that time, they farmed with mules and a two-row Ford tractor.

In 1955, the couple bought a grocery store next to Lakeside School on Highway 412 East. The store was rented from Joe Elmore. By 1964 business had grown to afford a new larger building a mile closer to Paragould and next to their home. Wooldridge Grocery was a favorite place for friends to buy food, fishing tackle, and gas, wash a car or just visit. Some customers stopped in for directions to Blytheville or Memphis, they usually got a "Harley Story" too.

They reared three children in the store: Kathy, Rickey and Randy. They all attended Lakeside and graduated from Greene County Tech School. Kathy earned a BSE from Arkansas State University.

The store was sold in 1981 to spend time with granddaughters Michaelina and Jana McFadden. Rebounding from retirement, Harley worked at Greene Acres Nursing Home for 11 years and Hester had a cleaning business. The car wash remained until 1998. In 1999 Harley started a new business: Commercial Cracking of Pecans.

The year 2000 finds the couple still traveling, fishing, peddling apples, cracking pecans and most of important of all: visiting with friends.

*Submitted by Hester Wooldridge*

**WRIGHT** – My grandmother, Margaret Paralee (Wright), Moore was born March 10,1878, in the Northeast part of Greene County. She was the daughter of William Jasper Wright and Mary Jane Starnes. William Jasper and his twin brother John Newton were born April, 30,1849, in Hickman County, Tennessee. They were the sons of Hezekiah B. Wright and Martha J. (Staires) Perry. Hezekiah had brought his family to Arkansas and eventually settled on their 250 acres of land that is now part of Breckenridge Twp and part of Northern Hurricane Twp.

William Jasper Wright married Mary Jane Starnes and they had four children. Marshall Barlow, born 1875; William Newton, born 1876; my grandmother, Margaret Paralee, "Maggie" (Moore) born 1878; and Henry Conway "Con". born 1880. Mary Jane was the daughter of Marshall and Paralee (Johnson) Starnes. She was born 1852 in Tennessee and lived there until she was 18 years old. She came to Arkansas with her family where she met and married William Jasper. William Jasper along with his parents and brother were charter members of the Baptist Church at Providence west of Marmaduke. Jasper died January 11, 1900, and Mary Jane died February 7,1890. Both are buried at Wright Cemetery.

Hezekiah B. Wright was born 1829 in Hickman County, Tennessee. After moving to Arkansas, he was very prominent in the community being a farmer and having a general merchandising business at Gainsville under the name of H. B. Wright and Company. He was elected coroner on the Democratic ticket in 1858. He belonged to the Masonic Fraternity, and was a Royal Arch Mason. He was the son of John Wright of South Carolina and Sarah (Barr) Wright of Kentucky. He had a brother Thompson born 1826 and a sister Rebecca. Hezekiah married a second time to a woman named Permelia E. (Ward) Wood, and they had eight children, Joseph D.; Franklin C., Alvin T., Emma M., Anna A., Revis, Hezekiah B. and Addie J. Addie J. died when she was two years and nine months old. Hezekiah B. Wright died January 24, 1922, he was 92 years old. Hezekiah, his first wife and most of his family are buried at the Wright Cemetery west of Marmaduke.

**WRIGHT** – Hezekiah Buren Wright first was born around Duck River in Hickman County, Tennessee on August 15, 1829, to John and Sarah (Barr) Wright. In 1848, he married Martha Jane (Stares) Perry, who was born in 1827 in North Carolina and had a child, Mary, by her first husband. In 1849, Hezekiah and Martha had twins, William Jasper and John Newton. In 1850, Hezekiah and his family was living in Humphrey County, Tennessee. Later that year they moved to Greene County, Arkansas in a horse drawn wagon settling first in Big Creek Township with his parents. In 1852, they purchased 250 acres of farmland in the now Breckenridge and Hurricane Township. He farmed this land for 70 years. With the knowledge of the business, wants of the people, and honorable dealing, he was successful in general merchandising at Old Gainesville of the H.B. Wright and Company firm. He was county coroner from 1858 until 1864, a Royal Arch Mason, and a Democrat.

When Hezekiah moved to Greene County, there were very few settlers, especially in the northern part of the county. He had to travel to Cape Girardeau, Missouri once a year to have corn ground, and to buy sugar, salt and coffee. The entire round trip was 250 miles of winding trail through the forest.

When Martha died on January 3, 1863, Hezekiah proceeded with her wishes to be buried on the homestead. Later when settlers came through with a sick baby that later died, they asked about local burial. Hezekiah let them also bury on the homestead, which is the start of Wright Cemetery.

In 1864, Hezekiah married Permelia E. (Ward) Wood, born January 7, 1842, in Tennessee widow of C. Wood. Somewhere in Illinois on August 21, 1864, Joseph D. was born. Their union resulted in seven more cildren born in Arkansas: Franklin C., Alvin T., Emma Mae, Anna A., Reavis, Addie Jewel, and Hezekiah Buren.

Joseph D. Wright second married Emma Rigney, who was born May 17, 1874. This union produced 12 children: A.D. (Gus), Lura, Car, Minnie, Anna, Delsie, Effie, Troy, Alvin, Oda and Alta. Emma died October 16, 1913. he was a member of Providence Baptist Church and died October 22, 1934. Both are buried at Wright Cemetery.

Franklin C. Wright second was born in 1867, married Ida Mae Culver (January 2, 1872 - December 31, 1955), was a member of Providence Baptist Church, and had seven children: Jewel, Dee, Florence, Cavie, Beulah, Ira and Carrie. Both are buried at Wright Cemetery.

Alvin Taylor Wright second was born in 1869. He married Ella Livesay in 1889. They had four children: Buel, Ollie who married Lawernce Pace in 1922, Clarence who married Edith Horton in 1928, and Albert.

Emma Mae Wright second was born May 3, 1872, and married James Starnes on January 5, 1893. Jim was born on February 4, 1871, in Lauderdale County, Tennessee to Marshall and Paralee (Johnson) Starnes. Jim and Emma were the parents of 11 children, but only six lived to adulthood. Their children were Avery, Claude Cicero, Nora, Telfair Conway, James Adron, Ernestene and Earlene. They were members of the Protestant Methodist Church. Later in life, they moved from near Marmaduke, Arkansas to the vicinity of Leonard in Clay County, Arkansas, where he continued to farm. Emma is said to have been very adept at playing the accordion and organ. She was an alto singer and loved reading poetry. Jim died September 20, 1911, in Rector, Arkansas and Emma died January 28, 1916. Both are buried at Wright Cemetery.

Anna Wright second was born in 1875. In 1897, she married Thomas Jackman born April 16, 1868. She had three children with Thomas: Earl, Clyde and Everett (Ebb). He died February 24, 1905. She married Thornton or T.G. Smoot in 1909 and had two children, Clifford and Orlie. T.G. died August 12, 1921-2. Anna died in 1927. All three are buried at Wright Cemetery.

Hezekiah Buren Wright second was born on May 28, 1884. He married Ruth Purcell in 1901. They had four children: Lonnie (1907-1907), Lennie (1908-1908), infant Wright (1909), and Leonard. Ruth died in 1914. He married Mary P. Ferguson in 1920 and had five children: Ormand, Willodean, LaVerne, Dorothy, and Audrey. Hezekiah died on January 5, 1961. Mary died on April 6, 1969. All six are buried at Wright Cemetery.

Two of the eight children born to Hezekiah and Permelia died before adulthood. Reavis was born November 3, 1881, and died January 9,

1898. Addie Jewel was born March 31, 1875, and died December 23, 1880. Both are buried at Wright Cemetery.

According to census records, other people lived in the home. In 1870, William J., 16; Sarah J., 12; and Margarett Pattoon, 12; were listed as orphans in the household. In 1880, Minerva Ring was listed as a servant. In 1900, David P. Johnson, 22; is listed as a farm laborer in the home. The 1870 census also shows Hezekiah had $1000 in real estate and $750 in personal property.

Hezekiah was of strong Baptist faith. Hezekiah, Permilia, John, and William were charter members of one of the oldest churches in Greene County, Providence Baptist Church. It was organized in 1866 or 1874. Hezekiah, saved and baptized by Elder James Miller, spent 57 years in the Bethlehem Baptist Association serving as treasurer and many other offices.

Permilla died on February 9, 1901, and was buried at Wright Cemetery. Hezekiah married Sarah Huckaby Vangilder in Rector, Arkansas on 16, 1902. Sarah was born in Tennessee around 1843 or 1844. The 1910 lists eight children with four living. She died in 1923.

Hezekiah died on January 24, 1922, following a brief illness. He was buried between Martha and Permilia at Wright Cemetery.

**WRIGHT/WHITAKER** – At the time of this writing, the summer of 1999, Frank and Bonnie Wright, the former Miss Bonnie Whitaker, live on the old Whitaker farm in the Spring Grove Community between Finch and Center Hill in Greene County and have lived in this area most all of their lives. Bonnie and her sister, Brenda (The Whitaker Sisters), were also known throughout the Northeast Arkansas area for their musical talents.

Bonnie is the daughter of Luther and Monra

*The Luther and Monra Whitaker Family from Spring Grove Community. Back row left to right: Parents; Monra and Luther L. Whitaker, Children; Jackie, Carlton and Larry. Front row left to right: Brenda, Richard, Betty Joyce and Bonnie.*

(Dunnam) Whitaker. Bonnie's brothers and sisters are Carlton of Cape Girardeau, Missouri, who was once a missionary to Morocco; Jackie who resides in east Paragould; Betty Joyce (Mrs. Charles Dowdy), a nurse, (deceased); Larry, who resides in Alexander Community; Brenda (Mrs. Danny Loftis) of Columbia, South Carolina and Richard, who resides in south Paragould. Luther Whitaker emigrated from Guntown, Lee County, Mississippi around 1920. Monra Dunnam's family was from Caldwell Community, which was on the north Craighead and south Greene County line near the Bono area. Monra and Luther met near Cardwell, Missouri and were married on November 14, 1931, at Leachville in Mississippi County, Arkansas.

Frank was born and raised on the Wright farm, barely a mile from where he and Bonnie currently live. His parents were Charlie Elmore Wright and Alma Culpepper Wright who were wed in Dunklin County, Missouri on January 6, 1940. His siblings include Ann Wright Dropiewski (deceased) who spent her adult life in the Livonia/Brighton, Michigan areas; Charlene, who married Bonnie's brother, Larry Whitaker; Larry Wright, who married June Ann Payne of Marmaduke and both teach school and reside in Mississippi County, Arkansas. Gary resides in Montgomery, Alabama and Roger, a dentist, who lives in Aberdeen, Mississippi.

Charlie's parents, Charlie L. Wright and Ollie

*The Charlie and Alma Wright Family from Spring Grove Community. Back row left to right: Roger, Ann, Frank, Gary and Larry. Front row left to right: Charlene, (parents) Alma and Charlie Wright.*

Lee (Bailey) Wright emigrated to Greene County from Hickman County, Kentucky shortly after 1900. Alma's parents, Jeff Thomas Culpepper and Annie Florence (Peterson) Culpepper also lived in the Spring Grove Community in Greene County for several years after retirement. They had spent several years in the Detroit, Michigan area, but were originally from Clay County, Arkansas.

Frank also has two aunts (sisters of Alma Culpepper Wright), Mrs. Tillman Hester (formerly Lowanda Culpepper) and Mrs. George Monazym (formerly Dorothy Culpepper), who reside in the Alexander Community in Greene County. Bonnie's Aunt Grace (sister to Monra Dunnam) and husband, Harry Gramling, reside near the Walcott Community. Bonnie's Uncle R. L. Dunnam resides in the Finch community.

The Wrights are descended from the Easts, the Dunns, and the Baileys, who entered early western Kentucky from Virginia and claimed it from the wilderness. The Culpeppers are descended from early stock who migrated from England via Virginia, North Carolina and Tennessee to Northeastern Arkansas.

Neither the Wrights nor the Whitakers entered Greene County until after the turn of the 1900 century, however, they have left a lasting impact. Their descendants are a living legacy and the Whitakers, Wrights, Noels, Dowdys, Hesters, Dunnams and related kin attest to the hardy stock of pioneers which emigrated from those foreign lands so many years ago and carved a wonderful life out of the many wildernesses throughout this great country which became the Greene Counties of today.

**WULFEKUHLER** – The Fred Wulfekuhler family acquired majority interest in *Daily Press*, Inc. in July 1959 from Ed White Jr., president and owner of the Ed White Jr. Shoe Company. The remaining stock was purchased in 1962.

Fred and Oleatha Wulfekuhler moved to Paragould on July 29, 1959, his 41st birthday, with four children:
1. Susan
2. Jan
3. Kurt
4. Gail
5. Kristin (Nov 21, 1961 Paragould).

Fred's father, Conrad Wilhelm Wulfekuhler, a wholesale grocer, came to the United States in 1893 from Bad Rothenfelde, Germany. His mother, Gertrude, was the daughter of Otto and Anna Schmeckel, a Leavenworth, KS, grocer and farm owner.

Oleatha' parents were Rev. Hally Trent Clark and Ethel Altic Clark, from Ottawa, KS. Rev. Clark was an American Baptist minister who served several churches in Kansas, including Leavenworth, where Fred and Oleatha met. He also served pastorates in Nebraska and Wyoming, closing his career in Fort Lupton, CO.

Wulfekuhler, a native of Leavenworth, came to Paragould from Hutchinson, KS, where he began his professional newspaper career following military service. His last service assignment was manager of Armed Forces Radio Station WXLO, also known as the "Voice of Shangri-La," during WWII. The station was located on the Aleutian Island, Shemya.

Wulfekuhler graduated from Wentworth Mili-

*Fred Wulfekuhler.*

tary Academy's junior college in 1939 and from the University of Missouri at Kansas City in 1942, with a degree in political science. His first job out of school was with Proctor and Gamble in the advertising department.

Wulfekuhler joined the staff of the *Hutchinson News-Herald*, later the *Hutchinson News*, as a reporter-photographer in June 1946, shortly after being released from the Army. He was named picture editor in 1949, Sunday editor in 1951 and managing editor in 1957.

While Wulfekuhler was in Hutchinson, the

*The Wulfekuhler Family: Front Row: Kristin, Jan, Oleatha, Fred, Susan, Gail and Kurt. Back Row: Spouses: Robert Lile, Robert W. Smalling, F. Hopkins Kleihauer, F. Mac Bellingrath, and Birgitta Gabel.*

publisher, John P. Harris, built the first FM station in Kansas and Wulfekuhler filled in as a play-by-play sport's announcer when needed. Later he helped get the state's first CBS television station, KTVH, in operation. He also taught tennis summer evenings for the Hutchinson Recreation Department and coached the Hutchinson High

School and Junior College tennis teams to State Championships. The Junior Chamber of Commerce also named him "Man of the Year" for spearheading a drive to get the American Red Cross chapter in local hands and away from the St. Louis hierarchy.

The Wulfekuhlers visited Paragould for the first time in June 1959, after learning from May Brothers, the nation's oldest newspaper broker, that *Daily Press*, Inc, was for sale. Following the trip, the Wulfekuhlers returned to Hutchinson and began plans to purchase the newspaper.

In 1959, the *Daily Press* was located on West Court, just west of the Union Planters (then Security) Bank building. The press was an eight-page flatbed, replaced in 1962 with a 16 page Twin Cox-O-Type, which could print 16 pages at a time. It was one of four in the United States. The old press was sold to the Dumas, AR Clarion.

In 1974, a new building was built on the northeast corner of Hunt and U.S. Highway 49. A 24 page Goss Community offset press was installed along with a typesetting computer system, among the firsts for a daily newspaper in Arkansas.

One of Wulfekuhler's first additions to the newspaper in 1959 was an editorial page and an affirmation that there would be "no sacred cows or preferential treatment in news reporting". Prominent citizens and personal friends would receive no favors. His journalistic philosophy was "the truth is our profession" and "Lord, let us be doers not merely complainers".

He lobbied successfully for a United Fund, now the Greene County Community Fund; with his friend Ted Rand of radio station KDRS. Their support of a city manager form of government didn't fare so well. He also wrote many editorials in support of a new state constitution, championed in the Arkansas legislature by freshman Rep. David Pryor of Camden and Sen. Virgil Butler of Batesville. A Constitutional Convention in 1978 drafted a new constitution, but voters turned it down in 1980.

The *Daily Press*, during the Wulfekuhler era, was considered one of the best small dailies in Arkansas and won many state and national awards for editorial excellence. The University of Missouri School of Journalism rated it as the best newspaper under 10,000 circulations in the United States.

During the 30 years of ownership, all of the Wulfekuhler children worked part-time at the paper, proofreading, reporting and using a camera. Susan served as managing editor from 1983 to shortly before the paper was sold. *Daily Press*, Inc. was sold to the Paxton Media Group of Paducah, KY in the fall of 1989.

The Wulfekuhlers were active members of First United Methodist Church from 1959 to 1992. Fred taught the Men's Bible Class until 1992 when he and Oleatha moved from Paragould. He served as church lay leader for 25 years and was a Certified Lay Speaker. He and Oleatha also served as the church's lay delegates to annual conference for 10 years.

Fred was an active Rotarian for 47 years, serving as president of the Paragould Club in 1971-72. He also was named a Paul Harris Fellow. He was an avid tennis player and taught many youngsters in Hutchinson and Paragould how to play. He coached the Hutchinson High and Hutchinson Junior College tennis teams to state championships and coached the Paragould High School tennis team when it won two state championships with son, Kurt, winning the singles' titles.

Fred received the President's Award from the Arkansas Associated Press Managing Editors in 1989 for "his outstanding contributions to Arkansas journalism." Susan, Wulfekuhler's daughter, who was twice past president of the Arkansas APME, presented the award.

Wulfekuhler exercised leadership in state and national newspaper organizations. He served as a board member of the Mid-South Press Institute for eight years, was a Southern Newspaper Association board member three years and president of the Arkansas Press Association in 1979 after 19 years on the board of directors. He was a member of the National Press Association, Arkansas Press Association, American Society of Newspaper Editors and National Newspaper Photographer's Association. He was named to Who's Who of American Colleges and Universities while at the University of Missouri, Kansas City.

Four of the Wulfekuhler children, Susan, Kurt, Gail and Kristin graduated from Hendrix College in Conway. Jan got her degree from Arkansas State University.

Susan married F. Hopkins Kleihauer, a Chicago native, whom she met at Hendrix. They live in Cottage Grove, OR. She is a free-lance journalist and contributing editor to *Earth Light* magazine, an environmental publication, and Hop is self-employed.

Jan is married to Dr. Robert W. Smalling, son of the late Sam Smalling, retired Paragould High School principal and his wife, Jerry. Smalling is a doctor of optometry and past president of the Arkansas Optometry Society. He served as president of the Southern Council of Optometry, headquartered in Atlanta, in 2000. The Smallings live in Warren, AR, where she teaches school. They have three children and four grandchildren.

Kurt and his wife, Birgitta Gabel, a native Californian, are both clinical psychologists and live in Albuquerque, NM. They have two children.

Gail married F. Mac Bellingrath, a native of Pine Bluff. He is president of AVA, a vending operation that covers several areas of the state. Gail is very active in religious and community affairs. They have two children.

Kristin married Dr. Robert Lile of Little Rock, whom she met at Hendrix. Robert is a radiologist. Kristin is an avid photographer. She and Robert are also active bicyclists. They live in Loveland, CO.

Fred and Oleatha moved to Hot Springs Village, AR in 1992, where they live at 21 Galeon Way, on Lake Balboa. They have seven grandchildren and four great grandchildren.

**YEARGAIN** – Several generations of Yeargains will be mentioned in this article. Much of the information has been handed down through several generations, census, obituaries, funeral and cemetery records, letters, scrapbooks, court houses, Bibles and Union Hill Church records. Baptist and Methodist religion have prevailed through the ages with Ministers in both backgrounds. Family incomes have included farming, merchants, railroad, school teachers, bankers, doctors, horse traders, post masters, dry cleaning, saw mill, photography, blacksmiths and sales.

Andrew Yeargain came from Whales in the early 1700s. He married Oney Bowles in 1755 in Virginia. Their 11 children were Andrew, John, Sammuel, Benjamin, Jarrett Fletcher, Edward, James, Devereaux, Bartlett, William and Sarah.

Andrew was very involved and instrumental in promoting Methodism. The first Methodist Chapel built in Virgina was named Yeargains's Chapel about 1770. In 1780, conference was held at Baltimore, we find Rev. Andrew pastor of the Yadkin Circuit. He and Oney moved to North Carolina. They lived with Devereaux in Greenville, South Carolina as their final resting place.

Jarrett married Amelia. Their children were Benjamin, Devereaux, Bartlett Wesley, Henry, Hilary, Chesly, Patterson, Charlotte and Sarah. Benjamin A's first son, John Wesley was born 1817, Orange County, North Carolina. Benjamin, in January 1820, Orange County, married Susannah Moore. The identified children are Amelia, Nancy, Thomas, Mary, Benjamin, Sarah, Chesley, and Patterson. John Wesley had half brothers and sisters according to a letter written by Mildred Yeargain Hicks in 1977, a granddaughter.

John Wesley Yeargain married 1840 in Carroll County, Tennessee, Elizabeth Fowler. Children were Nancy born 1842, Lacy born 1844 and married in 1857, Frank Schooley of Kinmundy, Illinois. Andred G. born 1847 and married 1869 in Tennessee, Sarah Clementine Barnes. A son, John William was born 1870. John (Talley John) married Ada Croco January 1900 in Greene County. Both and a son, Charlie, are buried at Gainesville Cemetery. Daughters Mrytle married Oll Hamilton, Maymie married Homer Haney, and Pearl married John Nowell. Pearl and John's children are Carolyn and Delbert, the only grandchildren of Toby John and Ada. Carolyn married Donald William in 1961. Their children are Mark and Scott. 1994 Carolyn married Kenneth Cox. They live in Sikeston, Missouri and have three grandchildren, April and Dustin William live in Sikeston and Laudou William lives in Farmington, Missouri. Delbert married Linda Ward in 1962. Daughters, Cindy and Debbie. Delbert lives in Fenton, Missouri. Grandchildren Megan and Heather Brown live in Fenton, Missouri. Brett Nowell, Brian, Stephanie and Patricia Key live in Paragould, Arkansas. In 1882 Andrew G. married Sarah Higgins in Greene County, Arkansas who was 17 years younger than he. Their children were Mary Elizabeth who married Beldon Jaminson. Mildred married Clyde Hicks, Amy married Sidney Wineland, Lena married C. L. Jones, Clara married Joe Lee, Calvin-Gladys White, Hazel Elmer Weatherford, and Agnes died young.

Mary Louise born 1853 married Parrish

*Betty, Mildred, Amy, Lena, Hazel, Clara, Andrew G. and Sarah Yeargains.*

Greene Wilson, 20 years her senior in Stoddard, County, Missouri, 1871. This writer has a copy of a letter Parrish wrote Mary from Little Rock, Arkansas in 1880s. Children were Ben, John, Will, Nannie, Bettie and Maggie.

Miranda born 1857 married Abram K. Brown in Stoddard County 1883. Their children were Artie, Robert, James Azro, George, Pearl, Opal and two deceased. Information on John Wesley's first marriage family from a letter Mildred Yeargains Hicks wrote 1977.

John Wesley married 1858 in Weakley County, Tennessee, Caroline Moore Gentry. They settled in Stoddard County 1859 and owned propery until 1881. Their children are Robert Alexander, John James, Jordan Grant married Patsy Pierce, Emily married Stonewall White, Azro married Effie Seamore, Boyd married Julia Valentine and Ona married Will Hewitt. By 1883 John and Amelia lived in Greene County. They and many of their children and grandchildren are buried at Gainesville, Linwood and Providence Cemeteries. Their heirs sold to St. Louis, from Mountain and Southern Railroad Company 40 acres from $100.00 in November 1898.

*Left to right: Maymie, Ada, Mrytle, Pearl and John Yeargain. Taken in 1920.*

Carol Yeargain Tomlinson, daughter of Calvin, visited Uncle John and Aunt Ada with Mildred Yeargain Hicks as a child. She played the family organ and watched Ada make jelly.

Carolyn Nowell Cox has a four patch quilt top that grandmother Ada helped with 1950.

Today many generations of Andrew and Oney live or have lived in Greene County and surrounding states. 10 generations have been covered in this article.

**YOUNG** – Joseph L. Young (1846 PA) was the oldest of six children of Josiah H. and Mary Ann (Ellis) Young. Their family moved several times during his childhood, they started in Pennsylvania then moved to Allegany, NY, then to Oxford, WI and on to Wright County, MO. This is where Joseph, a young man of 23 and a minister, met and married Barbara Calhoun on May 20, 1869. Barbara was the daughter of George Washington and Rebecca (Sanders) Calhoun.

Joseph, like his father Josiah, was always trying to improve life for his family and decided it was time to move on once again. Barbara, who was tired of moving around, refused to be uprooted again. Joseph being determined loaded up the covered wagon and the children and told her to climb onboard or be left behind. Barbara being a devoted wife and mother, of course, climbed on. They moved from Douglas County, Mo and settled in Greene County, AR in mid 1884.

*Alvin Wesley Young early 1900s*

Joseph and Barbara had seven children:
1. Hattie
2. Mary J.
3. Lovinia "Vernie"
4. Alvin Wesley
5. Jerry M.
6. Brantley Sigel "Sig"
7. Elsie

Hattie (about 1871) died as a small child before the family left Missouri. Mary J. (1872-1889) was married to William F. Walton. Mary and their first child died during childbirth. Later that same year Lovinia "Vernie" (Aug 11, 1874-Jan 15, 1933) was left to raise her siblings in 1889 when her parents both passed away. William F. Walton being a widower married Vernie on June 3, 1890 and helped her to raise her siblings. William and Vernie had two children together, Galena (1899-1995) married James Bartley and Venetta (1895-1923) married William T. Bradford.

Alvin Wesley Young (Oct 11, 1876-Nov 6, 1927) worked in the sawmill of George Louden. George and Alvin became good friends. After George died, Alvin still helped around the sawmill. George's wife Hana (Williams) was left to raise their children. Alvin watched George's daughter Leila Maude Louden grow into a lovely young woman. They were married on June 27,1900, he being 23 and she 15. Alvin and Leila had eight children:

*Brantley Sigel "Sig" Young delivering cotton to Peach Orchard to be processed thru the cotton gin, late 1930s.*

1. Arthur Joe (1901-1982) married (1) Flora Belle Rice (2) Yulla Bell Fosset
2. Edith Barbara (1904-1912)
3. Clyde (1909-1975)
4. Delphin Demas (1907-1963) married Lola Annadale Wheeler
5. Melvin Wesley (1909-1975) married Ruth Maynard
6. Mildred Gladis (1911) married Charles Newten Stanage,
7. Ester Mary (1920) married Clyde Stanage
8. Elmer Warren (1921) married (1) Ada Gaynell Jones (2) Geraldine Fosset.

Jerry M. Young, the fifth child of Joseph and Barbara, lived a short life from 1877-1896.

Brantley Sigel "Sig" Young (Nov 14, 1882-Aug 11, 1953) was named after his mom's brother Brantley Sigel Calhoun. Sig

*Elsie Young Forehand early 1900s*

stayed with his sister Vernie after husband William passed away and helped her to raise her two children. Sig worked in the local sawmill. When he was a young man one of the smoke stacks fell on him. He was very lucky to have survived this accident. He later met and married Lela Abby Maynard (Mar 1, 1953- Feb 14, 1978); Lela was the daughter of Samuel Benton and Eva Victoria (Foshee) Maynard. Sig also was a farmer. Sig and Lela had five children:
1. Hazel Aileen (1927) married Harrison Wagner
2. Carl Lavaughn (1929- 1975) married Elwanda Ola Mryle Talor
3. Evalene (1931) married (1) Don Byers (2) Authur Roberts
4. Floyd (1934) married (1) Mildred Torgerson (2) Connie Louise Tooley
5. Patsy Jane (1938) married Gerald Wayne Boyd.

Elsie (Sept 28, 1885-Oct 15, 1950) was the last child born to Joseph and Barbara Young. Elsie married William Allen Forehand in 1909. Elsie and William worked farming to raise their family. They had eight children:
1. Hubert (1909-1987) married Lorene Wilson
2. Herbert (1910-1977)
3. Helen (1913) married Harold Compton
4. Lola (1915) married (1) Chester Cottles (2) Elton Cottles
5. Wanda (1918-1961) married Charles Compton
6. Zipporah (1920-1997) married Leo Laymon
7. Farabelle (1924)
8. Richard (1926-1999) married Mary Lane.

Joseph L. Young died Oct 15, 1889 and his wife Barbara died May 2, 1889, they are both buried in Wise Cemetery, Greene County, AR. Our Young's were a strong and hard working bunch. Many of their descendants still live in or around Greene County. Some are in the farming business,

*Brantley Sigel "Sig" Young early 1900s*

business owners, own rental properties in Greene County and others of us come back often to visit our roots.

*Submitted by Connie L. Young*

**YOUNG** – Katie Elizabeth Young (April 23, 1850 near Louisville KY) moved to Arkansas when she was a girl of seven years old. She was one of the pioneer citizens of Greene County, AR.

Katie met and married Malachi C. Snowden in about 1869. They settled in Forrest City, AR. They had three children, Albert Sidney, Alice Amelia and Samuel Issac. A story told by her grandson, Samuel Maurice "Uncle Morris" Snowden. When Katie was eight months pregnant with his father, she saddled a horse and carried her two children, Albert and Alice in the front. She was on a mission of mercy as one of her neighbors was ill and needed her help. It was dusk and as they traveled the lane, there was a panther stalking her. She told the children to remain quiet and still and look straight forward. As the terrified travelers arrived at their destination there was great relief in all their hearts. This writer thought this showed great courage, kindness to her neighbors and a generous heart. The spirit and stuff our pioneer women were made of.

Malachi had been a Confederate soldier in Captain R. W. Pitman's Company, 13 Regiment, Tennessee from June 4, 1861 to May 6, 1865. Malachi died of yellow fever in November of 1879 at the age of 40, in Forrest City, AR. (Source: Mortality schedule of Arkansas 1880, they list all deaths six months prior to 1880).

In 1888 Katie married James H. Rowe, also of Greene County. He had been a Confederate soldier in Company D, Davie's Regiment, Arkansas Cavalry. He was honorably discharged May 10, 1865. This information is from her widow's application filed August 3, 1915 and allowed $100, beginning Aug 13, 1915. James died Dec 28, 1896.

They had one daughter Ethel Mae Rowe (June 22, 1889). Ethel never married and died in Paragould on June 16, 1959. She is buried in Linwood Cemetery.

*Katie Elizabeth Young Snowden-Rowe, 1849-1923.*

In 1900 Katie was living in Cache Township in Greene County, AR. The other members of her household at this time were:
1. Sam Snowden, son (1879)
2. Ethel Rowe, daughter (1889)
3. Malachi Snowden, grandson, his father being, Albert Sidney Snowden (1896)
4. Fannie Young, sister (1846 KY)

Katie, known as "Aunt Kate" was a member of the Baptist Church. Katie died Sunday, Feb 3, 1924. She and her husband James H. Rowe are buried in Fairview Cemetery, across the road from the Fairview Baptist Church.

Her obituary states that she was survived by two daughters, Mrs. D. H. Faulkner and Miss Ethel Row, two sons, Albert Sidney Snowden and Samuel Isaac Snowden, also her brother George Young who resides near Finch, Greene County, AR. Funeral services were conducted at Fairview Church, Rev. H. J. Henry officiating.

*Submitted by Evelyn Euritha Wagner*

# INDEX

## SYMBOLS

1979 GRAND OPENING OF ED ROLESON JR.'S NEW FACILITY 41
1983 CENTENNIAL PARAGOULD PARADE 41
200TH ANNIVERSARY OF THE DECLARATION OF INDEPENDENCE 11

## A

ABBOTT 62
ABELL 60, 210
ABNEY 62, 114, 286
ABSHER 159
ACTION 19
ACUFF 46, 140, 216, 255, 293, 298
ADAMS 13, 19, 20, 43, 87, 95, 96, 99, 115, 119, 134, 140, 141, 154, 160, 174, 187, 209, 232, 238, 247, 257, 261, 295, 309, 311, 315, 332, 335, 339, 340
ADAMS NURSERY AND LANDSCAPING 43
ADDISON 52, 256
ADEN 25
ADERHOLDT 243
ADKINS 220
AGEE 92, 109, 263
AHLF 13, 262
AINLEY 141, 259
AINSWORTH 199
AKERS 320
AKIN 157
ALBIN 308
ALBRIGHT 119, 233
ALDEN 308
ALEXANDER 36, 53, 95, 188
ALEXANDER SCHOOL 95
ALFANO 205
ALFORD 265
ALL SAINTS' EPISCOPAL CHURCH 64
ALLEMAN 149
ALLEN 24, 43, 72, 79, 141, 142, 144, 161, 195, 207, 209, 250, 333, 340
ALLEN ENGINEERING CORPORATION 43
ALLEY 93
ALLISON 154, 169, 188, 203, 264
ALLRED 142, 177
ALMOND 125, 302
ALPHIN 209
ALSEY 79
ALSTADT 151
ALTHOFF 287
ALVEY 60
AMATO 280
AMERICAN RAILCAR 43
AMERICAN STATE BANK 28
AMICK 330
AMORINE 76, 184, 214, 346
AMOS 119
ANDERS 163, 270, 271, 273
ANDERSON 13, 24, 72, 75, 79, 92, 109, 120, 141, 142, 143, 146, 150, 157, 193, 208, 209, 216, 245, 248, 274, 279, 288, 305, 315, 318, 332
ANDIS 80
ANDRE 11
ANDREW 361
ANDREWS 16, 178, 187, 195, 205, 249, 270, 273
ANDRIESSON 327
ANNICE 154
ANTHONY 18
APLIN 220
APPLEGATE 68, 90
ARANT 25, 57, 207
ARCHER 208, 218, 344
ARCHIBALD 107, 118
ARGALL 250
ARKANSAS METHODIST HOSPITAL 43
ARMSTEAD 180
ARMSTRONG 119, 176, 186, 287, 298
ARNETT 356
ARNOLD 17, 74, 111, 118, 120, 143, 198, 238, 247, 276, 282, 292, 329, 333, 337, 348, 353
ARRINGTON 97
ARTHUR 112, 319
ASCHENBACH 216
ASHBY 74, 177, 288
ASHCRAFT 72, 198
ASHFORD 316
ASKINS 194, 198
ASWAD 272
ATCHESON 349
ATCHISON 13, 239, 256, 260
ATESBURY 250
ATKINS 47, 112, 125, 143, 144, 305
ATKINSON 200, 201
ATTEBERRY 258
ATWOOD 77, 173
AULD 169
AUSTIN 13, 15, 71, 111, 115, 116, 162, 179, 183, 213, 251, 255, 281, 321
AUTLER 194
AUTREY 16, 68, 100
AUTRY 23, 168, 333
AYERS 172, 290

## B

BABER 193
BACHAR 336
BAGUS 188
BAILEY 72, 77, 144, 145, 195, 265, 275, 360
BAIN 72, 75
BAINE 222, 238
BAINS 79
BAIR 294
BAIRD 46, 177, 281
BAKER 13, 216, 217, 245, 274, 277, 306, 307, 308, 323, 332
BALCOM 74
BALDRIDGE 86, 118, 284
BALDWIN 87
BALK 159
BALL 111, 112, 209, 270, 273
BALLARD 145, 322, 323
BALLINGER 288
BALTERRIA 333
BALWIN 203
BANDFIELD 97
BANDY 145, 264, 288
BANGESTER 88
BANK OF PARAGOULD 29
BANKS 255
BARBER 71, 253
BARD METHODIST CHURCH 83
BARD SCHOOL 95
BAREMORE 223
BARFIELD 140, 222
BARGER 87, 88, 145, 146, 273
BARHAM 250
BARKER 100, 107, 113, 114, 185, 286, 333, 335
BARKLEY 201, 337
BARKSDALE 47, 240
BARLOW 322
BARNES 152, 162, 281, 318, 322, 334, 342, 361
BARNETT 13, 141, 340
BARNHART 53, 166
BARNHILL 44, 68, 112, 116, 118, 146, 147, 148, 192, 209, 239, 250, 329, 355
BARR 147, 148, 263, 272, 347, 359
BARRETT 151, 193, 247, 248
BARRINGER 249
BARRON 13, 148, 298, 299, 349
BARROW 95, 122, 162, 165, 230
BARRY 125, 334
BARRY - KITCHENS HOME 125, 126
BARTHOLDI 12
BARTLETT 361
BARTLEY 362
BARTON 20, 100, 203, 318
BARTON SCHOOL 98
BASINGER 357
BASKINS 225
BASS 18, 100, 148, 168, 184, 233, 286, 307, 308
BATEMAN 95
BATES 257, 340
BATEY 16, 110, 207, 233, 268, 273
BATTEN 161
BATTENFIELD 237, 272
BATTEY 95
BATTLE 313
BATTLES 339
BATTON 118
BATY 13
BAUERS 304
BAUGH 97, 99, 245
BAURLE 205
BAYLESS 337
BAZZELL 177
BEACHER 263
BEAGLES 307
BEAL 141
BEALL 140, 141, 340
BEAN 148, 149, 154, 220, 306
BEANE 239, 251
BEARD 253, 257, 292, 303
BEARDEN 44, 269, 298
BEASLEY 90, 121, 195, 292, 323
BEASLY 155
BEATON 87, 97, 107, 121, 123, 149, 178, 329
BEATY 307
BEAUCHAMP 280
BEAUREGARD 193
BEAVER 13, 292
BEAVERT 309
BEBOUT 150
BECH 109
BECHLER 341
BECHTEL 277
BECK 87, 88, 174, 248, 341
BECKER 113, 114, 211, 224, 277
BECKHAM 289
BECKWITH 100
BEDFORD 204, 326
BEDNAR 151
BEECH GROVE 15
BEECH GROVE HIGH SCHOOL 95
BEECH GROVE SCHOOL 95, 96
BEECH GROVE UNITED METHODIST CHURCH 65
BEELER 254
BEETNER 344
BEISEL 119, 128
BEISING 149, 170
BELANGER 268
BELIEU 354
BELIEW 15, 338
BELIEW HILL 15
BELK 198
BELL 68, 72, 125, 283, 288
BELL - HALE HOME 125, 126
BELLINGRATH 361
BENBROOK 72, 75, 79
BENHAM 222
BENNER 257
BENNETT 111, 112, 121, 180, 186, 198, 305, 330
BENOIT 90
BENSKIN 323
BENSON 317, 329, 337
BENTLEY 298, 299, 309
BENTON 88, 109, 113, 134
BERDEN 192
BERGEN 46
BERGEY 187
BERKELEY 160, 161
BERNAL 333
BERRY 74, 87, 99, 245, 260
BERRYHILL 95
BERTCHIT 114
BERTIG 32, 44, 59, 131, 144, 149, 150
BETTIS 140
BETTS 97
BEVILL 196, 197
BICKLEY 86
BIG ROCK 23
BIG ROCKS 23
BIGGS 16, 20, 186, 209, 237, 281, 345
BILES 181
BILL 120, 304
BILLINGSLEY 307
BILLS 80, 93, 287
BINGHAM 144
BIRD 140, 283
BIRDWELL 156, 157
BIRMINGHAM 18, 149
BISE 306
BISHOP 13, 19, 21, 49, 95, 118, 135
BIVENS 56
BIVINS 56
BLACK 166, 228
BLACKBURN 95
BLACKFORD 83, 336
BLACKSHEAR 144, 149, 150
BLACKSHER 62
BLACKWOOD 20, 22, 87, 95, 100, 103, 108, 110, 112, 121, 154, 170, 189, 213, 214, 231, 295, 337
BLAGG 13
BLAIR 161, 216, 275, 334
BLAKE 119, 186
BLAKEWOOD 333
BLALOCK 44, 92, 102, 108, 110, 150, 179, 180, 252, 303, 331
BLAND 4, 5, 7, 24, 31, 44, 131, 134, 146, 150, 151, 168, 170, 175, 193, 199, 247, 250, 287, 288, 292, 295, 303, 327, 350
BLANKENSHIP 13, 54, 142, 168, 177, 245, 288
BLANTON 108
BLEIER 239
BLEVINS 168, 180, 331
BLISS 82
BLOCK 25, 32, 34, 44, 45, 75, 125, 128, 151, 152, 244, 305
BLOON 151
BLOSSOM 86, 125
BLOSSOM - MACK HOME 125, 126
BLOUNT 100
BLUCKER 174
BLUE 71, 74, 80
BLUE CANE SCHOOL 97
BLYTHE 202, 281
BO(W)LING 140
BOAZ 315
BOBBIE HOUSTON'S CAFÉ 49
BOBBIT 95, 97, 112, 307, 308
BOBBITT 187, 219, 246, 337
BOBO 112, 122, 152, 153, 154, 178, 225, 335
BOBO SCHOOL 95, 96
BOCKMAN 311
BODE 111, 223
BOGAN 47, 119, 165, 358

BOGARD 254
BOGGAN 358
BOGGS 52, 131, 210
BOGNER 341
BOHANING 153
BOHANNAN 21
BOHANNING 153
BOHANNON 68
BOLDING 206
BOLICK 252, 341
BOLIN 228
BOLING 66, 88, 112, 128, 187
BOLLING 296
BOLLINGER 213
BOLTON 223
BOMAR 153, 154, 204, 215
BOND 21, 97, 100, 107, 119, 323, 337
BONDS 13, 281
BONE 102, 104, 146, 165, 237, 296
BONHAM 49
BONHAN 148
BONNER 232
BOON 11, 75
BOONE 13, 21, 62, 72, 79, 99, 107, 118, 119, 160, 179, 182, 183, 240, 295, 313, 348, 350
BOOTEN 99
BOOTH 90, 280
BOOZER 154, 184, 223, 298, 315, 358
BORING 333
BOROVSKY 177
BORROW 22
BOSQUE 209
BOSTIC 105
BOSTON 216
BOTTOM 111, 112
BOUCHER 267
BOUDY 258
BOULDIN 25, 52
BOULTON 52
BOUNDS 98
BOWDEN 35, 36, 100
BOWEN 79
BOWERS 33, 44, 59, 105, 209, 329
BOWLES 318, 361
BOWLIN 13, 16, 78, 154, 186, 232, 301, 349, 350
BOWLING 322
BOWMAN 168, 178, 213
BOWSER 340
BOX 332
BOYD 23, 65, 83, 95, 99, 100, 154, 155, 157, 170, 174, 196, 252, 259, 282, 308, 317, 349, 362
BOZARTH 52
BOZZARD 217
BRAASCH 253
BRACKEN 103, 245, 288
BRACKENRIDGE 281

BRADBURN 95
BRADDOCK 150, 151
BRADEN 107, 244, 318
BRADFORD 189, 319, 321, 362
BRADLEY 350
BRADLY 97
BRADSHAW 199
BRADSHER 7, 52, 107, 128, 266, 308, 329, 354
BRADY 318, 323
BRAHAM 325, 326
BRAMLETT 100, 113, 229
BRANCH 11, 25, 96, 108, 118, 125, 155, 178, 180, 250, 257, 266, 351, 352, 353
BRANCH - WRAPE HOME 125, 126
BRAND 172, 336, 343
BRANDON 83, 95, 112, 155, 156, 239
BRANNON 213, 214, 299
BRANOM 14
BRASHEARS 198, 265, 304, 346
BRASHER 156, 194, 340
BRASHERS 198, 265
BRASS 141
BRASWELL 318
BRATTON 16
BRAUN 304, 330
BRAY 148, 212, 346, 347
BRAZIL 51, 131, 156, 244
BREAZEALE 175
BRECHER 304
BRECKENRIDGE 15, 24, 65, 95, 99, 145, 198, 270, 271, 272, 315, 350, 351, 354
BRECKINRIDGE 250
BREKENRIDGE 198
BRENGARD 61, 303, 318
BRENNEISE 244
BRENNEISEN 131, 244, 250
BRENT 250
BRENTLY 312
BRENTS 23, 214, 231
BREWER 32, 76, 97, 107, 120, 148, 156, 157, 178, 278, 319, 329, 352, 353, 354
BREWINGTON 117, 120, 323
BRICKA 322
BRICKELL 68
BRIDGE 176
BRIDGES 13, 53, 68, 108, 118, 119, 157, 158, 165, 166, 245, 246, 285
BRIGGS 119, 250
BRIGHT 288

BRIGHTON SCHOOL 96, 97
BRINKLEY 167, 225, 288, 317
BRINTON 45, 224
BRITTON 79
BROADAWAY 35, 36
BROCK 233, 333
BROCKETT 179
BROGDEN 318, 321
BROILES 76
BRONSON 104
BROOKBANK 241
BROOKFIELD 10, 158, 159, 182, 344
BROOKS 13, 80, 86, 107, 141, 159, 221, 250, 261, 311, 331
BROOMS 344
BROUGHTON 348
BROWN 13, 25, 35, 36, 95, 107, 118, 120, 140, 159, 160, 168, 181, 185, 194, 209, 210, 211, 215, 218, 223, 226, 234, 240, 245, 259, 272, 274, 275, 282, 343, 356, 357, 361
BROWNE 248
BROWNING 13, 53, 159, 160, 161, 249
BROWNS CHAPEL BAPTIST CHURCH 66
BROWN'S CHAPEL SCHOOL 96, 98
BROYLES 128
BRUCE 13, 176, 221, 333
BRUE 44
BRUMLY 101
BRUMMET 321
BRUMMETT 92, 109
BRUNE 239
BRUNNER 76
BRUSHY RIDGE SCHOOL 96, 99
BRUSNER 248
BRUST 322, 324
BRYAN TOWNSHIP 20
BRYANT 6, 7, 37, 90, 140, 161, 162, 196, 222, 223, 227, 230, 233, 237, 265
BRYMER 243
BRYSON 162, 254, 255
BUCHANAN 19, 99, 100, 101, 107, 115, 116, 158, 176, 219, 317
BUCHHOLZ 240
BUCHMAN 53, 54, 209
BUCK 49, 191
BUCKANAN 99
BUEHLING 301
BUELL 337
BULAR 329
BULLIN 109, 181

BULLINGER 61
BULLINGTON 164, 271
BULLOCK 188
BUMPERS 222
BUNCH 122, 168
BURCH 158
BUREN 359
BURFOOT 154
BURFORD 331
BURGESS 163, 171, 175, 287, 333, 347
BURKE 287
BURKEEN 163, 164, 210, 270, 317, 320
BURKETT 252
BURMINGHAM 318
BURNER 278
BURNETT 151
BURNHAM 72
BURNS 97, 287, 288, 322
BURR 249
BURRIS 278
BURROUGHS 107, 163, 174, 321, 324, 325, 326
BURROW 56, 97, 318
BURTON 20, 49, 71, 75, 92, 109, 155, 176, 221, 339, 355
BUSBY 5, 7, 48, 56, 104, 140, 147, 148, 163, 164, 244, 270, 271, 281, 296, 320
BUSH 349
BUSHAND 309
BUSSICK 352
BUTLER 13, 21, 24, 61, 87, 100, 119, 157, 164, 247, 248, 252, 253, 266, 271, 272, 282, 303, 354, 361
BYCHETT 250
BYERS 25, 362
BYRD 148, 164, 212, 236, 268, 269, 294
BYRN 140
BYRON 206

C

CABRERA 74
CACHE 20
CACHE BOTTOMS 20, 24
CACHE RIVER 20
CACHE TOWNSHIP 20
CADENHEAD 164, 165, 180, 237
CAGLE 204
CAIN 262
CAINS 207
CAIRS 56
CALDWELL 97, 99, 111, 297, 298, 310, 311
CALDWELL CHAPEL SCHOOL 97, 99
CALEEL 326

CALHOUN 362
CALLAWAY 335
CALVERT 7, 89, 95, 250
CALVIN 131
CAMBELL 105
CAMMON 154, 236
CAMP 119, 153, 249
CAMP GROUND UNITED METHODIST CHURCH 67
CAMPBELL 22, 53, 74, 100, 134, 158, 159, 164, 165, 183, 245, 246, 270, 279, 284, 288, 295, 304, 343, 344, 345, 349
CAMPGROUND SCHOOL 91
CAMREN 84
CANDLESS 341
CANNON 276, 344
CANTRELL 206
CANTWELL 144
CANZADA 335
CAPPS 14, 51, 182, 183, 184
CAPTON 308
CAR 333
CARAGHAN 334
CARDIN 324
CARDWELL 247, 256
CAREY 156
CARLILE 74
CARLSON 186
CARLTON 355
CARMACK 19, 95
CARMICHAEL 180
CARMIKLE 105
CARNEY 122
CAROTHERS 180
CARPENTER 72, 108, 154, 165, 166, 220, 257, 277, 343
CARR 87, 107, 207, 209, 252, 267
CARRAWAY 155
CARRIER 308
CARRIGAN 321
CARROLL 60, 166
CARRUTHERS 180
CARSON 147, 148
CARTER 74, 80, 93, 105, 111, 114, 151, 163, 250, 251, 262, 274, 318, 334, 355
CARTWRIGHT 296
CARVELL 219
CARVER 95
CARY 157
CASE 25, 288, 333
CASEBOLT 56
CASEY 95, 218, 301
CASH 280
CASHON 247, 248
CASTEEL 205, 216, 217
CASTLE 221
CASTLEBERRY 72, 75, 79, 251, 287
CASTON 249
CATE 142

CATES 151, 259
CATHEY 13, 20, 34, 35, 44, 59, 87, 95, 97, 99, 140, 159, 175, 257
CATSOULIS 185
CATWALK 16
CECIL 206
CEDAR HILL 15
CELENSKY 306
CENTER HILL 15
CENTER HILL CHURCH OF CHRIST 80
CERSTVIK 177
CHADWICK 16, 270
CHAFFIN 199
CHAMBERLIN 96, 223
CHAMBERS 352
CHAMP 260
CHANCE 334
CHANDLER 114, 142, 163, 171, 243, 321, 323, 326
CHANEY 152
CHAPLAIN 75
CHAPMAN 60, 99, 262, 298
CHAPPEL 323
CHARLES 100
CHASE 174
CHEATHAM 207
CHERRY 72, 75, 79, 151, 198, 222
CHESSER 25, 357
CHESTNUT 13, 324
CHILD ART STUDIO 45
CHILDERS 13, 18, 111, 166, 167, 176, 201, 298, 300
CHILDRESS 25, 228, 337, 349
CHILDS 74
CHILES 256
CHILTON 281
CHITWOOD 13
CHRIST UNITED METHODIST CHURCH 83
CHUNN 57, 58, 167, 293, 319
CHURCH 174, 282
CHURCHILL 277
CISSELL 170
CITY BARBER SHOP 45
CITY LIGHT AND WATER 30
CLARDY 97
CLARIDA 97
CLARK 13, 16, 24, 49, 52, 54, 83, 86, 105, 107, 137, 145, 148, 155, 158, 167, 168, 169, 170, 172, 174, 176, 180, 184, 188, 192, 194, 225, 228, 235, 248, 249, 250, 259, 260, 262, 268, 271, 272, 276, 280, 285, 288, 290, 291, 295, 315, 330, 344,

360
**CLARKE** 180, 250
**CLARK'S CHAPEL SCHOOL** 99, 100
**CLAY** 160
**CLAYBOURNE** 329
**CLAYBROOK** 68
**CLAYPOLE** 207
**CLAYTON** 5, 13, 52, 60, 78, 90, 99, 149, 170, 207, 257
**CLEABORN** 232
**CLEAVELAND** 349
**CLEMENS** 208
**CLEMENT** 208, 209, 213, 278
**CLEMENTS** 154, 170, 171, 177, 213, 229, 232, 233, 247, 291
**CLEMETS** 90
**CLEVELAND** 13, 171, 298
**CLIFFORD** 23, 171, 172, 197
**CLIFTON** 6, 102, 104, 105, 172, 236, 252, 265, 333, 334, 344
**CLINE** 76, 121, 172, 178, 184, 200, 213, 231, 233, 250, 316, 321
**CLINES** 177
**CLINTON** 234, 284
**CLOPTON** 21, 119
**CLOWER** 93
**CLUBB** 77
**CLUCK** 327
**CLYNE** 176, 251
**COATES** 34, 60, 165, 175
**COBAL** 143
**COBB** 13, 202, 238, 260, 276
**COBBS** 349
**COBLE** 276
**COBURN** 349, 358
**COCHRAN** 301
**COCHRANE** 224
**COCKES** 13
**CODDRINGTON** 161
**CODY** 53
**COE** 176
**COFFEE** 232, 337
**COFFEL** 292
**COFFEY** 326
**COFFMAN** 15, 16, 175, 176, 198, 251, 292
**COFFMAN COMMUNITY** 16
**COGGINS** 356
**COLBATH** 172
**COLBERT** 35, 36, 148
**COLE** 17, 59, 60, 97, 99, 107, 113, 142, 162, 165, 173, 174, 186, 194, 221, 243, 245, 274, 283, 284, 318, 321, 323, 326, 336, 347
**COLEMAN** 99, 111, 144, 201, 239, 340

**COLLAR** 51, 174, 299
**COLLEY** 71, 206, 209
**COLLIER** 13, 88, 174, 175, 196, 250, 254
**COLLING** 196
**COLLINS** 22, 44, 46, 59, 151, 175, 205, 206, 275, 292, 333
**COLLINS THEATRE** 46
**COLMER** 185
**COLMORE** 251
**COLN** 90
**COMBS** 198
**COMMISSARY** 16
**COMMISSARY COMMUNITY** 16
**COMMISSARY SCHOOL** 99, 100
**COMPTON** 197, 362
**CONDRY** 157
**CONE** 17, 18, 169
**CONGER** 86
**CONGLETON** 216, 217
**CONKLIN** 315
**CONNELL** 163, 354
**CONNELLY** 146
**CONNELLY SCHOOL** 99, 101
**CONNER** 71, 210, 323
**CONRAD** 288
**CONSTABLE** 161
**CONWAY** 325
**CONYERS** 83
**COOK** 13, 18, 36, 52, 70, 89, 90, 99, 167, 175, 176, 206, 209, 217, 246, 247, 251, 267, 276, 294, 304, 307, 308, 315, 350
**COOL** 199
**COOPER** 13, 75, 80, 88, 97, 102, 107, 116, 121, 140, 161, 176, 177, 250, 251, 252, 253, 296, 298, 332, 333, 348, 356
**COOPER SCHOOL** 100, 101
**COPELAND** 56, 84, 104, 208
**CORBETT** 166
**CORBIN** 283
**CORBY** 333
**CORDER** 303
**CORGAN** 327
**CORINTH CHURCH** 85
**CORLEY** 199
**CORNER CAFÉ** 46
**CORNISH** 141, 295
**CORNWALLIS** 10, 11
**CORZINE** 251
**COSSEY** 142, 177
**COSTEN** 13
**COTHERN** 13, 76, 83, 95, 112, 230, 317
**COTHREN** 20, 87, 122, 165, 177, 186, 213, 292, 310

**COTTLES** 362
**COTTON** 59, 92, 250
**COTTON BELT SCHOOL** 100, 101, 102
**COUCH** 291
**COUNTS** 168, 213, 344
**COURTNEY** 78, 165
**COUSAR** 201
**COVINGTON** 176, 248, 338
**COWAN** 327
**COWDEN** 288
**COWELL** 277
**COWEN** 140, 166
**COX** 44, 48, 50, 75, 80, 89, 99, 106, 107, 116, 118, 119, 131, 153, 177, 178, 179, 201, 238, 241, 246, 254, 257, 259, 261, 262, 273, 278, 283, 311, 313, 316, 335, 342, 347, 361, 362
**COY** 25, 186
**COZART** 179, 222, 273
**CRABTREE** 209
**CRAFT** 13, 176
**CRAFTON** 88, 120, 145
**CRAIG** 15, 65, 112, 178, 245, 261, 281
**CRANE** 264, 349
**CRAVEN** 15
**CRAVER** 49, 224
**CRAWFORD** 13, 128, 150, 169, 179, 180, 216, 250
**CRAWLEY** 182
**CREEL** 301
**CREMEENS** 80
**CRENSHAW** 86
**CREWS** 44, 161, 354
**CRIBBS** 86, 209, 280
**CRICK** 231
**CRIDER** 165
**CRISP** 84
**CRITES** 235
**CRITZ** 144
**CROCE** 180
**CROCKER** 81, 315, 353
**CROCKETT** 116, 161, 165, 180, 188, 261, 338, 339
**CROCO** 361
**CROFFARD** 252
**CROFT** 22, 100, 101, 180, 181, 207, 220, 237, 315, 317
**CROFT COLLEGE** 93, 101
**CROFT SCHOOL** 100, 102
**CROLEY** 182
**CROLLEY** 182
**CRONAN** 324
**CROSS** 153, 207, 212, 274, 275
**CROSS ROADS SCHOOL** 101, 103

**CROSSNO** 83, 87, 217
**CROTTS** 111
**CROUCH** 259
**CROW** 13, 195, 196, 284
**CROWDER** 238
**CROWELL** 145, 181, 246
**CROWLEY** 10, 15, 22, 23, 24, 71, 76, 102, 121, 159, 177, 180, 181, 182, 183, 184, 214, 215, 219, 230, 231, 237, 238, 251, 252, 267, 284, 306, 317, 338, 341, 357
**CROWLEY'S RIDGE** 23
**CROWLEY'S RIDGE ACADEMY** 101, 104
**CROWLEY'S RIDGE COLLEGE** 93
**CROWLEY'S RIDGE STATE PARK** 10, 23
**CRUM** 123
**CRUSE** 119, 224, 297, 298, 358
**CRUTCHFIELD** 46
**CUDD** 107, 354
**CULBERTSON** 269
**CULLEN** 97, 228
**CULLEY** 228
**CULLINS** 190
**CULP** 265, 288
**CULPEPPER** 360
**CULVER** 359
**CUMMINGS** 316
**CUMMINS** 110
**CUNNINGHAM** 24, 25, 49, 100, 102, 145, 180, 184, 187, 261, 328
**CUPP** 16, 20, 83, 84, 88, 122, 140, 154, 160, 184, 185, 186, 203, 219, 232, 237, 272, 288, 342
**CUPPLES** 13, 86, 120
**CURETON** 208
**CURRY** 161, 313, 335, 356
**CURSE** 262
**CURTIS** 288
**CUSHMAN** 334
**CUTHBERTSON** 194

**D**

**DABBS** 198
**DACUS** 20, 28, 87, 97, 117, 121, 154, 186, 187, 221, 230, 232, 247, 251, 276, 301, 305, 355
**DAGGETT** 336
**DAHLING** 192
**DAHLQUIST** 290
**DAILY** 254
**DALTON** 103, 268, 339

**DAMERON** 160
**DAMMANN** 304
**DANFORD** 335
**DANIEL** 261, 301
**DANIEL(S)** 140
**DANIELS** 25, 174, 233, 333, 338
**DANNER** 317
**DANTIN** 204
**DARELS** 116
**DARR** 176, 243, 292
**DAUGHHETEE** 46, 210, 272
**DAUGHTREY** 313
**DAULTON** 225
**DAVENPORT** 148, 187, 332
**DAVID** 340
**DAVIDSON** 24, 95, 110, 114, 187, 188, 194, 258, 259, 316, 328, 332
**DAVIES** 13, 184, 187, 190, 197, 344
**DAVIS** 15, 70, 95, 104, 160, 168, 172, 176, 177, 179, 186, 188, 189, 192, 196, 199, 220, 221, 227, 232, 234, 243, 245, 253, 272, 275, 293, 299, 300, 318, 321, 330, 338, 343, 344, 349, 354
**DAWSON** 176, 283
**DAY** 99, 110, 189, 262, 309
**DE BON** 146
**DE FAUSIDE** 203
**DE LA PLAINE** 16
**DE LURYEA** 175
**DEA** 171
**DEAKIN** 131
**DEAN** 152, 296
**DEARIN** 333
**DEARING** 177
**DEASON** 14, 23, 260
**DEBAUN** 79
**DEBOARD** 23
**DEBOE** 13
**DEBOIS** 79
**DEBOLT** 243
**DEBONS** 119, 189
**DECK** 192
**DECKARD** 176
**DECORATION DAY** 6
**DEHART** 99, 198, 270
**DELAPLAINE** 16, 17
**DELAPLAINE BAPTIST CHURCH** 80
**DELK** 323
**DELURYEA** 53
**DEMENT** 221
**DEMOSS** 19
**DENBOW** 252
**DENHAM** 71, 107, 203
**DENMAN SCHOOL** 101, 103
**DENMON** 333
**DENNING** 290
**DENNIS** 20, 117, 154,

184, 185, 190, 230, 257, 295, 301, 350
**DENNISANE** 350
**DENTON** 151
**DEPEW** 13
**DEPRIEST** 25
**DEROE** 61
**DESMOND** 257
**DESPAIN** 90
**DETRICH** 121
**DEVANE** 81
**DEVERS** 313
**DEVOLL** 229, 251
**DEVORE** 105, 344
**DIAL** 190, 196, 261
**DIAMOND** 337
**DICKENSON** 16, 95
**DICKERSON** 278, 316
**DICKEY** 61, 68, 251
**DICKINSON** 25, 250, 270
**DICKMAN** 287
**DICKSON** 47, 97, 140, 192
**DICKSON MEMORIAL HOSPITAL** 47
**DICKY** 324
**DIFFEY** 264
**DIGGS** 13, 14, 25, 78, 112, 118, 155, 169, 190, 191, 192, 234, 235, 240, 253, 261, 267, 283, 285, 350
**DILES** 291
**DILLIN** 264
**DILLINGHAM** 112
**DILLMAN** 47, 192, 340
**DILLON** 72, 140
**DILLS** 53
**DINWIDDIE** 167
**DINWOOD** 167
**DISTRETTI** 186
**DIXIE SCHOOL** 113
**DIXON** 13, 14, 61, 140, 250
**DODD** 107, 212, 248, 264, 277, 281
**DODDS** 192, 193, 247, 350
**DODGE** 92, 109, 146, 163, 193, 345
**DODSON** 337
**DOERFUL** 304
**DOGGETT** 266
**DOHOGNE** 61
**DOLLAR** 13, 269, 304, 316
**DOLLARS** 25
**DOLLINS** 19, 47, 107, 119, 193, 216, 316
**DOLLINS FURNITURE** 47
**DOLLISON** 206
**DON PERKEY'S SHOES** 53
**DONAGHEY** 189
**DONALD** 150
**DONALDSON** 224, 244, 249, 250
**DONAVAN** 261

DONOVAN 264
DOOLEY 120, 235
DORSEY 147
DORTCH 25, 84, 118, 193, 194, 234, 252, 266, 287, 319, 342
DORTH 234
DOUGHTY 171, 180, 333
DOUGLAS 71, 211
DOVER 15, 16, 70, 100, 116, 119, 120, 149, 154, 157, 158, 241, 242, 257, 284, 285, 293, 321, 350
DOWDY 13, 123, 189, 335, 338, 360
DOWELL 61, 89
DOWLER 24, 194, 308
DOWNS 105, 121, 145, 270, 297
DOYLE 154
DOYNE 250
DR. PEPPER BOTTLING CO. 31
DRAFFEN 331
DRAKE 144
DRANE 267
DRAPER 229
DREMAN 90
DRILLING 158
DRISKEL 99
DRISKELL 72
DRITTLES 233
DROPE 338
DROPIEWSKI 360
DRUMMOND 246
DUBOIS 72, 75
DUBUIS 189
DUDLEY 28
DUFF 343
DUFFEL 268
DUFFELL 83
DUFORD 356
DUHIGG 179
DUKE 160
DUKES 164
DULANEY 265, 355
DUNAVANT 248
DUNBAR 339
DUNCAN 84, 142, 161, 263, 269
DUNIGAN 114
DUNLAP 345
DUNN 194, 215, 323, 330, 360
DUNNAM 96, 97, 99, 360
DUNNING 346, 347
DUPLER 306
DURHAM 257
DUTCH 344
DYER 88, 146, 176, 279

E

EAGAN 57
EAGLE 123
EAKER 13, 24, 52, 195, 327, 328
EAKERS 128
EARLE 140
EARNHEART 233
EARP 24
EASON 174, 239
EAST SIDE BAPTIST CHURCH 81
EASTEP 149, 274, 329
EASTER 13, 307, 308, 318
EASTMAN 145
EAYSON 154
ED ROLESON JR., INC. 41
EDGAR 330
EDGIN 281
EDISON 75
EDMINSTON 294
EDMISTON 140, 293
EDMONDS 68, 301
EDRINGTON 154, 195, 237, 344
EDWARD 196
EDWARDS 18, 75, 97, 99, 105, 112, 140, 154, 176, 186, 187, 202, 208, 222, 233, 237, 238, 288, 296, 308, 309, 315, 321, 337, 349, 351, 352
EIGER 54
EISENHOWER 221, 292
ELBERT 151
ELDER 140
ELDRIDGE 191
ELENANDER 114
ELKINS 199, 268, 269, 300
ELLEDGE 209
ELLINGRON 196
ELLINGTON 18, 83, 95, 99, 100, 110, 128, 161, 162, 167, 188, 190, 196, 223, 229, 251, 292, 318, 336
ELLINOR 162
ELLIOT 154
ELLIOTT 251, 286
ELLIS 44, 97, 171, 195, 196, 209, 279, 280, 298, 325, 362
ELMORE 46, 95, 155, 159, 276, 337, 359
ELROD 236
EMERSON 37, 349
EMMER 72
EMMERT 321
EMMONS 87, 88, 109
EMORINE 237
EMPFIELD 196
EMPFIELDS 197
EMRAH 75, 79
EMRICH 247
ENGLAND 313
ENGLERT 174
ENSOR 119
EPHRUSSI 291
EPSABA 17
EPSABA COMMUNITY 17
EPSABA SCHOOL 92
ERNEST 284
ERNST 165
ERWIN 97, 146, 265
ESINGER 23
ESPER 324, 326
ESTES 20, 84
ETHERIDGE 250
EUBANK 268
EUBANKS 13, 74, 87, 111, 140, 146, 174, 197, 198, 206, 210, 215, 217, 226, 229, 237, 238, 251, 268, 270, 272, 282, 290
EUDALY 249, 250
EUGENE 121
EVANS 14, 51, 97, 99, 107, 163, 198, 199, 265, 277, 293, 296, 313, 325, 333, 348, 356, 357, 358
EVELAND 103, 296
EVENING SHADE SCHOOL 101, 104
EVENING STAR SCHOOL 105
EVETT 326, 344
EVEY 340

F

FAGG 123
FAHR 13, 95, 199, 277
FAIRCHILD 144
FAISON 250
FALLON 140
FANNING 207
FARLEY 16, 99, 102, 104, 116, 199, 200, 231, 278, 321, 347
FARMER 13, 198, 358
FARRAR 87, 121, 167, 200, 201, 314, 328
FARREL 97
FARRELL 68, 78, 201, 202, 206, 358
FARRIS 144
FARROW 250
FARTHING 294
FAUBUS 93
FAUGHN 195
FAUGHT 122
FAULKNER 13, 25, 83, 97, 100, 102, 105, 112, 113, 152, 154, 156, 165, 185, 202, 237, 250, 303, 321, 349, 363
FAUSTENIA'S 47
FEAR 221
FEARS 162, 177, 208, 270, 334
FELKINS 323
FELTY 83, 202, 203, 278, 299
FERGUSON 153, 154, 245, 256, 284, 359
FERRELL 80, 103, 287, 321
FICKEN 218
FIELD 307
FIELDER 18, 21, 22, 140, 185, 237, 241
FIELDING 284
FIELDS 112, 318
FILES 18, 108
FILMER 250
FINCH 17, 18, 25, 105, 114, 250, 279
FINCH BAPTIST CHURCH 81
FINCH COMMUNITY 17
FINCH SCHOOL 105, 107
FINDLEY 323
FINK 267
FINKE 267
FINLEY 13, 180
FIRST BAPTIST CHURCH OF PARAGOULD 68
FIRST NATIONAL BANK 32
FIRST PRESBYTERIAN CHURCH 69
FIRST UNITED METHODIST CHURCH OF PARAGOULD 70
FISHEL 335
FISHER 53, 140, 269, 290
FISK 329
FITCH 107
FITZGERALD 13, 64, 165, 202, 293, 321, 343, 347
FITZNICOLL 161
FLAKE 250
FLANERY 54, 188, 338, 339
FLANNERY 121
FLEEMAN 57, 253
FLEISCHER 228
FLEMON 206, 333
FLETCHER 13, 18, 46, 105, 107, 110, 131, 159, 187, 190, 227, 243, 261, 262, 283, 311, 324, 333, 342, 357, 361
FLIGOR 251
FLOOD 250
FLORA 149, 170, 323
FLORES 325
FLORIAN 189
FLOWERS 52
FLOYD 123, 271
FLURNOY 217
FLUTY 97
FOLIGER 105
FONDREN 317
FONTAINE 18
FORBESS 171
FORBIS 144
FORBUS 109
FORD 13, 30, 32, 44, 71, 79, 88, 111, 112, 115, 156, 205, 209, 221, 229, 235, 247, 258, 263, 299, 301, 312, 316
FOREHAND 103, 362
FORESYTH 203
FORESYTHE 203, 229, 230
FORKUM 96
FORREST 249, 254, 261
FORRESTER 259
FORSCHY 112
FORSYTH 203
FORSYTHE 203, 250
FORTENBERRY 194, 205
FORTSON 225
FOSHEE 258, 259, 362
FOSSET 362
FOSSETT 103
FOSTER 13, 79, 97, 203, 204, 302, 329, 330, 355
FOUCHE 250
FOWLER 81, 97, 140, 166, 201, 209, 361
FOX 154, 195, 204, 280, 292, 318, 330
FRAIR 15
FRAMER 175
FRANCIS 24
FRANK 148, 198, 353
FRANKE 224
FRANKLIN 148, 168, 290
FRANKOWSKI 267
FRANKS 140, 245, 349
FRANZ 168
FRASURE 105
FRAZIAR 294
FRED 107
FREDERKING 338
FREDRICK 323
FREE 88, 324, 325
FREEMAN 13, 25, 74, 119, 176, 186, 263, 275, 358
FREIDMAN 44
FRENCH 97, 103, 107, 112, 149, 204, 205, 212, 233, 236, 279, 287, 329, 355
FRETS 107
FREY 7, 146
FRIAR 65, 187, 209, 350
FRIARS' SCHOOL 95
FRICKE 118, 120, 335, 341
FRIELAND 86
FRIELDS 205, 238
FRIERSON 295
FRITZ SCHOOL 106, 107
FROCK 335
FRUCHEY 205, 273
FRY 119, 144, 263
FRYAR 215
FRYER 198
FUCHS 101
FULK 140
FULKERSON 175, 205, 206, 208, 209, 275, 292
FULLER 160, 268, 280, 315
FULTON 77
FUNK 155, 198
FUQUA 345, 348
FURBY 293
FURGERSON 148, 297
FUTREL 231
FUTRELL 7, 16, 34, 99, 102, 125, 167, 168, 177, 197, 206, 211, 217, 257, 268, 270, 271, 290

G

GABEL 361
GABLE 251
GAGE 265
GAILEY 205
GAILON 206
GAINESVILLE 18
GAITHER 18, 257
GALBREATH 144
GALE 304
GALEY 205
GALLERY 323
GALLOP 90
GALLOWAY 301
GAMBILL 233, 339, 355
GAMMA 179
GANDER 76
GANDY 293
GARDENER 317
GARDINER 173
GARDNER 13, 22, 44, 101, 113, 118, 131, 136, 181, 197, 199, 206, 207, 218, 237, 238, 264, 265, 333, 339, 340, 355
GARDY 196
GARLAND 226
GARMRATH 207, 208, 293, 319
GARMROTH 207, 232, 288
GARNER 6, 21, 44, 102, 105, 118, 128, 198, 200, 205, 208, 209, 213, 217, 221, 277, 298, 301
GARNETT 277
GARRETT 166
GASKILL 25, 155, 166
GASSAWAY 213
GATES 52, 80, 112, 209
GATEWOOD 120, 175, 205, 329
GATHINGS 175, 216, 292
GATLIN 25, 54, 72, 79, 84, 140, 155, 203, 318
GATZ 32, 44, 59, 150

GAY 14, 237, 250
GAZAWAY 33, 52
GAZAWAY ACE HOME IMPROVEMENT CENTER 33
GEER 101, 317
GENTRY 207, 209, 283, 361
GEORGE 142, 342
GERALDEZ 185
GERBER 36
GERDES 5, 21, 116, 118, 119, 120, 146, 149, 159, 209, 252, 253, 274, 304, 329, 338, 340
GERMAN 269
GETSON 101, 111, 112, 209, 223, 296
GIBBS 72, 75, 79, 97, 118, 295
GIBSON 95, 99, 100, 105, 154, 177, 190, 204, 229, 230, 337, 338, 345, 350
GILBERT 102, 109, 157, 173, 174, 240, 349
GILES 153
GILG 19
GILL 18, 105, 107, 264
GILLEAN 111
GILLESPIE 283
GILLETT 313
GILLIAM 25, 45, 99, 172, 208, 250, 260
GILMORE 99, 179
GILUM 233
GINGER 167, 168, 286, 315, 330
GINN 289, 290
GINNETT 185
GIPSON 215
GISINER 251
GIST 131, 156
GIVAN 209
GIVENS 313
GLADISH 164, 227, 271, 273, 281
GLASS 107
GLASSCOCK 153, 207, 339
GLASSGO 78
GLASSGOW 212
GLEGHORN 18, 167, 176
GLENN 52, 125, 194, 209, 210, 256
GLENN - SKAGGS HOME 125, 127
GLISSON 19, 107, 111
GLOVER 163, 251
GOALBY 340
GODFREY 308
GODINET 279
GOEBEL 210, 211
GOEDECKE 226
GOEHRING 221
GOFF 301
GOGUE 262

GOINS 23, 24, 99, 101, 137, 145, 167, 177, 210, 211, 212, 264, 271, 272, 320
GOLDEN 330
GOLDMAN 119, 209, 240
GONSER 52, 194
GOOCH 302
GOOD 13, 140, 212
GOODLOE 154
GOODMAN 60, 295, 324
GOODSON 18, 125, 144
GOODSON - ATKINS HOME 125, 127
GOODWIN 34, 35, 36, 44, 155, 175, 201
GOODWIN, MOORE, COLBERT, BROADAWAY AND GRAY, LLP 34
GORDON 97, 166, 196, 205, 212, 213, 261, 266, 296
GOSHA 145
GOSSAGE 145
GOTT 236
GOUGE 107
GOULD 62, 65, 71, 72, 87, 118, 202, 306
GOURLEY 261
GOVANS 232
GOWEN 319
GRABER 25
GRACE UNITED GENERAL BAPTIST CHURCH 83, 84
GRADY 101, 196, 213, 317
GRAFFISH 239
GRAFTENREED 83
GRAHAM 119, 221, 296, 324
GRAMBLING 216
GRAMLING 22, 23, 24, 28, 53, 76, 87, 102, 141, 172, 174, 177, 182, 183, 184, 190, 203, 206, 213, 214, 215, 216, 225, 228, 231, 232, 251, 278, 316, 333, 341, 344, 360
GRANDE 65
GRANDSTAFF 325
GRANT 112, 172, 193
GRANTHAM 232
GRAVES 61, 107, 222, 223, 348
GRAY 23, 25, 35, 36, 84, 112, 145, 146, 215, 259, 295, 344
GRAYSON 186, 246, 267, 281, 296, 350
GREEN 25, 71, 100, 111, 116, 150, 165, 166, 193, 197, 198, 204, 215, 216, 252, 289, 304, 316, 333, 340, 343, 355

GREENE 10, 11, 119, 123, 190, 196, 208, 216, 353
GREENE ACRES NURSING HOME 48
GREENE COUNTY SCHOOL 116
GREENE COUNTY TECH HIGH SCHOOL 95, 121
GREENWAY 71, 74, 83, 99, 101, 105, 116, 148, 178, 188, 214, 261, 286, 334, 337
GREENWOOD 308
GREER 164, 205, 232, 271, 273, 333
GREGG 35
GREGORY 16, 62, 76, 87, 123, 163, 177, 214, 216, 255, 323
GREGSON 176
GRENADE 78
GRETICHER 128
GREY 105
GRIER 332
GRIERSON 344
GRIFFIN 70, 72, 76, 79, 84, 171, 177, 209, 257, 285
GRIFFIN MEMORIAL UNITED METHODIST CHURCH 84
GRIFFITH 75, 215
GRIGGRY 343
GRIGGS 88, 286
GRILLS 329, 339
GRIMES 21, 105, 166, 200, 249
GRIMMETT 336
GRISSOM 277
GRIZZARD 125
GROGAN 145
GROOMS 15, 62, 90, 99, 102, 172, 229, 241, 321, 330, 333, 343
GROSS 119, 192, 216
GROTY 287
GROVER 276
GRUBBS 199
GRUMB 306
GRUMBLES 337
GSCHWEND 335
GUEST 99, 268
GUIER 227
GUINN 179, 228
GUM GROVE SCHOOL 95
GUNN 200
GUNTER 103, 296
GURLEY 254
GUTHRIE 227
GWINNER 298
GWYN 177

**H**

HAAS 100

HABA 305
HABERLING 167
HADDON 160
HADLEY 234
HAFFEY 61
HAGAN 170
HAGER 75
HAGGARD 5, 257, 343
HAGGARTY 297
HAGOOD 216, 217
HAHN 223
HAILEY 169, 251
HAINE 140
HAIRRELL 201
HAISLIP 303
HAIZLIP 44, 59
HALE 41, 75, 125, 271, 272, 338
HALEY 145, 317
HALFORD 162
HALL 13, 16, 23, 25, 62, 68, 101, 102, 140, 142, 163, 167, 168, 197, 198, 217, 218, 219, 220, 237, 239, 255, 256, 268, 283, 294, 328, 333, 340
HALLER 120, 335, 338
HALLEY 251, 284
HALLIDAY 18, 19
HALLIDAY COMMUNITY 18
HALLIDAY SCHOOL 107, 108
HALLY 213
HALSTEAD 112
HAMASAKI 280
HAMBLIN 79, 272
HAMET 183
HAMETT 107
HAMILTON 25, 35, 40, 44, 49, 125, 149, 180, 212, 231, 259, 276, 278, 290, 291, 361
HAMILTON HARDWARE 49
HAMLIN 210
HAMM 97, 161
HAMMETT 156, 157, 250
HAMMICK 191
HAMMON 226, 261
HAMMOND 44, 88, 109, 125, 248, 250, 261, 315, 327
HAMMOND HOME 125, 127
HAMMONDS 70
HAMPTON 15, 86, 87, 107, 113, 118, 119, 125, 134, 154, 218, 248, 258, 265, 329, 330, 353
HANCOCK 18, 96, 144, 186, 303
HAND 101
HANELINE 21, 120, 166

HANEMANN 285
HANEY 99, 361
HANEY SCHOOL 111
HANKINS 39
HANKS 218, 219
HANSBROUGH 52, 57, 79, 152, 301
HANSIL 220
HARD 264
HARDEE 146
HARDIMAN 95
HARDIN 142, 166, 247
HARDING 128, 161, 277
HARDY 348
HARGRAVE 84
HARGROVE 18, 140
HARLAN 199
HARLEY 281
HARLOW 58, 99
HARMON 175, 176, 320, 324, 335
HARMS 218, 252, 253
HARPER 322, 338
HARRALSTON 172
HARREL 152
HARRELL 148
HARRELSON 177
HARRINGTON 275, 276, 298
HARRIS 49, 52, 76, 87, 96, 112, 119, 125, 172, 174, 177, 180, 200, 207, 217, 218, 219, 220, 225, 226, 238, 245, 252, 253, 275, 294, 317, 320, 328, 343, 344, 360
HARRIS - MCKENZIE HOME 125, 127
HARRIS BARBER SHOP 49
HARRISON 295, 325, 337, 341, 347
HARRUP 250
HART 13, 59, 86, 87, 88, 100, 111, 153, 220, 223, 227, 248, 261, 338
HARTLEY 68
HARTWICK 296
HARVEY 13, 93, 97, 100, 199, 220, 221, 292, 320, 323
HARVEY'S CHAPEL SCHOOL 107
HARVILL 221, 275, 309, 334
HARVY 324
HASS 13, 111, 118, 121
HASTINGS 143
HASTY 184
HATCH 156
HATCHER 264
HATHCOCK 13
HATLEY 221
HATLY 252
HATTON 238
HAVEN 146

HAVENS 54, 205
HAWES 340
HAWK 105, 165
HAWKINS 21, 128, 149, 221, 248, 329
HAWKS 327
HAWL 217
HAWLEY 304
HAY 179, 221, 222, 237
HAYDEN 291
HAYES 156, 260, 292, 340, 348
HAYGOOD 109, 288
HAYLEY 220
HAYMORE 168
HAYNES 44, 59, 112, 140, 156, 209, 234, 288, 312
HAYS 131, 157, 264, 340, 354
HAZLEWOOD 61
HAZZARD 7, 52
HEAD 177
HEAGLER 23, 24
HEARD 187, 249
HEATH 6, 7, 37, 95, 96, 112, 125, 161, 162, 212, 222, 223, 227, 231
HEATH - GRIZZARD HOME 125, 127
HEATH - MACK HOME 125, 127
HEATH FUNERAL HOME 37
HECHT 206, 333
HEDGEPETH 113
HEDGER 235
HEDGES 162, 257
HEFNER 18
HELD 145
HELLER 238
HELLMAN 322, 324
HELTON 120
HELVERING 284
HELVERINGS 165
HELWIG 340
HEMMINGWAY 101
HEMPEL 253
HENDERSON 90, 107, 176, 296, 339
HENDRIX 95, 120, 223, 274, 345, 352
HENLEY 13, 118
HENN 209
HENNARD 204
HENRIE 340
HENRY 250, 363
HENSHAW 250
HENSLEY 159, 175
HENSON 13, 112, 118, 172, 210, 272, 283, 320, 344, 345
HERAL 112, 146, 209, 223, 224
HERGET 7, 25, 45, 59, 61, 62, 128, 224
HERITAGE 25
HERONS 118
HERREN 18, 22, 71, 105, 148, 171, 187, 196, 260, 286

HERRICK 160
HERRIN 187
HERRING 296
HERRINGTON 344
HERRON 62, 250
HESS 165
HESSON 101
HESTER 23, 52, 81, 95, 97, 100, 119, 143, 159, 167, 177, 214, 221, 224, 225, 236, 277, 302, 341, 346, 357, 360
HEWITT 362
HEZEKIAH 359
HIBBARD 111, 112, 146, 160, 223
HICKMAN 95
HICKS 34, 46, 47, 146, 152, 171, 194, 197, 223, 352, 355, 361, 362
HICKSON 264
HIDE 181
HIGDON 163
HIGGINS 49, 71, 89, 110, 111, 121, 128, 148, 172, 201, 206, 233, 241, 260, 266, 281, 286, 321, 361
HIGGINS - OWENS HOME 128, 129
HIGH 286
HIGHFILL 25, 60, 78, 128, 155, 156, 176, 183, 239, 251, 359
HIGHFILL - KNOX HOME 128, 129
HIGHT 116
HIGHTOWER 296, 300
HILBURN 13
HILDRETH 177, 340
HILL 52, 62, 83, 95, 97, 107, 123, 146, 160, 210, 223, 225, 226, 234, 245, 250, 283, 285, 286, 321, 330, 338
HILLBURN 78, 79
HILLIS 207
HILLS 253
HINK 218
HINKLE 289, 290, 301
HINMAN 87
HINSON 156, 179
HINTON 250
HIRSCH 240
HITCHCOCK 180, 294
HOADLEY 226
HOBBS 191, 330
HOBBY 152
HOBGOOD 318
HOCKELL 324, 325
HODGE 100, 103
HODGES 23, 24
HODLEY 115, 116
HOELSCHER 226, 252, 253, 329
HOENSHELL 274
HOFFER 197

HOFFLINGER 145
HOFFMAN 209
HOFLINGER 82, 94, 226, 227
HOGAN 154, 350
HOGGARD 121, 199, 227
HOKE 256
HOLBERT 297
HOLCOMB 41, 81, 119, 152, 176, 270, 338
HOLDEN 145, 177, 310
HOLDER 223
HOLIFIELD 92, 107, 173, 227, 343
HOLIMAN 240
HOLIWAY 47
HOLKER 66
HOLLAND 7, 30, 72, 75, 79, 100, 104, 172, 227, 228, 276, 335, 343
HOLLIFIELD 344
HOLLIGAN 16
HOLLINGSWORTH 258
HOLLIS 47, 86, 110, 193, 294, 304
HOLLOMAN 175
HOLLOWAY 294, 330
HOLLOWELL 72
HOLMES 100, 228
HOLOBAUGH 300
HOLONECK 45
HOLSOMBECK 331
HOLSTEN 161
HOLT 21, 70, 72, 75, 79, 84, 86, 215, 250, 256, 257
HOLTZCLAW 245
HONEN 306
HONEY 95, 112, 116, 118, 260, 287
HOOD 140, 279
HOOKER 19, 71, 194, 232, 282, 316, 318, 319
HOOKER SWITCH 19
HOOKS 309
HOOPER 14, 62, 144, 296, 336
HOOTEN 165, 228
HOOTON 214, 228
HOPE 290
HOPGOOD 97
HOPKINS 13, 16, 87, 99, 110, 128, 164, 237, 276, 290, 294, 298
HOPPER 13, 71, 120, 197, 243, 262, 288
HOPSON 236
HORN 77, 238, 263, 331
HORNE 188, 228, 229, 233, 251, 278, 321, 331, 353
HORNER 268
HORRELL 188
HORTON 18, 87, 95,
96, 99, 105, 116, 131, 140, 151, 154, 304, 359
HOSEY 158
HOSKINS 83, 128, 155, 229, 331
HOSKINS-MERIWETHER HOME 128, 129
HOTS 172, 317, 320
HOUGHTON 229
HOUSE 59, 213, 329, 336, 340, 341
HOUSMAN 244
HOUSTON 49, 50, 121, 170, 186, 187, 188, 216, 236, 246, 247, 274, 345
HOVIS 280
HOWARD 87, 95, 102, 116, 161, 203, 208, 210, 211, 216, 265, 297, 358
HOWDER 194
HOWE 13, 19, 100, 120, 151, 173, 332, 342
HOWELL 80, 100, 155, 186, 187, 228, 276, 311, 337
HOWERTON 75, 79
HOWTON 203, 229, 230
HOYER 16, 87, 110, 271, 277, 338
HUBBELL 204
HUBBERT 295
HUBENER 51
HUCKABAY 119, 120, 159, 187, 188, 240
HUCKABEE 141, 296
HUCKABY 336, 355, 360
HUDDLESTON 162
HUDGEINS 21
HUDGENS 19, 352
HUDGINS 206, 333, 337
HUFFINE 13, 234, 259, 274
HUFFINES 49
HUFFMAN 87, 227, 321, 323, 324, 349
HUFFORD 111, 120, 335
HUGGANS 359
HUGH 275
HUGHES 23, 60, 88, 96, 121, 128, 148, 183, 184, 214, 215, 230, 231, 232, 241, 245, 256, 297, 341
HUGHES - LITTLE HOME 128, 129
HUGHSON 188
HULL 77
HULSEY 201
HUMPHREY 251
HUNT 19, 47, 99, 119, 144, 214, 216, 232, 255, 256, 316
HUNTER 13, 45, 148, 167, 168, 243, 275,
286, 315, 340
HUNTSMAN 321, 323
HURD 74
HURST 68, 250
HUSTON 161, 327
HUTCHERSON 225, 300
HUTCHINS 22, 78, 116, 154, 165, 170, 176, 183, 185, 213, 228, 229, 230, 232, 233, 251, 320, 323, 342
HUTCHISON 86
HUTSON 224
HYATT 100, 248, 327, 335
HYDAS 325
HYDE 18, 25, 46, 71, 105, 107, 115, 116, 148, 168, 178, 179, 216, 233, 275, 286, 292, 309, 321, 333, 334, 347
HYNEMAN 224
HYZDU 333

I

IGARISHI 205
IISON 100
IMMANUEL BAPTIST CHURCH 84
INGRAM 40, 111, 250
INMAN 61, 246
INNESS 25
IRVINE 179
IRVING 93, 213
IRWIN 275
ISHAMEL 233
ISHMAEL 233, 238, 297, 298, 315, 318, 320, 355
ISOM 72, 76, 100, 233, 234, 337
IVIE 145, 237, 295
IVY 90, 209, 250

J

J & S WOODCRAFTS, INC. 38
J. D. BLOCK HOME 125, 126, 133
J. MARION FUTRELL HOME 125, 126
JACKLIN 82
JACKMAN 21, 162, 250, 255, 359
JACKSON 13, 16, 21, 24, 52, 53, 59, 76, 78, 84, 86, 88, 95, 96, 99, 102, 110, 111, 112, 118, 121, 128, 134, 154, 156, 166, 175, 197, 221, 224, 225, 226, 228, 232, 234, 235, 236, 252, 254, 263, 269, 279, 290, 294, 305, 307, 309, 333, 338, 347, 351, 352, 353
JACKSON - HERGET HOME 128, 129

286, 315, 340
HUNTSMAN 321, 323
JACKSON COLLEGE 95
JACKSON'S COM-MISSARY 16
JACOB 253, 254, 266
JACOBS 221
JAKUBIK 60
JAMERSON 236
JAMES 103, 205, 218, 236, 332
JAMESON 95, 224, 236
JAMINSON 361
JAMISON 15, 71, 329, 339, 353
JANES 188
JARETT 100
JARMAN 131, 280
JARRETT 100, 175, 243
JARVIS 118, 120, 204
JASPER 359
JAYES 19
JEFFERY 218
JENKINS 2, 6, 13, 50, 62, 222
JENKINS LAMP AND SHADE MANU-FACTURING, INC. 50
JENNE 60
JENNINGS 235, 251
JERNIGAN 25, 92, 100, 150, 236, 355
JESPERSEN 236
JETER 263, 289
JETT 273
JETTON 15, 57, 74, 87, 99, 232, 237, 272, 329, 330, 347
JEWISON 236
JOHNS 15, 16, 71, 101, 102, 181, 237, 339
JOHNSON 13, 16, 25, 52, 58, 68, 77, 87, 88, 90, 95, 99, 105, 134, 140, 141, 142, 147, 150, 157, 161, 162, 165, 177, 180, 186, 205, 207, 220, 221, 225, 235, 236, 237, 238, 239, 249, 250, 251, 253, 255, 262, 264, 277, 281, 288, 291, 297, 305, 315, 321, 324, 325, 327, 328, 329, 333, 340, 348, 350, 359, 360
JOHNSTON 21, 70, 83, 99, 118, 140, 190, 193, 196, 213, 239, 249, 297, 298, 315, 346
JOINER 228
JONES 49, 57, 66, 78, 84, 87, 95, 98, 99, 107, 111, 114, 118, 121, 122, 128, 144, 145, 146, 147, 148, 153, 160, 164, 174,
175, 177, 182, 187, 188, 192, 194, 230, 235, 237, 239, 240, 245, 247, 253, 261, 266, 279, 281, 288, 296, 298, 300, 309, 320, 334, 335, 337, 346, 349, 362
JONES RIDGE 23
JONES RIDGE SCHOOL 108, 109
JORDAN 49, 72, 75, 161, 173, 240, 330
JORDEN 271
JORDON 79, 178, 194, 250
JOSEPH 240
JOY 25
JOYNER 228
JUDD 112
JUDKINS 250
JULIAN 264
JUMPER 18, 87, 337
JUNE 1981 – 150YEAR HOMECOMING OF THE PINE KNOTT 71
JUSTES 280
JUSTICE 100, 192, 210, 240, 241, 272

K

KAPELMAN 209
KAPPELMAN 209, 340
KAPPLEMANN 304
KARCHER 250
KARLMEIER 226
KARMEIER 226
KASPER 306
KASSERMAN 97
KASTNER 256
KATTERHENRY 287
KAUBLE 335
KAY 61, 165
KEASLER 50, 51, 241, 242
KEASLER BODY COMPANY 50
KEATING 279
KECK 356
KEE 45, 319, 352
KEEKER 288
KEELING 175, 195, 206, 255
KEELOR 242, 243, 288
KEENEY 298
KEITH 172, 310, 333, 339
KELLER 240, 329
KELLEY 32, 97, 99, 118
KELLIM 105
KELLY 100, 224, 259, 311
KELSO 217, 219, 220
KEMP 145
KEMPNER 144, 149
KENMAN 340

KENNAMORE 321
KENNEDY 13, 21, 75, 116, 154, 176, 261, 263
KENNEMORE 163, 167, 215, 243, 262, 321, 323, 325, 326
KENNETT 45, 128, 243
KENNETT - BEISEL - MITCHELL HOME 128, 129
KENNEY 178
KENT 336
KEOWN 308
KERLEY 219
KERSEY 219, 259
KEUTER 260
KEY 108, 110, 113, 154, 157, 165, 277, 288, 319, 344
KIBLER 88
KIDD 25
KIDWELL 267
KIEFFNER 88
KIERSKY 245
KIESTLER 97, 199
KIFER 112
KILBEY 250
KILKREECE 357
KILLIAN 52, 102, 209, 261
KILLIGREW 208
KILTZ 97
KIMBALL 181
KIMBROUGH 26, 135, 146, 157, 243, 244
KINDER 265
KING 70, 77, 176, 198, 205, 238, 257, 259, 266, 271, 272, 282, 303, 324, 342, 350
KINGSTON 100, 249
KINON 341
KINTE 49
KIRBY 140, 147
KIRCHOFF 44, 60, 82, 125, 159
KIRK 51, 131, 156, 244
KIRK AND BRAZIL CONSTRUCTION COMPANY 51
KIRKENDALL 281
KIRKLAND 250
KIRSCH 32, 34, 131, 144, 152, 159, 244, 266, 305, 312
KIRSH 61
KISSINGER 168
KITCHEN 13, 161
KITCHENS 125, 152, 180, 232
KLEIHAUER 361
KLINGENSMITH 205
KNIGHT 45, 116, 118, 165, 166, 175, 199, 219, 220, 272, 353
KNOLLY 183
KNOPPE 60

KNOTT 279
KNOWLES 239
KNOX 119, 128, 249
KOLB 257
KOREAN WAR 13
KOSTOPULOS 151
KOSTOWSKI 74
KOTTERHENRICH 287
KRECHTING 272
KRISTE 306
KRUPA 157
KUETER 25, 82, 145
KUMMER 198
KURANER 264
KURTZ 327
KUYKENDALL 13, 76, 230, 231, 250, 267
KYZER 283

**L**

L.W. BALDWIN ELEMENTARY SCHOOL 119
LACEWELL 113, 150
LACEY 52, 80, 103, 244, 245
LACHOWSKY 189
LACKEY 270
LACKNER 196
LACONURE 109
LACY 194
LADD 191
LADIGO 284
LADY 119, 245, 295, 349
LAFE 19, 20
LAFE HIGH SCHOOL 120
LAFFERETY 211
LAFFERTY 167, 210, 211, 271
LAFFOON 57, 245
LAIRD 61
LAKE 113
LAKESIDE SCHOOL 108
LAM 97, 99, 107, 158, 245, 246, 293
LAMAN 151, 169, 170
LAMAND 97
LAMB 20, 22, 95, 97, 99, 112, 123, 140, 148, 154, 155, 170, 175, 183, 186, 187, 190, 246, 247, 261, 267, 283, 294, 295, 296, 311, 328, 337, 342, 355
LAMBERT 25, 168, 273
LAMBERTH 97
LAMPKINS 210
LAN 50
LANCASTER 224, 225, 310, 357
LANCE 101, 111, 223
LAND 22, 204
LANDERS 264, 334
LANDRUM 4, 53, 109, 121, 128, 131, 142, 151, 161, 193, 196, 211, 247, 248, 249, 327
LANDRUM SCHOOL 92, 108, 109
LANDRUS 121
LANDS 154, 161, 162
LANE 23, 24, 38, 92, 155, 185, 248, 291, 362
LANGE 12, 25, 340
LANGFORD 223
LANGHAM 320
LANGLEY 35, 36, 154, 164, 254, 334, 350
LANGRUM 163
LANGSTON 25, 165
LANKFORD 169
LANN 79
LARGENT 229, 345
LARKIN 249
LARUE 259, 260
LASHLEY 92, 104, 109
LASTER 148
LATCH 84
LATHER 250
LATHERMAN 16
LATIMER 146
LATOOF 204
LATTA 178
LAUBACH 53
LAUCHSTAEDT 226
LAUNCY 243
LAWLESS 99
LAWRENCE 89, 154, 159, 236, 248, 249
LAWSON 13, 134, 161, 205, 243, 249, 250
LAX 21, 157
LAY 249, 250
LAYER 97
LAYL 216, 247
LAYMAN 13, 22, 170
LAYMON 362
LAYMOND 119
LAYNE 288
LAYTON 145, 180
LEA 151
LEACH 176, 177, 249
LEATH 74
LEATHERWOOD 318
LEDER 226
LEE 14, 18, 35, 90, 111, 121, 159, 204, 215, 220, 226, 244, 245, 252, 274, 284, 298
LEGITT 53
LEIRER 287
LEISHMAN 198
LELAND 290
LEMASTER 264
LEMMON 226
LEMMONS 71, 74, 80, 93, 101, 110, 116, 148, 177, 181, 245
LEMONS 115, 121, 317
LENDERMAN 71, 76,

83, 177, 265, 339, 346
LENZY 157
LEPLEY 356
LEROY 89
LESTER 209
LETSON 254
LETTERMAN 220
LETURNO 245
LEVAUX 240
LEVINE 18
LEVINS 83, 95
LEWIS 19, 74, 83, 87, 108, 151, 169, 198, 199, 233, 250, 268, 279, 288, 340
LIBERTY CHURCH OF CHRIST 81
LIBHART 206, 333
LIDDELL 124, 354
LIDDLE 179
LIDEL 88
LIEBLONG 32, 353
LIGHT 20, 59, 81, 119, 146, 197, 215, 230, 237, 250, 321
LIGHT BAPTIST CHURCH 85
LIGHTFOOT 250
LIGON 149, 232, 250, 269
LIKE 101, 209, 275
LILE 36, 361
LINAM 24
LINCOLN 97, 153, 217
LINDEL 291
LINDEN 7, 52
LINDERMAN 100
LINDLEY 97, 131, 215, 304
LINDLY 99
LINDSEY 25, 209
LINGO 72, 75, 79
LINKE 128
LINKLETTER 93
LIPSCOMB 36, 51, 68, 128, 244, 250, 330, 333
LITTLE 99, 128, 154, 155, 172, 199, 201, 206, 239, 250, 251, 302, 356
LITTLEPAGE 267, 295
LITTLETON 160, 255
LIVELY 199, 337
LIVESAY 21, 119, 293, 303, 359
LIVINGSTON 13
LLOYD 78, 95, 99, 119, 131, 168, 176, 198, 223, 226, 229, 251, 332
LOAR 199
LOCKART 310
LOCKRIDGE 160, 318
LOCKWOOD 44, 252, 327
LOFTIN 250, 288
LOFTIS 360

LOFTUS 175
LOGAN 94, 216
LOLLICK 181
LOLULYMA 19
LOMAX 326
LONG 80, 99, 140, 262, 296
LOOKDOO 259
LOONEY 239, 296, 321
LOPEZ 44, 59
LORADO 20
LORENZ 289
LORRANCE 177
LOUDEN 362
LOULYMA 19
LOUY 177
LOVE 250, 307
LOVEALL 237
LOVELACE 18, 115, 156, 173, 261, 337
LOVELADY 6, 7, 13, 15, 25, 52, 65, 95, 102, 104, 172, 193, 252, 270, 342, 344, 350, 351
LOVELL 101
LOWE 25, 32, 290, 333, 339, 340
LOWMAN 340
LOWRY 326
LOYD 178
LUCAS 248
LUCUS 160
LUEKER 218, 226, 252, 253, 304, 340, 341
LUMLEY 140
LUNDY 46
LUSCHER 180
LUSK 39
LUSTER 23
LUTEN 331
LUTER 52, 128
LUTER - MCPHERSON HOME 128, 130
LUTY 166
LUYET 189
LYCURTIS 319
LYERLY 190
LYLE 71
LYLES 13
LYNCH 109, 279
LYNN 25, 100, 226, 262, 297, 335
LYON 174, 299
LYONS 309
LYTLE 201

**M**

M. F. BLOCK INSURANCE, INCORPORATED 44
MABERRY 194, 195
MABREY 75
MABRY 72, 297, 318, 320
MACARTHUR 302
MACK 35, 44, 61, 118, 125, 181, 240, 244, 278, 305, 313, 314

MACKENZIE 203
MACKEY 149, 170
MACKINTOSH 262
MACMILLAN 155
MACNEILL 260
MADDOX 206, 253, 273
MADOX 227
MAERKER 297
MAGALLON 336
MAGERS 344
MAHAN 253, 254, 266, 323
MAJOR 230
MAJORS 99, 116, 184, 230
MALIN 19, 107
MALLARD 338
MALONE 335
MALTRAVERS 160
MANCHESTER 97, 107, 121
MANDRELL 333
MANGRUM 43, 110, 175, 214, 228, 233, 292, 337
MANN 162, 216, 223, 226, 254, 255, 256
MANOR 120
MARCHBANKS 281, 282
MARKHAM 131
MARKO 206
MARKS 295
MARKUM 237
MARLAR 25, 72, 75, 79
MARMADUKE 20, 21, 86
MARMADUKE HIGH SCHOOL 124
MARMADUKE METHODIST CHURCH 85, 86
MARMADUKE PICNIC 7
MARMADUKE SCHOOL 110, 120
MARR 340
MARRET 349
MARROW 163, 237
MARSHALL 25, 97, 150, 202, 229, 256, 313
MARTEN 185
MARTIAU 160
MARTIN 5, 18, 44, 62, 82, 95, 99, 101, 104, 107, 112, 113, 121, 140, 149, 154, 177, 181, 190, 194, 208, 248, 256, 257, 266, 270, 274, 286, 316, 320, 324, 332
MARTZ 341
MASON 13, 172, 173, 344
MASSENGILL 281
MASSEY 77, 80, 197, 207, 268
MASTER 281
MASTERS 219

MASTERSON 257, 258
MATALENA 355
MATHIS 274
MATTHEW 227
MATTHEWS 237
MATTINGLY 297
MATTIX 183, 190, 337
MAXFIELD 154
MAXWELL 13, 45, 107, 119, 142, 322
MAY 72, 75, 79, 113, 177, 258, 270, 316, 317, 329
MAYBERRY 90, 110, 226
MAYNARD 258, 259, 362
MAYNE 274
MAYNESS 154
MCABEE 304
MCADAMS 353
MCALLISTER 119
MCANINCH 44, 144
MCANTOSH 198
MCARTHUR 258
MCBEE 120, 223
MCBRIDE 46, 90, 107, 150, 161, 162, 223
MCCAIN 279
MCCALISTER 62
MCCALL 156, 206
MCCANDISH 340
MCCANDLESS 252
MCCARDLE 141
MCCARROLL 145
MCCARTER 320
MCCARTNEY 292
MCCASKAY 147
MCCAUGHEN 194
MCCAULEY 78
MCCAWAN 279
MCCHESNEY 311
MCCLAIN 153
MCCLARIN 344
MCCLELLAND 177, 259, 260, 308
MCCLERKIN 78, 118
MCCLUNEY 121
MCCLUNG 85
MCCLURE 57, 71, 95, 99, 100, 102, 107, 116, 128, 160, 185, 204, 205, 212, 213, 257, 260, 263, 338
MCCLURE - HIGHFILL HOME 128, 130
MCCOMB 356
MCCONE 176
MCCONKEY 277
MCCORD 13, 97, 162, 255
MCCORMICK 260, 261
MCCOWAN 279, 280
MCCOWN 280
MCCOY 260
MCCRACKEN 249, 281
MCCUBBIN 348
MCCULLAR 251
MCCULLARS 140
MCCULLOCH 261
MCCULLOUGH 59, 276
MCCURTRY 119
MCDANIEL 30, 44, 66, 72, 74, 78, 79, 89, 99, 100, 118, 140, 148, 154, 165, 168, 175, 178, 183, 186, 194, 206, 222, 224, 234, 246, 261, 276, 283, 298, 306, 332, 349, 358
MCDONALD 82, 88, 107, 119, 125, 199, 202, 215, 245, 289, 295, 312
MCDONAUGH 146
MCDONOUGH 146
MCDOW 154
MCDOWELL 118, 329
MCELRATH 320
MCELWEE 118, 145, 289
MCELWEECE 116
MCELWRATH 333
MCEWEN 176
MCFADDEN 48, 74, 359
MCFALL 221, 261
MCFARLAND 141, 250, 259, 344
MCGARRAUGH 316, 330
MCGAUGHEY 266
MCGEE 123, 136, 181, 253, 263, 310
MCGEHEE 213
MCGILL 147
MCGINNIS 11, 84, 205
MCGINTY 197
MCGIVNEY 60
MCGLOTHERN 95
MCGOWAN 92, 100, 109, 287
MCGRAW 239, 261, 262
MCGREW 178, 335
MCGUE 123
MCGUIRE 165, 166, 303
MCHANEY 21, 57, 99, 109, 112, 113, 154, 220, 261, 274, 299, 302, 350
MCHENRY 280
MCINTOSH 151, 250, 262, 280
MCIVER 176
MCKEITHEN 307
MCKELVEY 86, 87, 92, 97, 113, 157, 175, 218, 236, 244, 298, 309
MCKENZIE 57, 125, 305, 333
MCKEOWN 253
MCKINNEY 176, 194, 253
MCKINNON 159
MCKINZIE 16
MCKNELLY 209, 223
MCKNIGHT 289, 290
MCLAUGHLIN 99, 176, 345
MCLENDON 283
MCLERKIN 262
MCMACKIN 181
MCMAINS 233
MCMENAMIN 156, 271, 272
MCMILLON 50, 83, 95, 97, 99, 276, 355
MCMURRAY 199
MCMURRY 58
MCMURTRY 13
MCNEAL 242
MCNEIL 99, 100, 224, 303
MCNIEL 83, 95
MCNIFF 140
MCNUTT 113
MCPHERSON 68, 120, 128, 292, 302, 306, 359
MCQUAID 94
MCRAE 260
MCSPADDEN 25, 262, 263, 321, 323
MCTAGGART 327
MCWHIRTER 113
MCWORTER 78
MEADOR 13
MEADOWS 15, 21, 24, 74, 118, 194
MEADOW'S GROVE 24
MEADOWS GROVE SCHOOL 95
MEALER 277
MEARS 104
MEDARIS 170
MEDICI 6
MEDSKER 25, 237, 347
MEEKER 211
MEEKS 221
MEIER 356
MEISER 32, 59, 61
MELDOREN 287
MELLON 76, 182
MELTON 224, 240, 345
MELVIN 192
MERCER 95
MERCHANT 352
MEREDITH 136, 263, 309, 310, 330
MERIDETH 22, 109, 120, 263
MERIWETHER 30, 44, 59, 128, 244, 263, 264, 305
MERRIET 323
MERRILL 244
MERRIMAN 324
MERRIWETHER 131
MERTZ 167, 340
MESCHE 256
METCALF 176
METHENY 137, 148, 168, 172, 264, 271, 272, 344
METTS 349
MEYER 218, 226
MEYERS 304
MEYRICK 144
MICENHAAMMER 258
MICK 90, 266
MICKEY 250
MICKLER 245
MIDDLETON 21, 44, 348
MIDGETT 209
MIDKIFF 329
MIER 307
MIFFLIN 120, 341
MILAM 335
MILBURN 329
MILENDER 349
MILES 87, 88, 206, 252, 292, 318, 341
MILLAY 187
MILLER 13, 83, 86, 97, 100, 107, 108, 113, 118, 119, 120, 121, 144, 149, 152, 153, 158, 170, 178, 180, 181, 186, 188, 190, 196, 212, 218, 220, 229, 235, 236, 237, 245, 250, 251, 260, 261, 265, 266, 292, 308, 309, 318, 321, 330, 332, 333, 337, 340, 352, 355, 360
MILLER SCHOOL 92, 108, 110
MILLS 118, 310, 318
MILNER 247
MIMS 268, 298
MINKS 204
MINNIS 303
MINTO 333
MINTON 309, 310
MINYARD 323
MISENHIMER 53
MITCHELL 7, 32, 44, 59, 64, 105, 114, 128, 150, 170, 180, 228, 241, 253, 254, 261, 266, 267, 268, 282, 286, 301, 321
MITCHEM 13
MIZE 144
MIZELL 260
MOBBS 97, 324
MOBLEY 281, 283
MOCK 24, 137, 165, 271, 272, 302
MOHMMAD 322
MOLDER 253
MOLENEAUX 215
MONAZYM 360
MONEA CHRISTIAN COLLEGE 93
MONEY 84
MONK 36
MONROE 288, 335
MONTEITH 88, 145, 146, 175
MONTGOMERY 72, 75, 79, 268, 297, 346
MONTGOMRY 268
MONTIETH 16
MOON 214, 323
MOONEY 75, 197, 198, 215, 250
MOORE 13, 20, 35, 36, 76, 86, 90, 95, 97, 105, 156, 197, 206, 209, 214, 217, 238, 239, 262, 264, 266, 268, 279, 281, 282, 294, 296, 297, 317, 318, 319, 329, 334, 336, 349, 359, 361
MOORMAN 169
MOOSE 75
MORELAND 7, 24
MOREY 70
MORGAN 25, 62, 71, 80, 128, 144, 154, 164, 176, 186, 203, 224, 228, 268, 269, 276, 278, 282, 316, 317, 341
MORGAN-BLOCK HOME 128, 130
MORNING STAR METHODIST CHURCH 86
MORNING STAR SCHOOL 108
MORRIS 7, 52, 60, 97, 114, 158, 167, 168, 174, 176, 182, 257, 269, 270, 278, 288, 295
MORRISON 119, 134, 140, 142, 174, 177
MORROW 7, 16, 24, 45, 104, 115, 137, 163, 164, 167, 168, 197, 198, 205, 210, 211, 217, 233, 239, 261, 262, 264, 265, 270, 271, 272, 273, 301, 320, 330, 332, 333, 334, 357
MORTEN 299
MORTON 273, 274, 293
MOSBY 194
MOSELEY 144
MOSES 88
MOSKY 188
MOSLEY 223, 248
MOSS 134, 168, 169, 197, 232, 274
MOTHERSHED 274, 345
MOUNCE 96, 140
MOUNDS SCHOOL 121
MOUSER 209, 337
MT. CARMEL SCHOOL 92
MUELLER 19, 52, 95, 96, 105, 110, 119, 181, 226, 274, 277, 303, 304
MULBERRY GROVE 11
MULLINS 245, 303, 308
MUNDREON 239
MUNSEY 338
MURPHY 61, 207, 288, 321
MURRAY 153
MUSE 301
MUSKA 265
MYDGETT 250
MYER 13
MYERS 13, 99, 162, 329
MYHAM 119
MYRICK 143, 144, 145, 183, 221, 274, 275

N

NADUA 340
NALL 255
NAMORS 259
NANNEY 239
NAPIER 25, 347
NAQUIN 204
NASH 75
NATION 238
NEAL 103, 141, 219, 234, 313
NEARNE 182
NEECE 209
NEELY 175, 217, 275, 276, 298, 321, 349
NEGRON 206, 333
NEGUS 325
NEISWONGER 142
NELSON 72, 140, 221, 288, 289
NESLER 119
NESS 302, 350
NETHERLAND 220
NETHING 335, 338
NETTLES 95, 239, 261, 263, 308, 310, 337, 357
NEW HOME SCHOOL 95, 110, 111
NEW LIBERTY METHODIST CHURCH 87
NEWBERRY 18, 19, 20, 100, 105, 112, 122, 153, 174, 185, 186, 187, 231, 237, 239, 276, 283, 299, 301, 327, 328
NEWBERRY SCHOOL 110, 111
NEWBOLES 337
NEWCOMB 168
NEWELL 265
NEWMAN 18, 150, 151, 206
NEWSOM 17, 71, 81, 95, 109, 115, 116, 128, 143, 154, 180, 190, 205, 220, 225, 250, 260, 276, 277, 294, 337, 346, 350
NEWSOME 17, 18, 95, 107

NEWTON 120, 150, 335
NEYMAN 333
NICHOLES 177
NICHOLS 257
NICKOLS 178, 257
NIEMANN 324, 326
NIMROD 191
NIPPER 228
NIX 200, 257, 334
NIXON 306
NOBLE 176, 177
NOBLIN 211
NOCKOLS 257
NOEL 13, 19, 95, 100, 166, 189, 193, 236, 249, 277, 342, 360
NOLAN 60
NOLAND 243
NOLES 142, 174, 187, 299
NOONER 229
NORMAN 95, 214, 275, 277, 278, 308, 352, 353
NORRIS 205, 239
NORSWORTHY 290
NORTH 95
NORTH END SCHOOL 110, 112
NORTHEAST ARKANSAS REGIONAL LIBRARY 51
NORTHEAST ARKANSAS TRIBUNE 39
NORTHEN 56, 57
NORTHERN 57
NORTON 89, 99, 110, 148, 192, 249, 306
NORVELL 349
NORVILLE 344
NORWOOD 99, 202, 250, 278
NOWELL 278, 353, 361
NUNALLY 209
NUNN 131, 235
NUNN - TRICE HOME 130, 131
NUNNERY 155, 278
NUTT 20, 90, 140, 154, 176, 187, 191, 212, 278, 279, 280, 295, 304, 307, 342
NUTTY 346

O

OAK GROVE HIGH SCHOOL 91, 92
OAK GROVE SCHOOL 92, 113
OBRIANT 79
O'BRIEN 332
O'BRISSELL 250
O'BRYANT 75
O'CONNER 232
O'CONNOR 232
O'CRUAOLAOIC 182
O'DANIEL 340
ODELL 96
O'DELL 99, 186, 187, 247

ODOM 280
OGDEN 112, 323
OGG 270
OGLES 13
OGLESBY 223
O'KEAN SCHOOL 111, 112
OKLE 210
OLD BETHEL SCHOOL 111, 113
OLD DIXIE SCHOOL 113, 114
OLD GULF STATION 48
OLD GUNNELL SCHOOL 119
OLDHAM 28, 53, 160
OLIPHANT 213
OLIVARES 340
OLIVE 205
OLIVER 44, 119
OLLERMAN 236
OLLIS 338
OLSEN 228
OLSON 229
OMMEN 19, 335
O'NEAL 52
ORICK 60, 104, 105, 172, 198, 208, 280, 344
ORR 281, 352
ORTCUTTER 334
OSADCHUK 284
OSBAN 75
OSBORN 335, 345, 355
OSBORNE 333
OSSEN 325
OSTEEN 176, 251
O'STEEN 239, 281
OSWALD 340
OTEY 250, 300
OVERALL 293
OVERBAY 25, 164, 271, 281
OVERBURY 281
OVERMAN 16
OVERSHINE 280
OVERTON 212, 213
OWEN 15, 56, 76, 99, 131, 140, 174, 198, 218, 238
OWEN - MERRIWETHER HOME 130, 131
OWENS 87, 97, 118, 120, 128, 131, 162, 171, 198, 246, 252, 281, 282, 289, 333
OWENS' CHAPEL 87
OXLEY 334

P

PACE 49, 95, 204, 205, 207, 359
PACK 99, 178, 196
PAEY 68
PAFF 116
PAGE 160, 168, 259, 277
PAINTER 288
PALESTINE SCHOOL 113

PALMER 186, 211, 278, 351
PANHORST 209, 226, 252, 253, 304
PANISKO 249
PANNELL 86, 113, 218, 265, 267, 282
PAPACHRISTON 338
PARAGOULD 14, 25
PARAGOULD DOORS 52
PARAMORE 306
PARHAM 140, 327
PARHM 239
PARISH 123, 316
PARKER 49, 84, 86, 112, 166, 249, 259, 260, 264, 265, 273, 332, 333
PARKHURST 275
PARKINSON 13, 51, 241
PARKS 120, 229
PARMENTER 95
PARRIS 202
PARRISH 13
PARSON 165
PARSONS 161
PARTAIN 340
PARTEN 273
PARTLOW 30, 282, 283, 316
PASCAL 123
PASISATTE 258
PATE 68, 229
PATILLO 187
PATTEN 229, 263
PATTERSON 166, 240, 258, 265, 279, 298, 299
PATTISHALL 97
PATTON 90, 147, 161, 256, 260
PATTOON 360
PATTY 216
PAUL 145
PAULDING 12
PAULSEN 296
PAYNE 13, 18, 83, 96, 100, 107, 119, 157, 163, 175, 189, 283, 292, 297, 349, 360
PEARCE 154, 229, 232, 258, 278
PEAVYHOUSE 121
PECK 232, 253, 254, 294
PEEBLES 228
PEEL 257
PEELER 13, 274
PEEVEHOUSE 22
PEGG 83, 96, 283, 320, 335, 355
PEMBERTON 194, 330
PENDERGRASS 218
PENN 175, 192
PENNEY 229, 233, 251, 283, 348
PENNINGTON 59
PENNY 17, 174, 226, 283, 296

PENRY 308
PENTECOST 345
PEOPLES BANK 52
PEPPER 30
PERCIFUL 90
PERDEW 313
PERKEY 53, 165, 284
PERKINS 112, 249, 250
PERMENTER 169, 250
PERRY 25, 196, 301, 359
PERSHING 160
PERSIAN GULF (DESERT STORM) 13
PETERMAN 166
PETERS 176
PETERSON 82, 239, 254, 360
PETTUS 64
PEVEHOUSE 23, 125, 183, 213, 214, 284, 317, 320
PEWITT 247
PHELPS 89, 251
PHILHOURS 25, 131
PHILHOURS - BERTIG HOME 130, 131
PHILIPS 164
PHILLIP 344
PHILLIPS 6, 7, 44, 48, 49, 52, 72, 99, 100, 101, 113, 114, 118, 119, 120, 157, 158, 160, 171, 175, 176, 184, 192, 209, 210, 220, 241, 262, 284, 285, 286, 297
PHOFF 118
PICKARD 61
PICKENS 279
PICKNEY 255
PIERCE 13, 96, 119, 180, 274, 296, 362
PIERCEALL 145, 229, 251
PIERSSON 325
PIGG 246
PIGUE 61
PILLOTT 243
PILLOW 18, 25, 45, 52, 71, 116, 128, 148, 168, 172, 174, 188, 193, 205, 209, 216, 232, 233, 271, 272, 286, 287, 320, 337
PINE 141
PINE KNOT SCHOOL 115, 116, 121
PINE KNOTT CHURCH OF CHRIST 71
PINEDA 131
PINT KNOT SCHOOL 116
PIPKINS 85
PIPPINS 218
PITCHER 121, 330
PITMAN 107, 323, 324

PITTS 197, 318, 349
PLEASANT HILL METHODIST CHURCH 87, 115
PLEASANT HILL SCHOOL 115, 116, 117
PLOUVIER 250
POE 45, 186, 267, 287
POGUE 271, 272
POINDEXTER 53, 241, 242
POLK 207
POLLOCK 141, 340
PONDER 7, 122
POOLE 21, 97, 99, 118, 167
POPLAR BLUFF 24
POPPE 151, 287, 295
PORTER 46, 264, 274
PORTERFIELD 158
PORTING 247
POST OAK SCHOOL 116, 117
POTTER 62, 78, 89, 141, 177, 211, 275, 294, 296, 342, 344, 354, 355
POTTS 166, 348
POUNDS 177
POWELL 78, 93, 152, 175, 302, 358
POWERS 99, 120, 147, 216, 222, 290, 306, 355
PRANGER 163, 287, 288
PRATER 67
PRATT 18, 100, 186, 259, 279, 304, 307, 308, 350
PRATTON 288
PREMO 227
PRESLEY 60, 335
PRESSON 97
PREVO 259
PRICE 19, 72, 119, 121, 140, 173, 196, 206, 289, 290, 296, 315
PRIDEMORE 105
PRINCE 13, 68, 90, 210, 243, 254, 287, 288
PRITCHETT 151, 288, 295
PROCTOR 168
PROFFER 331
PROVIDENCE 21
PROVIDENCE COMMUNITY 21
PROVINCE 143
PRUET 72, 117, 125, 128, 131, 145, 288, 289
PRUETT 49, 70, 72, 101, 288, 338
PRUETT'S CHAPEL CHURCH 117
PRUETT'S CHAPEL METHODIST CHURCH 72

PRUETT'S CHAPEL SCHOOL 117
PRUITT 206, 298, 333, 340
PRYOR 36, 171, 229, 232, 233, 361
PSALMONDS 88
PUCKETT 213, 289, 328
PULLEY 145
PURCELL 272, 289, 290, 359
PURDUE 297
PURDY 111
PURETT 269
PURNELL 161
PURRMAN 196, 197
PURVINE 140
PYLAND 77
PYLE 99

Q

QUALLS 177, 249
QUEEN 208
QUESENBERRY 348
QUINN 61, 173, 174

R

RACHUBKA 322
RADATZ 311
RADCLIFFE 344
RAE 295
RAGLAN 278
RAGLE 118, 329
RAGLIN 321
RAGSDALE 209, 261, 263, 310
RAGSDALL 102
RAGSDELL 112, 154, 270
RAINBOLT 245
RAINES 290
RAINEY 72, 278
RAINWATER 44, 79, 149, 238, 290, 291, 330
RAISH 324
RALEIGH 228
RALEY 60, 291, 321
RAMER 87, 118, 120, 291, 319, 329
RAMER'S CHAPEL UNITED METHODIST CHURCH 87
RAMER'S SCHOOL 116, 118
RAMPY 180
RAMSEY 21, 112, 118, 158
RAND 44, 59, 361
RANDAL 160
RANDALL 260
RANDLEMAN 97, 290
RANDLES 308
RANKIN 165
RAPLEY 264
RASBERRY 97, 98, 101, 107, 110, 111, 117, 120, 123, 336
RATTON 151, 175, 193, 291, 292

RAVER 180
RAWLINGS 250
RAWLS 345
RAY 158, 195, 196, 205, 272, 279, 282, 295, 302, 352
RAYNES 179
RAZORBACK CONCRETE COMPANY 40
REA 295
READ 123
REAGAN 58
REBUCK 321
RECORDS 61
RECTOR 180
REDDICK 140, 190, 195, 196, 204, 218, 252, 273, 292, 293, 296, 318, 326, 341, 345
REDDICK SCHOOL 117, 118
REDWINE 221
REECE 277
REED 65, 76, 118, 167, 177, 181, 258, 293, 294, 307, 309, 310
REEDER 287
REEDY 336
REEKS 188
REESE 249
REEVES 120, 177, 208, 210, 211, 217, 231, 341
REID 103, 258, 288, 324
REILLY 210, 211
REINHART 233, 319
REISER 154, 350
REISKAMP 175
REMAGAN 311
REMELEY 100
REMY 185
RENFROE 217, 219, 220, 294
RENSHAW 88
RESENDEZ 325
RETHERFORD 268, 294
REY 214
REYNOLDS 31, 44, 59, 68, 84, 111, 121, 123, 146, 166, 250, 254, 263, 288, 291, 294, 295, 301, 331
RHEA 87, 90, 96, 160, 170, 196, 267, 280, 295, 296, 307, 308
RHINE 52, 96, 105, 110, 119, 277, 282, 286, 296
RHODES 53
RICE 111, 200, 209, 296, 298, 330, 362
RICHARDS 99
RICHARDSON 7, 23, 24, 44, 88, 90, 99, 101, 102, 118, 120, 145, 201, 210, 211, 256, 348

RICHBERG 179
RICHEY 25
RICHMOND 125
RICKEY 112, 146, 223
RICKMAN 172, 232, 338
RIDDICK 344
RIDER 60
RIDGE 273
RIDLEY 250
RIECK 51, 241
RIGGS 168, 177
RIGGSBEE 119, 253
RIGHTNOWAR 294
RIGNEY 359
RILEY 13, 88, 92, 100, 150, 221, 288, 326
RING 82, 256, 360
RIPPY 95, 97, 99, 292, 293, 296
RISNER 219, 305
RITCHEY 149, 297
RITTER 46, 128, 260, 294, 295
RIZZOTTO 137, 271, 272
ROACH 150
ROBB 16, 22, 308, 309, 334, 342
ROBBINS 49, 131, 221, 287
ROBBINS - KIRSCH HOME 131, 132
ROBBS 88
ROBBS CHAPEL 88
ROBBS CHAPEL BAPTIST CHURCH 87
ROBERT 17, 165
ROBERTS 19, 83, 92, 116, 140, 148, 150, 151, 166, 174, 199, 200, 209, 210, 213, 215, 220, 238, 249, 270, 272, 281, 315, 316, 327, 328, 332, 333, 340, 351, 362
ROBERTSON 13, 183, 184, 205, 215, 262, 306, 357
ROBESON 13, 297
ROBINETTE 252
ROBINS 282
ROBINSON 15, 16, 22, 95, 99, 100, 119, 123, 171, 199, 215, 221, 233, 238, 272, 297, 298, 315, 318, 320, 330, 351, 357
ROCKWELL 39
ROCKWOOD 161, 249, 250
RODGERS 199, 310
ROE 72
ROGERS 14, 16, 46, 51, 61, 88, 99, 107, 112, 118, 122, 145, 148, 174, 176, 185, 208, 223, 226, 231, 240, 248, 251, 253, 265, 280, 282, 288, 298, 299, 300, 301, 318, 328, 342

ROLESON 41, 119, 321
RONEY 56
ROOF 252
ROOKER 105, 109, 165, 209, 343
ROONEY 235, 300
ROOSEVELT 321
ROOTS 317
ROSE 68, 108, 154, 192, 282, 340
ROSEMOND 68
ROSENTHAL 119
ROSS 97, 149, 154, 204, 232, 236, 276, 289, 300, 301, 322
ROSWELL 233, 311, 327
ROTH 209
ROTHE 223
ROUSSEAU 90, 154, 350
ROW 79, 363
ROWDEN 114
ROWE 13, 75, 80, 99, 120, 138, 148, 155, 167, 197, 202, 203, 208, 215, 239, 289, 301, 313, 319, 321, 322, 347, 355, 362, 363
ROWEN 75, 105
ROWLAND 25, 52, 117, 154, 216, 275, 301, 302, 343
ROWLANDS 185
ROWLETTE 324
ROY 175, 177, 186, 187, 304
ROZNOS 211
RUDDER 274
RUDI 25, 302
RUDISAL 152
RUDISILL 152
RUEHLE 349
RUMMEL 146
RUNYAN 107
RUPP 253
RUSHER 120
RUSHING 231
RUSSEL 23, 72
RUSSELL 20, 75, 79, 101, 176, 209, 250, 268, 302, 312, 313, 314, 324
RUSSOM 217, 259
RUST 97, 180
RUTER 211
RUTH 352
RUTHERFORD 294, 296, 355
RUTLEDGE 21, 118, 156, 202, 303, 304, 353
RUTTER 308
RYALS 174
RYAN 140, 154, 187, 215, 303
RYLES 195, 320
RYLEY 227
RYMON 252

S

SAIN 52
SALE 355
SAMMONS 113
SAMPLES 68
SAMPSON 345
SAMUEL 48, 61, 211, 240
SAMUELS 53, 54
SANDERS 77, 100, 155, 239, 272, 288, 303, 304, 362
SANDLIN 74, 271
SANDO 281
SANDUSKY 152
SANFORD 97, 160, 161, 199, 249
SANGER 340
SAPP 341
SATER 344
SAUER 230
SAUNDERS 325
SAURHEAVER 320
SAVILLO 323
SAWYER 298
SAYE 192
SCAGGS 118
SCATTER CREEK 21
SCATTER CREEK COMMUNITY 21
SCATTER CREEK SCHOOL 118, 119
SCHAFF 62, 96
SCHANDA 84
SCHECK 252
SCHEER 120, 164, 253, 304, 341
SCHEFSLER 326
SCHERF 271
SCHICK 253
SCHIMMING 111
SCHISLER 186, 267, 279, 304, 305
SCHIVNER 83
SCHLACERMAN 287
SCHLAKE 226
SCHLERSEMERFER 268
SCHMECKEL 360
SCHMUCKER 60
SCHMUECKER 13
SCHNEIDER 149
SCHNIVVING 24
SCHOOLEY 361
SCHRAMM 297
SCHREIT 12, 25, 57, 144, 305
SCHUESSLER 305
SCHUG 62, 89, 90, 306
SCHUGTOWN CHURCH 89
SCHUGTOWN METHODIST CHURCH 89
SCHULLY 326
SCHULTZ 61
SCHUNK 335
SCHUTT 226
SCHWAMB 222, 223, 306, 307

SCHYBOARD 96
SCOBEY 15, 315
SCOFIELD 250
SCOTT 18, 52, 70, 87, 98, 122, 140, 157, 158, 194, 205, 206, 211, 250, 256, 279, 280, 295, 298, 307, 308, 315, 325, 336, 344
SCUDDER 152
SEACHORD 268, 269
SEAL 244
SEAMORE 362
SEARS 177, 191, 232, 308, 356, 358
SEATS 257
SEAY 121, 123, 154, 166, 186, 190, 213, 214, 225, 230, 231
SECURITY – UNION PLANTERS BANK 53
SEE 75
SELECTMAN 65
SELF 22, 155, 308, 309
SELLARS 268
SENTER 309
SERRANO 344
SEVENTH AND MUELLER CHURCH OF CHRIST 74
SEVIER 350
SHADE 340
SHAKESPEARE 146
SHAMCO METAL RECYCLING 53
SHANE 185, 282, 309, 321, 332
SHANNON 194
SHARKEY 158, 183, 344
SHARP 14, 51, 260, 318
SHARPE 233, 251
SHARROCK 296
SHATLEY 13, 95
SHAVER 147, 148, 153, 176, 251, 318
SHAW 269
SHEARE 337
SHEARER 100, 222, 248, 249, 275
SHEDD 196
SHEER 19
SHEETS 185
SHEFFIELD 216, 217, 232
SHEHORN 109
SHELBY 30, 145, 150, 262
SHELTON 18, 75, 142, 196, 246, 273, 292, 318, 358
SHEPARD 163, 175, 292
SHEPHARD 232
SHEPHERD 109, 136, 263, 309, 310, 312
SHEPHERT 109
SHEPPARD 250, 304

SHERBOURNE 250
SHERIDAN 125
SHERMAN 196
SHERRIN 181
SHEWMAKER 22, 272, 317, 333, 348
SHIELDS 78, 234
SHILCUTT 156
SHILLCUT 156
SHILOH UNITED METHODIST CHURCH 75
SHIPMAN 12, 25, 76, 280
SHIPP 159, 310, 311
SHIRLEY 160, 165, 310
SHIVELY 337
SHOALS 16
SHOCK 200
SHOEMAKER 177
SHOOK 283
SHORT 74, 96, 121, 122, 154
SHOTTS 351, 352, 353
SHOULTZ 287
SHOUSE 313
SHRABLE 205, 273
SHRADER 296
SHREVE 249, 250
SHRITE 288
SHULTZ 188, 338
SIBERT 22, 112
SICKENDIECK 209
SIDEBOTTOM 46
SIDNEY 243
SIFFORD 209
SIGLER 268, 340
SIGMAN 248
SIKES 2, 107
SILKWOOD 166
SILLIN 189
SIMMONS 72, 75, 79, 116, 118, 248, 249, 252, 276, 327, 335
SIMMS 150
SIMONS 25
SIMPSON 18, 61, 86, 116, 120, 168, 170, 171, 180, 200, 201, 224, 245, 251, 265, 268, 302, 307, 308, 311, 312, 313, 314, 315, 322, 323, 324, 325, 326, 336
SIMS 107, 115, 119, 140, 166, 170, 171, 183, 212, 217, 218, 238, 271, 272, 285, 286, 295, 298, 315, 318, 321
SINGLETON 62, 203
SIPERT 201
SIPES 177
SISCO 172, 280
SISK 45, 304
SKAGGS 7, 86, 95, 110, 125, 217, 336
SKELTON 58, 336
SKINNER 256
SKOKOS 350
SLATTON 88, 165, 239, 355

SLAVINS 295
SLAW 308
SLINKER 289
SLOAN 7, 11, 14, 18, 30, 52, 134, 307, 315
SMALLEN 53
SMALLING 361
SMALLWOOD 250
SMELSER 15, 16, 167, 168, 270, 273, 312, 315, 316, 320, 333
SMITH 11, 16, 21, 22, 23, 25, 45, 46, 52, 74, 80, 81, 87, 90, 92, 93, 97, 99, 100, 101, 102, 104, 105, 107, 109, 110, 113, 116, 117, 119, 120, 123, 124, 125, 137, 140, 142, 144, 145, 147, 148, 152, 160, 163, 165, 166, 168, 172, 185, 192, 193, 194, 195, 198, 200, 203, 204, 206, 207, 208, 209, 210, 211, 223, 224, 228, 229, 230, 233, 243, 245, 246, 249, 250, 254, 256, 258, 261, 263, 266, 269, 271, 272, 276, 277, 278, 280, 283, 292, 293, 294, 301, 304, 309, 311, 316, 317, 318, 319, 320, 321, 323, 329, 332, 333, 336, 339, 343, 344, 349, 350, 351
SMOOT 83, 99, 117, 176, 359
SMOTHERMAN 176, 259
SMOTHERS 121
SNEEL 168
SNEERINGER 257
SNETSINGER 134
SNIDER 331
SNOW 224, 281, 349
SNOWBALL 323
SNOWDEN 158, 163, 200, 243, 262, 263, 312, 321, 322, 323, 324, 325, 326, 344, 362, 363
SNYDER 149, 204, 256, 292, 326
SOLLIS 188
SONGER 18, 326
SONNENBERG 232
SORRELL 213
SOUERS 334
SOUTHARD 273
SOUTHERD 227
SOUTHERLAND 79
SOUTHSIDE SCHOOL 119
SOWARD 79
SPAIN 13, 90, 148, 174, 177, 192, 219, 252

SPANN 250
SPARKS 5, 7, 147, 148, 164, 190, 244, 271, 278, 281, 298
SPARS 118
SPEAKER 79
SPEAR 79, 279, 280
SPEARS 280, 294
SPEER 168, 230, 280
SPEERS 252, 280
SPELLMEYER 340
SPENCE 92, 100, 146, 252, 327
SPENCER 119, 147, 325
SPENSER 250
SPERRY 250
SPIKES 144
SPILLMAN 87, 167, 168, 177, 213, 216, 237, 264
SPITZER 304
SPIVEY 160
SPRAGGINS 160, 161
SPRAGUE 97
SPRINGLES 119
SPRINGMAN 23
SPROLES 325
SPURLOCK 160
SRAJT 305
SRITE 288
SRUM 65
ST. FRANCIS RIVER 10
ST. GERTRUDE'S SELECT SCHOOL 94
ST. JOHN'S CHURCH 88
ST. JOHN'S LUTHERAN CHURCH 88
ST. MARY'S CEMETERY 82
ST. MARY'S CHURCH IN PARAGOULD, ARKANSAS 73
ST. MARY'S SCHOOL 94
ST. PAUL CHURCH 89
STACEY 259
STACK 301
STACY 54, 176
STACY & COMPANY HAIR AND NAIL SALON 54
STAGE 128
STAGGS 13, 107
STAIRES 118, 359
STAIRN 180
STALCOP 327
STALCUP 177, 247, 248
STALEY 238, 239
STALLCUP 15, 70, 95, 187, 327, 328
STALLINGS 257, 308
STAMPS 165
STANAGE 362
STANFILL 318
STANFORD 17, 21, 22, 120, 174, 217, 219, 328
STANFORD CONSOLIDATED SCHOOL 119
STANFORD HIGH SCHOOL 120
STANFORD SCHOOL 118, 119
STANLEY 148, 154, 257, 296, 350
STAPLETON 207, 219, 340
STARES 359
STARLIN 99
STARLING 102, 221, 237, 259, 317
STARNES 7, 21, 24, 87, 95, 97, 117, 118, 119, 121, 149, 166, 291, 328, 329, 333, 359
STARR 101
STARRETT 331
STATEN 111
STAUB 165, 338
STAUDT 82
STAYTON 111
STEARNS 119
STEDMAN 30, 154, 221, 224, 295, 350
STEELE 209, 309
STEINBERG 22, 125, 179, 230, 349
STELL 109
STEPHENS 87, 118, 149, 158, 209, 226, 281, 291, 319, 324, 325, 329, 339, 344, 348, 352
STEPP 57, 339
STEVENS 100, 168, 185, 188, 195, 204, 225, 227, 238, 270, 273, 290, 291, 292, 297, 324, 329, 330
STEVENSON 15, 45, 84, 92, 116, 150, 188, 218, 330, 347, 358
STEVESON 250
STEWART 72, 88, 147, 209, 301, 318, 352, 357
STEYER 61, 330
STICKLER 194, 330, 331
STIDHAM 131
STIDHAM - LANDRUM HOME 131, 132
STIMMSON 109
STIMSON 92, 108, 109, 150, 229, 236, 309, 331, 332
STOBAUGH 202
STOBUCK 346
STODDARD 97
STOKES 97, 264
STOLTE 274
STONE 112, 169, 176, 186, 202, 203, 204, 250, 300

STONEWALL 22
STONEWALL SCHOOL 118, 119
STOREY 44, 236
STORMES 225
STORY 259
STOUT 19, 166, 199
STOVALL 144
STOVER 13
STRAIT 252
STRATTON 44
STRAUB 13, 94, 210, 291
STRAUGHAN 67
STRAWMATT 236
STRICKLAND 226
STRICKLIN 106, 114, 119, 331
STRINGER 265
STRONG 182, 183
STROPE 107, 273
STROUD 88, 272
STROUGHMATT 224
STUARD 250
STUART 59, 148, 222, 224, 249, 267, 289, 290, 337, 358
STUBBLEFIELD 54, 296
STUCK 44
STUDEBAKER 209
STURGES 323
STURSA 158, 344
STURY 167
STUTES 86, 109, 218, 265, 309, 331, 332
STUTTS 109
STUTZ 118
SUDDATH 289
SUDDETH 333
SUDDUTH 340
SUDMEYER 304
SUFTIN 184, 337
SULLINGER 13, 221
SULLIVAN 34, 173, 199, 355
SUMMERS 121, 203, 316
SUMMITT 195
SUMPTER 248, 323
SUNLITE CASUAL FURNITURE 54
SUTFIN 23, 177, 183, 184, 239
SUTIN 177
SUTOWSKI 226
SUTTLE 79
SUTTON 13, 75
SVAGLIC 330
SVALODA 305
SVOBODA 304
SWAFFORD 173, 174, 241, 254
SWAIN 174, 198
SWAN 174
SWICEGOOD 295, 307
SWIGERT 90
SWIHART 81
SWINDEL 321
SWINDLE 15, 34, 86, 109, 123, 140, 142, 176, 229, 233, 246, 274, 284, 294, 332
SWINK 344
SWORD 230
SZABO 249

T

TALBERT 349
TALOR 362
TANKERSLEY 350
TANNEHILL 305
TANNER 113
TANSIL 134
TANT 71
TAPP 350
TAPPAN 193, 350
TARRANCE 15
TARRY 88
TASSEY 320
TATE 160, 200, 220, 350
TATUM 102, 214, 276, 308
TAUNTON 319
TAYLOR 13, 15, 16, 25, 49, 54, 65, 70, 72, 75, 79, 83, 92, 99, 100, 101, 119, 131, 177, 189, 198, 199, 206, 211, 221, 236, 241, 271, 272, 273, 296, 298, 301, 303, 312, 315, 320, 332, 333, 334, 340, 350, 351
TAYLOR HOME 131, 132
TEAGUE 334
TEDDER 76, 145, 167, 241, 334
TELEFLORA 54
TENNECO AUTOMOTIVE 42
TENNESSEE 244
TENNISON 23, 87, 95, 100, 178, 273, 334, 335, 337
TENNYSON 23, 100, 159, 321
TERRELL 336
TERRY 111, 114, 120, 188, 323, 335, 338
TETRICK 248
TEXTER 352
THACKER 176
THADDEUS 327
THAXTON 241
THETFORD 202, 303, 353, 354
THIRD AVENUE BAPTIST CHURCH 90
THOLEN 335
THOMAS 74, 110, 120, 157, 158, 160, 175, 184, 192, 206, 207, 230, 253, 260, 296, 297, 335, 340
THOMASON 45, 46, 83, 87, 95, 167, 192, 201, 263, 314, 315, 332, 336, 346, 347

THOMASSON 195
THOMEN 24, 296
THOMPSON 7, 17, 18, 21, 24, 48, 68, 71, 72, 75, 77, 79, 83, 86, 92, 95, 96, 99, 105, 110, 112, 113, 116, 119, 120, 148, 167, 168, 176, 180, 181, 184, 190, 192, 193, 207, 208, 214, 225, 245, 248, 249, 256, 258, 261, 264, 277, 281, 292, 295, 298, 309, 312, 329, 336, 337, 342, 355
THOMSON 239
THORNE 97, 202, 263
THORNTON 59, 303
THORP 188
THRELKELD 205
THROCKMORTON 161
THURMAN 92, 148, 216, 272
THURMOND 88
TIERMANN 253
TIGG 21
TILLMAN 13, 46, 87, 112, 145, 154
TIMBERLAKE 257
TINSLEY 121, 154, 229
TIPPETT 263
TIPTON 235
TOALSON 163
TODD 112, 134, 221, 239, 278
TODDSVILLE SCHOOL 120
TOELKEN 19, 226, 335, 338, 341
TOKIO 22
TOKIO CHURCH 90
TOKIO COMMUNITY 22
TOKIO SCHOOL 120
TOLER 116
TOLL 238, 315
TOLLESON 25, 280
TOMASON 100
TOMES 265
TOMHAFE 287
TOMLIN 199
TOMLINSON 46, 47, 189, 362
TOMPKINS 99
TOOLEY 362
TOOMB 87
TOOMBS 79, 83, 141, 188, 338
TORGERSON 362
TORRENCE 272
TOVEY 161
TOWELL 74
TOWER 121
TOWER SCHOOL 120, 121
TOWERY 170, 267, 295
TOWLES 206, 207

TOWNSEND 306
TOWNSLEY 349
TRACER 349
TRACY 234
TRADING BARN 55
TRAMMEL 310
TRANTHAM 13, 100, 107, 118, 166, 329, 339
TRAVIS 192, 214, 247, 312
TRAYWICK 340
TREADWAY 71, 115, 119, 233, 339
TREATY OF PARIS 11
TREECE 107, 172, 178, 179, 293
TRICE 32, 44, 59, 131, 140, 206, 339, 340
TRIPLETT 232
TRIPP 211
TRITCH 20, 55, 89, 120, 218, 252, 253, 294, 304, 335, 340, 341
TRITSCH 340
TROTTER 254
TROUT 103
TROVER 229
TROW 313
TROXLER 159
TROZLER 90
TRUE 209, 239, 281
TRULLINGER 257
TUBB 46
TUCKER 154, 254, 289, 297, 315, 331, 337
TUGGLE 111
TURMAN 176
TURNBOW 231, 341
TURNER 15, 55, 61, 96, 97, 121, 151, 233, 261
TURNER DAIRIES, INC. 55
TURNER HOLDINGS, L.L.C. 55
TURPIN 159, 184, 357
TWEEDY 250
TYLER 54, 166, 296
TYNER 95, 143, 185, 186, 229, 231, 233, 342, 355

## U

UNDERWOOD 122, 228, 245
UNION STATION 55
UPPER LAFE SCHOOL 120
USERY 236
UTHOFF 245
UTTER 74
UTZ 286

## V

VAIL 175, 292
VALAUDINGHAM 180
VALENTINE 159, 199, 202, 312, 362
VALLEY FORGE 11
VAN MORTEN 300
VAN SCHAICK 344
VAN SYOC 344
VAN-HOOK 144
VANAMAN 164, 281
VANARDSDALE 303
VANCLEVE 274
VANDERBILT 336
VANDERVOORT 55
VANDERVOORT HOTEL 55
VANDIVER 240
VANGILDER 254, 292, 345, 348, 355, 360
VANHORN 151, 180
VANNOY 257
VANOVER 77
VARDEMAN 245
VARNER 121, 142, 237
VARVIL 165, 193, 342
VARVILL 343
VAUGHN 23, 32, 118, 121, 140, 209, 250, 260, 268, 275, 276, 296, 337, 355
VAUGHTER 209
VEAZEY 177
VELLANCE 351
VERBEYCK 128
VERNON 75, 79
VESPUSIUS 337
VICKREY 274
VICKROY 166
VIETNAM WAR 13
VILLAGE SCHOOL 120, 121
VILLINES 75
VINCENT 99, 107, 189, 340
VINES 13, 105, 165, 172, 227, 275, 343
VINING 101
VINSON 318
VIRGIN 78, 79, 99
VLACO 288
VOIGHT 296
VOLK 326
VOLNER 25
VON BRAUN 146
VOWELL 86, 99, 107, 118, 218

## W

W. S. PRUET HOME 131, 132
WADDEL 340
WADDELL 164, 270
WADDY 248
WADE 61, 72, 75, 79, 90, 125
WADKINS 198
WADLEY 16, 88, 250
WAFFORD 176
WAGGONER 344, 349
WAGNER 105, 158, 159, 163, 172, 200, 201, 243, 258, 263, 268, 302, 303, 311, 312, 314, 315, 321, 322, 323, 324, 325, 326, 336, 344, 362, 363
WAGSTER 53
WAHL 341
WAINWRIGHT 258
WAITS 24
WALCOTT 22
WALCOTT BAPTIST CHURCH 82
WALCOTT SCHOOL 116, 121, 122
WALDEN 21, 24, 83, 86, 113, 118, 150, 154, 156, 157, 184, 218, 265, 337, 341
WALDRUM 119, 292, 343
WALKER 6, 13, 97, 100, 112, 119, 140, 181, 195, 212, 235, 237, 242, 243, 250, 253, 288, 344, 355, 356, 357
WALL 22, 23, 24, 32, 61, 76, 131, 169, 231, 247, 250
WALLACE 75, 219, 241, 261, 264, 304, 349
WALLDRUM 185
WALLIS 99, 210, 252, 253
WALLS 22, 123, 155, 296
WALNUT GROVE SCHOOL 121, 122
WALNUT RIDGE SCHOOL 123
WALPOLE 278
WALSH 161, 281, 296
WALTERS 13, 92, 213, 235, 236, 238, 250, 306
WALTON 103, 211, 227, 265, 362
WAMBLE 281
WAMOCK 25
WAR BETWEEN THE STATES 13
WAR FOR INDEPENDENCE 10
WARBRITTON 19
WARD 62, 100, 119, 120, 123, 210, 224, 265, 272, 276, 283, 294, 318, 359, 361
WARE 151
WARMICK 181
WARNER 147
WARNICUTT 348
WARREN 76, 78, 113, 159, 182, 184, 199, 207, 209
WARREN'S CHAPEL METHODIST EPISCOPAL CHURCH, SOUTH 76
WARRICK 188
WARWICK 166
WASH 322
WASHINGTON 10, 11, 62, 97, 131, 151, 233, 251, 345
WASHINGTON-OWENS HOME 131, 132
WATERS 72, 75, 79, 350
WATKINS 69, 165, 174, 283
WATLEY 120
WATSON 13, 19, 25, 30, 56, 62, 72, 74, 75, 76, 79, 87, 96, 101, 118, 154, 161, 163, 167, 168, 198, 267, 286, 290, 304, 315, 326, 330, 343, 345, 349
WATSON BROTHERS 56
WATSON'S FASHION BOUTIQUE 56
WATWOOD 13
WAYLAND 357
WAYNE 260
WEATHERFORD 13, 173, 345
WEATHERLY 119, 140, 202, 250, 309
WEAVER 111, 252, 274, 327, 347
WEBB 77, 78, 123, 143, 164, 174, 212, 215, 216, 224, 225, 236, 239, 257, 278, 345, 346, 358
WEBER 178
WEBSTER 101, 261
WEDDINGTON 21, 118, 194
WEEKS 308
WEGNER 120, 226, 335
WELCH 215, 246, 252, 253, 278, 334, 346
WELLING 257
WELLS 24, 33, 52, 114, 116, 246, 333, 337, 346, 347, 348
WELSHANS 219
WELTI 335
WESLEY 159
WESSELL 28, 44, 59, 161
WESSON 77, 228
WEST 13, 54, 58, 72, 75, 79, 83, 92, 111, 177, 188, 256, 337, 338
WEST VIEW BAPTIST CHURCH 77
WESTFALL 340
WESTHOUSE 145
WESTWOOD 303
WETHERLY 109
WHATLEY 247
WHEELER 142, 154, 160, 173, 272, 274, 317, 320, 362
WHIPPLE 251
WHISTLE 349
WHITAKER 360
WHITBY 273
WHITE 7, 16, 56, 57, 104, 119, 131, 144, 151, 154, 160, 179, 185, 194, 207, 217, 221, 232, 253, 262, 273, 281, 284, 296, 301, 329, 332, 333, 348, 355, 360, 362
WHITE - HAYS HOME 131, 132
WHITE OAK SCHOOL 107, 121, 123
WHITE PRINTING COMPANY, INCORPORATED 56
WHITEHEAD 164, 206, 207, 344
WHITEHURST 79
WHITESIDE 292
WHITFIELD 154
WHITLEY 219
WHITLOCK 15, 281
WHITNEY 77, 262, 310, 349
WHITSETT 62, 340
WHITSITT 62
WHITSON 288
WHITTEN 62, 245, 349
WHITTENBERG 144
WHITTINGTON 161
WHITTON 13
WHITWORTH 164, 168, 257, 269
WIDEMAN 275
WIDMER 83
WIGGINS 205
WIGGINTON 49
WILBORN 281
WILBOURN 59, 131, 340
WILCOCKSON 119, 176, 270, 328
WILCOX 95, 122, 223
WILCOXSON 247, 342
WILEY 23, 182, 183, 184
WILFONG 294
WILHELM 164
WILHITE 308
WILKERSON 93, 249, 261, 326
WILKIN 219
WILKINS 74, 257
WILKINSON 80, 101, 103, 105, 109, 121, 296
WILLARD 329
WILLBANKS 19
WILLCOCKSON 96, 97, 99, 116, 118, 148, 154, 190, 201, 230, 247, 273, 275, 283, 287, 336, 337, 349, 350
WILLCOX 190
WILLCOXEN 20
WILLETT 258
WILLEY 261
WILLHITE 295
WILLIAM 361
WILLIAMS 10, 13, 15, 62, 65, 75, 79, 81, 85, 95, 96, 99, 100, 102, 108, 119, 121, 125, 145, 146, 151, 155, 156, 157, 166, 173, 174, 175, 184, 186, 194, 198, 200, 204, 220, 221, 223, 233, 236, 238, 239, 252, 253, 259, 261, 270, 273, 275, 278, 281, 288, 290, 295, 306, 307, 308, 319, 326, 329, 335, 339, 346, 347, 348, 350, 351, 352, 353, 354, 355, 362
WILLIAMSON 68, 72, 79, 96, 99, 107, 112, 118, 192, 282, 285, 303, 349
WILLINGHAM 23
WILLIS 243, 305, 315
WILLS 75, 114, 275
WILSON 13, 21, 28, 75, 79, 99, 116, 119, 120, 165, 172, 173, 174, 179, 180, 194, 195, 198, 217, 219, 232, 233, 243, 265, 279, 280, 282, 288, 299, 328, 331, 333, 345, 361, 362
WIMBERLY 121
WINBERRY 72, 84
WINCE 286
WINCHESTER 329
WINDER 113
WINELAND 89
WINFORD 13
WINN 19, 65, 77, 83, 96, 99, 100, 119, 165, 186, 243, 354, 355
WINSTEAD 205
WINTZ 226
WISE 25, 68, 226, 294, 355
WISEMAN 286
WISENFELS 349
WITCHER 44, 59, 167, 168
WITT 187, 193, 269, 290
WITTE 209
WOFFORD 123
WOGMAN 13
WOLF 119, 240
WOLFORD 335
WOOD 18, 52, 68, 78, 81, 83, 95, 96, 99, 100, 105, 107, 124, 144, 148, 159, 160, 181, 185, 188, 192, 194, 216, 224, 227, 242, 243, 249, 262, 268, 288, 294, 308,

313, 334, 345, 348, 356, 357, 358, 359
**WOOD SCHOOL** 121, 123
**WOODALL** 274
**WOODARD** 119, 245
**WOODBRIDGE** 333
**WOODROME** 324
**WOODS** 72, 75, 78, 79, 107, 119, 189, 236, 251, 257
**WOOD'S CHAPEL SCHOOL** 121, 124
**WOOD'S CHAPEL UNITED METHODIST CHURCH** 78, 79
**WOODSIDE** 7
**WOODSMALL** 349
**WOODSON** 119, 122, 224, 226, 286
**WOODWARD** 74, 223, 333
**WOOLDRIDGE** 193, 252, 290, 302, 311, 359
**WOOLRIDGE** 341
**WOOLSEY** 203
**WOOLVERTON** 196
**WOOSLEY** 30
**WORD** 259, 260
**WORLDS** 121
**WORLEY** 97
**WORRELL** 336
**WORTHAM** 54, 145
**WOUBILMAN** 151
**WRAPE** 32, 44, 60, 125, 262, 324
**WRAY** 16, 295
**WREN** 289
**WRENN** 277
**WRIGHT** 14, 21, 32, 38, 44, 49, 56, 68, 72, 75, 79, 96, 148, 184, 187, 204, 268, 269, 278, 297, 303, 329, 340, 348, 359, 360
**WRING** 77
**WULFEKUHLER** 52, 360
**WWI** 13
**WWII** 13
**WYATT** 52, 57, 58, 118, 140, 164, 233, 268, 319, 348
**WYATT BROTHERS FURNITURE, INCORPORATED** 57
**WYLIE** 248
**WYNN** 95, 100
**WYNNE** 336
**WYSE** 70, 113

**Y**

**YANCEY** 352
**YANTIS** 119
**YARBORY** 355
**YARBOUR** 186
**YARBROUGH** 72, 172, 200, 355
**YARNELL** 235
**YATES** 13, 68, 141, 188, 283, 309, 338, 339
**YEAGER** 50, 56
**YEARGAIN** 46, 47, 180, 361
**YEARGIN** 119
**YEARTA** 358
**YEATES** 334
**YODER** 236
**YONESHIGE** 312, 336
**YOPP** 99, 118, 119, 321
**YORK** 159, 283
**YOUNG** 88, 103, 131, 148, 178, 248, 258, 296, 321, 323, 324, 327, 354, 362, 363
**YOUNG - COX HOME** 131, 133
**YOW** 169

**Z**

**ZATLIN** 272
**ZIMMERMAN** 99
**ZITMAN** 54
**ZOLK** 79
**ZOLLINER** 19
**ZOLLNER** 108, 189
**ZOLMAN** 252
**ZOLNER** 56

Henry Trice Home, built 1893

The Block Mansion

*The Big Snow of 1918*

*Location of Belk Simpson Company*